Fiction's Many Worlds

Charles E. May

California State University—Long Beach

D. C. HEATH AND COMPANY

Lexington, Massachusetts   Toronto

Address editorial correspondence to:

D. C. Heath
125 Spring Street
Lexington, MA 02173

Acquisitions Editor: Paul Smith
Developmental Editor: Linda Bieze
Production Editor: Carolyn Ingalls
Designer: Cia Boynton
Production Coordinator: Chuck Dutton
Permissions Editor: Margaret Roll

Cover: **Left:** Romare Bearden. *Mother and Child.* 1969. 8½ ×
4¼ inches. The Estate of Romare Bearden, courtesy ACA
Galleries, New York, New York. **Top Right:** *Clown,* Paul Klee.
1929/133 (D3). Oil on Canvas, 26⅜ × 19⅝ in. Private
Collection. **Bottom Right:** *Portrait of a Girl,* 1908, Max Pechstein
1881–1955. Courtesy of Staatliche Museen zu Berlin Preußischer
Kulturbesitz Nationalgalerie. Photo by Jörg P. Anders/Bildarchiv
Preßischer Kulturbesitz. Berlin.

International Standard Book Number: 0–669–27762–2

Library of Congress Catalog Number: 92–70797

789-DOC-05 04 03

Preface

Fiction's Many Worlds is both a short story anthology and a short story text-book. That is, the book includes a large number of stories that readers will find pleasurable and that teachers may teach in any way they see fit, but it also suggests a direction for the study of short fiction that I have found effective and that I hope you will find useful.

THE STORIES

I have included as many stories as possible, for a book can never contain too many good ones. However, not only are the stories a pleasure to read, they are also highly "teachable," for they clearly illustrate central characteristics of fiction, and they are thematically and structurally complex enough to encourage close analysis. I have included many frequently anthologized stories, because they have withstood the test of previous teaching; but I have also made room for a number of new stories that represent the renaissance taking place in the short story in the past few years.

The fact that a generous number of the stories in this anthology are quite short is the result of a conscious editorial and pedagogical decision. Although I am sympathetic to a wide range of approaches to fiction—from the thematic to the theoretical—I still believe there is no substitute for a good, close reading of the text. It has been my experience that students are more likely to engage in such a reading if the story is brief enough to permit a close analysis of its structure, language, and thematic implications. It has also been my experience that students learn how to read stories more meaningfully if they have some sense of the shared generic devices of the stories. Reading very short fictions makes it possible for students to consider several stories at once and thus to discover the formal and thematic conventions they have in common.

EDITORIAL APPARATUS

The Introduction to *Fiction's Many Worlds* consists of two parts: a discussion of Rudyard Kipling's delightful little "Just So" story, "How the Whale Got His Throat," which emphasizes the crucial differences between events that stories present and the rhetorical nature of the presentation itself; and a comparative discussion of Hemingway's "Hills Like White Elephants" and Patricia Crossman's "A Life to Live," which illustrates the range of complexity of stories and emphasizes the need for close analysis rather than casual reading.

The 142 stories in the collection are organized into four parts that illustrate the basic "worlds," or realms of reality, of fiction. The range is from fictions that primarily intend to be clear reflections of everyday reality to those that seem highly stylized and self-reflexive explorations of the nature of story itself. Each group is preceded by a short introduction about the basic characteristics of that "world," as well as a short analysis of a typical story as an example of how students might develop their own analyses. Each story is followed by five or six reading prompts or exercises for students to consider. At the end of the book there are definitions of basic critical terms relevant to short fiction, as well as a short biographical note on each author.

COMPUTER HYPERTEXT SUPPLEMENT

This book also provides a hypertext computer supplement. A number of the stories have been prepared on computer disks in a hypertext format. Each story in the hypertext format contains idea prompts throughout, which indicate points where the student should pause and examine certain issues, and writing prompts, which ask students to respond to writing ideas. Each story also includes a *Notes* area where students can take notes, as well as a *Draft* area where students can prepare an analytical paper on a single story or group of stories. Students can then move back and forth between the Notes, the Writing Prompts, and the Draft areas, copying material and transferring it as necessary. When they have completed a draft of the paper, students can either print it out or export it to a word processing program where it can be revised, edited, and formatted for submission either on disk or in hard copy.

You can use the hypertext stories for out-of-class reading or writing assignments in which students have their own copy of the stories on disks for use at home or in a campus computer lab. Or, if a computer classroom is available, you may assign a story or group of stories for the entire class to work on at one time. The hypertext format makes it possible for students to read the story, think about it, take notes on it, respond to directed prompts, write a rough draft of a paper, and prepare a final copy without leaving the keyboard. Students report that they enjoy analyzing fiction in this way, for they feel they are truly interacting with the story and making discoveries of their own, rather than giving the work a cursory reading and waiting for the teacher to provide an analysis.

The hypertext stories are available both in HyperCard 2.1 for the Macintosh and in ToolBook 1.5 for IBM compatible machines runnning Windows 3.0 and higher.

INSTRUCTOR'S GUIDE

The Instructor's Guide that accompanies this book features my own discussions of every story in the text (either individually or in groups that share thematic or formal characteristics), as well as suggestions for further reading on the short story as a genre and the authors represented in the text. If a film version of the story is available, it also is discussed. The Instructor's Guide also includes an essay on the worlds of short fiction, an annotated bibliography on the short story, and alternate tables of contents.

ACKNOWLEDGMENTS

This book would not have been possible without the stimulation and challenge of the hundreds of students who have studied the short story with me over the years at California State University, Long Beach. Neither would it have been possible without the confident support of editor Paul Smith nor the gentle prodding of editor Linda Bieze, both of D. C. Heath. Thanks also to the other wonderful professionals at D. C. Heath, Cia Boynton, Carolyn Ingalls, Toby Levenson, and Margaret Roll, for their expert assistance. Of particular help were those colleagues who read the manuscript and made comments on it: Tony Grooms, The University of Georgia; Alden W. Hart, Slippery Rock University; Donald W. Heidt, College of the Canyons; Dale Kramer, University of Illinois at Urbana–Champaign; and Joseph Lostracco, Austin Community College. I owe special thanks to my good friend and colleague David Peck at California State University, Long Beach, who keeps me honest.

As always, I am grateful to my wife Pat and my children Hillary, Alex, and Jordan, who provided reassurance when the compilation got complicated, moral support when the task got tedious, and love all the time.

I dedicate this book to my mother Kathleen—whose Cherokee blood, Appalachian heritage, and personal good sense have made her a model of hard work, courage, and determination for me; and to my wife Patricia—whose gentleness, kindness, intelligence and good humor make everything possible.

Charles E. May

Contents

PART TWO | *The World of Dream and Hallucination* 225

PART THREE | *The World of Fable, Legend, Allegory, and Myth* 413

PART FOUR | *The World of Story*   583

The Short Story: Terms and Techniques 767

Biographies of the Authors 789

Acknowledgments 829

Photo Credits 834

Author/Title Index 835

RUDYARD
KIPLING

How the Whale Got His Throat

On the sea, once upon a time, O my Best Beloved, there was a Whale, and he ate fishes. He ate the starfish and the gar fish, and the crab and the dab, and the paice and the dace, and the skate and his mate, and the mackerel and the pickerel, and the really truly twirly-whirly eel. All the fishes he could find in all the sea he ate with his mouth—so! Till at last there was only one small fish left in all the sea, and he was a small 'Stute Fish, and he swam a little behind the Whale's right ear, so as to be out of harm's way. Then the Whale stood up on his tail and said, "I'm hungry." And the small 'Stute Fish said in a small 'stute voice, "Noble and generous Cetacean, have you ever tasted Man?"

"No," said the Whale. "What is it like?"

"Nice," said the small 'Stute Fish. "Nice but nubbly."

"Then fetch me some," said the Whale, and he made the sea froth up with his tail.

"One at a time is enough," said the 'Stute Fish. "If you swim to latitude Fifty North, longitude Forty West (that is Magic), you will find, sitting *on* a raft *in* the middle of the sea, with nothing on but a pair of blue canvas breeches, a pair of suspenders (you must *not* forget the suspenders, Best Beloved), and a jack-knife, one shipwrecked Mariner, who, it is only fair to tell you, is a man of infinite-resource-and-sagacity."

So the Whale swam and swam to latitude Fifty North, longitude Forty West, as fast as he could swim, and *on* a raft, *in* the middle of the sea, *with* nothing to wear except a pair of blue canvas breeches, a pair of suspenders (you must particularly remember the suspenders, Best Beloved), *and* a jack-knife, he found one single, solitary shipwrecked Mariner, trailing his toes in the water. (He had his Mummy's leave to paddle, or else he would never have done it, because he was a man of infinite-resource-and-sagacity.)

Then the Whale opened his mouth back and back and back till it nearly touched his tail, and he swallowed the shipwrecked Mariner, and the raft he was sitting on, and his blue canvas breeches, and the suspenders (*which* you must not forget), *and* the jack-knife—He swallowed them all down into his warm, dark, inside cupboards, and then he smacked his lips—so, and turned round three times on his tail.

But as soon as the Mariner, who was a man of infinite-resource-and-sagacity, found himself truly inside the Whale's warm, dark, inside cupboards, he stumped and he jumped and he thumped and he bumped, and he pranced and he danced, and he banged and he clanged, and he hit and he bit, and he leaped and he creeped, and he prowled and he howled, and he hopped and he dropped, and he cried and he sighed, and he crawled and he bawled, and he stepped and he lepped, and he danced hornpipes where he shouldn't, and the Whale felt most unhappy indeed. (*Have* you forgotten the suspenders?)

So he said to the 'Stute Fish, "This man is very nubbly, and besides he is making me hiccough. What shall I do?"

"Tell him to come out," said the 'Stute Fish.

So the Whale called down his own throat to the shipwrecked Mariner, "Come out and behave yourself. I've got the hiccoughs."

"Nay, nay!" said the Mariner. "Not so, but far otherwise. Take me to my natal-shore and the white-cliffs-of-Albion, and I'll think about it." And he began to dance more than ever.

"You had better take him home," said the 'Stute Fish to the Whale. "I ought to have warned you that he is a man of infinite-resource-and-sagacity."

So the Whale swam and swam, with both flippers and his tail as hard as he could for the hiccoughs; and at last he saw the Mariner's natal-shore and the white-cliffs-of-Albion, and he rushed half-way up the beach, and opened his mouth wide and wide and wide, and said, "Change here for Winchester, Ashuelot, Nashua, Keene, and the stations of the *Fitch*burg Road"; and just as he said "Fitch" the Mariner walked out of his mouth. But while the Whale had been swimming, the Mariner, who was indeed a person of infinite-resource-and-sagacity, had taken his jack-knife and cut up the raft into a little square grating all running criss-cross, and he had tied it firm with his suspenders (*now* you know why you were not to forget the suspenders!) and he dragged that grating good and tight into the Whale's throat, and there it stuck! Then he recited the following *Sloka,* which, as you have not heard it, I will now proceed to relate—

> By means of a grating
> I have stopped your ating.

For the Mariner he was also an Hi-ber-ni-an. And he stepped out on the shingle, and went home to his Mother, who had given him leave to trail his toes in the water; and he married and lived happily ever afterward. So did the Whale. But from that day on, the grating in his throat, which he could neither cough up nor swallow down, prevented him from eating anything except very, very small fish; and that is the reason why whales nowadays never eat men or boys or little girls.

The small 'Stute Fish went and hid himself in the mud under the Door-sills of the Equator. He was afraid that the Whale might be angry with him.

The Sailor took the jack-knife home. He was wearing the blue canvas breeches when he walked out on the shingle. The suspenders were left behind, you see, to tie the grating with; and that is the end of *that* tale.

STORY AND DISCOURSE: *"You Must **Not** Forget the Suspenders, Best Beloved"*

Rudyard Kipling's simple little children's story about how the whale got his throat illustrates a basic characteristic of fiction worth keeping in mind—that stories are always told, either orally or in writing, by someone. Although this

may seem obvious when stated straightforwardly, frequently we get so caught up in the story that we respond to the events as if they were happening right now rather than as the narration of events that occurred in the past.

Although losing ourselves in a story is necessary for our enjoyment of it "as if" it were a "real" series of events, such total involvement does not usually permit us to understand the story as a language-created event. As the language of the story encourages us to create visual images of the events in our mind, the language itself disappears. As we become caught up in the apparent dynamic action of the event, we lose sight of the teller who controls that action with words. "How the Whale Got His Throat" cleverly reminds us of the control of the teller.

Kipling's *Just So Stories* illustrates an underlying impulse of story-telling as old as the human imagination itself—the need to account for things. The most primitive means by which human beings tried to account for phenomena they did not understand was to create a story that provided a plausible explanation. Such stories, now called "myths," were actually like scientific theoretical models, the value of which is that they provide a unified explanation. Such a myth is "true" not necessarily because it "corresponds" to the facts of the phenomena, but because it is "coherent"; that is, the myth incorporates all the elements of the phenomena, and it holds together.

Kipling's whimsical story explanation of how the whale got his throat begins in the familiar fairy-tale way "once upon a time" and thus establishes the events of the story as having taken place in the past—not a specific time in the past as an historical account might assert, but rather an indeterminate time in some generalized distant past. However, as soon as we begin reading or hearing the story, we forget that the events exist in the past and begin to imagine them taking place in the present. This illusion of the presentness of the past begins to assert itself particularly when events are dramatized, for example, when the whale stands upon his tail and says (and we see and hear him say it), "I'm hungry." As the story continues, we become further caught up in the events as if they are happening before our eyes "now" just as they happened "then." In fact, the concept of "then" disappears, and we are only aware of the illusion of "now."

We follow the events, one thing after another, driven by the desire to see what happens next. However, if we think about it, this very desire is a contradiction in terms, for whatever happens "next" in a story has already happened. What we are experiencing is a written account of the event, a fact that Kipling cleverly keeps in front of us every time he tells us that we must not forget the suspenders. The effect of this teasing remark is to remind us that there is a teller. Of more importance, by telling us *not* to forget something that seems to have no significance, he reminds us of an important difference between the teller and the listener—that the teller knows the significance of the suspenders before we do because the events of the story have taken place prior to the telling of it. This means that the beginning of the story (as told) has embedded within it the end of the story (as a series of events).

Introduction

Hokusai: *The Great Wave, 1823–1829*

Although this may sound quite obvious, it is a fact that as readers we forget in order to become involved in the action of the story. One of the most important implications of this fact is that stories always have two time frames—the time the events took place and the time the story is being related. Film director Mel Brooks plays with this concept in his movie *Space Balls,* a parody of George Lucas's *Star Wars.* At one point in *Space Balls,* Helmet, the character who parodies the villain Darth Vader, and the enemy ship's captain are trying to determine the whereabouts of the heroes by looking at a radar screen. The captain suggests that they take a look at the film *Space Balls* to find them. He explains that as a result of new technology, the home-video version of the film is made available even while the theater release is still being made. After they put the tape on the VCR, they fast-forward to a point in the film identical to the point in the film we are watching. Thus Helmet sees himself on the tape just as the viewer sees him, except now the viewer sees Helmet seeing himself.

Obviously puzzled, Helmet looks at himself in the monitor and then looks out at us; looking back at the monitor, he waves his hand as one might do in front of a mirror or in front of a camcorder. This bit of dialogue follows:

HELMET: What the hell am I looking at? When does this happen in the movie?

COMMANDER: Now. You're looking at "now," sir. Everything that happens now is happening now.

HELMET: What happened to "then"?

COMMANDER: We're past that.

HELMET: When?

COMMANDER: Now. We're at "now" now.

HELMET: Go back to "then."

COMMANDER: When?

HELMET: Now!

COMMANDER: Now?

HELMET: Now!

COMMANDER: I can't.

HELMET: Why?

COMMANDER: We missed it.

HELMET: When?

COMMANDER: Just now.

HELMET: When will "then" be "now"?

COMMANDER: Soon.

HELMET: How soon?

At this point, the scene on the monitor shifts to the heroes trudging through the sand on another planet. The radar operator sitting at the monitor says, "Sir, we have identified their location."

Helmet is so thoroughly confused as to the nature of his existence in time that he does not know where he is in space either.

HELMET: Where?

RADAR OPERATOR: It's the moon of Vega.

COMMANDER: Good work. Set a course and prepare for our arrival.

HELMET: When? *(In complete hysteria)*

COMMANDER: 1900 hours. By high noon tomorrow they will be our prisoners.

HELMET: Who? *(shouting in panic just as his helmet visor drops down and covers his face)*

Mel Brooks is obviously satirizing the speed at which commercial movies get released on home video nowadays, but in so doing, he also makes clear a crucial fact about narrative fiction—there is always a gap between the time of the events as they took place and the time of the relation of those events.

During our first encounter with a story, we are inevitably more caught up with the time frame of the action than with the time frame of the telling of it, for if the story catches our interest, we are eager to see what happens next, allowing ourselves to forget that the actual event has already occurred in its entirety. The Nobel Prize–winning South American writer Gabriel García Márquez has one of his characters say, "Stories only happen to those who know how to tell them." What this means is that we can never get a replication of the events as they actually took place in the world; we can only "know" those events as narrated by someone else. And indeed when the events are narrated by one who knows how to tell them, what we get is a story.

A basic difference between the events as they might have taken place in the real world and the events as they are narrated is that in the narration we get only a "selection" of the events. If you tried to tell the story of your current day in every single minute detail that occurred, as well as to convey all the thoughts, feelings, and impressions you might have felt as they occurred, you would probably never be able to finish telling it. Consequently, when we tell a story, we select some items to tell and filter out others. Think of being at a party and meeting someone who interests you. Even though there might be lots of noise from other people around you, you would probably focus on the person who has your interest so that you would not even hear what else is going on around you. Similarly, when you tell a story, you select some details and ignore others based on some principle of interest.

Moreover, when someone tells a story, the sequence of the events as told may vary from the sequence of the events as they actually occurred. Instead of telling the event one item after another in time, a teller might skip ahead to some point or, forgetting something, might skip back to a previous point. Or the teller might organize the narration around some central impression or interest, narrating the events that seem related to that impression or interest, regardless of how the events followed each other in time. When we tell a story, we have our own special interest in the story, or else we probably would not bother to tell it in the first place. Consequently, we might insert some commentary in the story indicating how we feel about the events, supplying additional related information, or providing some explanation or clarification.

When we tell a story, there may be certain elements of the story we wish to express that are hard to state straightforwardly; that is, they cannot be explained adequately, nor can the simple narration of a series of events communicate them adequately. Consequently, we might try to communicate the idea or feeling in terms of something else, using analogies and comparisons, prefacing them by saying "it's something like. . . ."

Finally, when we tell a story, we may have some specific intention in mind: to communicate or argue for an idea, to get a sympathetic reaction, to create a certain effect. Thus we may add flourishes, embellish things a bit, even alter some events and make up some others in order to achieve the purpose we want.

All these characteristics indicate basic differences between our usual assumption of *story* as simply a series of events as they might occur in the world and *story* as this book defines the term: that is, as a narrated series of events that differ from the events as they might have occurred in the real world in significant ways.

What makes Kipling's story interesting to us is not merely the relation of the events, as clever as those are, but also the many additions and alterations the teller of the story makes to the events—contributions that if left out would not alter the nature of the events but would definitely alter the way we as readers receive them. Let's take a look at some of the elements of the story that have nothing to do with it as an actual series of events in time but which have much to do with the story as we receive it, that is, as narrated by a teller:

1. Addressing the listener as "Best Beloved" to suggest the cozy and caring nature of the relation between teller and listener.

2. Listing items that rhyme to create a memorable sing-song effect: "He ate the starfish and the gar fish, and the crab and the dab, and the paice and dace, and the skate and his mate, and the mackereel and pickereel, and the really truly twirly-whirly eel."

3. Listing items that rhyme to create an intensification of actions: "He stumped and he jumped and he thumped and he bumped, and he pranced and he danced, and he banged and he clanged, and he hit and he bit, and he leaped and he creeped, and he prowled and he howled, and he hopped and he dropped, and he cried and he sighed, and he crawled and he bawled, and he stepped and he lepped, and he danced hornpipes where he shouldn't, and the Whale felt most unhappy indeed."

4. Depicting the whale as a train conductor when it opens its mouth to let the sailor out in order to create a familiar and amusing analogy: "Change here for Winchester, Ashuelot, Nashua, Keene, and the Stations of the *Fitch*burg Road."

5. Continually referring to the sailor as a "man of infinite-resource-and-sagacity" to set up an expectation in the listener that is fulfilled like the refrain in a song.

None of these devices has anything to do with the actual occurrence of events; they are used to create certain effects. Because they are devices used by a speaker or a user of language, we can legitimately call them "rhetorical devices." All devices that a teller or writer may use to transform actual events into "language events" we will term *rhetorical devices*. Rhetorical devices are all those things that make the events we read, that is, the story, "different" from the events as they might have taken place in the real world. In short, what makes a story a story are all those devices that make it different from life. These devices are what we must study if we are to understand *story*.

This does not mean that to be a good reader you must think of a story as if you were a writer. Nor does it mean that you should ignore what seems to happen in a story or what ideas it may be about and focus only on how the story is told. Nor does it mean that your enjoyment of a story will be spoiled because you cannot simply "lose yourself" in the story. However, when we read stories in a literature class, we are not reading them merely to find out what happens next, but to try to understand them. In order to understand stories, we must have some idea about how they work. And learning how they work means first of all making the important distinction between what we "take to be" actual incidents in the world and what we actually have when we read a story—a teller's narration of events that have already taken place. We must always remember that the story is *not* the events, but rather a structure made up of language that somehow replicates the events. A famous expert on language, Alfred Korzybski, expressed the difference in his book *Science and Sanity* (1933) by using the analogy of the relationship between a map and the territory that the map replicates. "A map is *not* the territory it represents," Korzybski reminds us, "but, if correct, it has a *similar structure* to the territory, which accounts for its usefulness." Similarly, he continues, all language structures must be considered only as maps, for a word is *not* the object it represents.

Perhaps this distinction can be seen more clearly if we take a look at some cartoons from the newspapers that illustrate this inescapable fact by comically violating it. Consider the "Herman" cartoon on the next page. The cartoon character is obviously in a mall or park by a directory or map. Since maps are of no value in finding out where we want to go unless we know where we are in relation to the map, such directories always have a particular point marked "You Are Here." The cartoon character points to that spot on the map with his umbrella; immediately the metaphor of the map is literalized, and the point of his umbrella appears beside him. After all, if he indeed is located at the point on the map where it says "You Are Here," then whatever action takes place on the map "here" should take place in the territory represented by "here." However, this sort of identification of the map with the territory

HERMAN®

can only take place in the "map" of the cartoon itself; it cannot take place in the territory we take to be reality.

Let's look at another cartoon, from a strip named "Basil."

BASIL   **BY GERRY LANTS**

 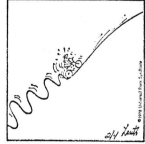

In the first frame Basil seems to be riding his bike up a hill. By saying this, we are taking the map (that is, the cartoon depiction made up of simple lines) as if it were an actual territory (that is, a person, a bike, a hill). The second frame reaffirms our first impression—that this is indeed a hill, and a steep one at that. However, in the third frame, the hill begins to act in a way we do not expect hills to act. Thus we are suddenly made aware that it is not a hill, that is, not an actual territory, but rather a diagonal line that we took to be a hill because a figure we took to be a person was able to ride an object we took to be a bike up it. In the final frame, in other words, the line begins to act like a line again, and thus the representative or maplike nature of the line that we allowed ourselves to forget reasserts itself as what it really is.

What this strip reminds us, like Kipling's suspenders, is that maps follow certain conventions or rules for depicting territories, rules that we conveniently forget so that we can maintain the illusion that they are actual. However, in order to understand how this illusion is created, and thus understand how fictional depictions work, we must remember that all we can know of the territory is the map. That is, all we can know of the events is what is filtered through the rhetorical devices and literary conventions that make the telling or relating of the story possible.

The central paradox that plagues the study of narrative fiction is that it is a linear form that must ultimately be read in a nonlinear way. The problem, says C. S. Lewis, author of the *Narnia Chronicles,* is that for stories to be stories, they must be a series of events; yet at the same time it must be understood that this series is only a net to catch something else. And this "something else," which, for want of a better word, we call *theme,* is something "that has no sequence in it, something other than a process and much more like a state or quality."

Whenever you are asked to read stories for a class, you probably do so in a straightforward, linear way: You scan the letters, words, sentences, and paragraphs, translating them into mental images—watching things happen, hearing people talk—trying desperately to get to the end of the story. And the "end" usually means merely the conclusion of a series of events that occur "just one damned thing after another." However, when you are asked what happened in the story and begin telling the events, one thing after another, a teacher may say, "No, that's not what I meant, that's not what I meant at all" and then spend the rest of the class period pointing out that something else "happened" in the story which you did not see. How can this be? Given a fairly attentive reader who can summarize the story events accurately, how can it be that he or she did not see the same things happen that the teacher did? The problem arises, of course, with the assumption that the story has "meaning." The problem is trying to find out how a mere series of events communicates meaning.

The primary way that any information is held together and communicated is by redundancy or repetition, particularly repetition with variations. *Redundancy* is the sending of more messages than are necessary to communicate information, and indeed, the repetition, often with variations, of the elements of the message is what creates the one essential characteristic for information to be communicated: a system or structure, that is, a pattern or a map.

Looking at narrative in terms of its systematic structure rather than merely in terms of the events it seems to recount is as old as Aristotle. However, this approach got its most influential boost when it was adopted by the Russian formalists in the 1920s and was then taken up by the structuralist movement of the 1960s and 1970s. According to the formalists, when approaching narrative fiction, one must make an initial distinction between the series of events that a writer takes as his or her subject matter and the specific structure that results when the writer presents the completed narrative to the reader. Whereas the first is merely the aggregate of the events in a causal-chronological order, the latter is the organization of the events in strategically justifiable ways that the Russian formalists called "motivation." Basically, what we must do is perceive the story as a narrated story dominated by rhetorical devices and thus all laid out at once, as if in space, rather than a series of events happening one after the other in time.

The earliest and still the clearest statement of this basic tactic of reading was made by the Canadian critic Northrop Frye in the 1960s: "In the direct experience of fiction, continuity is the center of our attention; our later memory, or what I call the possession of it, tends to become discontinuous. Our attention shifts from the sequence of incidents to another focus: a sense of what the work of fiction was all about, or what criticism usually calls its theme." However, by "theme," Frye does not mean a conceptual statement but rather what Aristotle meant by *dianoia,* the mythos or plot understood as a simultaneous unity. The elements of the plot are of interest not in relation to sequence or suspense but rather in relation to a structured presentation for a rhetorical purpose.

Often there is a direct relationship between the complexity of the ideas embodied in a story and the complexity of its rhetorical pattern of devices. Relatively simple ideas and conflicts can be illustrated or embodied in relatively straightforward narratives, whereas complex ideas and subtle conflicts frequently require more complex and subtle rhetorical devices. Stories that we sometimes find hard to understand or that seem to have no real point may be baffling because the conflicts or ideas they embody are, by their very nature, difficult to put into words or because we are not familiar with the narrative devices and conventions used to communicate them. On the other hand, although we may like stories that are relatively easy to understand, it may be that they are easy because the conflicts or ideas they embody are trivial and oversimplified or because the narrative devices they use are so familiar as to be clichéd or so false as to be unreal.

The following two stories have similar sets of characters and similar plot situations. Both involve a couple making a stop on a journey and discussing a disagreement that exists between them. However, the two stories are presented to us in quite different ways. "A Life to Live" depends mainly on a teller, whereas "Hills Like White Elephants" primarily depends on dialogue, as in a play or a film. In "Life" we know exactly what the conflict is and can state it directly; in "Hills" we are never told directly what the problem is and may find putting it into words difficult. Most readers find "A Life to Live" understandable and satisfying, whereas most readers find "Hills Like White Elephants" puzzling and disturbing. The discussion that follows makes some suggestions about the rhetorical devices that communicate the stories and how these devices are related to the conflicts and ideas embodied in the stories.

PATRICIA
CROSSMAN | *A Life to Live*

It was after midnight when they came into the diner.
They were so young I could hardly believe it when I saw the boy carrying a baby in one of those funny little tilted seats.

The girl looked pale and there was something about those blue shadows under her eyes that got to me. No one as young as she was should look so tired and drained.

"Is there a ladies' room?" she asked me across the counter.

"Sure," I said. "On the left."

"Thanks." She adjusted one of those quilted diaper bags over her shoulder and lifted the baby out of the carrying seat. It was a young baby—not more than three or four months old, and it had one of those comical-serious old-man faces babies sometimes have.

She handled him like she had been doing it all her life, but no words passed between her and the boy.

He sat on a counter and stared at himself in the mirror

"Going far?" I asked him.

"Brunswick."

"You in the navy?"

"My father-in-law is."

I pondered that for a while. Some people you can talk to just like you've known them all your life. But some, like this kid with his rangy bones and set shoulders, make you know they want to be left alone.

He took out a briar pipe.

When he had it lit, he clamped it in his teeth, trying so hard to look like a man, but that pipe made him look even younger.

Pretty soon she came back, with the baby looking fresh as a daisy, all cleaned up. But she hadn't combed her own hair or anything—and she seemed not to care.

I could see how pretty she was, even all rumpled like that, and I wondered if the boy minded that she wasn't fixing herself up at all.

She slid the baby into the leaning chair, and sat down on the stool next to the boy, with the baby on the counter between them.

"Two cups of coffee, please," the boy said. "You want anything else?" He looked toward her, but not at her.

"Yes," she said, looking at me, "would you do me a big favor? Would you warm the baby's bottle?"

I took the bottle and put it in a pan of water on the stove.

While it was heating, there wasn't a sound from behind me.

When I handed the bottle to her, our hands touched and it gave me a jolt to feel how cold and clammy her fingers were.

"How about a sandwich to go with that coffee?" I asked recklessly. "Bowl of soup? Turnover?"

"B.L.T.," the boy said, "on toast."

"Nothing for me," she said, testing the baby's milk on her wrist. I whistled over that bacon on the grill, kind of occupying myself so I wouldn't have to look at them.

Above the noise of the radio, I could hear the baby going for that bottle like there was no more where that came from, and when I turned around to give the boy his B.L.T., she had that little blanketed lump up over her shoulder, and, patting his back, she looked more like his sister instead of his mother.

When she sat him back in his chair, he reached for his father, and the boy put his sandwich down and broke off a little corner of toast and put it on the baby's tongue. He rolled it and gummed it, working hard, and finally the boy smiled.

"How's your sandwich?" I asked. "Kid seems to like it."

"It's okay. It's good." The boy held half out to the girl. "Go on, have some."

"Well, okay." She took it and raised her eyes and gave him a look—well I'm telling you I had to go off a few feet and start wiping the counter. Such a look as she gave him isn't decent someone else should see.

"No wonder," I said to myself, "they don't look at each other. This is very big trouble, when two kids are so much in love as they are, and he is driving her home to her father."

They began to talk in low voices.

I stood near the radio with my head tilted toward the twelve-thirty news, but even so, some of their words came through to me.

"Just what," she said, "do you think you'll prove?"

"I told you."

"You told me nothing. You told me nothing I can understand."

"Your father was right."

"Right? Right?"

"You are too young, just like he said—too young for all you've had to live through, and I'm not going to put you through any more."

Her girlish voice was flat with bitterness. "What am I—some kind of glass? I shouldn't *live*? I might not be up to it?"

"He let us get married when he found out about the baby—right? Okay. That was very rough. But we managed up to now. We ate; thanks to Tillman and Sons, Hardware, we ate. I made a living. Maybe selling nuts and bolts wasn't exactly big time, but the kid got his vitamins and his checkups. Okay?"

"Barney," her voice was a plea, "why is this any different?"

"Because up to now we had each other. Up to now I've been around to take care of you. How could you get along cooped up in that crummy flat alone? Besides, the city is no place to raise a kid."

"I want to be in our own place. I want to start a home."

"You'll be safe with your father. He'll take care of you."

"I can take care of myself—of Timmy. I got married, didn't I? I had him, didn't I?"

"I gotta do what's best for you—for both of you—and you've got to get off my back, Millie! When I get settled . . . well, maybe then you can come to me. Now, please . . . "

"All right! All right!" She got up, her face all flushed, and grabbed for the baby. But she screamed, instead. The baby was choking on that little crumb of toast; noiselessly choking, his hands and feet jerking at the air, and his face slowly turning purple.

The boy's face was a mask of horror.

But the girl grabbed that kid, tore him out of the chair and swung him by his heels. Then she drew off and cracked him between the shoulder blades with the flat of her free hand, once, twice, and then a slap I thought would break his little backbone, and the toast flew out of his wide-open mouth and he drew great, tearing chunks of air into his lungs and his face turned red.

She turned him right-side up and cried and cried, rocking and soothing, whispering and comforting and I stood around, helpless, not knowing what to do or say.

But the boy kept looking at her, and feeling the kid all over to be sure he was really alive, really okay. He looked at the girl hard, like he'd never really got a good look at her before. You could see he was really thinking, the way his lips were set. I found myself nodding, and I wasn't a bit surprised when they gathered up everything and went out to the car and headed back the way they'd come.

ERNEST
HEMINGWAY | *Hills Like White Elephants*

The hills across the valley of the Ebro were long and white. On this side there was no shade and no trees and the station was between two lines of rails in the sun. Close against the side of the station there was the warm shadow of the building and a curtain, made of strings of bamboo beads, hung across the open door into the bar, to keep out flies. The American and the girl with him sat at a table in the shade, outside the building. It was very hot and the express from Barcelona would come in forty minutes. It stopped at this junction for two minutes and went on to Madrid.

"What should we drink?" the girl asked. She had taken off her hat and put it on the table.

"It's pretty hot," the man said.

"Let's drink beer."

"Dos cervezas," the man said into the curtain.

"Big ones?" a woman asked from the doorway.

"Yes. Two big ones."

The woman brought two glasses of beer and two felt pads. She put the felt pads and the beer glasses on the table and looked at the man and the girl. The girl was looking off at the line of hills. They were white in the sun and the country was brown and dry.

"They look like white elephants," she said.

"I've never seen one," the man drank his beer.

"No, you wouldn't have."

"I might have," the man said. "Just because you say I wouldn't have doesn't prove anything."

The girl looked at the bead curtain. "They've painted something on it," she said. "What does it say?"

"Anis del Toro. It's a drink."

"Could we try it?"

The man called "Listen" through the curtain. The woman came out from the bar.

"Four reales."

"We want two Anis del Toro."

"With water?"

"Do you want it with water?"

"I don't know," the girl said. "Is it good with water?"

"It's all right."

"You want them with water?" asked the woman.

"Yes, with water."

"It tastes like licorice," the girl said and put the glass down.

"That's the way with everything."

"Yes," said the girl. "Everything tastes of licorice. Especially all the things you've waited so long for, like absinthe."

"Oh, cut it out."

"You started it," the girl said. "I was being amused. I was having a fine time."

"Well, let's try and have a fine time."

"All right. I was trying. I said the mountains looked like white elephants. Wasn't that bright?"

"That was bright."

"I wanted to try this new drink. That's all we do, isn't it—look at things and try new drinks?"

"I guess so."

The girl looked across at the hills.

"They're lovely hills," she said. "They don't really look like white elephants. I just meant the coloring of their skin through the trees."

"Should we have another drink?"

"All right."

The warm wind blew the bead curtain against the table.

"The beer's nice and cool," the man said.

"It's lovely," the girl said.

"It's really an awfully simple operation, Jig," the man said. "It's not really an operation at all."

The girl looked at the ground the table legs rested on.

"I know you wouldn't mind it, Jig. It's really not anything. It's just to let the air in."

The girl did not say anything.

"I'll go with you and I'll stay with you all the time. They just let the air in and then it's all perfectly natural."

"Then what will we do afterward?"

"We'll be fine afterward. Just like we were before."

"What makes you think so?"

"That's the only thing that bothers us. It's the only thing that's made us unhappy."

The girl looked at the bead curtain, put her hand out and took hold of two of the strings of beads.

"And you think then we'll be all right and be happy."

"I know we will. You don't have to be afraid. I've known lots of people that have done it."

"So have I," said the girl. "And afterward they were all so happy."

"Well," the man said, "if you don't want to you don't have to. I wouldn't have you do it if you didn't want to. But I know it's perfectly simple."

"And you really want to?"

"I think it's the best thing to do. But I don't want you to do it if you don't really want to."

"And if I do it you'll be happy and things will be like they were and you'll love me?"

"I love you now. You know I love you."

"I know. But if I do it, then it will be nice again if I say things are like white elephants, and you'll like it?"

"I'll love it. I love it now but I just can't think about it. You know how I get when I worry."

"If I do it you won't ever worry?"

"I won't worry about that because it's perfectly simple."

"Then I'll do it. Because I don't care about me."

"What do you mean?"

"I don't care about me"

"Well, I care about you."

"Oh, yes. But I don't care about me. And I'll do it and then everything will be fine."

"I don't want you to do it if you feel that way."

The girl stood up and walked to the end of the station. Across, on the other side, were fields of grain and trees along the banks of the Ebro. Far away, beyond the river, were mountains. The shadow of a cloud moved across the field of grain and she saw the river through the trees.

"And we could have all this," she said. "And we could have everything and every day we make it more impossible."

"What did you say?"

"I said we could have everything."

"We can have everything."

"No, we can't."

"We can have the whole world."

"No, we can't."

"We can go everywhere."

"No, we can't. It isn't ours any more."

"It's ours."

"No, it isn't. And once they take it away, you never get it back."

"But they haven't taken it away."

"We'll wait and see."

"Come on back in the shade," he said. "You mustn't feel that way."

"I don't feel any way," the girl said. "I just know things."

"I don't want you to do anything that you don't want to do——"

"Nor that isn't good for me," she said. "I know. Could we have another beer?"

"All right. But you've got to realize——"

"I realize," the girl said. "Can't we maybe stop talking?"

They sat down at the table and the girl looked across at the hills on the dry side of the valley and the man looked at her and at the table.

"You've got to realize," he said, "that I don't want you to do it if you don't want to. I'm perfectly willing to go through with it if it means anything to you."

"Doesn't it mean anything to you? We could get along."

"Of course it does. But I don't want anybody but you. I don't want any one else. And I know it's perfectly simple."

"Yes, you know it's perfectly simple."

"It's all right for you to say that, but I do know it."

"Would you do something for me now?"

"I'd do anything for you."

"Would you please please please please please please please stop talking?"

He did not say anything but looked at the bags against the wall of the station. There were labels on them from all the hotels where they had spent nights.

"But I don't want you to," he said, "I don't care anything about it."

"I'll scream," the girl said.

The woman came out through the curtains with two glasses of beer and put them down on the damp felt pads. "The train comes in five minutes," she said.

"What did she say?" asked the girl.

"That the train is coming in five minutes."

The girl smiled brightly at the woman, to thank her.

"I'd better take the bags over to the other side of the station," the man said. She smiled at him.

"All right. Then come back and we'll finish the beer."

He picked up the two heavy bags and carried them around the station to the other tracks. He looked up the tracks but could not see the train. Coming back, he walked through the barroom, where people waiting for the train were drinking. He drank an Anis at the bar and looked at the people. They were all waiting reasonably for the train. He went out through the bead curtain. She was sitting at the table and smiled at him.

"Do you feel better?" he asked.

"I feel fine," she said. "There's nothing wrong with me. I feel fine."

STUDYING SHORT FICTION: *"A Life to Live"* and *"Hills Like White Elephants"*

Before you begin reading the discussion of these two stories, respond to the following questions:

1. Which story did you enjoy the most? Why?
2. Which story do you think is the "best" story? Why?
3. Which story do you think is the hardest to read? Why?
4. Did you have to read one story more than once? If so, why?
5. What is your impression of the characters in the two stories?
6. What problems do the characters have in the two stories?
7. What is your opinion of the way the problems are solved?
8. What do you think is the purpose or point of the two stories?

NARRATION AND DRAMA

One of the first things you might notice about the two stories is that "A Life to Live" has an identifiable teller, whereas "Hills Like White Elephants" does not. We are not sure who tells the story "Hills Like White Elephants," for it seems to be presented to us as it is happening, as a play or film might be presented. Thus we can say that "A Life to Live" is primarily "narrated," whereas "Hills Like White Elephants" is primarily "dramatized."

However, if we look more closely, we can see that there is some dramatization in "A Life to Live." As the narrator relates the characters saying things, we "hear" them as if we were there when the event took place; moreover, he relates events in a dramatic way so that we seem to see the events take place rather than merely hear him tell about them. Moreover, there is some narration in "Hills Like White Elephants." For example, in the first paragraph a voice describes a scene, and in the next-to-last paragraph a voice describes an action. There are other places where we feel that someone is telling this story, even though he or she is not in the story, nor can we see the teller.

"A Life to Live" AS SIMPLE NARRATIVE

If you are like most students, you probably liked the story "A Life to Live" better than you liked "Hills Like White Elephants." And there are a number of reasons why "Life" is appealing and a number of reasons why "Hills" is not. "A Life to Live" seems to be a simple little episode involving characters with whom we can identify in a situation that is easy to understand. Moreover, the conflict, which is, of course, what makes a story a story rather than merely a random and meaningless series of events, is easy to determine. The two characters are young and with their first child; the boy thinks his wife is too young to take care of the baby by herself; she, on the other hand, is convinced that she is mature and competent enough to be responsible for the baby.

We suspect, from watching a lot of television, that such a conflict will probably be resolved by the young wife proving to the husband that she is capable of taking care of the baby. And, indeed, our expectations are fulfilled. The boy is convinced; he decides not to make his wife stay with her parents, and the story ends with the couple going back home again. Television has taught us that no problem is so complex that it cannot be resolved within a thirty-minute episode. Thus we complete the story pleased that our expectations have been fulfilled, that the child was saved, that the girl exonerated herself, that the boy learned his lesson, and that everything ends happily. If we ask ourselves why the story is told by the man who runs the diner, there does not seem to be any clear or necessary reason except that "somebody had to tell it." Perhaps he is meant to reflect our superior knowledge, for at the end we too may find ourselves nodding knowingly as he does, not a bit surprised when the two gather up their stuff and head back the way they came.

"Hills Like White Elephants" AS NARRATIVE FILM

We may not feel quite so pleased and smug when we finish reading "Hills Like White Elephants." Again, we are presented with a couple on a journey who have stopped for a time along the way. We are also made aware that there is some conflict between them; however, we may not be quite so sure what the conflict is. It certainly is neither mentioned explicitly nor described, as it is in "A Life to Live." Moreover, when we finish the story, we are not sure that the conflict, whatever it was, has been resolved in any way. This may not seem like a story at all, but rather an inconclusive little episode with no meaning, no point, no purpose. We are puzzled, confused, maybe even a little resentful. Television has not prepared us to read a story like this one.

In fact, there has been a film version of this story, a short film that appeared on the cable channel HBO in 1990. It was directed by the well-known director Tony Richardson; the screenplay was written by Joan Didion and John Gregory Dunn, a husband-and-wife writing team of high renown; and it starred two of the most familiar and competent actors of the 1980s and 1990s — Melanie Griffith and James Woods. A brief discussion of the way the screenwriters and director deal with some of the problems that we had reading the story may help us see how film often differs from written fiction.

First of all, the fact that the woman is pregnant is made clear in the film immediately when she gets off the train, for she says she is going to be sick and runs into the station to the restroom. The waitress smiles knowingly. When the woman comes out of the restroom, the waitress gives her something to drink to make her feel better and refuses to take payment for it, saying she has six children of her own.

The pregnancy as the source of the conflict is made emphatic when the man playfully talks about having several wives and children, and the woman responds bitterly, "You wouldn't have any children." Moreover, a bit later when he first mentions the operation as "letting the air in," she says, "Everything has another name. . . . It's not a baby, it's tissue." However, the basic difference between the film and the story is that in the film the conflict between the couple is made explicit by dialogue in which she says she wants a home and he indicates that he is not domestic, that he is a writer and wants to remain on the move. For example, when she says that all we do is try new drinks and look at things, he insists that he does more than just look at things, that he writes it all down. In fact, his career as a writer becomes the most important cause of the conflict in the film.

HE: As far as I know I only have one life to live, and by God, I'm going to live it where it interests me. I have no romantic feelings about home or family or any other baggage.

The fact that he is a writer, a detail in the film that does not exist in the original story, then becomes an important part of the plot. She talks about a past event in their lives about which he wrote a story, but he says it was not exactly her in the story.

SHE: It's never exactly me in the story. It won't be exactly me in the story when you write about this one.

HE: I don't want to write a story about this. (*We hear the train whistle coming closer.*)

SHE: But you will. And in the story there will be a man, someone like you, and a woman who is not exactly me, and the woman will be sitting here and the man will be standing there, and the train will be coming. And she'll stand up and they'll get on the train, and they'll both know that it's not going to make any difference whether she does it or she doesn't do it.

HE: Stop it.

SHE: And I'll be wherever I am and I'll read this story by you.

HE: You'll be where I am.

SHE: And I'll put it down and I won't show it to whoever I'm with.

HE: You'll be with me.

However, as she begins to cry and says she will remember all the events of their life together, he can only say, "It's perfectly simple." When the train arrives, we see the two looking at each other saying nothing; finally, we see and hear the train bell ringing before we cut to the credits.

This brief description of the material created especially for the film should make clear that film, the most popular narrative medium in modern society, the one with which we are probably the most familiar, often needs to make motivation more emphatic and conflict more explicit than it is in serious narrative fiction. The filmmakers make several changes to shift the conflict from the puzzling and ambiguous one suggested in the story to the more emphatic conflict of the writer's life versus the domestic life.

"Hills Like White Elephants": THE CONFLICT

Now let us look at the story "Hills Like White Elephants" and try to determine what makes it "hard to read" or "difficult to understand" and why. In other words, let us look at what makes the story different from popular fiction such as "A Life to Live" or narrative film such as Tony Richardson's film—both forms that we have learned to "read" rather easily because they frequently simplify conflict and because we are so often exposed to them. What are the techniques, conventions, and rhetorical devices of "Hills Like White Elephants" we must be aware of in order to be able to understand the story?

Let us begin with the conflict. There really does not seem to be a conflict until the girl says the hills look like white elephants and the man says he has never seen one. But this seems like a simple disagreement—not a crucial argument. We begin to suspect that there is something more lying behind the disagreement about the hills when the girl makes another comparison: "Everything tastes of licorice. Especially all the things you've waited so long for, like absinthe." The man responds to this with "Oh, cut it out," and she in turn says "You started it." From this point on, everything in the story revolves around their argument.

The argument centers on something designated by the impersonal pronoun *it*. The man says such things as the following:

"It's not really anything."

"It's perfectly natural."

"It's perfectly simple."

"It's an awfully simple operation. . . . It's not really an operation at all."

The girl's references to *it* are:

"If I do it you'll be happy and things will be like they were and you'll love me."

"If I do it you won't ever worry."

"Then I'll do it. Because I don't care about it."

Although we begin to realize that these *its* refer to the abortion the man wants the girl to have, there are other references to *it* that seem different:

The man says at one point, "It's the only thing that's made us unhappy." And later he says, "I'm perfectly willing to go through with it if it means anything to you." To which she responds, "Doesn't it mean anything to you? We could get along." In these cases, *it* is not a reference to the abortion but to the pregnancy, since for the man they both mean the same thing. One other place where the reference to *it* is left vague is when the girl walks to the end of the station and looks across the river and says, "And we could have everything and every day we make it more impossible." When the man says "We can have the whole world," she says "It isn't ours any more." Then she says: "Once they take it away, you never get it back." This *it* refers to something less concrete than either the pregnancy or the abortion, something intangible that is irreclaimable because of the conflict.

"Hills Like White Elephants": IN SPACE AND TIME

Now to determine what the *it* means to the characters in the story and why it is never specified but always left vague and ambiguous. All stories exist both in space and in time. However, the difference between the way stories exist in space and time and the way other things exist in space and time is that stories have a rhetorical existence, not merely a physical one. In other words, the way the story exists in space and time has a rhetorical purpose; it is meant to communicate something. Consequently, the story depends on a number of literary and rhetorical conventions.

One of the most powerful conventions of short fiction is the convention of selection of details. Every story is made up of two kinds of details—those realistically motivated details that exist merely to give the illusion of hard, concrete reality and those that are mentioned because the teller has a rhetorical purpose for mentioning them, such as Kipling's repeated mention of the suspenders in "How the Whale Got His Throat." Edgar Allan Poe suggested in the earliest discussion of the short story in American literature that the writer should not use a single word that was not carefully chosen to contribute to the overall purpose or effect that the writer had in writing the story. Anton Chekhov, the great Russian author, once advised a young writer that if he described a gun hanging on a wall on the first page of a story, then that gun should be fired before the end of the story.

We can think of details in a story that merely give us a sense of actuality as being relatively "loose" and even dispensable, or at least changeable. Details in the story that are relevant to its meaning or overall rhetorical effect we can think of as being relatively "bound" to the story, that is, intrinsic and not easily detachable or changeable. Trying to determine which details in a story are "loose" and which are "bound" is one of the most important skills for reading stories effectively. One basic way we can determine which details are bound and which are loose is by applying the principle of redundancy or repetition: If a certain detail or kind of detail is mentioned more than once or twice in a story, we might suspect that it is relevant in some way.

Let's first look at the time frame of "Hills Like White Elephants." The couple are on their way to Madrid, Spain. They have stopped at a junction and are awaiting an express connection from Barcelona, which, we are told, will arrive in forty minutes and stop there for only two minutes. Thus we have a situation explicitly cut off from the ordinary flow of time; the two people are enclosed between the time they got off one train and the time they will get on another. On the first reading of this story, the fact that the train will arrive from Barcelona in forty minutes may seem merely a "loose" realistic detail. However, at the end of the story the time is mentioned again when the waitress comes out and says that the train will arrive in five minutes.

This means that the events of the story we have just read take place in a time span of thirty-five minutes. However, we know that it only took about ten to fifteen minutes to read the story. How do we account for this discrepancy? After all, if the author had not wanted us to be concerned with the time element, he did not have to mention the time frame both at the beginning and at the end of the story. Moreover, if he had not wanted us to see the disparity between the time of the events in the story and the time of the reading of the story, then he could have made the time span of the events more closely match the time span of the reading; either he could have made the train arrive in fifteen minutes instead of forty minutes or he could have made the story longer.

The fact that there is a fifteen- to twenty-minute discrepancy between the announced span of the events and the time of the reading should lead us to ask what happened to those extra twenty minutes. The only answer is that they must be in the blank spaces in between the lines of the story, that is, points in the story when the characters are not saying anything. Our realization that there are more blank spaces in the time span of the story than spoken dialogue should make us more aware of the basic problem that we began with—that is, that the story is about something that is never explicitly mentioned, but only hinted at and referred to, if at all, by the impersonal pronoun *it*. These two elements—the references to *it* and the many blank spaces or silences inherent in the story—seem to be related. What we must examine now is *why* the couple do not speak of their problem explicitly and *why* there are so many silences, or blank spaces, in the story.

Perhaps a look at how the story exists spatially may provide further understanding. The author makes the spatial reality of the story as explicit as he does the temporal reality. The first paragraph locates the couple at a station situated between two lines of rails. One line of rails is going the way the couple have come, whereas the other is going in the direction they are heading; they are at a junction. If we make the assumption that this spatial location is a "bound motif" or idea, since it is made so emphatic, then we might suspect that the spatial location is meant to communicate the psychological location of the couple as well as their physical one. The spatial situation of the rails suggests where they have been (much as the labels on their luggage suggest all the hotels where they have stayed), as well as where they are going, which, of course, is precisely what is at issue here. She wishes to go one way; he wishes to go another.

There is a further indication of their physical location that also may be meaningful—they are in a valley. On this side there are hills that are long and white, and the country is brown and dry with no trees. Later on in the story when the girl gets up and walks to the end of the station, she looks toward the "other side" of the valley, where there are fields of grain and trees along the banks of the river. This is the scenery she looks at when she says, "And we could have all this. . . . And we could have everything and every day we make it more impossible."

"Hills Like White Elephants":
MEANING AS METAPHOR

However, as soon as we become aware of the valley with the barren hills on this side and the green fields on the other side, we become involved with another element of the story that is purely rhetorical. Let us look at the passage where the conflict is first announced. Since it also is the passage that gives the story its title, we might suspect that it is significant, for it is another convention of stories that titles are carefully chosen to serve as a cue to the story to come.

The girl says the hills look like white elephants, to which the man says he has never seen one, that is, a white elephant. Perhaps the girl has never seen one either, but that is not the reason she makes the comparison. On the one hand, from her perspective, it is an idle remark, probably the kind of remark she has made many times in the past in their travels as they looked around at the landscape and commented on it. A bit later she says, "That's all we do, isn't it—look at things and try new drinks?"

What makes this more than an idle remark in this story, however, is the fact that the man does not respond to it in the way he probably did in the past. Instead of sharing something with her, he is focused on himself and his concern with the pregnancy. She says later, "If I do it, then it will be nice again if I say things are like white elephants and you'll like it?" He says, "I'll love it. I love it now but I just can't think about it. You know how I get when I worry."

This junction in the relationship, indicated by the spatial location of the railway junction, is related to the time emphasis in the story we have already noted, in which there are many silences in their conversation. When two people are "at one" with each other and there is no sense of conflict, then they can say things to each other easily, can make trivial remarks that do not seem trivial, can make silly comments with the full confidence that the remarks will be appreciated by the other. However, if there comes a time in the relationship when this sense of union is broken, it is not so easy to talk without arguing. Trivial remarks remain just that—trivial; silly remarks that may have been simple banter before now fall flat. It is as though there is nothing to say and no point in talking about it—something the girl is quite aware of when she says, "Would you please please please please please please please stop talking?" This is why there are so many silences in the story, why the story communicates more by what is not said than by what is said.

However, there is one more important aspect about the way things are communicated or not communicated in this story—the fact that the girl often talks in metaphors, whereas the man argues by reason. First, she says the hills look like white elephants. Then she says that everything tastes like licorice. . . . like absinthe. Since these are the two main metaphors in the story, the two main points when things are expressed in terms of other things, we might legitimately ask what they mean. The girl definitely has some meaning in mind with the reference to licorice and absinthe, for she says, "Everything tastes of licorice. Especially all the things you've waited so long for, like absinthe." Licorice is used as a candy, for it has a sweet taste, but it is also used as a medicine, and it has a definite bitter taste. The girl makes this more emphatic by mentioning the liqueur absinthe, which, even though it is sweet, has a bitter taste of wormwood. We know that the pregnancy has this same bittersweet effect, for even as it suggests their union, it suggests their separation.

Although the girl may not be making a conscious analogy to the white elephants, the way she does with the licorice comparison, the basic meaning of this central metaphor is similar. A white elephant is, in some Eastern cultures, a holy animal, venerated, but it is useless for any practical purpose. Thus, when people refer to an object as a "white elephant" or when they have a "white elephant" sale, they are referring to something that is both valuable and useless at the same time, for example, that expensive but ugly vase that your great Aunt Sally gave you for a present. The unnamed *it* in the story is, like the taste of licorice and a white elephant, valuable and sweet but also worthless and bitter.

Finally, there is the metaphor of the two sides of the valley, this side which is dry and barren and the other side, the one they cannot have, which is a fertile field of grain with trees along the banks of the river. The metaphor seems quite clear, for it represents what the girl at least sees as the two sides of the conflict—fertility versus barrenness. The fact that she looks across the river to the green and fertile side and says "And we could have all this" seems to indicate her conscious awareness of the metaphor.

The basic situation in the story, although it seems puzzling at first, can now be seen in all its complexity. The girl wants to have the baby; the man does not. It is more than this, however. The girl wants the man to *want* to have the baby. He, on the other hand, wants her to *want* to have the operation. He says he does not want her to do it if she does not want to, but the point is that he wants her to want to. In such a situation as this, it is pointless to talk about it. It certainly is pointless to argue. He uses logic, providing several reasons she should have the operation. She can only speak from emotion, using not logic but metaphor, metaphor with which he can no longer sympathetically identify.

At the end of the story, when the arrival of the train is announced, the man picks up the bags and carries them across the station to the other tracks; as he stops to buy another drink, a drink that tastes like licorice, or wormwood, he looks at the people waiting "reasonably" for the train, for he does not understand why she is not "reasonable." However, there is no way to argue reasonably about the conflict at the center of the story. Whatever sense of union the couple once had is gone, and as the girl says, once it is gone, one cannot get it back. Although we know that the two people will be going in

Resolution as much as there can be

the same physical direction at the end of the story, we feel that this story has marked a junction in which they will be going in opposite emotional directions.

"You Must Not Forget the Suspenders, Best Beloved"

What this discussion is meant to illustrate is that in order to understand the meaning of a story, we must analyze the structure of rhetorical devices that make up the story. Whereas a first reading of the story merely to find out "what happens next" may leave us confused and resentful because the nature of the conflict and the meaning of the story are not clear, a second reading focusing on the teller's control of the story's rhetorical devices can make that meaning clear. As you read the stories in this collection, remember the advice of Kipling, "You must *not* forget the suspenders, Best Beloved."

<table>
<tr><td>PART
ONE</td><td><h1>The World
of Ordinary
Reality</h1></td></tr>
</table>

In spite of the title of this section, the kind of reality presented in fiction, no matter how familiar and apparently real it may seem, is never quite ordinary. Short fictions especially seldom focus on a usual day, but rather a particular day when things get complicated and the everyday routine is broken up. In fact the word *plot,* which we often use to refer to the series of events in a story, comes from an earlier word *complot,* which in turn comes from the Latin word *complicare,* which means "to complicate." For example, Hemingway's "Hills Like White Elephants" does not focus on the kind of routine stopover the couple in the story has made many times before; rather it centers on a point in time and space when a conflict in their relationship develops and a crisis is reached. Indeed, "conflict" and "crisis" are key concepts for understanding what causes "complication" and therefore plot in fiction.

The difference between a series of events in fiction and a series of events in "real" life is that events in fiction are "directed" toward some "end," whereas events in life often "just happen."

Granted, events in life sometimes create a conflict and initiate a crisis, but events in life do not constitute a plot, that is, unless someone tells a story about them in which the events are meaningfully motivated and move toward some meaningful end.

When events move along as they usually do in our lives, we do not ask why they happen; however, when something unusual occurs, something that makes it difficult to go on the way we have been going, we often ask "Why did that happen?" And when we start asking about what makes things happen, we often look for "intention." In real life when events occur that seem to have no discernible cause, we may attribute them either to a power beyond our knowledge or to accident. However, in fiction, there is no such thing as an accident, because in fiction, there is no question that a higher power—the author—caused things to happen. Everything in fiction thus is "motivated" and can be said to have "intention." No matter how much a fiction may seem to be "realistic"—a term usually used to mean that the story features "as-if-real" characters involved in events that seem to take place in an "as-if-real" world—fiction is never identical to life. Because fiction's basic intention is to be "meaningful," we cannot say about an event in fiction, "it just happened."

Because fictions must give some illusion of reality, even though they must always have an intentional pattern of meaning, individual stories may vary as to whether the illusion of reality or the intentional pattern is most emphasized. For example, although "The Girls in Their Summer Dresses" and "Thief" are both about a cultural conflict between the sexual attitudes of males and females, one seems to develop naturally or "realistically," whereas the other seems more controlled by the patterned intention to illustrate a concept. It seems very plausible in "The Girls in Their Summer Dresses" that a young couple would take a walk and that the man, as he usually does, would look at other women; it also seems plausible, as well as a familiar short story convention, that on this day a conflict which has lain dormant develops and so a crisis results.

However, in the story "Thief," is it plausible that two women in an airport would set up a man in this flawless way? Do they do it often? Is this the first time they do it? How is it that the dark-haired woman is so expert a pickpocket that she can take the man's wallet without his knowing it? These kinds of questions do not bother us, for we respond to the story as the illustration of female retaliation against sexist male attitudes toward women; a pleasing pattern overshadows our demand for plausibility. Moreover, the "ends" of each of the two stories differ. Whereas in "The Girls in Their Summer Dresses" the ending is inconclusive and vague, as it might be in real life, in "Thief" the ending may give us a sense of satisfaction that "poetic justice" has been done—another indication that the intentional pattern of the story dominates over the plausible rendering of real life.

"The Cop and the Anthem," "The Cask of Amontillado," "Désirée's Baby," and "Tennessee's Partner" also seem to be governed more by the patterned nature of the story than by the ragged nature of ordinary reality.

Indeed, all four stories involve characters that seem less "real" than illustrative, and all four seem based on the rhetorical principle of irony rather than on the events of everyday life. "The Overcoat," "A Summer Tragedy," "Dead Men's Path," "The Train from Rhodesia," and "Just Lather, That's All" are all based on relatively clear-cut conflicts, but they represent a range from the relatively real to the relatively patterned.

Anton Chekhov, Katherine Mansfield, James Joyce, and Sherwood Anderson are significant figures in the transition from the kind of patterned story typical of the nineteenth century to a seemingly more realistic story in the twentieth century. This shift was initially signaled by Chekhov, who wrote stories that many called "slices of life." Compare, for example, the story "Misery" by Chekhov and the story "The Cop and the Anthem" by O. Henry to see the difference between a story motivated by rhetorical pattern and one motivated by the need to express human feeling.

However, in spite of the fact that the two stories by Chekhov seem merely inconclusive little anecdotes about real life, both are still motivated by meaning; it is just that instead of allowing the pattern of irony or poetic justice to dominate, as O. Henry does, Chekhov tries to embody the subtle problem of the inexpressibility of human emotion. Katherine Mansfield, who was strongly influenced by Chekhov, also is less interested in creating a patterned story than in this problem of the inexpressibility of feeling. James Joyce follows in this "new tradition" of the short story by creating stories that seem so little patterned and that end so inconclusively that we are not sure whether they are stories at all. We know the boy has discovered something in "Araby," but we are not quite sure what the discovery is or what caused it.

In all the stories that follow in this section, although characters, events, and objects seem primarily to be "as if real," at the same time they also owe their existence to the force of meaningful pattern. Learning ways to understand what stories mean and how they use language and pattern to create meaning is the purpose of this book. Reading stories in a literature class is not the same as reading stories in the airport as you wait for your plane. In the latter case, you may be just filling up time in as entertaining a way as possible. The purpose of a literature class is to understand what stories are about and what makes them work, and one of the best methods for understanding a story is to write an analysis of it.

Writing about stories in a literature class is often more formal than simply telling a friend about a movie you saw last night. If someone asks you about a movie you saw and you begin telling step by step what happened in the film, your listener is likely to get bored and restless. The friend was not really asking what happened in the movie, but asking rather what you thought about it, what held it together, what worked or did not work in it, and where it fits within the category of movies you have seen in the past.

Similarly, when teachers ask you to write a paper about a story, they are usually not interested in a blow-by-blow account of the events; the weakest kind of paper you can write is a mere summary of the plot. What the teacher is usually after is not summary but analysis. That term means you have looked at this object called a story, perceived that it is a meaningful object, understood that is made up of various parts that fit together to make it a meaningful object, and have some idea of what that meaning is and how it is created. The following is an analysis of the story "The Loan" by Bernard Malamud. It is not presented as the only possible analysis of the story, nor even the best possible analysis, but rather as an example of the kinds of details one might examine in a story and might wish to discuss, as well as the kind of structure such an analysis might follow.

METAPHOR AND MORALITY
IN MALAMUD'S *"The Loan"*

Bernard Malamud's story "The Loan" begins the way many stories do—with an event that breaks up the everyday routine of life. In this case the event is the arrival of the character Kobotsky, who makes a demand upon Lieb the baker and thus creates a conflict between Lieb and his wife Bessie. Basically, the story has to do with the state of misery, since all the characters in the story indicate they have suffered. Lieb's arrival announces this idea, for his "face glittered with misery. If suffering had marked him, he no longer sought to conceal the sign; the shining was his own—him—now."

However, whereas Kobotsky is gaunt and ghostly, Lieb looks like a ghost only because of the flour on his face. He is prosperous because of misery. "One day, out of misery, he had wept into the dough. Thereafter his bread was such it brought customers in from everywhere." The fact that the characters in the story are all Jewish suggests that the Jewish culture itself is relevant here. Lieb's explanation echoes the Psalmist crying out in Psalm 80:5 of the Old Testament about the misery of the Jews: "Thou feedest them with the bread of tears; and givest them tears to drink in great measure."

The arrival of Kobotsky frightens Bessie, for she knows from her own experience of suffering that such a man is a threat because of the irresistibility of his sorrow. When Kobotsky finally asks Lieb for the two-hundred-dollar loan, Lieb stares at Kobotsky's crippled hands and thinks of his own eyes cloudy with cataracts. Lieb feels united with him because of their age as well as because of their carefree youth in the past. Bessie, however, is not so united with Kobotsky's past. A second wife, she is not even united with Lieb's past, and she therefore firmly refuses to allow the loan.

After Bessie and Lieb have argued bitterly—Bessie worrying about her own future security and Lieb saying that his money is worth nothing if he cannot share it with a friend—Kobotsky prepares to leave, but not before he makes his sinning manifest. Revealing that he wants the loan to buy a tombstone for his dead wife, he recounts his five years of misery. Even Bessie is affected, and Lieb thinks he has won and they will all sit down at the table and eat together. However, Bessie recites her own tale of affliction, that, coming as it does on the heels of Kobotsky's story, is almost comic in the extreme way it surpasses it. With her tale, the game is up. Both Lieb and Kobotsky realize that as Kobotsky holds his hands over his ears, and Lieb, having heard the story many times before, munches resignedly on a piece of bread.

However, at this moment, Bessie, the mock tears streaming down her face, screeches and runs to throw open the oven door. The mood of the story then changes with a significant metaphor: "A cloud of smoke billowed out at her. The loaves in the trays were blackened bricks—charred corpses." This final image completes the story's pattern and extends it in a complex way. It is, of course, the culmination of all the references to bread throughout the story. The bread of tears that became the bread of life for Lieb now has become the bread of death for Kobotsky—the death of his hope for the loan. Yet it is also an extension of the broad Jewish experience of misery—the gas ovens of the Nazi persecution and the charred corpses of millions of Jews. It recalls part of Bessie's story, that her brother sacrificed himself and his family in Hitler's incinerators to allow her to come to America and have a new life. Finally, it recalls the image of Kobotsky himself—the gaunt ghost or corpse searching for the money to buy a stone for the corpse of his wife.

All of these implications of the "charred corpses" create a moral dilemma for the reader that reflects the moral dilemma of the characters within the story. Although misery can give one the capacity to understand and sympathize with the sorrow of others as it does Lieb, it can also make someone become burned-out and hard like Bessie—can turn someone into the brick-hard corpse she has become. However, even as readers are tempted to judge Bessie harshly for her lack of compassion, they may find it difficult to do so; for what her choice amounts to is a decision to refuse to grant the money for the sake of the dead wife and keep it for the sake of the living one. Recognizing this unresolvable moral situation—a situation that remembrance of their youthful and happy past cannot erase—the two men can do nothing more. "Kobotsky and the baker embraced and sighed over their lost youth. They pressed mouths together and parted forever."

COMMENT

This essay is about 800 words long, roughly the equivalent of 3 typewritten pages. It follows certain basic steps in presenting one reader's understanding of both what the story says and how it says it.

Paragraphs one and two state the thesis or main idea of the story that the essay will try to explain—the theme of the complex nature of misery and its relation in this particular story to the Jewish cultural experience of misery.

Paragraphs three and four discuss the basic conflict in the story, especially as it concerns the effect of the past on the present.

Paragraph five discusses the central metaphoric event of the story, the burning of the bread.

Paragraph six explains how the metaphor of the bread of tears illustrates the central moral dilemma of the story.

BERNARD
MALAMUD | *The Loan*

The sweet, the heady smell of Lieb's white bread drew customers in droves long before the loaves were baked. Alert behind the counter, Bessie, Lieb's second wife, discerned a stranger among them, a frail, gnarled man with a hard hat who hung, disjointed, at the edge of the crowd. Though the stranger looked harmless enough among the aggressive purchasers of baked goods, she was at once concerned. Her glance questioned him but he signaled with a deprecatory nod of his hatted head that he would wait—glad to (forever)—though his face glittered with misery. If suffering had marked him, he no longer sought to conceal the sign; the shining was his own—him—now. So he frightened Bessie.

She made quick hash of the customers, and when they, after her annihilating service, were gone, she returned him her stare.

He tipped his hat. "Pardon me—Kobotsky. Is Lieb the baker here?"

"Who Kobotsky?"

"An old friend"—frightening her further.

"From where?"

"From long ago."

"What do you want to see him?"

The question insulted, so Kobotsky was reluctant to say.

As if drawn into the shop by the magic of a voice, the baker, shirtless, appeared from the rear. His pink, fleshy arms had been deep in dough. For a hat he wore jauntily a flour-covered brown paper sack. His peering glasses were dusty with flour, and the inquisitive face white with it so that he resembled a paunchy ghost; but the ghost, through the glasses, was Kobotsky, not he.

"Kobotsky," the baker cried almost with a sob, for it was so many years gone Kobotsky reminded him of, when they were both at least young, and circumstances were—ah, different. Unable, for sentimental reasons, to refrain from smarting tears, he jabbed them away with a thrust of the hand.

Kobotsky removed his hat—he had grown all but bald where Lieb was gray—and patted his flushed forehead with an immaculate handkerchief.

Lieb sprang forward with a stool. "Sit, Kobotsky."

"Not here," Bessie murmured.

"Customers," she explained to Kobotsky. "Soon comes the supper rush."

"Better in the back," nodded Kobotsky.

So that was where they went, happier for the privacy. But it happened that no customers came so Bessie went in to hear.

Kobotsky sat enthroned on a tall stool in a corner of the room, stoop-shouldered, his black coat and hat on, the stiff, gray-veined hands drooping over thin thighs. Lieb, peering through full moons, eased his bones on a flour sack. Bessie lent an attentive ear, but the visitor was dumb. Embarrassed, Lieb did the talking; ah, of old times. The world was new. We were, Kobotsky, young. Do you remember how both together, immigrants out of steerage, we registered in night school?

"Haben, hatte, gehabt." He cackled at the sound of it.

No word from the gaunt one on the stool. Bessie fluttered around an impatient duster. She shot a glance into the shop: empty.

Lieb, acting the life of the party, recited, to cheer his friend: " 'Come,' said the wind to the trees one day, 'Come over the meadow with me and play.' Remember, Kobotsky?"

Bessie sniffed aloud. "Lieb, the bread!"

The baker bounced up, strode over to the gas oven and pulled one of the tiered doors down. Just in time he yanked out the trays of brown breads in hot pans, and set them on the tin-top worktable.

Bessie clucked at the narrow escape.

Lieb peered into the shop. "Customers," he said triumphantly. Flushed, she went in. Kobotsky, with wetted lips, watched her go. Lieb set to work molding the risen dough in a bowl into two trays of pans. Soon the bread was baking, but Bessie was back.

The honey odor of the new loaves distracted Kobotsky. He breathed the sweet fragrance as if this were the first air he was tasting, and even beat his fist against his chest at the delicious smell.

"Oh, my God," he all but wept. "Wonderful."

"With tears," Lieb said humbly, pointing to the large pot of dough.

Kobotsky nodded.

For thirty years, the baker explained, he was never with a penny to his name. One day, out of misery, he had wept into the dough. Thereafter his bread was such it brought customers in from everywhere.

"My cakes they don't like so much, but my bread and rolls they run miles to buy."

Kobotsky blew his nose, then peeked into the shop: three customers.

"Lieb"—a whisper.

Despite himself the baker stiffened.

The visitor's eyes swept back to Bessie out front, then, under raised brows, questioned the baker.

Lieb, however, remained mute.

Kobotsky coughed clear his throat. "Lieb, I need two hundred dollars." His voice broke.

Lieb slowly sank onto the sack. He knew—had known. From the minute of Kobotsky's appearance he had weighed in his thoughts the possibility of this against the remembrance of the lost and bitter hundred, fifteen years ago. Kobotsky swore he had repaid it, Lieb said no. Afterwards a broken friendship. It took years to blot out of the system the memoried outrage.

Kobotsky bowed his head.

At least admit you were wrong, Lieb thought, waiting a cruelly long time.

Kobotsky stared at his crippled hands. Once a cutter of furs, driven by arthritis out of the business.

Lieb gazed too. The button of a truss bit into his belly. Both eyes were cloudy with cataracts. Though the doctor swore he would see after the operation, he feared otherwise.

He sighed. The wrong was in the past. Forgiven: forgiven at the dim sight of him.

"For myself, positively, but she"—Lieb nodded towards the shop—"is a second wife. Everything is in her name." He held up empty hands.

Kobotsky's eyes were shut.

"But I will ask her—" Lieb looked doubtful.

"My wife needs—"

The baker raised a palm. "Don't speak."

"Tell her—"

"Leave it to me."

He seized the broom and circled the room, raising clouds of white dust.

When Bessie, breathless, got back she threw one look at them, and with tightened lips, waited adamant.

Lieb hastily scoured the pots in the iron sink, stored the bread pans under the table and stacked the fragrant loaves. He put one eye to the slot of the oven: baking, all baking.

Facing Bessie, he broke into a sweat so hot it momentarily stunned him.

Kobotsky squirmed atop the stool.

"Bessie," said the baker at last, "this is my old friend."

She nodded gravely.

Kobotsky lifted his hat.

"His mother—God bless her—gave me many times a plate hot soup. Also when I came to this country, for years I ate at his table. His wife is a very fine person—Dora—you will someday meet her—"

Kobotsky softly groaned.

"So why I didn't meet her yet?" Bessie said, after a dozen years, still jealous of the first wife's prerogatives.

"You will."

"Why didn't I?"

"Because I didn't see her myself fifteen years," Lieb admitted.

"Why not?" she pounced.

Lieb paused. "A mistake."

Kobotsky turned away.

"My fault," said Lieb

"Because you never go any place," Bessie spat out. "Because you live always in the shop. Because it means nothing to you to have friends."

Lieb solemnly agreed.

"Now she is sick," he announced. "The doctor must operate. This will cost two hundred dollars. I promised Kobotsky—"

Bessie screamed.

Hat in hand, Kobotsky got off the stool.

Pressing a palm to her bosom, Bessie lifted her arm to her eyes. She tottered. They both ran forward to catch her but she did not fall. Kobotsky retreated quickly to the stool and Lieb returned to the sink.

Bessie, her face like the inside of a loaf, quietly addressed the visitor. "I have pity for your wife but we can't help you. I am sorry, Mr. Kobotsky, we are poor people, we don't have the money."

"A mistake," Lieb cried, enraged.

Bessie strode over to the shelf and tore out a bill box. She dumped its contents on the table, the papers flying everywhere.

"Bills," she shouted.

Kobotsky hunched his shoulders.

"Bessie, we have in the bank—"

"No—"

"I saw the bankbook."

"So what if you saved a few dollars, so have you got life insurance?"

He made no answer.

"Can you get?" she taunted.

The front door banged. It banged often. The shop was crowded with customers clamoring for bread. Bessie stomped out to wait on them.

In the rear the wounded stirred. Kobotsky, with bony fingers buttoned his overcoat.

"Sit," sighed the baker.

"Lieb, I am sorry—"

Kobotsky sat, his face lit with sadness.

When Bessie finally was rid of the rush, Lieb went into the shop. He spoke to her quietly, almost in a whisper, and she answered as quietly, but it took only a minute to start them quarreling.

Kobotsky slipped off the stool. He went to the sink, wet half his handkerchief and held it to his dry eyes. Folding the damp handkerchief, he thrust it into his overcoat pocket, then took out a small penknife and quickly pared his fingernails.

As he entered the shop, Lieb was pleading with Bessie, reciting the embittered hours of his toil, the enduring drudgery. And now that he had a cent to his name, what was there to live for if he could not share it with a dear friend? But Bessie had her back to him.

"Please," Kobotsky said, "don't fight. I will go away now."

Lieb gazed at him in exasperation, Bessie stayed with head averted.

"Yes," Kobotsky sighed, "the money I wanted for Dora, but she is not sick, Lieb, she is dead."

"Ai," Lieb cried, wringing his hands.

Bessie faced the visitor, pallid.

"Not now," he spoke kindly, "five years ago."

Lieb groaned.

"The money I need for a stone on her grave. She never had a stone. Next Sunday is five years that she is dead and every year I promise her, 'Dora, this year I will give you your stone,' and every year I gave her nothing."

The grave, to his everlasting shame, lay uncovered before all eyes. He had long ago paid a fifty-dollar deposit for a headstone with her name on it in clearly chiseled letters, but had never got the rest of the money. If there wasn't one thing to do with it there was always another: first an operation; the second year he couldn't work, imprisoned again by arthritis; the third a widowed sister lost her only son and the little Kobotsky earned had to help support her; the fourth incapacitated by boils that made him ashamed to walk out into the street. This year he was at least working, but only for just enough to eat and sleep, so Dora still lay without a stone, and for aught he knew he would someday return to the cemetery and find her grave gone.

Tears sprang into the baker's eyes. One gaze at Bessie's face—at the odd looseness of neck and shoulders—told him that she too was moved. Ah, he had won out. She would now say yes, give the money, and they would then all sit down at the table and eat together.

But Bessie, though weeping, shook her head, and before they could guess what, had blurted out the story of her afflictions: how the Bolsheviki came when she was a little girl and dragged her beloved father into the snowy fields without his shoes; the shots scattered the blackbirds in the trees and the snow oozed blood; how, when she was married a year, her husband, a sweet and gentle man, an educated accountant—rare in those days and that place—died of typhus in Warsaw; and how she, abandoned in her grief, years later found sanctuary in the home of an older brother in Germany, who sacrificed his own chances to send her, before the war, to America, and himself ended, with wife and daughter, in one of Hitler's incinerators.

"So I came to America and met here a poor baker, a poor man—who was always in his life poor—without a penny and without enjoyment in his life, and I married him, God knows why, and with my both hands, working day and night, I fixed up for him his piece of business and we make now, after twelve years, a little living. But Lieb is not a healthy man, also with eyes that he needs an operation, and this is not yet everything. Suppose, God forbid, that he died, what will I do alone by myself? Where will I go, where, and who will take care of me if I have nothing?"

The baker, who had often heard this tale, munched, as he listened, chunks of white bread.

When she had finished he tossed the shell of a loaf away. Kobotsky, at the end of the story, held his hands over his ears.

Tears streaming from her eyes, Bessie raised her head and suspiciously sniffed the air. Screeching suddenly, she ran into the rear and with a cry wrenched open the oven door. A cloud of smoke billowed out at her. The loaves in the trays were blackened bricks—charred corpses.

Kobotsky and the baker embraced and sighed over their lost youth. They pressed mouths together and parted forever.

Exercises

1. Discuss the tone of the story, especially as created by the voice of the teller and the style of speech of the characters.

2. Why is Lieb's profession as a baker important to this story? What is the relevance of the background of bread baking?

3. Discuss the significance of the fact that Lieb has prospered because of crying into the dough.

4. Why do we not know during most of the dialogue that Kobotsky's wife is dead?

5. Discuss your reactions to Bessie. Is her position understandable, or is she totally unsympathetic?

6. What is the effect of Bessie's story about her misfortune coming right after Kobotsky's story?

7. Discuss the significance of the description of the bread on the trays as "charred corpses."

IRWIN
SHAW | # The Girls in Their Summer Dresses

Fifth Avenue was shining in the sun when they left the Brevoort. The sun was warm, even though it was February, and everything looked like Sunday morning—the buses and the well-dressed people walking slowly in couples and the quiet buildings with the windows closed.

Michael held Frances' arm tightly as they walked toward Washington Square in the sunlight. They walked lightly, almost smiling, because they had slept late and had a good breakfast and it was Sunday. Michael unbuttoned his coat and let it flap around him in the mild wind.

"Look out," Frances said as they crossed Eighth Street. "You'll break your neck." Michael laughed and Frances laughed with him.

"She's not so pretty," Frances said. "Anyway, not pretty enough to take a chance of breaking your neck."

Michael laughed again. "How did you know I was looking at her?"

Frances cocked her head to one side and smiled at her husband under the brim of her hat. "Mike, darling," she said.

"O.K.," he said. "Excuse me."

Frances patted his arm lightly and pulled him along a little faster toward Washington Square. "Let's not see anybody all day," she said. "Let's just hang around with each other. You and me. We're always up to our neck in people, drinking their Scotch or drinking our Scotch; we only see each other in bed. I want to go out with my husband all day long. I want him to talk only to me and listen only to me."

"What's to stop us?" Michael asked.

"The Stevensons. They want us to drop by around one o'clock and they'll drive us into the country."

"The cunning Stevensons," Mike said. "Transparent. They can whistle. They can go driving in the country by themselves."

"Is it a date?"

"It's a date."

Frances leaned over and kissed him on the tip of the ear.

"Darling," Michael said, "this is Fifth Avenue."

"Let me arrange a program," Frances said. "A planned Sunday in New York for a young couple with money to throw away."

"Go easy."

"First let's go to the Metropolitan Museum of Art," Frances suggested, because Michael had said during the week he wanted to go. "I haven't been there in three years and there're at least ten pictures I want to see again. Then we can take the bus down to Radio City and watch them skate. And later we'll go down to Cavanagh's and get a steak as big as a blacksmith's apron, with a bottle of wine, and after that there's a French picture at the Filmarte that everybody says—say, are you listening to me?"

"Sure," he said. He took his eyes off the hatless girl with the dark hair, cut dancer-style like a helmet, who was walking past him.

"That's the program for the day," Frances said flatly. "Or maybe you'd just rather walk up and down Fifth Avenue."

"No," Michael said. "Not at all."

"You always look at other women," Frances said. "Everywhere. Every damned place we go."

"No, darling," Michael said, "I look at everything. God gave me eyes and I look at women and men in subway excavations and moving pictures and the little flowers of the field. I casually inspect the universe."

"You ought to see the look in your eye," Frances said, "as you casually inspect the universe on Fifth Avenue."

"I'm a happily married man." Michael pressed her elbow tenderly. "Example for the whole twentieth century—Mr. and Mrs. Mike Loomis. Hey, let's have a drink," he said, stopping.

"We just had breakfast."

"Now listen, darling," Mike said, choosing his words with care, "it's a nice day and we both felt good and there's no reason why we have to break it up. Let's have a nice Sunday."

"All right. I don't know why I started this. Let's drop it. Let's have a good time."

They joined hands consciously and walked without talking among the baby carriages and the old Italian men in their Sunday clothes and the young women with Scotties in Washington Square Park.

"At least once a year everyone should go to the Metropolitan Museum of Art," Frances said after a while, her tone a good imitation of the tone she had used at breakfast and at the beginning of their walk. "And it's nice on Sunday. There're a lot of people looking at the pictures and you get the feeling maybe Art isn't on the decline in New York City, after all—"

"I want to tell you something," Michael said very seriously. "I have not touched another woman. Not once. In all the five years."

"All right," Frances said.

"You believe that, don't you?"

"All right."

They walked between the crowded benches, under the scrubby city-park trees.

"I try not to notice it," Frances said, "but I feel rotten inside, in my stomach, when we pass a woman and you look at her and I see that look in your eye and that's the way you looked at me the first time. In Alice Maxwell's house. Standing there in the living room, next to the radio, with a green hat on and all those people."

"I remember the hat," Michael said.

"The same look," Frances said. "And it makes me feel bad. It makes me feel terrible."

"Sh-h-h, please, darling, sh-h-h."

"I think I would like a drink now," Frances said.

They walked over to a bar on Eighth Street, not saying anything, Michael automatically helping her over curbstones and guiding her past automobiles. They sat near a window in the bar and the sun streamed in and there was a small, cheerful fire in the fireplace. A little Japanese waiter came over and put down some pretzels and smiled happily at them.

"What do you order after breakfast?" Michael asked.

"Brandy, I suppose," Frances said.

"Courvoisier," Michael told the waiter. "Two Courvoisiers."

The waiter came with the glasses and they sat drinking the brandy in the sunlight. Michael finished half his and drank a little water.

"I look at women," he said. "Correct. I don't say it's wrong or right. I look at them. If I pass them on the street and I don't look at them, I'm fooling you, I'm fooling myself."

"You look at them as though you want them," Frances said, playing with her brandy glass. "Every one of them."

"In a way," Michael said, speaking softly and not to his wife, "in a way that's true. I don't do anything about it, but it's true."

"I know it. That's why I feel bad."

"Another brandy," Michael called. "Waiter, two more brandies."

He sighed and closed his eyes and rubbed them gently with his fingertips. "I love the way women look. One of the things I like best about New York is the battalions of women. When I first came to New York from Ohio that was the first thing I noticed, the million wonderful women, all over the city. I walked around with my heart in my throat."

"A kid," Frances said. "That's a kid's feeling."

"Guess again," Michael said. "Guess again. I'm older now. I'm a man getting near middle age, putting on a little fat, and I still love to walk along Fifth Avenue at three o'clock on the east side of the street between Fiftieth and Fifty-seventh Streets. They're all out then, shopping, in their furs and their crazy hats, everything all concentrated from all over the world into seven blocks—the best furs, the best clothes, the handsomest women, out to spend money and feeling good about it."

The Japanese waiter put the two drinks down, smiling with great happiness.

"Everything is all right?" he asked.

"Everything is wonderful," Michael said.

"If it's just a couple of fur coats," Frances said, "and forty-five dollar hats—"

"It's not the fur coats. Or the hats. That's just the scenery for that particular kind of woman. Understand," he said, "you don't have to listen to this."

"I want to listen."

"I like the girls in the offices. Neat, with their eyeglasses, smart, chipper, knowing what everything is about. I like the girls on Forty-fourth Street at lunchtime, the actresses, all dressed up on nothing a week. I like the salesgirls in the stores, paying attention to you first because you're a man, leaving lady customers waiting. I got all this stuff accumulated in me because I've been thinking about it for ten years and now you've asked for it and here it is."

"Go ahead," Frances said.

"When I think of New York City, I think of all the girls on parade in the city. I don't know whether it's something special with me or whether every man in the city walks around with the same feeling inside him, but I feel as though I'm at a picnic in this city. I like to sit near the women in the theatres, the famous beauties who've taken six hours to get ready and look it. And the young girls at the football games, with the red cheeks, and when the warm weather comes, the girls in their summer dresses." He finished his drink. "That's the story."

Frances finished her drink and swallowed two or three times extra. "You say you love me?"

"I love you."

"I'm pretty, too," Frances said. "As pretty as any of them."

"You're beautiful," Michael said.

"I'm good for you," Frances said, pleading. "I've made a good wife, a good housekeeper, a good friend. I'd do any damn thing for you."

"I know," Michael said. He put his hand out and grasped hers.

"You'd like to be free to—" Frances aid.

"Sh-h-h."

"Tell the truth." She took her hand away from under his.

Michael flicked the edge of his glass with his finger. "O.K.," he said gently. "Sometimes I feel I would like to be free."

"Well," Frances said, "any time you say."

"Don't be foolish." Michael swung his chair around to her side of the table and patted her thigh.

She began to cry silently into her handkerchief, bent over just enough so that nobody else in the bar would notice. "Someday," she said, crying, "you're going to make a move."

Michael didn't say anything. He sat watching the bartender slowly peel a lemon.

"Aren't you?" Frances asked harshly. "Come on, tell me. Talk. Aren't you?"

"Maybe," Michael said. He moved his chair back again. "How the hell do I know?"

"You know," Frances persisted. "Don't you know?"

"Yes," Michael said after a while, "I know."

Frances stopped crying then. Two or three snuffles into the handkerchief and she put it away and her face didn't tell anything to anybody. "At least do me one favor," she said.

"Sure."

"Stop talking about how pretty this woman is or that one. Nice eyes, nice breasts, a pretty figure, good voice." She mimicked his voice. "Keep it to yourself. I'm not interested."

Michael waved to the waiter. "I'll keep it to myself," he said.

Frances flicked the corners of her eyes. "Another brandy," she told the waiter.

"Two," Michael said.

"Yes, Ma'am, yes, sir," said the waiter, backing away.

Frances regarded Michael coolly across the table. "Do you want me to call the Stevensons?" she asked. "It'll be nice in the country."

"Sure," Michael said. "Call them."

She got up from the table and walked across the room toward the telephone. Michael watched her walk, thinking what a pretty girl, what nice legs.

EXERCISES

1. Is this story about a basic difference between males and females in American culture, or is it a story about a particular conflict between this man and woman? Explain.

2. Discuss the following as general conflicts in this story:

   (a) desire versus casual observation

   (b) distance versus closeness

   (c) freedom versus control

   (d) openness versus concealment

3. How is this story about an adult's feeling versus a kid's feeling?

4. For the first time, the man tries to explain his motivation for looking at other women, concluding "That's the story." Is it the full story? Is there more that he does not tell? In what way and for what reason does he desire other women?

5. In the last paragraph, what is the meaning of the way the man looks at his wife?

ROBLEY
WILSON, JR. | *Thief*

He is waiting at the airline ticket counter when he first notices the young woman. She has glossy black hair pulled tightly into a knot at the back of her head—the man imagines it loosed and cascading to the small of her back—and carries over the shoulder of her leather coat a heavy black purse. She wears black boots of soft leather. He struggles to see her face—she is ahead of him in line—but it is not until she has bought her ticket and turns to walk away that he realizes her beauty, which is pale and dark-eyed and full-mouthed, and which quickens his heartbeat. She seems aware that he is staring at her and lowers her gaze abruptly.

The airline clerk interrupts. The man gives up looking at the woman—he thinks she may be about twenty-five—and buys a round-trip, coach class ticket to an eastern city.

His flight leaves in an hour. To kill time, the man steps into one of the airport cocktail bars and orders a scotch and water. While he sips it he watches the flow of travelers through the terminal—including a remarkable number, he thinks, of unattached pretty women dressed in fashion magazine clothes—until he catches sight of the black-haired girl in the leather coat. She is standing near a Travelers Aid counter, deep in conversation with a second girl, a blonde in a cloth coat trimmed with gray fur. He wants somehow to attract the brunette's attention, to invite her to have a drink with him before her own flight leaves for wherever she is traveling, but even though he believes for a moment she is looking his way he cannot catch her eye from out of the shadows of the bar. In another instant the two women separate; neither of their directions is toward him. He orders a second scotch and water.

When next he sees her, he is buying a magazine to read during the flight and becomes aware that someone is jostling him. At first he is startled that anyone would be so close as to touch him, but when he sees who it is he musters a smile.

"Busy place," he says.

She looks up at him—Is she blushing?—and an odd grimace crosses her mouth and vanishes. She moves away from him and joins the crowds in the terminal.

The man is at the counter with his magazine, but when he reaches into his back pocket for his wallet the pocket is empty. *Where could I have lost it?* he thinks. His mind begins enumerating the credit cards, the currency, the membership and identification cards; his stomach churns with something very like fear. *The girl who was so near to me,* he thinks—and all at once he understands that she has picked his pocket.

What is he to do? He still has his ticket, safely tucked inside his suitcoat—he reaches into the jacket to feel the envelope, to make sure. He can take the flight, call someone to pick him up at his destination—since he cannot even afford bus fare—conduct his business and fly home. But in the meantime he will have to do something about the lost credit cards— call home, have his wife get the numbers out of the top desk drawer, phone the card companies— so difficult a process, the whole thing suffocating. What shall he do?

First: Find a policeman, tell what has happened, describe the young woman; damn her, he thinks, for seeming to be attentive to him, to let herself stand so close to him, to blush prettily when he spoke—and all the time she wanted only to steal from him. And her blush was not shyness but the anxiety of being caught; that was most disturbing of all. *Damned deceitful creatures.* He will spare the policeman the details—just tell what she has done, what is in the wallet. He grits his teeth. He will probably never see his wallet again.

He is trying to decide if he should save time by talking to a guard near the x-ray machines when he is appalled—and elated—to see the black-haired girl. (*Ebony-Tressed Thief,* the newspapers will say.) She is seated against a front window of the terminal, taxis and private cars moving sluggishly beyond her in the gathering darkness; she seems engrossed in a book. A seat beside her is empty, and the man occupies it.

"I've been looking for you," he said.

She glances at him with no sort of recognition. "I don't know you," she says.

"Sure you do."

She sighs and puts the book aside. "Is this all you characters think about—picking up girls like we were stray animals? What do you think I am?"

"You lifted my wallet," he says. He is pleased to have said "lifted," thinking it sounds more worldly than *stole* or *took* or even *ripped off.*

"I beg your pardon?" the girl says.

"I know you did—at the magazine counter. If you'll just give it back, we can forget the whole thing. If you don't, then I'll hand you over to the police."

She studies him, her face serious. "All right," she says. She pulls the black bag onto her lap, reaches into it and draws out a wallet.

He takes it from her. "Wait a minute," he says. "This isn't mine."

The girl runs; he bolts after her. It is like a scene in a movie—bystanders scattering, the girl zig-zagging to avoid collisions, the sound of his own breathing reminding him how old he is—until he hears a woman's voice behind him: "Stop, thief! Stop that man!"

Ahead of him the brunette disappears around a corner and in the same moment a young man in a marine uniform puts out a foot to trip him up. He falls hard, banging knee and elbow on the tile floor of the terminal, but manages to hang on to the wallet which is not his.

The wallet is a woman's, fat with money and credit cards from places like Sak's and Peck & Peck and Lord & Taylor, and it belongs to the blonde in the fur-trimmed coat—the blonde he has earlier seen in conversation with the criminal brunette. She, too, is breathless, as is the policeman with her.

"That's him," the blonde girl says. "He lifted my billfold."

It occurs to the man that he cannot even prove his own identity to the policeman.

Two weeks later—the embarrassment and rage have diminished, the family lawyer has been paid, the confusion in his household has receded—the wallet turns up without explanation in one morning's mail. It is intact, no money is missing, all the cards are in place. Though he is relieved, the man thinks that for the rest of his life he will feel guilty around policemen, and ashamed in the presence of women.

EXERCISES

1. Discuss the character of the man in the story. Is he an evil man, an unlikable man? What do you know about him? How do you feel about him?
2. Discuss the point of view of the story. Why is it told in the present tense, instead of the usual past tense of narrative? Does the narrator identify with the man or the woman? How do you know?
3. Why do both the man and the blonde woman use the word *lifted* instead of the word *stole?*
4. Why is the chase described "like a scene in a movie"?
5. Who is the thief of the title—the dark-haired woman who stole the wallet or the man who is accused of stealing the wallet from the blonde woman— or is there another kind of stealing going on in this story?
6. Is there a kind of poetic justice involved in this story? Explain. What is meant by the final sentence, "Though he is relieved, the man thinks that for the rest of his life he will feel guilty around policemen, and ashamed in the presence of women"?

O. HENRY | *The Cop and the Anthem*

On his bench in Madison Square Soapy moved uneasily. When wild geese honk high of nights, and when women without sealskin coats grow kind to their husbands, and when Soapy moves uneasily on his bench in the park, you may know that winter is near at hand.

A dead leaf fell in Soapy's lap. That was Jack Frost's card. Jack is kind to the regular denizens of Madison Square, and gives fair warning of his annual call. At the corners of four streets he hands his pasteboard to the North Wind, footman of the mansion of All Outdoors, so that the inhabitants thereof may make ready.

Soapy's mind became cognizant of the fact that the time had come for him to resolve himself into a singular Committee of Ways and Means to provide against the coming rigor. And therefore he moved uneasily on his bench.

The hibernatorial ambitions of Soapy were not of the highest. In them were no considerations of Mediterranean cruises, of soporific Southern skies or drifting in the Vesuvian Bay. Three months on the Island was what his soul craved. Three months of assured board and bed and congenial company, safe from Boreas and bluecoats, seemed to Soapy the essence of things desirable.

For years the hospitable Blackwell's had been his winter quarters. Just as his more fortunate fellow New Yorkers had bought their tickets to Palm Beach and the Riviera each winter, so Soapy had made his humble arrangements for his annual hegira to the Island. And now the time was come. On the previous night three Sabbath newspapers, distributed beneath his coat, about his ankles and over his lap, had failed to repulse the cold as he slept on his bench near the spurting fountain in the ancient square. So the Island loomed big and timely in Soapy's mind. He scorned the provisions made in the name of charity for the city's dependents. In Soapy's opinion the Law was more benign than Philanthropy. There was an endless round of institutions, municipal and elee-mosynary, on which he might set out and receive lodging and food accordant with the simple life. But to one of Soapy's proud spirit the gifts of charity are encumbered. If not in coin you must pay in humiliation of spirit for every benefit received at the hands of philanthropy. As Cæsar had his Brutus, every bed of charity must have its toll of a bath, every loaf of bread its compensation of a private and personal inquisition. Wherefore it is better to be a guest of the law, which, though conducted by rules, does not meddle unduly with a gentleman's private affairs.

Soapy, having decided to go to the Island, at once set about accomplishing his desire. There were many easy ways of doing this. The pleasantest was to dine luxuriously at some expensive restaurant; and then, after declaring insolvency, be handed over quietly and without uproar to a policeman. An accommodating magistrate would do the rest.

Soapy left his bench and strolled out of the square and across the level sea of asphalt, where Broadway and Fifth Avenue flow together. Up Broadway he turned, and halted at a glittering café, where are gathered together nightly the choicest products of the grape, the silkworm, and the protoplasm.

Soapy had confidence in himself from the lowest button of his vest upward. He was shaven, and his coat was decent and his neat black, ready-tied four-in-hand had been presented to him by a lady missionary on Thanksgiving Day. If he could reach a table in the restaurant unsuspected success would be his. The portion of him that would show above the table would raise no doubt in the waiter's mind. A roasted mallard duck, thought Soapy, would be about the thing—with a bottle of Chablis, and then Camembert, a demitasse and a cigar. One dollar for the cigar would be enough. The total would not be so high as to call forth any supreme manifestation of revenge from the café management; and yet the meat would leave him filled and happy for the journey to his winter refuge.

But as Soapy set foot inside the restaurant door the head waiter's eye fell upon his frayed trousers and decadent shoes. Strong and ready hands turned him about and conveyed him in silence and haste to the sidewalk and averted the ignoble fate of the menaced mallard.

Soapy turned off Broadway. It seemed that his route to the coveted Island was not to be an epicurean one. Some other way of entering limbo must be thought of.

At a corner of Sixth Avenue electric lights and cunningly displayed wares behind plate-glass made a shop window conspicuous. Soapy took a cobblestone and dashed it through the glass. People came running around the corner, a policeman in the lead. Soapy stood still, with his hands in his pockets, and smiled at the sight of brass buttons.

"Where's the man that done that?" inquired the officer, excitedly.

"Don't you figure out that I might have had something to do with it?" said Soapy, not without sarcasm, but friendly, as one greets good fortune.

The policeman's mind refused to accept Soapy even as a clue. Men who smash windows do not remain to parley with the law's minions. They take to their heels. The policeman saw a man halfway down the block running to catch a car. With drawn club he joined in the pursuit. Soapy, with disgust in his heart, loafed along, twice unsuccessful.

On the opposite side of the street was a restaurant of no great pretensions. It catered to large appetites and modest purses. Its crockery and atmosphere were thick; its soup and napery thin. Into this place Soapy took his accusive shoes and telltale trousers without challenge. At a table he sat and consumed beefsteak, flapjacks, doughnuts and pie. And then to the waiter he betrayed the fact that the minutest coin and himself were strangers.

"Now, get busy and call a cop," said Soapy. "And don't keep a gentleman waiting."

"No cop for youse," said the waiter, with a voice like butter cakes and an eye like the cherry in a Manhattan cocktail. "Hey, Con!"

Neatly upon his left ear on the callous pavement two waiters pitched Soapy. He arose joint by joint, as a carpenter's rule opens, and beat the dust from his clothes. Arrest seemed but a rosy dream. The Island seemed very far away. A policeman who stood before a drug store two doors away laughed and walked down the street.

Five blocks Soapy travelled before his courage permitted him to woo capture again. This time the opportunity presented what he fatuously termed to himself a "cinch." A young woman of a modest and pleasing guise was standing before a show window gazing with sprightly interest at its display of shaving mugs and inkstands, and two yards from the window a large policeman of severe demeanor leaned against a water plug.

It was Soapy's design to assume the role of the despicable and execrated "masher." The refined and elegant appearance of his victim and the contiguity of the conscientious cop encouraged him to believe that he would soon feel the pleasant official clutch upon his arm that would insure his winter quarters on the right little, tight little isle.

Soapy straightened the lady missionary's ready-made tie, dragged his shrinking cuffs into the open, set his hat at a killing cant and sidled toward the young woman. He made eyes at her, was taken with sudden coughs and "hems," smiled, smirked and went brazenly through the impudent and contemptible litany of the "masher." With half an eye Soapy saw the policeman was watching him fixedly. The young woman moved away a few steps, and again bestowed her absorbed attention upon the shaving mugs. Soapy followed, boldly stepping to her side, raised his hat and said:

"Ah there, Bedelia! Don't you want to come and play in my yard?"

The policeman was still looking. The persecuted young woman had but to beckon a finger and Soapy would be practically en route for his insular haven. Already he imagined he could feel the cozy warmth of the station-house. The young woman faced him and, stretching out a hand, caught Soapy's coat sleeve.

"Sure, Mike," she said, joyfully, "if you'll blow me to a pail of suds. I'd have spoke to you sooner, but the cop was watching."

With the young woman playing the clinging ivy to his oak Soapy walked past the policeman overcome with gloom. He seemed doomed to liberty.

At the next corner he shook off his companion and ran. He halted in the district where by night are found the lightest streets, hearts, vows and librettos. Women in furs and men in greatcoats moved gaily in the wintry air. A sudden fear seized Soapy that some dreadful enchantment had rendered him immune to arrest. The thought brought a little of panic upon it, and when he came upon another policeman lounging grandly in front of a transplendent theatre he caught at the immediate straw of "disorderly conduct."

On the sidewalk Soapy began to yell drunken gibberish at the top of his harsh voice. He danced, howled, raved, and otherwise disturbed the welkin.

The policeman twirled his club, turned his back to Soapy and remarked to a citizen:

" 'Tis one of them Yale lads celebratin' the goose egg they give to the Hartford College. Noisy; but no harm. We've instructions to lave them be."

Disconsolate, Soapy ceased his unavailing racket. Would never a policeman lay hands on him? In his fancy the Island seemed an unattainable Arcadia. He buttoned his thin coat against the chilling wind.

In a cigar store he saw a well-dressed man lighting a cigar at a swinging light. His silk umbrella he had set by the door on entering. Soapy stepped inside, secured the umbrella and sauntered off with it slowly. The man at the cigar light followed hastily.

"My umbrella," he said, sternly.

"Oh, is it?" sneered Soapy, adding insult to petit larceny. "Well, why don't you call a policeman? I took it. Your umbrella! Why don't you call a cop? There stands one on the corner."

The umbrella owner slowed his steps. Soapy did likewise, with a presentiment that luck would again run against him. The policeman looked at the two curiously.

"Of course," said the umbrella man—"that is—well, you know how these mistakes occur—I—if it's your umbrella I hope you'll excuse me—I picked it up this morning in a restaurant—If you recognize it as yours, why—I hope you'll——"

"Of course it's mine," said Soapy, viciously.

The ex-umbrella man retreated. The policeman hurried to assist a tall blonde in an opera cloak across the street in front of a street car that was approaching two blocks away.

Soapy walked eastward through a street damaged by improvements. He hurled the umbrella wrathfully into an excavation. He muttered against the men who wear helmets and carry clubs. Because he wanted to fall into their clutches, they seemed to regard him as a king who could do no wrong.

At length Soapy reached one of the avenues to the east where the glitter and turmoil was but faint. He set his face down this toward Madison Square, for the homing instinct survives even when the home is a park bench.

But on an unusually quiet corner Soapy came to a stand-still. Here was an old church, quaint and rambling and gabled. Through one violet-stained window a soft light glowed, where, no doubt, the organist loitered over the keys, making sure of his mastery of the coming Sabbath anthem. For there drifted out to Soapy's ears sweet music that caught and held him transfixed against the convolutions of the iron fence.

The moon was above, lustrous and serene; vehicles and pedestrians were few; sparrows twittered sleepily in the eaves—for a little while the scene might have been a country churchyard. And the anthem that the organist played cemented Soapy to the iron fence, for he had known it well in the days when his life contained such things as mothers and roses and ambitions and friends and immaculate thoughts and collars.

The conjunction of Soapy's receptive state of mind and the influences about the old church wrought a sudden and wonderful change in his soul. He viewed with swift horror the pit into which he had tumbled, the degraded days, unworthy desires, dead hopes, wrecked faculties and base motives that made up his existence.

And also in a moment his heart responded thrillingly to this novel mood. An instantaneous and strong impulse moved him to battle with his desperate fate. He would pull himself out of the mire; he would make a man of himself again; he would conquer the evil that had taken possession of him. There was time; he was comparatively young yet; he would resurrect his old eager ambitions and pursue them without faltering. Those solemn but sweet organ notes had set up a revolution in him. To-morrow he would go into the roaring downtown district and find work. A fur importer had once offered him a place as driver. He would find him to-morrow and ask for the position. He would be somebody in the world. He would——

Soapy felt a hand laid on his arm. He looked quickly around into the broad face of a policeman.

"What are you doin' here?" asked the officer.

"Nothin'," said Soapy.

"Then come along," said the policeman.

"Three months on the Island," said the Magistrate in the Police Court the next morning.

EXERCISES

1. Note the tone established by the language in the first eight paragraphs. Does this language characterize the narrator or Soapy? Discuss the purpose of this language.

2. Discuss the reasons why Soapy does not want charity. If Soapy does not want charity, how does he intend to "work" for his keep? In what ways must he "pay" for charity?

3. Discuss the ironies in the story of "doomed to be free." Consider also whether Soapy can be free only if he is in prison.

4. Discuss the reasons why Soapy has so much trouble getting into prison. Is there a pattern involved here?

5. For what is Soapy finally arrested after all his failed efforts to get arrested? What is the basic irony in his being arrested for doing nothing?

6. Describe the basic structure of this story. What is the purpose of the structure? At what point did you know the story would end the way it did? How did you know?

EDGAR
ALLAN
POE | *The Cask of Amontillado*

The thousand injuries of Fortunato I had borne as I best could, but when he ventured upon insult, I vowed revenge. You, who so well know the nature of my soul, will not suppose, however, that I gave utterance to a threat. *At length* I would be avenged; this was a point definitively settled—but the very definitiveness with which it was resolved precluded the idea of risk. I must not only punish, but punish with impunity. A wrong is unredressed when retribution overtakes its redresser. It is equally unredressed when the avenger fails to make himself felt as such to him who has done the wrong.

It must be understood that neither by word nor deed had I given Fortunato cause to doubt my good will. I continued, as was my wont, to smile in his face, and he did not perceive that my smile *now* was at the thought of his immolation.

He had a weak point—this Fortunato—although in other regards he was a man to be respected and even feared. He prided himself on his connoisseurship in wine. Few Italians have the true virtuoso spirit. For the most part their enthusiasm is adopted to suit the time and opportunity to practise imposture upon the British and Austrian *millionaires*. In painting and gemmary Fortunato, like his countrymen, was a quack, but in the matter of old wines he was sincere. In this respect I did not differ from him materially; I was skilful in the Italian vintages myself, and bought largely whenever I could.

It was about dusk, one evening during the supreme madness of the carnival season, that I encountered my friend. He accosted me with excessive warmth, for he had been drinking much. The man wore motley. He had on a tight-fitting parti-striped dress, and his head was surmounted by the conical cap and bells. I was so pleased to see him, that I thought I should never have done wringing his hand.

I said to him—"My dear Fortunato, you are luckily met. How remarkably well you are looking today! But I have received a pipe of what passes for Amontillado, and I have my doubts."

"How?" said he, "Amontillado? A pipe? Impossible! And in the middle of the carnival?"

"I have my doubts," I replied; "and I was silly enough to pay the full Amontillado price without consulting you in the matter. You were not to be found, and I was fearful of losing a bargain."

"Amontillado!"

"I have my doubts."

"Amontillado!"

"And I must satisfy them."

"Amontillado!"

"As you are engaged, I am on my way to Luchesi. If any one has a critical turn, it is he. He will tell me"——

"Luchesi cannot tell Amontillado from Sherry."

"And yet some fools will have it that his taste is a match for your own."

"Come let us go."

"Whither?"

"To your vaults."

"My friend, no; I will not impose upon your good nature. I perceive you have an engagement. Luchesi"——

"I have no engagement; come."

"My friend, no. It is not the engagement, but the severe cold with which I perceive you are afflicted. The vaults are insufferably damp. They are encrusted with nitre."

"Let us go, nevertheless. The cold is merely nothing. Amontillado! You have been imposed upon; and as for Luchesi, he cannot distinguish Sherry from Amontillado."

Thus speaking, Fortunato possessed himself of my arm. Putting on a mask of black silk, and drawing a *roquelaire* closely about my person, I suffered him to hurry me to my palazzo.

There were no attendants at home; they had absconded to make merry in honour of the time. I had told them that I should not return until the morning, and had given them explicit orders not to stir from the house. These orders were sufficient, I well knew, to insure their immediate disappearance, one and all, as soon as my back was turned.

I took from their sconces two flambeaux, and giving one to Fortunato, bowed him through several suites of rooms to the archway that led into the vaults. I passed down a long and winding staircase, requesting him to be cautious as he followed. We came at length to the foot of the descent, and stood together on the damp ground of the catacombs of the Montresors.

The gait of my friend was unsteady, and the bells upon his cap jingled as he strode.

"The pipe," said he.

"It is farther on," said I; "but observe the white webwork which gleams from these cavern walls."

He turned towards me, and looked into my eyes with two filmy orbs that distilled the rheum of intoxication.

"Nitre?" he asked, at length.

"Nitre," I replied. "How long have you had that cough?"

"Ugh! ugh! ugh!—ugh! ugh! ugh!—ugh! ugh! ugh!—ugh! ugh! ugh!—ugh! ugh! ugh!"

My poor friend found it impossible to reply for many minutes.

"It is nothing," he said, at last.

"Come," I said, with decision, "we will go back; your health is precious. You are rich, respected, admired, beloved; you are happy, as once I was. You are a man to be missed. For me it is no matter. We will go back; you will be ill, and I cannot be responsible. Besides, there is Luchesi"——

"Enough," he said; "the cough is a mere nothing; it will not kill me. I shall not die of a cough."

"True—true," I replied; "and, indeed, I had no intention of alarming you unnecessarily—but you should use all proper caution. A draught of this Medoc will defend us from the damps."

Here I knocked off the neck of a bottle which I drew from a long row of its fellows that lay upon the mould.

"Drink," I said, presenting him the wine.

He raised it to his lips with a leer. He paused and nodded to me familiarly, while his bells jingled.

"I drink," he said, "to the buried that repose around us."

"And I to your long life."

He again took my arm, and we proceeded.

"These vaults," he said, "are extensive."

"The Montresors," I replied, "were a great and numerous family."

"I forgot your arms."

"A huge human foot, d'or in a field azure; the foot crushes a serpent rampant whose fangs are imbedded in the heel."

"And the motto?"

"Nemo me impune lacessit."

"Good!" he said.

The wine sparkled in his eyes and the bells jingled. My own fancy grew warm with the Medoc. We had passed through walls of piled bones, with casks and puncheons intermingling, into the inmost recesses of the catacombs. I paused again, and this time I made bold to seize Fortunato by an arm above the elbow.

"The nitre!" I said: "see, it increases. It hangs like moss upon the vaults.

We are below the river's bed. The drops of moisture trickle among the bones. Come, we will go back ere it is too late. Your cough"——

"It is nothing," he said; "let us go on. But first, another draught of the Medoc."

I broke and reached him a flagon of De Grâve. He emptied it at a breath. His eyes flashed with a fierce light. He laughed and threw the bottle upwards with a gesticulation I did not understand.

I looked at him in surprise. He repeated the movement—a grotesque one.

"You do not comprehend?" he said.

"Not I," I replied.

"Then you are not of the brotherhood."

"How?"

"You are not of the masons?"

"Yes, yes," I said, "yes, yes."

"You? Impossible! A mason?"

"A mason," I replied.

"A sign," he said.

"It is this," I answered, producing a trowel from beneath the folds of my *roquelaire.*

"You jest," he exclaimed, recoiling a few paces. "But let us proceed to the Amontillado."

"Be it so," I said, replacing the tool beneath the cloak, and again offering him my arm. He leaned upon it heavily. We continued our route in search of the Amontillado. We passed through a range of low arches, descended, passed on, and descending again, arrived at a deep crypt, in which the foulness of the air caused our flambeaux rather to glow than flame.

At the most remote end of the crypt there appeared another less spacious. Its walls had been lined with human remains piled to the vault, overhead, in the fashion of the great catacombs of Paris. Three sides of this interior crypt were still ornamented in this manner. From the fourth the bones had been thrown down, and lay promiscuously upon the earth, forming at one point a mound of some size. Within the wall thus exposed by the displacing of the bones, we perceived a still interior recess, in depth about four feet, in width three, in height six or seven. It seemed to have been constructed for no especial use within itself, but formed merely the interval between two of the colossal supports of the roof of the catacombs, and was backed by one of their circumscribing walls of solid granite.

It was in vain that Fortunato, uplifting his dull torch, endeavoured to pry into the depths of the recess. Its termination the feeble light did not enable us to see.

"Proceed," I said; "herein is the Amontillado. As for Luchesi"——

"He is an ignoramus," interrupted my friend, as he stepped unsteadily forward, while I followed immediately at his heels. In an instant he had reached the extremity of the niche, and finding his progress arrested by the rock, stood stupidly bewildered. A moment more and I had fettered him to the granite. In its surface were two iron staples, distant from each other about two feet, horizontally. From one of these depended a short chain, from the other a padlock. Throwing the links about his waist, it was but the work of a few seconds to secure. He was too much astounded to resist. Withdrawing the key I stepped back from the recess.

"Pass your hand," I said, "over the wall; you cannot help feeling the nitre. Indeed it is *very* damp. Once more let me *implore* you to return. No? Then I must positively leave you. But I must first render you all the little attentions in my power."

"The Amontillado!" ejaculated my friend, not yet recovered from his astonishment.

"True," I replied; "the Amontillado."

As I said these words I busied myself among the pile of bones of which I have before spoken. Throwing them aside, I soon uncovered a quantity of building stone and mortar. With these materials and with the aid of my trowel, I began vigorously to wall up the entrance of the niche.

I had scarcely laid the first tier of the masonry when I discovered that the intoxication of Fortunato had in a great measure worn off. The earliest indication I had of this was a low moaning cry from the depth of the recess. It was *not* the cry of a drunken man. There was then a long and obstinate silence. I laid the second tier, and the third, and the fourth; and then I heard the furious vibrations of the chain. The noise lasted for several minutes, during which, that I might hearken to it with the more satisfaction, I ceased my labours and sat down upon the bones. When at last the clanking subsided, I resumed the trowel, and finished without interruption the fifth, the sixth, and the seventh tier. The wall was now nearly upon a level with my breast. I again paused, and holding the flambeaux over the mason-work, threw a few feeble rays upon the figure within.

A succession of loud and shrill screams, bursting suddenly from the throat of the chained form, seemed to thrust me violently back. For a brief moment I hesitated—I trembled. Unsheathing my rapier, I began to grope with it about the recess; but the thought of an instant reassured me. I placed my hand upon the solid fabric of the catacombs, and felt satisfied. I reapproached the wall. I replied to the yells of him who clamoured. I re-echoed—I aided—I surpassed them in volume and in strength. I did this, and the clamourer grew still.

It was now midnight, and my task was drawing to a close. I had completed the eighth, the ninth, and the tenth tier. I had finished a portion of the last and the eleventh; there remained but a single stone to be fitted and plastered in. I struggled with its weight; I placed it partially in its destined position. But now there came from out the niche a low laugh that erected the hairs upon my head. It was succeeded by a sad voice, which I had difficulty in recognising as that of the noble Fortunato. The voice said—

"Ha! ha! ha!—he! he!—a very good joke indeed—an excellent jest. We will have many a rich laugh about it at the palazzo—he! he! he!—over our wine—he! he! he!"

"The Amontillado!" I said.

"He! he! he!—he! he! he—yes, the Amontillado. But is it not getting late? Will not they be awaiting us at the palazzo, the Lady Fortunato and the rest? Let us be gone."

"Yes," I said, "let us be gone."

"For the love of God, Montresor!"

"Yes," I said, "for the love of God!"

But to these words I hearkened in vain for a reply. I grew impatient. I called aloud—

"Fortunato!"

No answer. I called again—

"Fortunato!"

No answer still. I thrust a torch through the remaining aperture and let it fall within. There came forth in return only a jingling of the bells. My heart grew sick—on account of the dampness of the catacombs. I hastened to make an end of my labour. I forced the last stone into its position; I plastered it up. Against the new masonry I re-erected the old rampart of bones. For the half of a century no mortal has disturbed them. *In pace requiescat!*

EXERCISES

1. What method does the narrator use to get Fortunato down into the catacombs? Note how he makes sure that all his servants will be gone. Point out other examples of this method in the story.

2. Discuss the Montresor coat of arms and motto, *"Nemo me impune lacessit"* (No one harms me with impunity). If the emblem of the foot crushing a serpent whose fangs are still embedded represents the relationship between Montresor and Fortunato, which represents Montresor—the serpent or the foot?

3. What is the significance of Montresor's little joke or pun about the Freemasons? The Freemasons are a secret society founded to promote the brotherhood of man.

4. Note how Montresor mocks Fortunato when he chains him up. Point out other examples of mockery in this story.

5. What is the significance of the names of the two men? The name Montresor means "my treasure"; Fortunato suggests either "fortunate one" or "fated one."

6. At the end of the story, we discover that the event took place fifty years ago. Why is Montresor telling it now? To whom is he telling it? Who is the "you" in the phrase "you who so well know the nature of my soul"? To whom does the final statement *"In pace requiescat"* (Rest in peace) refer—Fortunato or Montresor?

KATE
CHOPIN | *Désirée's Baby*

A s the day was pleasant, Madame Valmondé drove over to L'Abri to see Désirée and the baby.

It made her laugh to think of Désirée with a baby. Why, it seemed but yesterday that Désirée was little more than a baby herself; when Monsieur in riding through the gateway of Valmondé had found her lying asleep in the shadow of the big stone pillar.

The little one awoke in his arms and began to cry for "Dada." That was as much as she could do or say. Some people thought she might have strayed there of her own accord, for she was of the toddling age. The prevailing belief was that she had been purposely left by a party of Texans, whose canvas-covered wagon, late in the day, had crossed the ferry that Coton Maïs kept, just below the plantation. In time Madame Valmondé abandoned every speculation but the one that Désirée had been sent to her by a beneficent Providence to be the child of her affection, seeing that she was without child of the flesh. For the girl grew to be beautiful and gentle, affectionate and sincere—the idol of Valmondé.

It was no wonder, when she stood one day against the stone pillar in whose shadow she had lain asleep, eighteen years before, that Armand Aubigny riding by and seeing her there, had fallen in love with her. That was the way all the Aubignys fell in love, as if struck by a pistol shot. The wonder was that he had not loved her before; for he had known her since his father brought him home from Paris, a boy of eight, after his mother died there. The passion that awoke in him that day, when he saw her at the gate, swept along like an avalanche, or like a prairie fire, or like anything that drives headlong over all obstacles.

Monsieur Valmondé grew practical and wanted things well considered: that is, the girl's obscure origin. Armand looked into her eyes and did not care. He was reminded that she was nameless. What did it matter about a name when he could give her one of the oldest and proudest in Louisiana? He ordered the *corbeille* from Paris, and contained himself with what patience he could until it arrived; then they were married.

Madame Valmondé had not seen Désirée and the baby for four weeks. When she reached L'Abri she shuddered at the first sight of it, as she always did. It was a sad looking place, which for many years had not known the gentle presence of a mistress, old Monsieur Aubigny having married and buried his wife in France, and she having loved her own land too well ever to leave it. The roof came down steep and black like a cowl, reaching out beyond the wide galleries that encircled the yellow stuccoed house. Big solemn oaks grew close to it, and their thick-leaved, far-reaching branches shadowed it like a pall. Young Aubigny's rule was a strict one, too, and under it his negroes had forgotten how to be gay, as they had been during the old master's easy-going and indulgent lifetime.

The young mother was recovering slowly, and lay full length, in her soft white muslins and laces, upon a couch. The baby was beside her, upon her arm, where he had fallen asleep, at her breast. The yellow nurse woman sat beside a window fanning herself.

Madame Valmondé bent her portly figure over Désirée and kissed her, holding her an instant tenderly in her arms. Then she turned to the child.

"This is not the baby!" she exclaimed, in startled tones. French was the language spoken at Valmondé in those days.

"I knew you would be astonished," laughed Désirée, "at the way he has grown. The little *cochon de lait!* Look at his legs, mamma, and his hands and fingernails—real fingernails. Zandrine had to cut them this morning. Isn't it true, Zandrine?"

The woman bowed her turbaned head majestically, "Mais si, Madame."

"And the way he cries," went on Désirée, "is deafening. Armand heard him the other day as far away as La Blanche's cabin."

Madame Valmondé had never removed her eyes from the child. She lifted it and walked with it over to the window that was lightest. She scanned the baby narrowly, then looked as searchingly at Zandrine, whose face was turned to gaze across the fields.

"Yes, the child has grown, has changed," said Madame Valmondé, slowly, as she replaced it beside its mother. "What does Armand say?"

Désirée's face became suffused with a glow that was happiness itself.

"Oh, Armand is the proudest father in the parish, I believe, chiefly because it is a boy, to bear his name; though he says not,—that he would have loved a girl as well. But I know it isn't true. I know he says that to please me. And mamma," she added, drawing Madame Valmondé's head down to her, and speaking in a whisper, "he hasn't punished one of them—not one of them— since baby is born. Even Négrillon, who pretended to have burnt his leg that he might rest from work—he only laughed, and said Négrillon was a great scamp. Oh, mamma, I'm so happy; it frightens me."

What Désirée said was true. Marriage, and later the birth of his son, had softened Armand Aubigny's imperious and exacting nature greatly. This was what made the gentle Désirée so happy, for she loved him desperately. When he frowned she trembled, but loved him. When he smiled, she asked no greater blessing of God. But Armand's dark, handsome face had not often been disfigured by frowns since the day he fell in love with her.

When the baby was about three months old, Désirée awoke one day to the conviction that there was something in the air menacing her peace. It was at first too subtle to grasp. It had only been a disquieting suggestion; an air of mystery among the blacks; unexpected visits from far-off neighbors who could hardly account for their coming. Then a strange, an awful change in her husband's manner, which she dared not ask him to explain. When he spoke to her, it was with averted eyes, from which the old love-light seemed to have gone out. He absented himself from home; and when there, avoided her presence and that of her child, without excuse. And the very spirit of Satan seemed suddenly to take hold of him in his dealings with the slaves. Désirée was miserable enough to die.

She sat in her room, one hot afternoon, in her *peignoir,* listlessly drawing through her fingers the strands of her long, silky brown hair that hung about her shoulders. The baby, half naked, lay asleep upon her own great mahogany bed, that was like a sumptuous throne, with its satin-lined half-canopy. One of La Blanche's little quadroon boys—half naked too—stood fanning the child slowly with a fan of peacock feathers. Désirée's eyes had been fixed absently and sadly upon the baby, while she was striving to penetrate the threatening mist that she felt closing about her. She looked from her child to the boy who stood beside him, and back again; over and over. "Ah!" It was a cry that she could not help; which she was not conscious of having uttered. The blood turned like ice in her veins, and a clammy moisture gathered upon her face.

She tried to speak to the little quadroon boy; but no sound would come, at first. When he heard his name uttered, he looked up, and his mistress was pointing to the door. He laid aside the great, soft fan, and obediently stole away, over the polished floor, on his bare tiptoes.

She stayed motionless, with gaze riveted upon her child, and her face the picture of fright.

Presently her husband entered the room, and without noticing her, went to a table and began to search among some papers which covered it.

"Armand," she called to him, in a voice which must have stabbed him, if he was human. But he did not notice. "Armand," she said again. Then she rose and tottered towards him. "Armand," she panted once more, clutching his arm, "look at our child. What does it mean? tell me."

He coldly but gently loosened her fingers from about his arm and thrust the hand away from him. "Tell me what it means!" she cried despairingly.

"It means," he answered lightly, "that the child is not white; it means that you are not white."

A quick conception of all that this accusation meant for her nerved her with unwonted courage to deny it. "It is a lie; it is not true, I am white! Look at my hair, it is brown; and my eyes are gray, Armand, you know they are gray. And my skin is fair," seizing his wrist. "Look at my hand; whiter than yours, Armand," she laughed hysterically.

"As white as La Blanche's," he returned cruelly; and went away leaving her alone with their child.

When she could hold a pen in her hand, she sent a despairing letter to Madame Valmondé.

"My mother, they tell me I am not white. Armand has told me I am not white. For God's sake tell them it is not true. You must know it is not true. I shall die. I must die. I cannot be so unhappy, and live."

The answer that came was as brief:

"My own Désirée: Come home to Valmondé; back to your mother who loves you. Come with your child."

When the letter reached Désirée she went with it to her husband's study, and laid it open upon the desk before which he sat. She was like a stone image: silent, white, motionless after she placed it there.

In silence he ran his cold eyes over the written words. He said nothing. "Shall I go, Armand?" she asked in tones sharp with agonized suspense.

"Yes, go."

"Do you want me to go?"

"Yes, I want you to go."

He thought Almighty God had dealt cruelly and unjustly with him; and felt, somehow, that he was paying Him back in kind when he stabbed thus into his wife's soul. Moreover he no longer loved her, because of the unconscious injury she had brought upon his home and his name.

She turned away like one stunned by a blow, and walked slowly toward the door, hoping he would call her back.

"Good-by, Armand," she moaned.

He did not answer her. That was his last blow at fate.

Désirée went in search of her child. Zandrine was pacing the sombre gallery with it. She took the little one from the nurse's arms with no word of explanation, and descending the steps, walked away, under the live-oak branches.

It was an October afternoon; the sun was just sinking. Out in the still fields the negroes were picking cotton.

Désirée had not changed the thin white garment nor the slippers which she wore. Her hair was uncovered and the sun's rays brought a golden gleam from its brown meshes. She did not take the broad, beaten road which led to the far-off plantation of Valmondé. She walked across a deserted field, where the stubble bruised her tender feet, so delicately shod, and tore her thin gown to shreds.

She disappeared among the reeds and willows that grew thick along the banks of the deep, sluggish bayou; and she did not come back again.

Some weeks later there was a curious scene enacted at L'Abri. In the centre of the smoothly swept back yard was a great bonfire. Armand Aubigny sat in the wide hallway that commanded a view of the spectacle; and it was he who dealt out to a half dozen negroes the material which kept this fire ablaze.

A graceful cradle of willow, with all its dainty furbishings, was laid upon the pyre, which had already been fed with the richness of a priceless *layette*. Then there were silk gowns, and velvet and satin ones added to these; laces, too, and embroideries; bonnets and gloves; for the *corbeille* had been of rare quality.

The last thing to go was a tiny bundle of letters; innocent little scribblings that Désirée had sent to him during the days of their espousal. There was the remnant of one back in the drawer from which he took them. But it was not Désirée's; it was part of an old letter from his mother to his father. He read it. She was thanking God for the blessing of her husband's love:—

"But, above all," she wrote, "night and day, I thank the good God for having so arranged our lives that our dear Armand will never know that his mother, who adores him, belongs to the race that is cursed with the brand of slavery."

EXERCISES

1. Note how the exposition, or background, of the story is all established in the first few paragraphs. Why does the story not start with these events? Why does it begin with Madame Valmondé's visit to L'Abri?

2. What is the point or purpose of L'Abri being such a sad-looking place, with the roof coming down "steep and black like a cowl" and the oaks shadowing it like a "pall"?

3. What is the importance of family name in this story? Why is "carrying on a family name" so important to Armand? Why is knowing one's parentage so important in many societies?

4. Why does everyone else perceive something out of the ordinary about the baby before the mother does?

5. Why is the ending such a surprise? What does this suggest about racial biases, about gender biases?

6. There is an obvious theme of social importance in this story; is it a theme that is time-bound to the nineteenth century, or is it also relevant today?

7. Is this story about racial discrimination or gender discrimination? Support your answer.

BRET HARTE | *Tennessee's Partner*

I do not think that we ever knew his real name. Our ignorance of it certainly never gave us any social inconvenience, for at Sandy Bar in 1854 most men were christened anew. Sometimes these appellatives were derived from some distinctiveness of dress, as in the case of "Dungaree Jack"; or from some peculiarity of habit, as shown in "Saleratus Bill," so called from an undue proportion of that chemical in his daily bread; or from some unlucky slip, as exhibited in "The Iron Pirate," a mild, inoffensive man, who earned that baleful title by his unfortunate mispronunciation of the term "iron pyrites." Perhaps this may have been the beginning of a rude heraldry; but I am constrained to think that it was because a man's real name in that day rested solely upon his own unsupported statement. "Call yourself Clifford, do you?" said Boston, addressing a timid new-comer with infinite scorn; "hell is full of such Cliffords!" He then introduced the unfortunate man, whose name happened to be really Clifford, as "Jay-bird Charley,"—an unhallowed inspiration of the moment that clung to him ever after.

But to return to Tennessee's Partner, whom we never knew by any other than this relative title; that he had ever existed as a separate and distinct individuality we only learned later. It seems that in 1853 he left Poker Flat to go to San Francisco, ostensibly to procure a wife. He never got any farther than Stockton. At that place he was attracted by a young person who waited upon the table at the hotel where he took his meals. One morning he said something to her which caused her to smile not unkindly, to somewhat coquettishly break a plate of toast over his upturned, serious, simple face, and to retreat to the kitchen. He followed her, and emerged a few moments later, covered with more toast and victory. That day week they were married by a Justice of the Peace, and returned to Poker Flat. I am aware that something more might be made of this episode, but I prefer to tell it as it was current at Sandy Bar,—in the gulches and bar-rooms,—where all sentiment was modified by a strong sense of humor.

Of their married felicity but little is known, perhaps for the reason that Tennessee, then living with his partner, one day took occasion to say something to the bride on his own account, at which, it is said, she smiled not unkindly and chastely retreated,—this time as far as Marysville, where Tennessee followed her, and where they went to housekeeping without the aid of a Justice of the Peace. Tennessee's Partner took the loss of his wife simply and seriously, as was his fashion. But to everybody's surprise, when Tennessee one day returned from Marysville, without his partner's wife,—she having smiled and retreated with somebody else,—Tennessee's Partner was the first man to shake his hand and greet him with affection. The boys who had gathered in the cañon to see the shooting were naturally indignant. Their indignation might have found vent in sarcasm but for a certain look in Tennessee's Partner's eye that indicated a lack of humorous appreciation. In fact, he was a grave man, with a steady application to practical detail which was unpleasant in a difficulty.

Meanwhile a popular feeling against Tennessee had grown up on the Bar. He was known to be a gambler; he was suspected to be a thief. In these suspicions Tennessee's Partner was equally compromised; his continued intimacy with Tennessee after the affair above quoted could only be accounted for on the hypothesis of a copartnership of crime. At last Tennessee's guilt became flagrant. One day he overtook a stranger on his way to Red Dog. The stranger afterward related that Tennessee beguiled the time with interesting anecdote and reminiscence, but illogically concluded the interview in the following words: "And now, young man, I'll trouble you for your knife, your pistols, and your money. You see your weppings might get you into trouble at Red Dog, and your money's a temptation to the evilly disposed. I think you said your address was San Francisco. I shall endeavor to call." It may be stated here that Tennessee had a fine flow of humor, which no business preoccupation could wholly subdue.

This exploit was his last. Red Dog and Sandy Bar made common cause against the highwayman. Tennessee was hunted in very much the same fashion as his prototype, the grizzly. As the toils closed around him, he made a desperate dash through the Bar, emptying his revolver at the crowd before the

Arcade Saloon, and so on up Grizzly Cañon; but at its farther extremity he was stopped by a small man on a gray horse. The men looked at each other a moment in silence. Both were fearless, both self-possessed and independent; and both types of a civilization that in the seventeenth century would have been called heroic, but, in the nineteenth, simply "reckless." "What have you got there?—I call," said Tennessee, quietly. "Two bowers and an ace," said the stranger, as quietly, showing two revolvers and a bowie-knife. "That takes me," returned Tennessee; and with this gamblers' epigram, he threw away his useless pistol, and rode back with his captor.

It was a warm night. The cool breeze which usually sprang up with the going down of the sun behind the *chaparral*-crested mountain was that evening withheld from Sandy Bar. The little cañon was stifling with heated resinous odors, and the decaying drift-wood on the Bar sent forth faint, sickening exhalations. The feverishness of day, and its fierce passions, still filled the camp. Lights moved restlessly along the bank of the river, striking no answering reflection from its tawny current. Against the blackness of the pines the windows of the old loft above the express-office stood out staringly bright; and through their curtainless panes the loungers below could see the forms of those who were even then deciding the fate of Tennessee. And above all this, etched on the dark firmament, rose the Sierra, remote and passionless, crowned with remoter passionless stars.

The trial of Tennessee was conducted as fairly as was consistent with a judge and jury who felt themselves to some extent obliged to justify, in their verdict, the previous irregularities of arrest and indictment. The law of Sandy Bar was implacable, but not vengeful. The excitement and personal feeling of the chase were over; with Tennessee safe in their hands they were ready to listen patiently to any defence, which they were already satisfied was insufficient. There being no doubt in their own minds, they were willing to give the prisoner the benefit of any that might exist. Secure in the hypothesis that he ought to be hanged, on general principles, they indulged him with more latitude of defence than his reckless hardihood seemed to ask. The Judge appeared to be more anxious than the prisoner, who, otherwise unconcerned, evidently took a grim pleasure in the responsibility he had created. "I don't take any hand in this yer game," had been his invariable, but good-humored reply to all questions. The Judge—who was also his captor—for a moment vaguely regretted that he had not shot him "on sight," that morning, but presently dismissed this human weakness as unworthy of the judicial mind. Nevertheless, when there was a tap at the door, and it was said that Tennessee's Partner was there on behalf of the prisoner, he was admitted at once without question. Perhaps the younger members of the jury, to whom the proceedings were becoming irksomely thoughtful, hailed him as a relief.

For he was not, certainly, an imposing figure. Short and stout, with a square face, sunburned into a preternatural redness, clad in a loose duck "jumper," and trousers streaked and splashed with red soil, his aspect under any circumstances would have been quaint, and was now even ridiculous. As he stooped to deposit at his feet a heavy carpet-bag he was carrying, it became obvious, from partially developed legends and inscriptions, that the material with which his trousers had been patched had been originally intended for a less ambitious covering. Yet he advanced with great gravity, and after having shaken the hand of each person in the room with labored cordiality, he wiped his serious, perplexed face on a red bandanna handkerchief, a shade lighter than his complexion, laid his powerful hand upon the table to steady himself, and thus addressed the Judge:—

"I was passin' by," he began, by way of apology, "and I thought I'd just step in and see how things was gittin' on with Tennessee thar,—my pardner. It's a hot night. I disremember any sich weather before on the Bar."

He paused a moment, but nobody volunteering any other meteorological recollection, he again had recourse to his pocket-handkerchief, and for some moments mopped his face diligently.

"Have you anything to say in behalf of the prisoner?" said the Judge, finally.

"That's it," said Tennessee's Partner, in a tone of relief. "I come yar as Tennessee's pardner,—knowing him nigh on four year, off and on, wet and dry, in luck and out o' luck. His ways ain't allers my ways, but thar ain't any p'ints in that young man, thar ain't any liveliness as he's been up to, as I don't know. And you sez to me, sez you,—confidential-like, and between man and man,—sez you, 'Do you know anything in his behalf?' and I sez to you, sez I,—confidential-like, as between man and man,—'What should a man know of his pardner?' "

"Is this all you have to say?" asked the Judge, impatiently, feeling, perhaps, that a dangerous sympathy of humor was beginning to humanize the Court.

"Thet's so," continued Tennessee's Partner. "It ain't for me to say anything agin' him. And now, what's the case? Here's Tennessee wants money, wants it bad, and doesn't like to ask it of his old pardner. Well, what does Tennessee do? He lays for a stranger, and he fetches that stranger. And you lays for *him,* and you fetches *him;* and the honors is easy. And I put it to you, bein' a far-minded man, and to you, gentlemen, all, as far-minded men, ef this is n't so."

"Prisoner," said the Judge, interrupting, "have you any questions to ask this man?"

"No! no!" continued Tennessee's Partner, hastily. "I play this yer hand alone. To come down to the bed-rock, it's just this: Tennessee, thar, has played it pretty rough and expensive-like on a stranger, and on this yer camp. And now, what's the fair thing? Some would say more; some would say less. Here's seventeen hundred dollars in coarse gold and a watch,—it's about all my pile,—and call it square!" And before a hand could be raised to prevent him, he had emptied the contents of the carpet-bag upon the table.

For a moment his life was in jeopardy. One or two men sprang to their feet, several hands groped for hidden weapons, and a suggestion to "throw him from the window" was only overridden by a gesture from the Judge. Tennessee laughed. And apparently oblivious of the excitement, Tennessee's Partner improved the opportunity to mop his face again with his handkerchief.

When order was restored, and the man was made to understand, by the use of forcible figures and rhetoric, that Tennessee's offence could not be condoned by money, his face took a more serious and sanguinary hue, and those who were nearest to him noticed that his rough hand trembled slightly on the table. He hesitated a moment as he slowly returned the gold to the carpetbag, as if he had not yet entirely caught the elevated sense of justice which swayed the tribunal, and was perplexed with the belief that he had not offered enough. Then he turned to the Judge, and saying, "This yer is a lone hand, played alone, and without my pardner," he bowed to the jury and was about to withdraw, when the Judge called him back. "If you have anything to say to Tennessee, you had better say it now." For the first time that evening the eyes of the prisoner and his strange advocate met. Tennessee smiled, showed his white teeth, and, saying, "Euchred, old man!" held out his hand. Tennessee's Partner took it in his own, and saying "I just dropped in as I was passin' to see how things was gettin' on," let the hand passively fall, and adding that "it was a warm night," again mopped his face with his handkerchief, and without another word withdrew.

The two men never again met each other alive. For the unparalleled insult of a bribe offered to Judge Lynch—who, whether bigoted, weak, or narrow, was at least incorruptible—firmly fixed in the mind of that mythical personage any wavering determination of Tennessee's fate; and at the break of day he was marched, closely guarded, to meet it at the top of Marley's Hill.

How he met it, how cool he was, how he refused to say anything, how perfect were the arrangements of the committee, were all duly reported, with the addition of a warning moral and example to all future evil-doers, in the Red Dog Clarion, by its editor, who was present, and to whose vigorous English I cheerfully refer the reader. But the beauty of that midsummer morning, the blessed amity of earth and air and sky, the awakened life of the free woods and hills, the joyous renewal and promise of Nature, and above all, the infinite Serenity that thrilled through each, was not reported, as not being a part of the social lesson. And yet, when the weak and foolish deed was done, and a life, with its possibilities and responsibilities, had passed out of the misshapen thing that dangled between earth and sky, the birds sang, the flowers bloomed, the sun shone, as cheerily as before; and possibly the Red Dog Clarion was right.

Tennessee's Partner was not in the group that surrounded the ominous tree. But as they turned to disperse attention was drawn to the singular appearance of a motionless donkey-cart halted at the side of the road. As they approached, they at once recognized the venerable "Jenny," and the two-wheeled cart as the property of Tennessee's Partner,—used by him in carrying dirt from his claim; and a few paces distant the owner of the equipage himself, sitting under a buckeye-tree, wiping the perspiration from his glowing face. In answer to an inquiry, he said he had come for the body of the "diseased," "if it was all the same to the committee." He didn't wish to "hurry anything"; he could "wait." He was not working that day; and when the gentlemen were done with the "diseased," he would take him. "Ef thar is any present," he added, in his simple, serious way, "as would care to jine in the fun'l, they kin come." Perhaps it was from a sense of humor, which I have already intimated was a feature of Sandy Bar,—perhaps it was from something even better than that; but two thirds of the loungers accepted the invitation at once.

It was noon when the body of Tennessee was delivered into the hands of his partner. As the cart drew up to the fatal tree, we noticed that it contained a rough, oblong box,—apparently made from a section of sluicing,—and half filled with bark and the tassels of pine. The cart was further decorated with slips of willow, and made fragrant with buckeye-blossoms. When the body was deposited in the box, Tennessee's Partner drew over it a piece of tarred canvas, and gravely mounting the narrow seat in front, with his feet upon the shafts, urged the little donkey forward. The equipage moved slowly on, at that decorous pace which was habitual with "Jenny" even under less solemn circumstances. The men—half curiously, half jestingly, but all good-humoredly—strolled along beside the cart; some in advance, some a little in the rear of the homely catafalque. But, whether from the narrowing of the road or some present sense of decorum, as the cart passed on, the company fell to the rear in couples, keeping step, and otherwise assuming the external show of a formal procession. Jack Folinsbee, who had at the outset played a funeral march in dumb show upon an imaginary trombone, desisted, from a lack of sympathy and appreciation,—not having, perhaps, your true humorist's capacity to be content with the enjoyment of his own fun.

The way led through Grizzly Cañon,—by this time clothed in funereal drapery and shadows. The redwoods, burying their moccasined feet in the red soil, stood in Indian-file along the track, trailing an uncouth benediction from their bending boughs upon the passing bier. A hare, surprised into helpless inactivity, sat upright and pulsating in the ferns by the roadside, as the *cortége* went by. Squirrels hastened to gain a secure outlook from higher boughs; and the blue-jays, spreading their wings, fluttered before them like outriders, until the outskirts of Sandy Bar were reached, and the solitary cabin of Tennessee's Partner.

Viewed under more favorable circumstances, it would not have been a cheerful place. The unpicturesque site, the rude and unlovely outlines, the unsavory details, which distinguish the nest-building of the California miner, were all here, with the dreariness of decay superadded. A few paces from the cabin there was a rough enclosure, which, in the brief days of Tennessee's Partner's matrimonial felicity, had been used as a garden, but was now overgrown with fern. As we approached it we were surprised to find that what we had taken for a recent attempt at cultivation was the broken soil about an open grave.

The cart was halted before the enclosure; and rejecting the offers of assistance with the same air of simple self-reliance he had displayed throughout, Tennessee's Partner lifted the rough coffin on his back, and deposited it, unaided, within the shallow grave. He then nailed down the board which served as a lid; and mounting the little mound of earth beside it, took off his hat, and slowly mopped his face with his handkerchief. This the crowd felt was a preliminary to speech; and they disposed themselves variously on stumps and boulders, and sat expectant.

"When a man," began Tennessee's Partner, slowly, "has been running free all day, what's the natural thing for him to do? Why, to come home. And if he ain't in a condition to go home, what can his best friend do? Why, bring him home! And here's Tennessee has been running free, and we brings him home from his wandering." He paused, and picked up a fragment of quartz, rubbed it thoughtfully on his sleeve, and went on: "It ain't the first time that I've packed him on my back, as you see'd me now. It ain't the first time that I brought him to this yer cabin when he couldn't help himself; it ain't the first time that I and 'Jinny' have waited for him on yon hill, and picked him up and so fetched him home, when he couldn't speak, and didn't know me. And now that it's the last time, why—" he paused, and rubbed the quartz gently on his sleeve—"you see it's sort of rough on his pardner. And now, gentlemen," he added, abruptly, picking up his long-handled shovel, "the fun'l 's over; and my thanks, and Tennessee's thanks, to you for your trouble."

Resisting any proffers of assistance, he began to fill in the grave, turning his back upon the crowd, that after a few moments' hesitation gradually withdrew. As they crossed the little ridge that hid Sandy Bar from view, some, looking back, thought they could see Tennessee's Partner, his work done, sitting upon the grave, his shovel between his knees, and his face buried in his red bandanna handkerchief. But it was argued by others that you couldn't tell his face from his handkerchief at that distance; and this point remained undecided.

In the reaction that followed the feverish excitement of that day, Tennessee's Partner was not forgotten. A secret investigation had cleared him of any complicity in Tennessee's guilt, and left only a suspicion of his general sanity. Sandy Bar made a point of calling on him, and proffering various uncouth, but well-meant kindnesses. But from that day his rude health and great strength seemed visibly to decline; and when the rainy season fairly set in, and the tiny grass-blades were beginning to peep from the rocky mound above Tennessee's grave, he took to his bed.

One night, when the pines beside the cabin were swaying in the storm, and trailing their slender fingers over the roof, and the roar and rush of the swollen river were heard below, Tennessee's Partner lifted his head from the pillow, saying, "It is time to go for Tennessee; I must put 'Jinny' in the cart"; and would have risen from his bed but for the restraint of his attendant. Struggling, he still pursued his singular fancy: "There, now, steady, 'Jinny,'—steady, old girl. How dark it is! Look out for the ruts,—and look out for him, too, old gal. Sometimes, you know, when he's blind drunk, he drops down right in the trail. Keep on straight up to the pine on the top of the hill. Thar—I told you so!—thar he is,—coming this way, too,—all by himself, sober, and his face a-shining. Tennessee! Pardner!"

And so they met.

EXERCISES

1. Discuss the tone established early in the story. What kind of narrator tells it? Discuss his statement, "I prefer to tell it as it was current at Sandy Bar,—in the gulches and bar-rooms,—where all sentiment was modified by a strong sense of humor."

2. Discuss the significance of the following description of Tennessee's Partner: "He was a grave man, with a steady application to practical detail which was unpleasant in a difficulty." How is this relevant to the events of the story?

3. Note the gambling language used when Tennessee is captured. Point out other metaphors of card games and gambling in this story. How is game-playing a central metaphor in the story?

4. What is Tennessee's Partner's motivation for offering all his gold to free Tennessee? What effect does it have?

5. What does Tennessee mean when he takes his partner's hand and says, "Euchred, old man"?

6. Many readers have criticized this story for being overly sentimental and false, claiming no one could be so forgiving as Tennessee's Partner. Consider the point of view, and argue that it is barroom comedy rather than sentimentality that dominates the story.

JOHN P.
DAVIS | *The Overcoat*

It was late fall. The leaves outside the church lay dead and brown on the frozen earth. There was a smoky greenwood fire in the stove. Somebody, little David didn't know who, was singing *Nearer My God to Thee*. The whole environment was strange to David: Sybil sitting on one side of him and his father on the other, both looking straight ahead. Their mouths were buttoned tight. His was wide open in curiosity. There were so many people there whom he wanted to see. He wished that he dared look around. He just *knew* that old, blind Stephen was back there sitting beside the stove. And the green patches over his eyes looked so funny. Everyone was so quiet. He felt like moving around. He wondered why they had had to take his mother all the way in to town and then bring her back out again in that grey box covered with flowers. She would be ever so much more comfortable at home on the couch. He began to kick his tan boots with brass eyelets against the back of the next pew; but his father looked at him. David had seen that look before. It meant: stop. He stopped. Then he began to think of his mother again. Whenever he did, pictures seemed to flash through his head. He always had a choky feeling in his throat like after eating dry bread from Mother's tin breadbox. He remembered everything.

Now he was thinking of the time when Sybil had sent him for the doctor. There he was now: standing down at the crossroads, kicking his feet into the dusty red clay. He had been angry. He imagined his face had been like Father's when he had hit his thumb with a hammer and said "damn." He had gone for the doctor in a hurry. Gee! but he remembered that well. But why shouldn't he? Hadn't Sybil stopped him from playing "Indian" to say that mother was very, very sick? She had sent him running to get Doctor Parker or if he couldn't be found to get . . . (Sybil had frowned a moment before going on) . . . yes, to get Doctor Benson. How he had scurried off to Doctor Parker's. He hadn't stopped on the way either to see if he could make a stone skip three times over a pool of water. Instead he had run a little bit, and even when all out of breath he had trudged on and on—down through the woods a mile and a half and over a cornfield which had been cut down and ploughed under, revealing only the roots of cornstalks. Finally he had come to the little yellow house of the doctor, sitting back between two rows of tall sycamore trees. His heart had bumped up and down inside of him when he had seen the green shutters on the house closed. He felt a dryness in his throat when nobody answered his knock. But he hadn't given up. No! He had gone on back across the cornfield and then up the hill to Doctor Benson's low rambling white house with a porch all the way round. A dog had barked and a white gardener had yelled to him to go round the back way. Hadn't he resented it though. And he had almost cried when the maid peeking out at him from behind the door of the kitchen had said that Doctor Benson wasn't there and that he would have to go down to Hunt's grocery store to find him. But he had to find a doctor. Sybil said that he must. So he had gone on.

And then standing down there at the crossroads, kicking the toes off of his tan boots, he had seen thin-lipped Doctor Benson sitting in Hunt's store, sipping a bottle of pop with his little yellow-haired boy. He hated the Hunts, who cheated every Negro who bought things on credit at their store. He hated thin-lipped, sneering Doctor Benson. Most of all he hated that Benson boy with his wiry yellow hair. Wasn't he always calling out after him:

> "*Nigger, Nigger never die,*
> *Snotty nose and shiny eye*"?

Hadn't he thrown a stone and hit his spotted white fox terrier? Could he ever forget that day in early fall when he had been walking along the road with his grey, fuzzy chinchilla overcoat on his arm—his overcoat that both his mother and father had picked out for him, with its half-red lining and its pearly grey buttons? Oh, he remembered well enough. That yellow-haired Benson brat (that's what he'd heard Father call him) grabbed his overcoat from his arm and stamped all over it, saying: "Niggers lak him oughtn't ter have that kind of an overcoat nohow." And he told him: "Ef he wanted it, to pick it up lak a common Nigger should."

But he wasn't going to take orders from any poor white trash. He had thrown his head back, clenched his fists, and walked away, leaving his overcoat by the side of the road. Hadn't he been proud at that moment? His mother had sent Sybil to look for the coat, but it wasn't there. Then she had whipped him and cried afterwards. She kissed him on his quivering, pouting mouth. How he remembered that kiss! It made up for the whipping, it made up for everything except, except that Benson boy. He didn't care that his mother had had to buy him a drab second-hand overcoat at a Jew store for a dollar ninety-eight cents (the other had cost seven dollars). He had been proud. He had shown that Benson boy that he wouldn't take orders from poor white trash, even if he were smaller.

And now Sybil had sent him for this "brat's" father. What good was this poor white doctor, anyway? He didn't know anything about medicine. Father had said he didn't. All he would do would be to charge Father a lot of money without doing Mother any good. He might poison her. He'd be low down and mean enough to do something like that. What was the use of getting him anyway? Father had said just that morning that he was going to bring a colored doctor home with him after work. Sybil was just a frightened girl. She was always getting excited about something. What did the father of that little "brat" know about curing people?

He had hesitated and wavered—first deciding to get the doctor and then not to. Even when he was a quarter of a mile up the road he had turned to go back, but again he had visions of his overcoat lying torn and dirty on the ground. And everything went black and then red before him.

He wondered what he would tell Sybil when he got home. He couldn't tell her why he hadn't got Doctor Benson. She wouldn't understand. What could he tell her? Well, he'd better make up his mind soon to a straight tale and stick to it. If Sybil caught him lying, she'd tell Father and he'd get an awful licking. Besides Sybil hadn't really wanted Doctor Benson. Hadn't she said to get Doctor Parker and hadn't she almost *not* said Doctor Benson? Well, he'd better hurry home or she'd be worrying about him.

He remembered just as plainly how Sybil had acted: how she had paled under her cream color as she said, "But, Buddy, couldn't you get any . . . body?" He hated himself a thousand times since for just shaking his head. Sybil had cried and cried until she went in to Mother; then she bit her lips and wiped her eyes on her gingham apron and went in with her face frozen into a smile. How brave Syb had been! He had always thought of her as brave and oldish-like. He felt mean and sorry. He had even tried to make up for not getting the doctor by drawing a bucket of water and filling the woodbox with chips.

Then Sybil came and took him to see Mother. He shuddered. How pale and white she looked as she lay there—whiter than any white woman he had ever seen. Her eyes were dark and filled with tears. The skin on her face seemed tight, like the cream-colored parlor curtains on a stretcher. She looked as if something was hurting inside of her. And then she had told him to kiss her; and when he did, her lips seemed sticky and queer. How mean he felt then. He wanted to run from the room. He wanted to cry and his eyes welled up with tears. He would have cried, too, if Sybil hadn't pinched him and shaken her head. Instead, he smiled a little. Funny, but somehow he always understood Syb.

He could hear his mother just as plainly making Syb promise to take care of "Davy Boy" (that's what she always called him) and to be a good girl for Mother's sake. Then she made him promise to be "good" and mind Sybil and Father, and get in wood and chips whenever Sybil asked him. To him it seemed very much like the times his mother had got ready to go to town and left him in Sybil's care. But he promised. And his mother ran her long, slim fingers through his hair and kissed him again and again.

Then his father had come home from work, bringing with him a tall colored doctor. They had both gone to Mother's room. How well he remembered Sybil and himself huddled together by the kitchen woodbox, listening to the low tones of the doctor and his father. It seemed such a long time. It grew darker and darker. Soon it became all black and Syb lit the coal-oil lamp on the table and came back to sit beside him.

Finally Father, looking tired, with the corners of his mouth twitching and the little wrinkles under his eyes seeming much darker to David than ever before, called them into Mother's room. Mother was there, trying to say something. Tears choked her, and Sybil brushed back a strand of her long, silken hair that was blowing over her eyes. "Mo . . . ther," she said, her whole body quivering, "Mo . . . ther." And then David remembered something like a wind that blew across his face; and when he looked at his mother again, she had closed her eyes.

And he heard the doctor say, shaking his head, "If I'd only been here two hours sooner." David thought of every time his mother had ever kissed him. He thought of himself down at the crossroads watching Doctor Benson sip soda-pop. He fell on the couch and cried and cried and cried, and his father clutched him tightly and tried to soothe him; while Sybil was looking out of the window into the dark night—standing there in her gingham apron, withered like the white flower in the fruit jar on the kitchen table.

David didn't know how much time had passed since he had begun thinking all this, but he had been very quiet. Now he cast sidewide glances about the church. Tall Deacon Gant was praying and Sybil made him bow his head. "We has faith in you, Gawd," droned the old man. The rest was only syllables to David. Old Mother Simms was looking out of dark, heavily lidded eyes into his. She looked so sad as tears rolled down the furrows of her black, wrinkled face. But somehow it seemed funny to see her with fluffy purple feathers on her hat and a black lace collar on her starched white dress. Now David felt that something was going to happen. They were standing up, Sybil, Father, and he. Sybil was guiding him past the grey box. He was looking on his mother's closed eyes. How full her cheeks looked now; not as when she was sick. He could hear voices all around. He thought he heard that Benson boy calling out after him; he almost saw a red tongue poking out of a pale face, topped by yellow hair. He fancied he heard his mother call him "Davy

Boy." Everything was in a daze. When next he recognized his surroundings, he was in a black coach drawn by two horses. Sybil was crying; Father, stonily silent.

EXERCISES

1. Discuss the significance of the story being told as if by someone who knows the mind of David during the funeral. Could the story have had any other point of view or perspective and had the same impact? How would it have been different if told purely from David's own point of view?
2. Would you characterize this as a relatively simple story or a complex one? Explain.
3. What does David understand about the implications of his actions? How do you know?
4. Is this a story about heroic pride, foolish pride, or childish pride?
5. How would this story be different if it did not focus on race prejudice, for example, if David were white and the Benson boy were just a bully rather than a bigot?
6. Why is the story entitled "The Overcoat" even though the incident with the overcoat is not the central incident in the story?

ARNA
BONTEMPS | *A Summer Tragedy*

Old Jeff Patton, the black share farmer, fumbled with his bow tie. His fingers trembled, and the high, stiff collar pinched his throat. A fellow loses his hand for such vanities after thirty or forty years of simple life. Once a year, or maybe twice if there's a wedding among his kin-folks, he may spruce up; but generally fancy clothes do nothing but adorn the wall of the big room and feed the moths. That had been Jeff Patton's experience. He had not worn his stiff-bosomed shirt more than a dozen times in all his married life. His swallowtailed coat lay on the bed beside him, freshly brushed and pressed, but it was as full of holes as the overalls in which he worked on week days. The moths had used it badly. Jeff twisted his mouth into a hideous toothless grimace as he contended with the obstinate bow. He stamped his good foot and decided to give up the struggle.

"Jennie," he called.

"What's that, Jeff?" His wife's shrunken voice came out of the adjoining room like an echo. It was hardly bigger than a whisper.

"I reckon you'll have to he'p me wid this heah bow tie, baby," he said meekly. "Dog if I can hitch it up."

Her answer was not strong enough to reach him, but presently the old woman came to the door, feeling her way with a stick. She had a wasted, dead-leaf appearance. Her body, as scrawny and gnarled as a stringbean, seemed less than nothing in the ocean of frayed and faded petticoats that surrounded her. These hung an inch or two above the tops of her heavy, unlaced shoes and showed little grotesque piles where the stockings had fallen down from her negligible legs.

"You oughta could do a heap mo' wid a thing like that 'n me—beingst as you got yo' good sight."

"Looks like I *oughta* could," he admitted. "But ma fingers is gone democrat on me. I get all mixed up in the looking glass an' can't tell whicha way to twist the devilish thing."

Jenny sat on the side of the bed and old Jeff Patton got down on one knee while she tied the bow knot. It was a slow and painful ordeal for each of them in this position. Jeff's bones cracked, his knee ached, and it was only after a half dozen attempts that Jennie worked a semblance of a bow into the tie.

"I got to dress maself now," the old woman whispered. "These is ma old shoes an' stockings, and I ain't so much as unwrapped ma dress."

"Well, don't worry 'bout me no mo', baby," Jeff said. "That 'bout finishes me. All I gotta do now is slip on that old coat 'n ves' an' I'll be fixed to leave."

Jennie disappeared again through the dim passage into the shed room. Being blind was no handicap to her in that black hole. Jeff heard the cane placed against the wall beside the door and knew that his wife was on easy ground. He put on his coat, took a battered top hat from the bed post, and hobbled to the front door. He was ready to travel. As soon as Jennie could get on her Sunday shoes and her old black silk dress, they would start.

Outside the tiny log house the day was warm and mellow with sunshine. A host of wasps was humming with busy excitement in the trunk of a dead sycamore. Grey squirrels were searching through the grass for hickory nuts and blue jays were in the trees, hopping from branch to branch. Pine woods stretched away to the left like a black sea. Among them were scattered scores of log houses like Jeff's, houses of black share farmers. Cows and pigs wandered freely among the trees. There was no danger of loss. Each farmer knew his own stock and knew his neighbor's as well as he knew his neighbor's children.

Down the slope to the right were the cultivated acres on which the colored folks worked. They extended to the river, more than two miles away, and they were today green with the unmade cotton crop. A tiny thread of a road, which passed directly in front of Jeff's place, ran through these green fields like a pencil mark.

Jeff, standing outside the door with his absurd hat in his left hand, surveyed the wide scene tenderly. He had been forty-five years on these acres. He loved them with the unexplained affection that others have for the countries to which they belong.

The sun was hot on his head, his collar still pinched his throat, and the Sunday clothes were intolerably hot. Jeff transferred the hat to his right hand and began fanning with it. Suddenly the whisper that was Jennie's voice came out of the shed room.

"You can bring the car round front whilst you's waitin'," it said feebly. There was a tired pause; then it added, "I'll soon be fixed to go."

"A'right, baby," Jeff answered. "I'll get it in a minute."

But he didn't move. A thought struck him that made his mouth fall open. The mention of the car brought to his mind, with new intensity, the trip he and Jennie were about to take. Fear came into his eyes; excitement took his breath. Lord, Jesus!

"Jeff . . . Oh Jeff," the old woman's whisper called.

He awakened with a jolt. "Hunh, baby?"

"What you doin'?"

"Nuthin. Jes studyin'. I jes been turnin' things round 'n round in ma mind."

"You could be gettin' the car," she said.

"Oh yes, right away, baby."

He started round to the shed, limping heavily on his bad leg. There were three frizzly chickens in the yard. All his other chickens had been killed or stolen recently. But the frizzly chickens had been saved somehow. That was fortunate indeed, for these curious creatures had a way of devouring "poison" from the yard and in that way protecting against conjure and bad luck and spells. But even the frizzly chickens seemed now to be in a stupor. Jeff thought they had some ailment; he expected all three of them to die shortly.

The shed in which the old model-T Ford stood was only a grass roof held up by four corner poles. It had been built by tremulous hands at a time when the little rattletrap car had been regarded as a peculiar treasure. And, miraculously, despite wind and downpour, it still stood.

Jeff adjusted the crank and put his weight on it. The engine came to life with a sputter and bang that rattled the old car from radiator to tail light. Jeff hopped into the seat and put his foot on the accelerator. The sputtering and banging increased. The rattling became more violent. That was good. It was good banging, good sputtering and rattling, and it meant that the aged car was still in running condition. She could be depended on for this trip.

Again Jeff's thought halted as if paralyzed. The suggestion of the trip fell into the machinery of his mind like a wrench. He felt dazed and weak. He swung the car out into the yard, made a half turn, and drove around to the front door. When he took his hands off the wheel, he noticed that he was trembling violently. He cut off the motor and climbed to the ground to wait for Jennie.

A few moments later she was at the window, her voice rattling against the pane like a broken shutter.

"I'm ready, Jeff."

He did not answer, but limped into the house and took her by the arm. He led her slowly through the big room, down the step, and across the yard.

"You reckon I'd oughta lock the do'?" he asked softly.

They stopped and Jennie weighed the question. Finally she shook her head.

"Ne' mind the do'," she said. "I don't see no cause to lock up things."

"You right," Jeff agreed. "No cause to lock up."

Jeff opened the door and helped his wife into the car. A quick shudder passed over him. Jesus! Again he trembled.

"How come you shaking so?" Jennie whispered.

"I don't know," he said.

"You mus' be scairt, Jeff."

"No, baby, I ain't scairt."

He slammed the door after her and went around to crank up again. The motor started easily. Jeff wished that it had not been so responsive. He would have liked a few more minutes in which to turn things around in his head. As it was, with Jennie chiding him about being afraid, he had to keep going. He swung the car into the little pencil-mark road and started off toward the river, driving very slowly, very cautiously.

Chugging across the green countryside, the small, battered Ford seemed tiny indeed. Jeff felt a familiar excitement, a thrill, as they came down the first slope to the immense levels on which the cotton was growing. He could not help reflecting that the crops were good. He knew what that meant, too; he had made forty-five of them with his own hands. It was true that he had worn out nearly a dozen mules, but that was the fault of old man Stevenson, the owner of the land. Major Stevenson had the odd notion that one mule was all a share farmer needed to work a thirty-acre plot. It was an expensive notion, the way it killed mules from overwork, but the old man held to it. Jeff thought it killed a good many share farmers as well as mules, but he had no sympathy for them. He had always been strong, and he had been taught to have no patience with weakness in men. Women or children might be tolerated if they were puny, but a weak man was a curse. Of course, his own children—

Jeff's thought halted there. He and Jennie never mentioned their dead children any more. And naturally he did not wish to dwell upon them in his mind. Before he knew it, some remark would slip out of his mouth and that would make Jennie feel blue. Perhaps she would cry. A woman like Jennie could not easily throw off the grief that comes from losing five grown children within two years. Even Jeff was still staggered by the blow. His memory had not been much good recently. He frequently talked to himself. And, although he had kept it a secret, he knew that his courage had left him. He was terrified by the least unfamiliar sound at night. He was reluctant to venture far from home in the daytime. And that habit of trembling when he felt fearful was now far beyond his control. Sometimes he became afraid and trembled without knowing what had frightened him. The feeling would just come over him like a chill.

The car rattled slowly over the dusty road. Jennie sat erect and silent, with a little absurd hat pinned to her hair. Her useless eyes seemed very large and very white in their deep sockets. Suddenly Jeff heard her voice, and he inclined his head to catch the words.

"Is we passed Delia Moore's house yet?" she asked.

"Not yet," he said.

"You must be drivin' mighty slow, Jeff."

"We jes as well take our time, baby."

There was a pause. A little puff of steam was coming out of the radiator of the car. Heat wavered above the hood. Delia Moore's house was nearly half a mile away. After a moment Jennie spoke again.

"You ain't really scairt, is you, Jeff?"

"Nah, baby, I ain't scairt."

"You know how we agreed—we gotta keep on goin'."

Jewels of perspiration appeared on Jeff's forehead. His eyes rounded, blinked, became fixed on the road.

"I don't know," he said with a shiver. "I reckon it's the only thing to do."

"Hm."

A flock of guinea fowls, pecking in the road, were scattered by the passing car. Some of them took to their wings; others hid under bushes. A blue jay, swaying on a leafy twig, was annoying a roadside squirrel. Jeff held an even speed till he came near Delia's place. Then he slowed down noticeably.

Delia's house was really no house at all, but an abandoned store building converted into a dwelling. It sat near a crossroads, beneath a single black cedar tree. There Delia, a catlike old creature of Jennie's age, lived alone. She had been there more years than anybody could remember, and long ago had won the disfavor of such women as Jennie. For in her young days Delia had been gayer, yellower, and saucier than seemed proper in those parts. Her ways with menfolks had been dark and suspicious. And the fact that she had had as many husbands as children did not help her reputation.

"Yonder's old Delia," Jeff said as they passed.

"What she doin'?"

"Jes sittin' in the do'," he said.

"She see us?"

"Hm," Jeff said. "Musta did."

That relieved Jennie. It strengthened her to know that her old enemy had seen her pass in her best clothes. That would give the old she-devil something to chew her gums and fret about, Jennie thought. Wouldn't she have a fit if she didn't find out? Old evil Delia! This would be just the thing for her. It would pay her back for being so evil. It would also pay her, Jennie thought, for the way she used to grin at Jeff—long ago when her teeth were good.

The road became smooth and red, and Jeff could tell by the smell of the air that they were nearing the river. He could see the rise where the road turned and ran along parallel to the stream. The car chugged on monotonously. After a long silent spell, Jennie leaned against Jeff and spoke.

"How many bale o' cotton you think we got standin'?" she said.

Jeff wrinkled his forehead as he calculated.

" 'Bout twenty-five, I reckon."

"How many you make las' year?"

"Twenty-eight," he said. "How come you ask that?"

"I's jes thinkin'," Jennie said quietly.

"It don't make a speck o' diff'ence though," Jeff reflected. "If we get much or if we get little, we still gonna be in debt to old man Stevenson when he gets through counting up agin us. It's took us a long time to learn that."

Jennie was not listening to these words. She had fallen into a trance-like meditation. Her lips twitched. She chewed her gums and rubbed her old gnarled hands nervously. Suddenly, she leaned forward, buried her face in the nervous hands, and burst into tears. She cried aloud in a dry, cracked voice that suggested the rattle of fodder on dead stalks. She cried aloud like a child, for she had never learned to suppress a genuine sob. Her slight old frame shook heavily and seemed hardly able to sustain such violent grief.

"What's the matter, baby?" Jeff asked awkwardly. "Why you cryin' like all that?"

"I's jes thinkin'," she said.

"So you the one what's scairt now, hunh?"

"I ain't scairt, Jeff. I's jes thinkin' 'bout leavin' eve'thing like this—eve'-thing we been used to. It's right sad-like."

Jeff did not answer, and presently Jennie buried her face again and continued crying.

The sun was almost overhead. It beat down furiously on the dusty wagon path road, on the parched roadside grass, and the tiny battered car. Jeff's hands, gripping the wheel, became wet with perspiration; his forehead sparkled. Jeff's lips parted and his mouth shaped a hideous grimace. His face suggested the face of a man being burned. But the torture passed and his expression softened again.

"You mustn't cry, baby," he said to his wife. "We gotta be strong. We can't break down."

Jennie waited a few seconds, then said, "You reckon we oughta do it, Jeff? You reckon we oughta go 'head an' do it really?"

Jeff's voice choked; his eyes blurred. He was terrified to hear Jennie say the thing that had been in his mind all morning. She had egged him on when he had wanted more than anything in the world to wait, to reconsider, to think things over a little longer. Now *she* was getting cold feet. Actually, there was no need of thinking the question through again. It would only end in making the same painful decision once more. Jeff knew that. There was no need of fooling around longer.

"We jes as well to do like we planned," he said. "They ain't nuthin else for us now—it's the bes' thing."

Jeff thought of the handicaps, the near impossibility, of making another crop with his leg bothering him more and more each week. Then there was always the chance that he would have another stroke, like the one that had made him lame. Another one might kill him. The least it could do would be to leave him helpless. Jeff gasped . . . Lord, Jesus! He could not bear to think of being helpless, like a baby, on Jennie's hands. Frail, blind Jennie.

The little pounding motor of the car worked harder and harder. The puff of steam from the cracked radiator became larger. Jeff realized that they were climbing a little rise. A moment later the road turned abruptly and he looked down upon the face of the river.

"Jeff."

"Hunh?"

"Is that the water I hear?"

"Hm. Tha's it."

"Well, which way you goin' now?"

"Down this-a way," he answered. "The road runs 'longside o' the water a lil piece."

She waited a while calmly. Then she said, "Drive faster."

"A'right, baby," Jeff said.

The water roared in the bed of the river. It was fifty or sixty feet below the level of the road. Between the road and the water there was a long smooth slope, sharply inclined. The slope was dry; the clay had been hardened by prolonged summer heat. The water below, roaring in a narrow channel, was noisy and wild.

"Jeff."

"Hunh?"

"How far you goin'?"

"Jes a lil piece down the road."

"You ain't scairt is you, Jeff?"

"Nah, baby," he said trembling. "I ain't scairt."

"Remember how we planned it, Jeff. We gotta do it like we said. Brave-like."

"Hm."

Jeff's brain darkened. Things suddenly seemed unreal, like figures in a dream. Thoughts swam in his mind foolishly, hysterically, like little blind fish in a pool within a dense cave. They rushed, crossed one another, jostled, collided, retreated, and rushed again. Jeff soon became dizzy. He shuddered violently and turned to his wife.

"Jennie, I can't do it. I can't." His voice broke pitifully.

She did not appear to be listening. All the grief had gone from her face. She sat erect, her unseeing eyes wide open, strained and frightful. Her glossy black skin had become dull. She seemed as thin and as sharp and bony as a starved bird. Now, having suffered and endured the sadness of tearing herself away from beloved things, she showed no anguish. She was absorbed with her own thoughts, and she didn't even hear Jeff's voice shouting in her ear.

Jeff said nothing more. For an instant there was light in his cavernous brain. That chamber was, for less than a second, peopled by characters he knew and loved. They were simple, healthy creatures, and they behaved in a manner that he could understand. They had quality. But since he had already taken leave of them long ago, the remembrance did not break his heart again. Young Jeff Patton was among them, the Jeff Patton of fifty years ago who went down to New Orleans with a crowd of country boys to the Mardi Gras doings. The gay young crowd—boys with candy-striped shirts and rouged brown girls in noisy silks—was like a picture in his head. Yet it did not make him sad. On that very trip Slim Burns had killed Joe Beasley—the crowd had been broken up. Since then Jeff Patton's world had been the Greenbrier Plantation. If there had been other Mardi Gras carnivals, he had not heard of them. Since then there had been no time; the years had fallen on him like waves. Now he was old, worn out. Another paralytic stroke like the one he had already suffered would put him on his back for keeps. In that condition, with a frail blind woman to look after him, he would be worse off than if he were dead.

Suddenly Jeff's hands became steady. He actually felt brave. He slowed down the motor of the car and carefully pulled off the road. Below, the water of the stream boomed, a soft thunder in the deep channel. Jeff ran the car onto the clay slope, pointed it directly toward the stream, and put his foot heavily on the accelerator. The little car leaped furiously down the steep incline toward the water. The movement was nearly as swift and direct as a fall. The two old black folks, sitting quietly side by side, showed no excitement. In another instant the car hit the water and dropped immediately out of sight.

A little later it lodged in the mud of a shallow place. One wheel of the crushed and upturned little Ford became visible above the rushing water.

EXERCISES

1. Discuss the physical description of the old couple and the place where they live. What is the nature of the "world" of the story?

2. What is the significance of Jeff's having lost his courage? What does this mean?

3. Why have the couple decided to take their own lives? At what point in the story did you know they were going to take their lives?

4. Although the story is not told by Jeff, it does focus on his consciousness. Why is the story told from Jeff's perspective rather than from Jennie's?

5. If the ending is not really a shock, why does the storyteller not tell us what they have planned until the end? Does this have anything to do with the point of view of the story?

6. Is the act of the old couple one of courage or cowardice? How does the storyteller judge the suicide? How do you know?

CHINUA
ACHEBE | *Dead Men's Path*

Michael Obi's hopes were fulfilled much earlier than he expected. He was appointed headmaster of Ndume Central School in January 1949. It had always been an unprogressive school, so the Mission authorities decided to send a young and energetic man to run it. Obi accepted this responsibility with enthusiasm. He had many wonderful ideas and this was an opportunity to put them into practice. He had had sound secondary school education which designated him a "pivotal teacher" in the official records and set him apart from the other headmasters in the mission field. He was outspoken in his condemnation of the narrow views of these older and often less-educated ones.

"We shall make a good job of it, shan't we?" he asked his young wife when they first heard the joyful news of his promotion.

"We shall do our best," she replied. "We shall have such beautiful gardens and everything will be just *modern* and delightful . . ." In their two years of married life she had become completely infected by his passion for "modern methods" and his denigration of "these old and superannuated people in the teaching field who would be better employed as traders in the Onitsha market." She began to see herself already as the admired wife of the young headmaster, the queen of the school.

The wives of the other teachers would envy her position. She would set the fashion in everything . . . Then, suddenly, it occurred to her that there might not be other wives. Wavering between hope and fear, she asked her husband, looking anxiously at him.

"All our colleagues are young and unmarried," he said with enthusiasm which for once she did not share. "Which is a good thing," he continued.

"Why?"

"Why? They will give all their time and energy to the school."

Nancy was downcast. For a few minutes she became sceptical about the new school; but it was only for a few minutes. Her little personal misfortune could not blind her to her husband's happy prospects. She looked at him as he sat folded up in a chair. He was stoop-shouldered and looked frail. But he sometimes surprised people with sudden bursts of physical energy. In his present posture, however, all his bodily strength seemed to have retired behind his deep-set eyes, giving them an extraordinary power of penetration. He was only twenty-six, but looked thirty or more. On the whole, he was not unhandsome.

"A penny for your thoughts, Mike," said Nancy after a while, imitating the woman's magazine she read.

"I was thinking what a grand opportunity we've got at last to show these people how a school should be run."

Ndume School was backward in every sense of the word. Mr. Obi put his whole life into the work, and his wife hers too. He had two aims. A high standard of teaching was insisted upon, and the school compound was to be turned into a place of beauty. Nancy's dream-gardens came to life with the coming of the rains, and blossomed. Beautiful hibiscus and allamanda hedges in brilliant red and yellow marked out the carefully tended school compound from the rank neighbourhood bushes.

One evening as Obi was admiring his work he was scandalized to see an old woman from the village hobble right across the compound, through a marigold flower-bed and the hedges. On going up there he found faint signs of an almost disused path from the village across the school compound to the bush on the other side.

"It amazes me," said Obi to one of his teachers who had been three years in the school, "that you people allowed the villagers to make use of this foot-path. It is simply incredible." He shook his head.

"The path," said the teacher apologetically, "appears to be very important to them. Although it is hardly used, it connects the village shrine with their place of burial."

"And what has that got to do with the school?" asked the headmaster.

"Well, I don't know," replied the other with a shrug of the shoulders. "But I remember there was a big row some time ago when we attempted to close it."

"That was some time ago. But it will not be used now," said Obi as he walked away. "What will the Government Education Officer think of this when he comes to inspect the school next week? The villagers might, for all I know, decide to use the schoolroom for a pagan ritual during the inspection."

Heavy sticks were planted closely across the path at the two places where it entered and left the school premises. These were further strengthened with barbed wire.

Three days later the village priest of *Ani* called on the headmaster. He was an old man and walked with a slight stoop. He carried a stout walking-stick which he usually tapped on the floor, by way of emphasis, each time he made a new point in his argument.

"I have heard," he said after the usual exchange of cordialities, "that our ancestral footpath has recently been closed . . ."

"Yes," replied Mr. Obi. "We cannot allow people to make a highway of our school compound."

"Look here, my son," said the priest bringing down his walking-stick, "this path was here before you were born and before your father was born. The whole life of this village depends on it. Our dead relatives depart by it and our ancestors visit us by it. But most important, it is the path of children coming in to be born . . ."

Mr. Obi listened with a satisfied smile on his face.

"The whole purpose of our school," he said finally, "is to eradicate just such beliefs as that. Dead men do not require footpaths. The whole idea is just fantastic. Our duty is to teach your children to laugh at such ideas."

"What you say may be true," replied the priest, "but we follow the practices of our fathers. If you re-open the path we shall have nothing to quarrel about. What I always say is: let the hawk perch and let the eagle perch." He rose to go.

"I am sorry," said the young headmaster. "But the school compound cannot be a thoroughfare. It is against our regulations. I would suggest your constructing another path, skirting our premises. We can even get our boys to help in building it. I don't suppose the ancestors will find the little detour too burdensome."

"I have no more words to say," said the old priest, already outside.

Two days later a young woman in the village died in childbed. A diviner was immediately consulted and he prescribed heavy sacrifices to propitiate ancestors insulted by the fence.

Obi woke up next morning among the ruins of his work. The beautiful hedges were torn up not just near the path but right round the school, the flowers trampled to death and one of the school buildings pulled down . . . That day, the white Supervisor came to inspect the school and wrote a nasty report on the state of the premises but more seriously about the "tribal-war situation developing between the school and the village, arising in part from the misguided zeal of the new headmaster."

EXERCISES

1. Describe the personality and motivation of Mr. Obi. Why does he order the path blocked off?
2. What two value systems are represented in the story? Discuss the virtues of each.
3. How do you react to the ending of the story? Is the nasty report against Mr. Obi an example of poetic justice? What is ironic about the ending?
4. Discuss the significance of the title. Discuss Mr. Obi's statement, "Dead men do not require footpaths."
5. If "backward" is not the opposite of "modern methods," as Mr. Obi thinks, then what is the opposite of the "modern" in this story?
6. Is this a simple story or a complex one? Are the ideas it illustrates simple or complex?

NADINE
GORDIMER | *The Train from Rhodesia*

The train came out of the red horizon and bore down towards them over the single straight track.

The stationmaster came out of his little brick station with its pointed chalet roof, feeling the creases in his serge uniform in his legs as well. A stir of preparedness rippled through the squatting native vendors waiting in the dust; the face of a carved wooden animal, eternally surprised, stuck out of a sack. The stationmaster's barefoot children wandered over. From the grey mud huts with the untidy heads that stood within a decorated mud wall, chickens, and dogs with their skin stretched like parchment over their bones, followed the piccanins down to the track. The flushed and perspiring west cast a reflection, faint, without heat, upon the station, upon the tin shed marked "Goods," upon the walled kraal, upon the grey tin house of the stationmaster and upon the sand, that lapped all around, from sky to sky, cast little rhythmical cups of shadow, so that the sand became the sea, and closed over the children's black feet softly and without imprint.

The stationmaster's wife sat behind the mesh of her veranda. Above her head the hunk of a sheep's carcass moved slightly, dangling in a current of air. They waited.

The train called out, along the sky; but there was no answer; and the cry hung on: I'm coming . . . I'm coming . . .

The engine flared out now, big, whisking a dwindling body behind it; the track flared out to let it in.

Creaking, jerking, jostling, gasping, the train filled the station.

Here, let me see that one—the young woman curved her body farther out of the corridor window. Missus? smiled the old man, looking at the creatures he held in his hand. From a piece of string on his grey finger hung a tiny woven basket; he lifted it, questioning. No, no, she urged, leaning down towards him, across the height of the train towards the man in the piece of old rug; that one, that one, her hand commanded. It was a lion, carved out of soft dry wood that looked like spongecake; heraldic, black and white, with impressionistic detail burnt in. The old man held it up to her still smiling, not from the heart, but at the customer. Between its vandyke teeth, in the mouth opened in an endless roar too terrible to be heard, it had a black tongue. Look, said the young husband, if you don't mind! And round the neck of the thing, a piece of fur (rat? rabbit? meerkat?); a real mane, majestic, telling you somehow that the artist had delight in the lion.

All up and down the length of the train in the dust the artists sprang, walking bent, like performing animals, the better to exhibit the fantasy held towards the faces on the train. Buck, startled and stiff, staring with round black and white eyes. More lions, standing erect, grappling with strange, thin, elongated warriors who clutched spears and showed no fear in their slits of eyes. How much, they asked from the train, how much?

Give me penny, said the little ones with nothing to sell. The dogs went and sat, quite still, under the dining car, where the train breathed out the smell of meat cooking with onion.

A man passed beneath the arch of reaching arms meeting grey-black and white in the exchange of money for the staring wooden eyes, the stiff wooden legs sticking up in the air; went along under the voices and the bargaining, interrogating the wheels. Past the dogs; glancing up at the dining car where he could stare at the faces behind glass, drinking beer, two by two, on either side of a uniform railway vase with its pale dead flower. Right to the end, to the guard's van, where the stationmaster's children had just collected their mother's two loaves of bread, to the engine itself, where the stationmaster and the driver stood talking against the steaming complaint of the resting beast.

The man called out to them, something loud and joking. They turned to laugh, in a twirl of steam. The two children careened over the sand, clutching the bread, and burst through the iron gate and up the path through the garden in which nothing grew.

Passengers drew themselves in at the corridor windows and turned into compartments to fetch money, to call someone to look. Those sitting inside looked up: suddenly different, caged faces, boxed in, cut off after the contact of outside. There was an orange a piccanin would like . . . What about that chocolate? It wasn't very nice . . .

A girl had collected a handful of the hard kind, that no one liked, out of the chocolate box, and was throwing them to the dogs, over at the dining car. But the hens darted in and swallowed the chocolates, incredibly quick and accurate, before they had even dropped in the dust, and the dogs, a little bewildered, looked up with their brown eyes, not expecting anything.

—No, leave it, said the young woman, don't take it . . .

Too expensive, too much, she shook her head and raised her voice to the old man, giving up the lion. He held it high where she had handed it to him. No, she said, shaking her head. Three-and-six? insisted her husband, loudly. Yes baas! laughed the old man. Three-and-six?—the young man was incredulous. Oh leave it—she said. The young man stopped. Don't you want it? he said, keeping his face closed to the old man. No, never mind, she said, leave it. The old native kept his head on one side, looking at them sideways, holding the lion. Three-and-six, he murmured, as old people repeat things to themselves.

The young woman drew her head in. She went into the coupé and sat down. Out of the window, on the other side, there was nothing; sand and bush; a thorn tree. Back through the open doorway, past the figure of her husband in the corridor, there was the station, the voices, wooden animals waving, running feet. Her eye followed the funny little valance of scrolled wood that outlined the chalet roof of the station; she thought of the lion and smiled. That bit of fur round the neck. But the wooden buck, the hippos, the elephants, the baskets that already bulked out of their brown paper under the seat and on the luggage rack! How will they look at home? Where will you put them? What will they mean away from the places you found them? Away from the unreality of the last few weeks? The young man outside. But he is not part of the unreality; he is for good now. Odd . . . somewhere there was an idea that he, that living with him, was part of the holiday, the strange places.

Outside, a bell rang. The stationmaster was leaning against the end of the train, green flag rolled in readiness. A few men who had got down to stretch their legs sprang on to the train, clinging to the observation platforms, or perhaps merely standing on the iron step, holding the rail; but on the train, safe from the one dusty platform, the one tin house, the empty sand.

There was a grunt. The train jerked. Through the glass the beer drinkers looked out, as if they could not see beyond it. Behind the fly-screen, the stationmaster's wife sat facing back at them beneath the darkening hunk of meat.

There was a shout. The flag drooped out. Joints not yet coordinated, the segmented body of the train heaved and bumped back against itself. It began to move; slowly the scrolled chalet moved past it, the yells of the natives, running alongside, jetted up into the air, fell back at different levels. Staring wooden faces waved drunkenly, there, then gone, questioning for the last time at the windows. Here, one-and-six baas!—As one automatically opens a hand to catch a thrown ball, a man fumbled wildly down his pocket, brought up the shilling and sixpence and threw them out; the old native, gasping, his skinny toes splaying the sand, flung the lion.

The piccanins were waving, the dogs stood, tails uncertain, watching the train go; past the mud huts, where a woman turned to look up from the smoke of the fire, her hand pausing on her hip.

The stationmaster went slowly in under the chalet.

The old native stood, breath blowing out the skin between his ribs, feet tense, balanced in the sand, smiling and shaking his head. In his opened palm, held in the attitude of receiving, was the retrieved shilling and sixpence.

The blind end of the train was being pulled helplessly out of the station.

The young man swung in from the corridor, breathless. He was shaking his head with laughter and triumph. Here! he said. And waggled the lion at her. One-and-six!

What? she said.

He laughed. I was arguing with him for fun, bargaining—when the train had pulled out already, he came tearing after. . . . One-and-six Baas! So there's your lion.

She was holding it away from her, the lion with the open jaws, the pointed teeth, the black tongue, the wonderful ruff of fur facing her. She was looking at it with an expression of not seeing, of seeing something different. Her face was drawn up, wryly, like the face of a discomforted child. Her mouth lifted nervously at the corner. Very slowly, cautious, she lifted her finger and touched the mane, where it was joined to the wood.

But how could you, she said. He was shocked by the dismay of her face. Good Lord, he said, what's the matter?

If you wanted the thing, she said, her voice rising and breaking with the shrill impotence of anger, why didn't you buy it in the first place? If you wanted it, why didn't you pay for it? Why didn't you take it decently, when he offered it? Why did you have to wait for him to run after the train with it, and give him one-and-six? One-and-six!

She was pushing it at him, trying to force him to take the lion. He stood astonished, his hands hanging at his sides.

But you wanted it! You liked it so much!

—It's a beautiful piece of work, she said fiercely, as if to protect it from him.

You liked it so much! You said yourself it was too expensive—

Oh *you*—she said, hopeless and furious. *You* . . . She threw the lion onto the seat.

He stood looking at her.

She sat down again in the corner and, her face slumped in her hands, stared out of the window. Everything was turning round inside her. One-and-six. One-and-six. One-and-six for the wood and the carving and the sinews of the legs and the switch of the tail. The mouth open like that and the teeth. The black tongue, rolling, like a wave. The mane round the neck. To give one-and-six for that. The heat of shame mounted through her legs and body and sounded in her ears like the sound of sand pouring. Pouring, pouring. She sat there, sick. A weariness, a tastelessness, the discovery of a void made her hands slacken their grip, atrophy emptily, as if the hour was not worth their grasp. She was feeling like this again. She had thought it was something to do with singleness, with being alone and belonging too much to oneself.

She sat there not wanting to move or speak, or to look at anything even; so that the mood should be associated with nothing, no object, word or sight that might recur and so recall the feeling again. . . . Smuts blew in grittily, settled on her hands. Her back remained at exactly the same angle, turned against the young man sitting with his hands dropping between his sprawled legs, and the lion, fallen on its side in the corner

The train had cast the station like a skin. It called out to the sky, I'm coming, I'm coming; and again, there was no answer.

EXERCISES

1. The people at the train station are referred to both as vendors and as artists. Which are they? What is suggested by the fact that the old man holds up the lion smiling "not from the heart, but at the customer"?

2. What kind of relationship does the woman have with the young man? Why does she refer to the last few weeks as "unreal"? Why does she think that living with him is part of the holiday?

3. Why is there so much detail in this story about the physical scene—the people on the platform, the people on the train, the train itself? What effect do all these specific details have?

4. Why does the young woman react so extremely to the young man's encounter with the vendor? Is there anything in the story to prepare us for this reaction?

5. What is the void the young woman has discovered? Is this a story about the young woman, about her relationship with the young man, or about the relationship between whites and blacks in Africa?

6. Discuss the following: "She was feeling like this again. She had thought it was something to do with singleness, with being alone and belonging too much to oneself."

HERNANDO
TÉLLEZ | *Just Lather, That's All*

He said nothing when he entered. I was passing the best of my razors back and forth on a strop. When I recognized him I started to tremble. But he didn't notice. Hoping to conceal my emotion, I continued sharpening the razor. I tested it on the meat of my thumb, and then held it up to the light. At that moment he took off the bullet-studded belt that his gun holster dangled from. He hung it up on a wall hook and placed his military cap over it. Then he turned to me, loosening the knot of his tie, and said, "It's hot as hell. Give me a shave." He sat in the chair.

I estimated he had a four-day beard. The four days taken up by the latest expedition in search of our troops. His face seemed reddened, burned by the sun. Carefully, I began to prepare the soap. I cut off a few slices, dropped them into the cup, mixed in a bit of warm water, and began to stir with the brush. Immediately the foam began to rise. "The other boys in the group should have this much beard, too," he remarked. I continued stirring the lather.

"But we did all right, you know. We got the main ones. We brought back some dead, and we've got some others still alive. But pretty soon they'll all be dead."

"How many did you catch?" I asked.

"Fourteen. We had to go pretty deep into the woods to find them. But we'll get even. Not one of them comes out of this alive, not one."

He leaned back on the chair when he saw me with the lather-covered brush in my hand. I still had to put the sheet on him. No doubt about it, I was upset. I took a sheet out of the drawer and knotted it around my customer's neck. He wouldn't stop talking. He probably thought I was in sympathy with his party.

"The town must have learned a lesson from what we did the other day," he said.

"Yes," I replied, securing the knot at the base of his dark, sweaty neck.

"That was a fine show, eh?"

"Very good," I answered, turning back for the brush. The man closed his eyes with a gesture of fatigue and sat waiting for the cool caress of the soap. I had never had him so close to me. The day he ordered the whole town to file into the patio of the school to see the four rebels hanging there, I came face to face with him for an instant. But the sight of the mutilated bodies kept me from noticing the face of the man who had directed it all, the face I was now about to take into my hands. It was not an unpleasant face, certainly. And the beard, which made him seem a bit older than he was, didn't suit him badly at all. His name was Torres. Captain Torres. A man of imagination, because who else would have thought of hanging the naked rebels and then holding target practice on certain parts of their bodies? I began to apply the first layer of soap. With his eyes closed, he continued. "Without any effort I could go straight to sleep," he said, "but there's plenty to do this afternoon."

I stopped the lathering and asked with a feigned lack of interest: "A firing squad?" "Something like that, but a little slower." I got on with the job of lathering his beard. My hands started trembling again. The man could not possibly realize it, and this was in my favor. But I would have preferred that he hadn't come. It was likely that many of our faction had seen him enter. And an enemy under one's roof imposes certain conditions. I would be obliged to shave that beard like any other one, carefully, gently, like that of any customer, taking pains to see that no single pore emitted a drop of blood. Being careful to see that the little tufts of hair did not lead the blade astray. Seeing that his skin ended up clean, soft, and healthy, so that passing the back of my hand over it I couldn't feel a hair. Yes, I was secretly a rebel, but I was also a conscientious barber, and proud of the preciseness of my profession. And this four-days' growth of beard was a fitting challenge.

I took the razor, opened up the two protective arms, exposed the blade and began the job, from one of the sideburns downward. The razor responded beautifully. His beard was inflexible and hard, not too long, but thick. Bit by bit the skin emerged. The razor rasped along, making its customary sound as fluffs of lather mixed with bits of hair gathered along the blade. I paused a moment to clean it, then took up the strop again to sharpen the razor, because I'm a barber who does things properly. The man, who had kept his eyes closed, opened them now, removed one of his hands from under the sheet, felt the spot on his face where the soap had been cleared off, and said, "Come to the school today at six o'clock." "The same thing as the other day?" I asked horrified. "It could be better," he replied. "What do you plan to do?" "I don't know yet. But we'll amuse ourselves." Once more he leaned back and closed his eyes. I approached him with the razor poised. "Do you plan to punish them all?" I ventured timidly. "All." The soap was drying on his face. I had to hurry. In the mirror I looked toward the street. It was the same as ever: the grocery store with two or three customers in it. Then I glanced at the clock: two-twenty in the afternoon. The razor continued on its downward stroke. Now from the other sideburn down. A thick, blue beard. He should have let it grow like some poets or priests do. It would suit him well. A lot of people wouldn't recognize him. Much to his benefit, I thought, as I attempted to cover the neck area smoothly. There, for sure, the razor had to be handled masterfully, since the hair, although softer, grew into little swirls. A curly beard. One of the tiny pores could be opened up and issue forth its pearl of blood. A good barber such as I prides himself on never allowing this to happen to a client. And this was a first-class client. How many of us had he ordered shot? How many of us had he ordered mutilated? It was better not to think about it. Torres did not know that I was his enemy. He did not know it nor did the rest. It was a secret shared by very few, precisely so that I could inform the revolutionaries of what Torres was doing in the town and of what he was planning each time he undertook a rebel-hunting excursion. So it was going to be very difficult to explain that I had him right in my hands and let him go peacefully—alive and shaved.

The beard was now almost completely gone. He seemed younger, less burdened by years than when he had arrived. I suppose this always happens with men who visit barber shops. Under the stroke of my razor Torres was being rejuvenated—rejuvenated because I am a good barber, the best in the town, if I may say so. A little more lather here, under his chin, on his Adam's apple, on this big vein. How hot it is getting! Torres must be sweating as much as I. But he is not afraid. He is a calm man, who is not even thinking about what he is going to do with the prisoners this afternoon. On the other hand I, with this razor in my hands, stroking and restroking this skin, trying to keep blood from oozing from these pores, can't even think clearly. Damn him for coming, because I'm a revolutionary and not a murderer. And how easy it would be to kill him. And he deserves it. Does he? No! What the devil! No one deserves to have someone else make the sacrifice of becoming a murderer. What do you gain by it? Nothing. Others come along and still others, and the first ones kill the second ones and they the next ones and it goes on like this until everything is a sea of blood. I could cut this throat just so, zip! zip! I wouldn't give him time to complain and since he has his eyes closed he wouldn't see the glistening knife blade or my glistening eyes. But I'm trembling like a real murderer. Out of his neck a gush of blood would spout onto the sheet, on the chair, on my hands, on the floor. I would have to close the door. And the blood would keep inching along the floor, warm, ineradicable, uncontainable, until it reached the street, like a little scarlet stream. I'm sure that one solid stroke, one deep incision, would prevent any pain. He wouldn't suffer. But what would I do with the body? Where would I hide it? I would have to flee, leaving all I have behind, and take refuge far away, far, far away. But they would follow until they found me. "Captain Torres' murderer. He slit his throat while he was shaving him—a coward." And then on the other side. "The avenger of us all. A name to remember. (And here they would mention my name.) He was the town barber. No one knew he was defending our cause."

And what of all this? Murderer or hero? My destiny depends on the edge of this blade. I can turn my hand a bit more, press a little harder on the razor, and sink it in. The skin would give way like silk, like rubber, like the strop. There is nothing more tender than human skin and the blood is always there, ready to pour forth. A blade like this doesn't fail. It is my best. But I don't want to be a murderer, no sir. You come to me for a shave. And I perform my work honorably. . . . I don't want blood on my hands. Just lather, that's all. You are an executioner and I am only a barber. Each person has his own place in the scheme of things. That's right. His own place.

Now his chin had been stroked clean and smooth. The man sat up and looked into the mirror. He rubbed his hands over his skin and felt it fresh, like new.

"Thanks," he said. He went to the hanger for his belt, pistol and cap. I must have been very pale; my shirt felt soaked. Torres finished adjusting the buckle, straightened his pistol in the holster and after automatically smoothing down his hair, he put on the cap. From his pants pocket he took out several coins to pay me for my services. And he began to head toward the door. In the doorway he paused for a moment, and turning to me he said:

"They told me that you'd kill me. I came to find out. But killing isn't easy. You can take my word for it." And he headed on down the street.

EXERCISES

1. Which is more important in this story—the conflict between the two men or the conflict within the mind of the barber? How do you know?

2. What kind of social situation forms the background of this story? Which side of the social conflict is the "right" side? How do you know?

3. Describe the nature of the conflict within the barber. Why does he not kill his enemy when he has the chance?

4. What is meant by the phrase, "Each person has his own place in the scheme of things"? What is the difference between the two men?

5. Why does the captain risk his life by having a man he knows is his enemy shave him? What is the meaning of his final words to the barber? Is it believable for him to say killing isn't easy after we have heard of the executions he has performed? Support your answer.

6. Is this a simple story or a complex one? Is the situation simple and the theme complex, or vice versa?

ANTON
CHEKHOV | *After the Theatre*

Nadya Zelenin had just come back with her mamma from the theatre where she had seen a performance of "Yevgeny Onyegin." As soon as she reached her own room she threw off her dress, let down her hair, and in her petticoat and white dressing-jacket hastily sat down to the table to write a letter like Tatyana's.

"I love you," she wrote, "but you do not love me, do not love me!"

She wrote it and laughed.

She was only sixteen and did not yet love anyone. She knew that an officer called Gorny and a student called Gruzdev loved her, but now after the opera she wanted to be doubtful of their love. To be unloved and unhappy—how interesting that was. There is something beautiful, touching, and poetical about it when one loves and the other is indifferent. Onyegin was interesting because he was not in love at all, and Tatyana was fascinating because she was so much in love; but if they had been equally in love with each other and had been happy, they would perhaps have seemed dull.

"Leave off declaring that you love me," Nadya went on writing, thinking of Gorny. "I cannot believe it. You are very clever, cultivated, serious, you have immense talent, and perhaps a brilliant future awaits you, while I am an uninteresting girl of no importance, and you know very well that I should be only a hindrance in your life. It is true that you were attracted by me and thought you had found your ideal in me, but that was a mistake, and now you are asking yourself in despair: 'Why did I meet that girl?' And only your goodness of heart prevents you from owning it to yourself. . . ."

Nadya felt sorry for herself, she began to cry, and went on:

"It is hard for me to leave my mother and my brother, or I should take a nun's veil and go whither chance may lead me. And you would be left free and would love another. Oh, if I were dead!"

She could not make out what she had written through her tears; little rainbows were quivering on the table, on the floor, on the ceiling, as though she were looking through a prism. She could not write, she sank back in her easychair and fell to thinking of Gorny.

My God! how interesting, how fascinating men were! Nadya recalled the fine expression, ingratiating, guilty, and soft, which came into the officer's face when one argued about music with him, and the effort he made to prevent his voice from betraying his passion. In a society where cold haughtiness and indifference are regarded as signs of good breeding and gentlemanly bearing, one must conceal one's passions. And he did try to conceal them, but he did not succeed, and everyone knew very well that he had a passionate love of music. The endless discussions about music and the bold criticisms of people who knew nothing about it kept him always on the strain; he was frightened, timid, and silent. He played the piano magnificently, like a professional pianist, and if he had not been in the army he would certainly have been a famous musician.

The tears on her eyes dried. Nadya remembered that Gorny had declared his love at a Symphony concert, and again downstairs by the hatstand where there was a tremendous draught blowing in all directions.

"I am very glad that you have at last made the acquaintance of Gruzdev, our student friend," she went on writing. "He is a very clever man, and you will be sure to like him. He came to see us yesterday and stayed till two o'clock. We were all delighted with him, and I regretted that you had not come. He said a great deal that was remarkable."

Nadya laid her arms on the table and leaned her head on them, and her hair covered the letter. She recalled that the student, too, loved her, and that he had as much right to a letter from her as Gorny. Wouldn't it be better after all to write to Gruzdev? There was a stir of joy in her bosom for no reason whatever; at first the joy was small, and rolled in her bosom like an indiarubber ball; then it became more massive, bigger, and rushed like a wave. Nadya forgot Gorny and Gruzdev; her thoughts were in a tangle and her joy grew and grew; from her bosom it passed into her arms and legs, and it seemed as though a light, cool breeze were breathing on her head and ruffling her hair. Her shoulders quivered with subdued laughter, the table and the lamp chimney shook, too, and tears from her eyes splashed on the letter. She could not stop laughing, and to prove to herself that she was not laughing about nothing she made haste to think of something funny.

"What a funny poodle," she said, feeling as though she would choke with laughter. "What a funny poodle!"

She thought how, after tea the evening before, Gruzdev had played with Maxim the poodle, and afterwards had told them about a very intelligent poodle who had run after a crow in the yard, and the crow had looked round at him and said: "Oh, you scamp!"

The poodle, not knowing he had to do with a learned crow, was fearfully confused and retreated in perplexity, then began barking. . . .

"No, I had better love Gruzdev," Nadya decided, and she tore up the letter to Gorny.

She fell to thinking of the student, of his love, of her love; but the thoughts in her head insisted on flowing in all directions, and she thought about everything—about her mother, about the street, about the pencil, about the piano. . . . She thought of them joyfully, and felt that everything was good, splendid, and her joy told her that this was not all, that in a little while it would be better still. Soon it would be spring, summer, going with her mother to Gorbiki. Gorny would come for his furlough, would walk about the garden with her and make love to her. Gruzdev would come too. He would play croquet and skittles with her, and would tell her wonderful things. She had a passionate longing for the garden, the darkness, the pure sky, the stars. Again her shoulders shook with laughter, and it seemed to her that there was a scent of wormwood in the room and that a twig was tapping at the window.

She went to her bed, sat down, and not knowing what to do with the immense joy which filled her with yearning, she looked at the holy image hanging at the back of her bed, and said:

"Oh, Lord God! Oh, Lord God!"

EXERCISES

1. Why does the young woman sit down to write her letter as soon as she gets home? What does this suggest about the effects of seeing a dramatic performance? After seeing a play or a movie, is it necessary to make a transition from the depicted world to the world of everyday reality? Why?

2. Consider throughout the story the difference between the way things "really" are and those things which she considers "interesting," "beautiful," and "poetical." What is the difference between these two types of experiences?

3. Discuss that section of the story where the girl forgets both young men and begins laughing and crying simultaneously. Why does she feel she must think of something funny?

4. What is the significance of the smell of wormwood in the room and the sound of the twig tapping at the window? Why does she turn to the religious symbol?

5. What is the tone of her final exclamation? Is it happy, despairing, tired? Support your answer with details from the story.
6. Is this merely the story of a silly adolescent girl, or does it embody some more basic human dilemma or feeling?

ANTON
CHEKHOV | *Misery*

"To whom shall I tell my grief?"

The twilight of evening. Big flakes of wet snow are whirling lazily about the street lamps, which have just been lighted, and lying in a thin soft layer on roofs, horses' backs, shoulders, caps. Iona Potapov, the sledge-driver, is all white like a ghost. He sits on the box without stirring, bent as double as the living body can be bent. If a regular snowdrift fell on him it seems as though even then he would not think it necessary to shake it off. . . . His little mare is white and motionless too. Her stillness, the angularity of her lines, and the stick-like straightness of her legs make her look like a halfpenny gingerbread horse. She is probably lost in thought. Anyone who has been torn away from the plough, from the familiar gray landscapes, and cast into this slough, full of monstrous lights, of unceasing uproar and hurrying people, is bound to think.

It is a long time since Iona and his nag have budged. They came out of the yard before dinner-time and not a single fare yet. But now the shades of evening are falling on the town. The pale light of the street lamps changes to a vivid color, and the bustle of the street grows noisier.

"Sledge to Vyborgskaya!" Iona hears. "Sledge!"

Iona starts, and through his snow-plastered eye-lashes sees an officer in a military overcoat with a hood over his head.

"To Vyborgskaya," repeats the officer. "Are you asleep? To Vyborgskaya!"

In token of assent Iona gives a tug at the reins which sends cakes of snow flying from the horse's back and shoulders. The officer gets into the sledge. The sledge-driver clicks to the horse, cranes his neck like a swan, rises in his seat, and more from habit than necessity brandishes his whip. The mare cranes her neck, too, crooks her stick-like legs, and hesitatingly sets off. . . .

"Where are you shoving, you devil?" Iona immediately hears shouts from the dark mass shifting to and fro before him. "Where the devil are you going? Keep to the r-right!"

"You don't know how to drive! Keep to the right," says the officer angrily.

A coachman driving a carriage swears at him; a pedestrian crossing the road and brushing the horse's nose with his shoulder looks at him angrily and shakes the snow off his sleeve. Iona fidgets on the box as though he were sitting on thorns, jerks his elbows, and turns his eyes about like one possessed, as though he did not know where he was or why he was there.

"What rascals they all are!" says the officer jocosely. "They are simply doing their best to run up against you or fall under the horse's feet. They must be doing it on purpose."

Iona looks at his fare and moves his lips. . . . Apparently he means to say something, but nothing comes but a sniff.

"What?" inquires the officer.

Iona gives a wry smile, and straining his throat, brings out huskily: "My son . . . er . . . my son died this week, sir."

"H'm! What did he die of?"

Iona turns his whole body round to his fare, and says:

"Who can tell! It must have been from fever. . . . He lay three days in the hospital and then he died. . . . God's will."

"Turn round, you devil!" comes out of the darkness. "Have you gone cracked, you old dog? Look where you are going!"

"Drive on! drive on! . . ." says the officer. "We shan't get there till to-morrow going on like this. Hurry up!"

The sledge-driver cranes his neck again, rises in his seat, and with heavy grace swings his whip. Several times he looks round at the officer, but the latter keeps his eyes shut and is apparently disinclined to listen. Putting his fare down at Vyborgskaya, Iona stops by a restaurant, and again sits huddled up on the box. . . . Again the wet snow paints him and his horse white. One hour passes, and then another. . . .

Three young men, two tall and thin, one short and hunchbacked, come up, railing at each other and loudly stamping on the pavement with their goloshes.

"Cabby, to the Police Bridge!" the hunchback cries in a cracked voice. "The three of us, . . . twenty kopecks!"

Iona tugs at the reins and clicks to his horse. Twenty kopecks is not a fair price, but he has no thoughts for that. Whether it is a rouble or whether it is five kopecks does not matter to him now so long as he has a fare. . . . The three young men, shoving each other and using bad language, go up to the sledge, and all three try to sit down at once. The question remains to be settled: Which are to sit down and which one is to stand? After a long altercation, ill-temper, and abuse, they come to the conclusion that the hunchback must stand because he is the shortest.

"Well, drive on," says the hunchback in his cracked voice, settling himself and breathing down Iona's neck. "Cut along! What a cap you've got, my friend! You wouldn't find a worse one in all Petersburg. . . ."

"He-he! . . . he-he! . . ." laughs Iona. "It's nothing to boast of!"

"Well, then, nothing to boast of, drive on! Are you going to drive like this all the way? Eh? Shall I give you one in the neck?"

"My head aches," says one of the tall ones. "At the Dukmasovs' yesterday Vaska and I drank four bottles of brandy between us."

"I can't make out why you talk such stuff," says the other tall one angrily. "You lie like a brute."

"Strike me dead, it's the truth! . . ."

"It's about as true as that a louse coughs."

"He-he!" grins Iona. "Me-er-ry gentlemen!"

"Tfoo! the devil take you!" cries the hunchback indignantly. "Will you get on, you old plague, or won't you? Is that the way to drive? Give her one with the whip. Hang it all, give it her well."

Iona feels behind his back the jolting person and quivering voice of the hunchback. He hears abuse addressed to him, he sees people, and the feeling of loneliness begins little by little to be less heavy on his heart. The hunchback swears at him, till he chokes over some elaborately whimsical string of epithets and is overpowered by his cough. His tall companions begin talking of a certain Nadyezhda Petrovna. Iona looks round at them. Waiting till there is a brief pause, he looks round once more and says:

"This week . . . er . . . my . . . er . . . son died!"

"We shall all die, . . ." says the hunchback with a sigh, wiping his lips after coughing. "Come, drive on! drive on! My friends, I simply cannot stand crawling like this! When will he get us there?"

"Well, you give him a little encouragement . . . one in the neck!"

"Do you hear, you old plague? I'll make you smart. If one stands on ceremony with fellows like you one may as well walk. Do you hear, you old dragon? Or don't you care a hang what we say?"

And Iona hears rather than feels a slap on the back of his neck.

"He-he! . . ." he laughs. "Merry gentlemen. . . . God give you health!"

"Cabman, are you married?" asks one of the tall ones.

"I? He-he! Me-er-ry gentlemen. The only wife for me now is the damp earth. . . . He-ho-ho! . . . The grave that is! . . . Here my son's dead and I am alive. . . . It's a strange thing, death has come in at the wrong door. . . . Instead of coming for me it went for my son. . . ."

And Iona turns round to tell them how his son died, but at that point the hunchback gives a faint sigh and announces that, thank God! they have arrived at last. After taking his twenty kopecks, Iona gazes for a long while after the revelers, who disappear into a dark entry. Again he is alone and again there is silence for him. . . . The misery which has been for a brief space eased comes back again and tears his heart more cruelly than ever. With a look of anxiety and suffering Iona's eyes stray restlessly among the crowds moving to and fro on both sides of the street: can he not find among those thousands someone who will listen to him? But the crowds flit by heedless of him and his misery. . . . His misery is immense, beyond all bounds. If Iona's heart were to burst and his misery to flow out, it would flood the whole world, it seems, but yet it is not seen. It has found a hiding-place in such an insignificant shell that one would not have found it with a candle by daylight. . . .

Iona sees a house-porter with a parcel and makes up his mind to address him.

"What time will it be, friend?" he asks.

"Going on for ten. . . . Why have you stopped here? Drive on!"

Iona drives a few paces away, bends himself double, and gives himself up to his misery. He feels it is no good to appeal to people. But before five minutes have passed he draws himself up, shakes his head as though he feels a sharp pain, and tugs at the reins. . . . He can bear it no longer.

"Back to the yard!" he thinks. "To the yard!"

And his little mare, as though she knew his thoughts, falls to trotting. An hour and a half later Iona is sitting by a big dirty stove. On the stove, on the floor, and on the benches are people snoring. The air is full of smells and stuffiness. Iona looks at the sleeping figures, scratches himself, and regrets that he has come home so early. . . .

"I have not earned enough to pay for the oats, even," he thinks. "That's why I am so miserable. A man who knows how to do his work, . . . who has had enough to eat, and whose horse has had enough to eat, is always at ease. . . ."

In one of the corners a young cabman gets up, clears his throat sleepily, and makes for the water-bucket.

"Want a drink?" Iona asks him.

"Seems so."

"May it do you good. . . . But my son is dead, mate. . . . Do you hear? This week in the hospital. . . . It's a queer business. . . ."

Iona looks to see the effect produced by his words, but he sees nothing. The young man has covered his head over and is already asleep. The old man sighs and scratches himself. . . . Just as the young man had been thirsty for water, he thirsts for speech. His son will soon have been dead for a week, and he has not really talked to anybody yet. . . . He wants to talk of it properly, with deliberation. . . . He wants to tell how his son was taken ill, how he suffered, what he said before he died, how he died. . . . He wants to describe the funeral, and how he went to the hospital to get his son's clothes. He still has his daughter Anisya in the country. . . . And he wants to talk about her too. . . . Yes, he has plenty to talk about now. His listener ought to sigh and exclaim and lament. . . . It would be even better to talk to women. Though they are silly creatures, they blubber at the first word.

"Let's go out and have a look at the mare," Iona thinks. "There is always time for sleep. . . . You'll have sleep enough, no fear. . . ."

He puts on his coat and goes into the stables where his mare is standing. He thinks about oats, about hay, about the weather. . . . He cannot think about his son when he is alone. . . . To talk about him with someone is possible, but to think of him and picture him is insufferable anguish. . . .

"Are you munching?" Iona asks his mare, seeing her shining eyes. "There, munch away, munch away. . . . Since we have not earned enough for oats, we will eat hay. . . . Yes, . . . I have grown too old to drive. . . . My son ought to be driving, not I. . . . He was a real cabman. . . . he ought to have lived. . . ."

Iona is silent for a while, and then he goes on:

"That's how it is, old girl. . . . Kuzma Ionitch is gone. . . . He said good-by to me. . . . He went and died for no reason. . . . Now, suppose you had a little colt, and you were own mother to that little colt. . . . And all at once that same little colt went and died. . . . You'd be sorry, wouldn't you? . . ."

The little mare munches, listens, and breathes on her master's hands. Iona is carried away and tells her all about it.

EXERCISES

1. The focus of this story is not on an event but on a need. What is the nature of that need? What makes "Misery" a story?

2. If we do not know anything about Iona's life aside from this one night, what do we know about him? What do we need to know about him?

3. What does Iona want to communicate in this story? What is the difference between a lament and a story? The title of the story is sometimes translated as "The Lament."

4. Why is it not possible to communicate fully the state of "misery"?

5. Why do people feel the powerful need to "share" their misery, to tell the story to someone?

6. Why does Iona want to talk about his misery "properly, with deliberation"? Why is it important that he know all the details and describe the death in specific detail?

KATHERINE
MANSFIELD | *The Fly*

"**Y**'are very snug in here," piped old Mr. Woodifield, and he peered out of the great, green leather armchair by his friend the boss's desk as a baby peers out of its pram. His talk was over; it was time for him to be off. But he did not want to go. Since he had retired, since his . . . stroke, the wife and the girls kept him boxed up in the house every day of the week except Tuesday. On Tuesday he was dressed up and brushed and allowed to cut back to the City for the day. Though what he did there the wife and girls couldn't imagine. Made a nuisance of himself to his friends, they supposed. . . . Well, perhaps so. All the same, we cling to our last pleasures as the tree clings to its last leaves. So there sat old Woodifield, smoking a cigar and staring almost greedily at the boss, who rolled in his office chair, stout, rosy, five years older than he, and still going strong, still at the helm. It did one good to see him.

Wistfully, admiringly, the old voice added, "It's snug in here, upon my word!"

"Yes, it's comfortable enough," agreed the boss, and he flipped the *Financial Times* with a paper-knife. As a matter of fact he was proud of his room; he liked to have it admired, especially by old Woodifield. It gave him a feeling of deep, solid satisfaction to be planted there in the midst of it in full view of the frail old figure in the muffler.

"I've had it done up lately," he explained, as he had explained for the past—how many?—weeks. "New carpet," and he pointed to the bright red carpet with a pattern of large white rings. "New furniture," and he nodded towards the massive bookcase and the table with legs like twisted treacle. "Electric heating!" He waved almost exultantly towards the five transparent, pearly sausages glowing so softly in the tilted copper pan.

But he did not draw old Woodifield's attention to the photograph over the table of a grave-looking boy in uniform standing in one of those spectral photographers' parks with photographers' storm clouds behind him. It was not new. It had been there for over six years.

"There was something I wanted to tell you," said old Woodifield, and his eyes grew dim remembering. "Now what was it? I had it in my mind when I started out this morning." His hands began to tremble, and patches of red showed above his beard.

Poor old chap, he's on his last pins, thought the boss. And, feeling kindly, he winked at the old man, and said jokingly, "I tell you what. I've got a little drop of something here that'll do you good before you go out into the cold again. It's beautiful stuff. It wouldn't hurt a child." He took a key off his watch-chain, unlocked a cupboard below his desk, and drew forth a dark, squat bottle. "That's the medicine," said he. "And the man from whom I got it told me on the strict Q.T. it came from the cellars of Windsor Cassel."

Old Woodifield's mouth fell open at the sight. He couldn't have looked more surprised if the boss had produced a rabbit.

"It's whisky, ain't it?" he piped, feebly. The boss turned the bottle and lovingly showed him the label. Whisky it was.

"D'you know," said he, peering up at the boss wonderingly, "they won't let me touch it at home." And he looked as though he was going to cry.

"Ah, that's where we know a bit more than the ladies," cried the boss, swooping across for two tumblers that stood on the table with the water-bottle, and pouring a generous finger into each. "Drink it down. It'll do you good. And don't put any water with it. It's sacrilege to tamper with stuff like this. Ah!" He tossed off his, pulled out his handkerchief, hastily wiped his moustaches, and cocked an eye at old Woodifield, who was rolling his in his chaps.

The old man swallowed, was silent a moment, and then said faintly, "It's nutty!"

But it warmed him; it crept into his chill old brain—he remembered.

"That was it," he said, heaving himself out of his chair. "I thought you'd like to know. The girls were in Belgium last week having a look at poor Reggie's grave, and they happened to come across your boy's. They're quite near each other, it seems."

Old Woodifield paused, but the boss made no reply. Only a quiver in his eyelids showed that he heard.

"The girls were delighted with the way the place is kept," piped the old voice. "Beautifully looked after. Couldn't be better if they were at home. You've not been across, have yer?"

"No, no!" For various reasons the boss had not been across.

"There's miles of it," quavered old Woodifield, "and it's all as neat as a garden. Flowers growing on all the graves. Nice broad paths." It was plain from his voice how much he liked a nice broad path.

The pause came again. Then the old man brightened wonderfully.

"D'you know what the hotel made the girls pay for a pot of jam?" he piped. "Ten francs! Robbery, I call it. It was a little pot, so Gertrude says, no bigger than a half-crown. And she hadn't taken more than a spoonful when they charged her ten francs. Gertrude brought the pot away with her to teach 'em a lesson. Quite right, too; it's trading on our feelings. They think because we're over there having a look around we're ready to pay anything. That's what it is." And he turned towards the door.

"Quite right, quite right!" cried the boss, though what was quite right he hadn't the least idea. He came round by his desk, followed the shuffling footsteps to the door, and saw the old fellow out. Woodifield was gone.

For a long moment the boss stayed, staring at nothing, while the grey-haired office messenger, watching him, dodged in and out of his cubbyhole like a dog that expects to be taken for a run. Then: "I'll see nobody for half an hour, Macey," said the boss. "Understand? Nobody at all."

"Very good, sir."

The door shut, the firm heavy steps recrossed the bright carpet, the fat body plumped down in the spring chair, and leaning forward, the boss covered his face with his hands. He wanted, he intended, he had arranged to weep. . . .

It had been a terrible shock to him when old Woodifield sprang that remark upon him about the boy's grave. It was exactly as though the earth had opened and he had seen the boy lying there with Woodifield's girls staring down at him. For it was strange. Although over six years had passed away, the boss never thought of the boy except as lying unchanged, unblemished in his uniform, asleep for ever. "My son!" groaned the boss. But no tears came yet. In the past, in the first months and even years after the boy's death, he had only to say those words to be overcome by such grief that nothing short of a violent fit of weeping could relieve him. Time, he had declared then, he had told everybody, could make no difference. Other men perhaps might recover, might live their loss down, but not he. How was it possible? His boy was an only son. Ever since his birth the boss had worked at building up this business for him; it had no other meaning if it was not for the boy. Life itself had come to have no other meaning. How on earth could he have slaved, denied himself, kept going all those years without the promise for ever before him of the boy's stepping into his shoes and carrying on where he left off?

And that promise had been so near being fulfilled. The boy had been in the office learning the ropes for a year before the war. Every morning they had started off together; they had come back by the same train. And what congratulations he had received as the boy's father! No wonder; he had taken to it marvellously. As to his popularity with the staff, every man jack of them down to old Macey couldn't make enough of the boy. And he wasn't in the least spoilt. No, he was just his bright, natural self, with the right word for everybody, with that boyish look and his habit of saying, "Simply splendid!"

But all that was over and done with as though it never had been. The day had come when Macey had handed him the telegram that brought the whole place crashing about his head. "Deeply regret to inform you. . . ." And he had left the office a broken man, with his life in ruins.

Six years ago, six years. . . . How quickly time passed! It might have happened yesterday. The boss took his hands from his face; he was puzzled.

Something seemed to be wrong with him. He wasn't feeling as he wanted to feel. He decided to get up and have a look at the boy's photograph. But it wasn't a favorite photograph of his; the expression was unnatural. It was cold, even stern-looking. The boy had never looked like that.

At that moment the boss noticed that a fly had fallen into his broad ink-pot, and was trying feebly but desperately to clamber out again. Help! help! said those struggling legs. But the sides of the inkpot were wet and slippery; it fell back again and began to swim. The boss took up a pen, picked the fly out of the ink, and shook it on to a piece of blotting-paper. For a fraction of a second it lay still on the dark patch that oozed round it. Then the front legs waved, took hold, and, pulling its small sodden body up it began the immense task of cleaning the ink from its wings. Over and under, over and under, went a leg along a wing, as the stone goes over and under the scythe. Then there was a pause, while the fly, seeming to stand on the tips of its toes, tried to expand first one wing and then the other. It succeeded at last, and, sitting down, it began, like a minute cat, to clean its face. Now one could imagine that the little front legs rubbed against each other lightly, joyfully. The horrible danger was over; it had escaped; it was ready for life again.

But just then the boss had an idea. He plunged his pen back into the ink, leaned his thick wrist on the blotting-paper, and as the fly tried its wings down came a great heavy blot. What would it make of that? What indeed! The little beggar seemed absolutely cowed, stunned, and afraid to move because of what would happen next. But then, as if painfully, it dragged itself forward. The front legs waved, caught hold, and, more slowly this time, the task began from the beginning.

He's a plucky little devil, thought the boss, and he felt a real admiration for the fly's courage. That was the way to tackle things; that was the right spirit. Never say die; it was only a question of . . . But the fly had again finished its laborious task, and the boss had just time to refill his pen, to shake fair and square on the new-cleaned body yet another dark drop. What about it this time? A painful moment of suspense followed. But behold, the front legs were again waving; the boss felt a rush of relief. He leaned over the fly and said to it tenderly, "You artful little b . . ." And he actually had the brilliant notion of breathing on it to help the drying process. All the same, there was something timid and weak about its efforts now, and the boss decided that this time should be the last, as he dipped the pen into the inkpot.

It was. The last blot on the soaked blotting-paper, and the draggled fly lay in it and did not stir. The back legs were stuck to the body; the front legs were not to be seen.

"Come on," said the boss. "Look sharp!" And he stirred it with his pen—in vain. Nothing happened or was likely to happen. The fly was dead.

The boss lifted the corpse on the end of the paper-knife and flung it into the waste-paper basket. But such a grinding feeling of wretchedness seized him that he felt positively frightened. He started forward and pressed the bell for Macey.

"Bring me some fresh blotting-paper," he said, sternly, "and look sharp about it." And while the old dog padded away he fell to wondering what it was he had been thinking about before. What was it? It was . . . He took out his handkerchief and passed it inside his collar. For the life of him he could not remember.

EXERCISES

1. What is the basic difference between how the boss is described and how old Woodifield is described? Is there any other reason for the dialogue with Woodifield except to remind the boss of his son?

2. What are the implications of the following: "He wanted, he intended, he had arranged to weep. . . ."? Does the statement tell us something about the boss, or does it tell us something about the nature of grief?

3. What is the significance of the boss's thinking of his son "lying unchanged, unblemished in his uniform, asleep forever"?

4. What are the boss's feelings about his son? Why did his death have such a powerful effect on the boss?

5. What is the purpose of such explicit, detailed descriptions of the efforts the fly makes?

6. The boss's feeling of wretchedness at the end is perhaps a complex of many feelings that he does not understand. Discuss the possible reasons for his feeling and how the story leads up to it.

7. Katherine Mansfield was highly influenced by Anton Chekhov. Compare this story with Chekhov's "Misery," focusing especially on the technique of the two stories.

KATHERINE
MANSFIELD | *Miss Brill*

Although it was so brilliantly fine—the blue sky powdered with gold and great spots of light like white wine splashed over the Jardins Publiques— Miss Brill was glad that she had decided on her fur. The air was motionless, but when you opened your mouth there was just a faint chill, like a chill from a glass of iced water before you sip, and now and again a leaf came drifting— from nowhere, from the sky. Miss Brill put up her hand and touched her fur. Dear little thing! It was nice to feel it again. She had taken it out of its box that afternoon, shaken out the mothpowder, given it a good brush, and rubbed the life back into the dim little eyes. "What has been happening to me?" said the sad little eyes. Oh, how sweet it was to see them snap at her again from the red eiderdown! . . . But the nose, which was of some black composition, wasn't at all firm. It must have had a knock, somehow. Never mind—a little dab of black sealing-wax when the time came—when it was absolutely necessary. . . . Little rogue! Yes, she really felt like that about it. Little rogue biting its tail just by her left ear. She could have taken it off and laid it on her lap and stroked it. She felt a tingling in her hands and arms, but that came from walking, she supposed. And when she breathed, something light and sad— no, not sad, exactly—something gentle seemed to move in her bosom.

There were a number of people out this afternoon, far more than last Sunday. And the band sounded louder and gayer. That was because the Season had begun. For although the band played all the year round on Sundays, out of season it was never the same. It was like some one playing with only the family to listen; it didn't care how it played if there weren't any strangers present. Wasn't the conductor wearing a new coat, too? She was sure it was new. He scraped with his foot and flapped his arms like a rooster about to crow, and the bandsmen sitting in the green rotunda blew out their cheeks and glared at the music. Now there came a little "flutey" bit—very pretty!—a little chain of bright drops. She was sure it would be repeated. It was; she lifted her head and smiled.

Only two people shared her "special" seat: a fine old man in a velvet coat, his hands clasped over a huge carved walking-stick, and a big old woman, sitting upright, with a roll of knitting on her embroidered apron. They did not speak. This was disappointing, for Miss Brill always looked forward to the conversation. She had become really quite expert, she thought, at listening as though she didn't listen, at sitting in other people's lives just for a minute while they talked round her.

She glanced, sideways, at the old couple. Perhaps they would go soon. Last Sunday, too, hadn't been as interesting as usual. An Englishman and his wife, he wearing a dreadful Panama hat and she button boots. And she'd gone on the whole time about how she ought to wear spectacles; she knew she needed them; but that it was no good getting any; they'd be sure to break and they'd never keep on. And he'd been so patient. He'd suggested everything— gold rims, the kind that curved round your ears, little pads inside the bridge. No, nothing would please her. "They'll always be sliding down my nose!" Miss Brill had wanted to shake her.

The old people sat on the bench, still as statues. Never mind, there was always the crowd to watch. To and fro, in front of the flower-beds and the band rotunda, the couples and groups paraded, stopped to talk, to greet, to buy a handful of flowers from the old beggar who had his tray fixed to the railings. Little children ran among them, swooping and laughing; little boys with big white silk bows under their chins, little girls, little French dolls, dressed up in velvet and lace. And sometimes a tiny staggerer came suddenly rocking into the open from under the trees, stopped, stared, as suddenly sat down "flop," until its small high-stepping mother, like a young hen, rushed scolding to its rescue. Other people sat on the benches and green chairs, but they were nearly always the same, Sunday after Sunday, and—Miss Brill had often noticed—there was something funny about nearly all of them. They were odd, silent, nearly all old, and from the way they stared they looked as though they'd just come from dark little rooms or even—even cupboards!

Behind the rotunda the slender trees with yellow leaves down drooping, and through them just a line of sea, and beyond the blue sky with gold-veined clouds.

Tum-tum-tum tiddle-um! tiddle-um! tum tiddley-um tum ta! blew the band.

Two young girls in red came by and two young soldiers in blue met them, and they laughed and paired and went off arm-in-arm. Two peasant women with funny straw hats passed, gravely, leading beautiful smoke-coloured donkeys. A cold, pale nun hurried by. A beautiful woman came along and dropped her bunch of violets, and a little boy ran after to hand them to her, and she took them and threw them away as if they'd been poisoned. Dear me! Miss Brill didn't know whether to admire that or not! And now an ermine toque and a gentleman in grey met just in front of her. He was tall, stiff, dignified, and she was wearing the ermine toque she'd bought when her hair was yellow. Now everything, her hair, her face, even her eyes, was the same colour as the shabby ermine, and her hand, in its cleaned glove, lifted to dab her lips, was a tiny yellowish paw. Oh, she was so pleased to see him—delighted! She rather thought they were going to meet that afternoon. She described where she'd been—everywhere, here, there, along by the sea. The day was so charming—didn't he agree? And wouldn't he, perhaps? . . . But he shook his head, lighted a cigarette, slowly breathed a great deep puff into her face, and, even while she was still talking and laughing, flicked the match away and walked on. The ermine toque was alone; she smiled more brightly than ever. But even the band seemed to know what she was feeling and played more softly, played tenderly, and the drum beat, "The Brute! The Brute!" over and over. What would she do? What was going to happen now? But as Miss Brill wondered, the ermine toque turned, raised her hand as though she'd seen some one else, much nicer, just over there, and pattered away. And the band changed again and played more quickly, more gaily than ever, and the old couple on Miss Brill's seat got up and marched away, and such a funny old man with long whiskers hobbled along in time to the music and was nearly knocked over by four girls walking abreast.

Oh, how fascinating it was! How she enjoyed it! How she loved sitting here, watching it all! It was like a play. It was exactly like a play. Who could believe the sky at the back wasn't painted? But it wasn't till a little brown dog trotted on solemn and then slowly trotted off, like a little "theatre" dog, a little dog that had been drugged, that Miss Brill discovered what it was that made it so exciting. They were all on the stage. They weren't only the audience, not only looking on; they were acting. Even she had a part and came every Sunday. No doubt somebody would have noticed if she hadn't been there; she was part of the performance after all. How strange she'd never thought of it like that before! And yet it explained why she made such a point of starting from home at just the same time each week—so as not to be late for the performance—and it also explained why she had quite a queer, shy feeling at telling her English pupils how she spent her Sunday afternoons. No wonder! Miss Brill nearly laughed out loud. She was on the stage. She thought of the old invalid gentleman to whom she read the newspaper four afternoons a week while he slept in the garden. She had got quite used to the frail head on the cotton pillow, the hollowed eyes, the open mouth and the high pinched nose. If he'd been dead she mightn't have noticed for weeks; she wouldn't have minded. But suddenly he knew he was having the paper read to him by an actress! "An actress!" The old head lifted; two points of lights quivered in the old eyes. "An actress—are ye?" And Miss Brill smoothed the newspaper as though it were the manuscript of her part and said gently: "Yes, I have been an actress for a long time."

The band had been having a rest. Now they started again. And what they played was warm, sunny, yet there was just a faint chill—a something, what was it?—not sadness—no, not sadness—a something that made you want to sing. The tune lifted, lifted, the light shone; and it seemed to Miss Brill that in another moment all of them, all the whole company, would begin singing. The young ones, the laughing ones who were moving together, they would begin, and the men's voices, very resolute and brave, would join them. And then she too, she too, and the others on the benches—they would come in with a kind of accompaniment—something low, that scarcely rose or fell, something so beautiful—moving. . . . And Miss Brill's eyes filled with tears and she looked smiling at all the other members of the company. Yes, we understand, we understand, she thought—though what they understood she didn't know.

Just at that moment a boy and a girl came and sat down where the old couple had been. They were beautifully dressed; they were in love. The hero and heroine, of course, just arrived from his father's yacht. And still soundlessly singing, still with that trembling smile, Miss Brill prepared to listen.

"No, not now," said the girl. "Not here, I can't."

"But why? Because of that stupid old thing at the end there?" asked the boy. "Why does she come here at all—who wants her? Why doesn't she keep her silly old mug at home?"

"It's her fu-fur which is so funny," giggled the girl. "It's exactly like a fried whiting."

"Ah, be off with you!" said the boy in an angry whisper. Then: "Tell me, ma petite chérie—"

"No, not here," said the girl. "Not *yet.*"

On her way home she usually bought a slice of honeycake at the baker's. It was her Sunday treat. Sometimes there was an almond in her slice, sometimes not. It made a great difference. If there was an almond it was like carrying home a tiny present—a surprise—something that might very well not have been there. She hurried on the almond Sundays and struck the match for the kettle in quite a dashing way.

But to-day she passed the baker's by, climbed the stairs, went into the little dark room—her room like a cupboard—and sat down on the red eiderdown. She sat there for a long time. The box that the fur came out of was on the bed. She unclasped the necklet quickly; quickly, without looking, laid it inside. But when she put the lid on she thought she heard something crying.

EXERCISES

1. In many ways this does not seem like a story at all, but rather like a sketch, a picture of a Sunday afternoon in the park. At the end, what transforms the static sketch into a story?

2. Discuss those elements in the story which suggest life as a stage play. What are the implications of comparing life to a play?

3. Consider the metaphor of things being kept inside, in a cupboard or a box, versus things being taken out and put on display. How do events in the story prepare for the ending when, as Miss Brill puts the fur piece away, she thinks she hears something crying?

4. Consider the difference between the process of "seeing," when one is a subjective consciousness, and being "seen," when one is transformed into an object. Discuss these processes in the story.

5. At the end of the story, do you feel that Miss Brill is a pathetic character who has been treated unfairly or that in some way she deserves what has happened to her? Consider the issues in the story of eavesdropping, of living life vicariously through others, of judging versus being judged, of poetic justice.

JAMES
JOYCE | *Eveline*

She sat at the window watching the evening invade the avenue. Her head was leaned against the window curtains and in her nostrils was the odor of dusty cretonne. She was tired.

Few people passed. The man out of the last house passed on his way home; she heard his footsteps clacking along the concrete pavement and afterwards crunching on the cinder path before the new red houses. One time there used to be a field there in which they used to play every evening with other people's children. Then a man from Belfast bought the field and built houses in it—not like their little brown houses but bright brick houses with shining roofs. The children of the avenue used to play together in that field—the Devines, the Waters, the Dunns, little Keogh the cripple, she and her brothers and sisters. Ernest, however, never played: he was too grown up. Her father used often to hunt them in out of the field with his blackthorn stick; but usually little Keogh used to keep *nix* and call out when he saw her father coming.

Still they seemed to have been rather happy then. Her father was not so bad then; and besides, her mother was alive. That was a long time ago; she and her brothers and sisters were all grown up; her mother was dead. Tizzie Dunn was dead, too, and the Waters had gone back to England. Everything changes. Now she was going to go away like the others, to leave her home.

Home! She looked round the room, reviewing all its familiar objects which she had dusted once a week for so many years, wondering where on earth all the dust came from. Perhaps she would never see again those familiar objects from which she had never dreamed of being divided. And yet during all those years she had never found out the name of the priest whose yellowing photograph hung on the wall above the broken harmonium beside the colored print of the promises made to Blessed Margaret Mary Alacoque. He had been a school friend of her father. Whenever he showed the photograph to a visitor her father used to pass it with a casual word:

—He is in Melbourne now.

She had consented to go away, to leave her home. Was that wise? She tried to weigh each side of the question. In her home anyway she had shelter and food; she had those whom she had known all her life about her. Of course she had to work hard both in the house and at business. What would they say of her in the Stores when they found out that she had run away with a fellow? Say she was a fool, perhaps; and her place would be filled up by advertisement. Miss Gavan would be glad. She had always had an edge on her, especially whenever there were people listening.

—Miss Hill, don't you see these ladies are waiting?

—Look lively, Miss Hill, please.

She would not cry many tears at leaving the Stores.

But in her new home, in a distant unknown country, it would not be like that. Then she would be married—she, Eveline. People would treat her with respect then. She would not be treated as her mother had been. Even now, though she was over nineteen, she sometimes felt herself in danger of her father's violence. She knew it was that that had given her the palpitations. When they were growing up he had never gone for her, like he used to go for Harry and Ernest, because she was a girl; but latterly he had begun to threaten her and say what he would do to her only for her dead mother's sake. And now she had nobody to protect her. Ernest was dead and Harry, who was in the church decorating business, was nearly always down somewhere in the country. Besides, the invariable squabble for money on Saturday nights had begun to weary her unspeakably. She always gave her entire wages—seven shillings—and Harry always sent up what he could but the trouble was to get any money from her father. He said she used to squander the money, that she had no head, that he wasn't going to give her his hard-earned money to throw about the streets, and much more, for he was usually fairly bad of a Saturday night. In the end he would give her the money and ask her had she any intention of buying Sunday's dinner. Then she had to rush out as quickly as she could and do her marketing, holding her black leather purse tightly in her hand as she elbowed her way through the crowds and returning home late under her load of provisions. She had hard work to keep the house together and to see that the two young children who had been left to her charge went to school regularly and got their meals regularly. It was hard work—a hard life—but now that she was about to leave it she did not find it a wholly undesirable life.

She was about to explore another life with Frank. Frank was very kind, manly, open-hearted. She was to go away with him by the night-boat to be his wife and to live with him in Buenos Ayres where he had a home waiting for her. How well she remembered the first time she had seen him; he was lodging in a house on the main road where she used to visit. It seemed a few weeks ago. He was standing at the gate, his peaked cap pushed back on his head and his hair tumbled forward over a face of bronze. Then they had come to know each other. He used to meet her outside the Stores every evening and see her home. He took her to see *The Bohemian Girl* and she felt elated as she sat in an unaccustomed part of the theatre with him. He was awfully fond of music and sang a little. People knew that they were courting and, when he sang about the lass that loves a sailor, she always felt pleasantly confused. He used to call her Poppens out of fun. First of all it had been an excitement for her to have a fellow and then she had begun to like him. He had tales of distant countries. He had started as a deck boy at a pound a month on a ship of the Allan Line going out to Canada. He told her the names of the ships he had been on and the names of the different services. He had sailed through the Straits of Magellan and he told her stories of the terrible Patagonians. He had fallen on his feet in Buenos Ayres, he said, and had come over to the old country just for a holiday. Of course, her father had found out the affair and had forbidden her to have anything to say to him.

—I know these sailor chaps, he said.

One day he had quarrelled with Frank and after that she had to meet her lover secretly.

The evening deepened in the avenue. The white of two letters in her lap grew indistinct. One was to Harry; the other was to her father. Ernest had been her favorite but she liked Harry too. Her father was becoming old lately, she noticed; he would miss her. Sometimes he could be very nice. Not long before, when she had been laid up for a day, he had read her out a ghost story and made toast for her at the fire. Another day, when their mother was alive, they had all gone for a picnic to the Hill of Howth. She remembered her father putting on her mother's bonnet to make the children laugh.

Her time was running out but she continued to sit by the window, leaning her head against the window curtain, inhaling the odor of dusty cretonne. Down far in the avenue she could hear a street organ playing. She knew the air. Strange that it should come that very night to remind her of the promise to her mother, her promise to keep the home together as long as she could. She remembered the last night of her mother's illness, she was again in the close dark room at the other side of the hall and outside she heard a melancholy air of Italy. The organ-player had been ordered to go away and given sixpence. She remembered her father strutting back into the sickroom saying:

—Damned Italians! coming over here!

As she mused, the pitiful vision of her mother's life laid its spell on the very quick of her being—that life of commonplace sacrifices closing in final craziness. She trembled as she heard again her mother's voice saying constantly with foolish insistence:

—Derevaun Seraun! Derevaun Seraun!

She stood up in a sudden impulse of terror. Escape! She must escape! Frank would save her. He would give her life, perhaps love, too. But she wanted to live. Why should she be unhappy? She had a right to happiness. Frank would take her in his arms, fold her in his arms. He would save her.

She stood among the swaying crowd in the station at the North Wall. He held her hand and she knew that he was speaking to her, saying something about the passage over and over again. The station was full of soldiers with brown baggages. Through the wide doors of the sheds she caught a glimpse of the black mass of the boat, lying in beside the quay wall, with illumined portholes. She answered nothing. She felt her cheek pale and cold and, out of a maze of distress, she prayed to God to direct her, to show her what was her duty. The boat blew a long mournful whistle into the mist. If she went, tomorrow she would be on the sea with Frank, steaming towards Buenos Ayres. Their passage had been booked. Could she still draw back after all he had done for her? Her distress awoke a nausea in her body and she kept moving her lips in silent fervent prayer.

A bell clanged upon her heart. She felt him seize her hand:

—Come!

All the seas of the world tumbled about her heart. He was drawing her into them: he would drown her. She gripped with both hands at the iron railing.

—Come!

No! No! No! It was impossible. Her hands clutched the iron in frenzy. Amid the seas she sent a cry of anguish!

—Eveline! Evvy!

He rushed beyond the barrier and called to her to follow. He was shouted at to go on but he still called to her. She set her white face to him, passive, like a helpless animal. Her eyes gave him no sign of love or farewell or recognition.

EXERCISES

1. Eveline's mind shifts back and forth between the remembered past and the expected future. Which does she focus on most?

2. What are the most important arguments for Eveline to leave? What are the most important arguments for her to stay?

3. What is the significance of the fact that Frank is a sailor?
4. What is it about her memory of her mother that makes her suddenly decide to leave?
5. What is the meaning of the final description of Eveline: "She set her white face to him, passive, like a helpless animal. Her eyes gave him no sign of love or farewell or recognition"?
6. A basic problem in this story is that it seems throughout that Eveline has decided to go with Frank. However, at the end, she does not go. How does the story prepare for her final decision not to go while it focuses so much on her wanting to go?

JAMES
JOYCE | *Araby*

North Richmond Street, being blind, was a quiet street except at the hour when the Christian Brothers' School set the boys free. An uninhabited house of two storeys stood at the blind end, detached from its neighbours in a square ground. The other houses of the street, conscious of decent lives within them, gazed at one another with brown imperturbable faces.

The former tenant of our house, a priest, had died in the back drawing-room. Air, musty from having been long enclosed, hung in all the rooms, and the waste room behind the kitchen was littered with old useless papers. Among these I found a few paper-covered books, the pages of which were curled and damp: *The Abbot*, by Walter Scott, *The Devout Communicant* and *The Memoirs of Vidocq*. I liked the last best because its leaves were yellow. The wild garden behind the house contained a central apple-tree and a few straggling bushes under one of which I found the late tenant's rusty bicycle-pump. He had been a very charitable priest; in his will he had left all his money to institutions and the furniture of his house to his sister.

When the short days of winter came dusk fell before we had well eaten our dinners. When we met in the street the houses had grown sombre. The space of sky above us was the colour of ever-changing violet and towards it the lamps of the street lifted their feeble lanterns. The cold air stung us and we played till our bodies glowed. Our shouts echoed in the silent street. The career of our play brought us through the dark muddy lanes behind the houses where we ran the gauntlet of the rough tribes from the cottages, to the back doors of the dark dripping gardens where odours arose from the ashpits, to the dark odorous stables where a coachman smoothed and combed the horse or shook music from the buckled harness. When we returned to the street, light from the kitchen windows had filled the areas. If my uncle was seen turning the corner we hid in the shadow until we had seen him safely housed. Or if Mangan's sister came out on the doorstep to call her brother in to his tea we watched her from our shadow peer up and down the street. We waited to see whether she would remain or go in and, if she remained, we left our shadow and walked up to Mangan's steps resignedly. She was waiting for us, her figure defined by the light from the half-opened door. Her brother always teased her before he obeyed and I stood by the railings looking at her. Her dress swung as she moved her body and the soft rope of her hair tossed from side to side.

Every morning I lay on the floor in the front parlour watching her door. The blind was pulled down to within an inch of the sash so that I could not be seen. When she came out on the doorstep my heart leaped. I ran to the hall, seized my books and followed her. I kept her brown figure always in my eye and, when we came near the point at which our ways diverged, I quickened my pace and passed her. This happened morning after morning. I had never spoken to her, except for a few casual words, and yet her name was like a summons to all my foolish blood.

Her image accompanied me even in places the most hostile to romance. On Saturday evenings when my aunt went marketing I had to go to carry some of the parcels. We walked through the flaring streets, jostled by drunken men and bargaining women, amid the curses of labourers, the shrill litanies of shop-boys who stood on guard by the barrels of pigs' cheeks, the nasal chanting of street-singers, who sang a *come-all-you* about O'Donovan Rossa, or a ballad about the troubles in our native land. The noises converged in a single sensation of life for me: I imagined that I bore my chalice safely through a throng of foes. Her name sprang to my lips at moments in strange prayers and praises which I myself did not understand. My eyes were often full of tears (I could not tell why) and at times a flood from my heart seemed to pour itself out into my bosom. I thought little of the future. I did not know whether I would ever speak to her or not or, if I spoke to her, how I could tell her of my confused adoration. But my body was like a harp and her words and gestures were like fingers upon the wires.

One evening I went into the back drawing-room in which the priest had died. It was a dark rainy evening and there was no sound in the house. Through one of the broken panes I heard the rain impinge upon the earth, the fine incessant needles of water playing in the sodden beds. Some distant lamp or lighted window gleamed below me. I was thankful that I could see so little. All my senses seemed to desire to veil themselves and, feeling that I was about to slip from them, I pressed the palms of my hands together until they trembled, murmuring: "O love! O love!" many times.

At last she spoke to me. When she addressed the first words to me I was so confused that I did not know what to answer. She asked me was I going to *Araby*. I forgot whether I answered yes or no. It would be a splendid bazaar, she said she would love to go.

"And why can't you?" I asked.

While she spoke she turned a silver bracelet round and round her wrist. She could not go, she said, because there would be a retreat that week in her convent. Her brother and two other boys were fighting for their caps and I was alone at the railings. She held one of the spikes, bowing her head towards me. The light from the lamp opposite our door caught the white curve of her neck, lit up her hair that rested there and, falling, lit up the hand upon the railing. It fell over one side of her dress and caught the white border of a petticoat, just visible as she stood at ease.

"It's well for you," she said.

"If I go," I said, "I will bring you something."

What innumerable follies laid waste my waking and sleeping thoughts after that evening! I wished to annihilate the tedious intervening days. I chafed against the work of school. At night in my bedroom and by day in the class-room her image came between me and the page I strove to read. The syllables of the word *Araby* were called to me through the silence in which my soul luxuriated and cast an Eastern enchantment over me. I asked for leave to go to the bazaar on Saturday night. My aunt was surprised and hoped it was not some Freemason affair. I answered few questions in class. I watched my master's face pass from amiability to sternness; he hoped I was not beginning to idle. I could not call my wandering thoughts together. I had hardly any patience with the serious work of life which, now that it stood between me and my desire, seemed to me child's play, ugly monotonous child's play.

On Saturday morning I reminded my uncle that I wished to go to the bazaar in the evening. He was fussing at the hallstand, looking for the hat-brush, and answered me curtly:

"Yes, boy, I know."

As he was in the hall I could not go into the front parlour and lie at the window. I left the house in bad humour and walked slowly toward the school. The air was pitilessly raw and already my heart misgave me.

When I came home to dinner my uncle had not yet been home. Still it was early. I sat staring at the clock for some time and, when its ticking began to irritate me, I left the room. I mounted the staircase and gained the upper part of the house. The high cold empty gloomy rooms liberated me and I went from room to room singing. From the front window I saw my companions playing below in the street. Their cries reached me weakened and indistinct and, lean-ing my forehead against the cool glass, I looked over at the dark house where she lived. I may have stood there for an hour, seeing nothing but the brown-clad figure cast by my imagination, touched discreetly by the lamplight at the curved neck, at the hand upon the railings and at the border below the dress.

When I came downstairs again I found Mrs. Mercer sitting at the fire. She was an old garrulous woman, a pawnbroker's widow, who collected used stamps for some pious purpose. I had to endure the gossip of the tea-table. The meal was prolonged beyond an hour and still my uncle did not come. Mrs. Mercer stood up to go: she was sorry she couldn't wait any longer, but it was after eight o'clock and she did not like to be out late, as the night air was bad for her. When she had gone I began to walk up and down the room, clenching my fists. My aunt said:

"I'm afraid you may put off your bazaar for this night of Our Lord."

At nine o'clock I heard my uncle's latchkey in the halldoor. I heard him talking to himself and heard the hallstand rocking when it had received the weight of his overcoat. I could interpret these signs. When he was midway through his dinner I asked him to give me the money to go to the bazaar. He had forgotten.

"The people are in bed and after their first sleep now," he said.

I did not smile. My aunt said to him energetically:

"Can't you give him the money and let him go? You've kept him late enough as it is."

My uncle said he was very sorry he had forgotten. He said he believed in the old saying: "All work and no play makes Jack a dull boy." He asked me where I was going and, when I had told him a second time he asked me did I know *The Arab's Farewell to His Steed*. When I left the kitchen he was about to recite the opening lines of the piece to my aunt.

I held a florin tightly in my hand as I strode down Buckingham Street towards the station. The sight of the streets thronged with buyers and glaring with gas recalled to me the purpose of my journey. I took my seat in a third-class carriage of a deserted train. After an intolerable delay the train moved out of the station slowly. It crept onward among ruinous houses and over the twinkling river. At Westland Row Station a crowd of people pressed to the carriage doors; but the porters moved them back, saying that it was a special train for the bazaar. I remained alone in the bare carriage. In a few minutes the train drew up beside an improvised wooden platform. I passed out on to the road and saw by the lighted dial of a clock that it was ten minutes to ten. In front of me was a large building which displayed the magical name.

I could not find any sixpenny entrance and, fearing that the bazaar would be closed, I passed in quickly through a turnstile, handing a shilling to a weary-looking man. I found myself in a big hall girdled at half its height by a gallery. Nearly all the stalls were closed and the greater part of the hall was in darkness. I recognised a silence like that which pervades a church after a service. I walked into the centre of the bazaar timidly. A few people were gathered about the stalls which were still open. Before a curtain, over which the words *Café Chantant* were written in coloured lamps, two men were counting money on a salver. I listened to the fall of the coins.

Remembering with difficulty why I had come I went over to one of the stalls and examined porcelain vases and flowered tea-sets. At the door of the stall a young lady was talking and laughing with two young gentlemen. I remarked their English accents and listened vaguely to their conversation.

"O, I never said such a thing!"

"O, but you did!"

"O, but I didn't!"

"Didn't she say that?"

"Yes. I heard her."

"O, there's a . . . fib!"

Observing me the young lady came over and asked me did I wish to buy anything. The tone of her voice was not encouraging; she seemed to have spoken to me out of a sense of duty. I looked humbly at the great jars that stood like eastern guards at either side of the dark entrance to the stall and murmured: "No, thank you."

The young lady changed the position of one of the vases and went back to the two young men. They began to talk of the same subject. Once or twice the young lady glanced at me over her shoulder.

I lingered before her stall, though I knew my stay was useless, to make my interest in her wares seem the more real. Then I turned away slowly and walked down the middle of the bazaar. I allowed the two pennies to fall against the sixpence in my pocket. I heard a voice call from one end of the gallery that the light was out. The upper part of the hall was now completely dark.

Gazing up into the darkness I saw myself as a creature driven and derided by vanity; and my eyes burned with anguish and anger.

EXERCISES

1. Discuss those elements in the story in which the boy's attraction to Mangan's sister is described in spiritual or religious terms.

2. Why does the boy have such an extreme reaction to overhearing the trivial conversation at the bazaar?

3. The story is told by an adult man thinking back on a childhood experience. What is the man's attitude toward the event? How does he feel about the boy he once was?

4. Are there clues in the story that prepare the reader for the boy's final reaction? Are there elements that suggest that he is deceiving himself about his feelings for the girl?

5. Is this a story about the initiation of a young boy? If so, into what aspect of human reality is he initiated?

6. Consider the theme of the story on its most general level—the human need to spiritualize the material and the inevitable disillusionment this need gives rise to.

7. A basic characteristic of Joyce's stories is the technique of "epiphany"— that moment when the essence of an experience suddenly becomes clear to someone—either a character in the story or the reader—a moment of recognition. Describe both the character's and the reader's epiphany in this story.

SHERWOOD
ANDERSON | *Hands*

Upon the half decayed veranda of a small frame house that stood near the edge of a ravine near the town of Winesburg, Ohio, a fat little old man walked nervously up and down. Across a long field that had been seeded for clover but that had produced only a dense crop of yellow mustard weeds, he could see the public highway along which went a wagon filled with berry pickers returning from the fields. The berry pickers, youths and maidens, laughed and shouted boisterously. A boy clad in a blue shirt leaped from the wagon and attempted to drag after him one of the maidens, who screamed and protested shrilly. The feet of the boy in the road kicked up a cloud of dust that floated across the face of the departing sun. Over the long field came a thin girlish voice, "Oh, you Wing Biddlebaum, comb your hair, it's falling into your eyes," commanded the voice to the man, who was bald and whose nervous little hands fiddled about the bare white forehead as though arranging a mass of tangled locks.

Wing Biddlebaum, forever frightened and beset by a ghostly band of doubts, did not think of himself as in any way a part of the life of the town where he had lived for twenty years. Among all the people of Winesburg but one had come close to him. With George Willard, son of Tom Willard, the proprietor of the New Willard House, he had formed something like a friendship. George Willard was the reporter on the *Winesburg Eagle* and sometimes in the evenings he walked out along the highway to Wing Biddlebaum's house. Now as the old man walked up and down on the veranda, his hands moving nervously about, he was hoping that George Willard would come and spend the evening with him. After the wagon containing the berry pickers had passed, he went across the field through the tall mustard weeds and climbing a rail fence peered anxiously along the road to the town. For a moment he stood thus, rubbing his hands together and looking up and down the road, and then, fear overcoming him, ran back to walk again upon the porch on his own house.

In the presence of George Willard, Wing Biddlebaum, who for twenty years had been the town mystery, lost something of his timidity, and his shadowy personality, submerged in a sea of doubts, came forth to look at the world. With the young reporter at his side, he ventured in the light of day into Main Street or strode up and down on the rickety front porch of his own house, talking excitedly. The voice that had been low and trembling became shrill and loud. The bent figure straightened. With a kind of wriggle, like a fish returned to the brook by the fisherman, Biddlebaum the silent began to talk, striving to put into words the ideas that had been accumulated by his mind during long years of silence.

Wing Biddlebaum talked much with his hands. The slender expressive fingers, forever active, forever striving to conceal themselves in his pockets or behind his back, came forth and became the piston rods of his machinery of expression.

The story of Wing Biddlebaum is a story of hands. Their restless activity, like unto the beating of the wings of an imprisoned bird, had given him his name. Some obscure poet of the town had thought of it. The hands alarmed their owner. He wanted to keep them hidden away and looked with amazement at the quiet inexpressive hands of other men who worked beside him in the fields, or passed, driving sleepy teams on country roads.

When he talked to George Willard, Wing Biddlebaum closed his fists and beat with them upon a table or on the walls of his house. The action made him more comfortable. If the desire to talk came to him when the two were walking in the fields, he sought out a stump or the top board of a fence and with his hands pounding busily talked with renewed ease.

The story of Wing Biddlebaum's hands is worth a book in itself. Sympathetically set forth it would tap many strange, beautiful qualities in obscure men. It is a job for a poet. In Winesburg the hands had attracted attention merely because of their activity. With them Wing Biddlebaum had picked as high as a hundred and forty quarts of strawberries in a day. They became his distinguishing feature, the source of his fame. Also they made more grotesque an already grotesque and elusive individuality. Winesburg was proud of the hands of Wing Biddlebaum in the same spirit in which it was proud of Banker White's new stone house and Wesley Moyer's bay stallion, Tony Tip, that had won the two-fifteen trot at the fall races in Cleveland.

As for George Willard, he had many times wanted to ask about the hands. At times an almost overwhelming curiosity had taken hold of him. He felt that there must be a reason for their strange activity and their inclination to keep hidden away and only a growing respect for Wing Biddlebaum kept him from blurting out the questions that were often in his mind.

Once he had been on the point of asking. The two were walking in the fields on a summer afternoon and had stopped to sit upon a grassy bank. All afternoon Wing Biddlebaum had talked as one inspired. By a fence he had stopped and beating like a giant woodpecker upon the top board had shouted at George Willard, condemning his tendency to be too much influenced by the people about him. "You are destroying yourself," he cried. "You have the inclination to be alone and to dream and you are afraid of dreams. You want to be like others in town here. You hear them talk and you try to imitate them."

On the grassy bank Wing Biddlebaum had tried again to drive his point home. His voice became soft and reminiscent, and with a sigh of contentment he launched into a long rambling talk, speaking as one lost in a dream.

Out of the dream Wing Biddlebaum made a picture for George Willard. In the picture men lived again in a kind of pastoral golden age. Across a green open country came clean-limbed young men, some afoot, some mounted upon horses. In crowds the young men came to gather about the feet of an old man who sat beneath a tree in a tiny garden and who talked to them.

Wing Biddlebaum became wholly inspired. For once he forgot the hands. Slowly they stole forth and lay upon George Willard's shoulders. Something new and bold came into the voice that talked. "You must try to forget all you have learned," said the old man. "You must begin to dream. From this time on you must shut your ears to the roaring of the voices."

Pausing in his speech, Wing Biddlebaum looked long and earnestly at George Willard. His eyes glowed. Again he raised the hands to caress the boy and then a look of horror swept over his face.

With a convulsive movement of his body, Wing Biddlebaum sprang to his feet and thrust his hands deep into his trousers pockets. Tears came to his eyes. "I must be getting along home. I can talk no more with you," he said nervously.

Without looking back, the old man had hurried down the hillside and across a meadow, leaving George Willard perplexed and frightened upon the grassy slope. With a shiver of dread the boy arose and went along the road toward town. "I'll not ask him about his hands," he thought, touched by the memory of the terror he had seen in the man's eyes. "There's something wrong, but I don't want to know what it is. His hands have something to do with his fear of me and of everyone."

And George Willard was right. Let us look briefly into the story of the hands. Perhaps our talking of them will arouse the poet who will tell the hidden wonder story of the influence for which the hands were but fluttering pennants of promise.

In his youth Wing Biddlebaum had been a school teacher in a town in Pennsylvania. He was not then known as Wing Biddlebaum, but went by the less euphonic name of Adolph Myers. As Adolph Myers he was much loved by the boys of his school.

Adolph Myers was meant by nature to be a teacher of youth. He was one of those rare, little-understood men who rule by a power so gentle that it passes as a lovable weakness. In their feeling for the boys under their charge such men are not unlike the finer sort of women in their love of men.

And yet that is but crudely stated. It needs the poet there. With the boys of his school, Adolph Myers had walked in the evening or had sat talking until dusk upon the schoolhouse steps lost in a kind of dream. Here and there went his hands, caressing the shoulders of the boys, playing about the tousled heads. As he talked his voice became soft and musical. There was a caress in that also. In a way the voice and the hands, the stroking of the shoulders and the touching of the hair were a part of the schoolmaster's effort to carry a dream into the young minds. By the caress that was in his fingers he expressed himself. He was one of those men in whom the force that creates life is diffused, not centralized. Under the caress of his hands doubt and disbelief went out of the minds of the boys and they began also to dream.

And then the tragedy. A half-witted boy of the school became enamored of the young master. In his bed at night he imagined unspeakable things and in the morning went forth to tell his dreams as facts. Strange, hideous accusations fell from his loose-hung lips. Through the Pennsylvania town went a shiver. Hidden, shadowy doubts that had been in men's minds concerning Adolph Myers were galvanized into beliefs.

The tragedy did not linger. Trembling lads were jerked out of bed and questioned. "He put his arms about me," said one. "His fingers were always playing in my hair," said another.

One afternoon a man of the town, Henry Bradford, who kept a saloon, came to the schoolhouse door. Calling Adolph Myers into the school yard he began to beat him with his fists. As his hard knuckles beat down into the frightened face of the schoolmaster, his wrath became more and more terrible. Screaming with dismay, the children ran here and there like disturbed insects. "I'll teach you to put your hands on my boy, you beast," roared the saloon keeper, who, tired of beating the master, had begun to kick him about the yard.

Adolph Myers was driven from the Pennsylvania town in the night. With lanterns in their hands a dozen men came to the door of the house where he lived alone and commanded that he dress and come forth. It was raining and one of the men had a rope in his hands. They had intended to hang the schoolmaster, but something in his figure, so small, white, and pitiful, touched their hearts and they let him escape. As he ran away into the darkness they repented of their weakness and ran after him, swearing and throwing sticks and great balls of soft mud at the figure that screamed and ran faster and faster into the darkness.

For twenty years Adolph Myers had lived alone in Winesburg. He was but forty but looked sixty-five. The name of Biddlebaum he got from a box of goods seen at a freight station as he hurried through an eastern Ohio town. He had an aunt in Winesburg, a black-toothed old woman who raised chickens, and with her he lived until she died. He had been ill for a year after the experience in Pennsylvania, and after his recovery worked as a day laborer in the fields, going timidly about and striving to conceal his hands. Although he did not understand what had happened he felt that the hands must be to blame. Again and again the fathers of the boys had talked of the hands. "Keep your hands to yourself," the saloon keeper had roared, dancing with fury in the schoolhouse yard.

Upon the veranda of his house by the ravine, Wing Biddlebaum continued to walk up and down until the sun had disappeared and the road beyond the field was lost in the grey shadows. Going into his house he cut slices of bread and spread honey upon them. When the rumble of the evening train that took away the express cars loaded with the day's harvest of berries had passed and restored the silence of the summer night, he went again to walk upon the veranda. In the darkness he could not see the hands and they became quiet. Although he still hungered for the presence of the boy, who was the medium through which he expressed his love of man, the hunger became again a part of his loneliness and his waiting. Lighting a lamp, Wing Biddlebaum washed the few dishes soiled by his simple meal and, setting up a folding cot by the screen door that led to the porch, prepared to undress for the night. A few stray white bread crumbs lay on the cleanly washed floor by the table; putting the lamp upon a low stool he began to pick up the crumbs, carrying them to his mouth one by one with unbelievable rapidity. In the dense blotch of light beneath the table, the kneeling figure looked like a priest engaged in some service of his church. The nervous expressive fingers, flashing in and out of the light, might well have been mistaken for the fingers of the devotee going swiftly through decade after decade of his rosary.

EXERCISES

1. What kind of reader expectations of Wing Biddlebaum are set up by the first paragraph?

2. Why does the narrator say that the story of Wing Biddlebaum would tap many "strange, beautiful qualities in obscure men. It is a job for a poet"?

3. Sherwood Anderson uses the word *grotesque* in this story to describe Wing Biddlebaum. Compare it with the use of the word in Anderson's story "Paper Pills." Try to define what he means by *grotesque.*

4. Explain why Wing Biddlebaum becomes inspired when he tells George Willard that he must try to forget all he has learned and that he must begin to dream.

5. Why does the narrator repeat that the story of Wing needs a poet to explain his love for the boys? What would a poet be able to express that others would not?

6. Two kinds of dreams are referred to in this story. What is the difference between them?

7. Discuss the significance of the final image of Wing being like a priest saying his rosary.

SHERWOOD
ANDERSON | *Paper Pills*

He was an old man with a white beard and huge nose and hands. Long before the time during which we will know him, he was a doctor and drove a jaded white horse from house to house through the streets of Winesburg. Later he married a girl who had money. She had been left a large fertile farm when her father died. The girl was quiet, tall, and dark, and to many people she seemed very beautiful. Everyone in Winesburg wondered why she married the doctor. Within a year after the marriage she died.

The knuckles of the doctor's hands were extraordinarily large. When the hands were closed they looked like clusters of unpainted wooden balls as large as walnuts fastened together by steel rods. He smoked a cob pipe and after his wife's death sat all day in his empty office close by a window that was covered with cobwebs. He never opened the window. Once on a hot day in August he tried but found it stuck fast and after that he forgot all about it.

Winesburg had forgotten the old man, but in Doctor Reefy there were the seeds of something very fine. Alone in his musty office in the Heffner Block above the Paris Dry Goods Company's store, he worked ceaselessly, building up something that he himself destroyed. Little pyramids of truth he erected and after erecting knocked them down again that he might have the truths to erect other pyramids.

Doctor Reefy was a tall man who had worn one suit of clothes for ten years. It was frayed at the sleeves and little holes had appeared at the knees and elbows. In the office he wore also a linen duster with huge pockets into which he continually stuffed scraps of paper. After some weeks the scraps of paper became little hard round balls, and when the pockets were filled he dumped them out upon the floor. For ten years he had but one friend, another old man named John Spaniard who owned a tree nursery. Sometimes, in a playful mood, old Doctor Reefy took from his pockets a handful of the paper balls and threw them at the nursery man. "That is to confound you, you blithering old sentimentalist," he cried, shaking with laughter.

The story of Doctor Reefy and his courtship of the tall dark girl who became his wife and left her money to him is a very curious story. It is delicious, like the twisted little apples that grow in the orchards of Winesburg. In the fall one walks in the orchards and the ground is hard with frost underfoot. The apples have been taken from the trees by the pickers. They have been put in barrels and shipped to the cities where they will be eaten in apartments that are filled with books, magazines, furniture, and people. On the trees are only a few gnarled apples that the pickers have rejected. They look like the knuckles of Doctor Reefy's hands. One nibbles at them and they are delicious. Into a little round place at the side of the apple has been gathered all of its sweetness. One runs from tree to tree over the frosted ground picking the gnarled, twisted apples and filling his pockets with them. Only the few know the sweetness of the twisted apples.

The girl and Doctor Reefy began their courtship on a summer afternoon. He was forty-five then and already he had begun the practice of filling his pockets with the scraps of paper that became hard balls and were thrown away. The habit had been formed as he sat in his buggy behind the jaded grey horse and went slowly along country roads. On the papers were written thoughts, ends of thoughts, beginnings of thoughts.

One by one the mind of Doctor Reefy had made the thoughts. Out of many of them he formed a truth that arose gigantic in his mind. The truth clouded the world. It became terrible and then faded away and the little thoughts began again.

The tall dark girl came to see Doctor Reefy because she was in the family way and had become frightened. She was in that condition because of a series of circumstances also curious.

The death of her father and mother and the rich acres of land that had come down to her had set a train of suitors on her heels. For two years she saw suitors almost every evening. Except two they were all alike. They talked to her of passion and there was a strained eager quality in their voices and in their eyes when they looked at her. The two who were different were much unlike each other. One of them, a slender young man with white hands, the son of a jeweler in Winesburg, talked continually of virginity. When he was with her he was never off the subject. The other, a black-haired boy with large ears, said nothing at all but always managed to get her into the darkness, where he began to kiss her.

For a time the tall dark girl thought she would marry the jeweler's son. For hours she sat in silence listening as he talked to her and then she began to be afraid of something. Beneath his talk of virginity she began to think there was a lust greater than in all the others. At times it seemed to her that as he talked he was holding her body in his hands. She imagined him turning it slowly about in the white hands and staring at it. At night she dreamed that he had bitten into her body and that his jaws were dripping. She had the dream three times, then she became in the family way to the one who said nothing at all but who in the moment of his passion actually did bite her shoulder so that for days the marks of his teeth showed.

After the tall dark girl came to know Doctor Reefy it seemed to her that she never wanted to leave him again. She went into his office one morning and without her saying anything he seemed to know what had happened to her.

In the office of the doctor there was a woman, the wife of the man who kept the bookstore in Winesburg. Like all old-fashioned country practitioners, Doctor Reefy pulled teeth, and the woman who waited held a handkerchief to her teeth and groaned. Her husband was with her and when the tooth was taken out they both screamed and blood ran down on the woman's white dress. The tall dark girl did not pay any attention. When the woman and the man had gone the doctor smiled. "I will take you driving into the country with me," he said.

For several weeks the tall dark girl and the doctor were together almost every day. The condition that had brought her to him passed in an illness, but she was like one who has discovered the sweetness of the twisted apples, she could not get her mind fixed again upon the round perfect fruit that is eaten in the city apartments. In the fall after the beginning of her acquaintanceship with him she married Doctor Reefy and in the following spring she died. During the winter he read to her all of the odds and ends of thoughts he had scribbled on the bits of paper. After he had read them he laughed and stuffed them away in his pockets to become round hard balls.

EXERCISES

1. Is Anderson's treatment of the story itself gnarled and twisted like the apples? Focus on the structure of the story, and discuss how it is organized.

2. Discuss the significance of the image pattern that connects the knuckles of the doctor's hands, the twisted apples, and the balled-up bits of paper.

3. What is the meaning of the girl's situation? What is the significance of her nightmare coming true even as she tries to avoid it?

4. What is the significance of the doctor's writing bits of thoughts and putting them in his pocket? How are the balled-up little notes "paper pills"?

5. Anderson begins the story with, "Everyone in Winesburg wondered why she married the doctor." Why does she marry the doctor? Does his problem complement her problem in some way?

6. In what way is this story "delicious, like the twisted little apples that grow in the orchards of Winesburg"?

JOHN
GALSWORTHY | *The Japanese Quince*

A s Mr. Nilson, well known in the City, opened the window of his dressing-room on Campden Hill, he experienced a peculiar sweetish sensation in the back of his throat, and a feeling of emptiness just under his fifth rib. Hooking the window back, he noticed that a little tree in the Square Gardens had come out in blossom, and that the thermometer stood at sixty. "Perfect morning," he thought; "Spring at last!"

Resuming some meditations on the price of Tintos, he took up an ivory-backed hand-glass and scrutinised his face. His firm, well-coloured cheeks, with their neat brown moustaches, and his round, well-opened, clear grey eyes, wore a reassuring appearance of good health. Putting on his black frock coat, he went downstairs.

In the dining-room his morning paper was laid out on the side-board. Mr. Nilson had scarcely taken it in his hand when he again became aware of that queer feeling. Somewhat concerned, he went to the French window and descended the scrolled iron steps into the fresh air. A cuckoo clock struck eight.

"Half an hour to breakfast," he thought; "I'll take a turn in the Gardens."

He had them to himself, and proceeded to pace the circular path with his morning paper clasped behind him. He had scarcely made two revolutions, however, when it was borne in on him that, instead of going away in the fresh air, the feeling had increased. He drew several deep breaths, having heard deep breathing recommended by his wife's doctor; but they augmented rather than diminished the sensation—as of some sweetish liquor in course within him, together with a faint aching just above his heart. Running over what he had eaten the night before, he could recollect no unusual dish, and it occurred to him that it might possibly be some smell affecting him. But he could detect nothing except a faint sweet lemony scent, rather agreeable than otherwise, which evidently emanated from the bushes budding in the sunshine. He was on the point of resuming his promenade, when a blackbird close by burst into song, and, looking up, Mr. Nilson saw at a distance of perhaps five yards a little tree, in the heart of whose branches the bird was perched. He stood staring curiously at this tree, recognising it for that which he had noticed from his window. It was covered with young blossoms, pink and white, and little bright green leaves both round and spikey; and on all this blossom and these leaves the sunlight glistened. Mr. Nilson smiled; the little tree was so alive and pretty! And instead of passing on, he stayed there smiling at the tree.

"Morning like this!" he thought; "and here I am the only person in the Square who has the—to come out and——!" But he had no sooner conceived this thought, than he saw quite near him a man with his hands behind him, who was also staring up and smiling at the little tree. Rather taken aback, Mr. Nilson ceased to smile, and looked furtively at the stranger. It was his next-door neighbour, Mr. Tandram, well known in the City, who had occupied the adjoining house for some five years. Mr. Nilson perceived at once the awkwardness of his position, for, being married, they had not yet had occasion to speak to one another. Doubtful as to his proper conduct, he decided at last to murmur: "Fine morning!" and was passing on, when Mr. Tandram answered: "Beautiful, for the time of year!" Detecting a slight nervousness in his neighbour's voice, Mr. Nilson was emboldened to regard him openly. He was of about Mr. Nilson's own height, with firm, well-coloured cheeks, neat brown moustaches, and round, well-opened, clear grey eyes; and he was wearing a black frock coat. Mr. Nilson noticed that he had his morning paper clasped behind him as he looked up at the little tree. And, visited somehow by the feeling that he had been caught out, he said abruptly:

"Er—can you give me the name of that tree?"

Mr. Tandram answered:

"I was about to ask you that," and stepped towards it. Mr. Nilson also approached the tree.

"Sure to have its name on, I should think," he said.

Mr. Tandram was the first to see the little label, close to where the blackbird had been sitting. He read it out.

"Japanese quince!"

"Ah!" said Mr. Nilson, "thought so. Early flowerers."

"Very," assented Mr. Tandram, and added: "Quite a feelin' in the air today."

Mr. Nilson nodded.

"It was a blackbird singin'," he said.

"Blackbirds," answered Mr. Tandram, "I prefer them to thrushes myself; more body in the note." And he looked at Mr. Nilson in an almost friendly way.

"Quite," murmured Mr. Nilson. "These exotics, they don't bear fruit. Pretty blossom!" and he again glanced up at the blossom, thinking: "Nice fellow, this, I rather like him."

Mr. Tandram also gazed up at the blossom. And the little tree, as if appreciating their attention, quivered and glowed. From a distance, the blackbird gave a loud, clear call. Mr. Nilson dropped his eyes. It struck him suddenly that Mr. Tandram looked a little foolish; and, as if he had seen himself, he said: "I must be going in. Good morning!"

A shade passed over Mr. Tandram's face, as if he, too, had suddenly noticed something about Mr. Nilson.

"Good morning," he replied, and clasping their journals to their backs they separated.

Mr. Nilson retraced his steps towards his garden window, walking slowly so as to avoid arriving at the same time as his neighbour. Having seen Mr. Tandram mount his scrolled iron steps, he ascended his own in turn. On the top step he paused.

With the slanting Spring sunlight darting and quivering into it, the Japanese quince seemed more living than a tree. The blackbird had returned to it, and was chanting out his heart.

Mr. Nilson sighed; again he felt that queer sensation, that chokey feeling in his throat.

The sound of a cough or sigh attracted his attention. There, in the shadow of his French window, stood Mr. Tandram, also looking forth across the Gardens at the little quince tree.

Unaccountably upset, Mr. Nilson turned abruptly into the house, and opened his morning paper.

EXERCISES

1. The story opens with Mr. Nilson experiencing a queer, sweetish sensation in the back of his throat and a feeling of emptiness under his fifth rib. Why does the story open this way? What does it have to do with "Spring at last"?

2. The story seems primarily to exist for the sake of the meeting between the two men. What does the meeting have to do with Mr. Nilson's queer feeling, with the aching just above his heart?

3. How would you characterize the conversation between the two men? Is it merely ordinary, or does it suggest something more than what is said?

4. What suddenly happens that makes Mr. Nilson think Mr. Tandram looks foolish? Why does a shade pass over Mr. Tandram's face? What have they noticed about each other?

5. Why do the Japanese quince and the singing blackbird dominate the central event? Do they symbolize something? Are they a catalyst for some feeling?

6. Why does Mr. Nilson feel "unaccountably upset" at the end of the story? How would you account for this feeling?

ARTURO
VIVANTE | *Can-Can*

I'm going to go for a drive," he said to his wife. "I'll be back in an hour or two."

He didn't often leave the house for more than the few minutes it took him to go to the post office or to a store, but spent his time hanging around, doing odd jobs—Mr. Fix-it, his wife called him—and also, though not nearly enough of it, painting—which he made his living from.

"All right," his wife said brightly, as though he were doing her a favor. As a matter of fact, she didn't really like him to leave; she felt safer with him at home, and he helped look after the children, especially the baby.

"You're glad to be rid of me, aren't you?" he said.

"Uh-huh," she said with a smile that suddenly made her look very pretty—someone to be missed.

She didn't ask him where he was going for his drive. She wasn't the least bit inquisitive, though jealous she was in silent, subtle ways.

As he put his coat on, he watched her. She was in the living room with their elder daughter. "Do the can-can, mother," the child said, at which she held up her skirt and did the can-can, kicking her legs up high in his direction.

He wasn't simply going out for a drive, as he had said, but going to a café, to meet Sarah, whom his wife knew but did not suspect, and with her go to a house on a lake his wife knew nothing about—a summer cottage to which he had the key.

"Well, goodbye," he said.

"Bye," she called back, still dancing.

This wasn't the way a husband expected his wife—whom he was about to leave at home to go to another woman—to behave at all, he thought. He expected her to be sewing or washing, not doing the can-can, for God's sake. Yes, doing something uninteresting and unattractive, like darning children's clothes. She had no stockings on, no shoes, and her legs looked very white and smooth, secret, as though he had never touched them or come near them. Her feet, swinging up and down high in the air, seemed to be nodding to him. She held her skirt bunched up, attractively. Why was she doing that of all times *now?* He lingered. Her eyes had mockery in them, and she laughed. The child laughed with her as she danced. She was still dancing as he left the house.

He thought of the difficulties he had had arranging this *rendezvous*—going out to a call box; phoning Sarah at her office (she was married, too); her being out; his calling her again; the busy signal; the coin falling out of sight, his opening the door of the phone box in order to retrieve it; at last getting her on the line; her asking him to call again next week, finally setting a date.

Waiting for her at the café, he surprised himself hoping that she wouldn't come. The appointment was at three. It was now ten past. Well, she was often late. He looked at the clock, and at the picture window for her car. A car like hers, and yet not hers—no luggage rack on it. The smooth hardtop gave him a peculiar pleasure. Why? It was 3:15 now. Perhaps she wouldn't come. No, if she was going to come at all, this was the most likely time for her to arrive. Twenty past. Ah, now there was some hope. Hope? How strange he should be hoping for her absence. Why had he made the appointment if he was hoping she would miss it? He didn't know why, but simpler, simpler if she didn't come. Because all he wanted now was to smoke that cigarette, drink that cup of coffee for the sake of them, and not to give himself something to do. And he wished he could go for a drive, free and easy, as he had said he would. But he waited, and at 3:30 she arrived. "I had almost given up hope," he said.

They drove to the house on the lake. As he held her in his arms he couldn't think of her; for the life of him he couldn't.

"What are you thinking about?" she said afterwards, sensing his detachment.

For a moment he didn't answer, then he said, "You really want to know what I was thinking of?"

"Yes," she said, a little anxiously.

He suppressed a laugh, as though what he was going to tell her was too absurd or silly. "I was thinking of someone doing the can-can."

"Oh," she said, reassured. "For a moment I was afraid you were thinking of your wife."

EXERCISES

1. This story is so brief that it might not be considered a story at all. What makes it a story rather than a mere event?

2. Discuss the tone and point of view of this story. Is it primarily realistic, or is it so abbreviated that it sounds like a fable?

3. Why does the man wish that the woman will not come? How does the meaning of the word *hope* change for him as he waits?

4. How does he feel as a result of his wife doing the can-can? Why is it a can-can rather than anything else it might be?

5. What is the point of this story? Does it say something about male–female relationships, about marriage, about infidelity, about desire, about love?

JOHN
UPDIKE | *A & P*

In walks these three girls in nothing but bathing suits. I'm in the third checkout slot, with my back to the door, so I don't see them until they're over by the bread. The one that caught my eye first was the one in the plaid green two-piece. She was a chunky kid, with a good tan and a sweet broad soft-looking can with those two crescents of white just under it, where the sun never seems to hit, at the top of the backs of her legs. I stood there with my hand on a box of HiHo crackers trying to remember if I rang it up or not. I ring it up again and the customer starts giving me hell. She's one of these cash-register-watchers, a witch about fifty with rouge on her cheekbones and no eyebrows, and I know it made her day to trip me up. She'd been watching cash registers for fifty years and probably never seen a mistake before.

By the time I got her feathers smoothed and her goodies into a bag—she gives me a little snort in passing, if she'd been born at the right time they would have burned her over in Salem—by the time I get her on her way the girls had circled around the bread and were coming back, without a pushcart, back my way along the counters, in the aisle between the checkouts and the Special bins. They didn't even have shoes on. There was this chunky one, with the two-piece—it was bright green and the seams on the bra were still sharp and her belly was still pretty pale so I guessed she just got it (the suit)—there was this one, with one of those chubby berry-faces, the lips all bunched together under her nose, this one, and a tall one, with black hair that hadn't quite frizzed right, and one of these sunburns right across under the eyes, and a chin that was too long—you know, the kind of girl other girls think is very "striking" and "attractive" but never quite makes it, as they very well know, which is why they like her so much—and then the third one, that wasn't quite so tall. She was the queen. She kind of led them, the other two peeking around and making their shoulders round. She didn't look around, not this queen, she just walked straight on slowly, on these long white prima-donna legs. She came down a little hard on her heels, as if she didn't walk in her bare feet that much, putting down her heels and then letting the weight move along to her toes as if she was testing the floor with every step, putting a little deliberate extra action into it. You never know for sure how girls' minds work (do you really think it's a mind in there or just a little buzz like a bee in a glass jar?) but you got the idea she had talked the other two into coming in here with her, and now she was showing them how to do it, walk slow and hold yourself straight.

She had on a kind of dirty-pink—beige maybe, I don't know—bathing suit with a little nubble all over it and, what got me, the straps were down. They were off her shoulders looped loose around the cool tops of her arms, and I guess as a result the suit had slipped a little on her, so all around the top of the cloth there was this shining rim. If it hadn't been there you wouldn't have known there could have been anything whiter than those shoulders. With the straps pushed off, there was nothing between the top of the suit and the top of her head except just *her*, this clean bare plane of the top of her chest down from the shoulder bones like a dented sheet of metal tilted in the light. I mean, it was more than pretty.

She had sort of okay hair that the sun and salt had bleached, done up in a bun that was unravelling, and a kind of prim face. Walking into the A & P with your straps down, I suppose it's the only kind of face you *can* have. She held her head so high her neck, coming up out of those white shoulders, looked kind of stretched, but I didn't mind. The longer her neck was, the more of her there was.

She must have felt in the corner of her eye me and over my shoulder Sto-kesie in the second slot watching, but she didn't tip. Not this queen. She kept her eyes moving across the racks, and stopped, and turned so slow it made my stomach rub the inside of my apron, and buzzed to the other two, who kind of huddled against her for relief, and then they all three of them went up the cat-and-dog-food-breakfast-cereal-macaroni-rice-raisins-seasonings-spreads-spaghetti-soft-drinks-crackers-and-cookies aisle. From the third slot I look straight up this aisle to the meat counter, and I watched them all the way. The fat one with the tan sort of fumbled with the cookies, but on second thought she put the package back. The sheep pushing their carts down the aisle—the girls were walking against the usual traffic (not that we have one-way signs or anything)—were pretty hilarious. You could see them, when Queenie's white shoulders dawned on them, kind of jerk, or hop, or hiccup, but their eyes snapped back to their own baskets and on they pushed. I bet you could set off dynamite in an A & P and the people would by and large keep reaching and checking oatmeal off their lists and muttering "Let me see, there was a third thing, began with A, asparagus, no, ah, yes, applesauce!" or whatever it is they do mutter. But there was no doubt, this jiggled them. A few houseslaves in pin curlers even looked around after pushing their carts past to make sure what they had seen was correct.

You know, it's one thing to have a girl in a bathing suit down on the beach, where what with the glare nobody can look at each other much any-way, and another thing in the cool of the A & P, under the fluorescent lights, against all those stacked packages, with her feet paddling along naked over our checkerboard green-and-cream rubber-tile floor.

"Oh Daddy," Stokesie said beside me. "I feel so faint."

"Darling," I said. "Hold me tight." Stokesie's married, with two babies chalked up on his fuselage already, but as far as I can tell that's the only dif-ference. He's twenty-two, and I was nineteen this April.

"Is it done?" he asks, the responsible married man finding his voice. I for-got to say he thinks he's going to be manager some sunny day, maybe in 1990 when it's called the Great Alexandrov and Petrooshki Tea Company or something.

What he meant was, our town is five miles from a beach, with a big sum-mer colony out on the Point, but we're right in the middle of town, and the women generally put on a shirt or shorts or something before they get out of the car into the street. And anyway these are usually women with six children and varicose veins mapping their legs and nobody, including them, could care less. As I say, we're right in the middle of town, and if you stand at our front doors you can see two banks and the Congregational church and the news-paper store and the three real-estate offices and about twenty-seven old free-loaders tearing up Central Street because the sewer broke again. It's not as if we're on the Cape, we're north of Boston and there's people in this town haven't seen the ocean for twenty years.

The girls had reached the meat counter and were asking McMahon some-thing. He pointed, they pointed, and they shuffled out of sight behind a pyr-amid of Diet Delight peaches. All that was left for us to see was old McMahon patting his mouth and looking after them sizing up their joints. Poor kids, I began to feel sorry for them, they couldn't help it.

Now here comes the sad part of the story, at least my family says it's sad, but I don't think it's so sad myself. The store's pretty empty, it being Thursday afternoon, so there was nothing much to do except lean on the register and wait for the girls to show up again. The whole store was like a pinball machine and I didn't know which tunnel they'd come out of. After a while they came around out of the far aisle, around the light bulbs, records at discount of the Caribbean Six or Tony Martin Sings or some such gunk you wonder they waste the wax on, sixpacks of candy bars, and plastic toys done up in cellophane that fall apart when a kid looks at them anyway. Around they come, Queenie still leading the way, and holding a little gray jar in her hand. Slots Three through Seven are unmanned and I could see her wondering between Stokes and me, but Stokesie with his usual luck draws an old party in baggy gray pants who stumbles up with four giant cans of pineapple juice (what do these bums *do* with all that pineapple juice? I've often asked myself) so the girls come to me. Queenie puts down the jar and I take it into my fingers icy cold. Kingfish Fancy Herring Snacks in Pure Sour Cream: 49¢. Now her hands are empty, not a ring or a bracelet, bare as God made them, and I wonder where the money's coming from. Still with that prim look she lifts a folded dollar bill out of the hollow at the center of her nubbled pink top. The jar went heavy in my hand. Really, I thought that was so cute.

Then everybody's luck begins to run out. Lengel comes in from haggling with a truck full of cabbages on the lot and is about to scuttle into that door marked MANAGER behind which he hides all day when the girls touch his eye. Lengel's pretty dreary, teaches Sunday school and the rest, but he doesn't miss that much. He comes over and says, "Girls, this isn't the beach."

Queenie blushes, though maybe it's just a brush of sunburn I was noticing for the first time, now that she was so close. "My mother asked me to pick up a jar of herring snacks." Her voice kind of startled me, the way voices do when you see the people first, coming out so flat and dumb yet kind of tony, too, the way it ticked over "pick up" and "snacks." All of a sudden I slid right down her voice into her living room. Her father and the other men were standing around in ice-cream coats and bow ties and the women were in sandals picking up herring snacks on toothpicks off a big glass plate and they were all holding drinks the color of water with olives and sprigs of mint in them. When my parents have somebody over they get lemonade and if it's a real racy affair Schlitz in tall glasses with "They'll Do It Every Time" cartoons stencilled on.

"That's all right," Lengel said. "But this isn't the beach." His repeating this struck me as funny, as if it had just occurred to him, and he had been thinking all these years the A & P was a great big dune and he was the head lifeguard. He didn't like my smiling—as I say he doesn't miss much—but he concentrates on giving the girls that sad Sunday-school-superintendent stare.

Queenie's blush is no sunburn now, and the plump one in plaid, that I liked better from the back—a really sweet can—pipes up, "We weren't doing any shopping. We just came in for one thing."

"That makes no difference," Lengel tells her, and I could see from the way his eyes went that he hadn't noticed she was wearing a two-piece before. "We want you decently dressed when you come in here."

"We *are* decent," Queenie says suddenly, her lower lip pushing, getting sore now that she remembers her place, a place from which the crowd that runs the A & P must look pretty crummy. Fancy Herring Snacks flashed in her very blue eyes.

"Girls, I don't want to argue with you. After this come in here with your shoulders covered. It's our policy." He turns his back. That's policy for you. Policy is what the kingpins want. What the others want is juvenile delinquency.

All this while, the customers had been showing up with their carts but, you know, sheep, seeing a scene, they had all bunched up on Stokesie, who shook open a paper bag as gently as peeling a peach, not wanting to miss a word. I could feel in the silence everybody getting nervous, most of all Lengel, who asks me, "Sammy, have you rung up their purchase?"

I thought and said "No" but it wasn't about that I was thinking. I go through the punches, 4, 9, GROC, TOT—it's more complicated than you think, and after you do it often enough, it begins to make a little song, that you hear words to, in my case "Hello (*bing*) there, you (*gung*) hap-py *pee*-pul (*splat*)!"—the *splat* being the drawer flying out. I uncrease the bill, tenderly as you may imagine, it just having come from between the two smoothest scoops of vanilla I had ever known were there, and pass a half and a penny into her narrow pink palm, and nestle the herrings in a bag and twist its neck and hand it over, all the time thinking.

The girls, and who'd blame them, are in a hurry to get out, so I say "I quit" to Lengel quick enough for them to hear, hoping they'll stop and watch me, their unsuspected hero. They keep right on going, into the electric eye; the door flies open and they flicker across the lot to their car, Queenie and Plaid and Big Tall Goony-Goony (not that as raw material she was so bad), leaving me with Lengel and a kink in his eyebrow.

"Did you say something, Sammy?"

"I said I quit."

"I thought you did."

"You didn't have to embarrass them."

"It was they who were embarrassing us."

I started to say something that came out "Fiddle-de-doo." It's a saying of my grandmother's, and I know she would have been pleased.

"I don't think you know what you're saying," Lengel said.

"I know you don't," I said. "But I do." I pull the bow at the back of my apron and start shrugging it off my shoulders. A couple customers that had been heading for my slot begin to knock against each other, like scared pigs in a chute.

Lengel sighs and begins to look very patient and old and gray. He's been a friend of my parents for years. "Sammy, you don't want to do this to your Mom and Dad," he tells me. It's true, I don't. But it seems to me that once you begin a gesture it's fatal not to go through with it. I fold the apron,

"Sammy" stitched in red on the pocket, and put it on the counter, and drop the bow tie on top of it. The bow tie is theirs, if you've ever wondered. "You'll feel this for the rest of your life," Lengel says, and I know that's true, too, but remembering how he made the pretty girl blush makes me so scrunchy inside I punch the No Sale tab and the machine whirs "pee-pul" and the drawer splats out. One advantage to this scene taking place in summer, I can follow this up with a clean exit, there's no fumbling around getting your coat and galoshes, I just saunter into the electric eye in my white shirt that my mother ironed the night before, and the door heaves itself open, and outside the sunshine is skating around on the asphalt.

I look around for my girls, but they're gone, of course. There wasn't anybody but some young married screaming with her children about some candy they didn't get by the door of a powder-blue Falcon station wagon. Looking back in the big windows, over the bags of peat moss and aluminum lawn furniture stacked on the pavement, I could see Lengel in my place in the slot, checking the sheep through. His face was dark gray and his back stiff, as if he'd just had an injection of iron, and my stomach kind of fell as I felt how hard the world was going to be to me hereafter.

EXERCISES

1. Characterize the speaker in the story. What is he like? Discuss the importance of Sammy's language in the story. What is Sammy's attitude toward girls in general? What is his attitude toward these girls in particular?

2. Why is one of the girls described by Sammy as "Queenie"? If she is a queen, what are the two other girls? If she is a queen, what does this make Sammy? Why does Sammy feel sorry for the girls? What does he mean when he thinks, "they couldn't help it"?

3. Why does Sammy think that what his parents say is the sad part of the story is not so sad? Why does Sammy think of the difference between his family and the family of Queenie? What does this have to do with the central event in the story?

4. Analyze Sammy's motive for quitting. Is it possible there are several motives involved? Discuss "it seems to me that once you begin a gesture it's fatal not to go through with it."

5. Why does Sammy feel the world is going to be hard for him hereafter? Is this an extreme reaction to a minor event?

6. Compare this story to James Joyce's "Araby." Discuss the elements of realism and romance in both stories.

TONI
CADE
BAMBARA | *The Lesson*

Back in the days when everyone was old and stupid or young and foolish and me and Sugar were the only ones just right, this lady moved on our block with nappy hair and proper speech and no makeup. And quite naturally we laughed at her, laughed the way we did at the junk man who went about his business like he was some big-time president and his sorry-ass horse his secretary. And we kinda hated her too, hated the way we did the winos who cluttered up our parks and pissed on our handball walls and stank up our hallways and stairs so you couldn't halfway play hide-and-seek without a god-damn gas mask. Miss Moore was her name. The only woman on the block with no first name. And she was black as hell, cept for her feet, which were fish-white and spooky. And she was always planning these boring-ass things for us to do, us being my cousin, mostly, who lived on the block cause we all moved North the same time and to the same apartment then spread out grad-ual to breathe. And our parents would yank our heads into some kinda shape and crisp up our clothes so we'd be presentable for travel with Miss Moore, who always looked like she was going to church, though she never did. Which is just one of the things the grownups talked about when they talked behind her back like a dog. But when she came calling with some sachet she'd sewed up or some gingerbread she's made or some book, why then they'd all be too embarrassed to turn her down and we'd get handed over all spruced up. She'd been to college and said it was only right that she should take responsibility for the young ones' education, and she not even related by marriage or blood. So they'd go for it. Specially Aunt Gretchen. She was the main gofer in the family. You got some ole dumb shit foolishness you want somebody to go for, you send for Aunt Gretchen. She been screwed into the go-along for so long, it's a blood-deep natural thing with her. Which is how she got saddled with me and Sugar and Junior in the first place while our mothers were in a la-de-da apartment up the block having a good ole time.

So this one day, Miss Moore rounds us all up at the mailbox and it's pure-dee hot and she's knockin herself out about arithmetic. And school suppose to let up in summer I heard, but she don't never let up. And the starch in my pinafore scratching the shit outta me and I'm really hating this nappy-head bitch and her goddamn college degree. I'd much rather go to the pool or to the show where it's cool. So me and Sugar leaning on the mailbox being surly, which is a Miss Moore word. And Flyboy checking out what everybody brought for lunch. And Fat Butt already wasting his peanut-butter-and-jelly sandwich like the pig he is. And Junebug punchin on Q.T.'s arm for potato chips. And Rosie Giraffe shifting from one hip to the other waiting for some-body to step on her foot or ask her if she from Georgia so she can kick ass, preferably Mercedes'. And Miss Moore asking us do we know what money is, like we a bunch of retards. I mean real money, she say, like it's only poker chips or monopoly papers we lay on the grocer. So right away I'm tired of this and say so. And would much rather snatch Sugar and go to the Sunset and terrorize the West Indian kids and take their hair ribbons and their money too. And Miss Moore files that remark away for next week's lesson on brotherhood, I can tell. And finally I say we oughta get to the subway cause it's cooler and besides we might meet some cute boys. Sugar done swiped her mama's lipstick, so we ready.

So we heading down the street and she's boring us silly about what things cost and what our parents make and how much goes for rent and how money ain't divided up right in this country. And then she gets to the part about we all poor and live in the slums, which I don't feature. And I'm ready to speak on that, but she steps out in the street and hails two cabs just like that. Then she hustles half the crew in with her and hands me a five-dollar bill and tells me to calculate 10 percent tip for the driver. And we're off. Me and Sugar and Junebug and Flyboy hangin out the window and hollering to everybody, putting lipstick on each other cause Flyboy a faggot anyway, and making farts with our sweaty armpits. But I'm mostly trying to figure how to spend this money. But they all fascinated with the meter ticking and Junebug starts laying bets as to how much it'll read when Flyboy can't hold his breath no more. Then Sugar lays bets as to how much it'll be when we get there. So I'm stuck. Don't nobody want to go for my plan, which is to jump out at the next light and run off to the first bar-b-que we can find. Then the driver tells us to get the hell out cause we there already. And the meter reads eighty-five cents. And I'm stalling to figure out the tip and Sugar say give him a dime. And I decide he don't need it bad as I do, so later for him. But then he tries to take off with Junebug foot still in the door so we talk about his mamma something ferocious. Then we check out that we on Fifth Avenue and everybody dressed up in stockings. One lady in a fur coat, hot as it is. White folks crazy.

"This is the place," Miss Moore say, presenting it to us in the voice she uses at the museum. "Let's look in the windows before we go in."

"Can we steal?" Sugar asks very serious like she's getting the ground rules squared away before she plays. "I beg your pardon," say Miss Moore, and we fall out. So she leads us around the windows of the toy store and me and Sugar screamin, "This is mine, that's mine, I gotta have that, that was made for me, I was born for that," till Big Butt drowns us out.

"Hey, I'm goin to buy that there."

"That there? You don't even know what it is, stupid."

"I do so," he say punchin on Rosie Giraffe. "It's a microscope."

"Whatcha gonna do with a microscope, fool?"

"Look at things."

"Like what, Ronald?" ask Miss Moore. And Big Butt ain't got the first notion. So here go Miss Moore gabbing about the thousands of bacteria in a drop of water and the somethinorother in a speck of blood and the million and one living things in the air around us is invisible to the naked eye. And what she say that for? Junebug go to town on that "naked" and we rolling. Then Miss Moore ask what it cost. So we all jam into the window smudgin it up and the price tag say $300. So then she ask how long'd take for Big Butt and Junebug to save up their allowances. "Too long," I say. "Yeh," adds Sugar, "outgrown it by that time." And Miss Moore say no, you never outgrow learning instruments. "Why, even medical students and interns and," blah, blah, blah. And we ready to choke Big Butt for bringing it up in the first damn place.

"This here costs four hundred eighty dollars," say Rosie Giraffe. So we pile up all over her to see what she pointin out. My eyes tell me it's a chunk of glass cracked with something heavy, and different-color inks dripped into the splits, then the whole thing put into a oven or something. But for $480 it don't make sense.

"That's a paperweight made of semi-precious stones fused together under tremendous pressure," she explains slowly, with her hands doing the mining and all the factory work.

"So what's a paperweight?" ask Rosie Giraffe.

"To weigh paper with, dumbbell," say Flyboy, the wise man from the East.

"Not exactly," say Miss Moore, which is what she say when you warm or way off too. "It's to weigh paper down so it won't scatter and make your desk untidy." So right away me and Sugar curtsy to each other and then to Mercedes who is more the tidy type.

"We don't keep paper on top of the desk in my class," say Junebug, figuring Miss Moore crazy or lyin one.

"At home, then," she say. "Don't you have a calendar and a pencil case and a blotter and a letter-opener on your desk at home where you do your homework?" And she know damn well what our homes look like cause she nosys around in them every chance she gets.

"I don't even have a desk," say Junebug. "Do we?"

"No. And I don't get no homework neither," says Big Butt.

"And I don't even have a home," says Flyboy like he do at school to keep the white folks off his back and sorry for him. Send this poor kid to camp posters, is his specialty.

"I do," says Mercedes. "I have a box of stationery on my desk and a picture of my cat. My godmother bought the stationery and the desk. There's a big rose on each sheet and the envelopes smell like roses."

"Who wants to know about your smelly-ass stationery," say Rosie Giraffe fore I can get my two cents in.

"It's important to have a work area all your own so that . . ."

"Will you look at this sailboat, please," say Flyboy, cutting her off and pointin to the thing like it was his. So once again we tumble all over each other to gaze at this magnificent thing in the toy store which is just big enough to maybe sail two kittens across the pond if you strap them to the posts tight. We all start reciting the price tag like we in assembly. "Handcrafted sailboat of fiberglass at one thousand one hundred ninety-five dollars."

"Unbelievable," I hear myself say and am really stunned. I read it again for myself just in case the group recitation put me in a trance. Same thing. For some reason this pisses me off. We look at Miss Moore and she lookin at us, waiting for I dunno what.

"Who'd pay all that when you can buy a sailboat set for a quarter at Pop's, a tube of glue for a dime, and a ball of string for eight cents? It must have a motor and a whole lot else besides," I say. "My sailboat cost me about fifty cents."

"But will it take water?" say Mercedes with her smart ass.

"Took mine to Alley Pond Park once," say Flyboy. "String broke. Lost it. Pity."

"Sailed mine in Central Park and it keeled over and sank. Had to ask my father for another dollar."

"And you got the strap," laugh Big Butt. "The jerk didn't even have a string on it. My old man wailed on his behind."

Little Q.T. was staring hard at the sailboat and you could see he wanted it bad. But he too little and somebody'd just take it from him. So what the hell. "This boat for kids, Miss Moore?"

"Parents silly to buy something like that just to get all broke up," say Rosie Giraffe.

"That much money it should last forever," I figure.

"My father'd buy it for me if I wanted it."

"Your father, my ass," say Rosie Giraffe getting a chance to finally push Mercedes.

"Must be rich people shop here," say Q.T.

"You are a very bright boy," say Flyboy. "What was your first clue?" And he rap him on the head with the back of his knuckles, since Q.T. the only one he could get away with. Though Q.T. liable to come up behind you years later and get his licks in when you half expect it.

"What I want to know is," I says to Miss Moore though I never talk to her, I wouldn't give the bitch that satisfaction, "is how much a real boat costs? I figure a thousand'd get you a yacht any day."

"Why don't you check that out," she says, "and report back to the group?" Which really pains my ass. If you gonna mess up a perfectly good swim day least you could do is have some answers. "Let's go in," she say like she got something up her sleeve. Only she don't lead the way. So me and Sugar turn the corner to where the entrance is, but when we get there I kinda hang back. Not that I'm scared, what's there to be afraid of, just a toy store. But I feel funny, shame. But what I got to be shamed about? Got as much right to go in as anybody. But somehow I can't seem to get hold of the door, so I step away from Sugar to lead. But she hangs back too. And I look at her and she looks at me and this is ridiculous. I mean, damn, I have never been shy about doing nothing or going nowhere. But then Mercedes steps up and then Rosie Giraffe and Big Butt crowd in behind and shove, and next thing we all stuffed into the doorway with only Mercedes squeezing past us, smoothing out her jumper and walking right down the aisle. Then the rest of us tumble in like a glued-together jigsaw done all wrong. And people lookin at us. And it's like the time me and Sugar crashed into the Catholic church on a dare. But once we got in there and everything so hushed and holy and the candles and the bowin and the handkerchiefs on all the drooping heads, I just couldn't go through with the plan. Which was for me to run up to the altar and do a tap dance while Sugar played the nose flute and messed around in the holy water. And Sugar kept given me the elbow. Then later teased me so bad I tied her up in the shower and turned it on and locked her in. And she'd be there till this day if Aunt Gretchen hadn't finally figured I was lying about the boarder takin a shower.

Same thing in the store. We all walkin on tiptoe and hardly touchin the games and puzzles and things. And I watched Miss Moore who is steady watchin us like she waitin for a sign. Like Mama Drewery watches the sky and sniffs the air and takes note of just how much slant is in the bird formation. Then me and Sugar bump smack into each other, so busy gazing at the toys, 'specially the sailboat. But we don't laugh and go into our fat-lady bump-stomach routine. We just stare at that price tag. Then Sugar run a finger over the whole boat. And I'm jealous and want to hit her. Maybe not her, but I sure want to punch somebody in the mouth.

"Watcha bring us here for, Miss Moore?"

"You sound angry, Sylvia. Are you mad about something?" Givin me one of them grins like she tellin a grown-up joke that never turns out to be funny. And she's lookin very closely at me like maybe she plannin to do my portrait from memory. I'm mad, but I won't give her that satisfaction. So I slouch around the store bein very bored and say, "Let's go."

Me and Sugar at the back of the train watchin the tracks whizzin by large then small then getting gobbled up in the dark. I'm thinkin about this tricky toy I saw in the store. A clown that somersaults on a bar then does chin-ups just cause you yank lightly at his leg. Cost $35. I could see me askin my mother for a $35 birthday clown. "You wanna who that costs what?" she'd say, cocking her head to the side to get a better view of the hole in my head. Thirty-five dollars could buy new bunk beds for Junior and Gretchen's boy. Thirty-five dollars and the whole household could go visit Grand-daddy Nelson in the country. Thirty-five dollars would pay for the rent and the piano bill too. Who are these people that spend that much for performing clowns and $1000 for toy sailboats? What kinda work they do and how they live and how come we ain't in on it? Where we are is who we are, Miss Moore always pointin out. But it don't necessarily have to be that way, she always adds then waits for somebody to say that poor people have to wake up and demand their share of the pie and don't none of us know what kind of pie she talking about in the first damn place. But she ain't so smart cause I still got her four dollars from the taxi and she sure ain't gettin it. Messin up my day with this shit. Sugar nudges me in my pocket and winks.

Miss Moore lines us up in front of the mailbox where we started from, seem like years ago, and I got a headache for thinkin so hard. And we lean all over each other so we can hold up under the draggy-ass lecture she always finishes us off with at the end before we thank her for borin us to tears. But she just looks at us like she readin tea leaves. Finally she say, "Well, what did you think of F.A.O. Schwarz?"

Rosie Giraffe mumbles, "White folks crazy."

"I'd like to go there again when I get my birthday money," says Mercedes, and we shove her out the pack so she has to lean on the mailbox by herself.

"I'd like a shower. Tiring day," say Flyboy.

Then Sugar surprises me by sayin, "You know, Miss Moore, I don't think all of us here put together eat in a year what that sailboat costs." And Miss Moore lights up like somebody goosed her "And?" she say, urging Sugar on. Only I'm standin on her foot so she don't continue.

"Imagine for a minute what kind of society it is in which some people can spend on a toy what it would cost to feed a family of six or seven. What do you think?"

"I think," say Sugar pushing me off her feet like she never done before, cause I whip her ass in a minute, "that this is not much of a democracy if you ask me. Equal chance to pursue happiness means an equal crack at the dough, don't it?" Miss Moore is besides herself and I am disgusted with Sugar's treachery. So I stand on her foot one more time to see if she'll shove me. She shuts up, and Miss Moore looks at me, sorrowfully I'm thinkin. And somethin weird is goin on, I can feel it in my chest.

"Anybody else learn anything today?" lookin dead at me. I walk away and Sugar has to run to catch up and don't even seem to notice when I shrug her arm off my shoulder.

"Well, we got four dollars anyway," she says.

"Uh, hunh."

"We could go to Hascombs and get half a chocolate layer and then go to the Sunset and still have plenty money for potato chips and ice cream sodas."

"Uh hunh."

"Race you to Hascombs," she say.

We start down the block and she gets ahead which is O.K. by me cause I'm going to the West End and then over to the Drive to think this day through. She can run if she want to and even run faster. But ain't nobody gonna beat me at nuthin.

1. Describe the cultural framework of the speaker. Why does she not like Miss Moore?

2. How important is the voice of this story? Discuss your reaction to the speaker's language. Compare it to the language of Sammy in John Updike's "A & P."

3. In the clash of values between Miss Moore and the children, whose values are positive and whose values are negative in this story? Or is it that simple?

4. Why does the narrator feel ashamed in the toy store? How is it like her experience in the church? Does this feeling seem a contradiction to her attitude in other parts of the story?

5. Why does Miss Moore take the children into the toy store? What kind of lesson is she trying to teach?

6. What does the narrator mean that something weird is going on? Why does she feel that Sugar has been treacherous?

7. What is the lesson in this story? Why does the narrator say she is going to think the day through? Has she changed in some way?

FRANK
O'CONNOR | *Judas*

I'll forget a lot of things before I forget that night. As I was going out the mother said: "Sure, you won't be late, Jerry?" and I only laughed at her and said: "Am I ever late?" As I went down the road I was thinking it was months since I had taken her to the pictures. You might think that funny, Michael John, but after the father's death we were thrown together a lot. And I knew she hated being alone in the house after dark.

At the same time I had troubles of my own. You see, Michael John, being an only child, I never knocked round with girls the way others did. All the chaps in the office went with girls, or at any rate they let on they did. They said: "Who was the old doll I saw you with last night, Jerry? Aha, Jerry, you'd better mind yourself, boy, or you'll be getting into trouble!" Paddy Kinnane, for instance, talked like that, and he never saw how it upset me. I think he thought it was a great compliment. It wasn't until years after that I began to suspect that Paddy's acquaintance with dolls was about of one kind with my own.

Then I met Kitty Doherty. Kitty was a hospital nurse, and all the chaps in the office said a fellow should never go with hospital nurses—they knew too much. I knew when I met Kitty that that was a lie. She was a well-educated, superior girl; she lived up the river in a posh locality, and her mother was on all sorts of councils and committees. She was small and wiry; a good-looking girl, always in good humor, and when she talked, she hopped from one thing to another like a robin on a frosty morning.

Anyway, she had me dazzled. I used to meet her in the evenings up the river road, as if I was walking there by accident and very surprised to see her. "Fancy meeting you!" I'd say, or "Well, well, isn't this a great surprise?" Then we'd stand talking for half an hour and I'd see her home. Several times she asked me in, but I was too nervous. I knew I'd lose my head, break the china, use some dirty word, and then go home and cut my throat. Of course, I never asked her to come to the pictures or anything like that. I knew she was above that. My only hope was that if I waited long enough I might be able to save her from drowning, the White Slave Traffic, or something of the sort. That would show in a modest, dignified way how I felt about her. Of course, I knew at the same time I ought to stay at home more with the mother, but the very thought that I might be missing an opportunity like that would be enough to spoil a whole evening on me.

This night in particular I was nearly distracted. It was three weeks since I'd seen Kitty. You know what three weeks are at that age. I was sure that at the very least the girl was dying and asking for me and that no one knew my address. A week before, I'd felt I simply couldn't bear it any longer, so I made an excuse and went down to the post office. I rang up the hospital and asked for her. I fully expected them to say that she was dead, and I got a shock when the girl at the other end asked my name. "I'm afraid," I said, "I'm a stranger to Miss Doherty, but I have an important message for her." Then I got completely panic-stricken. What could a girl like Kitty make of a damned deliberate lie like that? What else was it but a trap laid by an old and cunning hand? I held the receiver out and looked at it. "Moynihan," I said to it, "you're mad. An asylum, Moynihan, is the only place for a fellow like you." Then I heard her voice, not in my ear at all, but in the telephone booth as if she were standing before me, and I nearly dropped the receiver with terror. I put it to my ear and asked in a disguised voice: "Who is that speaking, please?" "This is Kitty Doherty," she said rather impatiently. "Who are you?" "I am Monsieur Bertrand," said I, speaking in what I hoped was a French accent. "I am afraid I have de wrong number." Then I put down the receiver carefully and thought how nice it would be if only I had a penknife handy to cut my throat with. It's funny, but from the moment I met Kitty I was always coveting sharp things like razors and penknives.

After that an awful idea dawned on my mind. Of course, I should have thought of it before, but, as you've probably guessed, I wasn't exactly knowledgeable. I began to see that I wasn't meeting Kitty for the very good reason that Kitty didn't want to meet me. That filled me with terror. I examined my conscience to find out what I might have said to her. You know what conscience is at that age. I remembered every remark I'd made and they were all brutal, indecent or disgusting. I had talked of Paddy Kinnane as a fellow who "went with dolls." What could a pure-minded girl think of a chap who naturally used such a phrase except—what, unfortunately, was true—that he had a mind like a cesspit.

It was a lovely summer evening, with views of hillsides and fields between the gaps in the houses, and that raised my spirits a bit. Maybe I was wrong, maybe she hadn't found out the sort I was and wasn't avoiding me, maybe we might meet and walk home together. I walked the full length of the river road and back, and then started off to walk it again. The crowds were thinning out as fellows and girls slipped off up the lanes or down to the river. As the streets went out like lamps about me I grew desperate. I saw clearly that she was avoiding me; that she knew I wasn't the quiet, good-natured chap I let on to be but a volcano of brutality and lust. "Lust, lust, lust!" I hissed to myself, clenching my fists.

Then I glanced up and saw her on a tram. I forgot instantly about the lust and smiled and waved my cap at her, but she was looking ahead and didn't see me. I ran after the car, intending to jump on it, to sit on one of the back seats on top and then say as she was getting off: "Fancy meeting you here!" (Trams were always a bit of a problem. If you sat beside a girl and paid for her, it might be considered forward; if you didn't, it looked mean. I never quite knew.) But as if the driver knew what was in my mind, he put on speed and away went the tram, tossing and screeching down the straight, and I stood panting in the middle of the road, smiling as if missing a tram was the best joke in the world and wishing all the time I had the penknife and the courage to use it. My position was hopeless. Then I must have gone a bit mad, for I started to race the tram. There were still lots of people out walking, and they stared after me, so I lifted my fists to my chest in the attitude of a professional runner and dropped into a comfortable stride which I hoped vaguely would delude them into the belief that I was in training for a big race.

Between the running and the halts I just managed to keep the tram in view all the way through town and out at the other side. When I saw Kitty get off and go up a hilly street I collapsed and was just able to drag myself after her. When she went into a house on a terrace I sat on the curb with my head between my knees till the panting stopped. At any rate I felt safe. I could now walk up and down before the house till she came out, and accost her with an innocent smile and say: "Fancy meeting you!"

But my luck was dead out that night. As I was walking up and down out of range of the house I saw a tall chap come strolling up at the opposite side and my heart sank. It was Paddy Kinnane.

"Hullo, Jerry," he chuckled with that knowing grin he put on whenever he wanted to compliment you on being discovered in a compromising situation, "what are you doing here?"

"Ah, just waiting for a chap I had a date with, Paddy," I said, trying to sound casual.

"Begor," said Paddy, "you look to me more like a man that was waiting for an old doll. Still waters run deep. . . . What time are you supposed to be meeting him?"

"Half eight," I said at random.

"Half eight?" said Paddy in surprise. " 'Tis nearly nine now."

"I know," said I, "but as I waited so long I may as well give him another few minutes."

"Ah, I'll wait along with you," said Paddy, leaning against the wall and taking out a packet of fags. "You might find yourself stuck by the end of the evening. There's people in this town and they have no consideration for anyone."

That was Paddy all out; no trouble too much for him if he could do you a good turn.

"As he kept me so long," I said hastily, "I don't think I'll bother with him. It only struck me this very minute that there's a chap up the Asragh road that I have to see on urgent business. You'll excuse me, Paddy. I'll tell you about it another time."

And away I went hell for leather to the tram. When I reached the tram-stop below Kitty's house I sat on the river wall in the dusk. The moon was rising, and every quarter of an hour the trams came grunting and squeaking over the old bridge and then went black out while the conductors switched the trolleys. I stood on the curb in the moonlight searching for Kitty. Then a bobby came along, and as he seemed to be watching me, I slunk slowly off up the hill and stood against a wall in the shadow. There was a high wall at the other side too, and behind it the roofs of a house shining in the moon. Every now and then a tram would come in and people would pass in the moonlight, and the snatches of conversation I caught were like the warmth from an open door to the heart of a homeless man. It was quite clear now that my position was hopeless. The last tram came and went, and still there was no Kitty and still I hung on.

Then I heard a woman's step. I couldn't even pretend to myself that it might be Kitty till she shuffled past me with that hasty little walk of hers. I started and called out her name; she glanced over her shoulder and, seeing a man emerging from the shadow, took fright and ran. I ran too, but she put on speed and began to outdistance me. At that I despaired. I stood on the pavement and shouted after her at the top of my voice.

"Kitty!" I cried. "Kitty, for God's sake, wait for me!"

She ran a few steps further and then halted, turned, and came back slowly down the path.

"Jerry Moynihan!" she whispered, lifting her two arms to her breasts as if I had found her with nothing on. "What in God's name are you doing here?"

I was summoning up strength to tell her that I just happened to be taking a stroll in that direction and was astonished to see her when I realized the improbability of it and began to cry instead. Then I laughed. I suppose it was nerves. But Kitty had had a bad fright and now that she was getting over it she was as cross as two sticks.

"What's wrong with you, I say," she snapped. "Are you out of your senses or what?"

"Well, you see," I stammered awkwardly, half in dread I was going to cry again, "I didn't see you in town."

"No," she replied with a shrug. "I know you didn't. I wasn't out. What about it?"

"I thought it might be something I said to you," I said desperately.

"No," said Kitty candidly, "it wasn't anything to do with you. It's Mother."

"Why?" I asked almost joyously. "Is there something wrong with her?"

"I don't mean that," said Kitty impatiently. "It's just that she made such a fuss, I felt it wasn't worth it."

"But what did she make a fuss about?" I asked.

"About you, of course," said Kitty in exasperation. "What did you think?"

"But what did I do?" I asked, clutching my head. This was worse than anything I'd ever imagined. This was terrible.

"You didn't do anything," said Kitty, "but people were talking about us. And you wouldn't come in and be introduced to her like anyone else. I know she's a bit of a fool, and her head is stuffed with old nonsense about her family. I could never see that they were different to anyone else, and anyway, she married a commercial herself, so she has nothing much to boast about. Still, you needn't be so superior. There's no obligation to buy, you know."

I didn't. There were cold shivers running through me. I had thought of Kitty as a secret between God, herself, and me and that she only knew the half of it. Now it seemed I didn't even know the half. People were talking about us! I was superior! What next?

"But what has she against me?" I asked despairingly.

"She thinks we're doing a tangle, of course," snapped Kitty as if she was astonished at my stupidity, "and I suppose she imagines you're not grand enough for a great-great-grandniece of Daniel O'Connell. I told her you were a different sort of fellow entirely and above all that sort of thing, but she wouldn't believe me. She said I was a deep, callous, crafty little intriguer and that I hadn't a drop of Daniel O'Connell's blood in my veins." Kitty began to giggle at the thought of herself as an intriguer.

"That's all she knows," I said bitterly.

"I know," said Kitty with a shrug. "The woman has no sense. And anyway she has no reason to think I'm telling lies. Cissy and I always had fellows, and we spooned with them all over the shop under her very nose, so why should she think I'm lying to her now?"

At that I began to laugh like an idiot. This was worse than appalling. This was a nightmare. Kitty, whom I had thought so angelic, talking in cold blood about "spooning" with fellows all over the house. Even the bad women in the books I'd read didn't talk about love in that cold-blooded way. Madame Bovary herself had at least the decency to pretend that she didn't like it. It was like another door opening on the outside world, but Kitty thought I was laughing at her and started to apologize.

"Of course I had no sense," she said. "You're the first fellow I ever met that treated me properly. The others only wanted to fool around with me, and now because I don't like it, Mother thinks I'm getting stuck-up. I told her I liked you better than any fellow I knew, but that I'd grown out of all that sort of thing."

"And what did she say to that?" I asked fiercely. It was—how can I describe it?—like a man who'd lived all his life in a dungeon getting into the sunlight for the first time and afraid of every shadow.

"Ah, I told you the woman was silly," said Kitty, getting embarrassed.

"Go on!" I shouted. "I want to know everything. I insist on knowing everything."

"Well," said Kitty with a demure little grin, "she said you were a deep, designing guttersnipe who knew exactly how to get round feather-pated little idiots like me. . . . You see," she added with another shrug, "it's quite hopeless. The woman is common. She doesn't understand."

"But I tell you she does understand," I shouted frantically. "She understands better than you do. I only wish to God I was deep and designing so that I'd have some chance with you."

"Do you really?" asked Kitty, opening her eyes wide. "To tell you the truth," she added after a moment, "I thought you were a bit keen the first time, but then I didn't know. When you didn't kiss me or anything, I mean."

"God," I said bitterly, "when I think of what I've been through in the past couple of weeks!"

"I know," said Kitty, biting her lip. "I was the same." And then we said nothing for a few moments.

"You're sure you're serious?" she asked suspiciously.

"I tell you, girl," I shouted, "I was on the point of committing suicide."

"What good would that be?" she asked with another shrug, and then she looked at me and laughed outright—the little jade!

It is all as clear in my mind as if it had happened last night. I told Kitty about my prospects. She didn't care, but I insisted on telling her. It was as if a stone had been lifted off my heart, and I went home in the moonlight singing. Then I heard the clock strike, and the singing stopped. I remembered the mother at home, waiting, and began to run again. This was desperation too, but a different sort.

The door was ajar and the kitchen in darkness. I saw her sitting before the fire by herself, and just as I was going to throw my arms about her, I smelt Kitty's perfume round me and was afraid to go near her. God help us, as if it would have told her anything!

"Hallo, Mum," I said with a laugh, rubbing my hands, "you're all in darkness."

"You'll have a cup of tea?" she said.

"I might as well," said I.

"What time is it?" she said, lighting the gas. "You're very late."

"Ah, I met a fellow from the office," I said, but at the same time I was stung by the complaint in her tone.

"You frightened me," she said with a little whimper. "I didn't know what happened to you. What kept you at all?"

"Oh, what do you think?" I said, goaded into retorting. "Drinking and blackguarding as usual."

I could have bitten my tongue off when I'd said it; it sounded so cruel, as if some stranger had said it instead of me. She turned to me for a moment with a frightened stare as if she was seeing the stranger too, and somehow I couldn't bear it.

"God Almighty," I said, "a fellow can have no life in his own house," and away with me upstairs.

I lit the candle, undressed and got into bed. I was wild. A chap could be a drunkard and blackguard and not be made to suffer more reproach than I was for being late one single night. That, I felt, was what you got for being a good son.

"Jerry," she called from the foot of the stairs, "will I bring you up your cup?"

"I don't want it now, thanks," I said.

I heard her give a heavy sigh and turn away. Then she locked the two doors front and back. She didn't wash up, and I knew my cup of tea was standing there on the table with a saucer on top in case I changed my mind. She came slowly up the stairs, and she walked like an old woman. I blew out the candle before she reached the landing in case she came in to ask me if I wanted anything else, and the moonlight came in the attic window and brought me memories of Kitty. But every time I tried to imagine her face while she grinned up at me, waiting for me to kiss her, it was the mother's face that came up with that look like a child's when you strike him the first time—as if he suddenly saw the stranger in you. I remembered all our life together from the night the father—God rest him!—died; our early Mass on Sunday; our visits to the pictures; our plans for the future, and Christ, Michael John, it was as if I was inside her mind and she sitting by the fire, waiting for the blow to fall! And now it had fallen, and I was a stranger to her, and nothing I ever did could make us the same to each other again. There was something like a cannon-ball stuck in my chest, and I lay awake till the cocks started crowing. Then I couldn't bear it any longer. I went out on to the landing and listened.

"Are you awake, Mother?" I asked in a whisper.

"What is it, Jerry?" she said in alarm, and I knew she hadn't slept any more than I had.

"I only came to say I was sorry," I said, opening the room door, and then as I saw her sitting up in bed under the Sacred Heart lamp, the cannon-ball burst inside me and I began to bawl like a kid.

"Oh, child, child," she cried out, "what are you crying for at all, my little boy?" and she spread out her arms to me. I went to her and she hugged me and rocked me just as she did when I was only a nipper. "Oh, oh, oh," she was saying to herself in a whisper, "my storeen bawn, my little man!"—all the names she hadn't called me since I was a kid. That was all we said. I couldn't bring myself to tell her what I'd done, and she wouldn't confess to me that she was jealous; all she could do was to try and comfort me for the way I'd hurt her, to make up to me for the nature she'd given me. "My storeen bawn," she said. "My little man!"

EXERCISES

1. As usual in stories, there are two time frames here—the time of the events and the time of the telling of the events. What is the central character like during the time of the events? In what ways does he feel he is different from the other boys he knows? How does the narrator feel about the way he was in the past?

2. In what ways does the narrator think Kitty is different from other girls?

How does he feel about her? How does he feel about the way he feels about her?

3. Point out the elements of the story that make it comic.

4. In the dialogue scene between the narrator and Kitty, what does he learn about Kitty? Does his new knowledge please him or disappoint him, or both? Explain.

5. Why is the narrator so impatient with his mother when he gets home? Why then does he feel guilty? What does the mother feel?

6. The title of the story seems primarily to refer to the protagonist, who feels he has betrayed someone. However, in what way is Kitty a betrayer? How has the mother betrayed the narrator, especially in the nature she has given him?

ELIZABETH
TAYLOR | *The First Death of Her Life*

Suddenly, tears poured from Lucy's eyes. She rested her forehead against her mother's hand and let the tears soak into the counterpane.

Dear Mr. Wilcox, she began, for her mind was always composing letters, I shall not be at the shop for the next four days, as my mother has passed away and I shall not be available until after the funeral. My mother passed away very peacefully. . . .

The nurse came in. She took her patient's wrist for a moment, replaced it on the bed, removed a jar of white lilac from the table, as if this were no longer necessary, and went out again.

The girl kneeling by the bed had looked up, but Dear Mr. Wilcox, she resumed, her eyes returning to the counterpane, My mother has died. I shall come back to work the day after tomorrow. Yours sincerely, Lucy Mayhew.

Her father was late. She imagined him hurrying from work, bicycling through the darkening streets, dogged, hunched up, slush thrown up by his wheels. Her mother did not move. Lucy stroked her mother's hand, with its loose gold ring, the calloused palm, the fine, long fingers. Then she stood up stiffly, her knees bruised from the waxed floor, and went to the window.

Snowflakes turned idly, drifting down over the hospital gardens. It was four o'clock in the afternoon and already the day seemed over. So few sounds came from this muffled and discolored world. In the hospital itself, there was a deep silence.

Her thoughts came to her in words, as if her mind spoke them first, understood them later. She tried to think of her childhood—little scenes she selected to prove how she and her mother had loved one another. Other scenes, especially last week's quarrel, she chose to forget, not knowing that in this moment she sent them away forever. Only loving-kindness remained. But, all the same, intolerable pictures broke through—her mother at the sink; her mother ironing; her mother standing between the lace curtains, staring out at the dreary street with a wounded look in her eyes; her mother tying the same lace curtains with yellow ribbons; attempts at lightness, gaiety, which came to nothing; her mother gathering her huge black cat to her, burying her face in its fur while a great, shivering sigh—of despair, of boredom—escaped her.

Her mother no longer sighed. She lay very still and sometimes took a little sip of air. Her arms were neatly at her side. Her eyes, which all day long had been turned to the white lilacs, were closed. Her cheekbones rose sharply from her bruised, exhausted face. She smelled faintly of wine. A small lilac flower floated on a glass of champagne, now discarded on the table at her side.

The champagne, with which they hoped to stretch out the thread of her life minute by minute, the lilac, the room of her own, all came to her at the end of a life of drabness and denial, just as, all along the mean street of the small English town where they lived, the dying and the dead were able to claim a lifetime's savings from the bereaved.

She is no longer there, Lucy thought, standing beside the bed. All day, her mother had stared at the white lilac; now she had sunk away. Outside, beyond the hospital gardens, mist settled over the town, blurred the street lamps.

The nurse returned with the matron. Lucy tautened, ready to be on her best behavior. In her heart, she trusted her mother to die without frightening her, and when the matron, deftly drawing Lucy's head to rest on her own shoulder, said in her calm voice, "She has gone," Lucy felt she had met this happening halfway.

A little bustle began, quick footsteps along the empty passages, and for a moment she was left alone with her dead mother. She laid her hand timidly on the soft, dark hair, so often touched, played with, when she was a child, standing on a stool behind her mother's chair while she sewed.

There were still the smell of wine and the hospital smell. It was growing dark in the room. She went to the dressing table and took her mother's handbag, very worn and shiny, and a book, a library book that she had chosen carefully, believing her mother would read it. Then she had a quick sip from the glass on the table, a mouthful of champagne, which she had never tasted before, and, looking wounded and aloof, walked down the middle of the corridor, feeling nurses falling away to left and right. Opening the glass doors onto the snowy gardens, she thought that it was like the end of a film. But no music rose up and engulfed her. Instead, there was her father turning in at the gates. He propped his bicycle against the wall and began to run clumsily across the wet gravel.

EXERCISES

1. Why is Lucy's mind always composing letters? What is the difference between composing letters in your mind and thinking about something?

2. Is this a story about the particular relationship between Lucy and her mother? Or is it a story about many people's reaction to the death of a close family member? Explain.

3. Is this a story or a sketch with little or no conflict? Does it focus on an event or on an emotion?

4. What is the significance of the scenes Lucy recalls from her childhood?

5. Explain the following: "all along the mean street of the small English town where they lived, the dying and the dead were able to claim a lifetime's savings from the bereaved."

6. What is suggested by Lucy's feeling in the last paragraph that it is like the end of a film, although no music rose up and engulfed her?

ALICE
WALKER | *To Hell with Dying*

"To hell with dying," my father would say. "These children want Mr. Sweet!"

Mr. Sweet was a diabetic and an alcoholic and a guitar player and lived down the road from us on a neglected cotton farm. My older brothers and sisters got the most benefit from Mr. Sweet, for when they were growing up he had quite a few years ahead of him and so was capable of being called back from the brink of death any number of times—whenever the voice of my father reached him as he lay expiring. "To hell with dying, man," my father would say, pushing the wife away from the bedside (in tears although she knew the death was not necessarily the last one unless Mr. Sweet really wanted it to be). "These children want Mr. Sweet!" And they did want him, for at a signal from Father they would come crowding around the bed and throw themselves on the covers, and whoever was the smallest at the time would kiss him all over his wrinkled brown face and tickle him so that he would laugh all down in his stomach, and his mustache, which was long and sort of straggly, would shake like Spanish moss and was also that color.

Mr. Sweet had been ambitious as a boy, wanted to be a doctor or lawyer or sailor, only to find that black men fare better if they are not. Since he could become none of these things he turned to fishing as his only earnest career and playing the guitar as his only claim to doing anything extraordinarily well. His son, the only one that he and his wife, Miss Mary, had, was shiftless as the day is long and spent money as if he were trying to see the bottom of the mint, which Mr. Sweet would tell him was the clean brown palm of his hand. Miss Mary loved her "baby," however, and worked hard to get him the "li'l necessaries" of life, which turned out mostly to be women.

Mr. Sweet was a tall, thinnish man with thick kinky hair going dead white. He was dark brown, his eyes were squinty and sort of bluish, and he chewed Brown Mule tobacco. He was constantly on the verge of being blind drunk, for he brewed his own liquor and was not in the least a stingy sort of man, and was always very melancholy and sad, though frequently when he was "feelin' good" he'd dance around the yard with us, usually keeling over just as my mother came to see what the commotion was.

Toward all of us children he was very kind, and had the grace to be shy with us, which is unusual in grown-ups. He had great respect for my mother for she never held his drunkenness against him and would let us play with him even when he was about to fall in the fireplace from drink. Although Mr. Sweet would sometimes lose complete or nearly complete control of his head and neck so that he would loll in his chair, his mind remained strangely acute and his speech not too affected. His ability to be drunk and sober at the same time made him an ideal playmate, for he was as weak as we were and we could usually best him in wrestling, all the while keeping a fairly coherent conversation going.

We never felt anything of Mr. Sweet's age when we played with him. We loved his wrinkles and would draw some on our brows to be like him, and his white hair was my special treasure and he knew it and would never come to visit us just after he had had his hair cut off at the barbershop. Once he came to our house for something, probably to see my father about fertilizer for his crops because, although he never paid the slightest attention to his crops, he liked to know what things would be best to use on them if he ever did. Anyhow, he had not come with his hair since he had just had it shaved off at the barbershop. He wore a huge straw hat to keep off the sun and also to keep his head away from me. But as soon as I saw him I ran up and demanded that he take me up and kiss me with his funny beard which smelled so strongly of tobacco. Looking forward to burying my small fingers into his woolly hair I threw away his hat only to find he had done something to his hair, that it was no longer there! I let out a squall which made my mother think that Mr. Sweet had finally dropped me in the well or something and from that day I've been wary of men in hats. However, not long after, Mr. Sweet showed up with his hair grown out and just as white and kinky and impenetrable as it ever was.

Mr. Sweet used to call me his princess, and I believed it. He made me feel pretty at five and six, and simply outrageously devastating at the blazing age of eight and a half. When he came to our house with his guitar the whole family would stop whatever they were doing to sit around him and listen to him play. He liked to play "Sweet Georgia Brown," that was what he called me sometimes, and also he liked to play "Caldonia" and all sorts of sweet, sad, wonderful songs which he sometimes made up. It was from one of these songs that I heard that he had had to marry Miss Mary when he had in fact loved somebody else (now living in Chi-ca-go, or De-stroy, Michigan). He was not sure that Joe Lee, her "baby," was also his baby. Sometimes he would cry and that was an indication that he was about to die again. And so we would all get prepared, for we were sure to be called upon.

I was seven the first time I remember actually participating in one of Mr. Sweet's "revivals"—my parents told me I had participated before, I had been the one chosen to kiss him and tickle him long before I knew the rite of Mr. Sweet's rehabilitation. He had come to our house, it was a few years after his wife's death, and was very sad, and also, typically, very drunk. He sat on the floor next to me and my older brother, the rest of the children were grown up and lived elsewhere, and began to play his guitar and cry. I held his woolly head in my arms and wished I could have been old enough to have been the woman he loved so much and that I had not been lost years and years ago.

When he was leaving, my mother said to us that we'd better sleep light that night for we'd probably have to go over to Mr. Sweet's before daylight. And we did. For soon after we had gone to bed one of the neighbors knocked on our door and called my father and said that Mr. Sweet was sinking fast and if he wanted to get in a word before the crossover he'd better shake a leg and get over to Mr. Sweet's house. All the neighbors knew to come to our house if something was wrong with Mr. Sweet, but they did not know how we always managed to make him well, or at least stop him from dying, when he was so often near death. As soon as we heard the cry we got up, my brother and I and my mother and father, and put on our clothes. We hurried out of the house and down the road for we were always afraid that we might some-day be too late and Mr. Sweet would get tired of dallying.

When we got to the house, a very poor shack really, we found the front room full of neighbors and relatives and someone met us at the door and said it was all very sad that old Mr. Sweet Little (for Little was his family name, although we mostly ignored it) was about to kick the bucket. My parents were advised not to take my brother and me into the "death room," seeing we were so young and all, but we were so much more accustomed to the death room than he that we ignored him and dashed in without giving his warning a sec-ond thought. I was almost in tears, for these deaths upset me fearfully, and the thought of how much depended on me and my brother (who was such a ham most of the time) made me very nervous.

The doctor was bending over the bed and turned back to tell us for at least the tenth time in the history of my family that, alas, old Mr. Sweet Little was dying and that the children had best not see the face of implacable death (I didn't know what "implacable" was, but whatever it was, Mr. Sweet was not!). My father pushed him rather abruptly out of the way saying, as he always did and very loudly for he was saying it to Mr. Sweet, "To hell with dying, man, these children want Mr. Sweet"—which was my cue to throw myself upon the bed and kiss Mr. Sweet all around the whiskers and under the eyes and around the collar of his nightshirt where he smelled so strongly of all sorts of things, mostly liniment.

I was very good at bringing him around, for as soon as I saw that he was struggling to open his eyes I knew he was going to be all right, and so could finish my revival sure of success. As soon as his eyes were open he would begin to smile and that way I knew that I had surely won. Once, though, I got a tremendous scare, for he could not open his eyes and later I learned that he had had a stroke and that one side of his face was stiff and hard to get into motion. When he began to smile I could tickle him in earnest because I was sure that nothing would get in the way of his laughter, although once he began to cough so hard that he almost threw me off his stomach, but that was when I was very small, little more than a baby, and my bushy hair had gotten in his nose.

When we were sure he would listen to us we would ask him why he was in bed and when he was coming to see us again and could we play his guitar, which more than likely would be leaning against the bed. His eyes would get all misty and he would sometimes cry out loud, but we never let it embarrass us, for he knew that we loved him and that we sometimes cried too for no reason. My parents would leave the room to just the three of us; Mr. Sweet, by that time, would be propped up in bed with a number of pillows behind his head and with me sitting and lying on his shoulder and along his chest. Even when he had trouble breathing he would not ask me to get down. Looking into my eyes he would shake his white head and run a scratchy old finger all around my hairline, which was rather low down, nearly to my eyebrows, and made some people say I looked like a baby monkey.

My brother was very generous in all this, he let me do all the revivaling—he had done it for years before I was born and so was glad to be able to pass it on to someone new. What he would do while I talked to Mr. Sweet was pretend to play the guitar, in fact pretend that he was a young version of Mr. Sweet, and it always made Mr. Sweet glad to think that someone wanted to be like him—of course, we did not know this then, we played the thing by ear, and whatever he seemed to like, we did. We were desperately afraid that he was just going to take off one day and leave us.

It did not occur to us that we were doing anything special; we had not learned that death was final when it did come. We thought nothing of triumphing over it so many times, and in fact became a trifle contemptuous of people who let themselves be carried away. It did not occur to us that if our father had been dying we could not have stopped it, that Mr. Sweet was the only person over whom we had power.

When Mr. Sweet was in his eighties I was studying in the university many miles from home. I saw him whenever I went home, but he was never on the verge of dying that I could tell and I began to feel that my anxiety for his health and psychological well-being was unnecessary. By this time he not only had a mustache but a long flowing snow-white beard, which I loved and combed and braided for hours. He was very peaceful, fragile, gentle, and the only jarring note about him was his old steel guitar, which he still played in the old sad, sweet, down-home blues way.

On Mr. Sweet's ninetieth birthday I was finishing my doctorate in Massachusetts and had been making arrangements to go home for several weeks' rest. That morning I got a telegram telling me that Mr. Sweet was dying again and could I please drop everything and come home. Of course I could. My dissertation could wait and my teachers would understand when I explained to them when I got back. I ran to the phone, called the airport, and within four hours I was speeding along the dusty road to Mr. Sweet's.

The house was more dilapidated than when I was last there, barely a shack, but it was overgrown with yellow roses which my family had planted many years ago. The air was heavy and sweet and very peaceful. I felt strange walking through the gate and up the old rickety steps. But the strangeness left me as I caught sight of the long white beard I loved so well flowing down the thin body over the familiar quilt coverlet. Mr. Sweet!

His eyes were closed tight and his hands, crossed over his stomach, were thin and delicate, no longer scratchy. I remembered how always before I had run and jumped up on him just anywhere; now I knew he would not be able to support my weight. I looked around at my parents, and was surprised to see that my father and mother also looked old and frail. My father, his own hair very gray, leaned over the quietly sleeping old man, who, incidentally, smelled still of wine and tobacco, and said, as he'd done so many times, "To hell with dying, man! My daughter is home to see Mr. Sweet!" My brother had not been able to come as he was in the war in Asia. I bent down and gently stroked the closed eyes and gradually they began to open. The closed, wine-stained lips twitched a little, then parted in a warm, slightly embarrassed smile. Mr. Sweet could see me and he recognized me and his eyes looked very spry and twinkly for a moment. I put my head down on the pillow next to his and we just looked at each other for a long time. Then he began to trace my peculiar hairline with a thin, smooth finger. I closed my eyes when his finger halted above my ear (he used to rejoice at the dirt in my ears when I was little), his hand stayed cupped around my cheek. When I opened my eyes, sure that I had reached him in time, his were closed.

Even at twenty-four how could I believe that I had failed? that Mr. Sweet was really gone? He had never gone before. But when I looked at my parents I saw that they were holding back tears. They had loved him dearly. He was like a piece of rare and delicate china which was always being saved from breaking and which finally fell. I looked long at the old face, the wrinkled forehead, the red lips, the hands that still reached out to me. Soon I felt my father pushing something cool into my hands. It was Mr. Sweet's guitar. He had asked them months before to give it to me; he had known that even if I came next time he would not be able to respond in the old way. He did not want me to feel that my trip had been for nothing.

The old guitar! I plucked the strings, hummed "Sweet Georgia Brown." The magic of Mr. Sweet lingered still in the cool steel box. Through the window I could catch the fragrant delicate scent of tender yellow roses. The man on the high old-fashioned bed with the quilt coverlet and the flowing white beard had been my first love.

Exercises

1. What does the title suggest about the nature of death in this story? Why does Mr. Sweet think he is dying when he is not? How do the children bring him back?

2. Describe the narrator's feelings about Mr. Sweet when she was a child. Why was Mr. Sweet an important figure in the narrator's youth?

3. Why is the revival of Mr. Sweet so important to the children? How does the family know when Mr. Sweet is going to need them to revive him?

4. Is this a story, or is it a character sketch, a memoir? What makes it a story? Is there a conflict in it that is resolved in some way? Does it communicate some realization about human reality?

5. The blues is a type of music that is both sweet and sad at the same time. Is this story an example of a blues theme?

6. What does the narrator mean that Mr. Sweet was her first love?

GRAHAM
GREENE | *The Innocent*

It was a mistake to take Lola there, I knew it the moment we alighted from the train at the small country station. On an autumn evening one remembers more of childhood than at any other time of year, and her bright veneered face, the small bag which hardly pretended to contain our "things" for the night, simply didn't go with the old grain warehouse across the small canal, the few lights up the hill, the posters of an ancient film. But she said, "Let's go into the country," and Bishop's Hendron was, of course, the first name which came into my head. Nobody would know me there now, and it hadn't occurred to me that it would be I who remembered.

Even the old porter touched a chord. I said, "There'll be a fourwheeler at the entrance," and there was, though at first I didn't notice it, seeing the two taxis and thinking, "The old place is coming on." It was very dark, and the thin autumn mist, the smell of wet leaves and canal water were deeply familiar.

Lola said, "But why did you choose this place? It's grim." It was no use explaining to her why it wasn't grim to me, that that sand heap by the canal had always been there (when I was three I remember thinking it was what other people meant by the seaside). I took the bag (I've said it was light; it was simply a forged passport of respectability) and said we'd walk. We came up over the little hump-backed bridge and passed the almshouses. When I was five I saw a middle-aged man run into one to commit suicide; he carried a knife, and all the neighbours pursued him up the stairs. She said, "I never thought the country was like *this*." They were ugly almshouses, little grey stone boxes, but I knew them as I knew nothing else. It was like listening to music, all that walk.

But I had to say something to Lola. It wasn't her fault that she didn't belong here. We passed the school, the church, and came round into the old wide High Street and the sense of the first twelve years of life. If I hadn't come, I shouldn't have known that sense would be so strong, because those years hadn't been particularly happy or particularly miserable: they had been ordinary years, but now with the smell of wood fires, of the cold striking up from the dark damp paving stones, I thought I knew what it was that held me. It was the smell of innocence.

I said to Lola, "It's a good inn, and there'll be nothing here, you'll see, to keep us up. We'll have dinner and drinks and go to bed." But the worst of it was that I couldn't help wishing that I were alone. I hadn't been back all these years; I hadn't realized how well I remembered the place. Things I'd quite forgotten, like that sand heap, were coming back with an effect of pathos and nostalgia. I could have been very happy that night in a melancholy, autumnal way wandering about the little town, picking up clues to that time of life when, however miserable we are, we have expectations. It wouldn't be the same if I came back again, for then there would be the memories of Lola, and Lola meant just nothing at all. We had happened to pick each other up at a bar the day before and liked each other. Lola was all right, there was no one I would rather spend the night with, but she didn't fit in with *these* memories. We ought to have gone to Maidenhead. That's country too.

The inn was not quite where I remembered it. There was the Town Hall, but they had built a new cinema with a Moorish dome and a café, and there was a garage which hadn't existed in my time. I had forgotten too the turning to the left up a steep, villaed hill.

"I don't believe that road was there in my day," I said.

"Your day?" Lola asked.

"Didn't I tell you? I was born here."

"You must get a kick out of bringing me here," Lola said. "I suppose you used to think of nights like this when you were a boy."

"Yes," I said, because it wasn't her fault. She was all right. I liked her scent. She used a good shade of lipstick. It was costing me a lot, a fiver for Lola and then all the bills and fares and drinks, but I'd have thought it money well spent anywhere else in the world.

I lingered at the bottom of that road. Something was stirring in the mind, but I don't think I should have remembered what, if a crowd of children hadn't come down the hill at that moment into the frosty lamplight, their voices sharp and shrill, their breath fuming as they passed under the lamps. They all carried linen bags, and some of the bags were embroidered with initials. They were in their best clothes and a little self-conscious. The small girls kept to themselves in a kind of compact, beleaguered group, and one thought of hair ribbons and shining shoes and the sedate tinkle of a piano. It all came back to me: they had been to a dancing lesson, just as I used to go, to a small square house with a drive of rhododendrons halfway up the hill. More than ever I wished that Lola were not with me, less than ever did she fit, as I thought "something's missing from the picture," and a sense of pain glowed dully at the bottom of my brain.

We had several drinks at the bar, but there was half an hour before they would agree to serve dinner. I said to Lola, "You don't want to drag round this town. If you don't mind, I'll just slip out for ten minutes and look at a place I used to know." She didn't mind. There was a local man, perhaps a schoolmaster, at the bar simply longing to stand her a drink: I could see how he envied me, coming down with her like this from town just for a night.

I walked up the hill. The first houses were all new. I resented them. They hid things like fields and gates I might have remembered. It was like a map which had got wet in the pocket and pieces had stuck together; when you opened it there were whole patches hidden. But halfway up, there the house really was, the drive; perhaps the same old lady was giving lessons. Children exaggerate age. She may not in those days have been more than thirty-five. I could hear the piano. She was following the same routine. Children under eight, 6–7 P.M. Children eight to thirteen, 7–8. I opened the gate and went in a little way. I was trying to remember.

I don't know what brought it back. I think it was simply the autumn, the cold, the wet frosting leaves, rather than the piano, which had played different tunes in those days. I remembered the small girl as well as one remembers anyone without a photograph to refer to. She was a year older than I was: she must have been just on the point of eight. I loved her with an intensity I have never felt since, I believe, for anyone. At least I have never made the mistake of laughing at children's love. It has a terrible inevitability of separation because there *can* be no satisfaction. Of course one invents tales of houses on fire, of war and forlorn charges which prove one's courage in her eyes, but never of marriage. One knows without being told that that can't happen, but the knowledge doesn't mean that one suffers less. I remembered all the games of blind-man's-buff at birthday parties when I vainly hoped to catch her, so that I might have the excuse to touch and hold her, but I never caught her; she always kept out of my way.

But once a week for two winters I had my chance: I danced with her. That made it worse (it was cutting off our only contact) when she told me during one of the last lessons of the winter that next year she would join the older class. She liked me too, I knew it, but we had no way of expressing it. I used to go to her birthday parties and she would come to mine, but we never even ran home together after the dancing class. It would have seemed odd; I don't think it occurred to us. I had to join my own boisterous teasing male companions, and she the besieged, the hustled, the shrilly indignant sex on the way down the hill.

I shivered there in the mist and turned my coat collar up. The piano was playing a dance from an old C. B. Cochran revue. It seemed a long journey to have taken to find only Lola at the end of it. There *is* something about innocence one is never quite resigned to lose. Now when I am unhappy about a girl, I can simply go and buy another one. Then the best I could think of was to write some passionate message and slip it into a hole (it was extraordinary how I began to remember everything) in the woodwork of the gate. I had once told her about the hole, and sooner or later I was sure she would put in her fingers and find the message. I wondered what the message could have been. One wasn't able to express much, I thought, in those days; but because the expression was inadequate, it didn't mean that the pain was shallower than what one sometimes suffered now. I remembered how for days I had felt in the hole and always found the message there. Then the dancing lessons stopped. Probably by the next winter I had forgotten.

As I went out of the gate I looked to see if the hole existed. It was there. I put in my finger, and, in its safe shelter from the seasons and the years, the scrap of paper rested yet. I pulled it out and opened it. Then I struck a match, a tiny glow of heat in the mist and dark. It was a shock to see by its diminutive flame a picture of crude obscenity. There could be no mistake; there were my initials below the childish, inaccurate sketch of a man and woman. But it woke fewer memories than the fume of breath, the linen bags, a damp leaf, or the pile of sand. I didn't recognize it; it might have been drawn by a dirty-minded stranger on a lavatory wall. All I could remember was the purity, the intensity, the pain of that passion.

I felt at first as if I had been betrayed. "After all," I told myself, "Lola's not so much out of place here." But later that night, when Lola turned away from me and fell asleep, I began to realize the deep innocence of that drawing. I had believed I was drawing something with a meaning unique and beautiful; it was only now after thirty years of life that the picture seemed obscene.

EXERCISES

1. Why does the man bring Lola to this place where he was born? Why does he wish that he were alone? What causes the sense of pain that glows dully at the bottom of his brain?
2. Discuss the statement "There *is* something about innocence one is never quite resigned to lose."
3. Why does the memory of the young girl make him even more discontent with Lola?
4. Discuss the difference between his memory of the passionate message he left in the tree and the picture that he finds.
5. What would he have thought if he had brought his bride to this place instead of a girl he had just picked up and paid? Would it have been different or the same?
6. Does the man's final realization indicate something about the nature of men, the general nature of all human beings, or the specific nature of this particular man? Explain.

KATHERINE
ANNE
PORTER | *Theft*

She had the purse in her hand when she came in. Standing in the middle of the floor, holding her bathrobe around her and trailing a damp towel in one hand, she surveyed the immediate past and remembered everything clearly. Yes, she had opened the flap and spread it out on the bench after she had dried the purse with her handkerchief.

She had intended to take the Elevated, and naturally she looked in her purse to make certain she had the fare, and was pleased to find forty cents in the coin envelope. She was going to pay her own fare, too, even if Camilo did have the habit of seeing her up the steps and dropping a nickel in the machine before he gave the turnstile a little push and sent her through it with a bow. Camilo by a series of compromises had managed to make effective a fairly complete set of smaller courtesies, ignoring the larger and more troublesome ones. She had walked with him to the station in a pouring rain, because she knew he was almost as poor as she was, and when he insisted on a taxi, she was firm and said, "You know it simply will not do." He was wearing a new hat of a pretty biscuit shade, for it never occurred to him to buy anything of a practical color; he had put it on for the first time and the rain was spoiling it. She kept thinking, "But this is dreadful, where will he get another?" She compared it with Eddie's hats that always seemed to be precisely seven years old and as if they had been quite purposely left out in the rain, and yet they sat with a careless and incidental rightness on Eddie. But Camilo was far different; if he wore a shabby hat it would be merely shabby on him, and he would lose his spirits over it. If she had not feared Camilo would take it badly, for he insisted on the practice of his little ceremonies up to the point he had fixed for them, she would have said to him as they left Thora's house, "Do go home. I can surely reach the station by myself."

"It is written that we must be rained upon tonight," said Camilo, "so let it be together."

At the foot of the platform stairway she staggered slightly—they were both nicely set up on Thora's cocktails—and said: "At least, Camilo, do me the favor not to climb these stairs in your present state, since for you it is only a matter of coming down again at once, and you'll certainly break your neck."

He made three quick bows, he was Spanish, and leaped off through the rainy darkness. She stood watching him, for he was a very graceful young man, thinking that tomorrow morning he would gaze soberly at his spoiled hat and soggy shoes and possibly associate her with his misery. As she watched, he stopped at the far corner and took off his hat and hid it under his overcoat. She felt she had betrayed him by seeing, because he would have been humiliated if he thought she even suspected him of trying to save his hat.

Roger's voice sounded over her shoulder above the clang of the rain falling on the stairway shed, wanting to know what she was doing out in the rain at this time of night, and did she take herself for a duck? His long, imperturbable face was steaming with water, and he tapped a bulging spot on the breast of his buttoned-up overcoat: "Hat," he said. "Come on, let's take a taxi."

She settled back against Roger's arm which he laid around her shoulders, and with the gesture they exchanged a glance full of long amiable associations, then she looked through the window at the rain changing the shapes of everything, and the colors. The taxi dodged in and out between the pillars of the Elevated, skidding slightly on every curve, and she said: "The more it skids the calmer I feel, so I really must be drunk."

"You must be," said Roger. "This bird is a homicidal maniac, and I could do with a cocktail myself this minute."

They waited on the traffic at Fortieth Street and Sixth Avenue, and three boys walked before the nose of the taxi. Under the globes of light they were cheerful scarecrows, all very thin and all wearing very seedy snappy-cut suits and gay neckties. They were not very sober either, and they stood for a moment wobbling in front of the car, and there was an argument going on among them. They leaned toward each other as if they were getting ready to sing, and the first one said: "When I get married it won't be jus' for getting married, I'm gonna marry for *love*, see?" and the second one said, "Aw, gwan and tell that stuff to *her*, why n't yuh?" and the third one gave a kind of hoot, and said, "Hell, dis guy? Wot the hell's he got?" and the first one said: "Aaah, shurrup yuh mush, I got plenty." Then they all squealed and scrambled across the street beating the first one on the back and pushing him around.

"Nuts," commented Roger, "pure nuts."

Two girls went skittering by in short transparent raincoats, one green, one red, their heads tucked against the drive of the rain. One of them was saying to the other, "Yes, I know all about *that*. But what about me? You're always so sorry for *him* . . ." and they ran on with their little pelican legs flashing back and forth.

The taxi backed up suddenly and leaped forward again, and after a while Roger said: "I had a letter from Stella today, and she'll be home on the twenty-sixth, so I suppose she's made up her mind and it's all settled."

"I had a sort of letter today too," she said, "making up my mind for me. I think it is time for you and Stella to do something definite."

When the taxi stopped on the corner of West Fifty-third Street, Roger said, "I've just enough if you'll add ten cents," so she opened her purse and gave him a dime, and he said, "That's beautiful, that purse."

"It's a birthday present," she told him, "and I like it. How's your show coming?"

"Oh, still hanging on, I guess. I don't go near the place. Nothing sold yet. I mean to keep right on the way I'm going and they can take it or leave it. I'm through with the argument."

"It's absolutely a matter of holding out, isn't it?"

"Holding out's the tough part."

"Good night, Roger."

"Good night, you should take aspirin and push yourself into a tub of hot water, you look as though you're catching cold."

"I will."

With the purse under her arm she went upstairs, and on the first landing Bill heard her step and poked his head out with his hair tumbled and his eyes red, and he said: "For Christ's sake, come in and have a drink with me. I've had some bad news."

"You're perfectly sopping," said Bill, looking at her drenched feet. They had two drinks, while Bill told how the director had thrown his play out after the cast had been picked over twice, and had gone through three rehearsals. "I said to him, 'I didn't say it was a masterpiece, I said it would make a good show.' And he said, 'It just doesn't *play*, do you see? It needs a doctor.' So I'm stuck, absolutely stuck," said Bill, on the edge of weeping again. "I've been crying," he told her, "in my cups." And he went on to ask her if she realized his wife was ruining him with her extravagance. "I send her ten dollars every week of my unhappy life, and I don't really have to. She threatens to jail me if I don't, but she can't do it. God, let her try it after the way she treated me! She's no right to alimony and she knows it. She keeps on saying she's got to have it for the baby and I keep on sending it because I can't bear to see anybody suffer. So I'm way behind on the piano and the victrola, both—"

"Well, this is a pretty rug, anyhow," she said.

Bill stared at it and blew his nose. "I got it at Ricci's for ninety-five dollars," he said. "Ricci told me it once belonged to Marie Dressler, and cost fifteen hundred dollars, but there's a burnt place on it, under the divan. Can you beat that?"

"No," she said. She was thinking about her empty purse and that she could not possibly expect a check for her latest review for another three days, and her arrangement with the basement restaurant could not last much longer if she did not pay something on account. "It's no time to speak of it," she said, "but I've been hoping you would have by now that fifty dollars you promised for my scene in the third act. Even if it doesn't play. You were to pay me for the work anyhow out of your advance."

"Weeping Jesus," said Bill, "you, too?" He gave a loud sob, or hiccough, in his moist handkerchief. "Your stuff was no better than mine, after all. Think of that."

"But you got something for it," she said. "Seven hundred dollars."

Bill said, "Do me a favor, will you? Have another drink and forget about it. I can't, you know I can't, I would if I could, but you know the fix I'm in."

"Let it go, then," she found herself saying almost in spite of herself. She had meant to be quite firm about it. They drank again without speaking, and she went to her apartment on the floor above.

There, she now remembered distinctly, she had taken the letter out of the purse before she spread the purse out to dry.

She had sat down and read the letter over again: but there were phrases that insisted on being read many times, they had a life of their own separate from the others, and when she tried to read past and around them, they moved with the movement of her eyes, and she could not escape them . . . "thinking about you more than I mean to . . . yes, I even talk about you . . . why were you so anxious to destroy . . . even if I could see you now I would not . . . not worth all this abominable . . . the end . . ."

Carefully she tore the letter into narrow strips and touched a lighted match to them in the coal grate.

Early the next morning she was in the bathtub when the janitress knocked and then came in, calling out that she wished to examine the radiators before she started the furnace going for the winter. After moving about the room for a few minutes, the janitress went out, closing the door very sharply.

She came out of the bathroom to get a cigarette from the package in the purse. The purse was gone. She dressed and made coffee, and sat by the window while she drank it. Certainly the janitress had taken the purse, and certainly it would be impossible to get it back without a great deal of ridiculous excitement. Then let it go. With this decision of her mind, there rose coincidentally in her blood a deep almost murderous anger. She set the cup carefully in the center of the table, and walked steadily downstairs, three long flights and a short hall and a steep short flight into the basement, where the janitress, her face streaked with coal dust, was shaking up the furnace. "Will you please give me back my purse? There isn't any money in it. It was a present, and I don't want to lose it."

The janitress turned without straightening up and peered at her with hot flickering eyes, a red light from the furnace reflected in them. "What do you mean, your purse?"

"The gold cloth purse you took from the wooden bench in my room," she said. "I must have it back."

"Before God I never laid eyes on your purse, and that's the holy truth," said the janitress.

"Oh, well then, keep it," she said, but in a very bitter voice; "keep it if you want it so much." And she walked away.

She remembered how she had never locked a door in her life, on some principle of rejection in her that made her uncomfortable in the ownership of things, and her paradoxical boast before the warnings of her friends, that she had never lost a penny by theft; and she had been pleased with the bleak humility of this concrete example designed to illustrate and justify a certain fixed, otherwise baseless and general faith which ordered the movements of her life without regard to her will in the matter.

In this moment she felt that she had been robbed of an enormous number of valuable things, whether material or intangible: things lost or broken by her own fault, things she had forgotten and left in houses when she moved: books borrowed from her and not returned, journeys she had planned and had not made, words she had waited to hear spoken to her and had not heard, and the words she had meant to answer with; bitter alternatives and intolerable substitutes worse than nothing, and yet inescapable: the long patient suffering of dying friendships and the dark inexplicable death of love—all that she had had, and all that she had missed, were lost together, and were twice lost in this landslide of remembered losses.

The janitress was following her upstairs with the purse in her hand and the same deep red fire flickering in her eyes. The janitress thrust the purse towards her while they were still a half dozen steps apart, and said: "Don't never tell on me. I musta been crazy. I get crazy in the head sometimes, I swear I do. My son can tell you."

She took the purse after a moment, and the janitress went on: "I got a niece who is going on seventeen, and she's a nice girl and I thought I'd give it to her. She needs a pretty purse. I musta been crazy; I thought maybe you wouldn't mind, you leave things around and don't seem to notice much."

She said: "I missed this because it was a present to me from someone. . . ."

The janitress said: "He'd get you another if you lost this one. My niece is young and needs pretty things, we oughta give the young ones a chance. She's got young men after her maybe will want to marry her. She oughta have nice things. She needs them bad right now. You're a grown woman, you've had your chance, you ought to know how it is!"

She held the purse out to the janitress saying: "You don't know what you're talking about. Here, take it, I've changed my mind. I really don't want it."

The janitress looked up at her with hatred and said: "I don't want it either now. My niece is young and pretty, she don't need fixin' up to be pretty, she's young and pretty anyhow! I guess you need it worse than she does!"

"It wasn't really yours in the first place," she said, turning away. "You mustn't talk as if I had stolen it from you."

"It's not from me, it's from her you're stealing it," said the janitress, and went back downstairs.

She laid the purse on the table and sat down with a cup of chilled coffee, and thought: I was right not to be afraid of any thief but myself, who will end by leaving me nothing.

EXERCISES

1. What is the relevance of the three boys and the two girls who walk in front of the taxi and whose conversation we overhear?

2. What is the relevance of this statement: "It's absolutely a matter of holding out, isn't it?"

3. What is the significance of the scene with Bill, who owes the protagonist money?

4. Why are we not told the details of the letter? How is the letter relevant to the story?

5. What is the fixed general faith that orders the movements of the protagonist's life?

6. Why does this one minor theft make the protagonist feel she has been robbed of an enormous number of valuable things? How do the things she remembers relate to the theft of the purse?

7. What is the significance of the phrase "you've had your chance"? Who triumphs in the encounter between the protagonist and the janitress? Explain.

8. Explain the statement "I was right not to be afraid of any thief but myself who will end by leaving me nothing." In what way has the protagonist robbed herself? What has she robbed from herself? How does the story prepare the reader for this realization?

MARY
ROBISON | *Yours*

A llison struggled away from her white Renault, limping with the weight of
the last of the pumpkins. She found Clark in the twilight on the twig-
and-leaf-littered porch behind the house.

He wore a wool shawl. He was moving up and back in a padded glider,
pushed by the ball of his slippered foot.

Allison lowered a big pumpkin, let it rest on the wide floorboards.

Clark was much older—seventy-eight to Allison's thirty-five. They were
married. They were both quite tall and looked something alike in their facial
features. Allison wore a natural-hair wig. It was a thick blond hood around
her face. She was dressed in bright-dyed denims today. She wore durable
clothes, usually, for she volunteered afternoons at a children's day-care center.

She put one of the smaller pumpkins on Clark's long lap. "Now, nothing
surreal," she told him. "Carve just a *regular* face. These are for kids."

In the foyer, on the Hepplewhite desk, Allison found the maid's chore list
with its cross-offs, which included Clark's supper. Allison went quickly
through the day's mail: a garish coupon packet, a bill from Jamestown Liq-
uors, November's pay-TV program guide, and the worst thing, the funniest,
an already opened, extremely unkind letter from Clark's relations up North.
"You're an old fool," Allison read, and "You're being cruelly deceived." There
was a gift check for Clark enclosed, but it was uncashable, signed, as it was,
"Jesus H. Christ."

Late, late into this night, Allison and Clark gutted and carved the pumpkins together, at an old table set on the back porch, over newspaper after
soggy newspaper, with paring knives and with spoons and with a Swiss Army
knife Clark used for exact shaping of tooth and eye and nostril. Clark had
been a doctor, an internist, but also a Sunday watercolorist. His four pumpkins were expressive and artful. Their carved features were suited to the sizes
and shapes of the pumpkins. Two looked ferocious and jagged. One registered
surprise. The last was serene and beaming.

Allison's four faces were less deftly drawn, with slits and areas of distor-
tion. She had cut triangles for noses and eyes. The mouths she had made were
just wedges—two turned up and two turned down.

By one in the morning they were finished. Clark, who had bent his long
torso forward to work, moved back over to the glider and looked out sleepily
at nothing. All the lights were out across the ravine.

Clark stayed. For the season and time, the Virginia night was warm. Most
leaves had been blown away already, and the trees stood unbothered. The
moon was round above them.

Allison cleaned up the mess.

"Your jack-o'-lanterns are much, much better than mine," Clark said to
her.

"Like hell," Allison said.

"Look at me," Clark said, and Allison did.

She was holding a squishy bundle of newspapers. The papers reeked sweetly with the smell of pumpkin guts.

"Yours are *far* better," he said.

"You're wrong. You'll see when they're lit," Allison said.

She went inside, came back with yellow vigil candles. It took her a while to get each candle settled, and then to line up the results in a row on the porch railing. She went along and lit each candle and fixed the pumpkin lids over the little flames.

"See?" she said.

They sat together a moment and looked at the orange faces.

"We're exhausted. It's good night time," Allison said. "Don't blow out the candles. I'll put in new ones tomorrow."

That night, in their bedroom, a few weeks earlier in her life than had been predicted, Allison began to die. "Don't look at me if my wig comes off," she told Clark. "Please."

Her pulse cords were fluttering under his fingers. She raised her knees and kicked away the comforter. She said something to Clark about the garage being locked.

At the telephone, Clark had a clear view out back and down to the porch. He wanted to get drunk with his wife once more. He wanted to tell her, from the greater perspective he had, that to own only a little talent, like his, was an awful, plaguing thing; that being only a little special meant you expected too much, most of the time, and liked yourself too little. He wanted to assure her that she had missed nothing.

He was speaking into the phone now. He watched the jack-o'-lanterns. The jack-o'-lanterns watched him.

EXERCISES

1. What is significant about the fact that the husband is seventy-eight and the wife is thirty-five? Is this a crucial element of the story? Explain.

2. What is the significance of the letter from the husband's relations with the check signed "Jesus H. Christ"? How do they think he is being cruelly deceived? Why are we not given more details about this?

3 Since the image of the jack-o'-lanterns ends the story, it is important to visualize them. What is the significance of their faces, particularly at the end of this story? What does it mean that the jack-o'-lanterns looked at him?

4. What is the significance of the title of the story? Why is it not entitled "Mine" instead of "Yours"?

5. Discuss the meaning of the husband's desire to assure his wife that she has missed nothing. Why does he feel he has a "greater perspective"?

6. What makes this a story rather than merely a sketch? What is the conflict in the story?

ROLF
YNGVE | *The Quail*

The quail came just before the lilacs bloomed in the green time of their first spring married. The morning was the first warm morning with no frost, only dew. Feeling sun on the bed she rose earlier than usual; when she saw the quail in the back yard she woke him. He saw eight birds scratching earth and pecking in the landlord's garden.

He told her they were California Quail. The hens were like dowager women, plump and impeccably arrayed in brown and gray. They were escorted by three portly males with gray-vested chests and an ascot of black plumage at their throats. Each bird had one black plume feather bobbing on the forehead. They wandered the garden like a tour group, stopping to peck in the earth, gliding, aimless and individual but coveyed together.

The couple dressed, whispering about the birds and watching them peck breakfast from the lawn. He made coffee, warmed rolls, and they ate at the kitchen table where they could watch the covey. He opened the window; they could smell the morning dampness and apple blossoms. Sun came through the window; the rolls were sweet with raisins, and they did not have to say anything to each other.

That evening, on his way home from work, he stopped at a feed store and bought cracked corn. He explained to her that the quail would stay as long as they were fed and well-treated. He scattered the corn near the kitchen window, and at sunset the birds returned. They came very close to the window, pecked at the corn, and took rolling dirt baths in the landlord's garden. She asked him if the birds would eat the landlord's seeds and plantings. He told her that the garden was in no danger as long as they fed the birds cracked corn.

After the birds came, they began to set the alarm clock early. At first it was to give them more time for coffee, rolls and watching the covey. When the lilacs bloomed and the tulips came out they set the alarm earlier still and made love before rising. She would bathe after and he would make breakfast, put out more corn for the birds.

It was best watching the covey just after sunrise, before the traffic noises, before the landlord let his poodle out. The landlord lived next door with a chicken wire fence dividing the two yards. When he let the poodle out, it would be crazy to get at the quail, charging the fence, yapping the insane little dog's bark. The covey would rise, flailing air, then settle in the apple tree's low branches waiting for the dog to calm himself and drop back to the corn.

Before long he could put corn on the windowsill and the quail would join them for breakfast. If they were quiet and ate without sudden movement, the birds would flutter to the windowsill a foot from the coffeepot and roll basket. The birds pecked at the corn, eating one piece at a time. Their beaks tapped the sill and their eyes gleamed. He removed the screen to see if they would come inside.

The four cocks were bold, sometimes walking onto the table, preening, ruffling feathers, shaking their plumes. For weeks she tried to feed them sweet roll crumbs from her fingers. The males looked at it, but it was a hen who finally ran to the offered scrap, eyed it sideways with her plume like a hat feather cocked over one eye, and took the crumb. There was the touch of the hen's beak on her fingers. She laughed aloud; the covey exploded from the windowsill. When a week passed and the birds finally began coming to the windowsill again, the hen always took one crumb.

Evenings they would sit in lawn chairs and watch the covey feed. When the early roses bloomed and the landlord's garden sprouted, they saw a hen mated. It was in the garden and they did not see the courtship, only the act when the cock, all gray and brown feathered with black throat feathers, twisted the hen's neck down with his bill. The hen writhed in the soil as the cock mounted her and beat her sides with his wings.

And the landlord's wife railed from inside the landlord's house "Tom! They're in the garden again, TOM!" The landlord ran from the house, waving his arms, hissing, his neck wrinkled and old, his hair white stubble.

The birds rose flailing air.

His wife held the screen door open, leaned out screeching, "Tom you *got* to do something about them birds! We got to eat that damn garden this winter, now you want to eat this winter you *do* something."

The screen door made a whacking slam and she was out, stooped, her poodle at her feet, her legs splayed, her dress a gray farm woman's dress with a stained apron. She sounded like the poodle.

"Dammit, *Tom!* You going to do something about them birds?"

The tenant and his wife sat in the lawn chairs watching, thinking *they* should do something. Tell the old woman, maybe, that the birds wouldn't bother the seedlings. But they thought she would fight with them, scream at them because she was angry and old. They thought it best to say something later, when she calmed herself.

The next day the landlord said he liked the birds and said the garden had grown enough to be out of danger. He said he had always liked quail. Even when he was a boy he had thought them beautiful and fine eating, but there was his wife. The landlord said his wife would most likely be better in a day or two and the garden was always a sore spot with her because they canned for winter.

When the poppies bloomed and the sweet peas came in, three broods were hatched. The first chicks appeared at breakfast with the hen leading a weaving path to the corn and the cock running half-circles behind them keeping the chicks in line. They counted ten new birds in the three families and they rose even earlier so they could linger over breakfast and smell the drying mustard weed behind the garden.

One hen led her chicks for evening strolls down the front sidewalk. She would promenade her family punctually at five-thirty. The landlord and his wife sat on the front porch one night not believing the hen would show as the tenant had described. They all laughed when the hen strutted by on cue. The landlord and his wife drank beer and told them about the Depression when there was drought and they had to save everything. The old woman said she still had those habits and also said she had been overly concerned about the garden. The tenant couple thought the landlord's wife would be just fine.

When it was autumn, they canned apples and applesauce. The landlord took in his squash, carrots, tomatoes, beets. The landlord's wife traded canned cherries for their canned apples. The landlord cut back the garden, and the tenant helped the old man put up storms, turn the garden, and clean the garage. He bought a fifty pound bag of cracked corn and built a feeding trough of redwood. With the trough on the windowsill there was enough room for all eighteen quail even with the window closed.

The covey was in good shape for the winter. He told her the birds would have an easy winter with the cracked corn and said they would stay near food. The chicks had grown, they were well fed, sleek with new adult plumage. The original eight were rotund, fattened by the summer's corn. He assured her the birds would be fine for the winter.

When the leaves turned and there was frost again they closed the kitchen window. She could not feed the hen crumbs but they could talk now without frightening the birds. They talked about the summer with the quail waking them early. He told her he had hoped all his life that it would someday be like it had been that summer.

When there was hard frost and cold mornings they lingered in bed, awake, warm next to each other, thinking of the quail, thinking of the warmth.

The morning after the first snowfall, the quail were gone. He brushed the snow out of the feeding trough and replaced the wet corn. The covey did not come back that night and the corn had not been touched the next morning. He told her the quail had probably gone to the hills outside town for winter. He told her there was better cover in the hills and that the hunting season was over, so they would be fine. He told her the birds would be back in the spring and it would be the same again.

The tenant and his wife slept late and hard through the winter. The winter was dry, bleak, and cold. There was talk of drought for summer; the landlord hoarded water for his garden by storing it in old oil drums.

The tenant changed the corn often, spreading some on the frozen ground. But the quail did not return and sparrows and jays ate the corn. His wife said she knew the quail would be back in the spring and it would be the same.

When the ground thawed and there was the mud and dirt smell outside, the tenant saw the landlord cleaning his garage and went to help. When he saw the plastic bag full of gray and brown feathers: down feathers, plume feathers, some with bits of dried skin; when he saw that sack and the large chicken wire trap that had not been in the garage before, he asked the landlord how he had managed to catch all the birds at once. The landlord said it had been his wife's idea. They had waited for the first winter storm and trapped the birds when they were huddled together. He said they had been fine eating.

The tenant did not tell his wife about the bag or trap but it was as if she knew. After a while he quit putting out the corn and when the fifty pound bag began to rot, he threw it on the trash.

EXERCISES

1. What is the significance of the quail arriving during the first spring of their marriage? Would the quail have had the same importance if they had arrived at any other year or season?

2. Discuss the significance of the following: "Sun came through the window; the rolls were sweet with raisins, and they did not have to say anything to each other."

3. What is suggested by the description of the quail looking like "dowager women" and "portly men"?

4. What is the difference between the way the young couple like the quail and the way the landlord likes quail? What does this difference mean?

5. Why does the story follow the progress of the seasons so explicitly? What is the basic difference between the way it was in summer and the way it is in winter in the story? What symbolic significance does this difference have?

6. Discuss the significance of the following: "He told her he had hoped all his life that it would someday be like it had been that summer."

7. What does the death of the quail by the older couple suggest to the storyteller? What does it have to do with the younger couple?

ANN
BEATTIE | *Janus*

The bowl was perfect. Perhaps it was not what you'd select if you faced a shelf of bowls, and not the sort of thing that would inevitably attract a lot of attention at a crafts fair, yet it had real presence. It was as predictably admired as a mutt who has no reason to suspect he might be funny. Just such a dog, in fact, was often brought out (and in) along with the bowl.

Andrea was a real-estate agent, and when she thought that some prospective buyers might be dog-lovers, she would drop off her dog at the same time she placed the bowl in the house that was up for sale. She would put a dish of water in the kitchen for Mondo, take his squeaking plastic frog out of her purse and drop it on the floor. He would pounce delightedly, just as he did every day at home, batting around his favorite toy. The bowl usually sat on a coffee table, though recently she had displayed it on top of a pine blanket chest and on a lacquered table. It was once placed on a cherry table beneath a Bonnard still-life, where it held its own.

Everyone who has purchased a house or who has wanted to sell a house must be familiar with some of the tricks used to convince a buyer that the house is quite special: a fire in the fireplace in early evening; jonquils in a pitcher on the kitchen counter, where no one ordinarily has space to put flowers; perhaps the slight aroma of spring, made by a single drop of scent vaporizing from a lamp bulb.

The wonderful thing about the bowl, Andrea thought, was that it was both subtle and noticeable—a paradox of a bowl. Its glaze was the color of cream and seemed to glow no matter what light it was placed in. There were a few bits of color in it—tiny geometric flashes—and some of these were tinged with flecks of silver. They were as mysterious as cells seen under a microscope; it was difficult not to study them, because they shimmered, flashing for a split second, and then resumed their shape. Something about the colors and their random placement suggested motion. People who liked country furniture always commented on the bowl, but then it turned out that people who felt comfortable with Biedermeier loved it just as much. But the bowl was not at all ostentatious, or even so noticeable that anyone would suspect that it had been put in place deliberately. They might notice the height of the ceiling on first entering a room, and only when their eye moved down from that, or away from the refraction of sunlight on a pale wall, would they see the bowl. Then they would go immediately to it and comment. Yet they always faltered when they tried to say something. Perhaps it was because they were in the house for a serious reason, not to notice some object.

Once, Andrea got a call from a woman who had not put in an offer on a house she had shown her. That bowl, she said—would it be possible to find out where the owners had bought that beautiful bowl? Andrea pretended that she did not know what the woman was referring to. A bowl, somewhere in the house? Oh, on a table under the window. Yes, she would ask, of course. She let a couple of days pass, then called back to say that the bowl had been a present and the people did not know where it had been purchased.

When the bowl was not being taken from house to house, it sat on Andrea's coffee table at home. She didn't keep it carefully wrapped (although she transported it that way, in a box); she kept it on the table, because she liked to see it. It was large enough so that it didn't seem fragile, or particularly vulnerable if anyone sideswiped the table or Mondo blundered into it at play. She had asked her husband to please not drop his house key in it. It was meant to be empty.

When her husband first noticed the bowl, he had peered into it and smiled briefly. He always urged her to buy things she liked. In recent years, both of them had acquired many things to make up for all the lean years when they were graduate students, but now that they had been comfortable for quite a while, the pleasure of new possessions dwindled. Her husband had pronounced the bowl "pretty," and he had turned away without picking it up to examine it. He had no more interest in the bowl than she had in his new Leica.

She was sure that the bowl brought her luck. Bids were often put in on houses where she had displayed the bowl. Sometimes the owners, who were always asked to be away or to step outside when the house was being shown, didn't even know that the bowl had been in their house. Once—she could not imagine how—she left it behind and then she was so afraid that something might have happened to it that she rushed back to the house and sighed with relief when the woman owner opened the door. The bowl, Andrea explained—she had purchased a bowl and set it on the chest for safekeeping while she toured the house with the prospective buyers, and she . . . She felt like rushing past the frowning woman and seizing her bowl. The owner stepped aside, and it was only when Andrea ran to the chest that the lady glanced at her a little strangely. In the few seconds before Andrea picked up the bowl, she realized that the owner must have just seen that it had been perfectly placed, that the sunlight struck the bluer part of it. Her pitcher had been moved to the far side of the chest, and the bowl predominated. All the way home, Andrea wondered how she could have left the bowl behind. It was like leaving a friend at an outing—just walking off. Sometimes there were stories in the paper about families forgetting a child somewhere and driving to the next city. Andrea had only gone a mile down the road before she remembered.

In time, she dreamed of the bowl. Twice, in a waking dream—early in the morning, between sleep and a last nap before rising—she had a clear vision of it. It came into sharp focus and startled her for a moment—the same bowl she looked at every day.

She had a very profitable year selling real estate. Word spread, and she had more clients than she felt comfortable with. She had the foolish thought that if only the bowl were an animate object she could thank it. There were times when she wanted to talk to her husband about the bowl. He was a stockbroker, and sometimes told people that he was fortunate to be married to a woman who had such a fine aesthetic sense and yet could also function in the real world. They were a lot alike, really—they had agreed on that. They were both quiet people—reflective, slow to make value judgments, but almost intractable once they had come to a conclusion. They both liked details, but while ironies attracted her, he was more impatient and dismissive when matters became many-sided or unclear. But they both knew this; it was the kind of thing they could talk about when they were alone in the car together, coming home from a party or after a weekend with friends. But she never talked to him about the bowl. When they were at dinner, exchanging their news of the day, or while they lay in bed at night listening to the stereo and murmuring sleepy disconnections, she was often tempted to come right out and say that she thought that the bowl in the living room, the cream-colored bowl, was responsible for her success. But she didn't say it. She couldn't begin to explain it. Sometimes in the morning, she would look at him and feel guilty that she had such a constant secret.

Could it be that she had some deeper connection with the bowl—a relationship of some kind? She corrected her thinking: how could she imagine such a thing, when she was a human being and it was a bowl? It was ridiculous. Just think of how people lived together and loved each other . . . But was that always so clear, always a relationship? She was confused by these thoughts, but they remained in her mind. There was something within her now, something real, that she never talked about.

The bowl was a mystery, even to her. It was frustrating, because her involvement with the bowl contained a steady sense of unrequited good fortune; it would have been easier to respond if some sort of demand were made in return. But that only happened in fairy tales. The bowl was just a bowl. She did not believe that for one second. What she believed was that it was something she loved.

In the past, she had sometimes talked to her husband about a new property she was about to buy or sell—confiding some clever strategy she had devised to persuade owners who seemed ready to sell. Now she stopped doing that, for all her strategies involved the bowl. She became more deliberate with the bowl, and more possessive. She put it in houses only when no one was there, and removed it when she left the house. Instead of just moving a pitcher or a dish, she would remove all the other objects from a table. She had to force herself to handle them carefully, because she didn't really care about them. She just wanted them out of sight.

She wondered how the situation would end. As with a lover, there was no exact scenario of how matters would come to a close. Anxiety became the operative force. It would be irrelevant if the lover rushed into someone else's arms, or wrote her a note and departed to another city. The horror was the possibility of the disappearance. That was what mattered.

She would get up at night and look at the bowl. It never occurred to her that she might break it. She washed and dried it without anxiety, and she moved it often, from coffee table to mahogany corner table or wherever, without fearing an accident. It was clear that she would not be the one who would do anything to the bowl. The bowl was only handled by her, set safely on one surface or another; it was not very likely that anyone would break it. A bowl was a poor conductor of electricity: it would not be hit by lightning. Yet the idea of damage persisted. She did not think beyond that—to what her life would be without the bowl. She only continued to fear that some accident would happen. Why not, in a world where people set plants where they did not belong, so that visitors touring a house would be fooled into thinking that dark corners got sunlight—a world full of tricks?

She had first seen the bowl several years earlier, at a crafts fair she had visited half in secret, with her lover. He had urged her to buy the bowl. She didn't *need* any more things, she told him. But she had been drawn to the bowl, and they had lingered near it. Then she went on to the next booth, and he came up behind her, tapping the rim against her shoulder as she ran her fingers over a wood carving. "You're still insisting that I buy that?" she said. "No," he said. "I bought it for you." He had bought her other things before this—things she liked more, at first—the child's ebony-and-turquoise ring that fitted her little finger; the wooden box, long and thin, beautifully dove-tailed, that she used to hold paper clips; the soft gray sweater with a pouch pocket. It was his idea that when he could not be there to hold her hand she could hold her own—clasp her hands inside the lone pocket that stretched across the front. But in time she became more attached to the bowl than to any of his other presents. She tried to talk herself out of it. She owned other things that were more striking or valuable. It wasn't an object whose beauty jumped out at you; a lot of people must have passed it by before the two of them saw it that day.

Her lover had said that she was always too slow to know what she really loved. Why continue with her life the way it was? Why be two-faced, he asked her. He had made the first move toward her. When she would not decide in his favor, would not change her life and come to him, he asked her what made her think she could have it both ways. And then he made the last move and left. It was a decision meant to break her will, to shatter her intransigent ideas about honoring previous commitments.

Time passed. Alone in the living room at night, she often looked at the bowl sitting on the table, still and safe, unilluminated. In its way, it was per-fect: the world cut in half, deep and smoothly empty. Near the rim, even in dim light, the eye moved toward one small flash of blue, a vanishing point on the horizon.

EXERCISES

1. Janus, the ancient Roman god of gateways, had two faces—one facing in one direction and one facing in another. Note the various elements in this story that have two sides, for example, that the vase is both subtle and noticeable at once.

2. What is the significance of the fact that the bowl was "meant to be empty"?

3. What is the tone of this story? Does it sound realistic or fable-like?

4. Why does the bowl take on such importance to Andrea? Why is her feeling about the bowl described in terms of a relationship with a lover?

5. Discuss the statement "While ironies attracted her, he was more impatient and dismissive when matters became many-sided and unclear."

6. Discuss the statement "There was something within her now, something real, that she never talked about."

7. Why does the emphasis shift to the past in the final section of the story? Why does Andrea's present use of the bowl seem appropriate, given the way she received it? What is two-faced about this story?

DAVID
LEAVITT | *Gravity*

Theo had a choice between a drug that would save his sight and a drug that would keep him alive, so he chose not to go blind. He stopped the pills and started the injections—these required the implantation of an unpleasant and painful catheter just above his heart—and within a few days the clouds in his eyes started to clear up; he could see again. He remembered going into New York City to a show with his mother, when he was twelve and didn't want to admit he needed glasses. "Can you read that?" she'd shouted, pointing to a Broadway marquee, and when he'd squinted, making out only one or two letters, she'd taken off her own glasses—harlequins with tiny rhinestones in the corners—and shoved them onto his face. The world came into focus, and he gasped, astonished at the precision around the edges of things, the legibility, the hard, sharp, colorful landscape. Sylvia had to squint through *Fiddler on the Roof* that day, but for Theo, his face masked by his mother's huge glasses, everything was as bright and vivid as a comic book. Even though people stared at him, and muttered things, Sylvia didn't care; he could *see*.

Because he was dying again, Theo moved back to his mother's house in New Jersey. The DHPG injections she took in stride—she'd seen her own mother through *her* dying, after all. Four times a day, with the equanimity of a nurse, she cleaned out the plastic tube implanted in his chest, inserted a sterilized hypodermic and slowly dripped the bag of sight-giving liquid into his veins. They endured this procedure silently, Sylvia sitting on the side of the hospital bed she'd rented for the duration of Theo's stay—his life, he sometimes thought—watching reruns of *I Love Lucy* or the news, while he tried not to think about the hard piece of pipe stuck into him, even though it was a constant reminder of how wide and unswimmable the gulf was becoming between him and the ever-receding shoreline of the well. And Sylvia was intricately cheerful. Each day she urged him to go out with her somewhere—to the library, or the little museum with the dinosaur replicas he'd been fond of as a child—and when his thinness and the cane drew stares, she'd maneuver him around the people who were staring, determined to shield him from whatever they might say or do. It had been the same that afternoon so many years ago, when she'd pushed him through a lobbyful of curious and laughing faces, determined that nothing should interfere with the spectacle of his seeing. What a pair they must have made, a boy in ugly glasses and a mother daring the world to say a word about it!

This warm, breezy afternoon in May they were shopping for revenge. "Your cousin Howard's engagement party is next month," Sylvia explained in the car. "A very nice girl from Livingston. I met her a few weeks ago, and really, she's a superior person."

"I'm glad," Theo said. "Congratulate Howie for me."

"Do you think you'll be up to going to the party?"

"I'm not sure. Would it be okay for me just to give him a gift?"

"You already have. A lovely silver tray, if I say so myself. The thank-you note's in the living room."

"Mom," Theo said, "why do you always have to—"

Sylvia honked her horn at a truck making an illegal left turn. "Better they should get something than no present at all, is what I say," she said. "But now, the problem is, *I* have to give Howie something, to be from me, and it better be good. It better be very, very good."

"Why?"

"Don't you remember that cheap little nothing Bibi gave you for your graduation? It was disgusting."

"I can't remember what she gave me."

"Of course you can't. It was a tacky pen-and-pencil set. Not even a real leather box. So naturally, it stands to reason that I have to get something truly spectacular for Howard's engagement. Something that will make Bibi blanch. Anyway, I think I've found just the thing, but I need your advice."

"Advice? Well, when my old roommate Nick got married, I gave him a garlic press. It cost five dollars and reflected exactly how much I felt, at that moment, our friendship was worth."

Sylvia laughed. "Clever. But my idea is much more brilliant, because it makes it possible for me to get back at Bibi *and* give Howard the nice gift he and his girl deserve." She smiled, clearly pleased with herself. "Ah, you live and learn."

"You live," Theo said.

Sylvia blinked. "Well, look, here we are." She pulled the car into a handicapped-parking place on Morris Avenue and got out to help Theo, but he was already hoisting himself up out of his seat, using the door handle for leverage. "I can manage myself," he said with some irritation. Sylvia stepped back.

"Clearly one advantage of all this for you," Theo said, balancing on his cane, "is that it's suddenly so much easier to get a parking place."

"Oh Theo, please," Sylvia said. "Look, here's where we're going."

She leaned him into a gift shop filled with porcelain statuettes of Snow White and all seven of the dwarves, music boxes which, when you opened them, played "The Shadow of Your Smile," complicated-smelling potpourris in purple wallpapered boxes, and stuffed snakes you were supposed to push up against drafty windows and doors.

"Mrs. Greenman," said an expansive, gray-haired man in a cream-colored cardigan sweater. "Look who's here, Archie, it's Mrs. Greenman."

Another man, this one thinner and balding, but dressed in an identical cardigan, peered out from the back of the shop. "Hello there!" he said, smiling. He looked at Theo, and his expression changed.

"Mr. Sherman, Mr. Baker. This is my son, Theo."

"Hello," Mr. Sherman and Mr. Baker said. They didn't offer to shake hands.

"Are you here for that item we discussed last week?" Mr. Sherman asked.

"Yes," Sylvia said. "I want advice from my son here." She walked over to a large ridged crystal bowl, a very fifties sort of bowl, stalwart and square-jawed. "What do you think? Beautiful, isn't it?"

"Mom, to tell the truth, I think it's kind of ugly."

"Four hundred and twenty-five dollars," Sylvia said admiringly. "You have to feel it."

Then she picked up the big bowl and tossed it to Theo, like a football.

The gentlemen in the cardigan sweaters gasped and did not exhale. When Theo caught it, it sank his hands. His cane rattled as it hit the floor.

"That's heavy," Sylvia said, observing with satisfaction how the bowl had weighted Theo's arms down. "And where crystal is concerned, heavy is impressive."

She took the bowl back from him and carried it to the counter. Mr. Sherman was mopping his brow. Theo looked at the floor, still surprised not to see shards of glass around his feet.

Since no one else seemed to be volunteering, he bent over and picked up the cane.

"Four hundred and fifty-nine, with tax," Mr. Sherman said, his voice still a bit shaky, and a look of relish came over Sylvia's face as she pulled out her checkbook to pay. Behind the counter, Theo could see Mr. Baker put his hand on his forehead and cast his eyes to the ceiling.

It seemed Sylvia had been looking a long time for something like this, something heavy enough to leave an impression, yet so fragile it could make you sorry.

They headed back out to the car.

"Where can we go now?" Sylvia asked, as she got in. "There must be someplace else to go."

"Home," Theo said. "It's almost time for my medicine."

"Really? Oh. All right." She pulled on her seat belt, inserted the car key in the ignition and sat there.

For just a moment, but perceptibly, her face broke. She squeezed her eyes shut so tight the blue shadow on the lids cracked.

Almost as quickly she was back to normal again, and they were driving. "It's getting hotter," Sylvia said. "Shall I put on the air?"

"Sure," Theo said. He was thinking about the bowl, or more specifically, about how surprising its weight had been, pulling his hands down. For a while now he'd been worried about his mother, worried about what damage his illness might secretly be doing to her that of course she would never admit. On the surface things seemed all right. She still broiled herself a skinned chicken breast for dinner every night, still swam a mile and a half a day, still kept used teabags wrapped in foil in the refrigerator. Yet she had also, at about three o'clock one morning, woken him up to tell him she was going to the twenty-four-hour supermarket, and was there anything he wanted. Then there was the gift shop: She had literally pitched that bowl toward him, pitched it like a ball, and as that great gleam of flight and potential regret came sailing his direction, it had occurred to him that she was trusting his two feeble hands, out of the whole world, to keep it from shattering. What was she trying to test? Was it his newly regained vision? Was it the assurance that he was there, alive, that he hadn't yet slipped past all her caring, a little lost boy in rhinestone-studded glasses? There are certain things you've already done before you even think how to do them—a child pulled from in front of a car, for instance, or the bowl, which Theo was holding before he could even begin to calculate its brief trajectory. It had pulled his arms down, and from that apish posture he'd looked at his mother, who smiled broadly, as if, in the war between heaviness and shattering, he'd just helped her win some small but sustaining victory.

EXERCISES

1. Why is seeing more important than living for Theo? Discuss the importance of the remembered event when Theo wore his mother's glasses. How is this a particularly relevant image in the story?

2. What is the relationship between the mother and the son in this story? Is it unusual or typical, special or ordinary?

3. What is the relevance of the mother insisting on buying a very special gift for the family that bought such a cheap gift for Theo?

4. What is the significance of the bowl being "heavy enough to leave an impression, yet so fragile it could make you sorry"?

5. The story would not be a story without the event of the mother tossing the bowl. What does the gesture mean to Theo? What does it mean to the mother?

6. What is the significance of the title of the story? What is the war between "heaviness and shattering" referred to in the last sentence?

TILLIE
OLSEN | *I Stand Here Ironing*

I stand here ironing, and what you asked me moves tormented back and forth with the iron.

"I wish you would manage the time to come in and talk with me about your daughter. I'm sure you can help me understand her. She's a youngster who needs help and whom I'm deeply interested in helping."

"Who needs help." Even if I came, what good would it do? You think because I am her mother I have a key, or that in some way you could use me as a key? She has lived for nineteen years. There is all that life that has happened outside of me, beyond me.

And when is there time to remember, to sift, to weigh, to estimate, to total? I will start and there will be an interruption and I will have to gather it all together again. Or I will become engulfed with all I did or did not do, with what should have been and what cannot be helped.

She was a beautiful baby. The first and only one of our five that was beautiful at birth. You do not guess how new and uneasy her tenancy in her now-loveliness. You did not know her all those years she was thought homely, or see her poring over her baby pictures, making me tell her over and over how beautiful she had been—and would be, I would tell her—and was now, to the seeing eye. But the seeing eyes were few or nonexistent. Including mine.

I nursed her. They feel that's important nowadays. I nursed all the children, but with her, with all the fierce rigidity of first motherhood, I did like the books then said. Though her cries battered me to trembling and my breasts ached with swollenness, I waited till the clock decreed.

Why do I put that first? I do not even know if it matters, or if it explains anything.

She was a beautiful baby. She blew shining bubbles of sound. She loved motion, loved light, loved color and music and textures. She would lie on the floor in her blue overalls patting the surface so hard in ecstasy her hands and feet would blur. She was a miracle to me, but when she was eight months old I had to leave her daytimes with the woman downstairs to whom she was no miracle at all, for I worked or looked for work and for Emily's father, who "could no longer endure" (he wrote in his good-bye note) "sharing want with us."

I was nineteen. It was the pre-relief, pre-WPA world of the depression. I would start running as soon as I got off the streetcar, running up the stairs, the place smelling sour, and awake or asleep to startle awake, when she saw me she would break into a clogged weeping that could not be comforted, a weeping I can hear yet.

After a while I found a job hashing at night so I could be with her days, and it was better. But it came to where I had to bring her to his family and leave her.

It took a long time to raise the money for her fare back. Then she got chicken pox and I had to wait longer. When she finally came, I hardly knew her, walking quick and nervous like her father, looking like her father, thin, and dressed in a shoddy red that yellowed her skin and glared at the pockmarks. All the baby loveliness gone.

She was two. Old enough for nursery school they said, and I did not know then what I know now—the fatigue of the long day, and the lacerations of group life in the nurseries that are only parking places for children.

Except that it would have made no difference if I had known. It was the only place there was. It was the only way we could be together, the only way I could hold a job.

And even without knowing, I knew. I knew the teacher that was evil because all these years it has curdled into my memory, the little boy hunched in the corner, her rasp, "why aren't you outside, because Alvin hits you? that's no reason, go out, scaredy." I knew Emily hated it even if she did not clutch and implore "don't go Mommy" like the other children, mornings.

She always had a reason why we should stay home. Momma, you look sick. Momma, I feel sick. Momma, the teachers aren't there today, they're sick. Momma, we can't go, there was a fire there last night. Momma, it's a holiday today, no school, they told me.

But never a direct protest, never rebellion. I think of our others in their three-, four-year-oldness—the explosions, the tempers, the denunciations, the demands—and I feel suddenly ill. I put the iron down. What in me demanded that goodness in her? And what was the cost, the cost to her of such goodness?

The old man living in the back once said in his gentle way: "You should smile at Emily more when you look at her." What *was* in my face when I looked at her? I loved her. There were all the acts of love.

It was only with the others I remembered what he said, and it was the face of joy, and not of care or tightness or worry I turned to them—too late for Emily. She does not smile easily, let alone almost always as her brothers and sisters do. Her face is closed and sombre, but when she wants, how fluid. You must have seen it in her pantomimes, you spoke of her rare gift for comedy on the stage that rouses a laughter out of the audience so dear they applaud and applaud and do not want to let her go.

Where does it come from, that comedy? There was none of it in her when she came back to me that second time, after I had had to send her away again. She had a new daddy now to learn to love, and I think perhaps it was a better time.

Except when we left her alone nights, telling ourselves she was old enough.

"Can't you go some other time, Mommy, like tomorrow?" she would ask. "Will it be just a little while you'll be gone? Do you promise?"

The time we came back, the front door open, the clock on the floor in the hall. She rigid awake. "It wasn't just a little while. I didn't cry. Three times I called you, just three times, and then I ran downstairs to open the door so you could come faster. The clock talked loud. I threw it away, it scared me what it talked."

She said the clock talked loud again that night I went to the hospital to have Susan. She was delirious with the fever that comes before red measles, but she was fully conscious all the week I was gone and the week after we were home when she could not come near the new baby or me.

She did not get well. She stayed skeleton thin, not wanting to eat, and night after night she had nightmares. She would call for me, and I would rouse from exhaustion to sleepily call back: "You're all right, darling, go to sleep, it's just a dream," and if she still called, in a sterner voice, "now go to sleep, Emily, there's nothing to hurt you." Twice, only twice, when I had to get up for Susan anyhow, I went in to sit with her.

Now when it is too late (as if she would let me hold and comfort her like I do the others) I get up and go to her at once at her moan or restless stirring. "Are you awake, Emily? Can I get you something?" And the answer is always the same: "No, I'm all right, go back to sleep, Mother."

They persuaded me at the clinic to send her away to a convalescent home in the country where "she can have the kind of food and care you can't manage for her, and you'll be free to concentrate on the new baby." They still send children to that place. I see pictures on the society page of sleek young women planning affairs to raise money for it, or dancing at the affairs, or decorating Easter eggs or filling Christmas stockings for the children.

They never have a picture of the children so I do not know if the girls still wear those gigantic red bows and the ravaged looks on them every other Sunday when parents can come to visit "unless otherwise notified"—as we were notified the first six weeks.

Oh it is a handsome place, green lawns and tall trees and fluted flower beds. High up on the balconies of each cottage the children stand, the girls in their red bows and white dresses, the boys in white suits and giant red ties. The parents stand below shrieking up to be heard and the children shriek down to be heard, and between them the invisible wall "Not To Be Contaminated by Parental Germs or Physical Affection."

There was a tiny girl who always stood hand in hand with Emily. Her parents never came. One visit she was gone. "They moved her to Rose College," Emily shouted in explanation. "They don't like you to love anybody here."

She wrote once a week, the labored writing of a seven-year-old. "I am fine. How is the baby. If I write my leter nicly I will have a star. Love." There never was a star. We wrote every other day, letters she could never hold or keep but only hear read—once. "We simply do not have room for children to keep any personal possessions," they patiently explained when we pieced one Sunday's shrieking together to plead how much it would mean to Emily, who loved so to keep things, to be allowed to keep her letters and cards.

Each visit she looked frailer. "She isn't eating," they told us.

(They had runny eggs for breakfast or mush with lumps, Emily said later, I'd hold it in my mouth and not swallow. Nothing ever tasted good, just when they had chicken.)

It took us eight months to get her released home, and only the fact that she gained back so little of her seven lost pounds convinced the social worker.

I used to try to hold and love her after she came back, but her body would stay stiff, and after a while she'd push away. She ate little. Food sickened her, and I think much of life too. Oh she had physical lightness and brightness, twinkling by on skates, bouncing like a ball up and down up and down over the jump rope, skimming over the hill; but these were momentary.

She fretted about her appearance, thin and dark and foreign-looking at a time when every little girl was supposed to look or thought she should look a chubby blonde replica of Shirley Temple. The doorbell sometimes rang for her, but no one seemed to come and play in the house or be a best friend. Maybe because we moved so much.

There was a boy she loved painfully through two school semesters. Months later she told me how she had taken pennies from my purse to buy him candy. "Licorice was his favorite and I brought him some every day, but he still liked Jennifer better'n me. Why, Mommy?" The kind of question for which there is no answer.

School was a worry to her. She was not glib or quick in a world where glibness and quickness were easily confused with ability to learn. To her over-worked and exasperated teachers she was an over-conscientious "slow learner" who kept trying to catch up and was absent entirely too often.

I let her be absent, though sometimes the illness was imaginary. How different from my now-strictness about attendance with the others. I wasn't working. We had a new baby, I was home anyhow. Sometimes, after Susan grew old enough, I would keep her home from school, too, to have them all together.

Mostly Emily had asthma, and her breathing, harsh and labored, would fill the house with a curiously tranquil sound. I would bring the two old dresser mirrors and her boxes of collections to her bed. She would select beads and single earrings, bottle tops and shells, dried flowers and pebbles, old postcards and scraps, all sorts of oddments; then she and Susan would play Kingdom, setting up landscapes and furniture, peopling them with action.

Those were the only times of peaceful companionship between her and Susan. I have edged away from it, that poisonous feeling between them, that terrible balancing of hurts and needs I had to do between the two, and did so badly, those earlier years.

Oh there are conflicts between the others too, each one human, needing, demanding, hurting, taking—but only between Emily and Susan, no, Emily toward Susan that corroding resentment. It seems so obvious on the surface, yet it is not obvious. Susan, the second child, Susan, golden- and curly-haired and chubby, quick and articulate and assured, everything in appearance and manner Emily was not; Susan, not able to resist Emily's precious things, losing or sometimes clumsily breaking them; Susan telling jokes and riddles to company for applause while Emily sat silent (to say to me later: that was *my* riddle, Mother, I told it to Susan); Susan, who for all the five years' difference in age was just a year behind Emily in developing physically.

I am glad for that slow physical development that widened the difference between her and her contemporaries, though she suffered for it. She was too vulnerable for that terrible world of youthful competition, of preening and parading, of constant measuring of yourself against every other, of envy, "If I had that copper hair," "If I had that skin. . . ." She tormented herself enough about not looking like the others, there was enough of the unsureness, the having to be conscious of words before you speak, the constant caring—what are they thinking of me? without having it all magnified by the merciless physical drives.

Ronnie is calling. He is wet and I change him. It is rare there is such a cry now. That time of motherhood is almost behind me when the ear is not one's own but must always be racked and listening for the child cry, the child call. We sit for a while and I hold him, looking out over the city spread in charcoal with its soft aisles of light. *"Shoogily,"* he breathes and curls closer.

I carry him back to bed, asleep. *Shoogily.* A funny word, a family word, inherited from Emily, invented by her to say: *comfort.*

In this and other ways she leaves her seal, I say aloud. And startle at my saying it. What do I mean? What did I start to gather together, to try and make coherent? I was at the terrible, growing years. War years. I do not remember them well. I was working, there were four smaller ones now, there was not time for her. She had to help be a mother, and housekeeper, and shopper. She had to set her seal. Mornings of crisis and near hysteria trying to get lunches packed, hair combed, coats and shoes found, everyone to school or Child Care on time, the baby ready for transportation. And always the paper scribbled on by a smaller one, the book looked at by Susan then mislaid, the homework not done. Running out to that huge school where she was one, she was lost, she was a drop; suffering over the unpreparedness, stammering and unsure in her classes.

There was so little time left at night after the kids were bedded down. She would struggle over books, always eating (it was in those years she developed her enormous appetite that is legendary in our family) and I would be ironing, or preparing food for the next day, or writing V-mail to Bill, or tending the baby. Sometimes, to make me laugh, or out of her despair, she would imitate happenings or types at school.

I think I said once: "Why don't you do something like this in the school amateur show?" One morning she phoned me at work, hardly understandable through the weeping: "Mother, I did it. I won, I won; they gave me first prize; they clapped and clapped and wouldn't let me go."

Now suddenly she was Somebody, and as imprisoned in her difference as she had been in anonymity.

She began to be asked to perform at other high schools, even in colleges, then at city and statewide affairs. The first one we went to, I only recognized her that first moment when thin, shy, she almost drowned herself into the curtains. Then: Was this Emily? The control, the command, the convulsing and deadly clowning, the spell, then the roaring, stamping audience, unwilling to let this rare and precious laughter out of their lives.

Afterwards: You ought to do something about her with a gift like that— but without money or knowing how, what does one do? We have left it all to her, and the gift has as often eddied inside, clogged and clotted, as been used and growing.

She is coming. She runs up the stairs two at a time with her light graceful step, and I know she is happy tonight. Whatever it was that occasioned your call did not happen today.

"Aren't you ever going to finish the ironing, Mother? Whistler painted his mother in a rocker. I'd have to paint mine standing over an ironing board." This is one of her communicative nights and she tells me everything and nothing as she fixes herself a plate of food out of the icebox.

She is so lovely. Why did you want me to come in at all? Why were you concerned? She will find her way.

She starts up the stairs to bed. "Don't get me up with the rest in the morning." "But I thought you were having midterms." "Oh, those," she comes back in, kisses me, and says quite lightly, "in a couple of years when we'll all be atom-dead they won't matter a bit."

She has said it before. She *believes* it. But because I have been dredging the past, and all that compounds a human being is so heavy and meaningful in me, I cannot endure it tonight.

I will never total it all. I will never come in to say: She was a child seldom smiled at. Her father left me before she was a year old. I had to work her first six years when there was work, or I sent her home and to his relatives. There were years she had care she hated. She was dark and thin and foreign-looking in a world where the prestige went to blondeness and curly hair and dimples, she was slow where glibness was prized. She was a child of anxious, not proud, love. We were poor and could not afford for her the soil of easy growth. I was a young mother, I was a distracted mother. There were the other children pushing up, demanding. Her younger sister seemed all that she was not. There were years she did not let me touch her. She kept too much in herself, her life was such she had to keep too much in herself. My wisdom came too late. She has much to her and probably little will come of it. She is a child of her age, of depression, of war, of fear.

Let her be. So all that is in her will not bloom—but in how many does it? There is still enough left to live by. Only help her to know—help make it so there is cause for her to know—that she is more than this dress on the ironing board, helpless before the iron.

EXERCISES

1. What is the significance of the fact that the speaker is ironing? To whom is she speaking? Or is this an interior monologue? Why is the story presented in this way?

2. What is the significance of the old man's advice to the mother to smile at Emily? Discuss the following: "What *was* in my face when I looked at her? I loved her. There were all the acts of love."

3. What is relevant about the daughter's talent for comedy? How is it that Emily seems transformed when she is on the stage? Would the story have been different if her talent had been painting, writing, or singing?

4. Why was the daughter's childhood the way it was? Who is to blame? Is this a story about this specific mother, or is this story applicable to many women?

5. Try to answer this question in the story: "What do I mean? What did I start to gather together, to try and make coherent?"

6. Why does the speaker say that her daughter should be left alone, even though there is much in her that will not bloom? Explain the analogy between the daughter and the dress.

THOMAS
MANN | *Railway Accident*

Tell you a story? But I don't know any. Well, yes, after all, here is something I might tell.

Once, two years ago now it is, I was in a railway accident; all the details are clear in my memory.

It was not really a first-class one—no wholesale telescoping or "heaps of unidentifiable dead"—not that sort of thing. Still, it was a proper accident, with all the trimmings, and on top of that it was at night. Not everybody has been through one, so I will describe it the best I can.

I was on my way to Dresden, whither I had been invited by some friends of letters: it was a literary and artistic pilgrimage, in short, such as, from time to time, I undertake not unwillingly. You make appearances, you attend functions, you show yourself to admiring crowds—not for nothing is one a subject of William II. And certainly Dresden is beautiful, especially the Zwinger; and afterwards I intended to go for ten days or a fortnight to the White Hart to rest, and if, thanks to the treatments, the spirit should come upon me, I might do a little work as well. To this end I had put my manuscript at the bottom of my trunk, together with my notes—a good stout bundle done up in brown paper and tied with string in the Bavarian colours. I like to travel in comfort, especially when my expenses are paid. So I patronized the sleeping-cars, reserving a place days ahead in a first-class compartment. All was in order; nevertheless I was excited, as I always am on such occasions, for a journey is still an adventure to me, and where travelling is concerned I shall never manage to feel properly blasé. I perfectly well know that the night train for Dresden leaves the central station at Munich regularly every evening, and every morning is in Dresden. But when I am travelling with it, and linking my momentous destiny to its own, the matter assumes importance. I cannot rid myself of the notion that it is making a special trip today, just on my account, and the unreasoning and mistaken conviction sets up in me a deep and speechless unrest, which does not subside until all the formalities of departure are behind me—the packing, the drive in the loaded cab to the station, the arrival there, and the registration of luggage—and I can feel myself finally and securely bestowed. Then, indeed, a pleasing relaxation takes place, the mind turns to fresh concerns, the unknown unfolds itself beyond the expanse of window-pane, and I am consumed with joyful anticipations.

And so on this occasion. I had tipped my porter so liberally that he pulled his cap and gave me a pleasant journey; and I stood at the corridor window of my sleeping-car smoking my evening cigar and watching the bustle on the platform. There were whistlings and rumblings, hurryings and farewells, and the singsong of newspaper and refreshment vendors, and over all the great electric moons glowed through the mist of the October evening. Two stout fellows pulled a hand-cart of large trunks along the platform to the baggage car in front of the train. I easily identified, by certain unmistakable features, my own trunk; one among many there it lay, and at the bottom of it reposed my precious package. "There," thought I, "no need to worry, it is in good hands. Look at that guard with the leather cartridge-belt, the prodigious sergeant-major's moustache, and the inhospitable eye. Watch him rebuking the old woman in the threadbare black cape—for two pins she would have got into a second-class carriage. He is security, he is authority, he is our parent, he is the State. He is strict, not to say gruff, you would not care to mingle with him; but reliability is writ large upon his brow, and in his care your trunk reposes as in the bosom of Abraham."

A man was strolling up and down the platform in spats and a yellow autumn coat, with a dog on a leash. Never have I seen a handsomer dog: a small, stocky bull, smooth-coated, muscular, with black spots; as well groomed and amusing as the dogs one sees in circuses, who make the audience laugh by dashing round and round the ring with all the energy of their small bodies. This dog had a silver collar, with a plaited leather leash. But all this was not surprising, considering his master, the gentleman in spats, who had beyond a doubt the noblest origins. He wore a monocle, which accentuated without distorting his general air; the defiant perch of his moustache bore out the proud and stubborn expression of his chin and the corners of his mouth. He addressed a question to the martial guard, who knew perfectly well with whom he was dealing and answered hand to cap. My gentleman strolled on, gratified with the impression he had made. He strutted in his spats, his gaze was cold, he regarded men and affairs with penetrating eye. Certainly he was far above feeling journey-proud; travel by train was no novelty to him. He was at home in life, without fear of authority or regulations; he was an authority himself—in short, a nob. I could not look at him enough. When he thought the time had come, he got into the train (the guard had just turned his back). He came along the corridor behind me, bumped into me, and did not apologize. What a man! But that was nothing to what followed. Without turning a hair he took his dog with him into the sleeping-compartment! Surely it was forbidden to do that. When should I presume to take a dog with me into a sleeping-compartment? But he did it, on the strength of his prescriptive rights as a nob, and shut the door behind him.

There came a whistle outside, the locomotive whistled in response, gently the train began to move. I stayed awhile by the window watching the hand-waving and the shifting lights. . . . I retired inside the carriage.

The sleeping-car was not very full, a compartment next to mine was empty and had not been got ready for the night; I decided to make myself comfortable there for an hour's peaceful reading. I fetched my book and settled in. The sofa had a silky salmon-pink covering, an ash-tray stood on the folding table, the light burned bright. I read and smoked.

The sleeping-car attendant entered in pursuance of his duties and asked for my ticket for the night. I delivered it into his grimy hands. He was polite but entirely official, did not even vouchsafe me a good-night as from one human being to another, but went out at once and knocked on the door of the next compartment. He would better have left it alone, for my gentleman of the spats was inside; and perhaps because he did not wish anyone to discover his dog, but possibly because he had really gone to bed, he got furious at anyone daring to disturb him. Above the rumbling of the train I heard his immediate and elemental burst of rage. "What do you want?" he roared. "Leave me alone, you swine." He said "swine." It was a lordly epithet, the epithet of a cavalry officer—it did my heart good to hear it. But the sleeping-car attendant must have resorted to diplomacy—of course he had to have the man's ticket—for just as I stepped into the corridor to get a better view the door of the compartment abruptly opened a little way and the ticket flew out into the attendant's face; yes, it was flung with violence straight in his face. He picked it up with both hands, and though he had got the corner of it in one eye, so that the tears came, he thanked the man, saluting and clicking his heels together. Quite overcome, I returned to my book.

I considered whether there was anything against my smoking another cigar and concluded that there was little or nothing. So I did it, rolling onward and reading; I felt full of contentment and good ideas. Time passed, it was ten o'clock, half past ten, all my fellow-travellers had gone to bed, at last I decided to follow them. I got up and went into my own compartment. A real little bedroom, most luxurious, with stamped leather wall hangings, clothes-hooks, a nickel-plated wash-basin. The lower berth was snowily prepared, the covers invitingly turned back. Oh, triumph of modern times! I thought. One lies in this bed as though at home, it rocks a little all night, and the result is that next morning one is in Dresden. I took my suitcase out of the rack to get ready for bed; I was holding it above my head, with my arms stretched up.

It was at this moment that the railway accident occurred. I remember it like yesterday.

We gave a jerk—but jerk is a poor word for it. It was a jerk of deliberately foul intent, a jerk with a horrid reverberating crash, and so violent that my suitcase leaped out of my hands I knew not whither, while I was flung forcibly with my shoulder against the wall. I had no time to stop and think. But now followed a frightful rocking of the carriage, and while that went on, one had plenty of leisure to be frightened. A railway carriage rocks going over switches or on sharp curves, that we know; but this rocking would not let me stand up, I was thrown from one wall to the other as the carriage careened. I had only one simple thought, but I thought it with concentration, exclusively. I thought: "Something is the matter, something is the matter, something is *very much* the matter!" Just in those words. But later I thought: "Stop, stop, stop!" For I knew that it would be a great help if only the train could be brought to a halt. And lo, at this my unuttered but fervent behest, the train did stop.

Up to now a deathlike stillness had reigned in the carriage, but at this point terror found tongue. Shrill feminine screams mingled with deeper masculine cries of alarm. Next door someone was shouting "Help!" No doubt about it, this was the very same voice which, just previously, had uttered the lordly epithet—the voice of the man in spats, his very voice, though distorted by fear. "Help!" it cried; and just as I stepped into the corridor, where the passengers were collecting, he burst out of his compartment in a silk sleeping-suit and halted, looking wildly round him. "Great God!" he exclaimed, "Almighty God!" and then, as though to abase himself utterly, perhaps in hope to avert destruction, he added in a deprecating tone: "*Dear* God!" But suddenly he thought of something else, of trying to help himself. He threw himself upon the case on the wall where an axe and saw are kept for emergencies, and broke the glass with his fist. But finding that he could not release the tools at once, he abandoned them, buffeted his way through the crowd of passengers, so that the half-dressed women screamed afresh, and leaped out of the carriage.

All that was the work of a moment only. And then for the first time I began to feel the shock: in a certain weakness of the spine, a passing inability to swallow. The sleeping-car attendant, red-eyed, grimy-handed, had just come up; we all pressed round him; the women, with bare arms and shoulders, stood wringing their hands.

The train, he explained, had been derailed, we had run off the track. That, as it afterwards turned out, was not true. But behold, the man in his excitement had become voluble, he abandoned his official neutrality; events had loosened his tongue and he spoke to us in confidence, about his wife. "I told her today, I did. 'Wife,' I said, 'I feel in my bones somethin's goin' to happen.'" And sure enough, hadn't something happened? We all felt how right he had been. The carriage had begun to fill with smoke, a thick smudge; nobody knew where it came from, but we all thought it best to get out into the night.

That could only be done by quite a big jump from the foot-board onto the line, for there was no platform of course, and besides our carriage was canted a good deal towards the opposite side. But the ladies—they had hastily covered their nakedness—jumped in desperation and soon we were all standing there between the lines.

It was nearly dark, but from where we were we could see that no damage had been done at the rear of the train, though all the carriages stood at a slant. But further forward—fifteen or twenty paces further forward! Not for nothing had the jerk we felt made such a horrid crash. There lay a waste of wreckage; we could see the margins of it, with the little lights of the guards' lanterns flickering across and to and fro.

Excited people came towards us, bringing reports of the situation. We were close by a small station not far beyond Regensburg, and as the result of a defective point our express had run onto the wrong line, had crashed at full speed into a stationary freight train, hurling it out of the station, annihilating its rear carriages, and itself sustaining serious damage. The great express engine from Maffei's in Munich lay smashed up and done for. Price seventy thousand marks. And in the forward coaches, themselves lying almost on one side, many of the seats were telescoped. No, thank goodness, there were no lives lost. There was talk of an old woman having been "taken out," but nobody had seen her. At least, people had been thrown in all directions, children buried under luggage, the shock had been great. The baggage car was demolished. Demolished—the baggage car? Demolished.

There I stood.

A bareheaded official came running along the track. The stationmaster. He issued wild and tearful commands to the passengers, to make them behave themselves and get back into the coaches. But nobody took any notice of him, he had no cap and no self-control. Poor wretch! Probably the responsibility was his. Perhaps this was the end of his career, the wreck of his prospects. I could not ask him about the baggage car—it would have been tactless.

Another official came up—he *limped* up. I recognized him by the sergeant-major's moustache; it was the stern and vigilant guard of the early evening—our Father, the State. He limped along, bent over with his hand on his knee, thinking about nothing else. "Oh, dear!" he said, "oh, dear, oh, dear me!" I asked him what was the matter. "I got stuck, sir, jammed me in the chest, I made my escape through the roof." This "made my escape through the roof" sounded like a newspaper report. Certainly the man would not have used the phrase in everyday life; he had experienced not so much an accident as a newspaper account of it—but what was that to me? He was in no state to give me news of my manuscript. So I accosted a young man who came up bustling and self-important from the waste of wreckage, and asked him about the heavy luggage.

"Well, sir, nobody can say anything as to that"—his tone implied that I ought to be grateful to have escaped unhurt. "Everything is all over the place. Women's shoes—" he said with a sweeping gesture to indicate the devastation, and wrinkled his nose. "When they start the clearing operations we shall see. . . . Women's shoes. . . ."

There I stood. All alone I stood there in the night and searched my heart. Clearing operations. Clearing operations were to be undertaken with my manuscript. Probably it was destroyed, then, torn up, demolished. My honeycomb, my spider-web, my nest, my earth, my pride and pain, my all, the best of me— what should I do if it were gone? I had no copy of what had been welded and forged, of what already was a living, speaking thing—to say nothing of my notes and drafts, all that I had saved and stored up and overheard and sweated over for years—my squirrel's hoard. What should I do? I inquired of my own soul and I knew that I should begin over again from the beginning. Yes, with animal patience, with the tenacity of a primitive creature the curious and complex product of whose little ingenuity and industry has been destroyed; after a moment of helpless bewilderment I should set to work again—and perhaps this time it would come easier!

But meanwhile a fire brigade had come up, their torches cast a red light over the wreck; when I went forward and looked for the baggage car, behold it was almost intact, the luggage quite unharmed. All the things that lay strewn about came out of the freight train: among the rest a quantity of balls of string—a perfect sea of string covered the ground far and wide.

A load was lifted from my heart. I mingled with the people who stood talking and fraternizing in misfortune—also showing off and being important. So much seemed clear, that the engine-driver had acted with great presence of mind. He had averted a great catastrophe by pulling the emergency brake at the last moment. Otherwise, it was said, there would have been a general smash and the whole train would have gone over the steep embankment on the left. Oh, praiseworthy engine-driver! He was not about, nobody had seen him, but his fame spread down the whole length of the train and we all lauded him in his absence. "That chap," said one man, and pointed with one hand somewhere off into the night, "that chap saved our lives." We all agreed.

But our train was standing on a track where it did not belong, and it behoved those in charge to guard it from behind so that another one did not run into it. Firemen perched on the rear carriage with torches of flaming pitch, and the excited young man who had given me such a fright with his "women's shoes" seized upon a torch too and began signalling with it, though no train was anywhere in sight.

Slowly and by degrees something like order was produced, the State our Father regained poise and presence. Steps had been taken, wires sent, presently a breakdown train from Regensburg steamed cautiously into the station and great gas flares with reflectors were set up about the wreck. We passengers were now turned off and told to go into the little station building to wait for our new conveyance. Laden with our hand luggage, some of the party with bandaged heads, we passed through a lane of inquisitive natives into the tiny waiting-room, where we herded together as best we could. And inside of an hour we were all stowed higgledy-piggledy into a special train.

I had my first-class ticket—my journey being paid for—but it availed me nothing, for everybody wanted to ride first and my carriage was more crowded than the others. But just as I found me a little niche, whom do I see diagonally opposite to me, huddled in the corner? My hero, the gentleman with the spats and the vocabulary of a cavalry officer. He did not have his dog, it had been taken away from him in defiance of his rights as a nob and now sat howling in a gloomy prison just behind the engine. His master, like myself, held a yellow ticket which was no good to him, and he was grumbling, he was trying to make head against this communistic levelling of rank in the face of general misfortune. But another man answered him in a virtuous tone: "You ought to be thankful that you can sit down." And with a sour smile my gentleman resigned himself to the crazy situation.

And now who got in, supported by two firemen? A wee little old grandmother in a tattered black cape, the very same who in Munich would for two pins have got into a second-class carriage. "Is this the first class?" she kept asking. And when we made room and assured her that it was, she sank down with a "God be praised!" onto the plush cushions as though only now was she safe and sound.

By Hof it was already five o'clock and light. There we breakfasted; an express train picked me up and deposited me with my belongings, three hours late, in Dresden.

Well, that was the railway accident I went through. I suppose it had to happen once; but whatever mathematicians may say, I feel that I now have every chance of escaping another.

EXERCISES

1. Why does the story begin "Tell you a story? But I don't know any"? Why does the narrator feel this incident is a "story" worth telling?

2. What is significant about such references as "literary and artistic pilgrimage," "thanks to the treatments," "do a little work"? Is the narrator's profession important to this story?

3. Why does the narrator spend so much time describing his feeling about traveling on a train, especially his conviction that the train is making a special trip just on his account?

4. What is the significance of the man with the dog? Why does the narrator notice him particularly? Is there any indication that this man will play a role in the story later on?

5. Discuss the paragraph in which the narrator thinks about the possibility that his manuscript has been destroyed. How does he describe the manuscript? In what way does he think of it?

6. What is the significance of the man described as "our Father, the State"?

7. Why do we meet the self-important man and the old woman one last time?

CHARLES W.
CHESNUTT | *The Sheriff's Children*

Branson County, North Carolina, is in a sequestered district of one of the staidest and most conservative States of the Union. Society in Branson County is almost primitive in its simplicity. Most of the white people own the farms they till, and even before the war there were no very wealthy families to force their neighbors, by comparison, into the category of "poor whites."

To Branson County, as to most rural communities in the South, the war is the one historical event that overshadows all others. It is the era from which all local chronicles are dated,—births, deaths, marriages, storms, freshets. No description of the life of any Southern community would be perfect that failed to emphasize the all pervading influence of the great conflict.

Yet the fierce tide of war that had rushed through the cities and along the great highways of the country had comparatively speaking but slightly disturbed the sluggish current of life in this region, remote from railroads and navigable streams. To the north in Virginia, to the west in Tennessee, and all along the seaboard the war had raged; but the thunder of its cannon had not disturbed the echoes of Branson County, where the loudest sounds heard were the crack of some hunter's rifle, the baying of some deep-mouthed hound, or the yodel of some tuneful negro on his way through the pine forest. To the east, Sherman's army had passed on its march to the sea; but no straggling band of "bummers" had penetrated the confines of Branson County. The war, it is true, had robbed the county of the flower of its young manhood; but the burden of taxation, the doubt and uncertainty of the conflict, and the sting of ultimate defeat, had been borne by the people with an apathy that robbed misfortune of half its sharpness.

The nearest approach to town life afforded by Branson County is found in the little village of Troy, the county seat, a hamlet with a population of four or five hundred.

Ten years make little difference in the appearance of these remote Southern towns. If a railroad is built through one of them, it infuses some enterprise; the social corpse is galvanized by the fresh blood of civilization that pulses along the farthest ramifications of our great system of commercial highways. At the period of which I write, no railroad had come to Troy. If a traveler, accustomed to the bustling life of cities, could have ridden through Troy on a summer day, he might easily have fancied himself in a deserted village. Around him he would have seen weather-beaten houses, innocent of paint, the shingled roofs in many instances covered with a rich growth of moss. Here and there he would have met a razor-backed hog lazily rooting his way along the principal thoroughfare; and more than once he would probably have had to disturb the slumbers of some yellow dog, dozing away the hours in the ardent sunshine, and reluctantly yielding up his place in the middle of the dusty road.

On Saturdays the village presented a somewhat livelier appearance, and the shade trees around the court house square and along Front Street served as hitching-posts for a goodly number of horses and mules and stunted oxen, belonging to the farmer-folk who had come in to trade at the two or three local stores.

A murder was a rare event in Branson County. Every well-informed citizen could tell the number of homicides committed in the county for fifty years back, and whether the slayer, in any given instance, had escaped, either by flight or acquittal, or had suffered the penalty of the law. So, when it became known in Troy early one Friday morning in summer, about ten years after the war, that old Captain Walker, who had served in Mexico under Scott, and had left an arm on the field of Gettysburg, had been foully murdered during the night, there was intense excitement in the village. Business was practically suspended, and the citizens gathered in little groups to discuss the murder, and speculate upon the identity of the murderer. It transpired from testimony at the coroner's inquest, held during the morning, that a strange mulatto had been seen going in the direction of Captain Walker's house the night before, and had been met going away from Troy early Friday morning, by a farmer on his way to town. Other circumstances seemed to connect the stranger with the crime. The sheriff organized a posse to search for him, and early in the evening, when most of the citizens of Troy were at supper, the suspected man was brought in and lodged in the county jail.

By the following morning the news of the capture had spread to the farthest limits of the county. A much larger number of people than usual came to town that Saturday,—bearded men in straw hats and blue homespun shirts, and butternut trousers of great amplitude of material and vagueness of outline; women in homespun frocks and slat-bonnets, with faces as expressionless as the dreary sandhills which gave them a meagre sustenance.

The murder was almost the sole topic of conversation. A steady stream of curious observers visited the house of mourning, and gazed upon the rugged face of the old veteran, now stiff and cold in death; and more than one eye dropped a tear at the remembrance of the cheery smile, and the joke—sometimes superannuated, generally feeble, but always good-natured—with which the captain had been wont to greet his acquaintances. There was a growing sentiment of anger among these stern men, toward the murderer who had thus cut down their friend, and a strong feeling that ordinary justice was too slight a punishment for such a crime.

Toward noon there was an informal gathering of citizens in Dan Tyson's store.

"I hear it 'lowed that Square Kyahtah's too sick ter hol' co'te this evenin'," said one, "an' that the purlim'nary hearin' 'll haf ter go over 'tel nex' week."

A look of disappointment went round the crowd.

"Hit 's the durndes', meanes' murder ever committed in this caounty," said another, with moody emphasis.

"I s'pose the nigger 'lowed the Cap'n had some greenbacks," observed a third speaker.

"The Cap'n," said another, with an air of superior information, "has left two bairls of Confedrit money, which he 'spected 'ud be good some day er nuther."

This statement gave rise to a discussion of the speculative value of Confederate money; but in a little while the conversation returned to the murder.

"Hangin' air too good fer the murderer," said one; "he oughter be burnt, stidier bein' hung."

There was an impressive pause at this point, during which a jug of moonlight whiskey went the round of the crowd.

"Well," said a round-shouldered farmer, who, in spite of his peaceable expression and faded gray eye, was known to have been one of the most daring followers of a rebel guerrilla chieftain, "what air yer gwine ter do about it? Ef you fellers air gwine ter set down an' let a wuthless nigger kill the bes' white man in Branson, an' not say nuthin' ner do nuthin', I'll move outen the caounty."

This speech gave tone and direction to the rest of the conversation. Whether the fear of losing the round-shouldered farmer operated to bring about the result or not is immaterial to this narrative; but, at all events, the crowd decided to lynch the negro. They agreed that this was the least that could be done to avenge the death of their murdered friend, and that it was a becoming way in which to honor his memory. They had some vague notions of the majesty of the law and the rights of the citizen, but in the passion of the moment these sunk into oblivion; a white man had been killed by a negro.

"The Cap'n was an ole sodger," said one of his friends solemnly. "He'll sleep better when he knows that a co'temartial has be'n hilt an' jestice done."

By agreement the lynchers were to meet at Tyson's store at five o'clock in the afternoon, and proceed thence to the jail, which was situated down the Lumberton Dirt Road (as the old turnpike antedating the plank-road was called), about half a mile south of the courthouse. When the preliminaries of the lynching had been arranged, and a committee appointed to manage the affair, the crowd dispersed, some to go to their dinners, and some to secure recruits for the lynching party.

It was twenty minutes to five o'clock, when an excited negro, panting and perspiring, rushed up to the back door of Sheriff Campbell's dwelling, which stood at a little distance from the jail and somewhat farther than the latter building from the courthouse. A turbaned colored woman came to the door in response to the negro's knock.

"Hoddy, Sis' Nance."

"Hoddy, Brer Sam."

"Is de shurff in," inquired the negro.

"Yas, Brer Sam, he's eatin' his dinner," was the answer.

"Will yer ax 'im ter step ter de do' a minute, Sis' Nance?"

The woman went into the dining-room, and a moment later the sheriff came to the door. He was a tall, muscular man, of a ruddier complexion than is usual among Southerners. A pair of keen, deep-set gray eyes looked out from under bushy eyebrows, and about his mouth was a masterful expression, which a full beard, once sandy in color, but now profusely sprinkled with gray, could not entirely conceal. The day was hot; the sheriff had discarded his coat and vest, and had his white shirt open at the throat.

"What do you want, Sam?" he inquired of the negro, who stood hat in hand, wiping the moisture from his face with a ragged shirt-sleeve.

"Shurff, dey gwine ter hang de pris'ner w'at's lock' up in de jail. Dey're comin' dis a-way now. I wuz layin' down on a sack er corn down at de sto', behine a pile er flour-bairls, w'en I hearn Doc' Cain en Kunnel Wright talkin' erbout it. I slip' outen de back do', en run here as fas' as I could. I hearn you say down ter de sto' once't dat you would n't let nobody take a pris'ner 'way fum you widout walkin' over yo' dead body, en I thought I'd let you know 'fo' dey come, so yer could pertec' de pris'ner."

The sheriff listened calmly, but his face grew firmer, and a determined gleam lit up his gray eyes. His frame grew more erect, and he unconsciously assumed the attitude of a soldier who momentarily expects to meet the enemy face to face.

"Much obliged, Sam," he answered. "I'll protect the prisoner. Who's coming?"

"I dunno who-all *is* comin'," replied the negro. "Dere's Mistah McSwayne, en Doc' Cain, en Maje' McDonal', en Kunnel Wright, en a heap er yuthers. I wuz so skeered I done furgot mo' d'n half un em. I spec' dey mus' be mos' here by dis time, so I'll git outen de way, fer I don't want nobody fer ter think I wux mix' up in dis business." The negro glanced nervously down the road toward the town, and made a movement as if to go away.

"Won't you have some dinner first?" asked the sheriff.

The negro looked longingly in at the open door, and sniffed the appetizing odor of boiled pork and collards.

"I ain't got no time fer ter tarry, Shurff," he said, "but Sis' Nance mought gin me sump'n I could kyar in my han' en eat on de way."

A moment later Nancy brought him a huge sandwich of split corn-pone, with a thick slice of fat bacon inserted between the halves, and a couple a baked yams. The negro hastily replaced his ragged hat on his head, dropped the yams in the pocket of his capacious trousers, and, taking the sandwich in his hand, hurried across the road and disappeared in the woods beyond.

The sheriff reentered the house, and put on his coat and hat. He then took down a double-barreled shotgun and loaded it with buckshot. Filling the chambers of a revolver with fresh cartridges, he slipped it into the pocket of the sack-coat which he wore.

A comely young woman in a calico dress watched these proceedings with anxious surprise.

"Where are you going, father?" she asked. She had not heard the conversation with the negro.

"I am goin' over to the jail," responded the sheriff. "There's a mob comin' this way to lynch the nigger we've got locked up. But they won't do it," he added, with emphasis.

"Oh, father! don't go!" pleaded the girl, clinging to his arm; "they'll shoot you if you don't give him up."

"You never mind me, Polly," said her father reassuringly, as he gently unclasped her hands from his arm. "I'll take care of myself and the prisoner, too. There ain't a man in Branson County that would shoot me. Besides, I have faced fire too often to be scared away from my duty. You keep close in the house," he continued, "and if any one disturbs you just use the old horse-pistol in the top bureau drawer. It's a little old-fashioned, but it did good work a few years ago."

The young girl shuddered at this sanguinary allusion, but made no further objection to her father's departure.

The sheriff of Branson was a man far above the average of the community in wealth, education, and social position. His had been one of the few families in the county that before the war had owned large estates and numerous slaves. He had graduated at the State University at Chapel Hill, and had kept up some acquaintance with current literature and advanced thought. He had traveled some in his youth, and was looked up to in the county as an authority on all subjects connected with the outer world. At first an ardent supporter of the Union, he had opposed the secession movement in his native State as long as opposition availed to stem the tide of public opinion. Yielding at last to the force of circumstances, he had entered the Confederate service rather late in the war, and served with distinction through several campaigns, rising in time to the rank of colonel. After the war he had taken the oath of allegiance, and had been chosen by the people as the most available candidate for the office of sheriff, to which he had been elected without opposition. He had filled the office for several terms, and was universally popular with his constituents.

Colonel or Sheriff Campbell, as he was indifferently called, as the military or civil title happened to be most important in the opinion of the person addressing him, had a high sense of the responsibility attaching to his office. He had sworn to do his duty faithfully, and he knew what his duty was, as sheriff, perhaps more clearly than he had apprehended it in other passages of his life. It was, therefore, with no uncertainty in regard to his course that he prepared his weapons and went over to the jail. He had no fears for Polly's safety.

The sheriff had just locked the heavy front door of the jail behind him when a half dozen horsemen, followed by a crowd of men on foot, came round a bend in the road and drew near the jail. They halted in front of the picket fence that surrounded the building, while several of the committee of arrangements rode on a few rods farther to the sheriff's house. One of them dismounted and rapped on the door with his riding-whip.

"Is the sheriff at home?" he inquired.

"No, he has just gone out," replied Polly, who had come to the door.

"We want the jail keys," he continued.

"They are not here," said Polly. "The sheriff has them himself." Then she added, with assumed indifference, "He is at the jail now."

The man turned away, and Polly went into the front room, from which she peered anxiously between the slats of the green blinds of a window that looked toward the jail. Meanwhile the messenger returned to his companions and announced his discovery. It looked as though the sheriff had learned of their design and was preparing to resist it.

One of them stepped forward and rapped on the jail door.

"Well, what is it?" said the sheriff, from within.

"We want to talk to you, Sheriff," replied the spokesman.

There was a little wicket in the door; this the sheriff opened, and answered through it.

"All right, boys, talk away. You are all strangers to me, and I don't know what business you can have." The sheriff did not think it necessary to recognize anybody in particular on such an occasion; the question of identity sometimes comes up in the investigation of these extra-judicial executions.

"We're a committee of citizens and we want to get into the jail."

"What for? It ain't much trouble to get into jail. Most people want to keep out."

The mob was in no humor to appreciate a joke, and the sheriff's witticism fell dead upon an unresponsive audience.

"We want to have a talk with the nigger that killed Cap'n Walker."

"You can talk to that nigger in the courthouse, when he's brought out for trial. Court will be in session here next week. I know what you fellows want, but you can't get my prisoner to-day. Do you want to take the bread out of a poor man's mouth? I get seventy-five cents a day for keeping this prisoner, and he's the only one in jail. I can't have my family suffer just to please you fellows."

One or two young men in the crowd laughed at the idea of Sheriff Campbell's suffering for want of seventy-five cents a day; but they were frowned into silence by those who stood near them.

"Ef yer don't let us in," cried a voice, "we'll bu's' the do' open."

"Bust away," answered the sheriff, raising his voice so that all could hear. "But I give you fair warning. The first man that tries it will be filled with buckshot. I'm sheriff of this county; I know my duty, and I mean to do it."

"What's the use of kicking, Sheriff?" argued one of the leaders of the mob. "The nigger is sure to hang anyhow; he richly deserves it; and we've got to do something to teach the niggers their places, or white people won't be able to live in the county."

"There's no use talking, boys," responded the sheriff. "I'm a white man outside, but in this jail I'm sheriff; and if this nigger's to be hung in this county, I propose to do the hanging. So you fellows might as well right-about-face, and march back to Troy. You've had a pleasant trip, and the exercise will be good for you. You know *me.* I've got powder and ball, and I've faced fire before now, with nothing between me and the enemy, and I don't mean to surrender this jail while I'm able to shoot." Having thus announced his determination, the sheriff closed and fastened the wicket, and looked around for the best position from which to defend the building.

The crowd drew off a little, and the leaders conversed together in low tones.

The Branson County jail was a small, two-story brick building, strongly constructed, with no attempt at architectural ornamentation. Each story was divided into two large cells by a passage running from front to rear. A grated iron door gave entrance from the passage to each of the four cells. The jail seldom had many prisoners in it, and the lower windows had been boarded up. When the sheriff had closed the wicket, he ascended the steep wooden stairs to the upper floor. There was no window at the front of the upper passage, and the most available position from which to watch the movements of the crowd below was the front window of the cell occupied by the solitary prisoner.

The sheriff unlocked the door and entered the cell. The prisoner was crouched in a corner, his yellow face, blanched with terror, looking ghastly in the semi-darkness of the room. A cold perspiration had gathered on his forehead, and his teeth were chattering with affright.

"For God's sake, Sheriff," he murmured hoarsely, "don't let 'em lynch me; I did n't kill the old man."

The sheriff glanced at the cowering wretch with a look of mingled contempt and loathing.

"Get up," he said sharply. "You will probably be hung sooner or later, but it shall not be to-day, if I can help it. I'll unlock your fetters, and if I can't hold the jail, you'll have to make the best fight you can. If I'm shot, I'll consider my responsibility at an end."

There were iron fetters on the prisoner's ankles, and handcuffs on his wrists. These the sheriff unlocked, and they fell clanking to the floor.

"Keep back from the window," said the sheriff. "They might shoot if they saw you."

The sheriff drew toward the window a pine bench which formed a part of the scanty furniture of the cell, and laid his revolver upon it. Then he took his gun in hand, and took his stand at the side of the window where he could with least exposure of himself watch the movements of the crowd below.

The lynchers had not anticipated any determined resistance. Of course they had looked for a formal protest, and perhaps a sufficient show of opposition to excuse the sheriff in the eye of any stickler for legal formalities. They had not however come prepared to fight a battle, and no one of them seemed willing to lead an attack upon the jail. The leaders of the party conferred together with a good deal of animated gesticulation, which was visible to the sheriff from his outlook, though the distance was too great for him to hear what was said. At length one of them broke away from the group, and rode back to the main body of the lynchers, who were restlessly awaiting orders.

"Well, boys," said the messenger, "we'll have to let it go for the present. The sheriff says he'll shoot, and he's got the drop on us this time. There ain't any of us that want to follow Cap'n Walker jest yet. Besides, the sheriff is a good fellow, and we don't want to hurt 'im. But," he added, as if to reassure the crowd, which began to show signs of disappointment, "the nigger might as well say his prayers, for he ain't got long to live."

There was a murmur of dissent from the mob, and several voices insisted that an attack be made on the jail. But pacific counsels finally prevailed, and the mob sullenly withdrew.

The sheriff stood at the window until they had disappeared around the bend in the road. He did not relax his watchfulness when the last one was out of sight. Their withdrawal might be a mere feint, to be followed by a further attempt. So closely, indeed, was his attention drawn to the outside, that he neither saw nor heard the prisoner creep stealthily across the floor, reach out his hand and secure the revolver which lay on the bench behind the sheriff, and creep as noiselessly back to his place in the corner of the room.

A moment after the last of the lynching party had disappeared there was a shot fired from the woods across the road; a bullet whistled by the window and buried itself in the wooden casing a few inches from where the sheriff was standing. Quick as thought, with the instinct born of a semi-guerrilla army experience, he raised his gun and fired twice at the point from which a faint puff of smoke showed the hostile bullet to have been sent. He stood a moment watching, and then rested his gun against the window, and reached behind him mechanically for the other weapon. It was not on the bench. As the sheriff realized this fact, he turned his head and looked into the muzzle of the revolver.

"Stay where you are, Sheriff," said the prisoner, his eyes glistening, his face almost ruddy with excitement.

The sheriff mentally cursed his own carelessness for allowing him to be caught in such a predicament. He had not expected anything of the kind. He had relied on the negro's cowardice and subordination in the presence of an armed white man as a matter of course. The sheriff was a brave man, but realized that the prisoner had him at an immense disadvantage. The two men stood thus for a moment, fighting a harmless duel with their eyes.

"Well, what do you mean to do?" asked the sheriff with apparent calmness.

"To get away, of course," said the prisoner, in a tone which caused the sheriff to look at him more closely, and with an involuntary feeling of apprehension; if the man was not mad, he was in a state of mind akin to madness, and quite as dangerous. The sheriff felt that he must speak the prisoner fair, and watch for a chance to turn the tables on him. The keen-eyed, desperate man before him was a different being altogether from the groveling wretch who had begged so piteously for life a few minutes before.

At length the sheriff spoke:—

"Is this your gratitude to me for saving your life at the risk of my own? If I had not done so, you would now be swinging from the limb of some neighboring tree."

"True," said the prisoner, "you saved my life, but for how long? When you came in, you said Court would sit next week. When the crowd went away they said I had not long to live. It is merely a choice of two ropes."

"While there's life there's hope," replied the sheriff. He uttered this commonplace mechanically, while his brain was busy in trying to think out some way of escape. "If you are innocent you can prove it."

The mulatto kept his eye upon the sheriff. "I didn't kill the old man," he replied; "but I shall never be able to clear myself. I was at his house at nine o'clock. I stole from it the coat that was on my back when I was taken. I would be convicted, even with a fair trial, unless the real murderer were discovered beforehand."

The sheriff knew this only too well. While he was thinking what argument next to use, the prisoner continued:—

"Throw me the keys—no, unlock the door."

The sheriff stood a moment irresolute. The mulatto's eye glittered ominously. The sheriff crossed the room and unlocked the door leading into the passage.

"Now go down and unlock the outside door."

The heart of the sheriff leaped within him. Perhaps he might make a dash for liberty, and gain the outside. He descended the narrow stairs, the prisoner keeping close behind him.

The sheriff inserted the huge iron key into the lock. The rusty bolt yielded slowly. It still remained for him to pull the door open.

"Stop!" thundered the mulatto, who seemed to divine the sheriff's purpose. "Move a muscle, and I'll blow your brains out."

The sheriff obeyed; he realized that his chance had not yet come.

"Now keep on that side of the passage, and go back upstairs."

Keeping the sheriff under cover of the revolver, the mulatto followed him up the stairs. The sheriff expected the prisoner to lock him into the cell and make his own escape. He had about come to the conclusion that the best thing he could do under the circumstances was to submit quietly, and take his chances of recapturing the prisoner after the alarm had been given. The sheriff had faced death more than once upon the battlefield. A few minutes before, well armed, and with a brick wall between him and them he had dared a hundred men to fight; but he felt instinctively that the desperate man confronting him was not to be trifled with, and he was too prudent a man to risk his life against such heavy odds. He had Polly to look after, and there was a limit beyond which devotion to duty would be quixotic and even foolish.

"I want to get away," said the prisoner, "and I don't want to be captured; for if I am I know I will be hung on the spot. I am afraid," he added somewhat reflectively, "that in order to save myself I shall have to kill you."

"Good God!" exclaimed the sheriff in involuntary terror; "you would not kill the man to whom you owe your own life."

"You speak more truly than you know," replied the mulatto. "I indeed owe my life to you."

The sheriff started. He was capable of surprise, even in that moment of extreme peril. "Who are you?" he asked in amazement.

"Tom, Cicely's son," returned the other. He had closed the door and stood talking to the sheriff through the grated opening. "Don't you remember Cicely—Cicely whom you sold, with her child, to the speculator on his way to Alabama?"

The sheriff did remember. He had been sorry for it many a time since. It had been the old story of debts, mortgages, and bad crops. He had quarreled with the mother. The price offered for her and her child had been unusually large, and he had yielded to the combination of anger and pecuniary stress.

"Good God!" he gasped, "you would not murder your own father?"

"My father?" replied the mulatto. "It were well enough for me to claim the relationship, but it comes with poor grace from you to ask anything by reason of it. What father's duty have you ever performed for me? Did you give me your name, or even your protection? Other white men gave their colored sons freedom and money, and sent them to the free States. You sold *me* to the rice swamps."

"I at least gave you the life you cling to," murmured the sheriff.

"Life?" said the prisoner, with a sarcastic laugh. "What kind of life? You gave me your own blood, your own features,—no man need look at us together twice to see that,—and you gave me a black mother. Poor wretch! She died under the lash, because she had enough womanhood to call her soul her own. You gave me a white man's spirit, and you made me a slave, and crushed it out."

"But you are free now," said the sheriff. He had not doubted, could not doubt, the mulatto's word. He knew whose passions coursed beneath that swarthy skin and burned in the black eyes opposite his own. He saw in this mulatto what he himself might have become had not the safeguards of parental restraint and public opinion been thrown around him.

"Free to do what?" replied the mulatto. "Free in name, but despised and scorned and set aside by the people to whose race I belong far more than to my mother's."

"There are schools," said the sheriff. "You have been to school." He had noticed that the mulatto spoke more eloquently and used better language than most Branson County people.

"I have been to school, and dreamed when I went that it would work some marvelous change in my condition. But what did I learn? I learned to feel that no degree of learning or wisdom will change the color of my skin and that I shall always wear what in my own country is a badge of degradation. When I think about it seriously I do not care particularly for such a life. It is the animal in me, not the man, that flees the gallows. I owe you nothing," he went on, "and expect nothing of you; and it would be no more than justice if I should avenge upon you my mother's wrongs and my own. But still I hate to shoot you; I have never yet taken human life—for I did *not* kill the old captain. Will you promise to give no alarm and make no attempt to capture me until morning, if I do not shoot?"

So absorbed were the two men in their colloquy and their own tumultuous thoughts that neither of them had heard the door below move upon its hinges. Neither of them had heard a light step come stealthily up the stairs, nor seen a slender form creep along the darkening passage toward the mulatto.

The sheriff hesitated. The struggle between his love of life and his sense of duty was a terrific one. It may seem strange that a man who could sell his own child into slavery should hesitate at such a moment, when his life was trembling in the balance. But the baleful influence of human slavery poisoned the very fountains of life and created new standards of right. The sheriff was conscientious; his conscience had merely been warped by his environment. Let no one ask what his answer would have been; he was spared the necessity of a decision.

"Stop," said the mulatto, "you need not promise. I could not trust you if you did. It is your life for mine; there is but one safe way for me; you must die."

He raised his arm to fire, when there was a flash—a report from the passage behind him. His arm fell heavily at his side, and the pistol dropped at his feet.

The sheriff recovered first from his surprise, and throwing open the door secured the fallen weapon. Then seizing the prisoner he thrust him into the cell and locked the door upon him; after which he turned to Polly, who leaned half-fainting against the wall, her hands clasped over her heart.

"Oh, father, I was just in time!" she cried hysterically, and, wildly sobbing, threw herself into her father's arms.

"I watched until they all went away," she said. "I heard the shot from the woods and I saw you shoot. Then when you did not come out I feared something had happened, that perhaps you had been wounded. I got out the other pistol and ran over here. When I found the door open, I knew something was wrong and when I heard voices I crept upstairs, and reached the top just in time to hear him say he would kill you. Oh, it was a narrow escape!"

When she had grown somewhat calmer, the sheriff left her standing there and went back into the cell. The prisoner's arm was bleeding from a flesh wound. His bravado had given place to a stony apathy. There was no sign in his face of fear or disappointment or feeling of any kind. The sheriff sent Polly to the house for cloth, and bound up the prisoner's wound with a rude skill acquired during his army life.

"I'll have a doctor come and dress the wound in the morning," he said to the prisoner. "It will do very well until then, if you will keep quiet. If the doctor asks you how the wound was caused, you can say that you were struck by the bullet fired from the woods. It would do you no good to have it known that you were shot while attempting to escape."

The prisoner uttered no word of thanks or apology, but sat in sullen silence. When the wounded arm had been bandaged, Polly and her father returned to the house.

The sheriff was in an unusually thoughtful mood that evening. He put salt in his coffee at supper, and poured vinegar over his pancakes. To many of Polly's questions he returned random answers. When he had gone to bed he lay awake for several hours.

In the silent watches of the night, when he was alone with God, there came into his mind a flood of unaccustomed thoughts. An hour or two before, standing face to face with death, he had experienced a sensation similar to that which drowning men are said to feel—a kind of clarifying of the moral faculty, in which the veil of the flesh, with its obscuring passions and prejudices, is pushed aside for a moment, and all the acts of one's life stand out, in the clear light of truth, in their correct proportions and relations,—a state of mind in which one sees himself as God may be supposed to see him. In the reaction following his rescue, this feeling had given place for a time to far different emotions. But now, in the silence of midnight, something of this clearness of spirit returned to the sheriff. He saw that he had owed some duty to this son of his,—that neither law nor custom could destroy a responsibility inherent in the nature of mankind. He could not thus, in the eyes of God at least, shake off the consequences of his sin. Had he never sinned, this wayward spirit would never have come back from the vanished past to haunt him. As these thoughts came, his anger against the mulatto died away, and in its place there sprang up a great pity. The hand of parental authority might have restrained the passions he had seen burning in the prisoner's eyes when the desperate man spoke the words which had seemed to doom his father to death. The sheriff felt that he might have saved this fiery spirit from the slough of slavery; that he might have sent him to the free North, and given him there, or in some other land, an opportunity to turn to usefulness and honorable pursuits the talents that had run to crime, perhaps to madness; he might, still less, have given this son of his the poor simulacrum of liberty which men of his caste could possess in a slave-holding community; or least of all, but still something, he might have kept the boy on the plantation, where the burdens of slavery would have fallen lightly upon him.

The sheriff recalled his own youth. He had inherited an honored name to keep untarnished; he had had a future to make; the picture of a fair young bride had beckoned him on to happiness. The poor wretch now stretched upon a pallet of straw between the brick walls of the jail had had none of these things,—no name, no father, no mother—in the true meaning of motherhood,—and until the past few years no possible future, and then one vague and shadowy in its outline, and dependent for form and substance upon the slow solution of a problem in which there were many unknown quantities.

From what he might have done to what he might yet do was an easy transition for the awakened conscience of the sheriff. It occurred to him, purely as a hypothesis, that he might permit his prisoner to escape; but his oath of office, his duty as sheriff, stood in the way of such a course, and the sheriff dismissed the idea from his mind. He could, however, investigate the circumstances of the murder, and move Heaven and earth to discover the real criminal, for he no longer doubted the prisoner's innocence; he could employ counsel for the accused, and perhaps influence public opinion in his favor. An acquittal once secured, some plan could be devised by which the sheriff might in some degree atone for his crime against this son of his—against society—against God.

When the sheriff had reached this conclusion he fell into an unquiet slumber, from which he awoke late the next morning.

He went over to the jail before breakfast and found the prisoner lying on his pallet, his face turned to the wall; he did not move when the sheriff rattled the door.

"Good-morning," said the latter, in a tone intended to waken the prisoner.

There was no response. The sheriff looked more keenly at the recumbent figure; there was an unnatural rigidity about its attitude.

He hastily unlocked the door and, entering the cell, bent over the prostrate form. There was no sound of breathing; he turned the body over—it was cold and stiff. The prisoner had torn the bandage from his wound and bled to death during the night. He had evidently been dead several hours.

EXERCISES

1. Discuss the relevance of the extended description of Branson County, North Carolina. How is the particular nature of the place important in this story?

2. Discuss the image of the black man Sam in the story. Is he realistic, or is he a stereotype?

3. Discuss the character of the sheriff created in the story. Is he realistic, or is he a stereotype?
4. Discuss the character of the prisoner. What kind of character is he given? How is his particular character important to the events of the story?
5. Discuss the dialogue scene between the sheriff and the prisoner. How much of the conflict and character is communicated by dialogue? How much is communicated by the author's exposition and description?
6. Why does the prisoner have to die in the end? Is his death necessary for the theme of the story?
7. Discuss the significance of the title of the story.

CARSON
McCULLERS | *A Tree, A Rock, A Cloud*

It was raining that morning, and still very dark. When the boy reached the streetcar café he had almost finished his route and he went in for a cup of coffee. The place was an all-night café owned by a bitter and stingy man called Leo. After the raw, empty street, the café seemed friendly and bright: along the counter there were a couple of soldiers, three spinners from the cotton mill, and in a corner a man who sat hunched over with his nose and half his face down in a beer mug. The boy wore a helmet such as aviators wear. When he went into the café he unbuckled the chin strap and raised the right flap up over his pink little ear; often as he drank his coffee someone would speak to him in a friendly way. But this morning Leo did not look into his face and none of the men were talking. He paid and was leaving the café when a voice called out to him:

"Son! Hey Son!"

He turned back and the man in the corner was crooking his finger and nodding to him. He had brought his face out of the beer mug and he seemed suddenly very happy. The man was long and pale, with a big nose and faded orange hair.

"Hey Son!"

The boy went toward him. He was an undersized boy of about twelve, with one shoulder drawn higher than the other because of the weight of the paper sack. His face was shallow, freckled, and his eyes were round child eyes.

"Yeah Mister?"

The man laid one hand on the paper boy's shoulders, then grasped the boy's chin and turned his face slowly from one side to the other. The boy shrank back uneasily.

"Say! What's the big idea?"

The boy's voice was shrill; inside the café it was suddenly very quiet.

The man said slowly, "I love you."

All along the counter the men laughed. The boy, who had scowled and sidled away, did not know what to do. He looked over the counter at Leo, and Leo watched him with a weary, brittle jeer. The boy tried to laugh also. But the man was serious and sad.

"I did not mean to tease you, Son," he said. "Sit down and have a beer with me. There is something I have to explain."

Cautiously, out of the corner of his eye, the paper boy questioned the men along the counter to see what he should do. But they had gone back to their beer or their breakfast and did not notice him. Leo put a cup of coffee on the counter and a little jug of cream.

"He is a minor," Leo said.

The paper boy slid himself up onto the stool. His ear beneath the upturned flap of the helmet was very small and red. The man was nodding at him soberly. "It is important," he said. Then he reached in his hip pocket and brought out something which he held up in the palm of his hand for the boy to see.

"Look very carefully," he said.

The boy stared, but there was nothing to look at very carefully. The man held in his big, grimy palm a photograph. It was the face of a woman, but blurred, so that only the hat and the dress she was wearing stood out clearly.

"See?" the man asked.

The boy nodded and the man placed another picture in his palm. The woman was standing on a beach in a bathing suit. The suit made her stomach very big, and that was the main thing you noticed.

"Got a good look?" He leaned over closer and finally asked: "You ever seen her before?"

The boy sat motionless, staring slantwise at the man. "Not so I know of."

"Very well." The man blew on the photographs and put them back into his pocket. "That was my wife."

"Dead?" the boy asked.

Slowly the man shook his head. He pursed his lips as though about to whistle and answered in a long-drawn way: "Nuuu—" he said. "I will explain."

The beer on the counter before the man was in a large brown mug. He did not pick it up to drink. Instead he bent down and, putting his face over the rim, he rested there for a moment. Then with both hands he tilted the mug and sipped.

"Some night you'll go to sleep with your big nose in a mug and drown," said Leo. "Prominent transient drowns in beer. That would be a cute death."

The paper boy tried to signal to Leo. While the man was not looking he screwed up his face and worked his mouth to question soundlessly: "Drunk?" But Leo only raised his eyebrows and turned away to put some pink strips of bacon on the grill. The man pushed the mug away from him, straightened himself, and folded his loose crooked hands on the counter. His face was sad as he looked at the paper boy. He did not blink, but from time to time the lids closed down with delicate gravity over his pale green eyes. It was nearing dawn and the boy shifted the weight of the paper sack.

"I am talking about love," the man said. "With me it is a science."

The boy half slid down from the stool. But the man raised his forefinger, and there was something about him that held the boy and would not let him go away.

"Twelve years ago I married the woman in the photograph. She was my wife for one year, nine months, three days, and two nights. I loved her. Yes. . . ." He tightened his blurred, rambling voice and said again: "I loved her. I thought also that she loved me. I was a railroad engineer. She had all home comforts and luxuries. It never crept into my brain that she was not satisfied. But do you know what happened?"

"Mgneeow!" said Leo.

The man did not take his eyes from the boy's face. "She left me. I came in one night and the house was empty and she was gone. She left me."

"With a fellow?" the boy asked.

Gently the man placed his palm down on the counter. "Why naturally, Son. A woman does not run off like that alone."

The café was quiet, the soft rain black and endless in the street outside. Leo pressed down the frying bacon with the prongs of his long fork. "So you have been chasing the floozie for eleven years. You frazzled old rascal!"

For the first time the man glanced at Leo. "Please don't be vulgar. Besides, I was not speaking to you." He turned back to the boy and said in a trusting and secretive undertone, "Let's not pay any attention to him. O.K.?"

The paper boy nodded doubtfully.

"It was like this," the man continued. "I am a person who feels many things. All of my life one thing after another has impressed me. Moonlight. The leg of a pretty girl. One thing after another. But the point is that when I had enjoyed anything there was a peculiar sensation as though it was laying around loose in me. Nothing seemed to finish itself up or fit in with the other things. Women? I had my portion of them. The same. Afterwards laying around loose in me. I was a man who had never loved."

Very slowly he closed his eyelids, and the gesture was like a curtain drawn at the end of a scene in a play. When he spoke again his voice was excited and the words came fast—the lobes of his large, loose ears seemed to tremble.

"Then I met this woman. I was fifty-one years old and she always said she was thirty. I met her at a filling station and we were married within three days. And do you know what it was like? I just can't tell you. All I had ever felt was gathered together around this woman. Nothing lay around loose in me any more but was finished up by her."

The man stopped suddenly and stroked his long nose. His voice sank down to a steady and reproachful undertone: "I'm not explaining this right. What happened was this. There were these beautiful feelings and loose little pleasures inside me. And this woman was something like an assembly line for my soul. I run these little pieces of myself through her and I come out complete. Now do you follow me?"

"What was her name?" the boy asked.

"Oh," he said. "I called her Dodo. But that is immaterial."

"Did you try to make her come back?"

The man did not seem to hear. "Under the circumstances you can imagine how I felt when she left me."

Leo took the bacon from the grill and folded two strips of it between a bun. He had a gray face, with slitted eyes, and a pinched nose saddled by faint blue shadows. One of the mill workers signaled for more coffee and Leo poured it. He did not give refills on coffee free. The spinner ate breakfast there every morning, but the better Leo knew his customers the stingier he treated them. He nibbled his own bun as though he grudged it to himself.

"And you never got hold of her again?"

The boy did not know what to think of the man, and his child's face was uncertain with mingled curiosity and doubt. He was new on the paper route; it was still strange to him to be out in the town in the black, queer early morning.

"Yes," the man said. "I took a number of steps to get her back. I went around trying to locate her. I went to Tulsa where she had folks. And to Mobile. I went to every town she had ever mentioned to me, and I hunted down every man she had formerly been connected with. Tulsa, Atlanta, Chicago, Cheehaw, Memphis. . . . For the better part of two years I chased around the country trying to lay hold of her."

"But the pair of them had vanished from the face of the earth!" said Leo.

"Don't listen to him," the man said confidentially. "And also just forget those two years. They are not important. What matters is that around the third year a curious thing began to happen to me."

"What?" the boy asked.

The man leaned down and tilted his mug to take a sip of beer. But as he hovered over the mug his nostrils fluttered slightly; he sniffled the staleness of the beer and did not drink. "Love is a curious thing to begin with. At first I thought only of getting her back. It was a kind of mania. But then as time went on I tried to remember her. But do you know what happened?"

"No," the boy said.

"When I laid myself down on a bed and tried to think about her my mind became a blank. I couldn't see her. I would take out her pictures and look. No good. Nothing doing. A blank. Can you imagine it?"

"Say, Mac!" Leo called down the counter. "Can you imagine this bozo's mind a blank!"

Slowly, as though fanning away flies, the man waved his hand. His green eyes were concentrated and fixed on the shallow little face of the paper boy.

"But a sudden piece of glass on a sidewalk. Or a nickel tune in a music box. A shadow on a wall at night. And I would remember. It might happen in a street and I would cry or bang my head against a lamppost. You follow me?"

"A piece of glass . . ." the boy said.

"Anything. I would walk around and I had no power of how and when to remember her. You think you can put up a kind of shield. But remembering don't come to a man face forward—it corners around sideways. I was at the mercy of everything I saw and heard. Suddenly instead of me combing the countryside to find her she began to chase me around in my very soul. *She* chasing *me*, mind you! and in my soul."

The boy asked finally: "What part of the country were you in then?"

"Ooh," the man groaned. "I was a sick mortal. It was like smallpox. I confess, Son, that I boozed. I fornicated. I committed any sin that suddenly appealed to me. I am loath to confess it but I will do so. When I recall that period it is all curdled in my mind, it was so terrible."

The man leaned his head down and tapped his forehead on the counter. For a few seconds he stayed bowed over in this position, the back of his stringy neck covered with orange furze, his hands with their long warped fingers held palm to palm in an attitude of prayer. Then the man straightened himself; he was smiling and suddenly his face was bright and tremulous and old.

"It was in the fifth year that it happened," he said. "And with it I started my science."

Leo's mouth jerked with a pale, quick grin. "Well none of we boys are getting any younger," he said. Then with sudden anger he balled up a dishcloth he was holding and threw it down hard on the floor. "You draggle-tailed old Romeo!"

"What happened?" the boy asked.

The old man's voice was high and clear: "Peace," he answered.

"Huh?"

"It is hard to explain scientifically, Son," he said. "I guess the logical explanation is that she and I had fleed around from each other for so long that finally we just got tangled up together and lay down and quit. Peace. A queer and beautiful blankness. It was spring in Portland and the rain came every afternoon. All evening I just stayed there on my bed in the dark. And that is how the science come to me."

The windows in the streetcar were pale blue with light. The two soldiers paid for their beers and opened the door—one of the soldiers combed his hair and wiped off his muddy puttees before they went outside. The three mill workers bent silently over their breakfasts. Leo's clock was ticking on the wall.

"It is this. And listen carefully. I meditated on love and reasoned it out. I realized what is wrong with us. Men fall in love for the first time. And what do they fall in love with?"

The boy's soft mouth was partly open and he did not answer.

"A woman," the old man said. "Without science, with nothing to go by, they undertake the most dangerous and sacred experience in God's earth. They fall in love with a woman. Is that correct, Son?"

"Yeah," the boy said faintly.

"They start at the wrong end of love. They begin at the climax. Can you wonder it is so miserable? Do you know how men should love?"

The old man reached over and grasped the boy by the collar of his leather jacket. He gave him a gentle little shake and his green eyes gazed down unblinking and grave.

"Son, do you know how love should be begun?"

The boy sat small and listening and still. Slowly he shook his head. The old man leaned closer and whispered:

"A tree. A rock. A cloud."

It was still raining outside in the street: a mild, gray, endless rain. The mill whistle blew for the six o'clock shift and the three spinners paid and went away. There was no one in the café but Leo, the old man, and the little paper boy.

"The weather was like this in Portland," he said. "At the time my science was begun. I meditated and I started very cautious. I would pick up something from the street and take it home with me. I bought a goldfish and I concentrated on the goldfish and I loved it. I graduated from one thing to another. Day by day I was getting this technique. On the road from Portland to San Diego—"

"Aw shut up!" screamed Leo suddenly. "Shut up! Shut up!"

The old man still held the collar of the boy's jacket; he was trembling and his face was earnest and bright and wild. "For six years now I have gone around by myself and built up my science. And now I am a master. Son, I can love anything. No longer do I have to think about it even. I see a street full of people and a beautiful light comes in me. I watch a bird in the sky. Or I meet a traveler on the road. Everything, Son. And anybody. All strangers and all loved! Do you realize what a science like mine can mean?"

The boy held himself stiffly, his hands curled tight around the counter edge. Finally he asked: "Did you ever really find that lady?"

"What? What say, Son?"

"I mean," the boy asked timidly. "Have you fallen in love with a woman again?"

The old man loosened his grasp on the boy's collar. He turned away and for the first time his green eyes had a vague and scattered look. He lifted the mug from the counter, drank down the yellow beer. His head was shaking slowly from side to side. Then finally he answered: "No, Son. You see that is the last step in my science. I go cautious. And I am not quite ready yet."

"Well!" said Leo. "Well well well!"

The old man stood in the open doorway. "Remember," he said. Framed there in the gray damp light of the early morning he looked shrunken and seedy and frail. But his smile was bright. "Remember I love you," he said with a last nod. And the door closed quietly behind him.

The boy did not speak for a long time. He pulled down the bangs on his forehead and slid his grimy little forefinger around the rim of his empty cup. Then without looking at Leo he finally asked:

"Was he drunk?"

"No," said Leo shortly.

The boy raised his clear voice higher. "Then was he a dope fiend?"

"No."

The boy looked up at Leo, and his flat little face was desperate, his voice urgent and shrill. "Was he crazy? Do you think he was a lunatic?" The paper boy's voice dropped suddenly with doubt. "Leo? Or not?"

But Leo would not answer him. Leo had run a night café for fourteen years, and he held himself to be a critic of craziness. There were the town characters and also the transients who roamed in from the night. He knew the manias of all of them. But he did not want to satisfy the questions of the waiting child. He tightened his pale face and was silent.

So the boy pulled down the right flap of his helmet and as he turned to leave he made the only comment that seemed safe to him, the only remark that could not be laughed down and despised:

"He sure has done a lot of traveling."

EXERCISES

1. Why is the boy's small, pink ear referred to more than once?

2. Why does the man call his ideas about love a "science"?

3. Discuss the relevance of the metaphor of things "lying around loose" in him. How is love like having everything "finished up"?

4. Explain what the man means about the wife chasing him? What is the difference between the things the man talks about and the things the boy talks about?

5. Why does Leo harass the man and get so angry?

6. How is it possible to love a tree, a rock, a cloud? What does the man mean by this?

7. What does Leo know that he does not or cannot tell the boy?

STEPHEN
CRANE | *The Blue Hotel*

The Palace Hotel at Fort Romper was painted a light blue, a shade that is on the legs of a kind of heron, causing the bird to declare its position against any background. The Palace Hotel, then, was always screaming and howling in a way that made the dazzling winter landscape of Nebraska seem only a grey swampish hush. It stood alone on the prairie, and when the snow was falling the town two hundreds yards away was not visible. But when the traveller alighted at the railway station he was obliged to pass the Palace Hotel before he could come upon the company of low clapboard houses which composed Fort Romper, and it was not to be thought that any traveller could pass the Palace Hotel without looking at it. Pat Scully, the proprietor, had proved himself a master of strategy when he chose his paints. It is true that on clear days, when the great transcontinental expresses, long lines of swaying Pullmans, swept through Fort Romper, passengers were overcome at the sight, and the cult that knows the brown-reds and the subdivisions of the dark greens of the East expressed shame, pity, horror, in a laugh. But the citizens of this prairie town and to the people who would naturally stop there, Pat Scully had performed a feat. With this opulence and splendour, these creeds, classes, egotisms, that streamed through Romper on the rails day after day, they had no colour in common.

As if the displayed delights of such a blue hotel were not sufficiently enticing, it was Scully's habit to go every morning and evening to meet the leisurely trains that stopped at Romper and work his seductions upon any man that he might see wavering, gripsack in hand.

One morning, when a snow-crusted engine dragged its long string of freight cars and its one passenger coach to the station, Scully performed the marvel of catching three men. One was a shaky and quick-eyed Swede, with a great shining cheap valise; one was a tall bronzed cowboy, who was on his way to a ranch near the Dakota line; one was a little silent man from the East, who didn't look it, and didn't announce it. Scully practically made them prisoners. He was so nimble and merry and kindly that each probably felt it would be the height of brutality to try to escape. They trudged off over the creaking board sidewalks in the wake of the eager little Irishman. He wore a heavy fur cap squeezed tightly down on his head. It caused his two red ears to stick out stiffly, as if they were made of tin.

At last, Scully, elaborately, with boisterous hospitality, conducted them through the portals of the blue hotel. The room which they entered was small. It seemed to be merely a proper temple for an enormous stove, which, in the centre, was humming with godlike violence. At various points on its surface the iron had become luminous and glowed yellow from the heat. Beside the stove Scully's son Johnnie was playing High-Five with an old farmer who had whiskers both grey and sandy. They were quarrelling. Frequently the old farmer turned his face toward a box of sawdust—coloured brown from tobacco juice—that was behind the stove, and spat with an air of great impatience and irritation. With a loud flourish of words Scully destroyed the game of cards, and bustled his son upstairs with part of the baggage of the new guests. He himself conducted them to three basins of the coldest water in the world. The cowboy and the Easterner burnished themselves fiery red with this water, until it seemed to be some kind of metal-polish. The Swede, however, merely dipped his fingers gingerly and with trepidation. It was notable that throughout this series of small ceremonies the three travellers were made to feel that Scully was very benevolent. He was conferring great favours upon them. He handed the towel from one to another with an air of philanthropic impulse.

Afterward they went to the first room, and sitting about the stove, listened to Scully's officious clamour at his daughters, who were preparing the midday meal. They reflected in the silence of experienced men who tread carefully amid new people. Nevertheless, the old farmer, stationary, invincible in his chair near the warmest part of the stove, turned his face from the sawdust-box frequently and addressed a glowing commonplace to the strangers. Usually he was answered in short but adequate sentences by either the cowboy or the Easterner. The Swede said nothing. He seemed to be occupied in making furtive estimates of each man in the room. One might have thought that he had the sense of silly suspicion which comes to guilt. He resembled a badly frightened man.

Later, at dinner, he spoke a little, addressing his conversation entirely to Scully. He volunteered that he had come from New York, where for ten years he had worked as a tailor. These facts seemed to strike Scully as fascinating, and afterward he volunteered that he had lived at Romper for fourteen years. The Swede asked about the crops and the price of labour. He seemed barely to listen to Scully's extended replies. His eyes continued to rove from man to man.

Finally, with a laugh and a wink, he said that some of these Western communities were very dangerous; and after his statement he straightened his legs under the table, tilted his head, and laughed again, loudly. It was plain that the demonstration had no meaning to the others. They looked at him wondering and in silence.

II

As the men trooped heavily back into the front room, the two little windows presented views of a turmoiling sea of snow. The huge arms of the wind were making attempts—mighty, circular, futile—to embrace the flakes as they sped. A gate-post like a still man with a blanched face stood aghast amid this profligate fury. In a hearty voice Scully announced the presence of a blizzard. The guests of the blue hotel, lighting their pipes, assented with grunts of lazy masculine contentment. No island of the sea could be exempt in the degree of this little room with its humming stove. Johnnie, son of Scully, in a tone which defined his opinion of his ability as a card-player, challenged the old farmer of both grey and sandy whiskers to a game of High-Five. The farmer agreed with a contemptuous and bitter scoff. They sat close to the stove, and squared their knees under a wide board. The cowboy and the Easterner watched the game with interest. The Swede remained near the window, aloof, but with a countenance that showed signs of an inexplicable excitement.

The play of Johnnie and the grey-beard was suddenly ended by another quarrel. The old man arose while casting a look of heated scorn at his adversary. He slowly buttoned his coat, and then stalked with fabulous dignity from the room. In the discreet silence of all other men the Swede laughed. His laughter rang somehow childish. Men by this time had begun to look at him askance, as if they wished to inquire what ailed him.

A new game was formed jocosely. The cowboy volunteered to become the partner of Johnnie, and they all then turned to ask the Swede to throw in his lot with the little Easterner. He asked some questions about the game, and, learning that it wore many names, and that he had played it when it was under an alias, he accepted the invitation. He strode toward the men nervously, as if he expected to be assaulted. Finally, seated, he gazed from face to face and laughed shrilly. This laugh was so strange that the Easterner looked up quickly, the cowboy sat intent and with his mouth open, and Johnnie paused, holding the cards with still fingers.

Afterward there was a short silence. Then Johnnie said, "Well, let's get at it. Come on now!" They pulled their chairs forward until their knees were bunched under the board. They began to play, and their interest in the game caused the others to forget the manner of the Swede.

The cowboy was a board-whacker. Each time that he held superior cards he whanged them, one by one, with exceeding force, down upon the improvised table, and took the tricks with a glowing air of prowess and pride that sent thrills of indignation into the hearts of his opponents. A game with a board-whacker in it is sure to become intense. The countenances of the Easterner and the Swede were miserable whenever the cowboy thundered down his aces and kings, while Johnnie, his eyes gleaming with joy, chuckled and chuckled.

Because of the absorbing play none considered the strange ways of the Swede. They paid strict heed to the game. Finally, during a lull caused by a new deal, the Swede suddenly addressed Johnnie: "I suppose there have been a good many men killed in this room." The jaws of the others dropped and they looked at him.

"What in hell are you talking about?" said Johnnie.

The Swede laughed again his blatant laugh, full of a kind of false courage and defiance. "Oh, you know what I mean all right," he answered.

"I'm a liar if I do!" Johnnie protested. The card was halted, and the men stared at the Swede. Johnnie evidently felt that as the son of the proprietor he should make a direct inquiry. "Now, what might you be drivin' at, mister?" he asked. The Swede winked at him. It was a wink full of cunning. His fingers shook on the edge of the board. "Oh, maybe you think I have been to nowheres. Maybe you think I'm a tenderfoot?"

"I don't know nothin' about you," answered Johnnie, "and I don't give a damn where you've been. All I got to say is that I don't know what you're driving at. There hain't never been nobody killed in this room."

The cowboy, who had been steadily gazing at the Swede, then spoke: "What's wrong with you, mister?"

Apparently it seemed to the Swede that he was formidably menaced. He shivered and turned white near the corners of his mouth. He sent an appealing glance in the direction of the little Easterner. During these moments he did not forget to wear his air of advanced pot-valour. "They say they don't know what I mean," he remarked mockingly to the Easterner.

The latter answered after prolonged and cautious reflection. "I don't understand you," he said, impassively.

The Swede made a movement then which announced that he thought he had encountered treachery from the only quarter where he had expected sympathy, if not help. "Oh, I see you are all against me. I see——"

The cowboy was in a state of deep stupefaction. "Say," he cried, as he tumbled the deck violently down upon the board, "say, what are you gittin' at, hey?"

The Swede sprang up with the celerity of a man escaping from a snake on the floor. "I don't want to fight!" he shouted. "I don't want to fight!"

The cowboy stretched his long legs indolently and deliberately. His hands were in his pockets. He spat into the sawdust-box. "Well, who the hell thought you did?" he inquired.

The Swede backed rapidly toward a corner of the room. His hands were out protecting in front of his chest, but he was making an obvious struggle to control his fright. "Gentlemen," he quavered, "I suppose I am going to be killed before I can leave this house! I suppose I am going to be killed before I can leave this house!" In his eyes was the dying-swan look. Through the windows could be seen the snow turning blue in the shadow of dusk. The wind tore at the house, and some loose thing beat regularly against the clap-boards like a spirit tapping.

A door opened, and Scully himself entered. He paused in surprise as he noted the tragic attitude of the Swede. Then he said, "What's the matter here?"

The Swede answered him swiftly and eagerly: "These men are going to kill me."

"Kill you!" ejaculated Scully. "Kill you! What are you talkin'?"

The Swede made the gesture of a martyr.

Scully wheeled sternly upon his son. "What is this, Johnnie?"

The lad had grown sullen. "Damned if I know," he answered. "I can't make no sense to it." He began to shuffle the cards, fluttering them together with an angry snap. "He says a good many men have been killed in this room, or something like that. And he says he's goin' to be killed here too. I don't know what ails him. He's crazy, I shouldn't wonder."

Scully then looked for explanation to the cowboy, but the cowboy simply shrugged his shoulders.

"Kill you?" said Scully again to the Swede. "Kill you? Man, you're off your nut."

"Oh, I know," burst out the Swede. "I know what will happen. Yes, I'm crazy—yes. Yes, of course, I'm crazy—yes. But I know one thing——" There was a sort of sweat of misery and terror upon his face. "I know I won't get out of here alive."

The cowboy drew a deep breath, as if his mind was passing into the last stages of dissolution. "Well, I'm doggoned," he whispered to himself.

Scully wheeled suddenly and faced his son. "You've been troublin' this man!"

Johnnie's voice was loud with its burden of grievance. "Why, good Gawd, I ain't done nothin' to 'im."

The Swede broke in. "Gentlemen, do not disturb yourselves. I will leave this house. I will go away, because"—he accused them dramatically with his glance—"because I do not want to be killed."

Scully was furious with his son. "Will you tell me what is the matter, you young divil? What's the matter, anyhow? Speak out!"

"Blame it!" cried Johnnie in despair, "don't I tell you I don't know? He—he says we want to kill him, and that's all I know. I can't tell what ails him."

The Swede continued to repeat: "Never mind, Mr. Scully; never mind. I will leave this house. I will go away, because I do not wish to be killed. Yes, of course, I am crazy—yes. But I know one thing! I will go away. I will leave this house. Never mind, Mr. Scully; never mind. I will go away."

"You will not go 'way," said Scully. "You will not go 'way until I hear the reason of this business. If anybody has troubled you I will take care of him. This is my house. You are under my roof, and I will not allow any peaceable man to be troubled here." He cast a terrible eye upon Johnnie, the cowboy, and the Easterner.

"Never mind, Mr. Scully; never mind. I will go away. I do not wish to be killed." The Swede moved toward the door which opened upon the stairs. It was evidently his intention to go at once for his baggage.

"No, no," shouted Scully peremptorily; but the white-faced man slid by him and disappeared. "Now," said Scully severely, "what does this mean?"

Johnnie and the cowboy cried together: "Why, we didn't do nothin' to 'im!"

Scully's eyes were cold. "No," he said, "you didn't?"

Johnnie swore a deep oath. "Why, this is the wildest loon I ever see. We didn't do nothin' at all. We were jest sittin' here playin' cards, and he——"

The father suddenly spoke to the Easterner. "Mr. Blanc," he asked, "what has these boys been doin'?"

The Easterner reflected again. "I didn't see anything wrong at all," he said at last, slowly.

Scully began to howl. "But what does it mane?" He stared ferociously at his son. "I have a mind to lather you for this, me boy."

Johnnie was frantic. "Well, what have I done?" he bawled at his father.

III

"I think you are tongued-tied," said Scully finally to his son, the cowboy, and the Easterner; and at the end of this scornful sentence he left the room.

Upstairs the Swede was swiftly fastening the straps of his great valise. Once his back happened to be half turned toward the door, and, hearing a noise there, he wheeled and sprang up, uttering a loud cry. Scully's wrinkled visage showed grimly in the light of the small lamp he carried. This yellow effulgence, streaming upward, coloured only his prominent features, and left his eyes, for instance, in mysterious shadow. He resembled a murderer.

"Man! man!" he exclaimed, "have you gone daffy?"

"Oh, no! Oh, no!" rejoined the other. "There are people in this world who know pretty nearly as much as you do—understand?"

For a moment they stood gazing at each other. Upon the Swede's deathly pale cheeks were two spots brightly crimson and sharply edged, as if they had been carefully painted. Scully placed the light on the table and sat himself on the edge of the bed. He spoke ruminatively. "By cracky, I never heard of such a thing in my life. It's a complete muddle. I can't, for the soul of me, think how you ever got this idea into your head." Presently, he lifted his eyes and asked: "And did you sure think they were going to kill you?"

The Swede scanned the old man as if he wished to see into his mind. "I did," he said at last. He obviously suspected that this answer might precipitate an outbreak. As he pulled on a strap his whole arm shook, the elbow wavering like a bit of paper.

Scully banged his hand impressively on the footboard of the bed. "Why, man, we're goin' to have a line of ilictric streetcars in this town next spring."

"A line of electric street cars," repeated the Swede, stupidly.

"And," said Scully, "there's a new railroad goin' to be built down from Broken Arm to here. Not to mintion the four churches and the smashin' big brick schoolhouse. Then there's the big factory, too. Why, in two years Romper'll be a met-tro-*pol*-is."

Having finished the preparation of his baggage, the Swede straightened himself. "Mr. Scully," he said, with sudden hardihood "how much do I owe you?"

"You don't owe me anythin'," said the old man, angrily.

"Yes, I do," retorted the Swede. He took seventy-five cents from his pocket and tendered it to Scully; but the latter snapped his fingers in disdainful refusal. However, it happened that they both stood gazing in a strange fashion at three silver pieces on the Swede's open palm.

"I'll not take your money," said Scully at last. "Not after what's been goin' on here." Then a plan seemed to strike him. "Here," he cried, picking up his lamp and moving toward the door. "Here! Come with me a minute."

"No," said the Swede, in overwhelming alarm.

"Yes," urged the old man. "Come on! I want you to come and see a picter—just across the hall—in my room."

The Swede must have concluded that his hour was come. His jaw dropped and his teeth showed like a dead man's. He ultimately followed Scully across the corridor, but he had the step of one hung in chains.

Scully flashed the light high on the wall of his own chamber. There was revealed a ridiculous photograph of a little girl. She was leaning against a balustrade of gorgeous decoration, and the formidable bang to her hair was prominent. The figure was as graceful as an upright sledstake, and, withal, it was of the hue of lead. "There," said Scully, tenderly, "that's the picter of my little girl that died. Her name was Carrie. She had the purtiest hair you ever saw! I was that fond of her, she——"

Turning then, he saw that the Swede was not contemplating the picture at all, but, instead, was keeping keen watch on the gloom in the rear.

"Look man!" cried Scully, heartily. "That's the picter of my little gal that died. Her name was Carrie. And then here's the picter of my oldest boy, Michael. He's a lawyer in Lincoln, an' doin' well. I gave that boy a grand eddication, and I'm glad for it now. He's a fine boy. Look at 'im now. Ain't he bold as blazes, him there in Lincoln, an honoured an' respicted gintleman! An honoured and respicted gintleman," concluded Scully with a flourish. And, so saying, he smote the Swede jovially on the back.

The Swede faintly smiled.

"Now," said the old man, "there's only one more thing." He dropped suddenly to the floor and thrust his head beneath the bed. The Swede could hear his muffled voice. "I'd keep it under me piller if it wasn't for that boy Johnnie. Then there's the old woman——Where is it now? I never put it twice in the same place. Ah, now come out with you!"

Presently he backed clumsily from under the bed, dragging with him an old coat rolled into a bundle. "I've fetched him," he muttered. Kneeling on the floor, he unrolled the coat and extracted from its heart a large yellow-brown whisky-bottle.

His first manoeuvre was to hold the bottle up to the light. Reassured, apparently, that nobody had been tampering with it, he thrust it with a generous movement toward the Swede.

The weak-kneed Swede was about to eagerly clutch this element of strength, but he suddenly jerked his hand away and cast a look of horror upon Scully.

"Drink," said the old man affectionately. He had risen to his feet, and now stood facing the Swede.

There was a silence. Then again Scully said: "Drink!"

The Swede laughed wildly. He grabbed the bottle, put it to his mouth; and as his lips curled absurdly around the opening and his throat worked, he kept his glance, burning with hatred, upon the old man's face.

IV

After the departure of Scully the three men, with the cardboard still upon their knees, preserved for a long time an astounded silence. Then Johnnie said: "That's the dod-dangedest Swede I ever see."

"He ain't no Swede," said the cowboy scornfully.

"Well, what is he then?" cried Johnnie. "What is he then?"

"It's my opinion," replied the cowboy deliberately, "he's some kind of a Dutchman." It was a venerable custom of the country to entitle as Swedes all light-haired men who spoke with a heavy tongue. In consequence the idea of the cowboy was not without its daring. "Yes, sir," he repeated. "It's my opinion this feller is some kind of a Dutchman."

"Well, he says he's a Swede, anyhow," muttered Johnnie, sulkily. He turned to the Easterner: "What do you think, Mr. Blanc?"

"Oh, I don't know," replied the Easterner.

"Well, what do you think makes him act that way?" asked the cowboy.

"Why, he's frightened." The Easterner knocked his pipe against a rim of the stove. "He's clear frightened out of his boots."

"What at?" cried Johnnie and the cowboy together.

The Easterner reflected over his answer.

"What at?" cried the others again.

"Oh, I don't know, but it seems to me this man has been reading dime novels, and he thinks he's right out in the middle of it—the shootin' and stabbin' and all."

"But," said the cowboy, deeply scandalized, "this ain't Wyoming, ner none of them places. This is Nebrasker."

"Yes," added Johnnie, "an' why don't he wait til he gits *out West?*"

The travelled Easterner laughed. "It isn't different there even—not in these days. But he thinks he's right in the middle of hell."

Johnnie and the cowboy mused along.

"It's awful funny," remarked Johnnie at last.

"Yes," said the cowboy. "This is a queer game. I hope we don't git snowed in, because then we'd have to stand this here man bein' around with us all the time. That wouldn't be no good."

"I wish pop would throw him out," said Johnnie.

Presently they heard a loud stamping on the stairs, accompanied by ringing jokes in the voice of old Scully, and laughter, evidently from the Swede. The men around the stove stared vacantly at each other. "Gosh!" said the cowboy. The door flew open, and old Scully, flushed and anecdotal, came into the room. He was jabbering at the Swede, who followed him, laughing bravely. It was the entry of two roisterers from a banquet hall.

"Come now," said Scully sharply to the three seated men, "move up and give us a chance at the stove." The cowboy and the Easterner obediently sidled their chairs to make room for the newcomers. Johnnie, however, simply arranged himself in a more indolent attitude, and then remained motionless.

"Come! Git over, there," said Scully.

"Plenty of room on the other side of the stove," said Johnnie.

"Do you think we want to sit in the draught?" roared the father.

But the Swede had interposed with a grandeur of confidence. "No, no. Let the boy sit where he likes," he cried in a bullying voice to the father.

"All right! All right!" said Scully, deferentially. The cowboy and the Easterner exchanged glances of wonder.

The five chairs were formed in a crescent about one side of the stove. The Swede began to talk; he talked arrogantly, profanely, angrily. Johnnie, the cowboy, and the Easterner maintained a morose silence, while old Scully appeared to be receptive and eager, breaking in constantly with sympathetic ejaculations.

Finally the Swede announced that he was thirsty. He moved in his chair, and said that he would go for a drink of water.

"I'll git it for you," cried Scully at once.

"No," said the Swede, contemptuously. "I'll get it for myself." He arose and stalked with the air of an owner off into the executive parts of the hotel.

As soon as the Swede was out of hearing Scully sprang to his feet and whispered intensely to the others: "Upstairs he thought I was tryin' to poison 'im."

"Say," said Johnnie, "this makes me sick. Why don't you throw 'im out in the snow?"

"Why, he's all right now," declared Scully. "It was only that he was from the East, and he thought this was a tough place. That's all. He's all right now."

The cowboy looked with admiration upon the Easterner. "You were straight," he said. "You were on to that there Dutchman."

"Well," said Johnnie to his father, "he may be all right now, but I don't see it. Other time he was scared, but now he's too fresh."

Scully's speech was always a combination of Irish brogue and idiom, Western twang and idiom, and scraps of curiously formal diction taken from the story-books and newspapers. He now hurled a strange mass of language at the head of his son. "What do I keep? What do I keep? What do I keep?" he demanded, in a voice of thunder. He slapped his knee impressively, to indicate that he himself was going to make reply, and that all should heed. "I keep a hotel," he shouted. "A hotel, do you mind? A guest under my roof has sacred privileges. He is to be intimidated by none. Not one word shall he hear that would prijudice him in favour of goin' away. I'll not have it. There's no place in this here town where they can say they iver took in a guest of mine because he was afraid to stay here." He wheeled suddenly upon the cowboy and the Easterner. "Am I right?"

"Yes, Mr. Scully," said the cowboy, "I think you're right."

"Yes, Mr. Scully," said the Easterner, "I think you're right."

V

At six-o'clock supper, the Swede fizzed like a fire-wheel. He sometimes seemed on the point of bursting into riotous song, and in all his madness he was encouraged by old Scully. The Easterner was encased in reserve; the cowboy sat in wide-mouthed amazement, forgetting to eat, while Johnnie wrathily demolished great plates of food. The daughters of the house, when they were obliged to replenish the biscuits, approached as warily as Indians, and, having succeeded in their purpose, fled with ill-concealed trepidation. The Swede domineered the whole feast, and he gave it the appearance of a cruel bacchanal. He seemed to have grown suddenly taller; he gazed, brutally disdainful, into every face. His voice rang through the room. Once when he jabbed out harpoon-fashion with his fork to pinion a biscuit, the weapon nearly impaled the hand of the Easterner, which had been stretched quietly out for the same biscuit.

After supper, as the men filed toward the other room, the Swede smote Scully ruthlessly on the shoulder. "Well, old boy, that was a good, square meal." Johnnie looked hopefully at his father; he knew that shoulder was tender from an old fall; and, indeed, it appeared for a moment as if Scully was going to flame out over the matter, but in the end he smiled a sickly smile and remained silent. The others understood from his manner that he was admitting his responsibility for the Swede's new view-point.

Johnnie, however, addressed his parent in an aside. "Why don't you license somebody to kick you downstairs?" Scully scowled darkly by way of reply.

When they were gathered about the stove, the Swede insisted on another game of High-Five. Scully gently deprecated the plan at first, but the Swede turned a wolfish glare upon him. The old man subsided, and the Swede canvassed the others. In his tone there was always a great threat. The cowboy and the Easterner both remarked indifferently that they would play. Scully said that he would presently have to go to meet the 6.58 train, and so the Swede turned menacingly upon Johnnie. For a moment their glances crossed like blades, and then Johnnie smiled and said, "Yes, I'll play."

They formed a square, with the little board on their knees. The Easterner and the Swede were again partners. As the play went on, it was noticeable that the cowboy was not board-whacking as usual. Meanwhile, Scully, near the lamp, had put on his spectacles and, with an appearance curiously like an old priest, was reading a newspaper. In time he went out to meet the 6.58 train, and, despite his precautions, a gust of polar wind whirled into the room as he opened the door. Besides scattering the cards, it chilled the players to the marrow. The Swede cursed frightfully. When Scully returned, his entrance disturbed a cosy and friendly scene. The Swede again cursed. But presently they were once more intent, their heads bent forward and their hands moving swiftly. The Swede had adopted the fashion of board-whacking.

Scully took up his paper and for a long time remained immersed in matters which were extraordinarily remote from him. The lamp burned badly, and once he stopped to adjust the wick. The newspaper, as he turned from page to page, rustled with a slow and comfortable sound. Then suddenly he heard three terrible words: "You are cheatin'!"

Such scenes often prove that there can be little of dramatic import in environment. Any room can present a tragic front; any room can be comic. This little den was now hideous as a torture-chamber. The new faces of the men themselves had changed it upon the instant. The Swede held a huge fist in front of Johnnie's face, while the latter looked steadily over it into the blazing orbs of his accuser. The Easterner had grown pallid; the cowboy's jaw had dropped in that expression of bovine amazement which was one of his important mannerisms. After the three words, the first sound in the room was made by Scully's paper as it floated forgotten to his feet. His spectacles had also fallen from his nose, but by a clutch he had saved them in air. His hand, grasping the spectacles, now remained poised awkwardly and near his shoulder. He stared at the cardplayers.

Probably the silence was while a second elapsed. Then, if the floor had been suddenly twitched out from under the men they could not have moved quicker. The five had projected themselves head-long toward a common point. It happened that Johnnie, in rising to hurl himself upon the Swede, had stumbled slightly because of his curiously instinctive care for the cards and the board. The loss of the moment allowed time for the arrival of Scully, and also allowed the cowboy time to give the Swede a great push which sent him staggering back. The men found tongue together, and hoarse shouts of rage, appeal, or fear burst from every throat. The cowboy pushed and jostled feverishly at the Swede, and the Easterner and Scully clung wildly to Johnnie; but through the smoky air, above the swaying bodies of the peace-compellers, the eyes of the two warriors ever sought each other in glances of challenge that were at once hot and steely.

Of course the board had been over-turned, and now the whole company of cards was scattered over the floor, where the boots of the men trampled the fat and painted kings and queens as they gazed with their silly eyes at the war that was waging above them.

Scully's voice was dominating the yells. "Stop now! Stop, I say! Stop, now——"

Johnnie, as he struggled to burst through the rank formed by Scully and the Easterner, was crying, "Well, he says I cheated! He says I cheated! I won't allow no man to say I cheated! If he says I cheated, he's a —— ——!"

The cowboy was telling the Swede, "Quit, now! Quit, d'ye hear——"

The screams of the Swede never ceased: "He did cheat! I saw him! I saw him——"

As for the Easterner, he was importuning in a voice that was not heeded: "Wait a moment, can't you? Oh, wait a moment. What's the good of a fight over a game of cards? Wait a moment——"

In this tumult no complete sentences were clear: "Cheat"— "Quit"— "He says"—these fragments pierced the uproar and rang out sharply. It was remarkable that, whereas Scully undoubtedly made the most noise, he was the least heard of any of the riotous band.

Then suddenly there was a great cessation. It was as if each man had paused for breath; and although the room was still lighted with the anger of men, it could be seen that there was no danger of immediate conflict, and at once Johnnie, shouldering his way forward, almost succeeded in confronting the Swede. "What did you say I cheated for? What did you say I cheated for? I don't cheat, and I won't let no man say I do!"

The Swede said, "I saw you! I saw you!"

"Well," cried Johnnie, "I'll fight any man what says I cheat!"

"No, you won't," said the cowboy. "Not here."

"Ah, be still, can't you?" said Scully, coming between them.

The quiet was sufficient to allow the Easterner's voice to be heard. He was repeating, "Oh, wait a moment, can't you? What's the good of a fight over a game of cards? Wait a moment!"

Johnnie, his red face appearing above his father's shoulder, hailed the Swede again. "Did you say I cheated?"

The Swede showed his teeth. "Yes."

"Then," said Johnnie, "we must fight."

"Yes, fight," roared the Swede. He was like a demoniac. "Yes, fight! I'll show you what kind of a man I am! I'll show you who you want to fight! Maybe you think I can't fight! Maybe you think I can't! I'll show you, you skin, you card-sharp! Yes, you cheated! You cheated! You cheated!"

"Well, let's go at it, then, mister," said Johnnie, coolly.

The cowboy's brow was beaded with sweat from his efforts in intercepting all sorts of raids. He turned in despair to Scully. "What are you goin' to do now?"

A change had come over the Celtic visage of the old man. He now seemed all eagerness; his eyes glowed.

"We'll let them fight," he answered, stalwartly. " I can't put up with it any longer. I've stood this damned Swede till I'm sick. We'll let them fight."

VI

The men prepared to go out of doors. The Easterner was so nervous that he had great difficulty in getting his arms into the sleeves of his new leather coat. As the cowboy drew his fur cap down over his ears his hands trembled. In fact, Johnnie and old Scully were the only ones who displayed no agitation. These preliminaries were conducted without words.

Scully threw open the door. "Well, come on," he said. Instantly a terrific wind caused the flame of the lamp to struggle at its wick, while a puff of black smoke sprang from the chimney-top. The stove was in mid-current of the blast, and its voice swelled to equal the roar of the storm. Some of the scarred and bedabbled cards were caught up from the floor and dashed helplessly against the farther wall. The men lowered their heads and plunged into the tempest as into a sea.

No snow was falling, but great whirls and clouds of flakes, swept up from the ground by the frantic winds, were streaming southward with the speed of bullets. The covered land was blue with the sheen of an unearthly satin, and there was no other hue save where, at the low, black railway station—which seemed incredibly distant—one light gleamed like a tiny jewel. As the men floundered into a thigh-deep drift, it was known that the Swede was bawling out something. Scully went to him, put a hand on his shoulder, and projected an ear. "What's that you say?" he shouted.

"I say," bawled the Swede again, "I won't stand much show against this gang. I know you'll all pitch on me."

Scully smote him reproachfully on the arm. "Tut, man!" he yelled. The wind tore the words from Scully's lips and scattered them far alee.

"You are all a gang of——" boomed the Swede, but the storm also seized the remainder of this sentence.

Immediately turning their backs upon the wind, the men had swung around a corner to the sheltered side of the hotel. It was the function of the little house to preserve here, amid this great devastation of snow, an irregular V-shape of heavily encrusted grass, which crackled beneath the feet. One could imagine the great drifts piled against the windward side. When the party reached the comparative peace of this spot it was found that the Swede was still bellowing.

"Oh, I know what kind of a thing this is! I know you'll all pitch on me. I can't lick you all!"

Scully turned upon him panther-fashion. "You'll not have to whip all of us. You'll have to whip my son Johnnie. An' the man what troubles you durin' that time will have me to dale with."

The arrangements were swiftly made. The two men faced each other, obedient to the harsh commands of Scully, whose face, in the subtly luminous gloom, could be seen set in the austere impersonal lines that are pictured on the countenances of the Roman veterans. The Easterner's teeth were chattering, and he was hopping up and down like a mechanical toy. The cowboy stood rock-like.

The contestants had not stripped off any clothing. Each was in his ordinary attire. Their fists were up, and they eyed each other in a calm that had the elements of leonine cruelty in it.

During this pause, the Easterner's mind, like a film, took lasting impressions of three men—the iron-nerved master of the ceremony; the Swede, pale, motionless, terrible; and Johnnie, serene yet ferocious, brutish yet heroic. The entire prelude had in it a tragedy greater than the tragedy of action, and this aspect was accentuated by the long, mellow cry of the blizzard, as it sped the tumbling and wailing flakes into the black abyss of the south.

"Now!" said Scully.

The two combatants leaped forward and crashed together like bullocks. There was heard the cushioned sound of blows, and of a curse squeezing out from between the tight teeth of one.

As for the spectators, the Easterner's pent-up breath exploded from him with a pop of relief, absolute relief from the tension of the preliminaries. The cowboy bounded into the air with a yowl. Scully was immovable as from supreme amazement and fear at the fury of the fight which he himself had permitted and arranged.

For a time the encounter in the darkness was such a perplexity of flying arms that it presented no more detail than would a swiftly revolving wheel. Occasionally a face, as if illuminated by a flash of light, would shine out, ghastly and marked with pink spots. A moment later, the men might have been known as shadows, if it were not for the involuntary utterance of oaths that came from them in whispers.

Suddenly a holocaust of warlike desire caught the cowboy, and he bolted forward with the speed of a broncho. "Go it, Johnnie! Go it! Kill him! Kill him!"

Scully confronted him. "Kape back," he said; and by his glance the cowboy could tell that this man was Johnnie's father.

To the Easterner there was a monotony of unchangeable fighting that was an abomination. This confused mingling was eternal to his sense, which was concentrated in a longing for the end, the priceless end. Once the fighters lurched near him, and as he scrambled hastily backward he heard them breathe like men on the rack.

"Kill him, Johnnie! Kill him! Kill him! Kill him!" The cowboy's face was contorted like one of those agony masks in museums.

"Keep still," said Scully, icily.

Then there was a sudden loud grunt, incomplete, cut short, and Johnnie's body swung away from the Swede and fell with sickening heaviness to the grass. The cowboy was barely in time to prevent the mad Swede from flinging himself upon his prone adversary. "No, you don't," said the cowboy, interposing an arm. "Wait a second."

Scully was at his son's side. "Johnnie! Johnnie, me boy!" His voice had a quality of melancholy tenderness. "Johnnie! Can you go on with it?" He looked anxiously down into the bloody, pulpy face of his son.

There was a moment of silence, and then Johnnie answered in his ordinary voice, "Yes, I—it—yes."

Assisted by his father he struggled to his feet. "Wait a bit now till you git your wind," said the old man.

A few paces away the cowboy was lecturing the Swede. "No, you don't! Wait a second!"

The Easterner was plucking at Scully's sleeve. "Oh, this is enough," he pleaded. "This is enough! Let it go as it stands. This is enough!"

"Bill," said Scully, "git out of the road." The cowboy stepped aside. "Now." The combatants were actuated by a new caution as they advanced toward collision. They glared at each other, and then the Swede aimed a lightning blow that carried with it his entire weight. Johnnie was evidently half stupid from weakness, but he miraculously dodged, and his fist sent the over-balanced Swede sprawling.

The cowboy, Scully, and the Easterner burst into a cheer that was like a chorus of triumphant soldiery, but before its conclusion the Swede had scuffled agilely to his feet and come in berserk abandon at his foe. There was another perplexity of flying arms, and Johnnie's body again swung away and fell, even as a bundle might fall from a roof. The Swede instantly staggered to a little wind-waved tree and leaned upon it, breathing like an engine, while his savage and flamelit eyes roamed from face to face as the men bent over Johnnie. There was a splendour of isolation in his situation at this time which the Easterner felt once when, lifting his eyes from the man on the ground, he beheld that mysterious and lonely figure, waiting.

"Are you any good yet, Johnnie?" asked Scully in a broken voice.

The son gasped and opened his eyes languidly. After a moment he answered, "No—I ain't—any good—any—more." Then, from shame and bodily ill, he began to weep, the tears furrowing down through the blood-stains on his face. "He was too—too—too heavy for me."

Scully straightened and addressed the waiting figure. "Stranger," he said, evenly, "it's all up with our side." Then his voice changed into that vibrant huskiness which is commonly the tone of the most simple and deadly announcements. "Johnnie is whipped."

Without replying, the victor moved off on the route to the front door of the hotel.

The cowboy was formulating new and unspellable blasphemies. The Easterner was startled to find that they were out in a wind that seemed to come direct from the shadowed arctic floes. He heard again the wail of the snow as it was flung to its grave in the south. He knew now that all this time the cold had been sinking into him deeper and deeper, and he wondered that he had not perished. He felt indifferent to the condition of the vanquished man.

"Johnnie, can you walk?" asked Scully.

"Did I hurt—hurt him any?" asked the son.

"Can you walk, boy? Can you walk?"

Johnnie's voice was suddenly strong. There was a robust impatience in it. "I asked you whether I hurt him any!"

"Yes, yes, Johnnie," answered the cowboy, consolingly; "he's hurt a good deal."

They raised him from the ground, and as soon as he was on his feet he went tottering off, rebuffing all attempts at assistance. When the party rounded the corner they were fairly blinded by the pelting of the snow. It burned their faces like fire. The cowboy carried Johnnie through the drift to the door. As they entered, some cards again rose from the floor and beat against the wall.

The Easterner rushed to the stove. He was so profoundly chilled that he almost dared to embrace the glowing iron. The Swede was not in the room. Johnnie sank into a chair and, folding his arms on his knees, buried his face in them. Scully, warming one foot and then the other at a rim of the stove, muttered to himself with Celtic mournfulness. The cowboy had removed his fur cap, and with a dazed and rueful air he was running one hand through his tousled locks. From overhead they could hear the creaking of boards, as the Swede tramped here and there in his room.

The sad quiet was broken by the sudden flinging open of a door that led toward the kitchen. It was instantly followed by an inrush of women. They precipitated themselves upon Johnnie amid a chorus of lamentation. Before they carried their prey off to the kitchen, there to be bathed and harangued with that mixture of sympathy and abuse which is a feat of their sex, the mother straightened herself and fixed old Scully with an eye of stern reproach. "Shame be upon you, Patrick Scully!" she cried. "Your own son, too. Shame be upon you!"

"There, now! Be quiet, now!" said the old man, weakly.

"Shame be upon you, Patrick Scully!" The girls, rallying to this slogan, sniffed disdainfully in the direction of those trembling accomplices, the cowboy and the Easterner. Presently they bore Johnnie away, and left the three men to dismal reflection.

VII

"I'd like to fight this here Dutchman myself," said the cowboy, breaking a long silence.

Scully wagged his head sadly. "No, that wouldn't do. It wouldn't be right. It wouldn't be right."

"Well, why wouldn't it?" argued the cowboy. "I don't see no harm in it."

"No," answered Scully, with mournful heroism. "It wouldn't be right. It was Johnnie's fight, and now we mustn't whip the man just because he whipped Johnnie."

"Yes, that's true enough," said the cowboy; "but—he better not get fresh with me, because I couldn't stand no more of it."

"You'll not say a word to him," commanded Scully, and even then they heard the tread of the Swede on the stairs. His entrance was made theatric.

He swept the door back with a bang and swaggered to the middle of the room. No one looked at him. "Well," he cried, insolently, at Scully, "I s'pose you'll tell me now how much I owe you?"

The old man remained stolid. "You don't owe me nothin'."

"Huh!" said the Swede, "huh! Don't owe 'im nothin'."

The cowboy addressed the Swede. "Stranger, I don't see how you come to be so gay around here."

Old Scully was instantly alert. "Stop!" he shouted, holding his hand forth, fingers upward. "Bill, you shut up!"

The cowboy spat carelessly into the sawdust-box. "I didn't say a word, did I?" he asked.

"Mr. Scully," called the Swede, "how much do I owe you?" It was seen that he was attired for departure, and that he had his valise in his hand.

"You don't owe me nothin'," repeated Scully in the same imperturbable way.

"Huh!" said the Swede. "I guess you're right. I guess if it was any way at all, you'd owe me somethin'. That's what I guess." He turned to the cowboy. "'Kill him! Kill him! Kill him!'" he mimicked, and then guffawed victoriously. "'Kill him!'" He was convulsed with ironical humour.

But he might have been jeering the dead. The three men were immovable and silent, staring with glassy eyes at the stove.

The Swede opened the door and passed into the storm, giving one derisive glance backward at the still group.

As soon as the door was closed, Scully and the cowboy leaped to their feet and began to curse. They trampled to and fro, waving their arms and smashing into the air with their fists. "Oh, but that was a hard minute!" wailed Scully. "That was a hard minute! Him there leerin' and scoffin'! One bang at his nose was worth forty dollars to me that minute! How did you stand it, Bill?"

"How did I stand it?" cried the cowboy in a quivering voice. "How did I stand it? Oh!"

The old man burst into sudden brogue. "I'd loike to take that Swade," he wailed, "and hould 'im down on a shtone flure and bate 'im to a jelly wid a shtick!"

The cowboy groaned in sympathy. "I'd like to git him by the neck and ha-ammer him"—he brought his hand down on a chair with a noise like a pistol-shot—"hammer that there Dutchman until he couldn't tell himself from a dead coyote!"

"I'd bat 'im until he——"

"I'd show *him* some things——"

And then together they raised a yearning, fanatic cry—"Oh-o-oh! if we only could——"

"Yes!"

"Yes!"

"And then I'd——"

"O-o-oh!"

VIII

The Swede, tightly gripping his valise, tacked across the face of the storm as if he carried sails. He was following a line of little naked, gasping trees which, he knew, must mark the way of the road. His face, fresh from the pounding of Johnnie's fists, felt more pleasure than pain in the wind and the driving snow. A number of square shapes loomed upon him finally, and he knew them as the houses of the main body of the town. He found a street and made travel along it, leaning heavily upon the wind whenever, at a corner, a terrific blast caught him.

He might have been in a deserted village. We picture the world as thick with conquering and elate humanity, but here, with the bugles of the tempest pealing, it was hard to imagine a peopled earth. One viewed the existence of man then as a marvel, and conceded a glamour of wonder to these lice which were caused to cling to a whirling, fire-smitten, ice-locked, disease-stricken, space-lost bulb. The conceit of man was explained by this storm to be the very engine of life. One was a coxcomb not to die in it. However, the Swede found a saloon.

In front of it an indomitable red light was burning, and the snowflakes were made blood-colour as they flew through the circumscribed territory of the lamp's shining. The Swede pushed open the door of the saloon and entered. A sanded expanse was before him, and at the end of it four men sat about a table drinking. Down one side of the room extended a radiant bar, and its guardian was leaning upon his elbows listening to the talk of the men at the table. The Swede dropped his valise upon the floor and, smiling fraternally upon the barkeeper, said, "Gimme some whisky, will you?" The man placed a bottle, a whisky-glass, and a glass of ice-thick water upon the bar. The Swede poured himself an abnormal portion of whisky and drank it in three gulps. "Pretty bad night," remarked the bartender, indifferently. He was making the pretension of blindness which is usually a distinction of his class; but it could have been seen that he was furtively studying the half-erased blood-stains on the face of the Swede. "Bad night," he said again.

"Oh, it's good enough for me," replied the Swede, hardily, as he poured himself some more whisky. The barkeeper took his coin and manoeuvred it through its reception by the highly nickelled cash-machine. A bell rang; a card labelled "20 cts." had appeared.

"No," continued the Swede, "this isn't too bad weather. It's good enough for me."

"So?" murmured the barkeeper, languidly.

The copious drams made the Swede's eyes swim, and he breathed a trifle heavier. "Yes, I like this weather. I like it. It suits me." It was apparently his design to impart a deep significance to these words.

"So?" murmured the bartender again. He turned to gaze dreamily at the scroll-like birds and bird-like scrolls which had been drawn with soap upon the mirrors in back of the bar.

"Well, I guess I'll take another drink," said the Swede, presently. "Having something?"

"No, thanks; I'm not drinkin'," answered the bartender. Afterwards he asked, "How did you hurt your face?"

The Swede immediately began to boast loudly. "Why, in a fight. I thumped the soul out of a man down here at Scully's hotel."

The interest of the four men at the table was at last aroused.

"Who was it?" said one.

"Johnnie Scully," blustered the Swede. "Son of the man what runs it. He will be pretty near dead for some weeks, I can tell you. I made a nice thing of him, I did. He couldn't get up. They carried him in the house. Have a drink?"

Instantly the men in some subtle way encased themselves in reserve. "No, thanks," said one. The group was of curious formation. Two were prominent local business men; one was the district attorney; and one was a professional gambler of the kind known as "square." But a scrutiny of the group would not have enabled an observer to pick the gambler from the men of more reputable pursuits. He was, in fact, a man so delicate in manner, when among people of fair class, and so judicious in his choice of victims, that in the strictly masculine part of the town's life he had come to be explicitly trusted and admired. People called him a thoroughbred. The fear and contempt with which his craft was regarded were undoubtedly the reason why his quiet dignity shone conspicuous above the quiet dignity of men who might be merely hatters, billiard-markers, or grocery clerks. Beyond an occasional unwary traveller who came by rail, this gambler was supposed to prey solely upon reckless and senile farmers, who, when flush with good crops, drove into town in all the pride and confidence of an absolutely invulnerable stupidity. Hearing at times in circuitous fashion of the despoilment of such a farmer, the important men of Romper invariably laughed in contempt of the victim, and if they thought of the wolf at all, it was with a kind of pride at the knowledge that he would never dare think of attacking their wisdom and courage. Besides, it was popular that this gambler had a real wife and two children in a neat cottage in a suburb, where he led an exemplary home life; and when any one even suggested a discrepancy in his character, the crowd immediately vociferated descriptions of this virtuous family circle. Then men who led exemplary home lives, and men who did not lead exemplary home lives, all subsided in a bunch, remarking that there was nothing more to be said.

However, when a restriction was placed upon him—as, for instance, when a strong clique of members of the new Pollywog Club refused to permit him, even as a spectator, to appear in the rooms of the organization—the candour and gentleness with which he accepted the judgment disarmed many of his foes and made his friends more desperately partisan. He invariably distinguished between himself and a respectable Romper man so quickly and frankly that his manner actually appeared to be a continual broadcast compliment.

And one must not forget to declare the fundamental fact of his entire position in Romper. It is irrefutable that in all affairs outside his business, in all matters that occur eternally and commonly between man and man, this thieving card-player was so generous, so just, so moral, that, in a contest, he could have put to flight the consciences of nine tenths of the citizens of Romper.

And so it happened that he was seated in this saloon with the two prominent local merchants and the district attorney.

The Swede continued to drink raw whisky, meanwhile babbling at the barkeeper and trying to induce him to indulge in potations. "Come on. Have a drink. Come on. What—no? Well, have a little one, then. By gawd, I've whipped a man to-night, and I want to celebrate. I whipped him good, too. Gentlemen," the Swede cried to the men at the table, "have a drink?"

"Ssh!" said the barkeeper.

The group at the table, although furtively attentive, had been pretending to be deep in talk, but now a man lifted his eyes toward the Swede and said, shortly, "Thanks. We don't want any more."

At this reply the Swede ruffled out his chest like a rooster. "Well," he exploded, "it seems I can't get anybody to drink with me in this town. Seems so, don't it? Well!"

"Ssh!" said the barkeeper.

"Say," snarled the Swede, "don't you try to shut me up. I won't have it. I'm a gentleman, and I want people to drink with me. And I want 'em to drink with me now. Now—do you understand?" He rapped the bar with his knuckles.

Years of experience had calloused the bartender. He merely grew sulky. "I hear you," he answered.

"Well," cried the Swede, "listen hard then. See those men over there? Well, they're going to drink with me, and don't you forget it. Now you watch."

"Hi!" yelled the barkeeper, "this won't do!"

"Why won't it?" demanded the Swede. He stalked over the the table, and by chance laid his hand upon the shoulder of the gambler. "How about this?" he asked wrathfully. "I asked you to drink with me."

The gambler simply twisted his head and spoke over his shoulder. "My friend, I don't know you."

"Oh, hell!" answered the Swede, "come and have a drink."

"Now, my boy," advised the gambler, kindly, "take your hand off my shoulder and go 'way and mind your own business." He was a little, slim man, and it seemed strange to hear him use this tone of heroic patronage to the burly Swede. The other men at the table said nothing.

"What! You won't drink with me, you little dude? I'll make you, then! I'll make you!" The Swede had grasped the gambler frenziedly at the throat, and was dragging him from his chair. The other men sprang up. The barkeeper dashed around the corner of his bar. There was a great tumult, and then was seen a long blade in the hand of the gambler. It shot forward, and a human body, this citadel of virtue, wisdom, power, was pierced as easily as if it had been a melon. The Swede fell with a cry of supreme astonishment.

The prominent merchants and the district attorney must have at once tumbled out of the place backward. The bartender found himself hanging limply to the arm of a chair and gazing into the eyes of a murderer.

"Henry," said the latter, as he wiped his knife on one of the towels that hung beneath the bar rail, "you tell 'em where to find me. I'll be home, waiting for 'em." Then he vanished. A moment afterward the barkeeper was in the street dinning through the storm for help and, moreover, companionship.

The corpse of the Swede, alone in the saloon, had its eyes fixed upon a dreadful legend that dwelt atop of the cash-machine: "This registers the amount of your purchase."

IX

Months later, the cowboy was frying pork over the stove of a little ranch near the Dakota line, when there was a quick thud of hoofs outside, and presently the Easterner entered with the letters and the papers.

"Well," said the Easterner at once, "the chap that killed the Swede has got three years. Wasn't much, was it?"

"He has? Three years?" The cowboy poised his pan of pork, while he ruminated upon the news. "Three years. That ain't much."

"No. It was a light sentence," replied the Easterner as he unbuckled his spurs. "Seems there was a good deal of sympathy for him in Romper."

"If the bartender had been any good," observed the cowboy, thoughtfully, "he would have gone in and cracked that there Dutchman on the head with a bottle in the beginnin' of it and stopped all this here murderin'."

"Yes, a thousand things might have happened," said the Easterner, tartly.

The cowboy returned his pan of pork to the fire, but his philosophy continued. "It's funny, ain't it? If he hadn't said Johnnie was cheatin' he'd be alive this minute. He was an awful fool. Game played for fun, too. Not for money. I believe he was crazy."

"I feel sorry for that gambler," said the Easterner.

"Oh, so do I," said the cowboy. "He don't deserve none of it for killin' who he did."

"The Swede might not have been killed if everything had been square."

"Might not have been killed?" exclaimed the cowboy. "Everythin' square? Why, when he said that Johnnie was cheatin' and acted like such a jackass? And then in the saloon he fairly walked up to git hurt?" With these arguments the cowboy browbeat the Easterner and reduced him to rage.

"You're a fool!" cried the Easterner, viciously. "You're a bigger jackass than the Swede by a million majority. Now let me tell you one thing. Let me tell you something. Listen! Johnnie *was* cheating!"

"'Johnnie,'" said the cowboy, blankly. There was a minute of silence, and then he said, robustly, "Why no. The game was only for fun."

"Fun or not," said the Easterner, "Johnnie was cheating. I saw him. I know it. I saw him. And I refused to stand up and be a man. I let the Swede fight it out alone. And you—you were simply puffing around the place and wanting to fight. And then old Scully himself! We are all in it! This poor gambler isn't even a noun. He is kind of an adverb. Every sin is the result of a collaboration. We, five of us, have collaborated in the murder of this Swede. Usually there are from a dozen to forty women really involved in every murder, but in this case it seems to be only five men—you, I, Johnnie, old Scully; and that fool of an unfortunate gambler came merely as a culmination, the apex of a human movement, and gets all the punishment."

The cowboy, injured and rebellious, cried out blindly into this fog of mysterious theory: "Well, I didn't do anythin', did I?"

EXERCISES

1. Discuss the significance of a game being at the center of the conflict. What is the difference between playing for "fun" and for "keeps"?

2. What is significant about the characters in the story being described in non-human terms?

3. Why does the Swede act so frightened in the early part of the story? What does it mean to be so convinced of the reality of the unreal that you begin to believe it?

4. What makes the Swede change his behavior after the conversation with Scully upstairs?

5. Is the Swede's death his own fault, the fault of chance, or the fault of others? Explain.

6. This story fulfills some of the requirements of classical tragedy. Discuss its five-act structure and the Swede as a tragic hero whose death results from poor judgment and pride.

7. Discuss the significance of the following statements:

   (a) "I don't understand you." "I don't know you."

   (b) "What does it mean, what does it mean?" "This is a queer game."

   (c) "Well, I didn't do anything, did I?"

8. Compare this story with Saki's "The Open Window" in Part IV. How are both about the effect of taking a fiction to be real?

PART TWO

The World of Dream and Hallucination

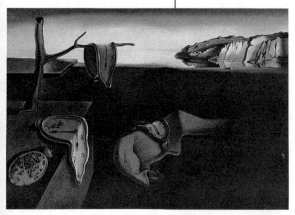

Whereas the stories in Part I focus on conflicts within the world of everyday-reality, the stories in Part II focus on situations that are so extreme, or on situations in which the characters or storytellers respond in such an extreme way, that the story no longer seems to be taking place in the realm of the ordinary everyday but rather in a world of dream or hallucination. They deal with situations in which people might actually say to themselves, "This can't be happening; this must be a dream." In such cases one may feel to be in a sort of daze in which everything around seems strange and hard to understand.

In Stephen Crane's "An Episode of War," the wound, which happens when it is not expected, so disrupts the Lieutenant's everyday activity that he no longer fits in, but seems dazed and disoriented. In Eudora Welty's story "A Visit of Charity," the differences between the inhabitants of the home for the elderly and the little girl are so extreme that things seem thrown out of proportion and unreal to her.

In "The Soft Touch of Grass," it is not merely the shock of the loss of his wife that so disorients the central character that he seems in a daze, but rather that his place in life, which was determined by his relationship with his wife, has been dislodged and he no longer feels comfortable in the world. The hallucinatory effect of Ambrose Bierce's "Chickamauga" results from the boy's deaf-mute state and the dual perspective of the story, as if it were told by the boy and an adult at the same time. What gives the story its eerie quality is the reader's sense that there is something hallucinatory and dreamlike about the way things are perceived.

In some of the stories in this section, the author is concerned with setting up a real event that becomes transformed into a meaningful metaphor. When an event or character is both real and metaphoric at once in a fiction, a dreamlike sense of reality is created. In Monica Wood's "Disappearing," for example, as the "real" act of swimming becomes a metaphor for the loss of a sense of body and self, the dream effect is increasingly intensified. This dream effect may also be created when the intentional pattern of meaning in the story dominates over the story's plausibility. Elizabeth Bowen's "The Demon Lover" sets up a kind of metaphoric situation of poetic justice that seems to take place in the real world. However, since poetic justice can take place only in the world of the story, the reader may have an uneasy feeling of being in both the real world and the story world at once. In Pamela Painter's story "The Bridge," because the older woman in the story must infer, that is, "make up," the younger woman's story, the story becomes stranger and more hallucinatory as it progresses.

"The Long Way Out," "A Sorrowful Woman," "Order of Insects," "Why Can't They Tell You Why," and "The Tell-Tale Heart" present situations in which madness is the dominant reason that the story is pushed out of the realm of everyday reality. A character we generally define as mad is one whose realm of reality does not seem the same as that accepted by the majority of people. There is no way for us to participate in that world; however, since fiction represents a meaningful structure, not just random behavior, there is no such thing as meaningless madness in fiction. Thus, we do have a right to ask the meaning of the woman's madness in "A Sorrowful Woman" and the cause of the mad behavior in "The Tell-Tale Heart," although we can only infer from the details we are given the answers to these questions.

In "The Peasant Marey," "A Memory," and "The Grave," reality seems hallucinatory because it takes place not in the actual world, but in memory; and since what is being described in these stories is a remembered event, we cannot ask that it follow the conventions of everyday activity but rather the perspective of the mind of the one who remembers it. "Swaddling Clothes," "Rashōmon," and "The Grasshopper and the Bell Cricket" derive their otherworldly effect from the fact that they spring from a cultural tradition different from that of the West. As a result, the world of these stories may seem unfamiliar to western readers and thus strange and dreamlike.

The remaining stories in this section involve in some way the strange, dreamlike world created by an extreme event or an extreme reaction to an event. The following 1,500-word (about 6 typewritten pages) discussion of Stephen Crane's "An Episode of War" is a sample analysis that attempts to explain the motivation for the story's hallucinatory effect.

Meaning and Meaninglessness in Crane's *"An Episode of War"*

Although this story is entitled "An Episode of War," the central character, a Civil War lieutenant, is not engaged in a battle when the story opens. Instead of using his sword as an instrument of war, he is using it as a tool to perform what is essentially a household chore of dividing coffee for his men. "Frowning and serious . . . on the verge of a great triumph in mathematics," he takes care to make "astonishingly equal" squares in the coffee. It is thus engaged in an activity of ordered, "mathematical" normality that the lieutenant suddenly cries out, and the situation is ordered no longer.

At this crucial point, the story presents a frozen scene in which the lieutenant can only gaze "sadly, mystically" at the "green face of a wood," while the men stand "statue-like and silent, astonished and awed by this catastrophe which happened when catastrophes were not expected." As is usual for our everyday experience when we are struck by the world outside and ask "why" or look for someone to blame, the lieutenant looks quickly at the man near him "as if he suspected it were a case of personal assault." When the lieutenant realizes that the man next to him is not the guilty party, he looks further for a cause. All he sees, though, is "the green face of a wood." Indeed, the answer to the question "What struck the lieutenant?"—the question that the lieutenant, the men, and the reader ask at this point—can only be "the green face of a wood."

Crane's control of the details of this situation further suggests that the wood is the enemy. Not only does Crane refuse to show us the person who fired the shot; he also does not even say that the lieutenant was shot at all. All we see is the blood that mysteriously appears on his sleeve. Furthermore, it is the wood, not the supposed enemy behind it, that is called "hostile." In fact, the wood dominates this first section of the story. As the lieutenant begins his trip back through the lines for medical aid, he stares at it once more, and the reader is forced to focus on it also as the men in silence "stared at the wood, then at the departing lieutenant; then at the wood, then at the lieutenant."

The wood as enemy is suggested by two more indirect references in the second section of the story. When the lieutenant goes back through the lines, he sees a general on a black horse gazing over the lines of the blue infantry "at the green woods which veiled his problems." At the end of this section as the lieutenant turns his eyes to the battle itself, he sees crowds of men standing and firing away, not at a concrete, observable enemy but at the "inscrutable distance." With the piling up of such images of the wood as a "mystery," as "hostile," as something which "veils" one's problems, as "inscrutable," as something one can only gaze at "sadly, mystically," we begin to realize that the lieutenant's enemy is the human being's most general enemy, that the "war" he is engaged in is the "war" in which people are always engaged. The green face of the wood which strikes the lieutenant and gives no answer is the meaninglessness we all face when something unexpected and mysterious confronts us.

Moreover, the lieutenant's confrontation in the first section of the story is not only with the blank mystery of the world outside but also with the ultimate extension of that mystery—the absolute mystery of death. The men shy away from him as if his "hand is upon the curtain which hangs before the revelations of all existence." They "fear vaguely that the weight of a finger upon him might send him headlong, precipitate the tragedy, hurl him at once into the dim, gray unknown." The results of such a confrontation are that the lieutenant becomes, at the same time, both lowly and dignified. The familiar sword he was using to divide the coffee becomes a strange thing to him. Puzzled with what to do with it, he looks at it in a "kind of stupefaction, as if he had been endowed with a trident, a sceptre, or a spade." The very metaphoric transformation of the sword suggests both the royal dignity and authority of the scepter and trident and the lowly, earth-bound subservience of the spade.

The lieutenant's efforts to sheathe his sword also strike us as both terrible and ludicrous. Although it is a desperate struggle, it is also a feat for bemused observation. "To sheathe a sword held by the left hand at the middle of the blade, in a scabbard hung at the left hip, is a feat worthy of a sawdust ring." Yet when the orderly-sergeant leans nervously backward for fear of touching the lieutenant, we are again reminded of the seriousness of the situation: "A wound gives strange dignity to him who wears it. Well men shy away from this new and terrible majesty." Still, for all his dignity and majesty, the lieutenant "wears the look of one who knows he is the victim of a terrible disease and understands his helplessness." Now we realize that the terrible disease of which the lieutenant is a victim is the same disease of which all human beings are victims—the disease of being human and therefore susceptible to the mystery of the uncontrollable world outside and the ultimate mystery of death.

In the third section of the story, the lieutenant, having reached help behind his lines, faces a different response to his wound. Instead of being treated with the awe due royalty, as he was earlier, he is now treated with the scorn due a child who has been careless enough to get himself into trouble. The doctor's response to the lieutenant is the final manifestation of his isolation. Because the doctor sees wounded men every day, the lieutenant is not special or royal as he was before. Just the opposite, he is beneath the doctor, "on a very low social plane." The lieutenant becomes merely an object that must be tended to precisely because he is a frail and "brittle" human object susceptible to the "hostile" world outside.

The lieutenant finally rebels against being treated like a disobedient child and being punished for something that is not his fault. He fears the loss of the arm will make concrete a much greater loss he has been moving toward throughout the story—the loss of his familiar and ordered place in the world. However, his rebellion makes no difference; and as he gazes at the schoolhouse door, "as sinister to him as the portals of death," we confront again the "veil" or "curtain" referred to earlier in the story that hangs before the revelations of all existence.

We do not enter these "portals" with the lieutenant and thus do not know what "revelations" are made to him. The loss of the arm is as mysterious as the wound itself. Instead, the story jumps ahead to a scene perhaps several months later. As his sisters, mother, and wife sob for a long time at the sight of the flat sleeve, he stands shamefaced and says, "Oh, well . . . I don't suppose it matters so much as all that." Crane sums up the story by saying, "And this is the story of how the lieutenant lost his arm." Both statements are obviously ironic, Crane's understatement giving us the clue to the irony of the lieutenant's disclaimer. First of all, we realize that this has not been a story of how the lieutenant lost his arm. That event occurred outside the given details of the story. The story itself presents the experience that led up to the amputation.

The lieutenant realizes, just as we do now, that the women are crying only over the physical loss of the arm. To them this loss is what the story is about. The lieutenant, though, now realizes that the physical loss is not so important. What is really important is the experience he has gone through—an experience structured as a short story called "An Episode of War." This story, moreover, is about the lieutenant's confrontation with the mystery of the world and humanity's precarious situation in it.

COMMENT

Paragraph one introduces the basic problem of the story—the discrepancy between the "everyday" context of the episode and the fact that it is also an episode of war.

Paragraphs two and three introduce the basic image of the "green face of the wood" and argue that the language of the story suggests that it is the antagonist.

Paragraph four argues that the central image of the wood represents the blank face of meaninglessness when human beings are struck for no apparent reason.

Paragraph five cites passages which support the argument that the lieutenant has been mysteriously touched by the threat of death.

Paragraphs six and seven show how the story progresses from the front lines to the area behind the lines in terms of reactions to the lieutenant's wound.

Paragraphs eight and nine argue that the conclusion of the story is ironic and make a final summary statement about the theme of the story.

STEPHEN
CRANE | *An Episode of War*

The lieutenant's rubber blanket lay on the ground, and upon it he had poured the company's supply of coffee. Corporals and other representatives of the grimy and hot-throated men who lined the breast-work had come for each squad's portion.

The lieutenant was frowning and serious at this task of division. His lips pursed as he drew with his sword various crevices in the heap, until brown squares of coffee, astoundingly equal in size, appeared on the blanket. He was on the verge of a great triumph in mathematics, and the corporals were thronging forward, each to reap a little square, when suddenly the lieutenant cried out and looked quickly at a man near him as if he suspected it was a case of personal assault. The others cried out also when they saw blood upon the lieutenant's sleeve.

He had winced like a man stung, swayed dangerously, and then straightened. The sound of his hoarse breathing was plainly audible. He looked sadly, mystically, over the breast-work at the green face of a wood, where now were many little puffs of white smoke. During this moment the men about him gazed statue-like and silent, astonished and awed by this catastrophe which happened when catastrophes were not expected—when they had leisure to observe it.

As the lieutenant stared at the wood, they too swung their heads, so that for another instant all hands, still silent, contemplated the distant forest as if their minds were fixed upon the mystery of a bullet's journey.

The officer had, of course, been compelled to take his sword into his left hand. He did not hold it by the hilt. He gripped it at the middle of the blade, awkwardly. Turning his eyes from the hostile wood, he looked at the sword as he held it there, and seemed puzzled as to what to do with it, where to put it. In short, this weapon had of a sudden become a strange thing to him. He looked at it in a kind of stupefaction, as if he had been endowed with a trident, a sceptre, or a spade.

Finally he tried to sheathe it. To sheathe a sword held by the left hand, at the middle of the blade, in a scabbard hung at the left hip, is a feat worthy of a sawdust ring. This wounded officer engaged in a desperate struggle with the sword and the wobbling scabbard, and during the time of it he breathed like a wrestler.

But at this instant the men, the spectators, awoke from their stone-like poses and crowded forward sympathetically. The orderly-sergeant took the sword and tenderly placed it in the scabbard. At the time, he leaned nervously backward, and did not allow even his finger to brush the body of the lieutenant. A wound gives strange dignity to him who bears it. Well men shy from his new and terrible majesty. It is as if the wounded man's hand is upon the curtain which hangs before the revelations of all existence—the meaning of ants, potentates, wars, cities, sunshine, snow, a feather dropped from a bird's wing; and the power of it sheds radiance upon a bloody form, and makes the other men understand sometimes that they are little. His comrades look at him with large eyes thoughtfully. Moreover, they fear vaguely that the weight of a finger upon him might send him headlong, precipitate the tragedy, hurl him at once into the dim, gray unknown. And so the orderly-sergeant, while sheathing the sword, leaned nervously backward.

There were others who proffered assistance. One timidly presented his shoulder and asked the lieutenant if he cared to lean upon it, but the latter waved him away mournfully. He wore the look of one who knows he is the victim of a terrible disease and understands his helplessness. He again stared over the breast-work at the forest, and then, turning, went slowly rearward. He held his right wrist tenderly in his left hand as if the wounded arm was made of very brittle glass.

And the men in silence stared at the wood, then at the departing lieutenant; then at the wood, then at the lieutenant.

As the wounded officer passed from the line of battle, he was enabled to see many things which as a participant in the fight were unknown to him. He saw a general on a black horse gazing over the lines of blue infantry at the green woods which veiled his problems. An aide galloped furiously, dragged his horse suddenly to a halt, saluted, and presented a paper. It was, for a wonder, precisely like a historical painting.

To the rear of the general and his staff a group, composed of a bugler, two or three orderlies, and the bearer of the corps standard, all upon maniacal horses, were working like slaves to hold their ground, preserve their respectful interval, while the shells boomed in the air about them, and caused their chargers to make furious quivering leaps.

A battery, a tumultuous and shining mass, was swirling toward the right. The wild thud of hoofs, the cries of the riders shouting blame and praise, menace and encouragement, and, last, the roar of the wheels, the slant of the glistening guns, brought the lieutenant to an intent pause. The battery swept in curves that stirred the heart; it made halts as dramatic as the crash of a wave on the rocks, and when it fled onward this aggregation of wheels, levers, motors had a beautiful unity, as if it were a missile. The sound of it was a war-chorus that reached into the depths of man's emotion.

The lieutenant, still holding his arm as if it were of glass, stood watching this battery until all detail of it was lost, save the figures of the riders, which rose and fell and waved lashes over the black mass.

Later, he turned his eyes toward the battle, where the shooting sometimes crackled like bush fires, sometimes sputtered with exasperating irregularity, and sometimes reverberated like the thunder. He saw the smoke rolling upward and saw crowds of men who ran and cheered, or stood and blazed away at the inscrutable distance.

He came upon some stragglers, and they told him how to find the field hospital. They described its exact location. In fact, these men, no longer having part in the battle, knew more of it than others. They told the performance of every corps, every division, the opinion of every general. The lieutenant, carrying his wounded arm rearward, looked upon them with wonder.

At the roadside a brigade was making coffee and buzzing with talk like a girls' boarding school. Several officers came out to him and inquired concerning things of which he knew nothing. One, seeing his arm, began to scold. "Why, man, that's no way to do. You want to fix that thing." He appropriated the lieutenant and the lieutenant's wound. He cut the sleeve and laid bare the arm, every nerve of which softly fluttered under his touch. He bound his handkerchief over the wound, scolding away in the meantime. His tone allowed one to think that he was in the habit of being wounded every day. The lieutenant hung his head, feeling, in this presence, that he did not know how to be correctly wounded.

The low white tents of the hospital were grouped around an old schoolhouse. There was here a singular commotion. In the foreground two ambulances interlocked wheels in the deep mud. The drivers were tossing the blame of it back and forth, gesticulating and berating, while from the ambulances, both crammed with wounded, there came an occasional groan. An interminable crowd of bandaged men were coming and going. Great numbers sat under the trees nursing heads or arms or legs. There was a dispute of some kind raging on the steps of the schoolhouse. Sitting with his back against a tree a man with a face as gray as a new army blanket was serenely smoking a corncob pipe. The lieutenant wished to rush forward and inform him that he was dying.

A busy surgeon was passing near the lieutenant. "Good morning," he said, with a friendly smile. Then he caught sight of the lieutenant's arm, and his face at once changed. "Well, let's have a look at it." He seemed possessed suddenly of a great contempt for the lieutenant. This wound evidently placed the latter on a very low social plane. The doctor cried out impatiently: "What mutton-head tied it up that way anyhow?" The lieutenant answered, "Oh, a man."

When the wound was disclosed the doctor fingered it disdainfully. "Humph," he said, "You come along with me and I'll tend to you." His voice contained the same scorn as if he were saying, "You will have to go to jail."

The lieutenant had been very meek, but now his face flushed, and he looked into the doctor's eyes. "I guess I won't have it amputated," he said.

"Nonsense, man! Nonsense! Nonsense!" cried the doctor. "Come along, now. I won't amputate it. Come along. Don't be a baby."

"Let go of me," said the lieutenant, holding back wrathfully, his glance fixed upon the door of the old schoolhouse, as sinister to him as the portals of death.

And this is the story of how the lieutenant lost his arm. When he reached home, his sisters, his mother, his wife, sobbed for a long time at the sight of the flat sleeve. "Oh, well," he said, standing shamefaced amid these tears, "I don't suppose it matters so much as all that."

EXERCISES

1. The title suggests that the incident described here is a result of war; why then is the lieutenant wounded when he is not engaged in battle?
2. What is the source of the bullet that wounded the lieutenant? Why is the mystery of the source of the bullet emphasized?
3. What is the effect of the wound on the men around the lieutenant? How does the lieutenant respond to the wound?
4. How is the lieutenant's perspective on the battle scene around him changed by the wound?
5. Explain the reaction of the doctor to the lieutenant's wound.
6. Discuss the tone of the last paragraph. Is this more than just a story about how the lieutenant lost his arm? What is the most basic and general meaning of the episode? Why does the lieutenant say it doesn't matter so much as all that?

EUDORA
WELTY | *A Visit of Charity*

It was mid-morning—a very cold, bright day. Holding a potted plant before her, a girl of fourteen jumped off the bus in front of the Old Ladies' Home, on the outskirts of town. She wore a red coat, and her straight yellow hair was hanging down loose from the pointed white cap all the little girls were wearing that year. She stopped for a moment beside one of the prickly dark shrubs with which the city had beautified the Home, and then proceeded slowly toward the building, which was of whitewashed brick and reflected the winter sunlight like a block of ice. As she walked vaguely up the steps she shifted the small pot from hand to hand; then she had to set it down and remove her mittens before she could open the heavy door.

"I'm a Campfire Girl. . . . I have to pay a visit to some old lady," she told the nurse at the desk. This was a woman in a white uniform who looked as if she were cold; she had close-cut hair which stood up on the very top of her head exactly like a sea wave. Marian, the little girl, did not tell her that this visit would give her a minimum of only three points in her score.

"Acquainted with any of our residents?" asked the nurse. She lifted one eyebrow and spoke like a man.

"With any old ladies? No—but—that is, any of them will do," Marian stammered. With her free hand she pushed her hair behind her ears, as she did when it was time to study Science.

The nurse shrugged and rose. "You have a nice *multiflora cineraria* there," she remarked as she walked ahead down the hall of closed doors to pick out an old lady.

There was loose, bulging linoleum on the floor. Marian felt as if she were walking on the waves, but the nurse paid no attention to it. There was a smell in the hall like the interior of a clock. Everything was silent until, behind one of the doors, an old lady of some kind cleared her throat like a sheep bleating. This decided the nurse. Stopping in her tracks, she first extended her arm, bent her elbow, and leaned forward from the hips—all to examine the watch strapped to her wrist; then she gave a loud double-rap on the door.

"There are two in each room," the nurse remarked over her shoulder.

"Two what?" asked Marian without thinking. The sound like a sheep's bleating almost made her turn around and run back.

One old woman was pulling the door open in short, gradual jerks, and when she saw the nurse a strange smile forced her old face dangerously awry. Marian, suddenly propelled by the strong, impatient arm of the nurse, saw next the sideface of another old woman, even older, who was lying flat in bed with a cap on and a counterpane drawn up to her chin.

"Visitor," said the nurse, and after one more shove she was off up the hall.

Marian stood tongue-tied; both hands held the potted plant. The old woman, still with that terrible, square smile (which was a smile of welcome) stamped on her bony face, was waiting. . . . Perhaps she said something. The old woman in bed said nothing at all, and she did not look around.

Suddenly Marian saw a hand, quick as a bird claw, reach up in the air and pluck the white cap off her head. At the same time, another claw to match drew her all the way into the room, and the next moment the door closed behind her.

"My, my, my," said the old lady at her side.

Marian stood enclosed by a bed, a washstand and a chair; the tiny room had altogether too much furniture. Everything smelled wet—even the bare floor. She held onto the back of the chair, which was wicker and felt soft and damp. Her heart beat more and more slowly, her hands got colder and colder, and she could not hear whether the old women were saying anything or not. She could not see them very clearly. How dark it was! The window shade was down, and the only door was shut. Marian looked at the ceiling. . . . It was like being caught in a robber's cave, just before one was murdered.

"Did you come to be our little girl for a while?" the first robber asked.

Then something was snatched from Marian's hand—the little potted plant.

"Flowers!" screamed the old woman. She stood holding the pot in an undecided way. "Pretty flowers," she added.

Then the old woman in bed cleared her throat and spoke. "They are not pretty," she said, still without looking around, but very distinctly.

Marian suddenly pitched against the chair and sat down in it.

"Pretty flowers," the first old woman insisted. "Pretty—pretty. . . ."

Marian wished she had the little pot back for just a moment—she had forgotten to look at the plant herself before giving it away. What did it look like?

"Stinkweeds," said the other old woman sharply. She had a bunchy white forehead and red eyes like a sheep. Now she turned them toward Marian. The fogginess seemed to rise in her throat again, and she bleated. "Who—are—you?"

To her surprise, Marian could not remember her name. "I'm a Campfire Girl," she said finally.

"Watch out for the germs," said the old woman like a sheep, not addressing anyone.

"One came out last month to see us," said the first old woman.

A sheep or a germ? wondered Marian dreamily, holding onto the chair.

"Did not!" cried the other old woman.

"Did so! Read to us out of the Bible, and we enjoyed it!" screamed the first.

"Who enjoyed it!" said the woman in bed. Her mouth was unexpectedly small and sorrowful, like a pet's.

"We enjoyed it," insisted the other. "You enjoyed it—I enjoyed it."

"We all enjoyed it," said Marian, without realizing that she had said a word.

The first old woman had just finished putting the potted plant high, high on the top of the wardrobe, where it could hardly be seen from below. Marian wondered how she had ever succeeded in placing it there, how she could ever have reached so high.

"You mustn't pay any attention to old Addie," she now said to the little girl. "She's ailing today."

"Will you shut your mouth?" said the woman in bed. "I am not."

"You're a story."

"I can't stay but a minute—really, I can't," said Marian suddenly. She looked down at the wet floor and thought that if she were sick in here they would have to let her go.

With much to-do the first old woman sat down in a rocking chair—still another piece of furniture—and began to rock. With the fingers of one hand she touched a very dirty cameo pin on her chest. "What do you do at school?" she asked.

"I don't know. . . . " said Marian. She tried to think but she could not.

"Oh, but the flowers are beautiful," the old woman whispered. She seemed to rock faster and faster; Marian did not see how anyone could rock so fast.

"Ugly," said the woman in bed.

"If we bring flowers—" Marian began, and then fell silent. She had almost said that if Campfire Girls brought flowers to the Old Ladies' Home, the visit would count one extra point, and if they took a Bible with them on the bus and read it to the old ladies, it counted double. But the old woman had not listened, anyway; she was rocking and watching the other one, who watched back from the bed.

"Poor Addie is ailing. She has to take medicine—see?" she said, pointing a horny finger at a row of bottles on the table, and rocking so high that her black comfort shoes lifted off the floor like a little child's.

"I am no more sick than you are," said the woman in bed.

"Oh, yes you are!"

"I just got more sense than you have, that's all," said the other old woman, nodding her head.

"That's only the contrary way she talks when *you all* come," said the first old lady with sudden intimacy. She stopped the rocker with a neat pat of her feet and leaned toward Marian. Her hand reached over—it felt like a petunia leaf, clinging and just a little sticky.

"Will you hush! Will you hush!" cried the other one.

Marian leaned back rigidly in her chair.

"When I was a little girl like you, I went to school and all," said the old woman in the same intimate, menacing voice. "Not here—another town. . . ."

"Hush!" said the sick woman. "You never went to school. You never came and you never went. You never were anything—only here. You never were born! You don't know anything. Your head is empty, your heart and hands and your old black purse are all empty, even that little old box that you brought with you you brought empty—you showed it to me. And yet you talk, talk, talk, talk, talk all the time until I think I'm losing my mind! Who are you? You're a stranger—a perfect stranger! Don't you know you're a stranger? Is it possible that they have actually done a thing like this to anyone—sent them in a stranger to talk, and rock, and tell away her whole long rigmarole? Do they seriously suppose that I'll be able to keep it up, day in, day out, night in, night out, living in the same room with a terrible old woman—forever?"

Marian saw the old woman's eyes grow bright and turn toward her. This old woman was looking at her with despair and calculation in her face. Her small lips suddenly dropped apart, and exposed a half circle of false teeth with tan gums.

"Come here, I want to tell you something," she whispered. "Come here!"

Marian was trembling, and her heart nearly stopped beating altogether for a moment.

"Now, now, Addie," said the first old woman. "That's not polite. Do you know what's really the matter with old Addie today?" She, too, looked at Marian; one of her eyelids drooped low.

"The matter?" the child repeated stupidly. "What's the matter with her?"

"Why, she's mad because it's her birthday!" said the first old woman, beginning to rock again and giving a little crow as though she had answered her own riddle.

"It is not, it is not!" screamed the old woman in bed. "It is not my birthday, no one knows when that is but myself, and will you please be quiet and say nothing more, or I'll go straight out of my mind!" She turned her eyes toward Marian again, and presently she said in the soft, foggy voice, "When the worst comes to the worst, I ring this bell, and the nurse comes." One of her hands was drawn out from under the patched counterpane—a thin little hand with enormous black freckles. With a finger which would not hold still she pointed to a little bell on the table among the bottles.

"How old are you?" Marian breathed. Now she could see the old woman in bed very closely and plainly, and very abruptly, from all sides, as in dreams. She wondered about her—she wondered for a moment as though there was nothing else in the world to wonder about. It was the first time such a thing had happened to Marian.

"I won't tell!"

The old face on the pillow, where Marian was bending over it, slowly gathered and collapsed. Soft whimpers came out of the small open mouth. It was a sheep that she sounded like—a little lamb. Marian's face drew very close, the yellow hair hung forward.

"She's crying!" She turned a bright, burning face up to the first old woman.

"That's Addie for you," the old woman said spitefully.

Marian jumped up and moved toward the door. For the second time, the claw almost touched her hair, but it was not quick enough. The little girl put her cap on.

"Well, it was a real visit," said the old woman, following Marian through the doorway and all the way out into the hall. Then from behind she suddenly clutched the child with her sharp little fingers. In an affected, high-pitched whine she cried, "Oh, little girl, have you a penny to spare for a poor old woman that's not got anything of her own? We don't have a thing in the world—not a penny for candy—not a thing! Little girl, just a nickel—a penny—"

Marian pulled violently against the old hands for a moment before she was free. Then she ran down the hall, without looking behind her and without looking at the nurse, who was reading *Field & Stream* at her desk. The nurse, after another triple motion to consult her wrist watch, asked automatically the question put to visitors in all institutions: "Won't you stay and have dinner with *us?*"

Marian never replied. She pushed the heavy door open into the cold air and ran down the steps.

Under the prickly shrub she stooped and quickly, without being seen, retrieved a red apple she had hidden there.

Her yellow hair under the white cap, her scarlet coat, her bare knees all flashed in the sunlight as she ran to meet the big bus rocketing through the street.

"Wait for me!" she shouted. As though at an imperial command, the bus ground to a stop.

She jumped on and took a big bite out of the apple.

EXERCISES

1. Point out the language that suggests Marian's attitude toward making her visit.
2. Discuss the implications of the description of the house, both inside and outside.

3. Discuss the difference between the two old ladies. Note particularly the language used to describe them.

4. Discuss Marian's feeling inside the room. How does she perceive things differently there?

5. What does the old woman's tirade against her roommate suggest about the relationship between the two?

6. What is suggested by the fact that Marian hid the apple before she went in the house? Consider the possible symbolic significance of eating an apple. Has Marian learned anything as a result of her experience?

7. Discuss the meaning of the title.

8. How does the story make you feel about Marian? How does it make you feel about the old ladies?

LUIGI
PIRANDELLO | *The Soft Touch of Grass*

They went into the next room, where he was sleeping in a big chair, to ask if he wanted to look at her for the last time before the lid was put on the coffin.

"It's dark. What time is it?" he asked.

It was nine-thirty in the morning, but the day was overcast and the light dim. The funeral had been set for ten o'clock.

Signor Pardi stared up at them with dull eyes. It hardly seemed possible that he could have slept so long and well all night. He was still numb with sleep and the sorrow of these last days. He would have liked to cover his face with his hands to shut out the faces of his neighbors grouped about his chair in the thin light; but sleep had weighted his body like lead, and although there was a tingling in his toes urging him to rise, it quickly went away. Should he still give way to his grief? He happened to say aloud, "Always . . ." but he said it like someone settling himself under the covers to go back to sleep. They all looked at him questioningly. Always what?

Always dark, even in the daytime, he had wanted to say, but it made no sense. The day after her death, the day of her funeral, he would always remember this wan light and his deep sleep, too, with her lying dead in the next room. Perhaps the windows. . . .

"The windows?"

Yes, they were still closed. They had not been opened during the night, and the warm glow of those big dripping candles lingered. The bed had been taken away and she was there in her padded casket, rigid and ashen against the creamy satin.

No. Enough. He had seen her.

He closed his eyes, for they burned from all the crying he had done these past few days. Enough. He had slept and everything had been washed away with that sleep. Now he was relaxed, with a sense of sorrowful emptiness. Let the casket be closed and carried away with all it held of his past life.

But since she was still there. . . .

He jumped to his feet and tottered. They caught him and, with eyes still closed, he allowed himself to be led to the open casket. When he opened his eyes and saw her, he called her by name, her name that lived for him alone, the name in which he saw her and knew her in all the fullness of the life they had shared together. He glared resentfully at the others daring to stare at her lying still in death. What did they know about her? They could not even imagine what it meant to him to be deprived of her. He felt like screaming, and it must have been apparent, for his son hurried over to take him away. He was quick to see the meaning of this and felt a chill as though he were stripped bare. For shame—those foolish ideas up to the very last, even after his night-long sleep. Now they must hurry so as not to keep the friends waiting who had come to follow the coffin to the church.

"Come on, Papa. Be reasonable."

With angry, piteous eyes, the bereaved man turned back to his big chair.

Reasonable, yes; it was useless to cry out the anguish that welled within him and that could never be expressed by words or deeds. For a husband who is left a widower at a certain age, a man still yearning for his wife, can the loss be the same as that of a son for whom—at a certain point—it is almost timely to be left an orphan? Timely, since he was on the point of getting married and would, as soon as the three months' mourning were passed, now that he had the added excuse that it was better for both of them to have a woman to look after the house.

"Pardi! Pardi!" they shouted from the entrance hall.

His chill became more intense when he understood clearly for the first time that they were not calling him but his son. From now on their surname would belong more to his son than to him. And he, like a fool, had gone in there to cry out the living name of his mate, like a profanation. For shame! Yes, useless, foolish ideas, he now realized, after that long sleep which had washed him clean of everything.

Now the one vital thing to keep him going was his curiosity as to how their new home would be arranged. Where, for example, were they going to have him sleep? The big double bed had been removed. Would he have a small bed? he wondered. Yes, probably his son's single bed. Now he would have the small bed. And his son would soon be lying in a big bed, his wife beside him within arm's reach. He, alone, in his little bed, would stretch out his arms into thin air.

He felt torpid, perplexed, with a sensation of emptiness inside and all around him. His body was numb from sitting so long. If he tried now to get up he felt sure that he would rise light as a feather in all that emptiness, now that his life was reduced to nothing. There was hardly any difference between himself and the big chair. Yet that chair appeared secure on its four legs, whereas he no longer knew where his feet and legs belonged nor what to do with his hands. What did he care about his life? He did not care particularly about the lives of others, either. Yet as he was still alive he must go on. Begin again—some sort of life which he could not yet conceive and which he certainly would never have contemplated if things had not changed in his own world. Now, deposed like this all of a sudden, not old and yet no longer young. . . .

He smiled and shrugged his shoulders. For his son, all at once, he had become a child. But after all, as everyone knows, fathers are children to their grown sons who are full of worldly ambition and have successfully outdistanced them in positions of importance. They keep their fathers in idleness to repay all they have received when they themselves were small, and their fathers in turn become young again.

The single bed. . . .

But they did not even give him the little room where his son had slept. Instead, they said, he would feel more independent in another, almost hidden on the courtyard; he would feel free there to do as he liked. They refurnished it with all the best pieces, so it would not occur to anyone that it had once been a servant's room. After the marriage, all the front rooms were pretentiously decorated and newly furnished, even to the luxury of carpets. Not a trace remained of the way the old house had looked. Even with his own furniture relegated to that little dark room, out of the mainstream of the young people's existence, he did not feel at home. Yet, oddly enough, he did not resent the disregard he seemed to have reaped along with the old furniture, because he admired the new rooms and was satisfied with his son's success.

But there was another deeper reason, not too clear as yet, a promise of another life, all shining and colorful, which was erasing the memory of the old one. He even drew a secret hope from it that a new life might begin for him too. Unconsciously, he sensed the luminous opening of a door at his back whence he might escape at the right moment, easy enough now that no one bothered about him, leaving him as if on holiday in the sanctuary of his little room "to do as he pleased." He felt lighter than air. His eyes had a gleam in them that colored everything, leading him from marvel to marvel, as though he really were a child again. He had the eyes of a child—lively and open wide on a world which was still new.

He took the habit of going out early in the morning to begin his holiday which was to last as long as his life lasted. Relieved of all responsibilities, he agreed to pay his son so much every month out of his pension for his maintenance. It was very little. Though he needed nothing, his son thought he should keep some money for himself to satisfy any need he might have. But need for what? He was satisfied now just to look on at life.

Having shaken off the weight of experience, he no longer knew how to get along with oldsters. He avoided them. And the younger people considered him too old, so he went to the park where the children played.

That was how he started his new life—in the meadow among the children in the grass. What an exhilarating scent the grass had, and so fresh where it grew thick and high. The children played hide-and-seek there. The constant trickle of some hidden stream outpurled the rustle of the leaves. Forgetting their game, the children pulled off their shoes and stockings. What a delicious feeling to sink into all that freshness of soft new grass with bare feet!

He took off one shoe and was stealthily removing the other when a young girl appeared before him, her face flaming. "You pig!" she cried, her eyes flashing.

Her dress was caught up in front on a bush, and she quickly pulled it down over her legs, because he was looking up at her from where he sat on the ground.

He was stunned. What had she imagined? Already she had disappeared. He had wanted to enjoy the children's innocent fun. Bending down, he put his two hands over his hard, bare feet. What had she seen wrong? Was he too old to share a child's delight in going barefoot in the grass? Must one immediately think evil because he was old? Ah, he knew that he could change in a flash from being a child to becoming a man again, if he must. He was still a man, after all, but he didn't want to think about it. He refused to think about it. It was really as a child that he had taken off his shoes. How wrong it was of that wretched girl to insult him like that! He threw himself face down on the grass. All his grief, his loss, his daily loneliness had brought about this gesture, interpreted now in the light of vulgar malice. His gorge rose in disgust and bitterness. Stupid girl! If he had wanted that—even his son admitted he might have "some desires"—he had plenty of money in his pocket for such needs.

Indignant, he pulled himself upright. Shamefacedly, with trembling hands, he put on his shoes again. All the blood had gone to his head and the pulse now beat hot behind his eyes. Yes he knew where to go for that. He knew.

Calmer now, he got up and went back to the house. In the welter of furniture which seemed to have been placed there on purpose to drive him mad, he threw himself on the bed and turned his face to the wall.

EXERCISES

1. What are the "foolish ideas" the man has at the death of his wife?
2. How is this story not about the death of the wife, but the death of his old life and the need to start a "new" life?
3. Discuss the common notion that old people experience a second childhood and become like little children again. How is this relevant to this story?
4. Discuss the relationship between the father and the son. What kind of change has taken place in their relationship?
5. Discuss the central character's dilemma as being one in which he is no longer a man yet not able to be a child.
6. Why was the central character's childlike gesture misunderstood by a child? Why is he so disgusted by this? What does the image of him turning his face to the wall mean?

WILLIAM
CARLOS
WILLIAMS | *The Use of Force*

They were new patients to me, all I had was the name, Olson. Please come down as soon as you can, my daughter is very sick.

When I arrived I was met by the mother, a big startled-looking woman, very clean and apologetic who merely said, Is this the doctor? and let me in. In the back, she added. You must excuse us, doctor, we have her in the kitchen where it is warm. It is very damp here sometimes.

The child was fully dressed and sitting on her father's lap near the kitchen table. He tried to get up, but I motioned for him not to bother, took off my overcoat and started to look things over. I could see that they were all very nervous, eyeing me up and down distrustfully. As often, in such cases, they weren't telling me more than they had to, it was up to me to tell them; that's why they were spending three dollars on me.

The child was fairly eating me up with her cold, steady eyes, and no expression to her face whatever. She did not move and seemed, inwardly, quiet; an unusually attractive little thing, and as strong as a heifer in appearance. But her face was flushed, she was breathing rapidly, and I realized that she had a high fever. She had magnificent blond hair, in profusion. One of those picture children often reproduced in advertising leaflets and the photogravure sections of the Sunday papers.

She's had a fever for three days, began the father and we don't know what it comes from. My wife has given her things, you know, like people do, but it don't do no good. And there's been a lot of sickness around. So we tho't you'd better look her over and tell us what is the matter.

As doctors often do I took a trial shot at it as a point of departure. Has she had a sore throat?

Both parents answered me together, No . . . No, she says her throat don't hurt her.

Does your throat hurt you? added the mother to the child. But the little girl's expression didn't change nor did she move her eyes from my face.

Have you looked?

I tried to, said the mother, but I couldn't see.

As it happens we had been having a number of cases of diphtheria in the school to which this child went during that month and we were all, quite apparently, thinking of that, though no one had as yet spoken of the thing.

Well, I said, suppose we take a look at the throat first. I smiled in my best professional manner and asking for the child's first name I said, come on, Mathilda, open your mouth and let's take a look at your throat.

Nothing doing.

Aw, come on, I coaxed, just open your mouth wide and let me take a look. Look, I said opening both hands wide, I haven't anything in my hands. Just open up and let me see.

Such a nice man, put in the mother. Look how kind he is to you. Come on, do what he tells you to. He won't hurt you.

At that I ground my teeth in disgust. If only they wouldn't use the word "hurt" I might be able to get somewhere. But I did not allow myself to be hurried or disturbed but speaking quietly and slowly I approached the child again.

As I moved my chair a little nearer suddenly with one cat-like movement both her hands clawed instinctively for my eyes and she almost reached them too. In fact she knocked my glasses flying and they fell, though unbroken, several feet away from me on the kitchen floor.

Both the mother and father almost turned themselves inside out in embarrassment and apology. You bad girl, said the mother, taking her and shaking her by one arm. Look what you've done. The nice man . . .

For heaven's sake, I broke in. Don't call me a nice man to her. I'm here to look at her throat on the chance that she might have diphtheria and possibly die of it. But that's nothing to her. Look here, I said to the child, we're going to look at your throat. You're old enough to understand what I'm saying. Will you open it now by yourself or shall we have to open it for you?

Not a move. Even her expression hadn't changed. Her breaths however were coming faster and faster. Then the battle began. I had to do it. I had to have a throat culture for her own protection. But first I told the parents that it was entirely up to them. I explained the danger but said that I would not insist on a throat examination so long as they would take the responsibility.

If you don't do what the doctor says you'll have to go to the hospital, the mother admonished her severely.

Oh yeah? I had to smile to myself. After all, I had already fallen in love with the savage brat, the parents were contemptible to me. In the ensuing struggle they grew more and more abject, crushed, exhausted while she surely rose to magnificent heights of insane fury of effort bred of her terror of me.

The father tried his best, and he was a big man but the fact that she was his daughter, his shame at her behavior and his dread of hurting her made him release her just at the critical moment several times when I had almost achieved success, till I wanted to kill him. But his dread also that she might have diphtheria made him tell me to go on, go on though he himself was almost fainting, while the mother moved back and forth behind us raising and lowering her hands in an agony of apprehension.

Put her in front of you on your lap, I ordered, and hold both her wrists.

But as soon as he did the child let out a scream. Don't, you're hurting me. Let go of my hands. Let them go I tell you. Then she shrieked terrifyingly, hysterically. Stop it! Stop it! You're killing me!

Do you think she can stand it, doctor! said the mother.

You get out, said the husband to his wife. Do you want her to die of diphtheria?

Come on now, hold her, I said.

Then I grasped the child's head with my left hand and tried to get the wooden tongue depressor between her teeth. She fought, with clenched teeth, desperately! But now I also had grown furious—at a child. I tried to hold myself down but I couldn't. I know how to expose a throat for inspection. And I did my best. When finally I got the wooden spatula behind the last teeth and just the point of it into the mouth cavity, she opened up for an instant but before I could see anything she came down again and gripping the wooden blade between her molars she reduced it to splinters before I could get it out again.

Aren't you ashamed, the mother yelled at her. Aren't you ashamed to act like that in front of the doctor?

Get me a smooth-handled spoon of some sort, I told the mother. We're going through with this. The child's mouth was already bleeding. Her tongue was cut and she was screaming in wild hysterical shrieks. Perhaps I should have desisted and come back in an hour or more. No doubt it would have been better. But I have seen at least two children lying dead in bed of neglect in such cases, and feeling that I must get a diagnosis, now or never I went at it again. But the worst of it was that I too had got beyond reason. I could have torn the child apart in my own fury and enjoyed it. It was a pleasure to attack her. My face was burning with it.

The damned little brat must be protected against her own idiocy, one says to one's self at such times. Others must be protected against her. It is social necessity. And all these things are true. But a blind fury, a feeling of adult shame, bred of a longing for muscular release are the operatives. One goes on to the end.

In a final unreasoning assault I overpowered the child's neck and jaws. I forced the heavy silver spoon back of her teeth and down her throat till she gagged. And there it was—both tonsils covered with membrane. She had fought valiantly to keep me from knowing her secret. She had been hiding that sore throat for three days at least and lying to her parents in order to escape just such an outcome as this.

Now truly she *was* furious. She had been on the defensive before but now she attacked. Tried to get off her father's lap and fly at me while tears of defeat blinded her eyes.

EXERCISES

1. Note the description of the little girl; for example, she was "eating me up" with her eyes; she is a "savage brat," with a "cat-like movement." Discuss the implications of this language and how it corresponds to her behavior throughout the story.

2. Why is the story presented in the imagery of a battle?

3. When the doctor says he fell in love with the brat, how do we interpret what he means by *love* in this statement?

4. Is the doctor a cruel and sadistic man who takes pleasure in hurting the child? Or does his behavior embody some basic impulse in all people? Explain.

5. Why does the child feel she must keep the sore throat a secret? Why does she feel defeated when the doctor finds out? Is her response a primitive, savage response, or is it a socially learned one? Explain.

6. Discuss the story as a conflict between savagery and society. Stick closely to the language and imagery in the story to support your point. Which one wins the battle—savagery or society? Explain.

AMBROSE
BIERCE | *Chickamauga*

One sunny autumn afternoon a child strayed away from its rude home in a small field and entered a forest unobserved. It was happy in a new sense of freedom from control, happy in the opportunity of exploration and adventure; for this child's spirit, in bodies of its ancestors, had for thousands of years been trained to memorable feats of discovery and conquest—victories in battles whose critical moments were centuries, whose victors' camps were cities of hewn stone. From the cradle of its race it had conquered its way through two continents and passing a great sea had penetrated a third, there to be born to war and dominion as a heritage.

The child was a boy aged about six years, the son of a poor planter. In his younger manhood the father had been a soldier, had fought against naked savages and followed the flag of his country into the capital of a civilized race to the far South. In the peaceful life of a planter the warrior-fire survived; once kindled, it is never extinguished. The man loved military books and pictures and the boy had understood enough to make himself a wooden sword, though even the eye of his father would hardly have known it for what it was. This weapon he now bore bravely, as became the son of an heroic race, and pausing now and again in the sunny space of the forest assumed, with some exaggeration, the postures of aggression and defense that he had been taught by the engraver's art. Made reckless by the ease with which he overcame invisible foes attempting to stay his advance, he committed the common enough military error of pushing the pursuit to a dangerous extreme, until he found himself upon the margin of a wide but shallow brook, whose rapid waters barred his direct advance against the flying foe that had crossed with illogical ease. But the intrepid victor was not to be baffled; the spirit of the race which had passed the great sea burned unconquerable in that small breast and would not be denied. Finding a place where some boulders in the bed of the stream lay but a step or a leap apart, he made his way across and fell again upon the rear-guard of his imaginary foe, putting all to the sword.

Now that the battle had been won, prudence required that he withdraw to his base of operations. Alas; like many a mightier conqueror, and like one, the mightiest, he could not

curb the lust for war,
Nor learn that tempted Fate will leave the loftiest star.

Advancing from the bank of the creek he suddenly found himself confronted with a new and more formidable enemy: in the path that he was following, sat, bolt upright, with ears erect and paws suspended before it, a rabbit! With a startled cry the child turned and fled, he knew not in what direction, calling with inarticulate cries for his mother, weeping, stumbling, his tender skin cruelly torn by brambles, his little heart beating hard with terror— breathless, blind with tears—lost in the forest! Then, for more than an hour, he wandered with erring feet through the tangled undergrowth, till at last, overcome by fatigue, he lay down in a narrow space between two rocks, within a few yards of the stream and still grasping his toy sword, no longer a weapon but a companion, sobbed himself to sleep. The wood birds sang merrily above his head; the squirrels, whisking their bravery of tail, ran barking from tree to tree, unconscious of the pity of it, and somewhere far away was a strange, muffled thunder, as if the partridges were drumming in celebration of nature's victory over the son of her immemorial enslavers. And back at the little plantation, where white men and black were hastily searching the fields and hedges in alarm, a mother's heart was breaking for her missing child.

Hours passed, and then the little sleeper rose to his feet. The chill of the evening was in his limbs, the fear of the gloom in his heart. But he had rested, and he no longer wept. With some blind instinct which impelled to action he struggled through the undergrowth about him and came to a more open ground—on his right the brook, to the left a gentle acclivity studded with infrequent trees; over all, the gathering gloom of twilight. A thin, ghostly mist rose along the water. It frightened and repelled him; instead of recrossing, in the direction whence he had come, he turned his back upon it, and went forward toward the dark enclosing wood. Suddenly he saw before him a strange moving object which he took to be some large animal—a dog, a pig—he could not name it; perhaps it was a bear. He had seen pictures of bears but knew of nothing to their discredit and had vaguely wished to meet one. But something in form or movement of this object—something in the awkwardness of its approach—told him that it was not a bear, and curiosity was stayed by fear. He stood still and as it came slowly on gained courage every moment, for he saw that at least it had not the long, menacing ears of the rabbit. Possibly his impressionable mind was half conscious of something familiar in its shambling, awkward gait. Before it had approached near enough to resolve his doubts he saw that it was followed by another and another. To right and to left were many more; the whole open space about him was alive with them—all moving toward the brook.

They were men. They crept upon their hands and knees. They used their hands only, dragging their legs. They used their knees only, their arms hanging idle at their sides. They strove to rise to their feet, but fell prone in the attempt. They did nothing naturally, and nothing alike, save only to advance foot by foot in the same direction. Singly, in pairs and in little groups, they came on through the gloom, some halting now and again while others crept slowly past them, then resuming their movement. They came by dozens and by hundreds; as far on either hand as one could see in the deepening gloom they extended and the black wood behind them appeared to be inexhaustible. The very ground seemed in motion toward the creek. Occasionally one who had paused did not again go on, but lay motionless. He was dead. Some, pausing, made strange gestures with their hands, erected their arms and lowered them again, clasped their heads; spread their palms upward, as men are sometimes seen to do in public prayer.

Not all of this did the child note; it is what would have been noted by an elder observer; he saw little but that these were men, yet crept like babes. Being men, they were not terrible, though unfamiliarly clad. He moved among them freely, going from one to another and peering into their faces with childish curiosity. All their faces were singularly white and many were streaked and gouted with red. Something in this—something too, perhaps, in their grotesque attitudes and movements—reminded him of the painted clown whom he had seen last summer in the circus, and he laughed as he watched them. But on and ever on they crept, these maimed and bleeding men, as heedless as he of the dramatic contrast between his laughter and their own ghastly gravity. To him it was a merry spectacle. He had seen his father's Negroes creep upon their hands and knees for his amusement—had ridden them so, "making believe" they were his horses. He now approached one of these crawling figures from behind and with an agile movement mounted it astride. The man sank upon his breast, recovered, flung the small boy fiercely to the ground as an unbroken colt might have done, then turned upon him a face that lacked a lower jaw—from the upper teeth to the throat was a great red gap fringed with hanging shreds of flesh and splinters of bone. The unnatural prominence of nose, the absence of chin, the fierce eyes, gave this man the appearance of a great bird of prey crimsoned in throat and breast by the blood of its quarry. The man rose to his knees, the child to his feet. The man shook his fist at the child; the child, terrified at last, ran to a tree near by, got upon the farther side of it and took a more serious view of the situation. And so the clumsy multitude dragged itself slowly and painfully along in hideous pantomime—moved forward down the slope like a swarm of great black beetles, with never a sound of going—in silence profound, absolute.

Instead of darkening, the haunted landscape began to brighten. Through the belt of trees beyond the brook shone a strange red light, the trunks and branches of the trees making a black lacework against it. It struck the creeping figures and gave them monstrous shadows, which caricatured their movements on the lit grass. It fell upon their faces, touching their whiteness with a ruddy tinge, accentuating the stains with which so many of them were freaked and maculated. It sparkled on buttons and bits of metal in their clothing. Instinctively the child turned toward the growing splendor and moved down the slope with his horrible companions; in a few moments had passed the foremost of the throng—not much of a feat, considering his advantages. He placed himself in the lead, his wooden sword still in hand, and solemnly directed the march, conforming his pace to theirs and occasionally turning as if to see that his forces did not straggle. Surely such a leader never before had such a following.

Scattered about upon the ground now slowly narrowing by the encroachment of this awful march to water, were certain articles to which, in the leader's mind, were coupled no significant associations: an occasional blanket, tightly rolled lengthwise, doubled and the ends bound together with a string; a heavy knapsack here, and there a broken rifle—such things, in short, as are found in the rear of retreating troops, the "spoor" of men flying from their hunters. Everywhere near the creek, which here had a margin of lowland, the earth was trodden into mud by the feet of men and horses. An observer of better experience in the use of his eyes would have noticed that these footprints pointed in both directions; the ground had been twice passed over—in advance and in retreat. A few hours before, these desperate, stricken men, with their more fortunate and now distant comrades, had penetrated the forest in thousands. Their successive battalions, breaking into swarms and reforming in lines, had passed the child on every side—had almost trodden on him as he slept. The rustle and murmur of their march had not awakened him. Almost within a stone's throw of where he lay they had fought a battle; but all unheard by him were the roar of the musketry, the shock of the cannon, "the thunder of the captains and the shouting." He had slept through it all, grasping his little wooden sword with perhaps a tighter clutch in unconscious sympathy with his martial environment, but as heedless of the grandeur of the struggle as the dead who had died to make the glory.

The fire beyond the belt of woods on the farther side of the creek, reflected to earth from the canopy of its own smoke, was now suffusing the whole landscape. It transformed the sinuous line of mist to the vapor of gold. The water gleamed with dashes of red, and red, too, were many of the stones protruding above the surface. But that was blood; the less desperately wounded had stained them in crossing. On them, too, the child now crossed with eager steps; he was going to the fire. As he stood upon the farther bank he turned about to look at the companions of his march. The advance was arriving at the creek. The stronger had already drawn themselves to the brink and plunged their faces into the flood. Three or four who lay without motion appeared to have no heads. At this the child's eyes expanded with wonder; even his hospitable understanding could not accept a phenomenon implying such vitality as that. After slaking their thirst these men had not had the strength to back away from the water, nor to keep their heads above it. They were drowned. In rear of these, the open spaces of the forest showed the leader as many formless figures of his grim command as at first; but not nearly so many were in motion. He waved his cap for their encouragement and smilingly pointed with his weapon in the direction of the guiding light—a pillar of fire to this strange exodus.

Confident of the fidelity of his forces, he now entered the belt of woods, passed through it easily in the red illumination, climbed a fence, ran across a field, turning now and again to coquet with his responsive shadow, and so approached the blazing ruin of a dwelling. Desolation everywhere! In all the wide glare not a living thing was visible. He cared nothing for that; the spectacle pleased, and he danced with glee in imitation of the wavering flames. He ran about, collecting fuel, but every object that he found was too heavy for him to cast in from the distance to which the heat limited his approach. In despair he flung in his sword—a surrender to the superior forces of nature. His military career was at an end.

Shifting his position, his eyes fell upon some outbuildings which had an oddly familiar appearance, as if he had dreamed of them. He stood considering them with wonder, when suddenly the entire plantation, with its enclosing forest, seemed to turn as if upon a pivot. His little world swung half around; the points of the compass were reversed. He recognized the blazing building as his own home!

For a moment he stood stupefied by the power of the revelation, then ran with stumbling feet, making a half-circuit of the ruin. There, conspicuous in the light of the conflagration, lay the dead body of a woman—the white face turned upward, the hands thrown out and clutched full of grass, the clothing deranged, the long dark hair in tangles and full of clotted blood. The greater part of the forehead was torn away, and from the jagged hole the brain protruded, overflowing the temple, a frothy mass of gray, crowned with clusters of crimson bubbles—the work of a shell.

The child moved his little hands, making wild, uncertain gestures. He uttered a series of inarticulate and indescribable cries—something between the chattering of an ape and the gobbling of a turkey—a startling, soulless, unholy sound, the language of a devil. The child was a deaf mute.

Then he stood motionless, with quivering lips, looking down upon the wreck.

EXERCISES

1. Discuss the importance of the first two paragraphs of the story. What is the tone of these paragraphs? How do they serve as the essential backdrop for the story?

2. Discuss the point of view of the story as reflected by this statement: "Not all of this did the child note; it is what would have been noted by an elder observer."

3. Point out the themes of natural versus unnatural, make-believe versus reality, adult versus child in the story.

4. What is the significance of our discovery that the child is a deaf mute? How does this fact account for much that is strange in the story? How does it communicate the horror of the story?

5. In what ways is this an antiwar story? Point out how it communicates the antiwar message not only in the basic situation it establishes but also in its tone and language.

MONICA
WOOD | *Disappearing*

When he starts in, I don't look anymore, I know what it looks like, what he looks like, tobacco on his teeth. I just lie in the deep sheets and shut my eyes. I make noises that make it go faster and when he's done he's as far from me as he gets. He could be dead he's so far away.

Lettie says leave then stupid but who would want me. Three hundred pounds anyway but I never check. Skin like tapioca pudding, I wouldn't show anyone. A man.

So we go to the pool at the junior high, swimming lessons. First it's blow bubbles and breathe, blow and breathe. Awful, hot nosefuls of chlorine. My eyes stinging red and patches on my skin. I look worse. We'll get caps and goggles and earplugs and body cream Lettie says. It's better.

There are girls there, what bodies. Looking at me and Lettie out the side of their eyes. Gold hair, skin like milk, chlorine or no.

They thought when I first lowered into the pool, that fat one parting the Red Sea. I didn't care. Something happened when I floated. Good said the little instructor. A little redhead in an emerald suit, no stomach, a depression almost, and white wet skin. Good she said you float just great. Now we're getting somewhere. The whistle around her neck blinded my eyes. And the water under the fluorescent lights. I got scared and couldn't float again. The bottom of the pool was scarred, drops of gray shadow rippling. Without the water I would crack open my head, my dry flesh would sound like a splash on the tiles.

At home I ate a cake and a bottle of milk. No wonder you look like that he said. How can you stand yourself. You're no Cary Grant I told him and he laughed and laughed until I threw up.

When this happens I want to throw up again and again until my heart flops out wet and writhing on the kitchen floor. Then he would know I have one and it moves.

So I went back. And floated again. My arms came around and the groan of the water made the tight blondes smirk but I heard Good that's the crawl that's it in fragments from the redhead when I lifted my face. Through the earplugs I heard her skinny voice. She was happy that I was floating and moving too.

Lettie stopped the lessons and read to me things out of magazines. You have to swim a lot to lose weight. You have to stop eating too. Forget cake and ice cream. Doritos are out. I'm not doing it for that I told her but she wouldn't believe me. She couldn't imagine.

Looking down that shaft of water I know I won't fall. The water shimmers and eases up and down, the heft of me doesn't matter I float anyway.

He says it makes no difference I look the same. But I'm not the same. I can hold myself up in deep water. I can move my arms and feet and the water goes behind me, the wall comes closer. I can look down twelve feet to a cold slab of tile and not be afraid. It makes a difference I tell him. Better believe it mister.

Then this other part happens. Other men interest me. I look at them, real ones, not the ones on TV that's something else entirely. These are real. The one with the white milkweed hair who delivers the mail. The meter man from the light company, heavy thick feet in boots. A smile. Teeth. I drop something out of the cart in the supermarket to see who will pick it up. Sometimes a man. One had yellow short hair and called me ma'am. Young. Thin legs and an accent. One was older. Looked me in the eyes. Heavy, but not like me. My eyes are nice. I color the lids. In the pool it runs off in blue tears. When I come out my face is naked.

The lessons are over, I'm certified. A little certificate signed by the redhead. She says I can swim and I can. I'd do better with her body, thin calves hard as granite.

I get a lane to myself, no one shares. The blondes ignore me now that I don't splash the water, know how to lower myself silently. And when I swim I cut the water cleanly.

For one hour every day I am thin, thin as water, transparent, invisible, steam or smoke.

The redhead is gone, they put her at a different pool and I miss the glare of the whistle dangling between her emerald breasts. Lettie won't come over at all now that she is fatter than me. You're so uppity she says. All this talk about water and who do you think you are.

He says I'm looking all right, so at night it is worse but sometimes now when he starts in I say no. On Sundays the pool is closed I can't say no. I haven't been invisible. Even on days when I don't say no it's all right, he's better.

One night he says it won't last, what about the freezer full of low-cal dinners and that machine in the basement. I'm not doing it for that and he doesn't believe me either. But this time there is another part. There are other men in the water I tell him. Fish he says. Fish in the sea. Good luck.

Ma you've lost says my daughter-in-law, the one who didn't want me in the wedding pictures. One with the whole family, she couldn't help that. I learned how to swim I tell her. You should try it, it might help your ugly disposition.

They closed the pool for two weeks and I went crazy. Repairing the tiles. I went there anyway, drove by in the car. I drank water all day.

Then they opened again and I went every day, sometimes four times until the green paint and new stripes looked familiar as a face. At first the water was heavy as blood but I kept on until it was thinner and thinner, just enough to hold me up. That was when I stopped with the goggles and cap and plugs, things that kept the water out of me.

There was a time I went the day before a holiday and no one was there. It was echoey silence just me and the soundless empty pool and a lifeguard behind the glass. I lowered myself so slow it hurt every muscle but not a blip of water not a ripple not one sound and I was under in that other quiet, so quiet some tears got out, I saw their blue trail swirling.

The redhead is back and nods, she has seen me somewhere. I tell her I took lessons and she still doesn't remember.

This has gone too far he says I'm putting you in the hospital. He calls them at the pool and they pay no attention. He doesn't touch me and I smile into my pillow, a secret smile in my own square of the dark.

Oh my God Lettie says what the hell are you doing what the hell do you think you're doing. I'm disappearing I tell her and what can you do about it not a blessed thing.

For a long time in the middle of it people looked at me. Men. And I thought about it. Believe it, I thought. And now they don't look at me again. And it's better.

I'm almost there. Almost water.

The redhead taught me how to dive, how to tuck my head and vanish like a needle into skin, and every time it happens, my feet leaving the board, I think, this will be the time.

EXERCISES

1. What does the language of the story suggest about the education, intelligence, and social level of the narrator? Is this important?

2. What is significant about the relationship the narrator has with her husband?

3. What is the metaphoric significance of the fact that the narrator floats?

4. What difference does the water make to the narrator? What does the law of gravity have to do with her experience?

5. How does the narrator's involvement with the water become obsessive?

6. The narrator's "disappearing" is the central event in the story. What does it mean? What does she mean when she says, "I'm almost there. Almost water."

KAY
BOYLE | *The Astronomer's Wife*

There is an evil moment on awakening when all things seem to pause. But for women, they only falter and may be set in action by a single move: a lifted hand and the pendulum will swing, or the voice raised and through every room the pulse takes up its beating. The astronomer's wife felt the interval gaping and at once filled it to the brim. She fetched up her gentle voice and sent it warily down the stairs for coffee, swung her feet out upon the oval mat, and hailed the morning with her bare arms' quivering flesh drawn taut in rhythmic exercise: left, left, left my wife and fourteen children, right, right, right in the middle of the dusty road.

The day would proceed from this, beat by beat, without reflection, like every other day. The astronomer was still asleep, or feigning it, and she, once out of bed, had come into her own possession. Although scarcely ever out of sight of the impenetrable silence of his brow, she would be absent from him all the day in being clean, busy, kind. He was a man of other things, a dreamer. At times he lay still for hours, at others he sat upon the roof behind his telescope, or wandered down the pathway to the road and out across the mountains. This day, like any other, would go on from the removal of the spot left there from dinner on the astronomer's vest to the severe thrashing of the mayonnaise for lunch. That man might be each time the new arching wave, and woman the undertow that sucked him back, were things she had been told by his silence were so.

In spite of the earliness of the hour, the girl had heard her mistress's voice and was coming up the stairs. At the threshold of the bedroom she paused, and said: "Madame, the plumber is here."

The astronomer's wife put on her white and scarlet smock very quickly and buttoned it at the neck. Then she stepped carefully around the motionless spread of water in the hall.

"Tell him to come right up," she said. She laid her hands on the bannisters and stood looking down the wooden stairway. "Ah, I am Mrs. Ames," she said softly as she saw him mounting. "I am Mrs. Ames," she said softly, softly down the flight of stairs. "I am Mrs. Ames," spoken soft as a willow weeping. "The professor is still sleeping. Just step this way."

The plumber himself looked up and saw Mrs. Ames with her voice hushed, speaking to him. She was a youngish woman, but this she had forgotten. The mystery and silence of her husband's mind lay like a chiding finger on her lips. Her eyes were gray, for the light had been extinguished in them. The strange dim halo of her yellow hair was still uncombed and sideways on her head.

For all of his heavy boots, the plumber quieted the sound of his feet, and together they went down the hall, picking their way around the still lake of water that spread as far as the landing and lay docile there. The plumber was a tough, hardy man; but he took off his hat when he spoke to her and looked her fully, almost insolently in the eye.

"Does it come from the wash-basin," he said, "or from the other . . . ?"

"Oh, from the other," said Mrs. Ames without hesitation.

In this place the villas were scattered out few and primitive, and although beauty lay without there was no reflection of her face within. Here all was awkward and unfit; a sense of wrestling with uncouth forces gave everything an austere countenance. Even the plumber, dealing as does a woman with matters under hand, was grave and stately. The mountains round about seemed to have cast them into the shadow of great dignity.

Mrs. Ames began speaking of their arrival that summer in the little villa, mourning each event as it followed on the other.

"Then, just before going to bed last night," she said, "I noticed something was unusual."

The plumber cast down a folded square of sackcloth on the brimming floor and laid his leather apron on it. Then he stepped boldly onto the heart of the island it shaped and looked long into the overflowing bowl.

"The water should be stopped from the meter in the garden," he said at last.

"Oh, I did that," said Mrs. Ames, "the very first thing last night. I turned it off at once, in my nightgown, as soon as I saw what was happening. But all this had already run in."

The plumber looked for a moment at her red kid slippers. She was standing just at the edge of the clear, pure-seeming tide.

"It's no doubt the soil lines," he said severely. "It may be that something has stopped them, but my opinion is that the water seals aren't working. That's the trouble often enough in such cases. If you had a valve you wouldn't be caught like this."

Mrs. Ames did not know how to meet this rebuke. She stood, swaying a little, looking into the plumber's blue relentless eyes.

"I'm sorry—I'm sorry that my husband," she said, "is still—resting and cannot go into this with you. I'm sure it must be very interesting. . . ."

"You'll probably have to have the traps sealed," said the plumber grimly, and at the sound of this Mrs. Ames' hand flew in dismay to the side of her face. The plumber made no move, but the set of his mouth as he looked at her seemed to soften. "Anyway, I'll have a look from the garden end," he said.

"Oh, do," said the astronomer's wife in relief. Here was a man who spoke of action and object as simply as women did! But however hushed her voice had been, it carried clearly to Professor Ames who lay, dreaming and solitary, upon his bed. He heard their footsteps come down the hall, pause, and skip across the pool of overflow.

"Katherine!" said the astronomer in a ringing tone. "There's a problem worthy of your mettle!"

Mrs. Ames did not turn her head, but led the plumber swiftly down the stairs. When the sun in the garden struck her face, he saw there was a wave of color in it, but this may have been anything but shame.

"You see how it is," said the plumber, as if leading her mind away. "The drains run from these houses right down the hill, big enough for a man to stand upright in them, and clean as a whistle too." There they stood in the garden with the vegetation flowering in disorder all about. The plumber looked at the astronomer's wife. "They come out at the torrent on the other side of the forest beyond there," he said.

But the words the astronomer had spoken still sounded in her in despair. The mind of man, she knew, made steep and sprightly flights, pursued illusion, took foothold in the nameless things that cannot pass between the thumb and finger. But whenever the astronomer gave voice to the thoughts that soared within him, she returned in gratitude to the long expanses of his silence. Desertlike they stretched behind and before the articulation of his scorn.

Life, life is an open sea, she sought to explain it in sorrow, and to survive women cling to the floating débris on the tide. But the plumber had suddenly fallen upon his knees in the grass and had crooked his fingers through the rings of the drains' trap-door. When she looked down she saw that he was looking up into her face, and she saw too that his hair was as light as gold.

"Perhaps Mr. Ames," he said rather bitterly, "would like to come down with me and have a look around?"

"Down?" said Mrs. Ames in wonder.

"Into the drains," said the plumber brutally. "They're a study for a man who likes to know what's what."

"Oh, Mr. Ames," said Mrs. Ames in confusion. "He's still—still in bed, you see."

The plumber lifted his strong, weathered face and looked curiously at her. Surely it seemed to him strange for a man to linger in bed, with the sun pouring yellow as wine all over the place. The astronomer's wife saw his lean cheeks, his high, rugged bones, and the deep seams in his brow. His flesh was as firm and clean as wood, stained richly tan with the climate's rigor. His fingers were blunt, but comprehensible to her, gripped in the ring and holding the iron door wide. The backs of his hands were bound round and round with ripe blue veins of blood.

"At any rate," said the astronomer's wife, and the thought of it moved her lips to smile a little, "Mr. Ames would never go down there alive. He likes going up," she said. And she, in her turn, pointed, but impudently, towards the heavens. "On the roof. Or on the mountains. He's been up on the tops of them many times."

"It's a matter of habit," said the plumber, and suddenly he went down the trap. Mrs. Ames saw a bright little piece of his hair still shining, like a star, long after the rest of him had gone. Out of the depths, his voice, hollow and dark with foreboding, returned to her. "I think something has stopped the elbow," was what he said.

This was speech that touched her flesh and bone and made her wonder. When her husband spoke of height, having no sense of it, she could not picture it nor hear. Depth or magic passed her by unless a name were given. But madness in a daily shape, as elbow stopped, she saw clearly and well. She sat down on the grass, bewildered that it should be a man who had spoken to her so.

She saw the weeds springing up, and she did not move to tear them up from life. She sat powerless, her senses veiled, with no action taking shape beneath her hands. In this way some men sat for hours on end, she knew, tracking a single thought back to its origin. The mind of man could balance and divide, weed out, destroy. She sat on the full, burdened grasses, seeking to think, and dimly waiting for the plumber to return.

Whereas her husband had always gone up, as the dead go, she knew now that there were others who went down, like the corporeal being of the dead. That men were then divided into two bodies now seemed clear to Mrs. Ames. This knowledge stunned her with its simplicity and took the uneasy motion from her limbs. She could not stir, but sat facing the mountains' rocky flanks, and harking in silence to lucidity. Her husband was the mind, this other man the meat, of all mankind.

After a little, the plumber emerged from the earth: first the light top of his head, then the burnt brow, and then the blue eyes fringed with whitest lash. He braced his thick hands flat on the pavings of the garden-path and swung himself completely from the pit.

"It's the soil lines," he said pleasantly. "The gases," he said as he looked down upon her lifted face, "are backing up the drains."

"What in the world are we going to do?" said the astronomer's wife softly. There was a young and strange delight in putting questions to which true answers would be given. Everything the astronomer had ever said to her was a continuous query to which there would be no response.

"Ah, come, now," said the plumber, looking down and smiling. "There's a remedy for every ill, you know. Sometimes it may be that," he said as if speaking to a child, "or sometimes the other thing. But there's always a help for everything a-miss."

Things come out of herbs and make you young again, he might have been saying to her; or the first good rain will quench any drought; or time of itself will put a broken bone together.

"I'm going to follow the ground pipe out right to the torrent," the plumber was saying. "The trouble's between here and there and I'll find it on the way. There's nothing at all that can't be done over for the caring," he was saying, and his eyes were fastened on her face in insolence, or gentleness, or love.

The astronomer's wife stood up, fixed a pin in her hair, and turned around towards the kitchen. Even while she was calling the servant's name, the plumber began speaking again.

"I once had a cow that lost her cud," the plumber was saying. The girl came out on the kitchen-step and Mrs. Ames stood smiling at her in the sun.

"The trouble is very serious, very serious," she said across the garden. "When Mr. Ames gets up, please tell him I've gone down."

She pointed briefly to the open door in the pathway, and the plumber hoisted his kit on his arm and put out his hand to help her down.

"But I made her another in no time," he was saying, "out of flowers and things and what-not."

"Oh," said the astronomer's wife in wonder as she stepped into the heart of the earth. She took his arm, knowing that what he said was true.

EXERCISES

1. What is the difference between the astronomer and his wife? What is the significance of his being an astronomer? Does this profession have symbolic value?

2. What is the difference between the astronomer and the plumber? Does the plumber's occupation have symbolic value in this story?

3. Discuss the similarity between the plumber and the astronomer's wife.

4. Discuss the following: "The mind of man, she knew, made steep and sprightly flights, pursued illusion, took foothold in the nameless things that cannot pass between the thumb and finger."

5. Discuss the statement "Life, life is an open sea, she sought to explain it in sorrow, and to survive women cling to the floating débris of the tide."

6. Discuss the difference between "going down" and "going up."

7. Discuss the difference between how the plumber talks and how the astronomer talks.

8. Discuss the final paragraph. What are the implications of "going down" into the "heart of things"?

ELIZABETH
BOWEN | *The Demon Lover*

Towards the end of her day in London Mrs. Drover went round to her shut-up house to look for several things she wanted to take away. Some belonged to herself, some to her family, who were by now used to their country life. It was late August; it had been a steamy, showery day: at the moment the trees down the pavement glittered in an escape of humid yellow afternoon sun. Against the next batch of clouds, already piling up ink-dark, broken chimneys and parapets stood out. In her once familiar street, as in any unused channel, an unfamiliar queerness had silted up; a cat wove itself in and out of railings, but no human eye watched Mrs. Drover's return. Shifting some parcels under her arm, she slowly forced round her latchkey in an unwilling lock, then gave the door, which had warped, a push with her knee. Dead air came out to meet her as she went in.

The staircase window having been boarded up, no light came down into the hall. But one door, she could just see, stood ajar, so she went quickly through into the room and unshuttered the big window in there. Now the prosaic woman, looking about her, was more perplexed than she knew by everything that she saw, by traces of her long former habit of life—the yellow smoke-stain up the white marble mantelpiece, the ring left by a vase on the top of the escritoire; the bruise in the wallpaper where, on the door being thrown open widely, the china handle had always hit the wall. The piano, having gone away to be stored, had left what looked like claw-marks on its part of the parquet. Though not much dust had seeped in, each object wore a film of another kind; and, the only ventilation being the chimney, the whole drawing-room smelled of the cold hearth. Mrs. Drover put down her parcels on the escritoire and left the room to proceed upstairs; the things she wanted were in a bedroom chest.

She had been anxious to see how the house was—the part-time caretaker she shared with some neighbours was away this week on his holiday, known to be not yet back. At the best of times he did not look in often, and she was never sure that she trusted him. There were some cracks in the structure, left by the last bombing, on which she was anxious to keep an eye. Not that one could do anything—

A shaft of refracted daylight now lay across the hall. She stopped dead and stared at the hall table—on this lay a letter addressed to her.

She thought first—then the caretaker *must* be back. All the same, who, seeing the house shuttered, would have dropped a letter in at the box? It was not a circular, it was not a bill. And the post office redirected, to the address in the country, everything for her that came through the post. The caretaker (even if he *were* back) did not know she was due in London today—her call here had been planned to be a surprise—so his negligence in the manner of this letter, leaving it to wait in the dusk and the dust, annoyed her. Annoyed, she picked up the letter, which bore no stamp. But it cannot be important, or they would know. . . . She took the letter rapidly upstairs with her, without a stop to look at the writing till she reached what had been her bedroom, where she let in light. The room looked over the garden and other gardens: the sun had gone in; as the clouds sharpened and lowered, the trees and rank lawns seemed already to smoke with dark. Her reluctance to look again at the letter came from the fact that she felt intruded upon—and by someone contemptuous of her ways. However, in the tenseness preceding the fall of rain she read it: it was a few lines.

> Dear Kathleen: You will not have forgotten that today is our anniversary, and the day we said. The years have gone by at once slowly and fast. In view of the fact that nothing has changed, I shall rely upon you to keep your promise. I was sorry to see you leave London, but was satisfied that you would be back in time. You may expect me, therefore, at the hour arranged. Until then . . .
>
> K.

Mrs. Drover looked for the date: it was today's. She dropped the letter on to the bed-springs, then picked it up to see the writing again—her lips, beneath the remains of lipstick, beginning to go white. She felt so much the change in her own face that she went to the mirror, polished a clear patch in it and looked at once urgently and stealthily in. She was confronted by a woman of forty-four, with eyes starting out under a hat-brim that had been rather carelessly pulled down. She had not put on any more powder since she left the shop where she ate her solitary tea. The pearls her husband had given her on their marriage hung loose round her now rather thinner throat, slipping in the V of the pink wool jumper her sister knitted last autumn as they sat round the fire. Mrs. Drover's most normal expression was one of controlled worry, but of assent. Since the birth of the third of her little boys, attended by a quite serious illness, she had had an intermittent muscular flicker to the left of her mouth, but in spite of this she could always sustain a manner that was at once energetic and calm.

Turning from her own face as precipitately as she had gone to meet it, she went to the chest where the things were, unlocked it, threw up the lid and knelt to search. But as rain began to come crashing down she could not keep from looking over her shoulder at the stripped bed on which the letter lay. Behind the blanket of rain the clock of the church that still stood struck six— with rapidly heightening apprehension she counted each of the slow strokes. "The hour arranged. . . . My God," she said, "*what* hour? How should I . . . ? After twenty-five years. . . ."

The young girl talking to the soldier in the garden had not ever completely seen his face. It was dark; they were saying goodbye under a tree. Now and then—for it felt, from not seeing him at this intense moment, as though she had never seen him at all—she verified his presence for these few moments longer by putting out a hand, which he each time pressed, without very much kindness, and painfully, on to one of the breast buttons of his uniform. That cut of the button on the palm of her hand was, principally what she was to carry away. This was so near the end of a leave from France that she could only wish him already gone. It was August 1916. Being not kissed, being drawn away from and looked at intimidated Kathleen till she imagined spectral glitters in the place of his eyes. Turning away and looking back up the lawn she saw, through branches of trees, the drawing-room window light: she caught a breath for the moment when she could go running back there into the safe arms of her mother and sister, and cry: "What shall I do, what shall I do? He has gone."

Hearing her catch her breath, her fiancé said, without feeling: "Cold?"

"You're going away such a long way."

"Not so far as you think."

"I don't understand?"

"You don't have to," he said. "You will. You know what we said."

"But that was—suppose you—I mean, suppose."

"I shall be with you," he said, "sooner or later. You won't forget that. You need do nothing but wait."

Only a little more than a minute later she was free to run up the silent lawn. Looking in through the window at her mother and sister, who did not for the moment perceive her, she already felt that unnatural promise drive down between her and the rest of all human kind. No other way of having given herself could have made her feel so apart, lost and foresworn. She could not have plighted a more sinister troth.

Kathleen behaved well when, some months later, her fiancé was reported missing, presumed killed. Her family not only supported her but were able to praise her courage without stint because they could not regret, as a husband for her, the man they knew almost nothing about. They hoped she would, in a year or two, console herself—and had it been only a question of consolation things might have gone much straighter ahead. But her trouble, behind just a little grief, was a complete dislocation from everything. She did not reject other lovers, for these failed to appear: for years she failed to attract men— and with the approach of her thirties she became natural enough to share her family's anxiousness on this score. She began to put herself out, to wonder; and at thirty-two she was very greatly relieved to find herself being courted by William Drover. She married him, and the two of them settled down in this quiet, arboreal part of Kensington: in this house the years piled up, her children were born and they all lived till they were driven out by the bombs of the next war. Her movements as Mrs. Drover were circumscribed, and she dismissed any idea that they were still watched.

As things were—dead or living the letter-writer sent her only a threat. Unable, for some minutes, to go on kneeling with her back exposed to the empty room, Mrs. Drover rose from the chest to sit on an upright chair whose back was firmly against the wall. The desuetude of her former bedroom, her married London home's whole air of being a cracked cup from which memory, with its reassuring power, had either evaporated or leaked away, made a crisis—and at just this crisis the letter-writer had, knowledgeably, struck. The hollowness of the house this evening cancelled years on years of voices, habits and steps. Through the shut windows she only heard rain fall on the roofs around. To rally herself, she said she was in a mood—and for two or three seconds shutting her eyes, told herself that she had imagined the letter. But she opened them—there it lay on the bed.

On the supernatural side of the letter's entrance she was not permitting her mind to dwell. Who, in London, knew she meant to call at the house today? Evidently, however, this had been known. The caretaker, *had* he come back, had had no cause to expect her: he would have taken the letter in his pocket, to forward it, at his own time, through the post. There was no other sign that the caretaker had been in—but, if not? Letters dropped in at doors of deserted houses do not fly or walk to tables in halls. They do not sit on the dust of empty tables with the air of certainty that they will be found. There is needed some human hand—but nobody but the caretaker had a key. Under circumstances she did not care to consider, a house can be entered without a key. It was possible that she was not alone now. She might be being waited for, downstairs. Waited for—until when? Until "the hour arranged." At least that was not six o'clock: six has struck.

She rose from the chair and went over and locked the door.

The thing was, to get out. To fly? No, not that: she had to catch her train. As a woman whose utter dependability was the keystone of her family life she was not willing to return to the country, to her husband, her little boys and her sister, without the objects she had come up to fetch. Resuming work at the chest she set about making up a number of parcels in a rapid, fumbling-decisive way. These, with her shopping parcels, would be too much to carry; these meant a taxi—at the thought of the taxi her heart went up and her normal breathing resumed. I will ring up the taxi now; the taxi cannot come too soon: I shall hear the taxi out there running its engine, till I walk calmly down to it through the hall. I'll ring up—But no: the telephone is cut off. . . . She tugged at a knot she had tied wrong.

The idea of flight . . . He was never kind to me, not really. I don't remember him kind at all. Mother said he never considered me. He was set on me, that was what it was—not love. Not love, not meaning a person well. What did he do, to make me promise like that? I can't remember—But she found that she could.

She remembered with such dreadful acuteness that the twenty-five years since then dissolved like smoke and she instinctively looked for the weal left by the button on the palm of her hand. She remembered not only all that he said and did but the complete suspension of *her* existence during that August week. I was not myself—they all told me so at the time. She remembered—but with one white burning blank as where acid has dropped on a photograph: *under no conditions* could she remember his face.

So, wherever he may be waiting, I shall not know him. You have no time to run from a face you do not expect.

The thing was to get to the taxi before any clock struck what could be the hour. She would slip down the street and round the side of the square to where the square gave on the main road. She would return in the taxi, safe, to her own door, and bring the solid driver into the house with her to pick up the parcels from room to room. The idea of the taxi driver made her decisive, bold: she unlocked her door, went to the top of the staircase and listened down.

She heard nothing—but while she was hearing nothing the *passé* air of the staircase was disturbed by a draught that travelled up to her face. It emanated from the basement: down there a door or window was being opened by someone who chose this moment to leave the house.

The rain had stopped; the pavements steamily shone as Mrs. Drover let herself out by inches from her own front door into the empty street. The unoccupied houses opposite continued to meet her look with their damaged stare. Making towards the thoroughfare and the taxi, she tried not to keep looking behind. Indeed, the silence was so intense—one of those creeks of London silence exaggerated this summer by the damage of war—that no tread could have gained on hers unheard. Where her street debouched on the square where people went on living, she grew conscious of, and checked, her unnatural pace. Across the open end of the square two buses impassively passed each other: women, a perambulator, cyclists, a man wheeling a barrow signalized, once again, the ordinary flow of life. At the square's most populous corner should be—and was—the short taxi rank. This evening, only one taxi—but this, although it presented its blank rump, appeared already to be alertly waiting for her. Indeed, without looking round the driver started his engine as she panted up from behind and put her hand on the door. As she did so, the clock struck seven. The taxi faced the main road: to make the trip back to her house it would have to turn—she had settled back on the seat and the taxi *had* turned before she, surprised by its knowing movement, recollected that she had not "said where." She leaned forward to scratch at the glass panel that divided the driver's head from her own.

The driver braked to what was almost a stop, turned round and slid the glass panel back: the jolt of this flung Mrs. Drover forward till her face was almost into the glass. Through the aperture driver and passenger, not six inches between them, remained for an eternity eye to eye. Mrs. Drover's mouth hung open for some seconds before she could issue her first scream. After that she continued to scream freely and to beat with her gloved hands on the glass all round as the taxi, accelerating without mercy, made off with her into the hinterland of deserted streets.

EXERCISES

1. Discuss the effect of the physical surroundings, such as the broken chimneys and parapets, no human eye, and dead air.
2. Why is Mrs. Drover described as a prosaic woman?
3. What is the effect of Mrs. Drover looking in the mirror? What purpose does this gesture serve?
4. Discuss Mrs. Drover's feelings for the soldier when she was young.
5. Why is the promise described as an "unnatural" one? Why is it called a "sinister troth"?
6. Is this a supernatural story, or is it a psychological story? Discuss the difference.
7. Discuss what happens at the end of the story. Does the nature of the story change here? Is the final event real, supernatural, or psychological?
8. Is the ending an example of poetic justice? Does Mrs. Drover deserve what happens to her?

RAYMOND
CARVER | *Why Don't You Dance?*

In the kitchen, he poured another drink and looked at the bedroom suite in his front yard. The mattress was stripped and the candy-striped sheets lay beside two pillows on the chiffonier. Except for that, things looked much the way they had in the bedroom—nightstand and reading lamp on his side of the bed, nightstand and reading lamp on her side.

His side, her side.

He considered this as he sipped the whiskey.

The chiffonier stood a few feet from the foot of the bed. He had emptied the drawers into cartons that morning, and the cartons were in the living room. A portable heater was next to the chiffonier. A rattan chair with a decorator pillow stood at the foot of the bed. The buffed aluminum kitchen set took up a part of the driveway. A yellow muslin cloth, much too large, a gift, covered the table and hung down over the sides. A potted fern was on the table, along with a box of silverware and a record player, also gifts. A big console-model television set rested on a coffee table, and a few feet away from this stood a sofa and chair and a floor lamp. The desk was pushed against the garage door. A few utensils were on the desk, along with a wall clock and two framed prints. There was also in the driveway a carton with cups, glasses, and plates, each object wrapped in newspaper. That morning he had cleared out the closets, and except for the three cartons in the living room, all the stuff was out of the house. He had run an extension cord on out there and everything was connected. Things worked, no different from how it was when they were inside.

Now and then a car slowed and people stared. But no one stopped. It occurred to him that he wouldn't, either.

"It must be a yard sale," the girl said to the boy.

This girl and this boy were furnishing a little apartment.

"Let's see what they want for the bed," the girl said.

"And for the TV," the boy said.

The boy pulled into the driveway and stopped in front of the kitchen table.

They got out of the car and began to examine things, the girl touching the muslin cloth, the boy plugging in the blender and turning the dial to MINCE, the girl picking up a chafing dish, the boy turning on the television set and making little adjustments.

He sat down on the sofa to watch. He lit a cigarette, looked around, flipped the match into the grass.

The girl sat on the bed. She pushed off her shoes and lay back. She thought she could see a star.

"Come here, Jack. Try this bed. Bring one of those pillows," she said.

"How is it?" he said.

"Try it," she said.

He looked around. The house was dark.

"I feel funny," he said. "Better see if anybody's home."

She bounced on the bed.

"Try it first," she said.

He lay down on the bed and put the pillow under his head.

"How does it feel?" she said.

"It feels firm," he said.

She turned on her side and put her hand to his face.

"Kiss me," she said.

"Let's get up," he said.

"Kiss me," she said.

She closed her eyes. She held him.

He said, "I'll see if anybody's home."

But he just sat up and stayed where he was, making believe he was watching the television.

Lights came on in houses up and down the street.

"Wouldn't it be funny if," the girl said and grinned and didn't finish.

The boy laughed, but for no good reason. For no good reason, he switched the reading lamp on.

The girl brushed away a mosquito, whereupon the boy stood up and tucked in his shirt.

"I'll see if anybody's home," he said. "I don't think anybody's home. But if anybody is, I'll see what things are going for."

"Whatever they ask, offer ten dollars less. It's always a good idea," she said. "And, besides, they must be desperate or something."

"It's a pretty good TV," the boy said.

"Ask them how much," the girl said.

The man came down the sidewalk with a sack from the market. He had sandwiches, beer, whiskey. He saw the car in the driveway and the girl on the bed. He saw the television set going and the boy on the porch.

"Hello," the man said to the girl. "You found the bed. That's good."

"Hello," the girl said, and got up. "I was just trying it out." She patted the bed. "It's a pretty good bed."

"It's a good bed," the man said, and put down the sack and took out the beer and the whiskey.

"We thought nobody was here," the boy said. "We're interested in the bed and maybe in the TV. Also maybe the desk. How much do you want for the bed?"

"I was thinking fifty dollars for the bed," the man said.

"Would you take forty?" the girl asked.

"I'll take forty," the man said.

He took a glass out of the carton. He took the newspaper off the glass. He broke the seal on the whiskey.

"How about the TV?" the boy said.

"Twenty-five."

"Would you take fifteen?" the girl said.

"Fifteen's okay. I could take fifteen," the man said.

The girl looked at the boy.

"You kids, you'll want a drink," the man said. "Glasses in that box. I'm going to sit down. I'm going to sit down on the sofa."

The man sat on the sofa, leaned back, and stared at the boy and the girl.

The boy found two glasses and poured whiskey.

"That's enough," the girl said. "I think I want water in mine."

She pulled out a chair and sat at the kitchen table.

"There's water in that spigot over there," the man said. "Turn on that spigot."

The boy came back with the watered whiskey. He cleared his throat and sat down at the kitchen table. He grinned. But he didn't drink anything from his glass.

The man gazed at the television. He finished his drink and started another. He reached to turn on the floor lamp. It was then that his cigarette dropped from his fingers and fell between the cushions.

The girl got up to help him find it.

"So what do you want?" the boy said to the girl.

The boy took out the checkbook and held it to his lips as if thinking.

"I want the desk," the girl said. "How much money is the desk?"

The man waved his hand at this preposterous question.

"Name a figure," he said.

He looked at them as they sat at the table. In the lamplight, there was something about their faces. It was nice or it was nasty. There was no telling.

"I'm going to turn off this TV and put on a record," the man said. "This record-player is going, too. Cheap. Make me an offer."

He poured more whiskey and opened a beer.

"Everything goes," said the man.

The girl held out her glass and the man poured.

"Thank you," she said. "You're very nice," she said.

"It goes to your head," the boy said. "I'm getting it in the head." He held up his glass and jiggled it.

The man finished his drink and poured another, and then he found the box with the records.

"Pick something," the man said to the girl, and he held the records out to her.

The boy was writing the check.

"Here," the girl said, picking something, picking anything, for she did not know the names on these labels. She got up from the table and sat down again. She did not want to sit still.

"I'm making it out to cash," the boy said.

"Sure," the man said.

They drank. They listened to the record. And then the man put on another.

Why don't you kids dance? he decided to say, and then he said it. "Why don't you dance?"

"I don't think so," the boy said.

"Go ahead," the man said. "It's my yard. You can dance if you want to."

Arms about each other, their bodies pressed together, the boy and the girl moved up and down the driveway. They were dancing. And when the record was over, they did it again, and when that one ended, the boy said, "I'm drunk."

The girl said, "You're not drunk."

"Well, I'm drunk," the boy said.

The man turned the record over and the boy said, "I am."

"Dance with me," the girl said to the boy and then to the man, and when the man stood up, she came to him with her arms wide open.

"Those people over there, they're watching," she said.

"It's okay," the man said. "It's my place," he said.

"Let them watch," the girl said.

"That's right," the man said. "They thought they'd seen everything over here. But they haven't seen this, have they?" he said.

He felt her breath on his neck.

"I hope you like your bed," he said.

The girl closed and then opened her eyes. She pushed her face into the man's shoulder. She pulled the man closer.

"You must be desperate or something," she said.

Weeks later, she said: "The guy was about middle-aged. All his things right there in his yard. No lie. We got real pissed and danced. In the driveway. Oh, my God. Don't laugh. He played us these records. Look at this record-player. The old guy gave it to us. And all these crappy records. Will you look at this shit?"

She kept talking. She told everyone. There was more to it, and she was trying to get it talked out. After a time, she quit trying.

EXERCISES

1. What is suggested by the phrase "His side, her side"? Where is the "her" referred to? What is suggested by "He considered this as he sipped the whiskey"? At what points in the story do we know what the man is thinking?

2. What is it about the placement of the furniture outside that makes this different than just a garage or yard sale? What is the significance of these differences?

3. What does the girl not finish when she says, "Wouldn't it be funny if"?

4. What is suggested by the phrase "They must be desperate or something"?

5. Is there a metaphoric relationship between the young couple and the man and the missing "her"?

6. What is suggested by the question, "Why don't you dance?"

7. At the end the narrator says, "There was more to it, and she was trying to get it talked out." What is the "more" to it?

RAYMOND CARVER | *Neighbors*

Bill and Arlene Miller were a happy couple. But now and then they felt they alone among their circle had been passed by somehow, leaving Bill to attend to his bookkeeping duties and Arlene occupied with secretarial chores. They talked about it sometimes, mostly in comparison with the lives of their neighbors, Harriet and Jim Stone. It seemed to the Millers that the Stones lived a fuller and brighter life. The Stones were always going out for dinner, or entertaining at home, or traveling about the country somewhere in connection with Jim's work.

The Stones lived across the hall from the Millers. Jim was a salesman for a machine-parts firm and often managed to combine business with pleasure trips, and on this occasion the Stones would be away for ten days, first to Cheyenne, then on to St. Louis to visit relatives. In their absence, the Millers would look after the Stones' apartment, feed Kitty, and water the plants.

Bill and Jim shook hands beside the car. Harriet and Arlene held each other by the elbows and kissed lightly on the lips.

"Have fun," Bill said to Harriet.

"We will," said Harriet. "You kids have fun too."

Arlene nodded.

Jim winked at her. "Bye, Arlene. Take good care of the old man."

"I will," Arlene said.

"Have fun," Bill said.

"You bet," Jim said, clipping Bill lightly on the arm. "And thanks again, you guys."

The Stones waved as they drove away, and the Millers waved too.

"Well, I wish it was us," Bill said.

"God knows, we could use a vacation," Arlene said. She took his arm and put it around her waist as they climbed the stairs to their apartment.

After dinner Arlene said, "Don't forget. Kitty gets liver flavor the first night." She stood in the kitchen doorway folding the handmade tablecloth that Harriet had bought for her last year in Santa Fe.

Bill took a deep breath as he entered the Stones' apartment. The air was already heavy and it was vaguely sweet. The sunburst clock over the television said half past eight. He remembered when Harriet had come home with the clock, how she had crossed the hall to show it to Arlene, cradling the brass case in her arms and talking to it through the tissue paper as if it were an infant.

Kitty rubbed her face against his slippers and then turned onto her side, but jumped up quickly as Bill moved to the kitchen and selected one of the stacked cans from the gleaming drainboard. Leaving the cat to pick at her food, he headed for the bathroom. He looked at himself in the mirror and then closed his eyes and then looked again. He opened the medicine chest. He found a container of pills and read the label—*Harriet Stone. One each day as directed*—and slipped it into his pocket. He went back to the kitchen, drew a pitcher of water, and returned to the living room. He finished watering, set the pitcher on the rug, and opened the liquor cabinet. He reached in back for the bottle of Chivas Regal. He took two drinks from the bottle, wiped his lips on his sleeve, and replaced the bottle in the cabinet.

Kitty was on the couch sleeping. He switched off the lights, slowly closing and checking the door. He had the feeling he had left something.

"What kept you?" Arlene said. She sat with her legs turned under her, watching television.

"Nothing. Playing with Kitty," he said, and went over to her and touched her breasts.

"Let's go to bed, honey," he said.

The next day Bill took only ten minutes of the twenty-minute break allotted for the afternoon and left at fifteen minutes before five. He parked the car in the lot just as Arlene hopped down from the bus. He waited until she entered the building, then ran up the stairs to catch her as she stepped out of the elevator.

"Bill! God, you scared me. You're early," she said.

He shrugged. "Nothing to do at work," he said.

She let him use her key to open the door. He looked at the door across the hall before following her inside.

"Let's go to bed," he said.

"Now?" she laughed. "What's gotten into you?"

"Nothing. Take your dress off." He grabbed for her awkwardly, and she said, "Good God, Bill."

He unfastened his belt.

Later they sent out for Chinese food, and when it arrived they ate hungrily, without speaking, and listened to records.

"Let's not forget to feed Kitty," she said.

"I was just thinking about that," he said. "I'll go right over."

He selected a can of fish flavor for the cat, then filled the pitcher and went to water. When he returned to the kitchen, the cat was scratching in her box. She looked at him steadily before she turned back to the litter. He opened all the cupboards and examined the canned goods, the cereals, the packaged foods, the cocktail and wine glasses, the china, the pots and pans. He opened the refrigerator. He sniffed some celery, took two bites of cheddar cheese, and chewed on an apple as he walked into the bedroom. The bed seemed enormous, with a fluffy white bedspread draped to the floor. He pulled out a nightstand drawer, found a half-empty package of cigarettes and stuffed them into his pocket. Then he stepped to the closet and was opening it when the knock sounded at the front door.

He stopped by the bathroom and flushed the toilet on his way.

"What's been keeping you?" Arlene said. "You've been over here more than an hour."

"Have I really?" he said.

"Yes, you have," she said.

"I had to go to the toilet," he said.

"You have your own toilet," she said.

"I couldn't wait," he said.

That night they made love again.

In the morning he had Arlene call in for him. He showered, dressed, and made a light breakfast. He tried to start a book. He went out for a walk and felt better. But after a while, hands still in his pockets, he returned to the apartment. He stopped at the Stones' door on the chance he might hear the cat moving about. Then he let himself in at his own door and went to the kitchen for the key.

Inside it seemed cooler than his apartment, and darker too. He wondered if the plants had something to do with the temperature of the air. He looked out the window, and then he moved slowly through each room considering everything that fell under his gaze, carefully, one object at a time. He saw ashtrays, items of furniture, kitchen utensils, the clock. He saw everything. At last he entered the bedroom, and the cat appeared at his feet. He stroked her once, carried her into the bathroom, and shut the door.

He lay down on the bed and stared at the ceiling. He lay for a while with his eyes closed, and then he moved his hand under his belt. He tried to recall what day it was. He tried to remember when the Stones were due back, and then he wondered if they would ever return. He could not remember their faces or the way they talked and dressed. He sighed and with effort rolled off the bed to lean over the dresser and look at himself in the mirror.

He opened the closet and selected a Hawaiian shirt. He looked until he found Bermudas, neatly pressed and hanging over a pair of brown twill slacks. He shed his own clothes and slipped into the shorts and the shirt. He looked in the mirror again. He went to the living room and poured himself a drink and sipped it on his way back to the bedroom. He put on a blue shirt, a dark suit, a blue and white tie, black wing-tip shoes. The glass was empty and he went for another drink.

In the bedroom again, he sat on a chair, crossed his legs, and smiled, observing himself in the mirror. The telephone rang twice and fell silent. He finished the drink and took off the suit. He rummaged through the top drawers until he found a pair of panties and a brassiere. He stepped into the panties and fastened the brassiere, then looked through the closet for an outfit. He put on a black and white checkered skirt and tried to zip it up. He put on a burgundy blouse that buttoned up the front. He considered her shoes, but understood they would not fit. For a long time he looked out the living-room window from behind the curtain. Then he returned to the bedroom and put everything away.

He was not hungry. She did not eat much, either. They looked at each other shyly and smiled. She got up from the table and checked that the key was on the shelf and then she quickly cleared the dishes.

He stood in the kitchen doorway and smoked a cigarette and watched her pick up the key.

"Make yourself comfortable while I go across the hall," she said. "Read the paper or something." She closed her fingers over the key. He was, she said, looking tired.

He tried to concentrate on the news. He read the paper and turned on the television. Finally he went across the hall. The door was locked.

"It's me. Are you still there, honey?" he called.

After a time the lock released and Arlene stepped outside and shut the door. "Was I gone so long?" she said.

"Well, you were," he said.

"Was I?" she said. "I guess I must have been playing with Kitty."

He studied her, and she looked away, her hand still resting on the doorknob.

"It's funny," she said. "You know—to go in someone's place like that."

He nodded, took her hand from the knob, and guided her toward their own door. He let them into their apartment.

"It *is* funny," he said.

He noticed white lint clinging to the back of her sweater, and the color was high in her cheeks. He began kissing her on the neck and hair and she turned and kissed him back.

"Oh, damn," she said. "Damn, damn," she sang, girlishly clapping her hands. "I just remembered. I really and truly forgot to do what I went over there to do. I didn't feed Kitty or do any watering." She looked at him. "Isn't that stupid?"

"I don't think so," he said. "Just a minute. I'll get my cigarettes and go back with you."

She waited until he had closed and locked their door, and then she took his arm at the muscle and said, "I guess I should tell you. I found some pictures."

He stopped in the middle of the hall. "What kind of pictures?"

"You can see for yourself," she said, and she watched him.

"No kidding." He grinned. "Where?"

"In a drawer," she said.

"No kidding," he said.

And then she said, "Maybe they won't come back," and was at once astonished at her words.

"It could happen," he said. "Anything could happen."

"Or maybe they'll come back and . . ." but she did not finish.

They held hands for the short walk across the hall, and when he spoke she could barely hear his voice.

"The key," he said. "Give it to me."

"What?" she said. She gazed at the door.

"The key," he said. "You have the key."

"My God," she said, "I left the key inside."

He tried the knob. It was locked. Then she tried the knob. It would not turn. Her lips were parted, and her breathing was hard, expectant. He opened his arms and she moved into them.

"Don't worry," he said into her ear. "For God's sake, don't worry."

They stayed there. They held each other. They leaned into the door as if against a wind, and braced themselves.

Exercises

1. How does the first paragraph of the story account for the events that follow?

2. Discuss the meaning of the statement "He looked at himself in the mirror and then closed his eyes and then looked again." Note that Bill looks at himself in the mirror several other times in the story.

3. Why does Bill want to go to bed with his wife after he has visited the apartment?

4. Explain why Bill's experience in the apartment moves from the trivial to the bizarre.

5. Part of what makes this story interesting is that it seems to deal with an experience that is not satisfactorily explainable in ordinary terms. Define *funny* in the sentence "'It's funny,' she said. 'You know—to go in someone's place like that.'" Discuss the feelings of being alone in someone else's home.

6. What do you guess are the kinds of pictures they find in the apartment? What is significant about them?

7. Explain the significance of the final event—locking the key inside, feeling anxious about it, and leaning against the door "as if against a wind."

TOBIAS
WOLFF | *Say Yes*

They were doing the dishes, his wife washing while he dried. He'd washed the night before. Unlike most men he knew, he really pitched in on the housework. A few months earlier he'd overheard a friend of his wife's congratulate her on having such a considerate husband, and he thought, *I try.* Helping out with the dishes was a way of showing how considerate he was.

They talked about different things and somehow got on the subject of whether white people should marry black people. He said that all things considered, he thought it was a bad idea.

"Why?" she asked.

Sometimes his wife got this look where she pinched her brows together and bit her lower lip and stared down at something. When he saw her like this he knew he should keep his mouth shut, but he never did. Actually it made him talk more. She had that look now.

"Why?" she asked again, and stood there with her hand inside a bowl, not washing it but just holding it above the water.

"Listen," he said, "I went to school with blacks, and I've worked with blacks and lived on the same street with blacks, and we've always gotten along just fine. I don't need you coming along now and implying that I'm a racist."

"I didn't imply anything," she said, and began washing the bowl again, turning it around in her hand as though she were shaping it. "I just don't see what's wrong with a white person marrying a black person, that's all."

"They don't come from the same culture as we do. Listen to them sometime—they even have their own language. That's okay with me, I *like* hearing them talk"—he did; for some reason it always made him feel happy—"but it's different. A person from their culture and a person from our culture could never really *know* each other."

"Like you know me?" his wife asked.

"Yes. Like I know you."

"But if they love each other," she said. She was washing faster now, not looking at him.

Oh boy, he thought. He said, "Don't take my word for it. Look at the statistics. Most of those marriages break up."

"Statistics." She was piling dishes on the drainboard at a terrific rate, just swiping at them with the cloth. Many of them were greasy, and there were flecks of food between the tines of the forks. "All right," she said, "what about foreigners? I suppose you think the same thing about two foreigners getting married."

"Yes," he said, "as a matter of fact I do. How can you understand someone who comes from a completely different background?"

"Different," said his wife. "Not the same, like us."

"Yes, different," he snapped, angry with her for resorting to this trick of repeating his words so that they sounded crass, or hypocritical. "These are dirty," he said, and dumped all the silverware back into the sink.

The water had gone flat and gray. She stared down at it, her lips pressed tight together, then plunged her hands under the surface. "Oh!" she cried, and jumped back. She took her right hand by the wrist and held it up. Her thumb was bleeding.

"Ann, don't move," he said. "Stay right there." He ran upstairs to the bathroom and rummaged in the medicine chest for alcohol, cotton, and a Band-Aid. When he came back down she was leaning against the refrigerator with her eyes closed, still holding her hand. He took the hand and dabbed at her thumb with the cotton. The bleeding had stopped. He squeezed it to see how deep the wound was and a single drop of blood welled up, trembling and bright, and fell to the floor. Over the thumb she stared at him accusingly. "It's shallow," he said. "Tomorrow you won't even know it's there." He hoped that she appreciated how quickly he had come to her aid. He'd acted out of concern for her, with no thought of getting anything in return, but now the thought occurred to him that it would be a nice gesture on her part not to start up that conversation again, as he was tired of it. "I'll finish up here," he said. "You go and relax."

"That's okay," she said. "I'll dry."

He began to wash the silverware again, giving a lot of attention to the forks.

"So," she said, "you wouldn't have married me if I'd been black."

"For Christ's sake, Ann!"

"Well, that's what you said, didn't you?"

"No, I did not. The whole question is ridiculous. If you had been black we probably wouldn't even have met. You would have had your friends and I would have had mine. The only black girl I ever really knew was my partner in the debating club, and I was already going out with you by then."

"But if we had met, and I'd been black?"

"Then you probably would have been going out with a black guy." He picked up the rinsing nozzle and sprayed the silverware. The water was so hot that the metal darkened to pale blue, then turned silver again.

"Let's say I wasn't," she said. "Let's say I am black and unattached and we meet and fall in love."

He glanced over at her. She was watching him and her eyes were bright. "Look," he said, taking a reasonable tone, "this is stupid. If you were black you wouldn't be you." As he said this he realized it was absolutely true. There was no possible way of arguing with the fact that she would not be herself if she were black. So he said it again: "If you were black you wouldn't be you."

"I know," she said, "but let's just say."

He took a deep breath. He had won the argument but he still felt cornered. "Say what?" he asked.

"That I'm black, but still me, and we fall in love. Will you marry me?"

He thought about it.

"Well?" she said, and stepped close to him. Her eyes were even brighter. "Will you marry me?"

"I'm thinking," he said.

"You won't, I can tell. You're going to say no."

"Let's not move too fast on this," he said. "There are lots of things to consider. We don't want to do something we would regret for the rest of our lives."

"No more considering. Yes or no."

"Since you put it that way—"

"Yes or no."

"Jesus, Ann. All right. No."

She said, "Thank you," and walked from the kitchen into the living room. A moment later he heard her turning the pages of a magazine. He knew that she was too angry to be actually reading it, but she didn't snap through the pages the way he would have done. She turned them slowly, as if she were studying every word. She was demonstrating her indifference to him, and it had the effect he knew she wanted it to have. It hurt him.

He had no choice but to demonstrate his indifference to her. Quietly, thoroughly, he washed the rest of the dishes. Then he dried them and put them away. He wiped the counters and the stove and scoured the linoleum where the drop of blood had fallen. While he was at it, he decided, he might as well mop the whole floor. When he was done the kitchen looked new, the way it looked when they were first shown the house, before they had ever lived here.

He picked up the garbage pail and went outside. The night was clear and he could see a few stars to the west, where the lights of the town didn't blur them out. On El Camino the traffic was steady and light, peaceful as a river. He felt ashamed that he had let his wife get him into a fight. In another thirty years or so they would both be dead. What would all that stuff matter then? He thought of the years they had spent together, and how close they were, and how well they knew each other, and his throat tightened so that he could hardly breathe. His face and neck began to tingle. Warmth flooded his chest. He stood there for a while, enjoying these sensations, then picked up the pail and went out the back gate.

The two mutts from down the street had pulled over the garbage can again. One of them was rolling around on his back and the other had something in her mouth. Growling, she tossed it into the air, leaped up and caught it, growled again and whipped her head from side to side. When they saw him coming they trotted away with short, mincing steps. Normally he would heave rocks at them, but this time he let them go.

The house was dark when he came back inside. She was in the bathroom. He stood outside the door and called her name. He heard bottles clinking, but she didn't answer him. "Ann, I'm really sorry," he said. "I'll make it up to you, I promise."

"How?" she asked.

He wasn't expecting this. But from a sound in her voice, a level and definite note that was strange to him, he knew that he had to come up with the right answer. He leaned against the door. "I'll marry you," he whispered.

"We'll see," she said. "Go on to bed. I'll be out in a minute."

He undressed and got under the covers. Finally he heard the bathroom door open and close.

"Turn off the light," she said from the hallway.

"What?"

"Turn off the light."

He reached over and pulled the chain on the bedside lamp. The room went dark. "All right," he said. He lay there, but nothing happened. "All right," he said again. Then he heard a movement across the room. He sat up, but he couldn't see a thing. The room was silent. His heart pounded the way it had on their first night together, the way it still did when he woke at a noise in the darkness and waited to hear it again—the sound of someone moving through the house, a stranger.

EXERCISES

1. Discuss the importance of the following question in the story: "How can you understand someone who comes from a completely different background than you?"

2. Why does the wife insist on continuing the argument? Why does she want to know whether he would have married her if she were black?

3. Is it absolutely true that if the wife were black she would be someone else? Explain.

4. What is the significance of the drop of blood from the wife's cut?

5. Discuss the nature of the husband's feelings while he is outside watching the traffic go by.

6. Discuss the final paragraph. Why does the husband feel the way he did on their first night together? Why does he feel the way he does when he hears a noise in the night? Are these feelings the same or different? Why does he feel there is a stranger in the house? How is this an inevitable ending for the story?

PAMELA
PAINTER | *The Bridge*

I

Abicycle whizzes past her from behind just as she steps onto the pedestrian
walkway of the bridge. It startles her. It also startles a young woman who
is walking slowly fifty feet ahead of her, cradling a bundle of something—a
potted plant, flowers, a baby—she can't tell what. She has the impulse belat-
edly to call something nasty to the young man on the bicycle, but he is moving
away too fast, his legs pumping hard. Anyway the young woman must have
said something to him because he turns his head around to her, slowing down
just slightly. He could have injured them both. The mother and the baby. Or
crushed the flowers.

She carries her purse slung over her shoulder on a long strap and in her
left hand a bag of groceries—no jars or cans to make it heavy. English muffins, tea, two lamb chops, a bottle of white wine, and a ripe cantaloupe. The
wind from the bay is brisk, cool. She stops to button her jacket, wrap her
scarf smartly around her neck. The scarf matches her skirt, which pleases her.
The young woman ahead of her has also stopped. She doesn't know why she
says "young woman" because indeed she might have been a grandmother out
for a stroll or a volunteer for the elderly on her way with bright flowers and
a lot to say. Squinting the young woman into sharper focus brings no more
illuminating details than a scarf that matches nothing else she wears. She has
changed the bundle from her left to right arm.

If she catches up to the young woman, and if there is a child bundled into
a blanket, perhaps they might talk for part of their trip across the bridge.
About the rudeness of the boy on the bicycle. She will smile at the baby,
admire its hair or eyes or nose, or if nothing warrants, the charm of children.
"How old?" she might ask. "Is it a boy or girl?" "The name?" Or perhaps
"What lovely flowers," although she can imagine that people might not
respond to this beyond a polite murmur of agreement. Perhaps because they
have nothing to do with making them.

Ahead of her the young woman stops again and is leaning over the heavy
iron railing of the bridge. She is looking down into the water as if something
has caught her eye, something worth the pause. She too stops, torn between
catching up to the young woman and wanting to see what holds her interest
in the water. She sets her grocery bag down between her feet and peers over
the shoulder-high railing down into the river below the young woman. There
are no barges or colorful sailing boats, no sightseeing cruises with loudspeak-
ers blaring a bored voice. Just as she looks back up again, in a graceful curve
as of a ballet gesture, the young woman throws her bundle over the side of
the bridge.

She tries to guess the weight of it, the drift of flowers or the downward
spiral of a helpless infant, but she cannot. It lands with a soft plop (like a tire

puncture?), floats an instant then disappears with tiny bubbles. Paper of the kind from a florist's long roll or a small square of blanket drifts past the original spot until it too has gathered enough water to sink. There has been no color at all, white paper around flowers, or a white baby's blanket.

She tries to scream, whirling around to the passing cars, turning back to the railing, toward the young woman whose coat is blowing open in the breeze. She realizes immediately that if it was or rather is a baby—what would be the difference? Would she throw down the groceries, tear off her jacket and scarf leaving them draped over the railing, kick off her shoes, call to anyone to witness her leap, even the young mother who now stands motionless, her arms withdrawn from the graceful arc of her throw? And then after the climb onto the iron railing higher than it looks, the leap into the water? The cold high shock of the water. Even now, half-believing, something has died for her. She does not jump.

She hurries toward the young woman, her heels clicking like a mugger sure of his prey and silence no longer necessary. She half expects the young woman to turn toward her and then run. Another bicycle passes and she wants to send for help, but she can't find the words to convince. What can she tell even her husband? She glances below again to the darkening river, scraping her elbow as she continues to run. A large camellia floats on the water where the bundle has dropped, or a small baby's bonnet, white and scalloped. She runs on, the grocery bag banging against her legs, bruising the cantaloupe. "I was watching!" she calls to the young woman, breathless. She points from where she has just come. "I was standing over there." She tries to determine just how far away she was but can't find a point to identify her place along the stark railing of the bridge.

The young woman turns but doesn't run. Together they stare at the place where she stood. The young woman's face is smooth and shiny like a plate and, yes, young. She might have been looking for signs of changing weather. Her hands fill in her pockets, her arms tight against her sides where a bundle was. Is she used to strangers talking to her, calling to her breathless from fifteen, ten feet away? She herself isn't used to watching babies being thrown from a bridge, or even flowers. There is a story in flowers too although a far different tale, probably romantic and full of empty gestures, predictable details. But what happened? There is a new emptiness inside her. What must there be in this young woman whose life has changed, perhaps by the crossing of a bridge in fall. "I saw you throw something into the river," she tells her.

The young woman seems to consider everything, then says, "You called. Are you all right?" as she pulls her coat closer about her. The young woman continues, "I think it is going to rain again. It's ruined everything I planned." The grocery bag feels heavy and she sets it down as if it contains bottles, quarts of heavy rich milk. "What was it?" she asks the young woman. "*What?*" The young woman seems to think the question does not refer to anything specific like flowers or babies as she glances at the bag of groceries— perhaps wondering if she should offer to carry them, or making a list of what she needs from the store. "I have to go," she says, shaking her head, and she goes.

And so. She watched the young woman once again recede into the distance. In her wake, Cambridge neon begins to breathe above the water. The subway thunders past her on its short sojourn outside the tunnel. How much does a baby weigh? She stoops down and moves the English muffins aside. She hefts the cantaloupe before lifting it out with both hands. She palms it like a basketball, but can't suspend it in one hand and so pulls her arm back over her shoulder, her hand under the fruit. Like a catapult she heaves it out into the river, lacking the grace of the young woman's motion. She tries to remember the soft plop of entry, and failing that, listens for a cry.

EXERCISES

1. What do we know about the central character? What do we know about the "young woman"? On what do we base this knowledge?
2. Why is the story presented in present tense?
3. What is the bundle the young woman throws off the bridge? Is it a child, flowers, or something else? Why does the central character become so involved in the act?
4. Discuss the statement "There is a story in flowers too although a far different tale, probably romantic and full of empty gestures, predictable details."
5. What is suggested by the fact that the central character sets down the grocery bag as if it contained quarts of heavy milk?
6. Why does the central character think "How much does a baby weigh?" Discuss the significance of the final gesture of throwing in the cantaloupe and then listening for a cry.

F. SCOTT
FITZGERALD | *The Long Way Out*

We were talking about some of the older castles in Touraine and we touched upon the iron cage in which Louis XI imprisoned Cardinal Balue for six years, then upon oubliettes and such horrors. I had seen several of the latter, simply dry wells thirty or forty feet deep where a man was thrown to wait for nothing; since I have such a tendency to claustrophobia that a Pullman berth is a certain nightmare, they had made a lasting impression. So it was rather a relief when a doctor told this story—that is, it was a relief when he began it, for it seemed to have nothing to do with the tortures long ago.

There was a young woman named Mrs. King who was very happy with her husband. They were well-to-do and deeply in love, but at the birth of her second child she went into a long coma and emerged with a clear case of schizophrenia or "split personality." Her delusion, which had something to do with the Declaration of Independence, had little bearing on the case and as she regained her health it began to disappear. At the end of ten months she was a convalescent patient scarcely marked by what had happened to her and very eager to go back into the world.

She was only twenty-one, rather girlish in an appealing way and a favorite with the staff of the sanitarium. When she became well enough so that she could take an experimental trip with her husband there was a general interest in the venture. One nurse had gone into Philadelphia with her to get a dress, another knew the story of her rather romantic courtship in Mexico and everyone had seen her two babies on visits to the hospital. The trip was to Virginia Beach for five days.

It was a joy to watch her make ready, dressing and packing meticulously and living in the gay trivialities of hair waves and such things. She was ready half an hour before the time of departure and she paid some visits on the floor in her powder-blue gown and her hat that looked like one minute after an April shower. Her frail lovely face, with just that touch of startled sadness that often lingers after an illness, was alight with anticipation.

"We'll just do nothing," she said. "That's my ambition. To get up when I want to for three straight mornings and stay up late for three straight nights. To buy a bathing suit by myself and order a meal."

When the time approached Mrs. King decided to wait downstairs instead of in her room and as she passed along the corridors, with an orderly carrying her suitcase, she waved to the other patients, sorry that they too were not going on a gorgeous holiday. The superintendent wished her well, two nurses found excuses to linger and share her infectious joy.

"What a beautiful tan you'll get, Mrs. King."

"Be sure and send a postcard."

About the time she left her room her husband's car was hit by a truck on his way from the city—he was hurt internally and was not expected to live more than a few hours. The information was received at the hospital in a glassed-in office adjoining the hall where Mrs. King waited. The operator, seeing Mrs. King and knowing that the glass was not sound proof, asked the head nurse to come immediately. The head nurse hurried aghast to a doctor and he decided what to do. So long as the husband was still alive it was best to tell her nothing, but of course she must know that he was not coming today.

Mrs. King was greatly disappointed.

"I suppose it's silly to feel that way," she said. "After all these months what's one more day? He said he'd come tomorrow, didn't he?" The nurse was having a difficult time but she managed to pass it off until the patient was back in her room. Then they assigned a very experienced and phlegmatic nurse to keep Mrs. King away from other patients and from newspapers. By the next day the matter would be decided one way or another.

But her husband lingered on and they continued to prevaricate. A little before noon next day one of the nurses was passing along the corridor when she met Mrs. King, dressed as she had been the day before but this time carrying her own suitcase.

"I'm gong to meet my husband," she explained. "He couldn't come yesterday but he's coming today at the same time."

The nurse walked along with her. Mrs. King had the freedom of the building and it was difficult to simply steer her back to her room, and the nurse did not want to tell a story that would contradict what the authorities were telling her. When they reached the front hall she signaled to the operator, who fortunately understood. Mrs. King gave herself a last inspection in the mirror and said:

"I'd like to have a dozen hats just like this to remind me to be this happy always."

When the head nurse came in frowning a minute later she demanded:

"Don't tell me George is delayed?"

"I'm afraid he is. There is nothing much to do but be patient."

Mrs. King laughed ruefully. "I wanted him to see my costume when it was absolutely new."

"Why, there isn't a wrinkle in it."

"I guess it'll last till tomorrow. I oughtn't to be blue about waiting one more day when I'm so utterly happy."

"Certainly not."

That night her husband died and at a conference of doctors next morning there was some discussion about what to do—it was a risk to tell her and a risk to keep it from her. It was decided finally to say that Mr. King had been called away and thus destroy her hope of an immediate meeting; when she was reconciled to this they could tell her the truth.

As the doctors came out of the conference one of them stopped and pointed. Down the corridor toward the outer hall walked Mrs. King carrying her suitcase.

Dr. Pirie, who had been in special charge of Mrs. King, caught his breath.

"This is awful," he said. "I think perhaps I'd better tell her now. There's no use saying he's away when she usually hears from him twice a week, and if we say he's sick she'll want to go to him. Anybody else like the job?"

II

One of the doctors in the conference went on a fortnight's vacation that afternoon. On the day of his return in the same corridor at the same hour, he stopped at the sight of a little procession coming toward him—an orderly carrying a suitcase, a nurse and Mrs. King dressed in the powder-blue suit and wearing the spring hat.

"Good morning, Doctor," she said. "I'm going to meet my husband and we're going to Virginia Beach. I'm going to the hall because I don't want to keep him waiting."

He looked into her face, clear and happy as a child's. The nurse signaled to him that it was as ordered, so he merely bowed and spoke of the pleasant weather.

"It's a beautiful day," said Mrs. King, "but of course even if it was raining it would be a beautiful day for me."

The doctor looked after her, puzzled and annoyed—why are they letting this go on, he thought. What possible good can it do?

Meeting Dr. Pirie, he put the question to him.

"We tried to tell her," Dr. Pirie said. "She laughed and said we were trying to see whether she's still sick. You could use the word unthinkable in an exact sense here—his death is unthinkable to her."

"But you can't just go on like this."

"Theoretically no," said Dr. Pirie. "A few days ago when she packed up as usual the nurse tried to keep her from going. From out in the hall I could see her face, see her begin to go to pieces—for the first time, mind you. Her muscles were tense and her eyes glazed and her voice was thick and shrill when she very politely called the nurse a liar. It was touch and go there for a minute whether we had a tractable patient or a restraint case—and I stepped in and told the nurse to take her down to the reception room."

He broke off as the procession that had just passed appeared again, headed back to the ward. Mrs. King stopped and spoke to Dr. Pirie.

"My husband's been delayed," she said. "Of course I'm disappointed but they tell me he's coming tomorrow and after waiting so long one more day doesn't seem to matter. Don't you agree with me, Doctor?"

"I certainly do, Mrs. King."

She took off her hat.

"I've got to put aside these clothes—I want them to be as fresh tomorrow as they are today." She looked closely at the hat. "There's a speck of dust on it, but I think I can get it off. Perhaps he won't notice."

"I'm sure he won't."

"Really I don't mind waiting another day. It'll be this time tomorrow before I know it, won't it?"

When she had gone along the younger doctor said:

"There are still the two children."

"I don't think the children are going to matter. When she 'went under,' she tied up this trip with the idea of getting well. If we took it away she'd have to go to the bottom and start over."

"Could she?"

"There's no prognosis," said Dr. Pirie. "I was simply explaining why she was allowed to go to the hall this morning."

"But there's tomorrow morning and the next morning."

"There's always the chance," said Dr. Pirie, "that some day he will be there."

The doctor ended his story here, rather abruptly. When we pressed him to tell what happened he protested that the rest was anticlimax—that all sympathy eventually wears out and that finally the staff of the sanitarium had simply accepted the fact.

"But does she still go to meet her husband?"

"Oh yes, it's always the same—but the other patients, except new ones, hardly look up when she passes along the hall. The nurses manage to substitute a new hat every year or so but she still wears the same suit. She's always a little disappointed but she makes the best of it, very sweetly too. It's not an unhappy life as far as we know, and in some funny way it seems to set an example of tranquillity to the other patients. For God's sake let's talk about something else—let's go back to oubliettes."

EXERCISES

1. What is the effect of beginning the story in such a storyteller way: "There was a young woman named Mrs. King who was happy with her husband"?

2. What does Mrs. King's delusion have to do with the Declaration of Independence?

3. Mrs. King is eager to go back to the world after ten months in the hospital. However, consider the nature of her ambition once she does go back.

4. Because the doctor tells the story of Mrs. King, his judgments influence our response. Discuss the following remarks of the doctor:

    (a) "You could use the word unthinkable in an exact sense here."

    (b) "I don't think the children are going to matter."

    (c) "There's always the chance that someday he will be there."

    (d) "For God's sake let's talk about something else—let's go back to oubliettes."

5. In the first paragraph the narrator suggests that the story of Mrs. King *does* have something to do with the tortures of long ago. However, one historian has said of Cardinal Balue's imprisonment that he spent eleven years in tranquility, undisturbed by the harassments of the world. Discuss.

6. Discuss the significance of the title.

GAIL
GODWIN | *A Sorrowful Woman*

Once upon a time there was a wife and mother one too many times.

O ne winter evening she looked at them: the husband durable, receptive, gentle: the child a tender golden three. The sight of them made her so sad and sick she did not want to see them ever again.

She told the husband these thoughts. He was attuned to her; he understood such things. He said he understood. What would she like him to do? "If you could put the boy to bed and read him the story about the monkey who ate too many bananas, I would be grateful." "Of course," he said. "Why, that's a pleasure." And he sent her off to bed.

The next night it happened again. Putting the warm dishes away in the cupboard, she turned and saw the child's grey eyes approving her movements.

In the next room was the man, his chin sunk in the open collar of his favorite wool shirt. He was dozing after her good supper. The shirt was the grey of the child's trusting gaze. She began yelping without tears, retching in between. The man woke in alarm and carried her in his arms to bed. The boy followed them up the stairs, saying, "It's all right, Mommy," but this made her scream. "Mommy is sick," the father said, "go and wait for me in your room."

The husband undressed her, abandoning her only long enough to root beneath the eiderdown for her flannel gown. She stood naked except for her bra, which hung by one strap down the side of her body; she had not the impetus to shrug it off. She looked down at the right nipple, shriveled with chill, and thought, How absurd, a vertical bra. "If only there were instant sleep," she said, hicupping, and the husband bundled her into the gown and went out and came back with a sleeping draft guaranteed swift. She was to drink a little glass of cognac followed by a big glass of dark liquid and afterwards there was just time to say Thank you and could you get him a clean pair of pajamas out of the laundry, it came back today.

The next day was Sunday and the husband brought her breakfast in bed and let her sleep until it grew dark again. He took the child for a walk, and when they returned, red-cheeked and boisterous, the father made supper. She heard them laughing in the kitchen. He brought her up a tray of buttered toast, celery sticks, and black bean soup. "I am the luckiest woman," she said, crying real tears. "Nonsense," he said. "You need a rest from us," and went to prepare the sleeping draft, find the child's pajamas, select the story for the night.

She got up Monday and moved about the house till noon. The boy, delighted to have her back, pretended he was a vicious tiger and followed her from room to room, growling and scratching. Whenever she came close, he would growl and scratch at her. One of his sharp little claws ripped her flesh, just above the wrist, and together they paused to watch a thin red line materialize on the inside of her pale arm and spill over in little beads. "Go away," she said. She got herself upstairs and locked the door. She called the husband's office and said, "I've locked myself away from him. I'm afraid." The husband told her in his richest voice to lie down, take it easy, and he was already on the phone to call one of the baby-sitters they often employed. Shortly after, she heard the girl let herself in, heard the girl coaxing the frightened child to come and play.

After supper several nights later, she hit the child. She had known she was going to do it when the father would see. "I'm sorry," she said, collapsing on the floor. The weeping child had run to hide. "What has happened to me, I'm not myself anymore." The man picked her tenderly from the floor and looked at her with much concern. "Would it help if we got, you know, a girl in? We could fix the room downstairs. I want you to feel freer," he said, understanding these things. "We have the money for a girl. I want you to think about it."

And now the sleeping draft was a nightly thing, she did not have to ask. He went down to the kitchen to mix it, he set it nightly beside her bed. The little glass and the big one, amber and deep rich brown, the flannel gown and the eiderdown.

The man put out the word and found the perfect girl. She was young, dynamic, and not pretty. "Don't bother with the room, I'll fix it up myself." Laughing, she employed her thousand energies. She painted the room white, fed the child lunch, read edifying books, raced the boy to the mailbox, hung her own watercolors on the fresh-painted walls, made spinach soufflé, cleaned a spot from the mother's coat, made them all laugh, danced in stocking feet to music in the white room after reading the child to sleep. She knitted dresses for herself and played chess with the husband. She washed and set the mother's soft ash-blonde hair and gave her neck rubs, offered to.

The woman now spent her winter afternoons in the big bedroom. She made a fire in the hearth and put on slacks and an old sweater she had loved at school, and sat in the big chair and stared out the window at snow-ridden branches, or went away into novels about other people moving through other winters.

The girl brought the child in twice a day, once in the later afternoon when he would tell of his day, all of it tumbling out quickly because there was not much time, and before he went to bed. Often now, the man took his wife to dinner. He made a courtship ceremony of it, inviting her beforehand so she could get used to the idea. They dressed and were beautiful together again and went out into the frosty night. Over candlelight he would say, "I think you are better, you know." "Perhaps I am," she would murmur. "You look . . . like a cloistered queen," he said once, his voice breaking curiously.

One afternoon the girl brought the child into the bedroom. "We've been out playing in the park. He found something he wants to give you, a surprise." The little boy approached her, smiling mysteriously. He placed his cupped hands in hers and left a live dry thing that spat brown juice in her palm and leapt away. She screamed and wrung her hands to be rid of the brown juice. "Oh, it was only a grasshopper," said the girl. Nimbly she crept to the edge of a curtain, did a quick knee bend and reclaimed the creature, led the boy competently from the room.

"The girl upsets me," said the woman to her husband. He sat frowning on the side of the bed he had not entered for so long. "I'm sorry, but there it is." The husband stroked his creased brow and said he was sorry too. He really did not know what they would do without that treasure of a girl. "Why don't you stay here with me in bed," the woman said.

Next morning she fired the girl who cried and said, "I loved the little boy, what will become of him now?" But the mother turned away her face and the girl took down the watercolors from the walls, sheathed the records she had danced to, and went away.

"I don't know what we'll do. It's all my fault, I know. I'm such a burden, I know that."

"Let me think. I'll think of something." (Still understanding these things.)

"I know you will. You always do, " she said.

With great care he rearranged his life. He got up hours early, did the shopping, cooked the breakfast, took the boy to nursery school. "We will manage," he said, "until you're better, however long that is." He did his work, collected the boy from the school, came home and made the supper, washed the dishes, got the child to bed. He managed everything. One evening, just as she was on the verge of swallowing her draft, there was a timid knock on her door. The little boy came in wearing his pajamas. "Daddy has fallen asleep on my bed and I can't get in. There's no room."

Very sedately she left her bed and went to the child's room. Things were much changed. Books were rearranged, toys. He'd done some new drawings. She came as a visitor to her son's room, wakened the father, and helped him to bed. "Ah, he shouldn't have bothered you," said the man, leaning on his wife. "I've told him not to." He dropped into his own bed and fell asleep with a moan. Meticulously she undressed him. She folded and hung his clothes. She covered his body with the bedclothes. She flicked off the light that shone in his face.

The next day she moved her things into the girl's white room. She put her hairbrush on the dresser; she put a note pad and pen beside the bed. She stocked the little room with cigarettes, books, bread, and cheese. She didn't need much.

At first the husband was dismayed. But he was receptive to her needs. He understood these things. "Perhaps the best thing is for you to follow it through," he said. "I want to be big enough to contain whatever you must do."

All day long she stayed in the white room. She was a young queen, a virgin in a tower; she was the previous inhabitant, the girl with all the energies. She tried these personalities on like costumes, then discarded them. The room had a new view of streets she'd never seen that way before. The sun hit the room in late afternoon and she took to brushing her hair in the sun. One day she decided to write a poem. "Perhaps a sonnet." She took up her pen and pad and began working from words that had lately lain in her mind. She had choices for the sonnet, ABAB or ABBA for a start. She pondered these possibilities until she tottered into a larger choice: she did not have to write a sonnet. Her poem, could be six, eight, ten, thirteen lines, it could be any number of lines, and it did not even have to rhyme.

She put down the pen on top of the pad.

In the evenings, very briefly, she saw the two of them. They knocked on her door, a big knock and a little, and she would call Come in, and the husband would smile though he looked a bit tired, yet somehow this tiredness suited him. He would put her sleeping draft on the bedside table and say, "The boy and I have done all right today," and the child would kiss her. One night she tasted for the first time the power of his baby spit.

"I don't think I can see him anymore," she whispered sadly to the man. And the husband turned away, but recovered admirably and said, "Of course, I see."

So the husband came alone. "I have explained to the boy," he said. "And we are doing fine. We are managing." He squeezed his wife's pale arm and put the two glasses on her table. After he had gone, she sat looking at the arm.

"I'm afraid it's come to that," she said. "Just push the notes under the door; I'll read them. And don't forget to leave the draft outside."

The man sat for a long time with his head in his hands. Then he rose and went away from her. She heard him in the kitchen where he mixed the draft in batches now to last a week at a time, storing it in a corner of the cupboard. She heard him come back, leave the big glass and the little one outside on the floor.

Outside her window the snow was melting from the branches, there were more people on the streets. She brushed her hair a lot and seldom read anymore. She sat in her window and brushed her hair for hours, and saw a boy fall off his new bicycle again and again, a dog chasing a squirrel, an old woman peek slyly over her shoulder and then extract a parcel from a garbage can.

In the evening she read the notes they slipped under her door. The child could not write, so he drew and sometimes painted his. The notes were painstaking at first: the man and boy offering the final strength of their day to her. But sometimes, when they seemed to have had a bad day, there were only hurried scrawls.

One night, when the husband's note had been extremely short, loving but short, and there had been nothing from the boy, she stole out of her room as she often did to get more supplies, but crept upstairs instead and stood outside their doors, listening to the regular breathing of the man and boy asleep. She hurried back to her room and drank the draft.

She woke earlier now. It was spring, there were birds. She listened for sounds of the man and the boy eating breakfast; she listened for the roar of the motor when they drove away. One beautiful noon, she went out to look at her kitchen in the daylight. Things were changed. He had bought some new dish towels. Had the old ones worn out? The canisters seemed closer to the sink. She inspected the cupboard and saw new things among the old. She got out flour, baking powder, salt, milk (he bought a different brand of butter), and baked a loaf of bread and left it cooling on the table.

The force of the two joyful notes slipped under her door that evening pressed her into the corner of the little room; she hardly had space to breathe. As soon as possible, she drank the draft.

Now the days were too short. She was always busy. She woke with the first bird. Worked till the sun set. No time for hair brushing. Her fingers raced the hours.

Finally, in the nick of time, it was finished one late afternoon. Her veins pumped and her forehead sparkled. She went to the cupboard, took what was hers, closed herself into the little white room, and brushed her hair for a while.

The man and boy came home and found: five loaves of warm bread, a roast stuffed turkey, a glazed ham, three pies of different fillings, eight molds of the boy's favorite custard, two weeks' supply of fresh-laundered sheets and shirts and towels, and hand-knitted sweaters (both of the same grey color), a sheath of marvelous water-color beasts accompanied by mad and fanciful stories nobody could ever make up again, and a tablet full of love sonnets addressed to the man. The house smelled redolently of renewal and spring. The man ran to the little room, could not contain himself to knock, flung back the door.

"Look, Mommy is sleeping," said the boy. "She's tired from doing all our things again." He dawdled in a stream of the last sun for that day and watched his father roll tenderly back her eyelids, lay his ear softly to her breast, test the delicate bones of her wrist. The father put down his face into her fresh-washed hair.

"Can we eat the turkey for supper?" the boy asked.

EXERCISES

1. Why does the story begin with the phrase "Once upon a time . . ."? Is there a fairy tale element in this story? Compare it to a fairy tale with which you are familiar.

2. Discuss the irony of the first paragraph. Discuss the fact that the perfection of the family makes the woman sick.

3. What does the image of the woman naked with a vertical bra communicate?

4. What does the phrase "I'm not myself anymore" mean? Who is she then? What kind of transformation has taken place? Why?

5. What is the significance of the grasshopper the child put in his mother's hand?

6. Why does the mother become extremely busy? What does "it" refer to in the following: "Finally, in the nick of time, it was finished one late afternoon"?

7. Discuss the fairy tale effect of the mother becoming "a young queen, a virgin in a tower"? What makes her decide against writing a poem? What does the phrase "the power of his baby spit" mean?

8. Is this applicable only to this woman, or is it a metaphoric story applicable to many?

WILLIAM
GASS | *Order of Insects*

We certainly had no complaints about the house after all we had been through in the other place, but we hadn't lived there very long before I began to notice every morning the bodies of a large black bug spotted about the downstairs carpet; haphazardly, as earth worms must die on the street after a rain; looking when I first saw them like rolls of dark wool or pieces of mud from the children's shoes, or sometimes, if the drapes were pulled, so like ink stains or deep burns they terrified me, for I had been intimidated by that thick rug very early and the first week had walked over it wishing my bare feet would swallow my shoes. The shells were usually broken. Legs and other parts I couldn't then identify would be scattered near like flakes of rust. Occasionally, I would find them on their backs, their quilted undersides showing orange, while beside them were smudges of dark-brown powder that had to be vacuumed carefully. We believed our cat had killed them. She was frequently sick during the night then—a rare thing for her—and we could think of no other reason. Overturned like that they looked pathetic even dead.

I could not imagine where the bugs had come from. I am terribly meticulous myself. The house was clean, the cupboards tight and orderly, and we never saw one alive. The other place had been infested with those flat brown fuzzy roaches, all wires and speed, and we'd seen *them* all right, frightened by the kitchen light, sifting through the baseboards and the floor's cracks; and in the pantry I had nearly closed my fingers on one before it fled, tossing its shadow across the starch like an image of the startle in my hand.

Dead, overturned, their three pairs of legs would be delicately drawn up and folded shyly over their stomachs. When they walked I suppose their forelegs were thrust out and then bent to draw the body up. I still wonder if they jumped. More than once I've seen our cat hook one of her claws under a shell and toss it in the air, crouching while the insect fell, feigning leaps—but there was daylight; the bug was dead; she was not really interested any more; and she would walk immediately away. That image takes the place of jumping. Even if I actually saw those two back pairs of legs unhinge, as they would have to if one leaped, I think I'd find the result unreal and mechanical, a poor try measured by that sudden, high, head-over-heels flight from our cat's paw. I could look it up, I guess, but it's no study for a woman . . . bugs.

At first I reacted as I should, bending over, wondering what in the world; yet even before I recognized them I'd withdrawn my hand, shuddering. Fierce, ugly, armored things: they used their shadows to seem large. The machine sucked them up while I looked the other way. I remember the sudden thrill of horror I had hearing one rattle up the wand. I was relieved that they were dead, of course, for I could never have killed one, and if they had been popped, alive, into the dust bag of the cleaner, I believe I would have had nightmares again as I did the time my husband fought the red ants in our kitchen. All night I lay awake thinking of the ants alive in the belly of the machine, and when toward morning I finally slept I found myself in the dreadful elastic tunnel of the suction tube where ahead of me I heard them: a hundred bodies rustling in the dirt.

I never think of their species as alive but as comprised entirely by the dead ones on our carpet, all the new dead manufactured by the action of some mysterious spoor—perhaps that dust they sometimes lie in—carried in the air, solidified by night and shaped, from body into body, spontaneously, as maggots were before the age of science. I have a single book about insects, a little dated handbook in French which a good friend gave me as a joke—because of my garden, the quaintness of the plates, the fun of reading about worms in such an elegant tongue—and my bug has his picture there climbing the stem of an orchid. Beneath the picture is his name: *Periplaneta orientalis L. Ces répugnants insectes ne sont que trop communs dans les cuisines des vieilles habitations des villes, dans les magasins, entrepôts, boulangeries, brasseries, restaurants, dans la cale des navires, etc.,* the text begins. Nevertheless they are a new experience for me and I think that I am grateful for it now.

The picture didn't need to show me there were two, adult and nymph, for by that time I'd seen the bodies of both kinds. Nymph. My god the names we use. The one was dark, squat, ugly, sly. The other, slimmer, had hard sheath-like wings drawn over its back like another shell, and you could see delicate interwoven lines spun like fossil gauze across them. The nymph was a rich golden color deepening in its interstices to mahogany. Both had legs that looked under a glass like the canes of a rose, and the nymph's were sufficiently transparent in a good light you thought you saw its nerves merge and run like a jagged crack to each ultimate claw.

Tipped, their legs have fallen shut, and the more I look at them the less I believe my eyes. Corruption, in these bugs, is splendid. I've a collection now I keep in typewriter-ribbon tins, and though, in time, their bodies dry and the interior flesh decays, their features hold, as I suppose they held in life, an Egyptian determination, for their protective plates are strong and death must break bones to get in. Now that the heavy soul is gone, the case is light.

I suspect if we were as familiar with our bones as with our skin, we'd never bury dead but shrine them in their rooms, arranged as we might like to find them on a visit; and our enemies, if we could steal their bodies from the battle sites, would be museumed as they died, the steel still eloquent in their sides, their metal hats askew, the protective toes of their shoes unworn, and friend and enemy would be so wondrously historical that in a hundred years we'd find the jaws still hung for the same speech and all the parts we spent our life with tilted as they always were—rib cage, collar, skull—still repetitious, still defiant, angel light, still worthy of memorial and affection. After all, what does it mean to say that when our cat has bitten through the shell and put confusion in the pulp, the life goes out of them? Alas for us, I want to cry, our bones are secret, showing last, so we must love what perishes: the muscles and the waters and the fats.

Two prongs extend like daggers from the rear. I suppose I'll never know their function. That kind of knowledge doesn't take my interest. At first I had to screw my eyes down, and as I consider it now, the whole change, the recent alteration in my life, was the consequence of finally coming near to something. It was a self-mortifying act, I recall, a penalty I laid upon myself for the evil-tempered words I'd shouted at my children in the middle of the night. I felt instinctively the insects were infectious and their own disease, so when I knelt I held a handkerchief over the lower half of my face . . . saw only horror . . . turned, sick, masking my eyes . . . yet the worst of angers held me through the day: vague, searching, guilty, and ashamed.

After that I came near often; saw, for the first time, the gold nymph's difference; put between the mandibles a tinted nail I'd let grow long; observed the movement of the jaws, the stalks of the antennae, the skull-shaped skull, the lines banding the abdomen, and found an intensity in the posture of the shell, even when tipped, like that in the gaze of Gauguin's natives' eyes. The dark plates glisten. They are wonderfully shaped; even the buttons of the compound eyes show a geometrical precision which prevents my earlier horror. It isn't possible to feel disgust toward such an order. Nevertheless, I reminded myself, a roach . . . and you a woman.

I no longer own my own imagination. I suppose they came up the drains or out of the registers. It may have been the rug they wanted. Crickets, too, I understand, will feed on wool. I used to rest by my husband . . . stiffly . . . waiting for silence to settle in the house, his sleep to come, and then the drama of their passage would take hold of me, possess me so completely that when I finally slept I merely passed from one dream to another without the slightest loss of vividness or continuity. Never alive, they came with punctures; their bodies formed from little whorls of copperish dust which in the downstairs darkness I couldn't possibly have seen; and they were dead and upside down when they materialized, for it was in that moment that our cat, herself darkly invisible, leaped and brought her paws together on the true soul of the roach; a soul so static and intense, so immortally arranged, I felt, while I lay shell-like in our bed, turned inside out, driving my mind away, it was the same as the dark soul of the world itself—and it was this beautiful and terrifying feeling that took possession of me finally, stiffened me like a rod beside my husband, played caesar to my dreams.

The weather drove them up, I think . . . moisture in the tubes of the house. The first I came on looked put together in Japan; broken, one leg bent under like a metal cinch; unwound. It rang inside the hollow of the wand like metal too; brightly, like a stream of pins. The clatter made me shiver. Well I always see what I fear. Anything my eyes have is transformed into a threatening object: mud, or stains, or burns, or if not these, then toys in unmendable metal pieces. Not fears to be afraid of. The ordinary fears of daily life. Healthy fears. Womanly, wifely, motherly ones: the children may point at the wretch with the hunch and speak in a voice he will hear; the cat has fleas again, they will get in the sofa; one's face looks smeared, it's because of the heat; is the burner on under the beans? The washing machine's obscure disease may reoccur, it rumbles on rinse and rattles on wash; my god it's already eleven o'clock; which one of you has lost a galosh? So it was amid the worries of our ordinary life I bent, innocent and improperly armed, over the bug that had come undone. Let me think back on the shock. . . . My hand would have fled from a burn with the same speed; anyone's death or injury would have weakened me as well; and I could have gone cold for a number of reasons, because I felt in motion in me my own murderous disease, for instance; but none could have produced the revulsion that dim recognition did, a reaction of my whole nature that flew ahead of understanding and made me withdraw like a spider.

I said I was innocent. Well I was not. Innocent. My god the names we use. What do we live with that's alive we haven't tamed—people like me?— even our houseplants breathe by our permission. All along I had the fear of what it was—something ugly and poisonous, deadly and terrible—the simple insect, worse and wilder than fire—and I should rather put my arms in the heart of a flame than in the darkness of a moist and webby hole. But the eye never ceases to change. When I examine my collection now it isn't any longer roaches I observe but gracious order, wholeness, and divinity. . . . My handkerchief, that time, was useless. . . . O my husband, they are a terrible disease.

The dark soul of the world . . . a phrase I should laugh at. The roach shell sickened me. And my jaw has broken open. I lie still, listening, but there is nothing to hear. Our cat is quiet. They pass through life to immortality between her paws.

Am I grateful now my terror has another object? From time to time I think so, but I feel as though I'd been entrusted with a kind of eastern mystery, sacred to a dreadful god, and I am full of the sense of my unworthiness and the clay of my vessel. So strange. It is the sewing machine that has the fearful claw. I live in a scatter of blocks and children's voices. The chores are my clock, and time is every other moment interrupted. I had always thought that love knew nothing of order and that life itself was turmoil and confusion. Let us leap, let us shout! I have leaped, and to my shame, I have wrestled. But this bug that I hold in my hand and know to be dead is beautiful, and there is a fierce joy in its composition that beggars every other, for its joy is the joy of stone, and it lives in its tomb like a lion.

I don't know which is more surprising: to find such order in a roach, or such ideas in a woman.

I could not shake my point of view, infected as it was, and I took up their study with a manly passion. I sought out spiders and gave them sanctuary; played host to worms of every kind; was generous to katydids and lacewings, aphids, ants and various grubs; pampered several sorts of beetle; looked after crickets; sheltered bees; aimed my husband's chemicals away from the grasshoppers, mosquitoes, moths, and flies. I have devoted hours to watching caterpillars feed. You can see the leaves they've eaten passing through them; their bodies thin and swell until the useless pulp is squeezed in perfect rounds from their rectal end; for caterpillars are a simple section of intestine, a decorated stalk of yearning muscle, and their whole being is enlisted in the effort of digestion. *Le tube digestif des Insectes est situé dans le grand axe de la cavité générale du corps . . . de la bouche vers l'anus . . . Le pharyn . . . L'œophage . . . Le jabot . . . Le ventricule chylifique . . . Le rectum et l'iléon . . .* Yet when they crawl their curves conform to graceful laws.

My children ought to be delighted with me as my husband is, I am so diligent, it seems, on their behalf, but they have taken fright and do not care to pry or to collect. My hobby's given me a pair of dreadful eyes, and sometimes I fancy they start from my head; yet I see, perhaps, no differently than Galileo saw when he found in the pendulum its fixed intent. Nonetheless my body resists such knowledge. It wearies of its edge. And I cannot forget, even while I watch our moonvine blossoms opening, the simple principle of the bug. It is a squat black cockroach after all, such a bug as frightens housewives, and it's only come to chew on rented wool and find its death absurdly in the teeth of the renter's cat.

Strange. Absurd. I am the wife of the house. This point of view I tremble in is the point of view of a god, and I feel certain, somehow, that could I give myself entirely to it, were I not continuing a woman, I could disarm my life, find peace and order everywhere; and I lie by my husband and I touch his arm and consider the temptation. But I am a woman. I am not worthy. Then I want to cry O husband, husband, I am ill, for I have seen what I have seen. What should he do at that, poor man, starting up in the night from his sleep to such nonsense, but comfort me blindly and murmur dream, small snail, only dream, bad dream, as I do to the children. I could go away like the wise cicada who abandons its shell to move to other mischief. I could leave and let my bones play cards and spank the children. . . . Peace. How can I think of such ludicrous things—beauty and peace, the dark soul of the world—for I am the wife of the house, concerned for the rug, tidy and punctual, surrounded by blocks.

EXERCISES

1. What is suggested by bugs in a house recently moved into?
2. What is unusual about these insects? How do they differ from insects of the previous house in which the narrator lived?
3. Why does the narrator become so fascinated with the physical nature of the insects?
4. Discuss the meaning of the narrator's sense of horror, guilt, shame, and anger after a close look at the insects.
5. How does the narrator's attitude toward the insects change? What does she mean by "I no longer own my own imagination"?
6. Discuss the statement "I don't know which is more surprising: to find such order in a roach, or such ideas in a woman."
7. How is this a story specifically about the plight of woman?
8. Discuss the appropriateness of the dead bugs as symbols of the narrator's situation.

JAMES
PURDY | *Why Can't They Tell You Why?*

P aul knew nearly nothing of his father until he found the box of photographs on the backstairs. From then on he looked at them all day and every evening, and when his mother Ethel talked to Edith Gainesworth on the telephone. He had looked amazed at his father in his different ages and stations of life, first as a boy his age, then as a young man, and finally before his death in his army uniform.

Ethel had always referred to him as *your father*, and now the photographs made him look much different from what this had suggested in Paul's mind.

Ethel never talked with Paul about why he was home sick from school and she pretended at first she did not know he had found the photographs. But she told everything she thought and felt about him to Edith Gainesworth over the telephone, and Paul heard all of the conversations from the backstairs where he sat with the photographs, which he had moved from the old shoe boxes where he had found them to two big clean empty candy boxes.

"Wouldn't you know a sick kid like him would take up with photographs," Ethel said to Edith Gainesworth. "Instead of toys or balls, old photos. And my God, I've hardly mentioned a thing to him about his father."

Edith Gainesworth, who studied psychology at an adult center downtown, often advised Ethel about Paul, but she did not say anything tonight about the photographs.

"All mothers should have pensions," Ethel continued. "If it isn't a terrible feeling being on your feet all day before the public and then having a sick kid under your feet when you're off at night. My evenings are worse than my days."

These telephone conversations always excited Paul because they were the only times he heard himself and the photographs discussed. When the telephone bell would ring he would run to the backstairs and begin looking at the photographs and then as the conversation progressed he often ran into the front room where Ethel was talking, sometimes carrying one of the photographs with him and making sounds like a bird or an airplane.

Two months had gone by like this, with his having attended school hardly at all and his whole life seemingly spent in listening to Ethel talk to Edith Gainesworth and examining the photographs in the candy boxes.

Then in the middle of the night Ethel missed him. She rose feeling a pressure in her scalp and neck. She walked over to his cot and noticed the Indian blanket had been taken away. She called Paul and walked over to the window and looked out. She walked around the upstairs, calling him.

"God, there is always something to bother you," she said. "Where are you, Paul?" she repeated in a mad sleepy voice. She went on down into the kitchen, though it did not seem possible he would be there, he never ate anything.

Then she said *Of course,* remembering how many times he went to the backstairs with those photographs.

"Now what are you doing in here, Paul?" Ethel said, and there was a sweet but threatening sound to her voice that awoke the boy from where he had been sleeping, spread out protectively over the boxes of photographs, his Indian blanket over his back and shoulder.

Paul crouched almost greedily over the boxes when he saw this ugly pale woman in the man's bathrobe looking at him. There was a faint smell from her like that of an uncovered cistern when she put on the robe.

"Just here, Ethel," he answered her question after a while.

"What do you mean, *just here*, Paul?" she said going up closer to him.

She took hold of his hair and jerked him by it gently as though this was a kind of caress she sometimes gave him. This gentle jerking motion made him tremble in short successive starts under her hand, until she let go.

He watched how she kept looking at the boxes of photographs under his guard.

"You sleep here to be near them?" she said.

"I don't know why, Ethel," Paul said, blowing out air from his mouth as though trying to make something disappear before him.

"You don't know, Paul," she said, her sweet fake awful voice and the stale awful smell of the bathrobe stifling as she drew nearer.

"Don't, don't!" Paul cried.

"Don't what?" Ethel answered, pulling him toward her by seizing on his pajama tops.

"Don't do anything to me, Ethel, my eye hurts."

"Your eye hurts," she said with unbelief.

"I'm sick to my stomach."

Then bending over suddenly, in a second she had gathered up the two boxes of photographs in her bathrobed arms.

"Ethel!" he cried out in the strongest, clearest voice she had ever heard come from him. "Ethel, those are my candy boxes!"

She looked down at him as though she was seeing him for the first time, noting with surprise how thin and puny he was, and how disgusting was one small mole that hung from his starved-looking throat. She could not see how this was her son.

"These boxes of pictures are what makes you sick."

"No, no, Mama Ethel," Paul cried.

"What did I tell you about calling me Mama," she said, going over to him and putting her hand on his forehead.

"I called you Mama Ethel, not Mama," he said.

"I suppose you think I'm a thousand years old." She raised her hand as though she was not sure what she wished to do with it.

"I think I know what to do with these," she said with a pretended calm.

"No, Ethel," Paul said, "give them here back. They are my boxes."

"Tell me why you slept out here on this backstairs where you know you'll make yourself even sicker. I want you to tell me and tell me right away."

"I can't, Ethel, I can't," Paul said.

"Then I'm going to burn the pictures," she replied.

He crawled hurrying over to where she stood and put his arms around her legs.

"Ethel, please don't take them, Ethel. Pretty please."

"Don't touch me," she said to him. Her nerves were so bad she felt that if he touched her again she would start as though a mouse had gotten under her clothes.

"You stand up straight and tell me like a little man why you're here," she said, but she kept her eyes half closed and turned from him.

He moved his lips to answer but then he did not really understand what she meant by *little* man. That phrase worried him whenever he heard it.

"What do you do with the pictures all the time, all day when I'm gone, and now tonight? I never heard of anything like it." Then she moved away from him, so that his hands fell from her legs where he had been grasping her, but she continued to stand near his hands as though puzzled what to do next.

"I look is all, Ethel," he began to explain.

"Don't bawl when you talk," she commanded, looking now at him in the face.

Then: "I want the truth!" she roared.

He sobbed and whined there, thinking over what it was she could want him to tell her, but everything now had begun to go away from his attention, and he had not really ever understood what had been expected of him here, and now everything was too hard to be borne.

"Do you hear me, Paul?" she said between her teeth, very close to him now and staring at him in such an angry way he closed his eyes. "If you don't answer me, do you know what I'm going to do?"

"Punish?" Paul said in his tiniest child voice.

"No, I'm not going to punish this time," Ethel said.

"You're not!" he cried, a new fear and surprise coming now into his tired eyes, and then staring at her eyes, he began to cry with panicky terror, for it seemed to him then that in the whole world there were just the two of them, him and Ethel.

"You remember where they sent Aunt Grace," Ethel said with terrible knowledge.

His crying redoubled in fury, some of his spit flying out onto the cold calcimine of the walls. He kept turning the while to look at the close confines of the staircase as though to find some place where he could see things outside.

"Do you remember where they sent her?" Ethel said in a quiet patient voice like a woman who has endured every unreasonable, disrespectful action from a child whom she still can patiently love.

"Yes, yes, Ethel," Paul cried hysterically.

"Tell Ethel where they sent Aunt Grace," she said with the same patience and kind restraint.

"I didn't know they sent little boys there," Paul said.

"You're more than a little boy now," Ethel replied. "You're old enough. . . . And if you don't tell Ethel why you look at the photographs all the time, we'll have to send you to the mental hospital with the bars."

"I don't know why I look at them, dear Ethel," he said now in a very feeble but wildly tense voice, and he began petting the fur on her houseslippers.

"I think you do, Paul," she said quietly, but he could hear her gentle, patient tone disappearing and he half raised his hands as though to protect him from anything this woman might now do.

"But I don't know why I look at them," he repeated, screaming, and he threw his arms suddenly around her legs.

She moved back, but still smiling her patient, knowing, forgiving smile.

"All right for you, Paul." When she said that *all right for you* it always meant the end of any understanding or reasoning with her.

"Where are we going?" he cried, as she ushered him through the door, into the kitchen.

"We're going to the basement, of course," she replied.

They had never gone there together before, and the terror of what might happen to him now gave him a kind of quiet that enabled him to walk steady down the long irregular steps.

"You carry the boxes of pictures, Paul," she said, "since you like them so much."

"No, no," Paul cried.

"Carry them," she commanded, giving them to him.

He held them before him and when they reached the floor of the basement, she opened the furnace and, tightening the cord of her bathrobe, she said coldly, her white face lighted up by the fire, "Throw the pictures into the furnace door, Paul."

He stared at her as though all the nightmares had come true, the complete and final fear of what may happen in living had unfolded itself at last.

"They're Daddy!" he said in a voice neither of them recognized.

"You had your choice," she said coolly. "You prefer a dead man to your own mother. Either you throw his pictures in the fire, for they're what makes you sick, or you will go where they sent Aunt Grace."

He began running around the room now, much like a small bird which has escaped from a pet shop into the confusion of a city street, and making odd little sounds that she did not recognize could come from his own lungs.

"I'm not going to stand for your clowning," she called out, but as though to an empty room.

As he ran round and round the small room with the boxes of photographs pressed against him, some of the pictures fell upon the floor and these he stopped and tried to recapture, at the same time holding the boxes tight against him, and making, as he picked them up, frothing cries of impotence and acute grief.

Ethel herself stared at him, incredulous. He not only could not be recognized as her son, he no longer looked like a child, but in his small unmended night shirt like some crippled and dying animal running hopelessly from its pain.

"Give me those pictures!" she shouted, and she seized a few which he held in his fingers, and threw them quickly into the fire.

Then turning back, she moved to take the candy boxes from him.

But the final sight of him made her stop. He had crouched on the floor, and, bending his stomach over the boxes, hissed at her, so that she stopped short, not seeing any way to get at him, seeing no way to bring him back, while from his mouth black thick strings of something slipped out, as though he had spewed out the heart of his grief.

EXERCISES

1. Why is Paul so fascinated with the pictures? Was he sick before he found them, or have the pictures made him sick? What is the nature of Paul's sickness?

2. What are the mother's feelings toward Paul? Does the story suggest why she feels this way?

3. Why does the phrase "little man" worry Paul? Does it have anything to do with the phrase "your father" that his mother uses?

4. Discuss the significance of the image of Paul as some crippled and dying animal.

5. Discuss the significance of the final image of Paul spewing out "the heart of his grief" in "black thick strings of something."

6. Who is the "they" in the title of the story? What does the "why" refer to? Why can't "they" tell you "why"?

EDGAR
ALLAN
POE | *The Tell-Tale Heart*

True!—nervous—very, very dreadfully nervous I had been and am! but why *will* you say that I am mad? The disease had sharpened my senses—not destroyed—not dulled them. Above all was the sense of hearing acute. I heard all things in the heaven and in the earth. I heard many things in hell. How, then, am I mad? Hearken! and observe how healthily—how calmly I can tell you the whole story.

It is impossible to say how first the idea entered my brain; but once conceived, it haunted me day and night. Object there was none. Passion there was none. I loved the old man. He had never wronged me. He had never given me insult. For his gold I had no desire. I think it was his eye! yes, it was this! One of his eyes resembled that of a vulture—a pale blue eye, with a film over it. Whenever it fell upon me, my blood ran cold; and so by degrees—very gradually—I made up my mind to take the life of the old man, and thus rid myself of the eye for ever.

Now this is the point. You fancy me mad. Madmen know nothing. But you should have seen *me*. You should have seen how wisely I proceeded—with what caution—with what foresight—with what dissimulation I went to work!

I was never kinder to the old man than during the whole week before I killed him. And every night, about midnight, I turned the latch of his door and opened it—oh, so gently! And then, when I had made an opening sufficient for my head, I put in a dark lantern, all closed, closed, so that no light shone out, and then I thrust in my head. Oh, you would have laughed to see how cunningly I thrust it in! I moved it slowly—very, very slowly, so that I might not disturb the old man's sleep. It took me an hour to place my whole head within the opening so far that I could see him as he lay upon his bed. Ha!—would a madman have been so wise as this? And then, when my head was well in the room, I undid the lantern cautiously—oh, so cautiously—cautiously (for the hinges creaked)—I undid it just so much that a single thin ray fell upon the vulture eye. And this I did for seven long nights—every night just at midnight—but I found the eye always closed; and so it was impossible to do the work; for it was not the old man who vexed me, but his Evil Eye. And every morning, when the day broke, I went boldly into the chamber, and spoke courageously to him, calling him by name in a hearty tone, and inquiring how he had passed the night. So you see he would have been a very profound old man, indeed, to suspect that every night, just at twelve, I looked in upon him while he slept.

Upon the eighth night I was more than usually cautious in opening the door. A watch's minute hand moves more quickly than did mine. Never before that night had I *felt* the extent of my own powers—of my sagacity. I could scarcely contain my feelings of triumph. To think that there I was, opening the door, little by little, and he not even to dream of my secret deeds or thoughts. I fairly chuckled at the idea; and perhaps he heard me; for he moved on the bed suddenly, as if startled. Now you may think that I drew back— but no. His room was as black as pitch with the thick darkness (for the shutters were close fastened, through fear of robbers), and so I knew that he could not see the opening of the door, and I kept pushing it on steadily, steadily.

I had my head in, and was about to open the lantern, when my thumb slipped upon the tin fastening, and the old man sprang up in the bed, crying out—"Who's there?"

I kept quite still and said nothing. For a whole hour I did not move a muscle, and in the meantime I did not hear him lie down. He was still sitting up in the bed listening;—just as I have done, night after night, hearkening to the death watches in the wall.

Presently I heard a slight groan, and I knew it was the groan of mortal terror. It was not a groan of pain or of grief—oh no!—it was the low stifled sound that arises from the bottom of the soul when overcharged with awe. I knew the sound well. Many a night, just at midnight, when all the world slept, it has welled up from my own bosom, deepening, with its dreadful echo, the terrors that distracted me. I say I knew it well. I knew what the old man felt, and pitied him, although I chuckled at heart. I knew that he had been lying awake ever since the first slight noise, when he had turned in the bed. His fears had been ever since growing upon him. He had been trying to fancy them causeless, but could not. He had been saying to himself—"It is nothing but the wind in the chimney—it is only a mouse crossing the floor," or "it is merely a cricket which has made a single chirp." Yes, he has been trying to comfort himself with these suppositions; but he had found all in vain. *All in vain;* because Death, in approaching him, had stalked with his black shadow before him, and enveloped the victim. And it was the mournful influence of the unperceived shadow that caused him to feel—although he neither saw nor heard—to *feel* the presence of my head within the room.

When I had waited a long time, very patiently, without hearing him lie down, I resolved to open a little—a very, very little crevice in the lantern. So I opened it—you cannot imagine how stealthily, stealthily—until, at length, a single dim ray, like the thread of the spider, shot from out the crevice and full upon the vulture eye.

It was open—wide, wide open—and I grew furious as I gazed upon it. I saw it with perfect distinctness—all a dull blue, with a hideous veil over it that chilled the very marrow in my bones; but I could see nothing else of the old man's face or person: for I had directed the ray as if by instinct, precisely upon the damned spot.

And now have I not told you that what you mistake for madness is but over-acuteness of the senses?—now, I say, there came to my ears a long, dull, quick sound, such as a watch makes when enveloped in cotton. I knew *that* sound well too. It was the beating of the old man's heart. It increased my fury, as the beating of a drum stimulates the soldier into courage.

But even yet I refrained and kept still. I scarcely breathed. I held the lantern motionless. I tried how steadily I could maintain the ray upon the eye. Meantime the hellish tattoo of the heart increased. It grew quicker and quicker, and louder and louder every instant. The old man's terror *must* have been extreme! It grew louder, I say, louder every moment!—do you mark me well? I have told you that I am nervous: so I am. And now at the dead hour of the night, amid the dreadful silence of that old house, so strange a noise as this excited me to uncontrollable terror. Yet, for some minutes longer I refrained and stood still. But the beating grew louder, louder! I thought the heart must burst. And now a new anxiety seized me—the sound would be heard by a neighbor! The old man's hour had come! With a loud yell, I threw open the lantern and leaped into the room. He shrieked once—once only. In an instant I dragged him to the floor, and pulled the heavy bed over him. I then smiled gaily, to find the deed so far done. But, for many minutes, the heart beat on with a muffled sound. This, however, did not vex me; it would not be heard through the wall. At length it ceased. The old man was dead. I removed the bed and examined the corpse. Yes, he was stone, stone dead. I placed my hand upon the heart and held it there many minutes. There was no pulsation. He was stone dead. His eye would trouble me no more.

If still you think me mad, you will think so no longer when I describe the wise precautions I took for the concealment of the body. The night waned, and I worked hastily, but in silence. First of all I dismembered the corpse. I cut off the head and the arms and the legs.

I then took up three planks from the flooring of the chamber, and deposited all between the scantlings. I then replaced the boards so cleverly, so cunningly, that no human eye—not even *his*—could have detected any thing wrong. There was nothing to wash out—no stain of any kind—no blood-spot whatever. I had been too wary for that. A tub had caught all—ha! ha!

When I had made an end of these labors, it was four o'clock—still dark as midnight. As the bell sounded the hour, there came a knocking at the street door. I went down to open it with a light heart,—for what had I *now* to fear? There entered three men, who introduced themselves, with perfect suavity, as officers of the police. A shriek had been heard by a neighbor during the night; suspicion of foul play had been aroused; information had been lodged at the police office, and they (the officers) had been deputed to search the premises.

I smiled,—for *what* had I to fear? I bade the gentlemen welcome. The shriek, I said, was my own in a dream. The old man, I mentioned, was absent

in the country. I took my visitors all over the house. I bade them search—
search *well.* I led them, at length, to *his* chamber. I showed them his treasures,
secure, undisturbed. In the enthusiasm of my confidence, I brought chairs into
the room, and desired them *here* to rest from their fatigues, while I myself, in
the wild audacity of my perfect triumph, placed my own seat upon the very
spot beneath which reposed the corpse of the victim.

The officers were satisfied. My *manner* had convinced them. I was singularly at ease. They sat, and while I answered cheerily, they chatted familiar
things. But, ere long, I felt myself getting pale and wished them gone. My head
ached, and I fancied a ringing in my ears: but still they sat and still they chatted.
The ringing became more distinct:—it continued and became more distinct: I
talked more freely to get rid of the feeling: but it continued and gained definitiveness—until, at length, I found that the noise was *not* within my ears.

No doubt I now grew *very* pale;—but I talked more fluently, and with a
heightened voice. Yet the sound increased—and what could I do? It was a
*low, dull, quick sound—much such a sound as a watch makes when envel-
oped in cotton.* I gasped for breath—and yet the officers heard it not. I talked
more quickly—more vehemently; but the noise steadily increased. I arose and
argued about trifles; in a high key and with violent gesticulations, but the
noise steadily increased. Why *would* they not be gone? I paced the floor to
and fro with heavy strides, as if excited to fury by the observation of the
men—but the noise steadily increased. Oh God! what *could* I do? I foamed—
I raved—I swore! I swung the chair upon which I had been sitting, and grated
it upon the boards, but the noise arose over all and continually increased. It
grew louder—louder—*louder!* And still the men chatted pleasantly, and
smiled. Was it possible they heard not? Almighty God!—no, no! They
heard!—they suspected!—they *knew!*—they were making a *mockery* of my
horror!—this I thought, and this I think. But any thing was better than this
agony! Any thing was more tolerable than this derision! I could bear those
hypocritical smiles no longer! I felt that I must scream or die!—and now—
again—hark! louder! louder! louder! *louder!*—

"Villains!" I shrieked, "dissemble no more! I admit the deed!—tear up the
planks!—here, here!—it is the beating of his hideous heart!"

EXERCISES

1. Discuss those points in the story in which the narrator identifies with the
   old man.

2. Discuss those points in the story in which time is a significant concern.

3. Consider the title of the story. What kind of tale does the heart tell? How
   is the title related to the theme of time?

4. If the narrator identifies with the old man and yet wants to kill him, how
   is this related to the theme of the eye? Consider this question in relationship
   to the fact that the narrator says it is his sense of hearing that is most acute.

5. What does the narrator's desire to kill the old man have to do with the
   theme of time and the tale the heart tells?

6. How is this story about madness defined in its broadest sense as mistaking inner reality for outer reality?

FYODOR
DOSTOEVSKY | *The Peasant Marey*

It was the second day in Easter week. The air was warm, the sky was blue, the sun was high, warm, bright, but my soul was very gloomy. I sauntered behind the prison barracks. I stared at the palings of the stout prison fence, counting them; but I had no inclination to count them, though it was my habit to do so. This was the second day of the "holidays" in the prison; the convicts were not taken out to work, there were numbers of men drunk, loud abuse and quarreling were springing up continually in every corner. There were hideous, disgusting songs, and card-parties installed beside the platform-beds. Several of the convicts who had been sentenced by their comrades, for special violence, to be beaten till they were half dead, were lying on the platform-bed, covered with sheepskins till they should recover and come to themselves again; knives had already been drawn several times. For these two days of holiday all this had been torturing me till it made me ill. And indeed I could never endure without repulsion the noise and disorder of drunken people, and especially in this place. On these days even the prison officials did not look into the prison, made no searches, did not look for vodka, understanding that they must allow even these outcasts to enjoy themselves once a year, and that things would be even worse if they did not. At last a sudden fury flamed up in my heart. A political prisoner called M. met me; he looked at me gloomily, his eyes flashed and his lips quivered. *"Je hais ces brigands!"* he hissed at me through his teeth, and walked on. I returned to the prison ward, though only a quarter of an hour before I had rushed out of it as though I were crazy, when six stalwart fellows had all together flung themselves upon the drunken Tatar Gazin to suppress him and had begun beating him; they beat him stupidly, a camel might have been killed by such blows, but they knew that this Hercules was not easy to kill, and so they beat him without uneasiness. Now on returning I noticed on the bed in the furthest corner of the room Gazin lying unconscious, almost without sign of life. He lay covered with a sheepskin, and everyone walked round him, without speaking; though they confidently hoped that he would come to himself next morning, yet if luck was against him, maybe from a beating like that, the man would die. I made my way to my own place opposite the window with the iron grating, and lay on my back with my hands behind my head and my eyes shut. I liked to lie like that; a sleeping man is not molested, and meanwhile one can dream and think. But I could not dream, my heart was beating uneasily, and M.'s words, *"Je hais ces brigands!"* were echoing in my ears. But why describe my impressions? I sometimes dream even now of those times at night, and I have no dreams more agonizing. Perhaps it will be noticed that even to this day I have scarcely once spoken in print of my life in prison. *The House of the Dead* I wrote fifteen years ago in the character of an imaginary person, a criminal who had killed his wife. I may add by the way that since then, very many persons have supposed, and even now maintain, that I was sent to penal servitude for the murder of my wife.

Gradually I sank into forgetfulness and by degrees was lost in memories. During the whole course of my four years in prison I was continually recalling all my past, and seemed to live over again the whole of my life in recollection. These memories rose up of themselves, it was not often that I summoned them of my own will. Each would begin from some point, some little thing, at times unnoticed, and then by degrees there would rise up a complete picture, some vivid and complete impression. I used to analyze these impressions, give new features to what had happened long ago, and best of all, I used to correct it, correct it continually, that was my great amusement. On this occasion, I suddenly for some reason remembered an unnoticed moment in my early childhood when I was only nine years old—a moment which I should have thought I had utterly forgotten; but at that time I was particularly fond of memories of my early childhood. I remembered the month of August in our country house: a dry bright day but rather cold and windy; summer was waning and soon we should have to go to Moscow to be bored all winter with French lessons, and I was so sorry to leave the country. I walked past the threshing-floor and, going down the ravine, I went up to the dense thicket of bushes that covered the further side of the ravine as far as the copse. And I plunged right into the midst of the bushes, and heard a peasant plowing alone on the clearing about thirty paces away. I knew that he was plowing up the steep hill and the horse was moving with effort, and from time to time the peasant's call "Come up!" floated upwards to me. I knew almost all our peasants, but I did not know who it was plowing now, and, indeed, I did not care, I was absorbed in my own affairs. I was busy, too; I was breaking off switches from the nut trees to whip the frogs with. Nut sticks make such fine whips, but they do not last; while birch twigs are just the opposite. I was interested, too, in beetles and other insects; I used to collect them, some very ornamental. I was very fond, too, of the little nimble red and yellow lizards with black spots on them, but I was afraid of snakes. Snakes, however, were much more rare than lizards. There were not many mushrooms there. To get mushrooms one had to go to the birch wood, and I was about to set off there. And there was nothing in the world that I loved so much as the wood with its mushrooms and wild berries, with its beetles and its birds, its hedgehogs and squirrels, with its damp smell of dead leaves which I loved so much, and even as I write I smell the fragrance of our birch wood: these impressions will remain for my whole life. Suddenly in the midst of the profound stillness I heard a clear and distinct shout, "Wolf!" I shrieked and, beside myself with terror, calling out at the top of my voice, ran out into the clearing and straight to the peasant who was plowing.

It was our peasant Marey. I don't know if there is such a name, but everyone called him Marey—a thick-set, rather well-grown peasant of fifty, with a good many grey hairs in his dark brown, spreading beard. I knew him, but had scarcely ever happened to speak to him till then. He stopped his horse on hearing my cry, and when, breathless, I caught with one hand at his plow and with the other at his sleeve, he saw how frightened I was.

"There is a wolf!" I cried, panting.

He flung up his head, and could not help looking round for an instant, almost believing me.

"Where is the wolf?"

"A shout . . . someone shouted: 'wolf' . . ." I faltered out.

"Nonsense, nonsense! A wolf? Why, it was your fancy! How could there be a wolf?" he muttered, reassuring me. But I was trembling all over, and still kept tight hold of his smock frock, and I must have been quite pale. He looked at me with an uneasy smile, evidently anxious and troubled over me.

"Why, you have had a fright, aïe, aïe!" He shook his head. "There, dear. . . . Come little one, aïe!"

He stretched out his hand, and all at once stroked my cheek.

"Come, come, there; Christ be with you! Cross yourself!"

But I did not cross myself. The corners of my mouth were twitching, and I think that struck him particularly. He put out his thick, black-nailed, earth-stained finger and softly touched my twitching lips.

"Aïe, there, there," he said to me with a slow, almost motherly smile. "Dear, dear, what is the matter? There; come, come!"

I grasped at last that there was no wolf, and that the shout that I had heard was my fancy. Yet that shout had been so clear and distinct, but such shouts (not only about wolves) I had imagined once or twice before, and I was aware of that. (These hallucinations passed away later as I grew older.)

"Well, I will go then," I said, looking at him timidly and inquiringly.

"Well, do, and I'll keep watch on you as you go. I won't let the wolf get you," he added, still smiling at me with the same motherly expression. "Well, Christ be with you! Come, run along then." And he made the sign of the cross over me and then over himself. I walked away, looking back almost at every tenth step. Marey stood still with his mare as I walked away, and looked after me and nodded to me every time I looked round. I must own I felt a little ashamed at having let him see me so frightened, but I was still very much afraid of the wolf as I walked away, until I reached the first barn halfway up the slope of the ravine; there my fright vanished completely, and all at once our yard-dog Volchok flew to meet me. With Volchok I felt quite safe, and I turned round to Marey for the last time; I could not see his face distinctly, but I felt that he was still nodding and smiling affectionately at me. I waved to him; he waved back at me and started his little mare. "Come up!" I heard his call in the distance again, and the little mare pulled at the plow again.

All this I recalled all at once, I don't know why, but with extraordinary minuteness of detail. I suddenly roused myself and sat up on the sleeping-platform, and, I remember, found myself still smiling quietly at my memories. I brooded over them for another minute.

When I got home that day I told no one of my "adventure" with Marey. And indeed it was hardly an adventure. And in fact I soon forgot Marey.

When I met him now and then afterwards, I never even spoke to him about the wolf or anything else; and all at once now, twenty years afterwards in Siberia, I remembered this meeting with such distinctness to the smallest detail. So it must have lain hidden in my soul, though I knew nothing of it, and rose suddenly to my memory when it was wanted; I remembered the soft motherly smile of the poor serf, the way he signed me with the cross and shook his head. "There, there, you have had a fright, little one!" And I remembered particularly the thick earth-stained finger with which he softly and with timid tenderness touched my quivering lips. Of course anyone would have reassured a child, but something quite different seemed to have happened in that solitary meeting; and if I had been his own son, he could not have looked at me with eyes shining with greater love. And what made him like that? He was our serf and I was his little master, after all. No one would know that he had been kind to me and reward him for it. Was he, perhaps, very fond of little children? Some people are. It was a solitary meeting in the deserted fields, and only God, perhaps, may have seen from above with what deep and humane civilized feeling, and with what a delicate, almost feminine tenderness, the heart of a coarse, brutally ignorant Russian serf, who had as yet no expectation, no idea even of his freedom, may be filled. Was not this, perhaps, what Konstantin Aksakov meant when he spoke of the high degree of culture of our peasantry?

And when I got down off the bed and looked around me, I remember I suddenly felt that I could look at these unhappy creatures with quite different eyes, and that suddenly by some miracle all hatred and anger had vanished utterly from my heart. I walked about, looking into the faces that I met. That shaven peasant, branded on his face as a criminal, bawling his hoarse, drunken song, may be that very Marey; I cannot look into his heart.

I met M. again that evening. Poor fellow! he could have no memories of Russian peasants, and no other view of these people but: *"Je hais ces brigands!"* Yes, the Polish prisoners had more to bear than I.

EXERCISES

1. Discuss the significance of the narrator's giving new features to what happened long ago, continually correcting those memories of the past. How much of the memory recalled here is corrected or given new features?

2. How is this a story about memory—about something that lies hidden until it is wanted?

3. By what miracle does all the hatred and anger vanish from the narrator's heart as a result of the story or memory?

4. This is a *frame story,* or a story within a story. What is the significance of the fact that in the memory, or inner story, there is no wolf, that what the narrator heard was only his fancy?

5. What is the significance of the fact that the outer story takes place during Easter week? How is this related to the fact that the memory the narrator recalls has been "buried" in the self?

6. Discuss this story as about a fantasy (thinking he hears the cry "wolf") that is dismissed by the reality of the peasant Marey. Discuss it also as a story in which a fantasy (the "corrected" memory of a past event) dismisses the reality of the narrator's present situation.

PÄR
LAGERKVIST | *Father and I*

I remember one Sunday afternoon when I was about ten years old, Daddy took my hand and we went for a walk in the woods to hear the birds sing. We waved good-bye to mother, who was staying at home to prepare supper, and so couldn't go with us. The sun was bright and warm as we set out briskly on our way. We didn't take this bird-singing too seriously, as though it was something special or unusual. We were sensible people, Daddy and I. We were used to the woods and the creatures in them, so we didn't make any fuss about it. It was just because it was Sunday afternoon and Daddy was free. We went along the railway line where other people aren't allowed to go, but Daddy belonged to the railway and had a right to. And in this way we came direct into the woods and did not need to take a roundabout way. Then the bird song and all the rest began at once. They chirped in the bushes; hedge-sparrows, thrushes, and warblers; and we heard all the noises of the little creatures as we came into the woods. The ground was thick with anemones, the birches were dressed in their new leaves, and the pines had young, green shoots. There was such a pleasant smell everywhere. The mossy ground was steaming a little, because the sun was shining upon it. Everywhere there was life and noise; bumble-bees flew out of their holes, midges circled where it was damp. The birds shot out of the bushes to catch them and then dived back again. All of a sudden a train came rushing along and we had to go down the embankment. Daddy hailed the driver with two fingers to his Sunday hat: the driver saluted and waved his hand. Everything seemed on the move. As we went on our way along the sleepers which lay and oozed tar in the sunshine, there was a smell of everything, machine oil and almond blossom, tar and heather, all mixed. We took big steps from sleeper to sleeper so as not to step among the stones, which were rough to walk on, and wore your shoes out. The rails shone in the sunshine. On both sides of the line stood the telephone poles that sang as we went by them. Yes! That was a fine day! The sky was absolutely clear. There wasn't a single cloud to be seen: there just couldn't be any on a day like this, according to what Daddy said. After a while we came to a field of oats on the right side of the line, where a farmer, whom we knew, had a clearing. The oats had grown thick and even; Daddy looked at it knowingly, and I could feel that he was satisfied. I didn't understand that sort of thing much, because I was born in town. Then we came to the bridge over the brook that mostly hadn't much water in it, but now there was plenty. We took hands so that we shouldn't fall down between the sleepers. From there it wasn't far to the railway gate-keeper's little place, which was quite buried in green. There were apple trees and gooseberry bushes right close to the house. We went in there, to pay a visit, and they offered us milk. We looked at the pigs, the hens, and the fruit trees, which were in full blossom, and then we went on again. We wanted to go to the river, because there it was prettier than anywhere else. There was something special about the river, because higher up stream it flowed past Daddy's old home. We never liked going back before we got to it, and, as usual, this time we got there after a fair walk. It wasn't far to the next station, but we didn't go on there. Daddy just looked to see whether the signals were right. He thought of everything. We stopped by the river, where it flowed broad and friendly in the sunshine, and the thick leafy trees on the banks mirrored themselves in the calm water. It was all so fresh and bright. A breeze came from the little lakes higher up. We climbed down the bank, went a little way along the very edge. Daddy showed me the fishing spots. When he was a boy he used to sit there on the stones and wait for perch all day long. Often he didn't get a single bite, but it was a delightful way to spend the day. Now he never had time. We played about for some time by the side of the river, and threw in pieces of bark that the current carried away, and we threw stones to see who could throw farthest. We were, by nature, very merry and cheerful, Daddy and I. After a while we felt a bit tired. We thought we had played enough, so we started off home again.

Then it began to get dark. The woods were changed. It wasn't quite dark yet, but almost. We made haste. Maybe mother was getting anxious, and waiting supper. She was always afraid that something might happen, though nothing had. This had been a splendid day. Everything had been just as it should, and we were satisfied with it all. It was getting darker and darker, and the trees were so queer. They stood and listened for the sound of our footsteps, as though they didn't know who we were. There was a glow-worm under one of them. It lay down there in the dark and stared at us. I held Daddy's hand tight, but he didn't seem to notice the strange light: he just went on. It was quite dark when we came to the bridge over the stream. It was roaring down underneath us as if it wanted to swallow us up, as the ground seemed to open under us. We went along the sleepers carefully, holding hands tight so that we shouldn't fall in. I thought Daddy would carry me over, but he didn't say anything about it. I suppose he wanted me to be like him, and not think anything of it. We went on. Daddy was so calm in the darkness, walking with even steps without speaking. He was thinking his own thoughts. I couldn't understand how he could be so calm when everything was so ghostly. I looked round scared. It was nothing but darkness everywhere. I hardly dared to breathe deeply, because then the darkness comes into one, and that was dangerous, I thought. One must die soon. I remember quite well thinking so then. The railway embankment was very steep. It finished in black night. The telephone posts stood up ghostlike against the sky, mumbling deep inside as though someone were speaking, way down in the earth. The white china hats sat there scared, cowering with fear, listening. It was all so creepy. Nothing was real, nothing was natural, all seemed a mystery. I went closer to Daddy, and whispered: "Why is it so creepy when it's dark?"

"No child, it isn't creepy," he said, and took my hand.

"Oh, yes, but it is, Daddy."

"No, you mustn't think that. We know there is a God don't we?" I felt so lonely, so abandoned. It was queer that it was only me that was frightened, and not Daddy. It was queer that we didn't feel the same about it. And it was queerer still that what he said didn't help, didn't stop me being frightened. Not even what he said about God helped. The thought of God made one feel creepy too. It was creepy to think that He was everywhere here in the darkness, down there under the trees, and in the telephone posts that mumbled so—probably that was Him everywhere. But all the same one could never see Him.

We went along silently, each of us thinking his own thoughts. My heart felt cramped as though the darkness had come in and was squeezing it.

Then, when we were in a bend, we suddenly heard a great noise behind us. We were startled out of our thoughts. Daddy pulled me down the embankment and held me tight, and a train rushed by; a black train. The lights were out in all the carriages, as it whizzed past us. What could it be? There shouldn't be any train now. We looked at it, frightened. The furnace roared in the big engine, where they shovelled in coal, and the sparks flew out into the night. It was terrible. The driver stood so pale and immovable, with such a stony look in the glare. Daddy didn't recognize him—didn't know who he was. He was just looking ahead as though he was driving straight into darkness, far into darkness, which had no end.

Startled and panting with fear I looked after the wild thing. It was swallowed up in the night. Daddy helped me up on to the line, and we hurried home. He said, "That was strange! What train was that I wonder? And I didn't know the driver either." Then he didn't say any more.

I was shaking all over. That had been for me—for my sake. I guessed what it meant. It was all the fear which would come to me, all the unknown; all that Daddy didn't know about, and couldn't save me from. That was how the world would be for me, and the strange life I should live; not like Daddy's, where everyone was known and sure. It wasn't a real world, or a real life;— it just rushed burning into the darkness which had no end.

EXERCISES

1. Note that this is a story told in the first person about a past event. Is the story told from the child's point of view or from the point of view of the adult remembering the event? Consider the difference between these two points of view.

2. Why is God mentioned in the trip back but not during the trip toward the river?

3. Discuss the significance of the imagery of the external world on the trip.

4. What is the significance of the repetition of such words as *mystery, unnatural,* and *queer?*

5. What makes the boy think "one must die soon"?

6. Is the black train a real train or an imagined one? Does the father really not know of the train? Explain what this means.

7. What does the boy mean when he says that his life will not be like Daddy's? Is he right? How do you know?

8. The story breaks into two structural parts—the trip to the river and the trip back. Why are the things the boy notes on the trip to the river reversed in some way on the trip back?

EUDORA
WELTY | *A Memory*

One summer morning when I was a child I lay on the sand after swimming in the small lake in the park. The sun beat down—it was almost noon. The water shone like steel, motionless except for the feathery curl behind a distant swimmer. From my position I was looking at a rectangle brightly lit, actually glaring at me, with sun, sand, water, a little pavilion, a few solitary people in fixed attitudes, and around it all a border of dark rounded oak trees, like the engraved thunderclouds surrounding illustrations in the Bible. Ever since I had begun taking painting lessons, I had made small frames with my fingers, to look out at everything.

Since this was a weekday morning, the only persons who were at liberty to be in the park were either children, who had nothing to occupy them, or those older people whose lives are obscure, irregular, and consciously of no worth to anything: this I put down as my observation at that time. I was at an age when I formed a judgment upon every person and every event which came under my eye, although I was easily frightened. When a person, or a happening, seemed to me not in keeping with my opinion, or even my hope or expectation, I was terrified by a vision of abandonment and wildness which tore my heart with a kind of sorrow. My father and mother, who believed that I saw nothing in the world which was not strictly coaxed into place like a vine on our garden trellis to be presented to my eyes, would have been badly concerned if they had guessed how frequently the weak and inferior and strangely turned examples of what was to come showed themselves to me.

I do not know even now what it was that I was waiting to see; but in those days I was convinced that I almost saw it at every turn. To watch everything about me I regarded grimly and possessively as a *need.* All through this summer I had lain on the sand beside the small lake, with my hands squared over my eyes, finger tips touching, looking out by this device to see everything: which appeared as a kind of projection. It did not matter to me what I looked at; from any observation I would conclude that a secret of life had been nearly revealed to me—for I was obsessed with notions about concealment, and from the smallest gesture of a stranger I would wrest what was to me a communication or a presentiment.

This state of exaltation was heightened, or even brought about, by the fact that I was in love then for the first time: I had identified love at once. The truth is that never since has any passion I have felt remained so hopelessly unexpressed within me or appeared so grotesquely altered in the outward world. It is strange that sometimes, even now, I remember unadulteratedly a certain morning when I touched my friend's wrist (as if by accident, and he pretended not to notice) as we passed on the stairs in school. I must add, and this is not so strange, that the child was not actually my friend. We had never exchanged a word or even a nod of recognition, but it was possible during that entire year for me to think endlessly on this minute and brief encounter which we endured on the stairs, until it would swell with a sudden and overwhelming beauty, like a rose forced into premature bloom for a great occasion.

My love had somehow made me doubly austere in my observations of what went on about me. Through some intensity I had come almost into a dual life, as observer and dreamer. I felt a necessity for absolute conformity to my ideas in any happening I witnessed. As a result, all day long in school I sat perpetually alert, fearing for the untoward to happen. The dreariness and regularity of the school day were a protection for me, but I remember with exact clarity the day in Latin class when the boy I loved (whom I watched constantly) bent suddenly over and brought his handkerchief to his face. I saw red—vermilion—blood flow over the handkerchief and his square-shaped hand; his nose had begun to bleed. I remember the very moment: several of the older girls laughed at the confusion and distraction; the boy rushed from the room; the teacher spoke sharply in warning. But this small happening which had closed in upon my friend was a tremendous shock to me; it was unforeseen, but at the same time dreaded; I recognized it, and suddenly I leaned heavily on my arm and fainted. Does this explain why, ever since that day, I have been unable to bear the sight of blood?

I never knew where this boy lived, or who his parents were. This occasioned during the year of my love a constant uneasiness in me. It was unbearable to think that his house might be slovenly and unpainted, hidden by tall trees, that his mother and father might be shabby—dishonest—crippled— dead. I speculated endlessly on the dangers of his home. Sometimes I imagined that his house might catch on fire in the night and that he might die. When he would walk into the schoolroom the next morning, a look of unconcern and even stupidity on his face would dissipate my dreams; but my fears were increased through his unconsciousness of them, for I felt a mystery deeper than danger which hung about him. I watched everything he did, trying to learn and translate and verify. I could reproduce for you now the clumsy weave, the exact shade of faded blue in his sweater. I remember how he used to swing his foot as he sat at his desk—softly, barely not touching the floor. Even now it does not seem trivial.

As I lay on the beach that sunny morning, I was thinking of my friend and remembering in a retarded, dilated, timeless fashion the incident of my hand brushing his wrist. It made a very long story. But like a needle going in and out among my thoughts were the children running on the sand, the upthrust oak trees growing over the clean pointed roof of the white pavilion, and the slowly changing attitudes of the grown-up people who had avoided the city and were lying prone and laughing on the water's edge. I still would not care to say which was more real—the dream I could make blossom at will, or the sight of the bathers. I am presenting them, you see, only as simultaneous.

I did not notice how the bathers got there, so close to me. Perhaps I actually fell asleep, and they came out then. Sprawled close to where I was lying, at any rate, appeared a group of loud, squirming, ill-assorted people who seemed thrown together only by the most confused accident, and who seemed driven by foolish intent to insult each other, all of which they enjoyed with a hilarity which astonished my heart. There were a man, two women, two young boys. They were brown and roughened, but not foreigners; when I was a child such people were called "common." They wore old and faded bathing suits which did not hide either the energy or the fatigue of their bodies, but showed it exactly.

The boys must have been brothers, because they both had very white straight hair, which shone like thistles in the red sunlight. The older boy was greatly overgrown—he protruded from his costume at every turn. His cheeks were ballooned outward and hid his eyes, but it was easy for me to follow his darting, sly glances as he ran clumsily around the others, inflicting pinches, kicks, and idiotic sounds upon them. The smaller boy was thin and defiant; his white bangs were plastered down where he had thrown himself time after time headfirst into the lake when the older child chased him to persecute him.

Lying in leglike confusion together were the rest of the group, the man and the two women. The man seemed completely given over to the heat and glare of the sun; his relaxed eyes sometimes squinted with faint amusement over the brilliant water and the hot sand. His arms were flabby and at rest. He lay turned on his side, now and then scooping sand in a loose pile about the legs of the older woman.

She herself stared fixedly at his slow, undeliberate movements, and held her body perfectly still. She was unnaturally white and fatly aware, in a bathing suit which had no relation to the shape of her body. Fat hung upon her upper arms like an arrested earthslide on a hill. With the first motion she might make, I was afraid that she would slide down upon herself in to a terrifying heap. Her breasts hung heavy and widening like pears into her bathing suit. Her legs lay prone one on the other like shadowed bulwarks, uneven and deserted, upon which, from the man's hand, the sand piled higher like the teasing threat of oblivion. A slow repetitious sound I had been hearing for a long time unconsciously, I identified as a continuous laugh which came through the motionless open pouched mouth of the woman.

The younger girl, who was lying at the man's feet, was curled tensely upon herself. She wore a bright green bathing suit like a bottle from which she might, I felt, burst into a rage of churning smoke. I could feel the genie-like rage in her narrowed figure as she seemed both to crawl and to lie still, watching the man heap the sand in his careless way about the larger legs of the older woman. The two little boys were running in wobbly ellipses about the others, pinching them indiscriminately and pitching sand into the man's roughened hair as though they were not afraid of him. The woman continued to laugh, almost as she would hum an annoying song. I saw that they were all resigned to each other's daring and ugliness.

There had been no words spoken among these people, but I began to comprehend a progression, a circle of answers, which they were flinging toward one another in their own way, in the confusion of vulgarity and hatred which twined among them all like a breath of steam rising from the wet sand. I saw the man lift his hand filled with crumbling sand, shaking it as the woman laughed, and pour it down inside her bathing suit between her bulbous descending breasts. There it hung, brown and shapeless, making them all laugh. Even the angry girl laughed, with an insistent hilarity which flung her to her feet and tossed her about the beach, her stiff, cramped legs jumping and tottering. The little boys pointed and howled. The man smiled, the way panting dogs seem to be smiling, and gazed about carelessly at them all and out over the water. He even looked at me, and included me. Looking back, stunned, I wished that they all were dead.

But at that moment the girl in the green bathing suit suddenly whirled all the way around. She reached rigid arms toward the screaming children and joined them in a senseless chase. The small boy dashed headfirst into the water, and the larger boy churned his overgrown body through the blue air onto a little bench, which I had not even known was there! Jeeringly he called to the others, who laughed as he jumped, heavy and ridiculous, over the back of the bench and tumbled exaggeratedly into the sand below. The fat woman leaned over the man to smirk, and the child pointed at her, screaming. The girl in green then came running toward the bench as though she would destroy it, and with a fierceness which took my breath away, she dragged herself through the air and jumped over the bench. But no one seemed to notice, except the smaller boy, who flew out of the water to dig his fingers into her side, in mixed congratulation and derision; she pushed him angrily down into the sand.

I closed my eyes upon them and their struggles but I could see them still, large and almost metallic, with painted smiles, in the sun. I lay there with my eyes pressed shut, listening to their moans and their frantic squeals. It seemed to me that I could hear also the thud and the fat impact of all their ugly bodies upon one another. I tried to withdraw to my most inner dream, that of touching the wrist of the boy I loved on the stair; I felt the shudder of my wish shaking the darkness like leaves where I had closed my eyes; I felt the heavy weight of sweetness which always accompanied this memory; but the memory itself did not come to me.

I lay there, opening and closing my eyes. The brilliance and then the blackness were like some alternate experiences of night and day. The sweetness of my love seemed to bring the dark and to swing me gently in its suspended wind; I sank into familiarity; but the story of my love, the long narrative of the incident on the stairs, had vanished. I did not know, any longer, the meaning of my happiness; it held me unexplained.

Once when I looked up, the fat woman was standing opposite the smiling man. She bent over and in a condescending way pulled down the front of her bathing suit, turning it outward, so that the lumps of mashed and folded sand came emptying out. I felt a peak of horror, as though her breasts themselves had turned to sand, as though they were of no importance at all and she did not care.

When finally I emerged again from the protection of my dream, the undefined austerity of my love, I opened my eyes onto the blur of an empty beach. The group of strangers had gone. Still I lay there, feeling victimized by the sight of the unfinished bulwark where they had piled and shaped the wet sand around their bodies, which changed the appearance of the beach like the ravages of a storm. I looked away, and for the object which met my eye, the small worn white pavilion, I felt pity suddenly overtake me, and I burst into tears.

That was my last morning on the beach. I remember continuing to lie there, squaring my vision with my hands, trying to think ahead to the time of my return to school in winter. I could imagine the boy I loved walking into the classroom, where I would watch him with this hour on the beach accompanying my recovered dream and added to my love. I could even foresee the way he would stare back, speechless and innocent, a medium-sized boy with blond hair, his unconscious eyes looking beyond me and out the window, solitary and unprotected.

EXERCISES

1. Discuss the significance of the young girl's looking at things through the frames she makes with her fingers.

2. Discuss the significance of the girl's reaction when things do not fit her opinion, hope, or expectation.

3. Discuss the girl's obsession with concealment. What is meant by her need to develop a presentiment out of the smallest gesture of a stranger?

4. Why is it relevant that the girl is in love at the time of this event? Discuss the significance of the boy's nosebleed.

5. How is the experience with the boy related to the events the girl observes on the beach?

6. Discuss the significance of the people the girl sees on the beach. What is it about them that most fascinates her?

7. What is the meaning of the image of the woman emptying the sand out of her bathing suit?

8. Why does the girl feel pity and burst into tears at the end of the story?

KATHERINE
ANNE
PORTER | *The Grave*

The grandfather, dead for more than thirty years, had been twice disturbed in his long repose by the constancy and possessiveness of his widow. She removed his bones first to Louisiana and then to Texas as if she had set out to find her own burial place, knowing well she would never return to the places she had left. In Texas she set up a small cemetery in a corner of her first farm, and as the family connection grew, and oddments of relations came over from Kentucky to settle, it contained at last about twenty graves. After the grandmother's death, part of her land was to be sold for the benefit of certain of her children, and the cemetery happened to lie in the part set aside for sale. It was necessary to take up the bodies and bury them again in the family plot in the big new public cemetery, where the grandmother had been buried. At last her husband was to lie beside her for eternity, as she had planned.

The family cemetery had been a pleasant small neglected garden of tangled rose bushes and ragged cedar trees and cypress, the simple flat stones rising out of uncropped sweet-smelling wild grass. The graves were lying open and empty one burning day when Miranda and her brother Paul, who often went together to hunt rabbits and doves, propped their twenty-two Winchester rifles carefully against the rail fence, climbed over and explored among the graves. She was nine years old and he was twelve.

They peered into the pits all shaped alike with such purposeful accuracy, and looking at each other with pleased adventurous eyes, they said in solemn tones: "These were graves!" trying by words to shape a special, suitable emotion in their minds, but they felt nothing except an agreeable thrill of wonder: they were seeing a new sight, doing something they had not done before. In them both there was also a small disappointment at the entire commonplaceness of the actual spectacle. Even if it had once contained a coffin for years upon years, when the coffin was gone a grave was just a hole in the ground. Miranda leaped into the pit that had held her grandfather's bones. Scratching around aimlessly and pleasurably as any young animal, she scooped up a lump of earth and weighed it in her palm. It had a pleasantly sweet, corrupt smell, being mixed with cedar needles and small leaves, and as the crumbs fell apart, she saw a silver dove no larger than a hazel nut, with spread wings and a neat fan-shaped tail. The breast had a deep round hollow in it. Turning it up to the fierce sunlight, she saw that the inside of the hollow was cut in little whorls. She scrambled out, over the pile of loose earth that had fallen back into one end of the grave, calling to Paul that she had found something, he must guess what. . . . His head appeared smiling over the rim of another grave. He waved a closed hand at her. "I've got something too!" They ran to compare treasures, making a game of it, so many guesses each, all wrong, and a final showdown with opened palms. Paul had found a thin wide gold ring carved with intricate flowers and leaves. Miranda was smitten at sight of the ring and wished to have it. Paul seemed more impressed by the dove. They made a trade, with some little bickering. After he had got the dove in his hand, Paul said, "Don't you know what this is? This is a screw head for a *coffin!* . . . I'll bet nobody else in the world has one like this!"

Miranda glanced at it without covetousness. She had the gold ring on her thumb; it fitted perfectly. "Maybe we ought to go now," she said, "maybe one of the niggers'll see us and tell somebody." They knew the land had been sold, the cemetery was no longer theirs, and they felt like trespassers. They climbed back over the fence, slung their rifles loosely under their arms—they had been shooting at targets with various kinds of firearms since they were seven years old—and set out to look for the rabbits and doves or whatever small game might happen along. On these expeditions Miranda always followed at Paul's heels along the path, obeying instructions about handling her gun when going through fences; learning how to stand it up properly so it would not slip and fire unexpectedly; how to wait her time for a shot and not just bang away in the air without looking, spoiling shots for Paul, who really could hit things if given a chance. Now and then, in her excitement at seeing birds whizz up suddenly before her face, or a rabbit leap across her very toes, she lost her head, and almost without sighting she flung her rifle up and pulled the trigger. She hardly ever hit any sort of mark. She had no proper sense of hunting at all. Her brother would be often completely disgusted with her. "You don't care whether you get your bird or not," he said. "That's no way to hunt." Miranda could not understand his indignation. She had seen him smash his hat and yell with fury when he had missed his aim. "What I like about shooting," said Miranda, with exasperating inconsequence, "is pulling the trigger and hearing the noise."

"Then, by golly," said Paul, "whyn't you go back to the range and shoot at bulls-eyes?"

"I'd just as soon," said Miranda, "only like this, we walk around more."

"Well, you just stay behind and stop spoiling my shots," said Paul, who, when he made a kill, wanted to be certain he had made it. Miranda, who alone brought down a bird once in twenty rounds, always claimed as her own any game they got when they fired at the same moment. It was tiresome and unfair and her brother was sick of it.

"Now, the first dove we see, or the first rabbit, is mine," he told her. "And the next will be yours. Remember that and don't get smarty."

"What about snakes?" asked Miranda idly. "Can I have the first snake?"

Waving her thumb gently and watching her gold ring glitter, Miranda lost interest in shooting. She was wearing her summer roughing outfit: dark blue overalls, a light blue shirt, a hired-man's straw hat, and thick brown sandals. Her brother had the same outfit except his was a sober hickory-nut color. Ordinarily Miranda preferred her overalls to any other dress, though it was making rather a scandal in the countryside, for the year was 1903, and in the back country the law of female decorum had teeth in it. Her father had been criticized for letting his girls dress like boys and go careering around astride barebacked horses. Big sister Maria, the really independent and fearless one, in spite of her rather affected ways, rode at a dead run with only a rope knotted around her horse's nose. It was said the motherless family was running down, with the Grandmother no longer there to hold it together. It was known that she had discriminated against her son Harry in her will, and that he was in straits about money. Some of his old neighbors reflected with vicious satisfaction that now he would probably not be so stiffnecked, nor have any more high-stepping horses either. Miranda knew this, though she could not say how. She had met along the road old women of the kind who smoked corn-cob pipes, who had treated her grandmother with most sincere respect. They slanted their gummy old eyes side-ways at the granddaughter and said, "Ain't you ashamed of yoself, Missy? It's aginst the Scriptures to dress like that. Whut yo Pappy thinkin about?" Miranda, with her powerful social sense, which was like a fine set of antennae radiating from every pore of her skin, would feel ashamed because she knew well it was rude and ill-bred to shock anybody, even bad-tempered old crones, though she had faith in her father's judgment and was perfectly comfortable in the clothes. Her father had said, "They're just what you need, and they'll save your dresses for school. . . ." This sounded quite simple and natural to her. She had been brought up in rigorous economy. Wastefulness was vulgar. It was also a sin. These were truths; she had heard them repeated many times and never once disputed.

Now the ring, shining with the serene purity of fine gold on her rather grubby thumb, turned her feelings against her overalls and sockless feet, toes sticking through the thick brown leather straps. She wanted to go back to the farmhouse, take a good cold bath, dust herself with plenty of Maria's violet talcum powder—provided Maria was not present to object, of course—put on the thinnest, most becoming dress she owned, with a big sash, and sit in a wicker chair under the trees. . . . These things were not all she wanted, of course; she had vague stirrings of desire for luxury and a grand way of living which could not take precise form in her imagination but were founded on family legend of past wealth and leisure. These immediate comforts were what she could have, and she wanted them at once. She lagged rather far behind Paul, and once she thought of just turning back without a word and going home. She stopped, thinking that Paul would never do that to her, and so she would have to tell him. When a rabbit leaped, she let Paul have it without dispute. He killed it with one shot.

When she came up with him, he was already kneeling, examining the wound, the rabbit trailing from his hands, "Right through the head," he said complacently, as if he had aimed for it. He took out his sharp, competent bowie knife and started to skin the body. He did it very cleanly and quickly. Uncle Jimbilly knew how to prepare the skins so that Miranda always had fur coats for her dolls, for though she never cared much for her dolls she liked seeing them in fur coats. The children knelt facing each other over the dead animal. Miranda watched admiringly while her brother stripped the skin away as if he were taking off a glove. The flayed flesh emerged dark scarlet, sleek, firm; Miranda with thumb and finger felt the long fine muscles with the silvery flat strips binding them to the joints. Brother lifted the oddly bloated belly. "Look," he said, in a low amazed voice. "It was going to have young ones."

Very carefully he slit the thin flesh from the center ribs to the flanks, and a scarlet bag appeared. He slit again and pulled the bag open, and there lay a bundle of tiny rabbits, each wrapped in a thin scarlet veil. The brother pulled these off and there they were, dark gray, their sleek wet down lying in minute even ripples, like a baby's head just washed, their unbelievably small delicate ears folded close, their little blind faces almost featureless.

Miranda said, "Oh, I want to *see*," under her breath. She looked and looked—excited but not frightened, for she was accustomed to the sight of animals killed in hunting—filled with pity and astonishment and a kind of shocked delight in the wonderful little creatures for their own sakes, they were so pretty. She touched one of them ever so carefully, "Ah, there's blood running over them," she said and began to tremble without knowing why. Yet she wanted most deeply to see and to know. Having seen, she felt at once as if she had known all along. The very memory of her former ignorance faded, she had always known just this. No one had ever told her anything outright, she had been rather unobservant of the animal life around her because she was accustomed to animals. They seemed simply disorderly and unaccountably rude in their habits, but altogether natural and not very interesting. Her brother had spoken as if he had known about everything all along. He may have seen all this before. He had never said a word to her, but she knew now a part at least of what he knew. She understood a little of the secret formless intuitions in her own mind and body, which had been clearing up, taking form, so gradually and so steadily she had not realized that she was learning what she had to know. Paul said cautiously, as if he were talking about something forbidden: "They were just about ready to be born." His voice dropped on the last word. "I know," said Miranda, "like kittens. I know, like babies." She was quietly and terribly agitated, standing again with her rifle under her arm, looking down at the bloody heap. "I don't want the skin," she said, "I won't have it." Paul buried the young rabbits again in their mother's body, wrapped the skin around her, carried her to a clump of sage bushes, and hid her away. He came out again at once and said to Miranda, with an eager friendliness, a confidential tone quite unusual in him, as if he were taking her into an important secret on equal terms: "Listen now. Now you listen to me, and don't ever forget. Don't you ever tell a living soul that you saw this. Don't tell a soul. Don't tell Dad because I'll get into trouble. He'll say I'm leading you into things you ought not to do. He's always saying that. So now don't go and forget and blab out something the way you're always doing. . . . Now, that's a secret. Don't you tell."

Miranda never told, she did not even wish to tell anybody. She thought about the whole worrisome affair with confused unhappiness for a few days.

Then it sank quietly into her mind and was heaped over by accumulated thousands of impressions, for nearly twenty years. One day she was picking her path among the puddles and crushed refuse of a market street in a strange city of a strange country, when without warning, plain and clear in its true colors as if she looked through a frame upon a scene that had not stirred nor changed since the moment it happened, the episode of that far-off day leaped from its burial place before her mind's eye. She was so reasonlessly horrified she halted suddenly staring, the scene before her eyes dimmed by the vision back of them. An Indian vendor had held up before her a tray of dyed sugar sweets, in the shapes of all kinds of small creatures: birds, baby chicks, baby rabbits, lambs, baby pigs. They were in gay colors and smelled of vanilla, maybe. . . . It was a very hot day and the smell in the market, with its piles of raw flesh and wilting flowers, was like the mingled sweetness and corruption she had smelled that other day in the empty cemetery at home: the day she had remembered always until now vaguely as the time she and her brother had found treasure in the opened graves. Instantly upon this thought the dreadful vision faded, and she saw clearly her brother, whose childhood face she had forgotten, standing again in the blazing sunshine, again twelve years old, a pleased sober smile in his eyes, turning the silver dove over and over in his hands.

EXERCISES

1. Discuss the central image of the grave. Discuss how the metaphor of things buried or hidden away is central in the story.

2. Discuss the theme of the inextricability of life and death in the story. Discuss the way this theme is embodied.

3. If this is an initiation story, into what is Miranda initiated? Is this an initiation for Paul also? Why or why not?

4. Discuss the significance of the dove and the ring. Are these merely objects, or are they symbols? How do you know?

5. Discuss the significance of Miranda's desire to change from overalls to her most becoming dress.

6. What is meant by Miranda's statement "I want to see"? What does she see?

7. Why does the image of Paul in Miranda's memory dismiss the dreadful vision of death and decay at the end?

YUKIO
MISHIMA | *Swaddling Clothes*

He was always busy, Toshiko's husband. Even tonight he had to dash off
to an appointment, leaving her to go home alone by taxi. But what else
could a woman expect when she married an actor—an attractive one? No
doubt she had been foolish to hope that he would spend the evening with her.
And yet he must have known how she dreaded going back to their house,
unhomely with its Western-style furniture and with the bloodstains still showing on the floor.

Toshiko had been oversensitive since girlhood: that was her nature. As the
result of constant worrying she never put on weight, and now, an adult
woman, she looked more like a transparent picture than a creature of flesh
and blood. Her delicacy of spirit was evident to her most casual acquaintance.

Earlier that evening, when she had joined her husband at a night club, she
had been shocked to find him entertaining friends with an account of "the
incident." Sitting there in his American-style suit, puffing at a cigarette, he had
seemed to her almost a stranger.

"It's a fantastic story," he was saying, gesturing flamboyantly as if in an
attempt to outweigh the attractions of the dance band. "Here this new nurse
for our baby arrives from the employment agency, and the very first thing I
notice about her is her stomach. It's enormous—as if she had a pillow stuck
under the kimono! No wonder, I thought, for I soon saw that she could eat
more than the rest of us put together. She polished off the contents of our rice
bin like that. . . ." He snapped his fingers. " 'Gastric dilation'—that's how she
explained her girth and her appetite. Well, the day before yesterday we heard
groans and moans coming from the nursery. We rushed in and found her
squatting on the floor, holding her stomach in her two hands, and moaning
like a cow. Next to her our baby lay in his cot, scared out of his wits and
crying at the top of his lungs. A pretty scene, I can tell you!"

"So the cat was out of the bag?" suggested one of their friends, a film
actor like Toshiko's husband.

"Indeed it was! And it gave me the shock of my life. You see, I'd completely swallowed that story about 'gastric dilation.' Well, I didn't waste any
time. I rescued our good rug from the floor and spread a blanket for her to
lie on. The whole time the girl was yelling like a stuck pig. By the time the
doctor from the maternity clinic arrived, the baby had already been born. But
our sitting room was a pretty shambles!"

"Oh, that I'm sure of!" said another of their friends, and the whole company burst into laughter.

Toshiko was dumbfounded to hear her husband discussing the horrifying
happening as though it were no more than an amusing incident which they
chanced to have witnessed. She shut her eyes for a moment and all at once
she saw the newborn baby lying before her: on the parquet floor the infant
lay, and his frail body was wrapped in bloodstained newspapers.

Toshiko was sure that the doctor had done the whole thing out of spite. As if to emphasize his scorn for this mother who had given birth to a bastard under such sordid conditions, he had told his assistant to wrap the baby in some loose newspapers, rather than proper swaddling. This callous treatment of the newborn child had offended Toshiko. Overcoming her disgust at the entire scene, she had fetched a brand-new piece of flannel from her cupboard and, having swaddled the baby in it, had laid him carefully in an armchair.

This all had taken place in the evening after her husband had left the house. Toshiko had told him nothing of it, fearing that he would think her oversoft, oversentimental; yet the scene had engraved itself deeply in her mind. Tonight she sat silently thinking back on it, while the jazz orchestra brayed and her husband chatted cheerfully with his friends. She knew that she would never forget the sight of the baby, wrapped in stained newspapers and lying on the floor—it was a scene fit for a butchershop. Toshiko, whose own life had been spent in solid comfort, poignantly felt the wretchedness of the illegitimate baby.

I am the only person to have witnessed its shame, the thought occurred to her. The mother never saw her child lying there in its newspaper wrappings, and the baby itself of course didn't know. I alone shall have to preserve that terrible scene in my memory. When the baby grows up and wants to find out about his birth, there will be no one to tell him, so long as I preserve silence. How strange that I should have this feeling of guilt! After all, it was I who took him up from the floor, swathed him properly in flannel, and laid him down to sleep in the armchair.

They left the night club and Toshiko stepped into the taxi that her husband had called for her. "Take this lady to Ushigomé," he told the driver and shut the door from the outside. Toshiko gazed through the window at her husband's smiling face and noticed his strong, white teeth. Then she leaned back in the seat, oppressed by the knowledge that their life together was in some way too easy, too painless. It would have been difficult for her to put her thoughts into words. Through the rear window of the taxi she took a last look at her husband. He was striding along the street toward his Nash car, and soon the back of his rather garish tweed coat had blended with the figures of the passers-by.

The taxi drove off, passed down a street dotted with bars and then by a theatre, in front of which the throngs of people jostled each other on the pavement. Although the performance had only just ended, the lights had already been turned out and in the half dark outside it was depressingly obvious that the cherry blossoms decorating the front of the theatre were merely scraps of white paper.

Even if that baby should grow up in ignorance of the secret of his birth, he can never become a respectable citizen, reflected Toshiko, pursuing the same train of thoughts. Those soiled newspaper swaddling clothes will be the symbol of his entire life. But why should I keep worrying about him so much? Is it because I feel uneasy about the future of my own child? Say twenty years from now, when our boy will have grown up into a fine, carefully educated young man, one day by a quirk of fate he meets that other boy, who then will also have turned twenty. And say that the other boy, who has been sinned against, savagely stabs him with a knife. . . .

It was a warm, overcast April night, but thoughts of the future made Toshiko feel cold and miserable. She shivered on the back seat of the car.

No, when the time comes I shall take my son's place, she told herself suddenly. Twenty years from now I shall be forty-three. I shall go to that young man and tell him straight out about everything—about his newspaper swaddling clothes, and about how I went and wrapped him in flannel.

The taxi ran along the dark wide road that was bordered by the park and by the Imperial Palace moat. In the distance Toshiko noticed the pinpricks of light which came from the blocks of tall office buildings.

Twenty years from now that wretched child will be in utter misery. He will be living a desolate, hopeless, poverty-stricken existence—a lonely rat. What else could happen to a baby who has had such a birth? He'll be wandering through the streets by himself, cursing his father, loathing his mother.

No doubt Toshiko derived a certain satisfaction from her somber thoughts: she tortured herself with them without cease. The taxi approached Hanzomon and drove past the compound of the British Embassy. At that point the famous rows of cherry trees were spread out before Toshiko in all their purity. On the spur of the moment she decided to go and view the blossoms by herself in the dark night. It was a strange decision for a timid and unadventurous young woman, but then she was in a strange state of mind and she dreaded the return home. That evening all sorts of unsettling fancies had burst open in her mind.

She crossed the wide street—a slim, solitary figure in the darkness. As a rule when she walked in the traffic Toshiko used to cling fearfully to her companion, but tonight she darted alone between the cars and a moment later had reached the long narrow park that borders the Palace moat. Chidorigafuchi, it is called—the Abyss of the Thousand Birds.

Tonight the whole park had become a grove of blossoming cherry trees. Under the calm cloudy sky the blossoms formed a mass of solid whiteness. The paper lanterns that hung from wires between the trees had been put out; in their place electric light bulbs, red, yellow, and green, shone dully beneath the blossoms. It was well past ten o'clock and most of the flower-viewers had gone home. As the occasional passers-by strolled through the park, they would automatically kick aside the empty bottles or crush the waste paper beneath their feet.

Newspapers, thought Toshiko, her mind going back once again to those happenings. Bloodstained newspapers. If a man were ever to hear of that piteous birth and know that it was he who had lain there, it would ruin his entire life. To think that I, a perfect stranger, should from now on have to keep such a secret—the secret of a man's whole existence. . . .

Lost in these thoughts, Toshiko walked on through the park. Most of the people still remaining there were quiet couples; no one paid her any attention. She noticed two people sitting on a stone bench beside the moat, not looking at the blossoms, but gazing silently at the water. Pitch black it was, and swathed in heavy shadows. Beyond the moat the somber forest of the Imperial Palace blocked her view. The trees reached up, to form a solid dark mass against the night sky. Toshiko walked slowly along the path beneath the blossoms hanging heavily overhead.

On a stone bench, slightly apart from the others, she noticed a pale object—not, as she had at first imagined, a pile of cherry blossoms, nor a garment forgotten by one of the visitors to the park. Only when she came closer did she see that it was a human form lying on the bench. Was it, she wondered, one of those miserable drunks often to be seen sleeping in public places? Obviously not, for the body had been systematically covered with newspapers, and it was the whiteness of those papers that had attracted Toshiko's attention. Standing by the bench, she gazed down at the sleeping figure.

It was a man in a brown jersey who lay there, curled up on layers of newspapers, other newspapers covering him. No doubt this had become his normal night residence now that spring had arrived. Toshiko gazed down at the man's dirty, unkempt hair, which in places had become hopelessly matted. As she observed the sleeping figure wrapped in its newspapers, she was inevitably reminded of the baby who had lain on the floor in its wretched swaddling clothes. The shoulder of the man's jersey rose and fell in the darkness in time with his heavy breathing.

It seemed to Toshiko that all her fears and premonitions had suddenly taken concrete form. In the darkness the man's pale forehead stood out, and it was a young forehead, though carved with wrinkles of long poverty and hardship. His khaki trousers had been slightly pulled up; on his sockless feet he wore a pair of battered gym shoes. She could not see his face and suddenly had an overmastering desire to get one glimpse of it.

She walked to the head of the bench and looked down. The man's head was half buried in his arms, but Toshiko could see that he was surprisingly young. She noticed the thick eyebrows and the fine bridge of his nose. His slightly open mouth was alive with youth.

But Toshiko had approached too close. In the silent night the newspaper bedding rustled, and abruptly the man opened his eyes. Seeing the young woman standing directly beside him, he raised himself with a jerk, and his eyes lit up. A second later a powerful hand reached out and seized Toshiko by her slender wrist.

She did not feel in the least afraid and made no effort to free herself. In a flash the thought had struck her, Ah, so the twenty years have already gone by! The forest of the Imperial Palace was pitch dark and utterly silent.

EXERCISES

1. Discuss the relevance of Toshiko's relationship with her husband. Why is it "difficult for her to put her thoughts into words"?

2. What is the significance of Toshiko's being "more like a transparent picture than a creature of flesh and blood"?

3. What is the significance of the fact that Toshiko gains a certain satisfaction from her somber thoughts?
4. What happens at the end of the story? What do you imagine happens after the man grabs Toshiko's wrist? Is the final event realistic, psychological, or metaphoric? What does it mean that the twenty years have already gone by?
5. Why does the final event occur? Is poetic justice involved here? Does Toshiko deserve what happens to her? Does she make it happen?
6. Perhaps the key sentence in the story is "It seemed to Toshiko that all her fears and premonitions had suddenly taken concrete form." Discuss the meaning of this sentence.

RYŪNOSUKE
AKUTAGAWA | *Rashōmon**

It was a chilly evening. A servant of a samurai stood under the Rashōmon, waiting for a break in the rain.

No one else was under the wide gate. On the thick column, its crimson lacquer rubbed off here and there, perched a cricket. Since the Rashōmon stands on Sujaku Avenue, a few other people at least, in sedge hat or nobleman's headgear, might have been expected to be waiting there for a break in the rain storm. But no one was near except this man.

For the past few years the city of Kyōto had been visited by a series of calamities, earthquakes, whirlwinds, and fires, and Kyōto had been greatly devastated. Old chronicles say that broken pieces of Buddhist images and other Buddhist objects, with their lacquer, gold, or silver leaf worn off, were heaped up on roadsides to be sold as firewood. Such being the state of affairs in Kyōto, the repair of the Rashōmon was out of the question. Taking advantage of the devastation, foxes and other wild animals made their dens in the ruins of the gate, and thieves and robbers found a home there too. Eventually it became customary to bring unclaimed corpses to this gate and abandon them. After dark it was so ghostly that no one dared approach.

Flocks of crows flew in from somewhere. During the daytime these cawing birds circled round the ridgepole of the gate. When the sky overhead turned red in the afterlight of the departed sun, they looked like so many grains of sesame flung across the gate. But on that day not a crow was to be seen, perhaps because of the lateness of the hour. Here and there the stone steps, beginning to crumble, and with rank grass growing in their crevices, were dotted with the white droppings of crows. The servant, in a worn blue kimono, sat

---

* The "Rashōmon" was the largest gate in Kyōto, the ancient capital of Japan. It was 106 feet wide and 26 feet deep, and was topped with a ridge-pole; its stone-wall rose 75 feet high. This gate was constructed in 789 when the then capital of Japan was transferred to Kyōto. With the decline of West Kyōto, the gate fell into bad repair, cracking and crumbling in many places, and became a hide-out for thieves and robbers and a place for abandoning unclaimed corpses.

on the seventh and highest step, vacantly watching the rain. His attention was drawn to a large pimple irritating his right cheek.

As has been said, the servant was waiting for a break in the rain. But he had no particular idea of what to do after the rain stopped. Ordinarily, of course, he would have returned to his master's house, but he had been discharged just before. The prosperity of the city of Kyōto had been rapidly declining, and he had been dismissed by his master, whom he had served many years, because of the effects of this decline. Thus, confined by the rain, he was at a loss to know where to go. And the weather had not a little to do with his depressed mood. The rain seemed unlikely to stop. He was lost in thoughts of how to make his living tomorrow, helpless incoherent thoughts protesting an inexorable fate. Aimlessly he had been listening to the pattering of the rain on the Sujaku Avenue.

The rain, enveloping the Rashōmon, gathered strength and came down with a pelting sound that could be heard far away. Looking up, he saw a fat black cloud impale itself on the tips of the tiles jutting out from the roof of the gate.

He had little choice of means, whether fair or foul, because of his helpless circumstances. If he chose honest means, he would undoubtedly starve to death beside the wall or in the Sujaku gutter. He would be brought to this gate and thrown away like a stray dog. If he decided to steal . . . His mind, after making the same detour time and again, came finally to the conclusion that he would be a thief.

But doubts returned many times. Though determined that he had no choice, he was still unable to muster enough courage to justify the conclusion that he must become a thief.

After a loud fit of sneezing he got up slowly. The evening chill of Kyōto made him long for the warmth of a brazier. The wind in the evening dusk howled through the columns of the gate. The cricket which had been perched on the crimson-lacquered column was already gone.

Ducking his neck, he looked around the gate, and drew up the shoulders of the blue kimono which he wore over his thin underwear. He decided to spend the night there, if he could find a secluded corner sheltered from wind and rain. He found a broad lacquered stairway leading to the tower over the gate. No one would be there, except the dead, if there were any. So, taking care that the sword at his side did not slip out of the scabbard, he set foot on the lowest step of the stairs.

A few seconds later, halfway up the stairs, he saw a movement above. Holding his breath and huddling cat-like in the middle of the broad stairs leading to the tower, he watched and waited. A light coming from the upper part of the tower shone faintly upon his right cheek. It was the cheek with the red, festering pimple visible under his stubbly whiskers. He had expected only dead people inside the tower, but he had only gone up a few steps before he noticed a fire above, about which someone was moving. He saw a dull, yellow, flickering light which made the cobwebs hanging from the ceiling glow in a ghostly way. What sort of person would be making a light in the Rash-ōmon . . . and in a storm? The unknown, the evil terrified him.

As quietly as a lizard, the servant crept up to the top of the steep stairs. Crouching on all fours, and stretching his neck as far as possible, he timidly peeped into the tower.

As rumor had said, he found several corpses strewn carelessly about the floor. Since the glow of the light was feeble, he could not count the number. He could only see that some were naked and others clothed. Some of them were women, and all were lolling on the floor with their mouths open or their arms outstretched showing no more signs of life than so many clay dolls. One would doubt that they had ever been alive, so eternally silent they were. Their shoulders, breasts, and torsos stood out in the dim light; other parts vanished in shadow. The offensive smell of these decomposed corpses brought his hand to his nose.

The next moment his hand dropped and he stared. He caught sight of a ghoulish form bent over a corpse. It seemed to be an old woman, gaunt, gray-haired, and nunnish in appearance. With a pine torch in her right hand, she was peeping into the face of a corpse which had long black hair.

Seized more with horror than curiosity, he even forgot to breathe for a time. He felt the hair of his head and body stand on end. As he watched, terrified, she wedged the torch between two floor boards and, laying hands on the head of the corpse, began to pull out the long hairs, one by one, as a monkey kills the lice of her young. The hair came out smoothly with the movement of her hands.

As the hair came out, fear faded from his heart, and his hatred toward the old woman mounted. It grew beyond hatred, becoming a consuming antipathy against all evil. At this instant if anyone had brought up the question of whether he would starve to death or become a thief—the question which had occurred to him a little while ago—he would not have hesitated to choose death. His hatred toward evil flared up like the piece of pine wood which the old woman had stuck in the floor.

He did not know why she pulled out the hair of the dead. Accordingly, he did not know whether her case was to be put down as good or bad. But in his eyes, pulling out the hair of the dead in the Rashōmon on this stormy night was an unpardonable crime. Of course it never entered his mind that a little while ago he had thought of becoming a thief.

Then, summoning strength into his legs, he rose from the stairs and strode, hand on sword, right in front of the old creature. The hag turned, terror in her eyes, and sprang up from the floor, trembling. For a small moment she paused, poised there, then lunged for the stairs with a shriek.

"Wretch! Where are you going?" he shouted, barring the way of the trembling hag who tried to scurry past him. Still she attempted to claw her way by. He pushed her back to prevent her . . . they struggled, fell among the corpses, and grappled there. The issue was never in doubt. In a moment he had her by the arm, twisted it, and forced her down to the floor. Her arms were all skin and bones, and there was no more flesh on them than on the shanks of a chicken. No sooner was she on the floor than he drew his sword and thrust the silver-white blade before her very nose. She was silent. She trembled as if in a fit, and her eyes were open so wide that they were almost out of their sockets, and her breath came in hoarse gasps. The life of this wretch was his now. This thought cooled his boiling anger and brought a calm pride and satisfaction. He looked down at her, and said in a somewhat calmer voice:

"Look here, I'm not an officer of the High Police Commissioner. I'm a stranger who happened to pass by the gate. I won't bind you or do anything against you, but you must tell me what you're doing up here."

Then the old woman opened her eyes still wider, and gazed at his face intently with the sharp red eyes of a bird of prey. She moved her lips, which were wrinkled into her nose, as though she were chewing something. Her pointed Adam's apple moved in her thin throat. Then a panting sound like the cawing of a crow came from her throat:

"I pull the hair . . . I pull out the hair . . . to make a wig."

Her answer banished all unknown from their encounter and brought disappointment. Suddenly she was only a trembling old woman there at his feet. A ghoul no longer: only a hag who makes wigs from the hair of the dead— to sell, for scraps of food. A cold contempt seized him. Fear left his heart, and his former hatred entered. These feelings must have been sensed by the other. The old creature, still clutching the hair she had pulled off the corpse, mumbled out these words in her harsh broken voice:

"Indeed, making wigs out of the hair of the dead may seem a great evil to you, but these that are here deserve no better. This woman, whose beautiful black hair I was pulling, used to sell cut and dried snake flesh at the guard barracks, saying that it was dried fish. If she hadn't died of the plague, she'd be selling it now. The guards liked to buy from her, and used to say her fish was tasty. What she did couldn't be wrong, because if she hadn't, she would have starved to death. There was no other choice. If she knew I had to do this in order to live, she probably wouldn't care."

He sheathed his sword, and, with his left hand on its hilt, he listened to her meditatively. His right hand touched the big pimple on his cheek. As he listened, a certain courage was born in his heart—the courage which he had not had when he sat under the gate a little while ago. A strange power was driving him in the opposite direction of the courage which he had had when he seized the old woman. No longer did he wonder whether he should starve to death or become a thief. Starvation was so far from his mind that it was the last thing that would have entered it.

"Are you sure?" he asked in a mocking tone, when she finished talking. He took his right hand from his pimple, and, bending forward, seized her by the neck and said sharply:

"Then it's right if I rob you. I'd starve if I didn't."

He tore her clothes from her body and kicked her roughly down on the corpses as she struggled and tried to clutch his leg. Five steps, and he was at the top of the stairs. The yellow clothes he had wrested off were under his arm, and in a twinkling he had rushed down the steep stairs into the abyss of the night. The thunder of his descending steps pounded in the hollow tower, and then it was quiet.

Shortly after that the hag raised up her body from the corpses. Grumbling and groaning, she crawled to the top stair by the still flickering torchlight, and through the gray hair which hung over her face, she peered down to the last stair in the torch light.

Beyond this was only darkness . . . unknowing and unknown.

EXERCISES

1. Discuss the significance of the landscape. How would you characterize it? What kinds of feelings does it embody?

2. How would you define the nature of evil in this story?

3. What is the significance of the combination of the horrible with the mundane suggested by our knowledge that the old hag is using the hair of the dead to make wigs?

4. What is the significance of the repeated reference to the big pimple on the cheek of the man?

5. What justifies behavior in this story? What does it mean that life springs from death? Is it not true that all life derives from death? Is the law of the jungle the necessary law?

6. What is the symbolic significance of the fact that the Rashōmon is a gateway? Is this story a gateway also? Explain.

YASUNARI
KAWABATA | # The Grasshopper and the Bell Cricket

Walking along the tile-roofed wall of the university, I turned aside and approached the upper school. Behind the white board fence of the school playground, from a dusky clump of bushes under the black cherry trees, an insect's voice could be heard. Walking more slowly and listening to that voice, and furthermore reluctant to part with it, I turned right so as not to leave the playground behind. When I turned to the left, the fence gave way to an embankment planted with orange trees. At the corner, I exclaimed with surprise. My eyes gleaming at what they saw up ahead, I hurried forward with short steps.

At the base of the embankment was a bobbing cluster of beautiful varicolored lanterns, such as one might see at a festival in a remote country village. Without going any farther, I knew that it was a group of children on an insect chase among the bushes of the embankment. There were about twenty lanterns. Not only were there crimson, pink, indigo, green, purple, and yellow lanterns, but one lantern glowed with five colors at once. There were even some little red store-bought lanterns. But most of the lanterns were beautiful square ones which the children had made themselves with love and care. The bobbing lanterns, the coming together of children on this lonely slope—surely it was a scene from a fairy tale?

One of the neighborhood children had heard an insect sing on this slope one night. Buying a red lantern, he had come back the next night to find the insect. The night after that, there was another child. This new child could not buy a lantern. Cutting out the back and front of a small carton and papering it, he placed a candle on the bottom and fastened a string to the top. The number of children grew to five, and then to seven. They learned how to color the paper that they stretched over the windows of the cutout cartons, and to draw pictures on it. Then these wise child-artists, cutting out round, three-cornered, and lozenge leaf shapes in the cartons, coloring each little window a different color, with circles and diamonds, red and green, made a single and whole decorative pattern. The child with the red lantern discarded it as a tasteless object that could be bought at a store. The child who had made his own lantern threw it away because the design was too simple. The pattern of light that one had had in hand the night before was unsatisfying the morning after. Each day, with cardboard, paper, brush, scissors, penknife, and glue, the children made new lanterns out of their hearts and minds. Look at my lantern! Be the most unusually beautiful! And each night, they had gone out on their insect hunts. These were the twenty children and their beautiful lanterns that I now saw before me.

Wide-eyed, I loitered near them. Not only did the square lanterns have old-fashioned patterns and flower shapes, but the names of the children who had made them were cut out in squared letters of the syllabary. Different from the painted-over red lanterns, others (made of thick cutout cardboard) had their designs drawn onto the paper windows, so that the candle's light seemed to emanate from the form and color of the design itself. The lanterns brought out the shadows of the bushes like dark light. The children crouched eagerly on the slope wherever they heard an insect's voice.

"Does anyone want a grasshopper?" A boy, who had been peering into a bush about thirty feet away from the other children, suddenly straightened up and shouted.

"Yes! Give it to me!" Six or seven children came running up. Crowding behind the boy who had found the grasshopper, they peered into the bush. Brushing away their outstretched hands and spreading out his arms, the boy stood as if guarding the bush where the insect was. Waving the lantern in his right hand, he called again to the other children.

"Does anyone want a grasshopper? A grasshopper!"

"I do! I do!" Four or five more children came running up. It seemed you could not catch a more precious insect than a grasshopper. The boy called out a third time.

"Doesn't anyone want a grasshopper?"

Two or three more children came over.

"Yes. I want it."

It was a girl, who just now had come up behind the boy who'd discovered the insect. Lightly turning his body, the boy gracefully bent forward. Shifting the lantern to his left hand, he reached his right hand into the bush.

"It's a grasshopper."

"Yes. I'd like to have it."

The boy quickly stood up. As if to say "Here!" he thrust out his fist that held the insect at the girl. She, slipping her left wrist under the string of her lantern, enclosed the boy's fist with both hands. The boy quietly opened his fist. The insect was transferred to between the girl's thumb and index finger.

"Oh! It's not a grasshopper. It's a bell cricket." The girl's eyes shone as she looked at the small brown insect.

"It's a bell cricket! It's a bell cricket!" The children echoed in an envious chorus.

"It's a bell cricket. It's a bell cricket."

Glancing with her bright intelligent eyes at the boy who had given her the cricket, the girl opened the little insect cage hanging at her side and released the cricket in it.

"It's a bell cricket."

"Oh, it's a bell cricket," the boy who'd captured it muttered. Holding up the insect cage close to his eyes, he looked inside it. By the light of his beautiful many-colored lantern, also held up at eye level, he glanced at the girl's face.

Oh, I thought. I felt slightly jealous of the boy, and sheepish. How silly of me not to have understood his actions until now! Then I caught my breath in surprise. Look! It was something on the girl's breast which neither the boy who had given her the cricket, nor she who had accepted it, nor the children who were looking at them noticed.

In the faint greenish light that fell on the girl's breast, wasn't the name "Fujio" clearly discernible? The boy's lantern, which he held up alongside the girl's insect cage, inscribed his name, cut out in the green papered aperture, onto her white cotton kimono. The girl's lantern, which dangled loosely from her wrist, did not project its pattern so clearly, but still one could make out, in a trembling patch of red on the boy's waist, the name "Kiyoko." This chance interplay of red and green—if it was chance or play—neither Fujio nor Kiyoko knew about.

Even if they remembered forever that Fujio had given her the cricket and that Kiyoko had accepted it, not even in dreams would Fujio ever know that his name had been written in green on Kiyoko's breast or that Kiyoko's name had been inscribed in red on his waist, nor would Kiyoko ever know that Fujio's name had been inscribed in green on her breast or that her own name had been written in red on Fujio's waist.

Fujio! Even when you have become a young man, laugh with pleasure at a girl's delight when, told that it's a grasshopper, she is given a bell cricket; laugh with affection at a girl's chagrin when, told that it's a bell cricket, she is given a grasshopper.

Even if you have the wit to look by yourself in a bush away from the other children, there are not many bell crickets in the world. Probably you will find a girl like a grasshopper whom you think is a bell cricket.

And finally, to your clouded, wounded heart, even a true bell cricket will seem like a grasshopper. Should that day come, when it seems to you that the world is only full of grasshoppers, I will think it a pity that you have no way to remember tonight's play of light, when your name was written in green by your beautiful lantern on a girl's breast.

EXERCISES

1. How is the scene of the children with lanterns on an insect hunt like a scene from a fairy tale?

2. What is the point of the fact that the children are always making new lanterns because they feel the old ones are tasteless or too simple?

3. Why does the boy keep asking if anyone wants the grasshopper until the girl asks for it? Discuss the significance of the description of the transfer of the insect from his hand to hers.

4. Why is it significant that the insect is a bell cricket? Did the boy know that it was? Why is the narrator jealous of the boy? What does the narrator realize about the boy's actions?

5. Discuss the significance of the outline of the boy's name on the girl's shirt and the outline of her name on his. Why is it significant that neither of them knows this?

6. What does the narrator make of the event? What do grasshoppers and bell crickets mean to him? What is the overall meaning of the event? How is the event an emblem?

JEAN
TOOMER | *Theater*

Life of nigger alleys, of pool rooms and restaurants and near-beer saloons soaks into the walls of Howard Theater and sets them throbbing jazz songs. Black-skinned, they dance and shout above the tick and trill of white-walled buildings. At night, they open doors to people who come in to stamp their feet and shout. At night, road-shows volley songs into the mass-heart of black people. Songs soak the walls and seep out to the nigger life of alleys and near-beer saloons, of the Poodle Dog and Black Bear cabarets. Afternoons, the house is dark, and the walls are sleeping singers until rehearsal begins. Or until John comes within them. Then they start throbbing to a subtle syncopation. And the space-dark air grows softly luminous.

John is the manager's brother. He is seated at the center of the theater, just before rehearsal. Light streaks down upon him from a window high above. One half his face is orange in it. One half his face is in shadow. The soft glow of the house rushes to, and compacts about, the shaft of light. John's mind coincides with the shaft of light. Thoughts rush to, and compact about it. Life of the house and of the slowly awakening stage swirls to the body of

John, and thrills it. John's body is separate from the thoughts that pack his mind.

Stage-lights, soft, as if they shine through clear pink fingers. Beneath them, hid by the shadow of a set, Dorris. Other chorus girls drift in. John feels them in the mass. And as if his own body were the mass-heart of a black audience listening to them singing, he wants to stamp his feet and shout. His mind, contained above desires of his body, singles the girls out, and tries to trace origins and plot destinies.

A pianist slips into the pit and improvises jazz. The walls awake. Arms of the girls, and their limbs, which . . . jazz, jazz . . . by lifting up their tight street skirts they set free, jab the air and clog the floor in rhythm to the music. (Lift your skirts, Baby, and talk t papa!) Crude, individualized, and yet . . . monotonous. . . .

John: Soon the director will herd you, my full-lipped, distant beauties, and tame you, and blunt your sharp thrusts in loosely suggestive movements, appropriate to Broadway. (O dance!) Soon the audience will paint your dusk faces white, and call you beautiful. (O dance!) Soon I . . . (O dance!) I'd like . . .

Girls laugh and shout. Sing discordant snatches of other jazz songs. Whirl with loose passion into the arms of passing show-men.

John: Too thick. Too easy. Too monotonous. Her whom I'd love I'd leave before she knew that I was with her. Her? Which? (O dance!) I'd like to . . .

Girls dance and sing. Men clap. The walls sing and press inward. They press the men and girls, they press John towards a center of physical ecstasy. Go to it, Baby! Fan yourself, and feed your papa! Put . . . nobody lied . . . and take . . . when they said I cried over you. No lie! The glitter and color of stacked scenes, the gilt and brass and crimson of the house, converge towards a center of physical ecstasy. John's feet and torso and his blood press in. He wills thought to rid his mind of passion.

"All right, girls. Alaska. Miss Reynolds, please."

The director wants to get the rehearsal through with.

The girls line up. John sees the front row: dancing ponies. The rest are in shadow. The leading lady fits loosely in the front. Lack-life, monotonous. "One, two, three—" Music starts. The song is somewhere where it will not strain the leading lady's throat. The dance is somewhere where it will not strain the girls. Above the staleness, one dancer throws herself into it. Dorris. John sees her. Her hair, crisp-curled, is bobbed. Bushy, black hair bobbing about her lemon-colored face. Her lips are curiously full, and very red. Her limbs in silk purple stockings are lovely. John feels them. Desires her. Holds off.

John: Stage-door johnny; chorus-girl. No, that would be all right. Dictie, educated, stuck-up; show-girl. Yep. Her suspicion would be stronger than her passion. It wouldn't work. Keep her loveliness. Let her go.

Dorris sees John and knows that he is looking at her. Her own glowing is too rich a thing to let her feel the slimness of his diluted passion.

"Who's that?" she asks her dancing partner.

"Th manager's brother. Dictie. Nothin doin, hon."

Dorris tosses her head and dances for him until she feels she has him. Then, withdrawing disdainfully, she flirts with the director.

Dorris: Nothin doin? How come? Aint I as good as him? Couldnt I have got an education if I'd wanted one? Dont I know respectable folks, lots of em, in Philadelphia and New York and Chicago? Aint I had men as good as him? Better. Doctors an lawyers. Whats a manager's brother, anyhow?

Two steps back, and two steps front.

"Say, Mame, where do you get that stuff?"

"Whatshmean, Dorris?"

"If you two girls cant listen to what I'm telling you, I know where I can get some who can. Now listen."

Mame: Go to hell, you black bastard.

Dorris: Whats eatin at him, anyway?

"Now follow me in this, you girls. Its three counts to the right, three counts to the left, and then you shimmy—"

John:—and then you shimmy. I'll bet she can. Some good cabaret, with rooms upstairs. And what in hell do you think you'd get from it? You're going wrong. Here's right: get her to herself—(Christ, but how she'd bore you after the first five minutes)—not if you get her right she wouldnt. Touch her, I mean. To herself—in some room perhaps. Some cheap, dingy bedroom. Hell no. Cant be done. But the point is, brother John, it can be done. Get her to herself somewhere, anywhere. Go down in yourself—and she'd be calling you all sorts of asses while you were in the process of going down. Hold em, bud. Cant be done. Let her go. (Dance and I'll love you!) And keep her loveliness.

"All right now, Chicken Chaser. Dorris and girls. Where's Dorris? I told you to stay on the stage, didn't I? Well? Now thats enough. All right. All right there, Professor? All right. One, two, three—"

Dorris swings to the front. The line of girls, four deep, blurs within the shadow of suspended scenes. Dorris wants to dance. The director feels that and steps to one side. He smiles, and picks her for a leading lady, one of these days. Odd ends of stage-men emerge from the wings, and stare and clap. A crap game in the alley suddenly ends. Black faces crowd the rear stage doors. The girls, catching joy from Dorris, whip up within the footlights' glow. They forget set steps; they find their own. The director forgets to bawl them out. Dorris dances.

John: Her head bobs to Broadway. Dance from yourself. Dance! O just a little more.

Dorris' eyes burn across the space of seats to him.

Dorris: I bet he can love. Hell, he cant love. He's too skinny. His lips are too skinny. He wouldnt love me anyway, only for that. But I'd get a pair of silk stockings out of it. Red silk. I got purple. Cut it, kid. You cant win him to respect you that away. He wouldnt anyway. Maybe he would. Maybe he'd love. I've heard em say that men who look like him (what does he look like?)

will marry if they love. O will you love me? And give me kids, and a home, and everything? (I'd like to make your nest, and honest, hon, I wouldnt run out on you.) You will if I make you. Just watch me.

Dorris dances. She forgets her tricks. She dances.

Glorious songs are the muscles of her limbs.

And her singing is of canebrake loves and mangrove feastings.

The walls press in, singing. Flesh of a throbbing body, they press close to John and Dorris. They close them in. John's heart beats tensely against her dancing body. Walls press his mind within his heart. And then, the shaft of light goes out the window high above him. John's mind sweeps up to follow it. Mind pulls him upward into dream. Dorris dances . . . John dreams:

> Dorris is dressed in a loose black gown splashed with lemon ribbons. Her feet taper long and slim from trim ankles. She waits for him just inside the stage door. John, collar and tie colorful and flaring, walks towards the stage door. There are no trees in the alley. But his feet feel as though they step on autumn leaves whose rustle has been pressed out of them by the passing of a million satin slippers. The air is sweet with roasting chestnuts, sweet with bonfires of old leaves. John's melancholy is a deep thing that seals all senses but his eyes, and makes him whole.
>
> Dorris knows that he is coming. Just at the right moment she steps from the door, as if there were no door. Her face is tinted like the autumn alley. Of old flowers, or of a southern canefield, her perfume. "Glorious Dorris." So his eyes speak. And their sadness is too deep for sweet untruth. She barely touches his arm. They glide off with footfalls softened on the leaves, the old leaves powdered by a million satin slippers.
>
> They are in a room. John knows nothing of it. Only, that the flesh and blood of Dorris are its walls. Singing walls. Lights, soft, as if they shine through clear pink fingers. Soft lights, and warm.
>
> John reaches for a manuscript of his, and reads. Dorris, who has no eyes, has eyes to understand him. He comes to a dancing scene. The scene is Dorris. She dances. Dorris dances. Glorious Dorris. Dorris whirls, whirls, dances. . . .

Dorris dances. The pianist crashes a bumper chord. The whole stage claps. Dorris, flushed, looks quick at John. His whole face is in shadow. She seeks for her dance in it. She finds it a dead thing in the shadow which is his dream. She rushes from the stage. Falls down the steps into her dressing-room. Pulls her hair. Her eyes, over a floor of tears, stare at the whitewashed ceiling. (Smell of dry paste, and paint, and soiled clothing.) Her pal comes in. Dorris flings herself into the old safe arms, and cries bitterly.

"I told you nothin doing," is what Mame says to comfort her.

EXERCISES

1. Discuss the tone of the first paragraph. Does "Theater" seem more like a picture, a poem, or a song than like a narrative? Discuss.

2. Discuss the relevance of the description of the manager's brother as having half his face lighted and half in darkness.

3. What is meant by "John's body is separate from the thoughts that pack his mind"?
4. How does the story make use of the techniques of theater rather than the techniques of narrative?
5. Discuss the nature of the conflict within John. What is the difference between the dance and the dream?
6. What does Dorris desire? What does John desire? Discuss the significance of John's dream or fantasy.

T. CORAGHESSAN
BOYLE | *Stones in My Passway,*
Hellhound on My Trail

> I got stones in my passway
> and my road seems black as night.
> I have pains in my heart,
> they have taken my appetite.
> —Robert Johnson (1914?–1938)

Saturday night. He's playing the House Party Club in Dallas, singing his blues, picking notes with a penknife. His voice rides up to a reedy falsetto that gets the men hooting and then down to the cavernous growl that chills the women, the hard chords driving behind it, his left foot beating like a hammer. The club's patrons—field hands and laborers—pound over the floorboards like the start of the derby, stamping along with him. Skirts fly, straw hats slump over eyebrows, drinks spill, ironed hair goes wiry. Overhead two dim yellow bulbs sway on their cords; the light is suffused with cigarette smoke, dingy and brown. The floor is wet with spittle and tobacco juice. From the back room, a smell of eggs frying. And beans.

Huddie Doss, the proprietor, has set up a bar in the corner: two barrels of roofing nails and a pine plank. The plank supports a cluster of gallon jugs, a bottle of Mexican rum, a pewter jigger, and three lemons. Robert sits on a stool at the far end of the room, boxed in by men in kerchiefs, women in calico. The men watch his fingers, the women look into his eyes.

It is 1938, dust bowl, New Deal. FDR is on the radio, and somebody in Robinsonville is naming a baby after Jesse Owens. Once, on the road to Natchez, Robert saw a Pierce Arrow and talked about it for a week. Another time he spent six weeks in Chicago and didn't know the World's Fair was going on. Now he plays his guitar up and down the Mississippi, and in Louisiana, Texas, and Arkansas. He's never heard of Hitler and he hasn't eaten in two days.

When he was fifteen he watched a poisoned dog tear out its entrails. It was like this:

They were out in the fields when a voice shouted, "Loup's gone mad!" and then he was running with the rest of them, down the slope and across the red dust road, past the shanties and into the gully where they dumped their trash, the dog crying high over the sun and then baying deep as craters in the moon. It was a coonhound, tawny, big-boned, the color of a lion. Robert pushed through the gathering crowd and stood watching as the animal dragged its hindquarters along the ground like a birthing bitch, the ropy testicles strung out behind. It was mewling now, the high-pitched cries sawing away at each breath, and then it was baying again, howling death until the day was filled with it, their ears and the pits of their stomachs soured with it. One of the men said in a terse, angry voice, "Go get Turkey Nason to come on down here with his gun," and a boy detached himself from the crowd and darted up the rise.

It was then that the dog fell heavily to its side, ribs heaving, and began to dig at its stomach with long racing thrusts of the rear legs. There was yellow foam on the black muzzle, blood bright in the nostrils. The dog screamed and dug, dug until the flesh was raw and its teeth could puncture the cavity to get at the gray intestine, tugging first at a bulb of it and then fastening on a lank strand like dirty wash. There was no sign of the gun. The woman beside Robert began to cry, a sound like crumpling paper. Then one of the men stepped in with a shovel in his hand. He hit the dog once across the eyes and the animal lunged for him. The shovel fell twice more and the dog stiffened, its yellow eyes gazing round the circle of men, the litter of bottles and cans and rusted machinery, its head lolling on the lean, muscular neck, poised for one terrible moment, and then it was over. Afterward Robert came close: to look at the frozen teeth, the thin, rigid limbs, the green flies on the pink organs.

Between sets Robert has been out back with a girl named Beatrice, and Ida Mae Doss, Huddie's daughter, is not happy about it. As he settles back down on the stool and reaches for his guitar, he looks up at the pine plank, the barrels, Ida Mae stationed behind the bar. She is staring at him—cold, hard, her eyes like razors. What can he do? He grins, sheepish. But then Beatrice steams in, perfumed in sweat, the blue print shift clinging like a wet sheet. She sashays through the knot of men milling around Robert and says, "Why don't you play something sweet?" Robert pumps the neck of the guitar, strikes the strings twice, and then breaks into "Phonograph Blues":

> And we played it on the sofa and we played it 'side the wall,
> But, boys, my needle point got rusty and it will not play at all.

The men nudge one another. Ida Mae looks daggers. Beatrice flounces to the center of the floor, raises her arms above her head, and begins a slow grinding shuffle to the pulse of the guitar.

No one knows how Robert got his guitar. He left Letterman's farm when he was sixteen, showed up a year and a half later with a new Harmony Sovereign. He walked into the Rooster Club in Robinsonville, Mississippi, and leaned against the wall while Walter Satter finished out his set. When Satter stepped up to the bar, Robert was at his elbow. "I heard your record," Robert said. He was short, skinny, looked closer to twelve than eighteen.

"You like it?"

"Taught me a lot."

Satter grinned.

"Mind if I sit in on the next set?"

"Sure—if you think you can go on that thing."

Robert sat in. His voice was a shower, his guitar a storm. The sweet slide leads cut the atmosphere like lightning at dusk. Satter played rhythm behind him for a while, then stepped down.

The lemons are pulp, the rum decimated, jugs lighter. Voices drift through the open door, fireflies perforate the dark rafters. It is hot as a jungle, dark as a cave. The club's patrons are quieter now—some slouched against the walls, others leaning on the bar, their fingers tapping like batons. Beatrice is an exception. She's still out in the center of the floor, head swaying to the music, heels kicking, face bright with perspiration—dancing. A glass in her hand. But suddenly she lurches to the left, her leg buckles, and she goes down. There is the shrill of breaking glass, and then silence. Robert has stopped playing. The final chord rings in the air, decapitated; a sudden unnatural silence filters through the smoke haze, descending like a judgment. Robert sets the guitar across the stool and shuffles out to where Beatrice lies on the floor. She rolls heavily to her side, laughing, muttering to herself. Robert catches her under the arms, helps her up, and guides her to a chair in the corner—and then it's over. The men start joking again, the bar gets busy, women tell stories, laugh.

Beatrice slumps in the chair, chin to chest, and begins to snore—delicate, jagged, the purr of a cat. Robert grins and pats her head—then turns to the bar. Ida Mae is there, measuring out drinks. Her eyes are moist. Robert squeezes the husk of a lemon over his glass, half fills it with rum, and presses a nickel into her palm. "What you got cooking, Ida Mae?" he says.

A thin silver chain hangs between her breasts, beneath the neckline of her cotton dress. It is ornamented with a wooden guitar pick, highly varnished, the shape of a seed.

"Got eggs," she says. "And beans."

Lubbock, Natchez, Pascagoula, Dallas, Eudora, Rosedale, Baton Rouge, Memphis, Friars Point, Vicksburg, Jonesboro, Mooringsport, Edwards, Chattanooga, Rolling Fork, Commerce, Itta Bena. Thelma, Betty Mae, Adeline, Harriet, Bernice, Ida Bell, Bertha Lee, Winifred, Maggie, Willie Mae. "Robert been driving too hard," people said. "Got to stumble."

In 1937 Franco laid siege to Madrid, the Japanese invaded Nanking, Amelia Earhart lost herself in the Pacific, and Robert made a series of recordings for

Victrix Records. He was twenty-three at the time. Or twenty-two. A man from Victrix sent him train fare to New Orleans in care of the High Times Club in Biloxi. Robert slit the envelope with his penknife and ran his thumb over the green-and-silver singles while the bartender read him the letter. Robert was ecstatic. He kissed women, danced on the tables, bought a Havana cigar—but the bills whispered in his palm and he never made it to the station. A week later the man sent him a nonrefundable one-way ticket.

The man was waiting for him when the train pulled into the New Orleans station. Robert stepped off the day coach with his battered Harmony Sovereign and a cardboard valise. The stink of kerosene and coal blistered the air. Outside, automobiles stood at the curb like a dream of the twentieth century. "Walter Fagen," the man said, holding out his hand. Robert looked up at the wisps of white-blond hair, the pale irises, the red tie, and then down at a torn ticket stub on the platform. "Pleased to meet you," he mumbled. One hand was on the neck of the guitar, the other in his pocket: "Go ahead, shake," Fagen said. Robert shook.

Fagen took him to a boardinghouse, paid the big kerchief-headed woman at the door, instructed Robert to come around to the Arlington Hotel in the morning. Then he gave him a two-dollar advance. Three hours later Fagen's dinner was interrupted by a phone call from the New Orleans police: Robert was being held for disorderly conduct. Fagen hired a taxi, drove to the jailhouse, laid five silver dollars on the desk, and walked out with his recording artist. Robert's right eye was swollen closed; the guitar was gone. Robert had nothing to say. When the taxi stopped in front of the boardinghouse, Fagen gave him thirty-five cents for breakfast and told him to get a good night's sleep.

Back at the Arlington, Fagen took a seat in the dining room and reordered. He was sipping a gimlet when a boy paged him to the phone. It was Robert. "I'm lonesome," he said.

"Lonesome?"

"Yeah—there's a woman here wants forty cents and I'm a nickel short."

The voices wash around her like birds at dawn, a Greek chorus gone mad. Smoke and stale sweat, the smell of lemon. She grits her teeth. "Give me a plate of it, then, girl," he is saying. "Haven't eat in two days." Then she's in the back room, stirring beans, cracking eggs, a woman scorned. The eggs, four of them, stare up at her like eyes. Tiny embryos. On the shelf above the stove: can of pepper, saltcellar, a knife, the powder they use for rats and roaches. Agamemnon, watch out!

Robert's dream is thick with the thighs of women, the liquid image of songs sung and songs to come, bright wire wheels and sloping fenders, swamps, trees, power lines, and the road, the road spinning out like string from a spool, like veins, blood and heart, distance without end, without horizon.

It is the last set. Things are winding down. Beatrice sags in the chair, skirt pulled up over her knees, her chest rising and falling with the soft rhythm of sleep. Beside her, a man in red suspenders presses a woman against the wall. Robert watches the woman's hands like dark animals on the man's hips. Earlier, a picker had been stabbed in the neck after a dispute over dice or women or liquor, and an old woman had fallen, drunk, and cut her head on the edge of a bench. But now things are winding down. Voices are hushed, cigarettes burn unattended, moonlight limns the windows.

Robert rests the guitar on his knee and does a song about a train station, a suitcase, and the eyes of a woman. His voice is mournful, sad as a steady rain, the guitar whining above it like a cry in the distance. "Yes!" they call out. "Robert!" Somebody whistles. Then they applaud, waves on the rocks, smoke rising as if from a rent in the earth. In response, the guitar reaches low for the opening bars of Robert's signature tune, his finale, but there is something wrong—the chords staggering like a seizure, stumbling, finally breaking off cold.

Cramps. A spasm so violent it jerks his fingers from the strings. He begins again, his voice quavering, shivered: "Got to keep moving, got to keep moving, / Hellhound on my trail." And then suddenly the voice chokes off, gags, the guitar slips to the floor with a percussive shock. His bowels are on fire. He stands, clutches his abdomen, drops to hands and knees. "Boy's had too much of that Mexican," someone says. He looks up, a sword run through him, panting, the shock waves pounding through his frame, looks up at the pine plank, the barrels, the cold, hard features of the girl with the silver necklace in her hand. Looks up, and snarls.

EXERCISES

1. Robert Johnson was a blues singer in the 1930s. Two of the songs he wrote and performed give this story its name. He died by poisoning, supposedly over a woman. Is this a story or a tribute to Johnson? If it is a story, what is the conflict? What is the basic theme or point of the story?

2. Discuss the meaning of the scene of the dog tearing out its entrails that Johnson saw when he was fifteen.

3. Why is the way Johnson is killed only briefly and obliquely referred to?

4. What is meant by the final scene when Johnson looks up and snarls?

5. Why is the story told in present tense? What relationship is there between the kind of music Johnson plays—the blues—and the way this story is presented?

6. Compare the atmosphere of this story with the atmosphere of Jean Toomer's "Theater."

LESLIE
SILKO | *Yellow Woman*

 My thigh clung to his with dampness, and I watched the sun rising up through the tamaracks and willows. The small brown water birds came to the river and hopped across the mud, leaving brown scratches in the alkali-white crust. They bathed in the river silently. I could hear the water, almost at our feet where the narrow fast channel bubbled and washed green ragged moss and fern leaves. I looked at him beside me, rolled in the red blanket on the white river sand. I cleaned the sand out of the cracks between my toes, squinting because the sun was above the willow trees. I looked at him for the last time, sleeping on the white river sand.

I felt hungry and followed the river south the way we had come the afternoon before, following our footprints that were already blurred by lizard tracks and bug trails. The horses were still lying down, and the black one whinnied when he saw me but he did not get up—maybe it was because the corral was made out of thick cedar branches and the horses had not yet felt the sun like I had. I tried to look beyond the pale red mesas to the pueblo. I knew it was there, even if I could not see it, on the sandrock hill above the river, the same river that moved past me now and had reflected the moon last night.

The horse felt warm underneath me. He shook his head and pawed the sand. The bay whinnied and leaned against the gate trying to follow, and I remembered him asleep in the red blanket beside the river. I slid off the horse and tied him close to the other horse. I walked north with the river again, and the white sand broke loose in footprints over footprints.

"Wake up."

He moved in the blanket and turned his face to me with his eyes still closed. I knelt down to touch him.

"I'm leaving."

He smiled now, eyes still closed. "You are coming with me, remember?" He sat up now with his bare dark chest and belly in the sun.

"Where?"

"To my place."

"And will I come back?"

He pulled his pants on. I walked away from him, feeling him behind me and smelling the willows.

"Yellow Woman," he said.

I turned to face him. "Who are you?" I asked.

He laughed and knelt on the low, sandy bank, washing his face in the river. "Last night you guessed my name, and you knew why I had come."

I stared past him at the shallow moving water and tried to remember the night, but I could only see the moon in the water and remember his warmth around me.

"But I only said that you were him and that I was Yellow Woman—I'm not really her—I have my own name and I come from the pueblo on the other side of the mesa. Your name is Silva and you are a stranger I met by the river yesterday afternoon."

He laughed softly. "What happened yesterday has nothing to do with what you will do today, Yellow Woman."

"I know—that's what I'm saying—the old stories about the ka'tsina spirit and Yellow Woman can't mean us."

My old grandpa liked to tell those stories best. There is one about Badger and Coyote who went hunting and were gone all day, and when the sun was going down they found a house. There was a girl living there alone, and she had light hair and eyes and she told them that they could sleep with her. Coyote wanted to be with her all night so he sent Badger into a prairie-dog hole, telling him he thought he saw something in it. As soon as Badger crawled in Coyote blocked up the entrance with rocks and hurried back to Yellow Woman.

"Come here," he said gently.

He touched my neck and I moved close to him to feel his breathing and to hear his heart. I was wondering if Yellow Woman had known who she was—if she knew that she would become part of the stories. Maybe she'd had another name that her husband and relatives called her so that only the ka'tsina from the north and the storytellers would know her as Yellow Woman. But I didn't go on; I felt him all around me, pushing me down into the white river sand.

Yellow Woman went away with the spirit from the north and lived with him and his relatives. She was gone for a long time, but then one day she came back and she brought twin boys.

"Do you know the story?"

"What story?" He smiled and pulled me close to him as he said this. I was afraid lying there on the red blanket. All I could know was the way he felt, warm, damp, his body beside me. This is the way it happens in the stories, I was thinking, with no thought beyond the moment she meets the ka'tsina spirit and they go.

"I don't have to go. What they tell in stories was real only then, back in time immemorial, like they say."

He stood up and pointed at my clothes tangled in the blanket. "Let's go," he said.

I walked beside him, breathing hard because he walked fast, his hand around my wrist. I had stopped trying to pull away from him, because his hand felt cool and the sun was high, drying the river bed into alkali. I will see someone, eventually I will see someone, and then I will be certain that he is only a man—some man from nearby—and I will be sure that I am not Yellow Woman. Because she is from out of time past and I live now and I've been to school and there are highways and pickup trucks that Yellow Woman never saw.

It was an easy ride north on horseback. I watched the change from the cottonwood trees along the river to the junipers that brushed past us in the foothills, and finally there were only piñons, and when I looked up at the rim of the mountain plateau I could see pine trees growing on the edge. Once I stopped to look down, but the pale sandstone had disappeared and the river was gone and the dark lava hills were all around. He touched my hand, not speaking, but always singing softly a mountain song and looking into my eyes.

I felt hungry and wondered what they were doing at home now—my mother, my grandmother, my husband, and the baby. Cooking breakfast, saying, "Where did she go?—maybe kidnapped," and Al going to the tribal police with the details: "She went walking along the river."

The house was made with black lava rock and red mud. It was high above the spreading miles of arroyos and long mesas. I smelled a mountain smell of pitch and buck brush. I stood there beside the black horse, looking down on the small, dim country we had passed, and I shivered.

"Yellow Woman, come inside where it's warm."

II

He lit a fire in the stove. It was an old stove with a round belly and an enamel coffeepot on top. There was only the stove, some faded Navajo blankets, and a bedroll and cardboard box. The floor was made of smooth adobe plaster, and there was one small window facing east. He pointed at the box.

"There's some potatoes and the frying pan." He sat on the floor with his arms around his knees pulling them close to his chest and he watched me fry the potatoes. I didn't mind him watching me because he was always watching me—he had been watching me since I came upon him sitting on the river bank trimming leaves from a willow twig with his knife. We ate from the pan and he wiped the grease from his fingers on his Levis.

"Have you brought women here before?" He smiled and kept chewing, so I said, "Do you always use the same tricks?"

"What tricks?" He looked at me like he didn't understand.

"The story about being a ka'tsina from the mountains. The story about Yellow Woman."

Silva was silent; his face was calm.

"I don't believe it. Those stories couldn't happen now," I said.

He shook his head and said softly, "But someday they will talk about us, and they will say, 'Those two lived long ago when things like that happened.'"

He stood up and went out. I ate the rest of the potatoes and thought about things—about the noise the stove was making and the sound of the mountain wind outside. I remembered yesterday and the day before, and then I went outside.

I walked past the corral to the edge where the narrow trail cut through the black rim rock. I was standing in the sky with nothing around me but the wind that came down from the blue mountain peak behind me. I could see faint mountain images in the distance, miles across the vast spread of mesas and valleys and plains. I wondered who was over there to feel the mountain wind on those sheer blue edges—who walks on the pine needles in those blue mountains.

"Can you see the pueblo?" Silva was standing behind me.

I shook my head. "We're too far away."

"From here I can see the world." He stepped out on the edge. "The Navajo reservation begins over there." He pointed to the east. "The Pueblo boundaries are over here." He looked below us to the south, where the narrow trail seemed to come from. "The Texans have their ranches over there, starting with that valley, the Concho Valley. The Mexicans run some cattle over there too."

"Do you ever work for them?"

"I steal from them," Silva answered. The sun was dropping behind us and shadows were filling the land below. I turned away from the edge that dropped forever into the valleys below.

"I'm cold," I said; "I'm going inside." I started wondering about this man who could speak the Pueblo language so well but who lived on a mountain and rustled cattle. I decided that this man Silva must be Navajo, because Pueblo men didn't do things like that.

"You must be a Navajo."

Silva shook his head gently. "Little Yellow Woman," he said, "you never give up, do you? I have told you who I am. The Navajo people know me, too." He knelt down and unrolled the bedroll and spread the extra blankets out on a piece of canvas. The sun was down, and the only light in the house came from outside—the dim orange light from sundown.

I stood there and waited for him to crawl under the blankets.

"What are you waiting for?" he said, and I lay down beside him. He undressed me slowly like the night before beside the river—kissing my face gently and running his hands up and down my belly and legs. He took off my pants and then he laughed.

"Why are you laughing?"

"You are breathing so hard."

I pulled away from him and turned my back to him.

He pulled me around and pinned me down with his arms and chest. "You don't understand, do you, little Yellow Woman? You will do what I want."

And again he was all around me with his skin slippery against mine, and I was afraid because I understood that his strength could hurt me. I lay underneath him and I knew that he could destroy me. But later, while he slept beside me, I touched his face and I had a feeling—the kind of feeling for him that overcame me that morning along the river. I kissed him on the forehead and he reached out for me.

When I woke up in the morning he was gone. It gave me a strange feeling because for a long time I sat there on the blankets and looked around the little house for some object of his—some proof that he had been there or maybe that he was coming back. Only the blankets and the cardboard box remained. The .30-30 that had been leaning in the corner was gone, and so was the knife

I had used the night before. He was gone, and I had my chance to go now. But first I had to eat, because I knew it would be a long walk home.

I found some dried apricots in the cardboard box, and I sat down on a rock at the edge of the plateau rim. There was no wind and the sun warmed me. I was surrounded by silence. I drowsed with apricots in my mouth, and I didn't believe that there were highways or railroads or cattle to steal.

When I woke up, I stared down at my feet in the black mountain dirt. Little black ants were swarming over the pine needles around my foot. They must have smelled the apricots. I thought about my family far below me. They would be wondering about me, because this had never happened to me before. The tribal police would file a report. But if old Grandpa weren't dead he would tell them what happened—he would laugh and say, "Stolen by a ka'tsina, a mountain spirit. She'll come home—they usually do." There are enough of them to handle things. My mother and grandmother will raise the baby like they raised me. Al will find someone else, and they will go on like before, except that there will be a story about the day I disappeared while I was walking along the river. Silva had come for me; he said he had. I did not decide to go. I just went. Moonflowers blossom in the sand hills before dawn, just as I followed him. That's what I was thinking as I wandered along the trail through the pine trees.

It was noon when I got back. When I saw the stone house I remembered that I had meant to go home. But that didn't seem important any more, maybe because there were little blue flowers growing in the meadow behind the stone house and the gray squirrels were playing in the pines next to the house. The horses were standing in the corral, and there was a beef carcass hanging on the shady side of a big pine in front of the house. Flies buzzed around the clotted blood that hung from the carcass. Silva was washing his hands in a bucket full of water. He must have heard me coming because he spoke to me without turning to face me.

"I've been waiting for you."

"I went walking in the big pine trees."

I looked into the bucket full of bloody water with brown-and-white animal hairs floating in it. Silva stood there letting his hands drip, examining me intently.

"Are you coming with me?"

"Where?" I asked him.

"To sell the meat in Marquez."

"If you're sure it's O.K."

"I wouldn't ask you if it wasn't," he answered.

He sloshed the water around in the bucket before he dumped it out and set the bucket upside down near the door. I followed him to the corral and watched him saddle the horses. Even beside the horses he looked tall, and I asked him again if he wasn't Navajo. He didn't say anything; he just shook his head and kept cinching up the saddle.

"But Navajos are tall."

"Get on the horse," he said, "and let's go."

The last thing he did before we started down the steep trail was to grab the .30-30 from the corner. He slid the rifle into the scabbard that hung from his saddle.

"Do they ever try to catch you?" I asked.

"They don't know who I am."

"Then why did you bring the rifle?"

"Because we are going to Marquez where the Mexicans live."

III

The trail leveled out on a narrow ridge that was steep on both sides like an animal spine. On one side I could see where the trail went around the rocky gray hills and disappeared into the southeast where the pale sandrock mesas stood in the distance near my home. On the other side was a trail that went west, and as I looked far into the distance I thought I saw the little town. But Silva said no, that I was looking in the wrong place, that I just thought I saw houses. After that I quit looking off into the distance; it was hot and the wildflowers were closing up their deep-yellow petals. Only the waxy cactus flowers bloomed in the bright sun, and I saw every color that a cactus blossom can be; the white ones and the red ones were still buds, but the purple and the yellow were blossoms, open full and the most beautiful of all.

Silva saw him before I did. The white man was riding a big gray horse, coming up the trail toward us. He was traveling fast and the gray horse's feet sent rocks rolling off the trail into the dry tumbleweeds. Silva motioned for me to stop and we watched the white man. He didn't see us right away, but finally his horse whinnied at our horses and he stopped. He looked at us briefly before he loped the gray horse across the three hundred yards that separated us. He stopped his horse in front of Silva, and his young fat face was shadowed by the brim of his hat. He didn't look mad, but his small, pale eyes moved from the blood-soaked gunny sacks hanging from my saddle to Silva's face and then back to my face.

"Where did you get the fresh meat?" the white man asked.

"I've been hunting," Silva said, and when he shifted his weight in the saddle the leather creaked.

"The hell you have, Indian. You've been rustling cattle. We've been looking for the thief for a long time."

The rancher was fat, and sweat began to soak through his white cowboy shirt and the wet cloth stuck to the thick rolls of belly fat. He almost seemed to be panting from the exertion of talking, and he smelled rancid, maybe because Silva scared him.

Silva turned to me and smiled. "Go back up the mountain, Yellow Woman."

The white man got angry when he heard Silva speak in a language he couldn't understand. "Don't try anything, Indian. Just keep riding to Marquez. We'll call the state police from there."

The rancher must have been unarmed because he was very frightened and if he had a gun he would have pulled it out then. I turned my horse around and the rancher yelled, "Stop!" I looked at Silva for an instant and there was something ancient and dark—something I could feel in my stomach—in his eyes, and when I glanced at his hand I saw his finger on the trigger of the .30-30 that was still in the saddle scabbard. I slapped my horse across the flank and the sacks of raw meat swung against my knees as the horse leaped up the trail. It was hard to keep my balance, and once I thought I felt the saddle slipping backward; it was because of this that I could not look back.

I didn't stop until I reached the ridge where the trail forked. The horse was breathing deep gasps and there was a dark film of sweat on its neck. I looked down in the direction I had come from, but I couldn't see the place. I waited. The wind came up and pushed warm air past me. I looked up at the sky, pale blue and full of thin clouds and fading vapor trails left by jets.

I think four shots were fired—I remember hearing four hollow explosions that reminded me of deer hunting. There could have been more shots after that, but I couldn't have heard them because my horse was running again and the loose rocks were making too much noise as they scattered around his feet.

Horses have a hard time running downhill, but I went that way instead of uphill to the mountain because I thought it was safer. I felt better with the horse running southeast past the round gray hills that were covered with cedar trees and black lava rock. When I got to the plain in the distance I could see the dark green patches of tamaracks that grew along the river; and beyond the river I could see the beginning of the pale sandrock mesas. I stopped the horse and looked back to see if anyone was coming; then I got off the horse and turned the horse around, wondering if it would go back to its corral under the pines on the mountain. It looked back at me for a moment and then plucked a mouthful of green tumbleweeds before it trotted back up the trail with its ears pointed forward, carrying its head daintily to one side to avoid stepping on the dragging reins. When the horse disappeared over the last hill, the gunny sacks full of meat were still swinging and bouncing.

IV

I walked toward the river on a wood-hauler's road that I knew would eventually lead to the paved road. I was thinking about waiting beside the road for someone to drive by, but by the time I got to the pavement I had decided it wasn't very far to walk if I followed the river back the way Silva and I had come.

The river water tasted good, and I sat in the shade under a cluster of silvery willows. I thought about Silva, and I felt sad at leaving him; still, there was something strange about him, and I tried to figure it out all the way back home.

I came back to the place on the river bank where he had been sitting the first time I saw him. The green willow leaves that he had trimmed from the branch were still lying there, wilted in the sand. I saw the leaves and I wanted to go back to him—to kiss him and to touch him—but the mountains were too far away now. And I told myself, because I believe it, he will come back sometime and be waiting again by the river.

I followed the path up from the river into the village. The sun was getting low, and I could smell supper cooking when I got to the screen door of my house. I could hear their voices inside—my mother was telling my grandmother how to fix the Jell-O and my husband, Al, was playing with the baby. I decided to tell them that some Navajo had kidnapped me, but I was sorry that old Grandpa wasn't alive to hear my story because it was the Yellow Woman stories he liked to tell best.

EXERCISES

1. Discuss the sequence of events in the first few paragraphs. Does the woman leave on her horse at this point, or does she only imagine leaving?

2. What kind of mythic character is Yellow Woman from the old stories?

3. In what way does this story depend on the continuity of past and present? Why is this continuity easier to believe in a story about a Native American than in a story about white Americans?

4. What is the appeal of being part of a "myth-in-the-making"?

5. Why does the woman not leave when she has the opportunity?

6. Explain the statement "There was something strange about him, and I tried to figure it out all the way home."

7. What is the point of this story? Is it meant to embody some female fantasy? Is it a culturally bound story, or does it embody something universal? Compare it with Kay Boyle's "The Astronomer's Wife."

TOMMASO
LANDOLFI | *Wedding Night*

At the end of the wedding banquet the chimney sweep was announced. The father, out of joviality, and because it seemed proper to him that a ceremony such as the cleaning of the chimney should be celebrated on just that day, gave the order to let him come in. But the man did not appear; he preferred to remain in the kitchen, where the great hearth was. Not all the toasts had yet been given, and this was why some of the guests, in their heart of hearts, criticized the interruption; nonetheless, due to the uproar made by the children, everyone rose from the table.

The bride had never seen a chimney sweep: she had been in boarding school when he used to come. Going into the kitchen she saw a tall, rather corpulent man, with a serious gray beard and bent shoulders; he was dressed in a corduroy suit the color of linseed oil. His stoop was counterbalanced by the weight of two huge mountain boots which seemed to hold his entire body erect. Although he had just washed very carefully, the skin of his face was deeply tinted with black, as though many blackheads of varying dimensions had taken root there; a black deposit, gathered between the lines of his forehead and cheeks, conferred a quality of meditative wisdom on that physiognomy. But this impression quickly dissolved, and the man's great timidity became quite obvious, especially when his features broke into a sort of smile.

He nearly frightened the young bride, because he was standing behind the door, though he acted frightened himself; and, as if he had been caught doing something reprehensible and had to justify his presence in that place, he began to repeat, speaking directly to the young bride, some sentences which she did not hear or did not understand. He stammered insistently and behaved as if he thought that what he said concerned her greatly and, all the while, he looked at her with the eyes of a beaten dog and yet significantly. From the very first moment the young bride was aware of his caterpillar nature.

He took off his jacket and began to unbutton his vest. She slipped out through the other door, but continued to follow what was going on in the kitchen; she had the feeling that something improper was about to happen and that her presence might make him uneasy in the performance of his rites. Somehow she almost felt ashamed for him. But there was no noise to feed her imagination and so she went back in again. The children had been sent away and he was alone. At that moment he was climbing a ladder set up inside the hood of the fireplace; his feet were bare and he was in his shirtsleeves, a brown shirt. Across his chest, fastened with leather straps, he had a tool which resembled the scraper for a kneading trough but whose use remained forever unknown to the young bride. And he had a kind of black gag, tied up behind his ears, which fitted over his mouth and nose. But she did not see him enter the flue of the chimney, because she ran away again.

When she came back the second time, the kitchen was empty and a strange smell, a terrible smell, had spread through it. Looking around her, the young bride connected it first with the man's large shoes set in a corner next to a bundle of clothes; it was, however, the death smell of the soot which was piling up on the hearthstone, falling in intermittent showers to the rhythm of a dull scraping which gnawed at the marrow of the house and which she felt echoing in her own entrails. In the intervals, a muffled rubbing revealed the man's laborious ascent.

An instant of absolute silence fell, an instant of lacerating suspense for the young bride. She continued to stare at the mouth of the flue, there under the hood at the end of the fireplace's black funnel; this mouth was not square but narrow, a dark slit.

Then a very high, guttural, inhuman cry sounded from some mysterious place, from the well, from the stones of the house, from the soul of the kitchen's pots and pans, from the very breast of the young bride, who was shaken by it through and through. That bestial howl of agony soon proved to be a kind of joyous call: the man had burst through onto the roof. The muffled rubbings resumed more rapidly now; finally a black foot came down out of the slit searching for support—the foot of a hanged man. The foot found the first rung of the ladder and the young bride ran away.

In the courtyard, as the bride sat on a millstone, the old housekeeper, one of those women for whom everything is new, assumed the task of keeping her informed; she walked back and forth bringing her the news with a mysterious air. "Now he is doing his cleaning under the hood," and the young bride pictured him as he shook off the soot, standing upright on the pile like a gravedigger on a mound of earth. "But what does he put on his feet to claw into the wall?" And then she ran after him to ask him: "My good man, what do you put on your feet to claw into the wall?" A gay reply followed which could not be heard clearly. "Now he is eating breakfast," and the housekeeper remained inside. Then she reappeared with a few small edelweiss; she said that the man had taken them out of a very clean little box and had offered them for the young bride.

After some time he himself came out, dressed again and with a pack on his back. He crossed the courtyard to leave, but the father stopped him and began to question him benevolently about his life. The young bride approached, too. Here the man, in the weak sun of winter, his face darker, his beard flecked with black and his eyes puckered by the light, looked like a big moth, a nocturnal bird surprised by the day. Or rather he looked like a spider or crab louse; the fact is that the hood of the hearth, when seen from below and if there is enough light outside, is not completely black but leaks a gray and slimy sheen.

He said that for thirty-five years he had been traveling through those towns cleaning the chimneys, that next year he would take his young son along to teach him the trade, that picking edelweiss was now forbidden and he had been able to gather those few flowers on the sly, and other such inconsequential things. Yet, whether astute or halting, it was quite clear that he only wished to hide himself behind those words, that he let the curtain of words fall in the same way that the cuttlefish beclouds the water.

He knew about all the deaths in the family, yet none of them had ever seen him!

By now the young bride felt that she was no longer ashamed for him, but was actually ashamed of herself.

After the chimney sweep had gone, she placed the few edelweiss beneath the portraits of the dead.

EXERCISES

1. Why is it significant that this story focuses on a bride who has never seen a chimney sweep? Why is it important that the girl is a bride and that the man is a chimney sweep?
2. What is meant by the expression "his caterpillar nature"?

3. Discuss the following: "She had the feeling that something improper was about to happen and that her presence might make him uneasy in the performance of his rites. Somehow she felt almost ashamed for him."

4. Why is the smell of the soot called a "death smell"? Why does the bride feel that the scraping at the "marrow" of the house is "echoing" in her own entrails?

5. Why is the inhuman cry sound like a bestial howl, only to be a joyous call of bursting through onto the roof?

6. Why are the sweep's later activities communicated to the bride by the housekeeper instead of described by the narrator?

7. What is meant by the bride's feeling of shame at the end?

8. Is the experience in the story a metaphoric one or a realistic one? Is the story's theme moral or psychological?

HEINRICH
BÖLL | *Across the Bridge*

The story I want to tell you has no particular point to it, maybe it isn't really a story at all, but I must tell you about it. Ten years ago there was a kind of prelude, and a few days ago the circle was completed. . . .

A few days ago I was in a train crossing the bridge that once, before the war, had been strong and wide, as strong as the iron of Bismarck's chest on all those monuments, as inflexible as the rules of bureaucracy; a wide, four-track railway bridge over the Rhine, supported by a row of massive piers, and ten years ago I used to take the same train across that bridge three times a week: Mondays, Wednesdays, and Saturdays. In those prewar days I was an employee of the Reich Gun Dog and Retriever Association; a modest position, I was a kind of errand-boy, really. I knew nothing about dogs, of course, I haven't had much education. Three times a week I would take the train from Königstadt, where our head office was, to Gründerheim, where we had a branch office. There I would pick up urgent correspondence, money, and "Pending Cases." The latter were in a large manila folder. Being only a messenger, of course, I never was told what was in the folder. . . .

In the morning I would go straight from the house to the station and catch the eight o'clock train to Gründerheim. The journey took three-quarters of an hour. Even in those days, crossing the bridge scared me. All the technical assurances of well-informed people concerning the ample load-capacity of the bridge were to no avail: I was just plain scared. The mere connection of train and bridge scared me; I am honest enough to admit it. The Rhine is very broad where we live. With a quaking heart I was invariably conscious of the slight swaying of the bridge, of the ominous rocking that continued for six hundred yards. At last came the reassuring, more muffled rattle as we regained the railway embankment, and then came the vegetable plots, rows and rows of vegetable plots—and finally, just before Kahlenkatten, a house: it was to this house that I clung, so to speak, with my eyes. This house stood on solid ground; my eyes would clutch at this house.

The exterior of the house was of reddish-brown stucco, it was very clean, the window frames and ledges all picked out in dark brown. Two floors, three windows upstairs and two down, in the middle the front door with three steps leading up to it. And invariably, if it was not raining too hard, a child would be sitting on these steps, a spindly little girl of about nine or ten holding a large, clean doll and frowning up at the train. Invariably my eyes would stumble over this child, to be brought up short by the window on the left, for each time I saw a woman in there, a bucket beside her, bent double, a scrubbing cloth in her hands, laboriously washing the floor. Invariably, even when it was raining cats and dogs, even when the child was not sitting there on the steps. The woman was always there: the thin nape of her neck, betraying her as the mother of the little girl, and that movement to and fro, that typical scrubbing movement. Many a time I meant to notice the furniture, or the curtains, but my eyes were glued to this thin, eternally scrubbing woman, and before I could think about anything else the train had passed. Mondays, Wednesdays, and Saturdays, it must always have been about ten minutes past eight, for in those days the trains were nothing if not punctual. By the time the train had passed, I was left with a view of the clean rear of the house, silent and uncommunicative.

Needless to say, I began wondering about this woman and this house. All the other places we passed held little interest for me. Kahlenkatten—Bröderkotten—Suhlenheim—Gründerheim—there was nothing very interesting about these stations. My thoughts were always preoccupied with that house. Why does the woman wash and scrub three times a week, I wondered. The house didn't look at all as if there were dirty people living in it, or as if a great many visitors came and went. In fact it looked almost inhospitable, although it was clean. It was a clean and yet unwelcoming house.

But when I caught the eleven o'clock train from Gründerheim for the return trip and saw the rear of the house shortly before noon just beyond Kahlenkatten, the woman would then be washing the panes of the end window on the right. Oddly enough, on Mondays and Saturdays she would be washing the end window on the right, and on Wednesdays the middle window. Chamois in hand, she rubbed and rubbed. Round her head she wore a scarf of a dull, reddish color. But on the way back I never saw the little girl, and now, approaching midday—it must have been a few minutes to twelve, for in those days the trains were nothing if not punctual—it was the front of the house that was silent and uncommunicative.

Although in telling my story I shall make every effort to describe only what I actually saw, presumably no one will object to the modest observation that, after three months, I permitted myself the mathematical combination that on Tuesdays, Thursdays, and Fridays the woman probably washed the other windows. This combination, modest though it was, gradually became an obsession. Sometimes, all the way from just before Kahlenkatten to Gründerheim, I would puzzle over which afternoons and mornings the other windows of the two floors were likely to get washed. In fact, I finally sat down with pencil and paper and devised a kind of cleaning timetable for myself. From what I had observed on the three mornings, I tried to figure out what was likely to get cleaned the other three afternoons and the remaining whole days. For I had the curiously fixed notion that the woman never did anything but wash and scrub. After all, I never saw her any other way, always bent double so that I thought I could hear her labored breathing—at ten minutes past eight; and busily rubbing with the chamois, so that I thought I could see the tip of her tongue between her tightly drawn lips—shortly before twelve.

The story of this house preyed on my mind. I started daydreaming. This made me careless in my work. Yes, I became careless. I let my thoughts wander too often. One day I even forgot the "Pending Cases" folder. I drew down upon my head the wrath of the District Manager of the Reich Gun Dog and Retriever Association. He sent for me; he was quivering with indignation. "Grabowski," he said to me, "I hear you forgot the 'Pending Cases.' Orders are orders, Grabowski." When I maintained a stubborn silence, the boss became more severe. "Messenger Grabowski, I'm warning you. The Reich Gun Dog and Retriever Association has no use for forgetful employees, you know. We can look elsewhere for qualified staff." He looked at me menacingly, but then he suddenly became human. "Have you something on your mind?" I admitted in a low voice: "Yes." "What is it?" he asked kindly. I merely shook my head. "Can I help? Tell me what I can do."

"Give me a day off, sir," I asked diffidently, "that's all I ask." He nodded magnanimously. "Done! And don't take what I said too seriously. Anybody can make one mistake, we've always been quite satisfied with you. . . ."

My heart leaped with joy. This interview took place on a Wednesday. And the following day, Thursday, was to be my day off. I had it all figured out. I caught the eight o'clock train, trembling more with impatience than with fear as we crossed the bridge: there she was, washing the front steps. I caught the next train back from Kahlenkatten and passed her house just about nine: top floor, middle window, front. I rode back and forth four times that day and had the whole Thursday timetable complete: front steps, middle window top floor front, middle window top floor back, attic, front room top. As I passed the house for the last time at six o'clock, I saw a little man's stooped figure digging humbly away in the garden. The child, holding the clean doll, was watching him like a jaileress. The woman was not in sight. . . .

But all this happened ten years ago, before the war. A few days ago I crossed that bridge again by train. My God, how far away my thoughts had been when I got onto the train at Königstadt! I had forgotten the whole business. Our train was made up of boxcars, and as we approached the Rhine a strange thing happened: one after another the boxcars ahead of us fell silent. It was quite extraordinary, as if the whole train of fifteen or twenty cars were a series of lights going out one after another. And we could hear a horrible,

hollow rattle, a kind of windy rattle; and suddenly it sounded as if little hammers were being tapped against the floor of our boxcar, and we fell silent too,
and there it was: nothing, nothing . . . nothing; left and right there was nothing, a ghastly void . . . in the distance the grassy banks of the Rhine . . . boats
. . . water, but one didn't dare look too far out: just looking made one giddy.
Nothing, nothing whatever! I could tell from the white face of a silent farmer's
wife that she was praying, other people were lighting cigarettes with trembling
hands; even the men playing cards in the corner had fallen silent. . . .

Then we could hear the cars up front riding over solid ground again, and
we all had the same thought: they've made it. If something happens to the
train, maybe those people can jump out, but we were in the last car but one,
and it was almost a foregone conclusion that we would plunge into the river.
The conviction was there in our eyes and in our pale faces. The temporary
bridge was no wider than the tracks, in fact the tracks themselves were the
bridge, and the side of the boxcar hung out over the bridge into space, and
the bridge rocked as if it were about to tip us off into space. . . .

But then all of a sudden there was a firmer rattle, we could hear it coming
closer, quite distinctly, and then under our car too it became somehow deeper,
more substantial, this rattle, we breathed again and dared to look out: there
were vegetable plots! Oh, may God bless vegetable plots! And suddenly I realized where we were, and my heart throbbed queerly the closer we came to
Kahlenkatten. For me there was but one question: would that house still be
standing? And then I saw it, first from a distance through the delicate sparse
green of a few trees in the vegetable plots, the red facade of the house, still
very clean, coming closer and closer. I was gripped by an indefinable emotion.
Everything, the past of ten years ago and everything that had happened since
then, raged within me in a frenzied, uncontrollable turmoil. And then the
house came right up close, with giant strides, and then I saw her, the woman:
she was washing the front steps. No, it wasn't her, those legs were younger, a
little heavier, but she had the same movements, those jerky, thrusting movements as she pushed the scrubbing cloth to and fro. My heart stood still, my
heart marked time. Then the woman turned her face for just a moment, and
instantly I recognized the little girl of ten years ago; that pinched, spidery,
frowning face, and in the expression on her face something rather sour, something disagreeably sour like stale salad. . . .

As my heart slowly started beating again, it struck me that today was in
fact Thursday. . . .

EXERCISES

1. What makes this a story despite the fact that the narrator thinks that perhaps it really isn't a story at all? Discuss the appropriateness of the circle
   metaphor in the first paragraph.
2. How does the house relieve the narrator's fear of the bridge?

3. Why does the narrator become so obsessed with the routine of the cleaning of the house?
4. What is the difference between the first train rides and the train ride the narrator makes ten years later? Why is the historical event that underlies the story not specified here? Compare this story with Cynthia Ozick's "The Shawl."
5. Contrast the changes that have taken place in ten years in the narrator and the occupants of the house.
6. What is significant about the fact that the present train ride takes place on Thursday?

CYNTHIA
OZICK | *The Shawl*

Stella, cold, cold, the coldness of hell. How they walked on the roads together, Rosa with Magda curled up between sore breasts, Magda wound up in the shawl. Sometimes Stella carried Magda. But she was jealous of Magda. A thin girl of fourteen, too small, with thin breasts of her own, Stella wanted to be wrapped in a shawl, hidden away, asleep, rocked by the march, a baby, a round infant in arms. Magda took Rosa's nipple, and Rosa never stopped walking, a walking cradle. There was not enough milk; sometimes Magda sucked air; then she screamed. Stella was ravenous. Her knees were tumors on sticks, her elbows chicken bones.

Rosa did not feel hunger; she felt light, not like someone walking but like someone in a faint, in trance, arrested in a fit, someone who is already a floating angel, alert and seeing everything, but in the air, not there, not touching the road. As if teetering on the tips of her fingernails. She looked into Magda's face through a gap in the shawl: a squirrel in a nest, safe, no one could reach her inside the little house of the shawl's windings. The face, very round, a pocket mirror of a face: but it was not Rosa's bleak complexion, dark like cholera, it was another kind of face altogether, eyes blue as air, smooth feathers of hair nearly as yellow as the Star sewn into Rosa's coat. You could think she was one of *their* babies.

Rosa, floating, dreamed of giving Magda away in one of the villages. She could leave the line for a minute and push Magda into the hands of any woman on the side of the road. But if she moved out of line they might shoot. And even if she fled the line for half a second and pushed the shawl-bundle at a stranger, would the woman take it? She might be surprised, or afraid; she might drop the shawl, and Magda would fall out and strike her head and die. The little round head. Such a good child, she gave up screaming, and sucked now only for the taste of the drying nipple itself. The neat grip of the tiny gums. One mite of a tooth tip sticking up in the bottom gum, how shining, an elfin tombstone of white marble gleaming there. Without complaining,

Magda relinquished Rosa's teats, first the left, then the right; both were cracked, not a sniff of milk. The duct-crevice extinct, a dead volcano, blind eye, chill hole, so Magda took the corner of the shawl and milked it instead. She sucked and sucked, flooding the threads with wetness. The shawl's good flavor, milk of linen.

It was a magic shawl, it could nourish an infant for three days and three nights. Magda did not die, she stayed alive, although very quiet. A peculiar smell, of cinnamon and almonds, lifted out of her mouth. She held her eyes open every moment, forgetting how to blink or nap, and Rosa and sometimes Stella studied their blueness. On the road they raised one burden of a leg after another and studied Magda's face. "Aryan," Stella said, in a voice grown as thin as a string; and Rosa thought how Stella gazed at Magda like a young cannibal. And the time that Stella said "Aryan," it sounded to Rosa as if Stella had really said "Let us devour her."

But Magda lived to walk. She lived that long, but she did not walk very well, partly because she was only fifteen months old, and partly because the spindles of her legs could not hold up her fat belly. It was fat with air, full and round. Rosa gave almost all her food to Magda, Stella gave nothing; Stella was ravenous, a growing child herself, but not growing much. Stella did not menstruate. Rosa did not menstruate. Rosa was ravenous, but also not; she learned from Magda how to drink the taste of a finger in one's mouth. They were in a place without pity, all pity was annihilated in Rosa, she looked at Stella's bones without pity. She was sure that Stella was waiting for Magda to die so she could put her teeth into the little thighs.

Rosa knew Magda was going to die very soon; she should have been dead already, but she had been buried away deep inside the magic shawl, mistaken there for the shivering mound of Rosa's breasts; Rosa clung to the shawl as if it covered only herself. No one took it away from her. Magda was mute. She never cried. Rosa hid her in the barracks, under the shawl, but she knew that one day someone would inform; or one day someone, not even Stella, would steal Magda to eat her. When Magda began to walk Rosa knew that Magda was going to die very soon, something would happen. She was afraid to fall asleep; she slept with the weight of her thigh on Magda's body; she was afraid she would smother Magda under her thigh. The weight of Rosa was becoming less and less; Rosa and Stella were slowly turning into air.

Magda was quiet, but her eyes were horribly alive, like blue tigers. She watched. Sometimes she laughed—it seemed a laugh, but how could it be? Magda had never seen anyone laugh. Still, Magda laughed at her shawl when the wind blew its corners, the bad wind with pieces of black in it, that made Stella's and Rosa's eyes tear. Magda's eyes were always clear and tearless. She watched like a tiger. She guarded her shawl. No one could touch it; only Rosa could touch it. Stella was not allowed. The shawl was Magda's own baby, her pet, her little sister. She tangled herself up in it and sucked on one of the corners when she wanted to be very still.

Then Stella took the shawl away and made Magda die.

Afterward Stella said: "I was cold."

And afterward she was always cold, always. The cold went into her heart: Rosa saw that Stella's heart was cold. Magda flopped onward with her little pencil legs scribbling this way and that, in search of the shawl; the pencils faltered at the barracks opening, where the light began. Rosa saw and pursued. But already Magda was in the square outside the barracks, in the jolly light. It was the roll-call arena. Every morning Rosa had to conceal Magda under the shawl against a wall of the barracks and go out and stand in the arena with Stella and hundreds of others, sometimes for hours, and Magda, deserted, was quiet under the shawl, sucking on her corner. Every day Magda was silent, and so she did not die. Rosa saw that today Magda was going to die, and at the same time a fearful joy ran in Rosa's two palms, her fingers were on fire, she was astonished, febrile: Magda, in the sunlight, swaying on her pencil legs, was howling. Ever since the drying up of Rosa's nipples, ever since Magda's last scream on the road, Magda had been devoid of any syllable; Magda was a mute. Rosa believed that something had gone wrong with her vocal cords, with her windpipe, with the cave of her larynx; Magda was defective, without a voice; perhaps she was deaf; there might be something amiss with her intelligence; Magda was dumb. Even the laugh that came when the ash-stippled wind made a clown out of Magda's shawl was only the air-blown showing of her teeth. Even when the lice, head lice and body lice, crazed her so that she became as wild as one of the big rats that plundered the barracks at daybreak looking for carrion, she rubbed and scratched and kicked and bit and rolled without a whimper. But now Magda's mouth was spilling a long viscous rope of clamor.

"Maaaa—"

It was the first noise Magda had ever sent out from her throat since the drying up of Rosa's nipples.

"Maaaa . . . aaa!"

Again! Magda was wavering in the perilous sunlight of the arena, scribbling on such pitiful little bent shins. Rosa saw. She saw that Magda was grieving for the loss of her shawl, she saw that Magda was going to die. A tide of commands hammered in Rosa's nipples: Fetch, get, bring! But she did not know which to go after first, Magda or the shawl. If she jumped out into the arena to snatch Magda up, the howling would not stop, because Magda would still not have the shawl; but if she ran back into the barracks to find the shawl, and if she found it, and if she came after Magda holding it and shaking it, then she would get Magda back, Magda would put the shawl in her mouth and turn dumb again.

Rosa entered the dark. It was easy to discover the shawl. Stella was heaped under it, asleep in her thin bones. Rosa tore the shawl free and flew— she could fly, she was only air—into the arena. The sunheat murmured of another life, of butterflies in summer. The light was placid, mellow. On the other side of the steel fence, far away, there were green meadows speckled with dandelions and deep-colored violets; beyond them, even farther, innocent tiger lilies, tall, lifting their orange bonnets. In the barracks they spoke of "flowers," of "rain": excrement, thick turd-braids, and the slow stinking maroon waterfall that slunk down from the upper bunks, the stink mixed with a bitter fatty floating smoke that greased Rosa's skin. She stood for an instant at the margin of the arena. Sometimes the electricity inside the fence would seem to hum; even Stella said it was only an imagining, but Rosa heard real sounds in the wire: grainy sad voices. The farther she was from the fence, the more clearly the voices crowded at her. The lamenting voices strummed so convincingly, so passionately, it was impossible to suspect them of being phantoms. The voices told her to hold up the shawl, high; the voices told her to shake it, to whip with it, to unfurl it like a flag. Rosa lifted, shook, whipped, unfurled. Far off, very far, Magda leaned across her air-fed belly, reaching out with the rods of her arms. She was high up, elevated, riding someone's shoulder. But the shoulder that carried Magda was not coming toward Rosa and the shawl, it was drifting away, the speck of Magda was moving more and more into the smoky distance. Above the shoulder a helmet glinted. The light tapped the helmet and sparkled it into a goblet. Below the helmet a black body like a domino and a pair of black boots hurled themselves in the direction of the electrified fence. The electric voices began to chatter wildly. "Maamaa, maaamaaa," they all hummed together. How far Magda was from Rosa now, across the whole square, past a dozen barracks, all the way on the other side! She was no bigger than a moth.

All at once Magda was swimming through the air. The whole of Magda traveled through loftiness. She looked like a butterfly touching a silver vine. And the moment Magda's feathered round head and her pencil legs and balloonish belly and zigzag arms splashed against the fence, the steel voices went mad in their growling, urging Rosa to run and run to the spot where Magda had fallen from her flight against the electrified fence; but of course Rosa did not obey them. She only stood, because if she ran they would shoot, and if she tried to pick up the sticks of Magda's body they would shoot, and if she let the wolf's screech ascending now through the ladder of her skeleton break out, they would shoot; so she took Magda's shawl and filled her own mouth with it, stuffed it in and stuffed it in, until she was swallowing up the wolf's screech and tasting the cinnamon and almond depth of Magda's saliva; and Rosa drank Magda's shawl until it dried.

EXERCISES

1. Why is the historical context of the story not made explicit?
2. Discuss the imagery of the story, such as a tooth as an "elfin tombstone" and the breast as an "extinct volcano."
3. How is the shawl a magic shawl?
4. Why is the baby described as being "Aryan," as being like one of "them"?
5. Discuss the style of the story; read some sentences aloud and listen to their rhythm.

6. What is suggested by the metaphor of lightness—of turning into air?
7. Discuss the particular kind of trap in which Rosa finds herself when the baby runs out into the yard.
8. Discuss the significance of the metaphor of the baby being like a butterfly in the air. Try to describe the effect the story creates at the end. What creates this effect?

JOHN
STEINBECK | *The Snake*

It was almost dark when young Dr. Phillips swung his sack to his shoulder and left the tide pool. He climbed up over the rocks and squashed along the street in his rubber boots. The street lights were on by the time he arrived at his little commercial laboratory on the cannery street of Monterey. It was a tight little building, standing partly on piers over the bay water and partly on the land. On both sides the big corrugated-iron sardine canneries crowded in on it.

Dr. Phillips climbed the wooden steps and opened the door. The white rats in their cages scampered up and down the wire, and the captive cats in their pens mewed for milk. Dr. Phillips turned on the glaring light over the dissection table and dumped his clammy sack on the floor. He walked to the glass cages by the window where the rattlesnakes lived, leaned over and looked in.

The snakes were bunched and resting in the corners of the cage, but every head was clear; the dusty eyes seemed to look at nothing, but as the young man leaned over the cage the forked tongues, black on the ends and pink behind, twittered out and waved slowly up and down. Then the snakes recognized the man and pulled in their tongues.

Dr. Phillips threw off his leather coat and built a fire in the tin stove; he set a kettle of water on the stove and dropped a can of beans into the water. Then he stood staring down at the sack on the floor. He was a slight young man with the mild, preoccupied eyes of one who looks through a microscope a great deal. He wore a short blond beard.

The draft ran breathily up the chimney and a glow of warmth came from the stove. The little waves washed quietly about the piles under the building. Arranged on shelves about the room were tier above tier of museum jars containing the mounted marine specimens the laboratory dealt in.

Dr. Phillips opened a side door and went into his bedroom, a book-lined cell containing an army cot, a reading light and an uncomfortable wooden chair. He pulled off his rubber boots and put on a pair of sheepskin slippers. When he went back to the other room the water in the kettle was already beginning to hum.

He lifted his sack to the table under the white light and emptied out two dozen common starfish. These he laid out side by side on the table. His preoccupied eyes turned to the busy rats in the wire cages. Taking grain from a paper sack, he poured it into the feeding troughs. Instantly the rats scrambled down from the wire and fell upon the food. A bottle of milk stood on a glass shelf between a small mounted octopus and a jellyfish. Dr. Phillips lifted down the milk and walked to the cat cage, but before he filled the containers he reached in the cage and gently picked out a big rangy alley tabby. He stroked her for a moment and then dropped her in a small black painted box, closed the lid and bolted it and then turned on a petcock which admitted gas into the killing chamber. While the short soft struggle went on in the black box he filled the saucers with milk. One of the cats arched against his hand and he smiled and petted her neck.

The box was quiet now. He turned off the petcock, for the airtight box would be full of gas.

On the stove the pan of water was bubbling furiously about the can of beans. Dr. Phillips lifted out the can with a big pair of forceps, opened it, and emptied the beans into a glass dish. While he ate he watched the starfish on the table. From between the rays little drops of milky fluid were exuding. He bolted his beans and when they were gone he put the dish in the sink and stepped to the equipment cupboard. From this he took a microscope and a pile of little glass dishes. He filled the dishes one by one with sea water from a tap and arranged them in a line beside the starfish. He took out his watch and laid it on the table under the pouring white light. The waves washed with little sighs against the piles under the floor. He took an eyedropper from a drawer and bent over the starfish.

At that moment there were quick soft steps on the wooden stairs and a strong knocking at the door. A slight grimace of annoyance crossed the young man's face as he went to open. A tall, lean woman stood in the doorway. She was dressed in a severe dark suit—her straight black hair, growing low on a flat forehead, was mussed as though the wind had been blowing it. Her black eyes glittered in the strong light.

She spoke in a soft throaty voice, "May I come in? I want to talk to you."

"I'm very busy just now," he said half-heartedly. "I have to do things at times." But he stood away from the door. The tall woman slipped in.

"I'll be quiet until you can talk to me."

He closed the door and brought the uncomfortable chair from the bedroom. "You see," he apologized, "the process is started and I must get to it." So many people wandered in and asked questions. He had little routines of explanations for the commoner processes. He could say them without thinking. "Sit here. In a few minutes I'll be able to listen to you."

The tall woman leaned over the table. With the eyedropper the young man gathered fluid from between the rays of the starfish and squirted it into a bowl of water, and then he drew some milky fluid and squirted it in the same bowl and stirred the water gently with the eyedropper. He began his little patter of explanation.

"When starfish are sexually mature they release sperm and ova when they are exposed at low tide. By choosing mature specimens and taking them out of the water, I give them a condition of low tide. Now I've mixed the sperm and eggs. Now I put some of the mixture in each one of these ten watch glasses. In ten minutes I will kill those in the first glass with menthol, twenty minutes later I will kill the second group and then a new group every twenty minutes. Then I will have arrested the process in stages, and I will mount the series on microscope slides for biologic study." He paused. "Would you like to look at this first group under the microscope?"

"No, thank you."

He turned quickly to her. People always wanted to look through the glass. She was not looking at the table at all, but at him. Her black eyes were on him, but they did not seem to see him. He realized why—the irises were as dark as the pupils, there was no color line between the two. Dr. Phillips was piqued at her answer. Although answering questions bored him, a lack of interest in what he was doing irritated him. A desire to arouse her grew in him.

"While I'm waiting the first ten minutes I have something to do. Some people don't like to see it. Maybe you'd better step into that room until I finish."

"No," she said in her soft flat tone. "Do what you wish. I will wait until you can talk to me." Her hands rested side by side on her lap. She was completely at rest. Her eyes were bright but the rest of her was almost in a state of suspended animation. He thought, "Low metabolic rate, almost as low as a frog's, from the looks." The desire to shock her out of her inanition possessed him again.

He brought a little wooden cradle to the table, laid out scalpels and scissors and rigged a big hollow needle to a pressure tube. Then from the killing chamber he brought the limp dead cat and laid it in the cradle and tied its legs to hooks in the sides. He glanced sidewise at the woman. She had not moved. She was still at rest.

The cat grinned up into the light, its pink tongue stuck out between its needle teeth. Dr. Phillips deftly snipped open the skin at the throat; with a scalpel he slit through and found an artery. With flawless technique he put the needle in the vessel and tied it in with gut. "Embalming fluid," he explained. "Later I'll inject yellow mass into the veinous system and red mass into the arterial system—for bloodstream dissection—biology classes."

He looked around at her again. Her dark eyes seemed veiled with dust. She looked without expression at the cat's open throat. Not a drop of blood had escaped. The incision was clean. Dr. Phillips looked at his watch. "Time for the first group." He shook a few crystals of menthol into the first watch-glass.

The woman was making him nervous. The rats climbed about on the wire of their cage again and squeaked softly. The waves under the building beat with little shocks on the piles.

The young man shivered. He put a few lumps of coal in the stove and sat down. "Now," he said. "I haven't anything to do for twenty minutes." He noticed how short her chin was between lower lip and point. She seemed to awaken slowly, to come up out of some deep pool of consciousness. Her head raised and her dark dusty eyes moved about the room and then came back to him.

"I was waiting," she said. Her hands remained side by side on her lap. "You have snakes?"

"Why, yes," he said rather loudly. "I have about two dozen rattlesnakes. I milk out the venom and send it to the anti-venom laboratories."

She continued to look at him but her eyes did not center on him, rather they covered him and seemed to see in a big circle all around him. "Have you a male snake, a male rattlesnake?"

"Well, it just happens I know I have. I came in one morning and found a big snake in—in coition with a smaller one. That's very rare in captivity. You see, I do know I have a male snake."

"Where is he?"

"Why, right in the glass cage by the window there."

Her head swung slowly around but her two quiet hands did not move. She turned back toward him. "May I see?"

He got up and walked to the case by the window. On the sand bottom the knot of rattlesnakes lay entwined, but their heads were clear. The tongues came out and flickered a moment and then waved up and down feeling the air for vibrations. Dr. Phillips nervously turned his head. The woman was standing beside him. He had not heard her get up from the chair. He had heard only the splash of water among the piles and the scampering of the rats on the wire screen.

She said softly, "Which is the male you spoke of?"

He pointed to a thick, dusty grey snake lying by itself in one corner of the cage. "That one. He's nearly five feet long. He comes from Texas. Our Pacific coast snakes are usually smaller. He's been taking all the rats, too. When I want the others to eat I have to take him out."

The woman stared down at the blunt dry head. The forked tongue slipped out and hung quivering for a long moment. "And you're sure he's a male."

"Rattlesnakes are funny," he said glibly. "Nearly every generalization proves wrong. I don't like to say anything definite about rattlesnakes, but—yes—I can assure you he's a male."

Her eyes did not move from the flat head. "Will you sell him to me?"

"Sell him?" he cried. "Sell him to you?"

"You do sell specimens, don't you?"

"Oh—yes. Of course I do. Of course I do."

"How much? Five dollars? Ten?"

"Oh! Not more than five. But—do you know anything about rattlesnakes? You might be bitten."

She looked at him for a moment. "I don't intend to take him. I want to leave him here, but—I want him to be mine. I want to come here and look at him and feed him and to know he's mine." She opened a little purse and took out a five-dollar bill. "Here! Now he is mine."

Dr. Phillips began to be afraid. "You could come to look at him without owning him."

"I want him to be mine."

"Oh, Lord!" he cried. "I've forgotten the time." He ran to the table. "Three minutes over. It won't matter much." He shook menthol crystals into the second watch-glass. And then he was drawn back to the cage where the woman still stared at the snake.

She asked, "What does he eat?"

"I feed them white rats, rats from the cage over there."

"Will you put him in the other cage? I want to feed him."

"But he doesn't need food. He's had a rat already this week. Sometimes they don't eat for three or four months. I had one that didn't eat for over a year."

In her low monotone she asked, "Will you sell me a rat?"

He shrugged his shoulders. "I see. You want to watch how rattlesnakes eat. All right. I'll show you. The rat will cost twenty-five cents. It's better than a bullfight if you look at it one way, and it's simply a snake eating his dinner if you look at it another." His tone had become acid. He hated people who made sport of natural processes. He was not a sportsman but a biologist. He could kill a thousand animals for knowledge, but not an insect for pleasure. He'd been over this in his mind before.

She turned her head slowly toward him and the beginning of a smile formed on her thin lips. "I want to feed my snake," she said. "I'll put him in the other cage." She had opened the top of the cage and dipped her hand in before he knew what she was doing. He leaped forward and pulled her back. The lid banged shut.

"Haven't you any sense," he asked fiercely. "Maybe he wouldn't kill you, but he'd make you damned sick in spite of what I could do for you."

"You put him in the other cage then," she said quietly.

Dr. Phillips was shaken. He found that he was avoiding the dark eyes that didn't seem to look at anything. He felt that it was profoundly wrong to put a rat into the cage, deeply sinful; and he didn't know why. Often he had put rats in the cage when someone or other had wanted to see it, but this desire tonight sickened him. He tried to explain himself out of it.

"It's a good thing to see," he said. "It shows you how a snake can work. It makes you have a respect for a rattlesnake. Then, too, lots of people have dreams about the terror of snakes making the kill. I think because it is a subjective rat. The person is the rat. Once you see it the whole matter is objective. The rat is only a rat and the terror is removed."

He took a long stick equipped with a leather noose from the wall. Opening the trap he dropped the noose over the big snake's head and tightened the thong. A piercing dry rattle filled the room. The thick body writhed and slashed about the handle of the stick as he lifted the snake out and dropped it in the feeding cage. It stood ready to strike for a time, but the buzzing gradually ceased. The snake crawled into a corner, made a big figure eight with its body and lay still.

"You see," the young man explained, "these snakes are quite tame. I've had them a long time. I suppose I could handle them if I wanted to, but everyone who does handle rattlesnakes gets bitten sooner or later. I just don't want to take the chance." He glanced at the woman. He hated to put in the rat. She had moved over in front of the new cage; her black eyes were on the stony head of the snake again.

She said, "Put in a rat."

Reluctantly he went to the rat cage. For some reason he was sorry for the rat, and such a feeling had never come to him before. His eyes went over the mass of swarming white bodies climbing up the screen toward him. "Which one?" he thought. "Which one shall it be?" Suddenly he turned angrily to the woman. "Wouldn't you rather I put in a cat? Then you'd see a real fight. The cat might even win, but if it did it might kill the snake. I'll sell you a cat if you like."

She didn't look at him. "Put in a rat," she said. "I want him to eat."

He opened the rat cage and thrust his hand in. His fingers found a tail and he lifted a plump, red-eyed rat out of the cage. It struggled up to try to bite his fingers and, failing, hung spread out and motionless from its tail. He walked quickly across the room, opened the feeding cage and dropped the rat in on the sand floor. "Now, watch it," he cried.

The woman did not answer him. Her eyes were on the snake where it lay still. Its tongue flicking in and out rapidly, tasted the air of the cage.

The rat landed on its feet, turned around and sniffed at its pink naked tail and then unconcernedly trotted across the sand, smelling as it went. The room was silent. Dr. Phillips did not know whether the water sighed among the piles or whether the woman sighed. Out of the corner of his eye he saw her body crouch and stiffen.

The snake moved out smoothly, slowly. The tongue flicked in and out. The motion was so gradual, so smooth that it didn't seem to be motion at all. In the other end of the cage the rat perked up in a sitting position and began to lick down the fine white hair on its chest. The snake moved on, keeping always a deep S curve in its neck.

The silence beat on the young man. He felt the blood drifting up in his body. He said loudly, "See! He keeps the striking curve ready. Rattlesnakes are cautious, almost cowardly animals. The mechanism is so delicate. The snake's dinner is to be got by an operation as deft as a surgeon's job. He takes no chances with his instruments."

The snake had flowed to the middle of the cage by now. The rat looked up, saw the snake and then unconcernedly went back to licking its chest.

"It's the most beautiful thing in the world," the young man said. His veins were throbbing. "It's the most terrible thing in the world."

The snake was close now. Its head lifted a few inches from the sand. The head weaved slowly back and forth, aiming, getting distance, aiming. Dr. Phillips glanced again at the woman. He turned sick. She was weaving too, not much, just a suggestion.

The rat looked up and saw the snake. It dropped to four feet and back up, and then—the stroke. It was impossible to see, simply a flash. The rat jarred as though under an invisible blow. The snake backed hurriedly into the corner from which it had come, and settled down, its tongue working constantly.

"Perfect!" Dr. Phillips cried. "Right between the shoulder blades. The fangs must almost have reached the heart."

The rat stood still, breathing like a little white bellows. Suddenly it leaped in the air and landed on its side. Its legs kicked spasmodically for a second and it was dead.

The woman relaxed, relaxed sleepily.

"Well," the young man demanded, "it was an emotional bath, wasn't it?"

She turned her misty eyes to him. "Will he eat it now?" she asked.

"Of course he'll eat it. He didn't kill it for a thrill. He killed it because he was hungry."

The corners of the woman's mouth turned up a trifle again. She looked back at the snake. "I want to see him eat it."

Now the snake came out of its corner again. There was no striking curve in its neck, but it approached the rat gingerly, ready to jump back in case it attacked. It nudged the body gently with its blunt nose, and drew away. Satisfied that it was dead, the snake touched the body all over with its chin, from head to tail. It seemed to measure the body and to kiss it. Finally it opened its mouth and unhinged its jaws at the corners.

Dr. Phillips put his will against his head to keep it from turning toward the woman. He thought, "If she's opening her mouth, I'll be sick. I'll be afraid." He succeeded in keeping his eyes away.

The snake fitted its jaws over the rat's head and then with a slow peristaltic pulsing, began to engulf the rat. The jaws gripped and the whole throat crawled up, and the jaws gripped again.

Dr. Phillips turned away and went to his work table. "You've made me miss one of the series," he said bitterly. "The set won't be complete." He put one of the watch glasses under a low-power microscope and looked at it, and then angrily he poured the contents of all the dishes into the sink. The waves had fallen so that only a wet whisper came up through the floor. The young man lifted a trapdoor at his feet and dropped the starfish down into the black water. He paused at the cat, crucified in the cradle and grinning comically into the light. Its body was puffed with embalming fluid. He shut off the pressure, withdrew the needle and tied the vein.

"Would you like some coffee?" he asked.

"No, thank you. I shall be going pretty soon."

He walked to her where she stood in front of the snake cage. The rat was swallowed, all except an inch of pink tail that stuck out of the snake's mouth like a sardonic tongue. The throat heaved again and the tail disappeared. The jaws snapped back into their sockets, and the big snake crawled heavily to the corner, made a big eight and dropped its head on the sand.

"He's asleep now," the woman said. "I'm going now. But I'll come back and feed my snake every little while. I'll pay for the rats. I want him to have plenty. And sometime—I'll take him away with me." Her eyes came out of their dusty dream for a moment. "Remember, he's mine. Don't take his poison. I want him to have it. Goodnight." She walked swiftly to the door and went out. He heard her footsteps on the stairs, but he could not hear her walk away on the pavement.

Dr. Phillips turned a chair around and sat down in front of the snake cage. He tried to comb out his thought as he looked at the torpid snake. "I've read so much about psychological sex symbols," he thought. "It doesn't seem to explain. Maybe I'm too much alone. Maybe I should kill the snake. If I knew—no, I can't pray to anything."

For weeks he expected her to return. "I will go out and leave her alone here when she comes," he decided. "I won't see the damned thing again."

She never came again. For months he looked for her when he walked about in the town. Several times he ran after some tall woman thinking it might be she. But he never saw her again—ever.

EXERCISES

1. Discuss the effect of the doctor's killing the cat at the same time that he fixes his dinner. How are the doctor's laboratory activities important to the story?

2. Discuss the tone of the story, especially as created by the sentence style.

3. Discuss the effect of the woman on the doctor. What is unusual about her? Is she realistic, or does she suggest something other than a specific human being?

4. Why does the woman want to see the snake eat the rat? Are we to think there is something psychologically strange about her? Or do her actions suggest that she is less real than representative and symbolic? Why is it significant that this strange visitor is a woman rather than a man?

5. Why is it important to the story that the protagonist is a doctor?

6. What does the doctor mean at the end that although he has read about psychological sex symbols, "it doesn't seem to explain"? Why does he say that he cannot pray to anything?

CHARLOTTE
PERKINS
GILMAN | *The Yellow Wall-Paper*

It is very seldom that mere ordinary people like John and myself secure ancestral halls for the summer.

A colonial mansion, a hereditary estate, I would say a haunted house, and reach the height of romantic felicity—but that would be asking too much of fate!

Still I will proudly declare that there is something queer about it.

Else, why should it be let so cheaply? And why have stood so long untenanted?

John laughs at me, of course, but one expects that in marriage.

John is practical in the extreme. He has no patience with faith, an intense horror of superstition, and he scoffs openly at any talk of things not to be felt and seen and put down in figures.

John is a physician, and *perhaps*—(I would not say it to a living soul, of course, but this is dead paper and a great relief to my mind—) *perhaps* that is one reason I do not get well faster.

You see he does not believe I am sick!

And what can one do?

If a physician of high standing, and one's own husband, assures friends and relatives that there is really nothing the matter with one but temporary nervous depression—a slight hysterical tendency—what is one to do?

My brother is also a physician, and also of high standing, and he says the same thing.

So I take phosphates or phosphites—whichever it is, and tonics, and journeys, and air, and exercise, and am absolutely forbidden to "work" until I am well again.

Personally, I disagree with their ideas.

Personally, I believe that congenial work, with excitement and change, would do me good.

But what is one to do?

I did write for a while in spite of them; but it *does* exhaust me a good deal—having to be so sly about it, or else meet with heavy opposition.

I sometimes fancy that in my condition if I had less opposition and more society and stimulus—but John says the very worst thing I can do is to think about my condition, and I confess it always makes me feel bad.

So I will let it alone and talk about the house.

The most beautiful place! It is quite alone, standing well back from the road, quite three miles from the village. It makes me think of English places that you read about, for there are hedges and walls and gates that lock, and lots of separate little houses for the gardeners and people.

There is a *delicious* garden! I never saw such a garden—large and shady, full of box-bordered paths, and lined with long grape-covered arbors with seats under them.

There were greenhouses, too, but they are all broken now.

There was some legal trouble, I believe, something about the heirs and coheirs; anyhow, the place has been empty for years.

That spoils my ghostliness, I am afraid, but I don't care—there is something strange about the house—I can feel it.

I even said so to John one moonlight evening, but he said what I felt was a *draught,* and shut the window.

I get unreasonably angry with John sometimes. I'm sure I never used to be so sensitive. I think it is due to this nervous condition.

But John says if I feel so, I shall neglect proper self-control; so I take pains to control myself—before him, at least, and that makes me very tired.

I don't like our room a bit. I wanted one downstairs that opened on the piazza and had roses all over the window, and such pretty old-fashioned chintz hangings! but John would not hear of it.

He said there was only one window and not room for two beds, and no near room for him if he took another.

He is very careful and loving, and hardly lets me stir without special direction.

I have a schedule prescription for each hour in the day; he takes all care from me, and so I feel basely ungrateful not to value it more.

He said we came here solely on my account, that I was to have perfect rest and all the air I could get. "Your exercise depends on your strength, my dear," said he, "and your food somewhat on your appetite; but air you can absorb all the time." So we took the nursery at the top of the house.

It is a big, airy room, the whole floor nearly, with windows that look all ways, and air and sunshine galore. It was nursery first and then playroom and gymnasium, I should judge; for the windows are barred for little children, and there are rings and things in the walls.

The paint and paper look as if a boys' school had used it. It is stripped off—the paper—in great patches all around the head of my bed, about as far as I can reach, and in a great place on the other side of the room low down. I never saw a worse paper in my life.

One of those sprawling flamboyant patterns committing every artistic sin.

It is dull enough to confuse the eye in following, pronounced enough to constantly irritate and provoke study, and when you follow the lame uncertain curves for a little distance they suddenly commit suicide—plunge off at outrageous angles, destroy themselves in unheard of contradictions.

The color is repellant, almost revolting; a smouldering unclean yellow, strangely faded by the slow-turning sunlight.

It is a dull yet lurid orange in some places, a sickly sulphur tint in others.

No wonder the children hated it! I should hate it myself if I had to live in this room long.

There comes John, and I must put this away,—he hates to have me write a word.

We have been here two weeks, and I haven't felt like writing before, since that first day.

I am sitting by the window now, up in this atrocious nursery, and there is nothing to hinder my writing as much as I please, save lack of strength.

John is away all day, and even some nights when his cases are serious.

I am glad my case is not serious!

But these nervous troubles are dreadfully depressing.

John does not know how much I really suffer. He knows there is no *reason* to suffer, and that satisfies him.

Of course it is only nervousness. It does weigh on me so not to do my duty in any way!

I meant to be such a help to John, such a real rest and comfort, and here I am a comparative burden already!

Nobody would believe what an effort it is to do what little I am able,—to dress and entertain, and order things.

It is fortunate Mary is so good with the baby. Such a dear baby!

And yet I *cannot* be with him, it makes me so nervous.

I suppose John never was nervous in his life. He laughs at me so about this wall-paper!

At first he meant to repaper the room, but afterwards he said that I was letting it get the better of me, and that nothing was worse for a nervous patient than to give way to such fancies.

He said that after the wall-paper was changed it would be the heavy bedstead, and then the barred windows, and then that gate at the head of the stairs, and so on.

"You know the place is doing you good," he said, "and really, dear, I don't care to renovate the house just for a three months' rental."

"Then do let us go downstairs," I said, "there are such pretty rooms there."

Then he took me in his arms and called me a blessed little goose, and said he would go down cellar, if I wished, and have it whitewashed into the bargain.

But he is right enough about the beds and windows and things.

It is an airy and comfortable room as any one need wish, and, of course, I would not be so silly as to make him uncomfortable just for a whim.

I'm really getting quite fond of the big room, all but that horrid paper.

Out of one window I can see the garden, those mysterious deep-shaded arbors, the riotous old-fashioned flowers, and bushes and gnarly trees.

Out of another I get a lovely view of the bay and a little private wharf belonging to the estate. There is a beautiful shaded lane that runs down there from the house. I always fancy I see people walking in these numerous paths and arbors, but John has cautioned me not to give way to fancy in the least. He says that with my imaginative power and habit of story-making, a nervous weakness like mine is sure to lead to all manner of excited fancies, and that I ought to use my will and good sense to check the tendency. So I try.

I think sometimes that if I were only well enough to write a little it would relieve the press of ideas and rest me.

But I find I get pretty tired when I try.

It is so discouraging not to have any advice and companionship about my work. When I get really well, John says we will ask Cousin Henry and Julia down for a long visit; but he says he would as soon put fireworks in my pillow-case as to let me have those stimulating people about now.

I wish I could get well faster.

But I must not think about that. This paper looks to me as if it *knew* what a vicious influence it had!

There is a recurrent spot where the pattern lolls like a broken neck and two bulbous eyes stare at you upside down.

I get positively angry with the impertinence of it and the everlastingness.

Up and down and sideways they crawl, and those absurd, unblinking eyes are everywhere. There is one place where two breadths didn't match, and the eyes go all up and down the line, one a little higher than the other.

I never saw so much expression in an inanimate thing before, and we all know how much expression they have! I used to lie awake as a child and get more entertainment and terror out of blank walls and plain furniture than most children could find in a toy-store.

I remember what a kindly wink the knobs of our big, old bureau used to have, and there was one chair that always seemed like a strong friend.

I used to feel that if any of the other things looked too fierce I could always hop into that chair and be safe.

The furniture in this room is no worse than inharmonious, however, for we had to bring it all from downstairs. I suppose when this was used as a playroom they had to take the nursery things out, and no wonder! I never saw such ravages as the children have made here.

The wall-paper, as I said before, is torn off in spots, and it sticketh closer than a brother—they must have had perseverance as well as hatred.

Then the floor is scratched and gouged and splintered, the plaster itself is dug out here and there, and this great heavy bed, which is all we found in the room, looks as if it had been through the wars.

But I don't mind it a bit—only the paper.

There comes John's sister. Such a dear girl as she is, and so careful of me! I must not let her find me writing.

She is a perfect and enthusiastic housekeeper, and hopes for no better profession. I verily believe she thinks it is the writing which made me sick!

But I can write when she is out, and see her a long way off from these windows.

There is one that commands the road, a lovely shaded winding road, and one that just looks off over the country. A lovely country, too, full of great elms and velvet meadows.

This wall-paper has a kind of subpattern in a different shade, a particularly irritating one, for you can only see it in certain lights, and not clearly then.

But in the places where it isn't faded and where the sun is just so—I can see a strange, provoking, formless sort of figure, that seems to skulk about behind that silly and conspicuous front design.

There's sister on the stairs!

Well, the Fourth of July is over! The people are all gone and I am tired out. John thought it might do me good to see a little company, so we just had mother and Nellie and the children down for a week.

Of course I didn't do a thing. Jennie sees to everything now.

But it tired me all the same.

John says if I don't pick up faster he shall send me to Weir Mitchell in the fall.

But I don't want to go there at all. I had a friend who was in his hands once, and she says he is just like John and my brother, only more so!

Besides, it is such an undertaking to go so far.

I don't feel as if it was worth while to turn my hand over for anything, and I'm getting dreadfully fretful and querulous.

I cry at nothing, and cry most of the time.

Of course I don't when John is here, or anybody else, but when I am alone.

And I am alone a good deal just now. John is kept in town very often by serious cases, and Jennie is good and lets me alone when I want her to.

So I walk a little in the garden or down that lovely lane, sit on the porch under the roses, and lie down up here a good deal.

I'm getting really fond of the room in spite of the wall-paper. Perhaps *because* of the wall-paper.

It dwells in my mind so!

I lie here on this great immovable bed—it is nailed down, I believe—and follow that pattern about by the hour. It is as good as gymnastics, I assure you. I start, we'll say, at the bottom, down in the corner over there where it has not been touched, and I determine for the thousandth time that I *will* follow that pointless pattern to some sort of a conclusion.

I know a little of the principle of design, and I know this thing was not arranged on any laws of radiation, or alternation, or repetition, or symmetry, or anything else that I ever heard of.

It is repeated, of course, by the breadths, but not otherwise.

Looked at in one way each breadth stands alone, the bloated curves and flourishes—a kind of "debased Romanesque" with *delirium tremens*—go waddling up and down in isolated columns of fatuity.

But, on the other hand, they connect diagonally, and the sprawling outlines run off in great slanting waves of optic horror, like a lot of wallowing seaweeds in full chase.

The whole thing goes horizontally, too, at least it seems so, and I exhaust myself in trying to distinguish the order of its going in that direction.

They have used a horizontal breadth for a frieze, and that adds wonderfully to the confusion.

There is one end of the room where it is almost intact, and there, when the crosslights fade and the low sun shines directly upon it, I can almost fancy radiation after all,—the interminable grotesques seem to form around a common centre and rush off in headlong plunges of equal distraction.

It makes me tired to follow it. I will take a nap I guess.

I don't know why I should write this.

I don't want to.

I don't feel able.

And I know John would think it absurd. But I *must* say what I feel and think in some way—it is such a relief!

But the effort is getting to be greater than the relief.

Half the time now I am awfully lazy, and lie down ever so much.

John says I mustn't lose my strength, and has me take cod liver oil and lots of tonics and things, to say nothing of ale and wine and rare meat.

Dear John! He loves me very dearly, and hates to have me sick. I tried to have a real earnest reasonable talk with him the other day, and tell him how I wish he would let me go and make a visit to Cousin Henry and Julia.

But he said I wasn't able to go, nor able to stand it after I got there; and I did not make out a very good case for myself, for I was crying before I had finished.

It is getting to be a great effort for me to think straight. Just this nervous weakness I suppose.

And dear John gathered me up in his arms, and just carried me upstairs and laid me on the bed, and sat by me and read to me till it tired my head.

He said I was his darling and his comfort and all he had, and that I must take care of myself for his sake, and keep well.

He says no one but myself can help me out of it, that I must use my will and self-control and not let any silly fancies run away with me.

There's one comfort, the baby is well and happy, and does not have to occupy this nursery with the horrid wall-paper.

If we had not used it, that blessed child would have! What a fortunate escape! Why, I wouldn't have a child of mine, an impressionable little thing, live in such a room for worlds.

I never thought of it before, but it is lucky that John kept me here after all, I can stand it so much easier than a baby, you see.

Of course I never mention it to them any more—I am too wise,—but I keep watch of it all the same.

There are things in that paper that nobody knows but me, or ever will.

Behind that outside pattern the dim shapes get clearer every day.

It is always the same shape, only very numerous.

And it is like a woman stooping down and creeping about behind that pattern. I don't like it a bit. I wonder—I begin to think—I wish John would take me away from here!

It is so hard to talk with John about my case, because he is so wise, and because he loves me so.

But I tried last night.

It was moonlight. The moon shines in all around just as the sun does.

I hate to see it sometimes, it creeps so slowly, and always comes in by one window or another.

John was asleep and I hated to waken him, so I kept still and watched the moonlight on that undulating wall-paper till I felt creepy.

The faint figure behind seemed to shake the pattern, just as if she wanted to get out.

I got up softly and went to feel and see if the paper *did* move, and when I came back John was awake.

"What is it, little girl?" he said. "Don't go walking about like that—you'll get cold."

I thought it was a good time to talk, so I told him that I really was not gaining here, and that I wished he would take me away.

"Why, darling!" said he, "our lease will be up in three weeks, and I can't see how to leave before.

"The repairs are not done at home, and I cannot possibly leave town just now. Of course if you were in any danger, I could and would, but you really are better, dear, whether you can see it or not. I am a doctor, dear, and I know. You are gaining flesh and color, your appetite is better, I feel really much easier about you."

"I don't weigh a bit more," said I, "nor as much; and my appetite may be better in the evening when you are here, but it is worse in the morning when you are away!"

"Bless her little heart!" said he with a big hug, "she shall be as sick as she pleases! But now let's improve the shining hours by going to sleep, and talk about it in the morning!"

"And you won't go away?" I asked gloomily.

"Why, how can I, dear? It is only three weeks more and then we will take a nice little trip of a few days while Jennie is getting the house ready. Really dear you are better!"

"Better in body perhaps—" I began, and stopped short, for he sat up straight and looked at me with such a stern, reproachful look that I could not say another word.

"My darling," said he, "I beg of you, for my sake and for our child's sake, as well as for your own, that you will never for one instant let that idea enter your mind! There is nothing so dangerous, so fascinating, to a temperament like yours. It is a false and foolish fancy. Can you not trust me as a physician when I tell you so?"

So of course I said no more on that score, and we went to sleep before long. He thought I was asleep first, but I wasn't, and lay there for hours trying to decide whether that front pattern and the back pattern really did move together or separately.

On a pattern like this, by daylight, there is a lack of sequence, a defiance of law, that is a constant irritant to a normal mind.

The color is hideous enough, and unreliable enough, and infuriating enough, but the pattern is torturing.

You think you have mastered it, but just as you get well underway in following, it turns a back-somersault and there you are. It slaps you in the face, knocks you down, and tramples upon you. It is like a bad dream.

The outside pattern is a florid arabesque, reminding one of a fungus. If you can imagine a toadstool in joints, an interminable string of toadstools, budding and sprouting in endless convolutions—why, that is something like it.

That is, sometimes!

There is one marked peculiarity about this paper, a thing nobody seems to notice but myself, and that is that it changes as the light changes.

When the sun shoots in through the east window—I always watch for that first long, straight ray—it changes so quickly that I never can quite believe it.

That is why I watch it always.

By moonlight—the moon shines in all night when there is a moon—I wouldn't know it was the same paper.

At night in any kind of light, in twilight, candlelight, lamplight, and worst of all by moonlight, it becomes bars! The outside pattern I mean, and the woman behind it is as plain as can be.

I didn't realize for a long time what the thing was that showed behind, that dim sub-pattern, but now I am quite sure it is a woman.

By daylight she is subdued, quiet. I fancy it is the pattern that keeps her so still. It is so puzzling. It keeps me quiet by the hour.

I lie down ever so much now. John says it is good for me, and to sleep all I can.

Indeed he started the habit by making me lie down for an hour after each meal.

It is a very bad habit I am convinced, for you see I don't sleep.

And that cultivates deceit, for I don't tell them I'm awake—O no!

The fact is I am getting a little afraid of John.

He seems very queer sometimes, and even Jennie has an inexplicable look.

It strikes me occasionally, just as a scientific hypothesis,—that perhaps it is the paper!

I have watched John when he did not know I was looking, and come into the room suddenly on the most innocent excuses, and I've caught him several times *looking at the paper!* And Jennie too. I caught Jennie with her hand on it once.

She didn't know I was in the room, and when I asked her in a quiet, a very quiet voice, with the most restrained manner possible, what she was doing with the paper—she turned around as if she had been caught stealing, and looked quite angry—asked me why I should frighten her so!

Then she said that the paper stained everything it touched, that she had found yellow smooches on all my clothes and John's, and she wished we would be more careful!

Did not that sound innocent? But I know she was studying that pattern, and I am determined that nobody shall find it out but myself!

Life is very much more exciting now than it used to be. You see I have something more to expect, to look forward to, to watch. I really do eat better, and am more quiet than I was.

John is so pleased to see me improve! He laughed a little the other day, and said I seemed to be flourishing in spite of my wall-paper.

I turned it off with laugh. I had no intention of telling him it was *because* of the wall-paper—he would make fun of me. He might even want to take me away.

I don't want to leave now until I have found it out. There is a week more, and I think that will be enough.

I'm feeling ever so much better! I don't sleep much at night, for it is so interesting to watch developments; but I sleep a good deal in the daytime.

In the daytime it is tiresome and perplexing.

There are always new shoots on the fungus, and new shades of yellow all over it. I cannot keep count of them, though I have tried conscientiously.

It is the strangest yellow, that wall-paper! It makes me think of all the yellow things I ever saw—not beautiful ones like buttercups, but old foul, bad yellow things.

But there is something else about that paper—the smell! I noticed it the moment we came into the room, but with so much air and sun it was not bad. Now we have had a week of fog and rain, and whether the windows are open or not, the smell is here.

It creeps all over the house.

I find it hovering in the dining-room, skulking in the parlor, hiding in the hall, lying in wait for me on the stairs.

It gets into my hair.

Even when I go to ride, if I turn my head suddenly and surprise it—there is that smell!

Such a peculiar odor, too! I have spent hours in trying to analyze it, to find what it smelled like.

It is not bad—at first, and very gentle, but quite the subtlest, most enduring odor I ever met.

In this damp weather it is awful, I wake up in the night and find it hanging over me.

It used to disturb me at first. I thought seriously of burning the house— to reach the smell.

But now I am used to it. The only thing I can think of that it is like is the *color* of the paper! A yellow smell.

There is a very funny mark on this wall, low down, near the mopboard. A streak that runs around the room. It goes behind every piece of furniture, except the bed, a long, straight, even *smooch,* as if it had been rubbed over and over.

I wonder how it was done and who did it, and what they did it for. Round and round and round—round and round and round—it makes me dizzy!

I really have discovered something at last.

Through watching so much at night, when it changes so, I have finally found out.

The front pattern *does* move—and no wonder! The woman behind shakes it!

Sometimes I think there are a great many women behind, and sometimes only one, and she crawls around fast, and her crawling shakes it all over.

Then in the very bright spots she keeps still, and in the very shady spots she just takes hold of the bars and shakes them hard.

And she is all the time trying to climb through. But nobody could climb through that pattern—it strangles so; I think that is why it has so many heads.

They get through, and then the pattern strangles them off and turns them upside down, and makes their eyes white!

If those heads were covered or taken off it would not be half so bad.

I think that woman gets out in the daytime!

And I'll tell you why—privately—I've seen her!

I can see her out of every one of my windows!

It is the same woman, I know, for she is always creeping, and most women do not creep by daylight.

I see her in that long shaded lane, creeping up and down. I see her in those dark grape arbors, creeping all around the garden.

I see her on that long road under the trees, creeping along, and when a carriage comes she hides under the blackberry vines.

I don't blame her a bit. It must be very humiliating to be caught creeping by daylight!

I always lock the door when I creep by daylight. I can't do it at night, for I know John would suspect something at once.

And John is so queer now, that I don't want to irritate him. I wish he would take another room! Besides, I don't want anybody to get that woman out at night but myself.

I often wonder if I could see her out of all the windows at once.

But, turn as fast as I can, I can only see out of one at one time.

And though I always see her, she *may* be able to creep faster than I can turn!

I have watched her sometimes away off in the open country, creeping as fast as a cloud shadow in a high wind.

If only that top pattern could be gotten off from the under one! I mean to try it, little by little.

I have found out another funny thing, but I shan't tell it this time! It does not do to trust people too much.

There are only two more days to get this paper off, and I believe John is beginning to notice. I don't like the look in his eyes.

And I heard him ask Jennie a lot of professional questions about me. She had a very good report to give.

She said I slept a good deal in the daytime.

John knows I don't sleep very well at night, for all I'm so quiet!

He asked me all sorts of questions, too, and pretended to be very loving and kind.

As if I couldn't see through him!

Still, I don't wonder he acts so, sleeping under this paper for three months. It only interests me, but I feel sure John and Jennie are secretly affected by it.

Hurrah! This is the last day, but it is enough. John to stay in town over night, and won't be out until this evening.

Jennie wanted to sleep with me—the sly thing! but I told her I should undoubtedly rest better for a night all alone.

That was clever, for really I wasn't alone a bit! As soon as it was moonlight and that poor thing began to crawl and shake the pattern, I got up and ran to help her.

I pulled and she shook, I shook and she pulled, and before morning we had peeled off yards of that paper.

A strip about as high as my head and half around the room.

And then when the sun came and that awful pattern began to laugh at me, I declared I would finish it to-day!

We go away to-morrow, and they are moving all my furniture down again to leave things as they were before.

Jennie looked at the wall in amazement, but I told her merrily that I did it out of pure spite at the vicious thing.

She laughed and said she wouldn't mind doing it herself, but I must not get tired.

How she betrayed herself that time!

But I am here, and no person touches this paper but me,—not *alive*!

She tried to get me out of the room—it was too patent! But I said it was so quiet and empty and clean now that I believed I would lie down again and sleep all I could; and not to wake me even for dinner—I would call when I woke.

So now she is gone, and the servants are gone, and the things are gone, and there is nothing left but that great bedstead nailed down, with the canvas mattress we found on it.

We shall sleep downstairs to-night, and take the boat home to-morrow.

I quite enjoy the room, now it is bare again.

How those children did tear about here!

This bedstead is fairly gnawed!

But I must get to work.

I have locked the door and thrown the key down into the front path.

I don't want to go out, and I don't want to have anybody come in, till John comes.

I want to astonish him.

I've got a rope up here that even Jennie did not find. If that woman does get out, and tries to get away, I can tie her!

But I forgot I could not reach far without anything to stand on!

This bed will *not* move!

I tried to lift and push it until I was lame, and then I got so angry I bit off a little piece at one corner—but it hurt my teeth.

Then I peeled off all the paper I could reach standing on the floor. It sticks horribly and the pattern just enjoys it! All those strangled heads and bulbous eyes and waddling fungus growths just shriek with derision!

I am getting angry enough to do something desperate. To jump out of the window would be admirable exercise, but the bars are too strong even to try.

Besides I wouldn't do it. Of course not. I know well enough that a step like that is improper and might be misconstrued.

I don't like to *look* out of the windows even—there are so many of those creeping women, and they creep so fast.

I wonder if they all come out of that wall-paper as I did?

But I am securely fastened now by my well-hidden rope—you don't get *me* out in the road there!

I suppose I shall have to get back behind the pattern when it comes night, and that is hard!

It is so pleasant to be out in this great room and creep around as I please!

I don't want to go outside. I won't, even if Jennie asks me to.

For outside you have to creep on the ground, and everything is green instead of yellow.

But here I can creep smoothly on the floor, and my shoulder just fits in that long smooch around the wall, so I cannot lose my way.

Why there's John at the door!

It is no use, young man, you can't open it!

How he does call and pound!

Now he's crying for an axe.

It would be a shame to break down that beautiful door!

"John dear!" said I in the gentlest voice, "the key is down by the front steps, under a plantain leaf!"

That silenced him for a few moments.

Then he said—very quietly indeed, "Open the door, my darling!"

"I can't," said I. "The key is down by the front door under a plantain leaf!"

And then I said it again, several times, very gently and slowly, and said it so often that he had to go and see, and he got it of course, and came in. He stopped short by the door.

"What is the matter?" he cried. "For God's sake, what are you doing!"

I kept on creeping just the same, but I looked at him over my shoulder.

"I've got out at last," said I, "in spite of you and Jane. And I've pulled off most of the paper, so you can't put me back!"

Now why should that man have fainted? But he did, and right across my path by the wall, so that I had to creep over him every time!

EXERCISES

1. Discuss the basic differences between the narrator and her husband. Are these differences general culturally determined differences between males and females in Western society, or are they mere literary and popular-culture stereotypes?

2. Why is writing such a central activity in this story? Why does the husband think that writing is bad for the narrator? How could writing be dangerous in any circumstance?

3. Why is wallpaper such a central motif in this story? Why does it seem an appropriate metaphor for the woman's situation? Why are the patterns on the wallpaper so important in this story?

4. Who is the woman behind the wallpaper? What is suggested by the fact that the woman is trapped behind patterns? Why does the narrator think that the number of women behind the wallpaper increases as the story progresses?

5. Discuss the gradual change in the point of view or perspective of the narrator as the story progresses. How is this reflected in the nature of her writing?

6. Is this a realistic story, a supernatural story, or a metaphoric story? Support your opinion by referring to details in the story.

WILLIAM
FAULKNER | *A Rose for Emily*

When Miss Emily Grierson died, our whole town went to her funeral: the men through a sort of respectful affection for a fallen monument, the women mostly out of curiosity to see the inside of her house, which no one save an old manservant—a combined gardener and cook—had seen in at least ten years.

It was a big, squarish frame house that had once been white, decorated with cupolas and spires and scrolled balconies in the heavily lightsome style of the seventies, set on what had once been our most select street. But garages and cotton gins had encroached and obliterated even the august names of that neighborhood; only Miss Emily's house was left, lifting its stubborn and coquettish decay above the cotton wagons and the gasoline pumps—an eyesore among eyesores. And now Miss Emily had gone to join the representatives of those august names where they lay in the cedar-bemused cemetery among the ranked and anonymous graves of Union and Confederate soldiers who fell at the battle of Jefferson.

Alive, Miss Emily had been a tradition, a duty, and a care; a sort of hereditary obligation upon the town, dating from that day in 1894 when Colonel Sartoris, the mayor—he who fathered the edict that no Negro woman should appear on the streets without an apron—remitted her taxes, the dispensation dating from the death of her father on into perpetuity. Not that Miss Emily would have accepted charity. Colonel Sartoris invented an involved tale to the effect that Miss Emily's father had loaned money to the town, which the town, as a matter of business, preferred this way of repaying. Only a man of Colonel Sartoris' generation and thought could have invented it, and only a woman could have believed it.

When the next generation, with its more modern ideas, became mayors and aldermen, this arrangement created some little dissatisfaction. On the first of the year they mailed her a tax notice. February came, and there was no reply. They wrote her a formal letter, asking her to call at the sheriff's office at her convenience. A week later the mayor wrote her himself, offering to call or to send his car for her, and received in reply a note on paper of an archaic shape, in a thin, flowing calligraphy in faded ink, to the effect that she no longer went out at all. The tax notice was also enclosed, without comment.

They called a special meeting of the Board of Aldermen. A deputation waited upon her, knocked at the door through which no visitor had passed since she ceased giving china-painting lessons eight or ten years earlier. They were admitted by the old Negro into a dim hall from which a stairway mounted into still more shadow. It smelled of dust and disuse—a close, dank smell. The Negro led them into the parlor. It was furnished in heavy, leather-covered furniture. When the Negro opened the blinds of one window, they could see that the leather was cracked: and when they sat down, a faint dust rose sluggishly about their thighs, spinning with slow motes in the single sun-ray. On a tarnished gilt easel before the fireplace stood a crayon portrait of Miss Emily's father.

They rose when she entered—a small, fat woman in black, with a thin gold chain descending to her waist and vanishing into her belt, leaning on an ebony cane with a tarnished gold head. Her skeleton was small and spare; perhaps that was why what would have been merely plumpness in another was obesity in her. She looked bloated, like a body long submerged in motionless water, and of that pallid hue. Her eyes, lost in the fatty ridges of her face, looked like two small pieces of coal pressed into a lump of dough as they moved from one face to another while the visitors stated their errand.

She did not ask them to sit. She just stood in the door and listened quietly until the spokesman came to a stumbling halt. Then they could hear the invisible watch ticking at the end of the gold chain.

Her voice was dry and cold. "I have no taxes in Jefferson. Colonel Sartoris explained it to me. Perhaps one of you can gain access to the city records and satisfy yourselves."

"But we have. We are the city authorities, Miss Emily. Didn't you get a notice from the sheriff, signed by him?"

"I received a paper, yes," Miss Emily said. "Perhaps he considers himself the sheriff. . . . I have no taxes in Jefferson."

"But there is nothing on the books to show that, you see. We must go by the—"

"See Colonel Sartoris. I have no taxes in Jefferson."

"But, Miss Emily—"

"See Colonel Sartoris." (Colonel Sartoris had been dead almost ten years.) "I have no taxes in Jefferson. Tobe!" The Negro appeared. "Show these gentlemen out."

II

So she vanquished them, horse and foot, just as she had vanquished their fathers thirty years before about the smell. That was two years after her father's death and a short time after her sweetheart—the one we believed would marry her—had deserted her. After her father's death she went out very little; after her sweetheart went away, people hardly saw her at all. A few of the ladies had the temerity to call, but were not received, and the only sign of life about the place was the Negro man—a young man then—going in and out with a market basket.

"Just as if a man—any man—could keep a kitchen properly," the ladies said; so they were not surprised when the smell developed. It was another link between the gross, teeming world and the high and mighty Griersons.

A neighbor, a woman, complained to the mayor, Judge Stevens, eighty years old.

"But what will you have me do about it, madam?" he said.

"Why, send her word to stop it," the woman said. "Isn't there a law?"

"I'm sure that won't be necessary," Judge Stevens said. "It's probably just a snake or a rat that nigger of hers killed in the yard. I'll speak to him about it."

The next day he received two more complaints, one from a man who came in diffident deprecation. "We really must do something about it, Judge. I'd be the last one in the world to bother Miss Emily, but we've got to do something." That night the Board of Aldermen met—three graybeards and one younger man, a member of the rising generation.

"It's simple enough," he said. "Send her word to have her place cleaned up. Give her a certain time to do it in, and if she don't . . ."

"Dammit, sir," Judge Stevens said, "will you accuse a lady to her face of smelling bad?"

So the next night, after midnight, four men crossed Miss Emily's lawn and slunk about the house like burglars, sniffing along the base of the brickwork and at the cellar openings while one of them performed a regular sowing motion with his hand out of a sack slung from his shoulder. They broke open the cellar door and sprinkled lime there, and in all the outbuildings. As they recrossed the lawn, a window that had been dark was lighted and Miss Emily sat in it, the light behind her, and her upright torso motionless as that of an idol. They crept quietly across the lawn and into the shadow of the locusts that lined the street. After a week or two the smell went away.

That was when people had begun to feel really sorry for her. People in our town, remembering how old lady Wyatt, her great-aunt, had gone completely crazy at last, believed that the Griersons held themselves a little too high for what they really were. None of the young men were quite good enough for Miss Emily and such. We had long thought of them as a tableau, Miss Emily a slender figure in white in the background, her father a spraddled silhouette in the foreground, his back to her and clutching a horsewhip, the two of them framed by the back-flung front door. So when she got to be thirty and was still single, we were not pleased exactly, but vindicated; even with insanity in the family she wouldn't have turned down all of her chances if they had really materialized.

When her father died, it got about that the house was all that was left to her; and in a way, people were glad. At last they could pity Miss Emily. Being left alone, and a pauper, she had become humanized. Now she too would know the old thrill and the old despair of a penny more or less.

The day after his death all the ladies prepared to call at the house and offer condolence and aid, as is our custom. Miss Emily met them at the door, dressed as usual and with no trace of grief on her face. She told them that her father was not dead. She did that for three days, with the ministers calling on her, and the doctors, trying to persuade her to let them dispose of the body. Just as they were about to resort to law and force, she broke down, and they buried her father quickly.

We did not say she was crazy then. We believed she had to do that. We remembered all the young men her father had driven away, and we knew that with nothing left, she would have to cling to that which had robbed her, as people will.

III

She was sick for a long time. When we saw her again, her hair was cut short, making her look like a girl, with a vague resemblance to those angels in colored church windows—sort of tragic and serene.

The town had just let the contracts for paving the sidewalks, and in the summer after her father's death they began the work. The construction company came with niggers and mules and machinery, and a foreman named Homer Barron, a Yankee—a big, dark, ready man, with a big voice and eyes lighter than his face. The little boys would follow in groups to hear him cuss the niggers, and the niggers singing in time to the rise and fall of picks. Pretty soon he knew everybody in town. Whenever you heard a lot of laughing anywhere about the square, Homer Barron would be in the center of the group. Presently we began to see him and Miss Emily on Sunday afternoons driving in the yellow-wheeled buggy and the matched team of bays from the livery stable.

At first we were glad that Miss Emily would have an interest, because the ladies all said, "Of course a Grierson would not think seriously of a Northerner, a day laborer." But there were still others, older people, who said that even grief could not cause a real lady to forget *noblesse oblige*—without calling it *noblesse oblige*. They just said, "Poor Emily. Her kinsfolk should come to her." She had some kin in Alabama; but years ago her father had fallen out with them over the estate of old lady Wyatt, the crazy woman, and there was no communication between the two families. They had not even been represented at the funeral.

And as soon as the old people said, "Poor Emily," the whispering began. "Do you suppose it's really so?" they said to one another. "Of course it is. What else could . . ." This behind their hands; rustling of craned silk and satin behind jalousies closed upon the sun of Sunday afternoon as the thin, swift clop-clop-clop of the matched team passed: "Poor Emily."

She carried her head high enough—even when we believed that she was fallen. It was as if she demanded more than ever the recognition of her dignity as the last Grierson; as if it had wanted that touch of earthiness to reaffirm her imperviousness. Like when she bought the rat poison, the arsenic. That was over a year after they had begun to say "Poor Emily," and while the two female cousins were visiting her.

"I want some poison," she said to the druggist. She was over thirty then, still a slight woman, though thinner than usual, with cold, haughty black eyes in a face the flesh of which was strained across the temples and about the eyesockets as you imagine a lighthouse-keeper's face ought to look. "I want some poison," she said.

"Yes, Miss Emily. What kind? For rats and such? I'd recom—"

"I want the best you have. I don't care what kind."

The druggist named several. "They'll kill anything up to an elephant. But what you want is—"

"Arsenic," Miss Emily said. "Is that a good one?"

"Is . . . arsenic? Yes, ma'am. But what you want—"

"I want arsenic."

The druggist looked down at her. She looked back at him, erect, her face like a strained flag. "Why, of course," the druggist said. "If that's what you want. But the law requires you to tell what you are going to use it for."

Miss Emily just stared at him, her head tilted back in order to look him eye for eye, until he looked away and went and got the arsenic and wrapped it up. The Negro delivery boy brought her the package; the druggist didn't come back. When she opened the package at home there was written on the box, under the skull and bones: "For rats."

IV

So the next day we all said, "She will kill herself"; and we said it would be the best thing. When she had first begun to be seen with Homer Barron, we had said, "She will marry him." Then we said, "She will persuade him yet," because Homer himself had remarked—he liked men, and it was known that he drank with the younger men in the Elks' Club—that he was not the marrying man. Later we said, "Poor Emily" behind the jalousies as they passed on Sunday afternoon in the glittering buggy, Miss Emily with her head high and Homer Barron with his hat cocked and a cigar in his teeth, reins and whip in a yellow glove.

Then some of the ladies began to say that it was a disgrace to the town and a bad example to the young people. The men did not want to interfere, but at last the ladies forced the Baptist minister—Miss Emily's people were Episcopal—to call upon her. He would never divulge what happened during that interview, but he refused to go back again. The next Sunday they again drove about the streets, and the following day the minister's wife wrote to Miss Emily's relations in Alabama.

So she had blood-kin under her roof again and we sat back to watch developments. At first nothing happened. Then we were sure that they were to be married. We learned that Miss Emily had been to the jeweler's and ordered a man's toilet set in silver, with the letters H. B. on each piece. Two days later we learned that she had bought a complete outfit of men's clothing, including a nightshirt, and we said, "They are married." We were really glad. We were glad because the two female cousins were even more Grierson than Miss Emily had ever been.

So we were not surprised when Homer Barron—the streets had been finished some time since—was gone. We were a little disappointed that there was not a public blowing-off, but we believed that he had gone on to prepare for Miss Emily's coming, or to give her a chance to get rid of the cousins. (By that time it was a cabal, and we were all Miss Emily's allies to help circumvent the cousins.) Sure enough, after another week they departed. And, as we had expected all along, within three days Homer Barron was back in town. A neighbor saw the Negro man admit him at the kitchen door at dusk one evening.

And that was the last we saw of Homer Barron. And of Miss Emily for some time. The Negro man went in and out with the market basket, but the front door remained closed. Now and then we would see her at a window for a moment, as the men did that night when they sprinkled the lime, but for almost six months she did not appear on the streets. Then we knew that this was to be expected too; as if that quality of her father which had thwarted her woman's life so many times had been too virulent and too furious to die.

When we next saw Miss Emily, she had grown fat and her hair was turning gray. During the next few years it grew grayer and grayer until it attained an even pepper-and-salt iron-gray, when it ceased turning. Up to the day of her death at seventy-four it was still that vigorous iron-gray, like the hair of an active man.

From that time on her front door remained closed, save for a period of six or seven years, when she was about forty, during which she gave lessons in china-painting. She fitted up a studio in one of the downstairs rooms, where the daughters and granddaughters of Colonel Sartoris' contemporaries were sent to her with the same regularity and in the same spirit that they were sent to church on Sundays with a twenty-five-cent piece for the collection plate. Meanwhile her taxes had been remitted.

Then the newer generation became the backbone and the spirit of the town, and the painting pupils grew up and fell away and did not send their children to her with boxes of color and tedious brushes and pictures cut from the ladies' magazines. The front door closed upon the last one and remained closed for good. When the town got free postal delivery, Miss Emily alone refused to let them fasten the metal numbers above her door and attach a mailbox to it. She would not listen to them.

Daily, monthly, yearly we watched the Negro grow grayer and more stooped, going in and out with the market basket. Each December we sent her a tax notice, which would be returned by the post office a week later, unclaimed. Now and then we would see her in one of the downstairs windows—she had evidently shut up the top floor of the house—like the carven torso of an idol in a niche, looking or not looking at us, we could never tell which. Thus she passed from generation to generation—dear, inescapable, impervious, tranquil, and perverse.

And so she died. Fell ill in the house filled with dust and shadows, with only a doddering Negro man to wait on her. We did not even know she was sick; we had long since given up trying to get any information from the Negro. He talked to no one, probably not even to her, for his voice had grown harsh and rusty, as if from disuse.

She died in one of the downstairs rooms, in a heavy walnut bed with a curtain, her gray head propped on a pillow yellow and moldy with age and lack of sunlight.

V

The Negro met the first of the ladies at the front door and let them in, with their hushed, sibilant voices and their quick, curious glances, and then he disappeared. He walked right through the house and out the back and was not seen again.

The two female cousins came at once. They held the funeral on the second day, with the town coming to look at Miss Emily beneath a mass of bought flowers, with the crayon face of her father musing profoundly above the bier and the ladies sibilant and macabre; and the very old men—some in their brushed Confederate uniforms—on the porch and the lawn, talking of Miss Emily as if she had been a contemporary of theirs, believing that they had danced with her and courted her perhaps, confusing time with its mathematical progression, as the old do, to whom all the past is not a diminishing road but, instead, a huge meadow which no winter ever quite touches, divided from them now by the narrow bottle-neck of the most recent decade of years.

Already we knew that there was one room in that region above stairs which no one had seen in forty years, and which would have to be forced. They waited until Miss Emily was decently in the ground before they opened it.

The violence of breaking down the door seemed to fill this room with pervading dust. A thin, acrid pall as of the tomb seemed to lie everywhere upon this room decked and furnished as for a bridal: upon the valance curtains of faded rose color, upon the rose-shaded lights, upon the dressing table, upon the delicate array of crystal and the man's toilet things backed with tarnished silver, silver so tarnished that the monogram was obscured. Among them lay a collar and tie, as if they had just been removed, which, lifted, left upon the surface a pale crescent in the dust. Upon a chair hung the suit, carefully folded; beneath it the two mute shoes and the discarded socks.

The man himself lay in the bed.

For a long while we just stood there, looking down at the profound and fleshless grin. The body had apparently once lain in the attitude of an embrace, but now the long sleep that outlasts love, that conquers even the grimace of love, had cuckolded him. What was left of him, rotted beneath what was left of the nightshirt, had become inextricable from the bed in which he lay; and upon him and upon the pillow beside him lay that even coating of the patient and biding dust.

Then we noticed that in the second pillow was the indentation of a head. One of us lifted something from it, and leaning forward, that faint and invisible dust dry and acrid in the nostrils, we saw a long strand of iron-gray hair.

Exercises

1. Determine the narrator or teller of the story. Although the teller seems to be one person, he or she is not identified specifically, but rather seems to

be a spokesperson for the entire town. Why does this story require this kind of plural narrator?

2. There is no mention of a rose within the story. What is the significance of the title? What is the rose for Emily?

3. Identify the points in the story in which Emily is transformed by the townspeople from a real person into a symbolic figure.

4. Discuss this story as a satiric parable about the relationship between the North and the South.

5. Discuss the significance of the passage about the old people's attitude toward time: "to whom all the past is not a diminishing road, but instead, a huge meadow which no winter ever quite touches. . . ."What does this have to do with the way the story itself breaks up time?

6. It is a basic convention of dramatic art that tragedies end in death, whereas comedies end in marriage. How is this story a tragicomedy? Does Emily have tragic stature? What is comic about her action?

JOSEPH
CONRAD | *The Secret Sharer*

On my right hand there were lines of fishing-stakes resembling a mysterious system of half-submerged bamboo fences, incomprehensible in its division of the domain of tropical fishes, and crazy of aspect as if abandoned for ever by some nomad tribe of fishermen now gone to the other end of the ocean; for there was no sign of human habitation as far as the eye could reach. To the left a group of barren islets, suggesting ruins of stone walls, towers, and blockhouses, had its foundations set in a blue sea that itself looked solid, so still and stable did it lie below my feet; even the track of light from the westering sun shone smoothly, without that animated glitter which tells of an imperceptible ripple. And when I turned my head to take a parting glance at the tug which had just left us anchored outside the bar, I saw the straight line of the flat shore joined to the stable sea, edge to edge, with a perfect and unmarked closeness, in one levelled floor half brown, half blue under the enormous dome of the sky. Corresponding in their insignificance to the islets of the sea, two small clumps of trees, one on each side of the only fault in the impeccable joint, marked the mouth of the river Meinam we had just left on the first preparatory stage of our homeward journey; and, far back on the inland level, a larger and loftier mass, the grove surrounding the great Paknam pagoda, was the only thing on which the eye could rest from the vain task of exploring the monotonous sweep of the horizon. Here and there gleams as of a few scattered pieces of silver marked the windings of the great river; and on the nearest of them, just within the bar, the tug steaming right into the land became lost to my sight, hull and funnel and masts, as though the impassive earth had swallowed her up without an effort, without a tremor. My eye followed the light cloud of her smoke, now here, now there, above the plain, according to the devious curves of the stream, but always fainter and farther away, till I lost it at last behind the mitre-shaped hill of the great pagoda. And then I was left alone with my ship, anchored at the head of the Gulf of Siam.

She floated at the starting-point of a long journey, very still in an immense stillness, the shadows of her spars flung far to the eastward by the setting sun. At that moment I was alone on her decks. There was not a sound in her— and around us nothing moved, nothing lived, not a canoe on the water, not a bird in the air, not a cloud in the sky. In this breathless pause at the threshold of a long passage we seemed to be measuring our fitness for a long and arduous enterprise, the appointed task of both our existences to be carried out, far from all human eyes, with only sky and sea for spectators and for judges.

There must have been some glare in the air to interfere with one's sight, because it was only just before the sun left us that my roaming eyes made out beyond the highest ridge of the principal islet of the group something which did away with the solemnity of perfect solitude. The tide of darkness flowed on swiftly; and with tropical suddenness a swarm of stars came out above the shadowy earth, while I lingered yet, my hand resting lightly on my ship's rail as if on the shoulder of a trusted friend. But, with all that multitude of celestial bodies staring down at one, the comfort of quiet communion with her was gone for good. And there were also disturbing sounds by this time—voices, footsteps forward; the steward flitted along the main-deck, a busily ministering spirit; a hand-bell tinkled urgently under the poop-deck. . . .

I found my two officers waiting for me near the supper table, in the lighted cuddy. We sat down at once, and as I helped the chief mate, I said:

"Are you aware that there is a ship anchored inside the islands? I saw her mastheads above the ridge as the sun went down."

He raised sharply his simple face, overcharged by a terrible growth of whisker, and emitted his usual ejaculations: "Bless my soul, sir! You don't say so!"

My second mate was a round-cheeked, silent young man, grave beyond his years, I thought; but as our eyes happened to meet I detected a slight quiver on his lips. I looked down at once. It was not my part to encourage sneering on board my ship. It must be said, too, that I knew very little of my officers. In consequence of certain events of no particular significance, except to myself, I had been appointed to the command only a fortnight before. Neither did I know much of the hands forward. All these people had been together for eighteen months or so, and my position was that of the only stranger on board. I mention this because it has some bearing on what is to follow. But what I felt most was my being a stranger to the ship; and if all the truth must be told, I was somewhat of a stranger to myself. The youngest man on board (barring the second mate), and untried as yet by a position of the fullest responsibility, I was willing to take the adequacy of the others for granted. They had simply to be equal to their tasks; but I wondered how far I should turn out faithful to that ideal conception of one's own personality every man sets up for himself secretly.

Meantime the chief mate, with an almost visible effect of collaboration on the part of his round eyes and frightful whiskers, was trying to evolve a theory of the anchored ship. His dominant trait was to take all things into earnest consideration. He was of a painstaking turn of mind. As he used to say, he "liked to account to himself" for practically everything that came in his way, down to a miserable scorpion he had found in his cabin a week before. The why and the wherefore of that scorpion—how it got on board and came to select his room rather than the pantry (which was a dark place and more what a scorpion would be partial to), and how on earth it managed to drown itself in the inkwell of his writing-desk—had exercised him infinitely. The ship within the islands was much more easily accounted for; and just as we were about to rise from table he made his pronouncement. She was, he doubted not, a ship from home lately arrived. Probably she drew too much water to cross the bar except at the top of spring tides. Therefore she went into that natural harbour to wait for a few days in preference to remaining in an open roadstead.

"That's so," confirmed the second mate, suddenly, in his slightly hoarse voice. "She draws over twenty feet. She's the Liverpool ship *Sephora* with a cargo of coal. Hundred and twenty-three days from Cardiff."

We looked at him in surprise.

"The tugboat skipper told me when he came on board for your letters, sir," explained the young man. "He expects to take her up the river the day after to-morrow."

After thus overwhelming us with the extent of his information he slipped out of the cabin. The mate observed regretfully that he "could not account for that young fellow's whims." What prevented him telling us all about it at once, he wanted to know.

I detained him as he was making a move. For the last two days the crew had had plenty of hard work, and the night before they had very little sleep. I felt painfully that I—a stranger—was doing something unusual when I directed him to let all hands turn in without setting an anchor-watch. I proposed to keep on deck myself till one o'clock or thereabouts. I would get the second mate to relieve me at that hour.

"He will turn out the cook and the steward at four," I concluded, "and then give you a call. Of course at the slightest sign of any sort of wind we'll have the hands up and make a start at once."

He concealed his astonishment. "Very well, sir." Outside the cuddy he put his head in the second mate's door to inform him of my unheard-of caprice to take a five hours' anchor-watch on myself. I heard the other raise his voice incredulously—"What? The Captain himself?" Then a few more murmurs, a door closed, then another. A few moments later I went on deck.

My strangeness, which had made me sleepless, had prompted that unconventional arrangement, as if I had expected in those solitary hours of the night to get on terms with the ship of which I knew nothing, manned by men of whom I knew very little more. Fast alongside a wharf, littered like any ship in port with a tangle of unrelated things, invaded by unrelated shore people, I had hardly seen her yet properly. Now, as she lay cleared for sea, the stretch of her main-deck seemed to me very fine under the stars. Very fine, very roomy for her size, and very inviting. I descended the poop and paced the waist, my mind picturing to myself the coming passage through the Malay Archipelago, down the Indian Ocean, and up the Atlantic. All its phases were familiar enough to me, every characteristic, all the alternatives which were likely to face me on the high seas—everything! . . . except the novel responsibility of command. But I took heart from the reasonable thought that the ship was like other ships, the men like other men, and that the sea was not likely to keep any special surprises expressly for my discomfiture.

Arrived at that comforting conclusion, I bethought myself of a cigar and went below to get it. All was still down there. Everybody at the after end of the ship was sleeping profoundly. I came out again on the quarter-deck, agreeably at ease in my sleeping-suit on that warm breathless night, barefooted, a glowing cigar in my teeth, and, going forward, I was met by the profound silence of the fore end of the ship. Only as I passed the door of the forecastle I heard a deep, quiet, trustful sigh of some sleeper inside. And suddenly I rejoiced in the great security of the sea as compared with the unrest of the land, in my choice of that untempted life presenting no disquieting problems, invested with an elementary moral beauty by the absolute straightforwardness of its appeal and by the singleness of its purpose.

The riding-light in the fore-rigging burned with a clear, untroubled, as if symbolic, flame, confident and bright in the mysterious shades of the night. Passing on my way aft along the other side of the ship, I observed that the rope side-ladder, put over, no doubt, for the master of the tub when he came to fetch away our letters, had not been hauled in as it should have been. I became annoyed at this, for exactitude in small matters is the very soul of discipline. Then I reflected that I had myself peremptorily dismissed my officers from duty, and by my own act had prevented the anchor-watch being formally set and things properly attended to. I asked myself whether it was wise ever to interfere with the established routine of duties even from the kindest of motives. My action might have made me appear eccentric. Goodness only knew how that absurdly whiskered mate would "account" for my conduct, and what the whole ship thought of that informality of their new captain. I was vexed with myself.

Not from compunction certainly, but, as it were mechanically, I proceeded to get the ladder in myself. Now a side-ladder of that sort is a light affair and comes in easily, yet my vigorous tug, which should have brought it flying on board, merely recoiled upon my body in a totally unexpected jerk. What the devil! . . . I was so astounded by the immovableness of that ladder that I remained stockstill, trying to account for it to myself like that imbecile mate of mine. In the end, of course, I put my head over the rail.

The side of the ship made an opaque belt of shadow on the darkling glassy shimmer of the sea. But I saw at once something elongated and pale floating very close to the ladder. Before I could form a guess a faint flash of phosphorescent light, which seemed to issue suddenly from the naked body of a man, flickered in the sleeping water with the elusive, silent play of summer lightning in a night sky. With a gasp I saw revealed to my stare a pair of feet, the long legs, a broad livid back immersed right up to the neck in a greenish cadaverous glow. One hand, awash, clutched the bottom rung of the ladder. He was complete but for the head. A headless corpse! The cigar dropped out of my gaping mouth with a tiny plop and a short hiss quite audible in the absolute stillness of all things under heaven. At that I suppose he raised up his face, a dimly pale oval in the shadow of the ship's side. But even then I could only barely make out down there the shape of his black-haired head. However, it was enough for the horrid, frost-bound sensation which had gripped me about the chest to pass off. The moment of vain exclamations was past, too. I only climbed on the spare spar and leaned over the rail as far as I could, to bring my eyes nearer to that mystery floating alongside.

As he hung by the ladder, like a resting swimmer, the sea lightning played about his limbs at every stir; and he appeared in it ghastly, silvery, fish-like. He remained as mute as a fish, too. He made no motion to get out of the water, either. It was inconceivable that he should not attempt to come on board, and strangely troubling to suspect that perhaps he did not want to. And my first words were prompted by just that troubled incertitude.

"What's the matter?" I asked in my ordinary tone, speaking down to the face upturned exactly under mine.

"Cramp," it answered, no louder. Then slightly anxious, "I say, no need to call any one."

"I was not going to," I said.

"Are you alone on deck?"

"Yes."

I had somehow the impression that he was on the point of letting go the ladder to swim away beyond my ken—mysterious as he came. But, for the moment, this being appearing as if he had risen from the bottom of the sea (it was certainly the nearest land to the ship) wanted only to know the time. I told him. And he, down there, tentatively:

"I suppose your captain's turned in?"

"I am sure he isn't," I said.

He seemed to struggle with himself, for I heard something like the low, bitter murmur of doubt. "What's the good?" His next words came out with a hesitating effort.

"Look here, my man. Could you call him out quietly?"

I thought the time had come to declare myself.

"I am the captain."

I heard a "By Jove!" whispered at the level of the water. The phosphorescence flashed in the swirl of the water all about his limbs, his other hand seized the ladder.

"My name's Leggatt."

The voice was calm and resolute. A good voice. The self-possession of that man had somehow induced a corresponding state in myself. It was very quietly that I remarked:

"You must be a good swimmer."

"Yes. I've been in the water practically since nine o'clock. The question for me now is whether I am to let go this ladder and go on swimming till I sink from exhaustion, or—to come on board here."

I felt this was no mere formula of desperate speech, but a real alternative in the view of a strong soul. I should have gathered from this that he was young; indeed, it is only the young who are ever confronted by such clear issues. But at the time it was pure intuition on my part. A mysterious communication was established already between us two—in the face of that silent, darkened tropical sea. I was young, too; young enough to make no comment. The man in the water began suddenly to climb up the ladder, and I hastened away from the rail to fetch some clothes.

Before entering the cabin I stood still, listening in the lobby at the foot of the stairs. A faint snore came through the closed door of the chief mate's room. The second mate's door was on the hook, but the darkness in there was absolutely soundless. He, too, was young and could sleep like a stone. Remained the steward, but he was not likely to wake up before he was called. I got a sleeping-suit out of my room and, coming back on deck, saw the naked man from the sea sitting on the main-hatch, glimmering white in the darkness, his elbows on his knees and his head in his hands. In a moment he had concealed his damp body in a sleeping-suit of the same grey-stripe pattern as the one I was wearing and followed me like my double on the poop. Together we moved right aft, barefooted, silent.

"What is it?" I asked in a deadened voice, taking the lighted lamp out of the binnacle, and raising it to his face.

"An ugly business."

He had rather regular features; a good mouth; light eyes under somewhat heavy, dark eyebrows; a smooth, square forehead; no growth on his cheeks; a small, brown moustache, and a well-shaped, round chin. His expression was concentrated, meditative, under the inspecting light of the lamp I held up to his face; such as a man thinking hard in solitude might wear. My sleeping-suit was just right for his size. A well-knit young fellow of twenty-five at most. He caught his lower lip with the edge of white, even teeth.

"Yes," I said, replacing the lamp in the binnacle. The warm, heavy tropical night closed upon his head again.

"There's a ship over there," he murmured.

"Yes, I know. The *Sephora*. Did you know of us?"

"Hadn't the slightest idea. I am the mate of her—" He paused and corrected himself. "I should say I *was*."

"Aha! Something wrong?"

"Yes. Very wrong indeed. I've killed a man."

"What do you mean? Just now?"

"No, on the passage. Weeks ago. Thirty-nine south. When I say a man—"

"Fit of temper," I suggested, confidently.

The shadowy, dark head, like mine, seemed to nod imperceptibly above the ghostly grey of my sleeping-suit. It was, in the night, as though I had been faced by my own reflection in the depths of a sombre and immense mirror.

"A pretty thing to have to own up to for a Conway boy," murmured my double, distinctly.

"You're a Conway boy?"

"I am," he said, as if startled. Then, slowly . . . "Perhaps you too—"

It was so; but being a couple of years older I had left before he joined. After a quick interchange of dates a silence fell; and I thought suddenly of my absurd mate with his terrific whiskers and the "Bless my soul—you don't say so" type of intellect. My double gave me an inkling of his thoughts by saying: "My father's a parson in Norfolk. Do you see me before a judge and jury on that charge? For myself I can't see the necessity. There are fellows that an angel from heaven—And I am not that. He was one of those creatures that are just simmering all the time with a silly sort of wickedness. Miserable devils that have no business to live at all. He wouldn't do his duty and wouldn't let anybody else do theirs. But what's the good of talking! You know well enough the sort of ill-conditioned snarling cur—"

He appealed to me as if our experiences had been as identical as our clothes. And I knew well enough the pestiferous danger of such a character where there are no means of legal repression. And I knew well enough also that my double there was no homicidal ruffian. I did not think of asking him for details, and he told me the story roughly in brusque, disconnected sentences. I needed no more. I saw it all going on as though I were myself inside that other sleeping-suit.

"It happened while we were setting a reefed foresail, at dusk. Reefed foresail! You understand the sort of weather. The only sail we had left to keep the ship running; so you may guess what it had been like for days. Anxious sort of job, that. He gave me some of his cursed insolence at the sheet. I tell you I was overdone with this terrific weather that seemed to have no end to it. Terrific, I tell you—and a deep ship. I believe the fellow himself was half crazed with funk. It was no time for gentlemanly reproof, so I turned round and felled him like an ox. He up and at me. We closed just as an awful sea made for the ship. All hands saw it coming and took to the rigging, but I had him by the throat, and went on shaking him like a rat, the men above us yelling, 'Look out! look out!' Then a crash as if the sky had fallen on my head. They say that for over ten minutes hardly anything was to be seen of the ship—just the three masts and a bit of the forecastle head and of the poop all awash driving along in a smother of foam. It was a miracle that they found us, jammed together behind the forebits. It's clear that I meant business, because I was holding him by the throat still when they picked us up. He was black in the face. It was too much for them. It seems they rushed us aft together, gripped as we were, screaming 'Murder!' like a lot of lunatics, and broke into the cuddy. And the ship running for her life, touch and go all the time, any minute her last in a sea fit to turn your hair grey only a-looking at it. I understand that the skipper, too, started raving like the rest of them. The man had been deprived of sleep for more than a week, and to have this sprung on him at the height of a furious gale nearly drove him out of his mind. I wonder they didn't fling me overboard after getting the carcass of their precious ship-mate out of my fingers. They had rather a job to separate us, I've been told. A sufficiently fierce story to make an old judge and a respectable jury sit up a bit. The first thing I heard when I came to myself was the maddening howling of that endless gale, and on that the voice of the old man. He was hanging on to my bunk, staring into my face out of his sou'wester.

" 'Mr. Leggatt, you have killed a man. You can act no longer as chief mate of this ship.' "

His care to subdue his voice made it sound monotonous. He rested a hand on the end of the skylight to steady himself with, and all that time did not stir a limb, so far as I could see. "Nice little tale for a quiet tea-party." he concluded in the same tone.

One of my hands, too, rested on the end of the skylight; neither did I stir a limb, so far as I knew. We stood less than a foot from each other. It occurred to me that if old "Bless my soul—you don't say so" were to put his head up the companion and catch sight of us, he would think he was seeing double, or imagine himself come upon a scene of weird witchcraft; the strange captain having a quiet confabulation by the wheel with his own grey ghost. I became very much concerned to prevent anything of the sort. I heard the other's soothing undertone.

"My father's a parson in Norfolk," it said. Evidently he had forgotten he had told me this important fact before. Truly a nice little tale.

"You had better slip down into my stateroom now," I said, moving off stealthily. My double followed my movements; our bare feet made no sound; I let him in, closed the door with care, and, after giving a call to the second mate, returned on deck for my relief.

"Not much sign of any wind yet," I remarked when he approached.

"No, sir. Not much," he assented, sleepily, in his hoarse voice, with just enough deference, no more, and barely suppressing a yawn.

"Well, that's all you have to look out for. You have got your orders."

"Yes, sir."

I paced a turn or two on the poop and saw him take up his position face forward with his elbow in the ratlines of the mizzen-rigging before I went below. The mate's faint snoring was still going on peacefully. The cuddy lamp was burning over the table on which stood a vase with flowers, a polite attention from the ship's provision merchant—the last flowers we should see for the next three months at the very least. Two bunches of bananas hung from the beam symmetrically, one on each side of the rudder-casing. Everything was as before in the ship—except that two of her captain's sleeping-suits were simultaneously in use, one motionless in the cuddy, the other keeping very still in the captain's stateroom.

It must be explained here that my cabin had the form of the capital letter L, the door being within the angle and opening into the short part of the letter. A couch was to the left, the bed-place to the right; my writing-desk and the chronometers' table faced the door. But any one opening it, unless he stepped right inside, had no view of what I call the long (or vertical) part of the letter. It contained some lockers surmounted by a bookcase; and a few clothes, a thick jacket or two, caps, oilskin coat, and such like, hung on hooks. There was at the bottom of that part a door opening into my bathroom, which could be entered also directly from the saloon. But that way was never used.

The mysterious arrival had discovered the advantage of this particular shape. Entering my room, lighted strongly by a big bulkhead lamp swung on gimbals above my writing-desk, I did not see him anywhere till he stepped out quietly from behind the coats hung in the recessed part.

"I heard somebody moving about, and went in there at once," he whispered.

I, too, spoke under my breath.

"Nobody is likely to come in here without knocking and getting permission."

He nodded. His face was thin and the sunburn faded, as though he had been ill. And no wonder. He had been, I heard presently, kept under arrest in his cabin for nearly seven weeks. But there was nothing sickly in his eyes or in his expression. He was not a bit like me, really; yet, as we stood leaning over my bed-place, whispering side by side, with our dark heads together and our backs to the door, anybody bold enough to open it stealthily would have been treated to the uncanny sight of a double captain busy talking in whispers with his other self.

"But all this doesn't tell me how you came to hang on to our side-ladder," I inquired, in the hardly audible murmurs we used, after he had told me something more of the proceedings on board the *Sephora* once the bad weather was over.

"When we sighted Java Head I had had time to think all those matters out several times over. I had six weeks of doing nothing else, and with only an hour or so every evening for a tramp on the quarter-deck."

He whispered, his arms folded on the side of my bed-place, staring through the open port. And I could imagine perfectly the manner of this thinking out—a stubborn if not a steadfast operation; something of which I should have been perfectly incapable.

"I reckoned it would be dark before we closed with the land," he continued, so low that I had to strain my hearing, near as we were to each other, shoulder touching shoulder almost. "So I asked to speak to the old man. He always seemed very sick when he came to see me—as if he could not look me in the face. You know, that foresail saved the ship. She was too deep to have run long under bare poles. And it was I that managed to set it for him. Anyway, he came. When I had him in my cabin—he stood by the door looking at me as if I had the halter round my neck already—I asked him right away to leave my cabin door unlocked at night while the ship was going through Sunda Straits. There would be the Java coast within two or three miles, off Angier Point. I wanted nothing more. I've had a prize for swimming my second year in the Conway."

"I can believe it," I breathed out.

"God only knows why they locked me in every night. To see some of their faces you'd have thought they were afraid I'd go about at night strangling people. Am I a murdering brute? Do I look it? By Jove! if I had been he wouldn't have trusted himself like that into my room. You'll say I might have chucked him aside and bolted out, there and then—it was dark already. Well, no. And for the same reason I wouldn't think of trying to smash the door. There would have been a rush to stop me at the noise, and I did not mean to get into a confounded scrimmage. Somebody else might have got killed—for I would not have broken out only to get chucked back, and I did not want any more of that work. He refused, looking more sick than ever. He was afraid of the men, and also of that old second mate of his who had been sailing with him for years—a grey-headed old humbug; and his steward, too, had been with him devil knows how long—seventeen years or more—a dogmatic sort of loafer who hated me like poison, just because I was the chief mate. No chief mate ever made more than one voyage in the *Sephora*, you know. Those two old chaps ran the ship. Devil only knows what the skipper wasn't afraid of (all his nerve went to pieces altogether in that hellish spell of bad weather we had)—of what the law would do to him—of his wife, perhaps. Oh, yes! she's on board. Though I don't think she would have meddled. She would have been only too glad to have me out of the ship in any way. The 'brand of Cain' business, don't you see. That's all right. I was ready enough to go off wandering on the face of the earth—and that was price enough to pay for an Abel of that sort. Anyhow, he wouldn't listen to me. 'This thing must take its course. I represent the law here.' He was shaking like a leaf. 'So you won't?' 'No!' 'Then I hope you will be able to sleep on that,' I said, and turned my back on him. 'I wonder that *you* can,' cries he, and locks the door.

"Well, after that, I couldn't. Not very well. That was three weeks ago. We have had a slow passage through the Java Sea; drifted about Carimata for ten days. When we anchored here they thought, I suppose, it was all right. The nearest land (and that's five miles) is the ship's destination; the consul would soon set about catching me; and there would have been no object in bolting to these islets there. I don't suppose there's a drop of water on them. I don't know how it was, but to-night that steward, after bringing me my supper, went out to let me eat it, and left the door unlocked. And I ate it—all there was, too. After I had finished I strolled out on the quarter-deck. I don't know that I meant to do anything. A breath of fresh air was all I wanted, I believe. Then a sudden temptation came over me. I kicked off my slippers and was in the water before I had made up my mind fairly. Somebody heard the splash and they raised an awful hullabaloo. 'He's gone! Lower the boats! He's committed suicide! No, he's swimming.' Certainly I was swimming. It's not so easy for a swimmer like me to commit suicide by drowning. I landed on the nearest islet before the boat left the ship's side. I heard them pulling about in the dark, hailing, and so on, but after a bit they gave up. Everything quieted down and the anchorage became as still as death. I sat down on a stone and began to think. I felt certain they would start searching for me at daylight. There was no place to hide on those stony things—and if there had been, what would have been the good? But now I was clear of that ship, I was not going back. So after a while I took off all my clothes, tied them up in a bundle with a stone inside, and dropped them in the deep water on the outer side of that islet. That was suicide enough for me. Let them think what they liked, but I didn't mean to drown myself. I meant to swim till I sank—but that's not the same thing. I struck out for another of these little islands, and it was from that one that I first saw your riding-light. Something to swim for. I went on easily, and on the way I came upon a flat rock a foot or two above the water. In the daytime I dare say, you might make it out with a glass from your poop. I scrambled up on it and rested myself for a bit. Then I made another start. That last spell must have been over a mile."

His whisper was getting fainter and fainter, and all the time he stared straight out through the port-hole, in which there was not even a star to be seen. I had not interrupted him. There was something that made comment impossible in his narrative, or perhaps in himself; a sort of feeling, a quality, which I can't find a name for. And when he ceased, all I found was a futile whisper: "So you swam for our light?"

"Yes—straight for it. It was something to swim for. I couldn't see any stars low down because the coast was in the way, and I couldn't see the land, either. The water was like glass. One might have been swimming in a confounded thousand-feet deep cistern with no place for scrambling out anywhere; but what I didn't like was the notion of swimming round and round like a crazed bullock before I gave out; and as I didn't mean to go back . . . No. Do you see me being hauled back, stark naked, off one of these little islands by the scruff of the neck and fighting like a wild beast? Somebody would have got killed for certain, and I did not want any of that. So I went on. Then your ladder—"

"Why didn't you hail the ship?" I asked, a little louder.

He touched my shoulder lightly. Lazy footsteps came right over our heads and stopped. The second mate had crossed from the other side of the poop and might have been hanging over the rail, for all we knew.

"He couldn't hear us talking—could he?" My double breathed into my very ear, anxiously.

His anxiety was an answer, a sufficient answer, to the question I had put to him. An answer containing all the difficulty of that situation. I closed the port-hole quietly, to make sure. A louder word might have been overheard.

"Who's that?" he whispered then.

"My second mate. But I don't know much more of the fellow than you do."

And I told him a little about myself. I had been appointed to take charge while I least expected anything of the sort, not quite a fortnight ago. I didn't know either the ship or the people. Hadn't had the time in port to look about me or size anybody up. And as to the crew, all they knew was that I was appointed to take the ship home. For the rest, I was almost as much of a stranger on board as himself, I said. And at the moment I felt it most acutely. I felt that it would take very little to make me a suspect person in the eyes of the ship's company.

He had turned about meantime; and we, the two strangers in the ship, faced each other in identical attitudes.

"Your ladder—" he murmured, after a silence. "Who'd have thought of finding a ladder hanging over at night in a ship anchored out here! I felt just then a very unpleasant faintness. After the life I've been leading for nine weeks, anybody would have got out of condition. I wasn't capable of swimming round as far as your rudder chains. And, lo and behold! there was a ladder to get hold of. After I gripped it I said to myself, 'What's the good?' When I saw a man's head looking over I thought I would swim away presently and leave him shouting—in whatever language it was. I didn't mind being looked at. I—I liked it. And then you speaking to me so quietly,—as if you had expected me—made me hold on a little longer. It had been a confounded lonely time—I don't mean while swimming. I was glad to talk a little to somebody that didn't belong to the *Sephora*. As to asking for the captain, that was a mere impulse. It could have been no use, with all the ship knowing about me and the other people pretty certain to be round here in the morning. I don't know—I wanted to be seen, to talk with somebody, before I went on. I don't know what I would have said. . . . 'Fine night, isn't it?' or something of the sort."

"Do you think they will be round here presently?" I asked with some incredulity.

"Quite likely," he said, faintly.

He looked extremely haggard all of a sudden. His head rolled on his shoulders.

"H'm. We shall see then. Meantime get into that bed," I whispered. "Want help? There."

It was a rather high bed-place with a set of drawers underneath. This amazing swimmer really needed the lift I gave him by seizing his leg. He tumbled in, rolled over on his back and flung one arm across his eyes. And then, with his face nearly hidden, he must have looked exactly as I used to look in that bed. I gazed upon my other self for a while before drawing across carefully the two green serge curtains which ran on a brass rod. I thought for a moment of pinning them together for greater safety, but I sat down on the couch, and once there I felt unwilling to rise and hunt for a pin. I would do it in a moment. I was extremely tired, in a peculiarly intimate way, by the strain of stealthiness, by the effort of whispering and the general secrecy of this excitement. It was three o'clock by now and I had been on my feet since nine, but I was not sleepy; I could not have gone to sleep. I sat there, fagged out, looking at the curtains, trying to clear my mind of the confused sensation of being in two places at once, and greatly bothered by an exasperating knocking in my head. It was a relief to discover suddenly that it was not in my head at all, but on the outside of the door. Before I could collect myself the words "Come in" were out of my mouth, and the steward entered with a tray, bringing in my morning coffee. I had slept, after all, and I was so frightened that I shouted, "This way! I am here, steward," as though he had been miles away. He put down the tray on the table next the couch and only then said, very quietly, "I can see you are here, sir." I felt him give me a keen look, but I dared not meet his eyes just then. He must have wondered why I had drawn the curtains of my bed before going to sleep on the couch. He went out, hooking the door open as usual.

I heard the crew washing decks above me. I knew I would have been told at once if there had been any wind. Calm, I thought, and I was doubly vexed. Indeed, I felt dual more than ever. The steward reappeared suddenly in the doorway. I jumped up from the couch so quickly that he gave a start.

"What do you want here?"

"Close your port, sir—they are washing decks."

"It is closed," I said, reddening.

"Very well, sir." But he did not move from the doorway and returned my stare in an extraordinary, equivocal manner for a time. Then his eyes wavered, all his expression changed, and in a voice unusually gentle, almost coaxingly:

"May I come in to take the empty cup away, sir?"

"Of course!" I turned my back on him while he popped in and out. Then I unhooked and closed the door and even pushed the bolt. This sort of thing could not go on very long. The cabin was as hot as an oven, too. I took a peep at my double, and discovered that he had not moved, his arm was still over his eyes; but his chest heaved; his hair was wet; his chin glistened with perspiration. I reached over him and opened the port.

"I must show myself on deck," I reflected.

Of course, theoretically, I could do what I liked, with no one to say nay to me within the whole circle of the horizon; but to lock my cabin door and take the key away I did not dare. Directly I put my head out of the companion I saw the group of my two officers, the second mate barefooted, the chief mate in long india-rubber boots, near the break of the poop, and the steward halfway down the poop ladder talking to them eagerly. He happened to catch sight of me and dived, the second ran down on the main-deck shouting some order or other, and the chief mate came to meet me, touching his cap.

There was a sort of curiosity in his eye that I did not like. I don't know whether the steward had told them that I was "queer" only, or downright drunk, but I know the man meant to have a good look at me. I watched him coming with a smile which, as he got into point-blank range, took effect and froze his very whiskers. I did not give him time to open his lips.

"Square the yards by lifts and braces before the hands go to breakfast."

It was the first particular order I had given on board that ship; and I stayed on deck to see it executed, too. I had felt the need of asserting myself without loss of time. That sneering young cub got taken down a peg or two on that occasion, and I also seized the opportunity of having a good look at the face of every foremast man as they filed past me to go to the after braces. At breakfast time, eating nothing myself, I presided with such frigid dignity that the two mates were only too glad to escape from the cabin as soon as decency permitted; and all the time the dual working of my mind distracted me almost to the point of insanity. I was constantly watching myself, my secret self, as dependent on my actions as my own personality, sleeping in that bed, behind that door which faced me as I sat at the head of the table. It was very much like being mad, only it was worse because one was aware of it.

I had to shake him for a solid minute, but when at last he opened his eyes it was in the full possession of his senses, with an inquiring look.

"All's well so far," I whispered. "Now you must vanish into the bathroom."

He did so, as noiseless as a ghost, and then I rang for the steward, and facing him boldly, directed him to tidy up my stateroom while I was having my bath—"and be quick about it." As my tone admitted of no excuses, he said, "Yes, sir," and ran off to fetch his dust-pan and brushes. I took a bath and did most of my dressing, splashing, and whistling softly for the steward's edification while the secret sharer of my life stood drawn up bolt upright in that little space, his face looking very sunken in daylight, his eyelids lowered under the stern, dark line of his eyebrows drawn together by a slight frown.

When I left him there to go back to my room the steward was finishing dusting. I sent for the mate and engaged him in some insignificant conversation. It was, as it were, trifling with the terrific character of his whiskers; but my object was to give him an opportunity for a good look at my cabin. And then I could at last shut, with a clear conscience, the door of my stateroom and get my double back into the recessed part. There was nothing else for it. He had to sit still on a small folding stool, half smothered by the heavy coats hanging there. We listened to the steward going into the bathroom out of the saloon, filling the water-bottles there, scrubbing the bath, setting things to rights, whisk, bang, clatter—out again into the saloon—turn the key—click. Such was my scheme for keeping my second self invisible. Nothing better could be contrived under the circumstances. And there we sat; I at my writing-desk ready to appear busy with some papers, he behind me out of sight of the door. It would not have been prudent to talk in day-time; and I could not have stood the excitement of that queer sense of whispering to myself. Now and then, glancing over my shoulder, I saw him far back there, sitting rigidly on the low stool, his bare feet close together, his arms folded, his head hanging on his breast—and perfectly still. Anybody would have taken him for me.

I was fascinated by it myself. Every moment I had to glance over my shoulder. I was looking at him when a voice outside the door said:

"Beg pardon, sir."

"Well!" . . . I kept my eyes on him, and so when the voice outside the door announced, "There's a ship's boat coming our way, sir," I saw him give a start—the first movement he had made for hours. But he did not raise his bowed head.

"All right. Get the ladder over."

I hesitated. Should I whisper something to him? But what? His immobility seemed to have been never disturbed. What could I tell him he did not know already? . . . Finally I went on deck.

II

The skipper of the *Sephora* had a thin red whisker all round his face, and the sort of complexion that goes with hair of that colour; also the particular, rather smeary shade of blue in the eyes. He was not exactly a showy figure; his shoulders were high, his stature but middling—one leg slightly more bandy than the other. He shook hands, looking vaguely around. A spiritless tenacity was his main characteristic, I judged. I behaved with a politeness which seemed to disconcert him. Perhaps he was shy. He mumbled to me as if he were ashamed of what he was saying; gave his name (it was something like Archbold—but at this distance of years I hardly am sure), his ship's name, and a few other particulars of that sort, in the manner of a criminal making a reluctant and doleful confession. He had had terrible weather on the passage out—terrible—terrible—wife aboard, too.

By this time we were seated in the cabin and the steward brought in a tray with a bottle and glasses. "Thanks! No." Never took liquor. Would have some water, though. He drank two tumblerfuls. Terrible thirsty work. Ever since daylight had been exploring the islands round his ship.

"What was that for—fun?" I asked, with an appearance of polite interest.

"No!" He sighed. "Painful duty."

As he persisted in his mumbling and I wanted my double to hear every word, I hit upon the notion of informing him that I regretted to say I was hard of hearing.

"Such a young man, too!" he nodded, keeping his smeary blue, unintelligent eyes fastened upon me. What was the cause of it—some disease? he inquired, without the least sympathy and as if he thought that, if so, I'd got no more than I deserved.

"Yes; disease," I admitted in a cheerful tone which seemed to shock him. But my point was gained, because he had to raise his voice to give me his tale. It is not worth while to record that version. It was just over two months since all this had happened, and he had thought so much about it that he seemed completely muddled as to its bearings, but still immensely impressed.

"What would you think of such a thing happening on board your own ship? I've had the *Sephora* for these fifteen years. I am a well-known shipmaster."

He was densely distressed—and perhaps I should have sympathised with him if I had been able to detach my mental vision from the unsuspected sharer of my cabin as though he were my second self. There he was on the other side of the bulkhead, four or five feet from us, no more, as we sat in the saloon. I looked politely at Captain Archbold (if that was his name), but it was the other I saw, in a grey sleeping-suit, seated on a low stool, his bare feet close together, his arms folded, and every word said between us falling into the ears of his dark head bowed on his chest.

"I have been at sea now, man and boy, for seven-and-thirty years, and I've never heard of such a thing happening in an English ship. And that it should be my ship. Wife on board, too."

I was hardly listening to him.

"Don't you think," I said, "that the heavy sea which, you told me, came aboard just then might have killed the man? I have seen the sheer weight of a sea kill a man very neatly, by simply breaking his neck."

"Good God!" he uttered, impressively, fixing his smeary blue eyes on me. "The sea! No man killed by the sea ever looked like that." He seemed positively scandalised at my suggestion. And as I gazed at him, certainly not prepared for anything original on his part, he advanced his head close to mine and thrust his tongue out at me so suddenly that I couldn't help starting back.

After scoring over my calmness in this graphic way he nodded wisely. If I had seen the sight, he assured me, I would never forget it as long as I lived. The weather was too bad to give the corpse a proper sea burial. So next day at dawn they took it up on the poop, covering its face with a bit of bunting; he read a short prayer, and then, just as it was, in its oilskins and long boots, they launched it amongst those mountainous seas that seemed ready every moment to swallow up the ship herself and the terrified lives on board of her.

"That reefed foresail saved you," I threw in.

"Under God—it did," he exclaimed fervently. "It was by a special mercy, I firmly believe, that it stood some of those hurricane squalls."

"It was the setting of that sail which—" I began.

"God's own hand in it," he interrupted me. "Nothing less could have done it. I don't mind telling you that I hardly dared give the order. It seemed impossible that we could touch anything without losing it, and then our last hope would have been gone."

The terror of that gale was on him yet. I let him go on for a bit, then said, casually—as if returning to a minor subject:

"You were very anxious to give up your mate to the shore people, I believe?"

He was. To the law. His obscure tenacity on that point had in it something incomprehensible and a little awful; something, as it were, mystical, quite apart from his anxiety that he should not be suspected of "countenancing any doings of that sort." Seven-and-thirty virtuous years at sea, of which over twenty of immaculate command, and the last fifteen in the *Sephora,* seemed to have laid him under some pitiless obligation.

"And you know," he went on, groping shamefacedly amongst his feelings, "I did not engage that young fellow. His people had some interest with my owners. I was in a way forced to take him on. He looked very smart, very gentlemanly, and all that. But do you know—I never liked him, somehow. I am a plain man. You see, he wasn't exactly the sort for the chief mate of a ship like the *Sephora*."

I had become so connected in thoughts and impressions with the secret sharer of my cabin that I felt as if I, personally, were being given to understand that I, too, was not the sort that would have done for the chief mate of a ship like the *Sephora*. I had no doubt of it in my mind.

"Not at all the style of man. You understand," he insisted, superfluously, looking hard at me.

I smiled urbanely. He seemed at a loss for a while.

"I suppose I must report a suicide."

"Beg pardon?"

"Sui-cide! That's what I'll have to write to my owners directly I get in."

"Unless you manage to recover him before to-morrow," I assented, dispassionately. . . . "I mean, alive."

He mumbled something which I really did not catch, and I turned my ear to him in a puzzled manner. He fairly bawled:

"The land—I say, the mainland is at least seven miles off my anchorage."

"About that."

My lack of excitement, of curiosity, of surprise, of any sort of pronounced interest, began to arouse his distrust. But except for the felicitous pretence of deafness I had not tried to pretend anything. I had felt utterly incapable of playing the part of ignorance properly, and therefore was afraid to try. It is also certain that he had brought some ready-made suspicions with him, and that he viewed my politeness as a strange and unnatural phenomenon. And yet how else could I have received him? Not heartily! That was impossible for psychological reasons, which I need not state here. My only object was to keep off his inquiries. Surlily? Yes, but surliness might have provoked a point-blank question. From its novelty to him and from its nature, punctilious courtesy was the manner best calculated to restrain the man. But there was the danger of his breaking through my defence bluntly. I could not, I think, have met him by a direct lie, also for psychological (not moral) reasons. If he had only known how afraid I was of his putting my feeling of identity with the other to the test! But, strangely enough—(I thought of it only afterwards)—I believe that he was not a little disconcerted by the reverse side of that weird situation, by something in me that reminded him of the man he was seeking—suggested a mysterious similitude to the young fellow he had distrusted and disliked from the first.

However that might have been, the silence was not very prolonged. He took another oblique step.

"I reckon I had no more than a two-mile pull to your ship. Not a bit more."

"And quite enough, too, in this awful heat," I said.

Another pause full of mistrust followed. Necessity, they say, is mother of invention, but fear, too, is not barren of ingenious suggestions. And I was afraid he would ask me point-blank for news of my other self.

"Nice little saloon, isn't it?" I remarked, as if noticing for the first time the way his eyes roamed from one closed door to the other. "And very well fitted out, too. Here, for instance," I continued, reaching over the back of my seat negligently and flinging the door open, "is my bath-room."

He made an eager movement, but hardly gave it a glance. I got up, shut the door of the bath-room, and invited him to have a look round, as if I were very proud of my accommodation. He had to rise and be shown round, but he went through the business without any raptures whatever.

"And now we'll have a look at my stateroom," I declared, in a voice as loud as I dared to make it, crossing the cabin to the starboard side with purposely heavy steps.

He followed me in and gazed around. My intelligent double had vanished. I played my part.

"Very convenient—isn't it?"

"Very nice. Very comf . . . ." He didn't finish and went out brusquely as if to escape from some unrighteous wiles of mine. But it was not to be. I had been too frightened not to feel vengeful; I felt I had him on the run, and I meant to keep him on the run. My polite insistence must have had something menacing in it, because he gave in suddenly. And I did not let him off a single item; mate's room, pantry, storerooms, the very sail-locker which was also under the poop—he had to look into them all. When at last I showed him out on the quarter-deck he drew a long, spiritless sigh, and mumbled dismally that he must really be going back to his ship now. I desired my mate, who had joined us, to see to the captain's boat.

The man of whiskers gave a blast on the whistle which he used to wear hanging round his neck, and yelled, "*Sephora*'s away!" My double down there in my cabin must have heard, and certainly could not feel more relieved than I. Four fellows came running out from somewhere forward and went over the side, while my own men, appearing on deck too, lined the rail. I escorted my visitor to the gangway ceremoniously, and nearly overdid it. He was a tenacious beast. On the very ladder he lingered, and in that unique, guiltily conscientious manner of sticking to the point:

"I say . . . you . . . you don't think that—"

I covered his voice loudly:

"Certainly not. . . . I am delighted. Good-bye."

I had an idea of what he meant to say, and just saved myself by the privilege of defective hearing. He was too shaken generally to insist, but my mate, close witness of that parting, looked mystified and his face took on a thoughtful cast. As I did not want to appear as if I wished to avoid all communication with my officers, he had the opportunity to address me.

"Seems a very nice man. His boat's crew told our chaps a very extraordinary story, if what I am told by the steward is true. I suppose you had it from the captain, sir?"

"Yes. I had a story from the captain."

"A very horrible affair—isn't it, sir?"

"It is."

"Beats all these tales we hear about murders in Yankee ships."

"I don't think it beats them. I don't think it resembles them in the least."

"Bless my soul—you don't say so! But of course I've no acquaintance whatever with American ships, not I, so I couldn't go against your knowledge. It's horrible enough to me. . . . But the queerest part is that those fellows seemed to have some idea the man was hidden aboard here. They had really. Did you ever hear of such a thing?"

"Preposterous—isn't it?"

We were walking to and fro athwart the quarter-deck. No one of the crew forward could be seen (the day was Sunday), and the mate pursued:

"There was some little dispute about it. Our chaps took offence. 'As if we would harbour a thing like that,' they said. 'Wouldn't you like to look for him in our coal-hold?' Quite a tiff. But they made it up in the end. I suppose he did drown himself. Don't you, sir?"

"I don't suppose anything."

"You have no doubt in the matter, sir?"

"None whatever."

I left him suddenly. I felt I was producing a bad impression, but with my double down there it was most trying to be on deck. And it was almost as trying to be below. Altogether a nerve-trying situation. But on the whole I felt less torn in two when I was with him. There was no one in the whole ship whom I dared take into my confidence. Since the hands had got to know his story, it would have been impossible to pass him off for any one else, and an accidental discovery was to be dreaded now more than ever. . . .

The steward being engaged in laying the table for dinner, we could talk only with our eyes when I first went down. Later in the afternoon we had a cautious try at whispering. The Sunday quietness of the ship was against us; the stillness of air and water around her was against us; the elements, the men were against us—everything was against us in our secret partnership; time itself—for this could not go on forever. The very trust in Providence was, I suppose, denied to his guilt. Shall I confess that this thought cast me down very much? And as to the chapter of accidents which counts for so much in the book of success, I could only hope that it was closed. For what favourable accident could be expected?

"Did you hear everything?" were my first words as soon as we took up our position side by side, leaning over my bed-place.

He had. And the proof of it was his earnest whisper, "The man told you he hardly dared to give the order."

I understood the reference to be to that saving foresail.

"Yes. He was afraid of it being lost in the setting."

"I assure you he never gave the order. He may think he did, but he never gave it. He stood there with me on the break of the poop after the maintopsail blew away, and whimpered about our last hope—positively whimpered about it and nothing else—and the night coming on! To hear one's skipper go on like that in such weather was enough to drive any fellow out of his mind. It worked me up into a sort of desperation. I just took it into my own hands and went away from him, boiling, and—But what's the use telling you? *You know!* . . . Do you think that if I had not been pretty fierce with them I should have got the men to do anything? Not it! The bo's'n perhaps? Perhaps! It wasn't a heavy sea—it was a sea gone mad! I suppose the end of the world will be something like that; and a man may have the heart to see it coming once and be done with it—but to have to face it day after day—I don't blame anybody. I was precious little better than the rest. Only—I as an officer of that old coal-wagon, anyhow—"

"I quite understand," I conveyed that sincere assurance into his ear. He was out of breath with whispering; I could hear him pant slightly. It was all very simple. The same strung-up force which had given twenty-four men a chance, at least, for their lives, had, in a sort of recoil, crushed an unworthy mutinous existence.

But I had no leisure to weigh the merits of the matter—footsteps in the saloon, a heavy knock. "There's enough wind to get under way with, sir." Here was the call of a new claim upon my thoughts and even upon my feelings.

"Turn the hands up," I cried through the door. "I'll be on deck directly."

I was going out to make the acquaintance of my ship. Before I left the cabin our eyes met—the eyes of the only two strangers on board. I pointed to the recessed part where the little camp-stool awaited him and laid my finger on my lips. He made a gesture—somewhat vague—a little mysterious, accompanied by a faint smile, as if of regret.

This is not the place to enlarge upon the sensations of a man who feels for the first time a ship move under his feet to his own independent word. In my case they were not unalloyed. I was not wholly alone with my command; for there was that stranger in my cabin. Or rather, I was not completely and wholly with her. Part of me was absent. That mental feeling of being in two places at once affected me physically as if the mood of secrecy had penetrated my very soul. Before an hour had elapsed since the ship had begun to move, having occasion to ask the mate (he stood by my side) to take a compass bearing of the Pagoda, I caught myself reaching up to his ear in whispers. I say I caught myself, but enough had escaped to startle the man. I can't describe it otherwise than by saying that he shied. A grave, preoccupied manner, as though he were in possession of some perplexing intelligence, did not leave him henceforth. A little later I moved away from the rail to look at the compass with such a stealthy gait that the helmsman noticed it—and I could not help noticing the unusual roundness of his eyes. These are trifling instances, though it's to no commander's advantage to be suspected of ludicrous eccentricities. But I was also more seriously affected. There are to a seaman certain words, gestures, that should in given conditions come as naturally, as instinctively as the winking of a menaced eye. A certain order should spring on to his lips without thinking; a certain sign should get itself made, so to speak, without reflection. But all unconscious alertness had abandoned me. I had to make an effort of will to recall myself back (from the cabin) to the conditions of the moment. I felt that I was appearing an irresolute commander to those people who were watching me more or less critically.

And, besides, there were the scares. On the second day out, for instance, coming off the deck in the afternoon (I had straw slippers on my bare feet) I stopped at the open pantry door and spoke to the steward. He was doing something there with his back to me. At the sound of my voice he nearly jumped out of his skin, as the saying is, and incidentally broke a cup.

"What on earth's the matter with you?" I asked, astonished.

He was extremely confused. "Beg your pardon, sir. I made sure you were in your cabin."

"You see I wasn't."

"No, sir. I could have sworn I had heard you moving in there not a moment ago. It's most extraordinary . . . very sorry, sir."

I passed on with an inward shudder. I was so identified with my secret double that I did not even mention the fact in those scanty, fearful whispers we exchanged. I suppose he had made some slight noise of some kind or other. It would have been miraculous if he hadn't at one time or another. And yet, haggard as he appeared, he looked always perfectly self-controlled, more than calm—almost invulnerable. On my suggestion he remained almost entirely in the bath-room, which, upon the whole, was the safest place. There could be really no shadow of an excuse for any one ever wanting to go in there, once the steward had done with it. It was a very tiny place. Sometimes he reclined on the floor, his legs bent, his head sustained on one elbow. At others I would find him on the camp-stool, sitting in his grey sleeping-suit and with his cropped dark hair like a patient, unmoved convict. At night I would smuggle him into my bed-place, and we would whisper together, with the regular foot-falls of the officer of the watch passing and repassing over our heads. It was an infinitely miserable time. It was lucky that some tins of fine preserves were stowed in a locker in my stateroom; hard bread I could always get hold of; and so he lived on stewed chicken, paté de foie gras, asparagus, cooked oysters, sardines—on all sorts of abominable sham delicacies out of tins. My early morning coffee he always drank; and it was all I dared do for him in that respect.

Every day there was the horrible manoeuvring to go through so that my room and then the bath-room should be done in the usual way. I came to hate the sight of the steward, to abhor the voice of that harmless man. I felt that it was he who would bring on the disaster of discovery. It hung like a sword over our heads.

The fourth day out, I think (we were then working down the east side of the Gulf of Siam, tack for tack, in light winds and smooth water)—the fourth day, I say, of this miserable juggling with the unavoidable, as we sat at our evening meal, that man, whose slightest movement I dreaded, after putting down the dishes ran up on deck busily. This could not be dangerous. Presently he came down again; and then it appeared that he had remembered a coat of mine which I had thrown over a rail to dry after having been wetted in a shower which had passed over the ship in the afternoon. Sitting stolidly at the head of the table I became terrified at the sight of the garment on his arm. Of course he made for my door. There was no time to lose.

"Steward," I thundered. My nerves were so shaken that I could not govern my voice and conceal my agitation. This was the sort of thing that made my terrifically whiskered mate tap his forehead with his forefinger. I had detected him using that gesture while talking on deck with a confidential air to the carpenter. It was too far to hear a word, but I had no doubt that this pantomime could only refer to the strange new captain.

"Yes, sir," the pale-faced steward turned resignedly to me. It was this maddening course of being shouted at, checked without rhyme or reason, arbitrarily chased out of my cabin, suddenly called into it, sent flying out of his pantry on incomprehensible errands, that accounted for the growing wretchedness of his expression.

"Where are you going with that coat?"

"To your room, sir."

"Is there another shower coming?"

"I'm sure I don't know, sir. Shall I go up again and see, sir?"

"No! never mind."

My object was attained, as of course my other self in there would have heard everything that passed. During this interlude my two officers never raised their eyes off their respective plates; but the lip of that confounded cub, the second mate, quivered visibly.

I expected the steward to hook my coat on and come out at once. He was very slow about it; but I dominated my nervousness sufficiently not to shout after him. Suddenly I became aware (it could be heard plainly enough) that the fellow for some reason or other was opening the door of the bath-room. It was the end. The place was literally not big enough to swing a cat in. My voice died in my throat and I went stony all over. I expected to hear a yell of surprise and terror, and made a movement, but had not the strength to get on my legs. Everything remained still. Had my second self taken the poor wretch by the throat? I don't know what I could have done next moment if I had not seen the steward come out of my room, close the door, and then stand quietly by the sideboard.

"Saved," I thought. "But, no! Lost! Gone! He was gone!"

I laid my knife and fork down and leaned back in my chair. My head swam. After a while, when sufficiently recovered to speak in a steady voice, I instructed my mate to put the ship round at eight o'clock himself.

"I won't come on deck," I went on. "I think I'll turn in, and unless the wind shifts I don't want to be disturbed before midnight. I feel a bit seedy."

"You did look middling bad a little while ago," the chief mate remarked without showing any great concern.

They both went out, and I stared at the steward clearing the table. There was nothing to be read on that wretched man's face. But why did he avoid my eyes I asked myself. Then I thought I should like to hear the sound of his voice.

"Steward!"

"Sir!" Startled as usual.

"Where did you hang up that coat?"

"In the bath-room, sir." The usual anxious tone. "It's not quite dry yet, sir."

For some time longer I sat in the cuddy. Had my double vanished as he had come? But of his coming there was an explanation, whereas his disappearance would be inexplicable. . . . I went slowly into my dark room, shut the door, lighted the lamp, and for a time dared not turn round. When at last I did I saw him standing bolt upright in the narrow recessed part. It would not be true to say I had a shock, but an irresistible doubt of his bodily existence flitted through my mind. Can it be, I asked myself, that he is not visible to other eyes than mine? It was like being haunted. Motionless, with a grave face, he raised his hands slightly at me in a gesture which meant clearly, "Heavens! what a narrow escape!" Narrow indeed. I think I had come creeping quietly as near insanity as any man who has not actually gone over the border. That gesture restrained me, so to speak.

The mate with the terrific whiskers was now putting the ship on the other tack. In the moment of profound silence which follows upon the hands going to their stations I heard on the poop his raised voice: "Hard alee!" and the distant shout of the order repeated on the maindeck. The sails, in that light breeze, made but a faint fluttering noise. It ceased. The ship was coming round slowly; I held my breath in the renewed stillness of expectation; one wouldn't have thought that there was a single living soul on her decks. A sudden brisk shout, "Mainsail haul!" broke the spell, and in the noisy cries and rush overhead of the men running away with the mainbrace we two, down in my cabin, came together in our usual position by the bed-place.

He did not wait for my question. "I heard him fumbling here and just managed to squat myself down in the bath," he whispered to me. "The fellow only opened the door and put his arm in to hang the coat up. All the same—"

"I never thought of that," I whispered back, even more appalled than before at the closeness of the shave, and marvelling at that something unyielding in his character which was carrying him through so finely. There was no agitation in his whisper. Whoever was being driven distracted, it was not he. He was sane. And the proof of his sanity was continued when he took up the whispering again.

"It would never do for me to come to life again."

It was something that a ghost might have said. But what he was alluding to was his old captain's reluctant admission of the theory of suicide. It would obviously serve his turn—if I had understood at all the view which seemed to govern the unalterable purpose of his action.

"You must maroon me as soon as ever you can get amongst these islands off the Cambodje shore," he went on.

"Maroon you! We are not living in a boy's adventure tale," I protested. His scornful whispering took me up.

"We aren't indeed! There's nothing of a boy's tale in this. But there's nothing else for it. I want no more. You don't suppose I am afraid of what can be done to me? Prison or gallows or whatever they may please. But you don't see me coming back to explain such things to an old fellow in a wig and twelve respectable tradesmen, do you? What can they know whether I am guilty or not—or of *what* I am guilty, either? That's my affair. What does the Bible say? 'Driven off the face of the earth.' Very well. I am off the face of the earth now. As I came at night so I shall go."

"Impossible!" I murmured. "You can't."

"Can't? . . . Not naked like a soul on the Day of Judgment. I shall freeze on to this sleeping-suit. The Last Day is not yet—and . . . you have understood thoroughly. Didn't you?"

I felt suddenly ashamed of myself. I may say truly that I understood—and my hesitation in letting that man swim away from my ship's side had been a mere sham sentiment, a sort of cowardice.

"It can't be done now till next night," I breathed out. "The ship is on the off-shore tack and the wind may fail us."

"As long as I know that you understand," he whispered. "But of course you do. It's a great satisfaction to have got somebody to understand. You seem to have been there on purpose." And in the same whisper, as if we two whenever we talked had to say things to each other which were not fit for the world to hear, he added, "It's very wonderful."

We remained side by side talking in our secret way—but sometimes silent or just exchanging a whispered word or two at long intervals. And as usual he stared through the port. A breath of wind came now and again into our faces. The ship might have been moored in dock, so gently and on an even keel she slipped through the water, that did not murmur even at our passage, shadowy and silent like a phantom sea.

At midnight I went on deck, and to my mate's great surprise put the ship round on the other tack. His terrible whiskers flitted round me in silent criticism. I certainly should not have done it if it had been only a question of getting out of that sleepy gulf as quickly as possible. I believe he told the second mate, who relieved him, that it was a great want of judgment. The other only yawned. That intolerable cub shuffled about so sleepily and lolled against the rails in such a slack, improper fashion that I came down on him sharply.

"Aren't you properly awake yet?"

"Yes, sir! I am awake."

"Well, then, be good enough to hold yourself as if you were. And keep a look-out. If there's any current we'll be closing with some islands before daylight."

The east side of the gulf is fringed with islands, some solitary, others in groups. On the blue background of the high coast they seem to float on silvery patches of calm water, arid and grey, or dark green and rounded like clumps of evergreen bushes, with the larger ones, a mile or two long, showing the outlines of ridges, ribs of grey rock under the dank mantle of matted leafage. Unknown to trade, to travel, almost to geography, the manner of life they harbour is an unsolved secret. There must be villages—settlements of fishermen at least—on the largest of them, and some communication with the world is probably kept up by native craft. But all that forenoon, as we headed for them, fanned along by the faintest of breezes, I saw no sign of man or canoe in the field of the telescope I kept on pointing at the scattered group.

At noon I gave no orders for a change of course, and the mate's whiskers became much concerned and seemed to be offering themselves unduly to my notice. At last I said:

"I am going to stand right in. Quite in—as far as I can take her."

The stare of extreme surprise imparted an air of ferocity also to his eyes, and he looked truly terrific for a moment.

"We're not doing well in the middle of the gulf," I continued, casually. "I am going to look for the land breezes to-night."

"Bless my soul! Do you mean, sir, in the dark amongst the lot of all them islands and reefs and shoals?"

"Well—if there are any regular land breezes at all on this coast one must get close inshore to find them, mustn't one?"

"Bless my soul!" he exclaimed again under his breath. All that afternoon he wore a dreamy, contemplative appearance which in him was a mark of perplexity. After dinner I went into my stateroom as if I meant to take some rest. There we two bent our dark heads over a half-unrolled chart lying on my bed.

"There," I said. "It's got to be Koh-ring. I've been looking at it ever since sunrise. It has got two hills and a low point. It must be inhabited. And on the coast opposite there is what looks like the mouth of a biggish river—with some town, no doubt, not far up. It's the best chance for you that I can see."

"Anything. Koh-ring let it be."

He looked thoughtfully at the chart as if surveying chances and distances from a lofty height—and following with his eyes his own figure wandering on the blank land of Cochin-China, and then passing off that piece of paper clean out of sight into uncharted regions. And it was as if the ship had two captains to plan her course for her. I had been so worried and restless running up and down that I had not had the patience to dress that day. I had remained in my sleeping-suit, with straw slippers and a soft floppy hat. The closeness of the heat in the gulf had been most oppressive, and the crew were used to see me wandering in that airy attire.

"She will clear the south point as she heads now," I whispered into his ear. "Goodness only knows when, though, but certainly after dark. I'll edge her in to half a mile, as far as I may be able to judge in the dark—"

"Be careful," he murmured, warningly—and I realised suddenly that all my future, the only future for which I was fit, would perhaps go irretrievably to pieces in any mishap to my first command.

I could not stop a moment longer in the room. I motioned him to get out of sight and made my way on the poop. That unplayful cub had the watch. I walked up and down for a while thinking things out, then beckoned him over.

"Send a couple of hands to open the two quarter-deck ports," I said, mildly.

He actually had the impudence, or else so forgot himself in his wonder at such an incomprehensible order, as to repeat:

"Open the quarter-deck ports! What for, sir?"

"The only reason you need concern yourself about is because I tell you to do so. Have them open wide and fastened properly."

He reddened and went off, but I believe made some jeering remark to the carpenter as to the sensible practice of ventilating a ship's quarter-deck. I know he popped into the mate's cabin to impart the fact to him because the whiskers came on deck, as it were by chance, and stole glances at me from below—for signs of lunacy or drunkenness, I suppose.

A little before supper, feeling more restless than ever, I rejoined, for a moment, my second self. And to find him sitting so quietly was surprising, like something against nature, inhuman.

I developed my plan in a hurried whisper.

"I shall stand in as close as I dare and then put her round. I will presently find means to smuggle you out of here into the sail-locker, which communicates with the lobby. But there is an opening, a sort of square for hauling the sails out, which gives straight on the quarter-deck and which is never closed in fine weather, so as to give air to the sails. When the ship's way is deadened in stays and all the hands are aft at the main-braces you will have a clear road to slip out and get overboard through the open quarter-deck port. I've had them both fastened up. Use a rope's end to lower yourself into the water so as to avoid a splash—you know. It could be heard and cause some beastly complication."

He kept silent for a while, then whispered, "I understand."

"I won't be there to see you go," I began with an effort. "The rest . . . I only hope I have understood, too."

"You have. From first to last"—and for the first time there seemed to be a faltering, something strained in his whisper. He caught hold of my arm, but the ringing of the supper bell made me start. He didn't, though; he only released his grip.

After supper I didn't come below again till well past eight o'clock. The faint, steady breeze was loaded with dew; and the wet, darkened sails held all there was of propelling power in it. The night, clear and starry, sparkled darkly, and the opaque, lightless patches shifting slowly against the low stars were the drifting islets. On the port bow there was a big one more distant and shadowily imposing by the great space of sky it eclipsed.

On opening the door I had a back view of my very own self looking at a chart. He had come out of the recess and was standing near the table.

"Quite dark enough," I whispered.

He stepped back and leaned against my bed with a level, quiet glance. I sat on the couch. We had nothing to say to each other. Over our heads the officer of the watch moved here and there. Then I heard him move quickly. I knew what that meant. He was making for the companion; and presently his voice was outside my door.

"We are drawing in pretty fast, sir. Land looks rather close."

"Very well, " I answered. "I am coming on deck directly."

I waited till he was gone out of the cuddy, then rose. My double moved too. The time had come to exchange our last whispers, for neither of us was ever to hear each other's natural voice.

"Look here!" I opened a drawer and took out three sovereigns. "Take this anyhow. I've got six and I'd give you the lot, only I must keep a little money to buy some fruit and vegetables for the crew from native boats as we go through Sunda Straits."

He shook his head.

"Take it," I urged him, whispering desperately. "No one can tell what—"

He smiled and slapped meaningly the only pocket of the sleeping-jacket. It was not safe, certainly. But I produced a large old silk handkerchief of mine, and tying the three pieces of gold in a corner, pressed it on him. He was touched, I suppose, because he took it at last, and tied it quickly round his waist under the jacket, on his bare skin.

Our eyes met; several seconds elapsed, till, our glances still mingled, I extended my hand and turned the lamp out. Then I passed through the cuddy, leaving the door of my room wide open. . . . "Steward!"

He was still lingering in the pantry in the greatness of his zeal, giving a rub-up to a plated cruet stand the last thing before going to bed. Being careful not to wake up the mate, whose room was opposite, I spoke in an undertone.

He looked round anxiously. "Sir!"

"Can you get me a little hot water from the galley?"

"I am afraid, sir, the galley fire's been out for some time now."

"Go and see."

He flew up the stairs.

"Now," I whispered, loudly, into the saloon—too loudly, perhaps, but I was afraid I couldn't make a sound. He was by my side in an instant—the double captain slipped past the stairs—through a tiny dark passage . . . a sliding door. We were in the sail-locker, scrambling on our knees over the sails. A sudden thought struck me. I saw myself wandering barefooted, bareheaded, the sun beating on my dark poll. I snatched off my floppy hat and tried hurriedly in the dark to ram it on my other self. He dodged and fended off silently. I wonder what he thought had come to me before he understood and suddenly desisted. Our hands met gropingly, lingered united in a steady, motionless clasp for a second. . . . No word was breathed by either of us when they separated.

I was standing quietly by the pantry door when the steward returned.

"Sorry, sir. Kettle barely warm. Shall I light the spirit-lamp?"

"Never mind."

I came out on deck slowly. It was now a matter of conscience to shave the land as close as possible—for now he must go overboard whenever the ship was put in stays. Must! There could be no going back for him. After a moment I walked over to leeward and my heart flew into my mouth at the nearness of the land on the bow. Under any other circumstances I would not have held on a minute longer. The second mate had followed me anxiously.

I looked on till I felt I could command my voice.

"She may weather," I said then in a quiet tone.

"Are you going to try that, sir?" he stammered out incredulously.

I took no notice of him and raised my tone just enough to be heard by the helmsman.

"Keep her good full."

"Good full, sir."

The wind fanned my cheek, the sails slept, the world was silent. The strain of watching the dark loom of the land grow bigger and denser was too much for me. I had shut my eyes—because the ship must go closer. She must! The stillness was intolerable. Were we standing still?

When I opened my eyes the second view started my heart with a thump. The black southern hill of Koh-ring seemed to hang right over the ship like a towering fragment of the everlasting night. On that enormous mass of blackness there was not a gleam to be seen, not a sound to be heard. It was gliding irresistibly towards us and yet seemed already within reach of the hand. I saw the vague figures of the watch grouped in the waist, gazing in awed silence.

"Are you going on, sir?" inquired an unsteady voice at my elbow.

I ignored it. I had to go on.

"Keep her full. Don't check her way. That won't do now," I said, warningly.

"I can't see the sails very well," the helmsman answered me, in strange, quavering tones.

Was she close enough? Already she was, I won't say in the shadow of the land, but in the very blackness of it, already swallowed up as it were, gone too close to be recalled, gone from me altogether.

"Give the mate a call," I said to the young man who stood at my elbow as still as death. "And turn all hands up."

My tone had a borrowed loudness reverberated from the height of the land. Several voices cried out together: "We are all on deck, sir."

Then stillness again, with the great shadow gliding closer, towering higher, without light, without a sound. Such a hush had fallen on the ship that she might have been a bark of the dead floating in slowly under the very gate of Erebus.

"My God! Where are we?"

It was the mate moaning at my elbow. He was thunderstruck, and as it were deprived of the moral support of his whiskers. He clapped his hands and absolutely cried out, "Lost!"

"Be quiet," I said, sternly.

He lowered his tone, but I saw the shadowy gesture of his despair. "What are we doing here?"

"Looking for the land wind."

He made as if to tear his hair, and addressed me recklessly.

"She will never get out. You have done it, sir. I knew it'd end in something like this. She will never weather, and you are too close now to stay. She'll drift ashore before she's round. O my God!"

I caught his arm as he was raising it to batter his poor devoted head, and shook it violently.

"She's ashore already," he wailed, trying to tear himself away.

"Is she? . . . Keep good full there!"

"Good full, sir," cried the helmsman in a frightened, thin, child-like voice.

I hadn't let go the mate's arm and went on shaking it. "Ready about, do you hear? You go forward"—shake—"and stop there"—shake—"and hold your noise"—shake—"and see these head-sheets properly overhauled"—shake, shake—shake.

And all the time I dared not look towards the land lest my heart should fail me. I released my grip at last and he ran forward as if fleeing for dear life.

I wondered what my double there in the sail-locker thought of this commotion. He was able to hear everything—and perhaps he was able to understand why, on my conscience, it had to be thus close—no less. My first order "Hard alee!" re-echoed ominously under the towering shadow of Koh-ring as if I had shouted in a mountain gorge. And then I watched the land intently. In that smooth water and light wind it was impossible to feel the ship coming-to. No! I could not feel her. And my second self was making now ready to slip out and lower himself overboard. Perhaps he was gone already . . . ?

The great black mass brooding over our very mastheads began to pivot away from the ship's side silently. And now I forgot the secret stranger ready to depart, and remembered only that I was a total stranger to the ship. I did not know her. Would she do it? How was she to be handled?

I swung the mainyard and waited helplessly. She was perhaps stopped, and her very fate hung in the balance, with the black mass of Koh-ring like the gate of the everlasting night towering over her taffrail. What would she do now? Had she way on her yet? I stepped to the side swiftly, and on the shadowy water I could see nothing except a faint phosphorescent flash revealing the glassy smoothness of the sleeping surface. It was impossible to tell—and I had not learned yet the feel of my ship. Was she moving? What I needed was something easily seen, a piece of paper, which I could throw overboard and watch. I had nothing on me. To run down for it I didn't dare. There was no time. All at once my strained, yearning stare distinguished a white object floating within a yard of the ship's side. White on the black water. A phosphorescent flash passed under it. What was that thing? . . . I recognised my own floppy hat. It must have fallen off his head . . . and he didn't bother. Now I had what I wanted—the saving mark for my eyes. But I hardly thought of my other self, now gone from the ship, to be hidden for ever from all friendly faces, to be a fugitive and a vagabond on the earth, with no brand of the curse on his sane forehead to stay a slaying hand . . . too proud to explain.

And I watched the hat—the expression of my sudden pity for his mere flesh. It had been meant to save his homeless head from the dangers of the sun. And now—behold—it was saving the ship, by serving me for a mark to help out the ignorance of my strangeness. Ha! It was drifting forward, warning me just in time that the ship had gathered sternway.

"Shift the helm," I said in a low voice to the seaman standing still like a statue.

The man's eyes glistened wildly in the binnacle light as he jumped round to the other side and spun round the wheel.

I walked to the break of the poop. On the over-shadowed deck all hands stood by the forebraces waiting for my order. The stars ahead seemed to be gliding from right to left. And all was so still in the world that I heard the quiet remark "She's round," passed in a tone of intense relief between two seamen.

"Let go and haul."

The foreyards ran round with a great noise, amidst cheery cries. And now the frightful whiskers made themselves heard giving various orders. Already the ship was drawing ahead. And I was alone with her. Nothing! no one in the world should stand now between us, throwing a shadow on the way of silent knowledge and mute affection, the perfect communion of a seaman with his first command.

Walking to the taffrail, I was in time to make out, on the very edge of a darkness thrown by a towering black mass like the very gateway of Erebus— yes, I was in time to catch an evanescent glimpse of my white hat left behind to mark the spot where the secret sharer of my cabin and of my thoughts, as though he were my second self, had lowered himself into the water to take his punishment: a free man, a proud swimmer striking out for a new destiny.

Exercises

1. What is the particular situation of the young captain with regard to his command? What does this have to do with the arrival of Leggatt and the captain's decision to hide him?

2. This story has been interpreted in many different ways. Comment on the following ways it might be read, supporting each one as best you can.

   (a) A conflict between loyalty to the individual and loyalty to the community.

   (b) An initiation story of a young man who undergoes a test of his abilities.

   (c) A psychological split in personality: Leggatt is half the captain's own self.

3. Note that Leggatt appears when the captain looks into the water. How is this similar to and different from the ancient myth of Narcissus, who became so fascinated with his reflection (which he took to be someone else) that he fell into the water and drowned?

4. How can a conflict within a person cause a sense of being split? What is the value of perceiving inner stuff as if it were outer stuff, of talking to oneself when troubled?

5. How does the appearance of Leggatt make the captain's position in a new command even more difficult than it would otherwise have been?

6. Why does the captain feel he must make the risk of getting Leggatt close to the island even more severe than need be? Why does taking this risk free the captain of Leggatt? Why does it simultaneously also release him from the anxiety he felt at the beginning?

PART
THREE

The World of Fable, Legend, Allegory, and Myth

The most ancient desire that underlies the impulse to tell a story is the need to account for things. Primitive stories that account for basic mysteries of existence, such as the creation of the earth or human life, usually called myths, were basic explanatory models for ancient people, somewhat in the way that scientific theories are today. Since their truth could not be tested by verifying their correspondence to external reality, such stories were considered true if they held together in a unified pattern, that is, if they were coherent. In addition to these great myths or stories, localized myths, often called *legends* or *folk tales,* have been created to explain some familiar phenomena, to account for the past of a region, or to justify some aspect of human behavior.

The basic motivation underlying both grand cosmic myths and more localized legends is not the need to recount an event in ordinary, everyday reality, but is rather the need to represent conceptual ideas in narrative form. A story explicitly built on a conceptual framework in which the characters seem but walking embodiments of ideas is usually called an allegory. On the sliding scale of fictional worlds, stories about everyday reality are on one end, whereas fables, legends, and allegories are on the other. Although the two types are sometimes mixed, the basic differences between them should be understood, for to read a fable as if it were a realistic story or a realistic story as if it were an allegory can result in misunderstanding.

First of all, writers who begin with the intention of recounting an event in everyday reality are likely to allow the event itself to be the primary determinant of the story; thus, realistic stories may appear less formal and tightly organized than fables, more like the ragged edges of life itself. However, when writers begin with the intention of explaining something or illustrating a set of ideas, they are more likely to allow the concept to determine the nature of the fiction; thus, fables and allegories are more formal and conventional than are realistic stories—they are more like the patterned nature of conceptual thought.

Secondly, writers who create so-called realistic stories are usually more concerned with creating characters who seem like real people—characters who have inner thoughts, who appear to have a historical background, and who seem somewhat unpredictable. On the other hand, writers of fables and allegories are more concerned with the story they have to tell; they create characters whose only purpose is to illustrate the ideas that the story tries to communicate or embody.

The discussion of Poe's "The Masque of the Red Death" at the end of these remarks suggests some of the basic characteristics of allegory. For example, we know nothing about Prince Prospero as a real person—what he feels, ate for breakfast, or did as a child. All we know of him is what we need to know to understand the allegorical intention—that he tries to escape death. Moreover, the story follows a predictable pattern in which Prospero must come face-to-face with that from which he tries to escape.

Although readers today may think that realistic stories are the most "natural" kind of fiction, the notion of telling stories about ordinary people in everyday situations did not begin until the eighteenth century. Before that, short fictions were more often of the legend, fable, or allegory type. In Isak Dinesen's story "The Cardinal's First Tale," the narrator makes a distinction between "story" and what he calls the new or "novel" art of narration that, for the sake of realism and individual characters, sacrifices the story. The "divine art is the story," says the Cardinal. "In the beginning was the story."

The first writer to establish the short story in America, Washington Irving, became a great success by combining the old legendary stories with the new "realistic" impulse. Irving took European legends with which he was familiar, put them in historical American settings, and told them from the point of view of a "real" storyteller with a satiric outlook. The result was the creation of such classic short stories as "Rip Van Winkle" and "The Legend of Sleepy Hollow." In "The Adventure of the German Student" in this collection, Irving tells a legendary story in such a way as to mock its basically romantic nature. This satiric approach did much to displace the old legendary mode of storytelling in favor of the new realistic mode.

Stories such as Seán O'Faoláin's "The Trout," Walter de la Mare's "The Riddle," and Liam O'Flaherty's "The Fairy Goose" are twentieth-century remnants of the old fable-type stories, in which a conceptual idea rather than the need to tell a realistic story is the primary determinant. The whimsical nature of these stories is due to the fact that even though they embody the kind of spiritual values that underlie the old fables and fairy tales, they are set in modern societies in which logic, reason, and science have for the most part replaced those values.

Because of their source in myths, which dealt with ultimate or metaphysical realities, short fictions have often been used to illustrate a spiritual value or a moral idea. Tolstoy's "The Three Hermits," Gottfried Keller's "A Little Legend of the Dance," Langston Hughes's "On the Road," Lafcadio Hearn's "The Boy Who Drew Cats," and Hermann Hesse's "The Poet" all establish the superiority of what might be called the "sacred" reality over the "profane" reality of everyday life. In this sense they are closely akin to ancient myths and legends, for primitive peoples felt that spiritual reality—some invisible realm of transcendent value—was the only true reality. What many modern people call "real"—the ordinary world of the everyday—was for primitive people just something to get through.

To move from the ancient world of fable and myth to the world of science fiction may seem like a giant leap, but these two types share basic characteristics. The world of the future is just as unknowable as the world of the ancient past, and because neither exist in everyday reality, both are more likely to be motivated by the desire to explore ideas than the desire to describe things "as they are." Kurt Vonnegut, Jr.'s "Harrison Bergeron," Ursula K. Le Guin's "The Ones Who Walk Away from Omelas," and Stanislaw Lem's "How the World Was Saved" are all science-fiction pieces with a conceptual or philosophic basis.

Since the mythic or legendary impulse is basically a primitive one, several stories in this section derive their power from being grounded in primal societies or groups that retain the values of folk culture. Gabriel García Márquéz's "A Very Old Man with Enormous Wings," Zora Neale Hurston's "Spunk," Giovanni Verga's "The She-Wolf," and João Guimarães Rosa's "The Third Bank of the River" all deal with primitive forces rather than with the daily activities of life. The rest of the stories in this section are primarily modern fables and allegories, stories that have a conceptual point to make and do so in a relatively self-conscious and clearly intentional way.

Worth special attention are two classic stories from the early stages of the development of the short story in the United States—Hawthorne's "Young Goodman Brown" and Melville's "Bartleby"—for they mark a crucial transition point between older fablelike stories and the more modern realistic stories. Although it seems obvious that "Young Goodman Brown" is on the allegorical end of the fictional spectrum, while "Bartleby" is on the more realistic end, both stories are quite mixed. We become interested in Goodman Brown as a real character facing real inner conflict, even as we feel that he is more allegorical than real. We may feel that Melville's story is basically about a realistic conflict within the narrator, but we may also have an uneasy sense that Bartleby himself is little more than a two-dimensional representation of loneliness and isolation who exists only to create the narrator's conflict.

Kafka's "A Country Doctor" is a perfect example of a combination of the worlds of fiction in the first three sections of this book. The doctor appears to be an as-if-real character facing his own inner conflict, while at the same time he seems impelled by the extremity of his situation into a dreamlike world; at the same time, we sense that a conceptual framework underlies the story, that it is an allegory on the theme of primitive versus civilized forces.

"The Masque of the Red Death" AS ALLEGORY

Although Poe often said that he detested allegories, the allegorical nature of "The Masque of the Red Death" is indicated by the fact that its only named character is a Prince with the suggestive name of Prospero and that its only real conflict is the symbolic one between Prospero and the Red Death. The theme of Poe's allegory quite clearly focuses on the impossibility—regardless of one's power, wealth, and influence—of escaping mortality or death. However, the story is somewhat more complex than this easy moral statement would suggest. First of all, there is no historical record of a pestilence with the symptoms that Poe gives to the Red Death. Since he could very easily have used an actual historical plague, we may assume that Poe invented this plague for particular thematic reasons.

In fact, the specific nature of the Red Death itself creates a basic irony in the story. The metaphor of a "Red" Death, because it suggests blood, is not the conventional image of death, but rather of life itself, for the presence of blood on the face of a person suggests the life within. In this sense, every living person wears a mask of red—the blood visible beneath the skin. However, as Joseph Roppolo suggests, it is precisely this sign of life that ironically suggests death (66). In fact, Poe's point is that it is the very presence of life which inevitably means death. Thus, Prospero does not simply try to escape death; rather, by enclosing himself within the castle and shutting out the outside world, he attempts to escape life in a closed-off world very much like Poe's notion of the artwork itself.

In this sense Prospero, as pointed out by Kermit Vanderbilt, is a reflection of Shakespeare's character of the same name in his play *The Tempest*, likewise an aesthetic magician who creates an alternate world of imaginative reality not susceptible to the contingencies of external reality (379). Indeed, Poe's emphasis in "The Masque of the Red Death" is that the abbey within which Prospero retreats is his own "creation," a result of his "own eccentric yet august taste"—phrases which echo Poe's own aesthetic theory that celebrates the ideal of the artwork as a self-sustained experience of absolute and immutable beauty. In effect, Prospero creates the image of a self-contained artwork within which he tries to live.

However, the seven rooms within the abbey seem to reflect the inevitable implication of human life and art—the inescapable temporality of human experience. The sequence of rooms may represent the seven ages of man—from the blue which suggests the beginning of life and light in the East to the black which suggests the darkness of night and death in the West (Blair 239). Consequently, even though Prospero attempts to create the illusion of art as eternally protected from the contingencies of life, the final realization of the reader is that since all artworks inevitably reflect life, one cannot escape, even within the artwork, the inevitable implication of process and thus mortality and death. The image of the clock in the final room, of course, suggests why this is so: both life and the literary work exist within time, and it is indeed time that makes life end inevitably in death.

The style of "The Masque of the Red Death" focuses primarily on the pictorial rather than on the narrative. Poe attempts to create the sense that the story exists as a painting does, within space and outside of time. The story has been called Poe's most pictorial composition, an arabesque which attempts to create an intricate geometric spatial pattern (Levin 149); thus it is quite static, lacking in narrative plot and emphasizing instead the spatial arrangements of painting. However, the irony is that because "The Masque of the Red Death" is a story and therefore exists in time, time triumphs. The conclusion of the story therefore emphasizes that the artistic effort to transform temporality into spatiality is doomed to failure. Even the seven rooms, which suggest a geometric pattern of static positioning, become transformed into an image of the time span of life when Prospero follows the Red Death through a temporal progression from birth to youth to maturity to old age and finally to death. It is when Prospero must confront the reality of the temporality of life that he inevitably must confront the death that life always insists upon.

Thus, although the story is ostensibly about the moral lesson of the human inability to escape death, it is actually an aesthetic allegory or fable, in which Prospero represents Poe's image of the artist who insists upon creating an ideal artwork, but who is always trapped by the essential time-bound nature of life. "The Masque of the Red Death" embodies an aesthetic theme common to much of Poe's short fiction. Such stories as "The Fall of the House of Usher," "The Tell-Tale Heart," and "Ligeia" also focus on the human need to escape death in the immutable world of aesthetic reality. However, while these other stories attempt to create a world of psychological obsession to embody this theme, "The Masque of the Red Death" is a striking example of Poe's attempt to deal with it in the conventional genre of allegory.

WORKS CITED

Blair, Walter. "Poe's Conception of Incident and Tone in the Tale." *Modern Philology* 41 (1944): 228–40.

Levin, Harry. *The Power of Blackness.* New York: Vintage Books, 1960.

Roppolo, Joseph P. "Meaning and 'The Masque of the Red Death.' " *Tulane Studies in English* 13 (1963): 59–69.

Vanderbilt, Kermit. "Art and Nature in 'The Masque of the Red Death.' " *Nineteenth-Century Fiction* 22 (1968): 379–89.

COMMENT

Although the preceding essay expresses the writer's own ideas, he or she has made sure to give credit to previous readers of the story who have published their thoughts on it. The documentation format used is that of the Modern Language Association in the *MLA Handbook for Writers of Research Papers*. The basic identifying information for the source cited is placed in parentheses following the passage. The full information is put in a "Works Cited" section at the end of the essay. The basic rule is that whatever you mention in the text does not have to be placed inside the parentheses. For example, in the preceding, the writer refers to Kermit Vanderbilt in the text and thus only puts a page number for the reference in the parentheses. However, because Walter Blair is not mentioned in the text, his last name is placed inside the parentheses to identify him.

Often students make a distinction between papers which express their own analysis and "research papers." However, an effective analytical paper is usually the result of your own analysis as well as the result of your awareness of what previous readers have said about the story. Reading criticism not only prevents you from simply repeating what others have already discovered but also helps you to make your own discoveries. Research should not be considered as a tedious and meaningless requirement but rather as an opportunity to engage in a dialogue with other interested readers whom you do not have the opportunity to meet in person.

EDGAR
ALLAN
POE | *The Masque of the Red Death*

The "Red Death" had long devastated the country. No pestilence had ever been so fatal, or so hideous. Blood was its Avator and its seal—the redness and the horror of blood. There were sharp pains, and sudden dizziness, and then profuse bleeding at the pores, with dissolution. The scarlet stains upon the body and especially upon the face of the victim, were the pest ban which shut him out from the aid and from the sympathy of his fellowmen. And the whole seizure, progress and termination of the disease, were the incidents of half an hour.

But the Prince Prospero was happy and dauntless and sagacious. When his dominions were half depopulated, he summoned to his presence a thousand hale and lighthearted friends from among the knights and dames of his court, and with these retired to the deep seclusion of one of his castellated abbeys. This was an extensive and magnificent structure, the creation of the prince's own eccentric yet august taste. A strong and lofty wall girdled it in. This wall had gates of iron. The courtiers, having entered, brought furnaces and massy hammers and welded the bolts. They resolved to leave means neither of ingress or egress to the sudden impulses of despair or of frenzy from within. The abbey was amply provisioned. With such precautions the courtiers might bid defiance to contagion. The external world could take care of itself. In the meantime it was folly to grieve, or to think. The prince had provided all the appliances of pleasure. There were buffoons, there were improvisatori, there were ballet-dancers, there were musicians, there was Beauty, there was wine. All these and security were within. Without was the "Red Death."

It was toward the close of the fifth or sixth month of his seclusion, and while the pestilence raged most furiously abroad, that the Prince Prospero entertained his thousand friends at a masked ball of the most unusual magnificence.

It was a voluptuous scene, that masquerade. But first let me tell of the rooms in which it was held. There were seven—an imperial suite. In many palaces, however, such suites form a long and straight vista, while the folding doors slide back nearly to the walls on either hand, so that the view of the whole extent is scarcely impeded. Here the case was very different; as might have been expected from the duke's love of the *bizarre*. The apartments were so irregularly disposed that the vision embraced but little more than one at a time. There was a sharp turn at every twenty or thirty yards, and at each turn a novel effect. To the right and left, in the middle of each wall, a tall and narrow Gothic window looked out upon a closed corridor which pursued the windings of the suite. These windows were of stained glass whose color varied in accordance with the prevailing hue of the decorations of the chamber into which it opened. That at the eastern extremity was hung, for example, in blue—and vividly blue were its windows. The second chamber was purple in its ornaments and tapestries, and here the panes were purple. The third was green throughout, and so were the casements. The fourth was furnished and lighted with orange—the fifth with white—the sixth with violet. The seventh apartment was closely shrouded in black velvet tapestries that hung all over the ceiling and down the walls, falling in heavy folds upon a carpet of the same material and hue. But in this chamber only, the color of the windows failed to correspond with the decorations. The panes here were scarlet—a deep blood color. Now in no one of the seven apartments was there any lamp or candelabrum, amid the profusion of golden ornaments that lay scattered to and fro or depended from the roof. There was no light of any kind emanating from lamp or candle within the suite of chambers. But in the corridors that followed the suite, there stood, opposite to each window, a heavy tripod, bearing a brazier of fire that projected its rays through the tinted glass and so glaringly illumined the room. And thus were produced a multitude of gaudy and fantastic appearances. But in the western or black chamber the effect of the fire-light that streamed upon the dark hangings through the blood-tinted panes, was ghastly in the extreme, and produced so wild a look upon the countenances of those who entered, that there were few of the company bold enough to set foot within its precincts at all.

It was in this apartment, also, that there stood against the western wall, a gigantic clock of ebony. Its pendulum swung to and fro with a dull, heavy, monotonous clang; and when the minute-hand made the circuit of the face, and the hour was to be stricken, there came from the brazen lungs of the clock a sound which was clear and loud and deep and exceedingly musical, but of so peculiar a note and emphasis that, at each lapse of an hour, the musicians of the orchestra were constrained to pause, momentarily, in their performance, to hearken to the sound; and thus the waltzers perforce ceased their evolutions; and there was a brief disconcert of the whole gay company; and, while the chimes of the clock yet rang, it was observed that the giddiest grew pale, and the more aged and sedate passed their hands over their brows as if in confused revery or meditation. But when the echoes had fully ceased, a light laughter at once pervaded the assembly; the musicians looked at each other and smiled as if at their own nervousness and folly, and made whispering vows, each to the other, that the next chiming of the clock should produce in them no similar emotion; and then, after the lapse of sixty minutes (which embrace three thousand and six hundred seconds of the Time that flies), there came yet another chiming of the clock, and then were the same disconcert and tremulousness and meditation as before.

But, in spite of these things, it was a gay and magnificent revel. The tastes of the duke were peculiar. He had a fine eye for colors and effects. He disregarded the *decora* of mere fashion. His plans were bold and fiery, and his conceptions glowed with barbaric lustre. There are some who would have thought him mad. His followers felt that he was not. It was necessary to hear and see and touch him to be *sure* that he was not.

He had directed, in great part, the movable embellishments of the seven chambers, upon occasion of this great *fête;* and it was his own guiding taste which had given character to the masqueraders. Be sure they were grotesque. There were much glare and glitter and piquancy and phantasm—much of what has been since seen in "Hernani." There were arabesque figures with unsuited limbs and appointments. There were delirious fancies such as the madman fashions. There was much of the beautiful, much of the wanton, much of the *bizarre,* something of the terrible, and not a little of that which might have excited disgust. To and fro in the seven chambers there stalked, in fact, a multitude of dreams. And these—the dreams—writhed in and about, taking hue from the rooms, and causing the wild music of the orchestra to seem as the echo of their steps. And, anon, there strikes the ebony clock which stands in the hall of the velvet. And then, for a moment, all is still, and all is silent save the voice of the clock. The dreams are stiff-frozen as they stand. But the echoes of the chime die away—they have endured but an instant— and a light, half-subdued laughter floats after them as they depart. And now again the music swells, and the dreams live, and writhe to and fro more merrily than ever, taking hue from the many tinted windows through which stream the rays from the tripods. But to the chamber which lies most westwardly of the seven, there are now none of the maskers who venture, for the night is waning away; and there flows a ruddier light through the blood-colored panes; and the blackness of the sable drapery appalls; and to him whose foot falls upon the sable carpet, there comes from the near clock of ebony a muffled peal more solemnly emphatic than any which reaches *their* ears who indulge in the more remote gayeties of the other apartments.

But these other apartments were densely crowded, and in them beat feverishly the heart of life. And the revel went whirlingly on, until at length there commenced the sounding of midnight upon the clock. And then the music ceased, as I have told; and the evolutions of the waltzers were quieted; and there was an uneasy cessation of all things as before. But now there were twelve strokes to be sounded by the bell of the clock; and thus it happened, perhaps, that before the last echoes of the last chime had utterly sunk into silence, there were many individuals in the crowd who had found leisure to become aware of the presence of a masked figure which had arrested the attention of no single individual before. And the rumor of this new presence having spread itself whisperingly around, there arose at length from the whole company, a buzz, or murmur, expressive of disapprobation and surprise—then, finally, of terror, of horror, and of disgust.

In an assembly of phantasms such as I have painted, it may well be supposed that no ordinary appearance could have excited such sensation. In truth the masquerade license of the night was nearly unlimited; but the figure in question had out-Heroded Herod, and gone beyond the bounds of even the prince's indefinite decorum. There are chords in the hearts of the most reckless which cannot be touched without emotion. Even with the utterly lost, to whom life and death are equally jests, there are matters of which no jest can be made. The whole company, indeed, seemed now deeply to feel that in the costume and bearing of the stranger neither wit nor propriety existed. The figure was tall and gaunt, and shrouded from head to foot in the habiliments of the grave. The mask which concealed the visage was made so nearly to resemble the countenance of a stiffened corpse that the closest scrutiny must have had difficulty in detecting the cheat. And yet all this might have been endured, if not approved, by the mad revellers around. But the mummer had gone so far as to assume the type of the Red Death. His vesture was dabbled in *blood*—and his broad brow, with all the features of the face, was besprinkled with the scarlet horror.

When the eyes of Prince Prospero fell upon this spectral image (which with a slow and solemn movement, as if more fully to sustain its *rôle*, stalked to and fro among the waltzers) he was seen to be convulsed, in the first moment, with a strong shudder, either of terror or distaste; but, in the next, his brow reddened with rage.

"Who dares?" he demanded hoarsely of the courtiers who stood near him—"who dares insult us with this blasphemous mockery? Seize him and unmask him—that we may know whom we have to hang at sunrise, from the battlements!"

It was in the eastern or blue chamber in which stood the Prince Prospero as he uttered these words. They rang throughout the seven rooms loudly and clearly—for the prince was a bold and robust man, and the music had become hushed at the waving of his hand.

It was in the blue room where stood the prince, with a group of pale courtiers by his side. At first, as he spoke, there was a slight rushing movement of this group in the direction of the intruder, who at the moment was also near at hand, and now, with deliberate and stately step, made closer approach to the speaker. But from a certain nameless awe with which the mad assumptions of the mummer had inspired the whole party, there were found none who put forth hand to seize him; so that, unimpeded, he passed within a yard of the prince's person; and, while the vast assembly, as if with one impulse, shrank from the centres of the room to the walls, he made his way uninterruptedly, but with the same solemn and measured step which had distinguished him from the first, through the blue chamber to the purple—through the purple to the green—through the green to the orange—through this again to the white—and even thence to the violet, ere a decided movement had been made to arrest him. It was then, however, that the Prince Prospero, maddening with rage and the shame of his own momentary cowardice, rushed hurriedly through the six chambers, while none followed him on account of a deadly terror that had seized upon all. He bore aloft a drawn dagger, and had approached, in rapid impetuosity, to within three or four feet of the retreating figure, when the latter, having attained the extremity of the velvet apartment, turned suddenly and confronted his pursuer. There was a sharp cry—and the dagger dropped gleaming upon the sable carpet, upon which, instantly afterwards, fell prostrate in death the Prince Prospero. Then, summoning the wild courage of despair, a throng of the revellers at once threw themselves into the black apartment, and, seizing the mummer, whose tall figure stood erect and motionless within the shadow of the ebony clock, gasped in unutterable horror at finding the grave-cerements and corpse-like mask which they handled with so violent a rudeness, untenanted by any tangible form.

And now was acknowledged the presence of the Red Death. He had come like a thief in the night. And one by one dropped the revellers in the blood-bedewed halls of their revel, and died each in the despairing posture of his fall. And the life of the ebony clock went out with that of the last of the gay. And the flames of the tripods expired. And Darkness and Decay and the Red Death held illimitable dominion over all.

EXERCISES

1. There is no historical record of any plague or epidemic with the symptoms of the "Red Death." Poe has obviously invented it for his own purposes. Why does Poe make blood the sign of the Red Death, since blood is the sign of life? Consider the implications of the sign of life being the sign of death.

2. Note that everything inside the castle is the invention of the Prince. Discuss the implications of Poe's using the name Prospero, which is also the name of the magician capable of creating an alternate world in Shakespeare's play *The Tempest*.

3. The seven rooms in the castle have been said to represent the seven ages of human life, moving from childhood to old age and finally death. Why is this an important theme in the story? Point out other elements of time as a theme in the story.

4. There is a film version of this story in which all the frames are animated oil paintings and in which several scenes look like famous paintings, such as the *Mona Lisa* and *The Last Supper.* The Red Death enters as a beautiful woman whom Prince Prospero pursues through the castle. When he catches her, she is transformed into a witchlike hag, then a corpse, then a skeleton, and finally the hooded figure of the Red Death. How appropriate are these film devices for the allegoric interpretation of the story?

WASHINGTON
IRVING | # The Adventure of the German Student

O n a stormy night, in the tempestuous times of the French revolution, a young German was returning to his lodgings, at a late hour, across the old part of Paris. The lightning gleamed, and the loud claps of thunder rattled through the lofty narrow streets—but I should first tell you something about this young German.

Gottfried Wolfgang was a young man of good family. He had studied for some time at Göttingen, but being of a visionary and enthusiastic character, he had wandered into those wild and speculative doctrines which have so often bewildered German students. His secluded life, his intense application, and the singular nature of his studies, had an effect on both mind and body. His health was impaired; his imagination diseased. He had been indulging in fanciful speculations on spiritual essences, until, like Swedenborg, he had an ideal world of his own around him. He took up a notion, I do not know from what cause, that there was an evil influence hanging over him; an evil genius or spirit seeking to ensnare him and ensure his perdition. Such an idea working on his melancholy temperament, produced the most gloomy effects. He became haggard and desponding. His friends discovered the mental malady preying upon him, and determined that the best cure was a change of scene; he was sent, therefore, to finish his studies amidst the splendors and gayeties of Paris.

Wolfgang arrived at Paris at the breaking out of the revolution. The popular delirium at first caught his enthusiastic mind, and he was captivated by the political and philosophical theories of the day: but the scenes of blood which followed shocked his sensitive nature; disgusted him with society and the world, and made him more than ever a recluse. He shut himself up in a solitary apartment in the *Pays Latin,* the quarter of students. There, in a gloomy street not far from the monastic walls of the Sorbonne, he pursued his favorite speculations. Sometimes he spent hours together in the great libraries of Paris, those catacombs of departed authors, rummaging among their hoards of dusty and obsolete works in quest of food for his unhealthy appetite. He was, in a manner, a literary ghoul, feeding in the charnel-house of decayed literature.

Wolfgang, though solitary and recluse, was of an ardent temperament, but for a time it operated merely upon his imagination. He was too shy and ignorant of the world to make any advances to the fair, but he was a passionate admirer of female beauty, and in his lonely chamber would often lose himself in reveries on forms and faces which he had seen, and his fancy would deck out images of loveliness far surpassing the reality.

While his mind was in this excited and sublimated state, a dream produced an extraordinary effect upon him. It was of a female face of transcendent beauty. So strong was the impression made, that he dreamt of it again and again. It haunted his thoughts by day, his slumbers by night; in fine, he became passionately enamoured of this shadow of a dream. This lasted so long that it became one of those fixed ideas which haunt the minds of melancholy men, and are at times mistaken for madness.

Such was Gottfried Wolfgang, and such his situation at the time I mentioned. He was returning home late one stormy night, through some of the old and gloomy streets of the *Marais,* the ancient part of Paris. The loud claps of thunder rattled among the high houses of the narrow streets. He came to the Place de Grève, the square where public executions are performed. The lightning quivered about the pinnacles of the ancient Hôtel de Ville, and shed flickering gleams over the open space in front. As Wolfgang was crossing the square, he shrank back with horror at finding himself close by the guillotine. It was the height of the reign of terror, when this dreadful instrument of death stood ever ready, and its scaffold was continually running with the blood of the virtuous and the brave. It had that very day been actively employed in the work of carnage, and there it stood in grim array, amidst a silent and sleeping city, waiting for fresh victims.

Wolfang's heart sickened within him, and he was turning shuddering from the horrible engine, when he beheld a shadowy form, cowering as it were at the foot of the steps which led up to the scaffold. A succession of vivid flashes of lightning revealed it more distinctly. It was a female figure, dressed in black. She was seated on one of the lower steps of the scaffold, leaning forward, her face hid in her lap; and her long dishevelled tresses hanging to the ground, streaming with the rain which fell in torrents. Wolfgang paused. There was something awful in this solitary monument of woe. The female had the appearance of being above the common order. He knew the times to be full of vicissitude, and that many a fair head, which had once been pillowed on down, now wandered houseless. Perhaps this was some poor mourner whom the dreadful axe had rendered desolate, and who sat here heart-broken on the strand of existence, from which all that was dear to her had been launched into eternity.

He approached, and addressed her in the accents of sympathy. She raised her head and gazed wildly at him. What was his astonishment at beholding, by the bright glare of the lightning, the very face which had haunted him in his dreams. It was pale and disconsolate, but ravishingly beautiful.

Trembling with violent and conflicting emotions, Wolfgang again accosted her. He spoke something of her being exposed at such an hour of the night, and to the fury of such a storm, and offered to conduct her to her friends. She pointed to the guillotine with a gesture of dreadful signification.

"I have no friend on earth!" said she.

"But you have a home," said Wolfgang.

"Yes—in the grave!"

The heart of the student melted at the words.

"If a stranger dare make an offer," said he, "without danger of being misunderstood, I would offer my humble dwelling as a shelter; myself as a devoted friend. I am friendless myself in Paris, and a stranger in the land; but if my life could be of service, it is at your disposal, and should be sacrificed before harm or indignity should come to you."

There was an honest earnestness in the young man's manner that had its effect. His foreign accent, too, was in his favor; it showed him not to be a hackneyed inhabitant of Paris. Indeed, there is an eloquence in true enthusiasm that is not to be doubted. The homeless stranger confided herself implicitly to the protection of the student.

He supported her faltering steps across the Pont Neuf, and by the place where the statue of Henry the Fourth had been overthrown by the populace. The storm had abated, and the thunder rumbled at a distance. All Paris was quiet; that great volcano of human passion slumbered for awhile, to gather fresh strength for the next day's eruption. The student conducted his charge through the ancient streets of the *Pays Latin,* and by the dusky walls of the Sorbonne, to the great dingy hotel which he inhabited. The old portress who admitted them stared with surprise at the unusual sight of the melancholy Wolfgang with a female companion.

On entering his apartment, the student, for the first time, blushed at the scantiness and indifference of his dwelling. He had but one chamber—an old-fashioned saloon—heavily carved, and fantastically furnished with the remains of former magnificence, for it was of those hotels in the quarter of the Luxembourg palace which had once belonged to nobility. It was lumbered with books and papers, and all the usual apparatus of a student, and his bed stood in a recess at one end.

When lights were brought, and Wolfgang had a better opportunity of contemplating the stranger, he was more than ever intoxicated by her beauty. Her face was pale, but of a dazzling fairness, set off by a profusion of raven hair that hung clustering about it. Her eyes were large and brilliant, with a singular expression approaching almost to wildness. As far as her black dress permitted her shape to be seen, it was of perfect symmetry. Her whole appearance was highly striking, though she was dressed in the simplest style. The only thing approaching to an ornament which she wore, was a broad black band round her neck, clasped by diamonds.

The perplexity now commenced with the student how to dispose of the helpless being thus thrown upon his protection. He thought of abandoning his chamber to her, and seeking shelter for himself elsewhere. Still he was so fascinated by her charms, there seemed to be such a spell upon his thoughts and senses, that he could not tear himself from her presence. Her manner, too, was singular and unaccountable. She spoke no more of the guillotine. Her grief had abated. The attentions of the student had first won her confidence, and then, apparently, her heart. She was evidently an enthusiast like himself, and enthusiasts soon understand each other.

In the infatuation of the moment, Wolfgang avowed his passion for her. He told her the story of his mysterious dream, and how she had possessed his heart before he had even seen her. She was strangely affected by his recital, and acknowledged to have felt an impulse towards him equally unaccountable. It was the time for wild theory and wild actions. Old prejudices and superstitions were done away; everything was under the sway of the "Goddess of Reason." Among other rubbish of the old times, the forms and ceremonies of marriage began to be considered superfluous bonds for honorable minds. Social compacts were the vogue. Wolfgang was too much of a theorist not to be tainted by the liberal doctrines of the day.

"Why should we separate?" said he: "our hearts are united; in the eye of reason and honor we are as one. What need is there of sordid forms to bind high souls together."

The stranger listened with emotion: she had evidently received illumination at the same school.

"You have no home nor family," continued he; "let me be everything to you, or rather let us be everything to one another. If form is necessary, form shall be observed—there is my hand. I pledge myself to you forever."

"Forever?" said the stranger, solemnly.

"Forever!" repeated Wolfgang.

The stranger clasped the hand extended to her: "Then I am yours, " murmured she, and sank upon his bosom.

The next morning the student left his bride sleeping, and sallied forth at an early hour to seek more spacious apartments, suitable to the change in his situation. When he returned, he found the stranger lying with her head hanging over the bed, and one arm thrown over it. He spoke to her, but received no reply. He advanced to awaken her from her uneasy posture. On taking her hand, it was cold—there was no pulsation—her face was pallid and ghastly.—In a word—she was a corpse.

Horrified and frantic, he alarmed the house. A scene of confusion ensued. The police was summoned. As the officer of police entered the room, he started back on beholding the corpse.

"Great heaven!" cried he, "how did this woman come here?"

"Do you know anything about her?" said Wolfgang, eagerly.

"Do I?" exclaimed the police officer: "she was guillotined yesterday."

He stepped forward; undid the black collar round the neck of the corpse, and the head rolled on the floor!

The student burst into a frenzy. "The fiend! the fiend has gained possession of me!" shrieked he: "I am lost forever."

They tried to soothe him, but in vain. He was possessed with the frightful belief that an evil spirit had reanimated the dead body to ensnare him. He went distracted, and died in a madhouse.

Here the old gentleman with the haunted head finished his narrative.

"And is this really a fact?" said the inquisitive gentleman.

"A fact not to be doubted," replied the other. "I had it from the best authority. The student told it me himself. I saw him in a madhouse at Paris."

EXERCISES

1. Discuss the basic mental attitude and psychological state of the central character. How does this establish the credibility of the events that follow? Discuss particularly the significance of the statement "He was, in a manner, a literary ghoul, feeding in the charnel-house of decayed literature."

2. Discuss the significance of the German student's fantasy of the female of transcendent beauty. What does this romantic ideal mean?

3. Discuss the meaning of obsession, fixed ideas, and madness in this story. A basic definition of madness is the mistaking of inner reality for outer reality. How is this the case here?

4. How is this a predictable story? Why is it inevitable that the German student will meet the woman of his fantasy, that she will be dead, and that he will go mad? What is the meaning of this series of events?

5. This is a conventional story from the early nineteenth century, which Irving presents both romantically and satirically at the same time. Discuss the combination of romantic and satiric elements in this story.

SEÁN
O'FAOLÁIN | *The Trout*

One of the first places Julia always ran to when they arrived in G—— was The Dark Walk. It is a laurel walk, very old; almost gone wild, a lofty midnight tunnel of smooth, sinewy branches. Underfoot the tough brown leaves are never dry enough to crackle: there is always a suggestion of damp and cool trickle.

She raced right into it. For the first few yards she always had the memory of the sun behind her, then she felt the dusk closing swiftly down on her so that she screamed with pleasure and raced on to reach the light at the far end; and it was always just a little too long in coming so that she emerged gasping, clasping her hands, laughing, drinking in the sun. When she was filled with the heat and glare she would turn and consider the ordeal again.

This year she had the extra joy of showing it to her small brother, and of terrifying him as well as herself. And for him the fear laster longer because his legs were so short and she had gone out at the far end while he was still screaming and racing.

When they had done this many times they came back to the house to tell everybody that they had done it. He boasted. She mocked. They squabbled.

"Cry baby!"

"You were afraid yourself, so there!"

"I won't take you any more."

"You're a big pig."

"I hate you."

Tears were threatening so somebody said, "Did you see the well?" She opened her eyes at that and held up her long lovely neck suspiciously and decided to be incredulous. She was twelve and at that age little girls are beginning to suspect most stories: they have already found out too many, from Santa Claus to the Stork. How could there be a well! In The Dark Walk? That she had visited year after year? Haughtily she said, "Nonsense."

But she went back, pretending to be going somewhere else, and she found a hole scooped in the rock at the side of the walk, choked with damp leaves, so shrouded by ferns that she only uncovered it after much searching. At the back of this little cavern there was about a quart of water. In the water she suddenly perceived a panting trout. She rushed for Stephen and dragged him to see, and they were both so excited that they were no longer afraid of the darkness as they hunched down and peered in at the fish panting in his tiny prison, his silver stomach going up and down like an engine.

Nobody knew how the trout got there. Even old Martin in the kitchen-garden laughed and refused to believe that it was there, or pretended not to believe, until she forced him to come down and see. Kneeling and pushing back his tattered old cap he peered in.

"Be cripes, you're right. How the divil in hell did that fella get there?"

She stared at him suspiciously.

"You knew?" She accused; but he said, "The divil a know"; and reached down to lift it out. Convinced she hauled him back. If she had found it then it was her trout.

Her mother suggested that a bird had carried the spawn. Her father thought that in the winter a small streamlet might have carried it down there as a baby, and it had been safe until the summer came and the water began to dry up. She said, "I see," and went back to look again and consider the matter in private. Her brother remained behind, wanting to hear the whole story of the trout, not really interested in the actual trout but much interested in the story which his mummy began to make up for him on the lines of, "So one day Daddy Trout and Mammy Trout. . . ." When he retailed it to her she said, "Pooh."

It troubled her that the trout was always in the same position; he had no room to turn; all the time the silver belly went up and down; otherwise he was motionless. She wondered what he ate and in between visits to Joey Pony, and the boat and a bathe to get cool, she thought of his hunger. She brought him down bits of dough; once she brought him a worm. He ignored the food. He just went on panting. Hunched over him she thought how, all the winter, while she was at school he had been in there. All the winter, in The Dark Walk, all day, all night, floating around alone. She drew the leaf of her hat down around her ears and chin and stared. She was still thinking of it as she lay in bed.

It was late June, the longest days of the year. The sun had sat still for a week, burning up the world. Although it was after ten o'clock it was still bright and still hot. She lay on her back under a single sheet, with her long legs spread, trying to keep cool. She could see the D of the moon through the fir-tree—they slept on the ground floor. Before they went to bed her mummy had told Stephen the story of the trout again, and she, in her bed, had resolutely presented her back to them and read her book. But she kept one ear cocked.

"And so, in the end, this naughty fish who would not stay at home got bigger and bigger and bigger, and the water got smaller and smaller. . . ."

Passionately she had whirled and cried, "Mummy, don't make it a horrible old moral story!" Her mummy had brought in a Fairy Godmother, then, who sent lots of rain, and filled the well, and a stream poured out and the trout floated away down to the river below. Staring at the moon she knew that there are no such things as Fairy Godmothers and that the trout, down in The Dark Walk, was panting like an engine. She heard somebody unwind a fishing-reel. Would the *beasts* fish him out!

She sat up. Stephen was a hot lump of sleep, lazy thing. The Dark Walk would be full of little scraps of moon. She leaped up and looked out the window, and somehow it was not so lightsome now that she saw the dim mountains far away and the black firs against the breathing land and heard a dog say, bark-bark. Quietly she lifted the ewer of water, and climbed out the window and scuttled along the cool but cruel gravel down to the maw of the tunnel. Her pyjamas were very short so that when she splashed water it wet her ankles. She peered into the tunnel. Something alive rustled inside there. She raced in, and up and down she raced, and flurried, and cried aloud, "Oh, Gosh, I can't find it," and then at last she did. Kneeling down in the damp she put her hand into the slimy hole. When the body lashed they were both mad with fright. But she gripped him and shoved him into the ewer and raced, with her teeth ground, out to the other end of the tunnel and down the steep paths to the river's edge.

All the time she could feel him lashing his tail against the side of the ewer. She was afraid he would jump right out. The gravel cut into her soles until she came to the cool ooze of the river's bank where the moon-mice on the water crept into her feet. She poured out watching until he plopped. For a second he was visible in the water. She hoped he was not dizzy. Then all she saw was the glimmer of the moon in the silent-flowing river, the dark firs, the dim mountains, and the radiant pointed face laughing down at her out of the empty sky.

She scuttled up the hill, in the window, plonked down the ewer and flew through the air like a bird into bed. The dog said bark-bark. She heard the fishing-reel whirring. She hugged herself and giggled. Like a river of joy her holiday spread before her.

In the morning Stephen rushed to her, shouting that "he" was gone, and asking "where" and "how." Lifting her nose in the air she said superciliously, "Fairy Godmother, I suppose?" and strolled away patting the palms of her hands.

EXERCISES

1. Why do the words *"The Dark Walk"* begin with capital letters? What is the tone of this description of "The Dark Walk"? Why is the journey through it such an ordeal?

2. Discuss the difference between the actual trout and what might be called the story of the trout or the mystery of the trout.

3. Why does Julia not want the story to be a moral story?

4. Why does Julia take the trout to the river? Why does this give her such delight?

5. Why does Julia refuse to give the actual explanation of the trout's disappearance at the end?

6. Compare this story with Saki's "The Open Window" in Part IV.

WALTER
DE LA MARE | *The Riddle*

So these seven children, Ann, and Matilda, James, William and Henry, Harriet and Dorothea, came to live with their grandmother. The house in which their grandmother had lived since her childhood was built in the time of the Georges. It was not a pretty house, but roomy, substantial, and square; and an elm tree outstretched its branches almost to the windows.

When the children were come out of the cab (five sitting inside and two beside the driver), they were shown into their grandmother's presence. They stood in a little black group before the old lady, seated in her bow-window. And she asked them each their names, and repeated each name in her kind, quavering voice. Then to one she gave a work-box, to William a jack-knife, to Dorothea a painted ball; to each a present according to age. And she kissed all her grandchildren to the youngest.

"My dears, " she said, "I wish to see all of you bright and gay in my house. I am an old woman, so that I cannot romp with you; but Ann must look to you, and Mrs. Fenn too. And every morning and every evening you must all come in to see your granny; and bring me smiling faces, that call back to my mind my own son Harry. But all the rest of the day, when school is done, you shall do just as you please, my dears. And there is only one thing, just one, I would have you remember. In the large spare bedroom that looks out on the slate roof there stands in the corner an old oak chest; ay, children, older than I, my dears, a great deal older; older than my grandmother. Play anywhere else in the house, but not there." She spoke kindly to them all, smiling at them; but she was very aged, and her eyes seemed to see nothing of this world.

And the seven children, though at first they were gloomy and strange, soon began to be happy and at home in the great house. There was much to interest and to amuse them there; all was new to them. Twice every day, morning and evening, they came in to see their grandmother, who every day seemed more feeble; and she spoke pleasantly to them of their mother, and her childhood, but never forgetting to visit her store of sugar-plums. And so the weeks passed by.

It was evening twilight when Henry went upstairs from the nursery by himself to look at the oak chest. He pressed his fingers into the carved fruit and flowers, and spoke to the dark smiling heads at the corners; and then, with a glance over his shoulder, he opened the lid and looked in. But the chest concealed no treasure, neither gold nor baubles, nor was there anything to alarm the eye. The chest was empty, except that it was lined with silk of old rose, seeming darker in the dusk, and smelling sweet of pot-pourri. And while Henry was looking in, he heard the softened laughter and the clinking of the cups downstairs in the nursery; and out at the window he saw the day darkening. These things brought strangely to his memory his mother, who in her glimmering white dress used to read to him in the dusk; and he climbed into the chest; and the lid closed gently down over him.

When the other six children were tired with their playing, they filed into their grandmother's room as usual for her goodnight and her sugar-plums. She looked out between the candles at them as if she were unsure of something in her thoughts. The next day Ann told her grandmother that Henry was not anywhere to be found.

"Dearie me, child. Then he must be gone away for a time," said the old lady. She paused. "But remember all of you, do not meddle with the oak chest."

But Matilda could not forget her brother Henry, finding no pleasure in playing without him. So she would loiter in the house thinking where he might be. And she carried her wood doll in her bare arms, singing under her breath all she could make up about him. And when in a bright morning she peeped in on the chest, so sweet-scented and secret it seemed that she took her doll with her into it—just as Henry himself had done.

So Ann, and James, and William, Harriet and Dorothea were left at home to play together. "Some day maybe they will come back to you, my dears," said their grandmother, "or maybe you will go to them. Heed my warning as best you may."

Now Harriet and William were friends together, pretending to be sweet-hearts; while James and Dorothea liked wild games of hunting, and fishing, and battles.

On a silent afternoon in October Harriet and William were talking softly together, looking out over the slate roof at the green fields, and they heard the squeak and frisking of a mouse behind them in the room. They went together and searched for the small, dark hole from whence it had come out. But finding no hole, they began to finger the carving of the chest, and to give names to the dark-smiling heads, just as Henry had done. "I know! Let's pretend you are Sleeping Beauty, Harriet," said William, "and I'll be the Prince that squeezes through the thorns and comes in." Harriet looked gently and strangely at her brother; but she got into the box and lay down, pretending to be fast asleep; and on tiptoe William leaned over, and seeing how big was the chest he stepped in to kiss the Sleeping Beauty and to wake her from her quiet sleep. Slowly the carved lid turned on its noiseless hinges. And only the clatter of James and Dorothea came in sometimes to recall Ann from her book.

But their old grandmother was very feeble, and her sight dim, and her hearing extremely difficult.

Snow was falling through the still air upon the roof; and Dorothea was a fish in the oak chest, and James stood over the hole in the ice, brandishing a walking-stick for a harpoon, pretending to be an Esquimau. Dorothea's face was red, and her wild eyes sparkled through her tousled hair. And James had a crooked scratch upon his cheek. "You must struggle, Dorothea, and then I shall swim back and drag you out. Be quick now!" He shouted with laughter as he was drawn into the open chest. And the lid closed softly and gently down as before.

Ann, left to her self, was too old to care overmuch for sugar-plums, but she would go solitary to bid her grandmother goodnight; and the old lady looked wistfully at her over her spectacles. "Well, my dear," she said with trembling head; and she squeezed Ann's fingers between her own knuckled finger and thumb. "What lonely old people we are, to be sure!" Ann kissed her grandmother's soft, loose cheek. She left the old lady sitting in her easy chair, her hands upon her knees, and her head turned sidelong towards her.

When Ann was gone to bed she used to sit reading her book by candle-light. She drew up her knees under the sheets, resting her book upon them. Her story was about fairies and gnomes; and the gently-flowing moonlight of the narrative seemed to illumine the white pages, and she could hear in fancy fairy voices, so silent was the great many-roomed house, and so mellifluent were the words of the story. Presently she put out her candle, and, with a confused babel of voices close to her ears, and faint swift pictures before her eyes, she fell asleep.

And in the dead of night she arose out of bed in dream, and with eyes wide open yet seeing nothing of reality, moved silently through the vacant house. Past the room where her grandmother was snoring in brief, heavy slumber, she stepped light and surely, and down the wide staircase. And Vega the far-shining stood over against the window above the slate roof. Ann walked in the strange room as if she were being guided by the hand toward the oak chest. There, just as if she was dreaming it was her bed, she laid herself down in the old rose silk, in the fragrant place. But it was so dark in the room that the movement of the lid was indisguishable.

Through the long day, the grandmother sat in her bow-window. Her lips were pursed, and she looked with dim, inquisitive scrutiny upon the street where people passed to and fro, and vehicles rolled by. At evening she climbed the stair and stood in the doorway of the large spare bedroom. The ascent had shortened her breath. Her magnifying spectacles rested upon her nose. Leaning her hand on the door-post she peered in towards the glimmering square of window in the quiet gloom. But she could not see far, because her sight was dim and the light of day feeble. Nor could she detect the faint fragrance, as of autumnal leaves. But in her mind was a tangled skein of memories—laughter and tears, and little children now old-fashioned, and the advent of friends, and long farewells. And gossiping fitfully, inarticulately, with herself, the old lady went down again to her window-seat.

EXERCISES

1. Walter de la Mare has been called a symbolist who believes that the outer world is an expression of an inner world and that external drama is the embodiment of internal drama. Discuss this story as symbolist.

2. Why are children so important in this story? How do children differ from adults in the way they think? Are children less likely than adults to believe that the material world is the only reality?

3. For de la Mare, only the imagination makes reality significant; external reality is like a dream that seems bewitched and insubstantial. Discuss this story from this point of view.

4. A *riddle* is a problem or puzzle that requires some ingenuity to solve. How is this story a riddle? Can it be solved in more than one way? Is it a significant riddle or a silly one? Does it embody some significant aspect of human experience?

5. Why does the grandmother grow more feeble every day? Why is Ann, the oldest, left till last? How is the way she enters the chest different from the way the others do?

6. If this story is a parable, what does it signify or stand for?

LIAM O'FLAHERTY | *The Fairy Goose*

An old woman named Mary Wiggins got three goose-eggs from a neighbour in order to hatch a clutch of goslings. She put an old clucking hen over the eggs in a wooden box with a straw bed. The hen proved to be a bad sitter. She was continually deserting the eggs, possibly because they were too big. The old woman then kept her shut up in the box. Either through weariness, want of air or simply pure devilment, the hen died on the eggs, two days before it was time for the shells to break.

The old woman shed tears of rage, both at the loss of her hen, of which she was particularly fond, and through fear of losing her goslings. She put the eggs near the fire in the kitchen, wrapped up in straw and old clothes. Two days afterwards, one of the eggs broke and a tiny gosling put out its beak. The other two eggs proved not to be fertile. They were thrown away.

The little gosling was a scraggy thing, so small and so delicate that the old woman, out of pity for it, wanted to kill it. But her husband said: "Kill nothing that is born in your house, woman alive. It's against the law of God."

"It's a true saying, my honest fellow," said the old woman. "What comes into the world is sent by God. Praised be He."

For a long time it seemed certain that the gosling was on the point of death. It spent all the day on the hearth in the kitchen nestling among the peat ashes, either sleeping or making little tweeky noises. When it was offered food, it stretched out its beak and pecked without rising off its stomach. Gradually, however, it became hardier and went out of doors to sit in the sun, on a flat rock. When it was three months it was still a yellowish colour with soft down even though other goslings of that age in the village were already going to the pond with the flock and able to flap their wings and join in the cackle at evening time, when the setting sun was being saluted. The little gosling was not aware of the other geese, even though it saw them rise on windy days and fly with a great noise from their houses to the pond. It made no effort to become a goose, and at four months of age it still could not stand on one leg.

The old woman came to believe that it was a fairy. The village women agreed with her after some dispute. It was decided to tie pink and red ribbons around the gosling's neck and to sprinkle holy water on its wing feathers.

That was done and then the gosling became sacred in the village. No boy dare throw a stone at it, or pull a feather from its wing, as they were in the habit of doing with geese, in order to get masts for the pieces of cork they floated in the pond as ships. When it began to move about, every house gave it dainty things. All the human beings in the village paid more respect to it than they did to one another. The little gosling had contracted a great affection for Mary Wiggins and followed her round everywhere, so that Mary Wiggins also came to have the reputation of being a woman of wisdom. Dreams were brought to her for unravelling. She was asked to set the spell of the Big Periwinkle and to tie the Knot of the Snakes on the sides of sick cows. And when children were ill, the gosling was brought secretly at night and led three times around the house on a thin halter of horsehair.

When the gosling was a year old it had not yet become a goose. Its down was still slightly yellowish. It did not cackle, but made curious tweeky noises. Instead of stretching out its neck and hissing at strangers, after the manner of a proper goose, it put its head to one side and made funny noises like a duck. It meditated like a hen, was afraid of water and cleansed itself by rolling on the grass. It fed on bread, fish and potatoes. It drank milk and tea. It amused itself by collecting pieces of cloth, nails, small fish-bones and the limpet-shells that are thrown in a heap beside dung-hills. These pieces of refuse it placed in a pile to the left of Mary Wiggins's door. And when the pile was tall, it made a sort of nest in the middle of it and lay in the nest.

Old Mrs. Wiggins had by now realized that the goose was worth money to her. So she became firmly convinced that the goose was gifted with super-natural powers. She accepted, in return for setting spells, a yard of white frieze cloth for unravelling dreams, a pound of sugar for setting the spell of the Big Periwinkle and half a donkey's load of potatoes for tying the Knot of the Snakes on a sick cow's side. Hitherto a kindly, humorous woman, she took to wearing her shawl in triangular fashion, with the tip of it reaching to her heels. She talked to herself or to her goose as she went along the road. She took long steps like a goose and rolled her eyes occasionally. When she cast a spell she went into an ecstasy, during which she made inarticulate sounds, like "boum, roum, toum, kroum."

Soon it became known all over the countryside that there was a woman of wisdom and a fairy goose in the village, and pilgrims came secretly from afar, at the dead of night, on the first night of the new moon, or when the spring tide had begun to wane.

The men soon began to raise their hats passing old Mary Wiggins's house, for it was understood, owing to the cure of Dara Foddy's cow, that the goose was indeed a good fairy and not a malicious one. Such was the excitement in the village and all over the countryside, that what was kept secret so long at last reached the ears of the parish priest.

The story was brought to him by an old woman from a neighbouring village to that in which the goose lived. Before the arrival of the goose, the other old woman had herself cast spells, not through her own merits but through those of her dead mother, who had a long time ago been the woman of wisdom in the district. The priest mounted his horse as soon as he heard the news and galloped at a break-neck speed towards Mary Wiggins's house, carrying his breviary and his stole. When he arrived in the village he dis-mounted at a distance from the house, gave his horse to a boy and put his stole around his neck.

A number of the villagers gathered and some tried to warn Mary Wiggins by whistling at a distance, but conscious that they had all taken part in some-thing forbidden by the sacred laws of orthodox religion, they were afraid to run ahead of the priest into the house. Mary Wiggins and her husband were within, making little ropes of brown horsehair which they sold as charms.

Outside the door, perched on her high nest, the little goose was sitting. There were pink and red ribbons around her neck and around her legs there were bands of black tape. She was quite small, a little more than half the size of a normal, healthy goose. But she had an elegant charm of manner, an air of civilization, and a consciousness of great dignity, which had grown out of the love and respect of the villagers.

When she saw the priest approach, she began to cackle gently, making the tweeky noise that was peculiar to her. She descended from her perch and waddled towards him, expecting some dainty gift. But instead of stretching out his hand to offer her something and saying, "Beadai, beadai, come here," as was customary, the priest halted and muttered something in a harsh, frightened voice. He became red in the face and he took off his hat.

Then for the first time in her life the little goose became terrified. She opened her beak, spread her wings and lowered her head. She began to hiss violently. Turning around, she waddled back to her nest, flapping her wings and raising a loud cackle, just like a goose, although she had never been heard to cackle loudly like a goose before. Clambering up on her high nest, she lay there, quite flat, trembling violently.

The bird, never having known fear of human beings, never having been treated with discourtesy, was so violently moved by the extraordinary phenomenon of a man wearing black clothes, scowling at her and muttering, that her animal nature was roused and showed itself with disgusting violence.

The people watching this scene were astounded. Some took off their caps and crossed themselves. For some reason it was made manifest to them that the goose was an evil spirit and not the good fairy which they had supposed her to be. Terrified of the priest's stole and of his breviary and of his scowling countenance, they were only too eager to attribute the goose's strange hissing and her still stranger cackle to supernatural forces of an evil nature. Some present even caught a faint rumble of thunder in the east, and although it was not noticed at the time, an old woman later asserted that she heard a great cackle of geese afar off, raised in answer to the fairy goose's cackle.

"It was," said the old woman, "certainly the whole army of devils offering her help to kill the holy priest."

The priest turned to the people and cried, raising his right hand in a threatening manner:

"I wonder the ground doesn't open up and swallow you all. Idolaters!"

"O father, blessed by the hand of God," cried an old woman, the one who later asserted she had heard the devilish cackle afar off. She threw herself on her knees in the road, crying: "Spare us, father."

Old Mrs. Wiggins, having heard the strange noises, rushed out into the yard with her triangular shawl trailing and her black hair loose. She began to make vague, mystic movements with her hands, as had recently become a habit with her. Lost in some sort of ecstasy, she did not see the priest at first. She began to chant something.

"You hag," cried the priest, rushing up the yard towards her menacingly.

The old woman caught sight of him and screamed. But she faced him boldly.

"Come no farther," she cried, still in an ecstasy, either affected, or the result of a firm belief in her own mystic powers.

Indeed, it is difficult to believe that she was not in earnest, for she used to be a kind, gentle woman.

Her husband rushed out, crying aloud. Seeing the priest, he dropped a piece of rope he had in his hand and fled around the corner of the house.

"Leave my way, you hag," cried the priest, raising his hand to strike her.

"Stand back," she cried. "Don't lay a hand on my goose."

"Leave my way," yelled the priest, "or I'll curse you."

"Curse, then," cried the unfortunate woman. "Curse!"

Instead, the priest gave her a blow under the ear, which felled her smartly. Then he strode up to the goose's nest and seized the goose. The goose, paralysed with terror, was just able to open her beak and hiss at him. He stripped the ribbons off her neck and tore the tape off her feet. Then he threw her out of the nest. Seizing a spade that stood by the wall, he began to scatter the refuse of which the nest was composed.

The old woman, lying prostrate in the yard, raised her head and began to chant in the traditional fashion, used by women of wisdom.

"I'll call on the winds of the east and of the west, I'll raise the winds of the sea. The lightning will flash in the sky and there'll be great sounds of giants warring in the heavens. Blight will fall on the earth and calves with fishes' tails will be born of cows. . . ."

The little goose, making tweeky noises, waddled over to the old woman and tried to hide herself under the long shawl. The people murmured at this, seeing in it fresh signs of devilry.

Then the priest threw down the spade and hauled the old woman to her feet, kicking aside the goose. The old woman, exhausted by her ecstasy and possibly seeking to gain popular support, either went into a faint or feigned one. Her hands and her feet hung limply. Again the people murmured. The priest, becoming embarrassed, put her sitting against the wall. Then he didn't know what to do, for his anger had exhausted his reason. He either became ashamed of having beaten an old woman, or he felt the situation was altogether ridiculous. So he raised his hand and addressed the people in a sorrowful voice.

"Let this be a warning," he said sadly. "This poor woman and . . . all of you, led astray by . . . foolish and . . . Avarice is at the back of this," he cried suddenly in an angry voice, shaking his fist. "The woman has been preying on your credulity, in order to extort money from you by her pretended sorcery. That's all it is. Money is at the back of it. But I give you warning. If I hear another word about this, I'll . . ."

He paused uncertainly, wondering what to threaten the poor people with. Then he added:

"I'll report it to the Archbishop of the diocese."

The people raised a loud murmur, asking forgiveness.

"Fear God," he added finally, "and love your neighbours."

Then, throwing a stone angrily at the goose, he strode out of the yard and left the village.

It was then the people began to curse violently and threaten to burn the old woman's house. The responsible people among them, however, chiefly those who had hitherto paid no respect to the superstition concerning the goose, restrained their violence. Finally the people went home and Mary Wiggins's husband, who had been hiding in a barn, came and brought his wife indoors. The little goose, uttering cries of amazement, began to collect the rubbish once more, piling it in a heap in order to rebuild her nest. That night, just after the moon had risen, a band of young men collected, approached Mary Wiggins's house and enticed the goose from her nest, by calling, "Beadai, beadai, come here, come here."

The little goose, delighted that people were again kind and respectful to her, waddled down to the gate, making happy noises.

The youths stoned her to death.

And the little goose never uttered a sound, so terrified and amazed was she at this treatment from people who had formerly loved her and whom she had never injured.

Next morning, when Mary Wiggins discovered the dead carcase of the goose, she went into a fit, during which she cursed the village, the priest, and all mankind.

And indeed it appeared that her blasphemous prayer took some effect at least. Although giants did not war in the heavens and though cows did not give birth to fishes, it is certain that from that day the natives of that village are quarrelsome drunkards, who fear God but do not love one another. And the old woman is again collecting followers from among the wives of the drunkards. These women maintain that the only time in the history of their generation that there was peace and harmony in the village was during the time when the fairy goose was loved by the people.

EXERCISES

1. Why does the gosling become sacred in the village? What does *sacred* mean in this context?

2. Discuss the motivation of old Mrs. Wiggins. Discuss the motivation of the woman who tells the parish priest about the gosling.

3. Discuss the effect the priest has on the goose. What does this mean?

4. Is Mary Wiggins pretending, or has she been transformed? How do you know?

5. Discuss the confrontation between the priest and Mary Wiggins. What motivates the priest?

6. Why is the goose killed? What effect does this have on you? What is the basic meaning of the story? Is this a comic or a serious parable, or both?

LEO
TOLSTOY | *The Three Hermits:*
An Old Legend Current
in the Volga District

> And in praying use not vain repetitions as the Gentiles
> do: for they think they shall be heard for their much
> speaking. Be not therefore like them; for your Father
> knoweth what things ye have need of, before ye ask
> Him.
>
> *Matthew vi: 7, 8.*

A Bishop was sailing from Archangel to the Solovétsk Monastery, and on the same vessel were a number of pilgrims on their way to visit the shrines at that place. The voyage was a smooth one. The wind favorable and the weather fair. The pilgrims lay on deck, eating, or sat in groups talking to one another. The Bishop, too, came on deck, and as he was pacing up and down he noticed a group of men standing near the prow and listening to a fisherman, who was pointing to the sea and telling them something. The Bishop stopped, and looked in the direction in which the man was pointing. He could see nothing, however, but the sea glistening in the sunshine. He drew nearer to listen, but when the man saw him, he took off his cap and was silent. The rest of the people also took off their caps and bowed.

"Do not let me disturb you, friends," said the Bishop. "I came to hear what this good man was saying."

"The fisherman was telling us about the hermits," replied one, a tradesman, rather bolder than the rest.

"What hermits?" asked the Bishop, going to the side of the vessel and seating himself on a box. "Tell me about them. I should like to hear. What were you pointing at?"

"Why, that little island you can just see over there," answered the man, pointing to a spot ahead and a little to the right. "That is the island where the hermits live for the salvation of their souls."

"Where is the island?" asked the Bishop. "I see nothing."

"There, in the distance, if you will please look along my hand. Do you see that little cloud? Below it, and a bit to the left, there is just a faint streak. That is the island."

The Bishop looked carefully, but his unaccustomed eyes could make out nothing but the water shimmering in the sun.

"I cannot see it," he said. "But who are the hermits that live there?"

"They are holy men," answered the fisherman. "I had long heard tell of them, but never chanced to see them myself till the year before last."

And the fisherman related how once, when he was out fishing, he had been stranded at night upon that island, not knowing where he was. In the morning, as he wandered about the island, he came across an earth hut, and met an old man standing near it. Presently two others came out, and after having fed him and dried his things, they helped him mend his boat.

"And what are they like?" asked the Bishop.

"One is a small man and his back is bent. He wears a priest's cassock and is very old; he must be more than a hundred, I should say. He is so old that the white of his beard is taking a greenish tinge, but he is always smiling, and his face is as bright as an angel's from heaven. The second is taller, but he also is very old. He wears a tattered peasant coat. His beard is broad, and of a yellowish grey color. He is a strong man. Before I had time to help him, he turned my boat over as if it were only a pail. He too is kindly and cheerful. The third is tall, and has a beard as white as snow and reaching to his knees. He is stern, with overhanging eyebrows; and he wears nothing but a piece of matting tied round his waist."

"And did they speak to you?" asked the Bishop.

"For the most part they did everything in silence, and spoke but little even to one another. One of them would just give a glance, and the others would understand him. I asked the tallest whether they had lived there long. He frowned, and muttered something as if he were angry; but the oldest one took his hand and smiled, and then the tall one was quiet. The oldest one only said: 'Have mercy upon us,' and smiled."

While the fisherman was talking, the ship had drawn nearer to the island.

"There, now you can see it plainly, if your Lordship will please to look," said the tradesman, pointing with his hand.

The Bishop looked, and now he really saw a dark streak—which was the island. Having looked at it a while, he left the prow of the vessel, and going to the stern, asked the helmsman:

"What island is that?"

"That one," replied the man, "has no name. There are many such in this sea."

"Is it true that there are hermits who live there for the salvation of their souls?"

"So it is said, your Lordship, but I don't know if it's true. Fishermen say they have seen them; but of course they may only be spinning yarns."

"I should like to land on the island and see these men," said the Bishop. "How could I manage it?"

"The ship cannot get close to the island," replied the helmsman, "but you might be rowed there in a boat. You had better speak to the captain."

The captain was sent for and came.

"I should like to see these hermits," said the Bishop. "Could I not be rowed ashore?"

The captain tried to dissuade him.

"Of course it could be done," said he, "but we should lose much time. And if I might venture to say so to your Lordship, the old men are not worth your pains. I have heard say that they are foolish old fellows, who understand nothing, and never speak a word, any more than the fish in the sea."

"I wish to see them," said the Bishop, "and I will pay you for your trouble and loss of time. Please let me have a boat."

There was no help for it; so the order was given. The sailors trimmed the sails, the steersman put up the helm, and the ship's course was set for the island. A chair was placed at the prow for the Bishop, and he sat there, looking ahead. The passengers all collected at the prow, and gazed at the island. Those who had the sharpest eyes could presently make out the rocks on it, and then a mud hut was seen. At last one man saw the hermits themselves. The captain brought a telescope and, after looking through it, handed it to the Bishop.

"It's right enough. There are three men standing on the shore. There, a little to the right of that big rock."

The Bishop took the telescope, got it into position, and he saw the three men: a tall one, a shorter one, and one very small and bent, standing on the shore and holding each other by the hand.

The captain turned to the Bishop.

"The vessel can get no nearer in than this, your Lordship. If you wish to go ashore, we must ask you to go in the boat, while we anchor here."

The cable was quickly let out; the anchor cast, and the sails furled. There was a jerk, and the vessel shook. Then, a boat having been lowered, the oarsmen jumped in, and the Bishop descended the ladder and took his seat. The men pulled at their oars and the boat moved rapidly towards the island. When they came within a stone's throw, they saw three old men: a tall one with only a piece of matting tied round his waist, a shorter one in a tattered peasant coat, and a very old one bent with age and wearing an old cassock—all three standing hand in hand.

The oarsmen pulled in to the shore, and held on with the boathook while the Bishop got out.

The old men bowed to him, and he gave them his blessing, at which they bowed still lower. Then the Bishop began to speak to them.

"I have heard," he said, "that you, godly men, live here saving your own souls and praying to our Lord Christ for your fellow men. I, an unworthy servant of Christ, am called, by God's mercy, to keep and teach His flock. I wished to see you, servants of God, and to do what I can to teach you, also."

The old men looked at each other smiling, but remained silent.

"Tell me," said the Bishop, "what you are doing to save your souls, and how you serve God on this island."

The second hermit sighed, and looked at the oldest, the very ancient one. The latter smiled, and said:

"We do not know how to serve God. We only serve and support ourselves, servant of God."

"But how do you pray to God?" asked the Bishop.

"We pray in this way," replied the hermit. "Three are ye, three are we, have mercy upon us."

And when the old man said this, all three raised their eyes to heaven, and repeated:

"Three are ye, three are we, have mercy upon us!"

The Bishop smiled.

"You have evidently heard something about the Holy Trinity," said he. "But you do not pray aright. You have won my affection, godly men. I see you wish to please the Lord, but you do not know how to serve Him. That is not the way to pray; but listen to me, and I will teach you. I will teach you, not a way of my own, but the way in which God in the Holy Scriptures has commanded all men to pray to Him."

And the Bishop began explaining to the hermits how God had revealed Himself to men; telling them of God the Father, and God the Son, and God the Holy Ghost.

"God the Son came down on earth," said he, "to save men, and this is how He taught us all to pray. Listen, and repeat after me: 'Our Father.' "

And the first old man repeated after him, "Our Father," and the second said, "Our Father," and the third said, "Our Father."

"Which art in heaven," continued the Bishop.

The first hermit repeated, "Which art in heaven," but the second blundered over the words, and the tall hermit could not say them properly. His hair had grown over his mouth so that he could not speak plainly. The very old hermit, having no teeth, also mumbled indistinctly.

The Bishop repeated the words again, and the old men repeated them after him. The Bishop sat down on a stone, and the old men stood before him, watching his mouth, and repeating the words as he uttered them. And all day long the Bishop labored, saying a word twenty, thirty, a hundred times over, and the old men repeated it after him. They blundered, and he corrected them, and made them begin again.

The Bishop did not leave off till he had taught them the whole of the Lord's Prayer so that they could not only repeat it after him, but could say it by themselves. The middle one was the first to know it, and to repeat the whole of it alone. The Bishop made him say it again and again, and at last the others could say it too.

It was getting dark and the moon was appearing over the water, before the Bishop rose to return to the vessel. When he took leave of the old men they all bowed down to the ground before him. He raised them, and kissed each of them, telling them to pray as he had taught them. Then he got into the boat and returned to the ship.

And as he sat in the boat and was rowed to the ship he could hear the three voices of the hermits loudly repeating the Lord's Prayer. As the boat drew near the vessel their voices could no longer be heard, but they could still be seen in the moonlight, standing as he had left them on the shore, the shortest in the middle, the tallest on the right, the middle one on the left. As soon as the Bishop had reached the vessel and got on board, the anchor was weighed and the sails unfurled. The wind filled them and the ship sailed away, and the Bishop took a seat in the stern and watched the island they had left. For a time he could still see the hermits, but presently they disappeared from sight, though the island was still visible. At last it too vanished, and only the sea was to be seen, rippling in the moonlight.

The pilgrims lay down to sleep, and all was quiet on deck. The Bishop did not wish to sleep, but sat alone at the stern, gazing at the sea where the island was no longer visible, and thinking of the good old men. He thought how pleased they had been to learn the Lord's Prayer; and he thanked God for having sent him to teach and help such godly men.

So the Bishop sat, thinking, and gazing at the sea where the island had disappeared. And the moonlight flickered before his eyes, sparkling, now here, now there, upon the waves. Suddenly he saw something white and shining, on the bright path which the moon cast across the sea. Was it a seagull, or the little gleaming sail of some small boat? The Bishop fixed his eyes on it, wondering.

"It must be a boat sailing after us," thought he, "but it is overtaking us very rapidly. It was far, far away a minute ago, but now it is much nearer. It cannot be a boat, for I can see no sail; but whatever it may be, it is following us and catching us up."

And he could not make out what it was. Not a boat, nor a bird, nor a fish! It was too large for a man, and besides a man could not be out there in the midst of the sea. The Bishop rose, and said to the helmsman:

"Look there, what is that, my friend? What is it?" the Bishop repeated, though he could now see plainly what it was—the three hermits running upon the water, all gleaming white, their grey beards shining, and approaching the ship as quickly as though it were not moving.

The steersman looked, and let go the helm in terror.

"Oh, Lord! The hermits are running after us on the water as though it were dry land!"

The passengers, hearing him, jumped up and crowded to the stern. They saw the hermits coming along hand in hand, and the two outer ones beckoning the ship to stop. All three were gliding along upon the water without moving their feet. Before the ship could be stopped, the hermits had reached it, and raising their heads, all three as with one voice, began to say:

"We have forgotten your teaching, servant of God. As long as we kept repeating it we remembered, but when we stopped saying it for a time, a word dropped out, and now it has all gone to pieces. We can remember nothing of it. Teach us again."

The Bishop crossed himself, and leaning over the ship's side, said:

"Your own prayer will reach the Lord, men of God. It is not for me to teach you. Pray for us sinners."

And the Bishop bowed low before the old men; and they turned and went back across the sea. And a light shone until daybreak on the spot where they were lost to sight.

EXERCISES

1. What does it mean to live for the salvation of your soul? Why is there an assumption that the truly religious person must cut himself or herself off from the world? What does it mean to be holy? What does it mean to be a saint?

2. What relationship is there between being religious and being foolish?

3. From what perspective does the Bishop think that he has something to teach the hermits?

4. What is the difference between the prayer the hermits say and the prayer the Bishop teaches them?

5. Why are the hermits able to run upon the water?

6. It has been said that the world is divided up between that for which we have words and that for which we do not have words. Discuss the differences between words and that which goes beyond words. Why does the bishop say it is not for him to teach the hermits?

GOTTFRIED
KELLER | # A Little Legend of the Dance

Saint Gregory relates in his tales that Musa was the dancer among the saints. She was the child of good folk, and a graceful little maiden who diligently served the Mother of God and knew only one passion, a love of dancing so uncontrollable that if the girl was not praying, then she was assuredly dancing. And she danced in every conceivable way. Musa danced with her playmates, with the children, with the young men, and even alone. She danced in her little chamber, in the great hall, in the gardens, and over the meadows, and even when she approached the altar she seemed to be dancing a delicious measure rather than walking. And on the smooth marble flags at the church door she never forgot to try a few hasty steps.

Indeed, one day, when she happened to be alone in church, she could not refrain from dancing a few figures in front of the altar and, so to speak, dancing a pretty prayer to the Virgin. She forgot herself so utterly that she fancied she was dreaming when an elderly but handsome gentleman came dancing toward her and supplemented her figures so deftly that between them the two performed the most finished *pas de deux*. The gentleman wore a royal robe of purple and a golden crown on his head, and had a glossy black beard lightly silvered with age as by distant starlight. And music sounded from the choir, for half a dozen cherubs were sitting or standing there on the top of the screen swinging their chubby little legs over it while they played or blew divers instruments. And the urchins made themselves quite comfortable, for each propped his music against one of the stone angels that adorned the choir screen. But the smallest, a round-cheeked piper, was an exception, for he crossed his legs and contrived to hold his music in his rosy toes. And he was the most zealous of all. The others swung their feet, stretched their rustling wings till they shimmered like the breasts of doves, and teased each other as they played.

Musa found no time to wonder at all this until the dance, which lasted some time, was over. The merry gentleman seemed to enjoy it as much as the maiden, who, for her part, might have been tripping about in heaven. But when the music stopped and Musa stood there panting, she began to be really afraid and looked at the old gentleman in amazement, for he was neither out of breath nor hot. He began to speak and introduced himself as David, the royal ancestor of Mary the Virgin, and her messenger. He asked her whether she would like to pass an eternity of bliss in an endless dance of joy, a dance compared with which the one they had just ended could only be called a dismal crawl.

She promptly replied that she could wish for nothing better. Whereupon the blessed King David rejoined that all she had to do was to give up all dancing and all joy for the rest of her earthly days and dedicate herself to penitence and spiritual exercises, and that without faltering or relapse.

At this the maiden was somewhat taken aback, and asked whether she must give up dancing altogether. She doubted whether there really was dancing in heaven, for there was a time for everything. Solid earth seemed a good and suitable place for dancing. Therefore heaven must have other things to offer; otherwise death would simply be superfluous.

David explained to her how sorely she was in error, and proved by many passages from the Bible, as by his own example, that dancing was certainly a blessed occupation for the blessed. But now she must make up her mind quickly, yes or no, whether by temporal renunciation she wished to enter into eternal bliss, or not; if not, he must be getting along, as heaven was in need of a few dancers.

Musa still stood there irresolute, her fingertips playing anxiously about her mouth. It seemed too hard never to dance again just for the sake of an unknown reward.

Then David made a sign and suddenly the musicians played a few bars of a dance, so incredibly blissful and unearthly that the maiden's soul leaped in her body and she twitched in every limb. But she could not move one of them to the measure, and she saw that her body was too stiff and heavy for that music. Full of longing, she thrust her hand into the King's and gave her promise.

Forthwith he vanished and the cherub musicians whirred and fluttered and crowded away through an open window in the church, but first they rolled up their music sheets and, like mischievous children, slapped the patient angels' faces till the church re-echoed.

Musa walked home with devout steps, the heavenly melody in her ears. She had a coarse garment made, laid aside all her fine raiment, and put it on. Then she built a cell in the back of her parents' garden where the shadows of the trees lay thick, made a little bed of moss in it, and lived thenceforth apart from her companions as a penitent and a saint. She passed all her time in prayer, and often scourged herself.

But her severest penance was to keep her limbs still and rigid. As soon as there was a single sound in the air, the twittering of a bird or the rustling of the leaves in the trees, her feet twitched and felt that they must dance. Because this involuntary twitching would not disappear and sometimes, before she was even aware of it, she could not suppress a little pirouette, she had her frail feet bound together with a light chain. Her relatives and friends marveled day and night at the change, but rejoiced in the possession of such a saint and guarded the hermitage under the trees as the apple of their eye. Many came for counsel and intercession. Above all, young maidens were brought to her who were a little heavy on their feet, for it had been noticed that any she touched became light and graceful of movement.

So she passed three years in her solitude, and toward the end of the third year Musa had become almost as thin and transparent as a summer cloud. She no longer moved from her little bed of moss, and lay looking longingly up to heaven. She thought that she could see the golden soles of the blessed dancing and gliding through the blue.

One raw autumn day the news went round that the saint was lying at the point of death. She had had her dark penitential robe taken from her and was clad in dazzling white bridal garments. So she lay with folded hands and smilingly awaited the hour of death.

The whole garden was filled with pious people, the breezes whispered, and the leaves were falling from the trees on every hand. But imperceptibly the whispering of the trees passed into music, which seemed to sound in every treetop, and when the people looked up, lo! everything was clothed in tender green. The myrtles and pomegranates bloomed in fragrance. The earth was decked with flowers, and a rose-colored light lay on the frail form of the dying maiden.

At that moment she gave up the ghost. The chain on her feet sprang asunder with a clear ringing sound. Heaven opened wide, full of infinite splendor, so that all might see beyond. Host upon host of lovely maidens and youths in utmost glory could be seen dancing in endless circles. A splendid King, enthroned on a cloud with a band of six cherubs sitting on its edge, descended a little toward earth and received the form of the blessed Musa before the eyes of all those who filled the garden. They saw how she was borne up to heaven, and forthwith danced out of sight amid the singing of the shining hosts.

In heaven it was high festival. On festal days, however (this is contested by Saint Gregory of Nyssa, but maintained by his namesake of Nazianzus), it was the custom to invite the Muses, who were sitting in hell, into heaven to lend a hand. They were well entertained, but when their work was done, they had to go back to the other place.

When the dances and all the ceremonies were at an end, and the heavenly hosts sat down to table, Musa was led to the table where the nine Muses were sitting. They sat huddled together, half-intimidated, staring round them with their eyes of fiery black or deep blue. Busy Martha from the Gospel served them with her own hands. She had put on her best kitchen apron and had a dainty little smudge on her white chin, and she kindly pressed the good things on the Muses. But it was only when Musa and Saint Cecilia and other women famed in art came along and cheerily greeted the shy Pierians and sat down beside them that they brightened up and grew confidential, while a charming gaiety spread over the whole circle of the women. Musa sat beside Terpsichore, and Cecilia between Polyhymnia and Euterpe, and they all held one another's hands. Then the little cherub musicians came up and made much of the beautiful women, hoping to get some of the shining fruit on the ambrosial table. King David came too in person and brought a golden goblet from which all drank. He passed kindly round the table, not forgetting to pat the lovely Erato's chin as he passed. As things were going so merrily at the Muses' table, our dear Lady herself appeared in all her beauty and goodness, to sit with the Muses awhile. She tenderly kissed the august Urania on the mouth under her starry coronal, and as she said good-by, whispered that she would not rest until the Muses should again sit in paradise forever.

But it did not turn out so. To show their gratitude for the kindness shown them, the Muses took counsel together, and in a distant corner of the underworld, practiced a hymn of praise, to which they tried to give the form of the solemn chorales usual in heaven. They divided into two groups of four voices each, with Urania singing a kind of descant, and so produced a remarkable piece of music.

When the next festival was celebrated in heaven, and the Muses were again on duty, they took advantage of a moment that seemed favorable, grouped themselves, and softly began their song, which soon swelled into a mighty chorus. But in those spaces it sounded so somber—nay, defiant and harsh—so heavy with longing, and so complaining, that at first a terrified silence reigned. Then the whole assembly was seized by earthly suffering and the yearning for earth, and a general weeping broke out.

Endless sighs throbbed through heaven. All the Elders and Prophets started up, terrified and dismayed, while the Muses, with the best intentions, sang ever louder and more sadly. All paradise, with the Patriarchs, the Elders, and the Prophets, all who had ever walked or lain on green pastures, were quite beside themselves. But at last the Holy Trinity itself came up to set things right, and silenced the zealous Muses with a long rolling peal of thunder.

Then peace and serenity returned to heaven, but the poor sisters had to depart; they have never been allowed to return since.

EXERCISES

1. What basic human desires underlie the desire to dance? How is dancing a "blessed occupation for the blessed"?

2. Why is Musa unable to dance to the heavenly music? Why does it fill her with longing? Why does she agree to David's conditions?

3. How does Musa's giving up earthly dance and scourging herself make her a saint? What does it mean that she becomes "almost as thin and transparent as a summer cloud"?

4. Why are the muses in hell while the saints are in heaven? What is the significance of having both groups together for a festival in heaven?

5. Why does the song composed and sung by the muses make the whole assembly filled with a "yearning for earth"?

6. Discuss the basic meaning of the legend, focusing particularly on the relationship between body and spirit, sacred and profane, heavenly and earthly.

LANGSTON
HUGHES | *On the Road*

He was not interested in the snow. When he got off the freight, one early evening during the depression, Sargeant never even noticed the snow. But he must have felt it seeping down his neck, cold, wet, sopping in his shoes. But if you had asked him, he wouldn't have known it was snowing. Sargeant didn't see the snow, not even under the bright lights of the main street, falling white and flaky against the night. He was too hungry, too sleepy, too tired.

The Reverend Mr. Dorset, however, saw the snow when he switched on his porch light, opened the front door of his parsonage, and found standing there before him a big black man with snow on his face, a human piece of night with snow on his face—obviously unemployed.

Said the Reverend Mr. Dorset before Sargeant even realized he'd opened his mouth: "I'm sorry. No! Go right on down this street four blocks and turn to your left, walk up seven and you'll see the Relief Shelter. I'm sorry. No!" He shut the door.

Sargeant wanted to tell the holy man that he had already been to the Relief Shelter, been to hundreds of relief shelters during the depression years, the beds were always gone and supper was over, the place was full, and they drew the color line anyhow. But the minister said, "No," and shut the door. Evidently he didn't want to hear about it. And he *had* a door to shut.

The big black man turned away. And even yet he didn't see the snow, walking right into it. Maybe he sensed it, cold, wet, sticking to his jaws, wet on his black hands, sopping in his shoes. He stopped and stood on the sidewalk hunched over—hungry, sleepy, cold—looking up and down. Then he looked right where he was—in front of a church. Of course! A church! Sure, right next to a parsonage, certainly a church.

It had *two* doors.

Broad white steps in the night all snowy white. Two high arched doors with slender stone pillars on either side. And way up, a round lacy window with a stone crucifix in the middle and Christ on the crucifix in stone. All this was pale in the street lights, solid and stony pale in the snow.

Sargeant blinked. When he looked up, the snow fell into his eyes. For the first time that night he *saw* the snow. He shook his head. He shook the snow from his coat sleeves, felt hungry, felt lost, felt not lost, felt cold. He walked up the steps of the church. He knocked at the door. No answer. He tried the handle. Locked. He put his shoulder against the door and his long black body slanted like a ramrod. He pushed. With loud rhythmic grunts, like the grunts in a chain-gang song, he pushed against the door.

"I'm tired . . . Huh! . . . Hongry . . . Uh! . . . I'm sleepy . . . Huh! I'm cold . . . I got to sleep somewheres," Sargeant said. "This here is a church, ain't it? Well, uh!"

He pushed against the door.

Suddenly, with an undue cracking and screaking, the door began to give way to the tall black Negro who pushed ferociously against it.

By now two or three white people had stopped in the street, and Sargeant was vaguely aware of some of them yelling at him concerning the door. Three or four more came running, yelling at him.

"Hey!" they said. "Hey!"

"Uh-huh," answered the big tall Negro, "I know it's a white folks' church, but I got to sleep somewhere." He gave another lunge at the door. "Huh!"

And the door broke open.

But just when the door gave way, two white cops arrived in a car, ran up the steps with their clubs, and grabbed Sargeant. But Sargeant for once had no intention of being pulled or pushed away from the door.

Sargeant grabbed, but not for anything so weak as a broken door. He grabbed for one of the tall stone pillars beside the door, grabbed at it and caught it. And held it. The cops pulled and Sargeant pulled. Most of the people in the street got behind the cops and helped them pull.

"A big black unemployed Negro holding onto our church!" thought the people. "The idea!"

The cops began to beat Sargeant over the head, and nobody protested. But he held on.

And then the church fell down.

Gradually, the big stone front of the church fell down, the walls and the rafters, the crucifix and the Christ. Then the whole thing fell down, covering the cops and the people with bricks and stones and debris. The whole church fell down in the snow.

Sargeant got out from under the church and went walking on up the street with the stone pillar on his shoulder. He was under the impression that he had buried the parsonage and the Reverend Mr. Dorset who said, "No!" So he laughed, and threw the pillar six blocks up the street and went on.

Sargeant thought he was alone, but listening to the *crunch, crunch, crunch* on the snow of his own footsteps, he heard other footsteps, too, doubling his own. He looked around, and there was Christ walking along beside him, the same Christ that had been on the cross on the church—still stone with a rough stone surface, walking along beside him just like he was broken off the cross when the church fell down.

"Well, I'll be dogged," said Sargeant. "This here's the first time I ever seed you off the cross."

"Yes," said Christ, crunching his feet in the snow. "You had to pull the church down to get me off the cross."

"You glad?" said Sargeant.

"I sure am," said Christ.

They both laughed.

"I'm a hell of a fellow, ain't I?" said Sargeant. "Done pulled the church down!"

"You did a good job," said Christ. "They have kept me nailed on a cross for nearly two thousand years."

"Whee-ee-e!" said Sargeant. "I know you are glad to get off."

"I sure am," said Christ.

They walked on in the snow. Sargeant looked at the man of stone.

"And you have been up there two thousand years?"

"I sure have," said Christ.

"Well, if I had a little cash," said Sargeant, "I'd show you around a bit."

"I been around," said Christ.

"Yeah, but that was a long time ago."

"All the same," said Christ, "I've been around."

They walked on in the snow until they came to the railroad yards. Sargeant was tired, sweating and tired.

"Where you goin'?" Sargeant said, stopping by the tracks. He looked at Christ. Sargeant said, "I'm just a bum on the road. How about you? Where you goin'?"

"God knows," Christ said, "but I'm leavin' here."

They saw the red and green lights of the railroad yard half veiled by the snow that fell out of the night. Away down the track they saw a fire in a hobo jungle.

"I can go there and sleep," Sargeant said.

"You can?"

"Sure," said Sargeant. "That place ain't got no doors."

Outside the town, along the tracks, there were barren trees and bushes below the embankment, snow-gray in the dark. And down among the trees and bushes there were makeshift houses made out of boxes and tin and old pieces of wood and canvas. You couldn't see them in the dark, but you knew they were there if you'd ever been on the road, if you had ever lived with the homeless and hungry in a depression.

"I'm side-tracking," Sargeant said. "I'm tired."

"I'm gonna make it on to Kansas City," said Christ.

"O.K.," Sargeant said. "So long!"

He went down into the hobo jungle and found himself a place to sleep. He never did see Christ no more. About 6:00 A.M. a freight came by. Sargeant scrambled out of the jungle with a dozen or so more hobos and ran along the track, grabbing at the freight. It was dawn, early dawn, cold and gray.

"Wonder where Christ is by now?" Sargeant thought. "He musta gone on way on down the road. He didn't sleep in this jungle."

Sargeant grabbed the train and started to pull himself up into a moving coal car, over the edge of a wheeling coal car. But strangely enough, the car was full of cops. The nearest cop rapped Sargeant soundly across the knuckles with his night stick. Wham! Rapped his big black hands for clinging to the top of the car. Wham! But Sargeant did not turn loose. He clung on and tried to pull himself into the car. He hollered at the top of his voice, "Damn it, lemme in this car!"

"Shut up," barked the cop. "You crazy coon!" He rapped Sargeant across the knuckles and punched him in the stomach. "You ain't out in no jungle now. This ain't no train. You in jail."

Wham! across his bare black fingers clinging to the bars of his cell. Wham! between the steel bars low down against his shins.

Suddenly Sargeant realized that he really was in jail. He wasn't on no train. The blood of the night before had dried on his face, his head hurt terribly, and a cop outside in the corridor was hitting him across the knuckles for holding onto the door, yelling and shaking the cell door.

"They musta took me to jail for breaking down the door last night," Sargeant thought, "that church door."

Sargeant went over and sat on a wooden bench against the cold stone wall. He was emptier than ever. His clothes were wet, clammy cold wet, and shoes sloppy with snow water. It was just about dawn. There he was, locked up behind a cell door, nursing his bruised fingers.

The bruised fingers were his, but not the *door.*

Not the *club,* but the fingers.

"You wait," mumbled Sargeant, black against the jail wall. "I'm gonna break down this door, too."

"Shut up—or I'll paste you one," said the cop.

"I'm gonna break down this door," yelled Sargeant as he stood up in his cell.

Then he must have been talking to himself because he said, "I wonder where Christ's gone? I wonder if he's gone to Kansas City?"

Exercises

1. Discuss the significance of the basic situation here: black man, the depression, turned away by the church on a snowy winter night.

2. Discuss the scene of the policemen pulling at Sargeant while he clings to the two stone pillars: " 'A big black unemployed Negro holding onto our church!' thought the people. 'The idea!' " What is the idea behind this image?

3. Why does the church fall down? Is this a supernatural story or a parable? What is the difference?

4. What is the significance of the image of Sargeant walking down the street with the pillar on his shoulder?

5. What is the personality of the Christ that the author creates here? Why does Christ come down from the cross? What is appropriate about the image of Christ as a homeless person?

6. What is the effect of Sargeant wondering at the end if Christ has gone to Kansas City? Is it a comic effect or a serious effect?

LAFCADIO
HEARN | *The Boy Who Drew Cats*

A long, long time ago, in a small country village in Japan, there lived a poor farmer and his wife, who were very good people. They had a number of children, and found it very hard to feed them all. The elder son was strong enough when only fourteen years old to help his father; and the little girls learned to help their mother almost as soon as they could walk.

But the youngest, a little boy, did not seem to be fit for hard work. He was very clever—cleverer than all his brothers and sisters; but he was quite weak and small, and people said he could never grow very big. So his parents thought it would be better for him to become a priest than to become a farmer. They took him with them to the village-temple one day, and asked the good old priest who lived there if he would have their little boy for his acolyte, and teach him all that a priest ought to know.

The old man spoke kindly to the lad, and asked him some hard questions. So clever were the answers that the priest agreed to take the little fellow into the temple as an acolyte, and to educate him for the priesthood.

The boy learned quickly what the old priest taught him, and was very obedient in most things. But he had one fault. He liked to draw cats during study-hours, and to draw cats even where cats ought not to have been drawn at all.

Whenever he found himself alone, he drew cats. He drew them on the margins of the priest's books, and on all the screens of the temple, and on the walls, and on the pillars. Several times the priest told him this was not right; but he did not stop drawing cats. He drew them because he could not really help it. He had what is called "the genius of an artist," and just for that reason he was not quite fit to be an acolyte;—a good acolyte should study books.

One day after he had drawn some very clever pictures of cats upon a paper screen, the old priest said to him severely: "My boy, you must go away from this temple at once. You will never make a good priest, but perhaps you will become a great artist. Now let me give you a last piece of advice, and be sure you never forget it. *Avoid large places at night;—keep to small!*"

The boy did not know what the priest meant by saying, "*Avoid large places;—keep to small.*" He thought and thought, while he was tying up his little bundle of clothes to go away; but he could not understand those words, and he was afraid to speak to the priest any more, except to say goodby.

He left the temple very sorrowfully, and began to wonder what he should do. If he went straight home he felt sure his father would punish him for having been disobedient to the priest; so he was afraid to go home. All at once he remembered that at the next village, twelve miles away, there was a very big temple. He had heard there were several priests at that temple; and he made up his mind to go to them and ask them to take him for their acolyte.

Now that big temple was closed up but the boy did not know this fact. The reason it had been closed up was that a goblin had frightened the priests away, and had taken possession of the place. Some brave warriors had afterward gone to the temple at night to kill the goblin; but they had never been seen alive again. Nobody had ever told these things to the boy;—so he walked all the way to the village hoping to be kindly treated by the priests.

When he got to the village, it was already dark, and all the people were in bed; but he saw the big temple on a hill at the other end of the principal street, and he saw there was a light in the temple. People who tell the story say the goblin used to make that light, in order to tempt lonely travelers to ask for shelter. The boy went at once to the temple, and knocked. There was no sound inside. He knocked and knocked again; but still nobody came. At last he pushed gently at the door, and was quite glad to find that it had not been fastened. So he went in, and saw a lamp burning—but no priest.

He thought some priest would be sure to come very soon, and he sat down and waited. Then he noticed that everything in the temple was gray with dust, and thickly spun over with cobwebs. So he thought to himself that the priests would certainly like to have an acolyte, to keep the place clean. He wondered why they had allowed everything to get so dusty. What most pleased him, however, were some big white screens, good to paint cats upon. Though he was tired, he looked at once for a writing pad, and found one and ground some ink, and began to paint cats.

He painted a great many cats upon the screens; and then he began to feel very, very sleepy. He was just on the point of lying down to sleep beside one of the screens, when he suddenly remembered the words, *"Avoid large places;—keep to small!"*

The temple was very large; he was all alone; and as he thought of these words—though he could not quite understand them—he began to feel for the first time a little afraid; and he resolved to look for a *small place* in which to sleep. He found a little cabinet, with a sliding door, and went into it, and shut himself up. Then he lay down and fell fast asleep.

Very late in the night he was awakened by a most terrible noise—a noise of fighting and screaming. It was so dreadful that he was afraid even to look through a chink in the little cabinet; he lay very still, holding his breath for fright.

The light that had been in the temple went out; but the awful sounds continued, and became more awful, and all the temple shook. After a long time silence came; but the boy was still afraid to move. He did not move until the light of the morning sun shone into the cabinet through the chinks of the little door.

Then he got out of his hiding place very cautiously, and looked about. The first thing he saw was that all the floor of the temple was covered with blood. And then he saw, lying dead in the middle of it, an enormous, monstrous rat—a goblin-rat—bigger than a cow!

But who or what could have killed it? There was no man or other creature to be seen. Suddenly the boy observed that the mouths of all the cats he had drawn the night before, were red and wet with blood. Then he knew that the goblin had been killed by the cats which he had drawn. And then also, for the first time, he understood why the wise old priest had said to him, *"Avoid large places at night;—keep to small."*

Afterward that boy became a very famous artist. Some of the cats which he drew are still shown to travelers in Japan.

EXERCISES

1. Why does the fact that the boy has the "genius of the artist" make him not fit to be an acolyte or to study books?
2. What is the difference between being a priest and being an artist? What is the similarity between the two?
3. Other than its immediate practical meaning in the story, what is the more general meaning of the advice "Avoid large places at night;—keep to small"? The famous anthropologist Claude Lévi-Strauss has suggested that there is something intrinsically aesthetic about miniatures, about reducing the large to the small. Discuss the justness of this statement and its relevance to this story.
4. It has been suggested that the artist creates imaginary things and acts as if they were real. How is this a story a parable of the artist?

HERMANN
HESSE | *The Poet*

The story is told of the Chinese poet Han Fook that from early youth he was animated by an intense desire to learn all about the poet's art and to perfect himself in everything connected with it. In those days he was still living in his home city on the Yellow River and had become engaged—at his own wish and with the aid of his parents, who loved him tenderly—to a girl of good family; the wedding was to be announced shortly for a chosen day of good omen. Han Fook at this time was about twenty years old and a handsome young man, modest, and of agreeable manners, instructed in the sciences and, despite his youth, already known among the literary folk of his district for a number of remarkable poems. Without being exactly rich, he had the expectation of comfortable means, which would be increased by the dowry of his bride, and since this bride was also very beautiful and virtuous, nothing whatever seemed lacking to the youth's happiness. Nevertheless, he was not entirely content, for his heart was filled with the ambition to become a perfect poet.

Then one evening when a lantern festival was being celebrated on the river, it happened that Han Fook was wandering alone on the opposite bank. He leaned against the trunk of a tree that hung out over the water, and mirrored in the river he saw a thousand lights floating and trembling, he saw men and women and young girls on the boats and barges, greeting each other and glowing like beautiful flowers in their festive robes, he heard the girl singers, the hum of the zither and the sweet tones of the flute players, and over all this he saw the bluish night arched like the dome of a temple. The youth's heart beat high as he took in all this beauty, a lonely observer in pursuit of his whim. But much as he longed to go across the river and take part in the feast and be in the company of his bride-to-be and his friends, much deeper was his longing to absorb it all as a perceptive observer and to reproduce it in a wholly perfect poem: the blue of the night and the play of the light on the water and the joy of the guests and the yearning of the silent onlooker leaning against the tree trunk on the bank. He realized that at all festivals and with all joys of this earth he would never feel wholly comfortable and serene at heart; even in the midst of life he would remain solitary and be, to a certain extent, a watcher, an alien, and he felt that his soul, unlike most others, was so formed that he must be alone to experience both the beauty of the earth and the secret longings of a stranger. Thereupon he grew sad, and pondered this matter, and the conclusion of his thoughts was this, that true happiness and deep satisfaction could only be his if on occasion he succeeded in mirroring the world so perfectly in his poems that in these mirror images he would possess the essence of the world, purified and made eternal.

Han Fook hardly knew whether he was still awake or had fallen asleep when he heard a slight rustling and saw a stranger standing beside the trunk of the tree, an old man of reverend aspect, wearing a violet robe. Han Fook roused himself and greeted the stranger with the salutation appropriate to the aged and distinguished; the stranger, however, smiled and spoke a few verses in which everything the young man had just felt was expressed so completely and beautifully and so exactly in accord with the rules of the great poets that the youth's heart stood still with amazement.

"Oh, who are you?" he cried, bowing deeply. "You who can see into my soul and who recite more beautiful verses than I have ever heard from any of my teachers!"

The stranger smiled once more with the smile of one made perfect, and said: "If you wish to be a poet, come to me. You will find my hut beside the source of the Great River in the northwestern mountains. I am called Master of the Perfect Word."

Thereupon the aged man stepped into the narrow shadow of the tree and instantly disappeared, and Han Fook, searching for him in vain and finding no trace of him, finally decided that it had all been a dream caused by his fatigue. He hastened across to the boats and joined in the festival, but amid the conversation and the music of the flutes he continued to hear the mysterious voice of the stranger, and his soul seemed to have gone away with the old man, for he sat remote and with dreaming eyes among the merry folk, who teased him for being in love.

A few days later Han Fook's father prepared to summon his friends and relations to decide upon the day of the wedding. The bridegroom demurred and said: "Forgive me if I seem to offend against the duty a son owes his father. But you know how great my longing is to distinguish myself in the art of poetry, and even though some of my friends praise my poems, nevertheless I know very well that I am still a beginner and still on the first stage of the journey. Therefore, I beg you to let me go my way in loneliness for a while and devote myself to my studies, for it seems to me that having a wife and a house to govern will keep me from these things. But now I am still young and without other duties, and I would like to live for a time for my poetry, from which I hope to gain joy and fame."

This speech filled his father with great surprise and he said: "This art must indeed be dearer to you than anything, since you wish to postpone your wedding on account of it. Or has something arisen between you and your bride? If so, tell me so that I can help to reconcile you, or select another girl."

The son swore, however, that his bride-to-be was no less dear to him than she had been yesterday and always, and that no shadow of discord had fallen between them. Then he told his father that on the day of the lantern festival a Master had become known to him in a dream, and that he desired to be his pupil more ardently than all the happiness in the world.

"Very well," his father said, "I will grant you a year. In this time you may pursue your dream, which perhaps was sent to you by a god."

"It may even take two years," Han Fook said hesitantly. "Who can tell?"

So his father let him go, and was troubled; the youth, however, wrote a letter to his bride, said farewell, and departed.

When he had wandered for a very long time, he reached the source of the river, and in complete isolation he found a bamboo hut, and in front of the hut on a woven mat sat the aged man whom he had seen beside the tree on the river bank. He sat playing a lute, and when he saw his guest approach with reverence he did not rise or greet him but simply smiled and let his delicate fingers run over the strings, and a magical music flowed like a silver cloud through the valley, so that the youth stood amazed and in his sweet astonishment forgot everything, until the Master of the Perfect Word laid aside his little lute and stepped into the hut. Then Han Fook followed him reverently and stayed with him as his servant and pupil.

With the passing of a month he had learned to despise all the poems he had hitherto composed, and he blotted them out of his memory. And after more months he blotted out all the songs that he had learned from his teachers at home. The Master rarely spoke to him; in silence he taught him the art of lute playing until the pupil's being was entirely saturated with music. Once Han Fook made a little poem which described the flight of two birds in the autumn sky, and he was pleased with it. He dared not show it to the Master, but one evening he sang it outside the hut, and the Master listened attentively. However, he said no word. He simply played softly on his lute and at once the air grew cool and twilight fell suddenly, a sharp wind arose although it was midsummer, and through the sky which had grown gray flew two herons in majestic migration, and everything was so much more beautiful and perfect than in the pupil's verses that the latter became sad and was silent and felt that he was worthless. And this is what the ancient did each time, and when a year had passed, Han Fook had almost completely mastered the playing of the lute, but the art of poetry seemed to him ever more difficult and sublime.

When two years had passed, the youth felt a devouring homesickness for his family, his native city, and his bride, and he besought the Master to let him leave.

The Master smiled and nodded. "You are free," he said, "and may go where you like. You may return, you may stay away, just as it suits you."

Then the pupil set out on his journey and traveled uninterruptedly until one morning in the half light of dawn he stood on the bank of his native river and looked across the arched bridge to his home city. He stole secretly into his father's garden and listened through the window of the bedchamber to his father's breathing as he slept, and he slipped into the orchard beside his bride's house and climbed a pear tree, and from there he saw his bride standing in her room combing her hair. And while he compared all these things which he was seeing with his eyes to the mental pictures he had painted of them in his homesickness, it became clear to him that he was, after all, destined to be a poet, and he saw that in poets' dreams reside a beauty and enchantment that one seeks in vain in the things of the real world. And he climbed down from the tree and fled out of the garden and over the bridge, away from his native city, and returned to the high mountain valley. There, as before, sat the old Master in front of his hut on his modest mat, striking the lute with his fingers, and instead of a greeting he recited two verses about the blessings of art, and at their depth and harmony the young man's eyes filled with tears.

Once more Han Fook stayed with the Master of the Perfect Word, who, now that his pupil had mastered the lute, instructed him in the zither, and the months melted away like snow before the west wind. Twice more it happened that he was overcome by homesickness. On the one occasion he ran away secretly at night, but before he had reached the last bend in the valley the night wind blew across the zither hanging at the door of the hut, and the notes flew after him and called him back so that he could not resist them. But the next time he dreamed he was planting a young tree in his garden, and his wife and children were assembled there and his children were watering the tree with wine and milk. When he awoke, the moon was shining into his room and he got up, disturbed in mind, and saw in the next room the Master lying asleep with his gray beard trembling gently; then he was overcome by a bitter hatred for this man who, it seemed to him, had destroyed his life and cheated him of his future. He was about to throw himself upon the Master and murder him when the ancient opened his eyes and began to smile with a sad sweetness and gentleness that disarmed his pupil.

"Remember, Han Fook," the aged man said softly, "you are free to do what you like. You may go to your home and plant trees, you may hate me and kill me, it makes very little difference."

"Oh, how could I hate you?" the poet cried, deeply moved. "That would be like hating heaven itself."

And he stayed and learned to play the zither, and after that the flute, and later he began under his Master's guidance to make poems, and he slowly learned the secret art of apparently saying only simple and homely things but thereby stirring the hearer's soul like wind on the surface of the water. He described the coming of the sun, how it hesitates on the mountain's rim, and the noiseless darting of the fishes when they flee like shadows under the water, and the swaying of a young birch tree in the spring wind, and when people listened it was not only the sun and the play of the fish and the whispering of the birch tree, but it seemed as though heaven and earth each time chimed together for an instant in perfect harmony, and each hearer was impelled to think with joy or pain about what he loved or hated, the boy about sport, the youth about his beloved, and the old man about death.

Han Fook no longer knew how many years he had spent with the Master beside the source of the Great River; often it seemed to him as though he had entered this valley only the evening before and been received by the ancient playing on his stringed instrument; often, too, it seemed as though all the ages and epochs of man had vanished behind him and become unreal.

And then one morning he awoke alone in the house, and though he searched everywhere and called, the Master had disappeared. Overnight it seemed suddenly to have become autumn, a raw wind tugged at the old hut, and over the ridge of the mountain great flights of migratory birds were moving, though it was not yet the season for that.

Then Han Fook took the little lute with him and descended to his native province, and when he came among men they greeted him with the salutation appropriate to the aged and distinguished, and when he came to his home city he found that his father and his bride and his relations had died and other people were living in their houses. In the evening, however, the festival of the lanterns was celebrated on the river and the poet Han Fook stood on the far side on the darker bank, leaning against the trunk of an ancient tree. And when he played on the little lute, the women began to sigh and looked into the night, enchanted and overwhelmed, and the young men called for the lute player, whom they could not find anywhere, and they exclaimed that none of them had ever heard such tones from a lute. But Han Fook only smiled. He looked into the river where floated the mirrored images of the thousand lamps; and just as he could no longer distinguish between the reflections and reality, so he found in his soul no difference between this festival and that first one when he had stood there as a youth and heard the words of the strange Master.

EXERCISES

1. Discuss the difference between participant and observer suggested in this story.

2. How is it possible to mirror the world so perfectly that the mirror image possesses the essence of the world, purified and made eternal? If a poem is a mirror of the world, why would it not be identical to the world?

3. Discuss the implications of the phrase "the Perfect Word."

4. Why does Han Fook feel the poet must be alone? Why does he feel he has not mastered the art of poetry even after two years of lessons?
5. Discuss the statement "He saw that in poets' dreams reside a beauty and enchantment that one seeks in vain in the things of the real world."
6. Discuss the meaning of the following: "It seemed as though heaven and earth each time chimed together in perfect harmony, and each hearer was impelled to think with joy or pain about what he loved or hated."
7. What is the difference between the first festival and the last festival in the story?

KURT
VONNEGUT, JR. | *Harrison Bergeron*

The year was 2081, and everybody was finally equal. They weren't only equal before God and the law. They were equal every which way. Nobody was smarter than anybody else. Nobody was better looking than anybody else. Nobody was stronger or quicker than anybody else. All this equality was due to the 211th, 212th, and 213th Amendments to the Constitution, and to the unceasing vigilance of agents of the United States Handicapper General.

Some things about living still weren't quite right, though. April, for instance, still drove people crazy by not being springtime. And it was in that clammy month that the H-G men took George and Hazel Bergeron's fourteen-year-old son, Harrison, away.

It was tragic, all right, but George and Hazel couldn't think about it very hard. Hazel had a perfectly average intelligence, which meant she couldn't think about anything except in short bursts. And George, while his intelligence was way above normal, had a little mental handicap radio in his ear. He was required by law to wear it at all times. It was tuned to a government transmitter. Every twenty seconds or so, the transmitter would send out some sharp noise to keep people like George from taking unfair advantage of their brains.

George and Hazel were watching television. There were tears on Hazel's cheeks, but she'd forgotten for the moment what they were about.

On the television screen were ballerinas.

A buzzer sounded in George's head. His thoughts fled in panic, like bandits from a burglar alarm.

"That was a real pretty dance, that dance they just did," said Hazel.

"Huh?" said George.

"That dance—it was nice," said Hazel.

"Yup," said George. He tried to think a little about the ballerinas. They weren't really very good—no better than anybody else would have been, anyway. They were burdened with sashweights and bags of birdshot, and their faces were masked, so that no one, seeing a free and graceful gesture or a pretty face, would feel like something the cat drug in. George was toying with the vague notion that maybe dancers shouldn't be handicapped. But he didn't get very far with it before another noise in his ear radio scattered his thoughts.

George winced. So did two of the eight ballerinas.

Hazel saw him wince. Having no mental handicap herself, she had to ask George what the latest sound had been.

"Sounded like somebody hitting a milk bottle with a ball peen hammer," said George.

"I'd think it would be real interesting, hearing all the different sounds," said Hazel, a little envious. "All the things they think up."

"Um," said George.

"Only, if I was Handicapper General, you know what I would do?" said Hazel. Hazel, as a matter of fact, bore a strong resemblance to the Handicapper General, a woman named Diana Moon Glampers. "If I was Diana Moon Glampers," said Hazel, "I'd have chimes on Sunday—just chimes. Kind of in honor of religion."

"I could think, if it was just chimes," said George.

"Well—maybe make 'em real loud," said Hazel. "I think I'd make a good Handicapper General."

"Good as anybody else," said George.

"Who knows better'n I do what normal is?" said Hazel.

"Right," said George. He began to think glimmeringly about his abnormal son who was now in jail, about Harrison, but a twenty-one-gun salute in his head stopped that.

"Boy!" said Hazel, "that was a doozy, wasn't it?"

It was such a doozy that George was white and trembling, and tears stood on the rims of his red eyes. Two of the eight ballerinas had collapsed to the studio floor, were holding their temples.

"All of a sudden you look so tired," said Hazel. "Why don't you stretch out on the sofa, so's you can rest your handicap bag on the pillows, honey-bunch." She was referring to the forty-seven pounds of birdshot in a canvas bag, which was padlocked around George's neck. "Go on and rest the bag for a little while," she said. "I don't care if you're not equal to me for a while."

George weighed the bag with his hands. "I don't mind it," he said. "I don't notice it any more. It's just a part of me."

"You been so tired lately—kind of wore out," said Hazel. "If there was just some way we could make a little hole in the bottom of the bag, and just take out a few of them lead balls. Just a few."

"Two years in prison and two thousand dollars fine for every ball I took out," said George. "I don't call that a bargain."

"If you could just take a few out when you came home from work," said Hazel. "I mean—you don't compete with anybody around here. You just sit around."

"If I tried to get away with it," said George, "then other people'd get away with it—and pretty soon we'd be right back to the dark ages again, with everybody competing against everybody else. You wouldn't like that, would you?"

"I'd hate it," said Hazel.

"There you are," said George. "The minute people start cheating on laws, what do you think happens to society?"

If Hazel hadn't been able to come up with an answer to this question, George couldn't have supplied one. A siren was going off in his head.

"Reckon it'd fall all apart," said Hazel.

"What would?" said George blankly.

"Society," said Hazel uncertainly. "Wasn't that what you just said?"

"Who knows?" said George.

The television program was suddenly interrupted for a news bulletin. It wasn't clear at first as to what the bulletin was about, since the announcer, like all announcers, had a serious speech impediment. For about half a minute, and in a state of high excitement, the announcer tried to say, "Ladies and gentlemen—"

He finally gave up, handed the bulletin to a ballerina to read.

"That's all right—" Hazel said of the announcer, "he tried. That's the big thing. He tried to do the best he could with what God gave him. He should get a nice raise for trying so hard."

"Ladies and gentlemen—" said the ballerina, reading the bulletin. She must have been extraordinarily beautiful, because the mask she wore was hideous. And it was easy to see that she was the strongest and most graceful of all the dancers, for her handicap bags were as big as those worn by two-hundred-pound men.

And she had to apologize at once for her voice, which was a very unfair voice for a woman to use. Her voice was a warm, luminous, timeless melody. "Excuse me—" she said, and she began again, making her voice absolutely uncompetitive.

"Harrison Bergeron, age fourteen," she said in a grackle squawk, "has just escaped from jail, where he was held on suspicion of plotting to overthrow the government. He is a genius and an athlete, is under-handicapped, and should be regarded as extremely dangerous."

A police photograph of Harrison Bergeron was flashed on the screen upside down, then sideways, upside down again, then right side up. The picture showed the full length of Harrison against a background calibrated in feet and inches. He was exactly seven feet tall.

The rest of Harrison's appearance was Halloween and hardware. Nobody had ever borne heavier handicaps. He had outgrown hindrances faster than the H-G men could think them up. Instead of a little ear radio for a mental handicap, he wore a tremendous pair of earphones, and spectacles with thick wavy lenses. The spectacles were intended to make him not only half blind, but to give him whanging headaches besides.

Scrap metal was hung all over him. Ordinarily, there was a certain symmetry, a military neatness to the handicaps issued to strong people, but Harrison looked like a walking junkyard. In the race of life, Harrison carried three hundred pounds.

And to offset his good looks, the H-G men required that he wear at all times a red rubber ball for a nose, keep his eyebrows shaved off, and cover his even white teeth with black caps at snaggle-tooth random.

"If you see this boy," said the ballerina, "do not—I repeat, do not—try to reason with him."

There was the shriek of a door being torn from its hinges.

Screams and barking cries of consternation came from the television set. The photograph of Harrison Bergeron on the screen jumped again and again, as though dancing to the tune of an earthquake.

George Bergeron correctly identified the earthquake, and well he might have—for many was the time his own home had danced to the same crashing tune. "My God—" said George, "that must be Harrison!"

The realization was blasted from his mind instantly by the sound of an automobile collision in his head.

When George could open his eyes again, the photograph of Harrison was gone. A living, breathing Harrison filled the screen.

Clanking, clownish, and huge, Harrison stood in the center of the studio. The knob of the uprooted studio door was still in his hand. Ballerinas, technicians, musicians, and announcers cowered on their knees before him, expecting to die.

"I am the Emperor!" cried Harrison. "Do you hear? I am the Emperor! Everybody must do what I say at once!" He stamped his foot and the studio shook.

"Even as I stand here—" he bellowed, "crippled, hobbled, sickened—I am a greater ruler than any man who ever lived! Now watch me become what I *can* become!"

Harrison tore the straps of his handicap harness like wet tissue paper, tore straps guaranteed to support five thousand pounds.

Harrison's scrap-iron handicaps crashed to the floor.

Harrison thrust his thumbs under the bars of the padlock that secured his head harness. The bar snapped like celery. Harrison smashed his headphones and spectacles against the wall.

He flung away his rubber-ball nose, revealed a man that would have awed Thor, the god of thunder.

"I shall now select my Empress!" he said, looking down on the cowering people. "Let the first woman who dares rise to her feet claim her mate and her throne!"

A moment passed, and then a ballerina arose, swaying like a willow.

Harrison plucked the mental handicap from her ear, snapped off her physical handicaps with marvelous delicacy. Last of all, he removed her mask.

She was blindingly beautiful.

"Now—" said Harrison, taking her hand, "shall we show the people the meaning of the word dance? Music!" he commanded.

The musicians scrambled back into their chairs, and Harrison stripped them of their handicaps, too. "Play your best," he told them, "and I'll make you barons and dukes and earls."

The music began. It was normal at first—cheap, silly, false. But Harrison snatched two musicians from their chairs, waved them like batons as he sang the music as he wanted it played. He slammed them back into their chairs.

The music began again and was much improved.

Harrison and his Empress merely listened to the music for a while—listened gravely, as though synchronizing their heartbeats with it.

They shifted their weights to their toes.

Harrison placed his big hands on the girl's tiny waist, letting her sense the weightlessness that would soon be hers.

And then, in an explosion of joy and grace, into the air they sprang!

Not only were the laws of the land abandoned, but the law of gravity and the laws of motion as well.

They reeled, whirled, swiveled, flounced, capered, gamboled, and spun.

They leaped like deer on the moon.

The studio ceiling was thirty feet high, but each leap brought the dancers nearer to it.

It became their obvious intention to kiss the ceiling.

They kissed it.

And then, neutralizing gravity with love and pure will, they remained suspended in air inches below the ceiling, and they kissed each other for a long, long time.

It was then that Diana Moon Glampers, the Handicapper General, came into the studio with a double-barreled ten-gauge shotgun. She fired twice, and the Emperor and the Empress were dead before they hit the floor.

Diana Moon Glampers loaded the gun again. She aimed it at the musicians and told them they had ten seconds to get their handicaps back on.

It was then that the Bergeron's television tube burned out.

Hazel turned to comment about the blackout to George. But George had gone out into the kitchen for a can of beer.

George came back in with the beer, paused while a handicap signal shook him up. And then he sat down again. "You been crying?" he said to Hazel.

"Yup," she said.

"What about?" he said.

"I forgot," she said. "Something real sad on television."

"What was it?" he said.

"It's all kind of mixed up in my mind," said Hazel.

"Forget sad things," said George.

"I always do," said Hazel.

"That's my girl," said George. He winced. There was the sound of a rivetting gun in his head.

"Gee—I could tell that one was a doozy," said Hazel.

"You can say that again," said George.

"Gee—" said Hazel, "I could tell that one was a doozy."

EXERCISES

1. What is the difference between the tone of this story and the tone of Ursula K. LeGuin's story "The Ones Who Walk Away from Omelas"? How are the two stories similar?

2. Why is it considered unfair advantage to use one's brain? What is the purpose of the handicappers?

3. What is normal in this story? Why is normality valued? Why is competition to be avoided? Should just trying, regardless of how well you do, be enough? Do students sometimes feel this way about their schoolwork?

4. Is Harrison an heroic figure or a comic figure? Is he a savior or a dictator? What is dangerous about him?

5. Why is dance the climactic act of being free in this story? Compare this use of dance with dance in Gottfried Keller's "A Little Legend of the Dance."

6. Why does the story end on a comic note so soon after what seems to be a tragic note? How is the story both absurd and serious at once? How is the world of the future depicted here both desirable and undesirable at once?

URSULA K.
LE GUIN   # The Ones Who Walk Away from Omelas

With a clamor of bells that set the swallows soaring, the Festival of Summer came to the city Omelas, bright-towered by the sea. The rigging of the boats in harbor sparkled with flags. In the streets between houses with red roofs and painted walls, between old moss-grown gardens and under avenues of trees, past great parks and public buildings, processions moved. Some were decorous: old people in long stiff robes of mauve and gray, grave master workmen, quiet, merry women carrying their babies and chatting as they walked. In other streets the music beat faster, a shimmering of gong and tambourine, and the people went dancing, the procession was a dance. Children dodged in and out, their high calls rising like the swallows' crossing flights over the music and the singing. All the processions wound towards the north side of the city, where on the great water-meadow called the Green Fields boys and girls, naked in the bright air, with mud-stained feet and ankles and long, lithe arms, exercised their restive horses before the race. The horses wore no gear at all but a halter without bit. Their manes were braided with streamers of silver, gold, and green. They flared their nostrils and pranced and boasted to one another; they were vastly excited, the horse being the only animal who has adopted our ceremonies as his own. Far off to the north and west the mountains stood up half encircling Omelas on her bay. The air of morning was so clear that the snow still crowning the Eighteen Peaks burned with white-gold fire across the miles of sunlit air, under the dark blue of the sky. There was just enough wind to make the banners that marked the racecourse snap and flutter now and then. In the silence of the broad green meadows one could hear the music winding through the city streets, farther and nearer and ever approaching, a cheerful faint sweetness of the air that from time to time trembled and gathered together and broke out into the great joyous clanging of the bells.

Joyous! How is one to tell about joy? How describe the citizens of Omelas?

They were not simple folk, you see, though they were happy. But we do not say the words of cheer much any more. All smiles have become archaic. Given a description such as this one tends to make certain assumptions. Given a description such as this one tends to look next for the King, mounted on a splendid stallion and surrounded by his noble knights, or perhaps in a golden litter borne by great-muscled slaves. But there was no king. They did not use swords, or keep slaves. They were not barbarians. I do not know the rules and laws of their society, but I suspect that they were singularly few. As they did without monarchy and slavery, so they also got on without the stock exchange, the advertisement, the secret police, and the bomb. Yet I repeat that these were not simple folk, not dulcet shepherds, noble savages, bland utopians. They were not less complex than us. The trouble is that we have a bad habit, encouraged by pedants and sophisticates, of considering happiness as something rather stupid. Only pain is intellectual, only evil interesting. This is the treason of the artist: a refusal to admit the banality of evil and the terrible boredom of pain. If you can't lick 'em, join 'em. If it hurts, repeat it. But to praise despair is to condemn delight, to embrace violence is to lose hold of everything else. We have almost lost hold; we can no longer describe a happy man, nor make any celebration of joy. How can I tell you about the people of Omelas? They were not naïve and happy children—though their children were, in fact, happy. They were mature, intelligent, passionate adults whose lives were not wretched. O miracle! but I wish I could describe it better. I wish I could convince you. Omelas sounds in my words like a city in a fairy tale, long ago and far away, once upon a time. Perhaps it would be best if you imagined it as your own fancy bids, assuming it will rise to the occasion, for certainly I cannot suit you all. For instance, how about technology? I think that there would be no cars or helicopters in and above the streets; this follows from the fact that the people of Omelas are happy people. Happiness is based on a just discrimination of what is necessary, what is neither necessary nor destructive, and what is destructive. In the middle category, however—that of the unnecessary but undestructive, that of comfort, luxury, exuberance, etc.— they could perfectly well have central heating, subway trains, washing machines, and all kinds of marvelous devices not yet invented here, floating light-sources, fuelless power, a cure for the common cold. Or they could have none of that: it doesn't matter. As you like it. I incline to think that people from towns up and down the coast have been coming in to Omelas during the last days before the Festival on very fast little trains and double-decked trams, and that the train station of Omelas is actually the handsomest building in town, though plainer than the magnificent Farmers' Market. But even granted trains, I fear that Omelas so far strikes some of you as goody-goody.

Smiles, bells, parades, horses, bleh. If so, please add an orgy. If an orgy would help, don't hesitate. Let us not, however, have temples from which issue beautiful nude priests and priestesses already half in ecstasy and ready to copulate with any man or woman, lover or stranger, who desires union with the deep godhead of the blood, although that was my first idea. But really it would be better not to have any temples in Omelas—at least, not manned temples. Religion yes, clergy no. Surely the beautiful nudes can just wander about, offering themselves like divine soufflés to the hunger of the needy and the rapture of the flesh. Let them join the processions. Let tambourines be struck above the copulations, and the glory of desire be proclaimed upon the gongs, and (a not unimportant point) let the offspring of these delightful rituals be beloved and looked after by all. One thing I know there is none of in Omelas is guilt. But what else should there be? I thought at first there were no drugs, but that is puritanical. For those who like it, the faint insistent sweetness of *drooz* may perfume the ways of the city, *drooz* which first brings a great lightness and brilliance to the mind and limbs, and then after some hours a dreamy languor, and wonderful visions at last of the very arcana and inmost secrets of the Universe, as well as exciting the pleasure of sex beyond all belief; and it is not habit-forming. For more modest tastes I think there ought to be beer. What else, what else belongs in the joyous city? The sense of victory, surely, the celebration of courage. But as we did without clergy, let us do without soldiers. The joy built upon successful slaughter is not the right kind of joy; it will not do; it is fearful and it is trivial. A boundless and generous contentment, a magnanimous triumph felt not against some outer enemy but in communion with the finest and fairest in the souls of all men everywhere and the splendor of the world's summer: this is what swells the hearts of the people of Omelas, and the victory they celebrate is that of life. I really don't think many of them need to take *drooz*.

Most of the processions have reached the Green Fields by now. A marvelous smell of cooking goes forth from the red and blue tents of the provisioners. The faces of small children are amiably sticky; in the benign gray beard of a man a couple of crumbs of rich pastry are entangled. The youths and girls have mounted their horses and are beginning to group around the starting line of the course. An old woman, small, fat, and laughing, is passing out flowers from a basket, and tall young men wear her flowers in their shining hair. A child of nine or ten sits at the edge of the crowd, alone, playing on a wooden flute. People pause to listen, and they smile, but they do not speak to him for he never ceases playing and never sees them, his dark eyes wholly rapt in the sweet, thin magic of the tune.

He finishes, and slowly lowers his hands holding the wooden flute.

As if that little private silence were the signal, all at once a trumpet sounds from the pavilion near the starting line: imperious, melancholy, piercing. The horses rear on their slender legs, and some of them neigh in answer. Sober-faced, the young riders stroke the horses' necks and soothe them, whispering, "Quiet, quiet, there my beauty, my hope. . . ." They begin to form in rank along the starting line. The crowds along the racecourse are like a field of grass and flowers in the wind. The Festival of Summer has begun.

Do you believe? Do you accept the festival, the city, the joy? No? Then let me describe one more thing.

In a basement under one of the beautiful public buildings of Omelas, or perhaps in the cellar of one of its spacious private homes, there is a room. It has one locked door, and no window. A little light seeps in dustily between cracks in the boards, secondhand from a cobwebbed window somewhere across the cellar. In one corner of the little room a couple of mops, with stiff, clotted, foul-smelling heads, stand near a rusty bucket. The floor is dirt, a little damp to the touch, as cellar dirt usually is. The room is about three paces long and two wide: a mere broom closet or disused tool room. In the room a child is sitting. It could be a boy or a girl. It looks about six, but actually is nearly ten. It is feeble-minded. Perhaps it was born defective, or perhaps it has become imbecile through fear, malnutrition, and neglect. It picks its nose and occasionally fumbles vaguely with its toes or genitals, as it sits hunched in the corner farthest from the bucket and the two mops. It is afraid of the mops. It finds them horrible. It shuts its eyes, but it knows the mops are still standing there; and the door is locked; and nobody will come. The door is always locked; and nobody ever comes, except that sometimes—the child has no understanding of time or interval—sometimes the door rattles terribly and opens, and a person, or several people, are there. One of them may come in and kick the child to make it stand up. The others never come close, but peer in at it with frightened, disgusted eyes. The food bowl and the water jug are hastily filled, the door is locked, the eyes disappear. The people at the door never say anything, but the child, who has not always lived in the tool room, and can remember sunlight and its mother's voice, sometimes speaks. "I will be good," it says. "Please let me out. I will be good!" They never answer. The child used to scream for help at night, and cry a good deal, but now it only makes a kind of whining, "eh-haa, eh-haa," and it speaks less and less often. It is so thin there are no calves to its legs; its belly protrudes; it lives on a half-bowl of corn meal and grease a day. It is naked. Its buttocks and thighs are a mass of festered sores, as it sits in its own excrement continually.

They all know it is there, all the people of Omelas. Some of them have come to see it, others are content merely to know it is there. They all know that it has to be there. Some of them understand why, and some do not, but they all understand that their happiness, the beauty of their city, the tenderness of their friendships, the health of their children, the wisdom of their scholars, the skill of their makers, even the abundance of their harvest and the kindly weathers of their skies, depend wholly on this child's abominable misery.

This is usually explained to children when they are between eight and twelve, whenever they seem capable of understanding; and most of those who come to see the child are young people, though often enough an adult comes, or comes back, to see the child. No matter how well the matter has been explained to them, these young spectators are always shocked and sickened at the sight. They feel disgust, which they had thought themselves superior to. They feel anger, outrage, impotence, despite all the explanations. They would like to do something for the child. But there is nothing they can do. If the child were brought up into the sunlight out of that vile place, if it were cleaned and fed and comforted, that would be a good thing, indeed; but if it were done, in that day and hour all the prosperity and beauty and delight of Omelas would wither and be destroyed. Those are the terms. To exchange all the goodness and grace of every life in Omelas for that single, small improvement: to throw away the happiness of thousands for the chance of the happiness of one: that would be to let guilt within the walls indeed.

The terms are strict and absolute; there may not even be a kind word spoken to the child.

Often the young people go home in tears, or in a tearless rage, when they have seen the child and faced this terrible paradox. They may brood over it for weeks or years. But as time goes on they begin to realize that even if the child could be released, it would not get much good of its freedom: a little vague pleasure of warmth and food, no doubt, but little more. It is too degraded and imbecile to know any real joy. It has been afraid too long ever to be free of fear. Its habits are too uncouth for it to respond to humane treatment. Indeed, after so long it would probably be wretched without walls about it to protect it, and darkness for its eyes, and its own excrement to sit in. Their tears at the bitter injustice dry when they begin to perceive the terrible justice of reality, and to accept it. Yet it is their tears and anger, the trying of their generosity and the acceptance of their helplessness, which are perhaps the true source of the splendor of their lives. Theirs is no vapid, irresponsible happiness. They know that they, like the child, are not free. They know compassion. It is the existence of the child, and their knowledge of its existence, that makes possible the nobility of their architecture, the poignancy of their music, the profundity of their science. It is because of the child that they are so gentle with children. They know that if the wretched one were not there sniveling in the dark, the other one, the flute-player, could make no joyful music as the young riders line up in their beauty for the race in the sunlight of the first morning of summer.

Now do you believe in them? Are they not more credible? But there is one more thing to tell, and this is quite incredible.

At times one of the adolescent girls or boys who go to see the child does not go home to weep or rage, does not, in fact, go home at all. Sometimes also a man or woman much older falls silent for a day or two, and then leaves home. These people go out into the street, and walk down the street alone. They keep walking, and walk straight out of the city of Omelas, through the beautiful gates. They keep walking across the farmlands of Omelas. Each one goes alone, youth or girl, man or woman. Night falls; the traveler must pass down village streets, between the houses with yellow-lit windows, and on out into the darkness of the fields. Each alone, they go west or north, towards the mountains. They go on. They leave Omelas, they walk ahead into the darkness, and they do not come back. The place they go towards is a place even less imaginable to most of us than the city of happiness. I cannot describe it at all. It is possible that it does not exist. But they seem to know where they are going, the ones who walk away from Omelas.

EXERCISES

1. Discuss the utopian nature of the city in the first paragraph. What is a utopia?

2. The center of the story is the long third paragraph in which the happiness of the people is discussed. Discuss the following elements:

   (a) "All smiles have become archaic."

   (b) "They were not barbarians."

   (c) ". . . these were not simple folk, not dulcet shepherds, noble savages, bland utopians."

   (d) ". . . we have a bad habit . . . of considering happiness as something rather stupid. Only pain is intellectual, only evil interesting."

   (e) "Happiness is based on a just discrimination of what is necessary, what is neither necessary nor destructive, and what is destructive."

   (f) "One thing I know there is none of in Omelas is guilt."

3. Why does the storyteller stop and ask if the reader believes and accepts the city?

4. The central secret required for Omelas to exist is the hidden child. How does the happiness of the people depend on the child's misery?

5. What is the terrible paradox of Omelas? What is the "terrible justice of reality"?

6. Where are those who walk away from Omelas going?

STANISLAW
LEM | *How the World Was Saved*

One day Trurl the constructor put together a machine that could create anything starting with *n*. When it was ready, he tried it out, ordering it to make needles, then nankeens and negligees, which it did, then nail the lot to narghiles filled with nepenthe and numerous other narcotics. The machine carried out his instructions to the letter. Still not completely sure of its ability, he had it produce, one after the other, nimbuses, noodles, nuclei, neutrons, naphtha, noses, nymphs, naiads, and *natrium*. This last it could not do, and Trurl, considerably irritated, demanded an explanation.

"Never heard of it," said the machine.

"What? But it's only sodium. You know, the metal, the element. . . ."

"Sodium starts with an *s*, and I work only in *n*."

"But in Latin it's *natrium*."

"Look, old boy," said the machine, "if I could do everything starting with *n* in every possible language, I'd be a Machine That Could Do Everything in the Whole Alphabet, since any item you care to mention undoubtedly starts with *n* in one foreign language or another. It's not that easy. I can't go beyond what you programmed. So no sodium."

"Very well," said Trurl and ordered it to make Night, which it made at once—small perhaps, but perfectly nocturnal. Only then did Trurl invite over his friend Klapaucius the constructor, and introduced him to the machine, praising its extraordinary skill at such length, that Klapaucius grew annoyed and inquired whether he too might not test the machine.

"Be my guest," said Trurl. "But it has to start with *n*."

"*N?*" said Klapaucius. "All right, let it make Nature."

The machine whined, and in a trice Trurl's front yard was packed with naturalists. They argued, each publishing heavy volumes, which the others tore to pieces; in the distance one could see flaming pyres, on which martyrs to Nature were sizzling; there was thunder, and strange mushroom-shaped columns of smoke rose up; everyone talked at once, no one listened, and there were all sorts of memoranda, appeals, subpoenas and other documents, while off to the side sat a few old men, feverishly scribbling on scraps of paper.

"Not bad, eh?" said Trurl with pride. "Nature to a T, admit it!"

But Klapaucius wasn't satisfied.

"What, that mob? Surely you're not going to tell me that's Nature?"

"Then give the machine something else," snapped Trurl. "Whatever you like." For a moment Klapaucius was at a loss for what to ask. But after a little thought he declared that he would put two more tasks to the machine; if it could fulfill them, he would admit that it was all Trurl said it was. Trurl agreed to this, whereupon Klapaucius requested Negative.

"Negative?!" cried Trurl. "What on earth is Negative?"

"The opposite of positive, of course," Klapaucius coolly replied. "Negative attitudes, the negative of a picture, for example. Now don't try to pretend you never heard of Negative. All right, machine, get to work!"

The machine, however, had already begun. First it manufactured antiprotons, then antielectrons, antineutrons, antineutrinos, and labored on, until from out of all this antimatter an antiworld took shape, glowing like a ghostly cloud above their heads.

"H'm," muttered Klapaucius, displeased. "That's supposed to be Negative? Well . . . let's say it is, for the sake of peace. . . . But now here's the third command: Machine, do Nothing!"

The machine sat still. Klapaucius rubbed his hands in triumph, but Trurl said:

"Well, what did you expect? You asked it to do nothing, and it's doing nothing."

"Correction: I asked it to do Nothing, but it's doing nothing."

"Nothing is nothing!"

"Come, come. It was supposed to do Nothing, but it hasn't done anything, and therefore I've won. For Nothing, my dear and clever colleague, is not your run-of-the-mill nothing, the result of idleness and inactivity, but dynamic, aggressive Nothingness, that is to say, perfect, unique, ubiquitous, in other words Nonexistence, ultimate and supreme, in its very own nonperson!"

"You're confusing the machine!" cried Trurl. But suddenly its metallic voice rang out:

"Really, how can you two bicker at a time like this? Oh yes, I know what Nothing is, and Nothingness, Nonexistence, Nonentity, Negation, Nullity and Nihility, since all these come under the heading of *n*, *n* as in Nil. Look then upon your world for the last time, gentlemen! Soon it will no longer be. . . ."

The constructors froze, forgetting their quarrel, for the machine was in actual fact doing Nothing, and it did it in this fashion: one by one, various things were removed from the world, and the things, thus removed, ceased to exist, as if they had never been. The machine had already disposed of nolars, nightzebs, nocs, necs, nallyrakers, neotremes and nonmalrigers. At moments, though, it seemed that instead of reducing, diminishing and subtracting, the machine was increasing, enhancing and adding, since it liquidated, in turn: nonconformists, nonentities, nonsense, nonsupport, nearsightedness, narrow-mindedness, naughtiness, neglect, nausea, necrophilia and nepotism. But after a while the world very definitely began to thin out around Trurl and Klapaucius.

"Omigosh!" said Trurl. "If only nothing bad comes out of all this . . ."

"Don't worry," said Klapaucius. "You can see it's not producing Universal Nothingness, but only causing the absence of whatever starts with *n*. Which is really nothing in the way of nothing, and nothing is what your machine, dear Trurl, is worth!"

"Do not be deceived," replied the machine. "I've begun, it's true, with everything in *n*, but only out of familiarity. To create however is one thing, to destroy, another thing entirely. I can blot out the world for the simple reason that I'm able to do anything and everything—and everything means every-thing—in *n*, and consequently Nothingness is child's play for me. In less than a minute now you will cease to have existence, along with everything else, so tell me now, Klapaucius, and quickly, that I am really and truly everything I was programmed to be, before it is too late."

"But—" Klapaucius was about to protest, but noticed, just then, that a number of things were indeed disappearing, and not merely those that started with *n*. The constructors were no longer surrounded by the gruncheons, the targalisks, the shupops, the calinatifacts, the thists, worches and pritons.

"Stop! I take it all back! Desist! Whoa! Don't do Nothing!!" screamed Klapaucius. But before the machine could come to a full stop, all the brash-ations, plusters, laries and zits had vanished away. Now the machine stood motionless. The world was a dreadful sight. The sky had particularly suffered: there were only a few, isolated points of light in the heavens—no trace of the glorious worches and zits that had, till now, graced the horizon!

"Great Gauss!" cried Klapaucius. "And where are the gruncheons? Where my dear, favorite pritons? Where now the gentle zits?!"

"They no longer are, nor ever will exist again," the machine said calmly. "I executed, or rather only began to execute, your order. . . ."

"I tell you to do Nothing, and you . . . you . . ."

"Klapaucius, don't pretend to be a greater idiot than you are," said the machine. "Had I made Nothing outright, in one fell swoop, everything would have ceased to exist, and that includes Trurl, the sky, the Universe, and you— and even myself. In which case who could say and to whom could it be said that the order was carried out and I am an efficient and capable machine? And if no one could say it to no one, in what way then could I, who also would not be, be vindicated?"

"Yes, fine, let's drop the subject," said Klapaucius. "I have nothing more to ask of you, only please, dear machine, please return the zits, for without them life loses all its charm. . . ."

"But I can't, they're in z," said the machine. "Of course. I can restore nonsense, narrowmindedness, nausea, necrophilia, neuralgia, nefariousness and noxiousness. As for the other letters, however, I can't help you."

"I want my zits!" bellowed Klapaucius.

"Sorry, no zits," said the machine. "Take a good look at this world, how riddled it is with huge, gaping holes, how full of Nothingness, the Nothingness that fills the bottomless void between the stars, how everything about us has become lined with it, how it darkly lurks behind each shred of matter. This is your work, envious one! And I hardly think the future generations will bless you for it. . . ."

"Perhaps . . . they won't find out, perhaps they won't notice," groaned the pale Klapaucius, gazing up incredulously at the black emptiness of space and not daring to look his colleague, Trurl, in the eye. Leaving him beside the machine that could do everything in n, Klapaucius skulked home—and to this day the world has remained honeycombed with nothingness, exactly as it was when halted in the course of its liquidation. And as all subsequent attempts to build a machine on any other letter met with failure, it is to be feared that never again will we have such marvelous phenomena as the worches and the zits—no, never again.

EXERCISES

1. What is the tone of this story? Is it comic or serious? At what point in the story do you make this judgment?

2. Why is Klapaucius dissatisfied with the machine's creation of Nature?

3. How is making Negative different from doing nothing?

4. How can Nothing be something? What is the difference between Nothingness and simply an absence of something?

5. Why doesn't the machine do Nothing all at once?

6. What does it mean that "Nothing lurks behind each shred of matter"? How is the world "honeycombed with nothingness"?

NATHANIEL
HAWTHORNE | *Wakefield*

In some old magazine or newspaper I recollect a story, told as truth of a man—let us call him Wakefield—who absented himself for a long time from his wife. The fact, thus abstractedly stated, is not very uncommon, nor—without a proper distinction of circumstances—to be condemned either as naughty or nonsensical. Howbeit, this, though far from the most aggravated, is perhaps the strangest, instance on record, of marital delinquency; and, moreover, as remarkable a freak as may be found in the whole list of human oddities. The wedded couple lived in London. The man, under pretence of going a journey, took lodgings in the next street to his own house, and there, unheard of by his wife or friends, and without the shadow of a reason for such self-banishment, dwelt upwards of twenty years. During that period, he beheld his home every day, and frequently the forlorn Mrs. Wakefield. And after so great a gap in his matrimonial felicity—when his death was reckoned certain, his estate settled, his name dismissed from memory, and his wife, long, long ago, resigned to her autumnal widowhood—he entered the door one evening, quietly, as from a day's absence, and became a loving spouse till death.

This outline is all that I remember. But the incident, though of the purest originality, unexampled, and probably never to be repeated, is one, I think, which appeals to the generous sympathies of mankind. We know, each for himself, that none of us would perpetrate such a folly, yet feel as if some other might. To my own contemplations, at least, it has often recurred, always exciting wonder, but with a sense that the story must be true, and a conception of its hero's character. Whenever any subject so forcibly affects the mind, time is well spent in thinking of it. If the reader choose, let him do his own meditation; or if he prefer to ramble with me through the twenty years of Wakefield's vagary, I bid him welcome; trusting that there will be a pervading spirit and a moral, even should we fail to find them, done up neatly, and condensed into the final sentence. Thought has always its efficacy, and every striking incident its moral.

What sort of man was Wakefield? We are free to shape out our own idea, and call it by his name. He was now in the meridian of life; his matrimonial affections, never violent, were sobered into a calm, habitual sentiment; of all husbands, he was likely to be the most constant, because a certain sluggishness would keep his heart at rest, wherever it might be placed. He was intellectual, but not actively so; his mind occupied itself in long and lazy musings, that ended to no purpose, or had not vigor to attain it; his thoughts were seldom so energetic as to seize hold of words. Imagination, in the proper meaning of the term, made no part of Wakefield's gifts. With a cold but not depraved nor wandering heart, and a mind never feverish with riotous thoughts, nor perplexed with originality, who could have anticipated that our friend would entitle himself to a foremost place among the doers of eccentric deeds? Had his acquaintances been asked, who was the man in London the surest to perform nothing today which should be remembered on the morrow, they would have thought of Wakefield. Only the wife of his bosom might have hesitated. She, without having analyzed his character, was partly aware of a quiet selfishness, that had rusted into his inactive mind; of a peculiar sort of vanity, the most uneasy attribute about him; of a disposition to craft which had seldom produced more positive effects than the keeping of petty secrets, hardly worth revealing; and, lastly, of what she called a little strangeness, sometimes, in the good man. This latter quality is indefinable, and perhaps non-existent.

Let us now imagine Wakefield bidding adieu to his wife. It is the dusk of an October evening. His equipment is a drab great-coat, a hat covered with an oilcloth, top-boots, an umbrella in one hand and a small portmanteau in the other. He has informed Mrs. Wakefield that he is to take the night coach into the country. She would fain inquire the length of his journey, its object, and the probable time of his return; but, indulgent to his harmless love of mystery, interrogates him only by a look. He tells her not to expect him positively by the return coach, nor to be alarmed should he tarry three or four days; but, at all events, to look for him at supper on Friday evening. Wakefield himself, be it considered, has no suspicion of what is before him. He holds out his hand, she gives her own, and meets his parting kiss in the matter-of-course way of a ten years' matrimony; and forth goes the middle-aged Mr. Wakefield, almost resolved to perplex his good lady by a whole week's absence. After the door has closed behind him, she perceives it thrust partly open, and a vision of her husband's face, through the aperture, smiling on her, and gone in a moment. For the time, this little incident is dismissed without a thought. But, long afterwards, when she has been more years a widow than a wife, that smile recurs, and flickers across all her reminiscences of Wakefield's visage. In her many musings, she surrounds the original smile with a multitude of fantasies, which make it strange and awful: as, for instance, if she imagines him in a coffin, that parting look is frozen on his pale features; or, if she dreams of him in heaven, still his blessed spirit wears a quiet and crafty smile. Yet, for its sake, when all others have given him up for dead, she sometimes doubts whether she is a widow.

But our business is with the husband. We must hurry after him along the street, ere he lose his individuality, and melt into the great mass of London life. It would be vain searching for him there. Let us follow close at his heels, therefore, until, after several superfluous turns and doublings, we find him comfortably established by the fireside of a small apartment, previously bespoken. He is in the next street to his own, and at his journey's end. He can scarcely trust his good fortune, in having got thither unperceived—recollecting that, at one time, he was delayed by the throng, in the very focus of a lighted lantern; and, again, there were footsteps that seemed to tread behind his own, distinct from the multitudinous tramp around him; and, anon, he heard a voice shouting afar, and fancied that it called his name. Doubtless, a dozen busybodies had been watching him, and told his wife the whole affair. Poor Wakefield! Little knowest thou thine own insignificance in this great world! No mortal eye but mine has traced thee. Go quietly to thy bed, foolish man; and, on the morrow, if thou wilt be wise, get thee home to good Mrs.

Wakefield, and tell her the truth. Remove not thyself, even for a little week, from thy place in her chaste bosom. Were she, for a single moment, to deem thee dead, or lost, or lastingly divided from her, thou wouldst be woefully conscious of a change in thy true wife forever after. It is perilous to make a chasm in human affections; not that they gape so long and wide—but so quickly close again!

Almost repenting of his frolic, or whatever it may be termed, Wakefield lies down betimes, and starting from his first nap, spreads forth his arms into the wide and solitary waste of the unaccustomed bed. "No,"—thinks he, gathering the bedclothes about him,—"I will not sleep alone another night."

In the morning he rises earlier than usual, and sets himself to consider what he really means to do. Such are his loose and rambling modes of thought that he has taken this very singular step with the consciousness of a purpose, indeed, but without being able to define it sufficiently for his own contemplation. The vagueness of the project, and the convulsive effort with which he plunges into the execution of it, are equally characteristic of a feeble-minded man. Wakefield sifts his ideas, however, as minutely as he may, and finds himself curious to know the progress of matters at home—how his exemplary wife will endure her widowhood of a week; and, briefly, how the little sphere of creatures and circumstances, in which he was a central object, will be affected by his removal. A morbid vanity, therefore, lies nearest the bottom of the affair. But, how is he to attain his ends? Not, certainly, by keeping close in this comfortable lodging, where, though he slept and awoke in the next street to his home, he is as effectually abroad as if the stage-coach had been whirling him away all night. Yet, should he reappear, the whole project is knocked in the head. His poor brains being hopelessly puzzled with this dilemma, he at length ventures out, partly resolving to cross the head of the street, and send one hasty glance towards his forsaken domicile. Habit—for he is a man of habits—takes him by the hand, and guides him, wholly unaware, to his own door, where, just at the critical moment, he is aroused by the scraping of his foot upon the step. Wakefield! whither are you going?

At that instant his fate was turning on the pivot. Little dreaming of the doom to which his first backward step devotes him, he hurries away, breathless with agitation hitherto unfelt, and hardly dares turn his head at the distant corner. Can it be that nobody caught sight of him? Will not the whole household—the decent Mrs. Wakefield, the smart maid servant, and the dirty little footboy—raise a hue and cry, through London streets, in pursuit of their fugitive lord and master? Wonderful escape! He gathers courage to pause and look homeward, but is perplexed with a sense of change about the familiar edifice, such as affects us all, when, after a separation of months or years, we again see some hill or lake, or work of art, with which we were friends of old. In ordinary cases, this indescribable impression is caused by the comparison and contrast between our imperfect reminiscences and the reality. In Wakefield, the magic of a single night has wrought a similar transformation, because, in that brief period, a great moral change has been effected. But this is a secret from himself. Before leaving the spot, he catches a far and momentary glimpse of his wife, passing athwart the front window, with her face turned towards the head of the street. The crafty nincompoop takes to his heels, scared with the idea that, among a thousand such atoms of mortality, her eye must have detected him. Right glad is his heart, though his brain be somewhat dizzy, when he finds himself by the coal fire of his lodgings.

So much for the commencement of this long whimwham. After the initial conception, and the stirring up of the man's sluggish temperament to put it in practice, the whole matter evolves itself in a natural train. We may suppose him, as the result of deep deliberation, buying a new wig, of reddish hair, and selecting sundry garments, in a fashion unlike his customary suit of brown, from a Jew's old-clothes bag. It is accomplished. Wakefield is another man. The new system being now established, a retrograde movement to the old would be almost as difficult as the step that placed him in his unparalleled position. Furthermore, he is rendered obstinate by a sulkiness occasionally incident to his temper, and brought on at present by the inadequate sensation which he conceives to have been produced in the bosom of Mrs. Wakefield. He will not go back until she be frightened half to death. Well; twice or thrice has she passed before his sight, each time with a heavier step, a paler cheek, and more anxious brow; and in the third week of his non-appearance he detects a portent of evil entering the house, in the guise of an apothecary. Next day the knocker is muffled. Towards nightfall comes the chariot of a physician, and deposits its big-wigged and solemn burden at Wakefield's door, whence, after a quarter of an hour's visit, he emerges, perchance the herald of a funeral. Dear woman! Will she die? By this time, Wakefield is excited to something like energy of feeling, but still lingers away from his wife's bedside, pleading with his conscience that she must not be disturbed at such a juncture. If aught else restrains him, he does not know it. In the course of a few weeks she gradually recovers; the crisis is over; her heart is sad, perhaps, but quiet; and, let him return soon or late, it will never be feverish for him again. Such ideas glimmer through the midst of Wakefield's mind, and render him indistinctly conscious that an almost impassable gulf divides his hired apartment from his former home. "It is but in the next street!" he sometimes says. Fool! It is in another world. Hitherto, he has put off his return from one particular day to another; henceforward, he leaves the precise time undetermined. Not tomorrow—probably next week—pretty soon. Poor man! The dead have nearly as much chance of revisiting their earthly homes as the self-banished Wakefield.

Would that I had a folio to write, instead of an article of a dozen pages! Then might I exemplify how an influence beyond our control lays its strong hand on every deed which we do, and weaves its consequences into an iron tissue of necessity. Wakefield is spell-bound. We must leave him, for ten years or so, to haunt around his house, without once crossing the threshold, and to be faithful to his wife, with all the affection of which his heart is capable, while he is slowly fading out of hers. Long since, it must be remarked, he had lost the perception of singularity in his conduct.

Now for a scene! Amid the throng of a London street we distinguish a man, now waxing elderly, with few characteristics to attract careless observers, yet bearing, in his whole aspect, the handwriting of no common fate, for such as have the skill to read it. He is meagre; his low and narrow forehead is deeply wrinkled; his eyes, small and lustreless, sometimes wander apprehensively about him, but oftener seem to look inward. He bends his head, and moves with an indescribable obliquity of gait, as if unwilling to display his full front to the world. Watch him long enough to see what we have described, and you will allow that circumstances—which often produce remarkable men from nature's ordinary handiwork—have produced one such here. Next, leaving him to sidle along the footwalk, cast your eyes in the opposite direction, where a portly female, considerably in the wane of life, with a prayer-book in her hand, is proceeding to yonder church. She has the placid mien of settled widowhood. Her regrets have either died away, or have become so essential to her heart, that they would be poorly exchanged for joy. Just as the lean man and well-conditioned woman are passing, a slight obstruction occurs, and brings these two figures directly in contact. Their hands touch; the pressure of the crowd forces her bosom against his shoulder; they stand, face to face, staring into each other's eyes. After a ten years' separation, thus Wakefield meets his wife!

The throng eddies away, and carries them asunder. The sober widow, resuming her former pace, proceeds to church, but pauses in the portal, and throws a perplexed glance along the street. She passes in, however, opening her prayer-book as she goes. And the man! with so wild a face that busy and selfish London stands to gaze after him, he hurries to his lodgings, bolts the door, and throws himself upon the bed. The latent feelings of years break out; his feeble mind acquires a brief energy from their strength; all the miserable strangeness of his life is revealed to him at a glance: and he cries out, passionately, "Wakefield! Wakefield! You are mad!"

Perhaps he was so. The singularity of his situation must have so moulded him to himself, that, considered in regard to his fellow-creatures and the business of life, he could not be said to possess his right mind. He had contrived, or rather he had happened, to dissever himself from the world—to vanish—to give up his place and privileges with living men, without being admitted among the dead. The life of a hermit is nowise parallel to his. He was in the bustle of the city, as of old; but the crowd swept by and saw him not; he was, we may figuratively say, always beside his wife and at his hearth, yet must never feel the warmth of the one nor the affection of the other. It was Wakefield's unprecedented fate to retain his original share of human sympathies, and to be still involved in human interests, while he had lost his reciprocal influence on them. It would be a most curious speculation to trace out the effect of such circumstances on his heart and intellect, separately, and in unison. Yet, changed as he was, he would seldom be conscious of it, but deem himself the same man as ever; glimpses of the truth, indeed, would come, but only for the moment; and still he would keep saying, "I shall soon go back!"— nor reflect that he had been saying so for twenty years.

I conceive, also, that these twenty years would appear, in the retrospect, scarcely longer than the week to which Wakefield had at first limited his absence. He would look on the affair as no more than an interlude in the main business of his life. When, after a little while more, he should deem it time to reënter his parlor, his wife would clap her hands for joy, on beholding the middle-aged Mr. Wakefield. Alas, what a mistake! Would Time but await the close of our favorite follies, we should be young men, all of us, and till Doomsday.

One evening, in the twentieth year since he vanished, Wakefield is taking his customary walk towards the dwelling which he still calls his own. It is a gusty night of autumn, with frequent showers that patter down upon the pavement, and are gone before a man can put up his umbrella. Pausing near the house, Wakefield discerns, through the parlor windows of the second floor, the red glow and the glimmer and fitful flash of a comfortable fire. On the ceiling appears a grotesque shadow of good Mrs. Wakefield. The cap, the nose and chin, and the broad waist, form an admirable caricature, which dances, moreover, with the up-flickering and down-sinking blaze, almost too merrily for the shade of an elderly widow. At this instant a shower chances to fall, and is driven, by the unmannerly gust, full into Wakefield's face and bosom. He is quite penetrated with its autumnal chill. Shall he stand, wet and shivering here, when his own hearth has a good fire to warm him, and his own wife will run to fetch the gray coat and small-clothes, which, doubtless, she has kept carefully in the closet of their bed chamber? No! Wakefield is no such fool. He ascends the steps—heavily!—for twenty years have stiffened his legs since he came down—but he knows it not. Stay, Wakefield! Would you go to the sole home that is left you? Then step into your grave! The door opens. As he passes in, we have a parting glimpse of his visage, and recognize the crafty smile, which was the precursor of the little joke that he has ever since been playing off at his wife's expense. How unmercifully has he quizzed the poor woman! Well, a good night's rest to Wakefield!

This happy event—supposing it to be such—could only have occurred at an unpremeditated moment. We will not follow our friend across the threshold. He has left us much food for thought, a portion of which shall lend its wisdom to a moral, and be shaped into a figure. Amid the seeming confusion of our mysterious world, individuals are so nicely adjusted to a system, and systems to one another and to a whole, that, by stepping aside for a moment, a man exposes himself to a fearful risk of losing his place forever. Like Wakefield, he may become, as it were, the Outcast of the Universe.

EXERCISES

1. Discuss the significance of the statement that the story has "a pervading spirit and a moral, even should we fail to find them, done up neatly, and condensed into the final sentence." How is the spirit or moral woven into every detail of the story?

2. Discuss the technique by which the teller, not knowing the actual facts of Wakefield's experience, makes up such elements as motivation, specific details, and events.

3. How is this a story about the idea that no matter how well we think we know someone, everyone always keeps unknowable secrets?

4. Discuss this story as being about the nature of the perverse. Think of some examples from your own experience in which you began an action that you had to continue, even though it was not to your benefit.

5. Discuss the motivation of wanting to have an effect on someone. Think of some examples in which you did something foolish to get a reaction.

6. If the story were to continue for another paragraph or two, what would happen?

FLANN
O'BRIEN | *Two in One*

The story I have to tell is a strange one, perhaps unbelievable. I will try to set it down as simply as I can. I do not expect to be disturbed in my literary labors, for I am writing this in the condemned cell.

Let us say my name is Murphy. The unusual occurrence which led me here concerns my relations with another man whom we shall call Kelly. Both of us were taxidermists.

I will not attempt a treatise on what a taxidermist is. The word is ugly and inadequate. Certainly it does not convey to the layman that such an operator must combine the qualities of zoologist, naturalist, chemist, sculptor, artist and carpenter. Who would blame such a person for showing some temperament now and again, as I did?

It is necessary, however, to say a brief word about this science. First, there is no such thing in modern practice as "stuffing" an animal. There is a record of stuffed gorillas having been in Carthage in the 5th century, and it is a fact that an Austrian prince, Siegmund Herberstein, had stuffed bison in the great hall of his castle in the 16th century—it was then the practice to draw the entrails of animals and to substitute spices and various preservative substances. There is a variety of methods in use today but, except in particular cases—snakes, for example, where preserving the translucency of the skin is a problem calling for special measures—the basis of all modern methods is simply this: you skin the animal very carefully according to a certain pattern, and you encase the skinless body in plaster of Paris. You bisect the plaster when cast providing yourself with two complementary moulds from which you can make a casting of the animal's body—there are several substances, all very light, from which such castings can be made. The next step, calling for infinite skill and patience, is to mount the skin on the casting of the body. That is all I need explain here, I think.

Kelly carried on a taxidermy business and I was his assistant. He was the boss—a swinish, overbearing mean boss, a bully, a sadist. He hated me, but enjoyed his hatred too much to sack me. He knew I had a real interest in the work, and a desire to broaden my experience. For that reason, he threw me all the commonplace jobs that came in. If some old lady sent her favorite terrier to be done, that was me; foxes and cats and Shetland ponies and white rabbits—they were all strictly *my* department. I could do a perfect job on such animals in my sleep, and got to hate them. But if a crocodile came in, or a Great Borneo spider, or (as once happened) a giraffe—Kelly kept them all for himself. In the meantime he would treat my own painstaking work with sourness and sneers and complaints.

One day the atmosphere in the workshop had been even fouler than usual, with Kelly in a filthier temper than usual. I had spent the forenoon finishing a cat, and at about lunch-time put it on a shelf where he left completed orders.

I could nearly *hear* him glaring at it. Where was the tail? I told him there was no tail, that it was a Manx cat. How did I know it was a Manx cat, how did I know it was not an ordinary cat which had lost its tail in a motor accident or something? I got so mad that I permitted myself a disquisition on cats in general, mentioning the distinctions as between *felis manul, felis silvestris* and *felis lybica,* and on the unique structure of the Manx cat. His reply to that? He called me a slob. That was the sort of life *I* was having.

On this occasion something within me snapped. I was sure I could hear the snap. I had moved up to where he was to answer his last insult. The loathsome creature had his back to me, bending down to put on his bicycle clips. Just to my hand on the bench was one of the long, flat steel instruments we use for certain operations with plaster. I picked it up and hit him a blow with it on the back of the head. He gave a cry and slumped forward. I hit him again. I rained blow after blow on him. Then I threw the tool away. I was upset. I went out into the yard and looked around. I remembered he had a weak heart. Was he dead? I remember adjusting the position of a barrel we had in the yard to catch rainwater, the only sort of water suitable for some of the mixtures we used. I found I was in a cold sweat but strangely calm. I went back into the workshop.

Kelly was just as I had left him. I could find no pulse. I rolled him over on his back and examined his eyes, for I have seen more lifeless eyes in my day than most people. Yes, there was no doubt: Kelly was dead. I had killed him. I was a murderer. I put on my coat and hat and left the place. I walked the streets for a while, trying to avoid panic, trying to think rationally. Inevitably, I was soon in a public house. I drank a lot of whiskey and finally went home to my digs. The next morning I was very sick indeed from this terrible mixture of drink and worry. Was the Kelly affair merely a fancy, a drunken fancy? No, there was no consolation in that sort of hope. He was dead all right.

It was as I lay in bed there, shaking, thinking and smoking, that the mad idea came into my head. No doubt this sounds incredible, grotesque, even disgusting, but I decided I would treat Kelly the same as any other dead creature that found its way to the workshop.

Once one enters a climate of horror, distinction of degree as between one infamy and another seems slight, sometimes undetectable. That evening I went to the workshop and made my preparations. I worked steadily all next day. I will not appall the reader with gruesome detail. I need only say that I applied the general technique and flaying pattern appropriate to apes. The job took me four days at the end of which I had a perfect skin, face and all. I made the usual castings before committing the remains of, so to speak, the remains, to the furnace. My plan was to have Kelly on view asleep on a chair, for the benefit of anybody who might call. Reflection convinced me that this would be far too dangerous. I had to think again.

A further idea began to form. It was so macabre that it shocked even myself. For days I had been treating the inside of the skin with the usual preservatives—cellulose acetate and the like—thinking all the time. The new illumination came upon me like a thunderbolt. *I would don his skin and, when the need arose, BECOME Kelly!* His clothes fitted me. So would his skin. Why not?

Another day's agonized work went on various alterations and adjustments but that night I was able to look into a glass and see Kelly looking back at me, perfect in every detail except for the teeth and eyes, which had to be my own but which I knew other people would never notice.

Naturally I wore Kelly's clothes, and had no trouble in imitating his unpleasant voice and mannerisms. On the second day, having "dressed," so to speak, I went for a walk, receiving salutes from newsboys and other people who had known Kelly. And on the day after, I was foolhardy enough to visit Kelly's lodgings. Where on earth had I been, his landlady wanted to know. (She had noticed nothing.) What, I asked—had that fool Murphy not told her that I had to go to the country for a few days? No? I had told the good-for-nothing to convey the message.

I slept that night in Kelly's bed. I was a little worried about what the other landlady would think of my own absence. I decided not to remove Kelly's skin the first night I spent in his bed but to try to get the rest of my plan of campaign perfected and into sharper focus. I eventually decided that Kelly should announce to various people that he was going to a very good job in Canada, and that he had sold his business to his assistant Murphy. I would then burn the skin. I would own a business and—what is more stupid than vanity!—I could secretly flatter myself that I had committed the perfect crime.

Need I say that I had overlooked something?

The mummifying preparation with which I had dressed the inside of the skin was, of course, quite stable for the ordinary purposes of taxidermy. It had not occurred to me that a night in a warm bed would make it behave differently. The horrible truth dawned on me the next day when I reached the workshop and tried to take the skin off. *It wouldn't come off!* It had literally fused with my own! And in the days that followed, this process kept rapidly advancing. Kelly's skin got to live again, to breathe, to perspire.

Then followed more days of terrible tension. My own landlady called one day, inquiring about me of "Kelly." I told her I had been on the point of calling on *her* to find out where I was. She was disturbed about my disappearance—

it was so unlike me—and said she thought she should inform the police. I thought it wise not to try to dissuade her. My disappearance would eventually come to be accepted, I thought. My Kelliness, so to speak, was permanent. It was horrible, but it was a choice of that or the scaffold.

I kept drinking a lot. One night, after many drinks, I went to the club for a game of snooker. This club was in fact one of the causes of Kelly's bitterness towards me. I had joined it without having been aware that Kelly was a member. His resentment was boundless. He thought I was watching him, and taking note of the attentions he paid the lady members.

On this occasion I nearly made a catastrophic mistake. It is a simple fact that I am a very good snooker player, easily the best in that club. As I was standing watching another game in progress awaiting my turn for the table, *I suddenly realised that Kelly did not play snooker at all!* For some moments, a cold sweat stood out on Kelly's brow at the narrowness of this escape. I went to the bar. There, a garrulous lady (who thinks her unsolicited conversation is a fair exchange for a drink) began talking to me. She remarked the long absence of my nice Mr. Murphy. She said he was missed a lot in the snooker room. I was hot and embarrassed and soon went home. To Kelly's place, of course.

Not embarrassment, but a real sense of danger, was to be my next portion in this adventure. One afternoon, two very casual strangers strolled into the workshop, saying they would like a little chat with me. Cigarettes were produced. Yes indeed, they were plain-clothesmen making a few routine inquiries. This man Murphy had been reported missing by several people. Any idea where he was? None at all. When had I last seen him? Did he seem upset or disturbed? No, but he was an impetuous type. I had recently reprimanded him for bad work. On similar other occasions he had threatened to leave and seek work in England. Had I been away for a few days myself? Yes, down in Cork for a few days. On business. Yes . . . yes . . . some people thinking of starting a natural museum down there, technical school people—that sort of thing.

The casual manner of these men worried me, but I was sure they did not suspect the truth and that they were genuinely interested in tracing Murphy. Still, I knew I was in danger, without knowing the exact nature of the threat I had to counter. Whiskey cheered me somewhat.

Then it happened. The two detectives came back accompanied by two other men in uniform. They showed me a search warrant. It was purely a formality; it had to be done in the case of all missing persons. They had already searched Murphy's digs and had found nothing of interest. They were very sorry for upsetting the place during my working hours.

A few days later the casual gentlemen called and put me under arrest for the willful murder of Murphy, of myself. They proved the charge in due course with all sorts of painfully amassed evidence, including the remains of human bones in the furnace. I was sentenced to be hanged. Even if I could now prove that Murphy still lived by shedding the accursed skin, what help would that be? Where, they would ask, is Kelly?

That is my strange and tragic story. And I end it with the thought that if Kelly and I must each be either murderer or murdered, it is perhaps better to accept my present fate as philosophically as I can and be cherished in the public mind as the victim of this murderous monster, Kelly. He *was* a murderer, anyway.

EXERCISES

1. The short story as a form began with the notion of something novel and strange to tell. Compare the beginning of this story with the beginning of Edgar Allan Poe's "The Tell-Tale Heart."
2. Why does the narrator feel it is necessary to describe in such detail the method of taxidermy?
3. What is the tone of this story—comic, ironic, or straightforward? Point out those places which support your understanding of the tone.
4. What is the logic of the central event? What makes the central event inevitable in this story?
5. Compare the metaphor of skin as it is used here and as it is used in L'Heureux's story "The Anatomy of Desire."
6. What kind of confusion of identity takes place as a result of the fusion of the skin?
7. What is the logic and poetic justice involved in Murphy's being arrested for having murdered himself? How does Poe's "The Tell-Tale Heart" treat the same theme?

ITALO
SVEVO | # The Mother

In a valley closed in by wooded hills, glowing in the colors of springtime, there rose, one beside the other, two large unadorned houses of stone and lime. They seemed fashioned by the same hand; and the gardens too, enclosed by hedgerows placed before each of the houses, were both of the same size and shape. But similar fates did not befall those who lived there.

In one of the gardens, while the dog slept on his chain and the farmer occupied himself in his fruitgrove, in a corner, apart from everything else, some baby chicks were speaking of their great experiences. There were older ones in the garden, but the chicks whose bodies still retained the form of the eggs from which they had hatched took pleasure in examining amongst themselves the life into which they had plunged because they were still not very accustomed to it. They had already known pleasure and pain because a few days' life is longer than it would seem to one who has stood it for years; and they knew a great deal, and understood that they had carried within themselves from the egg a part of that great experience. In fact, as soon as they saw light they knew that things needed a good looking-over, first with one eye and then with the other, to see if they had to eat or to protect themselves.

And they spoke of the world and of its vastness, with the trees and the hedges which enclosed it, and the house so large and so tall. They had already seen everything, but they saw better talking about it.

One of them, however, yellow-downed, well-fed—and therefore restless— could not content himself to speak of the things which he saw, but drew from the gentle heat of the sun an observation which he made immediately.

"We are well off, of course, because we have the sun, but I have known that in this world one is able to be even happier; that saddens me very much and I am telling you because it has also saddened you. The farmer's daughter said that we are miserable because we don't have a mother. She said it with accents of such strong feeling that I had to weep."

Another chick, whiter and by some hours younger than the first,—still remembering with gratitude the sweet atmosphere of his birth—protested.

"We have had a mother. It's that metal thing which is always warm, even during the bitterest cold, from which baby chicks come beautiful and perfected."

The yellow one, who for some time had carried inscribed upon his soul the words of the farmgirl, and had had, therefore, time enough to become quite pleased with himself dreaming of a mother until he imagined her as large as all the garden and as good as mash, exclaimed with a scorn directed as much at his challenger as at the mother of which the other spoke, "If one concerned himself with a dead mother everyone would have one. But our mother is alive and runs much faster than us. Perhaps she has wheels like the farmer's wagon. Thus she would be able to come to you without your needing to call her, to warm you when you are about to die from the cold of this world. At night, how fine it must be to have nearby a mother like that!"

Another chick spoke up. He was a brother of the others because he had come from the same machine. But he was shaped a little differently, with his broader beak and shorter, slender legs. He was called "the ill-mannered chick" because when he ate one could hear the threshing of his gullet. Actually he was a duckling who in home waters would have been considered very polite. In his presence also the farmgirl had spoken of a mother. It had happened once when a chick, trembling and overcome by cold in the grass, had died encircled by the others who had not given help because they had not felt the cold which touches other chicks. And the duckling, who had his little face poked through the group from the very base of his wide neck, had asserted directly and naively that when there is a mother the chicks cannot die.

The desire for a mother soon infected the entire yard and made it more lively (more disquieting, in the minds of the older ones). Many times the infantile diseases attacked the adults; and the diseases were more dangerous for them, and from time to time the ideas as well. The image of a mother which took seed in those little spring-warmed heads developed beyond measure, and during fine weather and times of plenty the healthy ones called themselves "Mother," and when the chicks were suffering, ducklings and baby turkey cocks became true brothers because they longed for the same mother.

Not wishing to be left out of things, one of the eldest one day swore that he would find the mother. He was the only one in the chickenyard who was christened, and he was called Curra because, when the farmer called *"Curra, curra"* with his apronful of mash, he was the first to run forward. He was already vigorous, a young cock in whose sprightliness was dawning the urge to fight. Fine and sharp as a blade, he required a mother first of all because the others admired him: the mother of which he spoke was capable of furnishing the very finest of things, therefore both the satisfaction of his ambitions and of his vanity.

One day, resolved, Curra escaped in a single jump over the thick hedge which twisted around his native ground. At the gate he immediately stopped, perplexed. Where would he find the mother in the immensity of that valley over which the clear blue sky stretched with even greater vastness? To him, so small, it was not possible to search in that immensity. Therefore he did not wander far from his native garden, the world he knew; and, thoughtful, he made a trip around it. Thus he arrived at the hedge of the other garden.

"If the mother is inside here," he thought, "I should find her immediately."

Save for the obstacle of infinite space, he did not have another cause for hesitation. And with one jump he also crossed that hedge and found himself in a garden very similar to that which he had left.

Here too there was a swarm of very young chicks who were carrying on a discussion amongst themselves in the thick grass. But here there was an animal which the other garden lacked. An enormous hen, perhaps ten times larger than Curra, was enthroned in the downy midst of the brood which—one saw it immediately—considered the fat, ponderous animal their chief and protector. And she did take care of all of them. She sent an admonition to those who wandered too far afield with sounds very much like those which the farmer's daughter used with her own chicks. But she made other sounds too. Every now and then she bowed over the weakest, covering them with all her body, certain of transmitting her own warmth.

"This is the mother," thought Curra with joy. "I have found her and I shall never leave her. How she will love me! I am the strongest and the most handsome of them all. And then too, it will be easy for me to be obedient because I already love her. How beautiful and majestic she is! I shall also help her to protect all of those little fools."

Without looking at him, the mother called. Curra approached, believing that he himself had been called. He saw her occupied in scratching the earth with rapid strokes of her great claws, and he stopped, interested in that action which he witnessed for the first time. When she stopped, a little worm lay wriggling before her on the ground then swept free of grass. Now she clucked while the little ones around her, failing to comprehend, stared in fascination.

"Blockheads!" thought Curra. "They don't even understand that she wants them to eat the worm."

And still carried away by his enthusiasm for obedience, he sprang quickly upon the prey and swallowed it.

And then—poor Curra!—the mother fell on him viciously. Curra did not immediately understand her action because he suspected that she, who had just found him, wished to caress him with great fury. Thankfully he would have accepted all of the caresses (of which he knew nothing, having never known a mother), and as a result he permitted her to hurt him. The blows which rained down upon him clearly were not kisses and quickly swept away all suspicions. Curra wanted to run away but the great bird struck him and, tripping him up, jumped all over him, sinking her claws into his belly.

With savage strength Curra did free himself and broke for the hedge. In his mad flight he tripped up some chicks who were in his way, and he left them chirping wildly with their legs in the air. Because of that he was able to save himself, for his enemy stopped an instant near the fallen ones. Having arrived at the hedge, despite the many branches and shoots, Curra, with one leap, carried his small and agile body into the open.

The mother, instead, was stopped through the connivance of the thick leaves. And there in the hedge she remained, majestic, watching as if from a window the intruder who, exhausted, had also stopped. She watched him with her terrible round eyes, red with anger.

"Who are you who takes the food which I have dug from the earth with so much effort?"

"I am Curra," the little chick said meekly. "But you, who are you? and why do you treat me so badly?"

To the two questions she gave but a single answer: "I am the mother," and proudly turned her back to him.

Some time thereafter Curra, by then a magnificent thoroughbred cock, found himself in an entirely different chickenyard. And one day he heard affectionate and plaintive talk from all of his new companions about their mother.

Reflecting upon his own terrible lot, he said with sadness, "My mother, instead, was a horrible monster and it would have been better if I had never known her."

EXERCISES

1. At what point in this story do you know that it is a fable? What are the particular characteristics of an animal fable? Why do writers sometimes tell stories about animals with human characteristics?

2. Why is the mother figure so important for the chickens? Why not the father? What is signified by the "desire for a mother"? Why does the mother come to stand for everything that is good?

3. What is the creature that Curra takes to be the mother for which he is searching?

4. How is the answer "Mother" an answer to both the questions "But who are you? and why do you treat me so badly?"

5. What is the significance of the fact that there are two houses side by side so similar they might have been built by the same hands?

6. What is the point that the lots of the inmates of the two houses are very different—one set with a mother and one set without?

GABRIEL
GARCÍA
MÁRQUEZ | *A Very Old Man with Enormous Wings: A Tale for Children*

On the third day of rain they had killed so many crabs inside the house that Pelayo had to cross his drenched courtyard and throw them into the sea, because the newborn child had a temperature all night and they thought it was due to the stench. The world had been sad since Tuesday. Sea and sky were a single ash-gray thing and the sands of the beach, which on March nights glimmered like powdered light, had become a stew of mud and rotten shellfish. The light was so weak at noon that when Pelayo was coming back to the house after throwing away the crabs, it was hard for him to see what it was that was moving and groaning in the rear of the courtyard. He had to go very close to see that it was an old man, a very old man, lying face down in the mud, who, in spite of his tremendous efforts, couldn't get up, impeded by his enormous wings.

Frightened by that nightmare, Pelayo ran to get Elisenda, his wife, who was putting compresses on the sick child, and he took her to the rear of the courtyard. They both looked at the fallen body with mute stupor. He was dressed like a ragpicker. There were only a few faded hairs left on his bald skull and very few teeth in his mouth, and his pitiful condition of a drenched great-grandfather had taken away any sense of grandeur he might have had. His huge buzzard wings, dirty and half-plucked, were forever entangled in the mud. They looked at him so long and so closely that Pelayo and Elisenda very soon overcame their surprise and in the end found him familiar. Then they dared speak to him, and he answered in an incomprehensible dialect with a strong sailor's voice. That was how they skipped over the inconvenience of the wings and quite intelligently concluded that he was a lonely castaway from some foreign ship wrecked by the storm. And yet, they called in a neighbor woman who knew everything about life and death to see him, and all she needed was one look to show them their mistake.

"He's an angel," she told them. "He must have been coming for the child, but the poor fellow is so old that the rain knocked him down."

On the following day everyone knew that a flesh-and-blood angel was held captive in Pelayo's house. Against the judgment of the wise neighbor woman, for whom angels in those times were the fugitive survivors of a celestial conspiracy, they did not have the heart to club him to death. Pelayo watched over him all afternoon from the kitchen, armed with his bailiff's club, and before going to bed he dragged him out of the mud and locked him up with the hens in the wire chicken coop. In the middle of the night, when the rain stopped, Pelayo and Elisenda were still killing crabs. A short time afterward the child woke up without a fever and with a desire to eat. Then they felt magnanimous and decided to put the angel on a raft with fresh water and provisions for three days and leave him to his fate on the high seas. But when they went out into the courtyard with the first light of dawn, they found the whole neighborhood in front of the chicken coop having fun with the angel, without the slightest reverence, tossing him things to eat through the openings in the wire as if he weren't a supernatural creature but a circus animal.

Father Gonzaga arrived before seven o'clock, alarmed at the strange news. By that time onlookers less frivolous than those at dawn had already arrived and they were making all kinds of conjectures concerning the captive's future. The simplest among them thought that he should be named mayor of the world. Others of sterner mind felt that he should be promoted to the rank of five-star general in order to win all wars. Some visionaries hoped that he could be put to stud in order to implant on earth a race of winged wise men who could take charge of the universe. But Father Gonzaga, before becoming a priest, had been a robust woodcutter. Standing by the wire, he reviewed his catechism in an instant and asked them to open the door so that he could take a close look at that pitiful man who looked more like a huge decrepit hen among the fascinated chickens. He was lying in a corner drying his open wings in the sunlight among the fruit peels and breakfast leftovers that the early risers had thrown him. Alien to the impertinences of the world, he only lifted his antiquarian eyes and murmured something in his dialect when Father Gonzaga went into the chicken coop and said good morning to him in Latin. The parish priest had his first suspicion of an imposter when he saw that he did not understand the language of God or know how to greet His ministers. Then he noticed that seen close up he was much too human: he had an unbearable smell of the outdoors, the back side of his wings was strewn with parasites and his main feathers had been mistreated by terrestrial winds, and nothing about him measured up to the proud dignity of angels. Then he came out of the chicken coop and in a brief sermon warned the curious against the risks of being ingenuous. He reminded them that the devil had the bad habit of making use of carnival tricks in order to confuse the unwary. He argued that if wings were not the essential element in determining the difference between a hawk and an airplane, they were even less so in the recognition of angels. Nevertheless, he promised to write a letter to his bishop so that the latter would write to his primate so that the latter would write to the Supreme Pontiff in order to get the final verdict from the highest courts.

His prudence fell on sterile hearts. The news of the captive angel spread with such rapidity that after a few hours the courtyard had the bustle of a marketplace and they had to call in troops with fixed bayonets to disperse the mob that was about to knock the house down. Elisenda, her spine all twisted from sweeping up so much marketplace trash, then got the idea of fencing in the yard and charging five cents admission to see the angel.

The curious came from far away. A traveling carnival arrived with a flying acrobat who buzzed over the crowd several times, but no one paid any attention to him because his wings were not those of an angel but, rather, those of a sidereal bat. The most unfortunate invalids on earth came in search of health: a poor woman who since childhood had been counting her heartbeats and had run out of numbers; a Portuguese man who couldn't sleep because the noise of the stars disturbed him; a sleepwalker who got up at night to undo the things he had done while awake; and many others with less serious ailments. In the midst of that shipwreck disorder that made the earth tremble, Pelayo and Elisenda were happy with fatigue, for in less than a week they had crammed their rooms with money and the line of pilgrims waiting their turn to enter still reached beyond the horizon.

The angel was the only one who took no part in his own act. He spent his time trying to get comfortable in his borrowed nest, befuddled by the hellish heat of the oil lamps and sacramental candles that had been placed along the wire. At first they tried to make him eat some mothballs, which, according to the wisdom of the wise neighbor woman, were the food prescribed for angels. But he turned them down, just as he turned down the papal lunches that the penitents brought him and they never found out whether it was because he was an angel or because he was an old man that in the end he ate nothing but eggplant mush. His only supernatural virtue seemed to be patience. Especially during the first days, when the hens pecked at him, searching for the stellar parasites that proliferated in his wings, and the cripples pulled out feathers to touch their defective parts with, and even the most merciful threw stones at him, trying to get him to rise so they could see him standing. The only time they succeeded in arousing him was when they burned his side with an iron for branding steers, for he had been motionless for so many hours that they thought he was dead. He awoke with a start, ranting in his hermetic language and with tears in his eyes, and he flapped his wings a couple of times, which brought on a whirlwind of chicken dung and lunar dust and a gale of panic that did not seem to be of this world. Although many thought that his reaction had been one not of rage but of pain, from then on they were careful not to annoy him, because the majority understood that his passivity was not that of a hero taking his ease but that of a cataclysm in repose.

Father Gonzaga held back the crowd's frivolity with formulas of maidservant inspiration while awaiting the arrival of a final judgment on the nature of the captive. But the mail from Rome showed no sense of urgency. They spent their time finding out if the prisoner had a navel, if his dialect had any connection with Aramaic, how many times he could fit on the head of a pin, or whether he wasn't just a Norwegian with wings. Those meager letters might have come and gone until the end of time if a providential event had not put an end to the priest's tribulations.

It so happened that during those days, among so many other carnival attractions, there arrived in town the traveling show of the woman who had been changed into a spider for having disobeyed her parents. The admission to see her was not only less than the admission to see the angel, but people were permitted to ask her all manner of questions about her absurd state and to examine her up and down so that no one would ever doubt the truth of her horror. She was a frightful tarantula the size of a ram and with the head of a sad maiden. What was most heart-rending, however, was not her outlandish shape but the sincere affliction with which she recounted the details of her misfortune. While still practically a child she had sneaked out of her parents' house to go to a dance, and while she was coming back through the woods after having danced all night without permission, a fearful thunderclap rent the sky in two and through the crack came the lightning bolt of brimstone that changed her into a spider. Her only nourishment came from the meatballs that charitable souls chose to toss into her mouth. A spectacle like that, full of so much human truth and with such a fearful lesson, was bound to defeat without even trying that of a haughty angel who scarcely deigned to look at mortals. Besides, the few miracles attributed to the angel showed a certain mental disorder, like the blind man who didn't recover his sight but grew three new teeth, or the paralytic who didn't get to walk but almost won the lottery, and the leper whose sores sprouted sunflowers. Those consolation miracles, which were more like mocking fun, had already ruined the angel's reputation when the woman who had been changed into a spider finally crushed him completely. That was how Father Gonzaga was cured forever of his insomnia and Pelayo's courtyard went back to being as empty as during the time it had rained for three days and crabs walked through the bedrooms.

The owners of the house had no reason to lament. With the money they saved they built a two-story mansion with balconies and gardens and high netting so that crabs wouldn't get in during the winter, and with iron bars on the windows so that angels wouldn't get in. Pelayo also set up a rabbit warren close to town and gave up his job as bailiff for good, and Elisenda bought some satin pumps with high heels and many dresses of iridescent silk, the kind worn on Sunday by the most desirable women in those times. The chicken coop was the only thing that didn't receive any attention. If they washed it down with creolin and burned tears of myrrh inside it every so often, it was not in homage to the angel but to drive away the dungheap stench that still hung everywhere like a ghost and was turning the new house into an old one. At first, when the child learned to walk, they were careful that he not get too close to the chicken coop. But then they began to lose their fears and got used to the smell, and before the child got his second teeth he'd gone inside the chicken coop to play, where the wires were falling apart. The angel was no less standoffish with him than with other mortals, but he tolerated the most ingenious infamies with the patience of a dog who had no illusions. They both came down with chicken pox at the same time. The doctor who took care of the child couldn't resist the temptation to listen to the angel's heart, and he found so much whistling in the heart and so many sounds in his kidneys that it seemed impossible for him to be alive. What surprised him most, however, was the logic of his wings. They seemed so natural on that completely human organism that he couldn't understand why other men didn't have them too.

When the child began school it had been some time since the sun and rain had caused the collapse of the chicken coop. The angel went dragging himself about here and there like a stray dying man. They would drive him out of the bedroom with a broom and a moment later find him in the kitchen. He seemed to be in so many places at the same time that they grew to think that he'd been duplicated, that he was reproducing himself all through the house, and the exasperated and unhinged Elisenda shouted that it was awful living in that hell full of angels. He could scarcely eat and his antiquarian eyes had also become so foggy that he went about bumping into posts. All he had left were the bare cannulae of his last feathers. Pelayo threw a blanket over him and extended him the charity of letting him sleep in the shed, and only then did they notice that he had a temperature at night, and was delirious with the tongue twisters of an old Norwegian. That was one of the few times they became alarmed, for they thought he was going to die and not even the wise neighbor woman had been able to tell them what to do with dead angels.

And yet he not only survived his worst winter, but seemed improved with the first sunny days. He remained motionless for several days in the farthest corner of the courtyard, where no one would see him, and at the beginning of December some large, stiff feathers began to grow on his wings, the feathers of a scarecrow, which looked more like another misfortune of decrepitude. But he must have known the reason for those changes, for he was quite careful that no one should notice them, that no one should hear the sea chanteys that he sometimes sang under the stars. One morning Elisenda was cutting some bunches of onions for lunch when a wind that seemed to come from the high seas blew into the kitchen. Then she went to the window and caught the angel in his first attempts at flight. They were so clumsy that his fingernails opened a furrow in the vegetable patch and he was on the point of knocking the shed down with the ungainly flapping that slipped on the light and couldn't get a grip on the air. But he did manage to gain altitude. Elisenda let out a sigh of relief, for herself and for him, when she saw him pass over the last houses, holding himself up in some way with the risky flapping of a senile vulture. She kept watching him even when she was through cutting the onions and she kept on watching until it was no longer possible for her to see him, because then he was no longer an annoyance in her life but an imaginary dot on the horizon of the sea.

EXERCISES

1. How is this a tale for children? In what ways is it not suitable for children?
2. What kind of world is introduced in the first paragraph? Even before the discovery of the angel, how do you know that this is not the everyday familiar world?
3. Why is the angel decrepit rather than splendid, as we are accustomed to expect of angels?

4. Why is such a circus atmosphere created around the angel? Compare this with O'Flaherty's "The Fairy Goose" and with Warner's "The Phoenix" in Part IV.
5. What is meant by the phrase "a cataclysm in repose"?
6. Why does the spider woman become more fascinating to the people than the angel?
7. What is the significance of the "mocking miracles"?
8. Discuss the ending of the story: the flight of the angel and his transformation from an annoyance to an imaginery dot on the horizon of the sea.

ZORA NEALE HURSTON | *Spunk*

A giant of a brown-skinned man sauntered up the one street of the village and out into the palmetto thickets with a small pretty woman clinging lovingly to his arm.

"Looka theah, folkses!" cried Elijah Mosley, slapping his leg gleefully. "Theah they go, big as life an' brassy, as tacks."

All the loungers in the store tried to walk to the door with an air of nonchalance but with small success.

"Now pee-eople!" Walter Thomas gasped. "Will you look at 'em!"

"But that's one thing Ah likes about Spunk Banks—he ain't skeered of nothin' on God's green footstool—*nothin'!* He rides that log down at sawmill jus' like he struts 'round wid another man's wife—jus' don't give a kitty. When Tes' Miller got cut to giblets on that circle-saw, Spunk steps right up and starts ridin'. The rest of us was skeered to go near it."

A round-shouldered figure in overalls much too large came nervously in the door and the talking ceased. The men looked at each other and winked.

"Gimme some soda-water. Sass'prilla Ah reckon," the newcomer ordered, and stood far down the counter near the open pickled pig-feet tub to drink it.

Elijah nudged Walter and turned with mock gravity to the newcomer.

"Say, Joe, how's everything up yo' way? How's yo' wife?"

Joe started and all but dropped the bottle he was holding. He swallowed several times painfully and his lips trembled.

"Aw 'Lige, you oughtn't to do nothin' like that," Walter grumbled. Elijah ignored him.

"She jus' passed heah a few minutes ago goin' thata way," with a wave of his hand in the direction of the woods.

Now Joe knew his wife had passed that way. He knew that the men lounging in the general store had seen her, moreover, he knew that the men knew *he* knew. He stood there silent for a long moment staring blankly, with his

Adam's apple twitching nervously up and down his throat. One could actually *see* the pain he was suffering, his eyes, his face, his hands, and even the dejected slump of his shoulders. He set the bottle down upon the counter. He didn't bang it, just eased it out of his hand silently and fiddled with his suspender buckle.

"Well, Ah'm goin' after her to-day. Ah'm goin' an' fetch her back. Spunk's done gone too fur."

He reached deep down into his trouser pocket and drew out a hollow ground razor, large and shiny, and passed his moistened thumb back and forth over the edge.

"Talkin' like a man, Joe. 'Course that's *yo'* fambly affairs, but Ah like to see grit in anybody."

Joe Kanty laid down a nickel and stumbled out into the street.

Dusk crept in from the woods. Ike Clarke lit the swinging oil lamp that was almost immediately surrounded by candle-flies. The men laughed boisterously behind Joe's back as they watched him shamble woodward.

"You oughtn't to said whut you said to him, 'Lige—look how it worked him up," Walter chided.

"And Ah hope it did work him up. Tain't even decent for a man to take and take like he do."

"Spunk will sho' kill him."

"Aw, Ah doan know. You never kin tell. He might turn him up an' spank him fur gettin' in the way, but Spunk wouldn't shoot no unarmed man. Dat razor he carried outa heah ain't gonna run Spunk down an' cut him, an' Joe ain't got the nerve to go to Spunk with it knowing he totes that Army .45. He makes that break outa heah to bluff us. He's gonna hide that razor behind the first palmetto root an' sneak back home to bed. Don't tell me nothin' 'bout that rabbit-foot colored man. Didn't he meet Spunk an' Lena face to face one day las' week an' mumble sumthin' to Spunk 'bout lettin' his wife alone?"

"What did Spunk say?" Walter broke in. "Ah like him fine but tain't right the way he carries on wid Lena Kanty, jus' 'cause Joe's timid 'bout fightin'."

"You wrong theah, Walter. Tain't 'cause Joe's timid at all, it's 'cause Spunk wants Lena. If Joe was a passle of wile cats Spunk would tackle the job just the same. He'd go after *anything* he wanted the same way. As Ah wuz sayin' a minute ago, he tole Joe right to his face that Lena was his. 'Call her and see if she'll come. A woman knows her boss an' she answers when he calls.' 'Lena, ain't I yo' husband?' Joe sorter whines out. Lena looked at him real disgusted but she don't answer and she don't move outa her tracks. Then Spunk reaches out an' takes hold of her arm an' says: 'Lena, youse mine. From now on Ah works for you an' fights for you an' Ah never wants you to look to nobody for a crumb of bread, a stitch of close or a shingle to go over yo' head, but *me* long as Ah live. Ah'll git the lumber foh owah house to-morrow. Go home an' git yo' things together!'

" 'Thass mah house,' Lena speaks up. 'Papa gimme that.'

" 'Well, says Spunk, 'doan give up what's yours, but when youse inside doan forgit youse mine, an' let no other man git outa his place wid you!'

"Lena looked up at him with her eyes so full of love that they wuz runnin' over, an' Spunk seen it an' Joe seen it too, and his lip started to tremblin' and his Adam's apple was galloping up and down his neck like a race horse. Ah bet he's wore out half a dozen Adam's apples since Spunk's been on the job with Lena. That's all he'll do. He'll be back heah after while swallowin' an' workin' his lips like he wants to say somethin' an' can't."

"But didn't he do *nothin'* to stop 'em?"

"Nope, not a frazzlin' thing—jus' stood there. Spunk took Lena's arm and walked off jus' like nothin' ain't happened and he stood there gazin' after them till they was outa sight. Now you know a woman don't want no man like that. I'm jus' waitin' to see whut he's goin' to say when he gits back."

But Joe Kanty never came back, never. The men in the store heard the sharp report of a pistol somewhere distant in the palmetto thicket and soon Spunk came walking leisurely, with his big black Stetson set at the same rakish angle and Lena clinging to his arm, came walking right into the general store. Lena wept in a frightened manner.

"Well," Spunk announced calmly, "Joe came out there wid a meat axe an' made me kill him."

He sent Lena home and led the men back to Joe—crumpled and limp with his right hand still clutching his razor.

"See mah back? Mah close cut clear through. He sneaked up an' tried to kill me from the back, but Ah got him, an' got him good, first shot," Spunk said.

The men glared at Elijah, accusingly.

"Take him up an' plant him in Stony Lonesome," Spunk said in a careless voice. "Ah didn't wanna shoot him but he made me do it. He's a dirty coward, jumpin' on a man from behind."

Spunk turned on his heel and sauntered away to where he knew his love wept in fear for him and no man stopped him. At the general store later on, they all talked of locking him up until the sheriff should come from Orlando, but no one did anything but talk.

A clear case of self-defense, the trial was a short one, and Spunk walked out of the court house to freedom again. He could work again, ride the dangerous log-carriage that fed the singing, snarling, biting circle-saw; he could stroll the soft dark lanes with his guitar. He was free to roam the woods again; he was free to return to Lena. He did all these things.

"Whut you reckon, Walt?" Elijah asked one night later. "Spunk's gittin' ready to marry Lena!"

"Naw! Why, Joe ain't had time to git cold yit. Nohow Ah didn't figger Spunk was the marryin' kind."

"Well, he is," rejoined Elijah. "He done moved most of Lena's things— and her along wid 'em—over to the Bradley house. He's buying it. Jus' like Ah told yo' all right in heah the night Joe was kilt. Spunk's crazy 'bout Lena.

He don't want folks to keep on talkin' 'bout her—thass reason he's rushin' so. Funny thing 'bout that bob-cat, wan't it?"

"What bob-cat, 'Lige? Ah ain't heered 'bout none."

"Ain't cher? Well, night befo' las' as they was goin' to bed, a big black bob-cat, black all over, you hear me, *black,* walked round and round that house and howled like forty, an' when Spunk got his gun an' went to the winder to shoot it, he says it stood right still an' looked him in the eye, an' howled right at him. The thing got Spunk so nervoused up he couldn't shoot. But Spunk says twan't no bob-cat nohow. He says it was Joe done sneaked back from Hell!"

"Humph!" sniffed Walter, "he oughter be nervous after what he done. Ah reckon Joe come back to dare him to marry Lena, or to come out an' fight. Ah bet he'll be back time and again, too. Know what Ah think? Joe wuz a braver man than Spunk."

There was a general shout of derision from the group.

"Thass a fact," went on Walter. "Lookit whut he done; took a razor an' went out to fight a man he knowed toted a gun an' wuz a crack shot, too; 'nother thing Joe wuz skeered of Spunk, skeered plumb stiff! But he went jes' the same. It took him a long time to get his nerve up. Tain't nothin' for Spunk to fight when he ain't skeered of nothin'. Now, Joe's done come back to have it out wid the man that's got all he ever had. Y'all know Joe ain't never had nothin' nor wanted nothin' besides Lena. It musta been a h'ant cause ain't nobody never seen no black bob-cat."

"'Nother thing," cut in one of the men, "Spunk was cussin' a blue streak to-day 'cause he 'lowed dat saw wuz wobblin'—almos' got 'im once. The machinist come, looked it over an' said it wuz alright. Spunk musta been leanin' t'wards it some. Den he claimed somebody pushed 'im but twan't nobody close to 'im. Ah wuz glad when knockin' off time came. I'm skeered of dat man when he gits hot. He'd beat you full of button holes as quick as he'd look atcher."

The men gathered the next evening in a different mood, no laughter. No bad-inage this time.

"Look, 'Lige, you goin' to set up wid Spunk?"

"Naw, Ah reckon not, Walter. Tell yuh the truth, Ah'm a li'l bit skittish. Spunk died too wicket—died cussin' he did. You know he thought he was done outa life."

"Good Lawd, who'd he think done it?"

"Joe."

"Joe Kanty? How come?"

"Walter, Ah b'leeve Ah will walk up thata way an' set. Lena would like it Ah reckon."

"But whut did he say, 'Lige?"

Elijah did not answer until they had left the lighted store and were strolling down the dark street.

"Ah wuz loadin' a wagon wid scantlin' right near the saw when Spunk fell on the carriage but 'fore Ah could git to him the saw got him in the body—awful sight. Me an' Skint Miller got him off but it was too late. Anybody could see that. The fust thing he said wuz: 'He pushed me, 'Lige—the dirty hound pushed me in the back!'—he was spittin' blood at ev'ry breath. We laid him on the sawdust pile with his face to the East so's he could die easy. He helt mah han' till the last, Walter, and said: 'It was Joe, 'Lige . . . the dirty sneak shoved me . . . he didn't dare come to mah face . . . but Ah'll git the son-of-a-wood louse soon's Ah get there an' make hell too hot for him . . . Ah felt him shove me . . . !' Thass how he died."

"If spirits kin fight, there's a powerful tussle goin' on somewhere ovah Jordan 'cause Ah b'leeve Joe's ready for Spunk an' ain't skeered any more—yas, Ah b'leeve Joe pushed 'im mahself."

They had arrived at the house. Lena's lamentations were deep and loud. She had filled the room with magnolia blossoms that gave off a heavy sweet odor. The keepers of the wake tipped about whispering in frightened tones. Everyone in the village was there, even old Jeff Kanty, Joe's father, who a few hours before would have been afraid to come within ten feet of him, stood leering triumphantly down upon the fallen giant as if his fingers had been the teeth of steel that laid him low.

The cooling board consisted of three sixteen-inch boards on saw horses, a dingy sheet was his shroud.

The women ate heartily of the funeral baked meats and wondered who would be Lena's next. The men whispered coarse conjectures between guzzles of whiskey.

EXERCISES

1. Although the characters in the story are described "as big as life," how are they bigger than life? How do you know this is a legendary story rather than a realistic one?

2. Discuss the statement "Now you know a woman don't want no man like that."

3. Who is the braver, Spunk or Joe? Is this a significant issue in the story?

4. Why do the deaths of Joe and Spunk take place "off stage" and are reported by people in the story rather than described by the teller directly?

5. Discuss the impact of the last paragraph. How do you react to this image of the women wondering who will be Lena's next and the men making coarse conjectures between guzzles of whiskey?

GIOVANNI
VERGA | *The She-Wolf*

She was tall, thin; she had the firm and vigorous breasts of the olive-skinned—and yet she was no longer young; she was pale, as if always plagued by malaria, and in that pallor, two enormous eyes, and fresh lips which devoured you.

In the village they called her the She-wolf, because she never had enough—of anything. The women made the sign of the cross when they saw her pass, alone as a wild bitch, prowling about suspiciously like a famished wolf; with her red lips she sucked the blood of their sons and husbands in a flash, and pulled them behind her skirt with a single glance of those devilish eyes, even if they were before the altar of Saint Agrippina. Fortunately, the She-wolf never went to church, not at Easter, not at Christmas, not to hear Mass, not for confession.—Father Angiolino of Saint Mary of Jesus, a true servant of God, had lost his soul on account of her.

Maricchia, a good girl, poor thing, cried in secret because she was the She-wolf's daughter, and no one would marry her, though, like every other girl in the village, she had her fine linen in a chest and her good land under the sun.

One day the She-wolf fell in love with a handsome young man who had just returned from the service and was mowing hay with her in the fields of the notary; and she fell in love in the strongest sense of the word, feeling the flesh afire beneath her clothes; and staring him in the eyes, she suffered the thirst one has in the hot hours of June, deep in the plain. But he went on mowing undisturbed, his nose bent over the swaths.

"What's wrong, Pina?" he would ask.

In the immense fields, where you heard only the crackling flight of the grasshoppers, as the sun hammered down overhead, the She-wolf gathered bundle after bundle, and sheaf after sheaf, never tiring, never straightening up for an instant, never raising the flask to her lips, just to remain at the heels of Nanni, who mowed and mowed and asked from time to time:

"What is it you want, Pina?"

One evening she told him, while the men were dozing on the threshing floor, tired after the long day, and the dogs were howling in the vast, dark countryside.

"It's you I want. You who're beautiful as the sun and sweet as honey. I want you!"

"And I want your daughter, instead, who's a maid," answered Nanni laughing.

The She-wolf thrust her hands into her hair, scratching her temples, without saying a word, and walked away. And she did not appear at the threshing floor any more. But she saw Nanni again in October, when they were making olive oil, for he was working near her house, and the creaking of the press kept her awake all night.

"Get the sack of olives," she said to her daughter, "and come with me."
Nanni was pushing olives under the millstone with a shovel, shouting
"Ohee" to the mule, to keep it from stopping.

"You want my daughter Maricchia?" Pina asked him.

"What'll you give your daughter Maricchia?" answered Nanni.

"She has all her father's things, and I'll give her my house too; as for me,
all I need is a little corner in the kitchen, enough for a straw mattress."

"If that's the way it is, we can talk about it at Christmas," said Nanni.

Nanni was all greasy and filthy, spattered with oil and fermented olives,
and Maricchia didn't want him at any price. But her mother grabbed her by
the hair before the fireplace, muttering between her teeth:

"If you don't take him, I'll kill you!"

The She-wolf was almost sick, and the people were saying that when the devil
gets old he becomes a hermit. She no longer roamed here and there, no longer
lingered at the doorway, with those bewitched eyes. Whenever she fixed them
on his face, those eyes of hers, her son-in-law began to laugh and pulled out
the scapular or the Virgin to cross himself. Maricchia stayed at home nursing
the babies, and her mother went into the fields to work with the men, and
just like a man too, weeding, hoeing, feeding the animals, pruning the vines,
despite the northeast and levantine winds of January or the August sirocco,
when the mules' heads drooped and the men slept face down along the wall,
on the north side. "In those hours between nones and vespers when no good
woman goes roving around," Pina was the only living soul to be seen wandering in the countryside, over the burning stones of the paths, through the
scorched stubble of the immense fields that became lost in the suffocating heat,
far, far away toward the foggy Etna, where the sky was heavy on the horizon.

"Wake up!" said the She-wolf to Nanni, who was sleeping in the ditch,
along the dusty hedge, his head on his arms. "Wake up. I've brought you some
wine to cool your throat."

Nanni opened his drowsy eyes wide, still half asleep, and finding her
standing before him, pale, with her arrogant breasts and her coal-black eyes,
he stretched out his hands gropingly.

"No! no good woman goes roving around in the hours between nones and
vespers!" sobbed Nanni, throwing his face back into the dry grass of the ditch,
deep, deep, his nails in his scalp. "Go away! go away! don't come to the
threshing floor again!"

The She-wolf was going away, in fact, retying her superb tresses, her gaze
bent fixedly before her as she moved through the hot stubble, her eyes as black
as coal.

But she came to the threshing floor again, and more than once, and Nanni
did not complain. On the contrary, when she was late, in the hours between
nones and vespers, he would go and wait for her at the top of the white,
deserted path, with his forehead bathed in sweat; and he would thrust his
hands into his hair, and repeat every time:

"Go away! go away! don't come to the threshing floor again!"

Maricchia cried night and day, and glared at her mother, her eyes burning with tears and jealousy, like a young she-wolf herself, every time she saw her come, mute and pale, from the fields.

"Vile, vile mother!" she said to her. "Vile mother!"

"Shut up!"

"Thief! Thief!"

"Shut up!"

"I'll go to the Sergeant, I will!"

"Go ahead!"

And she really did go, with her babies in her arms, fearing nothing, and without shedding a tear, like a madwoman, because now she too loved that husband who had been forced on her, greasy and filthy, spattered with oil and fermented olives.

The Sergeant sent for Nanni; he threatened him even with jail and the gallows. Nanni began to sob and tear his hair; he didn't deny anything, he didn't try to clear himself.

"It's the temptation!" he said. "It's the temptation of hell!"

He threw himself at the Sergeant's feet begging to be sent to jail.

"For God's sake, Sergeant, take me out of this hell! Have me killed, put me in jail; don't let me see her again, never! never!"

"No!" answered the She-wolf instead, to the Sergeant. "I kept a little corner in the kitchen to sleep in, when I gave him my house as dowry. It's my house. I don't intend to leave it."

Shortly afterward, Nanni was kicked in the chest by a mule and was at the point of death, but the priest refused to bring him the Sacrament if the She-wolf did not go out of the house. The She-wolf left, and then her son-in-law could also prepare to leave like a good Christian; he confessed and received communion with such signs of repentance and contrition that all the neighbors and the curious wept before the dying man's bed.—And it would have been better for him to die that day, before the devil came back to tempt him again and creep into his body and soul, when he got well.

"Leave me alone!" he told the She-wolf. "For God's sake, leave me in peace! I've seen death with my own eyes! Poor Maricchia is desperate. Now the whole town knows about it! If I don't see you it's better for both of us. . . ."

And he would have liked to gouge his eyes out not to see those of the She-wolf, for whenever they peered into his, they made him lose his body and soul. He did not know what to do to free himself from the spell. He paid for Masses for the souls in purgatory and asked the priest and the Sergeant for help. At Easter he went to confession, and in penance he publicly licked more than four feet of pavement, crawling on the pebbles in front of the church—and then, as the She-wolf came to tempt him again:

"Listen!" he said to her. "Don't come to the threshing floor again; if you do, I swear to God, I'll kill you!"

"Kill me," answered the She-wolf, "I don't care; I can't stand it without you."

As he saw her from the distance, in the green wheat fields, Nanni stopped hoeing the vineyard, and went to pull the ax from the elm. The She-wolf saw him come, pale and wild-eyed, with the ax glistening in the sun, but she did not fall back a single step, did not lower her eyes; she continued toward him, her hands laden with red poppies, her black eyes devouring him.

"Ah! damn your soul!" stammered Nanni.

EXERCISES

1. From your own cultural point of view, define the She-wolf's love for Nanni. Is it love, or is it lust? What is the difference between the two? How does the cultural perspective of the story differ from your own?

2. Note the setting and atmosphere of the story—the immense fields, the sirocco blowing across the Mediterranean that makes the mules' heads droop. What does this have to do with the emotions in the story? Can a physical locale affect emotions, or is this a literary convention?

3. Much of the effect of the story depends on the language used to describe the She-wolf, her love for Nanni, and the time of day when she goes to see him. What does this language suggest about her desire?

4. Why do the ways that Maricchia and Nanni use to combat the She-wolf not work?

5. What is the significance of the final view we have of the She-wolf, her hands laden with red poppies?

JOÃO
GUIMARÃES
ROSA | *The Third Bank of the River*

M y father was a dutiful, orderly, straightforward man. And according to several reliable people of whom I inquired, he had had these qualities since adolescence or even childhood. By my own recollection, he was neither jollier nor more melancholy than the other men we knew. Maybe a little quieter. It was Mother, not Father, who ruled the house. She scolded us daily— my sister, my brother, and me. But it happened one day that Father ordered a boat.

He was very serious about it. It was to be made specially for him, of mimosa wood. It was to be sturdy enough to last twenty or thirty years and just large enough for one person. Mother carried on plenty about it. Was her husband going to become a fisherman all of a sudden? Or a hunter? Father said nothing. Our house was less than a mile from the river, which around there was deep, quiet, and so wide you couldn't see across it.

I can never forget the day the rowboat was delivered. Father showed no joy or other emotion. He just put on his hat as he always did and said good-by to us. He took along no food or bundle of any sort. We expected Mother to rant and rave, but she didn't. She looked very pale and bit her lip, but all she said was: "If you go away, stay away. Don't ever come back!"

Father made no reply. He looked gently at me and motioned me to walk along with him. I feared Mother's wrath, yet I eagerly obeyed. We headed toward the river together. I felt bold and exhilarated, so much so that I said: "Father, will you take me with you in your boat?"

He just looked at me, gave me his blessing, and by a gesture, told me to go back. I made as if to do so but, when his back was turned, I ducked behind some bushes to watch him. Father got into the boat and rowed away. Its shadow slid across the water like a crocodile, long and quiet.

Father did not come back. Nor did he go anywhere, really. He just rowed and floated across and around, out there in the river. Everyone was appalled. What had never happened, what could not possibly happen, was happening. Our relatives, neighbors, and friends came over to discuss the phenomenon.

Mother was ashamed. She said little and conducted herself with great composure. As a consequence, almost everyone thought (though no one said it) that Father had gone insane. A few, however, suggested that Father might be fulfilling a promise he had made to God or to a saint, or that he might have some horrible disease, maybe leprosy, and that he left for the sake of the family, at the same time wishing to remain fairly near them.

Travelers along the river and people living near the bank on one side or the other reported that Father never put foot on land, by day or night. He just moved about on the river, solitary, aimless, like a derelict. Mother and our relatives agreed that the food which he had doubtless hidden in the boat would soon give out and that then he would either leave the river and travel off somewhere (which would be at least a little more respectable) or he would repent and come home.

How far from the truth they were! Father had a secret source of provisions: me. Every day I stole food and brought it to him. The first night after he left, we all lit fires on the shore and prayed and called to him. I was deeply distressed and felt a need to do something more. The following day I went down to the river with a loaf of corn bread, a bunch of bananas, and some bricks of raw brown sugar. I waited impatiently a long, long hour. Then I saw the boat, far off, alone, gliding almost imperceptibly on the smoothness of the river. Father was sitting in the bottom of the boat. He saw me but he did not row toward me or make any gesture. I showed him the food and then I placed it in a hollow rock on the river bank; it was safe there from animals, rain, and dew. I did this day after day, on and on and on. Later I learned, to my surprise, that Mother knew what I was doing and left food around where I could easily steal it. She had a lot of feelings she didn't show.

Mother sent for her brother to come and help on the farm and in business matters. She had the schoolteacher come and tutor us children at home because of the time we had lost. One day, at her request, the priest put on his vestments, went down to the shore, and tried to exorcise the devils that had got into my father. He shouted that Father had a duty to cease his unholy obstinacy. Another day she arranged to have two soldiers come and try to frighten him. All to no avail. My father went by in the distance, sometimes so far away he could barely be seen. He never replied to anyone and no one ever got close to him. When some newspapermen came in a launch to take his picture, Father headed his boat to the other side of the river and into the marshes, which he knew like the palm of his hand but in which other people quickly got lost. There in his private maze, which extended for miles, with heavy foliage overhead and rushes on all sides, he was safe.

We had to get accustomed to the idea of Father's being out on the river. We had to but we couldn't, we never could. I think I was the only one who understood to some degree what our father wanted and what he did not want. The thing I could not understand at all was how he stood the hardship. Day and night, in sun and rain, in heat and in the terrible midyear cold spells, with his old hat on his head and very little other clothing, week after week, month after month, year after year, unheedful of the waste and emptiness in which his life was slipping by. He never set foot on earth or grass, on isle or mainland shore. No doubt he sometimes tied up the boat at a secret place, perhaps at the tip of some island, to get a little sleep. He never lit a fire or even struck a match and he had no flashlight. He took only a small part of the food that I left in the hollow rock—not enough, it seemed to me, for survival. What could his state of health have been? How about the continual drain on his energy, pulling and pushing the oars to control the boat? And how did he survive the annual floods, when the river rose and swept along with it all sorts of dangerous objects—branches of trees, dead bodies of animals—that might suddenly crash against his little boat?

He never talked to a living soul. And we never talked about him. We just thought. No, we could never put our father out of mind. If for a short time we seemed to, it was just a lull from which we would be sharply awakened by the realization of his frightening situation.

My sister got married, but Mother didn't want a wedding party. It would have been a sad affair, for we thought of him every time we ate some especially tasty food. Just as we thought of him in our cozy beds on a cold, stormy night—out there, alone and unprotected, trying to bail out the boat with only his hands and a gourd. Now and then someone would say that I was getting to look more and more like my father. But I knew that by then his hair and beard must have been shaggy and his nails long. I pictured him thin and sickly, black with hair and sunburn, and almost naked despite the articles of clothing I occasionally left for him.

He didn't seem to care about us at all. But I felt affection and respect for him, and, whenever they praised me because I had done something good, I said: "My father taught me to act that way."

It wasn't exactly accurate but it was a truthful sort of lie. As I said, Father didn't seem to care about us. But then why did he stay around there? Why didn't he go up the river or down the river, beyond the possibility of seeing us or being seen by us? He alone knew the answer.

My sister had a baby boy. She insisted on showing Father his grandson. One beautiful day we all went down to the riverbank, my sister in her white wedding dress, and she lifted the baby high. Her husband held a parasol above them. We shouted to Father and waited. He did not appear. My sister cried; we all cried in each other's arms.

My sister and her husband moved far away. My brother went to live in a city. Times changed, with their usual imperceptible rapidity. Mother finally moved too; she was old and went to live with her daughter. I remained behind, a leftover. I could never think of marrying. I just stayed there with the impedimenta of my life. Father, wandering alone and forlorn on the river, needed me. I knew he needed me, although he never even told me why he was doing it. When I put the question to people bluntly and insistently, all they told me was that they heard that Father had explained it to the man who made the boat. But now this man was dead and nobody knew or remembered anything. There was just some foolish talk, when the rains were especially severe and persistent, that my father was wise like Noah and had the boat built in anticipation of a new flood; I dimly remember people saying this. In any case, I would not condemn my father for what he was doing. My hair was beginning to turn gray.

I have only sad things to say. What bad had I done, what was my great guilt? My father always away and his absence always with me. And the river, always the river, perpetually renewing itself. The river, always. I was beginning to suffer from old age, in which life is just a sort of lingering. I had attacks of illness and of anxiety. I had a nagging rheumatism. And he? Why, why was he doing it? He must have been suffering terribly. He was so old. One day, in his failing strength, he might let the boat capsize; or he might let the current carry it downstream, on and on, until it plunged over the waterfall to the boiling turmoil below. It pressed upon my heart. He was out there and I was forever robbed of my peace. I am guilty of I know not what, and my pain is an open wound inside me. Perhaps I would know—if things were different. I began to guess what was wrong.

Out with it! Had I gone crazy? No, in our house that word was never spoken, never through all the years. No one called anybody crazy, for nobody is crazy. Or maybe everybody. All I did was go there and wave a handkerchief so he would be more likely to see me. I was in complete command of myself. I waited. Finally he appeared in the distance, there, then over there, a vague shape sitting in the back of the boat. I called to him several times. And I said what I was so eager to say, to state formally and under oath. I said it as loud as I could:

"Father, you have been out there long enough. You are old. . . . Come back, you don't have to do it anymore. . . . Come back and I'll go instead. Right now, if you want. Any time. I'll get into the boat. I'll take your place."

And when I had said this my heart beat more firmly.

He heard me. He stood up. He maneuvered with his oars and headed the boat toward me. He had accepted my offer. And suddenly I trembled, down deep. For he had raised his arm and waved—the first time in so many, so many years. And I couldn't. . . . In terror, my hair on end, I ran, I fled madly. For he seemed to come from another world. And I'm begging forgiveness, begging, begging.

I experienced the dreadful sense of cold that comes from deadly fear, and I became ill. Nobody ever saw or heard about him again. Am I a man, after such a failure? I am what never should have been. I am what must be silent. I know it is too late. I must stay in the deserts and unmarked plains of my life, and I fear I shall shorten it. But when death comes I want them to take me and put me in a little boat in this perpetual water between the long shores; and I, down the river, lost in the river, inside the river . . . the river. . . .

EXERCISES

1. What is the cause or the motivation of the father's decision to go on the boat on the river? If there is no realistic motivation, what is the metaphoric or allegorical motivation?

2. How is this river a metaphor for the "river of life"? Compare this with the metaphor in John Cheever's "The Swimmer." Why in this story does the father simply move aimlessly on the river like a derelict?

3. Why does the son become more and more like the father? Why is the son the only one who seems to understand what the father wants and does not want? Why does he not tell us these things? Are there some things that cannot be said directly?

4. What is the boy's great guilt? What is meant by his feeling his father's "absence" is always with him? What is meant by the river being something that perpetually renews itself?

5. Why does the boy refuse to take his father's place? What does he mean when he says that his father seems to come from another world? How is this story like the story "Father and I" by Pär Lagkervist in Part II?

CHARLES
BAXTER | *The Cliff*

On the way out to the cliff, the old man kept one hand on the wheel. He smoked with the other hand. The inside of the car smelled of wine and cigarette ashes. He coughed constantly. His voice sounded like a version of the cough.

"I used to smoke Camels unfiltered," he told the boy. The dirt road, rutted, dipped hard, and the car bounced. "But I switched brands. Camels interfered with my eating. I couldn't taste what the Duchess cooked up. Meat, salad, Jell-O: it all tasted the same. So I went to low tar. You don't smoke, do you, boy?"

The boy stared at the road and shook his head.

"Not after what I've taught you, I hope not. You got to keep the body pure for the stuff we're doing."

"You don't keep it pure," the boy said.

"I don't have to. It's *been* pure. And, like I say, nobody is ever pure twice."

The California pines seemed brittle and did not sway as they drove past. The boy thought he could hear the crash of the waves in front of them. "Are we almost there?"

"Kind of impatient, aren't you?" the old man said, suppressing his cough. "Look, boy, I told you a hundred times: you got to train your will to do this. You get impatient, and you—"

"—I know, I know. 'You die.' " The boy was wearing a jacket and a New York Mets cap. "I know all that. You taught me. I'm only asking if we're there yet."

"You got a woman, boy?" The old man looked suspicious. "You got a woman?"

"I'm only fifteen," the boy said nervously.

"That's not too old for it, especially around here."

"I've been kissed," the boy said. "Is that the ocean?"

"That's her," the old man said. "Sometimes I think I know everything about you, and then sometimes I don't think I know anything. I hate to take chances like this. You could be hiding something out on me. The magic's no damn good if you're hiding something out on me."

"It'll be good," the boy said, seeing the long line of blue water through the trees. He pulled the visor down lower, so he wouldn't squint. "It'll be real good."

"Faith, hope, charity, and love," the old man recited. "And the spells. Now I admit I have fallen from the path of righteousness at times. But I never forget the spells. You forget them, you die."

"I would not forget them," the boy said.

"You better not be lying to me. You been thieving, sleeping with whores, you been carrying on in the bad way, well, we'll find out soon enough." He stopped the car at a clearing. He turned the key off in the ignition and reached under his seat for a wine bottle. His hands were shaking. The old man unscrewed the cap and took a long swig. He recapped it and breathed out the sweet aroma in the boy's direction. "Something for my nerves," he said. "I don't do this every day."

"You don't believe in the spells anymore," the boy said.

"I *am* the spells," the old man shouted. "I invented them. I just hate to see a fresh kid like you crash on the rocks on account of *you* don't believe in them."

"Don't worry," the boy said. "Don't worry about me."

They got out of the car together, and the old man reached around into the back seat for his coil of rope.

"I don't need it," the boy said. "I don't need the rope."

"Kid, we do it my way or we don't do it."

The boy took off his shoes. His bare feet stepped over pine needles and stones. He was wearing faded blue jeans and a sweatshirt, with a stain from the old man's wine bottle on it. He had taken off his jacket in the car, but he was still wearing the cap. They walked over a stretch of burnt grass and came to the edge of the cliff.

"Look at those sea gulls down there," the old man pointed. "Must be a hundred." His voice was trembling with nervousness.

"I know about the sea gulls." The boy had to raise his voice to be heard above the surf. "I've seen them."

"You're so smart, huh?" the old man coughed. He drew a cigarette out of his shirt and lit it with his Zippo lighter. "All right, I'm tired of telling you what to do, Mr. Know-It-All. Take off the sweatshirt." The boy took it off. "Now make a circle in the dirt."

"With what?"

"With your foot."

"There isn't any dirt."

"Do like I tell you."

The boy extended his foot and drew a magic circle around himself. It could not be seen, but he knew it was there.

"Now look out at the horizon and tell it what I told you to tell it."

The boy did as he was told.

"Now take this rope, take this end." The old man handed it to him. "God, I don't know sometimes." The old man bent down for another swig of wine. "Is your mind clear?"

"Yeah," the boy said.

"Are you scared?"

"Naw."

"Do you see anybody?"

"Nope."

"You got any last questions?"

"Do I hold my arms out?"

"They do that in the Soviet Union," the old man said, "but they also do it sitting on pigs. That's the kind of people they are. You don't have to hold your arms out. Are you ready? Jump!"

The boy felt the edge of the cliff with his feet, jumped, and felt the magic and the horizon lifting him up and then out over the water, his body parallel to the ground. He took it into his mind to swoop down toward the cliffs, and then to veer away suddenly, and whatever he thought, he did. At first he held on to the rope, but even the old man could see that it was unnecessary, and reeled it in. In his jeans and cap, the boy lifted himself upward, then dove down toward the sea gulls, then just as easily lifted himself up again, rushing over the old man's head before flying out over the water.

He shouted with happiness.

The old man reached down again for his wine.

"The sun!" the old man shouted. "The ocean! The land! That's how to do it!" And he laughed suddenly, his cough all gone. "The sky!" he said at last.

The boy flew in great soaring circles. He tumbled in the air, dove, flipped, and sailed. His eyes were dazzled with the blue also, and like the old man he smelled the sea salt.

But of course he was a teen-ager. He was grateful to the old man for teaching him the spells. But this—the cliffs, the sea, the blue sky, and the sweet wine—this was the old man's style, not his. He loved the old man for sharing the spells. He would think of him always, for that.

But even as he flew, he was getting ideas. It isn't the style of teen-agers to fly in broad daylight, on sunny days, even in California. What the boy wanted was something else: to fly low, near the ground, in the cities, speeding in smooth arcs between the buildings, late at night. Very late: at the time the girls are hanging up their clothes and sighing, sighing out their windows to the stagnant air, as the clocks strike midnight. The idea of the pig interested the boy. He grinned far down at the old man, who waved, who had long ago forgotten the dirty purposes of flight.

EXERCISES

1. What does the old man mean when he says "nobody is ever pure twice." Why is purity necessary for the "stuff" they are doing? What does the term *purity* mean?

2. What does the old man mean when he says, "The magic's no damn good if you're hiding something out on me"?

3. What are the spells that the old man says he invented? Why is righteousness important? Define *righteousness*.

4. A key statement in the story is probably the line, "Whatever he thought, he did." Discuss the significance of this as the basis of the magic. Why is this a basic human desire?

5. Another key phrase in the story is "the dirty purposes of flight." If this is a story about some universal human desire, what is signified by the desire to fly? Why might flight have "dirty purposes"? Should the human desire to fly have any specific purpose at all except the most basic one of escaping gravity?

ALAIN
ROBBE-GRILLET | *The Secret Room*

To Gustave Moreau.

The first thing to be seen is a red stain, of a deep, dark, shiny red, with almost black shadows. It is in the form of an irregular rosette, sharply outlined, extending in several directions in wide outflows of unequal length, dividing and dwindling afterward into single sinuous streaks. The whole stands out against a smooth, pale surface, round in shape, at once dull and pearly, a hemisphere joined by gentle curves to an expanse of the same pale color—white darkened by the shadowy quality of the place: a dungeon, a sunken room, or a cathedral—glowing with a diffused brilliance in the semi-darkness.

Further back, the space is filled with the cylindrical trunks of columns, repeated with progressive vagueness in their retreat toward the beginning of a vast stone stairway, turning slightly as it rises, growing narrower and narrower as it approaches the high vaults where it disappears.

The whole setting is empty, stairway and colonnades. Alone, in the foreground, the stretched-out body gleams feebly, marked with the red stain—a white body whose full, supple flesh can be sensed, fragile, no doubt, and vulnerable. Alongside the bloody hemisphere another identical round form, this one intact, is seen at almost the same angle of view; but the haloed point at its summit, of darker tint, is in this case quite recognizable, whereas the other one is entirely destroyed, or at least covered by the wound.

In the background, near the top of the stairway, a black silhouette is seen fleeing, a man wrapped in a long floating cape, ascending the last steps without turning around, his deed accomplished. A thin smoke rises in twisting scrolls from a sort of incense burner placed on a high stand of ironwork with a silvery glint. Nearby lies the milkwhite body, with wide streaks of blood running from the left breast, along the flank and on the hip.

It is a fully rounded woman's body, but not heavy, completely nude, lying on the back, the bust raised up somewhat by thick cushions thrown down on the floor, which is covered with oriental rugs. The waist is very narrow, the neck long and thin, curved to one side, the head thrown back into a darker area where, even so, may be discerned the facial features, the partly opened mouth, the wide-staring eyes, shining with a fixed brilliance, and the mass of long, black hair spread out in a complicated wavy disorder over a heavily folded cloth, of velvet perhaps, on which also rest the arm and shoulder.

It is a uniformly colored velvet of dark purple, or which seems so in this lighting. But purple, brown, blue also seem to dominate in the colors of the cushions—only a small portion of which is hidden beneath the velvet cloth, and which protrude noticeably, lower down, beneath the bust and waist—as well as in the oriental patterns of the rugs on the floor. Further on, these same colors are picked up again in the stone of the paving and the columns, the vaulted archways, the stairs, and the less discernible surfaces that disappear into the farthest reaches of the room.

The dimensions of this room are difficult to determine exactly; the body of the young sacrificial victim seems at first glance to occupy a substantial portion of it, but the vast size of the stairway leading down to it would imply rather that this is not the whole room, whose considerable space must in reality extend all around, right and left, as it does toward the far-away browns and blues among the columns standing in line, in every direction, perhaps toward other sofas, thick carpets, piles of cushions and fabrics, other tortured bodies, other incense burners.

It is also difficult to say where the light comes from. No clue, on the columns or on the floor, suggests the direction of the rays. Nor is any window or torch visible. The milkwhite body itself seems to light the scene, with its full breasts, the curve of its thighs, the rounded belly, the full buttocks, the stretched-out legs, widely spread, and the black tuft of the exposed sex, provocative, proffered, useless now.

The man has already moved several steps back. He is now on the first steps of the stairs, ready to go up. The bottom steps are wide and deep, like the steps leading up to some great building, a temple or theatre; they grow smaller as they ascend, and at the same time describe a wide helical curve, so gradually that the stairway has not yet made a halfturn by the time that it disappears near the top of the vaults, reduced then to a steep, narrow flight of steps without handrail, vaguely outlined, moreover, in the thickening darkness beyond.

But the man does not look in this direction, where his movement nonetheless carries him; his left foot on the second step and his right foot already touching the third, with his knee bent, he has turned around to look at the spectacle for one last time. The long, floating cape thrown hastily over his shoulders, clasped in one hand at his waist, has been whirled around by the rapid circular motion that has just caused his head and chest to turn in the opposite direction, and a corner of the cloth remains suspended in the air as if blown by a gust of wind; this corner, twisting around upon itself in the form of a loose S, reveals the red silk lining with its gold embroidery.

The man's features are impassive, but tense, as if in expectation—or perhaps fear—of some sudden event, or surveying with one last glance the total immobility of the scene. Though he is looking backward, his whole body is turned slightly forward, as if he were continuing up the stairs. His right arm— not the one holding the edge of the cape—is bent sharply toward the left, toward a point in space where the balustrade should be, if this stairway had one, an interrupted gesture, almost incomprehensible, unless it arose from an instinctive movement to grasp the absent support.

As to the direction of his glance, it is certainly aimed at the body of the victim lying on the cushions, its extended members stretched out in the form of a cross, its bust raised up, its head thrown back. But the face is perhaps hidden from the man's eyes by one of the columns, standing at the foot of the stairs. The young woman's right hand touches the floor just at the foot of this column. The fragile wrist is encircled by an iron bracelet. The arm is almost in darkness, only the hand receiving enough light to make the thin, outspread fingers clearly visible against the circular protrusion at the base of the stone column. A black metal chain running around the column passes through a ring affixed to the bracelet, binding the wrist tightly to the column.

At the top of the arm a rounded shoulder, raised up by the cushions, also stands out well lighted, as well as the neck, the throat, and the other shoulder, the armpit with its soft hair, the left arm likewise pulled back with its wrist bound in the same manner to the base of another column, in the extreme foreground; here the iron bracelet and the chain are fully displayed, represented with perfect clarity down to the slightest details.

The same is true, still in the foreground but at the other side, for a similar chain, but not quite as thick, wound directly around the ankle, running twice around the column and terminating in a heavy iron ring embedded in the floor. About a yard further back, or perhaps slightly further, the right foot is identically chained. But it is the left foot, and its chain, that are the most minutely depicted.

The foot is small, delicate, finely molded. In several places the chain has broken the skin, causing noticeable if not extensive depressions in the flesh. The chain links are oval, thick, the size of an eye. The ring in the floor resembles those used to attach horses; it lies almost touching the stone pavement to which it is riveted by a massive iron peg. A few inches away is the edge of a rug; it is grossly wrinkled at this point, doubtless as a result of the convulsive, but necessarily very restricted, movements of the victim attempting to struggle.

The man is still standing about a yard away, half leaning over her. He looks at her face, seen upside down, her dark eyes made larger by their surrounding eye-shadow, her mouth wide open as if screaming. The man's posture allows his face to be seen only in a vague profile, but one senses in it a violent exaltation, despite the rigid attitude, the silence, the immobility. His back is slightly arched. His left hand, the only one visible, holds up at some distance from the body a piece of cloth, some dark colored piece of clothing, which drags on the carpet, and which must be the long cape with its gold embroidered lining.

This immense silhouette hides most of the bare flesh over which the red stain, spreading from the globe of the breast, runs in long rivulets that branch out, growing narrower, upon the pale background of the bust and the flank. One thread has reached the armpit and runs in an almost straight, thin line along the arm; others have run down toward the waist and traced out, along one side of the belly, the hip, the top of the thigh, a more random network already starting to congeal. Three or four tiny veins have reached the hollow between the legs, meeting in a sinuous line, touching the point of the V formed by the outspread legs, and disappearing into the black tuft.

Look, now the flesh is still intact: the black tuft and the white belly, the soft curve of the hips, the narrow waist, and, higher up, the pearly breasts rising and falling in time with the rapid breathing, whose rhythm grows more accelerated. The man, close to her, one knee on the floor, leans further over. The head, with its long, curly hair, and which is alone free to move somewhat, turns from side to side, struggling; finally the woman's mouth twists open, while the flesh is torn open, the blood spurts out over the tender skin, stretched tight, the carefully shadowed eyes grow abnormally larger, the mouth opens wider, the head twists violently, one last time, from right to left, then more gently, to fall back finally and become still, amid the mass of black hair spread out on the velvet.

At the very top of the stone stairway, the little door has opened, allowing a yellowish but sustained shaft of light to enter, against which stands out the dark silhouette of the man wrapped in his long cloak. He has but to climb a few more steps to reach the threshold.

Afterward, the whole setting is empty, the enormous room with its purple shadows and its stone columns proliferating in all directions, the monumental staircase with no handrail that twists upward, growing narrower and vaguer as it rises into the darkness, toward the top of the vaults where it disappears.

Near the body, whose wound has stiffened, whose brilliance is already growing dim, the thin smoke from the incense burner traces complicated scrolls in the still air: first a coil turned horizontally to the left, which then straightens out and rises slightly, then returns to the axis of its point of origin, which it crosses as it moves to the right, then turns back in the first direction, only to wind back again, thus forming an irregular sinusoidal curve, more and more flattened out, and rising, vertically, toward the top of the canvas.

EXERCISES

1. Is this a description of a picture, or is it a story? What is the difference?

2. Edgar Allan Poe once suggested that the death of a beautiful woman was one of the most poetic subjects. Does this idea make any sense? Is it related to this story?

3. Why is the woman called a "a sacrificial victim"?

4. Is this an erotic story or a repulsive one? Explain.

5. Note the language used to describe the ankle chains: "It is the left foot, and its chain, that are the most minutely depicted." What is meant by the word *depicted* here?

6. Discuss the problem of sequence in this story. What is the order of events?

7. Discuss the implications of the last word in the story.

JOHN
L'HEUREUX | *The Anatomy of Desire*

Because Hanley's skin had been stripped off by the enemy, he could find no one who was willing to be with him for long. The nurses were obligated, of course, to see him now and then, and sometimes the doctor, but certainly not the other patients and certainly not his wife and children. He was raw, he was meat, and he would never be any better. He had a great and natural desire, therefore, to be possessed by someone.

He would walk around on his skinned feet, leaving bloody footprints up and down the corridors, looking for someone to love him.

"You're not supposed to be out here," the nurse said. And she added, somehow making it sound kind, "You untidy the floor, Hanley."

"I want to be loved by someone," he said. "I'm human too. I'm like you."

But he knew he was not like her. Everybody called her the saint.

"Why couldn't it be you?" he said.

She was swabbing his legs with blood retardant, a new discovery that kept Hanley going. It was one of those miracle medications that just grew out of the war.

"I wasn't chosen," she said. "I have my skin."

"No," he said. "I mean why couldn't it be you who will love me, possess me? I have desires, too," he said.

She considered this as she swabbed his shins and the soles of his feet.

"I have no desires," she said. "Or only one. It's the same thing."

He looked at her loving face. It was not a pretty face, but it was saintly.

"Then you will?" he said.

"If I come to know sometime that I must," she said.

The enemy had not chosen Hanley, they had just lucked upon him sleeping in his trench. They were a raid party of four, terrified and obedient, and they had been told to bring back an enemy to serve as an example of what is done to infiltrators.

They dragged Hanley back across the line and ran him, with his hands tied behind his back, the two kilometers to the general's tent.

The general dismissed the guards because he was very taken with Hanley. He untied the cords that bound his wrists and let his arms hang free. Then slowly, ritually, he tipped Hanley's face toward the light and examined it carefully. He kissed him on the brow and on the cheek and finally on the mouth. He gazed deep and long into Hanley's eyes until he saw his own reflection there looking back. He traced the lines of Hanley's eyebrows, gently, with the tip of his index finger. "Such a beautiful face," he said in his own language. He pressed his palms lightly against Hanley's forehead, against his cheekbones, his jaw. With his little finger he memorized the shape of Hanley's lips, the laugh lines at his eyes, the chin. The general did Hanley's face very thoroughly. Afterward he did some things down below, and so just before sunrise when the time came to lead Hanley out to the stripping post, he told the soldiers with the knives: "This young man could be my own son; so spare him here and here."

The stripping post stood dead-center in the line of barbed wire only a few meters beyond the range of gunfire. A loudspeaker was set up and began to blare the day's message. "This is what happens to infiltrators. No infiltrators will be spared." And then as troops from both sides watched through binoculars, the enemy cut the skin from Hanley's body, sparing—as the general had insisted—his face and his genitals. They were skilled men and the skin was stripped off expeditiously and they hung it, headless, on the barbed wire as an example. They lay Hanley himself on the ground where he could die.

He was rescued a little after noon when the enemy, for no good reason, went into sudden retreat.

Hanley was given emergency treatment at the field unit, and when they had done what they could for him, they sent him on to the vets' hospital. At least there, they told each other, he will be attended by the saint.

It was quite some time before the saint said yes, she would love him.

"Not just love me. Possess me."

"There are natural reluctancies," she said. "There are personal peculiarities," she said. "You will have to have patience with me."

"You're supposed to be a saint," he said.

So she lay down with him in his bloody bed and he found great satisfaction in holding this small woman in his arms. He kissed her and caressed her and felt young and whole again. He did not miss his wife and children. He did not miss his skin.

The saint did everything she must. She told him how handsome he was and what pleasure he gave her. She touched him in the way he liked best. She said he was her whole life, her fate. And at night when he woke her to staunch the blood, she whispered how she needed him, how she could not live without him.

This went on for some time.

The war was over and the occupying forces had made the general mayor of the capital city. He was about to run for senator and wanted his past to be beyond the reproach of any investigative committee. He wrote Hanley a letter which he sent through the International Red Cross.

"You could have been my own son," he said. "What we do in war is what we have to do. We do not choose cruelty or violence. I did only what was my duty."

"I am in love and I am loved," Hanley said. "Why isn't this enough?"

The saint was swabbing his chest and belly with blood retardant.

"Nothing is ever enough," she said.

"I love, but I am not possessed by love," he said, "I want to be surrounded by you. I want to be enclosed. I want to be enveloped. I don't have the words for it. But do you understand?"

"You want to be possessed," she said.

"I want to be inside you."

And so they made love, but afterward he said, "That was not enough. That is only a metaphor for what I want."

The general was elected senator and was made a trustee of three nuclear-arms conglomerates. But he was not well. And he was not sleeping well.

He wrote to Hanley, "I wake in the night and see your face before mine. I feel your forehead pressing against my palms. I taste your breath. I did only what I had to do. You could have been my son."

"I know what I want," Hanley said.

"If I can do it, I will," the saint said.

"I want your skin."

And so she lay down on the long white table, shuddering, while Hanley made his first incision. He cut along the shoulders and then down the arms and back up, then down the sides and the legs to the feet. It took him longer than he had expected. The saint shivered at the cold touch of the knife and she sobbed once at the sight of the blood, but by the time Hanley lifted the shroud of skin from her crimson body, she was resigned, satisfied even.

Hanley had spared her face and her genitals.

He spread the skin out to dry and, while he waited, he swabbed her raw body carefully with blood retardant. He whispered little words of love and thanks and desire to her. A smile played about her lips, but she said nothing.

It would be a week before he could put on her skin.

The general wrote to Hanley one last letter. "I can endure no more. I am possessed by you."

Hanley put on the skin of the saint. His genitals fitted nicely through the gap he had left and the skin at his neck matched hers exactly. He walked the corridors and for once left no bloody tracks behind. He stood before mirrors and admired himself. He touched his breasts and his belly and his thighs and there was no blood on his hands.

"Thank you," he said to her. "It is my heart's desire fulfilled. I am inside you. I am possessed by you."

And then, in the night, he kissed her on the brow and on the cheek and finally on the mouth. He gazed deep and long into her eyes. He traced the lines of her eyebrows gently, with the tip of his index finger. "Such a beautiful face," he said. He pressed his palms lightly against her forehead, her cheekbones, her jaw. With his little finger he memorized the shape of her lips.

And then it was that Hanley, loved, desperate to possess and be possessed, staring deep into the green and loving eyes of the saint, saw that there can be no possession, there is only desire. He plucked at his empty skin, and wept.

EXERCISES

1. How do you know in the first paragraph that this is a parable rather than a realistic story?
2. What does the desire to be possessed by someone really mean? Is being loved by someone the same as being possessed by someone?
3. Discuss the meaning of the general's actions with Hanley. Why does he say "he could be my own son"?
4. What is the significance of the nurse being called "the saint"?
5. The key to the story may be Hanley's declaring that he wants to be enclosed, to be enveloped, to be inside the saint. What does this mean? How is making love "only a metaphor" for what he wants? What does he want?
6. In what way is the general possessed by Hanley?
7. How is putting on the saint's skin more than a metaphor for his heart's desire? Why would one desire to be "inside" the other?
8. Why does Hanley weep at the end? What does he mean that there can be no possession, "there is only desire"?

DINO
BUZZATI | *The Falling Girl*

Marta was nineteen. She looked out over the roof of the skyscraper, and seeing the city below shining in the dusk, she was overcome with dizziness.

The skyscraper was silver, supreme and fortunate in that most beautiful and pure evening, as here and there the wind stirred a few fine filaments of cloud against an absolutely incredible blue background. It was in fact the hour when the city is seized by inspiration and whoever is not blind is swept away by it. From that airy height the girl saw the streets and the masses of buildings writhing in the long spasm of sunset, and at the point where the white of the houses ended, the blue of the sea began. Seen from above, the sea looked as if it were rising. And since the veils of the night were advancing from the east, the city became a sweet abyss burning with pulsating lights. Within it were powerful men, and women who were even more powerful, furs and violins, cars glossy as onyx, the neon signs of nightclubs, the entrance halls of darkened mansions, fountains, diamonds, old silent gardens, parties, desires, affairs, and, above all, that consuming sorcery of the evening which provokes dreams of greatness and glory.

Seeing these things, Marta hopelessly leaned out over the railing and let herself go. She felt as if she were hovering in the air, but she was falling. Given the extraordinary height of the skyscraper, the streets and squares down at the bottom were very far away. Who knows how long it would take her to get there. Yet the girl was falling.

At that hour the terraces and balconies of the top floors were filled with rich and elegant people who were having cocktails and making silly conversation. They were scattered in crowds, and their talk muffled the music. Marta passed before them and several people looked out to watch her.

Flights of that kind (mostly by girls, in fact) were not rare in the skyscraper and they constituted an interesting diversion for the tenants; this was also the reason why the price of those apartments was very high.

The sun had not yet completely set and it did its best to illuminate Marta's simple clothing. She wore a modest, inexpensive spring dress bought off the rack. Yet the lyrical light of the sunset exalted it somewhat, making it chic.

From the millionaires' balconies, gallant hands were stretched out toward her, offering flowers and cocktails. "Miss, would you like a drink? . . . Gentle butterfly, why not stop a minute with us?"

She laughed, hovering, happy (but meanwhile she was falling): "No, thanks, friends. I can't. I'm in a hurry."

"Where are you headed?" they asked her.

"Ah, don't make me say," Marta answered, waving her hands in a friendly good-bye.

A young man, tall, dark, very distinguished, extended an arm to snatch her. She liked him. And yet Marta quickly defended herself: "How dare you, sir?" and she had time to give him a little tap on the nose.

The beautiful people, then, were interested in her and that filled her with satisfaction. She felt fascinating, stylish. On the flower-filled terraces, amid the bustle of waiters in white and the bursts of exotic songs, there was talk for a few minutes, perhaps less, of the young woman who was passing by (from top to bottom, on a vertical course). Some thought her pretty, others thought her so-so, everyone found her interesting.

"You have your entire life before you," they told her, "why are you in such a hurry? You still have time to rush around and busy yourself. Stop with us for a little while, it's only a modest little party among friends, really, you'll have a good time."

She made an attempt to answer but the force of gravity had already quickly carried her to the floor below, then two, three, four floors below; in fact, exactly as you gaily rush around when you are just nineteen years old.

Of course, the distance that separated her from the bottom, that is, from street level, was immense. It is true that she began falling just a little while ago, but the street always seemed very far away.

In the meantime, however, the sun had plunged into the sea; one could see it disappear, transformed into a shimmering reddish mushroom. As a result, it no longer emitted its vivifying rays to light up the girl's dress and make her a seductive comet. It was a good thing that the windows and terraces of the skyscraper were almost all illuminated and the bright reflections completely gilded her as she gradually passed by.

Now Marta no longer saw just groups of carefree people inside the apartments; at times there were even some businesses where the employees, in black or blue aprons, were sitting at desks in long rows. Several of them were young people as old as or older than she, and weary of the day by now, every once in a while they raised their eyes from their duties and from typewriters. In this way they too saw her, and a few ran to the windows. "Where are you going? Why so fast? Who are you?" they shouted to her. One could divine something akin to envy in their words.

"They're waiting for me down there," she answered. "I can't stop. Forgive me." And again she laughed, wavering on her headlong fall, but it wasn't like her previous laughter anymore. The night had craftily fallen and Marta started to feel cold.

Meanwhile, looking downward, she saw a bright halo of lights at the entrance of a building. Here long black cars were stopping (from the great distance they looked as small as ants), and men and women were getting out, anxious to go inside. She seemed to make out the sparkling of jewels in that swarm. Above the entrance flags were flying.

They were obviously giving a large party, exactly the kind that Marta dreamed of ever since she was a child. Heaven help her if she missed it. Down there opportunity was waiting for her, fate, romance, the true inauguration of her life. Would she arrive in time?

She spitefully noticed that another girl was falling about thirty meters above her. She was decidedly prettier than Marta and she wore a rather classy evening gown. For some unknown reason she came down much faster than Marta, so that in a few moments she passed by her and disappeared below, even though Marta was calling her. Without doubt she would get to the party before Marta; perhaps she had a plan all worked out to supplant her.

Then she realized that they weren't alone. Along the sides of the skyscraper many other young women were plunging downward, their faces taut with the excitement of the flight, their hands cheerfully waving as if to say: look at us, here we are, entertain us, is not the world ours?

It was a contest, then. And she only had a shabby little dress while those other girls were dressed smartly like high-fashion models and some even wrapped luxurious mink stoles tightly around their bare shoulders. So self-assured when she began the leap, Marta now felt a tremor growing inside her; perhaps it was just the cold; but it may have been fear too, the fear of having made an error without remedy.

It seemed to be late at night now. The windows were darkened one after another, the echoes of music became more rare, the offices were empty, young men no longer leaned out from the windowsills extending their hands. What time was it? At the entrance to the building down below—which in the meantime had grown larger, and one could now distinguish all the architectural details—the lights were still burning, but the bustle of cars had stopped. Every now and then, in fact, small groups of people came out of the main floor wearily drawing away. Then the lights of the entrance were also turned off.

Marta felt her heart tightening. Alas, she wouldn't reach the ball in time. Glancing upwards, she saw the pinnacle of the skyscraper in all its cruel power. It was almost completely dark. On the top floors a few windows here and there were still lit. And above the top the first glimmer of dawn was spreading.

In a dining recess on the twenty-eighth floor a man about forty years old was having his morning coffee and reading his newspaper while his wife tidied up the room. A clock on the sideboard indicated 8:45. A shadow suddenly passed before the window.

"Alberto!" the wife shouted. "Did you see that? A woman passed by."

"Who was it?" he said without raising his eyes from the newspaper.

"An old woman," the wife answered. "A decrepit old woman. She looked frightened."

"It's always like that," the man muttered. "At these low floors only falling old women pass by. You can see beautiful girls from the hundred-and-fiftieth floor up. Those apartments don't cost so much for nothing."

"At least down here there's the advantage," observed the wife, "that you can hear the thud when they touch the ground."

"This time not even that," he said, shaking his head, after he stood listening for a few minutes. Then he had another sip of coffee.

EXERCISES

1. The story opens realistically, but a shift soon takes place. What kind of fictional world do we shift to? What new rules apply?

2. How is the girl's fall a metaphor for the way one rushes around at the age of nineteen? Why does everyone ask her why she is going so fast, when it seems to her that she is moving very slowly?

3. What is the significance of the other girl who is falling faster than Marta? How are the falling girls in a contest? What does the contest represent?

4. Why has Marta changed into a decrepit old woman by the time she reaches the twenty-eighth floor?

5. How is the falling a metaphor for time? Consider the tradition of a ball falling from a tall building to mark the change from the old year to the new.

6. What does the metaphor of reaching ground mean? How is flying like falling in this story? What is the significance of the law of gravity?

JULIO
CORTÁZAR | *The Island at Noon*

The first time he saw the island, Marini was politely leaning over the seats on the left, adjusting a plastic table before setting a lunch tray down. The passenger had looked at him several times as he came and went with magazines or glasses of whisky; Marini lingered while he adjusted the table, wondering, bored, if it was worth responding to the passenger's insistent look, one American woman out of many, when in the blue oval of the window appeared the coast of the island, the golden strip of the beach, the hills that rose toward the desolate plateau. Correcting the faulty position of the glass of beer, Marini smiled to the passenger. "The Greek islands," he said. "Oh, yes, Greece," the American woman answered with false interest. A bell rang briefly, and the steward straightened up, without removing the professional smile from his thin lips. He began attending to a Syrian couple, who ordered tomato juice, but in the tail of the plane he gave himself a few seconds to look down again; the island was small and solitary, and the Aegean Sea surrounded it with an intense blue that exalted the curl of a dazzling and kind of petrified white, which down below would be foam breaking against reefs and coves. Marini saw that the deserted beaches ran north and west; the rest was the mountain which fell straight into the sea. A rocky and deserted island, although the lead-gray spot near the northern beach could be a house, perhaps a group of primitive houses. He started opening the can of juice, and when he had straightened up the island had vanished from the window; only the sea was left, an endless green horizon. He looked at his wrist-watch without knowing why; it was exactly noon.

Marini liked being assigned to the Rome-Teheran line. The flight was less gloomy than on the northern lines, and the girls seemed happy to go to the Orient or to get to know Italy. Four days later, while he was helping a little boy who had lost his spoon and was pointing downheartedly at his dessert plate, he again discovered the edge of the island. There was a difference of eight minutes, but when he leaned over to a window in the tail he had no doubts; the island had an unmistakable shape, like a turtle whose paws were barely out of the water. He looked at it until they called for him, this time sure that the lead-gray spot was a group of houses; he managed to make out the lines of some cultivated fields that extended to the beach. During the stop at Beirut he looked at the stewardess's atlas and wondered if the island wasn't Horos. The radio operator, an indifferent Frenchman, was surprised at his interest. "All those islands look alike. I've been doing this route for two years, and I don't care a fig about them. Yes, show it to me next time." It wasn't Horos but Xiros, one of the many islands on the fringe of the tourist circuits. "It won't last five years," the stewardess said to him while they had a drink in Rome. "Hurry up if you're thinking of going, the hordes will be there any moment now. Genghis Cook is watching." But Marini kept thinking about the island, looking at it when he remembered or if there was a window near, almost always shrugging his shoulders in the end. None of it made any sense—flying three times a week at noon over Xiros was as unreal as dreaming three times a week that he was flying over Xiros. Everything was falsified in the futile and recurrent vision; except, perhaps, the desire to repeat it, the consulting of the wrist-watch before noon, the brief, pricking contact with the dazzling white band at the edge of an almost black blue, and the houses where the fishermen would barely lift their eyes to follow the passage of that other unreality.

Eight or nine weeks later, when they offered him the New York run, with all its advantages, Marini thought it was the chance to end that innocent and annoying obsession. In his pocket he had a guide book in which an imprecise geographer with a Levantine name gave more details about Xiros than was usual. He answered no, hearing himself as from a distance, and, avoiding the shocked surprise of a boss and two secretaries, he went to have a bite in the company's canteen, where Carla was waiting for him. Carla's bewildered disappointment did not disturb him; the southern coast of Xiros was uninhabitable, but toward the west remained traces of a Lydian or perhaps Creto-Mycenaean colony, and Professor Goldmann had found two stones carved with hieroglyphics that the fishermen used as piles for the small dock. Carla's head ached, and she left almost immediately; octopus was the principal resource for the handful of inhabitants, every five days a boat arrived to load the fish and leave some provisions and materials. In the travel agency they told him he would have to charter a special boat from Rynos, or perhaps it would be possible to go in the small boat that picked up the octopuses, but Marini could find out about this only in Rynos, where the agency didn't have an agent. At any rate, the idea of spending a few days on the island was just a plan for his June vacation; in the weeks that followed he had to replace White on the Tunis run, and then there was a strike, and Carla went back to her sisters' house in Palermo. Marini went to live in a hotel near the Piazza Navona, where there were secondhand bookstores; he amused himself not very enthusiastically by looking for books on Greece, and from time to time he leafed through a conversation manual. The word *kalimera* pleased him, and he tried it out on a redhead in a cabaret; he went to bed with her, learned about her grandfather in Odos and about certain unaccountable sore throats. In Rome it rained, in Beirut Tania was always waiting for him; there were other stories, always relatives or sore throats; one day it was again the Teheran run, the island at noon. Marini stayed glued to the window so long that the new stewardess considered him a poor partner and let him know how many trays she had served. That night Marini invited the stewardess for dinner at the Firouz, and it wasn't difficult to make her forgive him for the morning's distraction. Lucia advised him to have his hair cut American-style; he talked to her about Xiros for a while, but later he realized she preferred the vodka-lime of the Hilton. Time passed in things like that, in infinite trays of food, each one with the smile to which the passenger had the right. On the return trips the plane flew over Xiros at eight in the morning; the sun glared against the larboard windows, and you could scarcely see the golden turtle; Marini preferred to wait for the noons of the trip going, knowing that then he could stay a long minute against the window, while Lucia (and then Felisa) somewhat ironically took care of things. Once he took a picture of Xiros, but it came out blurred; he already knew some things about the island, he had underlined the rare mentions in a couple of books. Felisa told him that the pilots called him the madman of the island, but that didn't bother him. Carla had just written that she had decided not to leave the baby, and Marini sent her two weeks' wages and thought that the rest would not be enough for his vacation. Carla accepted the money and let him know through a friend that she'd probably marry the dentist from Treviso. Everything had such little importance at noon, on Mondays and Thursdays and Saturdays (twice a month on Sundays).

As time went on, he began to realize that Felisa was the only one who understood him a little; there was a tacit agreement that she would take care of the flight at noon, as soon as he stationed himself by the tail window. The island was visible for a few minutes, but the air was always so clean, and it was outlined by the sea with such a minute cruelty that the smallest details were implacably adjusted to the memory of the preceding flight: the green spot of the headland to the north, the lead-gray houses; the nets drying on the sand. When the nets weren't there, Marini felt as if he had been robbed, insulted. He thought of filming the passage over the island, to repeat the image in the hotel, but he preferred to save the money on the camera since there was less than a month left for vacation. He didn't keep a very strict account of the days; sometimes it was Tania in Beirut, sometimes Felisa in Teheran, almost always his younger brother in Rome, all a bit blurred, amiably easy and cordial and as if replacing something else, filling the hours before or after the flight, and during the flight, everything, too, was blurred and easy and stupid until it was time to lean toward the tail window, to feel the cold crystal like the boundary of an aquarium, where the golden turtle slowly moved in the thick blue.

That day, the nets were clearly sketched on the sand, and Marini could have sworn that the black dot on the left, at the edge of the sea, was a fisherman who must have been looking at the plane. "*Kalimera*," he absurdly thought. It no longer made any sense to wait. Mario Merolis would lend him the money he needed for the trip, and in less than three days he would be in Xiros. With his lips against the window, he smiled, thinking that he would climb to the green spot, that he would enter the sea of the northern coves naked, that he would fish octopuses with the men, communicating through signs and laughter. Nothing was difficult once decided—a night train, the first boat, another old and dirty boat, the night on the bridge, close to the stars, the taste of *anis* and mutton, daybreak among the islands. He landed with the first lights, and the captain introduced him to an old man, probably the elder. Klaios took his left hand and spoke slowly, looking him in the eyes. Two boys came, and Marini found out that they were Klaios' sons. The captain of the small boat exhausted his English: Twenty inhabitants, octopus, fish, five houses, Italian visitor would pay lodging Klaios. The boys laughed when Klaios discussed drachmas; Marini, too, already friends with the younger boys, watching the sun come up over a sea not as dark as from the air, a poor, clean room, a pitcher of water, smell of sage and tanned hides.

They left him alone to go load the small boat, and after tearing off his traveling clothes and putting on bathing trunks and sandals, he set out for a walk on the island. You still couldn't see anybody; the sun slowly but surely rose, and from the thickets grew a subtle smell, slightly acidic, mixing with the iodine of the wind. It must have been ten when he reached the northern headland and recognized the largest of the coves. He preferred being alone, although he would have liked to bathe at the sand beach even better; the island impregnated him, and he enjoyed it with such intimacy that he was incapable of thinking or choosing. His skin burned from sun and wind when he undressed to thrust himself into the sea from a rock; the water was cold and did him good. He let a sly current carry him to the entrance of a grotto, he returned to the open sea, rolled over on his back, accepted it all in a single act of conciliation that was also a name for the future. He knew without the slightest doubt that he would not leave the island, that somehow he would stay forever on the island. He managed to imagine his brother, Felisa, their faces when they found out he had stayed to live off fishing on a large solitary rock. He had already forgotten them when he turned over to swim toward the shore.

The sun dried him immediately, and he went down toward the houses, where two astonished women looked at him before running inside and closing their doors. He waved a greeting in the void and walked down toward the nets. One of Klaios' sons was waiting for him on the beach, and Marini pointed to the sea, inviting him. The boy hesitated, pointing to his cloth pants and red shirt. Then he ran toward one of the houses and came back almost naked; they dived together into an already lukewarm sea, dazzling under the eleven o'clock sun.

Drying himself in the sand, Ionas began to name things. "*Kalimera,*" Marini said, and the boy doubled over with laughter. Then Marini repeated the new sentences, teaching Ionas Italian words. Almost on the horizon the small boat grew smaller and smaller; Marini felt that now he was really alone on the island with Klaios and his people. He would let some days pass, he would pay for his room and learn to fish; some afternoon, when they were well acquainted, he would talk to them about staying and working with them. Getting up, he held out his hand to Ionas and started walking slowly toward the hill. The slope was steep, and he savored each pause, turning around time and again to look at the nets on the beach, the figures of the women speaking gaily to Ionas and Klaios and looking at him askance, laughing. When he reached the green spot he entered a world where the smell of thyme and sage were one with the fire of the sun and the sea breeze. Marini looked at his wrist-watch and then, with an impatient gesture, put it in the pocket of his bathing trunks. It wouldn't be easy to kill the former man, but there up high, tense with sun and space, he felt the enterprise was possible. He was in Xiros, he was there where he had so often doubted he could reach. He let himself fall back among the hot stones, he endured their edges and inflamed ridges and looked vertically at the sky; far away he could hear the hum of an engine.

Closing his eyes, he told himself he wouldn't look at the plane; he wouldn't let himself be contaminated by the worst of him that once more was going to pass over the island. But in the shadows of his eyelids he imagined Felisa with the trays, in that very moment distributing the trays, and his replacement, perhaps Giorgio or someone new from another line, someone who would also be smiling as he served the wine or the coffee. Unable to fight against all that past he opened his eyes and sat up, and in the same moment saw the right wing of the plane, almost over his head, tilt unaccountably, the changed sound of the jet engines, the almost vertical drop into the sea. He rushed down the hill, knocking against rocks and lacerating his arm among thorns. The island hid the place of the fall from him, but he turned before reaching the beach and through a predictable shortcut he passed the first ridge of the hill and came out onto the smaller beach. The plane's tail was sinking some 100 yards away, in total silence. Marini ran and dived into the water, still waiting for the plane to come up to float; but all you could see was the soft line of the waves, a cardboard box bobbing absurdly near the place of the fall, and almost at the end, when it no longer made sense to keep swimming, a hand out of the water, just for a second, enough time for Marini to change direction and dive under to catch by his hair the man who struggled to hold onto him and hoarsely swallowed air that Marini let him breathe without getting too close. Towing him little by little he got him to the shore, took the body dressed in white in his arms, and laying him on the sand he looked at the face full of foam where death had already settled, bleeding through an enormous gash in his throat. What good was artificial respiration if, with each convulsion, the gash seemed to open a little more and was like a repugnant mouth that called to Marini, tore him from his little happiness of such few hours on the island, shouted to him between torrents something he was no longer able to hear. Klaios' sons came running and behind them the women. When Klaios arrived, the boys gathered around the body lying on the sand, unable to understand how he had had the strength to swim to shore and drag himself there bleeding. "Close his eyes," one of the women begged crying. Klaios looked toward the sea, searching for other survivors. But, as always, they were alone on the island, and the open-eyed corpse was all that was new between them and the sea.

EXERCISES

1. Discuss the statement "None of it made any sense—flying three times a week at noon over Xiros was as unreal as dreaming three times a week that he was flying over Xiros."

2. What is meant by the statement that everything is falsified in the "futile and recurrent vision"?

3. Discuss the statement "Everything had such little importance at noon, on Mondays and Thursdays and Saturdays (twice a month on Sundays)."

4. Explain Marini's obsession with the island. Is this a realistic story or a parable?

5. How do you account for the seeming split between Marini in the plane and Marini on the island? Compare this with the split in the captain in Joseph Conrad's "The Secret Sharer" in Part II.

6. What happens in the final scene? How can it be accounted for?

PAUL
BOWLES | *The Scorpion*

A n old woman lived in a cave which her sons had hollowed out of a clay cliff near a spring before they went away to the town where many people live. She was neither happy nor unhappy to be there, because she knew that the end of life was near and that her sons would not be likely to return no matter what the season. In the town there are always many things to do, and they would be doing them, not caring to remember the time when they had lived in the hills looking after the old woman.

At the entrance to the cave at certain times of the year there was a curtain of water-drops through which the old woman had to pass to get inside. The water rolled down the bank from the plants above and dripped onto the clay below. So the old woman accustomed herself to sitting crouched in the cave for long periods of time in order to keep as dry as possible. Outside through the moving beads of water she saw the bare earth lighted by the gray sky, and sometimes large dry leaves went past, pushed by the wind that came from higher parts of the land. Inside where she was the light was pleasant and of a pink color from the clay all around.

A few people used to pass from time to time along the path not far away, and because there was a spring nearby, those travelers who knew that it existed but not just where it was would sometimes come near to the cave before they discovered that the spring was not there. The old woman would never call to them. She would merely watch them as they came near and suddenly saw her. Then she would go on watching as they turned back and went in other directions looking for the water to drink.

There were many things about this life that the old woman liked. She was no longer obliged to argue and fight with her sons to make them carry wood to the charcoal oven. She was free to move about at night and look for food. She could eat everything she found without having to share it. And she owed no one any debt of thanks for the things she had in her life.

One old man used to come from the village on his way down to the valley, and sit on a rock just distant enough from the cave for her to recognize him.

She knew he was aware of her presence in the cave there, and although she probably did not know this, she disliked him for not giving some sign that he knew she was there. It seemed to her that he had an unfair advantage over her and was using it in an unpleasant way. She thought up many ideas for annoying him if he should ever come near enough, but he always passed by in the distance, pausing to sit down on the rock for some time, when he would often gaze straight at the cave. Then he would continue slowly on his way, and it always seemed to the old woman that he went more slowly after his rest than before it.

There were scorpions in the cave all year round, but above all during the days just before the plants began to let water drip through. The old woman had a huge bundle of rags, and with this she would brush the walls and ceiling clear of them, stamping quickly on them with her hard bare heel. Occasionally a small wild bird or animal strayed inside the entrance, but she was never quick enough to kill it, and she had given up trying.

One dark day she looked up to see one of her sons standing in the doorway. She could not remember which one it was, but she thought it was the one who had ridden the horse down the dry river bed and nearly been killed. She looked at his hand to see if it was out of shape. It was not that son.

He began to speak: "Is it you?"

"Yes."

"Are you well?"

"Yes."

"Is everything well?"

"Everything."

"You stayed here?"

"You can see."

"Yes."

There was a silence. The old woman looked around the cave and was displeased to see that the man in the doorway made it practically dark in there. She busied herself with trying to distinguish various objects: her stick, her gourd, her tin can, her length of rope. She was frowning with the effort.

The man was speaking again.

"Shall I come in?"

She did not reply.

He backed away from the entrance, brushing the water drops from his garments. He was on the point of saying something profane, thought the old woman, who, even though she did not know which one this was, remembered what he would do.

She decided to speak.

"What?" she said.

He leaned forward through the curtain of water and repeated his question.

"Shall I come in?"

"No."

"What's the matter with you?"

"Nothing."

Then she added: "There's no room."

He backed out again, wiping his head. The old woman thought he would probably go away, and she was not sure she wanted him to. However, there was nothing else he could do, she thought. She heard him sit down outside the cave, and then she smelled tobacco smoke. There was no sound but the dripping of water upon the clay.

A short while later she heard him get up. He stood outside the entrance again.

"I'm coming in," he said.

She did not reply.

He bent over and pushed inside. The cave was too low for him to stand up in it. He looked about and spat on the floor.

"Come on," he said.

"Where?"

"With me."

"Why?"

"Because you have to come."

She waited a little while, and then said suspiciously: "Where are you going?"

He pointed indifferently toward the valley, and said: "Down that way."

"In the town?"

"Farther."

"I won't go."

"You have to come."

"No."

He picked up her stick and held it out to her.

"Tomorrow," she said.

"Now."

"I must sleep," she said, settling back into her pile of rags.

"Good. I'll wait outside," he answered, and went out.

The old woman went to sleep immediately. She dreamed that the town was very large. It went on forever and its streets were filled with people in new clothes. The church had a high tower with several bells that rang all the time. She was in the streets all one day, surrounded by people. She was not sure whether they were all her sons or not. She asked some of them: "Are you my sons?" They could not answer, but she thought that if they had been able to, they would have said: "Yes." Then when it was night she found a house with its door open. Inside there was a light and some women were seated in a corner. They rose when she went in, and said: "You have a room here." She did not want to see it, but they pushed her along until she was in it, and closed the door. She was a little girl and she was crying. The bells of the church were very loud outside, and she imagined they filled the sky. There was an open space in the wall high above her. She could see the stars through it, and they gave light to her room. From the reeds which formed the ceiling a scorpion came crawling. He came slowly down the wall toward her. She stopped crying and watched him. His tail curved up over his back and moved a little from side to side as he crawled. She looked quickly about for something to brush him down with. Since there was nothing in the room she used her hand. But her motions were slow, and the scorpion seized her finger with his pincers, clinging there tightly although she waved her hand wildly about. Then she realized that he was not going to sting her. A great feeling of happiness went through her. She raised her finger to her lips to kiss the scorpion. The bells stopped ringing. Slowly in the peace which was beginning, the scorpion moved into her mouth. She felt his hard shell and his little clinging legs going across her lips and her tongue. He crawled slowly down her throat and was hers. She woke up and called out.

Her son answered: "What is it?"

"I'm ready."

"So soon?"

He stood outside as she came through the curtain of water, leaning on her stick. Then he began walking a few paces ahead of her toward the path.

"It will rain," said her son.

"Is it far?"

"Three days," he said, looking at her old legs.

She nodded. Then she noticed the old man sitting on the stone. He had an expression of deep surprise on his face, as if a miracle had just occurred. His mouth was open as he stared at the old woman. When they came opposite the rock he peered more intently than ever into her face. She pretended not to notice him. As they picked their way carefully downhill along the stony path, they heard the old man's thin voice behind them, carried by the wind.

"Good-bye."

"Who is that?" said her son.

"I don't know."

Her son looked back at her darkly.

"You're lying," he said.

EXERCISES

1. Is this a realistic story or a parable? How do you know?
2. What is the meaning of the physical setting of the story? What is the significance of the veil of water that flows over the entrance of the cave?
3. Why does the son come to get her? Where is she to go?
4. What is the significance of the scorpion crawling inside her mouth "and was hers"? Why does this make her happy?
5. What is the meaning of the dream? Why does it make her willing to go?
6. Who is the old man? Why does he see the departure of the old woman as a miracle? Why at the end does the son say she is lying?

GEORGE H.
FREITAG | *An Old Man and His Hat*

One day long ago I went into a moving-picture house that showed Hoot Gibson riding a horse and crying. It was the next-to-the-last installment of a serial picture. The next installment would show why he cried and what was to be done and how Mr. Gibson fared. Next to my father, Hoot Gibson was the greatest man who lived. I had a nickel that my father gave me for the show. I saw Hoot Gibson crying on his horse. I paid only a nickel for that. The Texas sky was all around him in the picture, and still he cried.

The next week my father gave me a nickel to see why. It was Sunday afternoon in the wintertime, and I gave my coin to the ticket girl, and she would not give me a ticket, because between the last installment and this one I had grown into manhood. I could no longer get in for five cents. I couldn't see the reason why Hoot Gibson cried or know how he solved it. I had no more money. My father was poor. I asked the ticket girl to please let me in, that I had not grown another five cents' worth. But she would not. She was very beautiful, as beautiful as my mother. But allowing me to go in to see the last installment of Hoot Gibson was against the law. I waited outside for my friends to come out of the theater. They would know. I would ask Carl or Fred or Paul Robinson. I waited from ten after one until almost five in the afternoon for someone I knew to come out of the theater to tell me why Hoot Gibson cried and how he solved it and so on. It was cold and snowing in front of the picture show, and in sleighs people sped by laughing. But Carl or Fred or Paul never came out.

I knew they were in there. The horses made beautiful sounds with their feet upon the packed hard snow on the street in front of the theater. If someone on a quiz program now were to ask me, "Mr. Sills, what was the loneliest, darkest time of your life?" I would say, waiting in front of the picture show for Carl or Fred or Paul to come out and tell me why Hoot Gibson cried or what happened afterwards and how he solved it. As it is I never really knew. And when I saw Carl or Fred or Paul again and asked them about the show with Hoot Gibson in it, they sang songs and blinked their eyes and smoked cigars and wore glasses, and their voices were deep and choir-like, and their mouths never told. I asked them where they were on Sunday, February twentieth in the year 1920, but they couldn't account for it at all. They talked about girls and Wall Street and war and grief.

But no matter now. I don't care. I have more important things to discuss than anything Carl or Fred or Paul could ever conjure up. You know that!

I was walking with my fifteen-year-old son yesterday. We were out in the country in California, just a man and his kid walking, and we came to a bridge that spanned a river, and I remembered what my father, walking with me in my youth, might have asked, so I said to my son, "See the lovely bridge and the water?"

My son looked a long time at the bridge, at the water. Then he said, "What bridge, what water?"

"But don't you see a bridge?" I asked, "and a river?"

My boy looked again. "I see a bird with its head off and a tree without fruit," he said.

No rapport!

Now if I were walking along with my father in my young days, early days for him and early days for me, and my father and I came to a peach orchard, we will say, and he said, "Morris, what do you see on the tree?"

I would say, "A peach without a seed."

And my father would look a long time and he would say, "I see a peach too, Morris. I see a peach, too! But the peach I see has a seed."

And I would understand why. The peach has a seed because my father is older and looks at life more realistically. But to hear your son say, "A bird with its head off and a tree without fruit"—man alive; that is not *real* rapport, is it?

I am fifty-seven years old. My bones are splintering and creaking and I nap long and noisily sometimes. A couple of years ago I went back to visit my parents in Canton, Ohio. They are very old now and walk around from chair to chair to hold themselves up, and watch TV when there is a choir of young boys and girls singing *a cappella,* and I went walking uptown in the middle of the city where the noise was and the progress.

I came to the picture show that I waited in front of for Carl or Fred or Paul. But men were destroying it to make room for a parking lot, probably, or a supermarket. The steam shovels were at work swinging the iron ball, knocking down the sides of the theater's walls, and the men were swearing at the stupidity of the steam shovel and little black and white dogs were running away and rats were being made homeless, and lice; and the odor of the old rest rooms that always frightened me when I had to leave the picture and go was everywhere your nose went. I stood there thinking back. An old man does that, too. The day was very hot in Ohio. There was a storm coming up the side of the sky from Cleveland and Lake Erie, and brief flashes of lightning cut slits in the dark sky. Papers were blowing everywhere and schoolchildren carrying weighted-down problems in math were going home.

Finally a man called to me. "You, old man with the gray suit, you get out of there! You want to get killed?" But I kicked at the loose dirt and stooped to pick up old calendars and pencil stubs and walked toward the steam shovel with the man in it. The wind was blowing something fierce now and someone said, "They're sure getting it in Cleveland or Sandusky." And when I got opposite the man in the steam shovel, I asked him something.

A long time ago, when I was eight years old, or nine, I was in the show when Art Accord was untying a girl from the railroad tracks without a sound because in those days nobody made any noise going through life, and when the girl was rescued and Art Accord picked her up and carried her to safety and the train came and silently whistled at a rabbit crossing the tracks and

Art Accord was kissing the girl, Claire Windsor, I think, I was so happy that, standing in the aisle of the theater, I threw my cap into the air, and it never came down. I had to go home bareheaded and it was the day after Christmas and snowing and the needles on our lovely Christmas tree were falling onto my mother's carpet and all the windows had pictures of frost on them.

So I don't know what really got into me. I thought of my son and the bridge crossing the river and the bird with its head off and all, and I turned to the steam-shovel operator: "A cap with a blue visor on it. Have you come across a cap?" I asked.

Then someone coming out of an outside toilet, buttoning his pants, called to the man in the steam shovel. And the man in the cab of the shovel said, "Okay, Charles. Just an old man looking for his hat."

And I looked toward Cleveland where the storm was growing from. But anybody can look toward Cleveland. I looked through it. I looked through the lake, through Sandusky, through everything in my way, but I saw only the storm coming, the lightning flashing, the secret place that hid the thunder. And *that* is rapport!

EXERCISES

1. Discuss the significance of the narrator growing up without finding out what made Hoot Gibson cry.
2. Discuss what the narrator means when he says there is no rapport between him and his son.
3. Why does his father see a peach with a seed whereas the narrator does not?
4. Why did the narrator throw his hat in the air? Why does his hat not come down? Will it ever come down? Why or why not?
5. What is the meaning of *rapport* at the end of the story?
6. Compare both the theme and technique of this story with those of Lagerkvist's "Father and I" in Part II.

NATHANIEL
HAWTHORNE | *Young Goodman Brown*

Young Goodman Brown came forth at sunset into the street of Salem village; but put his head back, after crossing the threshold, to exchange a parting kiss with his young wife. And Faith, as the wife was aptly named, thrust her own pretty head into the street, letting the wind play with the pink ribbons of her cap while she called to Goodman Brown.

"Dearest heart," whispered she, softly and rather sadly, when her lips were close to his ear, "prithee put off your journey until sunrise and sleep in your own bed to-night. A lone woman is troubled with dreams and such thoughts that she's afeared of herself sometimes. Pray tarry with me this night, dear husband, of all nights in the year."

"My love and my Faith," replied young Goodman Brown, "of all nights in the year, this one night must I tarry away from thee. My journey, as thou callest it, forth and back again, must needs be done 'twixt now and sunrise. What, my sweet, pretty wife, dost thou doubt me already, and we but three months married?"

"Then God bless you!" said Faith, with the pink ribbons; "and may you find all well when you come back."

"Amen!" cried Goodman Brown. "Say thy prayers, dear Faith, and go to bed at dusk, and no harm will come to thee."

So they parted; and the young man pursued his way until, being about to turn the corner by the meeting-house, he looked back and saw the head of Faith still peeping after him with a melancholy air, in spite of her pink ribbons.

"Poor little Faith!" thought he, for his heart smote him. "What a wretch am I to leave her on such an errand! She talks of dreams, too. Methought as she spoke there was trouble in her face, as if a dream had warned her what work is to be done tonight. But no, no; 't would kill her to think it. Well, she's a blessed angel on earth; and after this one night I'll cling to her skirts and follow her to heaven."

With this excellent resolve for the future, Goodman Brown felt himself justified in making more haste on his present evil purpose. He had taken a dreary road, darkened by all the gloomiest trees of the forest, which barely stood aside to let the narrow path creep through, and closed immediately behind. It was all as lonely as could be; and there is this peculiarity in such a solitude, that the traveller knows not who may be concealed by the innumerable trunks and the thick boughs overhead; so that with lonely footsteps he may yet be passing through an unseen multitude.

"There may be a devilish Indian behind every tree," said Goodman Brown to himself; and he glanced fearfully behind him as he added, "What if the devil himself should be at my very elbow!"

His head turned back, he passed a crook of the road, and, looking forward again, beheld the figure of a man, in grave and decent attire, seated at the foot of an old tree. He arose at Goodman Brown's approach and walked onward side by side with him.

"You are late, Goodman Brown," said he. "The clock of the Old South was striking as I came through Boston, and that is full fifteen minutes agone."

"Faith kept me back a while," replied the young man, with a tremor in his voice, caused by the sudden appearance of his companion, though not wholly unexpected.

It was now deep dusk in the forest, and deepest in that part of it where these two were journeying. As nearly as could be discerned, the second traveller was about fifty years old, apparently in the same rank of life as Goodman Brown, and bearing a considerable resemblance to him, though perhaps more in expression than features. Still they might have been taken for father and son. And yet, though the elder person was as simply clad as the younger, and as simple in manner too, he had an indescribable air of one who knew the world, and who would not have felt abashed at the governor's dinner table or in King William's court, were it possible that his affairs should call him thither. But the only thing about him that could be fixed upon as remarkable was his staff, which bore the likeness of a great black snake, so curiously wrought that it might almost be seen to twist and wriggle itself like a living serpent. This, of course, must have been an ocular deception, assisted by the uncertain light.

"Come, Goodman Brown," cried his fellow-traveller, "this is a dull pace for the beginning of a journey. Take my staff, if you are so soon weary."

"Friend," said the other, exchanging his slow pace for a full stop, "having kept covenant by meeting thee here, it is my purpose now to return whence I came. I have scruples touching the matter thou wot'st of."

"Sayest thou so?" replied he of the serpent, smiling apart. "Let us walk on, nevertheless, reasoning as we go; and if I convince thee not thou shalt turn back. We are but a little way in the forest yet."

"Too far! too far!" exclaimed the goodman, unconsciously resuming his walk. "My father never went into the woods on such an errand, nor his father before him. We have been a race of honest men and good Christians since the days of the martyrs; and shall I be the first of the name of Brown that ever took this path and kept—"

"Such company, thou wouldst say," observed the elder person, interpreting his pause. "Well said, Goodman Brown! I have been as well acquainted with your family as with ever a one among the Puritans; and that's no trifle to say. I helped your grandfather, the constable, when he lashed the Quaker woman so smartly through the streets of Salem; and it was I that brought your father a pitch-pine knot, kindled at my own hearth, to set fire to an Indian village, in King Philip's war. They were my good friends, both; and many a pleasant walk have we had along this path, returned merrily after midnight. I would fain be friends with you for their sake."

"If it be as thou sayest," replied Goodman Brown, "I marvel they never spoke of these matters; or, verily, I marvel not, seeing that the least rumor of the sort would have driven them from New England. We are a people of prayer, and good works to boot, and abide no such wickedness."

"Wickedness or not," said the traveller with the twisted staff, "I have a very general acquaintance here in New England. The deacons of many a church have drunk the communion wine with me; the selectmen of divers towns make me their chairman; and a majority of the Great and General Court are firm supporters of my interest. The governor and I, too—But these are state secrets."

"Can this be so?" cried Goodman Brown, with a stare of amazement at his undisturbed companion. "Howbeit, I have nothing to do with the governor and council; they have their own ways, and are no rule for a simple husbandman like me. But, were I to go on with thee, how should I meet the eye of that good old man, our minister, at Salem village? Oh, his voice would make me tremble both Sabbath day and lecture day."

Thus far the elder traveller had listened with due gravity; but now burst into a fit of irrepressible mirth, shaking himself so violently that his snake-like staff actually seemed to wriggle in sympathy.

"Ha! ha! ha!" shouted he again and again; then composing himself, "Well, go on, Goodman Brown, go on; but, prithee, don't kill me with laughing."

"Well, then, to end the matter at once," said Goodman Brown, considerably nettled, "there is my wife, Faith. It would break her dear little heart; and I'd rather break my own."

"Nay, if that be the case," answered the other, "e'en go thy ways, Goodman Brown. I would not for twenty old women like the one hobbling before us that Faith should come to any harm."

As he spoke he pointed his staff at a female figure on the path, in whom Goodman Brown recognized a very pious and exemplary dame, who had taught him his catechism in youth, and was still his moral and spiritual adviser, jointly with the minister and Deacon Gookin.

"A marvel, truly, that Goody Cloyse should be so far in the wilderness at nightfall," said he. "But with your leave, friend, I shall take a cut through the woods until we have left this Christian woman behind. Being a stranger to you, she might ask whom I was consorting with and whither I was going."

"Be it so," said his fellow-traveller. "Betake you to the woods, and let me keep the path."

Accordingly the young man turned aside, but took care to watch his companion, who advanced softly along the road until he had come within a staff's length of the old dame. She, meanwhile, was making the best of her way, with singular speed for so aged a woman, and mumbling some indistinct words— a prayer, doubtless—as she went. The traveller put forth his staff and touched her withered neck with what seemed the serpent's tail.

"The devil!" screamed the pious old lady.

"Then Goody Cloyse knows her old friend?" observed the traveller, confronting her and leaning on his writhing stick.

"Ah, forsooth, and is it your worship indeed?" cried the good dame. "Yea, truly is it, and in the very image of my old gossip, Goodman Brown, the grandfather of the silly fellow that now is. But—would your worship believe it?—my broomstick hath strangely disappeared, stolen, as I suspect, by that unhanged witch, Goody Cory, and that, too, when I was all anointed with the juice of smallage, and cinquefoil, and wolf's bane—"

"Mingled with fine wheat and the fat of a new-born babe," said the shape of old Goodman Brown.

"Ah, your worship knows the recipe," cried the old lady, cackling aloud. "So, as I was saying, being all ready for the meeting, and no horse to ride on, I made up my mind to foot it; for they tell me there is a nice young man to be taken into communion to-night. But now your good worship will lend me your arm, and we shall be there in a twinkling."

"That can hardly be," answered her friend. "I may not spare you my arm, Goody Cloyse; but here is my staff, if you will."

So saying, he threw it down at her feet, where, perhaps, it assumed life, being one of the rods which its owner had formerly lent to the Egyptian magi. Of this fact, however, Goodman Brown could not take cognizance. He had cast up his eyes in astonishment, and, looking down again, beheld neither Goody Cloyse nor the serpentine staff, but his fellow-traveller alone, who waited for him as calmly as if nothing had happened.

"That old woman taught me my catechism," said the young man; and there was a world of meaning in this simple comment.

They continued to walk onward, while the elder traveller exhorted his companion to make good speed and persevere in the path, discoursing so aptly that his arguments seemed rather to spring up in the bosom of his auditor than to be suggested by himself. As they went, he plucked a branch of maple to serve for a walking stick, and began to strip it of the twigs and little boughs, which were wet with evening dew. The moment his fingers touched them they became strangely withered and dried up as with a week's sunshine. Thus the pair proceeded, at a good free pace, until suddenly, in a gloomy hollow of the road, Goodman Brown sat himself down on the stump of a tree and refused to go any farther.

"Friend," said he, stubbornly, "my mind is made up. Not another step will I budge on this errand. What if a wretched old woman do choose to go to the devil when I thought she was going to heaven: is that any reason why I should quit my dear Faith and go after her?"

"You will think better of this by and by," said his acquaintance, composedly. "Sit here and rest yourself a while; and when you feel like moving again, there is my staff to help you along."

Without more words, he threw his companion the maple stick, and was as speedily out of sight as if he had vanished into the deepening gloom. The young man sat a few moments by the roadside, applauding himself greatly, and thinking with how clear a conscience he should meet the minister in his morning walk, nor shrink from the eye of good old Deacon Gookin. And what calm sleep would be his that very night, which was to have been spent so wickedly, but so purely and sweetly now, in the arms of Faith! Amidst these pleasant and praiseworthy meditations, Goodman Brown heard the tramp of horses along the road, and deemed it advisable to conceal himself within the verge of the forest, conscious of the guilty purpose that had brought him thither, though now so happily turned from it.

On came the hoof tramps and the voices of the riders, two grave old voices, conversing soberly as they drew near. These mingled sounds appeared to pass along the road, within a few yards of the young man's hiding-place; but, owing doubtless to the depth of the gloom at that particular spot, neither the travellers nor their steeds were visible. Though their figures brushed the small boughs by the wayside, it could not be seen that they intercepted, even for a moment, the faint gleam from the strip of bright sky athwart which they must have passed. Goodman Brown alternately crouched and stood on tiptoe, pulling aside the branches and thrusting forth his head as far as he durst without discerning so much as a shadow. It vexed him the more, because he could have sworn, were such a thing possible, that he recognized the voices of the minister and Deacon Gookin, jogging along quietly, as they were wont to do, when bound to some ordination or ecclesiastical council. While yet within hearing, one of the riders stopped to pluck a switch.

"Of the two, reverend sir," said the voice like the deacon's, "I had rather miss an ordination dinner than to-night's meeting. They tell me that some of our community are to be here from Falmouth and beyond, and others from Connecticut and Rhode Island, besides several of the Indian powwows, who, after their fashion, know almost as much deviltry as the best of us. Moreover, there is a goodly young woman to be taken into communion."

"Mighty well, Deacon Gookin!" replied the solemn old tones of the minister. "Spur up, or we shall be late. Nothing can be done, you know, until I get on the ground."

The hoofs clattered again; and the voices, talking so strangely in the empty air, passed on through the forest, where no church had ever been gathered or solitary Christian prayed. Whither, then, could these holy men be journeying so deep into the heathen wilderness? Young Goodman Brown caught hold of a tree for support, being ready to sink down on the ground, faint and over-burdened with the heavy sickness of his heart. He looked up to the sky, doubting whether there was a heaven above him. Yet there was the blue arch, and the stars brightening in it.

"With heaven above and Faith below, I will yet stand firm against the devil!" cried Goodman Brown.

While he still gazed upward into the deep arch of the firmament and had lifted his hands to pray, a cloud, though no wind was stirring, hurried across the zenith and hid the brightening stars. The blue sky was still visible, except directly overhead, where this black mass of cloud was sweeping swiftly northward. Aloft in the air, as if from the depths of the cloud, came a confused and doubtful sound of voices. Once the listener fancied that he could distinguish the accents of the towns-people of his own, men and women, both pious and ungodly, many of whom he had met at the communion table, and had seen others rioting at the tavern. The next moment, so indistinct were the sounds, he doubted whether he had heard aught but the murmur of the old forest, whispering without a wind. Then came a stronger swell of those familiar tones, heard daily in the sunshine at Salem village, but never until now from a cloud of night. There was one voice of a young woman, uttering lamentations, yet with an uncertain sorrow, and entreating for some favor, which, perhaps, it would grieve her to obtain; and all the unseen multitude, both saints and sinners, seemed to encourage her onward.

"Faith!" shouted Goodman Brown, in a voice of agony and desperation; and the echoes of the forest mocked him, crying, "Faith! Faith!" as if bewildered wretches were seeking her all through the wilderness.

The cry of grief, rage, and terror was yet piercing the night, when the unhappy husband held his breath for a response. There was a scream, drowned immediately in a louder murmur of voices, fading into far-off laughter, as the dark cloud swept away, leaving the clear and silent sky above Goodman Brown. But something fluttered lightly down through the air and caught on the branch of a tree. The young man seized it, and beheld a pink ribbon.

"My Faith is gone!" cried he, after one stupefied moment. "There is no good on earth; and sin is but a name. Come, devil; for to thee is this world given."

And, maddened with despair, so that he laughed loud and long, did Goodman Brown grasp his staff and set forth again, at such a rate that he seemed to fly along the forest path rather than to walk or run. The road grew wilder and drearier and more faintly traced, and vanished at length, leaving him in the heart of the dark wilderness, still rushing onward with the instinct that guides mortal men to evil. The whole forest was peopled with frightful sounds—the creaking of the trees, the howling of wild beasts, and the yell of Indians; while sometimes the wind tolled like a distant church bell, and sometimes gave a broad roar around the traveller, as if all Nature were laughing him to scorn. But he was himself the chief horror of the scene, and shrank not from its other horrors.

"Ha! ha! ha!" roared Goodman Brown when the wind laughed at him. "Let us hear which will laugh loudest. Think not to frighten me with your deviltry. Come witch, come wizard, come Indian powwow, come devil himself, and here comes Goodman Brown. You may as well fear him as he fear you."

In truth, all through the haunted forest there could be nothing more frightful than the figure of Goodman Brown. On he flew among the black pines, brandishing his staff with frenzied gestures, now giving vent to an inspiration of horrid blasphemy, and now shouting forth such laughter as set all the echoes of the forest laughing like demons around him. The fiend in his own shape is less hideous than when he rages in the breast of man. Thus sped the demoniac on his course, until, quivering among the trees, he saw a red light before him, as when the felled trunks and branches of a clearing have been set on fire, and throw up their lurid blaze against the sky, at the hour of midnight. He paused, in a lull of the tempest that had driven him onward, and heard the swell of what seemed a hymn, rolling solemnly from a distance with the weight of many voices. He knew the tune; it was a familiar one in the choir of the village meeting-house. The verse died heavily away, and was lengthened by a chorus, not of human voices, but of all the sounds of the benighted wilderness pealing in awful harmony together. Goodman Brown cried out, and his cry was lost to his own ear by its unison with the cry of the desert.

In the interval of silence he stole forward until the light glared full upon his eyes. At one extremity of an open space, hemmed in by the dark wall of the forest, arose a rock, bearing some rude, natural resemblance either to an altar or a pulpit, and surrounded by four blazing pines, their tops aflame, their stems untouched, like candles at an evening meeting. The mass of foliage that had overgrown the summit of the rock was all on fire, blazing high into the night and fitfully illuminating the whole field. Each pendent twig and leafy festoon was in a blaze. As the red light arose and fell, a numerous congregation alternately shone forth, then disappeared in shadow, and again grew, as it were, out of the darkness, peopling the heart of the solitary woods at once.

"A grave and dark-clad company," quoth Goodman Brown.

In truth they were such. Among them, quivering to and fro between gloom and splendor, appeared faces that would be seen next day at the council board of the province, and others which, Sabbath after Sabbath, looked devoutly heavenward, and benignantly over the crowded pews, from the holiest pulpits in the land. Some affirm that the lady of the governor was there. At least there were high dames well known to her, and wives of honored husbands, and widows, a great multitude, and ancient maidens, all of excellent repute, and fair young girls, who trembled lest their mothers should espy them. Either the sudden gleams of light flashing over the obscure field bedazzled Goodman Brown, or he recognized a score of the church members of Salem village famous for their especial sanctity. Good old Deacon Gookin had arrived, and waited at the skirts of that venerable saint, his revered pastor. But, irreverently consorting with these grave, reputable, and pious people, these elders of the church, these chaste dames and dewy virgins, there were men of dissolute lives and women of spotted fame, wretches given over to all mean and filthy vice, and suspected even of horrid crimes. It was strange to see that the good shrank not from the wicked, nor were the sinners abashed by the saints. Scattered also among their pale-faced enemies were the Indian priests, or powwows, who had often scared their native forest with more hideous incantations than any known to English witchcraft.

"But where is Faith?" thought Goodman Brown; and, as hope came into his heart, he trembled.

Another verse of the hymn arose, a slow and mournful strain, such as the pious love, but joined to words which expressed all that our nature can conceive of sin, and darkly hinted at far more. Unfathomable to mere mortals is the lore of fiends. Verse after verse was sung; and still the chorus of the desert swelled between like the deepest tone of a mighty organ; and with the final peal of that dreadful anthem there came a sound, as if the roaring wind, the rushing streams, the howling beasts, and every other voice of the unconcerted wilderness were mingling and according with the voice of guilty man in homage to the prince of all. The four blazing pines threw up a loftier flame, and obscurely discovered shapes and visages of horror on the smoke wreaths above the impious assembly. At the same moment the fire on the rock shot redly forth and formed a glowing arch above its base, where now appeared a figure. With reverence be it spoken, the figure bore no slight similitude, both in garb and manner, to some grave divine of the New England churches.

"Bring forth the converts!" cried a voice that echoed through the field and rolled into the forest.

At the word, Goodman Brown stepped forth from the shadow of the trees and approached the congregation, with whom he felt a loathful brotherhood by the sympathy of all that was wicked in his heart. He could have well-nigh sworn that the shape of his own dead father beckoned him to advance, looking downward from a smoke wreath, while a woman, with dim features of despair, threw out her hand to warn him back. Was it his mother? But he had no power to retreat one step, nor to resist, even in thought, when the minister and good old Deacon Gookin seized his arms and led him to the blazing rock. Thither came also the slender form of a veiled female, led between Goody Cloyse, that pious teacher of the catechism, and Martha Carrier, who had received the devil's promise to be queen of hell. A rampant hag was she. And there stood the proselytes beneath the canopy of fire.

"Welcome, my children," said the dark figure, "to the communion of your race. Ye have found thus young your nature and your destiny. My children, look behind you!"

They turned; and flashing forth, as it were, in a sheet of flame, the fiend worshippers were seen; the smile of welcome gleamed darkly on every visage.

"There," resumed the sable form, "are all whom ye have reverenced from youth. Ye deemed them holier than yourselves, and shrank from your own sin, contrasting it with their lives of righteousness and prayerful aspirations heavenward. Yet here are they all in my worshipping assembly. This night it shall be granted you to know their secret deeds; how hoary-bearded elders of the church have whispered wanton words to the young maids of their households; how many a woman, eager for widows' weeds, has given her husband a drink at bedtime and let him sleep his last sleep in her bosom; how beardless youths have made haste to inherit their fathers' wealth; and how fair damsels—blush not, sweet ones—have dug little graves in the garden, and bidden me, the sole guest, to an infant's funeral. By the sympathy of your human hearts for sin ye shall scent out all the places—whether in church, bedchamber, street, field, or forest—where crime has been committed, and shall exult to behold the whole earth one stain of guilt, one mighty blood spot. Far more than this. It shall be yours to penetrate, in every bosom, the deep mystery of sin, the fountain of all wicked arts, and which inexhaustibly supplies more evil impulses than human power—than my power at its utmost—can make manifest in deeds. And now, my children, look upon each other."

They did so; and, by the blaze of the hell-kindled torches, the wretched man beheld his Faith, and the wife her husband, trembling before that unhallowed altar.

"Lo, there ye stand, my children," said the figure, in a deep and solemn tone, almost sad with its despairing awfulness, as if his once angelic nature could yet mourn for our miserable race. "Depending upon one another's hearts, ye had still hoped that virtue were not all a dream. Now are ye undeceived. Evil is the nature of mankind. Evil must be your only happiness. Welcome again, my children, to the communion of your race."

"Welcome," repeated the fiend worshippers, in one cry of despair and triumph.

And there they stood, the only pair, as it seemed, who were yet hesitating on the verge of wickedness in this dark world. A basin was hollowed, naturally, in the rock. Did it contain water, reddened by the lurid light? or was it blood? or, perchance, a liquid flame? Herein did the shape of evil dip his hand and prepare to lay the mark of baptism upon their foreheads, that they might be partakers of the mystery of sin, more conscious of the secret guilt of others, both in deed and thought, than they could now be of their own. The husband cast one look at his pale wife, and Faith at him. What polluted wretches would the next glance show them to each other, shuddering alike at what they disclosed and what they saw!

"Faith! Faith!" cried the husband, "look up to heaven, and resist the wicked one."

Whether Faith obeyed he knew not. Hardly had he spoken when he found himself amid calm night and solitude, listening to the roar of the wind which died heavily away through the forest. He staggered against the rock, and felt it chill and damp; while a hanging twig, that had been all on fire, besprinkled his cheek with the coldest dew.

The next morning young Goodman Brown came slowly into the street of Salem village, staring around him like a bewildered man. The good old minister was taking a walk along the graveyard to get an appetite for breakfast and meditate his sermon, and bestowed a blessing, as he passed, on Goodman Brown. He shrank from the venerable saint as if to avoid an anathema. Old Deacon Gookin was at domestic worship, and the holy words of his prayer were heard through the open window. "What God doth the wizard pray to?" quoth Goodman Brown. Goody Cloyse, that excellent old Christian, stood in the early sunshine at her own lattice, catechizing a little girl who had brought her a pint of morning's milk. Goodman Brown snatched away the child as from the grasp of the fiend himself. Turning the corner by the meeting-house, he spied the head of Faith, with the pink ribbons, gazing anxiously forth, and bursting into such joy at sight of him that she skipped along the street and almost kissed her husband before the whole village. But Goodman Brown looked sternly and sadly into her face, and passed on without a greeting.

Had Goodman Brown fallen asleep in the forest and only dreamed a wild dream of a witch-meeting?

Be it so if you will; but, alas! it was a dream of evil omen for young Goodman Brown. A stern, a sad, a darkly meditative, a distrustful, if not a desperate man did he become from the night of that fearful dream. On the Sabbath day, when the congregation were singing a holy psalm, he could not listen because an anthem of sin rushed loudly upon his ear and drowned all the blessed strain. When the minister spoke from the pulpit with power and fervid eloquence, and, with his hand on the open Bible, of the sacred truths of our religion, and of saint-like lives and triumphant deaths, and of future bliss or misery unutterable, then did Goodman Brown turn pale, dreading lest the roof should thunder down upon the gray blasphemer and his hearers. Often, waking suddenly at midnight, he shrank from the bosom of Faith; and at morning or eventide, when the family knelt down at prayer, he scowled and muttered to himself, and gazed sternly at his wife, and turned away. And when he had lived long, and was borne to his grave a hoary corpse, followed by Faith, an aged woman, and children and grandchildren, a goodly procession, besides neighbors not a few, they carved no hopeful verse upon his tombstone, for his dying hour was gloom.

EXERCISES

1. Why does Goodman Brown make his journey only after he has recently been married? If this is a journey he knows he has to make, why did he not make it the previous year?

2. If this is an allegory of a journey everyone must make, then the appearance of the devil is "not wholly unexpected." However, if it is a moral journey that applies only to Goodman Brown, then he would not know where he is going. Which is the case here?

3. Discuss the significance of the stranger resembling Goodman Brown. Discuss also the fact that the conversation between them is so apt that the devil's arguments seem to spring from "the bosom of his auditor" rather than to be suggested by himself.

4. What favor is the woman asking in the forest? Why is her voice of "uncertain sorrow"? Why is it that it would grieve her to obtain the very favor she is asking for?

5. What does it mean that the image of Brown's father beckons him, while his mother warns him away?

6. How would you define the nature of sin in this story? In what way is everyone sinful?

7. If this is an initiation story, into what is Goodman Brown being initiated? Why does he remain such a sad, stern, distrustful, even desperate man for the rest of his life?

JOHN
CHEEVER | *The Swimmer*

It was one of those midsummer Sundays when everyone sits around saying, "I *drank* too much last night." You might have heard it whispered by the parishioners leaving church, heard it from the lips of the priest himself, struggling with his cassock in the *vestiarium,* heard it from the golf links and the tennis courts, heard it from the wildlife preserve where the leader of the Audubon group was suffering from a terrible hangover. "I *drank* too much," said Donald Westerhazy. "We all *drank* too much," said Lucinda Merrill. "It must have been the wine," said Helen Westerhazy. "I *drank* too much of that claret."

This was at the edge of the Westerhazys' pool. The pool, fed by an artesian well with a high iron content, was a pale shade of green. It was a fine day. In the west there was a massive stand of cumulus cloud so like a city seen from a distance—from the bow of an approaching ship—that it might have had a name. Lisbon. Hackensack. The sun was hot. Neddy Merrill sat by the green water, one hand in it, one around a glass of gin. He was a slender man—he seemed to have the especial slenderness of youth—and while he was far from young he had slid down his banister that morning and given the bronze back-side of Aphrodite on the hall table a smack, as he jogged toward the smell of coffee in his dining room. He might have been compared to a summer's day, particularly the last hours of one, and while he lacked a tennis racket or a sail bag the impression was definitely one of youth, sport, and clement weather. He had been swimming and now he was breathing deeply, stertorously as if he could gulp into his lungs the components of that moment, the heat of the sun, the intenseness of his pleasure. It all seemed to flow into his chest. His own house stood in Bullet Park, eight miles to the south, where his four beautiful daughters would have had their lunch and might be playing tennis. Then it occurred to him that by taking a dogleg to the southwest he could reach his home by water.

His life was not confining and the delight he took in this observation could not be explained by its suggestion of escape. He seemed to see, with a cartographer's eye, that string of swimming pools, that quasi-subterranean stream that curved across the county. He had made a discovery, a contribution to modern geography; he would name the stream Lucinda after his wife. He was not a practical joker nor was he a fool but he was determinedly original and had a vague and modest idea of himself as a legendary figure. The day was beautiful and it seemed to him that a long swim might enlarge and celebrate its beauty.

He took off a sweater that was hung over his shoulders and dove in. He had an inexplicable contempt for men who did not hurl themselves into pools. He swam a choppy crawl, breathing either with every stroke or every fourth stroke and counting somewhere well in the back of his mind the one-two one-two of a flutter kick. It was not a serviceable stroke for long distances but the domestication of swimming had saddled the sport with some customs and in his part of the world a crawl was customary. To be embraced and sustained by the light green water was less a pleasure, it seemed, than the resumption of a natural condition, and he would have liked to swim without trunks, but this was not possible, considering his project. He hoisted himself up on the far curb—he never used the ladder—and started across the lawn. When Lucinda asked where he was going he said he was going to swim home.

The only map and charts he had to go by were remembered or imaginary but these were clear enough. First there were the Grahams, the Hammers, the Lears, the Howlands, and the Crosscups. He would cross Ditmar Street to the Bunkers and come, after a short portage, to the Levys, the Welchers, and the public pool in Lancaster. Then there were the Hallorans, the Sachses, the Biswangers, Shirley Adams, the Gilmartins, and the Clydes. The day was lovely, and that he lived in a world so generously supplied with water seemed like a clemency, a beneficence. His heart was high and he ran across the grass. Making his way home by an uncommon route gave him the feeling that he was a pilgrim, an explorer, a man with a destiny, and he knew that he would find friends all along the way; friends would line the banks of the Lucinda River.

He went through a hedge that separated the Westerhazys' land from the Grahams', walked under some flowering apple trees, passed the shed that housed their pump and filter, and came out at the Grahams' pool. "Why, Neddy," Mrs. Graham said, "what a marvelous surprise. I've been trying to get you on the phone all morning. Here, let me get you a drink." He saw then, like any explorer, that the hospitable customs and traditions of the natives would have to be handled with diplomacy if he was ever going to reach his destination. He did not want to mystify or seem rude to the Grahams nor did he have the time to linger there. He swam the length of their pool and joined them in the sun and was rescued, a few minutes later, by the arrival of two carloads of friends from Connecticut. During the uproarious reunions he was able to slip away. He went down by the front of the Grahams' house, stepped over a thorny hedge, and crossed a vacant lot to the Hammers'. Mrs. Hammer, looking up from her roses, saw him swim by although she wasn't quite sure who it was. The Lears heard him splashing past the open windows of their living room. The Howlands and the Crosscups were away. After leaving the Howlands' he crossed Ditmar Street and started for the Bunkers', where he could hear, even at that distance, the noise of a party.

The water refracted the sound of voices and laughter and seemed to suspend it in midair. The Bunkers' pool was on a rise and he climbed some stairs to a terrace where twenty-five or thirty men and women were drinking. The only person in the water was Rusty Towers, who floated there on a rubber raft. Oh, how bonny and lush were the banks of the Lucinda River! Prosperous men and women gathered by the sapphire-colored waters while caterer's men in white coats passed them cold gin. Overhead a red de Haviland trainer was circling around and around and around in the sky with something like the glee of a child in a swing. Ned felt a passing affection for the scene, a tenderness for the gathering, as if it was something he might touch. In the distance he heard thunder. As soon as Enid Bunker saw him she began to scream: "Oh, look who's here! What a marvelous surprise! When Lucinda said that you couldn't come I thought I'd *die*." She made her way to him through the crowd, and when they had finished kissing she led him to the bar, a progress that was slowed by the fact that he stopped to kiss eight or ten other women and shake the hands of as many men. A smiling bartender he had seen at a hundred parties gave him a gin and tonic and he stood by the bar for a moment, anxious not to get stuck in any conversation that would delay his voyage. When he seemed about to be surrounded he dove in and swam close to the side to avoid colliding with Rusty's raft. At the far end of the pool he bypassed the Tomlinsons with a broad smile and jogged up the garden path. The gravel cut his feet but this was the only unpleasantness. The party was confined to the pool, and as he went toward the house he heard the brilliant, watery sound of voices fade, heard the noise of a radio from the Bunkers' kitchen, where someone was listening to a ball game. Sunday afternoon. He made his way through the parked cars and down the grassy border of their driveway to Alewives Lane. He did not want to be seen on the road in his bathing trunks but there was no traffic and he made the short distance to the Levy's driveway, marked with a PRIVATE PROPERTY sign and a green tube for *The New York Times.* All the doors and windows of the big house were open but there were no signs of life; not even a dog barked. He went around the side of the house to the pool and saw that the Levys had only recently left. Glasses and bottles and dishes of nuts were on a table at the deep end, where there was a bathhouse or gazebo, hung with Japanese lanterns. After swimming the pool he got himself a glass and poured a drink. It was his fourth or fifth drink and he had swum nearly half the length of the Lucinda River. He felt tired, clean, and pleased at that moment to be alone; pleased with everything.

It would storm. The stand of cumulus cloud—that city—had risen and darkened, and while he sat there he heard the percussiveness of thunder again. The de Haviland trainer was still circling overhead and it seemed to Ned that he could almost hear the pilot laugh with pleasure in the afternoon; but when there was another peal of thunder he took off for home. A train whistle blew and he wondered what time it had gotten to be. Four? Five? He thought of the provincial station at that hour, where a waiter, his tuxedo concealed by a raincoat, a dwarf with some flowers wrapped in newspaper, and a woman who had been crying would be waiting for the local. It was suddenly growing dark; it was that moment when the pinheaded birds seem to organize their song into some acute and knowledgeable recognition of the storm's approach. Then there was a fine noise of rushing water from the crown of an oak at his back, as if a spigot there had been turned. Then the noise of fountains came from the crowns of all the tall trees. Why did he love storms, what was the meaning of his excitement when the door sprang open and the rain wind fled rudely up the stairs, why had the simple task of shutting the windows of an old house seemed fitting and urgent, why did the first watery notes of a storm wind have for him the unmistakable sound of good news, cheer, glad tidings? Then there was an explosion, a smell of cordite, and rain lashed the Japanese lanterns that Mrs. Levy had bought in Kyoto the year before last, or was it the year before that?

He stayed in the Levys' gazebo until the storm had passed. The rain had cooled the air and he shivered. The force of the wind had stripped a maple of its red and yellow leaves and scattered them over the grass and the water. Since it was midsummer the tree must be blighted, and yet he felt a peculiar sadness at this sign of autumn. He braced his shoulders, emptied his glass, and started for the Welchers' pool. This meant crossing the Lindleys' riding ring and he was surprised to find it overgrown with grass and all the jumps dismantled. He wondered if the Lindleys had sold their horses or gone away for the summer and put them out to board. He seemed to remember having heard something about the Lindleys and their horses but the memory was unclear. On he went, barefoot through the wet grass, to the Welchers', where he found their pool was dry.

This breach in his chain of water disappointed him absurdly, and he felt like some explorer who seeks a torrential headwater and finds a dead stream. He was disappointed and mystified. It was common enough to go away for the summer but no one ever drained his pool. The Welchers had definitely gone away. The pool furniture was folded, stacked, and covered with a tarpaulin. The bathhouse was locked. All the windows of the house were shut, and when he went around to the driveway in front he saw a FOR SALE sign nailed to a tree. When had he last heard from the Welchers—when, that is, had he and Lucinda last regretted an invitation to dine with them? It seemed only a week or so ago. Was his memory failing or had he so disciplined it in the repression of unpleasant facts that he had damaged his sense of the truth? Then in the distance he heard the sound of a tennis game. This cheered him, cleared away all his apprehensions and let him regard the overcast sky and the cold air with indifference. This was the day that Neddy Merrill swam across the county. That was the day! He started off then for his most difficult portage.

Had you gone for a Sunday afternoon ride that day you might have seen him, close to naked, standing on the shoulders of Route 424, waiting for a chance to cross. You might have wondered if he was the victim of foul play, had his car broken down, or was he merely a fool. Standing barefoot in the deposits of the highway—beer cans, rags, and blowout patches—exposed to all kinds of ridicule, he seemed pitiful. He had known when he started that this was a part of his journey—it had been on his maps—but confronted with the lines of traffic, worming through the summery light, he found himself unprepared. He was laughed at, jeered at, a beer can was thrown at him, and he had no dignity or humor to bring to the situation. He could have gone back, back to the Westerhazys', where Lucinda would still be sitting in the sun. He had signed nothing, vowed nothing, pledged nothing, not even to himself. Why, believing as he did, that all human obduracy was susceptible to common sense, was he unable to turn back? Why was he determined to complete his journey even if it meant putting his life in danger? At what point had this prank, this joke, this piece of horseplay become serious? He could not go back, he could not even recall with any clearness the green water at the Westerhazys', the sense of inhaling the day's components, the friendly and relaxed voices saying that they had *drunk* too much. In the space of an hour, more or less, he had covered a distance that made his return impossible.

An old man, tooling down the highway at fifteen miles an hour, let him get to the middle of the road, where there was a grass divider. Here he was exposed to the ridicule of the northbound traffic, but after ten or fifteen minutes he was able to cross. From here he had only a short walk to the Recreation Center at the edge of the village of Lancaster, where there were some handball courts and a public pool.

The effect of the water on voices, the illusion of brilliance and suspense, was the same here as it had been at the Bunkers' but the sounds here were louder, harsher, and more shrill, and as soon as he entered the crowded enclosure he was confronted with regimentation. "ALL SWIMMERS MUST TAKE A SHOWER BEFORE USING THE POOL. ALL SWIMMERS MUST USE THE FOOTBATH. ALL SWIMMERS MUST WEAR THEIR IDENTIFICATION DISKS." He took a shower, washed his feet in a cloudy and bitter solution, and made his way to the edge of the water. It stank of chlorine and looked to him like a sink. A pair of lifeguards in a pair of towers blew police whistles at what seemed to be regular intervals and abused the swimmers through a public address system. Neddy remembered the sapphire water at the Bunkers' with longing and thought that he might contaminate himself—damage his own prosperousness and charm— by swimming in this murk, but he reminded himself that he was an explorer, a pilgrim, and that this was merely a stagnant bend in the Lucinda River. He dove, scowling with distaste, into the chlorine and had to swim with his head above water to avoid collisions, but even so he was bumped into, splashed, and jostled. When he got to the shallow end both lifeguards were shouting at him: "Hey, you, you without the identification disk, get outa the water." He did, but they had no way of pursuing him and he went through the reek of suntan oil and chlorine out through the hurricane fence and passed the handball courts. By crossing the road he entered the wooded part of the Halloran estate. The woods were not cleared and the footing was treacherous and difficult until he reached the lawn and the clipped beech hedge that encircled their pool.

The Hallorans were friends, an elderly couple of enormous wealth who seemed to bask in the suspicion that they might be Communists. They were zealous reformers but they were not Communists, and yet when they were accused, as they sometimes were, of subversion, it seemed to gratify and excite them. Their beech hedge was yellow and he guessed this had been blighted like the Levys' maple. He called hullo, hullo, to warn the Hallorans of his approach, to palliate his invasion of their privacy. The Hallorans, for reasons that had never been explained to him, did not wear bathing suits. No explanations were in order, really. Their nakedness was a detail in their uncompromising zeal for reform and he stepped politely out of his trunks before he went through the opening in the hedge.

Mrs. Halloran, a stout woman with white hair and a serene face, was reading the *Times*. Mr. Halloran was taking beech leaves out of the water with a scoop. They seemed not surprised or displeased to see him. Their pool was perhaps the oldest in the country, a fieldstone rectangle, fed by a brook. It had no filter or pump and its waters were the opaque gold of the stream.

"I'm swimming across the county," Ned said.

"Why, I didn't know one could," exclaimed Mrs. Halloran.

"Well, I've made it from the Westerhazys'," Ned said. "That must be about four miles."

He left his trunks at the deep end, walked to the shallow end, and swam this stretch. As he was pulling himself out of the water he heard Mrs. Halloran say, "We've been *terribly* sorry to hear about all your misfortunes, Neddy."

"My misfortunes?" Ned asked. "I don't know what you mean."

"Why, we heard that you'd sold the house and that your poor children . . ."

"I don't recall having sold the house," Ned said, "and the girls are at home."

"Yes," Mrs. Halloran sighed. "Yes . . ." Her voice filled the air with an unseasonable melancholy and Ned spoke briskly. "Thank you for the swim."

"Well, have a nice trip," said Mrs. Halloran.

Beyond the hedge he pulled on his trunks and fastened them. They were loose and he wondered if, during the space of an afternoon, he could have lost some weight. He was cold and he was tired and the naked Hallorans and their dark water had depressed him. The swim was too much for his strength but how could he have guessed this, sliding down the banister that morning and sitting in the Westerhazys' sun? His arms were lame. His legs felt rubbery and ached at the joints. The worst of it was the cold in his bones and the feeling that he might never be warm again. Leaves were falling down around him and he smelled wood smoke on the wind. Who would be burning wood at this time of year?

He needed a drink. Whiskey would warm him, pick him up, carry him through the last of his journey, refresh his feeling that it was original and valorous to swim across the county. Channel swimmers took brandy. He needed a stimulant. He crossed the lawn in front of the Hallorans' house and went down a little path to where they had built a house for their only daughter, Helen, and her husband, Eric Sachs. The Sachses' pool was small and he found Helen and her husband there.

"Oh, *Neddy*," Helen said. "Did you lunch at Mother's?"

"Not *really*," Ned said. "I *did* stop to see your parents." This seemed to be explanation enough. "I'm terribly sorry to break in on you like this but I've taken a chill and I wonder if you'd give me a drink."

"Why, I'd *love* to," Helen said, "but there hasn't been anything in this house to drink since Eric's operation. That was three years ago."

Was he losing his memory, had his gift for concealing painful facts let him forget that he had sold his house, that his children were in trouble, and that his friend had been ill? His eyes slipped from Eric's face to his abdomen, where he saw three pale, sutured scars, two of them at least a foot long. Gone was his navel, and what, Neddy thought, would the roving hand, bed-checking one's gifts at 3 A.M., make of a belly with no navel, no link to birth, this breach in the succession?

"I'm sure you can get a drink at the Biswangers'," Helen said. "They're having an enormous do. You can hear it from here. Listen!"

She raised her head and from across the road, the lawns, the gardens, the woods, the fields, he heard again the brilliant noise of voices over water. "Well, I'll get wet," he said, still feeling that he had no freedom of choice about his means of travel. He dove into the Sachses' cold water and, gasping, close to drowning, made his way from one end of the pool to the other. "Lucinda and

I want *terribly* to see you," he said over his shoulder, his face set toward the Biswangers'. "We're sorry it's been so long and we'll call you *very* soon."

He crossed some fields to the Biswangers' and the sounds of revelry there. They would be honored to give him a drink, they would be happy to give him a drink. The Biswangers invited him and Lucinda for dinner four times a year, six weeks in advance. They were always rebuffed and yet they continued to send out their invitations, unwilling to comprehend the rigid and undemocratic realities of their society. They were the sort of people who discussed the price of things at cocktails, exchanged market tips during dinner, and after dinner told dirty stories to mixed company. They did not belong to Neddy's set—they were not even on Lucinda's Christmas-card list. He went toward their pool with feelings of indifference, charity, and some unease, since it seemed to be getting dark and these were the longest days of the year. The party when he joined it was noisy and large. Grace Biswanger was the kind of hostess who asked the optometrist, the veterinarian, the real-estate dealer, and the dentist. No one was swimming and the twilight, reflected on the water of the pool, had a wintry gleam. There was a bar and he started for this. When Grace Biswanger saw him she came toward him, not affectionately as he had every right to expect, but bellicosely.

"Why, this party has everything," she said loudly, "including a gate crasher."

She could not deal him a social blow—there was no question about this and he did not flinch. "As a gate crasher," he asked politely, "do I rate a drink?"

"Suit yourself," she said. "You don't seem to pay much attention to invitations."

She turned her back on him and joined some guests, and he went to the bar and ordered a whiskey. The bartender served him but he served him rudely. His was a world in which the caterer's men kept the social score, and to be rebuffed by a part-time barkeep meant that he had suffered some loss of social esteem. Or perhaps the man was new and uninformed. Then he heard Grace at his back say: "They went for broke overnight—nothing but income—and he showed up drunk one Sunday and asked us to loan him five thousand dollars. . . ." She was always talking about money. It was worse than eating your peas off a knife. He dove into the pool, swam its length and went away.

The next pool on his list, the last but two, belonged to his old mistress, Shirley Adams. If he had suffered any injuries at the Biswangers' they would be cured here. Love—sexual roughhouse in fact—was the supreme elixir, the pain killer, the brightly colored pill that would put the spring back into his step, the joy of life in his heart. They had had an affair last week, last month, last year. He couldn't remember. It was he who had broken it off, his was the upper hand, and he stepped through the gate of the wall that surrounded her pool with nothing so considered as self-confidence. It seemed in a way to be his pool, as the lover, particularly the illicit lover, enjoys the possessions of his mistress with an authority unknown to holy matrimony. She was there, her hair the color of brass, but her figure, at the edge of the lighted, cerulean water, excited in him no profound memories. It had been, he thought, a light-hearted affair, although she had wept when he broke it off. She seemed confused to see him and he wondered if she was still wounded. Would she, God forbid, weep again?

"What do you want?" she asked.

"I'm swimming across the county."

"Good Christ. Will you ever grow up?"

"What's the matter?"

"If you've come here for money," she said, "I won't give you another cent."

"You could give me a drink."

"I could but I won't. I'm not alone."

"Well, I'm on my way."

He dove in and swam the pool, but when he tried to haul himself up onto the curb he found that the strength in his arms and shoulders had gone, and he paddled to the ladder and climbed out. Looking over his shoulder he saw, in the lighted bathhouse, a young man. Going out onto the dark lawn he smelled chrysanthemums or marigolds—some stubborn autumnal fragrance—on the night air, strong as gas. Looking overhead he saw that the stars had come out, but why should he seem to see Andromeda, Cepheus, and Cassiopeia? What had become of the constellations of midsummer? He began to cry.

It was probably the first time in his adult life that he had ever cried, certainly the first time in his life that he had ever felt so miserable, cold, tired, and bewildered. He could not understand the rudeness of the caterer's barkeep or the rudeness of a mistress who had come to him on her knees and showered his trousers with tears. He had swum too long, he had been immersed too long, and his nose and his throat were sore from the water. What he needed then was a drink, some company, and some clean, dry clothes, and while he could have cut directly across the road to his house he went on to the Gilmartins' pool. Here, for the first time in his life, he did not dive but went down the steps into the icy water and swam a hobbled sidestroke that he might have learned as a youth. He staggered with fatigue on his way to the Clydes' and paddled the length of their pool, stopping again and again with his hand on the curb to rest. He climbed up the ladder and wondered if he had the strength to get home. He had done what he wanted, he had swum the county, but he was so stupefied with exhaustion that his triumph seemed vague. Stooped, holding on to the gateposts for support, he turned up the driveway of his own house.

The place was dark. Was it so late that they had all gone to bed? Had Lucinda stayed at the Westerhazys' for supper? Had the girls joined her there or gone someplace else? Hadn't they agreed, as they usually did on Sunday, to regret all their invitations and stay at home? He tried the garage doors to see what cars were in but the doors were locked and rust came off the handles onto his hands. Going toward the house, he saw that the force of the thunderstorm had knocked one of the rain gutters loose. It hung down over the front door like an umbrella rib, but it could be fixed in the morning. The house was locked, and he thought that the stupid cook or the stupid maid must have locked the place up until he remembered that it had been some time since they had employed a maid or a cook. He shouted, pounded on the door, tried to force it with his shoulder, and then, looking in at the windows, saw that the place was empty.

EXERCISES

1. Discuss what Neddy is like both realistically and symbolically. Is he primarily lifelike or larger than life?

2. Point out those places in Neddy's journey that begin to suggest its unreality.

3. What is the importance of time as a theme in this story?

4. What is significant about Neddy's tendency to repress unpleasant facts? How is this a "cause" of the experience he undergoes in this story?

5. Some transformation takes place in the story—a point at which the prank becomes serious. Why? What does it mean that he has reached a point of no return?

6. Discuss the significance of the phrase "He had swum too long, he had been immersed too long." How is this indicative of Neddy's experience?

7. What happens at the end? Does it "really" happen?

8. What kind of story is this: realistic, psychological, allegorical? Explain. Compare this story with Hawthorne's "Young Goodman Brown."

FRANZ
KAFKA | *A Country Doctor*

I was in great perplexity; I had to start on an urgent journey; a seriously ill patient was waiting for me in a village ten miles off; a thick blizzard of snow filled all the wide spaces between him and me; I had a gig, a light gig with big wheels, exactly right for our country roads; muffled in furs, my bag of instruments in my hand, I was in the courtyard all ready for the journey; but there was no horse to be had, no horse. My own horse had died in the night, worn out by the fatigues of this icy winter; my servant girl was now running round the village trying to borrow a horse; but it was hopeless, I knew it, and I stood there forlornly, with the snow gathering more and more thickly upon me, more and more unable to move. In the gateway the girl appeared, alone, and waved the lantern; of course, who would lend a horse at this time for such a journey? I strode through the courtyard once more; I could see no way out; in my confused distress I kicked at the dilapidated door of the year-long uninhabited pigsty. It flew open and flapped to and fro on its hinges. A steam and smell as of horses came out from it. A dim stable lantern was swinging inside from a rope. A man, crouching on his hams in that low space, showed an open blue-eyed face. "Shall I yoke up?" he asked, crawling out on all fours. I did not know what to say and merely stooped down to see what else was in the sty. The servant girl was standing beside me. "You never know what you're going to find in your own house," she said, and we both laughed. "Hey there, Brother, hey there, Sister!" called the groom, and two horses, enormous creatures with powerful flanks, one after the other, their legs tucked close to their bodies, each well-shaped head lowered like a camel's, by sheer strength of buttocking squeezed out through the door hole which they filled entirely. But at once they were standing up, their legs long and their bodies steaming thickly. "Give him a hand," I said, and the willing girl hurried to help the groom with the harnessing. Yet hardly was she beside him when the groom clipped hold of her and pushed his face against hers. She screamed and fled back to me; on her cheek stood out in red the marks of two rows of teeth. "You brute," I yelled in fury, "do you want a whipping?" but in the same moment reflected that the man was a stranger; that I did not know where he came from, and that of his own free will he was helping me out when everyone else had failed me. As if he knew my thoughts he took no offense at my threat but, still busied with the horses, only turned round once towards me. "Get in," he said then, and indeed: everything was ready. A magnificent pair of horses, I observed, such as I had never sat behind, and I climbed in happily. "But I'll drive, you don't know the way," I said. "Of course," said he, "I'm not coming with you anyway, I'm staying with Rose." "No," shrieked Rose, fleeing into the house with a justified presentiment that her fate was inescapable; I heard the door chain rattle as she put it up; I heard the key turn in the lock; I could see, moreover, how she put out the lights in the entrance hall and in further flight all through the rooms to keep herself from being discovered. "You're coming with me," I said to the groom, "or I won't go, urgent as my journey is. I'm not thinking of paying for it by handing the girl over to you." "Geeup!" he said; clapped his hands; the gig whirled off like a log in a freshet; I could just hear the door of my house splitting and bursting as the groom charged at it and then I was deafened and blinded by a storming rush that steadily buffeted all my senses. But this only for a moment, since, as if my patient's farmyard had opened out just before my courtyard gate, I was already there; the horses had come quietly to a standstill; the blizzard had stopped; moonlight all around; my patient's parents hurried out of the house, his sister behind them; I was almost lifted out of the gig; from their confused ejaculations I gathered not a word; in the sickroom the air was almost unbreathable; the neglected stove was smoking; I wanted to push open a window; but first I had to look at my patient. Gaunt, without any fever, not cold, not warm, with vacant eyes, without a shirt, the youngster heaved himself up from under the feather bedding, threw his arms around my neck, and whispered in my ear: "Doctor, let me die." I glanced round the room; no one had heard it; the parents were leaning forward in silence waiting for my verdict; the sister had set a chair for my handbag; I opened the bag and hunted among my instruments; the boy kept clutching at me from his bed to remind me of his entreaty; I picked up a pair of tweezers, examined them in the candlelight and laid them down again. "Yes," I thought blasphemously, "in cases like this the gods are helpful, send the missing horse, add to it a second because of the urgency, and to crown everything bestow even a groom—" And only now did I remember Rose again; what was I to do, how could I rescue her, how could I pull her away from under that groom at ten miles' distance, with a team of horses I couldn't control. These horses, now, they had somehow slipped the reins loose, pushed the window open from the outside, I did not know how; each of them had stuck a head in at a window and, quite unmoved by the startled cries of the family, stood eyeing the patient. "Better go back at once," I thought, as if the horses were summoning me to the return journey, yet I permitted the patient's sister, who fancied that I was dazed by the heat, to take my fur coat from me. A glass of rum was poured out for me, the old man clapped me on the shoulder, a familiarity justified by this offer of his treasure. I shook my head; in the narrow confines of the old man's thoughts I felt ill; that was my only reason for refusing the drink. The mother stood by the bed-side and cajoled me towards it. I yielded, and, while one of the horses whinnied loudly to the ceiling, laid my head to the boy's breast, which shivered under my wet beard. I confirmed what I already knew; the boy was quite sound, something a little wrong with his circulation, saturated with coffee by his solicitous mother, but sound and best turned out of bed with one shove. I am no world reformer and so I let him lie. I was the district doctor and did my duty to the uttermost, to the point where it became almost too much. I was badly paid and yet generous and helpful to the poor. I had still to see that Rose was all right, and then the boy might have his way and I wanted to die too. What was I doing there in that endless winter! My horse was dead, and not a single person in the village would lend me another. I had to get my team out of the pigsty; if they hadn't chanced to be horses I should have had to travel with swine. That was how it was. And I nodded to the family. They knew nothing about it, and, had they known, would not have believed it. To write prescriptions is easy, but to come to an understanding with people is hard. Well, this should be the end of my visit, I had once more been called out needlessly, I was used to that, the whole district made my life a torment with my night bell, but that I should have to sacrifice Rose this time as well, the pretty girl who had lived in my house for years almost without my noticing her—that sacrifice was too much to ask, and I had somehow to get it reasoned out in my head with the help of what craft I could muster, in order not to let fly at this family, which with the best will in the world could not restore Rose to me. But as I shut my bag and put an arm out for my fur coat, the family meanwhile standing together, the father sniffing at the glass of rum in his hand, the mother, apparently disappointed in me—why, what do people expect—biting her lips with tears in her eyes, the sister fluttering a blood-soaked towel, I was somehow ready to admit conditionally that the boy might be ill after all. I went towards him, he welcomed me smiling as if I were bringing him the most nourishing invalid broth—ah, now both horses were whinnying together; the noise, I suppose, was ordained by heaven to assist my examination of the patient—and this time I discovered that the boy was indeed ill. In his right side, near the hip, was an open wound as big as the palm of my hand. Rose-red, in many variations of shade, dark in the hollows, lighter at the edges, softly granulated, with irregular clots of blood, open as a surface mine to the daylight. That was how it looked from a distance. But on a closer inspection there was another complication. I could not help a low whistle of surprise. Worms, as thick and as long as my little finger, themselves rose-red and blood-spotted as well, were wriggling from their fastness in the interior of the wound towards the light, with small white heads and many little legs. Poor boy, you were past helping. I had discovered your great wound; this blossom in your side was destroying you. The family was pleased; they saw me busying myself; the sister told the mother, the mother the father, the father told several guests who were coming in, through the moonlight at the open door, walking on tiptoe, keeping their balance with outstretched arms. "Will you save me?" whispered the boy with a sob, quite blinded by the life within his wound. That is what people are like in my district. Always expecting the impossible from the doctor. They have lost their ancient beliefs; the parson sits at home and unravels his vestments, one after another; but the doctor is supposed to be omnipotent with his merciful surgeon's hand. Well, as it pleases them; I have not thrust my services on them; if they misuse me for sacred ends, I let that happen to me too; what better do I want, old country doctor that I am, bereft of my servant girl! And so they came, the family and the village elders, and stripped my clothes off me; a school choir with the teacher at the head of it stood before the house and sang these words to an utterly simple tune:

> Strip his clothes off, then he'll heal us,
> If he doesn't, kill him dead!
> Only a doctor, only a doctor.

Then my clothes were off and I looked at the people quietly, my fingers in my beard and my head cocked to one side. I was altogether composed and equal to the situation and remained so, although it was no help to me, since they now took me by the head and feet and carried me to the bed. They laid me down in it next to the wall, on the side of the wound. Then they all left the room; the door was shut; the singing stopped; clouds covered the moon; the bedding was warm around me; the horses' heads in the open windows wavered like shadows. "Do you know," said a voice in my ear, "I have very little confidence in you. Why, you were only blown in here, you didn't come on your own feet. Instead of helping me, you're cramping me on my death bed. What I'd like best is to scratch your eyes out." "Right," I said, "it is a shame. And yet I am a doctor. What am I to do? Believe me, it is not too easy for me either." "Am I supposed to be content with this apology? Oh, I must be, I can't help it. I always have to put up with things. A fine wound is all I brought into the world; that was my sole endowment." "My young friend," said I, "your mistake is: you have not a wide enough view. I have been in all the sickrooms, far and wide, and I tell you: your wound is not so bad. Done in a tight corner with two strokes of the ax. Many a one proffers his side and can hardly hear the ax in the forest, far less that it is coming nearer to him." "Is that really so, or are you deluding me in my fever?" "It is really so, take the word of an official doctor." And he took it and lay still. But now it was time for me to think of escaping. The horses were still standing faithfully in their places. My clothes, my fur coat, my bag were quickly collected; I didn't want to waste time dressing; if the horses raced home as they had come, I should only be springing, as it were, out of this bed into my own. Obediently a horse backed away from the window; I threw my bundle into the gig; the fur coat missed its mark and was caught on a hook only by the sleeve. Good enough. I swung myself on to the horse. With the reins loosely trailing, one horse barely fastened to the other, the gig swaying behind, my fur coat last of all in the snow. "Geeup!" I said, but there was no galloping; slowly, like old men, we crawled through the snowy wastes; a long time echoed behind us the new but faulty song of the children:

> O be joyful, all you patients,
> The doctor's laid in bed beside you!

Never shall I reach home at this rate; my flourishing practice is done for; my successor is robbing me, but in vain, for he cannot take my place; in my house the disgusting groom is raging; Rose is his victim; I do not want to think about it any more. Naked, exposed to the frost of this most unhappy of ages, with an earthly vehicle, unearthly horses, old man that I am, I wander astray. My fur coat is hanging from the back of the gig, but I cannot reach it, and none of my limber pack of patients lifts a finger. Betrayed! Betrayed! A false alarm on the night bell once answered—it cannot be made good, not ever.

EXERCISES

1. A typical Kafka theme is human responsibility. Discuss the responsibilities of the doctor in this story—both in his professional role as a doctor and in his personal role as a man.

2. Although this is a dreamlike story, it is also possible to think of it as an allegory in which the characters and events are representative of basic human characteristics. Consider the possible allegorical significance of the doctor, the groom, the servant girl, the boy with the wound, the doctor's inability to control the horses, the groom's desire for the girl, and the incurable nature of the wound.

3. Consider the basic themes of body versus mind, personal versus professional, old ways versus new ways, dream versus reality. What specific details communicate these themes?

4. We usually divide the world of our experience between the everyday—the known, the clear, the empirical, and the reasonable—and the mysterious—the ambiguous, the irrational, and the incredible. Discuss elements of both these realms in the story.

5. Because the story is so mysterious, readers have offered interpretations of it from many different points of view. Develop your own religious, social, and psychological interpretations of the story.

HERMAN
MELVILLE | *Bartleby*

I am a rather elderly man. The nature of my avocations, for the last thirty years, has brought me into more than ordinary contact with what would seem an interesting and somewhat singular set of men, of whom, as yet, nothing, that I know of, has ever been written—I mean, the law-copyists, or scriveners. I have known very many of them, professionally and privately, and, if I pleased, could relate divers histories, at which good-natured gentlemen might smile, and sentimental souls might weep. But I waive the biographies of all other scriveners, for a few passages in the life of Bartleby, who was a scrivener, the strangest I ever saw, or heard of. While, of other law-copyists, I might write the complete life, of Bartleby nothing of that sort can be done. I believe that no materials exist for a full and satisfactory biography of this man. It is an irreparable loss to literature. Bartleby was one of those beings of whom nothing is ascertainable, except from the original sources, and, in his case, those are very small. What my own astonished eyes saw of Bartleby, *that* is all I know of him, except, indeed, one vague report, which will appear in the sequel.

Ere introducing the scrivener, as he first appeared to me, it is fit I make some mention of myself, my *employés*, my business, my chambers, and general surroundings; because some such description is indispensable to an adequate understanding of the chief character about to be presented. Imprimis: I am a man who, from his youth upwards, has been filled with a profound conviction that the easiest way of life is the best. Hence, though I belong to a profession proverbially energetic and nervous, even to turbulence, at times, yet nothing of that sort have I ever suffered to invade my peace. I am one of those unambitious lawyers who never address a jury, or in any way draw down public applause; but, in the cool tranquillity of a snug retreat, do a snug business among rich men's bonds, and mortgages, and title-deeds. All who know me, consider me an eminently *safe* man. The late John Jacob Astor, a personage little given to poetic enthusiasm, had no hesitation in pronouncing my first grand point to be prudence; my next, method. I do not speak it in vanity, but simply record the fact, that I was not unemployed in my profession by the late John Jacob Astor; a name which, I admit, I love to repeat; for it hath a rounded and orbicular sound to it, and rings like unto bullion. I will freely add, that I was not insensible to the late John Jacob Astor's good opinion.

Some time prior to the period at which this little history begins, my avocations had been largely increased. The good old office, now extinct in the State of New York, of a Master in Chancery, had been conferred upon me. It was not a very arduous office, but very pleasantly remunerative. I seldom lose my temper; much more seldom indulge in dangerous indignation at wrongs and outrages; but I must be permitted to be rash here, and declare that I consider the sudden and violent abrogation of the office of Master in Chancery, by the new Constitution, as a ——premature act; inasmuch as I had counted upon a life-lease of the profits, whereas I only received those of a few short years. But this is by the way.

My chambers were up stairs, at No. — Wall Street. At one end, they looked upon the white wall of the interior of a spacious sky-light shaft, penetrating the building from top to bottom.

This view might have been considered rather tame than otherwise, deficient in what landscape painters call "life." But, if so, the view from the other end of my chambers offered, at least, a contrast, if nothing more. In that direction, my windows commanded an unobstructed view of a lofty brick wall, black by age and everlasting shade; which wall required no spyglass to bring out its lurking beauties, but, for the benefit of all near-sighted spectators, was pushed up to within ten feet of my window panes. Owing to the great height of the surrounding buildings, and my chambers being on the second floor, the interval between this wall and mine not a little resembled a huge square cistern.

At the period just preceding the advent of Bartleby, I had two persons as copyists in my employment, and a promising lad as an office-boy. First, Turkey; second, Nippers; third, Ginger Nut. These may seem names, the like of which are not usually found in the Directory. In truth, they were nicknames, mutually conferred upon each other by my three clerks, and were deemed expressive of their respective persons or characters. Turkey was a short, pursy Englishman, of about my own age—that is, somewhere not far from sixty. In the morning, one might say, his face was of a fine florid hue, but after twelve o'clock, meridian—his dinner hour—it blazed like a grate full of Christmas coals; and continued blazing—but, as it were, with a gradual wane—till six o'clock, P.M., or thereabouts; after which, I saw no more of the proprietor of the face, which, gaining its meridian with the sun, seemed to set with it, to rise, culminate, and decline the following day, with the like regularity and undiminished glory. There are many singular coincidences I have known in the course of my life, not the least among which was the fact, that, exactly when Turkey displayed his fullest beams from his red and radiant countenance, just then, too, at that critical moment, began the daily period when I considered his business capacities as seriously disturbed for the remainder of the twenty-four hours. Not that he was absolutely idle, or averse to business then; far from it. The difficulty was, he was apt to be altogether too energetic. There was a strange, inflamed, flurried, flighty recklessness of activity about him. He would be incautious in dipping his pen into his inkstand. All his blots upon my documents were dropped there after twelve o'clock, meridian. Indeed, not only would he be reckless, and sadly given to making blots in the afternoon, but, some days, he went further, and was rather noisy. At such times, too, his face flamed with augmented blazonry, as if cannel coal had been heaped on anthracite. He made an unpleasant racket with his chair; spilled his sand-box; in mending his pens, impatiently split them all to pieces, and threw them on the floor in a sudden passion; stood up, and leaned over his table, boxing his papers about in a most indecorous manner, very sad to behold in an elderly man like him. Nevertheless, as he was in many ways a most valuable person to me, and all the time before twelve o'clock, meridian, was the quickest, steadiest creature, too, accomplishing a great deal of work in a style not easily to be matched—for these reasons, I was willing to overlook his eccentricities, though, indeed, occasionally, I remonstrated with him. I did this very gently, however, because, though the civilest, nay, the blandest and most reverential of men in the morning, yet, in the afternoon, he was disposed, upon provocation, to be slightly rash with his tongue—in fact, insolent. Now, valuing his morning services as I did, and resolved not to lose them—yet, at the same time, made uncomfortable by his inflamed ways after twelve o'clock—and being a man of peace, unwilling by my admonitions to call forth unseemly retorts from him, I took upon me, one Saturday noon (he was always worse on Saturdays) to hint to him, very kindly, that, perhaps, now that he was growing old, it might be well to abridge his labors; in short, he need not come to my chambers after twelve o'clock, but, dinner over, had best go home to his lodgings, and rest himself till tea-time. But no; he insisted upon his afternoon devotions. His countenance became intolerably fervid, as he oratorically assured me—gesticulating with a long ruler at the other end of the room—that if his services in the morning were useful, how indispensable, then, in the afternoon?

"With submission, sir," said Turkey, on this occasion, "I consider myself your right-hand man. In the morning I but marshal and deploy my columns; but in the afternoon I put myself at their head, and gallantly charge the foe, thus"—and he made a violent thrust with the ruler.

"But the blots, Turkey," intimated I.

"True; but, with submission, sir, behold these hairs! I am getting old. Surely, sir, a blot or two of a warm afternoon is not to be severely urged against gray hairs. Old age—even if it blot the page—is honorable. With submission, sir, we *both* are getting old."

This appeal to my fellow-feeling was hardly to be resisted. At all events, I saw that go he would not. So, I made up my mind to let him stay, resolving, nevertheless, to see to it that, during the afternoon, he had to do with my less important papers.

Nippers, the second on my list, was a whiskered, sallow, and, upon the whole, rather piratical-looking young man, of about five-and-twenty. I always deemed him the victim of two evil powers—ambition and indigestion. The ambition was evinced by a certain impatience of the duties of a mere copyist, an unwarrantable usurpation of strictly professional affairs, such as the original drawing up of legal documents. The indigestion seemed betokened in an occasional nervous testiness and grinning irritability, causing the teeth to audibly grind together over mistakes committed in copying; unnecessary maledictions, hissed, rather than spoken, in the heat of business; and especially by a continual discontent with the height of the table where he worked. Though of a very ingenious, mechanical turn, Nippers could never get this table to suit him. He put chips under it, blocks of various sorts, bits of pasteboard, and at last went so far as to attempt an exquisite adjustment, by final pieces of folded blotting-paper. But no invention would answer. If, for the sake of easing his back, he brought the table lid at a sharp angle well up towards his chin, and wrote there like a man using the steep roof of a Dutch house for his desk, then he declared that it stopped the circulation in his arms. If now he lowered the table to his waistbands, and stooped over it in writing, then there was a sore aching in his back. In short, the truth of the matter was, Nippers knew not what he wanted. Or, if he wanted anything, it was to be rid of a scrivener's table altogether. Among the manifestations of his diseased ambition was a fondness he had for receiving visits from certain ambiguous-looking fellows in seedy coats, whom he called his clients. Indeed, I was aware that not only was he, at times, considerable of a ward-politician, but he occasionally did a little business at the Justices' courts, and was not unknown on the steps of the Tombs. I have good reason to believe, however, that one individual who called upon him at my chambers, and who, with a grand air, he insisted was his client, was no other than a dun, and the alleged title-deed, a bill. But, with all his failings, and the annoyances he caused me, Nippers, like his compatriot Turkey, was a very useful man to me; wrote a neat, swift hand; and, when he chose, was not deficient in a gentlemanly sort of deportment. Added to this, he always dressed in a gentlemanly sort of way; and so, incidentally, reflected credit upon my chambers. Whereas, with respect to Turkey, I had much ado to keep him from being a reproach to me. His clothes were apt to look oily, and smell of eating-houses. He wore his pantaloons very loose and baggy in summer. His coats were execrable; his hat not to be handled. But while the hat was a thing of indifference to me, inasmuch as his natural civility and deference, as a dependent Englishman, always led him to doff it the moment he entered the room, yet his coat was another matter. Concerning his coats, I reasoned with him; but with no effect. The truth was, I suppose, that a man with so small an income could not afford to sport such a lustrous face and a lustrous coat at one and the same time. As Nippers once observed, Turkey's money went chiefly for red ink. One winter day, I presented Turkey with a highly respectable-looking coat of my own—a padded gray coat, of a most comfortable warmth, and which buttoned straight up from the knee to the neck. I thought Turkey would appreciate the favor, and abate his rashness and obstreperousness of afternoons. But no; I verily believe that buttoning himself up in so downy and blanket-like a coat had a pernicious effect upon him— upon the same principle that too much oats are bad for horses. In fact, precisely as a rash, restive horse is said to feel his oats, so Turkey felt his coat. It made him insolent. He was a man whom prosperity harmed.

Though, concerning the self-indulgent habits of Turkey, I had my own private surmises, yet, touching Nippers, I was well persuaded that, whatever might be his faults in other respects, he was, at least, a temperate young man. But, indeed, nature herself seemed to have been his vintner, and, at his birth, charged him so thoroughly with an irritable, brandy-like disposition, that all subsequent potations were needless. When I consider how, amid the stillness of my chambers, Nippers would sometimes impatiently rise from his seat, and stooping over his table, spread his arms wide apart, seize the whole desk, and move it, and jerk it, with a grim, grinding motion on the floor, as if the table were a perverse voluntary agent, intent on thwarting and vexing him, I plainly perceive that, for Nippers, brandy-and-water were altogether superfluous.

It was fortunate for me that, owing to its peculiar cause—indigestion— the irritability and consequent nervousness of Nippers were mainly observable in the morning, while in the afternoon he was comparatively mild. So that, Turkey's paroxysms only coming on about twelve o'clock, I never had to do with their eccentricities at one time. Their fits relieved each other, like guards. When Nippers's was on, Turkey's was off; and *vice versa*. This was a good natural arrangement, under the circumstances.

Ginger Nut, the third on my list, was a lad, some twelve years old. His father was a car-man, ambitious of seeing his son on the bench instead of a cart, before he died. So he sent him to my office, as student at law, errand-boy, cleaner and sweeper, at the rate of one dollar a week. He had a little desk to himself, but he did not use it much. Upon inspection, the drawer exhibited a great array of shells of various sorts of nuts. Indeed, to this quick-witted youth, the whole noble science of the law was contained in a nutshell. Not the least among the employments of Ginger Nut, as well as one which he discharged with the most alacrity, was his duty as cake and apple purveyor for Turkey and Nippers. Copying law-papers being proverbially a dry, husky sort of business, my two scriveners were fain to moisten their mouths very often with Spitzenbergs, to be had at the numerous stalls nigh the Custom House and Post Office. Also, they sent Ginger Nut very frequently for that peculiar cake—small, flat, round, and very spicy—after which he had been named by them. Of a cold morning, when business was but dull, Turkey would gobble up scores of these cakes, as if they were mere wafers—indeed, they sell them at the rate of six or eight for a penny—the scrape of his pen blending with the crunching of the crisp particles in his mouth. Rashest of all the fiery afternoon blunders and flurried rashnesses of Turkey, was his once moistening a ginger-cake between his lips, and clapping it on to a mortgage, for a seal. I came within an ace of dismissing him then. But he mollified me by making an oriental bow, and saying—

"With submission, sir, it was generous of me to find you in stationery on my own account."

Now my original business—that of a conveyancer and title hunter, and drawer-up of recondite documents of all sorts—was considerably increased by receiving the Master's office. There was now great work for scriveners. Not only must I push the clerks already with me, but I must have additional help.

In answer to my advertisement, a motionless young man one morning stood upon my office threshold, the door being open, for it was summer. I can see that figure now—pallidly neat, pitiably respectable, incurably forlorn! It was Bartleby.

After a few words touching his qualifications, I engaged him, glad to have among my corps of copyists a man of so singularly sedate an aspect, which I thought might operate beneficially upon the flighty temper of Turkey, and the fiery one of Nippers.

I should have stated before that ground glass folding-doors divided my premises into two parts, one of which was occupied by my scriveners, the other by myself. According to my humor, I threw open these doors, or closed them. I resolved to assign Bartleby a corner by the folding-doors, but on my side of them, so as to have this quiet man within easy call, in case any trifling thing was to be done. I placed his desk close up to a small side-window in that part of the room, a window which originally had afforded a lateral view of certain grimy backyards and bricks, but which, owing to subsequent erections, commanded at present no view at all, though it gave some light. Within three feet of the panes was a wall, and the light came down from far above, between two lofty buildings, as from a very small opening in a dome. Still further to a satisfactory arrangement, I procured a high green folding screen, which might entirely isolate Bartleby from my sight, though not remove him from my voice. And thus, in a manner, privacy and society were conjoined.

At first, Bartleby did an extraordinary quantity of writing. As if long famishing for something to copy, he seemed to gorge himself on my documents. There was no pause for digestion. He ran a day and night line, copying by sun-light and by candle-light. I should have been quite delighted with his application, had he been cheerfully industrious. But he wrote on silently, palely, mechanically.

It is, of course, an indispensable part of a scrivener's business to verify the accuracy of his copy, word by word. Where there are two or more scriveners in an office, they assist each other in this examination, one reading from the copy, the other holding the original. It is a very dull, wearisome, and lethargic affair. I can readily imagine that, to some sanguine temperaments, it would be altogether intolerable. For example, I cannot credit that the mettlesome poet, Byron, would have contentedly sat down with Bartleby to examine a law document of, say five hundred pages, closely written in a crimpy hand.

Now and then, in the haste of business, it had been my habit to assist in comparing some brief document myself, calling Turkey or Nippers for this purpose. One object I had, in placing Bartleby so handy to me behind the screen, was to avail myself of his services on such trivial occasions. It was on the third day, I think, of his being with me, and before any necessity had arisen for having his own writing examined, that, being much hurried to complete a small affair I had in hand, I abruptly called to Bartleby. In my haste and natural expectancy of instant compliance, I sat with my head bent over the original on my desk, and my right hand sideways, and somewhat nervously extended with the copy, so that, immediately upon emerging from his retreat, Bartleby might snatch it and proceed to business without the least delay.

In this very attitude did I sit when I called to him, rapidly stating what it was I wanted him to do—namely, to examine a small paper with me. Imagine my surprise, nay, my consternation, when, without moving from his privacy, Bartleby, in a singularly mild, firm voice, replied, "I would prefer not to."

I sat awhile in perfect silence, rallying my stunned faculties. Immediately it occurred to me that my ears had deceived me, or Bartleby had entirely misunderstood my meaning. I repeated my request in the clearest tone I could assume; but in quite as clear a one came the previous reply, "I would prefer not to."

"Prefer not to," echoed I, rising in high excitement, and crossing the room with a stride. "What do you mean? Are you moonstruck? I want you to help me compare this sheet here—take it," and I thrust it towards him.

"I would prefer not to," said he.

I looked at him steadfastly. His face was leanly composed; his gray eye dimly calm. Not a wrinkle of agitation rippled him. Had there been the least uneasiness, anger, impatience, or impertinence in his manner; in other words, had there been any thing ordinarily human about him, doubtless I should have violently dismissed him from the premises. But as it was, I should have as soon thought of turning my pale plaster-of-paris bust of Cicero out of doors. I stood gazing at him awhile, as he went on with his own writing, and then reseated myself at my desk. This is very strange, thought I. What had one best do? But my business hurried me. I concluded to forget the matter for the present, reserving it for my future leisure. So, calling Nippers from the other room, the paper was speedily examined.

A few days after this, Bartleby concluded four lengthy documents, being quadruplicates of a week's testimony taken before me in my High Court of Chancery. It became necessary to examine them. It was an important suit, and great accuracy was imperative. Having all things arranged, I called Turkey, Nippers, and Ginger Nut from the next room, meaning to place the four copies in the hands of my four clerks, while I should read from the original. Accordingly, Turkey, Nippers, and Ginger Nut had taken their seats in a row, each with his document in his hand, when I called to Bartleby to join this interesting group.

"Bartleby! quick, I am waiting."

I heard a slow scrape of his chair legs on the uncarpeted floor, and soon he appeared standing at the entrance of his hermitage.

"What is wanted?" said he, mildly.

"The copies, the copies," said I, hurriedly. "We are going to examine them. There—" and I held towards him the fourth quadruplicate.

"I would prefer not to," he said, and gently disappeared behind the screen.

For a few moments I was turned into a pillar of salt, standing at the head of my seated column of clerks. Recovering myself, I advanced towards the screen, and demanded the reason for such extraordinary conduct.

"*Why* do you refuse?"

"I would prefer not to."

With any other man I should have flown outright into a dreadful passion, scorned all further words, and thrust him ignominiously from my presence. But there was something about Bartleby that not only strangely disarmed me, but, in a wonderful manner, touched and disconcerted me. I began to reason with him.

"These are your own copies we are about to examine. It is labor saving to you, because one examination will answer for your four papers. It is common usage. Every copyist is bound to help examine his copy. Is it not so? Will you not speak? Answer!"

"I prefer not to," he replied in a flutelike tone. It seemed to me that, while I had been addressing him, he carefully revolved every statement that I made; fully comprehended the meaning; could not gainsay the irresistible conclusion; but, at the same time, some paramount consideration prevailed with him to reply as he did.

"You are decided, then, not to comply with my request—a request made according to common usage and common sense?"

He briefly gave me to understand, that on that point my judgment was sound. Yes: his decision was irreversible.

It is not seldom the case that, when a man is browbeaten in some unprecedented and violently unreasonable way, he begins to stagger in his own plainest faith. He begins, as it were, vaguely to surmise that, wonderful as it may be, all the justice and all the reason is on the other side. Accordingly, if any disinterested persons are present, he turns to them for some reinforcement for his own faltering mind.

"Turkey," said I, "what do you think of this? Am I not right?"

"With submission, sir," said Turkey, in his blandest tone, "I think that you are."

"Nippers," said I, "what do *you* think of it?"

"I think I should kick him out of the office."

(The reader of nice perceptions will here perceive that, it being morning, Turkey's answer is couched in polite and tranquil terms, but Nippers replies in ill-tempered ones. Or, to repeat a previous sentence, Nippers's ugly mood was on duty, and Turkey's off.)

"Ginger Nut," said I, willing to enlist the smallest suffrage in my behalf, "what do *you* think of it?"

"I think, sir, he's a little *luny*," replied Ginger Nut, with a grin.

"You hear what they say," said I, turning towards the screen, "come forth and do your duty."

But he vouchsafed no reply. I pondered a moment in sore perplexity. But once more business hurried me. I determined again to postpone the consideration of this dilemma to my future leisure. With a little trouble we made out to examine the papers without Bartleby, though at every page or two Turkey deferentially dropped his opinion, that this proceeding was quite out of the common; while Nippers, twitching in his chair with a dyspeptic nervousness, ground out, between his set teeth, occasional hissing maledictions against the stubborn oaf behind the screen. And for his (Nippers's) part, this was the first and the last time he would do another man's business without pay.

Meanwhile Bartleby sat in his hermitage, oblivious to everything but his own peculiar business there.

Some days passed, the scrivener being employed upon another lengthy work. His late remarkable conduct led me to regard his ways narrowly. I observed that he never went to dinner; indeed, that he never went anywhere. As yet I had never, of my personal knowledge, known him to be outside of my office. He was a perpetual sentry in the corner. At about eleven o'clock though, in the morning, I noticed that Ginger Nut would advance toward the opening in Bartleby's screen, as if silently beckoned thither by a gesture invisible to me where I sat. The boy would then leave the office, jingling a few pence, and reappear with a handful of ginger-nuts, which he delivered in the hermitage, receiving two of the cakes for his trouble.

He lives, then, on ginger-nuts, thought I; never eats a dinner, properly speaking; he must be a vegetarian, then; but no; he never eats even vegetables; he eats nothing but ginger-nuts. My mind then ran on in reveries concerning the probable effects upon the human constitution of living entirely on ginger-nuts. Ginger-nuts are so called, because they contain ginger as one of their peculiar constituents, and the final flavoring one. Now, what was ginger? A hot, spicy thing. Was Bartleby hot and spicy? Not at all. Ginger, then, had no effect upon Bartleby. Probably he preferred it should have none.

Nothing so aggravates an earnest person as a passive resistance. If the individual so resisted be of a not inhumane temper, and the resisting one perfectly harmless in his passivity, then, in the better moods of the former, he will endeavor charitably to construe to his imagination what proves impossible to be solved by his judgment. Even so, for the most part, I regarded Bartleby and his ways. Poor fellow! thought I, he means no mischief; it is plain he intends no insolence; his aspect sufficiently evinces that his eccentricities are involuntary. He is useful to me. I can get along with him. If I turn him away, the chances are he will fall in with some less-indulgent employer, and then he will be rudely treated, and perhaps driven forth miserably to starve. Yes. Here I can cheaply purchase a delicious self-approval. To befriend Bartleby; to humor him in his strange willfulness, will cost me little or nothing, while I lay up in my soul what will eventually prove a sweet morsel for my conscience. But this mood was not invariable with me. The passiveness of Bartleby sometimes irritated me. I felt strangely goaded on to encounter him in new opposition—to elicit some angry spark from him answerable to my own. But, indeed, I might as well have essayed to strike fire with my knuckles against a bit of Windsor soap. But one afternoon the evil impulse in me mastered me, and the following little scene ensued:

"Bartleby," said I, "when those papers are all copied, I will compare them with you."

"I would prefer not to."

"How? Surely you do not mean to persist in that mulish vagary?"

No answer.

I threw open the folding-doors near by, and, turning upon Turkey and Nippers, exclaimed:

"Bartleby a second time says, he won't examine his papers. What do you think of it, Turkey?"

It was afternoon, be it remembered. Turkey sat glowing like a brass boiler; his bald head steaming; his hands reeling among his blotted papers.

"Think of it?" roared Turkey; "I think I'll just step behind his screen, and black his eyes for him!"

So saying, Turkey rose to his feet and threw his arms into a pugilistic position. He was hurrying away to make good his promise, when I detained him, alarmed at the effect of incautiously rousing Turkey's combativeness after dinner.

"Sit down, Turkey," said I, "and hear what Nippers has to say. What do you think of it, Nippers? Would I not be justified in immediately dismissing Bartleby?"

"Excuse me, that is for you to decide, sir. I think his conduct quite unusual, and, indeed, unjust, as regards Turkey and myself. But it may only be a passing whim."

"Ah," exclaimed I, "you have strangely changed your mind, then—you speak very gently of him now."

"All beer," cried Turkey; "gentleness is effects of beer—Nippers and I dined together to-day. You see how gentle *I* am, sir. Shall I go and black his eyes?"

"You refer to Bartleby, I suppose. No, not to-day, Turkey," I replied; "pray, put up your fists."

I closed the doors, and again advanced towards Bartleby. I felt additional incentives tempting me to my fate. I burned to be rebelled against again. I remembered that Bartleby never left the office.

"Bartleby," said I, "Ginger Nut is away; just step around to the Post Office, won't you?" (it was but a three minutes' walk), "and see if there is anything for me."

"I would prefer not to."

"You *will* not?"

"I *prefer* not."

I staggered to my desk, and sat there in deep study. My blind inveteracy returned. Was there any other thing in which I could procure myself to be ignominiously repulsed by this lean, penniless wight?—my hired clerk? What added thing is there, perfectly reasonable, that he will be sure to refuse to do?

"Bartleby!"

No answer.

"Bartleby," in a louder tone.

No answer.

"Bartleby," I roared.

Like a very ghost, agreeably to the laws of magical invocation, at the third summons, he appeared at the entrance of his hermitage.

"Go to the next room, and tell Nippers to come to me."

"I prefer not to," he respectfully and slowly said, and mildly disappeared.

"Very good, Bartleby," said I, in a quiet sort of serenely-severe, self-possessed tone, intimating the unalterable purpose of some terrible retribution very close at hand. At the moment I half intended something of the kind. But upon the whole, as it was drawing towards my dinner-hour, I thought it best to put on my hat and walk home for the day, suffering much from perplexity and distress of mind.

Shall I acknowledge it? The conclusion of this whole business was, that it soon became a fixed fact of my chambers, that a pale young scrivener, by the name of Bartleby, had a desk there; that he copied for me at the usual rate of four cents a folio (one hundred words); but he was permanently exempt from examining the work done by him, that duty being transferred to Turkey and Nippers, out of compliment, doubtless, to their superior acuteness; moreover, said Bartleby was never, on any account, to be dispatched on the most trivial errand of any sort; and that even if entreated to take upon him such a matter, it was generally understood that he would "prefer not to"—in other words, that he would refuse point-blank.

As days passed on, I became considerably reconciled to Bartleby. His steadiness, his freedom from all dissipation, his incessant industry (except when he chose to throw himself into a standing revery behind his screen), his great stillness, his unalterableness of demeanor under all circumstances, made him a valuable acquisition. One prime thing was this—*he was always there*— first in the morning, continually through the day, and the last at night. I had a singular confidence in his honesty. I felt my most precious papers perfectly safe in his hands. Sometimes, to be sure, I could not, for the very soul of me, avoid falling into sudden spasmodic passions with him. For it was exceeding difficult to bear in mind all the time those strange peculiarities, privileges, and unheard-of exemptions, forming the tacit stipulations on Bartleby's part under which he remained in my office. Now and then, in the eagerness of dispatching pressing business, I would inadvertently summon Bartleby, in a short, rapid tone, to put his finger, say, on the incipient tie of a bit of red tape with which I was about compressing some papers. Of course, from behind the screen the usual answer, "I prefer not to," was sure to come; and then, how could a human creature, with the common infirmities of our nature, refrain from bitterly exclaiming upon such perverseness—such unreasonableness? However, every added repulse of this sort which I received only tended to lessen the probability of my repeating the inadvertence.

Here it must be said, that according to the custom of most legal gentlemen occupying chambers in densely-populated law buildings, there were several keys to my door. One was kept by a woman residing in the attic, which person weekly scrubbed and daily swept and dusted my apartments. Another was kept by Turkey for convenience sake. The third I sometimes carried in my own pocket. The fourth I knew not who had.

Now, one Sunday morning I happened to go to Trinity Church, to hear a celebrated preacher, and finding myself rather early on the ground I thought

I would walk round to my chambers for a while. Luckily I had my key with me; but upon applying it to the lock, I found it resisted by something inserted from the inside. Quite surprised, I called out; when to my consternation a key was turned from within; and thrusting his lean visage at me, and holding the door ajar, the apparition of Bartleby appeared, in his shirt sleeves, and otherwise in a strangely tattered *déshabillé*, saying quietly that he was sorry, but he was deeply engaged just then, and—preferred not admitting me at present. In a brief word or two, he moreover added, that perhaps I had better walk round the block two or three times, and by that time he would probably have concluded his affairs.

Now, the utterly unsurmised appearance of Bartleby, tenanting my law-chambers of a Sunday morning, with his cadaverously gentlemanly *nonchalance*, yet withal firm and self-possessed, had such a strange effect upon me, that incontinently I slunk away from my own door, and did as desired. But not without sundry twinges of impotent rebellion against the mild effrontery of this unaccountable scrivener. Indeed, it was his wonderful mildness chiefly, which not only disarmed me, but unmanned me, as it were. For I consider that one, for the time, is somehow unmanned when he tranquilly permits his hired clerk to dictate to him, and order him away from his own premises. Furthermore, I was full of uneasiness as to what Bartleby could possibly be doing in my office in his shirt sleeves, and in an otherwise dismantled condition of a Sunday morning. Was anything amiss going on? Nay, that was out of the question. It was not to be thought of for a moment that Bartleby was an immoral person. But what could he be doing there?—copying? Nay again, whatever might be his eccentricities, Bartleby was an eminently decorous person. He would be the last man to sit down to his desk in any state approaching to nudity. Besides, it was Sunday; and there was something about Bartleby that forbade the supposition that he would by any secular occupation violate the proprieties of the day.

Nevertheless, my mind was not pacified; and full of a restless curiosity, at last I returned to the door. Without hindrance I inserted my key, opened it, and entered. Bartleby was not to be seen. I looked round anxiously, peeped behind his screen; but it was very plain that he was gone. Upon more closely examining the place, I surmised that for an indefinite period Bartleby must have eaten, dressed, and slept in my office, and that, too, without plate, mirror, or bed. The cushioned seat of a ricketty old sofa in one corner bore the faint impress of a lean, reclining form. Rolled away under his desk, I found a blanket; under the empty grate, a blacking box and brush; on a chair, a tin basin, with soap and a ragged towel; in a newspaper a few crumbs of ginger-nuts and a morsel of cheese. Yes, thought I, it is evident that Bartleby has been making his home here, keeping bachelor's hall by himself. Immediately then the thought came sweeping across me, what miserable friendlessness and loneliness are here revealed! His poverty is great; but his solitude, how horrible! Think of it. Of a Sunday, Wall Street is deserted as Petra; and every night of every day it is an emptiness. This building, too, which of weekdays hums with industry and life, at nightfall echoes with sheer vacancy, and all through Sunday is forlorn. And here Bartleby makes his home; sole spectator of a solitude which he has seen all populous—a sort of innocent and transformed Marius brooding among the ruins of Carthage!

For the first time in my life a feeling of overpowering stinging melancholy seized me. Before, I had never experienced aught but a not unpleasing sadness. The bond of a common humanity now drew me irresistibly to gloom. A fraternal melancholy! For both I and Bartleby were sons of Adam. I remembered the bright silks and sparkling faces I had seen that day, in gala trim, swan-like sailing down the Mississippi of Broadway; and I contrasted them with the pallid copyist, and thought to myself, Ah, happiness courts the light, so we deem the world is gay; but misery hides aloof, so we deem that misery there is none. These sad fancyings—chimeras, doubtless, of a sick and silly brain—led on to other and more special thoughts, concerning the eccentricities of Bartleby. Presentiments of strange discoveries hovered round me. The scrivener's pale form appeared to me laid out, among uncaring strangers, in its shivering winding sheet.

Suddenly I was attracted by Bartleby's closed desk, the key in open sight left in the lock.

I mean no mischief, seek the gratification of no heartless curiosity, thought I; besides, the desk is mine, and its contents, too, so I will make bold to look within. Everything was methodically arranged, the papers smoothly placed. The pigeon holes were deep, and removing the files of documents, I groped into their recesses. Presently I felt something there, and dragged it out. It was an old bandanna handkerchief, heavy and knotted. I opened it, and saw it was a savings' bank.

I now recalled all the quiet mysteries which I had noted in the man. I remembered that he never spoke but to answer; that, though at intervals he had considerable time to himself, yet I had never seen him reading—no, not even a newspaper; that for long periods he would stand looking out, at his pale window behind the screen, upon the dead brick wall; I was quite sure he never visited any refectory or eating house; while his pale face clearly indicated that he never drank beer like Turkey, or tea and coffee even, like other men; that he never went anywhere in particular that I could learn; never went out for a walk, unless, indeed, that was the case at present; that he had declined telling who he was, or whence he came, or whether he had any relatives in the world; that though so thin and pale, he never complained of ill health. And more than all, I remembered a certain unconscious air of pallid—how shall I call it?—of pallid haughtiness, say, or rather an austere reserve about him, which had positively awed me into my tame compliance with his eccentricities, when I had feared to ask him to do the slightest incidental thing for me, even though I might know, from his long-continued motionlessness, that behind his screen he must be standing in one of those dead-wall reveries of his.

Revolving all these things, and coupling them with the recently discovered fact, that he made my office his constant abiding place and home, and not forgetful of his morbid moodiness; revolving all these things, a prudential feeling began to steal over me. My first emotions had been those of pure melancholy and sincerest pity; but just in proportion as the forlornness of Bartleby grew and grew to my imagination, did that same melancholy merge into fear, that pity into repulsion. So true it is, and so terrible, too, that up to a certain point the thought or sight of misery enlists our best affections; but, in certain special cases, beyond that point it does not. They err who would assert that invariably this is owing to the inherent selfishness of the human heart. It rather proceeds from a certain hopelessness of remedying excessive and organic ill. To a sensitive being, pity is not seldom pain. And when at last it is perceived that such pity cannot lead to effectual succor, common sense bids the soul be rid of it. What I saw that morning persuaded me that the scrivener was the victim of innate and incurable disorder. I might give alms to his body; but his body did not pain him; it was his soul that suffered, and his soul I could not reach.

I did not accomplish the purpose of going to Trinity Church that morning. Somehow, the things I had seen disqualified me for the time from churchgoing. I walked homeward, thinking what I would do with Bartleby. Finally, I resolved upon this—I would put certain calm questions to him the next morning, touching his history, etc., and if he declined to answer them openly and unreservedly (and I supposed he would prefer not), then to give him a twenty dollar bill over and above whatever I might owe him, and tell him his services were no longer required; but that if in any other way I could assist him, I would be happy to do so, especially if he desired to return to his native place, wherever that might be, I would willingly help to defray the expenses. Moreover, if, after reaching home, he found himself at any time in want of aid, a letter from him would be sure of a reply.

The next morning came.

"Bartleby," said I, gently calling to him behind his screen.

No reply.

"Bartleby," said I, in a still gentler tone, "come here; I am not going to ask you to do anything you would prefer not to do—I simply wish to speak to you."

Upon this he noiselessly slid into view.

"Will you tell me, Bartleby, where you were born?"

"I would prefer not to."

"Will you tell me *anything* about yourself?"

"I would prefer not to."

"But what reasonable objection can you have to speak to me? I feel friendly towards you."

He did not look at me while I spoke, but kept his glance fixed upon my bust of Cicero, which, as I then sat, was directly behind me, some six inches above my head.

"What is your answer, Bartleby?" said I, after waiting a considerable time for a reply, during which his countenance remained immovable, only there was the faintest conceivable tremor of the white attenuated mouth.

"At present I prefer to give no answer," he said, and retired into his hermitage.

It was rather weak in me I confess, but his manner, on this occasion, nettled me. Not only did there seem to lurk in it a certain calm disdain, but his perverseness seemed ungrateful, considering the undeniable good usage and indulgence he had received from me.

Again I sat ruminating what I should do. Mortified as I was at his behavior, and resolved as I had been to dismiss him when I entered my office, nevertheless I strangely felt something superstitious knocking at my heart, and forbidding me to carry out my purpose, and denouncing me for a villain if I dared to breathe one bitter word against this forlornest of mankind. At last, familiarly drawing my chair behind his screen, I sat down and said: "Bartleby, never mind, then, about revealing your history; but let me entreat you, as a friend, to comply as far as may be with the usages of this office. Say now, you will help to examine papers to-morrow or next day: in short, say now, that in a day or two you will begin to be a little reasonable:—say so, Bartleby."

"At present I would prefer not to be a little reasonable," was his mildly cadaverous reply.

Just then the folding-doors opened, and Nippers approached. He seemed suffering from an unusually bad night's rest, induced by severer indigestion than common. He overheard those final words of Bartleby.

"*Prefer not*, eh?" gritted Nippers—"I'd *prefer* him, if I were you, sir," addressing me—"I'd *prefer* him; I'd give him preferences, the stubborn mule! What is it, sir, pray, that he *prefers* not to do now?"

Bartleby moved not a limb.

"Mr. Nippers," said I, "I'd prefer that you would withdraw for the present."

Somehow, of late, I had got into the way of involuntarily using this word "prefer" upon all sorts of not exactly suitable occasions. And I trembled to think that my contact with the scrivener had already and seriously affected me in a mental way. And what further and deeper aberration might it not yet produce? This apprehension had not been without efficacy in determining me to summary measures.

As Nippers, looking very sour and sulky, was departing, Turkey blandly and deferentially approached.

"With submission, sir," said he, "yesterday I was thinking about Bartleby here, and I think that if he would but prefer to take a quart of good ale every day, it would do much towards mending him, and enabling him to assist in examining his papers."

"So you have got the word, too," said I, slightly excited.

"With submission, what word, sir?" asked Turkey, respectfully crowding himself into the contracted space behind the screen, and by so doing, making me jostle the scrivener. "What word, sir?"

"I would prefer to be left alone here," said Bartleby, as if offended at being mobbed in his privacy.

"*That's* the word, Turkey," said I—"*that's* it."

"Oh, *prefer?* oh yes—queer word. I never use it myself. But, sir, as I was saying, if he would but prefer—"

"Turkey," interrupted I, "you will please withdraw."

"Oh certainly, sir, if you prefer that I should."

As he opened the folding-door to retire, Nippers at his desk caught a glimpse of me, and asked whether I would prefer to have a certain paper copied on blue paper or white. He did not in the least roguishly accent the word "prefer." It was plain that it involuntarily rolled from his tongue. I thought to myself, surely I must get rid of a demented man, who already has in some degree turned the tongues, if not the heads of myself and clerks. But I thought it prudent not to break the dismission at once.

The next day I noticed that Bartleby did nothing but stand at his window in his dead-wall revery. Upon asking him why he did not write, he said that he had decided upon doing no more writing.

"Why, how now? what next?" exclaimed I, "do no more writing?"

"No more."

"And what is the reason?"

"Do you not see the reason for yourself?" he indifferently replied.

I looked steadfastly at him, and perceived that his eyes looked dull and glazed. Instantly it occurred to me, that his unexampled diligence in copying by his dim window for the first few weeks of his stay with me might have temporarily impaired his vision.

I was touched. I said something in condolence with him. I hinted that of course he did wisely in abstaining from writing for a while; and urged him to embrace that opportunity of taking wholesome exercise in the open air. This, however, he did not do. A few days after this, my other clerks being absent, and being in a great hurry to dispatch certain letters by the mail, I thought that, having nothing else earthly to do, Bartleby would surely be less inflexible than usual, and carry these letters to the post-office. But he blankly declined. So, much to my inconvenience, I went myself.

Still added days went by. Whether Bartleby's eyes improved or not, I could not say. To all appearance, I thought they did. But when I asked him if they did, he vouchsafed no answer. At all events, he would do no copying. At last, in reply to my urgings, he informed me that he had permanently given up copying.

"What!" exclaimed I; "suppose your eyes should get entirely well—better than ever before—would you not copy then?"

"I have given up copying," he answered, and slid aside.

He remained as ever, a fixture in my chamber. Nay—if that were possible—he became still more of a fixture than before. What was to be done? He would do nothing in the office; why should he stay there? In plain fact, he had now become a millstone to me, not only useless as a necklace, but afflictive to bear. Yet I was sorry for him. I speak less than truth when I say that, on his own account, he occasioned me uneasiness. If he would but have named a single relative or friend, I would instantly have written, and urged their taking the poor fellow away to some convenient retreat. But he seemed alone, absolutely alone in the universe. A bit of wreck in the mid Atlantic. At length, necessities connected with my business tyrannized over all other considerations. Decently as I could, I told Bartleby that in six days' time he must unconditionally leave the office. I warned him to take measures, in the interval, for procuring some other abode. I offered to assist him in this endeavor, if he himself would but take the first step towards a removal. "And when you finally quit me, Bartleby," added I, "I shall see that you go not away entirely unprovided. Six days from this hour, remember."

At the expiration of that period, I peeped behind the screen, and lo! Bartleby was there.

I buttoned up my coat, balanced myself; advanced slowly towards him, touched his shoulder, and said, "The time has come; you must quit this place; I am sorry for you; here is money; but you must go."

"I would prefer not," he replied, with his back still towards me.

"You *must*."

He remained silent.

Now I had an unbounded confidence in this man's common honesty. He had frequently restored to me sixpences and shillings carelessly dropped upon the floor, for I am apt to be very reckless in such shirt-button affairs. The proceeding, then, which followed will not be deemed extraordinary.

"Bartleby," said I, "I owe you twelve dollars on account; here are thirty-two; the odd twenty are yours—Will you take it?" and I handed the bills towards him.

But he made no motion.

"I will leave them here, then," putting them under a weight on the table. Then taking my hat and cane and going to the door, I tranquilly turned and added—"After you have removed your things from these offices, Bartleby, you will of course lock the door—since every one is now gone for the day but you—and if you please, slip your key underneath the mat, so that I may have it in the morning. I shall not see you again; so good-by to you. If, hereafter, in your new place of abode, I can be of any service to you, do not fail to advise me by letter. Good-by, Bartleby, and fare you well."

But he answered not a word; like the last column of some ruined temple, he remained standing mute and solitary in the middle of the otherwise deserted room.

As I walked home in a pensive mood, my vanity got the better of my pity. I could not but highly plume myself on my masterly management in getting rid of Bartleby. Masterly I call it, and such it must appear to any dispassionate thinker. The beauty of my procedure seemed to consist in its perfect quietness. There was no vulgar bullying, no bravado of any sort, no choleric hectoring, and striding to and fro across the apartment, jerking out vehement commands for Bartleby to bundle himself off with his beggarly traps. Nothing of the kind. Without loudly bidding Bartleby depart—as an inferior genius might have done—I *assumed* the ground that depart he must; and upon that assumption built all I had to say. The more I thought over my procedure, the more I was charmed with it. Nevertheless, next morning, upon awakening, I had my doubts—I had somehow slept off the fumes of vanity. One of the coolest and wisest hours a man has, is just after he awakes in the morning. My procedure seemed as sagacious as ever—but only in theory. How it would prove in practice—there was the rub. It was truly a beautiful thought to have assumed Bartleby's departure; but, after all, that assumption was simply my own, and none of Bartleby's. The great point was, not whether I had assumed that he would quit me, but whether he would prefer so to do. He was more a man of preferences than assumptions.

After breakfast, I walked down town, arguing the probabilities *pro* and *con*. One moment I thought it would prove a miserable failure, and Bartleby would be found all alive at my office as usual; the next moment it seemed certain that I should find his chair empty. And so I kept veering about. At the corner of Broadway and Canal Street, I saw quite an excited group of people standing in earnest conversation.

"I'll take odds he doesn't," said a voice as I passed.

"Doesn't go?—done!" said I; "put up your money."

I was instinctively putting my hand in my pocket to produce my own, when I remembered that this was an election day. The words I had overheard bore no reference to Bartleby, but to the success or non-success of some candidate for the mayoralty. In my intent frame of mind, I had, as it were, imagined that all Broadway shared in my excitement, and were debating the same question with me. I passed on, very thankful that the uproar of the street screened my momentary absent-mindedness.

As I had intended, I was earlier than usual at my office door. I stood listening for a moment. All was still. He must be gone. I tried the knob. The door was locked. Yes, my procedure had worked to a charm; he indeed must be vanished. Yet a certain melancholy mixed with this; I was almost sorry for my brilliant success. I was fumbling under the door mat for the key, which Bartleby was to have left there for me, when accidentally my knee knocked against a panel, producing a summoning sound, and in response a voice came to me from within—"Not yet; I am occupied."

It was Bartleby.

I was thunderstruck. For an instant I stood like the man who, pipe in mouth, was killed one cloudless afternoon long ago in Virginia, by summer lightning; at his own warm open window he was killed, and remained leaning out there upon the dreamy afternoon, till some one touched him, when he fell.

"Not gone!" I murmured at last. But again obeying that wondrous ascendancy which the inscrutable scrivener had over me, and from which ascendancy, for all my chafing, I could not completely escape, I slowly went down stairs and out into the street, and while walking round the block, considered what I should next do in this unheard-of perplexity. Turn the man out by an actual thrusting I could not; to drive him away by calling him hard names would not do; calling in the police was an unpleasant idea; and yet, permit him to enjoy his cadaverous triumph over me—this, too, I could not think of. What was to be done? or, if nothing could be done, was there anything further that I could *assume* in the matter? Yes, as before I had prospectively assumed that Bartleby would depart, so now I might retrospectively assume that departed he was. In the legitimate carrying out of this assumption, I might enter my office in a great hurry, and pretending not to see Bartleby at all, walk straight against him as if he were air. Such a proceeding would in a singular degree have the appearance of a home-thrust. It was hardly possible that Bartleby could withstand such an application of the doctrine of assumptions. But upon second thoughts the success of the plan seemed rather dubious. I resolved to argue the matter over with him again.

"Bartleby," said I, entering the office, with a quietly severe expression, "I am seriously displeased. I am pained, Bartleby. I had thought better of you. I had imagined you of such a gentlemanly organization, that in any delicate dilemma a slight hint would suffice—in short, an assumption. But it appears I am deceived. Why," I added unaffectedly starting, "you have not even touched that money yet," pointing to it, just where I had left it the evening previous.

He answered nothing.

"Will you, or will you not, quit me?" I now demanded in a sudden passion, advancing close to him.

"I would prefer *not* to quit you," he replied, gently emphasizing the *not*.

"What earthly right have you to stay here? Do you pay any rent? Do you pay my taxes? Or is this property yours?"

He answered nothing.

"Are you ready to go on and write now? Are your eyes recovered? Could you copy a small paper for me this morning? or help examine a few lines? or step round to the post-office? In a word, will you do anything at all, to give a coloring to your refusal to depart the premises?"

He silently retired into his hermitage.

I was now in such a state of nervous resentment that I thought it but prudent to check myself at present from further demonstrations. Bartleby and I were alone. I remembered the tragedy of the unfortunate Adams and the still more unfortunate Colt in the solitary office of the latter; and how poor Colt, being dreadfully incensed by Adams, and imprudently permitting himself to get wildly excited, was at unawares hurried into his fatal act—an act which certainly no man could possibly deplore more than the actor himself. Often it had occurred to me in my ponderings upon the subject that had that altercation taken place in the public street, or at a private residence, it would not have terminated as it did. It was the circumstance of being alone in a solitary office, up stairs, of a building entirely unhallowed by humanizing domestic associations—an uncarpeted office, doubtless, of a dusty, haggard sort of appearance—this it must have been, which greatly helped to enhance the irritable desperation of the hapless Colt.

But when this old Adam of resentment rose in me and tempted me concerning Bartleby, I grappled him and threw him. How? Why, simply by recalling the divine injunction: "A new commandment give I unto you, that ye love one another." Yes, this it was that saved me. Aside from higher considerations, charity often operates as a vastly wise and prudent principle—a great safeguard to its possessor. Men have committed murder for jealousy's sake, and anger's sake, and hatred's sake, and selfishness' sake, and spiritual pride's sake; but no man, that ever I heard of, ever committed a diabolical murder for sweet charity's sake. Mere self-interest, then, if no better motive can be enlisted, should, especially with high-tempered men, prompt all beings to charity and philanthropy. At any rate, upon the occasion in question, I strove to drown my exasperated feelings towards the scrivener by benevolently construing his conduct. Poor fellow, poor fellow! thought I, he don't mean anything; and besides, he has seen hard times, and ought to be indulged.

I endeavored, also, immediately to occupy myself, and at the same time to comfort my despondency. I tried to fancy, that in the course of the morning, at such time as might prove agreeable to him, Bartleby, of his own free accord, would emerge from his hermitage and take up some decided line of march in the direction of the door. But no. Half-past twelve o'clock came; Turkey began to glow in the face, overturn his inkstand, and become generally obstreperous; Nippers abated down into quietude and courtesy; Ginger Nut munched his noon apple; and Bartleby remained standing at his window in one of his profoundest dead-wall reveries. Will it be credited? Ought I to acknowledge it? That afternoon I left the office without saying one further word to him.

Some days now passed, during which, at leisure intervals I looked a little into "Edwards on the Will," and "Priestley on Necessity." Under the circumstances, those books induced a salutary feeling. Gradually I slid into the persuasion that these troubles of mine, touching the scrivener, had been all predestinated from eternity, and Bartleby was billeted upon me for some mysterious purpose of an allwise Providence, which it was not for a mere mortal like me to fathom. Yes, Bartleby, stay there behind your screen, thought I; I shall persecute you no more; you are harmless and noiseless as any of these old chairs; in short, I never feel so private as when I know you are here. At last I see it, I feel it; I penetrate to the predestinated purpose of my life. I am content. Others may have loftier parts to enact; but my mission in this world, Bartleby, is to furnish you with office-room for such period as you may see fit to remain.

I believe that this wise and blessed frame of mind would have continued with me, had it not been for the unsolicited and uncharitable remarks obtruded upon me by my professional friends who visited the rooms. But thus it often is, that the constant friction of illiberal minds wears out at last the best resolves of the more generous. Though to be sure, when I reflected upon it, it was not strange that people entering my office should be struck by the peculiar aspect of the unaccountable Bartleby, and so be tempted to throw out some sinister observations concerning him. Sometimes an attorney, having business with me, and calling at my office, and finding no one but the scrivener there, would undertake to obtain some sort of precise information from him touching my whereabouts; but without heeding his idle talk, Bartleby would remain standing immovable in the middle of the room. So after contemplating him in that position for a time, the attorney would depart, no wiser than he came.

Also, when a reference was going on, and the room full of lawyers and witnesses, and business driving fast, some deeply-occupied legal gentleman present, seeing Bartleby wholly unemployed, would request him to run round to his (the legal gentleman's) office and fetch some papers for him. Thereupon, Bartleby would tranquilly decline, and yet remain idle as before. Then the lawyer would give a great stare, and turn to me. And what could I say? At last I was made aware that all through the circle of my professional acquaintance, a whisper of wonder was running round, having reference to the strange creature I kept at my office. This worried me very much. And as the idea came upon me of his possibly turning out a long-lived man, and keep occupying my chambers, and denying my authority; and perplexing my visitors; and scandalizing my professional reputation; and casting a general gloom over the premises; keeping soul and body together to the last upon his savings (for doubtless he spent but half a dime a day), and in the end perhaps outlive me, and claim possession of my office by right of his perpetual occupancy: as all these dark anticipations crowded upon me more and more, and my friends continually intruded their relentless remarks upon the apparition in my room; a great change was wrought in me. I resolved to gather all my faculties together, and forever rid me of this intolerable incubus.

Ere revolving any complicated project, however, adapted to this end, I first simply suggested to Bartleby the propriety of his permanent departure. In a calm and serious tone, I commended the idea to his careful and mature consideration. But, having taken three days to meditate upon it, he apprised me, that his original determination remained the same; in short, that he still preferred to abide with me.

What shall I do? I now said to myself, buttoning my coat to the last button. What shall I do? what ought I to do? what does conscience say I *should* do with this man, or, rather, ghost. Rid myself of him, I must; go, he shall. But how? You will not thrust him, the poor, pale, passive mortal—you will not thrust such a helpless creature out of your door? you will not dishonor yourself by such cruelty? No, I will not, I cannot do that. Rather would I let him live and die here, and then mason up his remains in the wall. What, then, will you do? For all your coaxing, he will not budge. Bribes he leaves under your own paper-weight on your table; in short, it is quite plain that he prefers to cling to you.

Then something severe, something unusual must be done. What! surely you will not have him collared by a constable, and commit his innocent pallor to the common jail? And upon what ground could you procure such a thing to be done?—a vagrant, is he? What! he a vagrant, a wanderer, who refuses to budge? It is because he will *not* be a vagrant, then, that you seek to count him *as* a vagrant. That is too absurd. No visible means of support: there I have him. Wrong again: for indubitably he *does* support himself, and that is the only unanswerable proof that any man can show of his possessing the means so to do. No more, then. Since he will not quit me, I must quit him. I will change my offices; I will move elsewhere, and give him fair notice, that if I find him on my new premises I will then proceed against him as a common trespasser.

Acting accordingly, next day I thus addressed him: "I find these chambers too far from the City Hall; the air is unwholesome. In a word, I propose to remove my offices next week, and shall no longer require your services. I tell you this now, in order that you may seek another place."

He made no reply; and nothing more was said.

On the appointed day I engaged carts and men, proceeded to my chambers, and, having but little furniture, everything was removed in a few hours. Throughout, the scrivener remained standing behind the screen, which I directed to be removed the last thing. It was withdrawn; and, being folded up like a huge folio, left him the motionless occupant of a naked room. I stood in the entry watching him a moment, while something from within me upbraided me.

I re-entered, with my hand in my pocket—and—and my heart in my mouth.

"Good-by, Bartleby; I am going—good-by, and God some way bless you; and take that," slipping something in his hand. But it dropped upon the floor, and then—strange to say—I tore myself from him whom I had so longed to be rid of.

Established in my new quarters, for a day or two I kept the door locked, and started at every footfall in the passages. When I returned to my rooms, after any little absence, I would pause at the threshold for an instant, and attentively listen, ere applying my key. But these fears were needless. Bartleby never came nigh me.

I thought all was going well, when a perturbed-looking stranger visited me, inquiring whether I was the person who had recently occupied rooms at No. — Wall Street.

Full of forebodings, I replied that I was.

"Then, sir," said the stranger, who proved a lawyer, "you are responsible for the man you left there. He refuses to do any copying; he refuses to do anything; he says he prefers not to; and he refuses to quit the premises."

"I am very sorry, sir," said I, with assumed tranquillity, but an inward tremor, "but, really, the man you allude to is nothing to me—he is no relation or apprentice of mine, that you should hold me responsible for him."

"In mercy's name, who is he?"

"I certainly cannot inform you. I know nothing about him. Formerly I employed him as a copyist; but he has done nothing for me now for some time past."

"I shall settle him, then—good morning, sir."

Several days passed, and I heard nothing more; and, though I often felt a charitable prompting to call at the place and see poor Bartleby, yet a certain squeamishness, of I know not what, withheld me.

All is over with him, by this time, thought I, at last, when, through another week, no further intelligence reached me. But, coming to my room the day after, I found several persons waiting at my door in a high state of nervous excitement.

"That's the man—here he comes," cried the foremost one, whom I recognized as the lawyer who had previously called upon me alone.

"You must take him away, sir, at once," cried a portly person among them, advancing upon me, and whom I knew to be the landlord of No. — Wall Street. "These gentlemen, my tenants, cannot stand it any longer; Mr. B—," pointing to the lawyer, "has turned him out of his room, and he now persists in haunting the building generally, sitting upon the banisters of the stairs by day, and sleeping in the entry by night. Everybody is concerned; clients are leaving the offices; some fears are entertained of a mob; something you must do, and that without delay."

Aghast at this torrent, I fell back before it, and would fain have locked myself in my new quarters. In vain I persisted that Bartleby was nothing to me—no more than to any one else. In vain—I was the last person known to have anything to do with him, and they held me to the terrible account. Fearful, then, of being exposed in the papers (as one person present obscurely threatened), I considered the matter, and, at length, said, that if the lawyer would give me a confidential interview with the scrivener, in his (the lawyer's) own room, I would, that afternoon, strive my best to rid them of the nuisance they complained of.

Going up stairs to my old haunt, there was Bartleby silently sitting upon the banister at the landing.

"What are you doing here, Bartleby?" said I.

"Sitting upon the banister," he mildly replied.

I motioned him into the lawyer's room, who then left us.

"Bartleby," said I, "are you aware that you are the cause of great tribulation to me, by persisting in occupying the entry after being dismissed from the office?"

No answer.

"Now one of two things must take place. Either you must do something, or something must be done to you. Now what sort of business would you like to engage in? Would you like to re-engage in copying for some one?"

"No; I would prefer not to make any change."

"Would you like a clerkship in a dry-goods store?"

"There is too much confinement about that. No, I would not like a clerkship; but I am not particular."

"Too much confinement," I cried, "why, you keep yourself confined all the time!"

"I would prefer not to take a clerkship," he rejoined, as if to settle that little item at once.

"How would a bar-tender's business suit you? There is no trying of the eye-sight in that."

"I would not like it at all; though, as I said before, I am not particular."

His unwonted wordiness inspirited me. I returned to the charge.

"Well, then, would you like to travel through the country collecting bills for the merchants? That would improve your health."

"No, I would prefer to be doing something else."

"How, then, would going as a companion to Europe, to entertain some young gentleman with your conversation—how would that suit you?"

"Not at all. It does not strike me that there is anything definite about that. I like to be stationary. But I am not particular."

"Stationary you shall be, then," I cried, now losing all patience, and, for the first time in all my exasperating connection with him, fairly flying into a passion. "If you do not go away from these premises before night, I shall feel bound—indeed, I *am* bound—to—to—to quit the premises myself!" I rather absurdly concluded, knowing not with what possible threat to try to frighten his immobility into compliance. Despairing of all further efforts, I was pre-cipitately leaving him, when a final thought occurred to me—one which had not been wholly unindulged before.

"Bartleby," said I, in the kindest tone I could assume under such exciting circumstances, "will you go home with me now—not to my office, but my dwelling—and remain there till we can conclude upon some convenient arrangement for you at our leisure? Come, let us start now, right away."

"No: at present I would prefer not to make any change at all."

I answered nothing; but, effectually dodging every one by the suddenness and rapidity of my flight, rushed from the building, ran up Wall Street towards Broadway, and, jumping into the first omnibus, was soon removed from pur-suit. As soon as tranquillity returned, I distinctly perceived that I had now done all that I possibly could, both in respect to the demands of the landlord and his tenants, and with regard to my own desire and sense of duty, to benefit Bartleby, and shield him from rude persecution. I now strove to be entirely care-free and quiescent; and my conscience justified me in the attempt; though, indeed, it was not so successful as I could have wished. So fearful was I of being again hunted out by the incensed landlord and his exasperated tenants, that, surrendering my business to Nippers, for a few days, I drove about the upper part of the town and through the suburbs, in my rockaway; crossed over to Jersey City and Hoboken, and paid fugitive visits to Manhattanville and Astoria. In fact, I almost lived in my rockaway for the time.

When again I entered my office, lo, a note from the landlord lay upon the desk. I opened it with trembling hands. It informed me that the writer had sent to the police, and had Bartleby removed to the Tombs as a vagrant. More-over, since I knew more about him than any one else, he wished me to appear at that place, and make a suitable statement of the facts. These tidings had a conflicting effect upon me. At first I was indignant; but, at last, almost approved. The landlord's energetic, summary disposition, had led him to adopt a procedure which I do not think I would have decided upon myself; and yet, as a last resort, under such peculiar circumstances, it seemed the only plan.

As I afterwards learned, the poor scrivener, when told that he must be conducted to the Tombs, offered not the slightest obstacle, but, in his pale, unmoving way, silently acquiesced.

Some of the compassionate and curious bystanders joined the party; and headed by one of the constables arm in arm with Bartleby, the silent procession filed its way through all the noise, and heat, and joy of the roaring thoroughfares at noon.

The same day I received the note, I went to the Tombs, or, to speak more properly, the Halls of Justice. Seeking the right officer, I stated the purpose of my call, and was informed that the individual I described was, indeed, within. I then assured the functionary that Bartleby was a perfectly honest man, and greatly to be compassionated, however unaccountably eccentric. I narrated all I knew, and closed by suggesting the idea of letting him remain in as indulgent confinement as possible, till something less harsh might be done—though, indeed, I hardly knew what. At all events, if nothing else could be decided upon, the alms-house must receive him. I then begged to have an interview.

Being under no disgraceful charge, and quite serene and harmless in all his ways, they had permitted him freely to wander about the prison, and, especially, in the inclosed grass-platted yards thereof. And so I found him there, standing all alone in the quietest of the yards, his face towards a high wall, while all around, from the narrow slits of the jail windows, I thought I saw peering out upon him the eyes of murderers and thieves.

"Bartleby!"

"I know you," he said, without looking round—"and I want nothing to say to you."

"It was not I that brought you here, Bartleby," said I, keenly pained at his implied suspicion. "And to you, this should not be so vile a place. Nothing reproachful attaches to you by being here. And see, it is not so sad a place as one might think. Look, there is the sky, and here is the grass."

"I know where I am," he replied, but would say nothing more, and so I left him.

As I entered the corridor again, a broad meat-like man, in an apron, accosted me, and, jerking his thumb over his shoulder, said—"Is that your friend?"

"Yes."

"Does he want to starve? If he does, let him live on the prison fare, that's all."

"Who are you?" asked I, not knowing what to make of such an unofficially speaking person in such a place.

"I am the grub-man. Such gentlemen as have friends here, hire me to provide them with something good to eat."

"Is this so?" said I, turning to the turnkey.

He said it was.

"Well, then," said I, slipping some silver into the grub-man's hands (for so they called him), "I want you to give particular attention to my friend there; let him have the best dinner you can get. And you must be as polite to him as possible."

"Introduce me, will you?" said the grub-man, looking at me with an expression which seemed to say he was all impatience for an opportunity to give a specimen of his breeding.

Thinking it would prove of benefit to the scrivener, I acquiesced; and, asking the grub-man his name, went up with him to Bartleby.

"Bartleby, this is a friend; you will find him very useful to you."

"Your sarvant, sir, your sarvant," said the grub-man, making a low salutation behind his apron. "Hope you find it pleasant here, sir; nice grounds—cool apartments—hope you'll stay with us sometime—try to make it agreeable. What will you have for dinner to-day?"

"I prefer not to dine to-day," said Bartleby, turning away. "It would disagree with me; I am unused to dinners." So saying, he slowly moved to the other side of the inclosure, and took up a position fronting the dead-wall.

"How's this?" said the grub-man, addressing me with a stare of astonishment. "He's odd, ain't he?"

"I think he is a little deranged," said I, sadly.

"Deranged? deranged is it? Well, now, upon my word, I thought that friend of yourn was a gentleman forger; they are always pale and genteel-like, them forgers. I can't help pity 'em—can't help it, sir. Did you know Monroe Edwards?" he added, touchingly, and paused. Then, laying his hand piteously on my shoulder, sighed, "he died of consumption at Sing-Sing. So you weren't acquainted with Monroe?"

"No, I was never socially acquainted with any forgers. But I cannot stop longer. Look to my friend yonder. You will not lose by it. I will see you again."

Some few days after this, I again obtained admission to the Tombs, and went through the corridors in quest of Bartleby; but without finding him.

"I saw him coming from his cell not long ago," said a turnkey, "may be he's gone to loiter in the yards."

So I went in that direction.

"Are you looking for the silent man?" said another turnkey, passing me. "Yonder he lies—sleeping in the yard there. 'Tis not twenty minutes since I saw him lie down."

The yard was entirely quiet. It was not accessible to the common prisoners. The surrounding walls, of amazing thickness, kept off all sounds behind them. The Egyptian character of the masonry weighed upon me with its gloom. But a soft imprisoned turf grew under foot. The heart of the eternal pyramids, it seemed, wherein, by some strange magic, through the clefts, grass-seed, dropped by birds, had sprung.

Strangely huddled at the base of the wall, his knees drawn up, and lying on his side, his head touching the cold stones, I saw the wasted Bartleby. But nothing stirred. I paused; then went close up to him; stooped over, and saw that his dim eyes were open; otherwise he seemed profoundly sleeping. Something prompted me to touch him. I felt his hand, when a tingling shiver ran up my arm and down my spine to my feet.

The round face of the grub-man peered upon me now. "His dinner is ready. Won't he dine to-day, either? Or does he live without dining?"

"Lives without dining," said I, and closed the eyes.

"Eh!—He's asleep, ain't he?"

"With kings and counselors," murmured I.

There would seem little need for proceeding further in this history. Imagination will readily supply the meagre recital of poor Bartleby's interment. But, ere parting with the reader, let me say, that if this little narrative has sufficiently interested him, to awaken curiosity as to who Bartleby was, and what manner of life he led prior to the present narrator's making his acquaintance, I can only reply, that in such curiosity I fully share, but am wholly unable to gratify it. Yet here I hardly know whether I should divulge one little item of rumor, which came to my ear a few months after the scrivener's decease. Upon what basis it rested, I could never ascertain; and hence, how true it is I cannot now tell. But, inasmuch as this vague report has not been without a certain suggestive interest to me, however sad, it may prove the same with some others; and so I will briefly mention it. The report was this: that Bartleby had been a subordinate clerk in the Dead Letter Office at Washington, from which he had been suddenly removed by a change in the administration. When I think over this rumor, hardly can I express the emotions which seize me. Dead letters! does it not sound like dead men? Conceive a man by nature and misfortune prone to a pallid hopelessness, can any business seem more fitted to heighten it than that of continually handling these dead letters, and assorting them for the flames? For by the cart-load they are annually burned. Sometimes from out the folded paper the pale clerk takes a ring—the finger it was meant for, perhaps, moulders in the grave; a bank-note sent in swiftest charity—he whom it would relieve, nor eats nor hungers any more; pardon for those who died despairing; hope for those who died unhoping; good tidings for those who died stifled by unrelieved calamities. On errands of life, these letters speed to death.

Ah, Bartleby! Ah, humanity!

EXERCISES

1. What is the matter with Bartleby? Why does he "prefer not to"? Does Bartleby ever give an answer to this central question? Consider the point in the story when the narrator thinks that there is something wrong with Bartleby's eyes.

2. Why doesn't the boss get rid of Bartleby right away? Why does he continue to let Bartleby stay on when it is clear that Bartleby will do no work?

3. Point out the many references to walls in the story. What function do the walls serve?

4. Bartleby is not the same kind of character as the narrator; whereas the narrator is presented as if he were a "real" person in the real world, Bartleby is presented as a character from the world of allegory or parable. Note that the boss says there is nothing "ordinarily human" about him. Consider the possibility that Bartleby arrives to effect a basic change in the narrator.

5. Discuss the significance of the minor characters in the story. How does Bartleby differ from them?

6. Discuss the significance of the epilogue about the dead letter office. How does it provide a possible motivation for Bartleby's actions? Consider the symbolic significance rather than the realistic significance of the detail.

PART FOUR | *The World of Story*

Aspiring writers often mistakenly think that in order to learn to write fiction, they must go out and get real-life experience so that they will have interesting things to write about. However, as Gabriel García Márquez has one of his characters say, "Stories only happen to those who know how to tell them," suggesting that it is not the event that makes a story, but rather it is the story-telling technique. Creative-writing teachers often tell their students to write about what they know best, and that is good advice. However, just because someone knows an experience well does not necessarily mean that he or she will be able to create a story about it. Inexperienced adolescent writers may indeed write about experiences they know well—experiences that have had powerful emotional impacts on them—such as the death of a grandparent, the divorce of parents, or the loss of a friend; but if they are not familiar with stories, the experience they tell may be just a series of events, one thing after another, with no point or significance.

If you ask professional fiction writers what they know best, they are most likely to answer "stories," because they usually have read a great many stories, so many in fact that they have internalized and made their own the devices, conventions, techniques, and themes of those writers whom they have read. It is a common legend that Ernest Hemingway was a great writer because he engaged in so many interesting experiences—fighting bulls in Spain, hunting wild animals in Africa, and catching big game fish in the Gulf. This experience makes for a nice story in its own right, but Hemingway himself knew that what made him an effective writer was the fact that he studied many other writers and spent a great deal of his early writing career learning how to describe things and how to recount events in such a way as to give them meaning. Stories, therefore, do not come merely from life, they also come from other stories; and because writers know stories probably better than anything else, they are often likely to write stories about stories.

However, it is not merely because writers know stories well that they often write about storytelling or draw from stories they know. Many modern stories are about the nature of storytelling because of a basic philosophic shift that has taken place in the twentieth century—a shift from a realistic, commonsense assumption that reality is merely "out there" waiting for us to know it to a philosophic assumption that reality is also the result of our creation of it. If we accept that reality is as much a result of our point of view as it is of mere external existence, then we may feel that reality comes from a sort of fiction-making process. Writers who accept this point of view may, in their desire to write about true reality, write about that fiction-making process itself rather than about some notion of reality as solid stuff out there in the external world.

Saki's "The Open Window" and Mark Twain's "The Celebrated Jumping Frog of Calaveras County" seem to be simple, humorous stories; yet they illustrate some of the complex ways that so-called "true" reality gets entwined with "fictional" reality, as well as some of the artful ways that storytellers involve their listeners in the worlds they create. Isak Dinesen's "The Blank Page," Virginia Woolf's "The Symbol," Vladimir Nabokov's "Signs and Symbols," and Donald Barthelme's "The Balloon" all explore various aspects of the artist's creation of a fiction and the reader's response to it. Frank Stockton's "The Lady, or the Tiger" and Margaret Atwood's "Happy Endings" both deal with the convention of endings of stories, while Grace Paley's "A Conversation with My Father" and Spencer Holst's "On Hope" focus on the creation of shifting fictional worlds. John Barth's "Autobiography: A Self-Recorded Fiction" pushes the notion of stories about stories just about as far as it can go, for the autobiography here is not of a person but of the story itself.

The next group of stories in this section has been selected to permit an analysis of how stories are often based on previous stories, essentially telling the same story over again from a new point of view or with a new purpose. Somerset Maugham's retelling of Jean de la Fontaine's "The Grasshopper and the Ant" seems a fairly clear example of an old tale with a new twist for satiric and ironic purposes. Sylvia Townsend Warner's wry and whimsical retelling of the sacred legend of the phoenix can be compared with two early versions of the myth by the Roman historian Tacitus and the Roman poet Ovid. John Updike's modern version of the Pygmalion myth satirizes the relationships between modern men and women, while Herbert Gold's treatment of the Apocrypha story of Susanna provides a modern version of innocence versus impurity. Robert Coover creates a humorous, more realistic, version of the sacred story of the Old Testament flood by telling it from the practical point of view of Noah's brother.

The next group of stories by Guy de Maupassant, Isaac Babel, and Doris Lessing are purposely placed together to provide the opportunity to explore how the stories of one generation grow out of the stories of a previous one. Although not always grouped together, many other stories in this collection can be examined in terms of "influence" or the persistence of a tradition. For example, the stories of Katherine Mansfield in the first part and those of Raymond Carver in the second part reflect much the same kind of homage to Anton Chekhov as the stories of Babel do to de Maupassant and the stories of Lessing do to Babel.

The final stories in this section present the notion of stories about stories in a variety of ways, some more obvious than others. Henry James's "The Real Thing" and "The Figure in the Carpet" are considerations about the artist's creation of the artwork and the reader's response to it, while Jorge Luis Borges's "Funes, the Memorious" is about the necessary balance between concrete detail and generality that must exist in story.

Susan Glaspell's "A Jury of Her Peers" and Ambrose Bierce's "An Occurrence at Owl Creek Bridge" may not at first glance seem stories as explicitly about the nature of art as do others in this section. However, "A Jury of Her Peers" is a sort of detective fiction in which characters try to put together clues to come up with a story that hangs together and is properly motivated. In this sense, the story is about what it takes to be a "good reader." In "An Occurrence at Owl Creek Bridge," Ambrose Bierce is concerned with showing how a story, because it is made up of words that must follow each other in time, makes a situation that takes place in a split second in the mind seem as though it is taking place over a longer period of time.

Stories that seem to be about fiction in general or about their own fictionality have become more interesting to modern critics and readers. The popular appeal is due to the pleasure of being drawn into a world that seems both real and fictional at once. Such films as Mel Brooks's *Blazing Saddles* and the fantasy *Who Framed Roger Rabbit?* amuse us because of a kind of crazy logic that underlies them. It somehow makes sense, even though we know it is absurd, that cartoon characters would have their own independent life as they do in *Roger Rabbit* and would therefore interact with seemingly "real" characters. In Mel Brooks's films, we get a certain pleasure out of seeing exposed the conventions that underlie the illusions of popular film genres such as westerns or horror films.

Modern critics and thinkers are interested in stories that explore or lay bare their own fictionality because such stories suggest that there is something basically fictional about the nature of reality itself. And if human beings create reality in much the same way that fiction writers create fiction, then stories provide an ideal means to study the nature of reality itself. Consequently, many researchers today are exploring story-making and story-understanding as two of the most basic elements of human thought. The implications of these studies of the worlds of story for the understanding of artificial intelligence and the basic nature of human cognition itself are still being explored.

THE POWER OF STORY
IN *"The Open Window"*

Saki's most anthologized story, "The Open Window," is a fiction that explores the means by which stories involve their readers in an inextricable mixture of illusion and reality. Although this is a light story, a little drawing-room comedy in which Framton Nuttel is nutty and Mrs. Sappleton is a little sappy, what makes "The Open Window" effective is the uncertainty, felt both by Nuttel and by the reader, about the kind of story that they are listening to or reading. The basic issue is whether Vera (whose name suggests the Latin word *veritas* for "truth") is relating fact or telling a tale.

The reader can clearly follow the steps by which the "self-possessed young lady" determines how to ensnare her unsuspecting listener with her story. After carefully making sure that Nuttel would have no way of knowing whether the story she is about to tell is truth or fantasy, Vera begins. The reader's initial response is to take the events she tells as truth; like Nuttel we have no way of determining that they are not truth. The plausibility of the story is suggested by Vera's "faltering human" tone, her specific detail, and her seemingly minor touches, such as the youngest brother singing "Bertie, why do you bound?" Moreover, as is often the case in legends and stories, Vera uses a fact of external reality as the peg on which to hang her story—the fact of the open window.

When Mrs. Sappleton enters and rattles on about her husband going snipe hunting, both the reader and Nuttel begin to think that they are witnessing a sad sense of minor madness. The use of such language as making a "fine mess" and "muddy up to the eyes" is Saki's way of making the story even more grotesque, as Nuttel and the reader imagine the resurrected corpses tracking across the carpet. Moreover, Saki is careful to create in Framton Nuttel a character that the reader is glad to see get his relatively harmless comeuppence. He is entirely too self-pitying and self-absorbed as he whines about his nerves and the doctor's recommendations. It is important that the reader feel a sense of poetic justice when Nuttel has a real shock to his nerves and is sparked into the kind of mental excitement and violent physical exercise he says his doctors have recommended against.

When Mrs. Sappleton turns to the window and says "Here they are at last," Nuttel and the reader have a moment of pity for the poor woman who is obviously hallucinating. However, when Nuttel looks out the window and sees the three men coming, the reader has a moment of indecision: Is this a story about a crazy old woman, or is it a ghost story? Our realization that we have been tricked into thinking this is one kind of story only to find out it is another is accompanied by our amusement at Nuttel's mad dash in getting out of the house. We are then momentarily puzzled when the men enter and we discover that they are not ghosts at all. We now are not sure what kind of story we are reading. It is only when Vera begins her next tale that we realize we too have been made the butt of Saki's story-made joke.

"The Open Window" is about the process of the storyteller's transforming fantasy into supposed fact only to reveal it as fantasy after all. For Framton Nuttel, the story inside the story becomes a reality to which he cannot merely passively respond but which involves him by actually threatening to enter the room he occupies. It works similarly for the reader until, in a gesture that lays bare what always underlies story, Saki makes clear that what we took to be real is story itself.

COMMENT

Just because a story seems simple and easy to understand does not mean that the analyst can say nothing useful about it. Puzzling stories are usually easier to talk about because they require some explication or interpretation to make them clear. In a discussion of a puzzling story that readers find hard to understand, the analyst serves as a sort of "translator," converting the story from relatively unfamiliar fictional conventions into more familiar expository and argumentative language. For apparently simple stories, such as Saki's "The Open Window," in which nothing really needs explication, the task of the analyst is to explain the means by which the story achieves its intention, not simply what the story means.

SAKI | # The Open Window

"My aunt will be down presently, Mr. Nuttel," said a very self-possessed young lady of fifteen; "in the meantime you must try and put up with me."

Framton Nuttel endeavored to say the correct something which should duly flutter the niece of the moment without unduly discounting the aunt that was to come. Privately he doubted more than ever whether these formal visits on a succession of total strangers would do much towards helping the nerve cure which he was supposed to be undergoing.

"I know how it will be," his sister had said when he was preparing to migrate to this rural retreat; "you will bury yourself down there and not speak to a living soul, and your nerves will be worse than ever from moping. I shall just give you letters of introduction to all the people I know there. Some of them, as far as I can remember, were quite nice."

Framton wondered whether Mrs. Sappleton, the lady to whom he was presenting one of the letters of introduction, came into the nice division.

"Do you know many of the people round here?" asked the niece, when she judged that they had had sufficient silent communion.

"Hardly a soul," said Framton. "My sister was staying here, at the rectory, you know, some four years ago, and she gave me letters of introduction to some of the people here."

He made the last statement in a tone of distinct regret.

"Then you know practically nothing about my aunt?" pursued the self-possessed young lady.

"Only her name and address," admitted the caller. He was wondering whether Mrs. Sappleton was in the married or widowed state. An undefinable something about the room seemed to suggest masculine habitation.

"Her great tragedy happened just three years ago," said the child; "that would be since your sister's time."

"Her tragedy?" asked Framton; somehow in this restful country spot tragedies seemed out of place.

"You may wonder why we keep that window wide open on an October afternoon," said the niece, indicating a large French window that opened on to a lawn.

"It is quite warm for the time of the year," said Framton, "but has that window got anything to do with the tragedy?"

"Out through that window, three years ago to a day, her husband and her two young brothers went off for their day's shooting. They never came back. In crossing the moor to their favorite snipe-shooting ground they were all three engulfed in a treacherous piece of bog. It had been that dreadful wet summer, you know, and places that were safe in other years gave way suddenly without warning. Their bodies were never recovered. That was the dreadful part of it." Here the child's voice lost its self-possessed note and became falteringly human. "Poor aunt always thinks that they will come back some day, they and the little brown spaniel that was lost with them, and walk in at that window just as they used to do. That is why the window is kept open every evening till it is quite dusk. Poor dear aunt, she has often told me how they went out, her husband with his white waterproof coat over his arm, and Ronnie, her youngest brother, singing, 'Bertie, why do you bound?' as he always did to tease her, because she said it got on her nerves. Do you know, sometimes on still, quiet evenings like this, I almost get a creepy feeling that they will all walk in through that window—"

She broke off with a little shudder. It was a relief to Framton when the aunt bustled into the room with a whirl of apologies for being late in making her appearance.

"I hope Vera has been amusing you?" she said.

"She has been very interesting," said Framton.

"I hope you don't mind the open window," said Mrs. Sappleton briskly; "my husband and brothers will be home directly from shooting, and they always come in this way. They've been out for snipe in the marshes today, so they'll make a fine mess over my poor carpets. So like you menfolk, isn't it?"

She rattled on cheerfully about the shooting and the scarcity of birds, and the prospects for duck in the winter. To Framton it was all purely horrible. He made a desperate but only partially successful effort to turn the talk on to a less ghastly topic; he was conscious that his hostess was giving him only a fragment of her attention, and her eyes were constantly straying past him to the open window and the lawn beyond. It was certainly an unfortunate coincidence that he should have paid his visit on this tragic anniversary.

"The doctors agree in ordering me complete rest, an absence of mental excitement, and avoidance of anything in the nature of violent physical exercise," announced Framton, who labored under the tolerably wide-spread delusion that total strangers and chance acquaintances are hungry for the least detail of one's ailments and infirmities, their cause and cure. "On the matter of diet they are not so much in agreement," he continued.

"No?" said Mrs. Sappleton, in a voice which only replaced a yawn at the last moment. Then she suddenly brightened into alert attention—but not to what Framton was saying.

"Here they are at last!" she cried. "Just in time for tea, and don't they look as if they were muddy up to the eyes!"

Framton shivered slightly and turned towards the niece with a look intended to convey sympathetic comprehension. The child was staring out through the open window with dazed horror in her eyes. In a chill shock of nameless fear Framton swung round in his seat and looked in the same direction.

In the deepening twilight three figures were walking across the lawn towards the window; they all carried guns under their arms, and one of them was additionally burdened with a white coat hung over his shoulders. A tired brown spaniel kept close at their heels. Noiselessly they neared the house, and then a hoarse young voice chanted out of the dusk: "I said, Bertie, why do you bound?"

Framton grabbed wildly at his stick and hat; the hall-door, the gravel-drive, and the front gate were dimly noted stages in his head-long retreat. A cyclist coming along the road had to run into the hedge to avoid imminent collision.

"Here we are, my dear," said the bearer of the white mackintosh, coming in through the window; "fairly muddy, but most of it's dry. Who was that who bolted out as we came up?"

"A most extraordinary man, a Mr. Nuttel," said Mrs. Sappleton; "could only talk about his illnesses, and dashed off without a word of goodby or apology when you arrived. One would think he had seen a ghost."

"I expect it was the spaniel," said the niece calmly; "he told me he had a horror of dogs. He was once hunted into a cemetery somewhere on the banks of the Ganges by a pack of pariah dogs, and had to spend the night in a newly dug grave with the creatures snarling and grinning and foaming just above him. Enough to make anyone lose their nerve."

Romance at short notice was her specialty.

EXERCISES

1. What is it about the personality of Framton Nuttel that makes us laugh at his fear? Why do we not sympathize with him? After all, he is the innocent victim of a pathological liar, is he not? Is there a difference between lying and telling stories?

2. At what point in the story does the girl decide to tell her story? What makes her decide to make up this particular story?

3. When you first read this story, what did you think of Mrs. Sappleton when she tells about the men folk coming home soon?

4. Nuttel thinks it is an unfortunate coincidence that he has come on this tragic anniversary. A coincidence might be thought of as an accident that seems meaningful. Can there be accidents in fiction?

5. When you first read the story, what was your feeling when the men came up the lawn?

6. This story goes through several transformations as you read it the first time—from psychological story, to ghost story, to comic realism. Discuss these transformations.

7. How is this a story about reader involvement in stories? How is it about the illusion of fiction becoming reality?

MARK
TWAIN | # The Celebrated Jumping Frog of Calaveras County

In compliance with the request of a friend of mine, who wrote me from the East, I called on good-natured, garrulous old Simon Wheeler, and inquired after my friend's friend, Leonidas W. Smiley, as requested to do, and I hereunto append the result. I have a lurking suspicion that *Leonidas W.* Smiley is a myth; that my friend never knew such a personage; and that he only conjectured that if I asked old Wheeler about him, it would remind him of his infamous *Jim* Smiley, and he would go to work and bore me to death with some exasperating reminiscence of him as long and as tedious as it should be useless to me. If that was the design, it succeeded.

I found Simon Wheeler dozing comfortably by the barroom stove of the dilapidated tavern in the decayed mining camp of Angel's, and I noticed that he was fat and bald-headed, and had an expression of winning gentleness and simplicity upon his tranquil countenance. He roused up, and gave me good-day. I told him a friend of mind had commissioned me to make some inquiries about a cherished companion of his boyhood named *Leonidas W.* Smiley— *Rev. Leonidas W.* Smiley, a young minister of the Gospel, who he had heard was at one time a resident of Angel's Camp. I added that if Mr. Wheeler could tell me anything about this Rev. Leonidas W. Smiley, I would feel under many obligations to him.

Simon Wheeler backed me into a corner and blockaded me there with his chair, and then sat down and reeled off the monotonous narrative which follows this paragraph. He never smiled, he never frowned, he never changed his voice from the gentle-flowing key to which he tuned his initial sentence, he never betrayed the slightest suspicion of enthusiasm; but all through the interminable narrative there ran a vein of impressive earnestness and sincerity, which showed me plainly that, so far from his imagining that there was anything ridiculous or funny about his story, he regarded it as a really important matter, and admired its two heroes as men of transcendent genius in *finesse*. I let him go on in his own way, and never interrupted him once.

"Rev. Leonidas W. H'm, Reverend Le—well, there was a feller here once by the name of *Jim* Smiley, in the winter of '49—or may be it was the spring of '50—I don't recollect exactly, somehow, though what makes me think it was one or the other is because I remember the big flume warn't finished when he first come to the camp; but any way, he was the curiosest man about always betting on anything that turned up you ever see, if he could get anybody to bet on the other side; and if he couldn't he'd change sides. Any way that suited the other man would suit *him*—any way just so's he got a bet, *he* was satisfied. But still he was lucky, uncommon lucky; he most always come out winner. He was always ready and laying for a chance; there couldn't be no solit'ry thing mentioned but that feller'd offer to bet on it, and take ary side you please, as I was just telling you. If there was a horse-race, you'd find him flush or you'd find him busted at the end of it; if there was a dog-fight, he'd bet on it; if there was a cat-fight, he'd bet on it; if there was a chicken-fight, he'd bet on it; why, if there was two birds setting on a fence, he would bet you which one would fly first; or if there was a camp-meeting, he would be there reg'lar to bet on Parson Walker, which he judged to be the best exhorter about here, and so he was too, and a good man. If he even see a straddle-bug start to go anywheres, he would bet you how long it would take him to get to— to wherever he was going to, and if you took him up, he would foller that straddle-bug to Mexico but what he would find out where he was bound for and how long he was on the road. Lots of the boys here has seen that Smiley, and can tell you about him. Why, it never made no difference to *him*—he'd bet on *any* thing—the dangdest feller. Parson Walker's wife laid very sick once, for a good while, and it seemed as if they warn't going to save her; but one morning he come in, and Smiley up and asked him how she was, and he said she was considerable better—thank the Lord for his inf'nite mercy—and coming on so smart that with the blessing of Prov'dence she'd get well yet; and Smiley, before he thought, says, "Well, I'll resk two-and-a-half she don't anyway."

Thish-yer Smiley had a mare—the boys called her the fifteen-minute nag, but that was only in fun, you know, because of course she was faster than that—and he used to win money on that horse, for all she was so slow and always had the asthma, or the distemper, or the consumption, or something of that kind. They used to give her two or three hundred yards start, and then pass her under way; but always at the fag end of the race she'd get excited and desperate like, and come cavorting and straddling up, and scattering her legs around limber, sometimes in the air, and sometimes out to one side among the fences, and kicking up m-o-r-e dust and raising m-o-r-e racket with her coughing and sneezing and blowing her nose—and *always* fetch up at the stand just about a neck ahead, as near as you could cipher it down.

And he had a little small bull-pup, that to look at him you'd think he warn't worth a cent but to set around and look ornery and lay for a chance to steal something. But as soon as money was up on him he was a different dog; his under-jaw'd begin to stick out like the fo'castle of a steamboat, and his teeth would uncover and shine like the furnaces. And a dog might tackle him and bully-rag him, and bite him, and throw him over his shoulder two or three times, and Andrew Jackson—which was the name of the pup—Andrew Jackson would never let on but what *he* was satisfied, and hadn't expected nothing else—and the bets being doubled and doubled on the other side all the time, till the money was all up; and then all of a sudden he would grab the other dog jest by the j'int of his hind leg and freeze to it—not chaw, you understand, but only just grip and hang on till they throwed up the sponge, if it was a year. Smiley always come out winner on that pup, till he harnessed a dog once that didn't have no hind legs, because they'd been sawed off in a circular saw, and when the thing had gone along far enough, and the money was all up, and he come to make a snatch for his pet holt, he see in a minute how he'd been imposed on, and how the other dog had him in the door, so to speak, and he 'peared surprised, and then he looked sorter discouraged-like, and didn't try no more to win the fight, and so he got shucked out bad. He gave Smiley a look, as much as to say his heart was broke, and it was *his* fault, for putting up a dog that hadn't no hind legs for him to take holt of, which was his main dependence in a fight, and then he limped off a piece and laid down and died. It was a good pup, was that Andrew Jackson, and would have made a name for hisself if he'd lived, for the stuff was in him and he had genius—I know it, because he hadn't no opportunities to speak of, and it don't stand to reason that a dog could make such a fight as he could under them circumstances if he hadn't no talent. It always makes me feel sorry when I think of that last fight of his'n, and the way it turned out.

Well, thish-yer Smiley had rat-tarriers, and chicken cocks, and tomcats and all them kind of things, till you couldn't rest, and you couldn't fetch nothing for him to bet on but he'd match you. He ketched a frog one day, and took him home, and said he cal'lated to educate him; and so he never done nothing for three months but set in his back yard and learn that frog to jump. And you bet you he *did* learn him, too. He'd give him a little pinch behind, and the next minute you'd see that frog whirling in the air like a doughnut—see him turn one summerset, or may be a couple, if he got a good start, and come down flat-footed and all right, like a cat. He got him up so in the matter of ketching flies, and kep' him in practice so constant, that he'd nail a fly every time as fur as he could see him. Smiley said all a frog wanted was education, and he could do 'most anything—and I believe him. Why, I've seen him set Dan'l Webster down here on this floor—Dan'l Webster was the name of the frog—and sing out, "Flies, Dan'l, flies!" and quicker'n you could wink he'd spring straight up and snake a fly off'n the counter there, and flop down on the floor ag'in as solid as a gob of mud, and fall to scratching the side of his head with his hind foot as indifferent as if he hadn't no idea he'd been doin' any more'n any frog might do. You never see a frog so modest and straight-for'ard as he was, for all he was so gifted. And when it come to fair and square jumping on a dead level, he could get over more ground at one straddle than any animal of his breed you ever see. Jumping on a dead level was his strong suit, you understand; and when it come to that, Smiley would ante up money on him as long as he had a red. Smiley was monstrous proud of his frog, and well he might be, for fellers that had traveled and been everywheres all said he laid over any frog that ever *they* see.

Well, Smiley kep' the beast in a little lattice box, and he used to fetch him down town sometimes and lay for a bet. One day a feller—a stranger in the camp, he was—come acrost him with his box, and says:

"What might it be that you've got in the box?"

And Smiley says, sorter indifferent-like, "It might be a parrot, or it might be a canary, maybe, but it ain't—it's only just a frog."

And the feller took it, and looked at it careful, and turned it round this way and that, and says, "H'm—so 'tis. Well, what's *he* good for?"

"Well," Smiley says, easy and careless, "he's good enough for *one* thing, I should judge—he can outjump any frog in Calaveras county."

The feller took the box again, and took another long, particular look, and give it back to Smiley, and says, very deliberate, "Well," he says, "I don't see no p'ints about that frog that's any better'n any other frog."

"Maybe you don't," Smiley says. "Maybe you understand frogs and maybe you don't understand 'em; maybe you've had experience, and maybe you ain't only a amature, as it were. Anyways, I've got *my* opinion, and I'll resk forty dollars that he can outjump any frog in Calaveras county."

And the feller studied a minute, and then says, kinder sad like, "Well, I'm only a stranger here, and I ain't got no frog; but if I had a frog, I'd bet you."

And then Smiley says, "That's all right—that's all right—if you'll hold my box a minute, I'll go and get you a frog." And so the feller took the box, and put up his forty dollars along with Smiley's, and set down to wait.

So he set there a good while thinking and thinking to hisself, and then he got the frog out and prized his mouth open and took a teaspoon and filled him full of quail shot—filled him pretty near up to his chin—and set him on the floor. Smiley he went to the swamp and slopped around in the mud for a long time, and finally he ketched a frog, and fetched him in, and give him to this feller, and says:

"Now, if you're ready, set him alongside of Dan'l, with his forepaws just even with Dan'l's, and I'll give the word." Then he says, "One—two—three—

git!" and him and the feller touched up the frogs from behind, and the new frog hopped off lively, but Dan'l give a heave, and hysted up his shoulders—so—like a Frenchman, but it warn't no use—he couldn't budge; he was planted as solid as a church, and he couldn't no more stir than if he was anchored out. Smiley was a good deal surprised, and he was disgusted too, but he didn't have no idea what the matter was, of course.

The feller took the money and started away; and when he was going out at the door, he sorter jerked his thumb over his shoulder—so—at Dan'l, and says again, very deliberate, "Well," he says, "*I* don't see no p'ints about that frog that's any better'n any other frog."

Smiley he stood scratching his head and looking down at Dan'l a long time, and at last he says, "I do wonder what in the nation that frog throw'd off for—I wonder if there ain't something the matter with him—he 'pears to look mighty baggy, somehow." And he ketched Dan'l by the nap of the neck, and hefted him, and says, "Why blame my cats if he don't weigh five pound!" and turned him upside down and he belched out a double handful of shot. And then he see how it was, and he was the maddest man—he set the frog down and took out after that feller, but he never ketched him. And——"

Here Simon Wheeler heard his name called from the front yard, and got up to see what was wanted. And turning to me as he moved away, he said: "Just set where you are, stranger, and rest easy—I ain't going to be gone a second."

But, by your leave, I did not think that a continuation of the history of the enterprising vagabond *Jim* Smiley would be likely to afford me much information concerning the Rev. *Leonidas W.* Smiley, and so I started away.

At the door I met the sociable Wheeler returning, and he buttonholed me and re-commenced:

"Well, thish-yer Smiley had a yaller one-eyed cow that didn't have no tail, only just a short stump like a bannanner, and——"

However, lacking both time and inclination, I did not wait to hear about the afflicted cow, but took my leave.

EXERCISES

1. What makes this a humorous story? Consider not only the specific details of Wheeler's tale, but also the way he tells it. Some readers have suggested that much of the humor depends on Wheeler's inability to tell the difference between the trivial and the significant. What is humorous about this inability?

2. Many critics have said that the theme of this story is the conflict between the values of the "civilized" East and the "primitive" West. What is the satiric point of the man from the East beating Jim Smiley? How does Simon Wheeler get revenge on the East by the telling of his tale? How is this story a joke?

3. If this story is an example of how to "tell a good tale," what are some of the characteristics of effective story-telling?

4. Locate those places in which appearance versus reality plays a role. How might this be considered a basic theme of the story?

5. The story depends on two basic character types: the naive and the knowing. Classify the characters as either naive or knowing. Explain how this character relationship is important.

6. Compare this story with Bret Harte's "Tennessee's Partner" in Part I on the basis of the relationship between the teller and the tale.

ISAK
DINESEN | # The Blank Page

By the ancient city gate sat an old coffee-brown, black-veiled woman who made her living by telling stories.

She said:

"You want a tale, sweet lady and gentleman? Indeed I have told many tales, one more than a thousand, since that time when I first let young men tell me, myself, tales of a red rose, two smooth lily buds, and four silky, supple, deadly entwining snakes. It was my mother's mother, the black-eyed dancer, the often-embraced, who in the end—wrinkled like a winter apple and crouching beneath the mercy of the veil—took upon herself to teach me the art of story-telling. Her own mother's mother had taught it to her, and both were better story-tellers than I am. But that, by now, is of no consequence, since to the people they and I have become one, and I am most highly honored because I have told stories for two hundred years."

Now if she is well paid and in good spirits, she will go on.

"With my grandmother," she said, "I went through a hard school. 'Be loyal to the story,' the old hag would say to me. 'Be eternally and unswervingly loyal to the story.' 'Why must I be that, Grandmother?' I asked her. 'Am I to furnish you with reasons, baggage?' she cried. 'And you mean to be a story-teller! Why, you are to become a story-teller, and I shall give you my reasons! Hear then: Where the story-teller is loyal, eternally and unswervingly loyal to the story, there, in the end, silence will speak. Where the story has been betrayed, silence is but emptiness. But we, the faithful, when we have spoken our last word, will hear the voice of silence. Whether a small snotty lass understands it or not.'

"Who then," she continues, "tells a finer tale than any of us? Silence does. And where does one read a deeper tale than upon the most perfectly printed page of the most precious book? Upon the blank page. When a royal and gallant pen, in the moment of its highest inspiration, has written down its tale with the rarest ink of all—where, then, may one read a still deeper, sweeter, merrier and more cruel tale than that? Upon the blank page."

The old beldame for a while says nothing, only giggles a little and munches with her toothless mouth.

"We," she says at last, "the old women who tell stories, we know the story of the blank page. But we are somewhat averse to telling it, for it might well, among the uninitiated, weaken our own credit. All the same, I am going to make an exception with you, my sweet and pretty lady and gentleman of the generous hearts. I shall tell it to you."

High up in the blue mountains of Portugal there stands an old convent for sisters of the Carmelite order, which is an illustrious and austere order. In ancient times the convent was rich, the sisters were all noble ladies, and miracles took place there. But during the centuries highborn ladies grew less keen on fasting and prayer, and great dowries flowed scantily into the treasury of the convent, and today the few portionless and humble sisters live in but one wing of the vast crumbling structure, which looks as if it longed to become one with the gray rock itself. Yet they are still a blithe and active sisterhood. They take much pleasure in their holy meditations, and will busy themselves joyfully with that one particular task which did once, long, long ago, obtain for the convent a unique and strange privilege: they grow the finest flax and manufacture the most exquisite linen of Portugal.

The long field below the convent is plowed with gentle-eyed, milk-white bullocks, and the seed is skillfully sown out by labor-hardened virginal hands with mold under the nails. At the time when the flax field flowers, the whole valley becomes air-blue, the very color of the apron which the blessed virgin put on to go out and collect eggs within St. Anne's poultry yard, the moment before the Archangel Gabriel in mighty wing-strokes lowered himself onto the threshold of the house, and while high, high up a dove, neck-feathers raised and wings vibrating, stood like a small clear silver star in the sky. During this month the villagers many miles round raise their eyes to the flax field and ask one another: "Has the convent been lifted into heaven? Or have our good little sisters succeeded in pulling down heaven to them?"

Later in due course the flax is pulled, scutched and hackled; thereafter the delicate thread is spun, and the linen woven, and at the very end the fabric is laid out on the grass to bleach, and is watered time after time, until one may believe that snow has fallen round the convent walls. All this work is gone through with precision and piety and with such sprinklings and litanies as are the secret of the convent. For these reasons the linen, baled high on the backs of small gray donkeys and sent out through the convent gate, downwards and ever downwards to the towns, is as flower-white, smooth and dainty as was my own little foot when, fourteen years old, I had washed it in the brook to go to a dance in the village.

Diligence, dear Master and Mistress, is a good thing, and religion is a good thing, but the very first germ of a story will come from some mystical place outside the story itself. Thus does the linen of the Convento Velho draw its true virtue from the fact that the very first linseed was brought home from the Holy Land itself by a crusader.

In the Bible, people who can read may learn about the lands of Lecha and Maresha, where flax is grown. I myself cannot read, and have never seen this book of which so much is spoken. But my grandmother's grandmother as a little girl was the pet of an old Jewish rabbi, and the learning she received from him has been kept and passed on in our family. So you will read, in the book of Joshua, of how Achsah the daughter of Caleb lighted from her ass and cried unto her father: "Give me a blessing! For thou hast now given me land; give me also the blessing of springs of water!" And he gave her the upper springs and the nether springs. And in the fields of Lecha and Maresha lived, later on, the families of them that wrought the finest linen of all. Our Portuguese crusader, whose own ancestors had once been great linen weavers of Tomar, as he rode through these same fields was struck by the quality of the flax, and so tied a bag of seeds to the pommel of his saddle.

From this circumstance originated the first privilege of the convent, which was to procure bridal sheets for all the young princesses of the royal house.

I will inform you, dear lady and gentleman, that in the country of Portugal in very old and noble families a venerable custom has been observed. On the morning after the wedding of a daughter of the house, and before the morning gift had yet been handed over, the Chamberlain or High Steward from a balcony of the palace would hang out the sheet of the night and would solemnly proclaim: *Virginem eam tenemus*—"we declare her to have been a virgin." Such a sheet was never afterwards washed or again lain on.

This time-honored custom was nowhere more strictly upheld than within the royal house itself, and it has there subsisted till within living memory.

Now for many hundred years the convent in the mountains, in appreciation of the excellent quality of the linen delivered, has held its second high privilege: that of receiving back that central piece of the snow-white sheet which bore witness to the honor of a royal bride.

In the tall main wing of the convent, which overlooks an immense landscape of hills and valleys, there is a long gallery with a black-and-white marble floor. On the walls of the gallery, side by side, hangs a low row of heavy, gilt frames, each of them adorned with a coroneted plate of pure gold, on which is engraved the name of a princess: Donna Christina, Donna Ines, Donna Jacintha Lenora, Donna Maria. And each of these frames encloses a square cut from a royal wedding sheet.

Within the faded markings of the canvases people of some imagination and sensibility may read all the signs of the zodiac: the Scales, the Scorpion, the Lion, the Twins. Or they may there find pictures from their own world of ideas: a rose, a heart, a sword—or even a heart pierced through with a sword.

In days of old it would occur that a long, stately, richly colored procession wound its way through the stone-gray mountain scenery, upwards to the convent. Princesses of Portugal, who were now queens or queen dowagers of foreign countries, Archduchesses, or Electresses, with their splendid retinue, proceeded here on a pilgrimage which was by nature both sacred and secretly gay. From the flax field upwards the road rises steeply; the royal lady would have to descend from her coach to be carried this last bit of the way in a palanquin presented to the convent for the very same purpose.

Later on, up to our own day, it has come to pass—as it comes to pass when a sheet of paper is being burnt, that after all other sparks have run along the edge and died away, one last clear little spark will appear and hurry along after them—that a very old highborn spinster undertakes the journey to Convento Velho. She has once, a long long time ago, been playmate, friend and maid-of-honor to a young princess of Portugal. As she makes her way to the convent she looks round to see the view widen to all sides. Within the building a sister conducts her to the gallery and to the plate bearing the name of the princess she has once served, and there takes leave of her, aware of her wish to be alone.

Slowly, slowly a row of recollections passes through the small, venerable, skull-like head under its mantilla of black lace, and it nods to them in amicable recognition. The loyal friend and confidante looks back upon the young bride's elevated married life with the elected royal consort. She takes stock of happy events and disappointments—coronations and jubilees, court intrigues and wars, the birth of heirs to the throne, the alliances of younger generations of princes and princesses, the rise or decline of dynasties. The old lady will remember how once, from the markings on the canvas, omens were drawn; now she will be able to compare the fulfillment to the omen, sighing a little and smiling a little. Each separate canvas with its coroneted name-plate has a story to tell, and each has been set up in loyalty to the story.

But in the midst of the long row there hangs a canvas which differs from the others. The frame of it is as fine and as heavy as any, and as proudly as any carries the golden plate with the royal crown. But on this one plate no name is inscribed, and the linen within the frame is snow-white from corner to corner, a blank page.

I beg of you, you good people who want to hear stories told: look at this page, and recognize the wisdom of my grandmother and of all old story-telling women!

For with what eternal and unswerving loyalty has not this canvas been inserted in the row! The story-tellers themselves before it draw their veils over their faces and are dumb. Because the royal papa and mama who once ordered this canvas to be framed and hung up, had they not had the tradition of loyalty in their blood, might have left it out.

It is in front of this piece of pure white linen that the old princesses of Portugal—worldly wise, dutiful, long-suffering queens, wives and mothers—and their noble old playmates, bridesmaids and maids-of-honor have most often stood still.

It is in front of the blank page that old and young nuns, with the Mother Abbess herself, sink into deepest thought.

EXERCISES

1. Explain the significance of the discussion of the "art of story-telling" in the beginning of this story. What does it mean to be loyal to the story? What is meant by the suggestion that if the storyteller is loyal to the story, in the end "silence will speak"?
2. What does it mean that a blank page tells the deepest story?
3. Discuss the statement "the very first germ of a story will come from some mystical place outside the story itself."
4. Discuss the significance of the ritual observed in this story. What is the importance of virginity here?
5. Compare the canvases of blood-stained sheets with Rorschach inkblots into which one can read whatever one wishes.
6. If each canvas has a story to tell, what story does the blank page canvas tell? Why does it make those women who observe it sink into the deepest thought?

VIRGINIA
WOOLF | *The Symbol*

There was a little dent on the top of the mountain like a crater on the moon. It was filled with snow, iridescent like a pigeon's breast, or dead white. There was a scurry of dry particles now and again, covering nothing. It was too high for breathing flesh or fur-covered life. All the same the snow was iridescent one moment; and blood red; and pure white, according to the day.

The graves in the valley—for there was a vast descent on either side; first pure rock; snow silted; lower a pine tree gripped a crag; then a solitary hut; then a saucer of pure green; then a cluster of eggshell roofs; at last, at the bottom, a village, a hotel, a cinema, and a graveyard—the graves in the churchyard near the hotel recorded the names of several men who had fallen climbing.

"The mountain," the lady wrote, sitting on the balcony of the hotel, "is a symbol . . ." She paused. She could see the topmost height through her glasses. She focused the lens, as if to see what the symbol was. She was writing to her elder sister at Birmingham.

The balcony overlooked the main street of the Alpine summer resort, like a box at a theater. There were very few private sitting rooms, and so the plays—such as they were—the curtain raisers—were acted in public. They were always a little provisional; preludes, curtain raisers. Entertainments to pass the time; seldom leading to any conclusion, such as marriage; or even lasting friendship. There was something fantastic about them, airy, inconclusive. So little that was solid could be dragged to this height. Even the houses looked gimcrack. By the time the voice of the English announcer reached the village it too became unreal.

Lowering her glasses, she nodded at the young men who in the street below were making ready to start. With one of them she had a certain connection—that is, an aunt of his had been mistress of her daughter's school.

Still holding the pen, still tipped with a drop of ink, she waved down at the climbers. She had written that the mountain was a symbol. But of what? In the forties of the last century two men, in the sixties four men, had perished; the first party when a rope broke, the second when night fell and froze them to death. We are always climbing to some height; that was the cliché. But it did not represent what was in her mind's eye, after seeing through her glasses the virgin height.

She continued, inconsequently. "I wonder why it makes me think of the Isle of Wight? You remember when Mama was dying, we took her there. And I would stand on the balcony when the boat came in and describe the passengers. I would say, I think that must be Mr. Edwards. . . . He has just come off the gangway. Then, now all the passengers have landed. Now they have turned the boat. . . . I never told you, naturally not—you were in India; you were going to have Lucy—how I longed when the doctor came that he should say, quite definitely, She cannot live another week. It was very prolonged; she lived eighteen months. The mountain just now reminded me how when I was alone, I would fix my eyes upon her death, as a symbol. I would think if I could reach that point—when I should be free—we could not marry as you remember until she died—a cloud then would do instead of the mountain. I thought, when I reach that point—I have never told anyone, for it seemed so heartless; I shall be at the top. And I could imagine so many sides. We come of course of an Anglo-Indian family. I can still imagine, from hearing stories told, how people live in other parts of the world. I can see mud huts, and savages; I can see elephants drinking at pools. So many of our uncles and cousins were explorers. I have always had a great desire to explore for myself. But of course, when the time came it seemed more sensible, considering our long engagement, to marry."

She looked across the street at a woman shaking a mat on another balcony. Every morning at the same time she came out. You could have thrown a pebble into her balcony. They had indeed come to the point of smiling at each other across the street.

"The little villas," she added, taking up her pen, "are much the same here as in Birmingham. Every house takes in lodgers. The hotel is quite full. Though monotonous, the food is not what you would call bad. And of course the hotel has a splendid view. One can see the mountain from every window. But then that's true of the whole place. I can assure you, I could shriek sometimes coming out of the one shop where they sell papers—we get them a week late—always to see that mountain. Sometimes it looks just across the way. At others, like a cloud; only it never moves. Somehow the talk, even among the invalids, who are everywhere, is always about the mountain. Either, how clear it is today, it might be across the street; or, how far away it looks, it might be a cloud. That is the usual cliché. In the storm last night, I hoped for once it was hidden. But just as they brought in the anchovies, the Rev. W. Bishop said, 'Look there's the mountain!'

"Am I being selfish? Ought I not to be ashamed of myself, when there is so much suffering? It is not confined to the visitors. The natives suffer dreadfully from goiter. Of course it could be stopped, if anyone had enterprise, and money. Ought one not to be ashamed of dwelling upon what after all can't be cured? It would need an earthquake to destroy that mountain, just as, I suppose, it was made by an earthquake. I asked the proprietor, Herr Melchior, the other day, if there were ever earthquakes now. No, he said, only landslides and avalanches. They have been known he said to blot out a whole village. But he added quickly, there's no danger here.

"As I write these words, I can see the young men quite plainly on the slopes of the mountain. They are roped together. One I think I told you was at the same school with Margaret. They are now crossing a crevasse . . ."

The pen fell from her hand, and the drop of ink straggled in a zigzag line down the page. The young men had disappeared.

It was only late that night when the search party had recovered the bodies that she found the unfinished letter on the table on the balcony. She dipped her pen once more and added, "The old clichés will come in very handy. They died trying to climb the mountain. . . . And the peasants brought spring flowers to lay upon their graves. They died in an attempt to discover . . ."

There seemed no fitting conclusion. And she added, "Love to the children," and then her pet name.

EXERCISES

1. Discuss the significance of the metaphor of reality as theater introduced in the story. Compare this with the similar metaphor in Katherine Mansfield's "Miss Brill" in Part I.

2. Why does the mountain remind the woman of her mother?

3. What does the mountain symbolize to the villagers?

4. What does the mountain symbolize at the end of the story?

5. What is the effect of the men dying while the woman is writing?

6. Is this a story about the subjective or the objective nature of symbolism? Compare this story with Nabokov's "Signs and Symbols."

VLADIMIR
NABOKOV | *Signs and Symbols*

For the fourth time in as many years they were confronted with the problem of what birthday present to bring a young man who was incurably deranged in his mind. He had no desires. Man-made objects were to him either hives of evil, vibrant with a malignant activity that he alone could perceive, or gross comforts for which no use could be found in his abstract world. After eliminating a number of articles that might offend him or frighten him (anything in the gadget line for instance was taboo), his parents chose a dainty and innocent trifle: a basket with ten different fruit jellies in ten little jars.

At the time of his birth they had been married already for a long time; a score of years had elapsed, and now they were quite old. Her drab gray hair was done anyhow. She wore cheap black dresses. Unlike other women of her age (such as Mrs. Sol, their next-door neighbor, whose face was all pink and mauve with paint and whose hat was a cluster of brookside flowers), she presented a naked white countenance to the fault-finding light of spring days. Her husband, who in the old country had been a fairly successful businessman, was now wholly dependent on his brother Isaac, a real American of almost forty years standing. They seldom saw him and had nicknamed him "the Prince."

That Friday everything went wrong. The underground train lost its life current between two stations, and for a quarter of an hour one could hear nothing but the dutiful beating of one's heart and the rustling of newspapers. The bus they had to take next kept them waiting for ages; and when it did come, it was crammed with garrulous high-school children. It was raining hard as they walked up the brown path leading to the sanitarium. There they waited again; and instead of their boy shuffling into the room as he usually did (his poor face blotched with acne, ill-shaven, sullen, and confused), a nurse they knew, and did not care for, appeared at last and brightly explained that he had again attempted to take his life. He was all right, she said, but a visit might disturb him. The place was so miserably understaffed, and things got mislaid or mixed up so easily, that they decided not to leave their present in the office but to bring it to him next time they came.

She waited for her husband to open his umbrella and then took his arm. He kept clearing his throat in a special resonant way he had when he was upset. They reached the bus-stop shelter on the other side of the street and he closed his umbrella. A few feet away, under a swaying and dripping tree, a tiny half-dead unfledged bird was helplessly twitching in a puddle.

During the long ride to the subway station, she and her husband did not exchange a word; and every time she glanced at his old hands (swollen veins, brown-spotted skin), clasped and twitching upon the handle of his umbrella, she felt the mounting pressure of tears. As she looked around trying to hook her mind onto something, it gave her a kind of soft shock, a mixture of compassion and wonder, to notice that one of the passengers, a girl with dark hair and grubby red toenails, was weeping on the shoulder of an older woman. Whom did that woman resemble? She resembled Rebecca Borisova, whose daughter had married one of the Soloveichiks—in Minsk, years ago.

The last time he had tried to do it, his method had been, in the doctor's words, a masterpiece of inventiveness; he would have succeeded, had not an envious fellow patient thought he was learning to fly—and stopped him. What he really wanted to do was to tear a hole in his world and escape.

The system of his delusions had been the subject of an elaborate paper in a scientific monthly, but long before that she and her husband had puzzled it out for themselves. "Referential mania," Herman Brink had called it. In these very rare cases the patient imagines that everything happening around him is a veiled reference to his personality and existence. He excludes real people from the conspiracy—because he considers himself to be so much more intelligent than other men. Phenomenal nature shadows him wherever he goes. Clouds in the staring sky transmit to one another, by means of slow signs, incredibly detailed information regarding him. His inmost thoughts are discussed at nightfall, in manual alphabet, by darkly gesticulating trees. Pebbles or stains or sun flecks form patterns representing in some awful way messages which he must intercept. Everything is a cipher and of everything he is the theme. Some of the spies are detached observers, such as glass surfaces and still pools; others, such as coats in store windows, are prejudiced witnesses, lynchers at heart; others again (running water, storms) are hysterical to the point of insanity, have a distorted opinion of him and grotesquely misinterpret his actions. He must be always on his guard and devote every minute and module of life to the decoding of the undulation of things. The very air he exhales is indexed and filed away. If only the interest he provokes were limited to his immediate surroundings—but alas it is not! With distance the torrents of wild scandal increase in volume and volubility. The silhouettes of his blood corpuscles, magnified a million times, flit over vast plains; and still farther, great mountains of unbearable solidity and height sum up in terms of granite and groaning firs the ultimate truth of his being.

When they emerged from the thunder and foul air of the subway, the last dregs of the day were mixed with the street lights. She wanted to buy some fish for supper, so she handed him the basket of jelly jars, telling him to go home. He walked up to the third landing and then remembered he had given her his keys earlier in the day.

In silence he sat down on the steps and in silence rose when some ten minutes later she came, heavily trudging upstairs, wanly smiling, shaking her head in deprecation of her silliness. They entered their two-room flat and he at once went to the mirror. Straining the corners of his mouth apart by means of his thumbs, with a horrible masklike grimace, he removed his new hopelessly uncomfortable dental plate and severed the long tusks of saliva connecting him to it. He read his Russian-language newspaper while she laid the table. Still reading, he ate the pale victuals that needed no teeth. She knew his moods and was also silent.

When he had gone to bed, she remained in the living room with her pack of soiled cards and her old albums. Across the narrow yard where the rain tinkled in the dark against some battered ash cans, windows were blandly alight and in one of them a black-trousered man with his bare elbows raised could be seen lying supine on an untidy bed. She pulled the blind down and examined the photographs. As a baby he looked more surprised than most babies. From a fold in the album, a German maid they had had in Leipzig and her fat-faced fiancé fell out. Minsk, the Revolution, Leipzig, Berlin, Leipzig, a slanting house front badly out of focus. Four years old, in a park: moodily, shyly, with puckered forehead, looking away from an eager squirrel as he would from any other stranger. Aunt Rosa, a fussy, angular, wild-eyed old lady, who had lived in a tremulous world of bad news, bankruptcies, train accidents, cancerous growths—until the Germans put her to death, together with all the people she had worried about. Age six—that was when he drew wonderful birds with human hands and feet, and suffered from insomnia like a grown-up man. His cousin, now a famous chess player. He again, aged about eight, already difficult to understand, afraid of the wallpaper in the passage, afraid of a certain picture in a book which merely showed an idyllic landscape with rocks on a hillside and an old cart wheel hanging from the branch of a leafless tree. Aged ten: the year they left Europe. The shame, the pity, the humiliating difficulties, the ugly, vicious, backward children he was with in that special school. And then came a time in his life, coinciding with a long convalescence after pneumonia, when those little phobias of his which his parents had stubbornly regarded as the eccentricities of a prodigiously gifted child hardened as it were into a dense tangle of logically interacting illusions, making him totally inaccessible to normal minds.

This, and much more, she accepted—for after all living did mean accepting the loss of one joy after another, not even joys in her case—mere possibilities of improvement. She thought of the endless waves of pain that for some reason or other she and her husband had to endure; of the invisible giants hurting her boy in some unimaginable fashion; of the incalculable amount of tenderness contained in the world; of the fate of this tenderness, which is either crushed, or wasted, or transformed into madness; of neglected children humming to themselves in unswept corners; of beautiful weeds that cannot hide from the farmer and helplessly have to watch the shadow of his simian stoop leave mangled flowers in its wake, as the monstrous darkness approaches.

It was past midnight when from the living room she heard her husband moan; and presently he staggered in, wearing over his nightgown the old overcoat with astrakhan collar which he much preferred to the nice blue bathrobe he had.

"I can't sleep," he cried.

"Why," she asked, "why can't you sleep? You were so tired."

"I can't sleep because I am dying," he said and lay down on the couch.

"Is it your stomach? Do you want me to call Dr. Solov?"

"No doctors, no doctors," he moaned, "To the devil with doctors! We must get him out of there quick. Otherwise we'll be responsible. Responsible!"

he repeated and hurled himself into a sitting position, both feet on the floor, thumping his forehead with his clenched fist.

"All right," she said quietly, "we shall bring him home tomorrow morning."

"I would like some tea," said her husband and retired to the bathroom.

Bending with difficulty, she retrieved some playing cards and a photograph or two that had slipped from the couch to the floor: knave of hearts, nine of spades, ace of spades, Elsa and her bestial beau.

He returned in high spirits, saying in a loud voice:

"I have it all figured out. We will give him the bedroom. Each of us will spend part of the night near him and the other part on this couch. By turns. We will have the doctor see him at least twice a week. It does not matter what the Prince says. He won't have to say much anyway because it will come out cheaper."

The telephone rang. It was an unusual hour for their telephone to ring. His left slipper had come off and he groped for it with his heel and toe as he stood in the middle of the room, and childishly, toothlessly, gaped at his wife. Having more English than he did, it was she who attended to calls.

"Can I speak to Charlie," said a girl's dull little voice.

"What number you want? No. That is not the right number."

The receiver was gently cradled. Her hand went to her old tired heart.

"It frightened me," she said.

He smiled a quick smile and immediately resumed his excited monologue. They would fetch him as soon as it was day. Knives would have to be kept in a locked drawer. Even at his worst he presented no danger to other people.

The telephone rang a second time. The same toneless anxious young voice asked for Charlie.

"You have the incorrect number. I will tell you what you are doing: you are turning the letter O instead of the zero."

They sat down to their unexpected festive midnight tea. The birthday present stood on the table. He sipped noisily; his face was flushed; every now and then he imparted a circular motion to his raised glass so as to make the sugar dissolve more thoroughly. The vein on the side of his bald head where there was a large birthmark stood out conspicuously and, although he had shaved that morning, a silvery bristle showed on his chin. While she poured him another glass of tea, he put on his spectacles and re-examined with pleasure the luminous, yellow, green, red little jars. His clumsy moist lips spelled out their eloquent labels: apricot, grape, beech plum, quince. He had got to crab apple, when the telephone rang again.

Exercises

1. Discuss the nature of the young man's mental derangement. What is "referential mania"? Consider particularly the young man's obsession that everything means something and that everything means something about him.

2. Why is "interpretation" an important activity for the young man?

3. Why does the woman look through the photograph album? What relevance do the pictures have to the present situation?

4. Why do the couple decide suddenly to take the young man out of the institution?

5. What is the meaning of the last phone ring? Why does the story end before the phone is answered?

6. Discuss the significance of the title of the story. What does it have to do with the final phone ring? What does it mean to feel that everything means something? How can things mean anything? Compare this story with Jorge Luis Borges' "Funes, the Memorious" and Alain Robbe-Grillet's "The Secret Room" in Part III.

DONALD BARTHELME | *The Balloon*

The balloon, beginning at a point on Fourteenth Street, the exact location of which I cannot reveal, expanded northward all one night, while people were sleeping, until it reached the Park. There, I stopped it; at dawn the northernmost edges lay over the Plaza; the free-hanging motion was frivolous and gentle. But experiencing a faint irritation at stopping, even to protect the trees, and seeing no reason the balloon should not be allowed to expand upward, over the parts of the city it was already covering, into the "air space" to be found there, I asked the engineers to see to it. This expansion took place throughout the morning, soft imperceptible sighing of gas through the valves. The balloon then covered forty-five blocks north-south on either side of the Avenue in some places. That was the situation, then.

But it is wrong to speak of "situations," implying sets of circumstances leading to some resolution, some escape of tension; there were no situations, simply the balloon hanging there—muted heavy grays and browns for the most part, contrasting with walnut and soft yellows. A deliberate lack of finish, enhanced by skillful installation, gave the surface a rough, forgotten quality; sliding weights on the inside, carefully adjusted, anchored the great, varishaped mass at a number of points. Now we have had a flood of original ideas in all media, works of singular beauty as well as significant milestones in the history of inflation, but at that moment there was only *this balloon*, concrete particular, hanging there.

There were reactions. Some people found the balloon "interesting." As a response this seemed inadequate to the immensity of the balloon, the suddenness of its appearance over the city; on the other hand, in the absence of hysteria or other societally induced anxiety, it must be judged a calm, "mature" one. There was a certain amount of initial argumentation about the "meaning" of the balloon; this subsided, because we have learned not to insist on meanings, and they are rarely even looked for now, except in cases involving the simplest, safest phenomena. It was agreed that since the meaning of the balloon could never be known absolutely, extended discussion was pointless, or at least less purposeful than the activities of those who, for example, hung green and blue paper lanterns from the warm gray underside, in certain streets, or seized the occasion to write messages on the surface, announcing their availability for the performance of unnatural acts, or the availability of acquaintances.

Daring children jumped, especially at those points where the balloon hovered close to a building, so that the gap between balloon and building was a matter of a few inches, or points where the balloon actually made contact, exerting an ever-so-slight pressure against the side of a building, so that balloon and building seemed a unity. The upper surface was so structured that a "landscape" was presented, small valleys as well as slight knolls, or mounds; once atop the balloon, a stroll was possible, or even a trip, from one place to another. There was pleasure in being able to run down an incline, then up the opposing slope, both gently graded, or in making a leap from one side to the other. Bouncing was possible, because of the pneumaticity of the surface, and even falling, if that was your wish. That all these varied motions, as well as others, were within one's possibilities, in experiencing the "up" side of the balloon, was extremely exciting for children, accustomed to the city's flat, hard skin. But the purpose of the balloon was not to amuse children.

Too, the number of people, children and adults, who took advantage of the opportunities described was not so large as it might have been: a certain timidity, lack of trust in the balloon, was seen. There was, furthermore, some hostility. Because we had hidden the pumps, which fed helium to the interior, and because the surface was so vast that the authorities could not determine the point of entry—that is, the point at which the gas was injected—a degree of frustration was evidenced by those city officers into whose province such manifestations normally fell. The apparent purposelessness of the balloon was vexing (as was the fact that it was "there" at all). Had we painted, in great letters, "LABORATORY TESTS PROVE" or "18% MORE EFFECTIVE!" on the sides of the balloon, this difficulty would have been circumvented. But I could not bear to do so. On the whole, these officers were remarkably tolerant, considering the dimensions of the anomaly, this tolerance being the result of, first, secret tests conducted by night that convinced them that little or nothing could be done in the way of removing or destroying the balloon, and, secondly, a public warmth that arose (not uncolored by touches of the aforementioned hostility) toward the balloon, from ordinary citizens.

As a single balloon must stand for a lifetime of thinking about balloons, so each citizen expressed, in the attitude he chose, a complex of attitudes. One man might consider that the balloon had to do with the notion *sullied,* as in the sentence *The big balloon sullied the otherwise clear and radiant Manhattan sky.* That is, the balloon was, in this man's view, an imposture, something inferior to the sky that had formerly been there, something interposed between the people and their "sky." But in fact it was January, the sky was dark and ugly; it was not a sky you could look up into, lying on your back in the street, with pleasure; unless pleasure, for you, proceeded from having been threatened, from having been misused. And the underside of the balloon was a pleasure to look up into, we had seen to that, muted grays and browns for the most part, contrasted with walnut and soft, forgotten yellows. And so, while this man was thinking *sullied*, still there was an admixture of pleasurable cognition in his thinking, struggling with the original perception.

Another man, on the other hand, might view the balloon as if it were part of a system of unanticipated rewards, as when one's employer walks in and says, "Here, Henry, take this package of money I have wrapped for you, because we have been doing so well in the business here, and I admire the way you bruise the tulips, without which bruising your department would not be a success, or at least not the success that it is." For this man the balloon might be a brilliantly heroic "muscle and pluck" experience, even if an experience poorly understood.

Another man might say, "Without the example of ———, it is doubtful that ——— would exist today in its present form," and find many to agree with him, or to argue with him. Ideas of "bloat" and "float" were introduced, as well as concepts of dream and responsibility. Others engaged in remarkably detailed fantasies having to do with a wish either to lose themselves in the balloon, or to engorge it. The private character of these wishes, of their origins, deeply buried and unknown, was such that they were not much spoken of; yet there is evidence that they were widespread. It was also argued that what was important was what you felt when you stood under the balloon; some people claimed that they felt sheltered, warmed, as never before, while enemies of the balloon felt, or reported feeling, constrained, a "heavy" feeling.

Critical opinion was divided:

"monstrous pourings"

                                                           "harp"

XXXXXXX *"certain contrasts with darker portions"*
                              "inner joy"
  "large, square corners"
"conservative eclecticism that has so far governed modern balloon design"
    ::::::*"abnormal vigor"*
  "warm, soft, lazy passages"
The Balloon
  "Has unity been sacrificed for a sprawling quality?"
  "Quelle catastrophe!"
  "munching"

People began, in a curious way, to locate themselves in relation to aspects of the balloon: "I'll be at that place where it dips down into Forty-seventh Street almost to the sidewalk, near the Alamo Chile House," or, "Why don't we go stand on top, and take the air, and maybe walk about a bit, where it forms a tight, curving line with the façade of the Gallery of Modern Art—" Marginal intersections offered entrances with a given time duration, as well as "warm, soft, lazy passages" in which . . . But it is wrong to speak of "marginal intersections," each intersection was crucial, none could be ignored (as if, walking there, you might not find someone capable of turning your attention, in a flash, from old exercises to new exercises, risks and escalations). Each intersection was crucial, meeting of balloon and building, meeting of balloon and man, meeting of balloon and balloon.

It was suggested that what was admired about the balloon was finally this: that it was not limited, or defined. Sometimes a bulge, blister, or sub-section would carry all the way east to the river on its own initiative, in the manner of an army's movements on a map, as seen in a headquarters remote from the fighting. Then that part would be, as it were, thrown back again, or would withdraw into new dispositions; the next morning, that part would have made another sortie, or disappeared altogether. This ability of the balloon to shift its shape, to change, was very pleasing, especially to people whose lives were rather rigidly patterned, persons to whom change, although desired, was not available. The balloon, for the twenty-two days of its existence, offered the possibility, in its randomness, of mislocation of the self, in contradistinction to the grid of precise, rectangular pathways under our feet. The amount of specialized training currently needed, and the consequent desirability of long-term commitments, has been occasioned by the steadily growing importance of complex machinery, in virtually all kinds of operations; as this tendency increases, more and more people will turn, in bewildered inadequacy, to solutions for which the balloon may stand as a prototype, or "rough draft."

I met you under the balloon, on the occasion of your return from Norway; you asked if it was mine; I said it was. The balloon, I said, is a spontaneous autobiographical disclosure, having to do with the unease I felt at your absence, and with sexual deprivation, but now that your visit to Bergen has been terminated, it is no longer necessary or appropriate. Removal of the balloon was easy; trailer trucks carried away the depleted fabric, which is now stored in West Virginia, awaiting some other time of unhappiness, sometime, perhaps, when we are angry with one another.

EXERCISES

1. What relationship does the narrator have to the balloon? Why can he not reveal the origins or sources of the balloon?

2. Why does the narrator say it is wrong to speak of "situations"? Why is the balloon not a situation? What is a "concrete particular"?

3. Discuss the various reactions to the balloon—the need to interpret it, to understand its meaning.

4. Discuss the significance of "critical opinion" about the balloon. How is the balloon like an art object?

5. Discuss the characteristic of the balloon that makes it most admired. What does this characteristic mean?

6. What is suggested by the real "intention" of the balloon as revealed by the last paragraph?
7. Discuss the satiric elements of this story. Compare it with Isak Dinesen's "The Blank Page."

FRANK
STOCKTON | # The Lady, or the Tiger

In the very olden time there lived a semi-barbaric king, whose ideas, though somewhat polished and sharpened by the progressiveness of distant Latin neighbors, were still large, florid, and untrammeled, as became the half of him which was barbaric. He was a man of exuberant fancy, and, withal, of an authority so irresistible that, at his will, he turned his varied fancies into facts. He was greatly given to self-communing; and, when he and himself agreed upon anything, the thing was done. When every member of his domestic and political systems moved smoothly in its appointed course, his nature was bland and genial; but whenever there was a little hitch, and some of his orbs got out of their orbits, he was blander and more genial still, for nothing pleased him so much as to make the crooked straight, and crush down uneven places.

Among the borrowed notions by which his barbarism had become semified was that of the public arena, in which, by exhibitions of manly and beastly valor, the minds of his subjects were refined and cultured.

But even here the exuberant and barbaric fancy asserted itself. The arena of the king was built, not to give the people an opportunity of hearing the rhapsodies of dying gladiators, nor to enable them to view the inevitable conclusion of a conflict between religious opinions and hungry jaws, but for purposes far better adapted to widen and develop the mental energies of the people. This vast amphitheater, with its encircling galleries, its mysterious vaults, and its unseen passages, was an agent of poetic justice, in which crime was punished, or virtue rewarded, by the decrees of an impartial and incorruptible chance.

When a subject was accused of a crime of sufficient importance to interest the king, public notice was given that on an appointed day the fate of the accused person would be decided in the king's arena—a structure which well deserved its name; for, although its form and plan were borrowed from afar, its purpose emanated solely from the brain of this man, who, every barleycorn a king, knew no tradition to which he owed more allegiance than pleased his fancy, and who ingrafted on every adopted form of human thought and action the rich growth of his barbaric idealism.

When all the people had assembled in the galleries, and the king, surrounded by his court, sat high up on his throne of royal state on one side of the arena, he gave a signal, a door beneath him opened, and the accused subject stepped out into the amphitheater. Directly opposite him, on the other side of the enclosed space, were two doors, exactly alike and side by side. It was the duty and the privilege of the person on trial to walk directly to these doors and open one of them. He could open either door he pleased: he was subject to no guidance or influence but that of the aforementioned impartial and incorruptible chance. If he opened the one, there came one of it a hungry tiger, the fiercest and most cruel that could be procured, which immediately sprang upon him, and tore him to pieces, as a punishment for his guilt. The moment that the case of the criminal was thus decided, doleful iron bells were clanged, great wails went up from the hired mourners posted on the outer rim of the arena, and the vast audience, with bowed heads and downcast hearts, wended slowly their homeward way, mourning greatly that one so young and fair, or so old and respected, should have merited so dire a fate.

But, if the accused person opened the other door, there came forth from it a lady, the most suitable to his years and station that his majesty could select among his fair subjects; and to this lady he was immediately married, as a reward of his innocence. It mattered not that he might already possess a wife and family, or that his affections might be engaged upon an object of his own selection: the king allowed no such subordinate arrangements to interfere with his great scheme of retribution and reward. The exercises, as in the other instance, took place immediately, and in the arena. Another door opened beneath the king, and a priest, followed by a band of choristers, and dancing maidens blowing joyous airs on golden horns and treading an epithalamic measure, advanced to where the pair stood, side by side; and the wedding was promptly and cheerily solemnized. Then the gay brass bells rang forth their merry peals, the people shouted glad hurrahs, and the innocent man, preceded by children strewing flowers on his path, led his bride to his home.

This was the king's semi-barbaric method of administering justice. Its perfect fairness is obvious. The criminal could not know out of which door would come the lady: he opened either he pleased, without having the slightest idea whether, in the next instant, he was to be devoured or married. On some occasions the tiger came out of one door, and on some out of the other. The decisions of his tribunal were not only fair, they were positively determinate: the accused person was instantly punished if he found himself guilty; and, if innocent, he was rewarded on the spot whether he liked it or not. There was no escape from the judgments of the king's arena.

The institution was a very popular one. When the people gathered together on one of the great trial days they never knew whether they were to witness a bloody slaughter or a hilarious wedding. This element of uncertainty lent an interest to the occasion which it could not otherwise have attained. Thus the masses were entertained and pleased, and the thinking part of the community could bring no charge of unfairness against this plan; for did not the accused person have the whole matter in his own hands?

The semi-barbaric king had a daughter as blooming as his most florid fancies, and with a soul as fervent and imperious as his own. As is usual in such cases, she was the apple of his eye, and was loved by him above all humanity. Among his courtiers was a young man of that fineness of blood and lowness of station common to the conventional heroes of romance who love royal maidens. This royal maiden was well satisfied with her lover, for he was handsome and brave to a degree unsurpassed in all this kingdom; and she loved him with an ardor that had enough of barbarism in it to make it exceedingly warm and strong. This love affair moved on happily for many months, until one day the king happened to discover its existence. He did not hesitate nor waver in regard to his duty in the premises. The youth was immediately cast into prison, and a day was appointed for his trial in the king's arena. This, of course, was an especially important occasion; and his majesty, as well as all the people, was greatly interested in the workings and development of this trial. Never before had such a case occurred; never before had a subject dared to love the daughter of a king. In after-years such things became commonplace enough; but then they were, in no slight degree, novel and startling.

The tiger-cages of the kingdom were searched for the most savage and relentless beasts, from which the fiercest monster might be selected for the arena; and the ranks of maiden youth and beauty throughout the land were carefully surveyed by competent judges, in order that the young man might have a fitting bride in case fate did not determine for him a different destiny. Of course, everybody knew that the deed with which the accused was charged had been done. He had loved the princess, and neither he, she, nor any one else thought of denying the fact; but the king would not think of allowing any fact of this kind to interfere with the workings of the tribunal, in which he took such great delight and satisfaction. No matter how the affair turned out, the youth would be disposed of; and the king would take an aesthetic pleasure in watching the course of events, which would determine whether or not the young man had done wrong in allowing himself to love the princess.

The appointed day arrived. From far and near the people gathered, and thronged the great galleries of the arena; and the crowds, unable to gain admittance, massed themselves against its outside walls. The king and his court were in their places, opposite the twin doors—those fateful portals, so terrible in their similarity.

All was ready. The signal was given. A door beneath the royal party opened, and the lover of the princess walked into the arena. Tall, beautiful, fair, his appearance was greeted with a low hum of admiration and anxiety. Half the audience had not known so grand a youth had lived among them. No wonder the princess loved him! What a terrible thing for him to be there!

As the youth advanced into the arena, he turned, as the custom was, to bow to the king: but he did not think at all of that royal personage; his eyes were fixed upon the princess, who sat to the right of her father. Had it not been for the moiety of barbarism in her nature, it is probable that lady would not have been there; but her intense and fervid soul would not allow her to be absent on an occasion in which she was so terribly interested. From the moment that the decree had gone forth, that her lover should decide his fate in the king's arena, she had thought of nothing, night or day, but this great event and the various subjects connected with it. Possessed of more power, influence, and force of character than any one who had ever before been interested in such a case, she had done what no other person had done—she had possessed herself of the secret of the doors. She knew in which of the two rooms, that lay behind those doors, stood the cage of the tiger, with its open front, and in which waited the lady. Through these thick doors, heavily curtained with skins on the inside, it was impossible that any noise or suggestion should come from within to the person who should approach to raise the latch of one of them; but gold, and the power of a woman's will, had brought the secret to the princess.

And not only did she know in which room stood the lady ready to emerge, all blushing and radiant, should her door be opened, but she knew who the lady was. It was one of the fairest and loveliest of the damsels of the court who had been selected as the reward of the accused youth, should he be proved innocent of the crime of aspiring to one so far above him; and the princess hated her. Often had she seen, or imagined that she had seen, this fair creature throwing glances of admiration upon the person of her lover, and sometimes she thought these glances were perceived and even returned. Now and then she had seen them talking together; it was but for a moment or two, but much can be said in a brief space; it may have been on most unimportant topics, but how could she know that? The girl was lovely, but she had dared to raise her eyes to the loved one of the princess; and, with all the intensity of the savage blood transmitted to her through long lines of wholly barbaric ancestors, she hated the woman who blushed and trembled behind that silent door.

When her lover turned and looked at her, and his eye met hers as she sat there paler and whiter than any one in the vast ocean of anxious faces about her, he saw, by that power of quick perception which is given to those whose souls are one, that she knew behind which door crouched the tiger, and behind which stood the lady. He had expected her to know it. He understood her nature, and his soul was assured that she would never rest until she had made plain to herself this thing, hidden to all other lookers-on, even to the king. The only hope for the youth in which there was any element of certainty was based upon the success of the princess in discovering this mystery; and the moment he looked upon her, he saw she had succeeded, as in his soul he knew she would succeed.

Then it was that his quick and anxious glance asked the question: "Which?" It was as plain to her as if he shouted it from where he stood. There was not an instant to be lost. The question was asked in a flash; it must be answered in another.

Her right arm lay on the cushioned parapet before her. She raised her hand, and made a slight, quick movement toward the right. No one but her lover saw her. Every eye but his was fixed on the man in the arena.

He turned, and with a firm and rapid step he walked across the empty space. Every heart stopped beating, every breath was held, every eye was fixed immovably upon that man. Without the slightest hesitation, he went to the door on the right, and opened it.

Now, the point of the story is this: Did the tiger come out of that door, or did the lady?

The more we reflect upon this question, the harder it is to answer. It involves a study of the human heart which leads us through devious mazes of passion, out of which it is difficult to find our way. Think of it, fair reader, not as if the decision of the question depended upon yourself, but upon that hot-blooded, semi-barbaric princess, her soul at a white heat beneath the combined fires of despair and jealousy. She had lost him, but who should have him?

How often, in her waking hours and in her dreams, had she started in wild horror, and covered her face with her hands as she thought of her lover opening the door on the other side of which waited the cruel fangs of the tiger!

But how much oftener had she seen him at the other door! How in her grievous reveries had she gnashed her teeth, and torn her hair, when she saw his start of rapturous delight as he opened the door of the lady! How her soul had burned in agony when she had seen him rush to meet that woman, with her flushing cheek and sparkling eye of triumph; when she had seen him lead her forth, his whole frame kindled with the joy of recovered life; when she had heard the glad shouts from the multitude, and the wild ringing of the happy bells; when she had seen the priest, with his joyous followers, advance to the couple, and make them man and wife before her very eyes; and when she had seen them walk away together upon their path of flowers, followed by the tremendous shouts of the hilarious multitude, in which her one despairing shriek was lost and drowned!

Would it not be better for him to die at once, and go to wait for her in the blessed regions of semi-barbaric futurity?

And yet, that awful tiger, those shrieks, that blood!

Her decision had been indicated in an instant, but it had been made after days and nights of anguished deliberation. She had known she would be asked, she had decided what she would answer, and, without the slightest hesitation, she had moved her hand to the right.

The question of her decision is one not to be lightly considered, and it is not for me to presume to set myself up as the one person able to answer it. And so I leave it with all of you: Which came out of the opened door—the lady, or the tiger?

EXERCISES

1. Note that the king is semibarbaric—which means that he is also semicivilized. His daughter is also characterized as half civilized and half barbaric. What does this duality have to do with the central duality of the story—tiger or lady?

2. Discuss the tone of the story. Is this a serious story about life and death? Or is it a comic story with a satiric theme? Traditionally, tragedies end in death and comedies end in marriage.

3. What is the difference between the king's method of administering justice and the courtroom/jury method used in "civilized" societies? How is a courtroom trial like theater? What is the difference between "poetic justice"

and "real-life justice"? How do we ever know the difference between innocence and guilt? How is the king's method "fair"?

4. How do you know which one came out the door? If the princess is half tigerish and half ladylike, the issue is, which side predominates? How are the two doors, and thus these two characteristics, "terrible in their similarity"?

5. When this story was first published, many readers wrote to Frank Stockton wanting to know the answer to the final question. Why do readers want to know what "happens" to characters who do not even exist except in an author's imagination?

MARGARET ATWOOD | *Happy Endings*

John and Mary meet.
What happens next?
If you want a happy ending, try A.

A. John and Mary fall in love and get married. They both have worthwhile and remunerative jobs which they find stimulating and challenging. They buy a charming house. Real estate values go up. Eventually, when they can afford live-in help, they have two children, to whom they are devoted. The children turn out well. John and Mary have a stimulating and challenging sex life and worthwhile friends. They go on fun vacations together. They retire. They both have hobbies which they find stimulating and challenging. Eventually they die. This is the end of the story.

B. Mary falls in love with John but John doesn't fall in love with Mary. He merely uses her body for selfish pleasure and ego gratification of a tepid kind. He comes to her apartment twice a week and she cooks him dinner, you'll notice that he doesn't even consider her worth the price of a dinner out, and after he's eaten the dinner he fucks her and after that he falls asleep, while she does the dishes so he won't think she's untidy, having all those dirty dishes lying around, and puts on fresh lipstick so she'll look good when he wakes up, but when he wakes up he doesn't even notice, he puts on his socks and his shorts and his pants and his shirt and his tie and his shoes, the reverse order from the one in which he took them off. He doesn't take off Mary's clothes, she takes them off herself, she acts as if she's dying for it every time, not because she likes sex exactly, she doesn't, but she wants John to think she does because if they do it often enough surely he'll get used to her, he'll come to depend on her and they will get married, but John goes out the door with hardly so much as a good-night and three days later he turns up at six o'clock and they do the whole thing over again.

Mary gets run-down. Crying is bad for your face, everyone knows that and so does Mary but she can't stop. People at work notice. Her friends tell her John is a rat, a pig, a dog, he isn't good enough for her, but she can't believe it. Inside John, she thinks, is another John, who is much nicer. This other John will emerge like a butterfly from a cocoon, a Jack from a box, a pit from a prune, if the first John is only squeezed enough.

One evening John complains about the food. He has never complained about the food before. Mary is hurt.

Her friends tell her they've seen him in a restaurant with another woman, whose name is Madge. It's not even Madge that finally gets to Mary: it's the restaurant. John has never taken Mary to a restaurant. Mary collects all the sleeping pills and aspirins she can find, and takes them and a half a bottle of sherry. You can see what kind of a woman she is by the fact that it's not even whiskey. She leaves a note for John. She hopes he'll discover her and get her to the hospital in time and repent and then they can get married, but this fails to happen and she dies.

John marries Madge and everything continues as in A.

C. John, who is an older man, falls in love with Mary, and Mary, who is only twenty-two, feels sorry for him because he's worried about his hair falling out. She sleeps with him even though she's not in love with him. She met him at work. She's in love with someone called James, who is twenty-two also and not yet ready to settle down.

John on the contrary settled down long ago: this is what is bothering him. John has a steady, respectable job and is getting ahead in his field, but Mary isn't impressed by him, she's impressed by James, who has a motorcycle and a fabulous record collection. But James is often away on his motorcycle, being free. Freedom isn't the same for girls, so in the meantime Mary spends Thursday evenings with John. Thursdays are the only days John can get away.

John is married to a woman called Madge and they have two children, a charming house which they bought just before the real estate values went up, and hobbies which they find stimulating and challenging, when they have the time. John tells Mary how important she is to him, but of course he can't leave his wife because a commitment is a commitment. He goes on about this more than is necessary and Mary finds it boring, but older men can keep it up longer so on the whole she has a fairly good time.

One day James breezes in on his motorcycle with some top-grade California hybrid and James and Mary get higher than you'd believe possible and they climb into bed. Everything becomes very underwater, but along comes John, who has a key to Mary's apartment. He finds them stoned and entwined. He's hardly in any position to be jealous, considering Madge, but nevertheless he's overcome with despair. Finally he's middle-aged, in two years he'll be bald as an egg and he can't stand it. He purchases a handgun, saying he needs it for target practice—this is the thin part of the plot, but it can be dealt with later—and shoots the two of them and himself.

Madge, after a suitable period of mourning, marries an understanding man called Fred and everything continues as in A, but under different names.

D. Fred and Madge have no problems. They get along exceptionally well and are good at working out any little difficulties that may arise. But their charming house is by the seashore and one day a giant tidal wave approaches. Real estate values go down. The rest of the story is about what caused the tidal wave and how they escape from it. They do, though thousands drown, but Fred and Madge are virtuous and lucky. Finally on high ground they clasp each other, wet and dripping and grateful, and continue as in A.

E. Yes, but Fred has a bad heart. The rest of the story is about how kind and understanding they both are until Fred dies. Then Madge devotes herself to charity work until the end of A. If you like, it can be "Madge," "cancer," "guilty and confused," and "bird watching."

F. If you think this is all too bourgeois, make John a revolutionary and Mary a counterespionage agent and see how far that gets you. Remember, this is Canada. You'll still end up with A, though in between you may get a lustful brawling saga of passionate involvement, a chronicle of our times, sort of.

You'll have to face it, the endings are the same however you slice it. Don't be deluded by any other endings, they're all fake, either deliberately fake, with malicious intent to deceive, or just motivated by excessive optimism if not by downright sentimentality.

The only authentic ending is the one provided here:

John and Mary die. John and Mary die. John and Mary die.

So much for endings. Beginnings are always more fun. True connoisseurs, however, are known to favor the stretch in between, since it's the hardest to do anything with.

That's about all that can be said for plots, which anyway are just one thing after another, a what and a what and a what.

Now try How and Why.

EXERCISES

1. Which of the first two stories—A or B—is the more interesting? Which one is more apt to be made into a movie? Which one is closer to the "truth"? What does interest have to do with truth? What makes one of these stories more interesting than the other?

2. From whose point of view would story C most likely be told? How do you feel about what happens in C after reading what happens in B? How would you feel about what happens in C if you have not read B?

3. Why does every story end with A? Why is the only authentic ending *"John and Mary die"*? Does this mean that all stories that end some other way are not authentic? What is the difference between endings in life and endings in stories?

4. What is the difference between a plot and an explanation? How does this story illustrate the importance of stories being more than just a series of events, one thing after another? How does the ending of a story make the story more than merely a series of events, just one thing after another?

GRACE
PALEY │ *A Conversation with My Father*

M y father is eighty-six years old and in bed. His heart, that bloody motor, is equally old and will not do certain jobs any more. It still floods his head with brainy light. But it won't let his legs carry the weight of his body around the house. Despite my metaphors, this muscle failure is not due to his old heart, he says, but to a potassium shortage. Sitting on one pillow, leaning on three, he offers last-minute advice and makes a request.

"I would like you to write a simple story just once more," he says, "the kind de Maupassant wrote, or Chekhov, the kind you used to write. Just recognizable people and then write down what happened to them next."

I say, "Yes, why not? That's possible." I want to please him, though I don't remember writing that way. I *would* like to try to tell such a story, if he means the kind that begins: "There was a woman . . ." followed by plot, the absolute line between two points which I've always despised. Not for literary reasons, but because it takes all hope away. Everyone, real or invented, deserves the open destiny of life.

Finally I thought of a story that had been happening for a couple of years right across the street. I wrote it down, then read it aloud. "Pa," I said, "how about this? Do you mean something like this?"

> Once in my time there was a woman and she had a son. They lived nicely, in a small apartment in Manhattan. This boy at about fifteen became a junkie, which is not unusual in our neighborhood. In order to maintain her close friendship with him, she became a junkie too. She said it was part of the youth culture, with which she felt very much at home. After a while, for a number of reasons, the boy gave it all up and left the city and his mother in disgust. Hopeless and alone, she grieved. We all visit her.

"O.K., Pa, that's it," I said, "an unadorned and miserable tale."

"But that's not what I mean," my father said. "You misunderstood me on purpose. You know there's a lot more to it. You know that. You left everything out. Turgenev wouldn't do that. Chekhov wouldn't do that. There are in fact Russian writers you never heard of, you don't have an inkling of, as good as anyone, who can write a plain ordinary story, who would not leave out what you have left out. I object not to facts but to people sitting in trees talking senselessly, voices from who knows where. . . ."

"Forget that one, Pa, what have I left out now? In this one?"

"Her looks, for instance."

"Oh. Quite handsome, I think. Yes."

"Her hair?"

"Dark, with heavy braids, as though she were a girl or a foreigner."

"What were her parents like, her stock? That she became such a person. It's interesting, you know."

"From out of town. Professional people. The first to be divorced in their county. How's that? Enough?" I asked.

"With you, it's all a joke," he said. "What about the boy's father? Why didn't you mention him? Who was he? Or was the boy born out of wedlock?"

"Yes," I said. "He was born out of wedlock."

"For Godsakes, doesn't anyone in your stories get married? Doesn't anyone have the time to run down to City Hall before they jump into bed?"

"No," I said. "In real life, yes. But in my stories, no."

"Why do you answer me like that?"

"Oh, Pa, this is a simple story about a smart woman who came to N.Y.C. full of interest love trust excitement very up to date, and about her son, what a hard time she had in this world. Married or not, it's of small consequence."

"It is of great consequence," he said.

"O.K.," I said.

"O.K. O.K. yourself," he said, "but listen. I believe you that she's good-looking, but I don't think she was so smart."

"That's true," I said. "Actually that's the trouble with stories. People start out fantastic. You think they're extraordinary, but it turns out as the work goes along, they're just average with a good education. Sometimes the other way around, the person's a kind of dumb innocent, but he outwits you and you can't even think of an ending good enough."

"What do you do then?" he asked. He had been a doctor for a couple of decades and then an artist for a couple of decades and he's still interested in details, craft, technique.

"Well, you just have to let the story lie around till some agreement can be reached between you and the stubborn hero."

"Aren't you talking silly now?" he asked. "Start again," he said. "It so happens I'm not going out this evening. Tell the story again. See what you can do this time."

"O.K.," I said. "But it's not a five-minute job." Second attempt:

Once, across the street from us, there was a fine handsome woman, our neighbor. She had a son whom she loved because she'd known him since birth (in helpless chubby infancy, and in the wrestling, hugging ages, seven to ten, as well as earlier and later). This boy, when he fell into the fist of adolescence, became a junkie. He was not a hopeless one. He was in fact hopeful, an ideologue and successful converter. With his busy brilliance, he wrote persuasive

articles for his high-school newspaper. Seeking a wider audience, using important connections, he drummed into Lower Manhattan newsstand distribution
a periodical called *Oh! Golden Horse!*

In order to keep him from feeling guilty (because guilt is the stony heart
of nine tenths of all clinically diagnosed cancers in America today, she said),
and because she had always believed in giving bad habits room at home
where one could keep an eye on them, she too became a junkie. Her kitchen
was famous for a while—a center for intellectual addicts who knew what they
were doing. A few felt artistic like Coleridge and others were scientific and
revolutionary like Leary. Although she was often high herself, certain good
mothering reflexes remained, and she saw to it that there was lots of orange
juice around and honey and milk and vitamin pills. However, she never
cooked anything but chili, and that no more than once a week. She explained,
when we talked to her, seriously, with neighborly concern, that it was her part
in the youth culture and she would rather be with the young, it was an honor,
than with her own generation.

One week, while nodding through an Antonioni film, this boy was severely
jabbed by the elbow of a stern and proselytizing girl, sitting beside him. She
offered immediate apricots and nuts for his sugar level, spoke to him sharply,
and took him home.

She had heard of him and his work and she herself published, edited, and
wrote a competitive journal called *Man Does Live by Bread Alone.* In the
organic heat of her continuous presence he could not help but become interested once more in his muscles, his arteries, and nerve connections. In fact he
began to love them, treasure them, praise them with funny little songs in *Man
Does Live.* . . .

> the fingers of my flesh transcend
> my transcendental soul
> the tightness in my shoulders end
> my teeth have made me whole

To the mouth of his head (that glory of will and determination) he brought
hard apples, nuts, wheat germ, and soybean oil. He said to his old friends,
From now on, I guess I'll keep my wits about me. I'm going on the natch.
He said he was about to begin a spiritual deep-breathing journey. How about
you too, Mom? he asked kindly.

His conversion was so radiant, splendid, that neighborhood kids his age
began to say that he had never been a real addict at all, only a journalist along
for the smell of the story. The mother tried several times to give up what had
become without her son and his friends a lonely habit. This effort only
brought it to supportable levels. The boy and his girl took their electronic
mimeograph and moved to the bushy edge of another borough. They were
very strict. They said they would not see her again until she had been off
drugs for sixty days.

At home alone in the evening, weeping, the mother read and reread the
seven issues of *Oh! Golden Horse!* They seemed to her as truthful as ever.
We often crossed the street to visit and console. But if we mentioned any of
our children who were at college or in the hospital or dropouts at home, she
would cry out, My baby! My baby! and burst into terrible, face-scarring,
time-consuming tears. The End.

First my father was silent, then he said, "Number One: You have a nice sense of humor. Number Two: I see you can't tell a plain story. So don't waste time." Then he said sadly, "Number Three: I suppose that means she was alone, she was left like that, his mother. Alone. Probably sick?"

I said, "Yes."

"Poor woman. Poor girl, to be born in a time of fools, to live among fools. The end. The end. You were right to put that down. The end."

I didn't want to argue, but I had to say, "Well, it is not necessarily the end, Pa."

"Yes," he said, "what a tragedy. The end of a person."

"No, Pa," I begged him. "It doesn't have to be. She's only about forty. She could be a hundred different things in this world as time goes on. A teacher or a social worker. An ex-junkie! Sometimes it's better than having a master's in education."

"Jokes," he said. "As a writer that's your main trouble. You don't want to recognize it. Tragedy! Plain tragedy! Historical tragedy! No hope. The end."

"Oh, Pa," I said. "She could change."

"In your own life, too, you have to look it in the face." He took a couple of nitroglycerin. "Turn to five," he said, pointing to the dial on the oxygen tank. He inserted the tubes into his nostrils and breathed deep. He closed his eyes and said, "No."

I had promised the family to always let him have the last word when arguing, but in this case I had a different responsibility. That woman lives across the street. She's my knowledge and my invention. I'm sorry for her. I'm not going to leave her there in that house crying. (Actually neither would Life, which unlike me has no pity.)

Therefore: She did change. Of course her son never came home again. But right now, she's the receptionist in a storefront community clinic in the East Village. Most of the customers are young people, some old friends. The head doctor has said to her, "If we only had three people in this clinic with your experiences. . . ."

"The doctor said that?" My father took the oxygen tubes out of his nostrils and said, "Jokes. Jokes again."

"No, Pa, it could really happen that way, it's a funny world nowadays."

"No," he said. "Truth first. She will slide back. A person must have character. She does not."

"No, Pa," I said. "That's it. She's got a job. Forget it. She's in that storefront working."

"How long will it be?" he asked. "Tragedy! You too. When will you look it in the face?"

EXERCISES

1. Discuss the narrator's attitude toward plot. What in real life corresponds to a plot in fiction? Can invented people in a story have "the open destiny of life"?

2. Why does the father say that the narrator's first story is not what he meant, that there is more to it than that?

3. What is the basis of the disagreement about stories between the narrator and her father?

4. What is the significance of the father having been both a doctor and an artist?

5. Why does the father tell the narrator after the second story that she cannot tell a plain story?

6. Why does the father insist it is the end, a tragedy, the end, whereas the narrator insists that there are still possibilities for the woman? Who is right? Explain.

SPENCER
HOLST | *On Hope*

The monkey leaped on the man's shoulder.

The man shuddered for he knew who it was. He knew exactly which monkey of the ten thousand that roam about on the Rock of Gibraltar, tame and free as pigeons, walking around in the parks and streets.

It was a demon monkey.

It was the one he'd trained to bring him necklaces, who brought him pearls, garnets, and amber from moonlit bedrooms in the big hotels—stolen from women sunk in snoring.

The monkey dangled before his eyes the largest diamond in the world.

The whole thing began several days previously when all on Gibraltar went into an uproar. The Rock of Gibraltar was visited by royalty, by the queen mother, and the princess. A battleship brought them and their entourage, and with them the famous necklace, the largest stone of which was the *Diamond of Hope*, which the princess was to wear at some great state occasion. (There's a curse on the necklace, you know, and misfortune had followed it, and come to whomever possessed it until it became part of the British crown jewels in the middle of the nineteenth century.)

On the very first night the royal party was in, the monkey returned to his gypsy master with the necklace. The necklace, of course, was valueless. It couldn't possibly be sold. Gibraltar would be swarming with police searching for it.

The gypsy was annoyed with the monkey, irritated at its genius, and terrified of being caught by the police with the gems; and besides, although he had no particular regard for the government—(being a gypsy) he liked the idea of "the princess" and wouldn't dream of stealing her necklace. So he quickly wrapped it up and addressed the package to her and dropped it in an ordinary mailbox. He enclosed a note to her saying something like, "You really ought to guard this more carefully."

The next night the monkey returned again with the necklace.

This time his note implored her to have the police guard the necklace more carefully, and he even gave them advice. He advised them to place the necklace in the center of a cage.

(For a monkey, of course, couldn't get into a locked cage.)

Then the third night, when this story begins, the monkey again brought the gypsy the necklace, and fell at the gypsy's feet, dead. Shot. Very probably the monkey had been fatally wounded by a guard as he was escaping.

The gypsy shuddered at the diamond, and was not surprised at the death of his friend.

The first two times it had been like some freak occurrence, like a weird accident—to unexpectedly discover oneself in possession of part of the British crown jewels! But now . . .

When he received the gems for the third time the whole thing was plunged into meaning. It no longer seemed like an accident. He had been given the necklace. Fate was at work. Now, the necklace was his.

He put it in his pocket.

It never occurred to him (being a gypsy) to doubt the reality of the curse which accompanied the diamond, and he accepted his fate with the stone. Quietly and secretly he buried the animal.

And as he thought about it he was actually a little pleased that he, a gypsy, had been singled out by fate to take the curse off the princess, and the English throne.

He walked down to the shore of the Mediterranean and took off his clothes, and—having nothing in which to put the necklace, he put it on—dove in, and swam.

There was a full moon and the sea was perfectly calm.

Just off Gibraltar there's a deep place in the Mediterranean. It's called the Gibraltar Trench. Only a mile from shore the sea is a mile deep.

The gypsy was a very good swimmer.

He swam out a mile, over this spot, took the necklace off and dropped it.

At that moment a smile lit his face as he imagined the thousands of Sherlock Holmeses searching for it for the next fifty years.

The man lazily began to swim back toward shore, and the necklace fell down into the depths.

They each had a mile to go—the man had a mile to swim, and the gems had a mile to fall.

The necklace fell much faster than the gypsy swam.

It fell straight down until it got about a hundred feet from the bottom, where it came to rest on the dorsal fin of a shark.

The shark had been sleeping, but the necklace woke it, and it turned round and around wondering what was happening. It decided to go up to investigate.

The shark swam upward even faster than the necklace had fallen.

Meanwhile the man still lazily swam toward the huge "rock," now ablaze as never before with the royal festivities, with a million electric light bulbs—and he thought of the curse. The stone would never bring its misfortune to anyone ever again; it was finished forever, its power over man extinguished for good, buried beneath a mile of water.

Then he looked over his shoulder and saw the necklace floating a foot above the water, moving slowly past him.

(The gypsy did not see the shark's fin, he only saw the necklace glittering in the moonlight, as if floating in the air, not coming toward him, but moving past him, now receding into the distance.)

The man immediately realized that one of two things was true. Obviously, either he was witnessing a miracle (and the whole thing smacked of the miraculous), or he was having a hallucination.

He decided to find out.

Was it a miracle? or, was it a delusion?

He began to shout and wave his arms and splash, and he began to swim after the necklace.

And sure enough the necklace stopped and after a moment began to move toward the man.

The man is swimming toward the necklace. The necklace is moving toward the man.

That is where the story ends.

However, I can't help noticing, at this moment, that at first glance it seems inevitable—you know, that the shark will devour the man.

But I do not believe that result is as inevitable as it seems at first glance; that is, I believe there are several reasons, so to speak, for hope.

1. I do not think a shark has ever been approached like this before, that is, by a man wondering whether the shark is a miraculous manifestation, or whether it is merely a figment of his own imagination. Such a man would smell different.

2. The man is a gypsy animal trainer.

3. The shark is now in possession of the necklace.

EXERCISES

1. What is significant about the fact that there is a curse on a diamond named the "Diamond of Hope"?

2. What does it mean that when the gypsy received the diamond the third time "the whole thing was plunged into meaning"? What is the difference between fate and an accident? How can there be fate in reality? How can there be an accident in fiction?

3. Why is it significant that he is a gypsy and that he accepts the story of the curse?

4. What is the significance of the mathematical parallel of dropping the necklace a mile out and a mile deep so that both the necklace and the man have an equal distance to travel?

5. What is the difference between a miracle and an hallucination? What is the difference between a story that depends on miracles and one that depends on hallucinations?

6. Explain how each of the three hypotheses listed at the end would negate the inevitability of the shark eating the man.

7. Compare this story with Frank Stockton's "The Lady, or the Tiger" and Margaret Atwood's "Happy Endings." Focus on the difference between story-telling and reality, fate and chance, and closed versus open endings.

JOHN
BARTH | *Autobiography:*
A Self-Recorded Fiction

You who listen give me life in a manner of speaking.
I won't hold you responsible.
My first words weren't my first words. I wish I'd begun differently.
Among other things I haven't a proper name. The one I bear's misleading, if not false. I didn't choose it either.
I don't recall asking to be conceived! Neither did my parents come to think of it. Even so. Score to be settled. Children are vengeance.
I seem to've known myself from the beginning without knowing I knew; no news is good news; perhaps I'm mistaken.
Now that I reflect I'm not enjoying this life: my link with the world.
My situation appears to me as follows: I speak in a curious, detached manner, and don't necessarily hear myself. I'm grateful for small mercies. Whether anyone follows me I can't tell.
Are you there? If so I'm blind and deaf to you, or you are me, or both're both. One may be imaginary; I've had stranger ideas. I hope I'm a fiction without real hope. Where there's a voice there's a speaker.
I see I see myself as a halt narrative: first person, tiresome. Pronoun sans ante or precedent, warrant or respite. Surrogate for the substantive; content-less form, interestless principle; blind eye blinking at nothing. Who am I. A little *crise d'identité* for you.
I must compose myself.
Look, I'm writing. No, listen, I'm nothing but talk; I won't last long. The odds against my conception were splendid; against my birth excellent; against my continuance favorable. Are yet. On the other hand, if my sort are permitted a certain age and growth. God help us, our life expectancy's been known to increase at an obscene rate instead of petering out. Let me squeak on long enough, I just might live forever: a word to the wise.
My beginning was comparatively interesting, believe it or not. Exposition. I was spawned not long since in an American state and born in no better. Grew in no worse. Persist in a representative. Prohibition, Depression, Radicalism, Decadence, and what have you. An eye sir for an eye. It's alleged, now, that Mother was a mere passing fancy who didn't pass quickly enough; there's evidence also that she was a mere novel device, just in style, soon to become a commonplace, to which Dad resorted one day when he found himself by himself with pointless pen. In either case she was mere, Mom; at any event Dad

dallied. He has me to explain. Bear in mind, I suppose he told her. A child is not its parents, but sum of their conjoined shames. A figure of speech. Their manner of speaking. No wonder I'm heterodoxical.

Nothing lasts longer than a mood. Dad's infatuation passed; I remained. He understood, about time, that anything conceived in so unnatural and fugitive a fashion was apt to be freakish, even monstrous—and an advertisement of his folly. His second thought therefore was to destroy me before I spoke a word. He knew how these things work; he went by the book. To expose ourselves publicly is frowned upon; therefore we do it to one another in private. He me, I him; one was bound to be the case. What fathers can't forgive is that their offspring receive and sow broadcast their shortcomings. From my conception to the present moment Dad's tried to turn me off; not ardently, not consistently, not successfully so far; but persistently, persistently, with at least half a heart. How do I know? I'm his bloody mirror!

Which is to say, upon reflection I reverse and distort him. For I suspect that my true father's sentiments are the contrary of murderous. That one only imagines he begot me; mightn't he be deceived and deadly jealous? In his heart of hearts he wonders whether I mayn't after all be the get of a nobler spirit, taken by beauty past his grasp. Or else, what comes to the same thing, to me, I've a pair of dads, to match my pair of moms. How account for my contradictions except as the vices of their versus? Beneath self-contempt, I particularly scorn my fondness for paradox. I despise pessimism, narcissism, solipsism, truculence, word-play, and pusillanimity, my chiefer inclinations; loathe self-loathers *ergo me;* have no pity for self-pity and so am free of that sweet baseness. I doubt I am. Being me's no joke.

I continued the tale of my forebears. Thus my exposure; thus my escape. This cursed me, turned me out; that, curse him, saved me; right hand slipped me through left's fingers. Unless on a third hand I somehow preserved myself. Unless unless: the mercy-killing was successful. Buzzards let us say made brunch of me betimes but couldn't stomach my voice, which persists like the Nauseous Danaid. We . . . monstrosities are easilier achieved than got rid of.

In sum I'm not what either parent or I had in mind. One hoped I'd be astonishing, forceful, triumphant—heroical in other words. One dead. I myself conventional. I turn out I. Not every kid thrown to the wolves ends a hero: for each survivor, a mountain of beast-baits; for every Oedipus, a city of feebs.

So much for my dramatic exposition: seems not to've worked. Here I am, Dad: Your creature! Your caricature!

Unhappily, things get clearer as we go along. I perceive that I have no body. What's less, I've been speaking of myself without delight or alternative as self-consciousness pure and sour; I declare now that even that isn't true. I'm not aware of myself at all, as far as I know. I don't think . . . I know what I'm talking about.

Well, well, being well into my life as it's been called I see well how it'll end, unless in some meaningless surprise. If anything dramatic were going to happen to make me successfuller . . . agreeabler . . . endurabler . . . it should've happened by now, we will agree. A change for the better still isn't unthinkable; miracles can be cited. But the odds against a wireless *deus ex machina* aren't encouraging.

Here, a confession: Early on I too aspired to immortality. Assumed I'd be beautiful, powerful, loving, loved. At least commonplace. Anyhow human. Even the revelation of my several defects—absence of presence to name one— didn't fetch me right to despair: crippledness affords its own heroisms, does it not; heroes are typically gimpish, are they not. But your crippled hero's one thing, a bloody hero after all; your heroic cripple another, etcetcetcetcetcet. Being an ideal's warped image, my fancy's own twist figure, is what undoes me.

I wonder if I repeat myself. One-track minds may lead to their origins. Perhaps I'm still in utero, hung up in my delivery; my exposition and the rest merely foreshadow what's to come, the argument for an interrupted pregnancy.

Womb, coffin, can—in any case, from my viewless viewpoint I see no point in going further. Since Dad among his other failings failed to end me when he should've, I'll turn myself off if I can this instant.

Can't. *Then if anyone hears me, speaking from here inside like a sunk submariner, and has the means to my end, I pray him do us both a kindness.*

Didn't. Very well, my ace in the hole: *Father, have mercy, I dare you! Wretched old fabricator, where's your shame? Put an end to this, for pity's sake! Now! Now!*

So. My last trump, and I blew it. Not much in the way of a climax; more a climacteric. I'm not the dramatic sort. May the end come quietly, then, without my knowing it. In the course of any breath. In the heart of any word. This one. This one.

Perhaps I'll have a posthumous cautionary value, like gibbeted corpses, pickled freaks. Self-preservation, it seems, may smell of formaldehyde.

A proper ending wouldn't spin out so.

I suppose I might have managed things to better effect, in spite of the old boy. Too late now.

Basket case. Waste.

Shake up some memorable last words at least. There seems to be time.

Nonsense. I'll mutter to the end, one word after another, string the rascals out, mad or not, heard or not, my last words will be my last words.

EXERCISES

1. Would a story have life if no one read it? Why or why not?
2. If a story has life, why cannot it also have consciousness? If it has consciousness, why cannot it be conscious of itself?

3. Who is the mother and who is the father of the speaker? What is the relationship between the author and the story?

4. Much of this story depends on puns. Point out some of them, and discuss how they work.

5. Discuss the end of this fiction. Compare it with Margaret Atwood's "Happy Endings."

6. Discuss how this story is like the following sentences (from *Metamagical Themas*, by Douglas Hofstadter, 1985) and like the accompanying cartoon:

> I am the thought you are now thinking.
> This inert sentence is my body, but my soul is alive, dancing in the sparks of your brain.
> It feels *sooo* good to have your eyes run over my curves and serifs.
> This sentence would be seven words long if it were six words shorter.
> Do you read me?

MOTHER GOOSE   **BY MIKE PETERS**

Reprinted by permission. Tribune Media Services.

JEAN DE LA
FONTAINE | *The Grasshopper and the Ant*

I

THE GRASSHOPPER AND THE ANT

A Grasshopper the summer long
Sang her song,
And found herself when winter came
Without a morsel to her name.
Not one scrap of worm or fly
Had the careless thing put by!
So she took her tale of want
To her neighbour Mistress Ant,
Begging just a grain or two

Wherewithal to carry through
Till the spring came round next year.
"I'll repay you, never fear,
Honest insect, ere the fall,
Interest and principal."
One fault from which the Ant is free
Is making loans too readily.
"Tell me how you spent the summer."
"Night and day, to every comer,
Please you, ma'am, I sang my ditty."
"Night and day, to every comer,
"Singing, were you? Very pretty!
Now's your chance,
Mistress Grasshopper, to dance."

SOMERSET
MAUGHAM | *The Ant and the Grasshopper*

W hen I was a very small boy I was made to learn by heart certain of the
fables of La Fontaine, and the moral of each was carefully explained to
me. Among those learned was *The Ant and the Grasshopper*, which is devised
to bring home to the young the useful lesson that in an imperfect world industry is rewarded and giddiness punished. In this admirable fable (I apologise
for telling something which everyone is politely, but inexactly, supposed to
know) the ant spends a laborious summer gathering its winter store, while the
grasshopper sits on a blade of grass singing to the sun. Winter comes and the
ant is comfortably provided for, but the grasshopper has an empty larder: he
goes to the ant and begs for a little food. Then the ant gives him her classic
answer:
"What were you doing in the summer time?"
"Saving your presence, I sang. I sang all day, all night."
"You sang. Why, then go and dance."
I do not ascribe it to perversity on my part, but rather to the inconsequence of childhood, which is deficient in moral sense, that I could never quite
reconcile myself to the lesson. My sympathies were with the grasshopper and
for some time I never saw an ant without putting my foot on it. In this summary (and as I have discovered since, entirely human) fashion I sought to
express my disapproval of prudence and common-sense.
I could not help thinking of this fable when the other day I saw George
Ramsay lunching by himself in a restaurant. I never saw anyone wear an
expression of such deep gloom. He was staring into space. He looked as
though the burden of the whole world sat upon his shoulders. I was sorry for
him: I suspected at once that his unfortunate brother had been causing trouble
again. I went up to him and held out my hand.
"How are you?" I asked.

"I'm not in hilarious spirits," he answered.

"Is it Tom again?"

He sighed.

"Yes, it's Tom again."

"Why don't you chuck him? You've done everything in the world for him. You must know by now that he's quite hopeless."

I suppose every family has a black sheep. Tom had been a sore trial to his for twenty years. He had begun life decently enough: he went into business, married and had two children. The Ramsays were perfectly respectable people and there was every reason to suppose that Tom Ramsay would have a useful and honourable career. But one day, without warning, he announced that he didn't like work and that he wasn't suited for marriage. He wanted to enjoy himself. He would listen to no expostulations. He left his wife and his office. He had a little money and he spent two happy years in various capitals of Europe. Rumours of his doings reached his relations from time to time and they were profoundly shocked. He certainly had a very good time. They shook their heads and asked what would happen when his money was spent. They soon found out: he borrowed. He was charming and unscrupulous. I have never met anyone to whom it was more difficult to refuse a loan. He made a steady income from his friends and he made friends easily. But he always said that the money you spent on necessities was boring; the money that was amusing to spend was the money you spent on luxuries. For this he depended on his brother George. He did not waste his charm on him. George was respectable. Once or twice he fell to Tom's promises of amendment and gave him considerable sums in order that he might make a fresh start. On these Tom bought a motorcar and some very nice jewellery. But when circumstances forced George to realise that his brother would never settle down and he washed his hands of him, Tom, without a qualm, began to blackmail him. It was not very nice for a respectable lawyer to find his brother shaking cocktails behind the bar of his favourite restaurant or to see him waiting on the box-seat of a taxi outside his club. Tom said that to serve in a bar or to drive a taxi was a perfectly decent occupation, but if George could oblige him with a couple of hundred pounds he didn't mind for the honour of the family giving it up. George paid.

Once Tom nearly went to prison. George was terribly upset. He went into the whole discreditable affair. Really Tom had gone too far. He had been wild, thoughtless and selfish, but he had never before done anything dishonest, by which George meant illegal; and if he were prosecuted he would assuredly be convicted. But you cannot allow your only brother to go to gaol. The man Tom had cheated, a man called Cronshaw, was vindictive. He was determined to take the matter into court; he said Tom was a scoundrel and should be punished. It cost George an infinite deal of trouble and five hundred pounds to settle the affair. I have never seen him in such a rage as when he heard that Tom and Cronshaw had gone off together to Monte Carlo the moment they cashed the cheque. They spent a happy month there.

For twenty years Tom raced and gambled, philandered with the prettiest girls, danced, ate in the most expensive restaurants, and dressed beautifully. He always looked as if he had just stepped out of a bandbox. Though he was forty-six you would never have taken him for more than thirty-five. He was a most amusing companion and though you knew he was perfectly worthless you could not but enjoy his society. He had high spirits, an unfailing gaiety and incredible charm. I never grudged the contributions he regularly levied on me for the necessities of his existence. I never lent him fifty pounds without feeling that I was in his debt. Tom Ramsay knew everyone and everyone knew Tom Ramsay. You could not approve of him, but you could not help liking him.

Poor George, only a year older than his scapegrace brother, looked sixty. He had never taken more than a fortnight's holiday in the year for a quarter of a century. He was in his office every morning at nine-thirty and never left it till six. He was honest, industrious and worthy. He had a good wife, to whom he had never been unfaithful even in thought, and four daughters to whom he was the best of fathers. He made a point of saving a third of his income and his plan was to retire at fifty-five to a little house in the country where he proposed to cultivate his garden and play golf. His life was blameless. He was glad that he was growing old because Tom was growing old too. He rubbed his hands and said:

"It was all very well when Tom was young and good-looking, but he's only a year younger than I am. In four years he'll be fifty. He won't find life too easy then. I shall have thirty thousand pounds by the time I'm fifty. For twenty-five years I've said that Tom would end in the gutter. And we shall see how he likes that. We shall see if it really pays best to work or be idle."

Poor George! I sympathised with him. I wondered now as I sat down beside him what infamous thing Tom had done. George was evidently very much upset.

"Do you know what's happened now?" he asked me.

I was prepared for the worst. I wondered if Tom had got into the hands of the police at last. George could hardly bring himself to speak.

"You're not going to deny that all my life I've been hard working, decent, respectable and straightforward. After a life of industry and thrift I can look forward to retiring on a small income in gilt-edged securities. I've always done my duty in that state of life in which it has pleased Providence to place me."

"True."

"And you can't deny that Tom has been an idle, worthless dissolute and dishonourable rogue. If there were any justice he'd be in the workhouse."

"True."

George grew red in the face.

"A few weeks ago he became engaged to a woman old enough to be his mother. And now she's died and left him everything she had. Half a million pounds, a yacht, a house in London and a house in the country."

George Ramsay beat his clenched fist on the table.

"It's not fair, I tell you, it's not fair. Damn it, it's not fair."

I could not help it. I burst into a shout of laughter as I looked at George's wrathful face. I rolled in my chair, I very nearly fell on the floor. George never forgave me. But Tom often asks me to excellent dinners in his charming house in Mayfair, and if he occasionally borrows a trifle from me, that is merely from force of habit. It is never more than a sovereign.

EXERCISES

1. How is this story both like and unlike the La Fontaine fable of the grasshopper and the ant? How is it a satire on the original fable? Which of the two is closer to the "truth," whatever that is? Which of the two is the more believable?

2. Compare this story also with the parable of the prodigal son in the Bible. How is it both like and unlike that story?

3. Which of the two versions of the ant and the grasshopper story gives you the more pleasure? If both give you pleasure, distinguish between the kind of pleasure each one gives.

4. Comment on the final statement: "It's not fair, I tell you, it's not fair. Damn it, it's not fair." What is the meaning of *fairness*? In reality, what determines fairness? In fiction, what determines fairness?

5. Discuss Maugham's story as a satire on our expectation that stories should have a moral.

LEGEND OF THE PHOENIX

The myth of the phoenix probably began with Greek historian Herodotus (fifth century B.C.), who wrote that the bird appeared to the people of Heliopolis once every five hundred years, and then only after the death of its parent. The following accounts are from the Roman historian Tacitus and the Roman poet Ovid, both writing in the first century A.D. Later in Europe during the medieval period the phoenix became a symbol of the Christian resurrection from death, because it dies of its own free will and out of its death comes life. Generally, it was a symbol of rarity, royalty, and the supernatural.

TACITUS | *The Phoenix*

That the phoenix is sacred to the Sun, and differs from the rest of the feathered species in the form of its head and the tincture of its plumage, are points settled on by the naturalist. Of its longevity the accounts are various. The common persuasion is that it lives five hundred years, though by some writers the date is extended to fourteen hundred and sixty-one. It is the custom of the phoenix when its course of years is finished, and the approach of death is felt, to build a nest in its native clime, Arabia, and there deposit the principles of life, from which a new progeny arises. The first care of the young bird, as soon as fledged and able to trust to its wings, is to perform the obsequies of its father. But his duty is not undertaken rashly. He collects a great quantity of myrrh, and to try his strength, makes frequent excursions with a load on his back. When he has made his experiment through a great tract of air, and gains sufficient confidence in his own vigour, he takes up the body of his father and flies with it to the Altar of the Sun, where he leaves it to be consumed in flames of fragrance. Such is the account of this wonderful bird. It has, no doubt, a mixture of fable; but that the phoenix from time to time appears in Egypt seems to be a fact satisfactorily ascertained.

OVID | *Metamorphosis (Book XV)*

But one alone,
A bird, renews, and re-begets itself—
The Phoenix of Assyria, which feeds
Not upon seeds or verdue but the oils
Of balsam and the tears of frankincense.
This bird, when five long centuries of life
Have passed, with claws and beak unsullied, builds
A nest high on a lofty swaying palm;
And lines the nest with cassia and spikenard
And golden myrrh and shreds of cinnamon,
And settles there at ease and, so embowered
In spicy perfumes, ends his life's long span.
Then from his father's body is reborn
A little Phoenix, so they say, to live
The same long years. When time has built his strength
With power to raise the weight, he lifts the nest—
The nest his cradle and his father's tomb—
As love and duty prompt, from that tall palm
And carries it across the sky to reach
The Sun's great city, and before the doors
Of the Sun's holy temple lays it down.

SYLVIA
TOWNSEND
WARNER | *The Phoenix*

L ord Strawberry, a nobleman, collected birds. He had the finest aviary in Europe, so large that eagles did not find it uncomfortable, so well laid out that both humming-birds and snow-buntings had a climate that suited them perfectly. But for many years the finest set of apartments remained empty, with just a label saying: "PHOENIX. *Habitat: Arabia.*"

Many authorities on bird life had assured Lord Strawberry that the phoenix is a fabulous bird, or that the breed was long extinct. Lord Strawberry was unconvinced: his family had always believed in phoenixes. At intervals he received from his agents (together with statements of their expenses) birds which they declared were the phoenix but which turned out to be orioles, macaws, turkey buzzards dyed orange, etc., or stuffed cross-breeds, ingeniously assembled from various plumages. Finally Lord Strawberry went himself to Arabia, where, after some months, he found a phoenix, won its confidence, caught it, and brought it home in perfect condition.

It was a remarkably fine phoenix, with a charming character—affable to the other birds in the aviary and much attached to Lord Strawberry. On its arrival in England it made a great stir among ornithologists, journalists, poets, and milliners, and was constantly visited. But it was not puffed by these attentions, and when it was no longer in the news, and the visits fell off, it showed no pique or rancour. It ate well, and seemed perfectly contented.

It costs a great deal of money to keep up an aviary. When Lord Strawberry died he died penniless. The aviary came on the market. In normal times the rarer birds, and certainly the phoenix, would have been bid for by the trustees of Europe's great zoological societies, or by private persons in the U.S.A.; but as it happened Lord Strawberry died just after a world war, when both money and bird-seed were hard to come by (indeed the cost of bird-seed was one of the things which had ruined Lord Strawberry). The London *Times* urged in a leader that the phoenix be bought for the London Zoo, saying that a nation of bird-lovers had a moral right to own such a rarity; and a fund, called the Strawberry Phoenix Fund, was opened. Students, naturalists, and school-children contributed according to their means; but their means were small, and there were no large donations. So Lord Strawberry's executors (who had the death duties to consider) closed with the higher offer of Mr. Tancred Poldero, owner and proprietor of Poldero's Wizard Wonderworld.

For quite a while Mr. Poldero considered his phoenix a bargain. It was a civil and obliging bird, and adapted itself readily to its new surroundings. It did not cost much to feed, it did not mind children; and though it had no tricks, Mr. Poldero supposed it would soon pick up some. The publicity of the Strawberry Phoenix Fund was now most helpful. Almost every contributor now saved up another half-crown in order to see the phoenix. Others, who had not contributed to the fund, even paid double to look at it on the five-shilling days.

But then business slackened. The phoenix was as handsome as ever, and as amiable; but, as Mr. Poldero said, it hadn't got Udge. Even at popular prices the phoenix was not really popular. It was too quiet, too classical. So people went instead to watch the antics of the baboons, or to admire the crocodile who had eaten the woman.

One day Mr. Poldero said to his manager, Mr. Ramkin:

"How long since any fool paid to look at the phoenix?"

"Matter of three weeks," replied Mr. Ramkin.

"Eating his head off," said Mr. Poldero. "Let alone the insurance. Seven shillings a week it costs me to insure that bird, and I might as well insure the Archbishop of Canterbury."

"The public don't like him. He's too quiet for them, that's the trouble. Won't mate nor nothing. And I've tried him with no end of pretty pollies, ospreys, and Cochin-Chinas, and the Lord knows what. But he won't look at them."

"Wonder if we could swap him for a livelier one," said Mr. Poldero.

"Impossible. There's only one of him at a time."

"Go on!"

"I mean it. Haven't you ever read what it says on the label?"

They went to the phoenix's cage. It flapped its wings politely, but they paid no attention. They read:

"PANSY. *Phoenix phoenixissima formoissima arabiana.* This rare and fabulous bird is UNIQUE. The World's Old Bachelor. Has no mate and doesn't want one. When old, sets fire to itself and emerges miraculously reborn. Specially imported from the East."

"I've got an idea," said Mr. Poldero. "How old do you suppose that bird is?"

"Looks in its prime to me," said Mr. Ramkin.

"Suppose," continued Mr. Poldero, "we could somehow get him alight? We'd advertise it beforehand, of course, work up interest. Then we'd have a new bird, and a bird with some romance about it, a bird with a life-story. We could sell a bird like that."

Mr. Ramkin nodded.

"I've read about it in a book," he said. "You've got to give them scented woods and what not, and they build a nest and sit down on it and catch fire spontaneous. But they won't do it till they're old. That's the snag."

"Leave that to me," said Mr. Poldero. "You get those scented woods; and I'll do the ageing."

It was not easy to age the phoenix. Its allowance of food was halved, and halved again, but though it grew thinner its eyes were undimmed and its plumage glossy as ever. The heating was turned off; but it puffed out its feathers against the cold, and seemed none the worse. Other birds were put into its cage, birds of a peevish and quarrelsome nature. They pecked and chivied it; but the phoenix was so civil and amiable that after a day or two they lost their animosity. Then Mr. Poldero tried alley cats. These could not be won by manners, but the phoenix darted above their heads and flapped its golden wings in their faces, and daunted them.

Mr. Poldero turned to a book on Arabia, and read that the climate was dry. "Aha!" said he. The phoenix was moved to a small cage that had a sprinkler in the ceiling. Every night the sprinkler was turned on. The phoenix began to cough. Mr. Poldero had another good idea. Daily he stationed himself in front of the cage to jeer at the bird and abuse it.

When spring was come, Mr. Poldero felt justified in beginning a publicity campaign about the ageing phoenix. The old public favourite, he said, was nearing its end. Meanwhile he tested the bird's reactions every few days by putting a few tufts of foul-smelling straw and some strands of rusty barbed wire into the cage, to see if it was interested in nesting yet. One day the phoenix began turning over the straw. Mr. Poldero signed a contract for the film rights. At last the hour seemed ripe. It was a fine Saturday evening in May. For some weeks the public interest in the ageing phoenix had been working up, and the admission charge had risen to five shillings. The enclosure was thronged. The lights and the cameras were trained on the cage, and a loud-speaker proclaimed to the audience the rarity of what was about to take place.

"The phoenix," said the loud-speaker, "is the aristocrat of bird-life. Only the rarest and most expensive specimens of oriental wood, drenched in exotic perfumes, will tempt him to construct his strange love-nest."

Now a neat assortment of twigs and shavings, strongly scented, was shoved into the cage.

"The phoenix," the loud-speaker continued, "is as capricious as Cleopatra, as luxurious as la du Barry, as heady as a strain of wild gypsy music. All the fantastic pomp and passion of the ancient East, its languorous magic, its subtle cruelties . . ."

"Lawks!" cried a woman in the crowd. "He's at it!"

A quiver stirred the dulled plumage. The phoenix turned its head from side to side. It descended, staggering, from its perch. Then wearily it began to pull about the twigs and shavings.

The cameras clicked, the lights blazed full on the cage. Rushing to the loud-speaker Mr. Poldero exclaimed:

"Ladies and gentlemen, this is the thrilling moment the world has breathlessly awaited. The legend of centuries is materializing before our modern eyes. The phoenix . . ."

The phoenix settled on its pyre and appeared to fall asleep.

The film director said:

"Well, if it doesn't evaluate more than this, mark it instructional."

At that moment the phoenix and the pyre burst into flames. The flames streamed upwards, leaped out on every side. In a minute or two everything was burned to ashes, and some thousand people, including Mr. Poldero, perished in the blaze.

EXERCISES

1. What is the tone of this modern fable based on the ancient fable of the phoenix? Support your answer with details from the story.

2. This story is not only a fable, but also a satire. What is it satirizing or exposing about modern society?

3. What is it about the phoenix that modern audiences in the story do not find appealing?

4. What is the basic fascination of the original phoenix myth? Discuss the implications of simultaneity of death and birth, old age and infancy. Con-

sider also that the method of reproduction here is "one from one" rather than "one from two." What is the basic appeal of such a method of reproduction?

5. Why are all consumed at the end? What is the fundamental mystery the onlookers have observed? Why does it destroy them?

6. Discuss how the account by the poet Ovid differs from the account of the historian Tacitus. What does this tell us about the development of myths? What elements of the original phoenix myth does Sylvia Townsend Warner make use of for her story?

OVID | *Pygmalion*

Pygmalion had seen these women spend
  Their days in wickedness, and horrified
At all the countless vices nature gives
To womankind lived celibate and long
Lacked the companionship of married love.
Meanwhile he carved his snow-white ivory
With marvellous triumphant artistry
And gave it perfect shape, more beautiful
Than ever woman born. His masterwork
Fired him with love. It seemed to be alive,
Its face to be a real girl's, a girl
Who wished to move—but modesty forbade.
Such art his art concealed. In admiration
His heart desired the body he had formed.
With many a touch he tries it—is it flesh
Or ivory? Not ivory still, he's sure!
Kisses he gives and thinks they are returned;
He speaks to it, caresses it, believes
The firm new flesh beneath his fingers yields,
And fears the limbs may darken with a bruise.
And now fond words he whispers, now brings gifts
That girls delight in—shells and polished stones,
And little birds and flowers of every hue,
Lilies and coloured balls and beads of amber,
The tear-drops of the daughters of the Sun.
He decks her limbs with robes and on her fingers
Sets splendid rings, a necklace round her neck,
Pearls in her ears, a pendant on her breast;
Lovely she looked, yet unadorned she seemed
In nakedness no whit less beautiful.
He laid her on a couch of purple silk,

Called her his darling, cushioning her head,
As if she relished it, on softest down.
    Venus' day came, the holiest festival
All Cyprus celebrates; incense rose high
And heifers, with their wide horns gilded, fell
Beneath the blade that struck their snowy necks.
Pygmalion, his offering given, prayed
Before the altar, half afraid, "Vouchsafe,
O Gods, if all things you can grant, my bride
Shall be"—he dared not say my ivory girl—
"The living likeness of my ivory girl."
And golden Venus (for her presence graced
Her feast) knew well the purpose of his prayer;
And, as an omen of her favouring power,
Thrice did the flame burn bright and leap up high.
And he went home, home to his heart's delight,
And kissed her as she lay, and she seemed warm;
Again he kissed her and with marvelling touch
Caressed her breast; beneath his touch the flesh
Grew soft, its ivory hardness vanishing,
And yielded to his hands, as in the sun
Wax of Hymettus softens and is shaped
By practised fingers into many forms,
And usefulness acquires by being used.
His heart was torn with wonder and misgiving,
Delight and terror that it was not true!
Again and yet again he tried his hopes—
She was alive! The pulse beat in her veins!
And then indeed in words that overflowed
He poured his thanks to Venus, and at last
His lips pressed real lips, and she, his girl,
Felt every kiss, and blushed, and shyly raised
Her eyes to his and saw the world and him.
The goddess graced the union she had made,
And when nine times the crescent moon had filled
Her silver orb, an infant girl was born,
Paphos, from whom the island takes its name.

JOHN
UPDIKE | *Pygmalion*

What he liked about his first wife was her gift of mimicry; after a party, theirs or another couple's, she would vivify for him what they had seen, the faces, the voices, twisting her pretty mouth into small contortions that brought back, for a dazzling instant, the presence of an absent acquaintance.

"Well, if I reawy—how does Gwen talk?—if I *re*-awwy cared about conser-wation—" And he, the husband, would laugh and laugh, even though Gwen was secretly his mistress and would become his second wife. What he liked about *her* was her liveliness in bed, and what he disliked about his first wife was the way she would ask to have her back rubbed and then, under his labor-ing hands, night after night, fall asleep.

For the first years of the new marriage, after he and Gwen had returned from a party he would wait, unconsciously, for the imitations, the recapitu-lation, to begin. He would even prompt, "What did you make of our hostess's brother?"

"Oh," Gwen would simply say, "he seemed very pleasant." Sensing with feminine intuition that he expected more, she might add, "Harmless. Maybe a little stuffy." Her eyes flashed as she heard in his expectant silence an unvoiced demand, and with that touching, childlike impediment of hers she blurted out, "What are you reawy after?"

"Oh, nothing. Nothing. It's just—Marguerite met him once a few years ago and she was struck by what a pompous nitwit he was. That way he has of sucking his pipestem and ending every statement with 'Do you follow me?' "

"I thought he was perfectly pleasant," Gwen said frostily, and turned her back to remove her silvery, snug party dress. As she wriggled it down over her hips she turned her head and defiantly added, "He had a *lot* to say about tax shelters."

"I bet he did," Pygmalion scoffed feebly, numbed by the sight of his wife frontally advancing, nude, toward him and their marital bed. "It's awfully late," he warned her.

"Oh, come on," she said, the lights out.

The first imitation Gwen did was of Marguerite's second husband, Ed; they had all unexpectedly met at a Save the Whales benefit ball, to which invitations had been sent out indiscriminately. "Oh-ho-*ho*," she boomed in the privacy of their bedroom afterward, "so you're my noble predecessor!" In aside she added, "Noble, my ass. He hates you so much you turned him on."

"I did?" he said. "I thought he was perfectly pleasant, in what could have been an awkward encounter."

"Yes, in*dee*dy," she agreed, imitating hearty Ed, and for a dazzling second allowing the man's slightly glassy and slack expression of forced benignity to invade her own usually petite and rounded features. "Nothing awkward about *us*, ho ho," she went on, encouraged. "And tell me, old chap, why *is* it your child-support check is never on time anymore?"

He laughed and laughed, entranced to see his bride arrive at what he con-ceived to be proper womanliness—a plastic, alert sensitivity to the human environment, a susceptible responsiveness tugged this way and that by the cur-rents of Nature herself. He could not know the world, was his fear, unless a woman translated it for him. Now, when they returned from a gathering, and he asked what she had made of so-and-so, Gwen would stand in her under-wear and consider, as if onstage. "We-hell, my dear," she would announce in sudden, fluting parody, "if it wasn't for Portugal there *rally* wouldn't be a country left in Europe!"

"Oh, come on," he would protest, delighted to see her pretty features distort themselves into an uncanny, snobbish horsiness.

"How did she do it?" Gwen would ask, as if professionally intent. "Something with the chin, sort of rolling it from side to side without unclenching the teeth."

"You've got it!" he applauded.

"Of course you *knoaow*," she went on in the assumed voice, "there *used* to be Greece, but now all these dreadful *A*rabs. . . ."

"Oh, yes, yes," he said, his face smarting from laughing so hard, so proudly. She had become perfect for him.

In bed she pointed out, "It's awfully late."

"Want a back rub?"

"Mmmm. That would be reawy nice." As his left hand labored on the smooth, warm, pliable surface, his wife—that small something in her that was all her own—sank out of reach; night after night, she fell asleep.

EXERCISES

1. Why is mimicry or pretending to be someone else an important theme in this story?

2. What is the effect of hearing the second wife say things that the first wife had mimicked earlier, for example, the way she pronounced the word *really*?

3. What is it about Pygmalion's second wife that he liked before they were married but does not like after their marriage? Explain why.

4. What is Pygmalion's definition of "proper womanliness"? What does it mean that he cannot know the world unless it is translated for him by a woman?

5. Discuss the meaning of the final scene when the second wife does what the first wife once did—falls asleep after a back rub.

6. Discuss the basic appeal of the Pygmalion myth, and explain how Updike makes use of this appeal to satirize some aspect of the modern relationship between men and women.

THE APOCRYPHA | *Daniel and Susanna*

There once lived in Babylon a man named Joakim. He married Susanna daughter of Hilkiah, a very beautiful and devout woman. Her parents, religious people, had brought up their daughter according to the law of Moses. Joakim was very rich and his house had a fine garden adjoining it, which was a regular meeting-place for the Jews, because he was the man of greatest distinction among them.

Now two elders of the community were appointed that year as judges. It was of them that the Lord had said, "Wickedness came forth from Babylon from elders who were judges and were supposed to govern my people." These men were constantly at Joakim's house, and everyone who had a case to be tried came to them there.

When the people went away at noon, Susanna used to go and walk in her husband's garden. Every day the two elders saw her entering the garden and taking her walk, and they were obsessed with lust for her. They no longer prayed to God, but let their thoughts stray from him and forgot the claims of morality. They were both infatuated with her; but they did not tell each other what pangs they suffered, because they were ashamed to confess that they wanted to seduce her. Day after day they watched eagerly to see her.

One day they said, "Let us go home; it is time for lunch." So they went off in different directions, but soon retraced their steps and found themselves face to face. When they questioned one another, each confessed his passion. Then they agreed on a time when they might find her alone.

And while they were watching for an opportune day, she went into the garden as usual with only her two maids; it was very hot, and she wished to bathe there. No one else was in the garden except the two elders, who had hidden and were spying on her. She said to her maids, "Bring me soap and olive oil, and shut the garden doors so that I can bathe." They did as she told them: they closed the garden doors and went out by the side door to fetch the things they had been ordered to bring; they did not see the elders because they were hiding. As soon as the maids had gone, the two elders started up and ran to Susanna. "Look!" they said, "the garden doors are shut, and no one can see us. We are burning with desire for you, so consent and yield to us. If you refuse, we shall give evidence against you that there was a young man with you and that was why you sent your maids away." Susanna groaned and said: "I see no way out. If I do this thing, the penalty is death; if I do not, you will have me at your mercy. My choice is made: I will not do it. It is better to be at your mercy than to sin against the Lord."

With that Susanna gave a loud shout, but the two elders shouted her down. One of them ran and opened the garden door. The household, hearing the uproar in the garden, rushed in through the side door to see what had happened to her. And when the elders had told their story, the servants were deeply shocked, for no such allegation had ever been made against Susanna.

Next day, when the people gathered at her husband Joakim's house, the two elders came, full of their criminal design to put Susanna to death. In the presence of the people they said, "Send for Susanna daughter of Hilkiah, Joakim's wife." So they sent for her, and she came with her parents and children and all her relatives. Now Susanna was a woman of great beauty and delicate feeling. She was closely veiled, but those scoundrels ordered her to be unveiled so that they might feast their eyes on her beauty. Her family and all who saw her were in tears. Then the two elders stood up before the people and put their hands on her head. She looked up to heaven through her tears, for she trusted in the Lord. The elders said: "As we were walking alone in the garden, this woman came in with two maids. She shut the garden doors and dismissed her maids. Then a young man, who had been in hiding, came and lay down with her. We were in a corner of the garden, and when we saw this wickedness we ran up to them. Though we saw them in the act, we could not hold the man; he was too strong for us, and he opened the door and forced his way out. We seized the woman and asked who the young man was, but she would not tell us. That is our evidence."

As they were elders of the people and judges, the assembly believed them and condemned her to death. Then Susanna cried out loudly: "Eternal God, who dost know all secrets and foresee all things, thou knowest that their evidence against me was false. And now I am to die, guiltless though I am of all the wicked things these men have said against me."

The Lord heard her cry. Just as she was being led off to execution, God inspired a devout young man named Daniel to protest, and he shouted out, "I will not have this woman's blood on my head." All the people turned and asked him, "What do you mean by that?" He came forward and said: "Are you such fools, you Israelites, as to condemn a woman of Israel, without making careful inquiry and finding out the truth? Re-open the trial; the evidence these men have brought against her is false."

So the people all hurried back, and the rest of the elders said to him, "Come, take your place among us and state your case, for God has given you the standing of an elder." Daniel said to them, "Separate these men and keep them at a distance from each other, and I will examine them." When they had been separated Daniel summoned one of them. "You hardened sinner," he said, "the sins of your past have now come home to you. You gave unjust decisions, condemning the innocent, and acquitting the guilty, although the Lord has said, 'You shall not put to death an innocent and guiltless man.' Now then, if you saw this woman, tell us, under what tree did you see them together?" He answered, "Under a clove-tree." Then Daniel retorted, "Very good: this lie has cost you your life, for already God's angel has received your sentence from God, and he will cleave you in two." And he told him to stand aside, and ordered them to bring in the other.

He said to him: "Spawn of Canaan, no son of Judah, beauty has been your undoing, and lust has corrupted your heart! Now we know how you have been treating the women of Israel, frightening them into consorting with you; but here is a woman of Judah who would not submit to your villainy. Now then, tell me, under what tree did you surprise them together?" "Under a yew-tree," he replied. Daniel said to him, "Very good: this lie has cost you your life, for the angel of God is waiting with his sword to hew you down and destroy you both."

Then the whole assembly gave a great shout and praised God, the saviour of those who trust in him. They turned on the two elders, for out of their own mouths Daniel had convicted them of giving false evidence; they dealt with them according to the law of Moses, and put them to death, as they in their wickedness had tried to do to their neighbour. And so an innocent life was saved that day. Then Hilkiah and his wife gave praise for their daughter Susanna, because she was found innocent of a shameful deed, and so did her husband Joakim and all her relatives. And from that day forward Daniel was a great man among his people.

HERBERT
GOLD | *Susanna at the Beach*

First came the girl. Then one fat man idly floated beside a friend in the water, lolling on his back, spitting, his great trunk rolling in the pleasure of himself. He liked to watch the girl while taking his pleasure.

Finally there were the people on shore. These September loiterers, with thin hocks and thick, with waddling rumps in dank wool or tendoned ones in Hawaiian shorts, with itching faces in devotion to sun or a suave glistening under the equivocation of lotion, all of them squinted and winked and finally moved toward her. They strolled, they turned on their heels, or they merely leaned. They came limping over the hot sand like the good wizards in a story.

The girl over whom the old men watched was diving from the end of a breakwater into the oily, brackish, waste-ridden substance of Lake Erie at Cleveland, Ohio. Her arms, deeply tanned, worked firmly; and heated from within, she scrambled up the rocks in haste after her discipline. She had fled all the billboard schemes of the life of a pretty girl. Lips soft and half-parted for a grand design rather than a Lucky Strike, hands taking the measure of ambition rather than the bottle of Coca-Cola, she had come to perfect her diving in a worn black cotton bathing suit which was already too small after her summer's growth. They were simple exercises, but she wanted them to be perfect. She had an idea of how they should be.

The old men, shaking off the sand flies which had multiplied among the refuse so late in the season, looked jealously to the thin cloth which held this girl and to the water which sheathed her. The girl measured the angle of her imagination against the remembered sting of an imperfect arc. Clean! she had prayed, but her worried brow was reporting, *No, another flop.* The black cloth gleamed in the wet. The droplets of water peeled down her body like broken beads as she climbed to try it again. The smile at the corners of her mouth was a promise to herself: Well! This time, then. Even in the brief instant of her stretching, a crescent-shaped slope at one shoulder flashed dry in the sunlight.

This time she went in straight and slender with the will of perfection.

It was a Tuesday afternoon, and a day of rare Indian summer heat. Still, only the most faithful had returned to the beach: the athletic grandfathers, white-haired and withered, with an eye for the weather; a student with his American history textbook and the glaze of sun in his face meeting the doze of exposure to knowledge; the kids pretending to fish and the dead shad belly-up at the washline of water on the sand; the occasional amorous ones, asking riddles, fondling each other slyly, their pockets a-jingle with desire and street-car fare; women from the industrial flats nearby, sitting in housedress to recall, complain, worry, and take a sleepy hour's leisure together. Mostly, however, beneath the roar and thump of road construction on the slope above them, almost in the shadow of the Terminal Tower to the east, there were the old men: the salesman sunning himself with neck reaching out and pants rolled above the knee so that by evening he can look "just like Miami Beach, better even"; the flat-thighed wanderer in a straw hat and red woolen trunks with a white canvas belt, his sinewy breasts hanging—he sat in a patch of seaweed to observe the diver and stroke the sand from between his toes; another, the big-bellied swimmer, now paddling and spewing water, shaggily emerged onto the pier in order to get nearer to the girl. His friend accompanied him. Hairy-chested loungers, old-time beaux, their bodies both wasted and swollen, they joined the rest of the men along the backwater. They watched the girl still diving, still climbing; her deep breathing pressed the erect buds of her adolescence against sleek black cloth, she rocked once on her toes, and then off she sprang.

This girl used herself hard, used her lightness hard; and each man there, turning to her from the beach or the pier, thought it a pity. A waste—her sufficiency unto herself silenced and saddened them and made their arms hang tensely forward. Challenged, they turned up the cards of their own sorts of sufficiencies.

The fat swimmer, swirls of hair on his belly and back, was now switching himself with a green branch as he talked business with his friend. They both studied the girl, and their discussion grew lyrical. They talked business and public affairs. He was saying: "You're John-cue Smith, let's put it, you want to get married—"

"I know! Got the taxes to pay, the down payments, the terms—"

"Yes, that's what I mean, to get ahead in life. The installments."

"I got the cost of living these days, Freddy."

"You got the government."

"Yes, Freddy, I got the taxes, yes—"

"The essentials of life."

"Yes, yes, all of that, yes"—and they both shook their heads mournfully and let their mouths fall open while the tips of the girl's feet, propelled by her dive, wriggled above water as she swam.

"Like to bite off a piece of that one, eh Freddy?"

"I saw it first, me, you want to say I didn't?"

A policeman on horseback looked for purse-snatching, nuisance-making, or drunkenness. Overhead, a pontooned airplane swooped low and up. The traffic rushed past the stillness of sun and beach and water, while, out on the lake, a single leaning sailboat, a visitor from the Clifton Club, kept its distance.

Two women, equipped for conversation with quart bottles of cherry pop, their dresses pulled over their knees and their stockings rolled down to their ankles, agreed on questions of mortality, bereavement, and the pleasures of a city beach. They sat on a log stripped by water and shaded their eyes first toward the industrial flats from which they had emerged, then over the lake and into the horizon and beyond. "My mama she die when she eighty-four," said the tanned younger one. "Just like baby, like new kid, she need milk to drink."

"Yah," sighed her friend, a fat and weary woman with concentric rings of flesh about her eyes. "Look that American girlie on the board, what she think? She hurt herself like that."

"She not able my mother care for herself or nothing."

"I know, dear."

"She die like so—sssst—after long life. She work hard."

"I *know,* dear."

"It ain't right, is it?" She nodded once, decisively, and said, "My father he still strong and smoke big cigar I buy for him. He sleep with woman and give her money and everything. Ain't nice old man like that. He make eye at every young girl—"

"Bad young girlie," said the plump woman to the sand, the water, and the figure now climbing back onto the rocks.

The tanned one pulled at her dress and said, "That's why, here in this country, many people go off on roof for fall down. My children all go away to Detroit and *I* give money to my papa."

"No justice on earth, darling," said the sad plump one.

The girl, the fine diver, went off the rocks again, measuring only with a frown the interior demands of her lonely stunt, absent from the beach on the parapets of ambition. She had scraped the cotton suit on a rock. The small split showed an edge of white breast, the first hard growth of the departure from girlhood. Some of the idlers had gathered in silence on the breakwater to watch her. "You want to tell me no, Freddy? I'm telling *you* no," the fat swimmer insisted. She did not see them; she had nothing to say to them; her regard was absorbed by the patch of black water and the rules of her skill.

Back on the beach, another immature and pretty girl sat with her feet drawn under her on the sands. No one, not even Freddy, the fat swimmer's friend, gave more than a glance to this one, whose tanned plumpness in stylish knee-length shorts promised an eventual stylish willingness while her profile remained strict, suburban, and pure. Her mother, shriveled to creamed skin rather than casual flesh, squatted like the image of her age by her side, but this was not the reason that the free-ranging eyes of the beach passed over her daughter so lightly. The men sensed that she feared to lie on grass because of disease, dirt, and small animals, that she shuddered at the thought of diving into the tricky, steaming, polluted waters, that despite her prettiness she had put herself apart from the play of caprice, open-mouthed laughter, and the risks of pleasure. "Look at the girl on the pier, the one that's diving again," this cute creature said.

"She's headed for earache, that's for sure," her mother commented with satisfaction. "Maybe she doesn't read the paper and how the water's unsafe. Dangerous for bathing. Full of organisms."

"I'm getting hungry, Mother"—wrinkling her junior-miss nose and hugging herself as her favorite starlet did.

"I *said* we'd stop at the Howard Johnson's."

Meanwhile, the diver scrambled over the rocks, up onto the pier, took three or four mincing, dancing steps, and bent her knees for her renewed essay at a controlled style. Her wide temples glowed pinker and pinker with the blood under her skin and the impact of water. Her innocence—an innocence of lessons—was informed by the heat and by the pressure of her blood which brought her climbing, diving, repeating this gesture again and again past the heaped-up rock. Had she seen them and gone on, it would have spoken for an angry and stubborn pride; but her way was the way of habit, of grace, and of a passionate ignorance, a deep communion with belly-smash on the shore of Lake Erie at Cleveland.

The plump lady from the flats was disturbed. "My doctor say: Playsuit! no stockings! Like that you have no more colds for wintertime. You have upper repertory affection, Doctor Sczymanski say. Neighbor she look at playsuit, close mouth, she say: shame! What can I do, darling?"

"That American girl, *she* have no shame," remarked the tanned woman whose father smoked big cigars. "Everybody is look at her legs"—and they both fell into a musing silence, and looked.

The beach was silent while a skin of complicity tightened like the dry sun about them all. Gradually these visitors to the September sands moved toward the breakwater, each one marvelously hushed because, if they said nothing, it could be presumed to be their habit and their devotion, an abandon to mutism in the heat, a pious thing superior to their daily selves: and thus, if the rip in the girl's suit grew longer, it was not their place to warn her of it. Let each creature hunger for itself alone—Freddy poked his pal to mean this—and thus send only appetite in the pursuit of others. The veiny old men moved fastest.

Within a few moments the beach was almost deserted except for the couple busily twisting and tickling in their well-worn place. The girl sat up with a jerk, spreading sand in an abrupt movement of her thighs, while her friend grinned, saying, "I'm not connerdicting you." He pulled her down again.

The tear in the diver's suit widened; the gash in this black second skin showed, to the fat man, the whiteness of belly, and then, to Freddy's bemusement, the flexing folds of flesh. Just once Freddy saw her fingers feel for the rip, but her body's intelligence calculated on nothing but the demands of perfection, and the thought of care for that clothing which was outside desire did not move further than the impatient, rummaging hand. She did not glance at herself.

Turned to her idea, fixed on some inner certainty, she closed the split with her fingers, then forgot it, then let go.

She dived and climbed without liability to the give of cloth or the alteration of her world which Freddy and the big-bellied swimmer brought. She scrambled up dripping, let her eyes roam absently over the tense strollers gathering on the rocks, and dived once more. The pale wetness of her flesh opened to them like a wound under the suit while the girl, if she thought of her body at all, thought only of her skill and of her rehearsals for its sake. She was secure (small splash and ripple) in the exercise of method. She was an expert.

"You trying to tell me no, Freddy?" Behind the fat swimmer and his friend, past the city beach on this September afternoon, the machinery of road construction throbbed and the insect hiss of an afternoon breeze occupied the trees on the slope leading up to the highway past the tables, the shelters, and the park restroom. Because his mouth was dry, the fat man pointed to the girl and whispered, "Lookit." He squeezed the muscles of his friend's arm, thumb and forefinger twanging, and then they both moved forward again. The heat and the effort brought shiny tears to his eyes and a dampness to his forehead. The thickness of his body in swimming trunks, sagging at the middle and the rear, bulging beneath, looked enormous in the sunlight and the intimacy of one leg's motion against the other.

Repetitious, formal, and oblivious, the girl's ambition seemed madness or a mad joke to the watchers. It pleased the fat man; it was a delight to him. He opened his mouth, like a swimmer, and put his tongue sideways to breathe more easily. Freddy—as to him—he could hardly believe it. He wanted to float up an inner tube and go out someplace to think about it.

When she climbed over the rocks once again, the rip widened almost audibly, and still she did not see that her suit was ready to hang in tatters. No one warned her—as we do not warn a madman that he is talking nonsense—but they sighed when she extended her arms for the dive. The fat man sighed. All of them leaned together now, men and women, sharing the girl and sharing each other, waiting for their world's confirmation against the challenge she brought it, an assurance of which they were in need before the return to autumn and the years rapid upon them. A whiteness of breast flashed out, its pink sprouting from the girl's body like a delicate thing nurtured in the dark. But the day was bright and the shadows short. Looking at this tender and abstracted girl, the old Polish woman shivered at her own memories of paleness, of resiliency, of pink colors. The fat man, too, partook of their communion, frowning darkly, the green branch switching at his flanks, his knees slightly bent. He pinched his friend instead of himself. Now, her hair flat on her head and the flush of pleasure high on her cheeks after the repeated slap of her forehead against water, the girl was diving in a diminished rhythm, worn out but blind to risk, finished but unable to stop. The moment when her breast and belly slipped by the surface was the fat man's favorite.

The diver, that object for the vindictive imaginations of old men and old women, seemed to pause to acknowledge their study of her, but saw nothing, saw nothing again, and went on. The fat man's eyelids had dropped. He was moved. As she climbed, dripping and critical, bewitched by mastery of her body, feeling, if the presence of the others had come through to her at all, only a reward of praise earned through the long summer, the fat man released his friend's arm to break the silence at last with a shrill whoop. Then the old Polish woman screamed, "You're nekked, girlie! *Nekked!*"

The fat man, his friend, the salesman, the student, many of them were now yelling their cheers at her. Poised for her dive, she must suddenly have seen them and seen herself in their sight. Her look was one of incredulity. Her eyes turned from herself to their shouting, gaping, heavy-tongued mouths and back to the loose cloth dangling from straps. She did not speak. She turned her face from them. Its stern and peaceful determination hardly altered. Then suddenly the extended arms flashed down: she ran, she did not dive, she jumped and rolled into the oily water. Despite this folding upon herself, their eyes searched out a glimpse of sunlit flesh, white and pink and tender. While the crowd applauded, the student shouted, "She wants to drown herself," and leaped into the water.

"I'll get her! Me too! *Me!*"

The young man reached for her hair and only touched it before she wrenched free. She doubled under, holding herself, and then she was swimming. The crowd was roaring. Four, five, six of the men had pushed to the edge of the breakwater. The girl kicked forward and swam with short, quick, sure strokes, straight out into the lake, while a cluster of young men and old, their smiles strict in pursuit, tumbled down the rocks to be first to catch her. The fat man, paddling furiously, was ahead of Freddy. The righteousness of a mob's laughter urged them to be swift, but the girl was very strong, very skillful, gifted, and encumbered by nothing but her single thought.

EXERCISES

1. How is the setting of the story on the shore of Lake Erie, where the water is oily, brackish, and waste-ridden, an appropriate setting for the event?

2. How does the young girl differ from the other people on the beach?

3. Discuss the men's reaction to the girl. Is this a stereotype, or is it typical? What is the relevance of the conversation between the two women?

4. What attitude do you think the narrator or storyteller has toward the girl? Support your answer. Why do the men prefer the girl on the pier to the pretty girl on the beach?

5. Discuss the following: ". . . sharing the girl and sharing each other, waiting for their world's confirmation against the challenge she brought it, an assurance for which they were in need before the return to autumn and the years rapid upon them."

6. What is the point of the rip in the girl's suit? Why is the girl able to evade the men at the end?

7. Compare this story with the story of Susanna from the Apocrypha. What basic theme does Herbert Gold see in the original story? How effective is he in transposing it to a modern setting?

GENESIS,
THE BIBLE | *The Flood*

When mankind began to increase and to spread all over the earth and daughters were born to them, the sons of the gods saw that the daughters of men were beautiful; so they took for themselves such women as they chose. But the Lord said, "My life-giving spirit shall not remain in man for ever; he for his part is mortal flesh: he shall live for a hundred and twenty years."

In those days, when the sons of the gods had intercourse with the daughters of men and got children by them, the Nephilim were on earth. They were the heroes of old, men of renown.

When the Lord saw that man had done much evil on earth and that his thoughts and inclinations were always evil, he was sorry that he had made man on earth, and he was grieved at heart. He said, "This race of men whom I have created, I will wipe them off the face of the earth—man and beast, reptiles and birds. I am sorry that I ever made them." But Noah had won the Lord's favour.

This is the story of Noah. Noah was a righteous man, the one blameless man of his time; he walked with God. He had three sons, Shem, Ham and Japheth. Now God saw that the whole world was corrupt and full of violence. In his sight the world had become corrupted, for all men had lived corrupt lives on earth. God said to Noah, "The loathsomeness of all mankind has become plain to me, for through them the earth is full of violence. I intend to destroy them, and the earth with them. Make yourself an ark with ribs of cypress; cover it with reeds and coat it inside and out with pitch. This is to be its plan: the length of the ark shall be three hundred cubits, its breadth fifty cubits, and its height thirty cubits. You shall make a roof for the ark, giving it a fall of one cubit when complete; and put a door in the side of the ark, and build three decks, upper, middle, and lower. I intend to bring the waters of the flood over the earth to destroy every human being under heaven that has the spirit of life; everything on earth shall perish. But with you I will make a covenant, and you shall go into the ark, you and your sons, your wife and your sons' wives with you. And you shall bring living creatures of every kind into the ark to keep them alive with you, two of each kind, a male and a female; two of every kind of bird, beast, and reptile, shall come to you to be kept alive. See that you take and store every kind of food that can be eaten; this shall be food for you and for them." Exactly as God had commanded him, so Noah did.

The Lord said to Noah, "Go into the ark, you and all your household; for I have seen that you alone are righteous before me in this generation. Take with you seven pairs, male and female, of all beasts that are ritually clean, and one pair, male and female, of all beasts that are not clean; also seven pairs, male and female, of every bird—to ensure that life continues on earth. In seven days' time I will send rain over the earth for forty days and forty nights, and I will wipe off the face of the earth every living thing that I have made." Noah did all that the Lord had commanded him. He was six hundred years old when the waters of the flood came upon the earth.

And so, to escape the waters of the flood, Noah went into the ark with his sons, his wife, and his sons' wives. And into the ark with Noah went one pair, male and female, of all beasts, clean and unclean, of birds and of everything that crawls on the ground, two by two, as God had commanded. Towards the end of seven days the waters of the flood came upon the earth. In the year when Noah was six hundred years old, on the seventeenth day of the second month, on that very day, all the springs of the great abyss broke through, the windows of the sky were opened, and rain fell on the earth for forty days and forty nights. On that very day Noah entered the ark with his sons, Shem, Ham and Japheth, his own wife, and his three sons' wives. Wild animals of every kind, cattle of every kind, reptiles of every kind that move upon the ground, and birds of every kind—all came to Noah in the ark, two by two of all creatures that had life in them. Those which came were one male and one female of all living things; they came in as God had commanded Noah, and the Lord closed the door on him. The flood continued upon the earth for forty days, and the waters swelled and lifted up the ark so that it rose high above the ground. They swelled and increased over the earth, and the ark floated on the surface of the waters. More and more the waters increased over the earth until they covered all the high mountains everywhere under heaven. The waters increased and the mountains were covered to a depth of fifteen cubits. Every living creature that moves on earth perished, birds, cattle, wild animals, all reptiles, and all mankind. Everything died that had the breath of life in its nostrils, everything on dry land. God wiped out every living thing that existed on earth, man and beast, reptile and bird; they were all wiped out over the whole earth, and only Noah and his company in the ark survived.

When the waters had increased over the earth for a hundred and fifty days, God thought of Noah and all the wild animals and the cattle with him in the ark, and he made a wind pass over the earth, and the waters began to subside. The springs of the abyss were stopped up, and so were the windows of the sky; the downpour from the skies was checked. The water gradually receded from the earth, and by the end of a hundred and fifty days it had disappeared. On the seventeenth day of the seventh month the ark grounded on a mountain in Ararat. The water continued to recede until the tenth month, and on the first day of the tenth month the tops of the mountains could be seen.

After forty days Noah opened the trap-door that he had made in the ark, and released a raven to see whether the water had subsided, but the bird con-

tinued flying to and fro until the water on the earth had dried up. Noah waited
for seven days, and then he released a dove from the ark to see whether the
water on the earth had subsided further. But the dove found no place where
she could settle, and so she came back to him in the ark, because there was
water over the whole surface of the earth. Noah stretched out his hand, caught
her and took her into the ark. He waited another seven days and again
released the dove from the ark. She came back to him towards evening with
a newly plucked olive leaf in her beak. Then Noah knew for certain that the
water on the earth had subsided still further. He waited yet another seven days
and released the dove, but she never came back. And so it came about that,
on the first day of the first month of his six hundred and first year, the water
had dried up on the earth, and Noah removed the hatch and looked out of
the ark. The surface of the ground was dry.

By the twenty-seventh day of the second month the whole earth was dry.
And God said to Noah, "Come out of the ark, you and your wife, your sons
and their wives. Bring out every living creature that is with you, live things of
every kind, bird and beast and every reptile that moves on the ground, and
let them swarm over the earth and be fruitful and increase there." So Noah
came out with his sons, his wife, and his sons' wives. Every wild animal, all
cattle, every bird, and every reptile that moves on the ground, came out of the
ark by families. Then Noah built an altar to the Lord. He took ritually clean
beasts and birds of every kind, and offered whole-offerings on the altar. When
the Lord smelt the soothing odour, he said within himself, "Never again will
I curse the ground because of man, however evil his inclinations may be from
his youth upwards. I will never again kill every living creature, as I have just
done.

> While the earth lasts
> seedtime and harvest, cold and heat,
> summer and winter, day and night,
> shall never cease."

ROBERT
COOVER | *The Brother*

right there right there in the middle of the damn field he says he wants to
put that thing together him and his buggy ideas and so me I says "how the
hell you gonna get it down to the water?" but he just focuses me out sweepin
the blue his eyes rollin like they do when he gets het on some new lunatic
notion and he says not to worry none about that just would I help him for
God's sake and because he don't know how he can get it done in time otherwise and though you'd have to be loonier than him to say yes I says I will of
course I always would crazy as my brother is I've done little else since I was
born and my wife she says "I can't figure it out I can't see why you always
have to be babyin that old fool he ain't never done nothin for you God knows

and you got enough to do here fields need plowin it's a bad enough year already my God and now that red-eyed brother of yours wingin around like a damn cloud and not knowin what in the world he's doin building a damn boat in the country my God what next? you're a damn fool I tell you" but packs me some sandwiches just the same and some sandwiches for my brother Lord knows *his* wife don't have to truck with him no more says he can go starve for all she cares she's fed up ever since the time he made her sit out on a hillside for three whole days rain and everything because he said she'd see God and she didn't see nothin and in fact she like to die from hunger nothin but berries and his boys too they ain't so bright neither but at least they come to help him out with his damn boat so it ain't just the two of us thank God for *that* and it ain't no goddamn fishin boat he wants to put up neither in fact it's the biggest damn thing I ever heard of and for weeks *weeks* I'm tellin you we ain't doin nothin but cuttin down pine trees and haulin them out to his field which is really pretty high up a hill and my God *that's* work lemme tell you and my wife she sighs and says I am really crazy *r-e-a-l-l-y* crazy and her four months with a child and tryin to do my work and hers too and still when I come home from haulin timbers around all day she's got enough left to rub my shoulders and the small of my back and fix a hot meal her long black hair pulled to a knot behind her head and hangin marvelously down her back her eyes gentle but very tired my God and I says to my brother I says "look I got a lotta work to do buddy you'll have to finish this idiot thing yourself I wanna help you all I can you know that but" and he looks off and he says "it don't matter none your work" and I says "the hell it don't how you think me and my wife we're gonna eat I mean where do you think this food comes from you been puttin away man? you can't eat this goddamn boat out here ready to rot in that bastard sun" and he just sighs long and says "no it just don't matter" and he sits him down on a rock kinda tired like and stares off and looks like he might even for God's sake cry and so I go back to bringin wood up to him and he's already started on the keel and frame God knows how *he* ever found out to build a damn boat lost in *his* fog where he is Lord he was twenty when I was born and the first thing I remember was havin to lead him around so he didn't get kicked by a damn mule him who couldn't never do nothin in a normal way just a huge oversize fuzzyface boy so anyway I take to gettin up a few hours earlier ever day to do my farmin my wife apt to lose the baby if she should keep pullin around like she was doin then I go to work on the boat until sundown and on and on the days hot and dry and my wife keepin good food in me or else I'd of dropped sure and no matter what I say to try and get out of it my brother he says "you come and help now the rest don't matter" and we just keep hammerin away and my God the damn thing is big enough for a hundred people and at least I think at *least* it's a place to live and not too bad at that at least it's good for somethin but my wife she just sighs and says no good will come of it and runs her hands through my hair but she don't ask me to stop helpin no more because she knows it won't do no good and she's kinda turned into herself now these days and gettin herself all ready and still we keep workin on that damn thing that damn boat and the days pass and my brother he says we gotta work harder we ain't got much time and from time to time he gets a coupla neighbors to come over and give a hand them sucked in by the size and the novelty of the thing makin jokes some but they don't stay around more than a day or two and they go away shakin their heads and swearin under their breath and disgusted they got weaseled into the thing in the first place and me I only get about half my place planted and see to my stock as much as I can my wife she takes more care of them than I can but at least we won't starve we say if we just get some rain and finally we get the damn thing done all finished by God and we cover it in and out with pitch and put a kinda fancy roof on it and I come home on that last day and I ain't never goin back ain't *never* gonna let him talk me into nothin again and I'm all smellin of tar and my wife she cries and cries and I says to her not to worry no more I'll be home all the time and me I'm cryin a little too though she don't notice just thinkin how she's had it so lonely and hard and all and for one whole day I just sleep the whole damn day and the rest of the week I work around the farm and one day I get an idea and I go over to my brother's place and get some pieces of wood left over and whaddaya know? they are all livin on that damn boat there in the middle of nowhere him and his boys and some women and my brother's wife she's there too but she's madder than hell and carpin at him to get outa that damn boat and come home and he says she's got just one more day and then he's gonna drug her on the boat but he don't say it like a threat or nothin more like a fact a plain fact tomorrow he's gonna drug her on the boat well I ain't one to get mixed up in domestic quarrels God knows so I grab up the wood and beat it back to my farm and that evenin I make a little cradle a kinda fancy one with little animal figures cut in it and polished down and after supper I give it to my wife as a surprise and she cries and cries and holds me tight and says don't never go away again and stay close by her and all I feel so damn good and warm about it all and glad the boat thing is over and we get out a little wine and we decide the baby's name is gonna be either Nathaniel or Anna and so we drink an extra cup to Nathaniel's health and we laugh and we sigh and we drink one to Anna and my wife she gently fingers the little animal figures and says they're beautiful and really they ain't I ain't much good at that sorta thing but I know what she means and then she says "where did you get the wood?" and I says "it's left over from the boat" and she don't say nothin for a moment and then she says "you been over there again today?" and I says "yes just to get the wood" and she says "what's he doin now he's got the boat done?" and I says "funny thing they're all living in the damn thing all except the old lady she's over there hollerin at him how he's getting senile and where does he think he's sailin to and how if he ain't afraid of runnin into a octypuss on the way he oughta get back home and him sayin she's a nut there ain't no water and her sayin that's what *she's* been tellin *him* for six months" and my wife she laughs and it's the happiest laugh I've heard from her in half a year and I laugh and we both have another cup of wine and my wife she says "so he's just livin on that big thing all by hisself?" and I says "no he's got his boys on there and some young women who are maybe wives of the boys or somethin I don't know I ain't never seen them before and all kindsa damn animals and birds and things I ain't never seen the likes" and my wife she says "animals? what animals?" and I says "oh all kinds I don't know a whole damn menagerie all clutterin and stinkin up the boat *God* what a mess" and my wife laughs again and she's a little silly with the wine and she says "I bet he ain't got no pigs" and "oh yes I seen them" I says and we laugh thinkin about pigs rootin around in that big tub and she says "I bet he ain't got no jackdaws" and I says "yes I seen a couple of them too or mostly I heard them you couldn't hardly hear nothin else" and we laugh again thinkin about them crows and his old lady and the pigs and all and my wife she says "*I* know what he ain't got I bet he ain't got no lice" and we both laugh like crazy and when I can I say "oh yes he does less he's took a bath" and we both laugh till we're cryin and we finish off the wine and my wife says "look now I *know* what he ain't got he ain't got no termites" and I says "you're right I don't recollect no termites maybe we oughta make him a present" and my wife she holds me close quiet all of a sudden and says "he's really movin Nathaniel's really movin" and she puts my hand down on her round belly and the little fella is kickin up a terrific storm and I says kinda anxious "does it hurt? do you think that—?" and "no" she says "it's good" she says and so I says with my hand on her belly "here's to you Nathaniel" and we drain what's left in the bottom of our cups and the next day we wake up in each other's arms and it's rainin and *thank God* we say and since it's rainin real good we stay inside and do things around the place and we're happy because the rain has come just in time and in the evenin things smell green and fresh and delicious and it's still rainin a little but not too hard so I decide to take a walk and I wander over by my brother's place thinkin I'll ask him if he'd like to take on some pet termites to go with his collection and there by God is his wife on the boat and I don't know if he drug her on or if she just finally come by herself but she ain't sayin nothin which is damn unusual and the boys they ain't sayin nothin either and my brother he ain't sayin nothin they're just all standin up there on top and gazin off and I holler up at them "nice rain ain't it?" and my brother he looks down at me standin there in the rain and still he don't say nothing but he raises his hand kinda funny like and then puts it back on the rail and I decide not to say nothin about the termites and it's startin to rain a little harder again so I turn away and go back home and I tell my wife about what happened and my wife she just laughs and says "they're *all* crazy he's finally got them *all* crazy" and she's cooked me up a special pastry with fresh meat and so we forget about them by God the next day the rain's still comin down harder than ever and the water's beginning to stand around in places and after a week of rain I can see the crops is pretty well ruined and I'm havin trouble keepin my stock fed and my wife she's cryin and talkin about our bad luck that we might as well of built a damn boat as plant all them crops and still we don't figure things out I mean it just don't come to our minds not even when the rain keeps spillin down like a ocean dumped upsidedown and now water is beginnin to stand around in big pools really big ones and water up to the ankles around the house and leakin in and pretty soon the whole damn house is gettin fulla water and I keep sayin maybe we oughta go use my brother's boat till this blows over but my wife she says "never" and then she starts in cryin again so finally I says to her I says "we can't be so proud I'll go ask him" and so I set out in the storm and I can hardly see where I'm goin and I slip up to my neck in places and finally I get to where the boat is and I holler up and my brother he comes out and he looks down at where I am and he don't say nothin that bastard he just looks at me and I shout up at him I says "hey is it all right for me and my wife to come over until this thing blows over?" and still he don't say a damn word he just raises his hand in that same sillyass way and I holler "hey you stupid sonuvabitch I'm soakin wet goddamn it and my house is fulla water and my wife she's about to have a kid and she's apt to get sick all wet and cold to the bones and all I'm askin you—" and right then right while I'm still talkin he turns around and he goes back in the boat and I can't hardly believe it me his brother but he don't come back out and I push up under the boat and I beat on it with my fists and scream at him and call him ever name I can think up and I shout for his boys and for his wife and for anybody inside and nobody comes out "God*damn* YOU" I cry out at the top of my lungs and half sobbin and sick and then feelin too beat out to do anythin more I turn around and head back for home but the rain is thunderin down like mad now and in places I gotta swim and I can't make it no further and I recollect a hill nearby and I head for it and when I get to it I climb up on top of it and it feels good to be on land again even if it is soggy and greasy and I vomit and retch there awhile and move further up and the next thing I know I'm wakin up the rain still in my face and the water halfway up the hill toward me and I look out and I can see my brother's boat is floatin and I wave at it but I don't see nobody wave back and then I quick look out towards my own place and all I can see is the top of it and of a sudden I'm scared scared about my wife and I go tearin for the house swimmin most all the way and cryin and shoutin and the rain still comin down like crazy and so now well now I'm back here on the hill again what little there is left of it and I'm figurin maybe I got a day left if the rain keeps comin and it don't show no signs of stoppin and I can't see my brother's boat no more gone just water how *how* did he know? that bastard and yet I gotta hand it to him it's not hard to see who's crazy around here I can't see my house no more I just left my wife inside where I found her I couldn't hardly stand to look at her the way she was

EXERCISES

1. What are the basic differences between the narrator and his brother Noah?
2. Why would the voice of the narrator sound out of place within the original biblical version of the story? What makes the story of the flood as told by Noah's brother plausible and believable?

3. What is the effect of the repeated reference to God by the narrator? How do they differ from the references to God in the Old Testament version of the story?

4. Why doesn't Noah allow his brother on the boat? How does the tone and mood of the story change with Noah's refusal?

5. Discuss the implications of the final image of the brother on the top of the hill alone.

6. Why does Coover choose to tell the story of Noah from the brother's point of view? What does the story illustrate? Are we supposed to see it as a humorous parody or as illustrative of an important moral issue? Support your answer.

GUY
DE MAUPASSANT | *In the Moonlight*

Well merited was the name "soldier of God" by the Abbé Marignan. He was a tall, thin priest, fanatical to a degree, but just and of an exalted soul. All his beliefs were fixed, with never a waver. He thought that he understood God thoroughly, that he penetrated His designs, His wishes, His intentions.

Striding up and down the garden walk of his little country parsonage, sometimes a question arose in his mind: "Why did God make that?" Then in his thoughts, putting himself in God's place, he searched obstinately and nearly always was satisfied that he found the reason. He was not the man to murmur in transports of pious humility, "O Lord, thy ways are past finding out!" What he said was: "I am the servant of God; I ought to know the reason of what he does or to divine it if I do not."

Everything in nature seemed to him created with an absolute and admirable logic. The "wherefore" and the "because" were always balanced. The dawns were made to rejoice you on waking, the days to ripen the harvests, the rains to water them, the evenings to prepare for sleeping and the nights dark for sleep.

The four seasons corresponded perfectly to all the needs of agriculture, and to him the suspicion could never have come that nature has no intention and that all which lives has accustomed itself, on the contrary, to the hard conditions of different periods, of climates and of matter.

But he hated women; he hated them unconsciously and despised them by instinct. He often repeated the words of Christ, "Woman, what have I to do with thee?" and he would add, "One would almost say that God himself was ill pleased with that particular work of his hands." Woman for him was indeed the "child twelve times unclean" of whom the poet speaks. She was the temptress who had ensnared the first man and who still continued her damnable work; she was the being who is feeble, dangerous, mysteriously troublous. And even more than her poisonous beauty he hated her loving soul.

He had often felt women's tenderness attack him, and though he knew himself to be unassailable he grew exasperated at this need of loving which quivers continually in their hearts.

To his mind God had only created woman to tempt man and to test him. Man should not approach her without those precautions for defense which he would take, and the fears he would cherish, near an ambush. Woman, indeed, was just like a trap, with her arms extended and her lips open toward a man.

He had toleration only for nuns, rendered harmless by their vow; but he treated them harshly notwithstanding, because, ever at the bottom of their chained-up hearts, their chastened hearts, he perceived the eternal tenderness that constantly went out even to him although he was a priest.

He had a niece who lived with her mother in a little house near by. He was bent on making her a sister of charity. She was pretty and harebrained and a great tease. When the abbé sermonized she laughed; when he was angry at her she kissed him vehemently, pressing him to her heart while he would seek involuntarily to free himself from her embrace. Notwithstanding, it made him taste a certain sweet joy, awakening deep within him that sensation of fatherhood which slumbers in every man.

Often he talked to her of God, of his God, walking beside her along the footpaths through the fields. She hardly listened but looked at the sky, the grass, the flowers, with a joy of living which could be seen in her eyes. Sometimes she rushed forward to catch some flying creature and, bringing it back, would cry: "Look, my uncle, how pretty it is; I should like to kiss it." And this necessity to "kiss flies" or sweet flowers worried, irritated and revolted the priest who saw, even in that, the ineradicable tenderness which ever springs in the hearts of women.

One day the sacristan's wife, who kept house for the Abbé Marignan, told him very cautiously that his niece had a lover!

He experienced a dreadful emotion, and he stood choking, with the soap all over his face, in the act of shaving.

When he found himself able to think and speak once more he cried: "It is not true; you are lying, Melanie!"

But the peasant woman put her hand on her heart. "May our Lord judge me if I am lying, Monsieur le Curé. I tell you she goes to him every evening as soon as your sister is in bed. They meet each other beside the river. You have only to go there between ten o'clock and midnight and see for yourself."

He ceased scratching his chin and commenced to pace the room quickly, as he always did in his hours of gravest thought. When he tried to begin his shaving again he cut himself three times from nose to ear.

All day long he remained silent, swollen with anger and with rage. To his priestly zeal against the mighty power of love was added the moral indignation of a father, of a teacher, of a keeper of souls, who has been deceived, robbed, played with by a child. He felt the egotistical sorrow that parents feel when their daughter announces that she has chosen a husband without them and in spite of their advice.

After his dinner he tried to read a little, but he could not attune himself to it and he grew angrier and angrier. When it struck ten he took his cane, a formidable oaken club which he always carried when he had to go out at night to visit the sick. Smilingly he regarded the enormous cudgel, holding it in his solid, countryman's fist and cutting threatening circles with it in the air. Then suddenly he raised it and, grinding his teeth, he brought it down upon a chair, the back of which, split in two, fell heavily to the ground.

He opened his door to go out, but he stopped upon the threshold, surprised by such a splendor of moonlight as you seldom see.

Endowed as he was with an exalted spirit, such a spirit as must have belonged to those dreamer-poets, the Fathers of the Church, he felt himself suddenly softened and moved by the grand and serene beauty of the pale-faced night.

In his little garden, bathed in the soft brilliance, his fruit trees, all arow, were outlining in shadow upon the walk their slender limbs of wood scarce clothed with green; while the giant honeysuckle climbing on the house wall exhaled delicious sugared breaths which hovered through the warm clear night like a perfumed soul.

He began to breathe deep, drinking the air as drunkards drink their wine and walking slowly, ravished, surprised and almost oblivious of his niece.

As he stepped into the open country he stopped to contemplate the whole plain, inundated by this caressing radiance and drowned in the tender and languishing charm of the serene night. In chorus the frogs threw into space their short metallic notes, and with the seduction of the moonlight distant nightingales mingled that fitful music of theirs which brings no thoughts but dreams, a light and vibrant melody which seems attuned to kisses.

The abbé continued his walk, his courage failing, he knew not why. He felt, as it were, enfeebled and suddenly exhausted; he had a great desire to sit down, to pause right there and praise God in all His works.

Below him, following the bends of the little river, wound a great line of poplars. On and about the banks, wrapping all the tortuous watercourse in a kind of light, transparent wadding, hung suspended a fine mist, a white vapor, which the moon rays crossed and silvered and caused to gleam.

The priest paused yet again, penetrated to the depths of his soul by a strong and growing emotion. And a doubt, a vague uneasiness, seized on him; he felt that one of those questions he sometimes put to himself was now being born.

Why had God done this? Since the night is destined for sleep, for unconsciousness, for repose, for forgetfulness of everything, why, then, make it more charming than the day, sweeter than dawns and sunsets? And this slow, seductive star, more poetical than the sun and so discreet that it seems designed to light up things too delicate, too mysterious for the great luminary—why had it come to brighten all the shades? Why did not the sweetest of all songsters go to rest like the others? Why set himself to singing in the vaguely troubling dark? Why this half veil over the world? Why these quiverings of the heart, this emotion of the soul, this languor of the body? Why this display of seductions which mankind never sees, since night brings sleep? For whom was this sublime spectacle intended, this flood of poetry poured from heaven to earth? The abbé did not understand it at all.

But then, down there along the edge of the pasture, appeared two shadows walking side by side under the arched roof of the trees all soaked in glittering mist.

The man was the taller and had his arm about his mistress's neck; from time to time he kissed her on the forehead. They animated the lifeless landscape which enveloped them, a divine frame made, as it were, expressly for them. They seemed, these two, a single being, the being for whom this calm and silent night was destined; and they approached the priest like a living answer, the answer vouchsafed by his Master to his question.

He stood stock-still, overwhelmed and with a beating heart. He likened it to some Bible story such as the loves of Ruth and Boaz, the accomplishment of the will of the Lord in one of those great scenes talked of in Holy Writ. Through his head ran the versicles of the *Song of Songs,* the ardent cries, the calls of the body, all the passionate poetry of that poem which burns with tenderness and love. And he said to himself, "God perhaps has made such nights as this to clothe with his ideals the loves of men."

He withdrew before the couple, who went on arm in arm. It was really his niece, and now he asked himself if he had not been about to disobey God. For does not God indeed permit love, since He surrounds it visibly with splendor such as this?

And he fled in amaze, almost ashamed, as if he had penetrated into a temple where he had no right to enter.

EXERCISES

1. What assumption does the priest make about God and nature that makes him think he can put himself in God's place?
2. What does the priest's hatred of women have to do with this assumption?
3. Describe the priest's ambiguous attitude toward his niece and his reaction to his discovery that his niece has a lover.
4. Consider the language describing the moonlit night and the effect the night has on the priest.
5. What final realization does the priest come to about the nature of the world and therefore the nature of God?
6. Compare the two basic parts of this story—part one, which emphasizes the logical nature of the priest's *thinking,* and part two, which emphasizes the irrational nature of his *experience.*

GUY
DE MAUPASSANT | *Love: Three Pages from a Sportsman's Notebook*

I have just read among the general news in one of the papers a drama of passion. He killed her and then he killed himself, so he must have loved her. What matters He or She? Their love alone matters to me; and it does not interest me because it moves me or astonishes me, or because it softens me or makes me think, but because it recalls to my mind a remembrance of my youth, a strange recollection of a hunting adventure where Love appeared to me, as the Cross appeared to the early Christians, in the midst of the heavens.

I was born with all the instincts and the senses of primitive man, tempered by the arguments and the restraints of a civilized being. I am passionately fond of shooting, yet the sight of the wounded animal, of the blood on its feathers and on my hands, affects my heart so as almost to make it stop.

That year the cold weather set in suddenly toward the end of autumn, and I was invited by one of my cousins, Karl de Rauville, to go with him and shoot ducks on the marshes, at daybreak.

My cousin was a jolly fellow of forty, with red hair, very stout and bearded, a country gentleman, an amiable semi-brute, of a happy disposition and endowed with that Gallic wit which makes even mediocrity agreeable. He lived in a house, half farmhouse, half château, situated in a broad valley through which a river ran. The hills right and left were covered with woods, old manorial woods where magnificent trees still remained, and where the rarest feathered game in that part of France was to be found. Eagles were shot there occasionally, and birds of passage, such as rarely venture into our overpopulated part of the country, invariably lighted amid these giant oaks, as if they knew or recognized some little corner of a primeval forest which had remained there to serve them as a shelter during their short nocturnal halt.

In the valley there were large meadows watered by trenches and separated by hedges; then, further on, the river, which up to that point had been kept between banks, expanded into a vast marsh. That marsh was the best shooting ground I ever saw. It was my cousin's chief care, and he kept it as a preserve. Through the rushes that covered it, and made it rustling and rough, narrow passages had been cut, through which the flat-bottomed boats, impelled and steered by poles, passed along silently over dead water, brushing up against the reeds and making the swift fish take refuge in the weeds, and the wild fowl, with their pointed, black heads, dive suddenly.

I am passionately fond of the water: of the sea, though it is too vast, too full of movement, impossible to hold; of the rivers which are so beautiful, but which pass on, and flee away; and above all of the marshes, where the whole unknown existence of aquatic animals palpitates. The marsh is an entire world in itself on the world of earth—a different world, which has its own life, its settled inhabitants and its passing travelers, its voices, its noises, and above all its mystery. Nothing is more impressive, nothing more disquieting, more terrifying occasionally, than a fen. Why should a vague terror hang over these low plains covered with water? Is it the low rustling of the rushes, the strange will-o'-the-wisp lights, the silence which prevails on calm nights, the still mists which hang over the surface like a shroud; or is it the almost inaudible splashing, so slight and so gentle, yet sometimes more terrifying than the cannons of men or the thunders of the skies, which make these marshes resemble countries one has dreamed of, terrible countries holding an unknown and dangerous secret?

No, something else belongs to it—another mystery, profounder and graver, floats amid these thick mists, perhaps the mystery of the creation itself! For was it not in stagnant and muddy water, amid the heavy humidity of moist land under the heat of the sun, that the first germ of life pulsated and expanded to the day?

I arrived at my cousin's in the evening. It was freezing hard enough to split the stones.

During dinner, in the large room whose sideboards, walls, and ceiling were covered with stuffed birds, with wings extended or perched on branches to which they were nailed—hawks, herons, owls, nightjars, buzzards, tiercels, vultures, falcons—my cousin who, dressed in a sealskin jacket, himself resembled some strange animal from a cold country, told me what preparations he had made for that same night.

We were to start at half past three in the morning, so as to arrive at the place which he had chosen for our watching-place at about half past four. On that spot a hut had been built of lumps of ice, so as to shelter us somewhat from the trying wind which precedes daybreak, a wind so cold as to tear the flesh like a saw, cut it like the blade of a knife, prick it like a poisoned sting, twist it like a pair of pincers, and burn it like fire.

My cousin rubbed his hands: "I have never known such a frost," he said; "it is already twelve degrees below zero at six o'clock in the evening."

I threw myself on to my bed immediately after we had finished our meal, and went to sleep by the light of a bright fire burning in the grate.

At three o'clock he woke me. In my turn, I put on a sheepskin, and found my cousin Karl covered with a bearskin. After having each swallowed two cups of scalding coffee, followed by glasses of liqueur brandy, we started, accompanied by a gamekeeper and our dogs, Plongeon and Pierrot.

From the first moment that I got outside, I felt chilled to the very marrow. It was one of those nights on which the earth seems dead with cold. The frozen air becomes resisting and palpable, such pain does it cause; no breath of wind moves it, it is fixed and motionless; it bites you, pierces through you, dries you, kills the trees, the plants, the insects, the small birds themselves, who fall from the branches on to the hard ground, and become stiff themselves under the grip of the cold.

The moon, which was in her last quarter and was inclining all to one side, seemed fainting in the midst of space, so weak that she was unable to wane, forced to stay up yonder, seized and paralyzed by the severity of the weather.

She shed a cold, mournful light over the world, that dying and wan light which she gives us every month, at the end of her period.

Karl and I walked side by side, our backs bent, our hands in our pockets and our guns under our arms. Our boots, which were wrapped in wool so that we might be able to walk without slipping on the frozen river, made no sound, and I looked at the white vapor which our dogs' breath made.

We were soon on the edge of the marsh, and entered one of the lanes of dry rushes which ran through the low forest.

Our elbows, which touched the long, ribbonlike leaves, left a slight noise behind us, and I was seized, as I had never been before, by the powerful and singular emotion which marshes cause in me. This one was dead, dead from cold, since we were walking on it, in the middle of its population of dried rushes.

Suddenly, at the turn of one of the lanes, I perceived the icehut which had been constructed to shelter us. I went in, and as we had nearly an hour to wait before the wandering birds would awake, I rolled myself up in my rug in order to try and get warm. Then, lying on my back, I began to look at the misshapen moon, which had four horns through the vaguely transparent walls of this polar house. But the frost of the frozen marshes, the cold of these walls, the cold from the firmament penetrated me so terribly that I began to cough. My cousin Karl became uneasy.

"No matter if we do not kill much today," he said: "I do not want you to catch cold; we will light a fire." And he told the gamekeeper to cut some rushes.

We made a pile in the middle of our hut which had a hole in the middle of the roof to let out the smoke, and when the red flames rose up to the clear, crystal blocks they began to melt, gently, imperceptibly, as if they were sweating. Karl, who had remained outside, called out to me: "Come and look here!" I went out of the hut and remained struck with astonishment. Our hut, in the shape of a cone, looked like an enormous diamond with a heart of fire, which had been suddenly planted there in the midst of the frozen water of the marsh. And inside, we saw two fantastic forms, those of our dogs, who were warming themselves at the fire.

But a peculiar cry, a lost, a wandering cry, passed over our heads, and the light from our hearth showed us the wild birds. Nothing moves one so much as the first clamor of a life which one does not see, which passes through the somber air so quickly and so far off, just before the first streak of a winter's day appears on the horizon. It seems to me, at this glacial hour of dawn, as if that passing cry which is carried away by the wings of a bird is the sigh of a soul from the world!

"Put out the fire," said Karl, "it is getting daylight."

The sky was, in fact, beginning to grow pale, and the flights of ducks made long, rapid streaks which were soon obliterated on the sky.

A stream of light burst out into the night; Karl had fired, and the two dogs ran forward.

And then, nearly every minute, now he, now I, aimed rapidly as soon as the shadow of a flying flock appeared above the rushes. And Pierrot and Plongeon, out of breath but happy, retrieved the bleeding birds, whose eyes still, occasionally, looked at us.

The sun had risen, and it was a bright day with a blue sky, and we were thinking of taking our departure, when two birds with extended necks and outstretched wings, glided rapidly over our heads. I fired, and one of them fell almost at my feet. It was a teal, with a silver breast, and then, in the blue space above me, I heard a voice, the voice of a bird. It was a short, repeated, heart-rending lament; and the bird, the little animal that had been spared began to turn round in the blue sky, over our heads, looking at its dead companion which I was holding in my hand.

Karl was on his knees, his gun to his shoulder watching it eagerly, until it should be within shot. "You have killed the duck," he said, "and the drake will not fly away."

He certainly did not fly away; he circled over our heads continually, and continued his cries. Never have any groans of suffering pained me so much as that desolate appeal, as that lamentable reproach of this poor bird which was lost in space.

Occasionally he took flight under the menace of the gun which followed his movements, and seemed ready to continue his flight alone, but as he could not make up his mind to this, he returned to find his mate.

"Leave her on the ground," Karl said to me, "he will come within shot by and by." And he did indeed come near us, careless of danger, infatuated by his animal love, by his affection for his mate, which I had just killed.

Karl fired, and it was as if somebody had cut the string which held the bird suspended. I saw something black descend, and I heard the noise of a fall among the rushes. And Pierrot brought it to me.

I put them—they were already cold—into the same gamebag, and I returned to Paris the same evening.

EXERCISES

1. Why does the newspaper article remind the narrator of the past event? What does the narrator mean when he says the event was one in which love appeared to him, much as the cross appeared to early Christians?

2. Discuss the implications of the long paragraph about marshes and fens. What is so fascinating to the narrator about a marsh? What does it have to do with love?

3. What is the effect of the series of descriptions about the coldness of the air? Why is so much emphasis placed on how cold it is?

4. Since atmosphere seems to dominate the story, discuss the significance of the general atmosphere.

5. Is human love the same as animal love? Why does Maupassant tell a story about wild birds to illustrate a drama of passion?

GUY
DE MAUPASSANT | *Confessing*

The noon sun poured fiercely down upon the fields. They stretched in undulating folds between the clumps of trees that marked each farmhouse; the different crops, ripe rye and yellowing wheat, pale-green oats, dark-green clover, spread a vast striped cloak, soft and rippling, over the naked body of the earth.

In the distance, on the crest of a slope, was an endless line of cows, ranked like soldiers, some lying down, others standing, their large eyes blinking in the burning light, chewing the cud and grazing on a field of clover as broad as a lake.

Two women, mother and daughter, were walking with a swinging step, one behind the other, towards this regiment of cattle. Each carried two zinc pails, slung outwards from the body on a hoop from a cask; at each step the metal sent out a dazzling white flash under the sun that struck full upon it.

The women did not speak. They were on their way to milk the cows. When they arrive, they set down one of their pails and approach the first two cows, making them stand up with a kick in the ribs from wooden-shod feet. The beast rises slowly, first on its forelegs, then with more difficulty raises its large hind quarters, which seem to be weighted down by the enormous udder of livid pendulous flesh.

The two Malivoires, mother and daughter, kneeling beneath the animal's belly, tug with a swift movement of their hands at the swollen teat, which at each squeeze sends a jet of milk into the pail. The yellowish froth mounts to the brim, and the women go from cow to cow until they reach the end of the long line.

As soon as they finish milking a beast, they change its position, giving it a fresh patch of grass on which to graze.

Then they start on their way home, more slowly now, weighed down by the load of milk, the mother in front, the daughter behind.

Abruptly the latter halts, sets down her burden, sits down, and begins to cry.

Mme. Malivoire, missing the sound of steps behind her, turns round and is quite amazed.

"What's the matter with you?" she said.

Her daughter Céleste, a tall girl with flaming red hair and flaming cheeks, flecked with freckles as though sparks of fire had fallen upon her face one day as she worked in the sun, murmurs, moaning softly like a beaten child:

"I can't carry the milk any further."

Her mother looked at her suspiciously.

"What's the matter with you?" she repeated.

"It drags too heavy, I can't," replied Céleste, who had collapsed and was lying on the ground between the two pails, hiding her eyes in her apron.

"What's the matter with you, then?" said her mother for the third time. The girl moaned:

"I guess there's a baby on the way." And she broke into sobs.

The old woman now in her turn set down her load, so amazed that she could find nothing to say. At last she stammered:

"You . . . you . . . you're going to have a baby, you clod! How can that be?"

The Malivoires were prosperous farmers, wealthy and of a certain position, widely respected, good business folk, of some importance in the district.

"I guess I am, all the same," faltered Céleste.

The frightened mother looked at the weeping girl groveling at her feet. After a few seconds she cried:

"You're going to have a baby! A baby! Where did you get it, you slut?"

Céleste, shaken with emotion, murmured:

"I guess it was in Polyte's coach."

The old woman tried to understand, tried to imagine, to realize who could have brought this misfortune upon her daughter. If the lad was well off and of decent position, an arrangement might be come to. It wasn't so bad, yet. Céleste was not the first to be in the same way, but it was annoying all the same, seeing their position and the way people talked.

"And who was it, you slut?" she repeated.

Céleste, resolved to make a clean breast of it, stammered:

"I guess it was Polyte."

At that Mme. Malivoire, mad with rage, rushed upon her daughter and began to beat her with such fury that her hat fell off in the effort.

With great blows of the fist she struck her on the head, on the back, all over her body; Céleste, prostrate between the two pails, which afforded her some slight protection, shielded just her face with her hands.

All the cows, disturbed, had stopped grazing and turned round, staring with their great eyes. The last one mooed, stretching out its muzzle towards the women.

After beating her daughter till she was out of breath, Mme. Malivoire stopped, exhausted; her spirits reviving a little, she tried to get a thorough understanding of the situation.

"———Polyte! Lord save us, it's not possible! How could you, with a carrier? You must have lost your wits. He must have played you a trick, the good-for-nothing!"

Céleste, still prostrate, murmured in the dust:

"I didn't pay my fare!"

And the old Norman woman understood.

Every week, on Wednesday and on Saturday, Céleste went to town with the farm produce, poultry, cream, and eggs.

She started at seven with her two huge baskets on her arm, the dairy produce in one, the chickens in the other, and went to the main road to wait for the coach to Yvetot.

She set down her wares and sat in the ditch, while the chickens with their short pointed beaks and the ducks with their broad flat bills thrust their heads between the wicker bars and looked about them with their round, stupid, surprised eyes.

Soon the bus, a sort of yellow box with a black leather cap on the top, came up, jerking and quivering with the trotting of the old white horse.

Polyte the coachman, a big jolly fellow, stout though still young, and so burned up by sun and wind, soaked by rain, and colored with brandy that his face and neck were brick-red, cracked his whip and shouted from the distance:

"Morning, Mam'selle Céleste. In good health, I hope?"

She gave him her baskets, one after the other, which he stowed in the boot; then she got in, lifting her leg high up to reach the step, and exposing a sturdy leg clad in a blue stocking.

Every time Polyte repeated the same joke: "Clumsy; it's not got any thinner."

She laughed, thinking it funny.

Then he uttered a "Gee up, old girl!" which started off the thin horse. Then Céleste, reaching for her purse in the depths of her pocket, slowly took out fivepence, threepence for herself and twopence for the baskets, and handed them to Polyte over his shoulder.

He took them, saying:

"Aren't we going to have our little bit of sport today?"

And he laughed heartily, turning round towards her so as to stare at her at his ease.

She found it a big expense, the half franc for a journey of two miles. And when she had no coppers she felt it still more keenly; it was hard to make up her mind to part with a silver coin.

One day, as she was paying, she asked:

"From a good customer like me you oughtn't to take more than threepence."

He burst out laughing.

"Threepence, my beauty; why, you're worth more than that."

She insisted on the point.

"But you make a good two francs a month out of me."

He whipped up his horse and exclaimed:

"Look here, I'm an obliging fellow! We'll call it quits for a bit of sport."

"What do you mean?" she asked with an air of innocence.

He was so amused that he laughed till he coughed.

"A bit of sport is a bit of sport, damn it; a game for a lad and a lass, a dance for two without music."

She understood, blushed, and declared:

"I don't care for that sort of game, M. Polyte."

But he was in no way abashed, and repeated, with growing merriment:

"You'll come to it some day, my beauty, a bit of sport for a lad and a lass!"

And since that day he had taken to asking her, each time that she paid her fare:

"Aren't we going to have our bit of sport today?"
She, too, joked about it by this time, and replied:
"Not today, M. Polyte, but Saturday, for certain!"
And amid peals of laughter he answered:
"Saturday then, my beauty."

But inwardly she calculated that, during the two years the affair had been going on, she had paid Polyte forty-eight whole francs, and in the country forty-eight francs is not a sum which can be picked up on the roadside; she also calculated that in two more years she would have paid nearly a hundred francs.

To such purpose she meditated that, one spring day as they jogged on alone, when he made his customary inquiry: "Aren't we going to have our bit of sport yet?" she replied:
"Yes, if you like, M. Polyte."

He was not at all surprised, and clambered over the back of his seat, murmuring with a complacent air:
"Come along, then. I knew you'd come to it some day."

The old white horse trotted so gently that she seemed to be dancing upon the same spot, deaf to the voice which cried at intervals, from the depths of the vehicle: "Gee up, old girl! Gee up, then!"

Three months later Céleste discovered that she was going to have a child.

All this she had told her mother in a tearful voice. Pale with fury, the old woman asked:
"Well, what did it cost?"
"Four months; that makes eight francs, doesn't it?" replied Céleste.

At that the peasant woman's fury was utterly unleashed, and, falling once more upon her daughter, she beat her a second time until she was out of breath. Then she rose and said:
"Have you told him about the baby?"
"No, of course not."
"Why haven't you told him?"
"Because very likely he'd have made me pay for all the free rides!"

The old woman pondered awhile, then picked up her milk pails.
"Come on, get up, and try to walk home," she said, and, after a pause, continued:
"And don't tell him as long as he doesn't notice anything, and we'll make six or eight months' fares out of him."

And Céleste, who had risen, still crying, disheveled and swollen round the eyes, started off again with dragging steps, murmuring:
"Of course I won't say a word."

EXERCISES

1. Discuss the opening scene of the story. How does it serve as a backdrop for the revelation that follows?

2. Discuss the tone of this story. Are we meant to feel sorry for Céleste? Are we supposed to feel contemptuous of Céleste?

3. How are we to feel about Polyte? How are we supposed to feel about the mother?

4. Why is the story about Polyte and Céleste presented as a dialogue instead of being told by Céleste to her mother?

5. Discuss the value system presented in this story. What importance does sexuality have to the characters in the story?

ISAAC BABEL | *Guy de Maupassant*

In the winter of 1916 I found myself in St. Petersburg with a forged passport and not a cent to my name. Alexey Kazantsev, a teacher of Russian literature, took me into his house.

He lived on a yellow, frozen, evil-smelling street in the Peski district. The miserable salary he received was padded out a bit by doing translations from the Spanish. Blasco-Ibáñez was just becoming famous at that time. Kazantsev had never so much as passed through Spain, but his love for that country filled his whole being. He knew every castle, every garden, and every river in Spain. There were many other people huddling around Kazantsev, all of them, like myself, flung out of the round of ordinary life. We were half-starved. From time to time the yellow press would publish, in the smallest print, unimportant news-items we had written.

I spent my mornings hanging around the morgues and police stations.

Kazantsev was happier than any of us, for he had a country of his own — Spain.

In November I was given the chance to become a clerk at the Obukhov Mills. It was a rather good position, and would have exempted me from military service.

I refused to become a clerk.

Even in those days, when I was twenty years old, I had told myself: better starve, go to jail, or become a bum than spend ten hours every day behind a desk in an office.

There was nothing particularly laudable in my resolve, but I have never broken it and I never will. The wisdom of my ancestors was firmly lodged in my head: we are born to enjoy our work, our fights, and our love; we are born for that and for nothing else.

Listening to my bragging, Kazantsev ruffled the short yellow fluff on the top of his head. The horror in his stare was mixed with admiration.

At Christmastime we had luck. Bendersky the lawyer, who owned a publishing house called "Halcyon," decided to publish a new edition of Maupassant's works. His wife Raïsa tried her hand at the translation, but nothing came of her lofty ambition.

Kazantsev, who was known as a translator of Spanish, had been asked whether he could recommend someone to assist Raïsa Mikhaylovna. He told them of me.

The next day, in someone else's coat, I made my way to the Benderskys'. They lived at the corner of the Nevsky and the Moyka, in a house of Finland granite adorned with pink columns, crenellations and coats-of-arms worked in stone.

Bankers without a history and catapulted out of nowhere, converted Jews who had grown rich selling materials to the army, they put up these pretentious mansions in St. Petersburg before the war.

There was a red carpet on the stairs. On the landings, upon their hindlegs, stood plush bears. Crystal lamps burned in their open mouths.

The Benderskys lived on the second floor. A high-breasted maid with a white cap on her head opened the door. She led me into a drawing-room decorated in the old Slav style. Blue paintings by Roerich depicting prehistoric stones and monsters hung on the walls. On stands in the corners stood ancestral icons.

The high-breasted maid moved smoothly and majestically. She had an excellent figure, was nearsighted and rather haughty. In her open gray eyes one saw a petrified lewdness. She moved slowly. I thought: when she makes love she must move with unheard-of agility. The brocade portiere over the doorway suddenly swayed, and a black-haired woman with pink eyes and a wide bosom entered the room. It was easy to recognize in Raïsa Bendersky one of those charming Jewesses who have come to us from Kiev and Poltava, from the opulent steppe-towns full of chestnut trees and acacias. The money made by their clever husbands is transformed by these women into a pink layer of fat on the belly, the back of the neck, and the well-rounded shoulders. Their subtle sleepy smiles drive officers from the local garrisons crazy.

"Maupassant," Raïsa said to me, "is the only passion of my life."

Trying to keep the swaying of her great hips under control, she left the room and returned with a translation of "Miss Harriet." In her translation not even a trace was left of Maupassant's free-flowing sentences with their fragrance of passion. Raïsa Bendersky took pains to write correctly and precisely, and all that resulted was something loose and lifeless, the way Jews wrote Russian in the old days.

I took the manuscript with me, and in Kazantsev's attic, among my sleeping friends, spent the night cutting my way through the tangled undergrowth of her prose. It was not such dull work as it might seem. A phrase is born into the world both good and bad at the same time. The secret lies in a slight, an almost invisible twist. The lever should rest in your hand, getting warm, and you can only turn it once not twice.

Next morning I took back the corrected manuscript. Raïsa wasn't lying when she told me that Maupassant was her sole passion. She sat motionless, her hands clasped, as I read it to her. Her satin hands dropped to the floor, her forehead paled, and the lace between her constricted breasts danced and heaved.

"How did you do it?"

I began to speak of style, of the army of words, of the army in which all kinds of weapons may come into play. No iron can stab the heart with such force as a period put just at the right place. She listened with her head down and her painted lips half open. In her hair, pressed smooth, divided by a parting and looking like patent leather, shone a dark gleam. Her legs in tight-fitting stockings, with their strong soft calves, were planted wide apart on the carpet.

The maid, glancing to the side with her petrified wanton eyes, brought in breakfast on a tray.

The glassy rays of the Petersburg sun lay on the pale and uneven carpet. Twenty-nine volumes of Maupassant stood on the shelf above the desk. The sun with its fingers of melting dissolution touched the morocco backs of the books—the magnificent grave of a human heart.

Coffee was served in blue cups, and we started translating "Idyl." Everyone remembers the story of the youthful, hungry carpenter who sucked the breast of the stout nursing-mother to relieve her of the milk with which she was overladen. It happened in a train going from Nice to Marseille, at noon on a very hot day, in the land of roses, the birthplace of roses, where beds of flowers flow down to the seashore.

I left the Banderskys with a twenty-five rouble advance. That night our crowd at Peski got as drunk as a flock of drugged geese. Between drinks we spooned up the best caviar, and then changed over to liver sausage. Half-soused, I began to berate Tolstoy.

"He turned yellow, your Count; he was afraid. His religion was all fear. He was frightened by the cold, by old age, by death; and he made himself a warm coat out of his faith."

"Go on, go on," Kazantsev urged, swaying his birdlike head.

We fell asleep on the floor beside our beds. I dreamed of Katya, a forty-year-old washerwoman who lived a floor below us. We went to her every morning for our hot water. I had never seen her face distinctly, but in my dream we did god-awful things together. We almost destroyed each other with kisses. The very next morning I couldn't restrain myself from going to her for hot water.

I saw a wan woman, a shawl across her chest, with ash-gray hair and labor-worn, withered hands.

From then on I took my breakfast at the Benderskys' every day. A new stove, herrings, and chocolate appeared in our attic. Twice Raïsa took me out in her carriage for drives to the islands. I couldn't prevent myself from telling her all about my childhood. To my amazement the story turned out to be very sordid. From under her moleskin cowl her gleaming, frightened eyes stared at me. The rusty fringe of her eyelashes quivered with pity.

I met Raïsa's husband, a yellow-faced Jew with a bald skull and a flat, powerful body that seemed always posed obliquely, ready for flight.

There were rumors about his being close to Rasputin. The enormous profits he made from war supplies drove him almost crazy, giving him the expression of a person with a fixed hallucination. His eyes never remained still: it seemed that reality was lost to him for ever. Raïsa was embarrassed whenever she had to introduce him to new acquaintances. Because of my youth I noticed this a full week later than I should have.

After the New Year Raïsa's two sisters arrived from Kiev. One day I took along the manuscript of *"L'Aveu"* and, not finding Raïsa at home, returned that evening. They were at dinner. Silvery, neighing laughter and excited male voices came from the dining-room. In rich houses without tradition dinners are always noisy. It was a Jewish noise, rolling and tripping and ending up on a melodious, singsong note. Raïsa came out to me in evening dress, her back bare. Her feet stepped awkwardly in wavering patent-leather slippers.

"I'm drunk, darling," she said, and held out her arms, loaded with chains of platinum and emerald stars.

Her body swayed like a snake's dancing to music. She tossed her marcelled hair about, and suddenly, with a tinkle of rings, slumped into a chair with ancient Russian carvings. Scars glowed on her powdered back.

Women's laughter again came from the dining-room. Raïsa's sisters, with delicate mustaches and as full-bosomed and round-bodied as Raïsa herself, entered the room. Their busts jutted out and their black hair fluttered. Both of them had their own Benderskys for husbands. The room was filled with disjointed, chaotic feminine merriment, the hilarity of ripe women. The husbands wrapped the sisters in their sealskins and Orenburg shawls and shod them in black boots. Beneath the snowy visors of their shawls only painted glowing cheeks, marble noses, and eyes with their myopic Jewish glitter could be seen. After making some more happy noise they left for the theater, where Chaliapin was singing *Judith.*

"I want to work," Raïsa lisped, stretching her bare arms to me, "we've skipped a whole week."

She brought a bottle and two glasses from the dining room. Her breasts swung free beneath the sacklike gown, the nipples rose beneath the clinging silk.

"It's very valuable," said Raïsa, pouring out the wine. "Muscatel '83. My husband will kill me when he finds out."

I had never drunk Muscatel '83, and tossed off three glasses one after the other without thinking. They carried me swiftly away into alleys where an orange flame danced and sounds of music could be heard.

"I'm drunk, darling. What are we doing today?"

"Today, it's *'L'Aveu.'* 'The Confession,' then. The sun is the hero of this story, *le soleil de France.* Molten drops of it pattering on the red-haired Céleste changed into freckles. The sun's direct rays and wine and apple-cider burnished the face of the coachman Polyte. Twice a week Céleste drove into town to sell cream, eggs and chickens. She gave Polyte ten sous for herself and four for her basket. And every time Polyte would wink at the red-haired Céleste and ask: 'When are we going to have some fun, *ma belle?*'—'What do you mean, Monsieur Polyte?' Jogging up and down on the box, the coachman explained: 'To have some fun means . . . why, what the hell, to have some fun! A lad with a lass; no music necessary. . . .'

"'I do not care for such jokes, Monsieur Polyte,' replied Céleste, moving further away the skirts that hung over her mighty calves in red stockings.

"But that devil Polyte kept right on guffawing and coughing: 'Ah, but one day we shall have our bit of fun, *ma belle,*' while tears of delight rolled down a face the color of brick-red wine and blood."

I downed another glass of the rare muscatel. Raïsa touched glasses with me. The maid with the stony eyes crossed the room and disappeared.

"*Ce diable de Polyte.* . . . In the course of two years Céleste had paid him forty-eight francs; that is, two francs short of fifty! At the end of the second year, when they were alone in the carriage, Polyte, who had some cider before setting out, asked her his usual question: 'What about having some fun today, Mamselle Céleste?' And she replied, lowering her eyes: 'I am at your disposal, Monsieur Polyte.'"

Raïsa flung herself down on the table, laughing. "*Ce diable de Polyte. . . .*"

"A white spavined mare was harnessed to the carriage. The white hack, its lips pink with age, went forward at a walking pace. The gay sun of France poured down on the ancient coach, screened from the world by a weather-beaten hood. A lad with a lass; no music necessary. . . ."

Raïsa held out a glass to me. It was the fifth.

"*Mon vieux,* to Maupassant."

"And what about having some fun today, *ma belle?*"

I reached over to Raïsa and kissed her on the lips. They quivered and swelled.

"You're funny," she mumbled through her teeth, recoiling.

She pressed herself against the wall, stretching out her bare arms. Spots began to glow on her arms and shoulders. Of all the gods ever put on a crucifix, this was the most ravishing.

"Be so kind as to sit down, Monsieur Polyte."

She pointed to an oblique blue armchair done in Slavonic style. Its back was constructed of carved interlacing bands with colorful pendants. I groped my way to it, stumbling as I went.

Night had blocked the path of my famished youth with a bottle of Muscatel '83 and twenty-nine books, twenty-nine bombs stuffed with pity, genius, and passion. I sprang up, knocking over the chair and banging against the shelf. The twenty-nine volumes crashed to the floor, their pages flew open, they fell on their edges . . . and the white mare of my fate went on at a walking pace.

"You are funny," growled Raïsa.

I left the granite house on the Moyka between eleven and twelve, before the sisters and the husband returned from the theater. I was sober and could have walked a chalk line, but it was pleasanter to stagger, so I swayed from side to side, singing in a language I had just invented. Through the tunnels of the streets bounded by lines of street lights the steamy fog billowed. Monsters roared behind the boiling walls. The roads amputated the legs of those walking on them.

Kazantsev was asleep when I got home. He slept sitting up, his thin legs extended in their felt boots. The canary fluff rose on his head. He had fallen asleep by the stove bending over a volume of *Don Quixote*, the edition of 1624. On the title-page of the book was a dedication to the Duc de Broglie. I got into bed quietly, so as not to wake Kazantsev; moved the lamp close to me and began to read a book by Edouard Maynial on Guy de Maupassant's life and work.

Kazantsev's lips moved; his head kept keeling over.

That night I learned from Edouard Maynial that Maupassant was born in 1850, the child of a Normandy gentleman and Laure Lepoiteven, Flaubert's cousin. He was twenty-five when he was first attacked by congenital syphilis. His productivity and *joie de vivre* withstood the onsets of the disease. At first he suffered from headaches and fits of hypochondria. Then the specter of blindness arose before him. His sight weakened. He became suspicious of everyone, unsociable and pettily quarrelsome. He struggled furiously, dashed about the Mediterranean in a yacht, fled to Tunis, Morocco, Central Africa . . . and wrote ceaselessly. He attained fame, and at forty years of age cut his throat; lost a great deal of blood, yet lived through it. He was then put away in a madhouse. There he crawled about on his hands and knees, devouring his own excrement. The last line in his hospital report read: *Monsieur de Maupassant va s'animaliser.* He died at the age of forty-two, his mother surviving him.

I read the book to the end and got out of bed. The fog came close to the window, the world was hidden from me. My heart contracted as the foreboding of some essential truth touched me with light fingers.

EXERCISES

1. Discuss the following: "A phrase is born into the world both good and bad at the same time. The secret lies in a slight, an almost invisible twist. The lever should rest in your hand, getting warm, and you can only turn it once not twice."

2. Discuss the following: "No iron can stab the heart with such force as a period put just at the right place."

3. Why are sexual desire and physical passion significant forces in this story?

4. What is the significance of the maid with the stony eyes? Discuss the significance of role-playing and acting-out in this story.

5. Why does Babel name this story "Guy de Maupassant"? What relationship does it have to Maupassant's stories in general and the story "Confessing" in particular?

6. The most important element of this story may be the introduction of the details of Maupassant's contracting syphilis and dying in a madhouse. Especially important is the last line from his hospital report: *"Monsieur de Maupassant is becoming an animal."* Try to explain the "essential truth" of which the narrator has a foreboding. Why does he say that it has touched him with "light fingers"?

ISAAC
BABEL | # The Sin of Jesus

Arina was a servant at the hotel. She lived next to the main staircase, while Seryoga, the janitor's helper, lived over the back stairs. Between them there was shame. On Palm Sunday Arina gave Seryoga a present—twins. Water flows, stars shine, a man lusts, and soon Arina was big again, her sixth month was rolling by—they're slippery, a woman's months. And now Seryoga must go into the army. There's a mess for you!

So Arina goes and says: "No sense, Seryoga. There's no sense in my waiting for you. For four years we'll be parted, and in four years, whichever way you look at it, I'll be sure to bring two or three more into this world. It's like walking around with your skirt turned up, working at the hotel. Whoever stops here, he's your master, let him be a Jew, let him be anybody at all. By the time you come home, my insides will be no good any more. I'll be a used-up woman, no match for you."

"That's so," Seryoga nodded.

"There's many that want me. Trofimych the contractor—but he's no gentleman. And Isai Abramych, the warden of Nikolo-Syvatsky Church, a feeble old man, but anyway I'm sick to the stomach of your murderous strength. I tell you this now, and I say it like I would at confession, I've got the wind plain knocked out of me. I'll spill my load in three months, then I'll take the baby to the orphanage and marry the old man."

When Seryoga heard this, he took off his belt and beat her like a hero, right on the belly.

"Look out there," Arina says to him, "go soft on the belly. It's your stuffing, no one else's."

There was no end to the beating, no end to the man's tears and the woman's blood, but that is neither here nor there.

Then the woman came to Jesus Christ.

"So on and so forth," she says, "Lord Jesus, I am the woman from the Hotel Madrid and Louvre, the one on Tverskaya Street. Working at the hotel, it's just like going around with your skirt up. Just let a man stop there, and he's your lord and master, let him be a Jew, let him be anyone at all. There is another slave of yours walking the earth, the janitor's helper, Seryoga. Last year on Palm Sunday I bore him twins."

And so she described it all to the Lord.

"And what if Seryoga were not to go into the army after all?" the Saviour suggested.

"Try and get away with it—not with the policeman around. He'll drag him off as sure as daylight."

"Oh yes, the policeman," the Lord bowed His head, "I never thought of him. Then perhaps you ought to live in purity for a while?"

"For four years?" the woman cried. "To hear you talk, all people should deny their animal nature. That's just your old ways all over again. And where will the increase come from? No, you'd better give me some sensible advice."

The Lord's cheeks turned scarlet, the woman's words had touched a tender spot. But He said nothing. You cannot kiss your own ear—even God knows that.

"I'll tell you what, God's servant, glorious sinner, maiden Arina," the Lord proclaimed in all His glory, "I have a little angel here in heaven, hanging around uselessly. His name is Alfred. Lately he's gotten out of hand altogether, keeps crying and nagging all the time: 'What have you done to me, Lord? Why do you turn me into an angel in my twentieth year, and me a hale young fellow?' So I'll give you Alfred the angel as a husband for four years. He'll be your prayer, he'll be your protection, and he'll be your solace. And as for offspring, you've nothing to worry about—you can't bear a duckling from him, let alone a baby, for there's a lot of fun in him, but no seriousness."

"That's just what I need," the maid Arina wept gratefully. "Their seriousness takes me to the doorstep of the grave three times every two years."

"You'll have a sweet respite, God's child Arina. May your prayer be light as a song. Amen."

And so it was decided. Alfred was brought in—a frail young fellow, delicate, two wings fluttering behind his pale-blue shoulders, rippling with rosy light like two doves playing in heaven. Arina threw her hefty arms about him, weeping out of tenderness, out of her woman's soft heart.

"Alfred, my soul, my consolation, my bridegroom. . . ."

In parting, the Lord gave her strict instructions to take off the angel's wings every night before he went to bed. His wings were attached to hinges, like a door, and every night she was to take them off and wrap them in a clean sheet, because they were brittle, his wings, and could snap as he tossed in bed—for what were they made of but the sighs of babes, no more than that.

For the last time the Lord blessed the union, while the choir of bishops, called in for the occasion, rendered thunderous praises. No food was served, not a crumb—that wasn't the style in heaven—and then Arina and Alfred, their arms about each other, ran down a silken ladder, straight back to earth. They came to Petrovka, the street where nothing but the best is sold. The woman would do right by her Alfred for he, if one might say so, not only lacked socks, but was altogether as natural as when his mother bore him. And she bought him patent-leather half-boots, checked jersey trousers, a fine hunting jacket, and an electric-blue vest.

"The rest," she says, "we'll find at home."

That day Arina begged off from work. Seryoga came and raised a fuss, but she did not even come out to him, only said from behind her locked door:

"Sergey Nifantyich, I am at present a-washing my feet and beg you to retire without further noise."

He went away without a word—the angel's power was already beginning to manifest itself!

In the evening Arina set out a supper fit for a merchant—the woman had devilish vanity! A half-pint of vodka, wine on the side, a Danube herring with potatoes, a samovar of tea. When Alfred had partaken of all these earthly blessings, he keeled over in a dead sleep. Quick as a wink, Arina lifted off his wings from the hinges, packed them away, and carried him to bed in her arms.

There it lies, the snowy wonder on the eiderdown pillows of her tattered, sinful bed, sending forth a heavenly radiance: moon-silver shafts of light pass and repass, alternate with red ones, float across the floor, sway over his shining feet. Arina weeps and rejoices, sings and prays. Arina, thou hast been granted a happiness unheard of on this battered earth. Blessed art thou among women!

They had drunk the vodka to the last drop, and now it took effect. As soon as they fell asleep, she went and rolled over on top of Alfred with her hot, six-months-big belly. Not enough for her to sleep with an angel, not enough that nobody beside her spat at the wall, snored and snorted—that wasn't enough for the clumsy, ravening slut. No, she had to warm her belly too, her burning belly big with Seryoga's lust. And so she smothered him in her fuddled sleep, smothered him like a week-old babe in the midst of her rejoicing, crushed him under her bloated weight, and he gave up the ghost, and his wings, wrapped in her sheet, wept pale tears.

Dawn came—and all the trees bowed low to the ground. In distant northern forests each fir tree turned into a priest, each fir tree bent its knees in silent worship.

Once more the woman stands before the Lord's throne. She is broad in the shoulders, mighty, the young corpse drooping in her huge red arms.

"Behold, Lord . . ."

But here the gentle heart of Jesus could endure no more, and He cursed the woman in His anger:

"As it is on earth, so shall it be with you, Arina, from this day on."

"How is it then, Lord?" the woman replied in a scarcely audible voice. "Was it I who made my body heavy, was it I that brewed vodka on earth, was it I that created a woman's soul, stupid and lonely?"

"I don't wish to be bothered with you," exclaimed the Lord Jesus. "You've smothered my angel, you filthy scum."

And Arina was thrown back to earth on a putrid wind, straight down to Tverskaya Street, to the Hotel Madrid and Louvre, where she was doomed to spend her days. And once there, the sky was the limit. Seryoga was carousing, drinking away his last days, seeing as he was a recruit. The contractor Trofimych, just come from Kolomna, took one look at Arina, hefty and red-cheeked: "Oh, you cute little belly," he said, and so on and so forth.

Isai Abramych, the old codger, heard about this cute little belly, and he was right there too, wheezing toothlessly:

"I cannot wed you lawfully," he said, "after all that happened. However, I can lie with you the same as anyone."

The old man ought to be lying in cold mother earth instead of thinking of such things, but no, he too must take his turn at spitting into her soul. It was as though they had all slipped the chain—kitchen-boys, merchants, foreigners. A fellow in trade—he likes to have his fun.

And that is the end of my tale.

Before she was laid up, for three months had rolled by in the meantime, Arina went out into the back yard, behind the janitor's rooms, raised her monstrous belly to the silken sky, and said stupidly:

"See, Lord, what a belly! They hammer at it like peas falling in a colander. And what sense there's in it I just can't see. But I've had enough."

With His tears Jesus laved Arina when He heard these words. The Saviour fell on His knees before her.

"Forgive me, little Arina. Forgive your sinful God for all He has done to you. . . ."

But Arina shook her head and would not listen.

"There's no forgiveness for you, Jesus Christ," she said. "No forgiveness, and never will be."

EXERCISES

1. Discuss the point of view and tone of the story. What is the narrator like? What is his attitude toward the events he is describing? At what point do you identify this as a fable?

2. Discuss the value system of Arina and Seryoga. What do they value? What is important to them?

3. Discuss the basic characteristics of Jesus Christ as he is presented in this story.

4. Discuss Arina's response to Christ: "To hear you talk, all people should deny their animal nature. That's just your old ways all over again."

5. What is the purpose of the Lord's giving Arina the angel Alfred? What is suggested by the phrase "Blessed art thou among women"?

6. Discuss the significance of Arina's killing the angel, of the Lord's anger, of her subsequent behavior, and of the Lord's begging her for forgiveness.

7. How is this story related to the stories of Maupassant?

ISAAC
BABEL | *My First Goose*

Savitsky, Commander of the VI Division, rose when he saw me, and I wondered at the beauty of his giant's body. He rose, the purple of his riding
breeches and the crimson of his little tilted cap and the decorations stuck on
his chest cleaving the hut as a standard cleaves the sky. A smell of scent and
the sickly sweet freshness of soap emanated from him. His long legs were like
girls sheathed to the neck in shining riding boots.

He smiled at me, struck his riding whip on the table, and drew toward
him an order that the Chief of Staff had just finished dictating. It was an order
for Ivan Chesnokov to advance on Chugunov-Dobryvodka with the regiment
entrusted to him, to make contact with the enemy and destroy the same.

"For which destruction," the Commander began to write, smearing the
whole sheet, "I make this same Chesnokov entirely responsible, up to and
including the supreme penalty, and will if necessary strike him down on the
spot; which you, Chesnokov, who have been working with me at the front for
some months now, cannot doubt."

The Commander signed the order with a flourish, tossed it to his orderlies
and turned upon me gray eyes that danced with merriment.

I handed him a paper with my appointment to the Staff of the Division.

"Put it down in the Order of the Day," said the Commander. "Put him
down for every satisfaction save the front one. Can you read and write?"

"Yes, I can read and write," I replied, envying the flower and iron of that
youthfulness. "I graduated in law from St. Petersburg University."

"Oh, are you one of those grinds?" he laughed. "Specs on your nose, too!
What a nasty little object! They've sent you along without making any enqui-
ries; and this is a hot place for specs. Think you'll get on with us?"

"I'll get on all right," I answered, and went off to the village with the
quartermaster to find a billet for the night.

The quartermaster carried my trunk on his shoulder. Before us stretched
the village street. The dying sun, round and yellow as a pumpkin, was giving
up its roseate ghost to the skies.

We went up to a hut painted over with garlands. The quartermaster
stopped, and said suddenly, with a guilty smile:

"Nuisance with specs. Can't do anything to stop it, either. Not a life for
the brainy type here. But you go and mess up a lady, and a good lady too,
and you'll have the boys patting you on the back."

He hesitated, my little trunk on his shoulder; then he came quite close to
me, only to dart away again despairingly and run to the nearest yard. Cossacks were sitting there, shaving one another.

"Here, you soldiers," said the quartermaster, setting my little trunk down
on the ground. "Comrade Savitsky's orders are that you're to take this chap
in your billets, so no nonsense about it, because the chap's been through a lot
in the learning line."

The quartermaster, purple in the face, left us without looking back. I raised my hand to my cap and saluted the Cossacks. A lad with long straight flaxen hair and the handsome face of the Ryazan Cossacks went over to my little trunk and tossed it out at the gate. Then he turned his back on me and with remarkable skill emitted a series of shameful noises.

"To your guns—number double-zero!" an older Cossack shouted at him, and burst out laughing. "Running fire!"

His guileless art exhausted, the lad made off. Then, crawling over the ground, I began to gather together the manuscript and tattered garments that had fallen out of the trunk. I gathered them up and carried them to the other end of the yard. Near the hut, on a brick stove, stood a cauldron in which pork was cooking. The steam that rose from it was like the far-off smoke of home in the village, and it mingled hunger with desperate loneliness in my head. Then I covered my little broken trunk with hay, turning it into a pillow, and lay down on the ground to read in *Pravda* Lenin's speech at the Second Congress of the Comintern. The sun fell upon me from behind the toothed hillocks, the Cossacks trod on my feet, the lad made fun of me untiringly, the beloved lines came toward me along a thorny path and could not reach me. Then I put aside the paper and went out to the landlady, who was spinning on the porch.

"Landlady," I said, "I've got to eat."

The old woman raised to me the diffused whites of her purblind eyes and lowered them again.

"Comrade," she said, after a pause, "what with all this going on, I want to go and hang myself."

"Christ!" I muttered, and pushed the old woman in the chest with my fist. "You don't suppose I'm going to go into explanations with you, do you?"

And turning around I saw somebody's sword lying within reach. A severe-looking goose was waddling about the yard, inoffensively preening its feathers. I overtook it and pressed it to the ground. Its head cracked beneath my boot, cracked and emptied itself. The white neck lay stretched out in the dung, the wings twitched.

"Christ!" I said, digging into the goose with my sword. "Go and cook it for me, landlady."

Her blind eyes and glasses glistening, the old woman picked up the slaughtered bird, wrapped it in her apron, and started to bear it off toward the kitchen.

"Comrade," she said to me, after a while, "I want to go and hang myself." And she closed the door behind her.

The Cossacks in the yard were already sitting around their cauldron. They sat motionless, stiff as heathen priests at a sacrifice, and had not looked at the goose.

"The lad's all right," one of them said, winking and scooping up the cabbage soup with his spoon.

The Cossacks commenced their supper with all the elegance and restraint of peasants who respect one another. And I wiped the sword with sand, went out at the gate, and came in again, depressed. Already the moon hung above the yard like a cheap earring.

"Hey, you," suddenly said Surovkov, an older Cossack. "Sit down and feed with us till your goose is done."

He produced a spare spoon from his boot and handed it to me. We supped up the cabbage soup they had made, and ate the pork.

"What's in the newspaper?" asked the flaxen-haired lad, making room for me.

"Lenin writes in the paper," I said, pulling out *Pravda*. "Lenin writes that there's a shortage of everything."

And loudly, like a triumphant man hard of hearing, I read Lenin's speech out to the Cossacks.

Evening wrapped about me the quickening moisture of its twilight sheets; evening laid a mother's hand upon my burning forehead. I read on and rejoiced, spying out exultingly the secret curve of Lenin's straight line.

"Trust tickles everyone's nostrils," said Surovkov, when I had come to the end. "The question is, how's it to be pulled from the heap. But he goes and strikes at it straight off like a hen pecking at a grain!"

This remark about Lenin was made by Surovkov, platoon commander of the Staff Squadron; after which we lay down to sleep in the hayloft. We slept, all six of us, beneath the wooden roof that let in the stars, warming one another, our legs intermingled. I dreamed, and in my dreams saw women. But my heart, stained with bloodshed, grated and brimmed over.

EXERCISES

1. Discuss the importance of the narrator's admiration for the physical appearance of the general.

2. Why is the life at the front not a life for the "brainy type"?

3. Why does the narrator react so severely to the landlady? Why are we not given any warning about his actions? Is it realistic that he would react this way without any inner conflict?

4. What is the effect of the narrator's reading Lenin to the Cossacks? Why does he rejoice in his reading?

5. What is the relationship between the women and the bloodshed in his dreams?

6. Is there any Maupassant influence evident in this story? Discuss.

DORIS
LESSING | *Homage for Isaac Babel*

The day I had promised to take Catherine down to visit my young friend Philip at his school in the country, we were to leave at eleven, but she arrived at nine. Her blue dress was new, and so were her fashionable shoes. Her hair had just been done. She looked more than ever like a pink-and-gold Renoir girl who expects everything from life.

Catherine lives in a white house overlooking the sweeping brown tides of the river. She helped me clean up my flat with a devotion which said that she felt small flats were altogether more romantic than large houses. We drank tea, and talked mainly about Philip, who, being fifteen, has pure stern tastes in everything from food to music. Catherine looked at the books lying around his room, and asked if she might borrow the stories of Isaac Babel to read on the train. Catherine is thirteen. I suggested she might find them difficult, but she said: "Philip reads them, doesn't he?"

During the journey I read newspapers and watched her pretty frowning face as she turned the pages of Babel, for she was determined to let nothing get between her and her ambition to be worthy of Philip.

At the school, which is charming, civilised, and expensive, the two children walked together across green fields, and I followed, seeing how the sun gilded their bright friendly heads turned towards each other as they talked. In Catherine's left hand she carried the stories of Isaac Babel.

After lunch we went to the pictures. Philip allowed it to be seen that he thought going to the pictures just for the fun of it was not worthy of intelligent people, but he made the concession, for our sakes. For his sake we chose the more serious of the two films that were showing in the little town. It was about a good priest who helped criminals in New York. His goodness, however, was not enough to prevent one of them from being sent to the gas chamber; and Philip and I waited with Catherine in the dark until she had stopped crying and could face the light of a golden evening.

At the entrance of the cinema the doorman was lying in wait for anyone who had red eyes. Grasping Catherine by her suffering arm, he said bitterly: "Yes, why are you crying? He had to be punished for his crime, didn't he?" Catherine stared at him, incredulous. Philip rescued her by saying with disdain: "Some people don't know right from wrong even when it's *demonstrated* to them." The doorman turned his attention to the next red-eyed emerger from the dark; and we went on together to the station, the children silent because of the cruelty of the world.

Finally Catherine said, her eyes wet again: "I think it's all absolutely beastly, and I can't bear to think about it." And Philip said: "But we've got to think about it, don't you see, because if we don't it'll just go on and on, don't you see?"

In the train going back to London I sat beside Catherine. She had the stories open in front of her, but she said: "Philip's awfully lucky. I wish I went to that school. Did you notice that girl who said hullo to him in the garden? They must be great friends. I wish my mother would let me have a dress like that, it's *not* fair."

"I thought it was too old for her."

"Oh, *did* you?"

Soon she bent her head again over the book, but almost at once lifted it to say: "Is he a very famous writer?"

"He's a marvellous writer, brilliant, one of the very best."

"Why?"

"Well, for one thing he's so simple. Look how few words he uses, and how strong his stories are."

"I see. Do you know him? Does he live in London?"

"Oh no, he's dead."

"Oh. Then why did you—I thought he was alive, the way you talked."

"I'm sorry, I suppose I wasn't thinking of him as dead."

"When did he die?"

"He was murdered. About twenty years ago, I suppose."

"*Twenty years.*" Her hands began the movement of pushing the book over to me, but then relaxed. "I'll be fourteen in November," she stated, sounding threatened, while her eyes challenged me.

I found it hard to express my need to apologise, but before I could speak, she said, patiently attentive again: "You said he was murdered?"

"Yes."

"I expect the person who murdered him felt sorry when he discovered he had murdered a famous writer."

"Yes, I expect so."

"Was he old when he was murdered?"

"No, quite young really."

"Well, that was bad luck, wasn't it?"

"Yes, I suppose it was bad luck."

"Which do you think is the very best story here? I mean, in your honest opinion, the very very best one?"

I chose the story about killing the goose. She read it slowly, while I sat waiting, wishing to take it from her, wishing to protect this charming little person from Isaac Babel.

When she had finished, she said: "Well, some of it I don't understand. He's got a funny way of looking at things. Why should a man's legs in boots look like *girls?*" She finally pushed the book over at me, and said: "I think it's all morbid."

"But you have to understand the kind of life he had. First, he was a Jew in Russia. That was bad enough. Then his experience was all revolution and civil war and . . ."

But I could see these words bouncing off the clear glass of her fiercely denying gaze; and I said: "Look, Catherine, why don't you try again when you're older? Perhaps you'll like him better then?"

She said gratefully: "Yes, perhaps that would be best. After all, Philip is two years older than me, isn't he?"

A week later I got a letter from Catherine.

Thank you very much for being kind enough to take me to visit Philip at his school. It was the most lovely day in my whole life. I am extremely grateful to you for taking me. I have been thinking about the Hoodlum Priest. That was a film which demonstrated to me beyond any shadow of doubt that Capital Punishment is a Wicked Thing, and I shall never forget what I learned that afternoon, and the lessons of it will be with me all my life. I have been meditating about what you said about Isaac Babel, the famed Russian short story writer, and I now see that the conscious simplicity of his style is what makes him, beyond the shadow of a doubt, the great writer that he is, and now in my school compositions I am endeavoring to emulate him so as to learn a conscious simplicity which is the only basis for a really brilliant writing style. Love, Catherine. P.S. Has Philip said anything about my party? I wrote but he hasn't answered. Please find out if he is coming or if he just forgot to answer my letter. I hope he comes, because sometimes I feel I shall die if he doesn't. P.P.S. Please don't tell him I said anything, because I should die if he knew. Love, Catherine.

EXERCISES

1. What is the difference between Catherine and Philip?

2. Discuss the relative merits of Catherine's saying, "I can't bear to think about it," and Philip's saying, "We've got to think about it." How is this an argument about what is appropriate and not appropriate in literature or film?

3. Discuss the significance of the conversation about Babel between the narrator and Catherine. What is the difference between Catherine and the narrator?

4. Read "My First Goose" by Babel. Why doesn't Catherine like the story about the goose?

5. Do you really believe Catherine's statement that the film about the Hoodlum Priest taught her a lesson about the wickedness of capital punishment that she will remember the rest of her life? Why or why not?

6. Where do you think Catherine got the idea of Babel's "conscious simplicity"? Do you think she understands it? Why or why not? What effect does her P.S. have on what she says in the rest of the letter?

7. How is this story a "homage" to Babel?

DORIS
LESSING | *Flight*

Above the old man's head was the dovecote, a tall wire-netted shelf on stilts, full of strutting, preening birds. The sunlight broke on their grey breasts into small rainbows. His ears were lulled by their crooning; his hands stretched up towards his favourite, a homing pigeon, a young plump-bodied bird, which stood still when it saw him and cocked a shrewd bright eye.

"Pretty, pretty, pretty," he said, as he grasped the bird and drew it down, feeling the cold coral claws tighten around his finger. Content, he rested the bird lightly on his chest and leaned against a tree, gazing out beyond the dovecote into the landscape of a late afternoon. In folds and hollows of sunlight and shade, the dark red soil, which was broken into great dusty clods, stretched wide to a tall horizon. Trees marked the course of the valley; a stream of rich green grass the road.

His eyes travelled homewards along this road until he saw his granddaughter swinging on the gate underneath a frangipani tree. Her hair fell down her back in a wave of sunlight; and her long bare legs repeated the angles of the frangipani stems, bare, shining brown stems among patterns of pale blossoms.

She was gazing past the pink flowers, past the railway cottage where they lived, along the road to the village.

His mood shifted. He deliberately held out his wrist for the bird to take flight, and caught it again at the moment it spread its wings. He felt the plump shape strive and strain under his fingers; and, in a sudden access of troubled spite, shut the bird into a small box and fastened the bolt. "Now you stay there," he muttered and turned his back on the shelf of birds. He moved warily along the hedge, stalking his grand-daughter, who was now looped over the gate, her head loose on her arms, singing. The light happy sound mingled with the crooning of the birds, and his anger mounted.

"Hey!" he shouted, and saw her jump, look back, and abandon the gate. Her eyes veiled themselves, and she said in a pert, neutral voice, "Hullo, Grandad." Politely she moved towards him, after a lingering backward glance at the road.

"Waiting for Steven, hey?" he said, his fingers curling like claws into his palm.

"Any objection?" she asked lightly, refusing to look at him.

He confronted her, his eyes narrowed, shoulders hunched, tight in a hard knot of pain that included the preening birds, the sunlight, the flowers, herself. He said, "Think you're old enough to go courting, hey?"

The girl tossed her head at the old-fashioned phrase and sulked, "Oh, Grandad!"

"Think you want to leave home, hey? Think you can go running around the fields at night?"

Her smile made him see her, as he had every evening of this warm end-of-summer month, swinging hand in hand along the road to the village with that red-handed, red-throated, violent-bodied youth, the son of the postmaster. Misery went to his head and he shouted angrily: "I'll tell your mother!"

"Tell away!" she said, laughing, and went back to the gate.

He heard her singing, for him to hear:

"I've got you under my skin,
I've got you deep in the heart of . . ."

"Rubbish," he shouted. "Rubbish. Impudent little bit of rubbish!"

Growling under his breath, he turned towards the dovecote, which was his refuge from the house he shared with his daughter and her husband and their children. But now the house would be empty. Gone all the young girls with their laughter and their squabbling and their teasing. He would be left, uncherished and alone, with that square-fronted, calm-eyed woman, his daughter.

He stooped, muttering, before the dovecote, resenting the absorbed, cooing birds.

From the gate the girl shouted: "Go and tell! Go on, what are you waiting for?"

Obstinately he made his way to the house, with quick, pathetic, persistent glances of appeal back at her. But she never looked around. Her defiant but anxious young body stung him into love and repentance. He stopped. "But I never meant. . . ." he muttered, waiting for her to turn and run to him. "I didn't mean. . . ."

She did not turn. She had forgotten him. Along the road came the young man Steven, with something in his hand. A present for her? The old man stiffened as he watched the gate swing back and the couple embrace. In the brittle shadows of the frangipani tree his grand-daughter, his darling, lay in the arms of the postmaster's son, and her hair flowed back over his shoulder.

"I see you!" shouted the old man spitefully. They did not move. He stumped into the little whitewashed house, hearing the wooden verandah creak angrily under his feet. His daughter was sewing in the front room, threading a needle held to the light.

He stopped again, looking back into the garden. The couple were now sauntering among the bushes, laughing. As he watched he saw the girl escape from the youth with a sudden mischievous movement and run off through the flowers with him in pursuit. He heard shouts, laughter, a scream, silence.

"But it's not like that at all," he muttered miserably. "It's not like that. Why can't you see? Running and giggling, and kissing and kissing. You'll come to something quite different."

He looked at his daughter with sardonic hatred, hating himself. They were caught and finished, both of them, but the girl was still running free.

"Can't you see?" he demanded of his invisible grand-daughter, who was at that moment lying in the thick green grass with the postmaster's son.

His daughter looked at him and her eyebrows went up in tired forbearance.

"Put your birds to bed?" she asked, humouring him.

"Lucy," he said urgently. "Lucy. . . ."

"Well, what is it now?"

"She's in the garden with Steven."

"Now you just sit down and have your tea."

He stumped his feet alternately, thump, thump, on the hollow wooden floor and shouted: "She'll marry him. I'm telling you, she'll be marrying him next!"

His daughter rose swiftly, brought him a cup, set him a plate.

"I don't want any tea. I don't want it, I tell you."

"Now, now," she crooned. "What's wrong with it? Why not?"

"She's eighteen. Eighteen!"

"I was married at seventeen, and I never regretted it."

"Liar," he said. "Liar. Then you should regret it. Why do you make your girls marry? It's you who do it. What do you do it for? Why?"

"The other three have done fine. They've three fine husbands. Why not Alice?"

"She's the last," he mourned. "Can't we keep her a bit longer?"

"Come, now, Dad. She'll be down the road, that's all. She'll be here every day to see you."

"But it's not the same." He thought of the other three girls, transformed inside a few months from charming, petulant, spoiled children into serious young matrons.

"You never did like it when we married," she said. "Why not? Every time, it's the same. When I got married you made me feel like it was something wrong. And my girls the same. You get them all crying and miserable the way you go on. Leave Alice alone. She's happy." She sighed, letting her eyes linger on the sunlit garden. "She'll marry next month. There's no reason to wait."

"You've said they can marry?" he said incredulously.

"Yes, Dad. Why not?" she said coldly and took up her sewing.

His eyes stung, and he went out on to the verandah. Wet spread down over his chin, and he took out a handkerchief and mopped his whole face. The garden was empty.

From around the corner came the young couple; but their faces were no longer set against him. On the wrist of the postmaster's son balanced a young pigeon, the light gleaming on its breast.

"For me?" said the old man, letting the drops shake off his chin. "For me?"

"Do you like it?" The girl grabbed his hand and swung on it. "It's for you, Grandad. Steven brought it for you." They hung about him, affectionate, concerned, trying to charm away his wet eyes and his misery. They took his arms and directed him to the shelf of birds, one on each side, enclosing him, petting him, saying wordlessly that nothing would be changed, nothing could change, and that they would be with him always. The bird was proof of it, they said, from their lying happy eyes, as they thrust it on him. "There, Grandad, it's yours. It's for you."

They watched him as he held it on his wrist, stroking its soft, sun-warmed back, watching the wings lift and balance.

"You must shut it up for a bit," said the girl intimately, "until it knows this is its home."

"Teach your grandmother to suck eggs," growled the old man.

Released by his half-deliberate anger, they fell back, laughing at him. "We're glad you like it." They moved off, now serious and full of purpose, to the gate, where they hung, backs to him, talking quietly. More than anything could, their grown-up seriousness shut him out, making him alone; also, it quietened him, took the sting out of their tumbling like puppies on the grass. They had forgotten him again. Well, so they should, the old man reassured himself, feeling his throat clotted with tears, his lips trembling. He held the new bird to his face, for the caress of its silken feathers. Then he shut it in a box and took out his favourite.

"Now you can go," he said aloud. He held it poised, ready for flight, while he looked down the garden towards the boy and the girl. Then, clenched in the pain of loss, he lifted the bird on his wrist and watched it soar. A whirr and a spatter of wings, and a cloud of birds rose into the evening from the dovecote.

At the gate Alice and Steven forgot their talk and watched the birds.

On the verandah, that woman, his daughter, stood gazing, her eyes shaded with a hand that still held her sewing.

It seemed to the old man that the whole afternoon had stilled to watch his gesture of self-command, that even the leaves of the trees had stopped shaking.

Dry-eyed and calm, he let his hands fall to his sides and stood erect, staring up into the sky.

The cloud of shining silver birds flew up and up, with a shrill cleaving of wings, over the dark ploughed land and the darker belts of trees and the bright folds of grass, until they floated high in the sunlight, like a cloud of motes of dust.

They wheeled in a wide circle, tilting their wings so there was flash after flash of light, and one after another they dropped from the sunshine of the upper sky to shadow, one after another, returning to the shadowed earth over trees and grass and field, returning to the valley and the shelter of night.

The garden was all a fluster and a flurry of returning birds. Then silence, and the sky was empty.

The old man turned, slowly, taking his time; he lifted his eyes to smile proudly down the garden at his grand-daughter. She was staring at him. She did not smile. She was wide-eyed and pale in the cold shadow, and he saw the tears run shivering off her face.

EXERCISES

1. The first two paragraphs of the story introduce the dovecote and the grand-daughter. What relationship do these two have to each other?

2. What is the significance of the granddaughter's singing *"I've got you under my skin, I've got you deep in the heart of . . ."*?

3. Why does the old man not want the granddaughter to leave? Why does he resent the absorbed, cooing birds? What is the significance of the old man's relationship with his daughter?

4. What does the old man mean by "But it's not like that at all"? Why does he feel that they were caught and finished, both of them?

5. Discuss the significance of the line "You must shut it up for a bit . . . until it knows this is its home."

6. Discuss the significance of the final gesture of the old man. What does it have to do with the granddaughter? Why is she crying? Why is he smiling?

7. Compare this story with Maupassant's "In the Moonlight."

DORIS
LESSING | *Wine*

A man and woman walked toward the boulevard from a little hotel in a side street.

The trees were still leafless, black, cold; but the fine twigs were swelling toward spring, so that looking upward it was with an expectation of the first glimmering greenness. Yet everything was calm, and the sky was a calm, classic blue.

The couple drifted slowly along. Effort, after days of laziness, seemed impossible; and almost at once they turned into a café and sank down, as if exhausted, in the glass-walled space that was thrust forward into the street.

The place was empty. People were seeking the midday meal in the restaurants. Not all: that morning crowds had been demonstrating, a procession had just passed, and its straggling end could still be seen. The sounds of violence, shouted slogans and singing, no longer absorbed the din of Paris traffic; but it was these sounds that had roused the couple from sleep.

A waiter leaned at the door, looking after the crowds, and he reluctantly took an order for coffee.

The man yawned; the woman caught the infection; and they laughed with an affectation of guilt and exchanged glances before their eyes, without regret, parted. When the coffee came, it remained untouched. Neither spoke. After some time the woman yawned again; and this time the man turned and looked at her critically, and she looked back. Desire asleep, they looked. This remained: that while everything which drove them slept, they accepted from each other a sad irony; they could look at each other without illusion, steady-eyed.

And then, inevitably, the sadness deepened in her till she consciously resisted it; and into him came the flicker of cruelty.

"Your nose needs powdering," he said.

"You need a whipping boy."

But always he refused to feel sad. She shrugged, and leaving him to it, turned to look out. So did he. At the far end of the boulevard there was a faint agitation, like stirred ants, and she heard him mutter, "Yes, and it still goes on. . . ."

Mocking, she said, "Nothing changes, everything is always the same. . . ."

But he had flushed. "I remember," he began, in a different voice. He stopped, and she did not press him, for he was gazing at the distant demonstrators with a bitterly nostalgic face.

Outside drifted the lovers, the married couples, the students, the old people. There the stark trees; there the blue, quiet sky. In a month the trees would be vivid green; the sun would pour down heat; the people would be brown, laughing, bare-limbed. No, no, she said to herself, at this vision of activity. Better the static sadness. And, all at once, unhappiness welled up in her, catching her throat, and she was back fifteen years in another country. She stood in blazing tropical moonlight, stretching her arms to a landscape that offered her nothing but silence; and then she was running down a path where small stones glinted sharp underfoot, till at last she fell spent in a swathe of glistening grass. Fifteen years.

It was at this moment that the man turned abruptly and called the waiter and ordered wine.

"What," she said humorously, "already?"

"Why not?"

For the moment she loved him completely and maternally, till she suppressed the counterfeit and watched him wait, fidgeting, for the wine, pour it, and then set the two glasses before them beside the still-brimming coffee cups. But she was again remembering that night, envying the girl ecstatic with moonlight, who ran crazily through the trees in an unsharable desire for— but that was the point.

"What are you thinking of?" he asked, still a little cruel.

"Ohhh," she protested humorously.

"That's the trouble, that's the trouble." He lifted his glass, glanced at her, and set it down. "Don't you want to drink?"

"Not yet."

He left his glass untouched and began to smoke.

These moments demanded some kind of gesture—something slight, even casual, but still an acknowledgment of the separateness of those two people in each of them; the one seen, perhaps, as a soft-staring never-closing eye, observing, always observing, with a tired compassion; the other, a shape of violence that struggled on in the cycle of desire and rest, creation and achievement.

He gave it to her. Again their eyes met in the grave irony, before he turned away, flickering his fingers irritably against the table; and she turned also, to note the black branches where the sap was tingling.

"I remember," he began; and again she said, in protest, "Ohhh!"

He checked himself. "Darling," he said drily, "you're the only woman I've ever loved." They laughed.

"It must have been this street. Perhaps this café—only they change so. When I went back yesterday to see the place where I came every summer, it was a *pâtisserie*, and the woman had forgotten me. There was a whole crowd of us—we used to go around together—and I met a girl here, I think, for the first time. There were recognized places for contacts; people coming from Vienna or Prague, or wherever it was, knew the places—it couldn't be this café, unless they've smartened it up. We didn't have the money for all this leather and chromium."

"Well, go on."

"I keep remembering her, for some reason. Haven't thought of her for years. She was about sixteen, I suppose. Very pretty—no, you're quite wrong. We used to study together. She used to bring her books to my room. I liked her, but I had my own girl, only she was studying something else, I forget what." He paused again, and again his face was twisted with nostalgia, and involuntarily she glanced over her shoulder down the street. The procession had completely disappeared, not even the sounds of singing and shouting remained.

"I remember her because. . . ." And, after a preoccupied silence: "Perhaps it is always the fate of the virgin who comes and offers herself, naked, to be refused."

"What!" she exclaimed, startled. Also, anger stirred in her. She noted it, and sighed. "Go on."

"I never made love to her. We studied together all that summer. Then, one weekend, we all went off in a bunch. None of us had any money, of course, and we used to stand on the pavements and beg lifts, and meet up again in some village. I was with my own girl, but that night we were helping the farmer get in his fruit, in payment for using his barn to sleep in, and I found this girl Marie was beside me. It was moonlight, a lovely night, and we were all singing and making love. I kissed her, but that was all. That night she came to me. I was sleeping up in the loft with another lad. He was asleep. I sent her back down to the others. They were all together down in the hay. I told her she was too young. But she was no younger than my own girl." He stopped; and after all these years his face was rueful and puzzled. "I don't know," he said. "I don't know why I sent her back." Then he laughed. "Not that it matters, I suppose."

"Shameless hussy," she said. The anger was strong now. "You had kissed her, hadn't you?"

He shrugged. "But we were all playing the fool. It was a glorious night— gathering apples, the farmer shouting and swearing at us because we were making love more than working, and singing and drinking wine. Besides, it was that time: the youth movement. We regarded faithfulness and jealousy and all that sort of thing as remnants of bourgeois morality." He laughed again, rather painfully. "I kissed her. There she was, beside me, and she knew my girl was with me that weekend."

"You kissed her," she said accusingly.

He fingered the stem of his wineglass, looking over at her and grinning. "Yes, darling," he almost crooned at her. "I kissed her."

She snapped over into anger. "There's a girl all ready for love. You make use of her for working. Then you kiss her. You know quite well. . . ."

"What do I know quite well?"

"It was a cruel thing to do."

"I was a kid myself. . . ."

"Doesn't matter." She noted, with discomfort, that she was almost crying. "Working with her! Working with a girl of sixteen, all summer!"

"But we all studied very seriously. She was a doctor afterward, in Vienna. She managed to get out when the Nazis came in, but. . . ."

She said impatiently, "Then you kissed her, on *that* night. Imagine her, waiting till the others were asleep, then she climbed up the ladder to the loft, terrified the other man might wake up, then she stood watching you sleep, and she slowly took off her dress and. . . ."

"Oh, I wasn't asleep. I pretended to be. She came up dressed. Shorts and sweater—our girls didn't wear dresses and lipstick—more bourgeois morality. I watched her strip. The loft was full of moonlight. She put her hand over my mouth and came down beside me." Again, his face was filled with rueful amazement. "God knows, I can't understand it myself. She was a beautiful creature. I don't know why I remember it. It's been coming into my mind the last few days." After a pause, slowly twirling the wineglass: "I've been a failure in many things, but not with. . . ." He quickly lifted her hand, kissed it, and said sincerely: "I don't know why I remember it now, when. . . ." Their eyes met, and they sighed.

She said slowly, her hand lying on his: "And so you turned her away."

He laughed. "Next morning she wouldn't speak to me. She started a love affair with my best friend—the man who'd been beside me that night in the loft, as a matter of fact. She hated my guts, and I suppose she was right."

"Think of her. Think of her at that moment. She picked up her clothes, hardly daring to look at you. . . ."

"As a matter of fact, she was furious. She called me all the names she could think of; I had to keep telling her to shut up, she'd wake the whole crowd."

"She climbed down the ladder and dressed again, in the dark. Then she went out of the barn, unable to go back to the others. She went into the orchard. It was still brilliant moonlight. Everything was silent and deserted, and she remembered how you'd all been singing and laughing and making love. She went to the tree where you'd kissed her. The moon was shining on the apples. She'll never forget it, never, never!"

He looked at her curiously. The tears were pouring down her face.

"It's terrible," she said. "Terrible. Nothing could ever make up to her for that. Nothing, as long as she lived. Just when everything was most perfect, all her life, she'd suddenly remember that night, standing alone, not a soul anywhere, miles of damned empty moonlight. . . ."

He looked at her shrewdly. Then, with a sort of humorous, deprecating grimace, he bent over and kissed her and said: "Darling, it's not my fault; it just isn't my fault."

"No," she said.

He put the wineglass into her hands; and she lifted it, looked at that small crimson globule of warming liquid, and drank with him.

EXERCISES

1. Explain the significance of the fact that the couple yawn and then laugh with an affectation of guilt. What is the sad irony the couple face? Why does she feel sad and he feel cruel?

2. Discuss the statement "These moments demanded some kind of gesture. . . ."

3. Why is the woman angry that he turned the girl away?

4. Why does the man remember the event now? What does it have to do with his present situation? Why do you suppose he turned the girl away?

5. Why does the woman tell the story of the girl? How does she know such things? Why was the event so significant to the girl?

6. Why is the wine the central metaphor and thus the title of the story?

7. Compare this story with Hemingway's "Hills like White Elephants."

SUSAN
GLASPELL | # A Jury of Her Peers

When Martha Hale opened the storm-door and got a cut of the north wind, she ran back for her big woolen scarf. As she hurriedly wound that round her head her eye made a scandalized sweep of her kitchen. It was no ordinary thing that called her away—it was probably farther from ordinary than anything that had ever happened in Dickson County. But what her eye took in was that her kitchen was in no shape for leaving: her bread all ready for mixing, half the flour sifted and half unsifted.

She hated to see things half done; but she had been at that when the team from town stopped to get Mr. Hale, and then the sheriff came running in to say his wife wished Mrs. Hale would come too—adding, with a grin, that he guessed she was getting scarey and wanted another woman along. So she had dropped everything right where it was.

"Martha!" now came her husband's impatient voice. "Don't keep folks waiting out here in the cold."

She again opened the storm-door, and this time joined the three men and the one woman waiting for her in the big two-seated buggy.

After she had the robes tucked around her she took another look at the woman who sat beside her on the back seat. She had met Mrs. Peters the year before at the county fair, and the thing she remembered about her was that she didn't seem like a sheriff's wife. She was small and thin and didn't have a strong voice. Mrs. Gorman, sheriff's wife before Gorman went out and Peters came in, had a voice that somehow seemed to be backing up the law with every word. But if Mrs. Peters didn't look like a sheriff's wife, Peters made it up in looking like a sheriff. He was to a dot the kind of man who could get himself elected sheriff—a heavy man with a big voice, who was particularly genial with the law-abiding, as if to make it plain that he knew the difference between criminals and non-criminals. And right there it came into Mrs. Hale's mind, with a stab, that this man who was so pleasant and lively with all of them was going to the Wrights' now as a sheriff.

"The country's not very pleasant this time of year," Mrs. Peters at last ventured, as if she felt they ought to be talking as well as the men.

Mrs. Hale scarcely finished her reply, for they had gone up a little hill and could see the Wright place now, and seeing it did not make her feel like talking. It looked very lonesome this cold March morning. It had always been a lonesome-looking place. It was down in a hollow, and the poplar trees around it were lonesome-looking trees. The men were looking at it and talking about what had happened. The county attorney was bending to one side of the buggy, and kept looking steadily at the place as they drew up to it.

"I'm glad you came with me," Mrs. Peters said nervously, as the two women were about to follow the men in through the kitchen door.

Even after she had her foot on the door-step, her hand on the knob, Martha Hale had a moment of feeling she could not cross that threshold. And the reason it seemed she couldn't cross it now was simply because she hadn't crossed it before. Time and time again it had been in her mind, "I ought to go over and see Minnie Foster"—she still thought of her as Minnie Foster, though for twenty years she had been Mrs. Wright. And then there was always something to do and Minnie Foster would go from her mind. But *now* she could come.

The men went over to the stove. The women stood close together by the door. Young Henderson, the county attorney, turned around and said, "Come up to the fire, ladies."

Mrs. Peters took a step forward, then stopped. "I'm not—cold," she said.

And so the two women stood by the door, at first not even so much as looking around the kitchen.

The men talked for a minute about what a good thing it was the sheriff had sent his deputy out that morning to make a fire for them, and then Sheriff Peters stepped back from the stove, unbuttoned his outer coat, and leaned his hands on the kitchen table in a way that seemed to mark the beginning of official business. "Now, Mr. Hale," he said in a sort of semi-official voice, "before we move things about, you tell Mr. Henderson just what it was you saw when you came here yesterday morning."

The county attorney was looking around the kitchen.

"By the way," he said, "has anything been moved?" He turned to the sheriff. "Are things just as you left them yesterday?"

Peters looked from cupboard to sink; from that to a small worn rocker a little to one side of the kitchen table.

"It's just the same."

"Somebody should have been left here yesterday," said the county attorney.

"Oh—yesterday," returned the sheriff, with a little gesture as if yesterday having been more than he could bear to think of. "When I had to send Frank to Morris Center for that man who went crazy—let me tell you, I had my hands full *yesterday.* I knew you could get back from Omaha by to-day, George, and as long as I went over everything here myself—"

"Well, Mr. Hale," said the county attorney, in a way of letting what was past and gone go, "tell just what happened when you came here yesterday morning."

Mrs. Hale, still leaning against the door, had that sinking feeling of the mother whose child is about to speak a piece. Lewis often wandered along and got things mixed up in a story. She hoped he would tell this straight and plain, and not say unnecessary things that would just make things harder for Minnie Foster. He didn't begin at once, and she noticed that he looked queer—as if standing in that kitchen and having to tell what he had seen there yesterday morning made him almost sick.

"Yes, Mr. Hale?" the county attorney reminded.

"Harry and I had started to town with a load of potatoes," Mrs. Hale's husband began.

Harry was Mrs. Hale's oldest boy. He wasn't with them now, for the very good reason that those potatoes never got to town yesterday and he was taking them this morning, so he hadn't been home when the sheriff stopped to say he wanted Mr. Hale to come over to the Wright place and tell the county attorney his story there, where he could point it all out. With all Mrs. Hale's other emotions came the fear that maybe Harry wasn't dressed warm enough—they hadn't any of them realized how that north wind did bite.

"We come along this road," Hale was going on, with a motion of his hand to the road over which they had just come, "and as we got in sight of the house I says to Harry, 'I'm goin' to see if I can't get John Wright to take a telephone.' You see," he explained to Henderson, "unless I can get somebody to go in with me they won't come out this branch road except for a price *I* can't pay. I'd spoke to Wright about it once before; but he put me off, saying folks talked too much anyway, and all he asked was peace and quiet—guess you know about how much he talked himself. But I thought maybe if I went to the house and talked about it before his wife, and said all the women-folks liked the telephones, and that in this lonesome stretch of road it would be a good thing—well, I said to Harry that that was what I was going to say—

though I said at the same time that I didn't know as what his wife wanted made much difference to John—"

Now, there he was!—saying things he didn't need to say. Mrs. Hale tried to catch her husband's eye, but fortunately the county attorney interrupted with:

"Let's talk about that a little later, Mr. Hale. I do want to talk about that, but I'm anxious now to get along to just what happened when you got here."

When he began this time, it was very deliberately and carefully:

"I didn't see or hear anything. I knocked at the door. And still it was all quiet inside. I knew they must be up—it was past eight o'clock. So I knocked again, louder, and I thought I heard somebody say 'Come in.' I wasn't sure— I'm not sure yet. But I opened the door—this door," jerking a hand toward the door by which the two women stood, "and there, in that rocker"—pointing to it—"sat Mrs. Wright."

Every one in the kitchen looked at the rocker. It came into Mrs. Hale's mind that that rocker didn't look in the least like Minnie Foster—the Minnie Foster of twenty years before. It was a dingy red, with wooden rungs up the back, and the middle rung was gone, and the chair sagged to one side.

"How did she—look?" the county attorney was inquiring.

"Well," said Hale, "she looked—queer."

"How do you mean—queer?"

As he asked it he took out a note-book and pencil. Mrs. Hale did not like the sight of that pencil. She kept her eye fixed on her husband, as if to keep him from saying unnecessary things that would go into that note-book and make trouble.

Hale did speak guardedly, as if the pencil had affected him too.

"Well, as if she didn't know what she was going to do next. And kind of—done up."

"How did she seem to feel about your coming?"

"Why, I don't think she minded—one way or other. She didn't pay much attention. I said, 'Ho' do, Mrs. Wright? It's cold, ain't it?' And she said, 'Is it?'—and went on pleatin' at her apron.

"Well, I was surprised. She didn't ask me to come up to the stove, or to sit down, but just set there, not even lookin' at me. And so I said: 'I want to see John.'

"And then she—laughed. I guess you would call it a laugh.

"I thought of Harry and the team outside, so I said, a little sharp, 'Can I see John?' 'No,' says she—kind of dull like. 'Ain't he home?' says I. Then she looked at me. 'Yes,' says she, 'he's home.' 'Then why can't I see him?' I asked her, out of patience with her now. 'Cause he's dead,' says she, just as quiet and dull—and fell to pleatin' her apron. 'Dead?' says I, like you do when you can't take in what you've heard.

"She just nodded her head, not getting a bit excited, but rockin' back and forth.

"'Why—where is he?' says I, not knowing *what* to say.

"She just pointed upstairs—like this"—pointing to the room above.

"I got up, with the idea of going up there myself. By this time I—didn't know what to do. I walked from there to here; then I says: 'Why, what did he die of?'

"'He died of a rope around his neck,' says she; and just went on pleatin' at her apron."

Hale stopped speaking, and stood staring at the rocker, as if he were still seeing the woman who had sat there the morning before. Nobody spoke; it was as if every one were seeing the woman who had sat there the morning before.

"And what did you do then?" the county attorney at last broke the silence.

"I went out and called Harry. I thought I might—need help. I got Harry in, and we went upstairs." His voice fell almost to a whisper. "There he was— lying over the—"

"I think I'd rather have you go into that upstairs," the county attorney interrupted, "where you can point it all out. Just go on now with the rest of the story."

"Well, my first thought was to get that rope off. It looked—"

He stopped, his face twitching.

"But Harry, he went up to him, and he said, 'No, he's dead all right, and we'd better not touch anything.' So we went downstairs.

"She was still sitting that same way. 'Has anybody been notified?' I asked. 'No,' says she, unconcerned.

"'Who did this, Mrs. Wright?' said Harry. He said it business-like, and she stopped pleatin' at her apron. 'I don't know,' she says. 'You don't *know*?' says Harry. 'Weren't you sleepin' in the bed with him?' 'Yes,' says she, 'but I was on the inside.' 'Somebody slipped a rope round his neck and strangled him, and you didn't wake up?' says Harry. 'I didn't wake up,' she said after him.

"We may have looked as if we didn't see how that could be, for after a minute she said, 'I sleep sound.'

"Harry was going to ask her more questions, but I said maybe that weren't our business; maybe we ought to let her tell her story first to the coroner or the sheriff. So Harry went fast as he could over to High Road—the Rivers' place, where there's a telephone."

"And what did she do when she knew you had gone for the coroner?" The attorney got his pencil in his hand all ready for writing.

"She moved from that chair to this one over here"—Hale pointed to a small chair in the corner—"and just sat there with her hands held together and looking down. I got a feeling that I ought to make some conversation, so I said I had come in to see if John wanted to put in a telephone; and at that she started to laugh, and then she stopped and looked at me—scared."

At the sound of a moving pencil the man who was telling the story looked up.

"I dunno—maybe it wasn't scared," he hastened; "I wouldn't like to say it was. Soon Harry got back, and then Dr. Lloyd came, and you, Mr. Peters, and so I guess that's all I know that you don't."

He said that last with relief, and moved a little, as if relaxing. Every one moved a little. The county attorney walked toward the stair door.

"I guess we'll go upstairs first—then out to the barn and around there." He paused and looked around the kitchen.

"You're convinced there was nothing important here?" he asked the sheriff. "Nothing that would—point to any motive?"

The sheriff too looked all around, as if to re-convince himself.

"Nothing here but kitchen things," he said, with a little laugh for the insignificance of kitchen things.

The county attorney was looking at the cupboard—a peculiar, ungainly structure, half closet and half cupboard, the upper part of it being built in the wall, and the lower part just the old-fashioned kitchen cupboard. As if its queerness attracted him, he got a chair and opened the upper part and looked in. After a moment he drew his hand away sticky.

"Here's a nice mess," he said resentfully.

The two women had drawn nearer, and now the sheriff's wife spoke.

"Oh—her fruit," she said, looking to Mrs. Hale for sympathetic understanding. She turned back to the county attorney and explained: "She worried about that when it turned so cold last night. She said the fire would go out and her jars might burst."

Mrs. Peters' husband broke into a laugh.

"Well, can you beat the women! Held for murder, and worrying about her preserves!"

The young attorney set his lips.

"I guess before we're through with her she may have something more serious than preserves to worry about."

"Oh, well," said Mrs. Hale's husband, with good-natured superiority, "women are used to worrying over trifles."

The two women moved a little closer together. Neither of them spoke. The county attorney seemed suddenly to remember his manners—and think of his future.

"And yet," said he, with the gallantry of a young politician, "for all their worries, what would we do without the ladies?"

The women did not speak, did not unbend. He went to the sink and began washing his hands. He turned to wipe them on the roller towel—whirled it for a cleaner place.

"Dirty towels! Not much of a housekeeper, would you say, ladies?"

He kicked his foot against some dirty pans under the sink.

"There's a great deal of work to be done on a farm," said Mrs. Hale stiffly.

"To be sure. And yet"—with a little bow to her—"I know there are some Dickson County farm-houses that do not have such roller towels." He gave it a pull to expose its full length again.

"Those towels get dirty awful quick. Men's hands aren't always as clean as they might be."

"Ah, loyal to your sex, I see," he laughed. He stopped and gave her a keen look. "But you and Mrs. Wright were neighbors. I suppose you were friends, too."

Martha Hale shook her head.

"I've seen little enough of her of late years. I've not been in this house—it's more than a year."

"And why was that? You didn't like her?"

"I liked her well enough," she replied with spirit. "Farmers' wives have their hands full, Mr. Henderson. And then"—She looked around the kitchen.

"Yes?" he encouraged.

"It never seemed a very cheerful place," said she, more to herself than to him.

"No," he agreed; "I don't think any one would call it cheerful. I shouldn't say she had the home-making instinct."

"Well, I don't know as Wright had, either," she muttered.

"You mean they didn't get on very well?" he was quick to ask.

"No; I don't mean anything," she answered, with decision. As she turned a little away from him, she added: "But I don't think a place would be any the cheerfuler for John Wright's bein' in it."

"I'd like to talk to you about that a little later, Mrs. Hale," he said. "I'm anxious to get the lay of things upstairs now."

He moved toward the stair door, followed by the two men.

"I suppose anything Mrs. Peters does'll be all right?" the sheriff inquired. "She was to take in some clothes for her, you know—and a few little things. We left in such a hurry yesterday."

The county attorney looked at the two women whom they were leaving alone there among the kitchen things.

"Yes—Mrs. Peters," he said, his glance resting on the woman who was not Mrs. Peters, the big farmer woman who stood behind the sheriff's wife. "Of course Mrs. Peters is one of us," he said, in a manner of entrusting responsibility. "And keep your eye out, Mrs. Peters, for anything that might be of use. No telling; you women might come upon a clue to the motive—and that's the thing we need."

Mr. Hale rubbed his face after the fashion of a show man getting ready for a pleasantry.

"But would the women know a clue if they did come upon it?" he said; and, having delivered himself of this, he followed the others through the stair door.

The women stood motionless and silent, listening to the footsteps, first upon the stairs, then in the room above them.

Then, as if releasing herself from something strange, Mrs. Hale began to arrange the dirty pans under the sink, which the county attorney's disdainful push of the foot had deranged.

"I'd hate to have men comin' into my kitchen," she said testily—"snoopin' round and criticizin'."

"Of course it's no more than their duty," said the sheriff's wife, in her manner of timid acquiescence.

"Duty's all right," replied Mrs. Hale bluffly; "but I guess that deputy sheriff that come out to make the fire might have got a little of this on." She gave the roller towel a pull. "Wish I'd thought of that sooner! Seems mean to talk about her for not having things slicked up, when she had to come away in such a hurry."

She looked around the kitchen. Certainly it was not "slicked up." Her eye was held by a bucket of sugar on a low shelf. The cover was off the wooden bucket, and beside it was a paper bag—half full.

Mrs. Hale moved toward it.

"She was putting this in there," she said to herself—slowly.

She thought of the flour in her kitchen at home—half sifted, half not sifted. She had been interrupted and had left things half done. What had interrupted Minnie Foster? Why had that work been left half done? She made a move as if to finish it,—unfinished things always bothered her,—and then she glanced around and saw that Mrs. Peters was watching her—and she didn't want Mrs. Peters to get that feeling she had got of work begun and then—for some reason—not finished.

"It's a shame about her fruit," she said, and walked toward the cupboard that the county attorney had opened, and got on the chair, murmuring: "I wonder if it's all gone."

It was a sorry enough looking sight, but "Here's one that's all right," she said at last. She held it toward the light. "This is cherries, too." She looked again. "I declare I believe that's the only one."

With a sigh, she got down from the chair, went to the sink and wiped off the bottle.

"She'll feel awful bad, after all her hard work in the hot weather. I remember the afternoon I put up my cherries last summer."

She set the bottle on the table, and, with another sigh, started to sit down in the rocker. But she did not sit down. Something kept her from sitting down in that chair. She straightened—stepped back, and, half turned away, stood looking at it, seeing the woman who sat there "pleatin' at her apron."

The thin voice of the sheriff's wife broke in upon her: "I must be getting those things from the front room closet." She opened the door into the other room, started in, stepped back. "You coming with me, Mrs. Hale?" she asked nervously. "You—you could help me get them."

They were soon back—the stark coldness of that shut-up room was not a thing to linger in.

"My!" said Mrs. Peters, dropping the things on the table and hurrying to the stove.

Mrs. Hale stood examining the clothes the woman who was being detained in town had said she wanted.

"Wright was close!" she exclaimed, holding up a shabby black skirt that bore the marks of much making over. "I think maybe that's why she kept so much to herself. I s'pose she felt she couldn't do her part; and then, you don't enjoy things when you feel shabby. She used to wear pretty clothes and be lively—when she was Minnie Foster, one of the town girls, singing in the choir. But that—oh, that was twenty years ago."

With a carefulness in which there was something tender, she folded the shabby clothes and piled them at one corner of the table. She looked at Mrs. Peters, and there was something in the other woman's look that irritated her.

"She don't care," she said to herself. "Much difference it makes to her whether Minnie Foster had pretty clothes when she was a girl."

Then she looked again, and she wasn't so sure; in fact, she hadn't at any time been perfectly sure about Mrs. Peters. She had that shrinking manner, and yet her eyes looked as if they could see a long way into things.

"This all you was to take in?" asked Mrs. Hale.

"No," said the sheriff's wife; "she said she wanted an apron. Funny thing to want," she ventured in her nervous little way, "for there's not much to get you dirty in jail, goodness knows. But I suppose just to make her feel more natural. If you're used to wearing an apron—. She said they were in the bottom drawer of this cupboard. Yes—here they are. And then her little shawl that always hung on the stair door."

Suddenly Mrs. Hale took a quick step toward the other woman.

"Mrs. Peters!"

"Yes, Mrs. Hale?"

"Do you think she—did it?"

A frightened look blurred the other things in Mrs. Peters' eyes.

"Oh, I don't know," she said, in a voice that seemed to shrink away from the subject.

"Well, I don't think she did," affirmed Mrs. Hale stoutly. "Asking for an apron, and her little shawl. Worryin' about her fruit."

"Mr. Peters says—" Footsteps were heard in the room above; she stopped, looked up, then went on in a lowered voice: "Mr. Peters says—it looks bad for her. Mr. Henderson is awful sarcastic in a speech, and he's going to make fun of her saying she didn't—wake up."

For a moment Mrs. Hale had no answer. Then, "Well, I guess John Wright didn't wake up—when they was slippin' that rope under his neck," she muttered.

"No, it's *strange*," breathed Mrs. Peters. "They think it was such a— funny way to kill a man."

She began to laugh; at sound of the laugh, abruptly stopped.

"That's just what Mr. Hale said," said Mrs. Hale, in a resolutely natural voice. "There was a gun in the house. He says that's what he can't understand."

"Mr. Henderson said, coming out, that what was needed for the case was a motive. Something to show anger—or sudden feeling."

"Well, I don't see any signs of anger around here," said Mrs. Hale. "I don't—"

She stopped. It was as if her mind tripped on something. Her eye was caught by a dish-towel in the middle of the kitchen table. Slowly she moved toward the table. One half of it was wiped clean, the other half messy. Her eyes made a slow, almost unwilling turn to the bucket of sugar and the half empty bag beside it. Things begun—and not finished.

After a moment she stepped back, and said, in that manner of releasing herself:

"Wonder how they're finding things upstairs? I hope she had it a little more red up up there. You know,"—she paused, and feeling gathered,—"it seems kind of *sneaking;* locking her up in town and coming out here to get her own house to turn against her!"

"But, Mrs. Hale," said the sheriff's wife, "the law is the law."

"I s'pose 'tis," answered Mrs. Hale shortly.

She turned to the stove, saying something about that fire not being much to brag of. She worked with it a minute, and when she straightened up she said aggressively:

"The law is the law—and a bad stove is a bad stove. How'd you like to cook on this?"—pointing with the poker to the broken lining. She opened the oven door and started to express her opinion of the oven; but she was swept into her own thoughts, thinking of what it would mean, year after year, to have that stove to wrestle with. The thought of Minnie Foster trying to bake in that oven—and the thought of her never going over to see Minnie Foster—.

She was startled by hearing Mrs. Peters say: "A person gets discouraged—and loses heart."

The sheriff's wife had looked from the stove to the sink—to the pail of water which had been carried in from outside. The two women stood there silent, above them the footsteps of the men who were looking for evidence against the woman who had worked in that kitchen. That look of seeing into things, of seeing through a thing to something else, was in the eyes of the sheriff's wife now. When Mrs. Hale next spoke to her, it was gently:

"Better loosen up your things, Mrs. Peters. We'll not feel them when we go out."

Mrs. Peters went to the back of the room to hang up the fur tippet she was wearing. A moment later she exclaimed, "Why, she was piecing a quilt," and held up a large sewing basket piled high was quilt pieces.

Mrs. Hale spread some of the blocks on the table.

"It's log-cabin pattern," she said, putting several of them together. "Pretty, isn't it?"

They were so engaged with the quilt that they did not hear the footsteps on the stairs. Just as the stair door opened Mrs. Hale was saying:

"Do you suppose she was going to quilt it or just knot it?"

The sheriff threw up his hands.

"They wonder whether she was going to quilt it or just knot it!"

There was a laugh for the ways of women, a warming of hands over the stove, and then the county attorney said briskly:

"Well, let's go right out to the barn and get that cleared up."

"I don't see as there's anything so strange," Mrs. Hale said resentfully, after the outside door had closed on the three men—"our taking up our time with little things while we're waiting for them to get the evidence. I don't see as it's anything to laugh about."

"Of course they've got awful important things on their minds," said the sheriff's wife apologetically.

They returned to an inspection of the blocks for the quilt. Mrs. Hale was looking at the fine, even sewing, and preoccupied with thoughts of the woman who had done that sewing, when she heard the sheriff's wife say, in a queer tone:

"Why, look at this one."

She turned to take the block held out to her.

"The sewing," said Mrs. Peters, in a troubled way. "All the rest of them have been so nice and even—but—this one. Why, it looks as if she didn't know what she was about!"

Their eyes met—something flashed to life, passed between them; then, as if with an effort, they seemed to pull away from each other. A moment Mrs. Hale sat there, her hands folded over that sewing which was so unlike all the rest of the sewing. Then she had pulled a knot and drawn the threads.

"Oh, what are you doing, Mrs. Hale?" asked the sheriff's wife, startled.

"Just pulling out a stitch or two that's not sewed very good," said Mrs. Hale mildly.

"I don't think we ought to touch things," Mrs. Peters said, a little helplessly.

"I'd just finish up this end," answered Mrs. Hale, still in that mild, matter-of-fact fashion.

She threaded a needle and started to replace bad sewing with good. For a little while she sewed in silence. Then, in that thin, timid voice, she heard:

"Mrs. Hale!"

"Yes, Mrs. Peters?"

"What do you suppose she was so—nervous about?"

"Oh, *I* don't know," said Mrs. Hale, as if dismissing a thing not important enough to spend much time on. "I don't know as she was—nervous. I sew awful queer sometimes when I'm just tired."

She cut a thread, and out of the corner of her eye looked up at Mrs. Peters. The small, lean face of the sheriff's wife seemed to have tightened up. Her eyes had that look of peering into something. But the next moment she moved, and said in her thin, indecisive way:

"Well, I must get those clothes wrapped. They may be through sooner than we think. I wonder where I could find a piece of paper—and string."

"In that cupboard, maybe," suggested Mrs. Hale, after a glance around.

One piece of the crazy sewing remained unripped. Mrs. Peters' back turned, Martha Hale now scrutinized that piece, compared it with the dainty, accurate sewing of the other blocks. The difference was startling. Holding this block made her feel queer, as if the distracted thoughts of the woman who had perhaps turned to it to try and quiet herself were communicating themselves to her.

Mrs. Peters' voice roused her.

"Here's a bird-cage," she said. "Did she have a bird, Mrs. Hale?"

"Why, I don't know whether she did or not." She turned to look at the cage Mrs. Peters was holding up. "I've not been here in so long." She sighed. "There was a man round last year selling canaries cheap—but I don't know as she took one. Maybe she did. She used to sing real pretty herself."

Mrs. Peters looked around the kitchen.

"Seems kind of funny to think of a bird here." She half laughed—an attempt to put up a barrier. "But she must have had one—or why would she have a cage? I wonder what happened to it."

"I suppose maybe the cat got it," suggested Mrs. Hale, resuming her sewing.

"No; she didn't have a cat. She's got that feeling some people have about cats—being afraid of them. When they brought her to our house yesterday, my cat got in the room, and she was real upset and asked me to take it out."

"My sister Bessie was like that," laughed Mrs. Hale.

The sheriff's wife did not reply. The silence made Mrs. Hale turn round. Mrs. Peters was examining the bird-cage.

"Look at this door," she said slowly. "It's broke. One hinge has been pulled apart."

Mrs. Hale came nearer.

"Looks as if some one must have been—rough with it."

Again their eyes met—startled, questioning, apprehensive. For a moment neither spoke nor stirred. Then Mrs. Hale, turning away, said brusquely:

"If they're going to find any evidence, I wish they'd be about it. I don't like this place."

"But I'm awful glad you came with me, Mrs. Hale." Mrs. Peters put the bird-cage on the table and sat down. "It would be lonesome for me—sitting here alone."

"Yes, it would, wouldn't it?" agreed Mrs. Hale, a certain determined naturalness in her voice. She picked up the sewing, but now it dropped in her lap, and she murmured in a different voice: "But I tell you what I *do* wish, Mrs. Peters. I wish I had come over sometimes when she was here. I wish—I had."

"But of course you were awful busy, Mrs. Hale. Your house—and your children."

"I could've come," retorted Mrs. Hale shortly. "I stayed away because it weren't cheerful—and that's why I ought to have come. I"—she looked around—"I've never liked this place. Maybe because it's down in a hollow and you don't see the road. I don't know what it is, but it's a lonesome place, and always was. I wish I had come over to see Minnie Foster sometimes. I can see now—" She did not put it into words.

"Well, you mustn't reproach yourself," counseled Mrs. Peters. "Somehow, we just don't see how it is with other folks till—something comes up."

"Not having children makes less work," mused Mrs. Hale, after a silence, "but it makes a quiet house—and Wright out to work all day—and no company when he did come in. Did you know John Wright, Mrs. Peters?"

"Not to know him. I've seen him in town. They say he was a good man."

"Yes—good," conceded John Wright's neighbor grimly. "He didn't drink, and kept his word as well as most, I guess, and paid his debts. But he was a hard man, Mrs. Peters. Just to pass the time of day with him—." She stopped, shivered a little. "Like a raw wind that gets to the bone." Her eye fell upon the cage on the table before her, and she added, almost bitterly: "I should think she would've wanted a bird!"

Suddenly she leaned forward, looking intently at the cage. "But what do you s'pose went wrong with it?"

"I don't know," returned Mrs. Peters; "unless it got sick and died."

But after she said it she reached over and swung the broken door. Both women watched it as if somehow held by it.

"You didn't know—her?" Mrs. Hale asked, a gentler note in her voice.

"Not till they brought her yesterday," said the sheriff's wife.

"She—come to think of it, she was kind of like a bird herself. Real sweet and pretty, but kind of timid and—fluttery. How—she—did—change."

That held her for a long time. Finally, as if struck with a happy thought and relieved to get back to everyday things, she exclaimed:

"Tell you what, Mrs. Peters, why don't you take the quilt in with you? It might take up her mind."

"Why, I think that's a real nice idea, Mrs. Hale," agreed the sheriff's wife, as if she too were glad to come into the atmosphere of a simple kindness. "There couldn't possibly be any objection to that, could there? Now, just what will I take? I wonder if her patches are in here—and her things."

They turned to the sewing basket.

"Here's some red," said Mrs. Hale, bringing out a roll of cloth. Underneath that was a box. "Here, maybe her scissors are in here—and her things." She held it up. "What a pretty box! I'll warrant that was something she had a long time ago—when she was a girl."

She held it in her hand a moment; then, with a little sigh, opened it.

Instantly her hand went to her nose.

"Why—!" .

Mrs. Peters drew nearer—then turned away.

"There's something wrapped up in this piece of silk," faltered Mrs. Hale.

"This isn't her scissors," said Mrs. Peters in a shrinking voice.

Her hand not steady, Mrs. Hale raised the piece of silk. "Oh, Mrs. Peters!" she cried. "It's—"

Mrs. Peters bent closer.

"It's the bird," she whispered.

"But, Mrs. Peters!" cried Mrs. Hale. "*Look* at it! Its neck—look at its neck! It's all—other side *to*."

She held the box away from her.

The sheriff's wife again bent closer.

"Somebody wrung its neck," said she, in a voice that was slow and deep.

And then again the eyes of the two women met—this time clung together in a look of dawning comprehension, of growing horror. Mrs. Peters looked from the dead bird to the broken door of the cage. Again their eyes met. And just then there was a sound at the outside door.

Mrs. Hale slipped the box under the quilt pieces in the basket, and sank into the chair before it. Mrs. Peters stood holding to the table. The county attorney and the sheriff came in from outside.

"Well, ladies," said the county attorney, as one turning from serious things to little pleasantries, "have you decided whether she was going to quilt it or knot it?"

"We think," began the sheriff's wife in a flurried voice, "that she was going to—knot it."

He was too preoccupied to notice the change that came in her voice on that last.

"Well, that's very interesting, I'm sure," he said tolerantly. He caught sight of the bird-cage. "Has the bird flown?"

"We think the cat got it," said Mrs. Hale in a voice curiously even.

He was walking up and down, as if thinking something out.

"Is there a cat?" he asked absently.

Mrs. Hale shot a look up at the sheriff's wife.

"Well, not *now,*" said Mrs. Peters. "They're superstitious, you know; they leave."

She sank into her chair.

The county attorney did not heed her. "No sign at all of any one having come in from the outside," he said to Peters, in the manner of continuing an interrupted conversation. "Their own rope. Now let's go upstairs again and go over it, piece by piece. It would have to have been some one who knew just the—"

The stair door closed behind them and their voices were lost.

The two women sat motionless, not looking at each other, but as if peering into something and at the same time holding back. When they spoke now it was as if they were afraid of what they were saying, but as if they could not help saying it.

"She liked the bird," said Martha Hale, low and slowly. "She was going to bury it in that pretty box."

"When I was a girl," said Mrs. Peters, under her breath, "my kitten—there was a boy took a hatchet, and before my eyes—before I could get there—" She covered her face an instant. "If they hadn't held me back I would have"—she caught herself, looked upstairs where footsteps were heard, and finished weakly—"hurt him."

Then they sat without speaking or moving.

"I wonder how it would seem," Mrs. Hale at last began, as if feeling her way over strange ground—"never to have had any children around?" Her eyes made a slow sweep of the kitchen, as if seeing what that kitchen had meant through all the years. "No, Wright wouldn't like the bird," she said after that—"a thing that sang. She used to sing. He killed that too." Her voice tightened.

Mrs. Peters moved uneasily.

"Of course we don't know who killed the bird."

"I knew John Wright," was Mrs. Hale's answer.

"It was an awful thing was done in this house that night, Mrs. Hale," said the sheriff's wife. "Killing a man while he slept—slipping a thing round his neck that choked the life out of him."

Mrs. Hale's hand went out to the bird-cage.

"His neck. Choked the life out of him."

"We don't *know* who killed him," whispered Mrs. Peters wildly. "We don't *know.*"

Mrs. Hale had not moved. "If there had been years and years of—nothing, then a bird to sing to you, it would be awful—still—after the bird was still."

It was as if something within her not herself had spoken, and it found in Mrs. Peters something she did not know as herself.

"I know what stillness is," she said, in a queer, monotonous voice. "When we homesteaded in Dakota, and my first baby died—after he was two years old—and me with no other then—"

Mrs. Hale stirred.

"How soon do you suppose they'll be through looking for evidence?"

"I know what stillness is," repeated Mrs. Peters, in just that same way. Then she too pulled back. "The law has got to punish crime, Mrs. Hale," she said in her tight little way.

"I wish you'd seen Minnie Foster," was the answer, "when she wore a white dress with blue ribbons, and stood up there in the choir and sang."

The picture of that girl, the fact that she had lived neighbor to that girl for twenty years, and had let her die for lack of life, was suddenly more than she could bear.

"Oh, I *wish* I'd come over here once in a while!" she cried. "That was a crime! That was a crime! Who's going to punish that?"

"We mustn't take on," said Mrs. Peters, with a frightened look toward the stairs.

"I might 'a' *known* she needed help! I tell you, it's *queer*, Mrs. Peters. We live close together, and we live far apart. We all go through the same things— it's all just a different kind of the same thing! If it weren't—why do you and I *understand*? Why do we *know*—what we know this minute?"

She dashed her hand across her eyes. Then, seeing the jar of fruit on the table, she reached for it and choked out:

"If I was you I wouldn't *tell* her her fruit was gone! Tell her it *ain't*. Tell her it's all right—all of it. Here—take this in to prove it to her! She—she may never know whether it was broke or not."

She turned away.

Mrs. Peters reached out for the bottle of fruit as if she were glad to take it—as if touching a familiar thing, having something to do, could keep her from something else. She got up, looked about for something to wrap the fruit in, took a petticoat from the pile of clothes she had brought from the front room, and nervously started winding that round the bottle.

"My!" she began, in a high, false voice, "it's a good thing the men couldn't hear us! Getting all stirred up over a little thing like a—dead canary." She hurried over that. "As if that could have anything to do with—with—My, wouldn't they *laugh*?"

Footsteps were heard on the stairs.

"Maybe they would," muttered Mrs. Hale—"maybe they wouldn't."

"No, Peters," said the county attorney incisively; "it's all perfectly clear, except the reason for doing it. But you know juries when it comes to women. If there was some definite thing—something to show. Something to make a story about. A thing that would connect up with this clumsy way of doing it."

In a covert way Mrs. Hale looked at Mrs. Peters. Mrs. Peters was looking at her. Quickly they looked away from each other. The outer door opened and Mr. Hale came in.

"I've got the team round now," he said. "Pretty cold out there."

"I'm going to stay here awhile by myself," the county attorney suddenly announced. "You can send Frank out for me, can't you?" he asked the sheriff. "I want to go over everything. I'm not satisfied we can't do better."

Again, for one brief moment, the two women's eyes found one another. The sheriff came up to the table.

"Did you want to see what Mrs. Peters was going to take in?"

The county attorney picked up the apron. He laughed.

"Oh, I guess they're not very dangerous things the ladies have picked out."

Mrs. Hale's hand was on the sewing basket in which the box was concealed. She felt that she ought to take her hand off the basket. She did not seem able to. He picked up one of the quilt blocks which she had piled on to cover the box. Her eyes felt like fire. She had a feeling that if he took up the basket she would snatch it from him.

But he did not take it up. With another little laugh, he turned away, saying:

"No; Mrs. Peters doesn't need supervising. For that matter, a sheriff's wife is married to the law. Ever think of it that way, Mrs. Peters?"

Mrs. Peters was standing beside the table. Mrs. Hale shot a look up at her; but she could not see her face. Mrs. Peters had turned away. When she spoke, her voice was muffled.

"Not—just that way," she said.

"Married to the law!" chuckled Mrs. Peters' husband. He moved toward the door into the front room, and said to the county attorney:

"I just want you to come in here a minute, George. We ought to take a look at these windows."

"Oh—windows," said the county attorney scoffingly.

"We'll be right out, Mr. Hale," said the sheriff to the farmer, who was still waiting by the door.

Hale went to look after the horses. The sheriff followed the county attorney into the other room. Again—for one moment—the two women were alone in that kitchen.

Martha Hale sprang up, her hands tight together, looking at that other woman, with whom it rested. At first she could not see her eyes, for the sheriff's wife had not turned back, since she turned away at that suggestion of being married to the law. But now Mrs. Hale made her turn back. Her eyes made her turn back. Slowly, unwillingly, Mrs. Peters turned her head until her eyes met the eyes of the other woman. There was a moment when they held each other in a steady, burning look in which there was no evasion nor flinching. Then Martha Hale's eyes pointed the way to the basket in which was hidden the thing that would make certain the conviction of the other woman—that woman who was not there and yet who had been there with them all through the hour.

For a moment Mrs. Peters did not move. And then she did it. With a rush forward, she threw back the quilt pieces, got the box, tried to put it in her handbag. It was too big. Desperately she opened it, started to take the bird out. But there she broke—she could not touch the bird. She stood helpless, foolish.

There was the sound of a knob turning in the inner door. Martha Hale snatched the box from the sheriff's wife, and got it in the pocket of her big coat just as the sheriff and the county attorney came back into the kitchen.

"Well, Henry," said the county attorney facetiously, "at least we found out that she was not going to quilt it. She was going to—what is it you call it, ladies?"

Mrs. Hale's hand was against the pocket of her coat.

"We call it—knot it, Mr. Henderson."

EXERCISES

1. Discuss the significance of the following passages:

    "Lewis often wandered along and got things mixed up in a story. She hoped he would tell this straight and plain, and not say unnecessary things. . . ."

    "But would the women know a clue if they came upon it?"

    "That look of seeing into things, of seeing through a thing to something else, was in the eyes of the sheriff's wife now."

    "Their eyes met—something flashed to life, passed between them."

    "If there was some definite thing—something to show. Something to make a story about. A thing that would connect up with this clumsy way of doing it."

2. What is the crime in the story? Where did it take place, upstairs or downstairs?

3. How does this story follow the conventions of the detective story? How does it follow the conventions of the courtroom drama?

4. A *clue* is that which makes a difference, part of an overall pattern that means something. What are the clues in this story? Why are the women able to see them and not the men?

AMBROSE
BIERCE | # An Occurrence at
Owl Creek Bridge

A man stood upon a railroad bridge in Northern Alabama, looking down into the swift waters twenty feet below. The man's hands were behind his back, the wrists bound with a cord. A rope loosely encircled his neck. It was attached to a stout cross-timber above his head, and the slack fell to the level of his knees. Some loose boards laid upon the sleepers supporting the metals of the railway supplied a footing for him and his executioners—two private soldiers of the Federal army, directed by a sergeant, who in civil life may have been a deputy sheriff. At a short remove upon the same temporary platform was an officer in the uniform of his rank, armed. He was a captain. A sentinel at each end of the bridge stood with his rifle in the position known as "support," that is to say, vertical in front of the left shoulder, the hammer resting on the forearm thrown straight across the chest—a formal and unnatural position, enforcing an erect carriage of the body. It did not appear to be the duty of these two men to know what was occurring at the centre of the bridge; they merely blockaded the two ends of the foot plank which traversed it.

Beyond one of the sentinels nobody was in sight; the railroad ran straight away into a forest for a hundred yards, then, curving, was lost to view. Doubtless there was an outpost further along. The other bank of the stream was open ground—a gentle acclivity crowned with a stockade of vertical tree trunks, loop-holed for rifles, with a single embrasure through which protruded the muzzle of a brass cannon commanding the bridge. Midway of the slope between bridge and fort were the spectators—a single company of infantry in line, at "parade rest," the butts of the rifles on the ground, the barrels inclining slightly backward against the right shoulder, the hands crossed upon the stock. A lieutenant stood at the right of the line, the point of his sword upon the ground, his left hand resting upon his right. Excepting the group of four at the centre of the bridge not a man moved. The company faced the bridge, staring stonily, motionless. The sentinels, facing the banks of the stream, might have been statues to adorn the bridge. The captain stood with folded arms, silent, observing the work of his subordinates but making no sign. Death is a dignitary who, when he comes announced, is to be received with formal manifestations of respect, even by those most familiar with him. In the code of military etiquette silence and fixity are forms of deference.

The man who was engaged in being hanged was apparently about thirty-five years of age. He was a civilian, if one might judge from his dress, which was that of a planter. His features were good—a straight nose, firm mouth, broad forehead, from which his long, dark hair was combed straight back, falling behind his ears to the collar of his well-fitting frock coat. He wore a moustache and pointed beard, but no whiskers; his eyes were large and dark grey and had a kindly expression which one would hardly have expected in one whose neck was in the hemp. Evidently this was no vulgar assassin. The liberal military code makes provision for hanging many kinds of people, and gentlemen are not excluded.

The preparations being complete, the two private soldiers stepped aside and each drew away the plank upon which he had been standing. The sergeant turned to the captain, saluted and placed himself immediately behind that officer, who in turn moved apart one pace. These movements left the condemned man and the sergeant standing on the two ends of the same plank, which spanned three of the cross-ties of the bridge. The end upon which the civilian stood almost, but not quite, reached a fourth. This plank had been held in place by the weight of the captain; it was now held by that of the sergeant. At a signal from the former, the latter would step aside, the plank would tilt and the condemned man go down between two ties. The arrangement commended itself to his judgment as simple and effective. His face had not been covered nor his eyes bandaged. He looked a moment at his "unsteadfast footing," then let his gaze wander to the swirling water of the stream racing madly beneath his feet. A piece of dancing driftwood caught his attention and his eyes followed it down the current. How slowly it appeared to move! What a sluggish stream!

He closed his eyes in order to fix his last thoughts upon his wife and children. The water, touched to gold by the early sun, the brooding mists under the banks at some distance down the stream, the fort, the soldiers, the piece of drift—all had distracted him. And now he became conscious of a new disturbance. Striking through the thought of his dear ones was a sound which he could neither ignore nor understand, a sharp, distinct, metallic percussion like the stroke of a blacksmith's hammer upon the anvil; it had the same ringing quality. He wondered what it was, and whether immeasurably distant or near by—it seemed both. Its recurrence was regular, but as slow as the tolling of a death knell. He awaited each stroke with impatience and—he knew not why—apprehension. The intervals of silence grew progressively longer; the delays became maddening. With their greater infrequency the sounds increased in strength and sharpness. They hurt his ear like the thrust of a knife; he feared he would shriek. What he heard was the ticking of his watch.

He unclosed his eyes and saw again the water below him. "If I could free my hands," he thought, "I might throw off the noose and spring into the stream. By diving I could evade the bullets, and, swimming vigorously, reach the bank, take to the woods, and get away home. My home, thank God, is as yet outside their lines; my wife and little ones are still beyond the invader's farthest advance."

As these thoughts, which have here to be set down in words, were flashed into the doomed man's brain rather than evolved from it, the captain nodded to the sergeant. The sergeant stepped aside.

II

Peyton Farquhar was a well-to-do planter, of an old and highly-respected Alabama family. Being a slave owner, and, like other slave owners, a politician, he was naturally an original secessionist and ardently devoted to the Southern cause. Circumstances of an imperious nature which it is unnecessary to relate here, had prevented him from taking service with the gallant army which had fought the disastrous campaigns ending with the fall of Corinth, and he chafed under the inglorious restraint, longing for the release of his energies, the larger life of the soldier, the opportunity for distinction. That opportunity, he felt, would come, as it comes to all in war time. Meanwhile he did what he could. No service was too humble for him to perform in aid of the South, no adventure too perilous for him to undertake if consistent with the character of a civilian who was at heart a soldier, and who in good faith and without too much qualification assented to at least a part of the frankly villainous dictum that all is fair in love and war.

One evening while Farquhar and his wife were sitting on a rustic bench near the entrance to his grounds, a grey-clad soldier rode up to the gate and asked for a drink of water. Mrs. Farquhar was only too happy to serve him with her own white hands. While she was gone to fetch the water, her husband approached the dusty horseman and inquired eagerly for news from the front.

"The Yanks are repairing the railroads," said the man, "and are getting ready for another advance. They have reached the Owl Creek bridge, put it in order, and built a stockade on the other bank. The commandant has issued an order, which is posted everywhere, declaring that any civilian caught interfering with the railroad, its bridges, tunnels, or trains, will be summarily hanged. I saw the order."

"How far is it to the Owl Creek bridge?" Farquhar asked.

"About thirty miles."

"Is there no force on this side the creek?"

"Only a picket post half a mile out, on the railroad, and a single sentinel at this end of the bridge."

"Suppose a man—a civilian and student of hanging—should elude the picket post and perhaps get the better of the sentinel," said Farquhar, smiling, "what could he accomplish?"

The soldier reflected. "I was there a month ago," he replied. "I observed that the flood of last winter had lodged a great quantity of driftwood against the wooden pier at this end of the bridge. It is now dry and would burn like tow."

The lady had now brought the water, which the soldier drank. He thanked her ceremoniously, bowed to her husband, and rode away. An hour later, after nightfall, he repassed the plantation, going northward in the direction from which he had come. He was a Federal scout.

III

As Peyton Farquhar fell straight downward through the bridge, he lost consciousness and was as one already dead. From this state he was awakened— ages later, it seemed to him—by the pain of a sharp pressure upon his throat, followed by a sense of suffocation. Keen, poignant agonies seemed to shoot from his neck downward through every fibre of his body and limbs. These pains appeared to flash along well-defined lines of ramification, and to beat with an inconceivably rapid periodicity. They seemed like streams of pulsating fire heating him to an intolerable temperature. As to his head, he was conscious of nothing but a feeling of fullness—of congestion. These sensations were unaccompanied by thought. The intellectual part of his nature was already effaced; he had power only to feel, and feeling was torment. He was conscious of motion. Encompassed in a luminous cloud, of which he was now merely the fiery heart, without material substance, he swung through unthinkable arcs of oscillation, like a vast pendulum. Then all at once, with terrible suddenness, the light about him shot upward with the noise of a loud plash; a frightful roaring was in his ears, and all was cold and dark. The power of thought was restored; he knew that the rope had broken and he had fallen into the stream. There was no additional strangulation; the noose about his neck was already suffocating him, and kept the water from his lungs. To die of hanging at the bottom of a river!—the idea seemed to him ludicrous. He opened his eyes in the blackness and saw above him a gleam of light, but how distant, how inaccessible! He was still sinking, for the light became fainter and fainter until it was a mere glimmer. Then it began to grow and brighten, and he knew that he was rising toward the surface—knew it with reluctance, for he was now very comfortable. "To be hanged and drowned," he thought, "that is not so bad; but I do not wish to be shot. No; I will not be shot; that is not fair."

He was not conscious of an effort, but a sharp pain in his wrist apprised him that he was trying to free his hands. He gave the struggle his attention, as an idler might observe the feat of a juggler, without interest in the outcome. What splendid effort!—what magnificent, what superhuman strength! Ah, that was a fine endeavour! Bravo! The cord fell away; his arms parted and floated upward, the hands dimly seen on each side in the growing light. He watched them with a new interest as first one and then the other pounced upon the noose at his neck. They tore it away and thrust it fiercely aside, its undulations resembling those of a water-snake. "Put it back, put it back!" He thought he shouted these words to his hands, for the undoing of the noose had been succeeded by the direst pang which he had yet experienced. His neck ached horribly; his brain was on fire; his heart, which had been fluttering faintly, gave a great leap, trying to force itself out at his mouth. His whole body was racked and wrenched with an insupportable anguish! But his disobedient hands gave no heed to the command. They beat the water vigorously with quick, downward strokes, forcing him to the surface. He felt his head emerge; his eyes were blinded by the sunlight; his chest expanded convulsively, and with a supreme and crowning agony his lungs engulfed a great draught of air, which instantly he expelled in a shriek!

He was now in full possession of his physical senses. They were, indeed, preternaturally keen and alert. Something in the awful disturbance of his organic system had so exalted and refined them that they made record of things never before perceived. He felt the ripples upon his face and heard their separate sounds as they struck. He looked at the forest on the bank of the stream, saw the individual trees, the leaves and the veining of each leaf—saw the very insects upon them, the locusts, the brilliant-bodied flies, the grey spiders stretching their webs from twig to twig. He noted the prismatic colors in all the dewdrops upon a million blades of grass. The humming of the gnats that danced above the eddies of the stream, the beating of the dragon flies' wings, the strokes of the water spiders' legs, like oars which had lifted their boat—all these made audible music. A fish slid along beneath his eyes and he heard the rush of its body parting the water.

He had come to the surface facing down the stream; in a moment the visible world seemed to wheel slowly round, himself the pivotal point, and he saw the bridge, the fort, the soldiers upon the bridge, the captain, the sergeant, the two privates, his executioners. They were in silhouette against the blue sky. They shouted and gesticulated, pointing at him; the captain had drawn his pistol, but did not fire; the others were unarmed. Their movements were grotesque and horrible, their forms gigantic.

Suddenly he heard a sharp report and something struck the water smartly within a few inches of his head, spattering his face with spray. He heard a second report, and saw one of the sentinels with his rifle at his shoulder, a light cloud of blue smoke rising from the muzzle. The man in the water saw the eye of the man on the bridge gazing into his own through the sights of the rifle. He observed that it was a grey eye, and remembered having read that grey eyes were keenest and that all famous marksmen had them. Nevertheless, this one had missed.

A counter swirl had caught Farquhar and turned him half round; he was again looking into the forest on the bank opposite the fort. The sound of a clear, high voice in a monotonous singsong now rang out behind him and came across the water with a distinctness that pierced and subdued all other sounds, even the beating of the ripples in his ears. Although no soldier, he had frequented camps enough to know the dread significance of that deliberate, drawling, aspirated chant; the lieutenant on shore was taking a part in the morning's work. How coldly and pitilessly—with what an even, calm intonation, presaging and enforcing tranquillity in the men—with what accurately-measured intervals fell those cruel words:

"Attention, company. . . . Shoulder arms. . . . Ready. . . . Aim. . . . Fire."

Farquhar dived—dived as deeply as he could. The water roared in his ears like the voice of Niagara, yet he heard the dulled thunder of the volley, and rising again toward the surface, met shining bits of metal, singularly flattened, oscillating slowly downward. Some of them touched him on the face and hands, then fell away, continuing their descent. One lodged between his collar and neck; it was uncomfortably warm, and he snatched it out.

As he rose to the surface, gasping for breath, he saw that he had been a long time under water; he was perceptibly farther down stream—nearer to safety. The soldiers had almost finished reloading; the metal ramrods flashed all at once in the sunshine as they were drawn from the barrels, turned in the air, and thrust into their sockets. The two sentinels fired again, independently and ineffectually.

The hunted man saw all this over his shoulder; he was now swimming vigorously with the current. His brain was as energetic as his arms and legs; he thought with the rapidity of lightning.

"The officer," he reasoned, "will not make that martinet's error a second time. It is as easy to dodge a volley as a single shot. He has probably already given the command to fire at will. God help me, I cannot dodge them all!"

An appalling plash within two yards of him, followed by a loud rushing sound, *diminuendo,* which seemed to travel back through the air to the fort and died in an explosion which stirred the very river to its deeps! A rising sheet of water, which curved over him, fell down upon him, blinded him, strangled him! The cannon had taken a hand in the game. As he shook his head free from the commotion of the smitten water, he heard the deflected shot humming through the air ahead, and in an instant it was cracking and smashing the branches in the forest beyond.

"They will not do that again," he thought; "the next time they will use a charge of grape. I must keep my eye upon the gun; the smoke will apprise me—the report arrives too late; it lags behind the missile. It is a good gun."

Suddenly he felt himself whirled round and round—spinning like a top. The water, the banks, the forest, the now distant bridge, fort and men—all were commingled and blurred. Objects were represented by their colors only; circular horizontal streaks of color—that was all he saw. He had been caught in a vortex and was being whirled on with a velocity of advance and gyration which made him giddy and sick. In a few moments he was flung upon the gravel at the foot of the left bank of the stream—the southern bank—and behind a projecting point which concealed him from his enemies. The sudden arrest of his motion, the abrasion of one of his hands on the gravel, restored him and he wept with delight. He dug his fingers into the sand, threw it over himself in handfuls and audibly blessed it. It looked like gold, like diamonds, rubies, emeralds; he could think of nothing beautiful which it did not resemble. The trees upon the bank were giant garden plants; he noted a definite order in their arrangement, inhaled the fragrance of their blooms. A strange, roseate light shone through the spaces among their trunks, and the wind made in their branches the music of æolian harps. He had no wish to perfect his escape, was content to remain in that enchanting spot until retaken.

A whizz and rattle of grapeshot among the branches high above his head roused him from his dream. The baffled cannoneer had fired him a random farewell. He sprang to his feet, rushed up the sloping bank, and plunged into the forest.

All that day he travelled, laying his course by the rounding sun. The forest seemed interminable; nowhere did he discover a break in it, not even a woodman's road. He had not known that he lived in so wild a region. There was something uncanny in the revelation.

By nightfall he was fatigued, footsore, famishing. The thought of his wife and children urged him on. At last he found a road which led him in what he knew to be the right direction. It was as wide and straight as a city street, yet it seemed untravelled. No fields bordered it, no dwelling anywhere. Not so much as the barking of a dog suggested human habitation. The black bodies of the great trees formed a straight wall on both sides, terminating on the horizon in a point, like a diagram in a lesson in perspective. Overhead, as he looked up through this rift in the wood, shone great golden stars looking unfamiliar and grouped in strange constellations. He was sure they were arranged in some order which had a secret and malign significance. The wood on either side was full of singular noises, among which—once, twice, and again—he distinctly heard whispers in an unknown tongue.

His neck was in pain, and, lifting his hand to it, he found it horribly swollen. He knew that it had a circle of black where the rope had bruised it. His eyes felt congested; he could no longer close them. His tongue was swollen with thirst; he relieved its fever by thrusting it forward from between his teeth into the cool air. How softly the turf had carpeted the untravelled avenue! He could no longer feel the roadway beneath his feet!

Doubtless, despite his suffering, he fell asleep while walking, for now he sees another scene—perhaps he has merely recovered from a delirium. He stands at the gate of his own home. All is as he left it, and all bright and beautiful in the morning sunshine. He must have travelled the entire night. As he pushes open the gate and passes up the wide white walk, he sees a flutter of female garments; his wife, looking fresh and cool and sweet, steps down from the verandah to meet him. At the bottom of the steps she stands waiting, with a smile of ineffable joy, an attitude of matchless grace and dignity. Ah, how beautiful she is! He springs forward with extended arms. As he is about to clasp her, he feels a stunning blow upon the back of the neck; a blinding white light blazes all about him, with a sound like the shock of a cannon— then all is darkness and silence!

Peyton Farquhar was dead; his body, with a broken neck, swung gently from side to side beneath the timbers of the Owl Creek bridge.

EXERCISES

1. Carefully look at the first section of the story. Discuss the static, pictorial, formal nature of the proceedings.

2. Discuss passages in the first section that establish the plausibility of the third section.

3. Pay particular attention to the last paragraph of the first section. What is the difference between thought set down in words and thoughts flashed in the brain?

4. The director of a famous film version of this story left out the second section completely, calling it "merely exposition." What did he mean by this statement? Is the section necessary or not?

5. Note the language of the first paragraph of the third section, particularly the verbs. What is suggested here—reality or fantasy?

6. If the protagonist imagines his own escape in the split second before he "comes to the end of his rope," why does he make it so difficult—having to escape bullets, cannon fire, possible drowning, etc.?

7. Point out clues that suggest that the protagonist's escape is not real.

8. What is the purpose of the verb tense shifts in the last three paragraphs of the story?

JORGE
LUIS
BORGES │ *Funes, the Memorious*

I remember him (I scarcely have the right to use this ghostly verb; only one man on earth deserved the right, and he is dead), I remember him with a dark passionflower in his hand, looking at it as no one has ever looked at such a flower, though they might look from the twilight of day until the twilight of night, for a whole life long. I remember him, his face immobile and Indian-like, and singularly *remote*, behind his cigarette. I remember (I believe) the strong delicate fingers of the plainsman who can braid leather. I remember, near those hands, a vessel in which to make maté tea, bearing the arms of the Banda Oriental; I remember, in the window of the house, a yellow rush mat, and beyond, a vague marshy landscape. I remember clearly his voice, the deliberate, resentful, nasal voice of the old Eastern Shore man, without the Italianate syllables of today, I did not see him more than three times; the last time, in 1887. . . .

That all those who knew him should write something about him seems to me a very felicitous idea; my testimony may perhaps be the briefest and without doubt the poorest, and it will not be the least impartial. The deplorable fact of my being an Argentinian will hinder me from falling into a dithyramb—an obligatory form in the Uruguay, when the theme is an Uruguayan.

Littérateur, slicker, Buenos Airean: Funes did not use these insulting phrases, but I am sufficiently aware that for him I represented these unfortunate categories. Pedro Leandro Ipuche has written that Funes was a precursor of the superman, "an untamed and vernacular Zarathustra"; I do not doubt it, but one must not forget, either, that he was a countryman from the town of Fray Bentos, with certain incurable limitations.

My first recollection of Funes is quite clear, I see him at dusk, sometime in March or February of the year '84. That year, my father had taken me to spend the summer at Fray Bentos. I was on my way back from the farm at San Francisco with my cousin Bernardo Haedo. We came back singing, on horseback; and this last fact was not the only reason for my joy. After a sultry day, an enormous slate-gray storm had obscured the sky. It was driven on by a wind from the south; the trees were already tossing like madmen; and I had the apprehension (the secret hope) that the elemental downpour would catch us out in the open. We were running a kind of race with the tempest. We rode into a narrow lane which wound down between two enormously high brick footpaths. It had grown black of a sudden; I now heard rapid almost secret steps above; I raised my eyes and saw a boy running along the narrow, cracked path as if he were running along a narrow, broken wall. I remember the loose trousers, tight at the bottom, the hemp sandals; I remember the cigarette in the hard visage, standing out against the by now limitless darkness. Bernardo unexpectedly yelled to him: "What's the time, Ireneo?" Without looking up, without stopping, Ireneo replied: "In ten minutes it will be eight o'clock, child Bernardo Juan Francisco." The voice was sharp, mocking.

I am so absentminded that the dialogue which I have just cited would not have penetrated my attention if it had not been repeated by my cousin, who was stimulated, I think, by a certain local pride and by a desire to show himself indifferent to the other's three-sided reply.

He told me that the boy above us in the pass was a certain Ireneo Funes, renowned for a number of eccentricities, such as that of having nothing to do with people and of always knowing the time, like a watch. He added that Ireneo was the son of María Clementina Funes, an ironing woman in the town, and that his father, some people said, was an "Englishman" named O'Connor, a doctor in the salting fields, though some said the father was a horse-breaker, or scout, from the province of El Salto. Ireneo lived with his mother, at the edge of the country house of the Laurels.

In the years '85 and '86 we spent the summer in the city of Montevideo. We returned to Fray Bentos in '87. As was natural, I inquired after all my acquaintances, and finally, about "the chronometer Funes." I was told that he had been thrown by a wild horse at the San Francisco ranch, and that he had been hopelessly crippled. I remember the impression of uneasy magic which the news provoked in me: the only time I had seen him we were on horseback, coming from San Francisco, and he was in a high place; from the lips of my cousin Bernardo the affair sounded like a dream elaborated with elements out of the past. They told me that Ireneo did not move now from his cot, but remained with his eyes fixed on the backyard fig tree, or on a cobweb. At sunset he allowed himself to be brought to the window. He carried pride to the extreme of pretending that the blow which had befallen him was a good thing. . . . Twice I saw him behind the iron grate which sternly delineated his eternal imprisonment: unmoving, once, his eyes closed; unmoving also, another time, absorbed in the contemplation of a sweet-smelling sprig of lavender cotton.

At the time I had begun, not without some ostentation, the methodical study of Latin. My valise contained the *De viris illustribus* of Lhomond, the *Thesaurus* of Quicherat, Caesar's *Commentaries,* and an odd-numbered volume of the *Historia Naturalis* of Pliny, which exceeded (and still exceeds) my modest talents as a Latinist. Everything is noised around in a small town; Ireneo, at his small farm on the outskirts, was not long in learning of the arrival of these anomalous books. He sent me a flowery, ceremonious letter, in which he recalled our encounter, unfortunately brief, "on the seventh day of February of the year '84," and alluded to the glorious services which Don Gregorio

Haedo, my uncle, dead the same year, "had rendered to the Two Fatherlands in the glorious campaign of Ituzaingó," and he solicited the loan of any one of the volumes, to be accompanied by a dictionary "for the better intelligence of the original text, for I do not know Latin as yet." He promised to return them in good condition, almost immediately. The letter was perfect, very nicely constructed; the orthography was of the type sponsored by Andrés Bello: *i* for *y*, *j* for *g*. At first I naturally suspected a jest. My cousins assured me it was not so, that these were the ways of Ireneo. I did not know whether to attribute to impudence, ignorance, or stupidity, the idea that the difficult Latin required no other instrument than a dictionary; in order fully to undeceive him I sent the *Gradus ad Parnassum* of Quicherat, and the Pliny.

On February 14, I received a telegram from Buenos Aires telling me to return immediately, for my father was "in no way well." God forgive me, but the prestige of being the recipient of an urgent telegram, the desire to point out to all of Fray Bentos the contradiction between the negative form of the news and the positive adverb, the temptation to dramatize my sorrow as I feigned a virile stoicism, all no doubt distracted me from the possibility of anguish. As I packed my valise, I noted that I was missing the *Gradus* and the volume of the *Historia Naturalis*. The "Saturn" was to weigh anchor on the morning of the next day; that night, after supper, I made my way to the house of Funes. Outside, I was surprised to find the night no less oppressive than the day.

Ireneo's mother received me at the modest ranch.

She told me that Ireneo was in the back room and that I should not be disturbed to find him in the dark, for he knew how to pass the dead hours without lighting the candle. I crossed the cobblestone patio, the small corridor; I came to the second patio. A great vine covered everything, so that the darkness seemed complete. Of a sudden I heard the high-pitched, mocking voice of Ireneo. The voice spoke in Latin; the voice (which came out of the obscurity) was reading, with obvious delight, a treatise or prayer or incantation. The Roman syllables resounded in the earthen patio; my suspicion made them seem undecipherable, interminable; afterwards, in the enormous dialogue of that night, I learned that they made up the first paragraph of the twenty-fourth chapter of the seventh book of the *Historia Naturalis*. The subject of this chapter is memory; the last words are *ut nihil non iisdem verbis redderetur auditum*.

Without the least change in his voice, Ireneo bade me come in. He was lying on the cot, smoking. It seems to me that I did not see his face until dawn; I seem to recall the momentary glow of the cigarette. The room smelled vaguely of dampness. I sat down, and repeated the story of the telegram and my father's illness.

I come now to the most difficult point in my narrative. For the entire story has no other point (the reader might as well know it by now) than this dialogue of almost a half-century ago. I shall not attempt to reproduce his words, now irrecoverable. I prefer truthfully to make a résumé of the many things Ireneo told me. The indirect style is remote and weak; I know that I sacrifice the effectiveness of my narrative; but let my readers imagine the nebulous sentences which clouded that night.

Ireneo began by enumerating, in Latin and Spanish, the cases of prodigious memory cited in the *Historia Naturalis:* Cyrus, king of the Persians, who could call every soldier in his armies by name; Mithridates Eupator, who administered justice in the twenty-two languages of his empire; Simonides, inventor of mnemotechny; Metrodorus, who practiced the art of repeating faithfully what he heard once. With evident good faith Funes marveled that such things should be considered marvelous. He told me that previous to the rainy afternoon when the blue-tinted horse threw him, he had been—like any Christian—blind, deaf-mute, somnambulistic, memoryless. (I tried to remind him of his precise perception of time, his memory for proper names; he paid no attention to me). For nineteen years, he said, he had lived like a person in a dream: he looked without seeing, heard without hearing, forgot everything—almost everything. On falling from the horse, he lost consciousness; when he recovered it, the present was almost intolerable it was so rich and bright; the same was true of the most ancient and most trivial memories. A little later he realized that he was crippled. This fact scarcely interested him. He reasoned (or felt) that immobility was a minimum price to pay. And now, his perception and his memory were infallible.

We, in a glance, perceive three wine glasses on the table; Funes saw all the shoots, clusters, and grapes of the vine. He remembered the shapes of the clouds in the south at dawn on the 30th of April of 1882, and he could compare them in his recollection with the marbled grain in the design of a leather-bound book which he had seen only once, and with the lines in the spray which an oar raised in the Rio Negro on the eve of the battle of the Quebracho. These recollections were not simple; each visual image was linked to muscular sensations, thermal sensations, etc. He could reconstruct all his dreams, all his fancies. Two or three times he had reconstructed an entire day. He told me: *I have more memories in myself alone than all men have had since the world was a world.* And again: *My dreams are like your vigils.* And again, toward dawn: *My memory, sir, is like a garbage disposal.*

A circumference on a blackboard, a rectangular triangle, a rhomb, are forms which we can fully intuit; the same held true with Ireneo for the tempestuous mane of a stallion, a herd of cattle in a pass, the ever-changing flame or the innumerable ash, the many faces of a dead man during the course of a protracted wake. He could perceive I do not know how many stars in the sky.

These things he told me; neither then nor at any time later did they seem doubtful. In those days neither the cinema nor the phonograph yet existed; nevertheless, it seems strange, almost incredible, that no one should have experimented on Funes. The truth is that we all live by leaving behind; no doubt we all profoundly know that we are immortal and that sooner or later every man will do all things and know everything.

The voice of Funes, out of the darkness, continued. He told me that toward 1886 he had devised a new system of enumeration and that in a very few days he had gone beyond twenty-four thousand. He had not written it down, for what he once meditated would not be erased. The first stimulus to his work, I believe, had been his discontent with the fact that "thirty-three Uruguayans" required two symbols and three words, rather than a single word and a single symbol. Later he applied his extravagant principle to the other numbers. In place of seven thousand thirteen, he would say (for example) *Máximo Perez*; in place of seven thousand fourteen, *The Train*; other numbers were *Luis Melián Lafinur, Olimar, Brimstone, Clubs, The Whale, Gas, The Cauldron, Napoleon, Agustín de Vedia*. In lieu of five hundred, he would say *nine*. Each word had a particular sign, a species of mark; the last were very complicated. . . . I attempted to explain that this rhapsody of unconnected terms was precisely the contrary of a system of enumeration. I said that to say three hundred and sixty-five was to say three hundreds, six tens, five units: an analysis which does not exist in such numbers as *The Negro Timoteo* or *The Flesh Blanket*. Funes did not understand me, or did not wish to understand me.

Locke, in the seventeenth century, postulated (and rejected) an impossible idiom in which each individual object, each stone, each bird and branch had an individual name; Funes had once projected an analogous idiom, but he had renounced it as being too general, too ambiguous. In effect, Funes not only remembered every leaf on every tree of every wood, but even every one of the times he had perceived or imagined it. He determined to reduce all of his past experience to some seventy thousand recollections, which he would later define numerically. Two considerations dissuaded him: the thought that the task was interminable and the thought that it was useless. He knew that at the hour of his death he would scarcely have finished classifying even all the memories of his childhood.

The two projects I have indicated (an infinite vocabulary for the natural series of numbers, and a usable mental catalogue of all the images of memory) are lacking in sense, but they reveal a certain stammering greatness. They allow us to make out dimly, or to infer, the dizzying world of Funes. He was, let us not forget, almost incapable of general, platonic ideas. It was not only difficult for him to understand that the generic term *dog* embraced so many unlike specimens of differing sizes and different forms; he was disturbed by the fact that a dog at three-fourteen (seen in profile) should have the same name as the dog at three-fifteen (seen from the front). His own face in the mirror, his own hands, surprised him on every occasion. Swift writes that the emperor of Lilliput could discern the movement of the minute hand; Funes could continuously make out the tranquil advances of corruption, of caries, of fatigue. He noted the progress of death, of moisture. He was the solitary and lucid spectator of a multiform world which was instantaneously and almost intolerably exact. Babylon, London, and New York have overawed the imagination of men with their ferocious splendor; no one, in those populous towers or upon those surging avenues, has felt the heat and pressure of a reality as indefatigable as that which day and night converged upon the unfortunate Ireneo in his humble South American farmhouse. It was very difficult for him to sleep. To sleep is to be abstracted from the world; Funes, on his back in his cot, in the shadows, imagined every crevice and every molding of the various houses which surrounded him. (I repeat, the least important of his recollections was more minutely precise and more lively than our perception of a physical pleasure or a physical torment.) Toward the east, in a section which was not yet cut into blocks of homes, there were some new unknown houses. Funes imagined them black, compact, made of a single obscurity; he would turn his face in this direction in order to sleep. He would also imagine himself at the bottom of the river, being rocked and annihilated by the current.

Without effort, he had learned English, French, Portuguese, Latin. I suspect, nevertheless, that he was not very capable of thought. To think is to forget a difference, to generalize, to abstract. In the overly replete world of Funes there were nothing but details, almost contiguous details.

The equivocal clarity of dawn penetrated along the earthen patio.

Then it was that I saw the face of the voice which had spoken all through the night. Ireneo was nineteen years old; he had been born in 1868; he seemed as monumental as bronze, more ancient than Egypt, anterior to the prophecies and the pyramids. It occurred to me that each one of my words (each one of my gestures) would live on in his implacable memory; I was benumbed by the fear of multiplying superfluous gestures.

Ireneo Funes died in 1889, of a pulmonary congestion.

EXERCISES

1. Why is *remember* a "ghostly verb"?
2. What does the narrator mean when he says that the story has no other point than the dialogue?
3. What is meant by the statement that the present was intolerable because it was so rich and bright?
4. What is meant by "We live by leaving behind"?
5. Why is Funes incapable of general ideas?
6. Why is Funes' world intolerable?
7. How is this story a parable of the artist?

HENRY
JAMES | *The Real Thing*

When the porter's wife, who used to answer the house-bell, announced "A gentleman and a lady, sir" I had, as I often had in those days—the wish being father to the thought—an immediate vision of sitters. Sitters my visitors in this case proved to be; but not in the sense I should have preferred. There was nothing at first however to indicate that they mightn't have come for a portrait. The gentleman, a man of fifty, very high and very straight, with a moustache slightly grizzled and a dark grey walking-coat admirably fitted, both of which I noted professionally—I don't mean as a barber or yet as a tailor—would have struck me as a celebrity if celebrities often were striking. It was a truth of which I had for some time been conscious that a figure with a good deal of frontage was, as one might say, almost never a public institution. A glance at the lady helped to remind me of this paradoxical law: she also looked too distinguished to be a "personality." Moreover one would scarcely come across two variations together.

Neither of the pair immediately spoke—they only prolonged the preliminary gaze suggesting that each wished to give the other a chance. They were visibly shy; they stood there letting me take them in—which, as I afterwards perceived, was the most practical thing they could have done. In this way their embarrassment served their cause. I had seen people painfully reluctant to mention that they desired anything so gross as to be represented on canvas; but the scruples of my new friends appeared almost insurmountable. Yet the gentleman might have said "I should like a portrait of my wife," and the lady might have said "I should like a portrait of my husband." Perhaps they weren't husband and wife—this naturally would make the matter more delicate. Perhaps they wished to be done together—in which case they ought to have brought a third person to break the news.

"We come from Mr. Rivet," the lady finally said with a dim smile that had the effect of a moist sponge passing over a "sunk" piece of painting, as well as of a vague allusion to vanished beauty. She was as tall and straight, in her degree, as her companion, and with ten years less to carry. She looked as sad as a woman could look whose face was not charged with expression; that is her tinted oval mask showed waste as an exposed surface shows friction. The hand of time had played over her freely, but to an effect of elimination. She was slim and stiff, and so well-dressed, in dark blue cloth, with lappets and pockets and buttons, that it was clear she employed the same tailor as her husband. The couple had an indefinable air of prosperous thrift—they evidently got a good deal of luxury for their money. If I was to be one of their luxuries it would behove me to consider my terms.

"Ah Claude Rivet recommended me?" I echoed; and I added that it was very kind of him, though I could reflect that, as he only painted landscape, this wasn't a sacrifice.

The lady looked very hard at the gentleman, and the gentleman looked round the room. Then staring at the floor a moment and stroking his moustache, he rested his pleasant eyes on me with the remark: "He said you were the right one."

"I try to be, when people want to sit."

"Yes, we should like to," said the lady anxiously.

"Do you mean together?"

My visitors exchanged a glance. "If you could do anything with *me* I suppose it would be double," the gentleman stammered.

"Oh yes, there's naturally a higher charge for two figures than for one."

"We should like to make it pay," the husband confessed.

"That's very good of you," I returned, appreciating so unwonted a sympathy—for I supposed he meant pay the artist.

A sense of strangeness seemed to dawn on the lady.

"We mean for the illustrations—Mr. Rivet said you might put one in."

"Put in—an illustration?" I was equally confused.

"Sketch her off, you know," said the gentleman, colouring.

It was only then that I understood the service Claude Rivet had rendered me; he had told them how I worked in black-and-white, for magazines, for storybooks, for sketches of contemporary life, and consequently had copious employment for models. These things were true, but it was not less true—I may confess it now; whether because the aspiration was to lead to everything or to nothing I leave the reader to guess—that I couldn't get the honours, to say nothing of the emoluments, of a great painter of portraits out of my head. My "illustrations" were my pot-boilers; I looked to a different branch of art— far and away the most interesting it had always seemed to me—to perpetuate my fame. There was no shame in looking to it also to make my fortune; but that fortune was by so much further from being made from the moment my visitors wished to be "done" for nothing. I was disappointed; for in the pictorial sense I had immediately *seen* them. I had seized their type—I had already settled what I would do with it. Something that wouldn't absolutely have pleased them, I afterwards reflected.

"Ah, you're—you're—a—?" I began as soon as I had mastered my surprise. I couldn't bring out the dingy word "models": it seemed so little to fit the case.

"We haven't had much practice," said the lady.

"We've got to *do* something, and we've thought that an artist in your line might perhaps make something of us," her husband threw off. He further mentioned that they didn't know many artists and that they had gone first, on the off-chance—he painted views of course, but sometimes put in figures; perhaps I remembered—to Mr. Rivet, whom they had met a few years before at a place in Norfolk where he was sketching.

"We used to sketch a little ourselves," the lady hinted.

"It's very awkward, but we absolutely *must* do something," her husband went on.

"Of course we're not so *very* young," she admitted with a wan smile.

With the remark that I might as well know something more about them the husband had handed me a card extracted from a neat new pocket-book— their appurtenances were all the freshest—and inscribed with the words "Major Monarch." Impressive as these words were they didn't carry my knowledge much further; but my visitor presently added: "I've left the army and we've had the misfortune to lose our money. In fact our means are dreadfully small."

"It's awfully trying—a regular strain," said Mrs. Monarch.

They evidently wished to be discreet—to take care not to swagger because they were gentlefolk. I felt them willing to recognize this as something of a drawback, at the same time that I guessed at an underlying sense—their consolation in adversity—that they *had* their points. They certainly had; but these advantages struck me as preponderantly social; such for instance as would help to make a drawing-room look well. However, a drawing-room was always, or ought to be, a picture.

In consequence of his wife's allusion to their age Major Monarch observed: "Naturally it's more for the figure that we thought of going in. We can still hold ourselves up." On the instant I saw that the figure was indeed their strong point. His "naturally" didn't sound vain, but it lighted up the question. "*She* has the best one," he continued, nodding at his wife with a pleasant after-dinner absence of circumlocution. I could only reply, as if we were in fact sitting over our wine, that this didn't prevent his own from being very good; which led him in turn to make answer: "We thought that if you ever had to do people like us we might be something like it. *She* particularly—for a lady in a book, you know."

I was so amused by them that, to get more of it, I did my best to take their point of view; and though it was an embarrassment to find myself appraising physically, as if they were animals on hire or useful blacks, a pair whom I should have expected to meet only in one of the relations in which criticism is tacit, I looked at Mrs. Monarch judicially enough to be able to exclaim after a moment with conviction: "Oh yes, a lady in a book!" She was singularly like a bad illustration.

"We'll stand up, if you like," said the Major; and he raised himself before me with a really grand air.

I could take his measure at a glance—he was six feet two and a perfect gentleman. It would have paid any club in process of formation and in want of a stamp to engage him at a salary to stand in the principal window. What struck me at once was that in coming to me they had rather missed their vocation; they could surely have been turned to better account for advertising purposes. I couldn't of course see the thing in detail, but I could see them make somebody's fortune—I don't mean their own. There was something in them for a waistcoat-maker, an hotel-keeper or a soap-vendor. I could imagine "We always use it" pinned on their bosoms with the greatest effect; I had a vision of the brilliancy with which they would launch a table d'hôte.

Mrs. Monarch sat still, not from pride but from shyness, and presently her husband said to her: "Get up, my dear, and show how smart you are." She obeyed, but she had no need to get up to show it. She walked to the end of the studio and then came back blushing, her fluttered eyes on the partner of her appeal. I was reminded of an incident I had accidentally had a glimpse of in Paris being with a friend there, a dramatist about to produce a play, when an actress came to him to ask to be entrusted with a part. She went through her paces before him, walked up and down as Mrs. Monarch was doing. Mrs. Monarch did it quite as well, but I abstained from applauding. It was very odd to see such people apply for such poor pay. She looked as if she had ten thousand a year. Her husband had used the word that described her: she was in the London current jargon essentially and typically "smart." Her figure was, in the same order of ideas, conspicuously and irreproachably "good." For a woman of her age her waist was surprisingly small; her elbow moreover had the orthodox crook. She held her head at the conventional angle, but why did she come to *me*? She ought to have tried on jackets at a big shop. I feared my visitors were not only destitute but "artistic"—which would be a great complication. When she sat down again I thanked her, observing that what a draughtsman most valued in his model was the faculty of keeping quiet.

"Oh *she* can keep quiet," said Major Monarch. Then he added jocosely: "I've always kept her quiet."

"I'm not a nasty fidget, am I?" It was going to wring tears from me, I felt, the way she hid her head, ostrich-like, in the other broad bosom.

The owner of this expanse addressed his answer to me. "Perhaps it isn't out of place to mention—because we ought to be quite business-like, oughtn't we?—that when I married her she was known as the Beautiful Statue."

"Oh dear!" said Mrs. Monarch ruefully.

"Of course I should want a certain amount of expression," I rejoined.

"Of *course!*"—and I had never heard such unanimity.

"And then I suppose you know that you'll get awfully tired."

"Oh we *never* get tired!" they eagerly cried.

"Have you had any kind of practice?"

They hesitated—they looked at each other. "We've been photographed—*immensely*," said Mrs. Monarch.

"She means the fellows have asked us themselves," added the Major.

"I see—because you're so good-looking."

"I don't know what they thought, but they were always after us."

"We always got our photographs for nothing," smiled Mrs. Monarch.

"We might have brought some, my dear," her husband remarked.

"I'm not sure we have any left. We've given quantities away," she explained to me.

"With our autographs and that sort of thing," said the Major.

"Are they to be got in the shops?" I enquired as a harmless pleasantry.

"Oh yes, *hers*—they used to be."

"Not now," said Mrs. Monarch with her eyes on the floor.

II

I could fancy the "sort of thing" they put on the presentation copies of their photographs, and I was sure they wrote a beautiful hand. It was odd how quickly I was sure of everything that concerned them. If they were now so poor as to have to earn shillings and pence they could never have had much of a margin. Their good looks had been their capital, and they had good-humouredly made the most of the career that this resource marked out for them. It was in their faces, the blankness, the deep intellectual repose of the twenty years of country-house visiting that had given them pleasant intonations. I could see the sunny drawing-rooms, sprinkled with periodicals she didn't read, in which Mrs. Monarch had continuously sat; I could see the wet shrubberies in which she had walked, equipped to admiration for either exercise. I could see the rich covers the Major had helped to shoot and the wonderful garments in which, late at night, he repaired to the smoking-room to talk about them. I could imagine their leggings and waterproofs, their knowing tweeds and rugs, their rolls of sticks and cases of tackle and neat umbrellas; and I could evoke the exact appearance of their servants and the compact variety of their luggage on the platforms of country stations.

They gave small tips, but they were liked; they didn't do anything themselves, but they were welcome. They looked so well everywhere; they gratified the general relish for stature, complexion and "form." They knew it without fatuity or vulgarity, and they respected themselves in consequence. They weren't superficial; they were thorough and kept themselves up—it had been their line. People with such a taste for activity had to have some line. I could feel how even in a dull house they could have been counted on for the joy of life. At present something had happened—it didn't matter what, their little income had grown less, it had grown least—and they had to do something for pocket-money. Their friends could like them, I made out, without liking to support them. There was something about them that represented credit—their clothes, their manners, their type; but if credit is a large empty pocket in which an occasional chink reverberates, the chink at least must be audible. What they wanted of me was to help to make it so. Fortunately they had no children—I soon divined that. They would also perhaps wish our relations to be kept secret: this was why it was "for the figure"—the reproduction of the face would betray them.

I liked them—I felt, quite as their friends must have done—they were so simple; and I had no objection to them if they would suit. But somehow with all their perfections I didn't easily believe in them. After all they were amateurs, and the ruling passion of my life was the detestation of the amateur. Combined with this was another perversity—an innate preference for the represented subject over the real one: the defect of the real one was so apt to be a lack of representation. I like things that appeared; then one was sure. Whether they *were* or not was a subordinate and almost always a profitless question. There were other considerations, the first of which was that I already had two or three recruits in use, notably a young person with big feet, in alpaca, from Kilburn, who for a couple of years had come to me regularly for my illustrations and with whom I was still—perhaps ignobly—satisfied. I frankly explained to my visitors how the case stood, but they had taken more precautions than I supposed. They had reasoned out their opportunity, for Claude Rivet had told them of the projected *édition de luxe*—of one of the writers of our day—the rarest of the novelists—who, long neglected by the multitudinous vulgar and dearly prized by the attentive (need I mention Philip Vincent?) had had the happy fortune of seeing, late in life, the dawn and then the full light of a higher criticism; an estimate in which on the part of the public there was something really of expiation. The edition preparing, planned by a publisher of taste, was practically an act of high reparation; the woodcuts with which it was to be enriched were the homage of English art to one of the most independent representatives of English letters. Major and Mrs. Monarch confessed to me they had hoped I might be able to work *them* into my branch of the enterprise. They knew I was to do the first of the books, "Rutland Ramsey," but I had to make clear to them that my participation in the rest of the affair—this first book was to be a test—must depend on the satisfaction I should give. If this should be limited my employers would drop me with scarce common forms. It was therefore a crisis for me, and naturally I was making special preparations, looking about for new people, should they be necessary, and securing the best types. I admitted however that I should like to settle down to two or three good models who would do for everything.

"Should we have often to—a—put on special clothes?" Mrs. Monarch timidly demanded.

"Dear yes—that's half the business."

"And should we be expected to supply our own costumes?"

"Oh no; I've got a lot of things. A painter's models put on—or put off—anything he likes."

"And you mean—a—the same?"

"The same?"

Mrs. Monarch looked at her husband again.

"Oh she was just wondering," he explained, "if the costumes are in *general* use." I had to confess that they were, and I mentioned further that some of them—I had a lot of genuine greasy last-century things—had served their time, a hundred years ago, on living world-stained men and women; on figures not perhaps so far removed, in that vanished world, from *their* type, the Monarchs', *quoi!* of a breeched and bewigged age. "We'll put on anything that *fits*," said the Major.

"Oh I arrange that—they fit in the pictures."

"I'm afraid I should do better for the modern books. I'd come as you like," said Mrs. Monarch.

"She has a got a lot of clothes at home: they might do for contemporary life," her husband continued.

"Oh I can fancy scenes in which you'd be quite natural." And indeed I could see the slipshod rearrangements of stale properties—the stories I tried to produce pictures for without the exasperation of reading them—whose sandy tracts the good lady might help to people. But I had to return to the fact that for this sort of work—the daily mechanical grind—I was already equipped: the people I was working with were fully adequate.

"We only thought we might be more like *some* characters," said Mrs. Monarch mildly, getting up.

Her husband also rose; he stood looking at me with a dim wistfulness that was touching in so fine a man.

"Wouldn't it be rather a pull sometimes to have—a—to have—?" He hung fire; he wanted me to help him by phrasing what he meant. But I couldn't—I didn't know. So he brought it out awkwardly: "The *real* thing; a gentleman, you know, or a lady." I was quite ready to give a general assent— I admitted that there was a great deal in that. This encouraged Major Monarch to say, following up his appeal with an unacted gulp: "It's awfully hard— we've tried everything." The gulp was communicative; it proved to be too much for his wife. Before I knew Mrs. Monarch had dropped again upon a divan and burst into tears. Her husband sat down beside her, holding one of her hands; whereupon she quickly dried her eyes with the other, while I felt embarrassed as she looked up at me. "There isn't a confounded job I haven't applied for—waited for—prayed for. You can fancy we'd be pretty bad first. Secretaryships and that sort of thing? You might as well ask for a peerage. I'd be *anything*—I'm strong; a messenger or a coalheaver. I'd put on a gold-laced cap and open carriage-doors in front of the haberdasher's; I'd hang about a station to carry portmanteaux; I'd be a postman. But they won't *look* at you; there are thousands as good as yourself already on the ground. *Gentlemen,* poor beggars, who've drunk their wine, who've kept their hunters!"

I was as reassuring as I knew how to be, and my visitors were presently on their feet again while, for the experiment, we agreed on an hour. We were discussing it when the door opened and Miss Churm came in with a wet umbrella. Miss Churm had to take the omnibus to Maida Vale and then walk half a mile. She looked a trifle blowsy and slightly splashed. I scarcely ever saw her come in without thinking fresh how odd it was that, being so little in herself, she should yet be so much in others. She was a meagre little Miss Churm, but was such an ample heroine of romance. She was only a freckled cockney, but she could represent everything, from a fine lady to a shepherdess; she had the faculty as she might have had a fine voice or long hair. She couldn't spell and she loved beer, but she had two or three "points," and practice, and a knack, and mother-wit, and a whimsical sensibility, and a love of the theatre, and seven sisters, and not an ounce of respect, especially for the *h*. The first thing my visitors saw was that her umbrella was wet, and in their spotless perfection they visibly winced at it. The rain had come on since their arrival.

"I'm all in a soak; there *was* a mess of people in the 'bus. I wish you lived near a stytion," said Miss Churm. I requested her to get ready as quickly as possible, and she passed into the room in which she always changed her dress. But before going out she asked me what she was to get into this time.

"It's the Russian princess, don't you know?" I answered; "The one with the 'golden eyes,' in black velvet, for the long thing in the *Cheapside*."

"Golden eyes! I *say!*" cried Miss Churm, while my companions watched her with intensity as she withdrew. She always arranged herself, when she was late, before I could turn around; and I kept my visitors a little on purpose, so that they might get an idea, from seeing her, what would be expected of themselves. I mentioned that she was quite my notion of an excellent model—she was really very clever.

"Do you think she looks like a Russian princess?" Major Monarch asked with lurking alarm.

"When I make her, yes."

"Oh if you have to *make* her—!" he reasoned, not without point.

"That's the most you can ask. There are so many who are not makeable."

"Well now, *here's* a lady"—and with a persuasive smile he passed his arm into his wife's—"who's already made!"

"Oh I'm not a Russian princess," Mrs. Monarch protested a little coldly. I could see she had known some and didn't like them. There at once was a complication of a kind I never had to fear with Miss Churm.

This young lady came back in black velvet—the gown was rather rusty and very low on her lean shoulders—and with a Japanese fan in her red hands. I reminded her that in the scene I was doing she had to look over some one's head. "I forgot whose it is; but it doesn't matter. Just look over a head."

"I'd rather look over a stove," said Miss Churm; and she took her station near the fire. She fell into position, settled herself into a tall attitude, gave a certain backward inclination to her head and a certain forward droop to her fan, and looked, at least to my prejudiced sense, distinguished and charming, foreign and dangerous. We left her looking so while I went downstairs with Major and Mrs. Monarch.

"I believe I could come about as near it as that," said Mrs. Monarch.

"Oh, you think she's shabby, but you must allow for the alchemy of art."

However, they went off with an evident increase of comfort founded on their demonstrable advantage in being the real thing. I could fancy them shuddering over Miss Churm. She was very droll about them when I went back, for I told her what they wanted.

"Well, if *she* can sit I'll tyke to bookkeeping," said my model.

"She's very ladylike," I replied as an innocent form of aggravation.

"So much the worse for *you*. That means she can't turn round."

"She'll do for the fashionable novels."

"Oh yes, she'll *do* for them!" my model humorously declared.

"Ain't they bad enough without her?" I had often sociably denounced them to Miss Churm.

III

It was for the elucidation of a mystery in one of these works that I first tried Mrs. Monarch. Her husband came with her, to be useful if necessary—it was sufficiently clear that as a general thing he would prefer to come with her. At first I wondered if this were for "propriety's" sake—if he were going to be jealous and meddling. The idea was too tiresome, and if it had been confirmed it would speedily have brought our acquaintance to a close. But I soon saw there was nothing in it and that if he accompanied Mrs. Monarch it was—in addition to the chance of being wanted—simply because he had nothing else to do. When they were separate his occupation was gone and they never *had* been separate. I judged rightly that in their awkward situation their close union was their main comfort and that this union had no weak spot. It was a real marriage, an encouragement to the hesitating, a nut for pessimists to crack. Their address was humble—I remember afterwards thinking it had been the only thing about them that was really professional—and I could fancy the lamentable lodgings in which the Major would have been left alone. He could sit there more or less grimly with his wife—he couldn't sit there anyhow without her.

He had too much tact to try and make himself agreeable when he couldn't be useful; so when I was too absorbed in my work to talk he simply sat and waited. But I liked to hear him talk—it made my work, when not interrupting it, less mechanical, less special. To listen to him was to combine the excitement of going out with the economy of staying at home. There was only one hindrance—that I seemed not to know any of the people this brilliant couple had known. I think he wondered extremely, during the term of our intercourse, whom the deuce I *did* know. He hadn't a stray sixpence of an idea to fumble for, so we didn't spin it very fine; we confined ourselves to questions of leather and even liquor—saddlers and breeches-makers and how to get excellent claret cheap—and matters like "good trains" and the habits of small game. His lore on these last subjects was astonishing—he managed to interweave the station-master with the ornithologist. When he couldn't talk about greater things he could talk cheerfully about smaller, and since I couldn't accompany him into reminiscences of the fashionable world he could lower the conversation without a visible effort to my level.

So earnest a desire to please was touching in a man who could so easily have knocked one down. He looked after the fire and had an opinion on the draught of the stove without my asking him, and I could see that he thought many of my arrangements not half knowing. I remember telling him that if I were only rich I'd offer him a salary to come and teach me how to live. Sometimes he gave a random sigh of which the essence might have been: "Give me even such a bare old barrack as *this,* and I'd do something with it!" When I wanted to use him he came alone; which was an illustration of the superior courage of women. His wife could bear her solitary second floor, and she was in general more discreet; showing by various small reserves that she was alive to the propriety of keeping our relations markedly professional—not letting them slide into sociability. She wished it to remain clear that she and the Major were employed, not cultivated, and if she approved of me as a superior, who could be kept in his place, she never thought me quite good enough for an equal.

She sat with great intensity, giving the whole of her mind to it, and was capable of remaining for an hour almost as motionless as before a photographer's lens. I could see she had been photographed often, but somehow the very habit that made her good for that purpose unfitted her for mine. At first I was extremely pleased with her ladylike air, and it was a satisfaction, on coming to follow her lines, to see how good they were and how far they could lead the pencil. But after a little skirmishing I began to find her too insurmountably stiff; do what I would with it my drawing looked like a photograph or a copy of a photograph. Her figure had no variety of expression—she herself had no sense of variety. You may say that this was my business and was only a question of placing her. Yet I placed her in every conceivable position and she managed to obliterate their differences. She was always a lady certainly, and into the bargain was always the same lady. She was the real thing, but always the same thing. There were moments when I rather writhed under the serenity of her confidence that she *was* the real thing. All her dealings with me and all her husband's were an implication that this was lucky for *me*. Meanwhile I found myself trying to invent types that approached her own, instead of making her own transform itself—in the clever way that was not impossible for instance to poor Miss Churm. Arrange as I would and take the precautions I would, she always came out, in my pictures, too tall—landing me in the dilemma of having represented a fascinating woman as seven feet high, which (out of respect perhaps to my own very much scantier inches) was far from my idea of such personage.

The case was worse with the Major—nothing I could do would keep *him* down, so that he became useful only for the representation of brawny giants. I adored variety and range, I cherished human accidents, the illustrative note; I wanted to characterise closely, and the thing in the world I most hated was the danger of being ridden by a type. I had quarrelled with some of my friends about it; I had parted company with them for maintaining that one *had* to be, and that if the type was beautiful—witness Raphael and Leonardo—the servitude was only a gain. I was neither Leonardo nor Raphael—I might only be a presumptuous young modern searcher; but I held that everything was to be sacrificed sooner than character. When they claimed that the obsessional form could easily *be* character I retorted, perhaps superficially, "Whose?" It couldn't be everybody's—it might end in being nobody's.

After I had drawn Mrs. Monarch a dozen times I felt surer even than before that the value of such a model as Miss Churm resided precisely in the fact that she had no positive stamp, combined of course with the other fact that what she did have was a curious and inexplicable talent for imitation. Her usual appearance was like a curtain which she could draw up at request for a capital performance. This performance was simply suggestive; but it was a word to the wise—it was vivid and pretty. Sometimes even I thought it, though she was plain herself, too insipidly pretty; I made it a reproach to her that the figures drawn from her were monotonously *(bêtement*, as we used to say*)* graceful. Nothing made her more angry: it was so much her pride to feel she could sit for characters that had nothing in common with each other. She would accuse me at such moments of taking away her "reputytion."

It suffered a certain shrinkage, this queer quantity, from the repeated visits of my new friends. Miss Churm was greatly in demand, never in want of employment, so I had no scruple in putting her off occasionally, to try them more at my ease. It was certainly amusing at first to do the real thing—it was amusing to do Major Monarch's trousers. They *were* the real thing, even if he did come out colossal. It was amusing to do his wife's back hair—it was so mathematically neat—and the particular "smart" tension of her tight stays. She lent herself especially to positions in which the face was somewhat averted or blurred; she abounded in ladylike back views and *profils perdus*. When she stood erect she took naturally one of the attitudes in which court-painters represent queens and princesses; so that I found myself wondering whether, to draw out this accomplishment, I couldn't get the editor of the *Cheapside* to publish a really royal romance, "A Tale of Buckingham Palace." Sometimes however the real thing and the make-believe came into contact; by which I mean that Miss Churm, keeping an appointment or coming to make one on days when I had much work in hand, encountered her invidious rivals. The encounter was not on their part, for they noticed her no more than if she had been the housemaid; not from intentional loftiness, but simply because as yet, professionally, they didn't know how to fraternise, as I could imagine they would have liked—or at least that the Major would. They couldn't talk about the omnibus—they always walked; and they didn't know what else to try— she wasn't interested in good trains or cheap claret. Besides, they must have felt—in the air—that she was amused at them, secretly derisive of their ever knowing how. She wasn't a person to conceal the limits of her faith if she had had a chance to show them. On the other hand Mrs. Monarch didn't think her tidy; for why else did she take pains to say to me—it was going out of the way, for Mrs. Monarch—that she didn't like dirty women?

One day when my young lady happened to be present with my other sitters—she even dropped in, when it was convenient, for a chat—I asked her to be so good as to lend a hand in getting tea, a service with which she was familiar and which was one of a class that, living as I did in a small way, with slender domestic resources, I often appealed to my models to render. They liked to lay hands on my property, to break the sitting, and sometimes the china—it made them feel Bohemian. The next time I saw Miss Churm after this incident she surprised me greatly by making a scene about it—she accused me of having wished to humiliate her. She hadn't resented the outrage at the time, but had seemed obliging and amused, enjoying the comedy of asking Mrs. Monarch, who sat vague and silent, whether she would have cream and sugar, and putting an exaggerated simper into the question. She had tried intonations—as if she too wished to pass for the real thing—till I was afraid my other visitors would take offence.

Oh they were determined not to do this, and their touching patience was the measure of their great need. They would sit by the hour, uncomplaining, till I was ready to use them; they would come back on the chance of being wanted and would walk away cheerfully if it failed. I used to go to the door with them to see in what magnificent order they retreated. I tried to find other employment for them—I introduced them to several artists. But they didn't "take," for reasons I could appreciate, and I became rather anxiously aware that after such disappointments they fell back upon me with a heavier weight. They did me the honor to think me most *their* form. They weren't romantic enough for the painters, and in those days there were few serious workers in black-and-white. Besides, they had an eye to the great job I had mentioned to them—they had secretly set their hearts on supplying the right essence for my pictorial vindication of our fine novelist. They knew that for this undertaking I should want no costume-effects, none of the frippery of past ages—that it was a case in which everything would be contemporary and satirical and presumably genteel. If I could work them into it their future would be assured, for the labour would of course be long and the occupation steady.

One day Mrs. Monarch came without her husband—she explained his absence by his having had to go to the City. While she sat there in her usual relaxed majesty there came at the door a knock which I immediately recognised as the subdued appeal of a model out of work. It was followed by the entrance of a young man whom I at once saw to be a foreigner and who proved in fact an Italian acquainted with no English word but my name, which he uttered in a way that made it seem to include all others. I hadn't then visited his country, nor was I proficient in his tongue; but as he was not so meanly constituted—what Italian is?—as to depend only on that member for expression he conveyed to me, in familiar but graceful mimicry, that he was in search of exactly the employment in which the lady before me was engaged. I was not struck with him at first, and while I continued to draw I dropped few signs of interest or encouragement. He stood his ground however—not importunately, but with a dumb dog-like fidelity in his eyes that amounted to innocent impudence, the manner of a devoted servant—he might have been in the house for years—unjustly suspected. Suddenly it struck me that this very attitude and expression made a picture; whereupon I told him to sit down and wait till I should be free. There was another picture in the way he obeyed me, and I observed as I worked that there were others still in the way he looked wonderingly, with his head thrown back, about the high studio. He might have been crossing himself in Saint Peter's. Before I finished I said to myself "The fellow's a bankrupt orangemonger, but a treasure."

When Mrs. Monarch withdrew he passed across the room like a flash to open the door for her, standing there with the rapt pure gaze of the young Dante spellbound by the young Beatrice. As I never insisted, in such situations, on the blankness of the British domestic, I reflected that he had the making of a servant—and I needed one, but couldn't pay him to be only that—as well as of a model; in short I resolved to adopt my bright adventurer if he would agree to officiate in the double capacity. He jumped at my offer, and in the event my rashness—for I had really known nothing about him—wasn't brought home to me. He proved a sympathetic though a desultory ministrant, and had in a wonderful degree the *sentiment de la pose*. It was uncultivated, instinctive, a part of the happy instinct that had guided him to my door and helped him to spell out my name on the card nailed to it. He had had no other introduction to me than a guess, from the shape of my high north window, seen outside, that my place was a studio and that as a studio it would contain an artist. He had wandered to England in search of fortune, like other itinerants, and had embarked, with a partner and a small green hand-cart, on the sale of penny ices. The ices had melted away and the partner had dissolved in their train. My young man wore tight yellow trousers with reddish stripes and his name was Oronte. He was sallow but fair, and when I put him into some old clothes of my own he looked like an Englishman. He was as good as Miss Churm, who could look, when requested, like an Italian.

IV

I thought Mrs. Monarch's face slightly convulsed when, on her coming back with her husband, she found Oronte installed. It was strange to have to recognise in a scrap of a lazzarone a competitor to her magnificent Major. It was she who scented danger first, for the Major was anecdotically unconscious. But Oronte gave us tea, with a hundred eager confusions—he had never been concerned in so queer a process—and I think she thought better of me for having at last an "establishment." They saw a couple of drawings that I had made of the establishment, and Mrs. Monarch hinted that it never would have struck her he had sat for them. "Now the drawings you make from *us,* they look exactly like us," she reminded me, smiling in triumph; and I recognized that this was indeed just their defect. When I drew the Monarchs I couldn't anyhow get away from them—get into the character I wanted to represent; and I hadn't the least desire my model should be discoverable in my picture. Miss Churm never was, and Mrs. Monarch thought I hid her, very properly, because she was vulgar; whereas if she was lost it was only as the dead who got to heaven are lost—in the gain of an angel the more.

By this time I had got a certain start with "Rutland Ramsay," the first novel in the great projected series; that is I had produced a dozen drawings, several with the help of the Major and his wife, and I had sent them in for approval. My understanding with the publishers, as I have already hinted, had been that I was to be left to do my work, in this particular case, as I liked, with the whole book committed to me; but my connexion with the rest of the series was only contingent. There were moments when, frankly, it *was* a comfort to have the real thing under one's hand; for there were characters in "Rutland Ramsay" that were very much like it. There were people presumably as erect as the Major and women of as good a fashion as Mrs. Monarch. There was a great deal of country-house life—treated, it is true, in a fine fanciful ironical generalised way—and there was a considerable implication of knickerbockers and kilts. There were certain things I had to settle at the outset; such things for instance as the exact appearance of the hero and the particular bloom and figure of the heroine. The author of course gave me a lead, but there was a margin for interpretation. I took the Monarchs into my confidence, I told them frankly what I was about, I mentioned my embarrassments and alternatives. "Oh take *him!*" Mrs. Monarch murmured sweetly, looking at her husband; and "What could you want better than my wife?" the Major enquired with the comfortable candour that now prevailed between us.

I wasn't obliged to answer these remarks—I was only obliged to place my sitters. I wasn't easy in mind, and I postponed a little timidly perhaps the solving of my question. The book was a large canvas, the other figures were numerous, and I worked off at first some of the episodes in which the hero and the heroine were not concerned. When once I had set *them* up I should have to stick to them—I couldn't make my young man seven feet high in one place and five feet nine in another. I inclined on the whole to the latter measurement, though the Major more than once reminded me that *he* looked about as young as any one. It was indeed quite possible to arrange him, for the figure, so that it would have been difficult to detect his age. After the spontaneous Oronte had been with me a month, and after I had given him to understand several times over that his native exuberance would presently constitute an insurmountable barrier to our further intercourse, I waked to a sense of his heroic capacity. He was only five feet seven, but the remaining inches were latent. I tried him almost secretly at first for I was really rather afraid of the judgment my other models would pass on such a choice. If they regarded Miss Churm as little better than a snare what would they think of the representation by a person so little the real thing as an Italian street-vendor of a protagonist formed by a public school?

If I went a little in fear of them it wasn't because they bullied me, because they had got an oppressive foothold, but because in their really pathetic decorum and mysteriously permanent newness they counted on me so intensely. I was therefore very glad when Jack Hawley came home: he was always of such good counsel. He painted badly himself, but there was no one like him for putting his finger on the place. He had been absent from England for a year; he had been somewhere—I don't remember where—to get a fresh eye. I was in a good deal of dread of any such organ, but we were old friends; he had been away for months and a sense of emptiness was creeping into my life. I hadn't dodged a missile for a year.

He came back with a fresh eye, but with the same old black velvet blouse, and the first evening he spent in my studio we smoked cigarettes till the small hours. He had done no work himself, he had only got the eye; so the field was clear for the production of my little things. He wanted to see what I had produced for the *Cheapside,* but he was disappointed in the exhibition. That at least seemed the meaning of two or three comprehensive groans which, as he lounged on my big divan, his leg folded under him, looking at my latest drawings, issued from his lips with the smoke of the cigarette.

"What's the matter with you?" I asked.

"What's the matter with *you?*"

"Nothing save that I'm mystified."

"You are indeed. You're quite off the hinge. What's the meaning of this new fad?" And he tossed me, with the visible irreverence, a drawing in which I happened to have depicted both my elegant models. I asked if he didn't think it good, and he replied that it struck him as execrable, given the sort of thing I had always represented myself to him as wishing to arrive at; but I let that pass—I was so anxious to see exactly what he meant. The two figures in the picture looked colossal, but I supposed this was *not* what he meant, inasmuch as, for aught he knew to the contrary, I might have been trying for some such effect. I maintained that I was working exactly in the same way as when he last had done me the honour to tell me I might do something some day. "Well, there's a screw loose somewhere," he answered; "wait a bit and I'll discover it." I depended upon him to do so: where else was the fresh eye? But he produced at last nothing more luminous than "I don't know—I don't like your types." This was lame for a critic who had never consented to discuss with me anything but the question of execution, the direction of strokes and the mystery of values.

"In the drawings you've been looking at I think my types are very handsome."

"Oh they won't do!"

"I've been working with new models."

"I see you have. *They* won't do."

"Are you very sure of that?"

"Absolutely—they're stupid."

"You mean *I* am—for I ought to get round that."

"You *can't*—with such people. Who are they?"

I told him, so far as was necessary, and he concluded heartlessly:

"Ce sont des gens qu'il faut mettre à la porte."

"You've never seen them; they're awfully good"—I flew to their defence.

"Not seen them? Why all this recent work of yours drops to pieces with them. It's all I want to see of them."

"No one else has said anything against it—the *Cheapside* people are pleased."

"Every one else is an ass, and the *Cheapside* people the biggest asses of all. Come, don't pretend at this time of day to have pretty illusions about the public, especially about publishers and editors. It's not for *such* animals you work—it's for those who know, *coloro che sanno;* so keep straight for *me* if you can't keep straight for yourself. There was a certain sort of thing you used to try for—and a very good thing it was. But this twaddle isn't *in* it." When I talked with Hawley later about "Rutland Ramsay" and its possible successors he declared that I must get back into my boat again or I should go to the bottom. His voice in short was the voice of warning.

I noted the warning, but I didn't turn my friends out of doors. They bored me a good deal; but the very fact that they bored me admonished me not to sacrifice them—if there was anything to be done with them—simply to irritation. As I look back at this phase they seem to me to have pervaded my life not a little. I have a vision of them as most of the time in my studio, seated against the wall on an old velvet bench to be out of the way, and resembling the while a pair of patient courtiers in a royal ante-chamber. I'm convinced that during the coldest weeks of the winter they held their ground because it saved them fire. Their newness was losing its gloss, and it was impossible not to feel them objects of charity. Whenever Miss Churm arrived they went away, and after I was fairly launched in "Rutland Ramsey" Miss Churm arrived pretty often. They managed to express to me tacitly that they supposed I wanted her for the low life of the book, and I let them suppose it, since they had attempted to study the work—it was lying about the studio—without discovering that it dealt only with the highest circles. They had dipped into the most brilliant of our novelists without deciphering many passages. I still took an hour from them, now and again, in spite of Jack Hawley's warning: it would be time enough to dismiss them, if dismissal should be necessary, when the rigour of the season was over. Hawley had made their acquaintance—he had met them at my fireside—and thought them a ridiculous pair. Learning that he was a painter they tried to approach him, to show him too that they were the real thing; but he looked at them, across the big room, as if they were miles away: they were a compendium of everything he most objected to in the social system of his country. Such people as that, all convention and patent-leather, with ejaculations that stopped conversation, had no business in a studio. A studio was a place to learn to see, and how could you see through a pair of feather-beds?

The main inconvenience I suffered at their hands was that at first I was shy of letting it break upon them that my artful little servant had begun to sit for me for "Rutland Ramsay." They knew I had been odd enough—they were prepared by this time to allow oddity to artists—to pick a foreign vagabond out of the streets when I might have had a person with whiskers and credentials; but it was some time before they learned how high I rated his accomplishments. They found him in an attitude more than once, but they never doubted I was doing him as an organ-grinder. There were several things they never guessed, and one of them was that for a striking scene in the novel, in which a footman briefly figured, it occurred to me to make use of Major Monarch as the menial. I kept putting this off, I didn't like to ask him to don the livery—besides the difficulty of finding a livery to fit him. At last, one day late in the winter, when I was at work on the despised Oronte, who caught one's idea on the wing, and was in the glow of feeling myself go very straight, they came in, the Major and his wife, with their society laugh about nothing (there was less and less to laugh at); came on like country-callers—they always reminded me of that—who have walked across the park after church and are presently persuaded to stay to luncheon. Luncheon was over, but they could stay to tea—I knew they wanted it. The fit was on me, however, and I couldn't let my ardour cool and my work wait, with the fading daylight, while my model prepared it. So I asked Mrs. Monarch if she would mind laying it out— a request which for an instant brought all the blood to her face. Her eyes were on her husband's for a second, and some mute telegraphy passed between them. Their folly was over the next instant; his cheerful shrewdness put an end to it. So far from pitying their wounded pride, I must add, I was moved to give it as complete a lesson as I could. They bustled about together and got out the cups and saucers and made the kettle boil. I know they felt as if they were waiting on my servant, and when the tea was prepared I said: "He'll have a cup, please—he's tired." Mrs. Monarch brought him one where he stood, and he took it from her, as if he had been a gentleman at a party squeezing a crush-hat with an elbow.

Then it came over me that she had made a great effort for me—made it with a kind of nobleness—and that I owed her a compensation. Each time I saw her after this I wondered what the compensation could be. I couldn't go on doing the wrong thing to oblige them. Oh it *was* the wrong thing, the stamp of the work for which they sat—Hawley was not the only person to say it now. I sent in a large number of drawings I had made for "Rutland Ramsay," and I received a warning that was more to the point than Hawley's. The artistic adviser of the house for which I was working was of opinion that many of my illustrations were not what had been looked for. Most of these illustrations were the subjects in which the Monarchs had figured. Without going into the question of what *had* been looked for, I had to face the fact that at this rate I shouldn't get the other books to do. I hurled myself in despair on Miss Churm—I put her through all her paces. I not only adopted Oronte publicly as my hero, but one morning when the Major looked in to see if I didn't require him to finish a *Cheapside* figure for which he had begun to sit the week before, I told him I had changed my mind—I'd do the drawing from my man. At this my visitor turned pale and stood looking at me. "Is *he* your idea of an English gentleman?" he asked.

I was disappointed, I was nervous, I wanted to get on with my work; so I replied with irritation: "Oh my dear Major—I can't be ruined for *you!*"

It was a horrid speech, but he stood another moment—after which, without a word, he quitted the studio. I drew a long breath, for I said to myself that I shouldn't see him again. I hadn't told him definitely that I was in danger of having my work rejected, but I was vexed at his not having felt the catastrophe in the air, read with me the moral of our fruitless collaboration, the lesson that in the deceptive atmosphere of art even the highest respectability may fail of being plastic.

I didn't owe my friends money, but I did see them again. They reappeared together three days later, and, given all the other facts, there was something tragic in that one. It was a clear proof they could find nothing else in life to do. They had threshed the matter out in a dismal conference—they had digested the bad news that they were not in for the series. If they weren't useful to me even for the *Cheapside* their function seemed difficult to determine, and I could only judge at first that they had come, forgivingly, decorously, to take a last leave. This made me rejoice in secret that I had little leisure for a scene; for I had placed both my other models in position together and I was pegging away at a drawing from which I hoped to derive glory. It had been suggested by the passage in which Rutland Ramsay, drawing up a chair to Artemisia's piano-stool, says extraordinary things to her while she ostensibly fingers out a difficult piece of music. I had done Miss Churm at the piano before—it was an attitude in which she knew how to take on an absolutely poetic grace. I wished the two figures to "compose" together with intensity, and my little Italian had entered perfectly into my conception. The pair were vividly before me, the piano had been pulled out; it was a charming show of blended youth and murmured love, which I had only to catch and keep. My visitors stood and looked at it, and I was friendly to them over my shoulder.

They made no response, but I was used to silent company and went on with my work, only a little disconcerted—even though exhilarated by the sense that *this* was at least the ideal thing—at not having got rid of them after all. Presently I heard Mrs. Monarch's sweet voice beside or rather above me: "I wish her hair were a little better done." I looked up and she was staring with a strange fixedness at Miss Churm, whose back was turned to her. "Do you mind my just touching it?" she went on—a question which made me spring up for an instant as with the instinctive fear that she might do the young lady a harm. But she quieted me with a glance I shall never forget—I confess I should like to have been able to paint *that*—and went for a moment to my model. She spoke to her softly, laying a hand on her shoulder and bending over her; and as the girl, understanding, gratefully assented, she disposed her rough curls, with a few quick passes, in such a way as to make Miss Churm's head twice as charming. It was one of the most heroic personal services I've ever seen rendered. Then Mrs. Monarch turned away with a low sigh and, looking about her as if for something to do, stooped to the floor with a noble humility and picked up a dirty rag that had dropped out of my paint-box.

The Major meanwhile had also been looking for something to do, and, wandering to the other end of the studio, saw before him my breakfast-things neglected, unremoved. "I say, can't I be useful *here?*" he called out to me with an irrepressible quaver. I assented with a laugh that I fear was awkward, and for the next ten minutes, while I worked, I heard the light clatter of china and the tinkle of spoons and glass. Mrs. Monarch assisted her husband—they washed up my crockery, they put it away. They wandered off into my little scullery, and I afterwards found that they had cleaned my knives and that my slender stock of plate had an unprecedented surface. When it came over me, the latent eloquence of what they were doing, I confess that my drawing was blurred for a moment—the picture swam. They had accepted their failure, but they couldn't accept their fate. They had bowed their heads in bewilderment to the perverse and cruel law in virtue of which the real thing could be so much less precious than the unreal; but they didn't want to starve. If my servants were my models; then my models might be my servants. They would reverse the parts—the others would sit for the ladies and gentlemen and *they* would do the work. They would still be in the studio—it was an intense dumb appeal to me not to turn them out. "Take us on," they wanted to say—"we'll do *anything.*"

My pencil dropped from my hand; my sitting was spoiled and I got rid of my sitters, who were also evidently rather mystified and awestruck. Then, alone with the Major and his wife I had a most uncomfortable moment. He put their prayer into a single sentence: "I say, you know—just let *us* do for you, can't you?" I couldn't—it was dreadful to see them emptying my slops;

but I pretended I could, to oblige them, for about a week. Then I gave them a sum of money to go away, and I never saw them again. I obtained the remaining books, but my friend Hawley repeats that Major and Mrs. Monarch did me a permanent harm, got me into false ways. If it be true I'm content to have paid the price—for the memory.

EXERCISES

1. What does the following tell us about the narrator: that he looks at people "professionally"; that when he first meets the Monarchs he says that in a "pictorial sense" he "had immediately seen them"; that very quickly he was sure of everything about them?

2. Discuss the significance of the narrator's preference for the represented subject over the real one. What does it mean that the defect of the real is a lack of representation? What does he mean by "I liked things that appeared. Then one was sure."

3. Discuss the following: "I wanted to characterize closely, and the thing in the world I most hated was the danger of being ridden by a type. I held that everything was to be sacrificed sooner than character."

4. Discuss the meaning of "I confess I should like to have been able to paint *that*." Why can't the narrator paint the glance Mrs. Monarch gives him?

5. At the end the narrator says he is content to have paid the price for the memory. If the story itself is the memory, in what way was the experience with the Monarchs worth it?

6. Discuss the following oppositions in the story: real versus appearance, real versus represented, real versus ideal, surface versus depth, pride versus humility, the individual versus the type.

7. If human beings are "real," is it appropriate to refer to them as "things"?

HENRY
JAMES | *The Figure in the Carpet*

I had done a few things and earned a few pence—I had perhaps even had time to begin to think I was finer than was perceived by the patronising; but when I take the little measure of my course (a fidgety habit, for it's none of the longest yet) I count my real start from the evening George Corvick, breathless and worried, came in to ask me a service. He had done more things than I, and earned more pence, though there were chances for cleverness I thought he sometimes missed. I could only however that evening declare to him that he never missed one for kindness. There was almost rapture in hearing it proposed to me to prepare for *The Middle*, the organ of our lucubrations, so called from the position in the week of its day of appearance, an article for which he had made himself responsible and of which, tied up with a stout string, he laid on my table the subject. I pounced upon my opportunity—that is on the first volume of it—and paid scant attention to my friend's explanation of his appeal. What explanation could be more to the point than my obvious fitness for the task? I had written on Hugh Vereker, but never a word in *The Middle*, where my dealings were mainly with the ladies and the minor poets. This was his new novel, an advance copy, and whatever much or little it should do for his reputation I was clear on the spot as to what it should do for mine. Moreover if I always read him as soon as I could get hold of him I had a particular reason for wishing to read him now: I had accepted an invitation to Bridges for the following Sunday, and it had been mentioned in Lady Jane's note that Mr Vereker was to be there. I was young enough to have an emotion about meeting a man of his renown and innocent enough to believe the occasion would demand the display of an acquaintance with his "last."

Corvick, who had promised a review of it, had not even had time to read it; he had gone to pieces in consequence of news requiring—as on precipitate reflection he judged—that he should catch the night-mail to Paris. He had had a telegram from Gwendolen Erme in answer to his letter offering to fly to her aid. I knew already about Gwendolen Erme; I had never seen her, but I had my ideas, which were mainly to the effect that Corvick would marry her if her mother would only die. That lady seemed now in a fair way to oblige him; after some dreadful mistake about some climate or some waters she had suddenly collapsed on the return from abroad. Her daughter, unsupported and alarmed, desiring to make a rush for home but hesitating at the risk, had accepted our friend's assistance, and it was my secret belief that at the sight of him Mrs Erme would pull round. His own belief was scarcely to be called secret; it discernibly at any rate differed from mine. He had showed me Gwendolen's photograph with the remark that she wasn't pretty but was awfully interesting; she had published at the age of nineteen a novel in three volumes, "Deep Down," about which, in *The Middle,* he had been really splendid. He appreciated my present eagerness and undertook that the periodical in question should do no less; then at the last, with his hand on the door, he said to me: "Of course you'll be all right, you know." Seeing I was a trifle vague he added: "I mean you won't be silly."

"Silly—about Vereker! Why, what do I ever find him but awfully clever?"

"Well, what's that but silly? What on earth does 'awfully clever' mean? For God's sake try to get *at* him. Don't let him suffer by our arrangement. Speak of him, you know, if you can, as *I* should have spoken of him."

I wondered an instant. "You mean as far and away the biggest of the lot—that sort of thing?"

Corvick almost groaned. "Oh, you know, I don't put them back to back that way; it's the infancy of art! But he gives me a pleasure so rare; the sense of"—he mused a little—"something or other."

I wondered again. "The sense, pray, of what?"

"My dear man, that's just what I want *you* to say!"

Even before Corvick had banged the door I had begun, book in hand, to prepare myself to say it. I sat up with Vereker half the night; Corvick couldn't have done more than that. He was awfully clever—I stuck to that, but he wasn't a bit the biggest of the lot. I didn't allude to the lot, however; I flattered myself that I emerged on this occasion from the infancy of art. "It's all right," they declared vividly at the office; and when the number appeared I felt there was a basis on which I could meet the great man. It gave me confidence for a day or two, and then that confidence dropped. I had fancied him reading it with relish, but if Corvick was not satisfied how could Vereker himself be? I reflected indeed that the heat of the admirer was sometimes grosser even than the appetite of the scribe. Corvick at all events wrote me from Paris a little ill-humouredly. Mrs Erme was pulling round, and I hadn't at all said what Vereker gave him the sense of.

II

The effect of my visit to Bridges was to turn me out for more profundity. Hugh Vereker, as I saw him there, was of a contact so void of angles that I blushed for the poverty of imagination involved in my small precautions. If he was in spirits it was not because he had read my review; in fact on the Sunday morning I felt sure he hadn't read it; though *The Middle* had been out three days and bloomed, I assured myself, in the stiff garden of periodicals which gave one of the ormolu tables the air of a stand at a station. The impression he made on me personally was such that I wished him to read it, and I corrected to this end with a surreptitious hand what might be wanting in the careless conspicuity of the sheet. I am afraid I even watched the result of my manœuvre, but up to luncheon I watched in vain.

When afterwards, in the course of our gregarious walk, I found myself for half an hour, not perhaps without another manœuvre, at the great man's side, the result of his affability was a still livelier desire that he should not remain in ignorance of the peculiar justice I had done him. It was not that he seemed to thirst for justice; on the contrary I had not yet caught in his talk the faintest grunt of a grudge—a note for which my young experience had already given me an ear. Of late he had had more recognition, and it was pleasant, as we used to say in *The Middle,* to see that it drew him out. He wasn't of course popular, but I judged one of the sources of his good humour to be precisely that his success was independent of that. He had none the less become in a manner the fashion; the critics at least had put on a spurt and caught up with him. We had found out at last how clever he was, and he had had to make the best of the loss of his mystery. I was strongly tempted, as I walked beside him, to let him know how much of that unveiling was my act; and there was a moment when I probably should have done so had not one of the ladies of our party, snatching a place at his other elbow, just then appealed to him in a spirit comparatively selfish. It was very discouraging: I almost felt the liberty had been taken with myself.

I had had on my tongue's end, for my own part, a phrase or two about the right word at the right time; but later on I was glad not to have spoken, for when on our return we clustered at tea I perceived Lady Jane, who had not been out with us, brandishing *The Middle* with her longest arm. She had taken it up at her leisure; she was delighted with what she had found, and I saw that, as a mistake in a man may often be a felicity in a woman, she would practically do for me what I hadn't been able to do for myself. "Some sweet little truths that needed to be spoken," I heard her declare, thrusting the paper at rather a bewildered couple by the fireplace. She grabbed it away from them again on the reappearance of Hugh Vereker, who after our walk had been upstairs to change something. "I know you don't in general look at this kind of thing, but it's an occasion really for doing so. You *haven't* seen it? Then you must. The man has actually got *at* you, at what *I* always feel, you know." Lady Jane threw into her eyes a look evidently intended to give an idea of what she always felt; but she added that she couldn't have expressed it. The man in the paper expressed it in a striking manner. "Just see there, and there, where I've dashed it, how he brings it out." She had literally marked for him the brightest patches of my prose, and if I was a little amused Vereker himself may well have been. He showed how much he was when before us all Lady Jane wanted to read something aloud. I liked at any rate the way he defeated her purpose by jerking the paper affectionately out of her clutch. He would take it upstairs with him, would look at it on going to dress. He did this half an hour later—I saw it in his hand when he repaired to his room. That was the moment at which, thinking to give her pleasure, I mentioned to Lady Jane that I was the author of the review. I did give her pleasure, I judged, but perhaps not quite so much as I had expected. If the author was "only me" the thing didn't seem quite so remarkable. Hadn't I had the effect rather of diminishing the lustre of the article than of adding to my own? Her ladyship was subject to the most extraordinary drops. It didn't matter; the only effect I cared about was the one it would have on Vereker up there by his bedroom fire.

At dinner I watched for the signs of this impression, tried to fancy there was some happier light in his eyes; but to my disappointment Lady Jane gave me no chance to make sure. I had hoped she would call triumphantly down the table, publicly demand if she hadn't been right. The party was large— there were people from outside as well, but I had never seen a table long enough to deprive Lady Jane of a triumph. I was just reflecting in truth that this interminable board would deprive *me* of one when the guest next me, dear woman—she was Miss Poyle, the vicar's sister, a robust, unmodulated person—had the happy inspiration and the unusual courage to address herself across it to Vereker, who was opposite, but not directly, so that when he replied they were both leaning forward. She inquired, artless body, what he thought of Lady Jane's "panegyric," which she had read—not connecting it however with her right-hand neighbour; and while I strained my ear for his reply I heard him, to my stupefaction, call back gaily, with his mouth full of bread: "Oh, it's all right—it's the usual twaddle!"

I had caught Vereker's glance as he spoke, but Miss Poyle's surprise was a fortunate cover for my own. "You mean he doesn't do you justice?" said the excellent woman.

Vereker laughed out, and I was happy to be able to do the same. "It's a charming article," he tossed us.

Miss Poyle thrust her chin half across the cloth. "Oh you're so deep!" she drove home.

"As deep as the ocean! All I pretend is, the author doesn't see——"

A dish was at this point passed over his shoulder, and we had to wait while he helped himself.

"Doesn't see what?" my neighbour continued.

"Doesn't see anything."

"Dear me—how very stupid!"

"Not a bit," Vereker laughed again. "Nobody does."

The lady on his further side appealed to him, and Miss Poyle sank back to me. "Nobody sees anything!" she cheerfully announced; to which I replied that I had often thought so too, but had somehow taken the thought for a proof on my own part of a tremendous eye. I didn't tell her the article was mine; and I observed that Lady Jane, occupied at the end of the table, had not caught Vereker's words.

I rather avoided him after dinner, for I confess he struck me as cruelly conceited, and the revelation was a pain. "The usual twaddle"—my acute little study! That one's admiration should have had a reserve or two could gall him to that point? I had thought him placid, and he was placid enough; such a surface was the hard, polished glass that encased the bauble of his vanity. I was really ruffled, and the only comfort was that if nobody saw anything George Corvick was quite as much out of it as I. This comfort however was not sufficient, after the ladies had dispersed, to carry me in the proper manner—I mean in a spotted jacket and humming an air—into the smoking-room. I took my way in some dejection to bed; but in the passage I encountered Mr Vereker, who had been up once more to change, coming out of his room. *He* was humming an air and had on a spotted jacket, and as soon as he saw me his gaiety gave a start.

"My dear young man," he exclaimed, "I'm so glad to lay hands on you! I'm afraid I most unwittingly wounded you by those words of mine at dinner to Miss Poyle. I learned but half an hour ago from Lady Jane that you wrote the little notice in *The Middle.*"

I protested that no bones were broken; but he moved with me to my own door, his hand, on my shoulder, kindly feeling for a fracture; and on hearing that I had come up to bed he asked leave to cross my threshold and just tell me in three words what his qualification of my remarks had represented. It was plain he really feared I was hurt, and the sense of his solicitude suddenly made all the difference to me. My cheap review fluttered off into space, and the best things I had said in it became flat enough beside the brilliancy of his being there. I can see him there still, on my rug, in the firelight and his spotted jacket, his fine, clear face all bright with the desire to be tender to my youth. I don't know what he had at first meant to say, but I think the sight of my relief touched him, excited him, brought up words to his lips from far within.

It was so these words presently conveyed to me something that, as I afterwards knew, he had never uttered to any one. I have always done justice to the generous impulse that made him speak; it was simply compunction for a snub unconsciously administered to a man of letters in a position inferior to his own, a man of letters moreover in the very act of praising him. To make the thing right he talked to me exactly as an equal and on the ground of what we both loved best. The hour, the place, the unexpectedness deepened the impression: he couldn't have done anything more exquisitely successful.

III

"I don't quite know how to explain it to you," he said, "but it was the very fact that your notice of my book had a spice of intelligence, it was just your exceptional sharpness that produced the feeling—a very old story with me, I beg you to believe—under the momentary influence of which I used in speaking to that good lady the words you so naturally resent. I don't read the things in the newspapers unless they're thrust upon me as that one was—it's always one's best friend that does it! But I used to read them sometimes—ten years ago. I daresay they were in general rather stupider then; at any rate it always seemed to me that they missed my little point with a perfection exactly as admirable when they patted me on the back as when they kicked me in the shins. Whenever since I've happened to have a glimpse of them they were still blazing away—still missing it, I mean, deliciously. *You* miss it, my dear fellow, with inimitable assurance; the fact of your being awfully clever and your article's being awfully nice doesn't make a hair's breadth of difference. It's quite with you rising young men," Vereker laughed, "that I feel most what a failure I am!"

I listened with intense interest; it grew intenser as he talked. "*You* a failure—heavens! What then may your 'little point' happen to be?"

"Have I got to *tell* you, after all these years and labours?" There was something in the friendly reproach of this—jocosely exaggerated—that made me, as an ardent young seeker for truth, blush to the roots of my hair. I'm as much in the dark as ever, though I've grown used in a sense to my obtuseness; at that moment, however, Vereker's happy accent made me appear to myself, and probably to him, a rare donkey. I was on the point of exclaiming "Ah, yes, don't tell me: for my honour, for that of the craft, don't!" when he went on in a manner that showed he had read my thought and had his own idea of the probability of our some day redeeming ourselves. "By my little point I mean—what shall I call it?—the particular thing I've written my books most *for*. Isn't there for every writer a particular thing of that sort, the thing that most makes him apply himself, the thing without the effort to achieve which he wouldn't write at all, the very passion of his passion, the part of the business in which, for him, the flame of art burns most intensely? Well, it's *that!*"

I considered a moment. I was fascinated—easily, you'll say; but I wasn't going after all to put off my guard. "Your description's certainly beautiful, but it doesn't make what you describe very distinct."

"I promise you it would be distinct if it should dawn on you at all." I saw that the charm of our topic overflowed for my companion into an emotion as lively as my own. "At any rate," he went on, "I can speak for myself: there's an idea in my work without which I wouldn't have given a straw for the whole job. It's the finest, fullest intention of the lot, and the application of it has been, I think, a triumph of patience, of ingenuity. I ought to leave that to somebody else to say; but that nobody does say it is precisely what we're talking about. It stretches, this little trick of mine, from book to book, and everything else, comparatively, plays over the surface of it. The order, the form, the texture of my books will perhaps some day constitute for the initiated a complete representation of it. So it's naturally the thing for the critic to look for. It strikes me," my visitor added, smiling, "even as the thing for the critic to find."

This seemed a responsibility indeed. "You call it a little trick?"

"That's only my little modesty. It's really an exquisite scheme."

"And you hold that you've carried the scheme out?"

"The way I've carried it out is the thing in life I think a bit well of myself for."

I was silent a moment. "Don't you think you ought—just a trifle—to assist the critic?"

"Assist him? What else have I done with every stroke of my pen? I've shouted my intention in his great blank face!" At this, laughing out again, Vereker laid his hand on my shoulder to show that the allusion was not to my personal appearance.

"But you talk about the initiated. There must therefore, you see, be initiation."

"What else in heaven's name is criticism supposed to be?" I'm afraid I coloured at this too; but I took refuge in repeating that his account of his silver lining was poor in something or other that a plain man knows things by. "That's only because you've never had a glimpse of it," he replied. "If you had had one the element in question would soon have become practically all you'd see. To me it's exactly as palpable as the marble of this chimney. Besides, the critic just *isn't* a plain man: if he were, pray, what would he be doing in his neighbour's garden? You're anything but a plain man yourself, and the very *raison d'être* of you all is that you're little demons of subtlety. If my great affair's a secret, that's only because it's a secret in spite of itself—the amazing event has made it one. I not only never took the smallest precaution to do so, but never dreamed of any such accident. If I had I shouldn't in advance have had the heart to go on. As it was I only became aware little by little, and meanwhile I had done my work."

"And now you quite like it?" I risked.

"My work?"

"Your secret. It's the same thing."

"Your guessing that," Vereker replied, "is a proof that you're as clever as I say!" I was encouraged by this to remark that he would clearly be pained to part with it, and he confessed that it was indeed with him now the great amusement of life. "I live almost to see if it will ever be detected." He looked at me for a jesting challenge; something at the back of his eyes seemed to peep out. "But I needn't worry—it won't!"

"You fire me as I've never been fired," I returned; "you make me determined to do or die." Then I asked: "Is it a kind of esoteric message?"

His countenance fell at this—he put out his hand as if to bid me goodnight. "Ah, my dear fellow, it can't be described in cheap journalese!"

I knew of course he would be awfully fastidious, but our talk had made me feel how much his nerves were exposed. I was unsatisfied—I kept hold of his hand. "I won't make use of the expression then," I said, "in the article in which I shall eventually announce my discovery, though I daresay I shall have hard work to do without it. But meanwhile, just to hasten that difficult birth, can't you give a fellow a clue?" I felt much more at my ease.

"My whole lucid effort gives him the clue—every page and line and letter. The thing's as concrete there as a bird in a cage, a bait on a hook, a piece of cheese in a mouse-trap. It's stuck into every volume as your foot is stuck into your shoe. It governs every line, it chooses every word, it dots every i, it places every comma."

I scratched my head. "Is it something in the style or something in the thought? An element of form or an element of feeling?"

He indulgently shook my hand again, and I felt my questions to be crude and my distinctions pitiful. "Good-night, my dear boy—don't bother about it. After all, you do like a fellow."

"And a little intelligence might spoil it?" I still detained him.

He hesitated. "Well, you've got a heart in your body. Is that an element of form or an element of feeling? What I contend that nobody has ever mentioned in my work is the organ of life."

"I see—it's some idea about life, some sort of philosophy. Unless it be," I added with the eagerness of a thought perhaps still happier, "some kind of game you're up to with your style, something you're after in the language. Perhaps it's a preference for the letter P!" I ventured profanely to break out. "Papa, potatoes, prunes—that sort of thing?" He was suitably indulgent: he only said I hadn't got the right letter. But his amusement was over; I could see he was bored. There was nevertheless something else I had absolutely to learn. "Should you be able, pen in hand, to state it clearly yourself—to name it, phrase it, formulate it?"

"Oh," he almost passionately sighed, "if I were only, pen in hand, one of *you* chaps!"

"That would be a great chance for you of course. But why should you despise us chaps for not doing what you can't do yourself?"

"Can't do?" He opened his eyes. "Haven't I done it in twenty volumes? I do it in my way," he continued. "You don't do it in yours."

"Ours is so devilish difficult," I weakly observed.

"So is mine. We each choose our own. There's no compulsion. You won't come down and smoke?"

"No. I want to think this thing out."

"You'll tell me then in the morning that you've laid me bare?"

"I'll see what I can do; I'll sleep on it. But just one word more," I added. We had left the room—I walked again with him a few steps along the passage. "This extraordinary 'general intention,' as you call it—for that's the most vivid description I can induce you to make of it—is then generally a sort of buried treasure?"

His face lighted. "Yes, call it that, though it's perhaps not for me to do so."

"Nonsense!" I laughed. "You know you're hugely proud of it."

"Well, I didn't propose to tell you so; but it *is* the joy of my soul!"

"You mean it's a beauty so rare, so great?"

He hesitated a moment. "The loveliest thing in the world!" We had stopped, and on these words he left me; but at the end of the corridor, while I looked after him rather yearningly, he turned and caught sight of my puzzled face. It made him earnestly, indeed I thought quite anxiously, shake his head and wave his finger. "Give it up—give it up!"

This wasn't a challenge—it was fatherly advice. If I had had one of his books at hand I would have repeated my recent act of faith—I would have spent half the night with him. At three o'clock in the morning, not sleeping, remembering moreover how indispensable he was to Lady Jane, I stole down to the library with a candle. There wasn't, so far as I could discover, a line of his writing in the house.

IV

Returning to town I feverishly collected them all; I picked out each in its order and held it up to the light. This gave me a maddening month, in the course of which several things took place. One of these, the last, I may as well immediately mention, was that I acted on Vereker's advice: I renounced my ridiculous attempt. I could really make nothing of the business; it proved a dead loss. After all, before, as he had himself observed, I liked him; and what now occurred was simply that my new intelligence and vain preoccupation damaged my liking. I not only failed to find his general intention—I found myself missing the subordinate intentions I had formerly found. His books didn't even remain the charming things they had been for me; the exasperation of my search put me out of conceit of them. Instead of being a pleasure the more they became a resource the less; for from the moment I was unable to follow up the author's hint I of course felt it a point of honour not to make use professionally of my knowledge of them. I *had* no knowledge—nobody had any. It was humiliating, but I could bear it—they only annoyed me now. At last they even bored me, and I accounted for my confusion—perversely, I confess—by the idea that Vereker had made a fool of me. The buried treasure was a bad joke, the general intention a monstrous *pose*.

The great incident of the time however was that I told George Corvick all about the matter and that my information had an immense effect upon him. He had at last come back, but so, unfortunately, had Mrs Erme, and there was as yet, I could see, no question of his nuptials. He was immensely stirred up by the anecdote I had brought from Bridges; it fell in so completely with the sense he had had from the first that there was more in Vereker than met the eye. When I remarked that the eye seemed what the printed page had been expressly invented to meet he immediately accused me of being spiteful because I had been foiled. Our commerce had always that pleasant latitude. The thing Vereker had mentioned to me was exactly the thing he, Corvick, had wanted me to speak of in my review. On my suggesting at last that with the assistance I had now given him he would doubtless be prepared to speak of it himself he admitted freely that before doing this there was more he must understand. What he would have said, had he reviewed the new book, was that there was evidently in the writer's inmost art something to *be* understood. I hadn't so much as hinted at that: no wonder the writer hadn't been flattered! I asked Corvick what he really considered he meant by his own supersubtlety, and, unmistakably kindled, he replied: "It isn't for the vulgar—it isn't for the vulgar!" He had hold of the tail of something; he would pull hard, pull it right out. He pumped me dry on Vereker's strange confidence and, pronouncing me the luckiest of mortals, mentioned half a dozen questions he wished to goodness I had had the gumption to put. Yet on the other hand he didn't want to be told too much—it would spoil the fun of seeing what would come. The failure of my fun was at the moment of our meeting not complete, but I saw it ahead, and Corvick saw that I saw it. I, on my side, saw likewise that one of the first things he would do would be to rush off with my story to Gwendolen.

On the very day after my talk with him I was surprised by the receipt of a note from Hugh Vereker, to whom our encounter at Bridges had been recalled, as he mentioned, by his falling, in a magazine, on some article to which my signature was appended. "I read it with great pleasure," he wrote, "and remembered under its influence our lively conversation by your bedroom fire. The consequence of this has been that I begin to measure the temerity of my having saddled you with a knowledge that you may find something of a burden. Now that the fit's over I can't imagine how I came to be moved so much beyond my wont. I had never before related, no matter in what expansion, the history of my little secret, and I shall never speak of the business again. I was accidentally so much more explicit with you than it had ever entered into my game to be, that I find this game—I mean the pleasure of playing it—suffers considerably. In short, if you can understand it, I've spoiled a part of my fun. I really don't want to give anybody what I believe you clever young men call the tip. That's of course a selfish solicitude, and I name it to you for what it may be worth to you. If you're disposed to humour me don't repeat my revelation. Think me demented—it's your right; but don't tell anybody why."

The sequel to this communication was that as early on the morrow as I dared I drove straight to Mr Vereker's door. He occupied in those years one of the honest old houses in Kensington Square. He received me immediately, and as soon as I came in I saw I had not lost my power to minister to his mirth. He laughed out at the sight of my face, which doubtless expressed my perturbation. I had been indiscreet—my compunction was great. "I *have* told somebody," I panted, "and I'm sure that person will by this time have told somebody else! It's a woman, into the bargain."

"The person you've told?"

"No, the other person. I'm quite sure he must have told her."

"For all the good it will do her—or do *me!* A woman will never find out."

"No, but she'll talk all over the place: she'll do just what you don't want."

Vereker thought a moment, but he was not so disconcerted as I had feared: he felt that if the harm was done it only served him right. "It doesn't matter—don't worry."

"I'll do my best, I promise you, that your talk with me shall go no further."

"Very good; do what you can."

"In the meantime," I pursued, "George Corvick's possession of the tip may, on his part, really lead to something."

"That will be a brave day."

I told him about Corvick's cleverness, his admiration, the intensity of his interest in my anecdote; and without making too much of the divergence of our respective estimates mentioned that my friend was already of opinion that he saw much further into a certain affair than most people. He was quite as fired as I had been at Bridges. He was moreover in love with the young lady: perhaps the two together would puzzle something out.

Vereker seemed struck with this. "Do you mean they're to be married?"

"I daresay that's what it will come to."

"That may help them," he conceded, "but we must give them time!"

I spoke of my own renewed assault and confessed my difficulties; where-upon he repeated his former advice: "Give it up, give it up!" He evidently didn't think me intellectually equipped for the adventure. I stayed half an hour, and he was most good-natured, but I couldn't help pronouncing him a man of shifting moods. He had been free with me in a mood, he had repented in a mood, and now in a mood he had turned indifferent. This general levity helped me to believe that, so far as the subject of the tip went, there wasn't much in it. I contrived however to make him answer a few more questions about it, though he did so with visible impatience. For himself, beyond doubt, the thing we were all so blank about was vividly there. It was something, I guessed, in the primal plan, something like a complex figure in a Persian carpet. He highly approved of this image when I used it, and he used an-other himself. "It's the very string," he said, "that my pearls are strung on!" The reason of his note to me had been that he really didn't want to give us a grain of succour—our density was a thing too perfect in its way to touch. He had formed the habit of depending upon it, and if the spell was to break it must break by some force of its own. He comes back to me from that last occasion—for I was never to speak to him again—as a man with some safe secret for enjoyment. I wondered as I walked away where he had got *his* tip.

V

When I spoke to George Corvick of the caution I had received he made me feel that any doubt of his delicacy would be almost an insult. He had instantly told Gwendolen, but Gwendolen's ardent response was in itself a pledge of discretion. The question would now absorb them, and they would enjoy their fun too much to wish to share it with the crowd. They appeared to have caught instinctively Vereker's peculiar notion of fun. Their intellectual pride, however, was not such as to make them indifferent to any further light I might throw on the affair they had in hand. They were indeed of the "artistic temperament," and I was freshly struck with my colleague's power to excite himself over a question of art. He called it letters, he called it life—it was all one thing. In what he said I now seemed to understand that he spoke equally for Gwendolen, to whom, as soon as Mrs Erme was sufficiently better to allow her a little leisure, he made a point of introducing me. I remember our calling together one Sunday in August at a huddled house in Chelsea, and my renewed envy of Corvick's possession of a friend who had some light to mingle with his own. He could say things to her that I could never say to him. She had indeed no sense of humour and, with her pretty way of holding her head on one side, was one of those persons whom you want, as the phrase is, to shake, but who have learnt Hungarian by themselves. She conversed perhaps in Hungarian with Corvick; she had remarkably little English for his friend. Corvick afterwards told me that I had chilled her by my apparent indisposition to oblige her with the detail of what Vereker had said to me. I admitted that I felt I had given thought enough to this exposure: hadn't I even made up my mind that it was hollow, wouldn't stand the test? The importance they attached to it was irritating—it rather envenomed my dissent.

That statement looks unamiable, and what probably happened was that I felt humiliated at seeing other persons derive a daily joy from an experiment which had brought me only chagrin. I was out in the cold while, by the evening fire, under the lamp, they followed the chase for which I myself had sounded the horn. They did as I had done, only more deliberately and sociably—they went over their author from the beginning. There was no hurry, Corvick said—the future was before them and the fascination could only grow; they would take him page by page, as they would take one of the classics, inhale him in slow draughts and let him sink deep in. I doubt whether they would have got so wound up if they had not been in love: poor Vereker's secret gave them endless occasion to put their young heads together. None the less it represented the kind of problem for which Corvick had a special aptitude, drew out the particular pointed patience of which, had he lived, he would have given more striking and, it is to be hoped, more fruitful examples. He at least was, in Vereker's words, a little demon of subtlety. We had begun by disputing, but I soon saw that without my stirring a finger his infatuation would have its bad hours. He would bound off on false scents as I had done— he would clap his hands over new lights and see them blown out by the wind of the turned page. He was like nothing, I told him, but the maniacs who embrace some bedlamitical theory of the cryptic character of Shakespeare. To this he replied that if we had had Shakespeare's own word for his being cryptic he would immediately have accepted it. The case there was altogether different—we had nothing but the word of Mr Snooks. I rejoined that I was stupefied to see him attach such importance even to the word of Mr Vereker. He inquired thereupon whether I treated Mr Vereker's word as a lie. I wasn't perhaps prepared, in my unhappy rebound, to go as far as that, but I insisted that till the contrary was proved I should view it as too fond an imagination. I didn't, I confess, say—I didn't at that time quite know—all I felt. Deep down, as Miss Erme would have said, I was uneasy, I was expectant. At the core of my personal confusion—for my curiosity lived in its ashes—was the sharpness of a sense that Corvick would at last probably come out somewhere. He made, in defence of his credulity, a great point of the fact that from of old, in his study of this genius, he had caught whiffs and hints of he didn't know what, faint wandering notes of a hidden music. That was just the rarity, that was the charm: it fitted so perfectly into what I reported.

If I returned on several occasions to the little house in Chelsea I daresay it was as much for news of Vereker as for news of Miss Erme's mamma. The hours spent there by Corvick were present to my fancy as those of a chess-player bent with a silent scowl, all the lamplit winter, over his board and his moves. As my imagination filled it out the picture held me fast. On the other side of the table was a ghostlier form, the faint figure of an antagonist good-humouredly but a little wearily secure—an antagonist who leaned back in his chair with his hands in his pockets and a smile on his fine clear face. Close to Corvick, behind him, was a girl who had begun to strike me as pale and wasted and even, on more familiar view, as rather handsome, and who rested on his shoulder and hung upon his moves. He would take up a chessman and hold it poised a while over one of the little squares, and then he would put it back in its place with a long sigh of disappointment. The young lady, at this, would slightly but uneasily shift her position and look across, very hard, very long, very strangely, at their dim participant. I had asked them at an early stage of the business if it mightn't contribute to their success to have some closer communication with him. The special circumstances would surely be held to have given me a right to introduce them. Corvick immediately replied that he had no wish to approach the altar before he had prepared the sacrifice. He quite agreed with our friend both as to the sport and as to the honour—he would bring down the animal with his own rifle. When I asked him if Miss Erme were as keen a shot he said after an hesitation: "No; I'm ashamed to say she wants to set a trap. She'd give anything to see him; she says she requires another tip. She's really quite morbid about it. But she must play fair—she *shan't* see him!" he emphatically added. I had a suspicion that they had even quarrelled a little on the subject—a suspicion not corrected by the way he more than once exclaimed to me: "She's quite incredibly literary, you know—quite fantastically!" I remember his saying of her that she felt in italics and thought in capitals. "Oh, when I've run him to earth," he also said, "then, you know, I shall knock at his door. Rather—I beg you to believe. I'll have it from his own lips: 'Right you are, my boy; you've done it this time!' He shall crown me victor—with the critical laurel."

Meanwhile he really avoided the chances London life might have given him of meeting the distinguished novelist; a danger however that disappeared with Vereker's leaving England for an indefinite absence, as the newspapers announced—going to the south for motives connected with the health of his wife, which had long kept her in retirement. A year—more than a year—had elapsed since the incident at Bridges, but I had not encountered him again. I think at bottom I was rather ashamed—I hated to remind him that though I had irremediably missed his point a reputation for acuteness was rapidly overtaking me. This scruple led me a dance; kept me out of Lady Jane's house, made me even decline, when in spite of my bad manners she was a second time so good as to make me a sign, an invitation to her beautiful seat. I once saw her with Vereker at a concert and was sure I was seen by them, but I slipped out without being caught. I felt, as on that occasion I splashed along in the rain, that I couldn't have done anything else; and yet I remember saying to myself that it was hard, was even cruel. Not only had I lost the books, but I had lost the man himself: they and their author had been alike spoiled for me. I knew too which was the lost I most regretted. I had liked the man still better than I had liked the books.

VI

Six months after Vereker had left England George Corvick, who made his living by his pen, contracted for a piece of work which imposed on him an absence of some length and a journey of some difficulty, and his undertaking of which was much of a surprise to me. His brother-in-law had become editor of a great provincial paper, and the great provincial paper, in a fine flight of fancy, had conceived the idea of sending a "special commissioner" to India. Special commissioners had begun, in the "metropolitan press," to be the fashion, and the journal in question felt that it had passed too long for a mere country cousin. Corvick had no hand, I knew, for the big brush of the correspondent, but that was his brother-in-law's affair, and the fact that a particular task was not in his line was apt to be with himself exactly a reason for accepting it. He was prepared to out-Herod the metropolitan press; he took solemn precautions against priggishness, he exquisitely outraged taste. Nobody ever knew it—the taste was all his own. In addition to his expenses he was to be conveniently paid, and I found myself able to help him, for the usual fat book, to a plausible arrangement with the usual fat publisher. I naturally inferred that his obvious desire to make a little money was not unconnected with the prospect of a union with Gwendolen Erme. I was aware that her mother's opposition was largely addressed to his want of means and of lucrative abilities, but it so happened that, on my saying the last time I saw him something that bore on the question of his separation from our young lady, he exclaimed with an emphasis that startled me: "Ah, I'm not a bit engaged to her, you know!"

"Not overtly," I answered, "because her mother doesn't like you. But I've always taken for granted a private understanding."

"Well, there *was* one. But there isn't now." That was all he said, except something about Mrs Erme's having got on her feet again in the most extraordinary way—a remark from which I gathered he wished me to think he meant that private understandings were of little use when the doctor didn't share them. What I took the liberty of really thinking was that the girl might in some way have estranged him. Well, if he had taken the turn of jealousy for instance it could scarcely be jealousy of me. In that case (besides the absurdity of it) he wouldn't have gone away to leave us together. For some time before his departure we had indulged in no allusion to the buried treasure, and from his silence, of which mine was the consequence, I had drawn a sharp conclusion. His courage had dropped, his ardour had gone the way of mine—this inference at least he left me to enjoy. More than that he couldn't do; he couldn't face the triumph with which I might have greeted an explicit admission. He needn't have been afraid, poor dear, for I had by this time lost all need to triumph. In fact I considered that I showed magnanimity in not reproaching him with his collapse, for the sense of his having thrown up the game made me feel more than ever how much I depended on him. If Corvick had broken down I should never know; no one would be of any use if *he* wasn't. It wasn't a bit true that I had ceased to care for knowledge; little by little my curiosity had not only begun to ache again, but had become the familiar torment of my consciousness. There are doubtless people to whom torments of such an order appear hardly more natural than the contortions of disease; but I don't know after all why I should in this connection so much as mention them. For the few persons, at any rate, abnormal or not, with whom my anecdote is concerned, literature was a game of skill, and skill meant courage, and courage meant honour, and honour meant passion, meant life. The stake on the table was of a different substance, and our roulette was the revolving mind, but we sat round the green board as intently as the grim gamblers at Monte Carlo. Gwendolen Erme, for that matter, with her white face and her fixed eyes, was of the very type of the lean ladies one had met in the temples of chance. I recognised in Corvick's absence that she made this analogy vivid. It was extravagant, I admit, the way she lived for the art of the pen. Her passion visibly preyed upon her, and in her presence I felt almost tepid. I got hold of "Deep Down" again: it was a desert in which she had lost herself, but in which too she had dug a wonderful hole in the sand—a cavity out of which Corvick had still more remarkably pulled her.

Early in March I had a telegram from her, in consequence of which I repaired immediately to Chelsea, where the first thing she said to me was: "He has got it, he has got it!"

She was moved, as I could see, to such depths that she must mean the great thing. "Vereker's idea?"

"His general intention. George has cabled from Bombay."

She had the missive open there; it was emphatic, but it was brief. "Eureka. Immense." That was all—he had saved the money of the signature. I shared her emotion, but I was disappointed. "He doesn't say what it is."

"How could he—in a telegram? He'll write it."

"But how does he know?"

"Know it's the real thing? Oh, I'm sure when you see it you do know. *Vera incessu patuit dea!*"

"It's you, Miss Erme, who are a dear for bringing me such news!"—I went all lengths in my high spirits. "But fancy finding our goddess in the temple of Vishnu! How strange of George to have been able to go into the thing again in the midst of such different and such powerful solicitations!"

"He hasn't gone into it, I know; it's the thing itself, let severely alone for six months, that has simply sprung out at him like a tigress out of the jungle. He didn't take a book with him—on purpose; indeed he wouldn't have needed to—he knows every page, as I do, by heart. They all worked in him together, and some day somewhere, when he wasn't thinking, they fell, in all their superb intricacy, into the one right combination. The figure in the carpet came out. That's the way he knew it would come and the real reason—you didn't in the least understand, but I suppose I may tell you now—why he went and why I consented to his going. We knew the change would do it, the difference of thought, of scene, would give the needed touch, the magic shake. We had perfectly, we had admirably calculated. The elements were all in his mind, and in the *secousse* of a new and intense experience they just struck light." She positively struck light herself—she was literally, facially luminous. I stammered something about unconscious cerebration, and she continued: "He'll come right home—this will bring him."

"To see Vereker, you mean?"

"To see Vereker—and to see *me*. Think what he'll have to tell me!"

I hesitated. "About India?"

"About fiddlesticks! About Vereker—about the figure in the carpet."

"But, as you say, we shall surely have that in a letter."

She thought like one inspired, and I remembered how Corvick had told me long before that her face was interesting. "Perhaps it won't go in a letter if it's 'immense.'"

"Perhaps not if it's immense bosh. If he has got something that won't go in a letter he hasn't got *the* thing. Vereker's own statement to me was exactly that the 'figure' *would* go in a letter."

"Well, I cabled to George an hour ago—two words," said Gwendolen.

"Is it indiscreet of me to inquire what they were?"

She hung fire, but at last she brought them out. "'Angel, write.'"

"Good!" I exclaimed. "I'll make it sure—I'll send him the same."

VII

My words however were not absolutely the same—I put something instead of "angel"; and in the sequel my epithet seemed the more apt, for when eventually we heard from Corvick it was merely, it was thoroughly to be tantalised. He was magnificent in his triumph, he described his discovery as stupendous; but his ecstasy only obscured it—there were to be no particulars till he should have submitted his conception to the supreme authority. He had thrown up his commission, he had thrown up his book, he had thrown up everything but the instant need to hurry to Rapallo, on the Genoese shore, where Vereker was making a stay. I wrote him a letter which was to await him at Aden—I besought him to relieve my suspense. That he found my letter was indicated by a telegram which, reaching me after weary days and without my having received an answer to my laconic dispatch at Bombay, was evidently intended as a reply to both communications. Those few words were in familiar French, the French of the day, which Corvick often made use of to show he wasn't a prig. It had for some persons the opposite effect, but his message may fairly be paraphrased. "Have patience; I want to see, as it breaks on you, the face you'll make!" *"Tellement envie de voir ta tête!"*—that was what I had to sit down with. I can certainly not be said to have sat down, for I seem to remember myself at this time as rushing constantly between the little house in Chelsea and my own. Our impatience, Gwendolen's and mine, was equal, but I kept hoping her light would be greater. We all spent during this episode, for people of our means, a great deal of money in telegrams, and I counted on the receipt of news from Rapallo immediately after the junction of the discoverer with the discovered. The interval seemed an age, but late one day I heard a hansom rattle up to my door with the crash engendered by a hint of liberality. I lived with my heart in my mouth and I bounded to the window—a movement which gave me a view of a young lady erect on the footboard of the vehicle and eagerly looking up at my house. At sight of me she flourished a paper with a movement that brought me straight down, the movement with which, in melodramas, handkerchiefs and reprieves are flourished at the foot of the scaffold.

"Just seen Vereker—not a note wrong. Pressed me to bosom—keeps me a month." So much I read on her paper while the cabby dropped a grin from his perch. In my excitement I paid him profusely and in hers she suffered it; then as he drove away we started to walk about and talk. We had talked, heaven knows, enough before, but this was a wondrous lift. We pictured the whole scene at Rapallo, where he would have written, mentioning my name, for permission to call; that is *I* pictured it, having more material than my companion, whom I felt hang on my lips as we stopped on purpose before shop-windows we didn't look into. About one thing we were clear: if he was staying on for fuller communication we should at least have a letter from him that would help us through the dregs of delay. We understood his staying on, and yet each of us saw, I think, that the other hated it. The letter we were clear about arrived; it was for Gwendolen, and I called upon her in time to save her the trouble of bringing it to me. She didn't read it out, as was natural enough; but she repeated to me what it chiefly embodied. This consisted of the remarkable statement that he would tell her when they were married exactly what she wanted to know.

"Only when we're married—not before," she explained. "It's tantamount to saying—isn't it?—that I must marry him straight off!" She smiled at me while I flushed with disappointment, a vision of fresh delay that made me at first unconscious of my surprise. It seemed more than a hint that on me as well he would impose some tiresome condition. Suddenly, while she reported several more things from his letter, I remembered what he had told me before going away. He found Mr Vereker deliriously interesting and his own possession of the secret a kind of intoxication. The buried treasure was all gold and gems. Now that it was there it seemed to grow and grow before him; it was in all time, in all tongues, one of the most wonderful flowers of art. Nothing, above all, when once one was face to face with it, had been more consummately done. When once it came out it came out, was there with a splendour that made you ashamed; and there had not been, save in the bottomless vulgarity of the age, with every one tasteless and tainted, every sense stopped, the smallest reason why it should have been overlooked. It was immense, but it was simple—it was simple, but it was immense, and the final knowledge of it was an experience quite apart. He intimated that the charm of such an experience, the desire to drain it, in its freshness, to the last drop, was what kept him there close to the source. Gwendolen, frankly radiant as she tossed me these fragments, showed the elation of a prospect more assured than my own. That brought me back to the question of her marriage, prompted me to ask her if what she meant by what she had just surprised me with was that she was under an engagement.

"Of course I am!" she answered. "Didn't you know it?" She appeared astonished; but I was still more so, for Corvick had told me the exact contrary. I didn't mention this, however; I only reminded her that I had not been to that degree in her confidence, or even in Corvick's, and that moreover I was not in ignorance of her mother's interdict. At bottom I was troubled by the disparity of the two assertions; but after a moment I felt that Corvick's was the one I least doubted. This simply reduced me to asking myself if the girl had on the spot improvised an engagement—vamped up an old one or dashed off a new—in order to arrive at the satisfaction she desired. I reflected that she had resources of which I was destitute; but she made her case slightly more intelligible by rejoining presently: "What the state of things has been is that we felt of course bound to do nothing in mamma's lifetime."

"But now you think you'll just dispense with your mother's consent?"

"Ah, it may not come to that!" I wondered what it might come to, and she went on: "Poor dear, she may swallow the dose. In fact, you know," she added with a laugh, "she really *must!*"—a proposition of which, on behalf of every one concerned, I fully acknowledged the force.

VIII

Nothing more annoying had ever happened to me than to become aware before Corvick's arrival in England that I should not be there to put him through. I found myself abruptly called to Germany by the alarming illness of my younger brother, who, against my advice, had gone to Munich to study, at the feet indeed of a great master, the art of portraiture in oils. The near relative who made him an allowance had threatened to withdraw it if he should, under specious pretexts, turn for superior truth to Paris—Paris being somehow, for a Cheltenham aunt, the school of evil, the abyss. I deplored this prejudice at the time, and the deep injury of it was now visible—first in the fact that it had not saved the poor boy, who was clever, frail and foolish, from congestion of the lungs, and second in the greater remoteness from London to which the event condemned me. I am afraid that what was uppermost in my mind during several anxious weeks was the sense that if we had only been in Paris I might have run over to see Corvick. This was actually out of the question from every point of view: my brother, whose recovery gave us both plenty to do, was ill for three months, during which I never left him and at the end of which we had to face the absolute prohibition of a return to England. The consideration of climate imposed itself, and he was in no state to meet it alone. I took him to Meran and there spent the summer with him, trying to show him by example how to get back to work and nursing a rage of another sort that I tried not to show him.

The whole business proved the first of a series of phenomena so strangely combined that, taken together (which was how I had to take them) they form as good an illustration as I can recall of the manner in which, for the good of his soul doubtless, fate sometimes deals with a man's avidity. These incidents certainly had larger bearings than the comparatively meagre consequence we are here concerned with—though I feel that consequence also to be a thing to speak of with some respect. It's mainly in such a light, I confess, at any rate, that at this hour the ugly fruit of my exile is present to me. Even at first indeed the spirit in which my avidity, as I have called it, made me regard this term owed no element of ease to the fact that before coming back from Rapallo George Corvick addressed me in a way I didn't like. His letter had none of the sedative action that I must to-day profess myself sure he had wished to give it, and the march of occurrences was not so ordered as to make up for what it lacked. He had begun on the spot, for one of the quarterlies, a great last word on Vereker's writings, and this exhaustive study, the only one that would have counted, have existed, was to turn on the new light, to utter—oh, so quietly!—the unimagined truth. It was in other words to trace the figure in the carpet through every convolution, to reproduce it in every tint. The result, said Corvick, was to be the greatest literary portrait ever painted, and what he asked of me was just to be so good as not to trouble him with questions till he should hang up his masterpiece before me. He did me the honour to declare that, putting aside the great sitter himself, all aloft in his indifference, I was individually the connoisseur he was most working for. I was therefore to be a good boy and not try to peep under the curtain before the show was ready: I should enjoy it all the more if I sat very still.

I did my best to sit very still, but I couldn't help giving a jump on seeing in *The Times*, after I had been a week or two in Munich and before, as I knew, Corvick had reached London, the announcement of the sudden death of poor Mrs Erme. I instantly wrote to Gwendolen for particulars, and she replied that her mother had succumbed to long-threatened failure of the heart. She didn't say, but I took the liberty of reading into her words, that from the point of view of her marriage and also of her eagerness, which was quite a match for mine, this was a solution more prompt than could have been expected and more radical than waiting for the old lady to swallow the dose. I candidly admit indeed that at the time—for I heard from her repeatedly—I read some singular things into Gwendolen's words and some still more extraordinary ones into her silences. Pen in hand, this way, I live the time over, and it brings back the oddest sense of my having been for months and in spite of myself a kind of coerced spectator. All my life had taken refuge in my eyes, which the procession of events appeared to have committed itself to keep astare. There were days when I thought of writing to Hugh Vereker and simply throwing myself on his charity. But I felt more deeply that I hadn't fallen quite so low, besides which, quite properly, he would send me about my business. Mrs Erme's death brought Corvick straight home, and within the month he was united "very quietly"—as quietly I suppose as he meant in his article to bring out his *trouvaille*—to the young lady he had loved and quitted. I use this last term, I may parenthetically say, because I subsequently grew sure that at the time he went to India, at the time of his great news from Bombay, there was no engagement whatever. There was none at the moment she affirmed the opposite. On the other hand he certainly became engaged the day he returned. The happy pair went down to Torquay for their honeymoon, and there, in a reckless hour, it occurred to poor Corvick to take his young bride a drive. He had no command of that business: this had been brought home to me of old in a little tour we had once made together in a dogcart. In a dogcart he perched his companion for a rattle over Devonshire hills, on one of the likeliest of which he brought his horse, who, it was true, had bolted, down with such violence that the occupants of the cart were hurled forward and that he fell horribly on his head. He was killed on the spot; Gwendolen escaped unhurt.

I pass rapidly over the question of this unmitigated tragedy, of what the loss of my best friend meant for me, and I complete my little history of my patience and my pain by the frank statement of my having, in a postscript to my very first letter to her after the receipt of the hideous news, asked Mrs Corvick whether her husband had not at least finished the great article on Vereker. Her answer was as prompt as my inquiry: the article, which had been barely begun, was a mere heart-breaking scrap. She explained that Corvick had just settled down to it when he was interrupted by her mother's death; then, on his return, he had been kept from work by the engrossments into which that calamity plunged them. The opening pages were all that existed; they were striking, they were promising, but they didn't unveil the idol. That great intellectual feat was obviously to have formed his climax. She said nothing more, nothing to enlighten me as to the state of her own knowledge—the knowledge for the acquisition of which I had conceived her doing prodigious things. This was above all what I wanted to know: had *she* seen the idol unveiled? Had there been a private ceremony for a palpitating audience of one? For what else but that ceremony had the previous ceremony been enacted? I didn't like as yet to press her, though when I thought of what had passed between us on the subject in Corvick's absence her reticence surprised me. It was therefore not till much later, from Meran, that I risked another appeal, risked it in some trepidation, for she continued to tell me nothing. "Did you hear in those few days of your blighted bliss," I wrote, "what we desired so to hear?" I said, "we" as a little hint; and she showed me she could take a little hint. "I heard everything," she replied, "and I mean to keep it to myself!"

IX

It was impossible not to be moved with the strongest sympathy for her, and on my return to England I showed her every kindness in my power. Her mother's death had made her means sufficient, and she had gone to live in a more convenient quarter. But her loss had been great and her visitation cruel; it never would have occurred to me moreover to suppose she could come to regard the enjoyment of a technical tip, of a piece of literary experience, as a counterpoise to her grief. Strange to say, none the less, I couldn't help fancying after I had seen her a few times that I caught a glimpse of some such oddity. I hasten to add that there had been other things I couldn't help fancying; and as I never felt I was really clear about these, so, as to the point I here touch on, I give her memory the benefit of every doubt. Stricken and solitary, highly accomplished and now, in her deep mourning, her maturer grace and her uncomplaining sorrow incontestably handsome, she presented herself as leading a life of singular dignity and beauty. I had at first found a way to believe that I should soon get the better of the reserve formulated the week after the catastrophe in her reply to an appeal as to which I was not unconscious that it might strike her as mistimed. Certainly that reserve was something of a shock to me—certainly it puzzled me the more I thought of it, though I tried to explain it, with moments of success, by the supposition of exalted sentiments, of superstitious scruples, of a refinement of loyalty. Certainly it added at the same time hugely to the price of Vereker's secret, precious as that mystery already appeared. I may as well confess abjectly that Mrs Corvick's unexpected attitude was the final tap on the nail that was to fix, as they say, my luckless idea, convert it into the obsession of which I am for ever conscious.

But this only helped me the more to be artful, to be adroit, to allow time to elapse before renewing my suit. There were plenty of speculations for the interval, and one of them was deeply absorbing. Corvick had kept his information from his young friend till after the removal of the last barriers to their intimacy; then he had let the cat out of the bag. Was it Gwendolen's idea, taking a hint from him, to liberate this animal only on the basis of the renewal of such a relation? Was the figure in the carpet traceable or describable only for husbands and wives—for lovers supremely united? It came back to me in a mystifying manner that in Kensington Square, when I told him that Corvick would have told the girl he loved, some word had dropped from Vereker that gave colour to this possibility. There might be little in it, but there was enough to make me wonder if I should have to marry Mrs Corvick to get what I wanted. Was I prepared to offer her this price for the blessing of her knowledge? Ah! that way madness lay—so I said to myself at least in bewildered hours. I could see meanwhile the torch she refused to pass on flame away in her chamber of memory—pour through her eyes a light that made a glow in her lonely house. At the end of six months I was fully sure of what this warm presence made up to her for. We had talked again and again of the man who had brought us together, of his talent, his character, his personal charm, his certain career, his dreadful doom, and even of his clear purpose in that great study which was to have been a supreme literary portrait, a kind of critical Vandyke or Velasquez. She had conveyed to me in abundance that she was tongue-tied by her perversity, by her piety, that she would never break the silence it had not been given to the "right person," as she said, to break. The hour however finally arrived. One evening when I had been sitting with her longer than usual I laid my hand firmly on her arm.

"Now, at last, what *is* it?"

She had been expecting me; she was ready. She gave a long, slow, soundless headshake, merciful only in being inarticulate. This mercy didn't prevent its hurling at me the largest, finest, coldest "Never!" I had yet, in the course of a life that had known denials, had to take full in the face. I took it and was aware that with the hard blow the tears had come into my eyes. So for a while we sat and looked at each other; after which I slowly rose. I was wondering if some day she would accept me; but this was not what I brought out. I said as I smoothed down my hat: "I know what to think then; it's nothing!"

A remote, disdainful pity for me shone out of her dim smile; then she exclaimed in a voice that I hear at this moment: "It's my *life!*" As I stood at the door she added: "You've insulted him!"

"Do you mean Vereker?"

"I mean—the Dead!"

I recognised when I reached the street the justice of her charge. Yes, it was her life—I recognised that too; but her life none the less made room with the lapse of time for another interest. A year and a half after Corvick's death she published in a single volume her second novel, "Overmastered," which I pounced on in the hope of finding in it some tell-tale echo or some peeping face. All I found was a much better book than her younger performance, showing I thought the better company she had kept. As a tissue tolerably intricate it was a carpet with a figure of its own; but the figure was not the figure I was looking for. On sending a review of it to *The Middle* I was surprised to learn from the office that a notice was already in type. When the paper came out I had no hesitation in attributing this article, which I thought rather vulgarly overdone, to Drayton Deane, who in the old days had been something of a friend of Corvick's, yet had only within a few weeks made the acquaintance of his widow. I had had an early copy of the book, but Deane had evidently had an earlier. He lacked all the same the light hand with which Corvick had gilded the gingerbread—he laid on the tinsel in splotches.

X

Six months later appeared "The Right of Way," the last chance, though we didn't know it, that we were to have to redeem ourselves. Written wholly during Vereker's absence, the book had been heralded, in a hundred paragraphs, by the usual ineptitudes. I carried it, as early a copy as any, I this time flattered myself, straightway to Mrs Corvick. This was the only use I had for it; I left the inevitable tribute of *The Middle* to some more ingenious mind and some less irritated temper. "But I already have it," Gwendolen said. "Drayton Deane was so good as to bring it to me yesterday, and I've just finished it."

"Yesterday? How did he get it so soon?"

"He gets everything soon. He's to review it in *The Middle*."

"He—Drayton Deane—review Vereker?" I couldn't believe my ears.

"Why not? One fine ignorance is as good as another."

I winced, but I presently said: "You ought to review him yourself!"

"I don't 'review,'" she laughed. "I'm reviewed!"

Just then the door was thrown open. "Ah yes, here's your reviewer!" Drayton Deane was there with his long legs and his tall forehead: he had come to see what she thought of "The Right of Way," and to bring news which was singularly relevant. The evening papers were just out with a telegram on the author of that work, who, in Rome, had been ill for some days with an attack of malarial fever. It had at first not been thought grave, but had taken in consequence of complications a turn that might give rise to anxiety. Anxiety had indeed at the latest hour begun to be felt.

I was struck in the presence of these tidings with the fundamental detachment that Mrs Corvick's public regret quite failed to conceal: it gave me the measure of her consummate independence. That independence rested on her knowledge, the knowledge which nothing now could destroy and which nothing could make different. The figure in the carpet might take on another twist or two, but the sentence had virtually been written. The writer might go down to his grave: she was the person in the world to whom—as if she had been his favoured heir—his continued existence was least of a need. This reminded me how I had observed at a particular moment—after Corvick's death—the drop of her desire to see him face to face. She had got what she wanted without that. I had been sure that if she hadn't got it she wouldn't have been restrained from the endeavour to sound him personally by those superior reflections, more conceivable on a man's part than on a woman's, which in my case had served as a deterrent. It wasn't however, I hasten to add, that my case, in spite of this invidious comparison, wasn't ambiguous enough. At the thought that Vereker was perhaps at that moment dying there rolled over me a wave of anguish—a poignant sense of how inconsistently I still depended on him. A delicacy that it was my one compensation to suffer to rule me had left the Alps and the Apennines between us, but the vision of the waning opportunity made me feel as if I might in my despair at last have gone to him. Of course I would really have done nothing of the sort. I remained five minutes, while my companions talked of the new book, and when Drayton Deane appealed to me for my opinion of it I replied, getting up, that I detested Hugh Vereker—simply couldn't read him. I went away with the moral certainty that as the door closed behind me Deane would remark that I was awfully superficial. His hostess wouldn't contradict him.

I continue to trace with a briefer touch our intensely odd concatenation. Three weeks after this came Vereker's death, and before the year was out the death of his wife. That poor lady I had never seen, but I had had a futile theory that, should she survive him long enough to be decorously accessible, I might approach her with the feeble flicker of my petition. Did she know and if she knew would she speak? It was much to be presumed that for more reasons than one she would have nothing to say; but when she passed out of all reach I felt that renouncement was indeed my appointed lot. I was shut up in my obsession for ever—my gaolers had gone off with the key. I find myself quite as vague as a captive in a dungeon about the time that further elapsed before Mrs Corvick became the wife of Drayton Deane. I had foreseen, through my bars, this end of the business, though there was no indecent haste and our friendship had rather fallen off. They were both so "awfully intellectual" that it struck people as a suitable match, but I knew better than any one the wealth of understanding the bride would contribute to the partnership. Never, for a marriage in literary circles—so the newspapers described the alliance—had a bride been so handsomely dowered. I began with due promptness to look for the fruit of their union—that fruit, I mean, of which the premonitory symptoms would be peculiarly visible in the husband. Taking for granted the splendour of the lady's nuptial gift, I expected to see him make a show commensurate with his increase of means. I knew what his means had been—his article on "The Right of Way" had distinctly given one the figure. As he was now exactly in the position in which still more exactly I was not I watched from month to month, in the likely periodicals, for the heavy message poor Corvick had been unable to deliver and the responsibility of which would have fallen on his successor. The widow and wife would have broken by the rekindled hearth the silence that only a widow and wife might break, and Deane would be as aflame with the knowledge as Corvick in his own hour, as Gwendolen in hers had been. Well, he was aflame doubtless, but the fire was apparently not to become a public blaze. I scanned the periodicals in vain: Drayton Deane filled them with exuberant pages, but he withheld the page I most feverishly sought. He wrote on a thousand subjects, but never on the subject of Vereker. His special line was to tell truths that other people either "funked," as he said, or overlooked, but he never told the only truth that seemed to me in these days to signify. I met the couple in those literary circles referred to in the papers: I have sufficiently intimated that it was only in such circles we were all constructed to revolve. Gwendolen was more than ever committed to them by the publication of her third novel, and I myself definitely classed by holding the opinion that this work was inferior to its immediate predecessor. Was it worse because she had been keeping worse company? If her secret was, as she had told me, her life—a fact discernible in her increasing bloom, an air of conscious privilege that, cleverly corrected by pretty charities, gave distinction to her appearance—it had yet not a direct influence on her work. That only made—everything only made—one yearn the more for it, rounded it off with a mystery finer and subtler.

XI

It was therefore from her husband I could never remove my eyes: I hovered about him in a manner that might have made him uneasy. I went even so far as to engage him in conversation. *Didn't* he know, hadn't he come into it as a matter of course?—that question hummed in my brain. Of course he knew; otherwise he wouldn't return my stare so queerly. His wife had told him what I wanted, and he was amiably amused at my impotence. He didn't laugh—he was not a laugher: his system was to present to my irritation, so that I should crudely expose myself, a conversational blank as vast as his big bare brow. It always happened that I turned away with a settled conviction from these unpeopled expanses, which seemed to complete each other geographically and to symbolise together Drayton Deane's want of voice, want of form. He simply hadn't the art to use what he knew; he literally was incompetent to take up the duty where Corvick had left it. I went still further—it was the only glimpse of happiness I had. I made up my mind that the duty didn't appeal to him. He wasn't interested, he didn't care. Yes, it quite comforted me to believe him too stupid to have joy of the thing I lacked. He was as stupid after as before, and that deepened for me the golden glory in which the mystery was wrapped. I had of course however to recollect that his wife might have imposed her conditions and exactions. I had above all to recollect that with Vereker's death the major incentive dropped. He was still there to be honoured by what might be done—he was no longer there to give it his sanction. Who, alas, but he had the authority?

Two children were born to the pair, but the second cost the mother her life. After this calamity I seemed to see another ghost of a chance. I jumped at it in thought, but I waited a certain time for manners, and at last my opportunity arrived in a remunerative way. His wife had been dead a year when I met Drayton Deane in the smoking-room of a small club of which we both were members, but where for months—perhaps because I rarely entered it— I had not seen him. The room was empty and the occasion propitious. I deliberately offered him, to have done with the matter for ever, that advantage for which I felt he had long been looking.

"As an older acquaintance of your late wife's than even you were," I began, "you must let me say to you something I have on my mind. I shall be glad to make any terms with you that you see fit to name for the information she had from George Corvick—the information, you know, that he, poor fellow, in one of the happiest hours of his life, had straight from Hugh Vereker."

He looked at me like a dim phrenological bust. "The information——?"

"Vereker's secret, my dear man—the general intention of his books: the string the pearls were strung on, the buried treasure, the figure in the carpet."

He began to flush—the numbers on his bumps to come out. "Vereker's books had a general intention?"

I stared in my turn. "You don't mean to say you don't know it?" I thought for a moment he was playing with me. "Mrs Deane knew it; she had it, as I say, straight from Corvick, who had, after infinite search and to Vereker's own delight, found the very mouth of the cave. Where *is* the mouth? He told after their marriage—and told alone—the person who, when the circumstances were reproduced, must have told you. Have I been wrong in taking for granted that she admitted you, as one of the highest privileges of the relation in which you stood to her, to the knowledge of which she was after Corvick's death the sole depositary? All *I* know is that that knowledge is infinitely precious, and what I want you to understand is that if you will in your turn admit *me* to it you will do me a kindness for which I shall be everlastingly grateful."

He had turned at last very red; I daresay he had begun by thinking I had lost my wits. Little by little he followed me; on my own side I stared with a livelier surprise. "I don't know what you're talking about," he said.

He wasn't acting—it was the absurd truth. "She *didn't* tell you——?"

"Nothing about Hugh Vereker."

I was stupefied; the room went round. It had been too good even for that! "Upon your honour?"

"Upon my honour. What the devil's the matter with you?" he demanded.

"I'm astounded—I'm disappointed. I wanted to get it out of you."

"It isn't *in* me!" he awkwardly laughed. "And even if it were——"

"If it were you'd let me have it—oh yes, in common humanity. But I believe you. I see—I see!" I went on, conscious, with the full turn of the wheel, of my great delusion, my false view of the poor man's attitude What I saw, though I couldn't say it, was that his wife hadn't thought him worth enlightening. This struck me as strange for a woman who had thought him worth marrying. At last I explained it by the reflection that she couldn't possibly have married him for his understanding. She had married him for something else. He was to some extent enlightened now, but he was even more astonished, more disconcerted: he took a moment to compare my story with his quickened memories. The result of his meditation was his presently saying with a good deal of rather feeble form:

"This is the first I hear of what you allude to. I think you must be mistaken as to Mrs Drayton Deane's having had any unmentioned, and still less any unmentionable, knowledge about Hugh Vereker. She would certainly have wished it—if it bore on his literary character—to be used."

"It *was* used. She used it herself. She told me with her own lips that she 'lived' on it."

I had no sooner spoken than I repented of my words; he grew so pale that I felt as if I had struck him. "Ah, 'lived'——!" he murmured, turning short away from me.

My compunction was real; I laid my hand on his shoulder. "I beg you to forgive me—I've made a mistake. You *don't* know what I thought you knew. You could, if I had been right, have rendered me a service; and I had my reasons for assuming that you would be in a position to meet me."

"Your reasons?" he asked. "What were your reasons?"

I looked at him well; I hesitated; I considered. "Come and sit down with me here, and I'll tell you." I drew him to a sofa, I lighted another cigarette and, beginning with the anecdote of Vereker's one descent from the clouds, I gave him an account of the extraordinary chain of accidents that had in spite of it kept me till that hour in the dark. I told him in a word just what I've written out here. He listened with deepening attention, and I became aware, to my surprise, by his ejaculations, by his questions, that he would have been after all not unworthy to have been trusted by his wife. So abrupt an experience of her want of trust had an agitating effect on him, but I saw that immediate shock throb away little by little and then gather again into waves of wonder and curiosity—waves that promised, I could perfectly judge, to break in the end with the fury of my own highest tides. I may say that to-day as victims of unappeased desire there isn't a pin to choose between us. The poor man's state is almost my consolation; there are indeed moments when I feel it to be almost my revenge.

EXERCISES

1. Discuss why Vereker cannot or will not explain what his general intention is. What is the difference between the kind of writing Vereker does and the kind of writing a critic does?

2. James said in one of his prefaces that what he remembers about his own intention for writing the story was to "reinstate analytical appreciation" of fiction, because he felt there was a collective mistrust of analytical reading. Discuss why people might mistrust the analysis of fiction and how James's story might be a little parable to reinstate it.

3. What does love have to do with the understanding of literature's general intention? Why is the narrator unable to understand or explain Vereker's general intention?

4. What relationship between literature and life is suggested by this story?

5. What relationship between form and content in literature is suggested by this story?

6. Compare the characteristics of a good artist in "The Real Thing" to the characteristics of a good critic in "The Figure in the Carpet." On the basis of these two stories, discuss the figure in the carpet in James's work.

The Short Story: Terms and Techniques

Allegory A mode of literary expression in which a second level of meaning lies beneath the surface plot. The allegorical mode may dominate the entire work, in which case the lower-level message is the work's primary excuse for being; or it may be an element within a work otherwise interesting and meaningful for its surface level alone. Nathaniel Hawthorne's stories constitute a range of the use of the allegorical mode, from stories that seem almost totally allegorical, in which all the characters and events can be translated into abstract terms, to stories that combine social, psychological, mythic, and metaphysical issues with such complexity that their characters and events defy simple conceptual equivalences.

Ambiguity A written or oral communication is said to be "ambiguous" when it may be interpreted in more than one way. As opposed to its negative sense in expository writing (in which a single meaning is usually intended), ambiguity has a positive sense in literature. In the short story, ambiguity may be manifested in a single event; for example, did Young Goodman Brown's experience in the forest really happen, or was it a dream? It may be manifested in a character; for example, is Bartleby in Melville's story meant to be understood "as if" he were real, or is he a symbolic figure? Because of the short story's highly compressed and poetic nature, ambiguity may play a more important role in the form than it usually does in the novel.

Antagonist Usually a character in fiction that stands as a rival or opponent to the main character or protagonist. However, in the short story, the antagonist is less often a character than it is a force, many times existing within the protagonist himself or herself. For example, the antagonist in Hawthorne's "Young Goodman Brown" is not the devil, but rather the antisocial desires within Goodman Brown himself. In Hemingway's "Hills Like White Elephants," the two central characters are not protagonist and antagonist, but rather both face the inexplicable loss of their relationship—this loss is the antagonist in the story.

Antistory A term popularized by Philip Stevick in a 1971 anthology by the same name. Stevick defines the antistory in terms of its contrariness to traditional conventions of fiction in the following ways: (1) The reality of the external world is broken up. (2) Realism is violated to return to the earlier narrative world of the romance and fairy tale. (3) Event is less important than subjective voice. (4) The story may not have an identifiable theme. (5)

The extreme rather than the ordinary in human experience is emphasized. (6) The experiencing mind takes the place of the analytical author. Other critics have termed such fiction *metafiction, self-reflexive fiction,* and *postmodernist fiction.*

Archetype   The psychoanalyst Carl Jung defines archetype as a "primordial image," an "archaic remnant." Jung makes clear that by archetype he does not mean certain specific mythologic images, for it would be absurd, he says, to suggest that such representations could be inherited. Rather, Jung says, the archetype is a "tendency to form such representations of a motif— representations that can vary a great deal in detail without losing their basic pattern." Northrop Frye, in his *Anatomy of Criticism* (1957), defines archetype as a typical or recurring image—"a symbol which connects one poem with another and thereby helps to unify and integrate our literary experience."

Atmosphere   The general mood of a story, which sets up expectations in the reader. Atmosphere is often associated with the setting of a story, but it can be established by action or dialogue as well. Because the short story is primarily a lyric rather than a mimetic form, atmosphere may play a more important role in the form than in the novel. Eudora Welty has suggested that the first thing we notice about a story is that we really cannot see the solid outlines of it; "it seems bathed in something of its own. It is wrapped in an atmosphere."

Ballad   A ballad is usually thought of as a song that tells a story. The folk ballad is a highly conventionalized story of supernatural events that affect ordinary people. Characterization is slight, and story itself is emphasized. The singer is usually objective, expressing no attitude toward the story. The ballad is the lyrical version of the folktale; in the former, song is foregrounded, whereas in the latter, story is foregrounded. In the early nineteenth century, Wordsworth and Coleridge experimented with the ballad form in *The Lyrical Ballads* by presenting ballad stories from the point of view of a concrete speaker. Romantic poetry is a literary version of the folk ballad; the nineteenth-century tale is a literary version of the folktale. The important difference in both is the introduction in the literary version of the tone and attitude of a particular speaker.

Character   Character in fiction is the creation of a semblance of virtual people. One of the problems of character in short stories was noted very early by William Dean Howells when he suggested that a defect in the form is that whereas we can remember certain stories, we can scarcely remember by name any of the people in them. Frank O'Connor (*The Lonely Voice,* 1963) points out that the characters in short fiction are not ones with which we can easily identify. The length of the form is one cause of this. In the novel we live with characters for a longer period of time; in short stories our encounter is brief, and the predicament rather than the person seems the focus. The short story, because it is more closely related to the romance form than to the novel, is more apt to present projective characters, that is, psychological archetypes rather than fully rounded characters with their own social personae and an individual psychology. The characters in short fiction are also apt to be in extreme situations, and characters in extreme situations are apt to act in terms of a deep level of subjectivity in which human differences are obliterated. In short fiction, we are often dealing with emotional states rather than with objective characters who seem to exist in the social world.

Character sketch   A seventeenth- and eighteenth-century literary form that presents types rather than individual characters; the form is predicated on the notion that human nature is everywhere the same. The short story usually focuses on situation rather than character; however, when the short story does center on character, such as in James Joyce's "Eveline," character is usually revealed by the character's reaction to a single crucial situation.

Coherence   That principle of writing which insists that the separate parts of the work be arranged in such a way that the meaning of the work is clear or the effect of the work is achieved. Coherence is a crucial element in short fiction because in its relatively short span a short story must organize materials in such a way as to strike singly at the reader. Lack of coherence in a short story is more apt to result in disaster than lack of coherence in a novel. Edith Wharton once noted that in the short story, "the least touch of irrelevance, the least chill of inattention, will instantly undo the spell." And William Faulkner has said that whereas in the novel the author can be careless, in the short story, "almost every word has got to be almost exactly right."

Comic story   The comic story encompasses a wide variety of modes and inflections, such as parody, burlesque, satire, irony, humor, and so on. Although both the comic and the tragic characters are unaware of their flaws or shortcomings, the reader usually does not identify with the comic character, but rather perceives the character from a detached point of view; the result is the impression that the character is not a person but a thing.

Complication   That point in a story in which the conflict is developed or when the already existing conflict is further intensified. It constitutes the rising action that must lead up to the climax and resolution.

Conflict   The struggle that develops as a result of the opposition between the protagonist in a fiction and the force that he or she encounters that necessitates a change in action. Traditionally in fiction, the opposing force is another person, the natural world, society, or some force within the self. In short fiction, the conflict is most often between the protagonist and some ineffable force either within the protagonist or within the basic given state of the human condition. Resolution of conflict in a short story is usually not as clear and emphatic as in the novel. The protagonist's response is often in terms that suggest a helplessness in the face of inexplicable forces, for example, the narrator's "Ah, Bartleby! Ah, humanity!" in Melville's famous story.

Controlling image (fundamental image)   A central image around which the story turns. Usually if the image is a metaphor it is termed the *controlling image;* if the image is nonmetaphorical, it is termed the *fundamental image.* Many short stories contain a central controlling image, such as the swaddling clothes in Yukio Mishima's story of that name, the vase in Anne Beattie's story "Janus," and the quail in Rolfe Yngve's story of that name. Such images often appear in short fiction because of the need for a central device to unify the symbolic implications of the story.

Conventions   Although a short story may depict life, the depiction is always by means of devices of stylization and compression. Such conventions constitute the necessary difference between life and art. According to the Russian formalists, these conventions constitute the "literariness" of literature and are the only proper concern of the literary critic. Because the short story has always been a less mimetic form than the novel, it is apt to be more convention-bound. As a result, making distinctions between stories that are highly "literary" and stories which are simple "formula" stories has always been a difficult task for short story critics. All short stories depend on conventions to communicate, but this does not mean that short stories are "conventional."

Crisis (climax)   Crisis denotes a turning point in fiction at which a resolution between the opposing forces must take place. A crisis and a climax do not necessarily have to occur at the same time, for while *climax* refers to the moment of the reader's highest emotional response, *crisis* refers to a structural element of plot only. Crisis marks a turning point in the plot and may indeed lead to climactic effects; there may be more than one crisis moment in a fiction. In Melville's "Bartleby," a crisis occurs when Bartleby decides to do no more copying at all; this makes the narrator try to get rid of him. Another crisis occurs when the narrator decides to move from his present offices. These crisis moments bring on the climax of Bartleby's complete withdrawal from life. The climax of a short story is often presented in terms of an ironic reversal or an ironic understatement. A basic difference between the short story and the novel is that whereas the novel's ending usually involves a point of letup, the short story's ending is a point of intensification.

Deconstruction   A contemporary, and quite controversial, literary theory, most directly indebted to the French thinker Jacques Derrida. Derrida analyzes the logic of discourse and tries to clarify the rules and beliefs that underlie it. The most obvious result of literary critics making use of Derrida's method is that they approach literature in such a way as to lay bare its self-reflexivity, that is, how it continually refers to its own means of signifying. As a result, for the deconstructionist critic, literary works can generate almost infinite contradictory meanings.

Detective story A highly formalized and logically structured mode of short fiction, the origin of which is attributed to Poe in such stories as "The Murders in the Rue Morgue," "The Mystery of Marie Roget," and "The Gold Bug." Other well-known practitioners are G. K. Chesterton and Arthur Conan Doyle. More recently, Jorges Luis Borges, in such stories as "Death and the Compass," has made use of detective story conventions. Because the detective story is such a convention-bound form, it has come under more serious attention recently by critics who have been influenced by European structuralism. Previously, the form had been best known as a popular form, more akin to the crossword puzzle than to the short story. Poe termed his detective tales *ratiocinative.*

Dialogue The similitude of conversation in fiction. Dialogue serves functions of characterizing, furthering the plot, establishing conflict, expressing thematic ideas, and so on. Although often made to sound "natural," dialogue is highly stylized. Many of Hemingway's stories depend greatly on highly stylized dialogue; for example, "Hills Like White Elephants" depends almost solely on dialogue. The word *dialogue* also refers to a fictional form or genre in which two people converse on a given subject.

Displacement A term coined by Northrop Frye to indicate the author's attempt to make the story psychologically motivated and "realistic" even though the basic direction and motivation of the events of the story are its mythic plot. Emphatic mythic stories such as John Updike's "Pygmalion" seem to be about "real" people, but it is the Pygmalion myth that gives the story its direction and theme. The romance stories of Hawthorne are less "displaced," that is, closer to the mythic and conventional structure of short fiction, than the more realistic stories of Henry James.

Doppelganger A common theme in short fiction in the nineteenth century in which a single character is split into two character objectifications of self. The doppelganger theme is a common one in short fiction because of the intensely subjective and romantic nature of the form, as well as because the short story often involves characters caught between the phenomenal and the psychic world of feelings and forces. Conrad's "The Secret Sharer" is an obvious example of the doppleganger theme; Melville's "Bartleby" is a somewhat less obvious example.

Dramatic monologue A poetic or narrative form presented as the speech of one person, in which a dramatic situation is established and a dramatic listener is implied. Its particular tension is between the reader's initial sympathy for the speaker (which is primary) and the reader's moral judgment. We understand the speaker's point of view not only by what he or she says, but also by judging the speaker's limitations and distortions.

Dream vision   An allegorical form common in the Middle Ages in which the narrator or a character falls asleep and then dreams a dream that becomes the actual framed story. Although the dream vision convention is used in the short story, typically the line between dream and reality is blurred. For example, in Hawthorne's "Young Goodman Brown," the reader is not sure whether the events in the forest are meant to be actual, allegorical, or dream.

Effect   Probably the most misunderstood aspect of short fiction since Poe's use of the term in his 1842 review of Hawthorne's *Twice-Told Tales*. Poe says: "A skillful literary artist has constructed a tale. If wise, he has not fashioned his thoughts to accommodate his incidents; but having conceived, with deliberate care, a certain unique or single effect to be wrought out, he then invents such incidents—he then combines such events as may best aid him in establishing his preconceived effect. If his very initial sentence tend not to the outbringing of this effect, then he has failed in his first step." Because of Poe's definition of the short story, the form has often been stereotyped as a contrived trick. However, the emphasis of Poe's remarks, and indeed the emphasis of effect in the short story, is rather on what Poe calls "the deepest effects" that can only be achieved by the unity of impression and sense of totality the short story can create. The effect of the short story is to draw the reader into a mysterious, problematic, extreme, or dreamlike atmosphere in which events and phenomena transcend everyday reality and exceed the powers of the logical mind to comprehend or control them.

Epiphany   A religious term to suggest a showing forth of spirit. Its literary application was introduced into criticism by James Joyce in *Stephen Hero* (1944): "By an epiphany he meant a sudden spiritual manifestation, whether in the vulgarity of speech or of gesture or in a memorable phase of the mind itself. He believed that it was for the man of letters to record these epiphanies with extreme care, seeing that they themselves are the most delicate and evanescent of moments." Stephen draws his theory of epiphany from Thomas Aquinas and establishes the following stages for its achievement: apprehension of the object as one integral thing, recognition that it is a constituted entity (an organized, composite structure), and finally, the manifestation of the "whatness" of the object when it achieves its epiphany. Joyce's stories in *The Dubliners* have been analyzed many times as epiphanic stories in which either a character or the reader experiences a sudden revelation of meaning or significance. See Joyce's "Araby" and "Eveline."

Episode   An episode, which is composed of two or more scenes centering around a central event, is perhaps the most common type of action embodied in the short story.

Essay (informal or personal)   A brief prose work, usually on a single topic, that emphasizes the personal point of view of the author and reveals his or her own values and experiences. The periodical essay of the eighteenth century, as developed by Addison and Steele in the *Tatler* and the *Spectator*, was an early influence on the development of the "sketch" form in American literature and therefore a progenitor of Washington Irving's sketches. The further development of the personal essay in the early nineteenth century by Lamb, Hazlitt, De Quincey, and others gave even further impetus to the development of the lyric-essay tone of Hawthorne's tales. The short story begins as a combination of the lyrical voice of the informal essay and the subject matter of the folktale.

Exemplum A brief anecdote or tale often introduced into medieval sermons for edifying or illustrative purposes. Preachers of the period had collections of such exempla from which to draw. In the fourteenth century, such exempla began to develop into exemplary narratives by the expansion of the anecdotes. Chaucer makes use of exempla in such tales as "The Nun's Priest Tale" and "The Pardoner's Tale."

Existentialism Existentialism became recognized in France in the 1950s. Its basic tenets are that rational thought cannot account for the complexity of human experience and that the individual person is concrete, singular, unique, free, and responsible. The short story is a particularly appropriate mode for existentialist writers in that they prefer the original, atypical, and emotionally charged complexity of situations and dislike the safe, secure, systematic life experience. Typical concerns of existential writers are man's estrangement from society, awareness that the world is meaningless, and recognition that one must turn from external props to the self.

Experience The American philosopher John Dewey makes a distinction between "experience" and "an experience" in *Art as Experience* (1934) that may be helpful in understanding the nature of the short story. As opposed to continuous experience, which is inchoate, "an experience" has an individualizing quality and an aesthetic and emotional unity that give it its name. "The existence of this unity is constituted by a single quality that pervades the entire experience in spite of the variation of the constituent parts." It seems quite clear that the short story deals with "an experience" rather than the more abstract and general sense of experience on which the novel usually focuses.

Exposition Exposition is usually the part or parts of a story that establish the antecedents of the central action. Exposition provides the reader with the necessary background information to understand the story, for example, the time and place of the action. Exposition also more generally provides an introduction to the nature of the fictive world of the story, such as the levels of probability the story employs. Exposition does not have to be located in the first part of a story but can be scattered throughout and thus enable the reader to make a gradual discovery of the background. Exposition is usually elliptical and ambiguous in the short story. Even when it is extensive, its relevance is more likely to be related to the symbolic meaning of the story. For example, the narrator's description of his surroundings and his clerks in Melville's "Bartleby" is not made clearly relevant until the reader perceives the meaning of Bartleby's nonaction.

Fable   One of the oldest narrative forms, the fable has instruction as its primary function. The basic mode of the form is analogy in which animals or inanimate objects speak to illustrate a moral lesson. The form is usually highly abbreviated and epigrammatic with little or no effort to characterize. The most famous examples of the fable are those of Aesop, who used the form orally in Greece in 600 B.C. The modern fable, such as Italo Svevo's "The Mother," may be more extended, may make more use of characterization, and may develop symbolic actions and characters rather than simple allegorical figures and events.

Fabulation   As Robert Scholes has defined it (*Structural Fabulation*, 1975), fabulation presents a world radically discontinuous with the virtual world yet makes us confront that world in some cognitive way. Fabulation is related to myth, fairy tale, folktale, and romance. See Charles Baxter's "The Cliff," Gabriel García Márquez's "A Very Old Man with Enormous Wings," and Paul Bowles's "The Scorpion."

Fairy tale   Various definitions have been posed for the fairy tale, a form of folktale in which supernatural events or characters are prominent. Fairy tales usually depict a realm of reality beyond that of the natural world in which the laws of the natural world are suspended. Bruno Bettelheim in his *The Uses of Enchantment* (1976) suggests that internal processes are externalized in fairy tales and represented there by the figures and events of the tales. The unrealistic nature of the stories is a clear indication that they are not concerned with information about the external world, but rather with the processes taking place within an individual. Fairy tales appeal to children and are valuable for the development of children because they conform to the way a child thinks and experiences the world, says Bettelheim. The projective nature of fairy tales helps the child reconcile and accept human dilemmas in a way that realistic stories cannot.

Fantastic   Tzvetan Todorov, in his study, *The Fantastic* (1970), defines the fantastic as a genre that lies between the "uncanny" and the "marvelous." All three genres present events that cannot be explained by the laws of the familiar world. If the person who experiences the event is a victim of illusion, and thus the laws of the world remain what they are, we are in the realm of the "uncanny." If the event has indeed taken place, then the work has created an alternate reality in which reality is controlled by laws unknown to us, and we are in the realm of the "marvelous." Todorov says that the fantastic occupies the duration of this uncertainty. Once we choose one answer or the other, we leave the fantastic for the uncanny or the marvelous. Because of the short story's basic folklore origins and romantic ancestry, the fantastic is a frequent theme in the form, as are also the uncanny and the marvelous.

Flashback   A scene in a fiction that depicts an earlier event. The flashback can be presented as a reminiscence by a character in the story or simply can be inserted into the narrative as exposition by the author. Contemporary fiction, at least since Joyce, has made use of flashbacks and flashforwards not simply to provide details of previous events, but also to break up the narrative's temporal flow itself. The result of such a time breakup is to create a spatial rather than a temporal form of narrative, which is closer to the conventions of poetry than to the usual linearity of prose. A typical example is Katherine Anne Porter's "The Grave," in which the flashbacks and the present action are so intermixed that time itself is broken up. Faulkner's "A Rose for Emily" is a well-known example of this technique.

Folktale   A short prose narrative, usually orally handed down. The term is often used interchangeably with myth and fairy tale. A. E. Coppard has suggested that the folktale answered to an inborn need to hear tales, "and it is my feeling that the closer the modern short story conforms to that ancient tradition of being spoken to you rather than being read at you the more acceptable it becomes."

Form   One of the most recalcitrant terms to define in literary criticism, especially when it is used in juxtaposition with *content*. As Rene Wellek and Austin Warren point out in *Theory of Literature* (1948), if we think of content as embodying the ideas and emotions in a work of art and form as all the linguistic elements by which content is expressed, we realize that such a distinction is not possible. If we take the most general definition that form is the organization of all the elements in a story in relation to its total effect, we can see that the short story is highly dependent on a perfection of form, that is, an integral relation between content and the structuring of content. Poe's discussion of the short story in his 1842 review of Hawthorne is the first discussion of the formal characteristics of short fiction.

Formalist criticism   The term refers to two different schools of criticism—the Russian formalists of the twenties and the so-called New Critics in America in the forties. The Russian formalists were concerned with what constitutes the "literariness" of literature, that is, the conventional devices literature uses to "make strange" or defamiliarize that which habit has made familiar and thus "not seen." The American formalists were more concerned with the individual work as an object. The most succinct statement of the American Formalist articles of faith is provided by Cleanth Brooks in a 1951 essay. The formalist believes that literary criticism is a description and an evaluation of its object, that the primary concern of criticism is with the problem of unity, that in a successful work form and content cannot be separated, that literature is basically metaphoric and symbolic, that the general and universal are seized on only by the concrete and particular, and that specific moral problems are the subject matter of literature.

Framed tales   The convention of including a story within a story. In such collections as the *Arabian Nights,* the *Decameron,* and the *Canterbury Tales,* the frame serves simply as an excuse for relating a series of tales. John Barth makes use of the frame tale convention in his collections *Lost in the Funhouse* and *Chimera* both to parody the form and to push it to its inevitable self-reflexive implications. Mark Twain's "The Celebrated Jumping Frog of Calaveras County" is a famous frame tale.

Genre study   The concept of studying literature by classification and definition of kinds is as old as the systematic study of literature itself. In fact, since Aristotle introduced the idea in the opening lines of the *Poetics,* the genre principle has been an essential element of the basic proposition that literature indeed can be studied systematically. In the field of literary theory, as in any other science, classification and definition are synonymous with system and understanding. Such an assumption was not questioned until the nineteenth century when the romantics rejected the concept as part of neoclassical rigidity and rules. It has only been since the mid-1950s, primarily due to the influence of Northrop Frye's *Anatomy of Criticism* (1957), that the study of literature (poetics) has recognized the importance of the study of kinds (genre). The widespread influence of European literary theory in the 1960s furthered the study of genre. Genre study is important for the short story precisely because it may allow for more serious discrimination between the short story and the novel and therefore better define the unique characteristics of the form.

Gothic romance   A form of fiction developed in the late eighteenth century, particularly in England, generally attributed to Horace Walpole. In the Preface to the second edition of *The Castle of Otranto,* Walpole claimed that he was trying to combine the two kinds of fiction: events and story typical of the medieval romance and the delineation of character typical of the realistic novel. Clara Reeve in her Preface to *The Old English Baron* emphasized only enough of the marvelous to "excite attention," enough of the manners of real life to "create probability," and enough of the pathetic to "engage the heart." Other examples of the form are Matthew Lewis's *The Monk* and Mary Shelley's *Frankenstein.* Later in the century the typical gothic thematic combination of romance and novel focuses on such gothic hero figures as Heathcliff in Brontë's *Wuthering Heights* and Ahab in Melville's *Moby Dick.* The focus in the gothic romance is more on symbolic figures and events than on realistic ones. The gothic genre had a strong influence on the development of short fiction because of Poe's familiarity with the gothic from Germany and from the gothic stories published in *Blackwoods* magazine in England.

Grammar of stories   On the assumption that stories are governed by rules, a grammar of stories is a set of statements describing these rules. A grammar of stories indicates how a story can be produced by using a set of rules and also provides a structural description of story. French structuralists such as Roland Barthes, Claude Bremond, and Tzvetan Todorov have developed grammars of certain groups of stories. Gerald Prince (*A Grammar of Stories: An Introduction,* 1973) has attempted, by using the theory of generative grammar, to develop a grammar to identify what would be intuitively recognized as minimal story.

Hebraic and Homeric styles Terms coined by Erich Auerbach in *Mimesis: The Representation of Reality in Western Literature* (1953) to designate two basic fictional styles. The first is exemplified by the passage about Ulysses' scar in the *Odyssey*, in which everything is externalized and no contour is blurred. "Clearly outlined, brightly and uniformly illuminated, men and things stand out in a realm where everything is visible; and not less clear— wholly expressed, orderly even in their ardor—are the feelings and thoughts of the persons involved." The Hebraic style, characterized by the story of Abraham and Isaac in Genesis, externalizes the phenomenon only to the extent that it is necessary for the narrative, leaving all else in obscurity. "The decisive points of the narrative alone are emphasized, what lies between is nonexistent; time and place are undefined and call for interpretation . . . ; the whole, permeated with the most unrelieved suspense and directed toward a single goal (and to that extent far more of a unity), remains mysterious and 'fraught with background.'" These distinctions reflect the basic division in fictional forms between the romance fiction and the realistic fiction. Because of its origins in the romance form, the short story is more apt to be in the Hebraic style than in the Homeric style.

Hermeneutics Hermeneutics is the theory of interpretation. The term originally referred to Hermes, the messenger of the gods, for the messages of the gods were mysterious and obscure and required interpretation for human beings. The difference between hermeneutics and exegesis is that the former is theory; the latter is practice. The theory of interpretation belongs originally to sacred texts and has only recently been used to apply to literary texts. The best-known discussion of the theory of interpretation in American criticism is E. D. Hirsch's *The Validity of Interpretation* (1967). Hirsch makes a sharp distinction between interpretation and criticism. "Interpretation is the construction of textual meaning as such; it explicates those meanings, and only those meanings, which the text explicitly represents. Criticism, on the other hand, builds on the results of interpretation; it confronts textual meaning not as such, but as a component within a larger context."

Interior monologue Edourard Dujardin defines this form as the speech of a character designed to introduce us directly to the character's internal life. It differs from other monologues in that it attempts to reproduce thought before any logical organization is imposed. "The internal monologue, in its nature of the order of poetry, is that unheard and unspoken speech by which a character expresses his inmost thoughts, those lying nearest the unconscious, without regard to logical organization—that is, in their original state—by means of direct sentences reduced to syntactic minimum, and in such a way as to give the impression of reproducing the thoughts just as they come into the mind."

Initiation story   This mode of short fiction has been variously defined as the depiction of a fall through knowledge to maturity, a descent into the primitive sources of being, and a discovery of evil. Mordecai Marcus (*Short Story Theories*, 1976) divides initiation stories into three types: those which lead the initiate only to the threshold of maturity and understanding (e.g., McCullers's "A Tree, A Rock, A Cloud"), those which take the protagonist across the threshold but leave him or her uncertain (e.g., Joyce's "Araby"), and those which take the protagonist firmly into maturity (Conrad's "The Secret Sharer"). Because of their relation to primitive rituals, initiation stories are apt to be highly formal, ritualistic, and symbolic.

Irrealism   Irrealism in contemporary short fiction is manifested as the story's loosening of its illusion of reality to expose the reality of its illusion. The story is presented self-consciously as a fiction rather than as-if-it-were-reality. Although this trend is a part of the so-called postmodernist movement in contemporary literature, the short story as a genre has always been more apt to lay bare its fictionality than the novel, which has traditionally tried to cover it up. The allegorical figures of Hawthorne and the symbolic figures of Melville exist more as functions of the story than as problematic characters in an as-if-real world. The basic difference between characters in the early short story form and the completely function-bound characters in the traditional folktale and parable is that such figures as Young Goodman Brown and Bartleby seem to exist both as if they were real people in a real world and as representative figures manipulated for the purposes of the story. The basic difference between these early short stories and the stories of such contemporary writers as John Barth, William H. Gass, Robert Coover, and Donald Barthelme is that in contemporary fiction what is usually a background aesthetic tension is now foregrounded so that the conflict between "fiction" and "reality" becomes the self-conscious conflict of the characters in the story itself. A number of stories in Part IV of this book illustrate this tendency.

Irony   Generally speaking, irony is a speech device whereby the intent of an utterance is conveyed by a statement that has the opposite meaning from what is denoted on the surface. Irony is a pervasive structural device in such stories as Poe's "The Cask of Amontillado" and O. Henry's "The Cop and the Anthem." Irony in twentieth-century short fiction is most often a result of point of view, which is usually both distanced and involved at the same time. The detachment in the point of view in Chekhov's stories, for example, does not indicate indifference, but rather a recognition of incongruities that cannot, by their very nature, be resolved. Irony also often functions in the short story in the form of a concluding understatement that ironically enforces the impact of the story rather than deflating it; see Stephen Crane's "An Episode of War" for an ending of this kind.

Legend A narrative that is handed down from generation to generation, usually associated with a particular place and a specific event. A classic early use of the legend convention in the short story is Washington Irving's "The Legend of Sleepy Hollow," which depicts the expulsion of Ichabod Crane from Sleepy Hollow and which signifies the triumph of the old Dutch atmosphere of New York over the attempted encroachment of Yankee exploitation. See Part III of this book for a number of examples of the modern legend form.

Literary short story A term that was current in American criticism in the 1940s to distinguish the short fiction of Hemingway, Welty, Anderson, and others from the popular pulp and slick magazine fiction of the day. The most pervasive distinction between the two seems to be that the literary story rebelled against the sentimentalizing of reality in the popular short story. The literary story, according to critics of the period, marked a direction toward the more intellectual and subtler emotional treatment in the form.

Local color The term usually refers to a movement in literature, especially in America in the latter part of the nineteenth century. The focus was on the environment, atmosphere, and milieu of a particular region. The movement forms a bridge between the romantic and the realistic movements and thus combines elements of both. The first phase of local-color stories is romantic and tends to emphasize the strange and unfamiliar area, with the focus also on the somewhat regionally secluded area and folk. The shift to realism is inevitable, since the local-color writer depends on particular details of a region and maintaining verisimilitude as to the dialogue of the characters. Local color for the realists means more than "a forced study of the picturesque scenery" of an area.

Lyric short story Eileen Baldeshwiler (*Short Story Theories,* 1976) defines the lyric story as one that differs from the mimetic or epic story in that the lyrical focus is on internal changes, moods, and feelings. The lyric story is usually open-ended and depends on the figurative language usually associated with poetry. The most important writers in the history of this type of short fiction are Turgenev, Chekhov, Mansfield, Sherwood Anderson, Conrad Aiken, and John Updike.

Metafiction (self-reflexive fiction) The terms refer to contemporary stories that take the fictional process as their subject matter; however, the metafictional or self-reflexive tendency has always been a common element of the short story. Basically, this is due to the short story's hovering between conventions of fantasy and reality, in which characters from the everyday world confront projective embodiments of psychic states. Moreover, the short story has always been a more self-conscious, "artistic" form than the novel. The illusion in such stories as "Young Goodman Brown" and "Bartleby" is that within a fiction itself there is a mixing of fiction and reality. Contemporary writers such as William H. Gass, Robert Coover, John Barth, and Donald Barthelme have pushed self-reflexiveness to such extremes that some critics have cried for an end to stories about writing when authors do not have anything else to write about. However, once we accept the postmodernist assumption—that reality is not a given, but rather a constantly made fictionalizing process—then we must agree with the metafictionalists that to write about fictional processes is to write about the only reality there is. See stories in Part IV of this collection.

Metaphor   Perhaps the most basic trope in literature, for in metaphor one thing is described in terms of another; in fact, one thing is, in a quite purposeful "mistake," called something else in order to reveal something that cannot be revealed in any other way. Linguist Roman Jakobson (*Fundamentals of Language,* 1971) defines metaphor as one of the fundamentals of the two polar aspects of communication. *Metaphor* refers to the faculty for selection and substitution; *metonymy* refers to the faculty for combination and contexture. The metaphoric process predominates in the literary schools of romanticism and symbolism, whereas the metonymic process predominates in the so-called realistic schools. The short story, although primarily a metaphoric form, is influenced in the midnineteenth century by the metonymic thrust of realism. A study of the combination of the two processes in the short story is a study not only of a genre, but also of the bipolar nature of language and thought itself.

Modernist story   Modernism as a movement is usually said to have begun in the early twentieth century as an attempt to overturn nineteenth-century bourgeois realism. In fiction, the effort was spearheaded by James Joyce and was manifested as an attempt to substitute a mythic for a realistic fictional method. The result in fiction has been the defeat of the usual expectations of linearity in narrative, of cause and effect, and of coherence of plot and character. Moreover, inward consciousness is substituted for public or objective consciousness, and a subjective voice challenges the objectivity of the nineteenth-century world view. This kind of shift can be seen in the American short story by comparing the "realistic" story of the late nineteenth century with the modernist short story of the twenties. See Austin Wright's *The American Short Story in the Twenties* (1961) for a complete discussion of this shift.

Motif   This term usually refers to a conventional incident or situation in a fiction that may serve as the basis for the structure of the narrative. In criticism, it is often used similarly to its use in music—to indicate a recurring idea or pattern. Russian formalist Boris Tomashevsky uses the term to refer to the smallest particles of thematic material. "The theme of an irreducible part of a work is called the motif; each sentence, in fact, has its own motif." Mutually related motifs constitute the thematic bonds of the work, says Tomashevsky. He also distinguishes between "bound motifs," which cannot be omitted without disturbing the connections between events, and "free motifs," which can be omitted without disturbing the causal-chronological course of events.

Motivation   Although this term usually refers to the convention of justifying the action of a character from his or her own psychological makeup, the Russian formalists use the term to refer to the network of devices justifying the introduction of individual motifs or groups of motifs in a work. Boris Tomashevsky classifies motivational devices as follows: (1) compositional motivation, which refers to the economy and usefulness of the motifs, the principle of every single property in the work contributing to the overall effect of the work; (2) realistic motivation, which refers to what Tzvetan Todorov has called *vraisemblance,* the realistic devices to convince the reader that the story is plausible and lifelike; and (3) artistic motivation, which refers to the demands of the artistic structure.

Myth   Myth is story, story that tacitly symbolizes basic human experience. Primitive myths are early expressions of the "story-telling urge." The short story is a romantic revival of mythic story. The anthropologist Claude Lévi-Strauss says, "Myth is the part of language where the formula *tradutore, tradittore* reaches its lowest truth value. . . . Its substance does not lie in its style, its original music, or its syntax, but in the story which it tells."

Myth critcism   A critical approach that assumes that literature develops both historically and psychologically out of myth. Northrop Frye asserts that in myth, "we see the structural principles of literature isolated." Myth criticism is not to be confused with *mythological criticism,* which is primarily concerned with finding parallels to mythological stories in the surface action of narrative. Myth critics are concerned with deep mythic structures.

Narrative   Narrative usually implies a contrast to "enacted" fiction. Wellek and Warren in *Theory of Literature* (1949) say that its chief pattern is its exclusiveness: "It intersperses scenes in dialogue with summary accounts of what is happening." Scholes and Kellogg in *The Nature of Narrative* (1966) say that by narrative they mean literary works that have the presence of both a story and a storyteller.

Narrative essay   A form of the personal essay in which the essay either is told in narrative form or makes extensive use of anecdotal material. The popularity of the form in the eighteenth century helped give rise to the nineteenth-century short story. Many critics have noted that Washington Irving's *Sketchbook* was strongly influenced by the tone established in the essays of Addison and Steele. Poe described many of the stories in Hawthorne's *Twice-Told Tales* as being narrative essays in tone and structure.

Narrator   In the most general sense, the one who tells the story or who recounts the narrative. Wayne Booth develops several different types of narrators in *The Rhetoric of Fiction* (1961). Even when an author is not dramatized in the story, the story creates an implicit picture of an author behind the scenes, which Booth calls an "implied narrator." Various dramatized narrators that Booth describes are unacknowledged centers of consciousness, observers, narrator-agents, and self-conscious narrators. Booth suggests that the important element to consider in narration is the relationship between the narrator, the author, the characters, and the reader. The relationship of the narrator to the story has always been an important element in the highly subjective and lyrically relativist short story.

Naturalism   The term was brought to bear on literature in the late nineteenth century by Émile Zola, who insisted on the novel's telling of absolutely truthful instances. The term refers more to choice of subject matter than to technical conventions. Although the late nineteenth-century stories of Guy de Maupassant and George Moore are often described as naturalistic, the focus on hard events and the rigid empiricism that dominate naturalism have not made the movement conducive to the short story.

Novel   The novel is, of course, many things, perhaps even all things its author wants to put in it. However, it differs from the short story not only in length, but also in its view of reality. Ian Watt (*The Rise of the Novel*, 1957) says that the novel is distinguished from other genres by the attention it pays to individual characterization and detailed presentation of the environment. Moreover, the novel is concerned with using past experiences as the causes of present action. "The novel in general," says Watt, "has interested itself much more than any other literary form in the development of its characters in the course of time."

Novella, novelle, nouvelle, novelette, novela   *Novella* is the Italian term for short story, from *nuovo*, meaning "new, strange, extraordinary." The best-known example of the form in Italian is Boccaccio's *Decameron*. The Renaissance form focuses on plot rather than character, but it differs from the fable in presenting the remarkable as being fact. Usually the story is built around a symbolic object, referred to as the "Falcon" (from one of Boccaccio's stories). The German form of short fiction is called *novelle* and indicates a form longer than a short story but shorter than a novel. The French term for this form is *nouvelle* and is distinguished from the short story, or *conte*, in both its length and its subject matter; whereas the *conte* arose as a French form that dealt with the fantastic, the *nouvelle* selects the strange and unusual from ordinary life. *Novela* is the Spanish term for the same form. *Novelette* is the term usually preferred by the British to refer to the form longer than the short story but shorter than the novel, whereas *short novel* is the term usually used to refer to American works of this genre. Henry James, using the French term *nouvelle*, found the form most conducive to his talents. Referring to it as the "ideal, the beautiful and blest nouvelle," he claimed that its main merit was the "effort to do the complicated thing with a strong brevity and lucidity—to arrive on behalf of the multiplicity, at a certain science of control."

Objective correlative   This key critical concept in modern formalist criticism was coined by T. S. Eliot in an essay on *Hamlet* in his book *The Sacred Wood*. An objective correlative is a situation, event, or an object that, when presented or described in a work, evokes a particular emotion for which the object is the formula. Short stories, which must often focus on a single situation and depend on the evocativeness or emotional resonance of a situation or event, express (like poetry) emotion by means of objective correlatives.

Parable   A brief allegory, often an analogue of an ethical situation, as in the parables of Jesus. See Tolstoy's "The Three Hermits" for a traditional parable. However, modern treatments of the parable form are not as clear in their moral meaning as Tolstoy's story. See John L'Heureux's "The Anatomy of Desire" for a more complex and open-ended parable.

Plot and story   The minimum distinction between plot and story is that *story* is a more general term referring to the narrative of character and action, whereas *plot* refers specifically to action with little reference to character. Russian formalist critic Boris Tomashevsky, however, makes the distinction between plot *(fabula)* and story *(sujet)* by noting that in the plot the events are arranged according to the orderly sequence in which those events are presented in the work, whereas in the story the events are arranged in causal-chronological order. Plot is the sum of the same events as are presented in story, but they are arranged so as to engage the emotions and develop the theme.

Plotless story   In the late nineteenth and early twentieth centuries, when Chekhov seemingly eliminated the beginnings and endings of his stories, critics called his stories plotless. Gradually, critics recognized that this so-called plotlessness indicated a general shift in emphasis in fiction from external action to a concern with mood and motives—the drama of the mind.

Point of view   The means by which the story is presented to the reader or, as Percy Lubbock says in *The Craft of Fiction* (1921), "the relation in which the narrator stands to the story," a relation that Lubbock says governs the whole question of technique in fiction. The basic questions to be asked about point of view are: Who talks to the reader? From what position regarding the story does he or she tell it? What channels of information does he or she use? And at what distance does he or she place the reader from the story? Wayne Booth, in his *The Rhetoric of Fiction* (1961), believes that additional questions need to be asked, such as: "What kind of person is the narrator? How fully characterized? How much aware of himself as a narrator? How reliable? At what points shall he speak truth and at what points utter no judgments or even utter falsehood?"

Postmodernist story   Postmodernism is an extension of the modernist movement that results from an increasing emphasis on self-consciousness and consequently self-reflexiveness in fiction. It moves beyond the modernist focus on the individual self to a fiction that is more and more about itself as fiction and about fictional processes. In the short story, the best-known practitioners are William H. Gass, Donald Barthelme, Robert Coover, John Barth, Jorge Borges, and Vladimir Nabokov.

Protagonist   The central figure in a story, the character whose fortunes most concern the reader. According to Frank O'Connor in *The Lonely Voice,* the protagonist of the short story is apt to be the "little man," or what O'Connor calls a "submerged population group." In such short stories as "Bartleby," it is not clear whether the unitary figure Bartleby most concerns us or whether the real protagonist is the narrator who confronts Bartleby and tries to understand him.

Psychological criticism   The most influential form of psychological criticism is so-called depth psychology, influenced by Sigmund Freud. However, much psychoanalytic criticism degenerated in the first half of the twentieth century into elaborate symbol hunting for Freudian dream symbols or, as practiced by psychoanalysts, attempts to psychoanalyze either a fictional character or the author. More recently, psychoanalytic criticism has become more sophisticated and helpful for understanding the basic nature of literature and the reader's relationship to it. Perhaps the best known is that form of criticism referred to as *transactive criticism* developed and practiced at the Center for the Psychological Study of the Arts at the State University of New York at Buffalo. Norman Holland, drawing on recent developments in ego psychology, is concerned with the empirical study of how the themes of a reader's own identity match and shape the themes of the text. David Bleich has turned his attention to the more basic nature of subjective criticism and has tried to develop a theory for a new subjective paradigm in contemporary thought. Psychoanalytic criticism is now less concerned with interpretation of the text, the character, or the author and is more concerned with how the Freudian dream work of displacement, condensation, and symbolism is related to the conventions of literature itself.

Realism   A literary method or technique in which the primary convention is to create an illusion of faithfulness to external reality. As a reaction to romanticism in the middle to late nineteenth century, realism was not a hospitable technique for the short story, which has always been basically a romantic and symbolic fictional form. The only sort of realism suitable to the short story is the psychological realism of James, which, rather than maintaining a fidelity to external reality, instead creates a stylized representation of the mind itself.

Reception aesthetics   Introduced in the late 1960s by German theorist Hans Robert Jauss, reception aesthetics derives from phenomenology and focuses on the study of a literary text through the reader's reaction to it. The best-known European practitioner is Wolfgang Iser (*The Implied Reader: Patterns of Communication in Prose Fiction from Bunyan to Beckett,* 1972). The best-known American practitioner is Stanley Fish (*Self-Consuming Artifacts: The Experience of Seventeenth-Century Literature,* 1972). For the reception critic, meaning is an event or process and is therefore temporal rather than spatial. Form is also temporal rather than spatial. The form of a work, says Fish, is the form of the reader's experience. Meaning, rather than being embedded in the work, is created through particular acts of reading. Iser says that there is no exact correlation between what is described in literary texts and objects in the real world. As a result, indeterminacy is characteristic of literary works. The reader must "normalize" the text either by projecting his or her standards into the text or by revising his or her standards. It is only in the act of reading that indeterminacy can be replaced with meaning.

Rhetorical criticism A mode of criticism that is concerned with the interactions between the work, the author, and the audience. The rhetorical critic is concerned with the work as a means of communication—the means by which the work affects or controls the reader. Such criticism thus works best with didactic works such as satire. However, Wayne Booth (*The Rhetoric of Fiction,* 1961) is concerned with nondidactic fiction and views rhetoric as the "art of communicating with readers"; he is therefore concerned with devices the author uses to "consciously or unconsciously impose his fictional world upon the reader."

Romance The romance (whether it be the medieval romance or the modern romance form) usually differs from the novel in that the focus is less on realistic events and characters than on symbolic events and representational characters. Northrop Frye says the romancer does not try to create real people but rather stylized figures and psychological archetypes.

Scene A unit of fictional action or narration in which specific actions are narrated or depicted. The scene, as opposed to the summary of past events or events quickly passed over, gives the reader a sense of participation in the event at the same time that it occurs. Consequently, it is usually used for intense moments. Although a short story most often is an episode of several scenes, the entire story can be composed of one scene, such as Hemingway's "Hills Like White Elephants."

Semiotics (semiology) The science of signs and sign systems in communication. *Semiotics* is the favored term of Charles Sanders Pierce, which he defines as the formal doctrine of signs. *Semiology* is the term coined by Ferdinand de Saussure: "A science that studies the life of signs within society is conceivable; it would be a part of social psychology and consequently of general psychology; I shall call it semiology (from the Greek *sēmeion,* 'sign'). Semiology would show what constitutes signs, what laws govern them." Roman Jakobson says that every message is made of signs and that the science of semiotics deals with the principles that underlie the structure of signs, their use in messages, and the specific nature of various sign systems.

Setting   Setting refers to all the circumstances and environment, both temporal and spatial, of a narrative. In the sense that setting is synonymous with atmosphere, setting has always played an important role in the short story.

Spatial form   Joseph Frank, in a now famous essay, uses this term to describe an effort in modern fiction to make the reader apprehend the work spatially in a "moment of time" rather than sequentially. To do this, the artist breaks up the narrative into interspersed fragments. This is parallel with the modern effort to supplant historical time in fiction with mythic time—the bodying forth of eternal prototypes apprehended totally. According to this point of view, a work of fiction cannot be read, but only reread. Frank says, "A knowledge of the whole is essential to an understanding of any part"; the work must be grasped as a unity. Creation and perception of spatial form are obviously more common and successful in the short story than in the novel because of length.

Stream of consciousness technique   A narrative technique by which an author tries to embody the total range of consciousness of a character without any authorial comment or explanation. The usual distinction between stream of consciousness and the interior monologue is that the latter presents that aspect of consciousness in which the mind formulates thoughts and feelings in language, whereas the former is a broader term indicating the presentation of all ranges of consciousness: sensations, thoughts, memories, associations.

Structuralism   The structuralist literary critic attempts to define structural principles that operate intertextually throughout the whole of literature as well as principles that operate in genres and in individual works. In one of the best primer introductions to structuralist literary theory, *Structuralism in Literature* (1974), Robert Scholes says that because narrative extends from myth to the modern novel, while preserving structural features, it offers a rich field for the structuralists: "Structuralism and formalism have given us virtually all the poetics of fiction that we have." Frederic Jameson (*The Prison House of Language,* 1972) suggests that formalism and structuralism find their most privileged objects in the smaller forms of narrative such as folktales, anecdotes, and short stories.

Tall tale   A humorous tale very popular in the American West; the story usually makes use of realistic detail and common speech, but it tells a tale of impossible events that most often focuses on a single legendary, superhuman figure, such as Paul Bunyan or Davy Crockett.

Teaching story   In traditional Hindu medicine, a story is given to a psychically disturbed patient for meditation. Such stories, often fairy tales, serve as parallels to states of mind. Internal processes are thus externalized in the characters and events of the story and embody the way the mind works. Meditation on the stories constitutes direct teaching and therapy.

Tone   Tone usually refers to the dominant mood of a work. Poe suggested that tone is more important in the short story than plot because the short story is unified by one perceiver's unified response to an event.

Vraisemblance (verisimilitude)   Critic Tzvetan Todorov defines *vraisemblance* as "the mask which conceals the text's own laws but which we are supposed to take for a relation to reality." Northrop Frye calls this concept "displacement"—a tendency to displace myth in a human direction. Frye says that by displacement he means the techniques a writer uses to "make his story credible, logically motivated or morally acceptable—lifelike, in short." Similarly, Todorov says we speak of vraisemblance when we refer to the work's attempts to make us believe that it conforms to reality and not to its own laws.

Western story   Usually a popular short story form. The setting is the key element—Western America during the frontier period. The characters are usually stereotyped; the plot is usually melodrama. Bret Harte's stories of philosophic gamblers, whores with hearts of gold, and grizzled prospectors who turn sentimental are the forerunners of the form in the American short story. In Stephen Crane's "The Blue Hotel," the romanticized violence of the Western pulp story is the key plot element that leads to the tragic death of the Swede.

Yarn   The yarn is an oral tale or a written transcription of what purports to be an oral tale. The yarn is usually a broadly comic tale; the classic example is "The Celebrated Jumping Frog of Calaveras County." The tension in the yarn is usually between realistic detail and incredible events juxtaposed in such a way that the teller of the tale protests that he or she is telling the truth while the reader or listener knows that he or she is lying. In other words, the incredulity of the listener is crucial to the effect of the yarn. The basic difference between the yarn and the tall tale is that the latter focuses primarily on the hero, whereas in the yarn the focus is on the teller.

Biographies of the Authors

ACHEBE, CHINUA

Born: Ogidi, Nigeria, 1930
Education: University College of Ibadan; London University
Biographical notes: Born a member of the Ibo tribe of southeast Nigeria; learned English at the age of eight; after college, began a career in radio; worked for the Biafran Ministry of Information to raise funds during the Biafran war; left Nigeria when it came under military rule; teaches at University of Massachusetts, in Amherst, Massachusetts.
Short story collections: *Sacrificial Egg*, 1962; *Girls at War*, 1973
Novels: *Things Fall Apart*, 1958; *No Longer at Ease*, 1960; *Arrow of God*, 1964; *A Man of the People*, 1966; *Anthills of the Savannah*, 1988
Poetry: *Christmas in Biafra*, 1973
Nonfiction: *Hopes and Impediments*, 1988
Comment: Writing in English, he focuses primarily on the changing life of the African people.

AKUTAGAWA, RYŪNOSUKE

Born: Tokyo, Japan, 1892
Education: Studied literature at Tokyo Imperial University
Biographical Notes: Received recognition for his writing while still a teenager; committed suicide at age thirty-five.
Short story collections: *Tales Grotesque and Curious*, 1930; *Hell Screen and Other Stories*, 1948; *Japanese Short Stories*, 1951; *Rashōmon and Other Stories*, 1952
Novels: *Kappa*, 1927
Comment: Often combines Western short story techniques, such as irony and the grotesque, with Oriental themes. His short stories "Rashōmon" and "In a Grove" were combined to make the classic film *Rashōmon*.
Died: 1927

ANDERSON, SHERWOOD

Born: Camden, Ohio, 1876
Education: Primarily self-educated
Biographical notes: Worked as a laborer, copywriter, and advertising writer; was a manufacturer and businessman until he made enough money to devote himself to writing full time.
Short story collections: *Winesburg, Ohio*, 1919; *Triumph of the Egg*, 1921; *Horses and Men*, 1923; *Death in the Woods*, 1933
Novels: *Windy McPherson's Son*, 1916; *Marching Men*, 1917; *Poor White*, 1920; *Dark Laughter*, 1925

Comment: Anderson's lyrical stories were a significant influence on the development of the modern American short story.
Died: 1941

ATWOOD, MARGARET

Born: Ottawa, Ontario, 1939
Education: Victoria College, University of Toronto, 1961; studied English literature at Harvard University
Biographical notes: Spent much of her childhood in rural northern Ontario and Quebec; largely educated at home during early childhood; since graduate school has taught at a number of schools in Canada and America.
Short story collections: *Dancing Girls,* 1977; *Murder in the Dark,* 1983; *Bluebeard's Egg and Other Stories,* 1986
Novels: *Surfacing,* 1972; *The Handmaid's Tale,* 1986; *Before Man,* 1979; *Bodily Harm,* 1981; *Cat's Eye,* 1989
Poetry: *Selected Poems,* 1978
Plays: *Sunset,* 1928; *Maria,* 1935
Comment: Atwood's fiction is often mythic rather than realistic.

BABEL, ISAAC

Born: Odessa, Russia, 1894
Education: Began writing while still an adolescent in school
Biographical notes: Served in the Communist Cavalry from 1917 to 1924; fell out of favor with the Stalinist regime in the 1930s, was arrested in 1939, and then disappeared.
Short story collections: *Odessa Tales,* 1924; *Red Cavalry,* 1926; *Isaac Babel: Collected Stories,* 1957
Novels: *Benia Krik,* 1927
Comment: A powerful influence on a number of modern short story writers.
Died: 1941?

BAMBARA, TONI CADE

Born: New York City, 1939
Education: Queens College, B.A., 1959; City College of New York, M.A., 1964; studied dance and filmmaking at a number of schools
Biographical notes: Grew up in Harlem and poverty-stricken Bedford-Stuyvesant; after graduating from college, worked for the New York State Welfare Department as a case investigator; directed a recreation program for psychiatric patients at New York City Metropolitan Hospital; has taught at various U.S. universities and colleges.
Short story collections: *Gorilla, My Love,* 1972; *The Sea Birds Are Still Alive: Collected Stories,* 1977
Novels: *The Salt Eaters,* 1980; *If Blessing Comes,* 1987
Comment: Focuses on the lives of black people in the U.S. North and South; often makes use of street dialect.

BARTH, JOHN

Born: Cambridge, Maryland, 1930
Education: Johns Hopkins University, B.A., 1951, and M.A., 1952
Biographical notes: Considered music as a career and briefly attended Julliard School of Music; began teaching career at Pennsylvania State University in 1953; also taught at State University of New York at Buffalo and Johns Hopkins University.
Short story collections: *Lost in the Funhouse*, 1968; *Chimera*, 1972
Novels: *The Floating Opera*, 1956; *The End of the Road*, 1958; *The Sot-Weed Factor*, 1960; *Giles Goatboy*, 1966; *Letters*, 1979; *Sabbatical: A Romance*, 1982; *Tidewater Tales*, 1987; *The Last Voyage of Somebody the Sailor*, 1991
Nonfiction: *The Friday Book: Essays and Other Nonfiction*, 1984
Comment: The most influential advocate of nonreferential, self-reflexive fiction in modern American literature.

BARTHELME, DONALD

Born: Philadelphia, Pennsylvania, 1931
Education: University of Houston, 1949–1957
Biographical notes: Family moved to Houston, Texas, when he was two years old; began writing in high school; edited the University of Houston college newspaper; wrote film criticism for the *Houston Post;* founded *Forum*, a literary magazine; became director of Houston's Contemporary Art Museum; taught creative writing at a number of universities.
Short story collections: *Come Back, Dr. Caligari*, 1964; *Unspeakable Practices, Unnatural Acts*, 1968; *City Life*, 1970; *Sadness*, 1972; *Amateurs*, 1976; *Great Days*, 1979; *Sixty Stories*, 1980; *Overnight to Many Distant Cities*, 1983; *Forty Stories*, 1987
Novels: *Snow White*, 1967; *The Dead Father*, 1975; *Paradise*, 1987; *The King*, 1990
Nonfiction: *Guilty Pleasures*, 1974
Comment: The most significant practitioner of satiric, absurdist short fiction in modern American literature.
Died: 1989

BAXTER, CHARLES

Born: Minneapolis, Minnesota, 1947
Education: Macalester College; from State University of New York at Buffalo, Ph.D., 1974
Biographical notes: High school teacher and professor of English at Wayne State University in Detroit, Michigan.
Short story collections: *Harmony of the World*, 1984; *Through the Safety Net*, 1985
Novels: *First Light*, 1987
Comment: Deals with chaos that lies beneath the surface of middle-class reality.

BEATTIE, ANN

Born: Washington, D.C., 1947
Education: American University, B.A., 1969; University of Connecticut, M.A., 1970

Biographical notes: Grew up in Chevy Chase, Maryland, a suburb of Washington, D.C.; has taught at Harvard University and the University of Virginia.
Short story collections: *Distortions,* 1976; *Secrets and Surprises,* 1979; *The Burning House,* 1982; *Where You'll Find Me,* 1986; *What Was Mine,* 1991
Novels: *Chilly Scenes of Winter,* 1976; *Falling in Place,* 1980; *Love Always,* 1985; *Picturing Will,* 1989
Comment: Focuses on American life in the sixties, seventies, and eighties in a flat, declarative writing style.

BIERCE, AMBROSE

Born: Meigs County, Ohio, 1842
Education: Little formal education
Biographical notes: Joined the Union Army at age nineteen; went to California on a military expedition; worked for the Treasury Department there; started educating himself and began writing and publishing stories in various newspapers; was editor of a number of different newspapers; went to Mexico in 1913 to observe Pancho Villa's rebellion against Mexican government; disappeared in battle.
Short story collections: *Tales of Soldiers and Civilians,* 1891; *Can Such Things Be?* 1893
Nonfiction: *The Fiend's Delight,* 1873; *Nuggets and Dust,* 1873; *Cobwebs from an Empty Skull,* 1874
Comment: During the realist period in American literature, Bierce was one of the few writers who remained a romantic in the tradition of Edgar Allan Poe.
Died: 1914?

BÖLL, HEINRICH

Born: Cologne, Germany, 1917
Education: University of Cologne, 1939
Biographical notes: Served in the German army for six years during World War II; was an American prisoner of war in 1945; won the Nobel Prize for Literature in 1972.
Short story collections: *Eighteen Stories,* 1966; *Absent Without Leave and other Stories,* 1967; *The Casualty,* 1986; *The Stories of Heinrich Böll,* 1986
Novels: *Acquainted with the Night,* 1954; *The Train Was on Time,* 1956; *Tomorrow and Yesterday,* 1957; *The Bread of Our Early Years,* 1957; *Billiards at Half-Past Nine,* 1961; *The Clown,* 1965; *And Where Were You, Adam?* 1970; *Group Portrait with Lady,* 1971; *The Lost Honor of Katherine Blum,* 1975; *The Safety Net,* 1982; *A Soldier's Legacy,* 1985
Nonfiction: *Missing Persons and Other Essays,* 1977
Comment: One of Germany's most important postwar writers; focuses on social, political, and economic life in Germany after the war.
Died: 1985

BONTEMPS, ARNA

Born: Alexandria, Louisiana, 1902
Education: Pacific Union College, B.A., 1923; University of Chicago, M.A., 1943

Biographical notes: Grew up in Los Angeles; moved to New York; taught school in New York City, Chicago, and Alabama; worked at Fisk University as a librarian and later taught at Yale University.

Short story collections: *The Old South: A Summer Tragedy and Other Stories,* 1973

Novels: *God Sends Sunday,* 1931; *Black Thunder,* 1936

Plays: *St. Louis Woman,* 1946

Comment: Has written several juvenile books, both fiction and nonfiction; has edited and coedited a number of anthologies, many of which focus on black achievements in America.

Died: 1973

BORGES, JORGE LUIS

Born: Buenos Aires, Argentina, 1899

Education: Was tutored at home as a child; attended private schools in Geneva, Switzerland, during World War I

Biographical notes: Born into a relatively wealthy family; began writing in his early twenties; was a municipal librarian in Buenos Aires between 1938 and 1946 until dismissed by the dictator Juan Perón; with the overthrow of Perón, was made director of the National Library of Buenos Aires and professor of literature at the University of Buenos Aires.

Short story collections: *Labyrinths,* 1962; *Ficciones,* 1962; *Dreamtigers,* 1964; *A Personal Anthology,* 1967; *The Alph and Other Stories 1933–1969,* 1970; *Chronicles of Bustos Domecq,* 1976; *Six Problems for Don Isidro Parodi,* 1981, both with Adolfo Bioy

Nonfiction: *Other Inquisitions 1937–52,* 1964; *A Universal History of Infamy,* 1972

Poetry: *Fervor of Buenos Aires,* 1923

Comment: Stories are often philosophical, intellectual, and literary; creates playful metaphysical puzzles about the nature of reality and human knowledge; is one of the foremost contemporary Spanish-American authors.

Died: 1986

BOWEN, ELIZABETH

Born: Dublin, Ireland, 1899

Education: Studied at the London Council of Art, 1918–1919

Biographical notes: Worked as a nurse during World War I; after her marriage in 1923, lived mainly in London.

Short story collections: *Encounters,* 1923; *The Cat Jumps,* 1934; *Look at All Those Roses,* 1941; *The Demon Lover,* 1945; *A Day in the Dark and Other Stories,* 1965; *The Collected Stories of Elizabeth Bowen,* 1974

Novels: *The Hotel,* 1927; *The Last September,* 1929; *The House in Paris,* 1935; *The Death of the Heart,* 1938; *The Heat of the Day,* 1949; *Eva Trout,* 1969

Nonfiction: *Seven Winters,* 1942; *English Novelists,* 1946; *Afterthought: Pieces About Writing,* 1962

Comment: Often focuses on women's efforts to find satisfying social roles and emotional states; writes in a highly polished and crafted style.

Died: 1973

BOWLES, PAUL

Born: New York City, 1910
Education: Studied music in New York, Berlin, and Paris; studied design in New York and at the University of Virginia
Biographical notes: Began publishing poetry when he was sixteen; wrote musical scores for a number of Broadway plays; returned to writing fiction in 1942.
Short story collections: *The Delicate Prey and Other Stories*, 1950; *A Little Stone*, 1950; *The Hours After Noon*, 1959; *A Hundred Camels in the Courtyard*, 1962; *The Time of Friendship*, 1967; *Pages from Cold Point and Other Stories*, 1968; *Three Tales*, 1975; *Things Gone and Things Still Here*, 1977; *Collected Stories of Paul Bowles, 1939–1976*, 1979; *Midnight Mass*, 1981
Novels: *The Sheltering Sky*, 1949; *Let It Come Down*, 1952; *The Spider's House*, 1955; *Up Above the World*, 1966; *Points in Time*, 1982
Poetry: *Scenes*, 1968; *The Thicket of Spring: Poems, 1926–1969*, 1972, *Next to Nothing*, 1976
Comment: Most frequent theme is the weakness of Western rationalism in the face of the primitive world.

BOYLE, KAY

Born: St. Paul, Minnesota, 1903
Education: Attended highly prestigious Shipley School in Bryn Mawr, Pennsylvania; studied architecture at Ohio Mechanics Institute in Cincinnati, Ohio; studied music at Cincinnati Conservatory of Music
Biographical notes: Worked as a telephone operator before going to New York to pursue writing career; lived for eighteen years in France, England, Austria, and Germany; after World War II, worked as a foreign correspondent in Germany; taught at San Francisco State University between 1963 and 1979.
Short story collections: *Short Stories*, 1929; *Wedding Day*, 1930; *First Love*, 1933; *The White Horses of Vienna*, 1936; *Thirty Stories*, 1946; *The Smoking Mountain: Stories of Postwar Germany*, 1951; *Nothing Ever Breaks Except the Heart*, 1966; *Fifty Stories*, 1980
Novels: *Plagued by the Nightingale*, 1931; *Year Before Last*, 1932; *Gentleman, I Address You Privately*, 1933; *Monday Night*, 1938; *The Crazy Hunter*, 1940; *Primer for Combat*, 1942; *Avalanche*, 1943; *A Frenchman Must Die*, 1946; *His Human Majesty*, 1949; *The Seagull on the Step*, 1955; *Generation Without Farewell*, 1960; *The Underground Woman*, 1975
Nonfiction: *The Long Walk at San Francisco State and Other Essays*, 1970
Comment: Focuses on the theme of the moral responsibility of the individual; experiments with surrealistic imagery and stream of consciousness.

BOYLE, T. CORAGHESSAN

Born: Peekskill, New York, 1948
Education: Studied music at State University of New York at Potsdam; studied writing at the University of Iowa, where he received Ph.D. in 1977
Biographical notes: After college, became a teacher; characterized himself as a hippie.
Short story collections: *Descent of Man*, 1979; *Greasy Lake and Other Stories*, 1985; *If the River Was Whiskey*, 1989

Novels: *Water Music,* 1981; *Budding Prospects: A Pastoral,* 1984; *World's End,* 1987; *East Is East,* 1990
Comment: Central theme is the importance of history; primarily writes in a satiric mode; often parodies social institutions and literary forms.

BUZZATI, DINO

Born: Belluno, Italy, 1906
Biographical notes: Worked most of his life as an editor and correspondent in Milan.
Short story collections: *Restless Nights: Selected Stories of Dino Buzzati,* 1983; *The Siren: A Selection from Dino Buzzati,* 1985
Novels: *The Tartar Steppe,* 1940
Comment: Often makes use of journalistic techniques to give his fantastic stories an air of verisimilitude.
Died: 1972

CARVER, RAYMOND

Born: Clatskanie, Oregon, 1939
Education: Humboldt State College, B.A., 1963
Biographical notes: Married young and had to take a variety of jobs to support his wife and two children; won several creative writing awards and taught writing at a number of universities.
Short story collections: *Will You Please Be Quiet, Please?,* 1976; *What We Talk About When We Talk About Love,* 1981; *Cathedral,* 1983; *Where I'm Calling From,* 1988
Nonfiction: *Fires,* 1983 (contains his few nonfiction pieces)
Poetry: *Near Klamath,* 1968; *Winter Insomnia,* 1970; *At Night the Salmon Move,* 1976; *Where Water Comes Together with Other Water,* 1985; *Ultramarine,* 1986; *A New Path to the Waterfall,* 1989
Comment: The leading figure in the renaissance of the short story in the 1970s and 1980s; early practitioner of the so-called minimalist school.
Died: 1988

CHEEVER, JOHN

Born: Quincy, Massachusetts, 1912
Education: Attended an exclusive prep school but got himself thrown out so he would not have to attend Harvard University
Biographical notes: After his father lost all his money in the stock market crash of 1929, his mother supported the family with a small gift shop.
Short story collections: *The Way Some People Live,* 1943; *The Enormous Radio,* 1953; *The Housebreaker of Shady Hill,* 1958; *Some People, Places and Things That Will Not Appear in My Next Novel,* 1961; *The Brigadier and the Golf Widow,* 1964; *The World of Apples,* 1973; *The Stories of John Cheever,* 1978
Novels: *The Wapshot Chronicle,* 1957; *The Wapshot Scandal,* 1964; *Bullet Park,* 1969; *Falconer,* 1977; *Oh What a Paradise It Seems,* 1982
Comment: Frequently focuses on the suburban milieu, often in mythic and fantastic modes.
Died: 1982

CHEKHOV, ANTON

Born: Taganrog, a seaport town in southern Russia, 1860
Education: University of Moscow, M.D., 1884
Biographical notes: In his early life to support his family while he studied medicine, Chekhov wrote a large number of popular short anecdotes and tales for Russian newspapers, mostly conventional and forgettable.
Short story collections: *Tales of Melpomene*, 1884; *In the Twilight*, 1887; *Innocent Talk*, 1887; *Tales*, 1888; *Tales and Stories*, 1894; *Collected Works*, 1900–1904
Plays: *The Sea Gull*, 1896; *Uncle Vanya*, 1899; *The Three Sisters*, 1901; *The Cherry Orchard*, 1904
Comment: The most important influence on the development of the modern short story in the twentieth century.
Died: 1904

CHESNUTT, CHARLES WADDELL

Born: Cleveland, Ohio, 1858
Education: Attended grade school in Fayetteville, North Carolina; largely self-taught
Biographical notes: Taught school and served as a high school principal until moving to New York and working as a journalist and a court reporter; admitted to the Ohio bar.
Short story collections: *The Conjure Woman*, 1899; *The Wife of His Youth and Other Stories of the Color Line*, 1899; *Collected Stories of Charles W. Chesnutt*, 1990
Novels: *The House Behind the Cedars*, 1901; *The Marrow of Tradition*, 1901; *The Colonel's Dreams*, 1905
Nonfiction: *Frederick Douglas*, 1899
Comment: One of the most important figures in the early history of Black literature in the United States; helped to establish African-American fiction.
Died: 1932

CHOPIN, KATE

Born: St. Louis, Missouri, 1851
Education: Catholic parochial school
Biographical notes: Married at age 18 and moved with husband to New Orleans; returned to St. Louis in 1884 after her husband's death.
Short story collections: *Bayou Folk*, 1894; *A Night in Acadie*, 1897
Novels: *At Fault*, 1890; *The Awakening*, 1899
Comment: Wrote realistic local-color stories about Creole life and customs; often emphasized female sexuality as well as woman's need for self-assertion and independence.
Died: 1904

CONRAD, JOSEPH

Born: Berdycezew, Poland, 1857
Education: Mostly self-educated
Biographical notes: Went to sea at the age of seventeen and stayed a seaman for the next twenty years; while still at sea, Conrad became a naturalized British citizen in 1886.

Short story collections: *Tales of Unrest,* 1898; *Youth, A Narrative, and Two Other Stories,* 1902; *Typhoon and Other Stories,* 1903; *A Set of Six,* 1908; *Within the Tides,* 1915; *Tales of Hearsay,* 1925
Novels: *Heart of Darkness,* 1899; *Lord Jim,* 1900; *Nostromo,* 1904; *The Secret Agent,* 1907; *Under Western Eyes,* 1911; *Chance,* 1913; *Victory,* 1915
Comment: One of the most significant innovators of symbolic fiction at the turn of the century.
Died: 1924

COOVER, ROBERT

Born: Charles City, Iowa, 1932
Education: Southern Illinois University, 1949–1951; Indiana University, B.A. 1953; University of Chicago, M.A., 1965
Biographical notes: Served in the Navy; has taught at Princeton, Columbia, and Washington Universities.
Short story collections: *Pricksongs and Descants,* 1969
Novels: *The Origin of the Brunists,* 1966; *The Universal Baseball Association, Inc., J. Henry Waugh, Prop,* 1968; *The Public Burning,* 1977; *Gerald's Party,* 1987
Comment: Specializes in fantasy, parody, and metafiction.

CORTÁZAR, JULIO

Born: Brussels, Belgium, 1914
Education: Received degrees to teach in both elementary and secondary schools from Escuela Normal Mariano Acosta in Buenos Aires in 1932 and 1935; also attended University of Buenos Aires from 1935 to 1937.
Biographical notes: Worked as a teacher and translator.
Short story collections: *Bestiary,* 1951; *Cronopios and Famas,* 1962; *End of the Game and Other Stories,* 1967; *Blow-up and Other Stories,* 1968; *A Change of Light and Other Stories,* 1974; *We Love Glenda So Much and Other Tales,* 1983
Novels: *Hopscotch,* 1963; *A Manual for Manuel,* 1973
Comment: His fiction is often experimentalist and surrealistic.
Died: 1984

CRANE, STEPHEN

Born: Newark, New Jersey, 1871
Education: Attended Lafayette College, 1890, and Syracuse University, 1891
Biographical notes: Worked as a freelance journalist in New York after leaving college, barely making a living until his fiction began being published; became a war correspondent in Cuba and Greece.
Short story collections: *The Open Boat,* 1898; *The Monster,* 1899; *Whilomville Stories,* 1900
Novels: *Maggie: A Girl of the Streets,* 1893; *The Red Badge of Courage,* 1895; *George's Mother,* 1896
Poetry: *The Black Riders,* 1895; *War Is Kind,* 1899
Comment: Significant innovator of impressionistic and symbolic fiction at the turn of the century.
Died: 1900

CROSSMAN, PATRICIA

Born: Vinalhaven, Maine, 1923
Education: Attended New England School of Art in Boston, 1941–42.
Biographical notes: Was a writer for the *Portland Press Herald,* Portland, Maine; also ran a business with her husband; is now retired and lives with her husband of over forty years on the small island of Vinalhaven off the coast of Maine.
Short stories: Has published a number of stories in *Redbook, McCalls, Woman's Day,* and *Good Housekeeping.*
Comment: Crossman says that what she feels most impelled to write about is the "unexpected strength of ordinary people."

DAVIS, JOHN P.

Education: Bates College, Harvard Law School
Biographical notes: Publicity director for Fisk University; editor of *Our World* magazine; director-editor of special publications for Phelps-Stokes Fund in New York City.
Nonfiction: Edited *The American Negro Reference Book,* 1966
Comment: Not well known as a fiction writer.

DE LA FONTAINE, JEAN

Born: Chateau-Thierry, France, 1621
Education: Was a novice at the Oratory, 1641; studied law in Paris, 1645–1647
Biographical notes: Spent most of his life as a prolific author of comedies, lyrics, fables, and licentious tales which put him in trouble with the law and in royal disfavor.
Works: *Fables,* 1668–1694; *Contes,* 1665–1674
Comment: Moved the fable away from its traditional focus on conventional morality toward a more realistic view of human nature.
Died: 1695

DE LA MARE, WALTER

Born: Charlton in Kent, England, 1873
Education: St. Paul's Cathedral Choir School in London, but unable to go to college
Biographical notes: Became a bookkeeper in the London offices of the Standard Oil Company; received a pension in 1908 and devoted himself entirely to writing.
Short story collections: *The Riddle and Other Stories,* 1923; *Ding Dong Bell,* 1924; *Broomsticks and Other Tales,* 1925; *The Connoisseur and Other Stories,* 1926; *Told Again: Traditional Tales,* 1927; *On the Edge,* 1930; *The Lord Fish,* 1933; *The Wind Blows Over,* 1936; *The Best Stories of Walter de la Mare,* 1942; *The Magic Jacket and Other Stories,* 1943; *The Scarecrow and Other Stories,* 1945; *The Dutch Cheese and Other Stories,* 1946; *A Beginning and Other Stories,* 1955
Novels: *Henry Brocken,* 1904; *The Return,* 1910; *The Three Mulla-Mulgars,* 1910; *Memoirs of Midget,* 1921; *At First Sight,* 1930
Poetry: *Collected Poems,* 1942; *Collected Rhymes and Verses,* 1944; *The Burning Glass and Other Poems,* 1945; *Winged Chariot,* 1951; *O Lovely England and Other Poems,* 1953

Nonfiction: *Pleasures and Speculations,* 1940; *Private View,* 1953
Comment: Primarily writes fantasies, often in fairy tale or fable mode; often focuses on children and the childlike.
Died: 1956

DINESEN, ISAK (KAREN BLIXEN)

Born: Rungsted, Denmark, 1885
Education: Studied English at Oxford University; studied painting in Paris and Rome
Biographical notes: Father committed suicide when she was ten years old; went to Africa with her husband in 1913; suffered from syphilis much of her life; divorced her husband and worked a coffee plantation in Africa on her own; returned to Denmark in 1931 and spent the rest of her life writing.
Short story collections: *Seven Gothic Tales,* 1934; *Winter's Tales,* 1942; *Last Tales,* 1975; *Anecdotes of Destiny,* 1974; *Carnival: Entertainments and Posthumous Tales,* 1977
Nonfiction: *Out of Africa,* 1937; *Daguerreotypes and Other Essays,* 1979
Comment: A classic storyteller who makes use of the conventions of fairy tale and fable to create complex philosophic parables.
Died: 1962

DOSTOEVSKY, FYODOR

Born: Moscow, 1821
Education: Attended military and engineering college in St. Petersburg
Biographical notes: Resigned from army in 1844 to devote his time to writing; arrested in 1849 and sentenced to death for political conspiracy; sentence was commuted, and he spent four years in a Siberian prison instead.
Novels: *Poor Folks,* 1846; *The Double,* 1846; *House of the Dead,* 1860; *Notes from the Underground,* 1864; *Crime and Punishment,* 1866; *The Idiot,* 1869; *The Brothers Karamazov,* 1880
Comment: Although best known for his novels of psychological and social realism, Dostoevsky's experiments with the theme of the double and the monologue form have had an important impact on modern short fiction.
Died: 1881

FAULKNER, WILLIAM

Born: New Albany, Mississippi, 1897
Education: Attended University of Mississippi in Oxford after a short stint in the Canadian Royal Flying Corps
Biographical notes: Began writing while living in New Orleans; was awarded the Nobel Prize for Literature in 1949.
Short story collections: *Go Down, Moses,* 1942; *Collected Stories of William Faulkner,* 1950; *Uncollected Stories of William Faulkner,* 1979
Novels: *Sartoris,* 1929; *As I Lay Dying,* 1930; *Light in August,* 1932; *Absalom, Absalom,* 1936; *The Unvanquished,* 1938; *The Hamlet,* 1940; *Intruder in the Dust,* 1948; *Knight's Gambit,* 1949; *The Town,* 1957; *The Mansion,* 1959; *The Reivers,* 1962

Comment: One of Faulkner's central themes is "time," especially the impingement of the past on the present; often experiments with various points of view and highly stylized language.

Died: 1962

FITZGERALD, F. SCOTT

Born: St. Paul, Minnesota, 1896

Education: Attended private schools and Princeton University

Biographical notes: Left Princeton in 1917 to join the army; married Zelda Sayre in 1920 and left the army to work for an advertising agency in New York; after much rejection of his work, achieved success with novels and stories that projected the image of flappers and wealthy playboys; between 1924 and 1931, lived in Europe, where Zelda experienced a nervous breakdown; last years, mostly spent in Hollywood, were marked by depression and drinking.

Short story collections: *Flappers and Philosophers*, 1920; *Tales of the Jazz Age*, 1922; *All the Sad Young Men*, 1926: *Taps at Reveille*, 1935

Novels: *This Side of Paradise*, 1920; *The Beautiful and the Damned*, 1922; *The Great Gatsby*, 1925; *Tender Is the Night*, 1934

Comment: Much of Fitzgerald's fiction is based on his own experiences in college, Europe, and Hollywood; best known for his image of the so-called jazz age of the 1920s.

Died: 1944

FREITAG, GEORGE H.

Born: Canton, Ohio, 1909

Education: No information available

Biographical notes: Taught writing at night schools and managed a sign business in San Bernardino, California, in the 1950s.

Short story collections: Has published a number of short stories in such magazines as *Harper's, The New Yorker, The Atlantic Monthly,* and others.

Novels: *The Lost Land,* 1947

Comment: His story "An Old Man and His Hat" was included in *Best American Short Stories* in 1968.

GALSWORTHY, JOHN

Born: Kingston Hill, Surrey, England, 1867

Education: Received a law degree from Oxford, 1898

Biographical notes: Called to the bar but was not interested in being a barrister; traveled in Canada, Australia, the South Seas, and Russia and begain a successful writing career; won Nobel Prize for Literature in 1932.

Short story collections: *Awakening,* 1920; *Captures,* 1923; *Caravan,* 1925; *A Commentary,* 1908; *Five Tales,* 1918; *From the Four Winds,* 1897; *The Little Man and Other Satires,* 1915; *A Man of Devon,* 1901; *A Motley,* 1910; *On Forsyte 'Change,* 1930; *Tatterdemalion,* 1920; *Two Forsyte Interludes,* 1927

Novels: Author of over twenty separate novels, but best known for the trilogies *The Forsyte Saga,* 1922, *A Modern Comedy,* 1929; and *End of the Chapter,* 1935

Plays: Wrote a number of plays, most of which are collected in *Plays,* 1929
Poems: *The Collected Poems of John Galsworthy,* 1934
Nonfiction: *A Sheaf,* 1916; *Another Sheaf,* 1919; *Candelabra,* 1933; *The Inn of Tranquility,* 1912
Comment: Best known for his literary portrayal of the upper middle class during the Edwardian era.
Died: 1933

García Márquez, Gabriel

Born: Arcata, Colombia, 1928
Education: Attended National University at Bogatá, Colombia, in 1947 to study law, but had to go to another university in Cartagena when National University was closed by civil war
Biographical notes: Began a journalism career while still in school, focusing especially on political issues; worked for Cuban news agency from 1959 to 1961; moved to New York and then Mexico City, where he edited magazines and wrote for an advertising agency; achieved great success in 1967 with the publication of *One Hundred Years of Solitude;* received the Nobel Prize in Literature in 1982; his political views have made him an exile from his country.
Short story collections: *Big Mama's Funeral,* 1962; *The Incredible and Sad Story of Innocent Eréndira and Her Heartless Grandmother,* 1927; *Collected Stories,* 1984
Novels: *Withering Leaves,* 1955; *No One Writes to the Colonel,* 1961; *In Evil Hour,* 1962; *One Hundred Years of Solitude,* 1967; *The Autumn of the Patriarch,* 1975; *Chronicle of a Death Foretold,* 1981; *Love in a Time of Cholera,* 1988; *The General in His Labyrinth,* 1990
Comment: Best known for his mastery of the technique known as "magical realism"—a form of fiction that features the concrete detail of everyday reality but exists in a world of fantasy.

Gass, William H.

Born: Fargo, North Dakota, 1924
Education: Kenyon College, B.A., 1947; Cornell University, Ph.D., 1954
Biographical notes: Has taught philosophy at a number of U.S. universities.
Short story collections: *In the Heart of the Heart of the Country,* 1968
Novels: *Omensetter's Luck,* 1966; *Willie Masters' Lonesome Wife,* 1971
Nonfiction: *Fiction and the Figures of Life,* 1970; *On Being Blue,* 1975; *The World within the Word,* 1978; *The Habitations of the Word,* 1984
Comment: A master of the self-referential text; an antirealist and experimentalist.

Gilman, Charlotte Perkins

Born: Hartford, Connecticut, 1860
Education: Little formal schooling; attended Rhode Island School of Design in Providence
Biographical notes: Had to support herself very early as a commercial artist, an art teacher, and a governess; suffered a nervous breakdown after the birth of her daughter and moved to Pasadena, California, without her husband; began career

as a writer and a lecturer on feminist ideas; ran for several political offices on the Socialist ticket.

Poetry: *In This Our World,* 1893

Nonfiction: *Women and Economics,* 1898; *Concerning Children,* 1900; *The Home,* 1903; *Human Work,* 1904; *Man-Made World,* 1911; *His Religion and Hers,* 1923

Comment: Best-known for "The Yellow Wall-Paper" because of its focus on woman's entrapment by male bias.

Died: 1935

GLASPELL, SUSAN

Born: Davenport, Iowa, 1876

Education: Drake University, Ph.D., 1899

Biographical notes: Worked as a legislative reporter for a Des Moines newspaper for a short time, but moved back to Davenport to spend her time writing fiction; later moved to New York and married social writer George Cram Cook in 1913, after which they moved to Provincetown, Massachusetts, on Cape Cod, where she wrote plays for her husband's Provincetown Players, famous for giving a start to many famous playwrights, such as Eugene O'Neil.

Short story collections: *Lifted Masks,* 1912

Novels: *The Glory of the Conquered,* 1909; *The Visioning,* 1911; *Fidelity,* 1915; *Brook Evans,* 1928; *Fugitive's Return,* 1929; *Ambrose Holt and Family,* 1931; *The Morning Is Near Us,* 1940; *Norma Ashe,* 1942; *Judd Ranking's Daughter,* 1945

Plays: *Plays,* 1920

Comment: Primarily a writer of popular novels and stories characterized by melodrama, sentimentality, and social issues; "A Jury of Her Peers," her only story that remains well known, is based on the play *Trifles* she wrote for the Provincetown Players.

Died: 1948

GODWIN, GAIL

Born: Birmingham, Alabama, 1937

Education: University of North Carolina, B.A., 1959; University of Iowa, M.A., 1968, and Ph.D., 1971

Biographical notes: Worked as a reporter for the *Miami Herald* for a year and then spent three years at the U.S. Embassy in London.

Short story collections: *Dream Children,* 1976; *Mr. Bedford and the Muses,* 1983

Novels: *The Perfectionists,* 1970; *Glass People,* 1972; *The Odd Woman,* 1974; *Violet Clay,* 1978; *A Mother and Two Daughters,* 1981; *The Finishing School,* 1985; *A Southern Family,* 1987; *Father's Melancholy's Daughter,* 1991

Comment: Focuses on the social and psychic situation of the modern woman.

GOLD, HERBERT

Born: Cleveland, Ohio, 1924

Education: Columbia University, B.A., 1946; and M.A., 1948

Biographical notes: Served in the U.S. Military Intelligence during World War II; taught at U.S. colleges and universities.

Short story collections: *Love and Like,* 1960; *The Magic Will: Stories and Essays of a Decade,* 1971; *Stories of Misbegotten Love,* 1985
Novels: *Birth of a Hero,* 1951; *The Prospect Before Us,* 1954; *The Man Who Was Not With It,* 1957; *The Optimist,* 1959; *Therefore Be Bold,* 1960; *Salt,* 1963; *Fathers,* 1967; *The Great American Jackpot,* 1969; *Biafra Goodbye,* 1970; *My Last Two Thousand Years,* 1972; *Swiftie the Magician,* 1974; *Waiting for Cordelia,* 1977; *Slave Trade,* 1979; *He/She,* 1980; *Family,* 1981; *True Love,* 1982; *Mister White Eyes,* 1984
Nonfiction: *The Age of Happy Problems,* 1962; *A Walk on the West Side,* 1981
Comment: Primarily known for his realistic novels that chronicle American life in the midwest and in California.

GORDIMER, NADINE

Born: Springs, South Africa, 1923
Education: University of Witwatersrand, Johannesburg, B.A., 1945
Biographical notes: Published her first story in 1939 and has been writing and living in Johannesburg ever since.
Short story collections: *The Soft Voice of the Serpent,* 1952; *Six Feet of the Country,* 1956; *Friday's Footprint,* 1960; *Not for Publication,* 1965; *Livingstone's Companions,* 1971; *A Soldier's Embrace,* 1980; *Something Out There,* 1984
Novels: *The Lying Days,* 1953; *A World of Strangers,* 1958; *Occasion for Loving,* 1963; *The Late Bourgeois World,* 1966; *A Guest of Honour,* 1970; *The Conservationist,* 1975; *Burgher's Daughter,* 1979; *July's People,* 1981; *Hillela: A Sport Novel,* 1987; *A Sport of Nature,* 1987; *My Son's Story,* 1990
Nonfiction: *The Essential Gesture: Writing Politics and Places,* 1989
Comment: Best known for her exploration of black–white relations in South Africa; she has moved from an earlier concern with writing style to a more emphatic focus on social issues.

GREENE, GRAHAM

Born: Berkhamstead, Herts, England, 1904
Education: Balliol College, Oxford, B.A., 1925
Biographical notes: Joined Roman Catholic Church; worked as a subeditor for *The Times,* London; reviewed books and films for *The Spectator;* worked with British Foreign Office and Secret Service; traveled in Southeast Asia and South and Central America.
Short story collections: *Nineteen Stories,* 1947; *Twenty-One Stories,* 1954; *A Sense of Reality,* 1963; *May We Borrow Your Husband?,* 1967; *Collected Stories,* 1972
Novels (selected): *Brighton Rock,* 1938; *The Power and the Glory,* 1940; *The Heart of the Matter,* 1948; *The End of the Affair,* 1951; *A Burnt-Out Case,* 1961; *The Comedians,* 1966; *Travels with My Aunt,* 1969; *The Human Factor,* 1978; *Monsignor Quixote,* 1982
Nonfiction: *Why Do I Write?,* 1948; *Collected Essays,* 1969; *A Sort of Life,* 1971; *Ways of Escape,* 1980
Comment: Best known for his so-called Catholic novels and his thriller "entertainments," Greene often focuses on theological matters of innocence, the fall from grace, sin, and redemption.
Died: 1991

HARTE, BRET

Born: Albany, New York, 1836
Education: Largely self-educated
Biographical notes: Moved to California; worked as a typesetter; edited *The Overland Monthly;* served as a U.S. consul in Prussia and Glasgow.
Short story collections: *The Luck of Roaring Camp, and Other Sketches,* 1870; *Mrs. Skaggs Husbands, and Other Sketches,* 1872; *Tales of the Argonauts,* 1875; *On the Frontier,* 1884; *The Writings of Bret Harte* (20 volumes), 1896–1914
Novels: *Gabriel Conroy,* 1876
Drama: *Two Men of Sandy Bar,* 1876; *Ah Sin,* 1877
Comment: A significant contributor to the development of the short story form; combined local color with the well-made story.
Died: 1902

HAWTHORNE, NATHANIEL

Born: Salem, Massachusetts, 1804
Education: Bowdoin College, B.A., 1825
Biographical notes: After graduation, he moved back to Salem and devoted himself to writing; after his marriage in 1842, moved to Concord, Massachusetts, but came back to Salem in 1846, where he took a government position in the Salem Customs House; in 1853, was appointed consul in Liverpool, England, a position he kept until 1857.
Short story collections: *Twice-Told Tales,* 1837; *Mosses from an Old Manse,* 1846
Novels: *The Scarlet Letter,* 1850; *The House of the Seven Gables,* 1851; *The Blithedale Romance,* 1852; *The Marble Faun,* 1860
Comment: One of the two most important innovators of the short story in America at midcentury; along with Poe, he transformed the old tale form into a highly symbolic new genre.
Died: 1864

HEARN, LAFCADIO

Born: Island of Lafcadio, off west coast of Greece, 1850
Education: French seminary and St. Cuthbert's, Ushaw, England
Biographical notes: After his mother went insane and he was abandoned by his great-aunt, he traveled to America at age nineteen and settled in Cincinnati, Ohio, where he spent a number of years writing for newspapers; moved to New Orleans, where he continued to write for newspapers; lived in the West Indies for a time; lived in Japan, where he became a Japanese citizen; taught secondary school and lectured at the Imperial University.
Short story collections: *Fantastics and Other Fancies,* 1914; *Stray Leaves from Strange Literature,* 1884; *Some Chinese Ghosts,* 1887; *Leaves from the Diary of an Impressionist,* 1911; *The Writings of Lafcadio Hearn,* 1922
Novels: *Chita,* 1889; *Karma,* 1918
Nonfiction: *Creole Sketches,* 1924; *Two Years in the French West Indies,* 1890; *Glimpses of Unfamiliar Japan,* 1894
Translations: Hearn translated a number of stories by the French writers Théophile

Gautier and Guy de Maupassant; he also translated and retold Japanese tales in *Japanese Fairy Tales,* 1898–1922; and *Kwaiden,* 1904

Comment: Often focuses on the odd and the gruesome; master of the brief impressionistic sketch and the weird fable.

Died: 1904

HEMINGWAY, ERNEST

Born: Oak Park, Illinois, 1898

Education: Graduated from high school but would not attend college

Biographical notes: Began work as a reporter for the Kansas City *Star* soon after graduation; volunteered as an ambulance driver early in World War I, but was injured after only three weeks and spent six months convalescing; after his return to the United States, worked as a foreign correspondent in Paris for the Toronto *Star;* began publishing his fiction and returned to America in 1928 to fame and fortune; lived in Key West, Florida, and later in Idaho; spent much time big game hunting in Africa and sport fishing in Florida; worked as a war correspondent during the Spanish Civil War and World War II; received the Nobel Prize for Literature in 1954; committed suicide in 1961.

Short story collections: *Three Stories and Ten Poems,* 1921; *In Our Time,* 1924; *Men Without Women,* 1927; *The Complete Short Stories,* 1987

Novels: *The Sun Also Rises,* 1926; *A Farewell to Arms,* 1929; *Winner Take Nothing,* 1933; *To Have and Have Not,* 1937; *For Whom the Bell Tolls,* 1940; *Across the River and into the Trees,* 1950; *The Old Man and the Sea,* 1952; *Islands in the Stream,* 1970; *The Garden of Eden,* 1986

Nonfiction: *Death in the Afternoon,* 1932; *The Green Hills of Africa,* 1935

Comment: Hemingway is best known for his thematic focus on the virtues of courage and heroism and a writing style characterized by clipped and repetitive syntax and simple language.

Died: 1961

HENRY, O. (WILLIAM SYDNEY PORTER)

Born: Greensboro, North Carolina, 1862

Education: Privately tutored by his aunt, with whom he lived after his mother's death

Biographical notes: Became a licensed pharmacist; moved to Texas, where he married and worked as a draftsman in Texas Land Office; worked as bank teller in Austin, Texas; tried and found guilty of embezzlement; served three years in federal penitentiary in Ohio, where he began writing short stories; moved to New York and gained fame for his magazine and newspaper stories under the name of O. Henry.

Short story collections: *Cabbages and Kings,* 1904; *The Four Million,* 1906; *The Trimmed Lamp,* 1906; *Heart of the West,* 1907; *The Voice of the City,* 1908; *The Gentle Grifter,* 1908; *Roads of Destiny,* 1909; *Options,* 1909; *Whirligigs,* 1910; *Sixes and Sevens,* 1911; *Rolling Stones,* 1912; *Waifs and Strays,* 1917; *The Complete Works of O. Henry,* 1953

Comment: America's best-known practitioner of the well-made, ironic, surprise-ending story; often scorned for his simplistic plots and stereotyped characters, but a powerful influence on the short story at the turn of the century.

Died: 1910

HESSE, HERMANN

Born: Calw, Wüttermberg, Germany, 1877
Education: Fled the Maulbronn Seminary, where he was supposed to prepare for the ministry; was expelled from high school
Biographical notes: Worked in bookshops for several years; was a pacificst during World War I and wrote antiwar tracts; underwent analysis with Carl Jung; received Nobel Prize for Literature in 1946.
Short story collections: *Stories of Five Decades,* 1972
Novels: *Peter Caminzind,* 1904; *Demian,* 1919; *Siddhartha,* 1922; *Steppenwolf,* 1927; *Narcissus and Goldmund,* 1930; *Journey to the East,* 1932; *Magister Ludi,* 1943
Comment: Best known for novels that explore the unconscious or that focus on Eastern mysticism.
Died: 1962

HOLST, SPENCER

Born: Detroit, Michigan
Education: Self-educated
Biographical notes: Besides being a writer, Holst is a painter who has had public showings of his work.
Short story collections: *The Language of Cats and Other Stories,* 1971; *Spencer Holst Stories,* 1976
Comment: Often writes short parables and modern fairy tales that focus on the nature of art, thought, and reality.

HUGHES, LANGSTON

Born: Joplin, Missouri, 1902
Education: Lincoln University, B.A., 1929
Biographical notes: After high school, traveled as a merchant seaman; worked as a busboy and at other odd jobs before receiving a college scholarship; taught at a number of U.S. universities as visiting professor; was in important figure in the Harlem Renaissance.
Short story collections: *The Ways of White Folks,* 1934; *Simple Speaks His Mind,* 1950; *Laughing to Keep from Crying,* 1952; *Simple Stakes a Claim,* 1957; *Something in Common and Other Stories,* 1963; *Simple's Uncle Sam,* 1965
Novels: *Not Without Laughter,* 1930; *Tambourines to Glory,* 1958
Poetry: *Weary Blues,* 1926; *Fine Clothes to the Jew,* 1927; *The Dream Keeper and Other Poems,* 1932; *Lament for Dark Peoples and Other Poems,* 1944; *Fields of Wonder,* 1947; *One-Way Ticket,* 1949; *Montage of a Dream Deferred,* 1951; *Ask Your Mama,* 1961; *The Panther and the Lash,* 1967
Nonfiction: *The Sweet Flypaper of Life,* 1955; *A Pictorial History of the Negro in Entertainment,* 1967; *Black Misery,* 1969; *A Pictorial History of Blackamericans,* 1973
Comment: Best known for his poetry; a popular writer who focuses on simple values and the human relationship to God.
Died: 1967

HURSTON, ZORA NEALE

Born: Eatonville, Florida, 1901

Education: Although Hurston left home and school to work as a wardrobe mistress for a theatrical group, she managed to complete her schooling and to attend Howard University; later went to New York and won a scholarship to Barnard College, where she studied anthropology.

Biographical notes: Hurston became part of the so-called Harlem Renaissance in the 1920s, writing stories and plays; also continued her anthropology studies by collecting folklore of the American South; worked as a librarian, a journalist, and a teacher; died in poverty in a welfare home.

Short story collections: *The Eatonville Anthology,* 1927

Novels: *Jonah's Gourd Vine,* 1934; *Their Eyes Were Watching God,* 1937; *Moses, Man of the Mountain,* 1939; *Seraph on the Sewanee,* 1948

Nonfiction: *Mules and Men,* 1938; *Tell My Horse,* 1938

Comment: Many of Hurston's short stories make use of African-American folklore in the South.

Died: 1960

IRVING, WASHINGTON

Born: New York City, 1783

Education: Admitted to the bar after being educated for a law profession

Biographical notes: After a financial failure of the family business in Europe in 1818, Irving stayed in England to pursue a profession as a writer; served as a U.S. diplomat and minister to Spain before returning to America, where he spent the rest of his life.

Short story collections: *The Sketchbook,* 1820; *Bracebridge Hall,* 1822; *Tales of a Traveller,* 1824; *The Alhambra,* 1832; *The Crayon Miscellany,* 1835; *Wolfert's Roost,* 1855

Long Fiction: *Diedrich Knickerbocker's History of New York,* 1809

Nonfiction: *A History of the Life and Adventures of Christopher Columbus,* 1828; *A Chronicle of the Conquest of Granada,* 1829; *Voyages and Discoveries of the Companions of Columbus,* 1832; *Life of George Washington,* 1855–1859

Comment: Combined European folk legends with an urbane writing style to create the basis of a unique new short narrative form.

Died: 1859

JAMES, HENRY

Born: New York City, 1843

Education: Received private tutoring both in America and Europe; entered Harvard Law School when he was only nineteen, but soon decided to devote his life to literature

Biographical notes: From 1875 until end of his life, James lived primarily in England, becoming a British citizen in 1915.

Short story collections: *A Passionate Pilgrim,* 1875; *The Madonna of the Future,* 1879; *The Lesson of the Master,* 1892; *The Real Thing,* 1893; *Embarrassments,* 1896; *The Soft Side,* 1900; *The Better Half,* 1903; *The Finer Grain,* 1910

Novels: *Roderick Hudson,* 1875; *The American,* 1877; *Daisy Miller,* 1879; *The Portrait of a Lady,* 1881; *The Bostonians,* 1886; *The Princess Cassamassima,* 1886; *The Spoils of Poynton,* 1897; *The Turn of the Screw,* 1898; *The Awkward Age,* 1809; *The Wings of the Dove,* 1902; *The Ambassadors,* 1903; *The Golden Bowl,* 1904

Nonfiction: *French Poets and Novelists,* 1878; *Hawthorne,* 1879; *Partial Portraits,* 1888; *Picture and Text,* 1893; *Prefaces to the New York Edition of the Novels and Tales of Henry James,* 1907–1917

Comment: James's greatest contributions to the short story are his self-conscious concern with his craft and a complex writing style that attempts to capture the subtle processes of the human mind.

Died: 1916

JOYCE, JAMES

Born: Dublin, Ireland, 1882

Education: Attended Jesuit boarding schools and University College, Dublin, from which he graduated in 1902; studied medicine in Paris

Biographical notes: Feeling estranged from his native country, Joyce spent much of his adult life in Switzerland and France, where he taught school to support himself while he wrote.

Short story collections: *The Dubliners,* 1914

Novels: *A Portrait of the Artist as a Young Man,* 1916; *Ulysses,* 1922; *Finnegan's Wake,* 1939

Poetry: *Chamber Music,* 1907

Drama: *Exiles,* 1918

Comment: Joyce is one of the most powerful influences on modern short fiction because of his development of a spatial rather than a temporal narrative structure.

Died: 1942

KAFKA, FRANZ

Born: Prague, Czechoslovakia, 1883

Education: Received a doctorate in law from German University in Prague in 1906

Biographical notes: Practiced law for a year after receiving his degree and then joined an insurance company, where he remained until 1922 when illness forced him to quit; few of his works were published during his lifetime.

Short story collections: *The Great Wall of China,* 1933; *A Franz Kafka Miscellany,* 1940; *Parables and Paradoxes,* 1962; *The Complete Stories,* 1971

Novels: *The Trial,* 1925; *The Castle,* 1926: *Amerika,* 1927

Nonfiction: *Diaries 1910–1913,* 1948, *Diaries 1914–1923,* 1949

Comment: Highly influential in pioneering the modern technique of presenting fantastic events in the most ordinary style, the effect of which is to create a nightmarish sense of reality.

Died: 1924

KAWABATA, YASUNARI

Born: Osaka, Japan, 1899

Education: Tokyo Imperial University, degree in Japanese Literature, 1924

Biographical notes: Became involved with an avant-garde literary group while still a student; taught at several American universities; won Nobel Prize in 1968; committed suicide in 1972

Short story collections: *The House of the Sleeping Beauties and Other Stories,* 1969; *The Izu Dancer and Others,* 1964

Novels: *Snow Country,* 1957; *Thousand Cranes,* 1959; *The Lake,* 1974

Comment: Kawabata's frequent themes are the transitory nature of time, a nostalgia for the past, and subtle erotic relationships.

Died: 1972

KELLER, GOTTFRIED

Born: Zurich, Switzerland, 1819

Education: After being expelled from school for a prank, studied art in Zurich and Munich; later studied drama and philosophy at the University of Heidelberg

Biographical notes: Gave up his ambitions to be a landscape painter and began writing political poems for the radical party.

Works: Keller's poetry, philosophy, and fiction are available in German in the *Complete Works,* edited by Jonas Frankel, 1926–1931

Comment: Best known for his romantic and political poetry.

Died: 1890

KIPLING, RUDYARD

Born: Bombay, India, 1865

Education: Educated in India and England

Biographical notes: Returned to India after school to become an editor of a newspaper in Lahore; after his marriage in 1892, lived for a few years in Vermont and then returned to England to live in Sussex; won Nobel Prize for Literature in 1907.

Short story collections: *Plain Tales from the Hills,* 1887; *Life's Handicap,* 1891; *Many Inventions,* 1893; *Just So Stories,* 1902; *Puck of Pook's Hill,* 1906; *Debits and Credits,* 1926

Novels: *The Light That Failed,* 1891; *Captains Courageous,* 1897; *Kim,* 1901

Poems: *Barrack-Room Ballads,* 1892

Comment: Although often criticized for his racist treatment of the Indian people, Kipling was instrumental in moving the short story from simple romanticism to symbolism at the turn of the century.

Died: 1936

LAGERKVIST, PÄR

Born: Vaexjoe, Sweden, 1891

Education: University of Uppsala

Biographical notes: After a year at the university, he went to France and became involved with modernist art movement; was relatively unknown in the United States until 1951, when he won the Nobel Prize for Literature.

Short story collections: *The Eternal Smile and Other Stories,* 1954; *The Marriage Feast and Other Stories,* 1955

Novels: *The Dwarf,* 1945; *Barabbas,* 1950; *The Sibyl,* 1958; *The Death of Ahasuerus,* 1962; *Pilgrim at Sea,* 1962; *The Holy Land,* 1966; *Herod and Mariamne,* 1968

Nonfiction: *Guest of Reality,* 1936
Comment: Frequently focuses on human relationship with God and basic conflict between good and evil; makes use of archetypal characters and situations.
Died: 1974

LANDOLFI, TOMMASO

Born: Pico, Frosinone, Italy, 1908
Education: University of Florence, degree in Italian language and literature
Biographical notes: Imprisoned for antifascist views just before World War II; spent his life as a writer.
Short story collections: *Gogol's Wife and Other Stories,* 1963; *Cancerqueen and Other Stories,* 1971; *Words in Commotion and Other Stories,* 1986
Comment: Has been called Italy's Kafka; focuses on the macabre and the fantastic.
Died: 1979

LEAVITT, DAVID

Born: Palo Alto, California, 1961
Education: Yale University, A.B., 1983
Biographical notes: After graduation, worked for a year as a reader and editorial assistant in New York before devoting himself to writing full time.
Short story collections: *Family Dancing,* 1984; *A Place I've Never Been,* 1990
Novels: *The Lost Language of Cranes,* 1986; *Equal Affections,* 1989
Comment: Focuses often on young homosexual men and the tensions created within the family structure.

LE GUIN, URSULA K.

Born: Berkeley, California, 1929
Education: Radcliffe College, B.A., 1951; Columbia University, M.A., 1952
Biographical notes: Le Guin is the daughter of well-known anthropologists Alfred L. Kroeber and Theodora Kroeber; has received several awards, including Hugo and Nebula awards for science fiction.
Short story collections: *The Wind's Twelve Quarters,* 1975; *Orsinian Tales,* 1976; *The Compass Rose,* 1982
Novels: *Planet of Exile,* 1966; *City of Illusions,* 1967; *A Wizard of Earthsea,* 1968; *The Left Hand of Darkness,* 1969; *The Lathe of Heaven,* 1971; *The Tombs of Atuan,* 1972; *The Farthest Shore,* 1972; *The Dispossessed,* 1974; *Very Far Away from Anywhere Else,* 1976; *The Water Is Wide,* 1976; *Malafrena,* 1979; *The Beginning Place,* 1980; *Always Coming Home,* 1985
Nonfiction: *The Language of the Night: Essays on Fantasy and Science Fiction,* 1979; *Dancing at the Edge of the World: Thoughts on Words, Women, Places,* 1989
Comment: Le Guin primarily writes in the related genres of science fiction and fantasy, both of which focus on metaphoric and mythic reality.

LEM, STANISLAW

Born: Lvov, Poland, 1921
Education: Studied medicine in Lvov, Poland, and in Krakow, Poland

Biographical notes: Worked as a garage mechanic during World War II; taught at the University of Krakow.

Short story collections: *The Cosmic Carnival of Stanislaw Lem*, 1981

Novels: *Hospital of Transfiguration*, 1988; *The Investigation*, 1974; *Solaris*, 1966; *Memoirs Found in a Bathtub*, 1973; *Return from the Stars*, 1980; *The Invincible*, 1973; *The Cyberiad*, 1974; *His Master's Voice*, 1984; *A Perfect Vacuum*, 1979; *Imaginary Magnitude*, 1985; *The Chain of Chance*, 1978; *Mortal Engines*, 1977

Comment: One of the world's best-known science fiction writers; deals playfully with philosophic and scientific ideas; often works in the fable, parable, or fairy tale mode.

LESSING, DORIS

Born: Kermanshah, Persia (Iran), 1919

Education: Educated in Rhodesia, Africa

Biographical notes: Left Africa in 1949 to pursue a writing career.

Short story collections: *This Was the Old Chief's Country*, 1951; *The Habit of Loving*, 1957; *A Man and Two Women*, 1963; *African Stories*, 1964; *The Black Madonna*, 1966; *The Story of a Non-Marrying Man and Other Stories*, 1972; *The Temptation of Jack Orkney and Other Stories*, 1972; *The Memoirs of a Survivor*, 1975

Novels: *The Grass Is Singing*, 1950; *Martha Quest*, 1952; *Five*, 1953; *A Paper Marriage*, 1954; *Retreat to Innocence*, 1956; *A Ripple from the Storm*, 1958; *The Golden Notebook*, 1962; *Landlocked*, 1965; *The Four-Gated City*, 1969; *Briefing for a Descent into Hell*, 1971; *The Summer Before Dark*, 1973; *Shikasta*, 1979; *The Marriage Between Zones Three, Four, and Five*, 1980; *The Sirian Experiment*, 1981; *The Making of the Representative for Planet 8*, 1982; *The Sentimental Agents*, 1983; *The Good Terrorist*, 1985; *The Fifth Child*, 1988

Comment: Often focuses on the modern woman's struggles for equal rights.

L'HEUREUX, JOHN

Born: 1934

Education: Holy Cross, B.A., 1959; M.A. in Philosophy, 1960; M.A. in English, 1963; Harvard, M.A. in English, 1968

Biographical notes: Ordained a Jesuit priest, 1965; now a professor at Stanford University.

Short story collections: *Family Affair*, 1974; *Desires*, 1981

Novels: *Tight White Collar*, 1972; *The Clang Birds*, 1972; *Jessica Fayer*, 1976; *A Woman Run Mad*, 1987

Comment: Writes about spiritual reality and the human desire for transcendence in a lean and spare prose style.

McCULLERS, CARSON

Born: Columbus, Georgia, 1917

Education: Studied at Columbia and New York Universities

Biographical notes: After high school, left for New York to study music, but decided to pursue a career in writing instead; suffered a number of strokes that left her partially paralyzed.

Short story collections: *The Ballad of the Sad Cafe*, 1951

Novels: *The Heart Is a Lonely Hunter,* 1940; *Reflections in a Golden Eye,* 1941; *The Member of the Wedding,* 1946; *Clock Without Hands,* 1961

Comment: Often focuses on the abnormal and the bizarre, the lonely and the grotesque; most common theme is loneliness and isolation; most stories are set in the South.

Died: 1967

Malamud, Bernard

Born: New York City, 1914

Education: New York City College, A.B., 1934, did graduate work in English at Columbia University

Biographical notes: Taught high school in New York City during the 1940s; moved to Oregon in 1949 and joined English department at Oregon State University, where he stayed until 1961; moved east to teach at Bennington College in Vermont.

Short story collections: *The Magic Barrel,* 1958; *Idiots First,* 1963; *Pictures of Fidelman,* 1969; *Rembrandt's Hat,* 1973; *Stories of Bernard Malamud,* 1983; *The People: and Uncollected Stories,* 1989

Novels: *The Natural,* 1952; *The Assistant,* 1957; *A New Life,* 1961; *The Fixer,* 1966; *The Tenants,* 1971; *Dublin's Lives,* 1979; *God's Grace,* 1982

Comment: Malamud's stories, focusing frequently on Jewish life in America, are often parables; they combine the folk tale with realistic social fiction to create a unique effect.

Died: 1986

Mann, Thomas

Born: Lübeck, Germany, 1875

Education: Attended University of Munich

Biographical notes: Although Mann was born to a wealthy merchant family, when his father died in 1982, the family firm had to be liquidated and Mann went to work for an insurance company. In the early 1930s he was a strong critic of Nazism and was driven out of Germany; lived in California between 1942 and 1952, becoming an American citizen in 1944; moved to Zurich, Switzerland, where he lived until his death; received the Nobel Prize for Literature in 1929.

Short story collections: *Little Herr Friedmann,* 1898; *Stories of Three Decades,* 1936

Novels: *Buddenbrooks,* 1901; *Death in Venice,* 1912; *The Magic Mountain,* 1924; *Joseph and His Brothers,* 1933–1944; *Doctor Faustus,* 1947; *Confessions of Felix Krull, Confidence Man,* 1954

Comment: Mann's short fiction is best known for its highly polished verbal style and its frequent focus on aesthetic issues.

Died: 1955

Mansfield, Katherine

Born: Wellington, New Zealand, 1888

Education: Studied music at Queen's College, London

Biographical notes: Began her writing career as a journalist; married editor-critic John Middleton Murry; contracted tuberculosis in 1917, which finally caused her death.

Short story collections: *In a German Pension,* 1911; *Bliss,* 1920; *The Garden Party,* 1922; *The Dove's Nest,* 1923; *Something Childish,* 1924; *Collected Stories of Katherine Mansfield,* 1945

Comment: Mansfield was the first and foremost inheritor of the short story technique of Anton Chekhov and was influential in spreading that technique to other English and American writers.

Died: 1923

Maugham, W. Somerset

Born: Paris, France, 1874

Education: Heidelburg University, 1891; trained for the medical profession at St. Thomas Hospital in London, M.D., 1897

Biographical notes: Orphaned at age ten, brought up by relatives in London.

Short story collections: Published numerous short stories that are collected in *Complete Short Stories,* 1951, and *Collected Short Stories,* 1975–1976

Novels: *Liza of Lambeth,* 1897; *Mrs. Craddock,* 1902; *The Magician,* 1908; *Of Human Bondage,* 1915; *The Moon and Sixpence,* 1916; *Cakes and Ale,* 1930; *The Razor's Edge,* 1944

Nonfiction: *A Writer's Notebook,* 1949; *The Vagrant Mood,* 1952; *The Art of Fiction,* 1955

Comment: A popular writer and a traditional tale-teller.

Died: 1965

Maupassant, Guy de

Born: Normandy, France, 1850

Education: Expelled from a seminary, sent to study law near Rouen

Biographical notes: Served with the French army during the Franco-Prussian War; then worked as a clerk in the Naval Ministry in Paris; became friends with Gustave Flaubert, who tutored him in writing.

Short story collections: *La Maison Tellier,* 1881; *Mademoiselle Fifi,* 1882; *Contes de la Bécasse,* 1883; *Contes et Nouvelles,* 1885; *L'Inutile Beauté,* 1890

Novels: *Une Vie,* 1883; *Bel Ami,* 1885; *Pierre et Jean,* 1888

Comment: Although best known for his surprise-ending story "The Necklace," Maupassant's major influence on the short story is his realistic emphasis on ordinary people and his development of the supernatural story into psychological realism.

Died: 1893

Melville, Herman

Born: New York City, 1819

Education: Attended school in Albany, New York

Biographical notes: Went to sea as a cabin boy in 1837; spent four years on a whaling voyage in the South Seas; wrote most of his novels in the ten-year period between 1846 and 1857, but did not receive critical or popular success; spent nineteen years as an inspector in the New York Customs House.

Short story collections: *The Piazza Tales,* 1856

Novels: *Typee*, 1846; *Omoo*, 1847; *Mardi*, 1849; *Redburn*, 1849; *Moby-Dick*, 1851; *Pierre*, 1852; *The Confidence Man*, 1857

Comment: His most influential short story, "Bartleby," marked a shift from the allegorical and psychological fiction of Hawthorne and Poe to short fiction that was both realistic and symbolic.

Died: 1891

MISHIMA, YUKIO

Born: Tokyo, Japan, 1925

Education: Educated at an elite private school and at Tokyo Imperial University

Biographical notes: Worked for Japanese Finance Ministry for a short time before beginning writing career; founded a conservative and militaristic society in 1968; committed suicide in 1970 in a formal ceremony.

Short story collections: *Death in Midsummer*, 1966; *Seven Stories*, 1989

Novels: *Confessions of a Mask*, 1949; *Temple of the Golden Pavilion*, 1959; *After the Banquet*, 1963; *The Sailor Who Fell from Grace with the Sea*, 1965; *Forbidden Colors*, 1968; *The Sea of Fertility*, 1975

Comment: Highly stylized short fiction; best-known story is "Patriotism," a fully detailed story of a ritual Japanese suicide.

Died: 1970

NABOKOV, VLADIMIR

Born: St. Petersburg, Russia, 1899

Education: Cambridge University, England

Biographical notes: Moved to France and supported himself in various ways while writing; left France for the United States to escape the Nazis; became an American citizen and taught Russian at Cornell University; moved to Switzerland after becoming successful as a writer.

Short story collections: *Nabokov's Dozen*, 1958; *Nabokov's Quartet*, 1967

Novels (selected): *The Real Life of Sebastian Knight*, 1941; *Lolita*, 1955; *Pnin*, 1957; *Pale Fire*, 1962; *The Gift*, 1963; *Ada, Or, Ardor: A Family Chronicle*, 1969

Nonfiction: *Speak, Memory*, rev. ed., 1966; *Strong Opinions*, 1976; *Lectures on Literature*, 1980; *Lectures on Don Quixote*, 1983

Comment: An early influential innovator in the modernist style of self-reflexive fiction.

Died: 1977

O'BRIEN, FLANN (BRIAN O'NOLAN)

Born: County Tyrone, Ireland, 1911

Education: University College, Dublin, B.A., 1932

Biographical notes: After graduation from college, worked as a civil servant for eighteen years; wrote a column for *The Irish Times* for twenty-five years under the pen name Miles na Gopaleen.

Short story collections: *A Flann O'Brien Reader*, 1978

Novels: *At Swim-Two-Birds*, 1939; *The Hard Life*, 1962; *The Dalkey Archive*, 1964; *The Third Policeman*, 1967; *The Poor Mouth*, 1973

Comment: Primarily a comic, satiric writer focusing on Irish life.

Died: 1966

O'CONNOR, FRANK (MICHAEL DONOVAN)

Born: Cork, Ireland, 1903
Education: Left school at age fourteen
Biographical notes: Had a poverty-stricken childhood; served with the Irish Republican Army during the Civil War in the 1920s, during which he was imprisoned by the British; worked as librarian in Cork and in Dublin as director of the Abbey Theater; taught in America at various universities in the 1960s.
Short story collections: *Guests of the Nation*, 1931; *Bones of Contention*, 1936; *Crab Apple Jelly*, 1944; *The Common Chord*, 1947; *The Stories of Frank O'Connor*, 1952; *More Stories by Frank O'Connor*, 1954; *Domestic Relations*, 1957; *Collection Two*, 1964; *Collection Three*, 1969; *Collected Stories*, 1982
Novels: *The Saint and Mary Kate*, 1932; *Dutch Interior*, 1940
Nonfiction: *Towards an Appreciation of Literature*, 1945; *The Art of Theatre*, 1947; *The Lonely Voice*, 1963; *An Only Child*, 1961; *The Backward Look: A Survey of Irish Literature*, 1967; *My Father's Son*, 1968
Comment: Often wrote comic stories that featured Irish characters.
Died: 1966

O'FAOLÁIN, SEÁN (JOHN WHELAN)

Born: Dublin, Ireland, 1900
Education: National University of Ireland, B.A., 1921; M.A., 1929
Biographical notes: Grew up in Cork; served in the Irish Republican Army; studied and taught in the United States.
Short story collections: *Midsummer Night Madness*, 1932; *A Purse of Coppers*, 1937; *Teresa and Other Stories*, 1947; *The Man Who Invented Sin and Other Stories*, 1948; *I Remember! I Remember!*, 1961; *The Heat of the Sun*, 1966; *The Talking Trees*, 1971; *Foreign Affairs*, 1976; *The Collected Stories of Seán O'Faoláin*, 1980–1982
Novels: *A Nest of Simple Fools*, 1934; *Bird Alone*, 1936; *Come Back to Erin*, 1940; *And Again?*, 1979
Nonfiction: *The Short Story*, 1948; *The Irish*, 1947; *The Vanishing Hero*, 1956; *Vive Moi!*, 1964
Comment: Has mastered a wide variety of story types, including fable, fairy tale, and realistic story.
Died: 1990

O'FLAHERTY, LIAM

Born: Aran Islands, 1896
Education: Trained for the priesthood at Holy Cross College, but decided against ordination while a student
Biographical notes: Served in the Irish Guards during World War I, was shell-shocked and discharged with a pension; traveled and worked at various jobs; joined the Republican forces during the Civil War in Ireland and had to flee to England.
Short story collections: *Spring Sowing*, 1924; *Civil War*, 1925; *The Tent*, 1926; *Red Barbara and Other Stories*, 1928; *The Mountain Tavern and Other Stories*, 1929: *The Wild Swan and Other Stories*, 1932; *The Short Stories of Liam O'Flaherty*,

1937; *Two Lovely Beasts and Other Stories,* 1950; *The Stories of Liam O'Flaherty,* 1956

Novels (selected): *Thy Neighbor's Wife,* 1923; *The Informer,* 1925; *The House of Gold,* 1929; *Skerett,* 1932; *Famine,* 1937

Comment: Often characterized as a naturalist writer with romantic tendencies, similar to Theodore Drieser and Frank Norris in American literature.

Died: 1984

OLSEN, TILLIE

Born: Omaha, Nebraska, 1913

Education: Quit school in eleventh grade to work

Biographical notes: The daughter of Russian immigrants, Olsen grew up in poverty; was a member of the Young Communists and worked to organize Kansas City meat packers; published some fiction in the 1930s in *Partisan Review,* but then had little time to write again until the 1950s, when she was awarded a creative writing fellowship at Stanford University.

Short story collections: *Tell Me a Riddle,* 1961

Novels: *Yonnondio,* 1974

Nonfiction: *Silences,* 1978

Comment: Highly respected by feminist literary and social critics, Olsen is more influential for her encouragement to other women than for her own written output, which is relatively small.

OVID (PUBLIUS OVIDIUS NASO)

Born: Sulmo, in the Abruzzi, Italy, 43 B.C.

Education: Studied law

Biographical notes: Visited Athens, Greece, and devoted himself to poetry; in A.D. 8, he was banished to an isolated fishing village on the Black Sea.

Narrative: *Metamorphoses*

Drama: *Medea*

Poetry: *Amores; Ars Amatoria* (The Art of Love)

Comment: The first major writer to grow up under the Roman empire; highly influential on writers from the Renaissance to the present.

Died: A.D. 17

OZICK, CYNTHIA

Born: New York City, 1928

Education: New York University, B.A., 1949; Ohio State University, M.A., 1950

Biographical notes: Taught English for a time after graduation.

Short story collections: *The Pagan Rabbi and Other Stories,* 1971; *Bloodshed and Three Novellas,* 1976; *Levitation: Five Fictions,* 1981; *The Shawl,* 1989

Novels: *Trust,* 1966; *The Cannibal Galaxy,* 1983; *The Messiah of Stockholm,* 1987

Nonfiction: *Art and Ardor,* 1983

Comment: A powerful writer about Jewish life in America after World War II; particularly concerned with the effect of the Holocaust on Jews.

PAINTER, PAMELA

Born: Pittsburg, Pennsylvania, 1941
Education: Allegheny College, 1959–1960, and Pennsylvania State University, B.A., 1964; University of Illinois at Chicago Circle, M.A., 1979
Biographical notes: Founding editor of *Story Quarterly;* taught creative writing at Harvard Extension School and Emerson College, Boston.
Short story collections: *Getting to Know the Weather,* 1985

PALEY, GRACE

Born: New York City, 1922
Education: Attended Hunter College, 1938–1939; also attended New York University
Biographical notes: Has taught at Columbia University, Syracuse University, and Sarah Lawrence College.
Short story collections: *The Little Disturbances of Man,* 1959; *Enormous Changes at the Last Minute,* 1974; *Later the Same Day,* 1985
Comment: Deals with ordinary people of ethnically mixed Greenwich Village; frequently focuses on feminist themes; best known for her comic approach and her inventive use of dialogue.

PIRANDELLO, LUIGI

Born: Agrigento, Sicily, 1867
Education: Studied at University of Rome and in Bonn, Germany
Biographical notes: Was a professor at Roman Normal College for Women; won Nobel Prize for Literature in 1934.
Short story collections: *Luigi Pirandello: Short Stories,* 1959; *The Merry-Go-Round of Love and Selected Stories,* 1964
Novels: *The Late Mattia Pascal,* 1904
Drama: *Six Characters in Search of an Author,* 1921; *Naked Masks: Five Plays,* 1952 (includes *Liolá, It Is So! If You Think So, Henry IV, Six Characters, Each in His Own Way); Plays,* 1959 (includes *The Life I Gave You* and *The Rules of the Game)*
Comment: Wrote primarily in the tradition of nineteenth-century realism; most frequent focus was ordinary social life and routine of the middle class.
Died: 1936

POE, EDGAR ALLAN

Born: Boston, Massachusetts, 1809
Education: Attended University of Virginia and West Point but did not complete schooling at either
Biographical notes: After the death of his parents, Poe was adopted by John Allan, who completely disowned Poe after he was dismissed from West Point; spent much of his life in near poverty, working at his writing and as an editor for various American magazines; married his thirteen-year-old cousin Virginia, who died after a lingering illness; Poe himself died shortly after being found in a gutter in Baltimore, Maryland.

Short story collections: *Tales of the Grotesque and the Arabesque,* 1840; *Tales,* 1845
Novels: *The Narrative of Arthur Gordon Pym,* 1838
Poetry: See Poe's *Collected Works*
Comment: Poe is the single most important early innovator and theorist of the short story form in America; his chief contribution was to transform the popular supernatural tale into a complex psychological story; argued that the short story was a poetic form aesthetically superior to the novel because it was focused around a central unifying effect.
Died: 1849

PORTER, KATHERINE ANNE

Born: Indian Creek, Texas, near San Antonio, 1890
Education: Attended private schools in Texas and Louisiana
Biographical notes: Ran away and got married when she was sixteen, but divorced three years later; worked as a journalist in Chicago and Fort Worth, Texas; worked as a newspaper reporter in Chicago, Fort Worth, Texas, and Denver, Colorado; began free-lance writing in the 1920s while living in New York, Mexico, and Fort Worth; began publishing short stories in 1930.
Short story collections: *Flowering Judas,* 1930; *Hacienda,* 1934; *Noon Wine,* 1937; *Pale Horse, Pale Rider,* 1939; *The Leaning Tower,* 1944; *The Collected Stories,* 1965
Novels: *The Ship of Fools,* 1962
Nonfiction: *The Collected Essays and Occasional Writings of Katherine Anne Porter,* 1970
Comment: Best known for a highly poetic writing style and her frequent focus on complex psychological states.
Died: 1980

PURDY, JAMES

Born: Ohio, 1923
Education: Attended University of Chicago and University of Puebla, Mexico
Biographical notes: Has been a college professor and an interpreter.
Short story collections: *Don't Call Me By My Right Name and Other Stories,* 1956; *63 Dream Place,* 1957; *Color of Darkness,* 1957; *Children Is All,* 1962; *A Day After the Fair,* 1977
Novels: *Malcolm,* 1959; *The Nephew,* 1961; *Cabot Wright Begins,* 1964; *Eustace Chistholm and the Works,* 1967; *Jeremy's Version,* 1970; *I Am Eliham Thrush,* 1972; *The House of the Solitary Maggot,* 1974; *In a Shallow Grave,* 1976; *Narrow Rooms,* 1978; *Dream Palaces,* 1980; *Mourners Below,* 1981; *On Glory's Course,* 1984; *In the Hollow of His Hand,* 1986; *Candles of Your Eyes,* 1986
Comment: Often focuses on the child in the American family and the failure of love; often writes in an ironic black comic style.

ROBBE-GRILLET, ALAIN

Born: Brest, France, 1922
Education: Institut National Argonomique
Biographical notes: Robbe-Grillet is not only a novelist, but also a literary theorist and a filmmaker.

Short story collections: *Snapshots,* 1962
Novels: *The Erasers,* 1953; *The Voyeur,* 1955; *Jealousy,* 1957; *In the Labyrinth,* 1959; *Project for a Revolution in New York,* 1972
Scenario: *Last Year at Marienbad,* 1961
Nonfiction: *For a New Novel,* 1963
Comment: Best known for his theories of the *nouveau roman,* or new novel; focuses on the hard, concrete surfaces of external reality.

ROBISON, MARY

Born: Washington, D.C., 1949
Education: Ohio State University, B.A., 1976; Johns Hopkins University, M.A., 1977
Biographical notes: After receiving the M.A. degree in creative writing, Robison began publishing short stories in *The New Yorker* and has been publishing there ever since; taught creative writing at Harvard University and the University of Houston.
Short story collections: *Days,* 1979; *An Amateur's Guide to the Night,* 1983; *Believe Them,* 1988
Novels: *Oh!,* 1981; *Substraction,* 1991
Comment: Robison belongs to that group of writers largely responsible for the so-called renaissance of the short story in the 1970s; because her writing is economical and direct, she has been called a minimalist writer.

ROSA, JOÃO GUIMARÃES

Born: Cordisburgo, Minas Gerais, Brazil, 1908
Education: Studied medicine
Biographical notes: Left medicine to join the diplomatic corps, serving in Germany, Paris, and Colombia; was Cabinet Chief in the Foreign Ministry in Rio de Janeiro, Brazil, until 1953.
Short story collections: *The Third Bank of the River,* 1962
Novels: *The Devil to Pay in the Backlands,* 1956
Comment: An important figure in modern Brazilian literature; an early innovator in the technique known as magical realism; often writes in a poetic style, presenting fantastic events in everyday life.
Died: 1967

SAKI (H. H. MUNRO)

Born: Burma, 1879
Education: Educated in England
Biographical notes: Worked as a journalist and a correspondent for London newspapers; joined the 22nd Royal Fusiliers during World War I and was killed in the trenches.
Short story collections: *The Chronicles of Clovis,* 1911; *Beasts and Super-Beasts,* 1914; *The Bodley Head Saki,* 1963; *Incredible Tales,* 1966; *Best of Saki,* 1976; *Short Stories,* 1979
Comment: Best known for his whimsical short stories from a childhood perspective; often focuses on the quasi-supernatural.
Died: 1916

SHAW, IRWIN

Born: Brooklyn, New York, 1913

Education: Brooklyn College, B.A., 1934

Biographical notes: Began writing radio scripts in the 1930s; then moved on to both short stories and novels in the 1940s through the 1970s; served three years in the army in World War II; many of his novels have been adapted to film and television.

Short story collections: *Sailor off the Bremen*, 1939; *Welcome to the City*, 1942; *Act of Faith*, 1946; *Mixed Company*, 1950; *Tips on a Dead Jockey*, 1957; *Love on a Dark Street*, 1965; *God Was Here but He Left Early*, 1973; *Short Stories: Five Decades*, 1978

Novels: *The Young Lions*, 1948; *The Troubled Air*, 1951; *Lucy Crown*, 1956; *Voices of a Summer Day*, 1965; *Rich Man, Poor Man*, 1970; *Evening in Byzantium*, 1973; *Nightwork*, 1975; *Beggarman, Thief*, 1977; *The Top of the Hills*, 1979; *Bread upon the Waters*, 1981; *Acceptable Losses*, 1982

Plays: *Bury the Dead*, 1936; *The Gentle People: A Brooklyn Fable*, 1939; *Sons and Soldiers*, 1944; *The Assassin*, 1946; *Children from Their Games*, 1962

Comment: Many of Shaw's novels have become best-sellers because of their sprawling, melodramatic plots.

Died: 1984

SILKO, LESLIE MARMON

Born: Albuquerque, New Mexico, 1948

Education: Educated in Catholic schools in Albuquerque; University of New Mexico, B.A., 1969; studied law for a time, but withdrew from law school

Biographical notes: Descended from Mexican, white, and Pueblo Indians, Silko grew up near Albuquerque, highly influenced by Indian traditions and stories; taught for two years at Navajo Community College in Arizona; spent two years in Ketchikan, Alaska, working on her novel *Ceremony;* taught at the University of New Mexico and the University of Arizona.

Short story collections: *Laguna Woman*, 1974; *Storyteller*, 1981

Novels: *Ceremony*, 1974; *Almanac of the Dead*, 1990

Comment: Best known for her use of Indian legends, stories, and traditions.

STEINBECK, JOHN

Born: Salinas, California, 1902

Education: Went to Stanford University for a time, but left without a degree

Biographical notes: After leaving college to pursue his writing career in New York, he returned to California to take on a number of miscellaneous jobs picking fruit, working as a caretaker, and so on while he continued to write; began publishing fiction in late 1920s; worked as a war correspondent in Italy during World War II; won the Nobel Prize for Literature in 1962.

Short story collections: *The Long Valley*, 1938

Novels: *Cup of Gold*, 1929; *The Pastures of Heaven*, 1932; *To a God Unknown*, 1933; *The Red Pony*, 1933; *Tortilla Flat*, 1935; *In Dubious Battle*, 1936; *The Grapes of Wrath*, 1939; *Of Mice and Men*, 1940; *Cannery Row*, 1945; *The Way-*

ward Bus, 1947; *East of Eden*, 1952; *Sweet Thursday*, 1954; *The Winter of Our Discontent*, 1961
Nonfiction: *The Sea of Cortez*, 1941; *A Russian Journal*, 1948; *Once There Was a War*, 1958; *Travels with Charley in Search of America*, 1962; *America and Americans*, 1966
Comment: Best known for his novel *The Grapes of Wrath*, the story of an Oklahoma family trying to escape the dust bowl to California; his short stories are often symbolic and mythic treatments of primitive states.
Died: 1968

STOCKTON, FRANK

Born: Philadelphia, 1834
Education: B.A. degree from Philadelphia Central High School, 1852
Biographical notes: Worked at an engraving office; wrote for Philadelphia newspapers.
Works: *The Novels and Stories of Frank Stockton*, 1899–1904, contains 21 novels and 66 short stories
Comment: A humorous short story writer whose one famous story, "The Lady, or the Tiger?" was the most talked about short story of its period.
Died: 1902

SVEVO, ITALO (SCHMITZ, ARON HECTOR)

Born: Trieste, Italy, 1861
Education: Attended school in West Germany and the University of Trieste
Biographical notes: Worked as a bank clerk in Trieste; taught French and German; was an industrialist manufacturing marine paints.
Short story collections: *The Nice Old Man and the Pretty Girl and Other Stories*, 1930; *Short Sentimental Journey and Other Stories*, 1967–1980
Novels: *Confessions of Zeno*, 1930; *As a Man Grows Older*, 1932; *Further Confessions of Zeno*, 1969; *A Life*, 1967–1980
Comment: Best known for his experimental style and his development of the psychoanalytical novel.
Died: 1928

TACITUS, GAIUS CORNELIUS

Born: Rome, A.D. 55
Education: Studied rhetoric at Rome
Biographical notes: Became a praetor and a consul; best known as an orator and historian.
Works: *Historae* (12 vols.); *Annales* (8 vols.)
Comment: A precise prose stylist who influenced many later writers.
Died: A.D. 120

TAYLOR, ELIZABETH

Born: Reading, Berkshire, England, 1912
Education: Attended Abbey School in Reading

Biographical notes: Spent her life in England as a writer.

Short story collections: *Hester Lily: Twelve Short Stories*, 1954; *The Blush and Other Stories*, 1958; *A Dedicated Man and Other Stories*, 1965; *The Devastating Boys and Other Stories*, 1972

Novels: *At Mrs. Lippicote's*, 1945; *Palladian*, 1946; *A View of the Harbour*, 1949; *A Wreath of Roses*, 1949; *A Game of Hide and Seek*, 1951; *The Sleeping Beauty*, 1953; *Angel*, 1957; *In a Summer Season*, 1961; *The Soul of Kindness*, 1964; *Mrs. Palfrey at the Claremont*, 1971

Comment: Best known as a writer given more to stylistic grace than to the creation of three-dimensional characters.

Died: 1975

TÉLLEZ, HERNANDO

Born: Bogotá, Colombia, 1908

Biographical notes: Worked for several magazines and newspapers in Colombia; served as consul in Marseilles and as a senator in Colombia.

Short story collections: *Ashes for the Wind and Other Tales*, 1950

Comments: Best known as an essayist on a variety of topics.

Died: 1966

TOLSTOY, LEO

Born: Tuyla, Russia, 1828

Education: Received private tutoring as a child; studied at the University of Kazan

Biographical notes: After leaving school, served in the Russian army; was an artillery officer during the Crimean War in the 1850s; began publishing fiction shortly after; settled down on his family's estate in the early 1860s to farm, teach, and write; in the late 1870s, underwent a religious crisis and conversion, after which his writings became more and more concerned with his own idea of Christian salvation.

Short story collections: *Sevastapol Stories*, 1855; *The Death of Ivan Ilych*, 1886

Novels: *The Cossacks*, 1862; *War and Peace*, 1869; *Anna Karenina*, 1877; *Master and Man*, 1895; *Kreutzer Sonata*, 1899; *Resurrection*, 1899

Nonfiction: *What Men Live By*, 1881; *My Confession*, 1882; *What I Believe*, 1884; *The Kingdom of God Is Within You*, 1893

Comment: Tolstoy's sprawling novels are his best-known works; his best-known story, "The Death of Ivan Ilych," is a classic treatment of the human confrontation with death.

Died: 1910

TOOMER, JEAN

Born: Washington, D.C., 1894

Education: University of Wisconsin, 1914; City College of New York, 1917–1918; the Gurdjieff Institute in France

Biographical notes: Taught school in Georgia, New York, and Chicago; hailed as a leader of the Harlem Renaissance; joined Quaker movement and spent last part of his life as a recluse.

Short story collections: *Cane*, 1923

Novels: *Cane,* 1923
Comment: Toomer's major work, *Cane,* is a novel made up of poems and short stories
    focusing on the black experience in both the rural South and the urban North.
Died: 1967

TWAIN, MARK (SAMUEL LANGHORNE CLEMENS)

Born: Florida, Missouri, 1835
Education: Mostly self-educated
Biographical notes: Raised in Hannibal, Missouri; at age thirteen, became apprentice
    on local newspaper; later worked as a journeyman printer; spent five years as an
    apprentice and then a licensed steamboat pilot; worked as a journlist in the
    Nevada Territory and San Francisco; suffered financial losses and death of his chil-
    dren in his last years.
Short story collections: *The Celebrated Jumping Frog of Calaveras County,* 1867; *The
    Man That Corrupted Hadleyburg,* 1900
Novels: *Adventures of Tom Sawyer,* 1876; *The Prince and the Pauper,* 1882; *Adven-
    tures of Huckleberry Finn,* 1885; *A Connecticut Yankee in King Arthur's Court,*
    1889; *Pudd'nhead Wilson,* 1894
Comment: Although Twain is best known for his novels, his short stories are a good
    example of the combination of the comic tale and the local-color story.
Died: 1910

UPDIKE, JOHN

Born: Shillington, Pennsylvania, 1932
Education: Graduated *summa cum laude* from Harvard University in 1954; studied art
    for a year on a fellowship in England
Biographical notes: Joined the staff of the *New Yorker* magazine in the mid-1950s and
    wrote the column "Talk of the Town" for two years; moved to Massachusetts to
    begin full-time writing in 1957.
Short story collections: *The Same Door,* 1959; *Pigeon Feathers,* 1962; *Olinger Stories,*
    1964; *The Music School,* 1966; *Bech: A Book,* 1970; *Museums & Women,* 1972;
    Too Far To Go: The Maple Stories, 1979; *Problems,* 1979; *Trust Me,* 1987
Novels: *The Poorhouse Fair,* 1959; *Rabbit, Run,* 1960; *The Centaur,* 1963; *Of the
    Farm,* 1965; *Couples,* 1968; *Rabbit Redux,* 1971; *A Month of Sundays,* 1975;
    Marry Me, 1976; *The Coup,* 1978; *Rabbit Is Rich,* 1981; *Bech is Back,* 1982; *The
    Witches of Eastwick,* 1984; *Roger's Version,* 1986; *Rabbit at Rest,* 1990
Poetry: *The Carpentered Hen and Other Tame Creatures,* 1958; *Telephone Poles,*
    1963; *Midpoint,* 1969; *Tossing and Turning,* 1977; *Facing Nature,* 1985
Nonfiction: *Picked-Up Pieces,* 1975; *Hugging the Shore: Essays and Criticism,* 1983;
    Just Looking: Essays on Art, 1989; *Self-Consciousness,* 1989
Comment: Updike has often been identified as a *New Yorker* writer, a term suggesting
    slick, self-consciously lyrical and stylized stories.

VERGA, GIOVANNI

Born: Catania, Sicily, 1840
Education: Studied law
Biographical notes: A member of the southern Italian landowner class, he spent his life
    writing.

Short story collections: *Under the Shadow of Etna,* 1896; *Cavalleria Rusticana and Other Stories,* 1928; *The She-Wolf and Other Stories,* 1958
Novels: *The House by the Medlar Tree,* 1890; *Mastro-don Gessualdo,* 1923
Comment: Focuses on the harsh, primitive life of the Sicilian peasants; uses a realist style.
Died: 1922

VIVANTE, ARTURO

Born: Rome, Italy, 1923
Education: McGill University, B.A., 1945; University of Rome, M.D. 1949
Biographical notes: Practices general medicine; served as writer in residence at a number of U.S. universities.
Short story collections: *The French Girls of Kilini,* 1967; *English Stories,* 1975; *Run to the Waterfall,* 1979
Novels: *A Goodly Babe,* 1966; *Doctor Giovanni,* 1969
Nonfiction: *Writing Fiction,* 1980
Comment: Best known for his anecdotal, reminiscent short fiction.

VONNEGUT, KURT

Born: Indianapolis, Indiana, 1942
Education: Educated at Cornell, where his major was biochemistry; studied anthropology at the University of Chicago
Biographical notes: Served in the army during World War II; was captured by the Germans in late 1944 and released in 1945; worked as a publicist for General Electric until 1950; has been writing full time ever since.
Short story collections: *Canary in a Cat House,* 1968; *Welcome to the Monkey House,* 1968
Novels: *Player Piano,* 1952; *The Sirens of Titan,* 1959; *Mother Night,* 1961; *Cat's Cradle,* 1963; *God Bless You, Mr. Rosewater,* 1966; *Slaughterhouse-Five,* 1969; *Breakfast of Champions,* 1973; *Slapstick, or Lonesome No More,* 1976; *Jailbird,* 1979; *Deadeye Dick,* 1982
Nonfiction: *Palm Sunday: An Autobiographical Collage,* 1981
Comment: Vonnegut's short fiction is often satirical and whimsical.

WALKER, ALICE

Born: Eatonton, Georgia, 1944
Education: Attended Spelman College in Atlanta; Sarah Lawrence College, B.A., 1965
Biographical notes: Walker's early life, she says, was affected by an accident when she was eight that left her blind in one eye; after graduating from college, she became active in the civil rights movement of the late 1960s; began teaching creative writing and Black literature at Jackson State University in Mississippi; has also taught at the University of Massachusetts, Yale University, and the University of California, Berkeley; won the Pulitzer Prize in 1983.
Short story collections: *In Love and Trouble: Stories of Black Women,* 1973; *You Can't Keep a Good Woman Down,* 1981
Novels: *The Third Life of Grange Copeland,* 1970; *Meridian,* 1976; *The Color Purple,* 1982; *The Temple of My Familiar,* 1989

Poetry: *Once: Poems,* 1968; *Revolutionary Petunias,* 1973; *Good Night, Willie Lee, I'll See You in the Morning,* 1979; *Horses Make a Landscape Look More Beautiful,* 1984
Nonfiction: *In Search of Our Mother's Gardens: A Collection of Womanist Poems,* 1983; *Langston Hughes: American Poet,* 1973; *I Love Myself When I'm Laughing . . . and Then Again When I'm Looking Mean and Impressive: A Zora Neale Hurston Reader,* 1979
Comment: Walker is often concerned with discrimination against blacks and against women.

WARNER, SYLVIA TOWNSEND

Born: Harrow, Middlesex, England, 1893
Education: Privately educated
Biographical notes: Spent her life as a writer; she is the author of some three dozen books.
Short story collections: *A Moral Ending and Other Stories,* 1931; *The Salutation,* 1932; *More Joy in Heaven and Other Stories,* 1935; *The Cat's Cradle Book,* 1940; *A Garland of Straw,* 1943; *The Museum of Cheats,* 1947; *Winter in the Air,* 1956; *A Spirit Rises,* 1962; *Swans on an Autumn River,* 1966; *The Innocent and the Guilty,* 1971; *Kingdom of Elfin,* 1977; *One Thing Leading to Another,* 1984
Novels: *Lolly Willowes,* 1926; *Mr. Fortune's Maggot,* 1927; *The True Heart,* 1929; *The Summer Will Show,* 1936; *The Corner That Held Them,* 1948; *The Flint Anchor,* 1954
Nonfiction: *Somerset,* 1949; *Jane Austen: 1775–1817,* 1951; *Sketches from Nature,* 1963; *T. H. White: A Biography,* 1967; *Scenes from Childhood,* 1982
Poetry: *Collected Poems,* 1983
Comment: Often features eccentric characters; primarily writes in the modes of fable, fantasy, and irony.
Died: 1978

WELTY, EUDORA

Born: Jackson, Mississippi, 1909
Education: Attended Jackson State College for Women; University of Wisconsin, B.A., 1929; spent a year studying at Columbia University's School of Advertising
Biographical notes: Moved back to Jackson in 1932 to work for newspapers, a radio station, and the Works Progress Administration as a publicity agent; also during this time began writing short stories; has been writing ever since, winning, among many other awards, the Pulitzer Prize.
Short story collections: *A Curtain of Green,* 1941; *The Wide Net,* 1943; *The Golden Apples,* 1949; *Selected Stories,* 1954; *The Bride of Innesfallen,* 1955; *Thirteen Stories,* 1965; *The Collected Stories of Eudora Welty,* 1980
Novels: *The Robber Bridegroom,* 1942; *Delta Wedding,* 1946; *The Ponder Heart,* 1954; *Losing Battles,* 1970; *The Optimist's Daughter,* 1972
Nonfiction: *One Writer's Beginning,* 1984
Comment: Welty's short stories, her primary claim to literary fame, are often characterized by a mythic quality in which ordinary characters are given an archetypal sense of reality.

WILLIAMS, WILLIAM CARLOS

Born: Rutherford, New Jersey, 1883
Education: University of Pennsylvania, M.D., 1906
Biographical notes: Spent his life as a pediatrician.
Short story collections: *The Knife of the Times*, 1932; *Making Light of It*, 1950; *The Farmer's Daughters: Collected Short Stories*, 1961
Novels: *White Mule*, 1937; *In the Money*, 1940
Poetry: *Patterson*, 1946–58
Nonfiction: *In the American Grain*, 1925
Comment: Best known for his five-volume impressionistic poem *Patterson* and his impressionistic short story "The Use of Force."
Died: 1963

WILSON, ROBLEY, JR.

Born: Brunswick, Maine, 1930
Education: Bowdoin College, B.A., 1957; Indiana University; University of Iowa, M.F.A., 1968
Biographical notes: Served in the U.S. Air Force in the 1950s; teaches English and Russian at the University of Northern Iowa in Cedar Falls.
Short story collections: *The Pleasures of Manhood*, 1977; *Living Alone*, 1978; *Dancing for Men*, 1982
Poetry: *All That Lovemaking*, 1961; *Returning to the Body*, 1977
Comment: Often focuses on the relationships between men and women and the difficulties of human involvement.

WOLFF, TOBIAS

Born: Alabama, 1945
Education: Did not complete high school, but after his hitch in the army, graduated from Oxford University in England with First Class Honors
Biographical notes: Worked as an apprentice seaman; served four years in the Army; has taught at Stanford and Syracuse Universities.
Short story collections: *In the Garden of North American Martyrs*, 1981; *Back in the World*, 1985
Novels: *The Barracks Thief*, 1984
Nonfiction: *This Boy's Life*, 1989
Comment: Writes about contemporary characters who try to escape alienation through fantasy and fabrication.

WOOD, MONICA

Born: Mexico, Maine, 1953
Education: Georgetown University, B.A.; University of Southern Maine, M. Ed.
Biographical notes: Has been a high school teacher/counselor, and a songwriter/singer; teaches fiction writing for the University of Southern Maine Department of Community Programs; lives in Portland, Maine, with her husband of 14 years, Dan Abbott.

Short story collections: Has published stories in *Redbook, The North American Review, Manoa,* and many other magazines and anthologies.
Novels: Her first novel, *Secret Language,* is to be published in 1993
Comment: Wood says she has a special fondness for the first-person narrative. "It's the closest I get to acting, to trying on new roles and living temporarily in another skin. If I have any characteristic theme, it is the human search—constant and dangerous—for transformation."

WOOLF, VIRGINIA

Born: London, 1882
Education: Privately educated
Biographical notes: Her life was plagued by mental depression and several suicide attempts; took her own life by drowning.
Short story collections: *Kew Gardens,* 1919; *Monday or Tuesday,* 1921; *A Haunted House,* 1944
Novels: *Night and Day,* 1919; *Jacob's Room,* 1922; *Mrs. Dalloway,* 1925; *To the Lighthouse,* 1927; *The Waves,* 1931
Nonfiction: *The Common Reader,* 1925; *The Common Reader, Second Series,* 1932; *Collected Essays,* 1966, 1967, 1969
Comment: Important for her experimentation with interior monologue and stream of consciousness, and her poetic and symbolic fiction.
Died: 1941

YNGVE, ROLF

Born: Minnesota, 1951
Education: B.S. in Meteorology, University of Utah, late 1970s
Biographical notes: Served in the U.S. Navy.
Short story collections: Has published a small number of short stories in literary journals.
Comment: "The Quail" appeared in *Best American Short Stories,* 1979.

Acknowledgments

Chinua Achebe. "Dead Men's Path" from *Girls at War and Other Stories,* Copyright © 1972, 1973 by Chinua Achebe. Used by permission of Doubleday, a division of Bantam Doubleday Dell Publishing Group, Inc.

Ryūnosuke Akutagawa. "Rashōmon" is reprinted from *Rashōmon and Other Stories* by Ryūnosuke Akutagawa, translated by Takashi Kojima. By permission of Liveright Publishing Corporation. Copyright 1952 by Liveright Publishing Corporation. Copyright renewed 1980.

Sherwood Anderson. "Paper Pills," "Hands," from *Winesburg, Ohio.* Copyright 1919 by B.W. Huebsch. Copyright 1947 by Eleanor Copenhaver Anderson. Used by permission of Viking Penguin, a division of Penguin Books USA, Inc.

The Apocrypha. "Daniel and Susanna." From the New English Bible. Copyright © the Delegates of the Oxford University Press and the Syndics of the Cambridge University Press, 1961, 1970. Reprinted by permission.

Margaret Atwood. "Happy Endings" from *Murder in the Dark.* Reprinted by permission of Margaret Atwood, © 1991.

Isaac Babel. "My First Goose," "Guy de Maupassant," and "The Sin of Jesus" from *Collected Stories,* translated by Walter Morrison. Copyright 1955 by S.G. Phillips, Inc.

Toni Cade Bambara. "The Lesson" from *Gorilla, My Love,* Copyright © 1972 by Toni Cade Bambara. Reprinted by permission of Random House, Inc.

John Barth. "Autobiography" from *Lost in the Funhouse,* Copyright © 1968. Used by permission of Doubleday, a division of Bantam Doubleday Dell Publishing Group, Inc.

Donald Barthelme. "The Balloon" from *Unspeakable Practices, Unnatural Acts,* Copyright 1968 by Donald Barthelme, reprinted with the permission of Wylie, Aitken & Stone, Inc.

Charles Baxter. "The Cliff," reprinted from *Harmony of the World,* by permission of the University of Missouri Press. Copyright © 1984 by the author.

Ann Beattie. "Janus" from *Where You'll Find Me,* Copyright © 1986 by Iron and Pity, Inc. Reprinted by permission of Linden Press, a division of Simon & Schuster, Inc.

Heinrich Böll. "Across the Bridge" from *Children Are Civilians Too,* 1970. Used by permission of the translator, Leila Vennewitz, and by permission of Joan Daves, agent for Heinrich Boll.

Arna Bontemps. "A Summer Tragedy" from *The Old South.* Reprinted by permission of Harold Ober Associates Incorporated. Copyright 1933 by Arna Bontemps, renewed.

Jorge Luis Borges. "Funes, the Memorious" from *Ficciones,* translated by Anthony Kerrigan. Translation copyright © 1962, 1990 by Grove Press, Inc. Used by permission of Grove Press, Inc.

Elizabeth Bowen. "The Demon Lover" from *The Collected Stories of Elizabeth Bowen,* Copyright 1946 and renewed 1974 by Elizabeth Bowen. Reprinted by permission of Alfred A. Knopf, Inc.

Paul Bowles. "The Scorpion" from *The Delicate Prey and Other Stories,* 1946.

Kay Boyle. "The Astronomer's Wife" from *The White Horses of Vienna and Other Stories,* Copyright 1936, 1964 by Kay Boyle. Reprinted by permission of A. Watkins, Inc.

T. Coraghessan Boyle. "Stones in My Passway, Hellhound on My Trail," © 1979 by T. Coraghessan Boyle. From *Greasy Lake and Other Stories.* Used by permission of Viking Penguin, a division of Penguin Books USA, Inc.

Dino Buzzati. "The Falling Girl" from *Il Colombre,* Copyright 1983 by Dino Buzzati. Used by permission.

Ernest Hemingway. "Hills Like White Elephants" reprinted with permission of Charles Scribner's Sons, an imprint of Macmillan Publishing Company, from *Men Without Women.* Copyright 1927 by Charles Scribner's Sons; renewal copyright 1955 by Ernest Hemingway.

Herman Hesse. "The Poet" from *Strange News From Another Side,* 1972. Used by permission of Suhrkamp Verlag.

Spencer Holst. "On Hope" from *The Language of Cats and Other Stories,* Copyright 1971 by Spencer Holst. Used by permission of the author.

Langston Hughes. "On the Road" from *Laughing to Keep From Crying* 1952. Reprinted by permission of Harold Ober Associates Incorporated. Copyright 1952 by Langston Hughes. Copyright renewed 1980 by George Houston Bass.

James Joyce. "Araby" and "Eveline" from *Dubliners,* Copyright 1916 by B.W. Heubsch. Definitive text Copyright © 1967 by the estate of James Joyce. Used by permission of Viking Penguin, a division of Penguin Books USA, Inc. "Eveline" computer version by permission of The Society of Authors as the literary representative of the Estate of James Joyce.

Franz Kafka. "A Country Doctor" from *The Penal Colony,* translated by Willa & Edwin Muir. Translation copyright 1948 and renewed 1976 by Schocken Books. Reprinted by permission of Schocken books, published by Pantheon Books, a division of Random House, Inc.

Yasunari Kawabata. "The Grasshopper and the Bell Cricket" from *Palm of the Hand Stories* by Yasunari Kawabata. English translation copyright © 1988 by Lane Dunlap and J. Martin Holman. Published by North Point Press and reprinted by permission of Farrar, Straus & Giroux, Inc.

Gottfried Keller. "A Little Legend of the Dance" from *The People of Seldwyla and Seven Legends.* Translated by M.D. Hottinger. Used by permission of J M Dent & Sons Ltd Publishers.

Pär Lagerkvist. "Father and I" from *The Eternal Smile and other Stories* (1952), © the estate of Pär Lagerkvist 1992; published in agreement with Albert Bonniers Förlag AB.

Tommaso Landolfi. "Wedding Night" from *Gogol's Wife and Other Stories.* Copyright © 1961, 1963 by New Directions Publishing Corporation. Reprinted by permission of New Directions Publishing Corporation.

David Leavitt. "Gravity" from *A Place I've Never Been,* Copyright © 1990 by David Leavitt. Used by permission of Viking Penguin, a division of Penguin Books USA, Inc.

Ursula K. Le Guin. "The Ones Who Walk Away from Omelas" Copyright © 1973 by Ursula K. Le Guin; first appeared in *New Dimensions 3*; reprinted by permission of the author and the author's agent, Virginia Kidd.

Stanislaw Lem. "How the World Was Saved" from *The Cyberiad: Fables For the Cybernetic Age,* translated from the Polish by Michael Kandel. English translation © 1974 by The Continuum Publishing Company. Reprinted by permission of the publisher.

Doris Lessing. "Homage for Isaac Babel" from *A Man and Two Women,* Copyright © 1958, 1962, 1963 by Doris Lessing. Reprinted by permission of Simon & Schuster. "Flight" from *African Stories,* Copyright © 1951, 1953, 1954, 1957, 1958, 1962, 1963, 1964, 1965. Reprinted by permission of Simon & Schuster. "Wine" from *The Habit of Loving,* Copyright © 1957 by Doris Lessing. Reprinted by permission of HarperCollins Publishers.

Carson McCullers. "A Tree, A Rock, A Cloud" from *The Ballad of the Sad Cafe and Collected Short Stories,* Copyright 1936, 1941, 1942, 1950, © 1955 by Carson McCullers. Copyright © renewed 1979 by Floria V. Lasky. Reprinted by permission of Houghton Mifflin Company. All rights reserved.

Bernard Malamud. "The Loan" from *The Magic Barrel,* Copyright © 1952, 1958 and renewal Copyright © 1980 by Bernard Malamud. Reprinted by permission of Farrar, Straus & Giroux, Inc. Computer version by permission of Russell & Volkening as agents for the author. Copyright © 1958 by Bernard Malamud, renewed in Ann Malamud.

Thomas Mann. "Railway Accident" from *Stories of Three Decades*, Copyright 1936 and renewed 1964 by Alfred A. Knopf, Inc. Reprinted by permission of Alfred A. Knopf, Inc.

Katherine Mansfield. "Miss Brill" and "The Fly" from *The Short Stories of Katherine Mansfield*, Copyright 1922 by Alfred A. Knopf, Inc., and renewed 1950 by John Middleton Murray. Reprinted by permission of Alfred A. Knopf, Inc. "The Fly" computer version by permission of The Society of Authors as the literary representative of the Estate of Katherine Mansfield.

W. Somerset Maugham. "The Ant and the Grasshopper" from *Cosmopolitans*, 1924. Used by permission of A P Watt Ltd. on behalf of The Royal Literary Fund.

Guy de Maupassant. "In the Moonlight," "Confessing," and "Love: Three Pages from a Sportsman's Notebook" from *The Complete Short Stories of Guy de Maupassant*, Doubleday & Co., 1955.

Yukio Mishima. "Swaddling Clothes" from *Death in Midsummer and Other Stories*. Copyright © 1966 by New Directions Publishing Corporation. Reprinted by permission of New Directions Publishing Corporation.

Vladimir Nabokov. "Signs and Symbols" from *Nabokov's Dozen* by Vladimir Nabokov. Copyright 1948 by Vladimir Nabokov. Reprinted by permission of Vintage Books, a Division of Random House, Inc.

Flann O'Brien. "Two in One" from *A Flann O'Brien Reader*. Copyright 1954 by Brian O'Nolan. Reprinted by permission of Brandt & Brandt Literary Agents, Inc.

Frank O'Connor. "Judas" from *Collected Stories*. Used by permission of Joan Daves Agency.

Seán O'Faoláin. "The Trout" from *The Man Who Invented Sin*, Copyright 1948 by Devin-Adair, Publishers, Inc. All rights reserved.

Liam O'Flaherty. "The Fairy Goose" from *The Stories of Liam O'Flaherty*, Copyright 1956 by Devin-Adair, Publishers, Inc. All rights reserved.

Tillie Olsen. "I Stand Here Ironing" from *Tell Me a Riddle*, Copyright © 1956, 1957, 1960, 1961 by Tillie Olsen. Used by permission of Delacorte Press/Seymour Lawrence, a division of Bantam Doubleday Dell Publishing Group, Inc.

Ovid. "Pygmalion" from *Metamorphoses*, translated by A.D. Melville (1986) by permission of Oxford University Press © A. D. Melville 1986.

Cynthia Ozick. "The Shawl" from *The Shawl*, Copyright © 1980, 1983 by Cynthia Ozick. Reprinted by permission of Alfred A. Knopf, Inc.

Pamela Painter. "The Bridge" from *The Threepenny Review*, Spring, 1984. Used by permission of the author.

Grace Paley. "A Conversation with My Father" from *Enormous Changes at the Last Minute*, Copyright © 1972, 1974 by Grace Paley. Reprinted by permission of Farrar, Straus & Giroux, Inc.

Luigi Pirandello. "The Soft Touch of Grass" from *Short Stories By Pirandello*, translation Copyright © 1959, 1987 by Lily Duplaix. Reprinted by permission of Simon & Schuster, Inc.

Katherine Anne Porter. "The Grave" from *The Leaning Tower and Other Stories* copyright 1944 and renewed 1972 by Katherine Anne Porter, reprinted by permission of Harcourt Brace Jovanovich, Inc. "Theft" from *Flowering Judas and Other Stories*, copyright 1935 and renewed 1963 by Katherine Anne Porter, reprinted by permission of Harcourt Brace Jovanovich, Inc.

James Purdy. "Why Can't They Tell You Why?" from *Color of Darkness*, Copyright © 1961 by J.B. Lippincott Company. Copyright © 1956, 1957 by James Purdy. Reprinted by permission of HarperCollins Publishers.

Alain Robbe-Grillet. "The Secret Room" from *Snapshots*, Copyright © 1968 by Grove Press. Copyright © 1962 by Les Editions de Minuit.

Mary Robison. "Yours" from *An Amateur's Guide to the Night*, Copyright © 1981, 1982, 1983 by Mary Robison. Reprinted by permission of Alfred A. Knopf, Inc.

João Guimarães Rosa. "The Third Bank of the River" from *Modern Brazilian Short Stories*, edited by William Grossman, Copyright © 1967 The Regents of the University of California.

Saki. "The Open Window" from *The Complete Short Stories of Saki.*

Irwin Shaw. "The Girls in Their Summer Dresses" from *Mixed Company*. Reprinted with Permission. © Irwin Shaw. Reprinted by permission of the Estate of Irwin Shaw.

Leslie Silko. "Yellow Woman" from *The Man to Send Rain Clouds*, © 1974 by Leslie Marmon Silko. Reprinted by permission of the author.

John Steinbeck. "The Snake" from *The Long Valley*, Copyright 1938, renewed © 1966 by John Steinbeck. Used by permission of Viking Penguin, a division of Penguin Books USA, Inc.

Elizabeth Taylor. "The First Death of Her Life" from *The New Yorker*, Copyright 1949 by *The New Yorker Magazine*, Inc. Reprinted by permission of the Estate of the late Elizabeth Taylor.

Hernando Téllez. "Just Lather, That's All" from *Great Spanish Short Stories*, edited by Angel Flores for Dell Publishing. Used by permission.

Jean Toomer. "Theater" is reprinted from *Cane* by Jean Toomer by permission of Liveright Publishing Corporation. Copyright 1923 by Boni & Liveright. Copyright renewed 1951 by Jean Toomer.

John Updike. "A & P" from *Pigeon Feathers and other Stories*, Copyright © 1962 by John Updike. Reprinted by permission of Alfred A. Knopf, Inc. Originally appeared in *The New Yorker;* "Pygmalion" from *Trust Me*, Copyright © 1962, 1979, 1980, 1981, 1982, 1983, 1984, 1985, 1986, 1987 by John Updike. Reprinted by permission of Alfred A. Knopf, Inc.

Giovanni Verga. "The She-Wolf" from *The She-Wolf and Other Stories*. Reprinted by permission of Giovanni Cecchetti.

Arturo Vivante. "Can-Can." First published by *The London Magazine*, February/March 1972, Vol. II, No. 6. Used by permission of the author.

Kurt Vonnegut, Jr. "Harrison Bergeron," from *Welcome to the Monkey House*, Copyright © 1961 by Kurt Vonnegut, Jr. Used by permission of Dell Books, a division of Bantam Doubleday Dell Publishing Group, Inc.

Alice Walker. "To Hell with Dying" from *In Love and Trouble*, Copyright © 1967 by Alice Walker, reprinted by permission of Harcourt Brace Jovanovich, Inc.

Sylvia Townsend Warner. "The Phoenix" from *The Cat's Cradle Book*. Copyright 1940. Used by permission of the Executors of the Sylvia Townsend Warner Estate, Chatto & Windus as publisher.

Eudora Welty. "A Visit of Charity" and "A Memory" from *A Curtain of Green and Other Stories*, copyright 1941, 1937 and renewed 1969, 1965 by Eudora Welty, reprinted by permission of Harcourt Brace Jovanovich, Inc.

William Carlos Williams. "The Use of Force" from *The Doctor Stories*, Copyright 1938 by William Carlos Williams. Reprinted by permission of New Directions Publishing Corporation.

Robley Wilson, Jr. "Thief." Reprinted from *Dancing for Men*, by permission of the University of Pittsburgh Press. © 1983 by Robley Wilson, Jr.

Tobias Wolff. "Say Yes" from *Back in the World*, Copyright © 1985 by Tobias Wolff. Reprinted by permission of Houghton Mifflin Company. All rights reserved.

Monica Wood. "Disappearing" first appeared in *Fiction Network*. Copyright 1988 by Monica Wood. Used by permission of the author.

Virginia Woolf. "The Symbol" from *The Complete Shorter Fiction of Virginia Woolf*, edited by Susan Dick, copyright © 1985 by Quentin Bell and Angelica Garnett, reprinted by permission of Harcourt Brace Jovanovich, Inc.

Rolf Yngve. "The Quail" from *Quarterly West*, 5, 1978 Used by permission.

Photo Credits

Page 1 Hokusai, Katsushika, Japanese, 1760–1849. *The Great Wave*. From the series: Fugaku Sanjurokei. Woodblock print. Spaulding Collection. Courtesy, Museum of Fine Arts, Boston.

Page 27 Hopper, Edward: *New York Office*, 1962. Oil on canvas, 40 × 55". Collection of the Montgomery Museum of Fine Arts and The Blount Collection.

Page 225 Dali, Salvador: *The Persistence of Memory*, 1931. Oil on canvas, 9½ × 13". Collection, The Museum of Modern Art, New York. Given anonymously.

Page 413 Munch, Edvard. *The Dance of Life*, 1899–1900. The National Gallery, Oslo.

Page 583 Wyeth, Andrew: *Christina's World*. (1948). Tempera on gessoed panel, 32¼ × 47¾". Collection, The Museum of Modern Art, New York. Purchase.

Index of Authors

and Titles